# U.S.

## A NARRATIVE HISTORY

## VOLUME 1: TO 1877

# A NARRATIVE HISTORY

## VOLUME 1: TO 1877

### Eighth Edition


**James West Davidson**

**Brian DeLay**
*University of California, Berkeley*

**Christine Leigh Heyrman**
*University of Delaware*

**Mark H. Lytle**
*Bard College*

**Michael B. Stoff**
*University of Texas, Austin*

Mc
Graw
Hill
Education

U.S.: A NARRATIVE HISTORY, VOLUME 1: TO 1877, EIGHTH EDITION
Published by McGraw-Hill Education, 2 Penn Plaza, New York, NY 10121. 

This book is printed on acid-free paper.

2 3 4 5 6 7 8 9 LMN 21 20 19 18

ISBN 978-1-259-71227-2

MHID 1-259-71227-3

Portfolio Manager: *Jason Seitz*

Lead Product Developer: *Dawn Groundwater*

Product Developer: *Sara Gordus*

Marketing Manager: *Will Walter*

Lead Content Project Manager: *Susan Trentacosti*

Content Project Manager: *George Theofanopoulos*

Buyer: *Laura Fuller*

Design: *Egzon Shaqiri*

Content Licensing Specialist: *Ann Marie Jannette*

Cover Image: *©McGraw-Hill Education*

Compositor: *Aptara®, Inc.*

Typeface: *STIXGeneral Regular 10/12*



Library of Congress Control Number: 2017950177



mheducation.com/highered

# WHAT'S NEW IN U.S.

## SOME HIGHLIGHTS:

- >> **A THEMATIC TIMELINE** at the beginning of each chapter is a new feature that previews key events and the themes connecting them.
- >> **MAKE A CASE** questions in each chapter challenge students to take an evidence-based stand on a debated issue.
- >> **EVERY CHAPTER** has been revised to reflect new trends in scholarship.
- >> **CHAPTER 7, THE AMERICAN PEOPLE AND THE AMERICAN REVOLUTION,** includes a new section about the varied roles of women in the Revolutionary War, and the discussion of the contribution of the French in the war has been expanded.

- >> **CHAPTER 9, THE EARLY REPUBLIC,** is now illustrated with a photo of the Broadway phenomenon *Hamilton*, and new discussions look at Saint Domingue's slave rebellions, France's abolition of slavery, and Napoleon's incursion in the Western Hemisphere.
- >> **CHAPTER 10, THE OPENING OF AMERICA,** now includes the slave trade between the Upper South and the Deep South after the international slave trade ended in 1808.
- >> **CHAPTER 12, AFIRE WITH FAITH,** increases coverage of black abolitionists, while **CHAPTER 13, THE OLD SOUTH,** has more on slavery and slave revolts in South America and the Caribbean.



# U.S. BRIEF CONTENTS

# Contents

©Richard A. Cooke/Getty Images

©Rafael Valls Gallery, London, UK/Bridgeman Images

©Medioimages/Photodisc/Getty Images RF

## 3 COLONIZATION & CONFLICT IN THE SOUTH 1600–1750

NIEUW AMSTERDAM OFTE NUE NIEUW IORX OPT TEYLANT MAN

©Peter Newark American Pictures/Bridgeman Images

## 4 COLONIZATION & CONFLICT IN THE NORTH 1600–1700

Courtesy Palace of the Governors Photo Archives (NMHM/DCA) neg. 158345



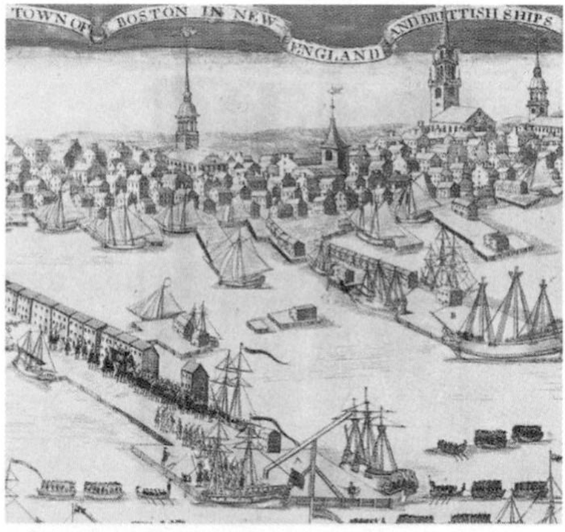

TOWN OF BOSTON IN NEW ENGLAND AND BRITTISH SHIPS


©Bettmann/Getty Images

CHARLES TOWN
BOSTON
©Peter Newark American Pictures/Bridgeman Images

## 7 THE AMERICAN PEOPLE AND THE AMERICAN REVOLUTION 1775–1783

Courtesy of Winterthur Museum

## 8 CRISIS AND CONSTITUTION 1776–1789

©Collection of the New-York Historical Society/Bridgeman Images

©Collection of the New-York Historical Society, USA/ Bridgeman Images

# 11 THE RISE OF DEMOCRACY 1824–1840

Source: Library of Congress, Prints and Photographs Division [LC-DIG-pga-05966]

# 12 AFIRE WITH FAITH 1820–1850

©Bridgeman Images

## 13 THE OLD SOUTH 1820–1860

©Photo Researchers, Inc/Alamy

## 14 WESTERN EXPANSION AND THE RISE OF THE SLAVERY ISSUE 1820–1850

Source: Library of Congress, Prints and Photographs Division [LC-DIG-ppmsca-37270]

## 16 THE CIVIL WAR AND THE REPUBLIC 1861–1865

Source: Library of Congress, Prints and Photographs Division [LC-USZC4-13286]

## 17 RECONSTRUCTING THE UNION 1865–1877

# Out of many stories, one *U.S.*

From five distinguished scholars comes one approachable and compelling narrative. *U.S.: A Narrative History* tells the stories of the American people in a concise and visually appealing way. The engaging narrative, crafted by a team of authors representing different eras, regions, topics, and approaches, showcases the diversity and complexity of the American past and guides students to develop a more nuanced understanding of our present and future.

This extremely readable program provides opportunities to engage with and uncover the history of America by leveraging the tools and practices that historians use to illuminate the past. The approachable narrative is supported by a comprehensive set of learning activities found in Connect: American History. By harnessing the power of Connect, your students will get the help they need, when and how they need it, so that your class time can be more rewarding for your students and you.

# Primary Sources Help Students Think Critically about History

Primary sources help students think critically about history and expose them to contrasting perspectives of key events. The Eighth Edition of *U.S.: A Narrative History* provides three different ways to use primary source documents in your course.

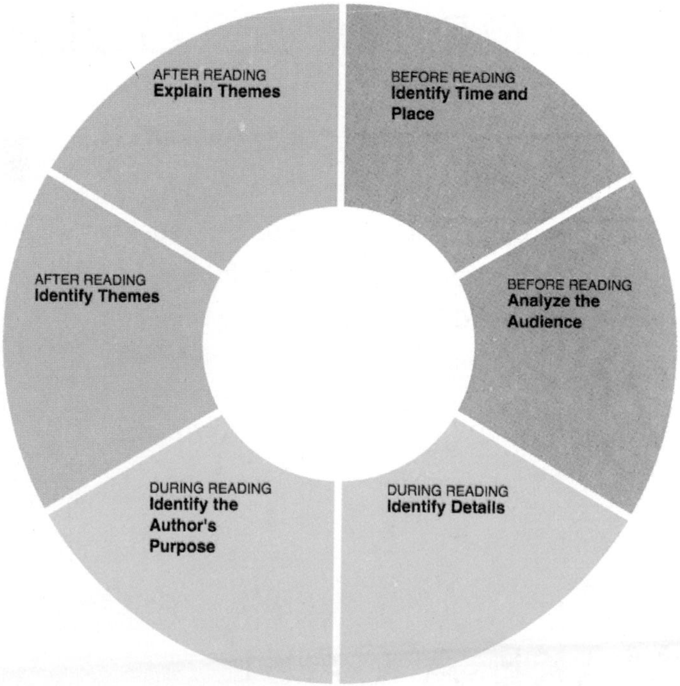

BEFORE READING
Identify Time and Place
BEFORE READING
Analyze the Audience
DURING READING
Identify Details
DURING READING
Identify the Author's Purpose
AFTER READING
Identify Themes
AFTER READING
Explain Themes


**Power of Process for Primary Sources is a critical thinking tool for reading and writing about primary sources.** As part of Connect History, McGraw-Hill Education's learning platform Power of Process contains a database of over 400 searchable primary sources in addition to the capability for instructors to upload their own sources. Instructors can then select a series of strategies for students to use to analyze and comment on a source. The Power of Process framework helps students develop essential academic skills such as understanding, analyzing, and synthesizing readings and visuals such as maps, leading students toward higher order thinking and writing.

**Features that offer contrasting perspectives or showcase historical artifacts.** Within the print or eBook, the Eighth Edition of *U.S.: A Narrative History* offers the following features:

# MANY HISTORIES

Two primary source documents offer contrasting perspectives on key events for analysis and discussion. Introductions and Thinking Critically questions frame the documents. For example, how did Spaniards and Aztecs differ in their account of first contact? Or, what were the arguments used to justify the internment of Japanese Americans during WWII and how did they compare to the experiences of those imprisoned?

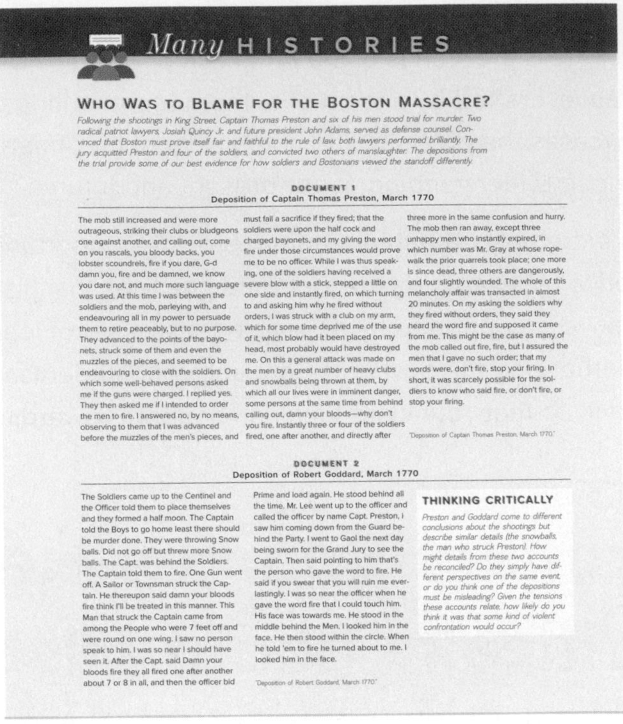

*Many* HISTORIES

WHO WAS TO BLAME FOR THE BOSTON MASSACRE?

*Following the shootings in King Street, Captain Thomas Preston and six of his men stood trial for murder. Two radical patriot lawyers, Josiah Quincy Jr. and future president John Adams, served as defense counsel. Convinced that Boston must prove itself fair and faithful to the rule of law, both lawyers performed brilliantly. The jury acquitted Preston and four of the soldiers, and convicted two others of manslaughter. The depositions from the trial provide some of our best evidence for how soldiers and Bostonians viewed the standoff differently.*

**DOCUMENT 1**
**Deposition of Captain Thomas Preston, March 1770**

The mob still increased and were more outrageous, striking their clubs or bludgeons one against another, and calling out, come on you rascals, you bloody backs, you lobster scoundrels, fire if you dare, G-d damn you, fire and be damned, we know you dare not, and much more such language was used. At this time I was between the soldiers and the mob, parleying with, and endeavouring all in my power to persuade them to retire peaceably, but to no purpose. They advanced to the points of the bayonets, struck some of them and even the muzzles of the pieces, and seemed to be endeavouring to close with the soldiers. On which some well-behaved persons asked me if the guns were charged. I replied yes. They then asked me if I intended to order the men to fire. I answered no, by no means, observing to them that I was advanced before the muzzles of the men's pieces, and must fall a sacrifice if they fired; that the soldiers were upon the half cock and charged bayonets, and my giving the word fire under those circumstances would prove me to be no officer. While I was thus speaking, one of the soldiers having received a severe blow with a stick, stepped a little on one side and instantly fired, on which turning to and asking him why he fired without orders, I was struck with a club on my arm, which for some time deprived me of the use of it, which blow had it been placed on my head, most probably would have destroyed me. On this a general attack was made on the men by a great number of heavy clubs and snowballs being thrown at them, by which all our lives were in imminent danger, some persons at the same time from behind calling out, damn your bloods—why don't you fire. Instantly three or four of the soldiers fired, one after another, and directly after three more in the same confusion and hurry. The mob then ran away, except three unhappy men who instantly expired, in which number was Mr. Gray at whose ropewalk the prior quarrels took place; one more is since dead, three others are dangerously, and four slightly wounded. The whole of this melancholy affair was transacted in almost 20 minutes. On my asking the soldiers why they fired without orders, they said they heard the word fire and supposed it came from me. This might be the case as many of the mob called out fire, fire, but I assured the men that I gave no such order; that my words were, don't fire, stop your firing. In short, it was scarcely possible for the soldiers to know who said fire, or don't fire, or stop your firing.

"Deposition of Captain Thomas Preston, March 1770."

**DOCUMENT 2**
**Deposition of Robert Goddard, March 1770**

The Soldiers came up to the Centinel and the Officer told them to place themselves and they formed a half moon. The Captain told the Boys to go home least there should be murder done. They were throwing Snow balls. Did not go off but threw more Snow balls. The Capt. was behind the Soldiers. The Captain told them to fire. One Gun went off. A Sailor or Townsman struck the Captain. He thereupon said damn your bloods fire think I'll be treated in this manner. This Man that struck the Captain came from among the People who were 7 feet off and were round on one wing. I saw no person speak to him. I was so near I should have seen it. After the Capt. said Damn your bloods fire they all fired one after another about 7 or 8 in all, and then the officer bid Prime and load again. He stood behind all the time. Mr. Lee went up to the officer and called the officer by name Capt. Preston, I saw him coming down from the Guard behind the Party. I went to Gaol the next day being sworn for the Grand Jury to see the Captain. Then said pointing to him that's the person who gave the word to fire. He said if you swear that you will ruin me everlastingly. I was so near the officer when he gave the word fire that I could touch him. His face was towards me. He stood in the middle behind the Men. I looked him in the face. He then stood within the circle. When he told 'em to fire he turned about to me. I looked him in the face.

"Deposition of Robert Goddard, March 1770"

**THINKING CRITICALLY**

*Preston and Goddard come to different conclusions about the shootings but describe similar details (the snowballs, the man who struck Preston). How might details from these two accounts be reconciled? Do they simply have different perspectives on the same event, or do you think one of the depositions must be misleading? Given the tensions these accounts relate, how likely do you think it was that some kind of violent confrontation would occur?*

# HISTORIAN'S TOOLBOX

These feature boxes, which alternate with Many Histories, showcase historical images and artifacts, asking students to focus on visual evidence and examine material culture. Introductions and Thinking Critically questions frame the images.

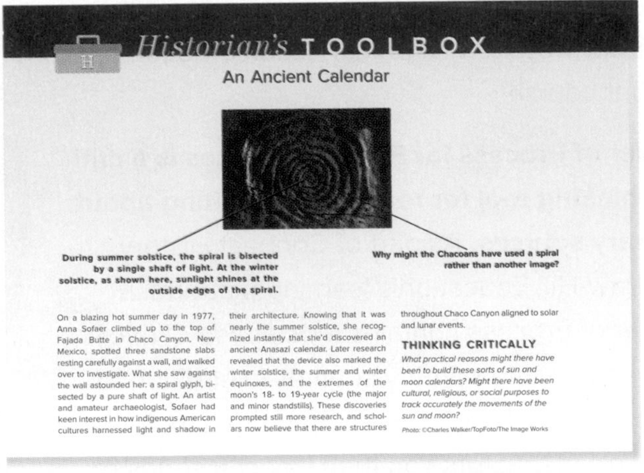

*Historian's* TOOLBOX

An Ancient Calendar

**During summer solstice, the spiral is bisected by a single shaft of light. At the winter solstice, as shown here, sunlight shines at the outside edges of the spiral.**

**Why might the Chacoans have used a spiral rather than another image?**

On a blazing hot summer day in 1977, Anna Sofaer climbed up to the top of Fajada Butte in Chaco Canyon, New Mexico, spotted three sandstone slabs resting carefully against a wall, and walked over to investigate. What she saw against the wall astounded her: a spiral glyph, bisected by a pure shaft of light. An artist and amateur archaeologist, Sofaer had keen interest in how indigenous American cultures harnessed light and shadow in their architecture. Knowing that it was nearly the summer solstice, she recognized instantly that she'd discovered an ancient Anasazi calendar. Later research revealed that the device also marked the winter solstice, the summer and winter equinoxes, and the extremes of the moon's 18- to 19-year cycle (the major and minor standstills). These discoveries prompted still more research, and scholars now believe that there are structures throughout Chaco Canyon aligned to solar and lunar events.

**THINKING CRITICALLY**

*What practical reasons might there have been to build these sorts of sun and moon calendars? Might there have been cultural, religious, or social purposes to track accurately the movements of the sun and moon?*

Photo: ©Charles Walker/TopFoto/The Image Works

# MAKE A CASE

Ideal for class discussion or writing, these questions help students learn to form a historical argument by asking them to weigh in on debated issues and give evidence for their answer.

## Make a Case

Do you think religion was only a surface justification or a primary motivation for the religious wars and rivalries of the sixteenth century? What sorts of evidence would help you make a compelling argument either way?

**Select primary source documents that meet the unique needs of your course.** No two history courses are the same. Using McGraw-Hill Education's Create allows you to quickly and easily create custom course materials with cross-disciplinary content and other third-party sources.

- **CHOOSE YOUR OWN CONTENT:** Create a book that contains only the chapters you want, in the order you want. Create will even renumber the pages for you!
- **ADD READINGS:** Use our American History Collections to include primary sources, or Taking Sides: Annual Editions. Add your own original content, such as syllabus or History major requirements!
- **CHOOSE YOUR FORMAT**: Print or eBook? Softcover, spiral-bound, or loose-leaf? Black-and-white or color? Perforated, three-hole punched, or regular paper?
- **CUSTOMIZE YOUR COVER:** Pick your own cover image and include your name and course information right on the cover. Students will know they're purchasing the right book—and using everything they purchase!
- **REVIEW YOUR CREATION:** When you are all done, you'll receive a free PDF review copy in just minutes! To get started, go to create.mheducation.com and register today.

# Map Tools to Promote Student Learning

Using Connect History and more than 100 maps, students can learn the course material more deeply and study more effectively than ever before.

Interactive maps give students a hands-on understanding of geography. *U.S.: A Narrative History* offers over 30 interactive maps that support geographical as well as historical thinking. These maps appear in

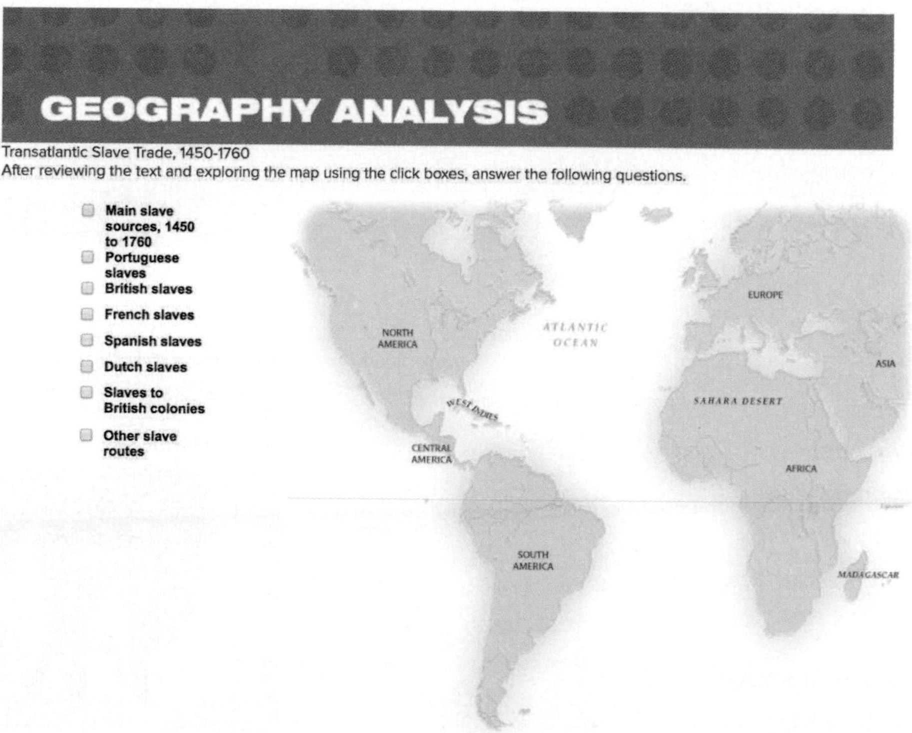
GEOGRAPHY ANALYSIS
Transatlantic Slave Trade, 1450-1760
After reviewing the text and exploring the map using the click boxes, answer the following questions.
Main slave sources, 1450 to 1760
Portuguese slaves
British slaves
French slaves
Spanish slaves
Dutch slaves
Slaves to British colonies
Other slave routes
NORTH AMERICA
ATLANTIC OCEAN
EUROPE
ASIA
WEST INDIES
SAHARA DESERT
CENTRAL AMERICA
AFRICA
SOUTH AMERICA
MADAGASCAR

both the eBook and Connect History exercises. For some interactive maps, students click on the boxes in the map legend to see changing boundaries, visualize migration routes, or analyze war battles and election results. With others, students manipulate a slider to help them better understand change over time. New interactive maps feature advanced navigation features, including zoom, as well as audio and textual animation.

A complete list of maps can be found in a separate section of the frontmatter.

# SmartBook Tailors Content to the Individual Student

Mc Graw Hill Education SMARTBOOK™

As part of McGraw-Hill Education's Connect History, SmartBook prepares students for class, guiding them through the chapters and highlighting what they need to learn to help them study more efficiently and effectively. SmartBook is proven to strengthen memory recall, keep students in class, and boost grades.

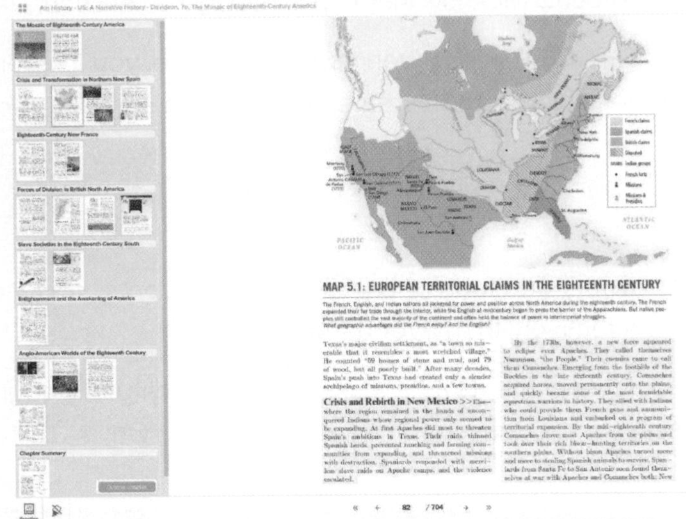

MAP 5.1: EUROPEAN TERRITORIAL CLAIMS IN THE EIGHTEENTH CENTURY
Crisis and Rebirth in New Mexico


By helping students master core concepts ahead of time, SmartBook enables instructors to spend more meaningful time in the classroom. Through real-time reports, instructors can also track class or individual student performance on chapter topics or completion of chapter readings.

# Critical Missions Promote Critical Thinking

*What would your students do if they were senators voting on the impeachment of Andrew Johnson? Or if they were advisers to Harry Truman, helping him decide whether to drop the atomic bomb?*

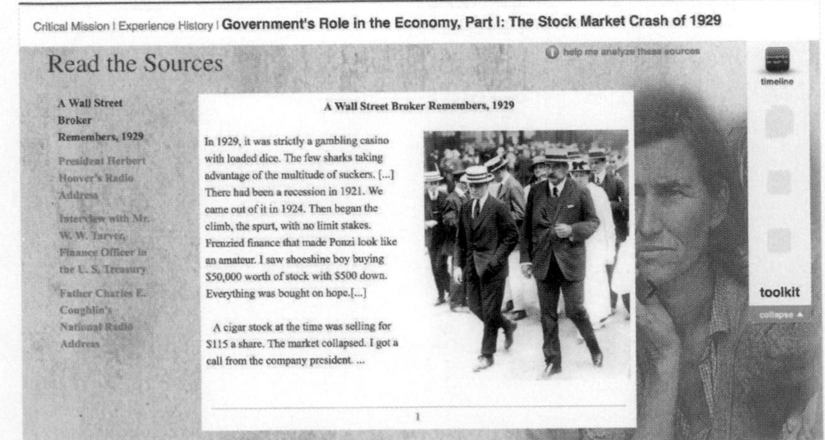

Critical Mission | Experience History | Government's Role in the Economy, Part I: The Stock Market Crash of 1929
Read the Sources
help me analyze these sources
timeline
A Wall Street Broker Remembers, 1929
President Herbert Hoover's Radio Address
Interview with Mr. W. W. Tarver, Finance Officer in the U. S. Treasury
Father Charles E. Coughlin's National Radio Address
A Wall Street Broker Remembers, 1929
In 1929, it was strictly a gambling casino with loaded dice. The few sharks taking advantage of the multitude of suckers. [...] There had been a recession in 1921. We came out of it in 1924. Then began the climb, the spurt, with no limit stakes. Frenzied finance that made Ponzi look like an amateur. I saw shoeshine boy buying $50,000 worth of stock with $500 down. Everything was bought on hope.[...]
A cigar stock at the time was selling for $115 a share. The market collapsed. I got a call from the company president. ...
1
toolkit
collapse


An immersive activity that shows students how to work with primary sources and develop a historical argument, Critical Missions help students feel like active participants in a series of transformative moments in history. As advisers to key historical figures, they read and analyze primary sources, interpret maps and timelines, and write recommendations. As a follow-up activity in each Critical Mission, students learn to think like historians by conducting a retrospective analysis from a contemporary perspective.

# List of MAPS

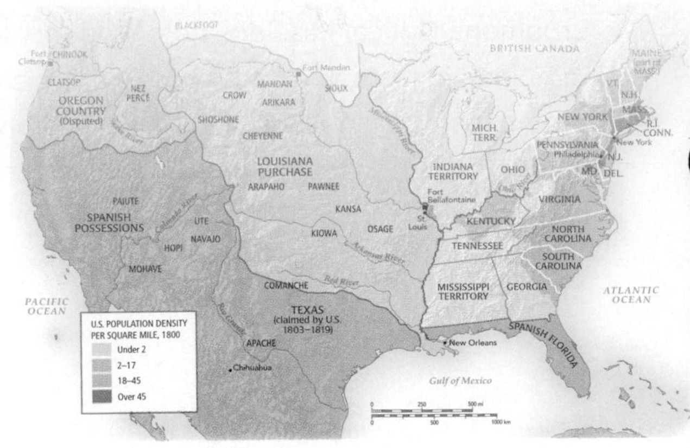

U.S. population density per square mile, 1800
Spanish possessions
Oregon Country
Louisiana Purchase
Expedition of Lewis and Clark, 1804–1806
Expeditions by Zebulon Pike, 1805–1807
BRITISH CANADA
OREGON COUNTRY (Disputed)
LOUISIANA PURCHASE
SPANISH POSSESSIONS
TEXAS (claimed by U.S. 1803–1819)
SPANISH FLORIDA
INDIANA TERRITORY
MICH. TERR.
MISSISSIPPI TERRITORY
NEW YORK
PENNSYLVANIA
OHIO
VIRGINIA
KENTUCKY
TENNESSEE
NORTH CAROLINA
SOUTH CAROLINA
GEORGIA
PACIFIC OCEAN
ATLANTIC OCEAN
Gulf of Mexico
U.S. POPULATION DENSITY PER SQUARE MILE, 1800
Under 2
2–17
18–45
Over 45




A map of the United States appears on the inside front cover, while a world map appears on the inside back cover.

# List of AUTHOR-SELECTED PRIMARY SOURCE DOCUMENTS IN POWER OF PROCESS

Power of Process for Primary Sources is a critical thinking tool for reading and writing about primary sources. As part of Connect History, McGraw-Hill Education's learning platform, Power of Process contains a database of over 400 searchable primary sources in addition to the capability for instructors to upload their own sources. Instructors can then select a series of strategies for students to use to analyze and comment on a source. The Power of Process framework helps students develop essential academic skills such as understanding, analyzing, and synthesizing readings and visuals such as maps, leading students toward higher order thinking and writing.

The following primary source documents, carefully selected by the authors to coordinate with this chapter, are available in the Power of Process assignment type within Connect History at http://connect.mheducation.com.

# Acknowledgments

We would like to express our deep appreciation to the following individuals who contributed to the development of our U.S. history programs:

**Reviewers of *U.S.: A Narrative History***

Mary Adams, *City College of San Francisco*

Jennifer Allen, *Brookhaven College*

Janet Allured, *McNeese State University*

Diana Barnes, *Youngstown State University*

Chris Bell, *Edmonds Community College*

James Blain, *McNeese State University*

Roger Bowerman, *Glendale Community College*

Jeffrey Brown, *New Mexico State University*

Ann Chirhart, *Indiana State University*

Bradley Clampitt, *East Central University*

Patty Colman, *Moorpark College*

Michael Colomaio, *Alfred State University*

Tonia Compton, *Columbia College, Columbia*

Clarissa Confer, *California University of Pennsylvania*

Cara Converse, *Moorpark College*

Cassandra Cookson, *Lee College*

William Cooley, *Walsh University*

Aaron Cowen, *Slippery Rock University*

David Cullen, *Collins College, Plano*

David Dalton, *College of the Ozarks*

Brandon Franke, *Blinn College*

Christos Frentzos, *Austin Peay State University*

Timothy Fritz, *Mount St. Mary's University*

Tabetha Garman, *North East State University*

George Gastil, *Grossmont College*

Michael Gattis, *Faulkner State Community College*

Frank Gilbert, *Southeastern Oklahoma State University*

Jim Good, *Lone Star College, North Harris*

Patricia Gower, *University of the Incarnate Word*

Charles Grear, *Prairie View A&M*

Devethia Guillory, *Prairie View A&M*

Debra Haber, *Middle Tennessee State University–Murfreesboro*

Christopher Haight, *University of Houston*

Debbie Hargis, *Odessa College*

Sahalie Hashim, *The University of Texas at Dallas*

Aran Heaney, *Alfred State College*

Tom Heiting, *Odessa College*

Jennifer Helgren, *University of the Pacific*

Jay Hester, *Sierra College*

Lucy Hoffman, *Greenville Technical College*

Kelly Hopkins, *University of Houston, Houston*

Justin Horton, *Thomas Nelson Community College*

Chresancio Jackson, *Louisiana Delta Community College*

Cynthia Jurisson, *University of Chicago Lab School*

Carol Keller, *San Antonio College*

Richard Kitchen, *New Mexico Military Institute*

Dennis Kortheuer, *California State University, Long Beach*

Pat Ledbetter, *Texas College*

Mary Lewis, *Jacksonville College*

Tammi Littrel, *Chadron State College*

Philbert Martin, *San Jacinto College, South*

Bob McConaughy, *Austin Community College*

Suzanne McFadden, *Austin Community College*

John William Meador, *Central New Mexico Community College, Montoya*

Greg Miller, *Hillsborough Community College, Dale Mabry*

James Mills, *University of Texas, Brownsville*

Russell Mitchell, *Tarrant County College, Southeast*

Michael Namorato, *University of Mississippi*

Bret Nelson,
*San Jacinto College, North*

Michael Noble,
*Eastfield College*

Shannon O'Bryan,
*Greenville Technical College*

Alison Ollinger-Riefstahl,
*Mercyhurst Northeast College*

Kathryn Ostrofsky,
*Angelo State University*

Stephen Patnodes,
*Farmingdale State University*

Susan Richards,
*Central New Mexico Community College Albuquerque*

Edward Richey,
*University of North Texas*

Joaquin Riveya-Martinez,
*Texas State University, San Marcos*

Stephen Rockenbach,
*Virginia State University*

Norman Rodriguez,
*John Wood Community College*

Ronald Romanchek,
*Eastfield College*

Todd Romero,
*University of Houston*

Michele Rotunda,
*Rutgers University, Newark*

Donald Seals,
*Kilgore College*

Steven Short,
*Collin College*

Richard Sorrel,
*Brookdale Community College*

Maureen Melvin Sowa,
*Bristol Community College*

Jodi Steeley,
*Merced Community College*

Curtis Thomas,
*Richland College*

Rita Thomas,
*Northern Kentucky University*

Richard Trimble,
*Ocean County College*

Ruth Truss,
*University of Montevallo*

Salli Vargis,
*Georgia Perimeter College*

William Wantland,
*Mount Vernon Nazarene University*

Tom Wells,
*Weatherford College*

Chad Wooley,
*Tarrant County College*

Nancy Young,
*University of Houston*

# About the Authors

**James West Davidson** received his Ph.D. from Yale University. A historian who has pursued a full-time writing career, his works include *After the Fact: The Art of Historical Detection* (with Mark H. Lytle), *The Logic of Millennial Thought: Eighteenth-Century New England*, and *Great Heart: The History of a Labrador Adventure* (with John Rugge). He is co-editor with Michael Stoff of the *Oxford New Narratives in American History*, which includes his study *'They Say': Ida B. Wells and the Reconstruction of Race*. Most recently he wrote *A Little History of the United States.*

**Brian DeLay** received his Ph.D. from Harvard and is an Associate Professor of History at the University of California, Berkeley. He is a frequent guest speaker at teacher workshops across the country and has won several prizes for his book *War of a Thousand Deserts: Indian Raids and the U.S.-Mexican War*. His current book project, *Shoot the State*, explores the connection between guns, freedom, and domination around the Western Hemisphere, from the American Revolution through World War II.

**Christine Leigh Heyrman** is the Robert W. and Shirley P. Grimble Professor of American History at the University of Delaware. She received her Ph.D. in American Studies from Yale University. The author of *Commerce and Culture: The Maritime Communities of Colonial Massachusetts, 1690–1750*, she received the Bancroft Prize for her second book, *Southern Cross: The Beginnings of the Bible Belt,* and the Parkman Prize for her third, *American Apostles: When Evangelicals Entered the World of Islam.*

**Mark H. Lytle,** a Ph.D. from Yale University, is the Lyford Paterson and Mary Gray Edwards Professor of History Emeritus at Bard College. He served two years as Mary Ball Washington Professor of American History at University College Dublin, in Ireland. His publications include *The Origins of the Iranian-American Alliance, 1941–1953, After the Fact: The Art of Historical Detection* (with James West Davidson), *America's Uncivil Wars: The Sixties Era from Elvis to the Fall of Richard Nixon*, and most recently, *The Gentle Subversive: Rachel Carson, Silent Spring, and the Rise of the Environmental Movement*. His forthcoming book, *The All-Consuming Nation*, considers the tension between the post–World War II consumer democracy and its environmental costs.

**Michael B. Stoff** is Associate Professor of History and University Distinguished Teaching Professor at the University of Texas at Austin. The recipient of a Ph.D. from Yale University, he has been honored many times for his teaching, most recently with the University of Texas systemwide Regents Outstanding Teaching Award. In 2008, he was named an Organization of American Historians Distinguished Lecturer. He is the author of *Oil, War, and American Security: The Search for a National Policy on Foreign Oil, 1941–1947*, co-editor (with Jonathan Fanton and R. Hal Williams) of *The Manhattan Project: A Documentary Introduction to the Atomic Age*, and series co-editor (with James West Davidson) of the *Oxford New Narratives in American History*. He is currently working on a narrative of the bombing of Nagasaki.

# 1 The First Civilizations of North America

From the air, this serpentine mound fashioned thousands of years ago still stands out in bold relief. Located in southern Ohio, it extends from the snake's coiled tail at the left of the photo to the open mouth at the top right. The snake's tail points toward the winter solstice sunrise, while the mouth is oriented to the summer solstice sunrise.



## >> An American Story

## THE POWER OF A HIDDEN PAST

Stories told about the past have power over both the present and the future. Until recently most students were taught that American history began several centuries ago—with the "discovery" of America by Columbus, or with the English colonization of Jamestown and Plymouth.

^ This bottle in the shape of a nursing mother and child was created near Cahokia sometime between 1200 and 1400 CE, perhaps in a village where such crafts were practiced. It was buried in a tomb, most likely of a high-ranking individual.
©The Detroit Institute of Arts/St. Louis Museum of Science & Natural History/Bridgeman Images

History books ignored or trivialized the continent's precontact history. But the reminders of that hidden past are everywhere. Scattered across the United States are thousands of ancient archaeological sites and hundreds of examples of monumental architecture, still imposing even after centuries of erosion, looting, and destruction.

Man-made earthen mounds, some nearly 5,000 years old, exist throughout eastern North America in a bewildering variety of shapes and sizes. Many are easily mistaken for modest hills, but others evoke wonder. In present-day Louisiana an ancient town with earthworks took laborers an estimated 5 million work hours to construct. In Ohio a massive serpent effigy snakes for a quarter mile across the countryside, its head aligned to the summer solstice. In Illinois a vast, earthen construct covers 16 acres at its base and once reached as high as a 10-story building.

Observers in the colonial and revolutionary eras looked on such sites as curiosities and marvels. George Washington, Thomas Jefferson, and other prominent Americans collected ancient artifacts, took a keen interest in the excavation of mounds, and speculated about the Indian civilizations that created them. Travelers explored these strange mounds, trying to imagine the peoples who had built them. In 1795 the Reverend James Smith traced the boundaries of a mound wall that was strategically placed to protect a neck of land along a looping river bend in the Ohio valley. "The wall at present is so mouldered down that a man could easily ride over it. It is however about 10 feet, as near as I can judge, in perpendicular height. . . . In one place I observe a breach in the wall about 60 feet wide, where I suppose the gate formerly stood through which the people passed in and out of this stronghold." Smith was astonished by the size of the project. "Compared with this," he exclaimed, "what feeble and insignificant works are those of Fort Hamilton or Fort Washington! They are no more in comparison to it than a rail fence is to a brick wall."

But in the 1830s and 1840s, as Americans sought to drive Indians west of the Mississippi and then confine them on smaller and smaller reservations, many began thinking differently about the continent's ancient sites. Surely the simple and "savage" people just then being expelled from American life could not have constructed such inspiring monuments. Politicians, writers, and even some influential scientists dismissed the claim that North America's ancient architecture had been built by the ancestors of contemporary Indians and instead attributed the mounds to peoples of Europe, Africa, or Asia—Hindus, perhaps, or Israelites, Egyptians, or Japanese. Many nineteenth-century Americans found special comfort in a tale about King Madoc from Wales, who supposedly shipwrecked in the Americas in the twelfth century and had left behind a small but ingenious population of Welsh pioneers who built the mysterious mounds before being overrun by Indians. The Welsh hypothesis seemed to offer poetic justice, because it implied that nineteenth-century Indians were only receiving a fitting punishment for what their ancestors had done to the remarkable mound builders from Wales.

These fanciful tales were discredited in the late nineteenth and early twentieth centuries. In recent decades archaeologists working across the Americas have discovered in more detail how native peoples built the Western Hemisphere's ancient architecture. They have also helped to make clear the degree to which prejudice and politics have blinded European Americans to the complexity, wonder, and significance of America's history before 1492. At least 15,000 years of human habitation in North America allowed a broad range of cultures to develop, based on agriculture as well as hunting and gathering. In North America a population in the millions spoke hundreds of languages. Cities evolved as well as towns and farms, exhibiting great diversity in their cultural, political, economic, and religious organization. <<

## THEMATIC TIMELINE

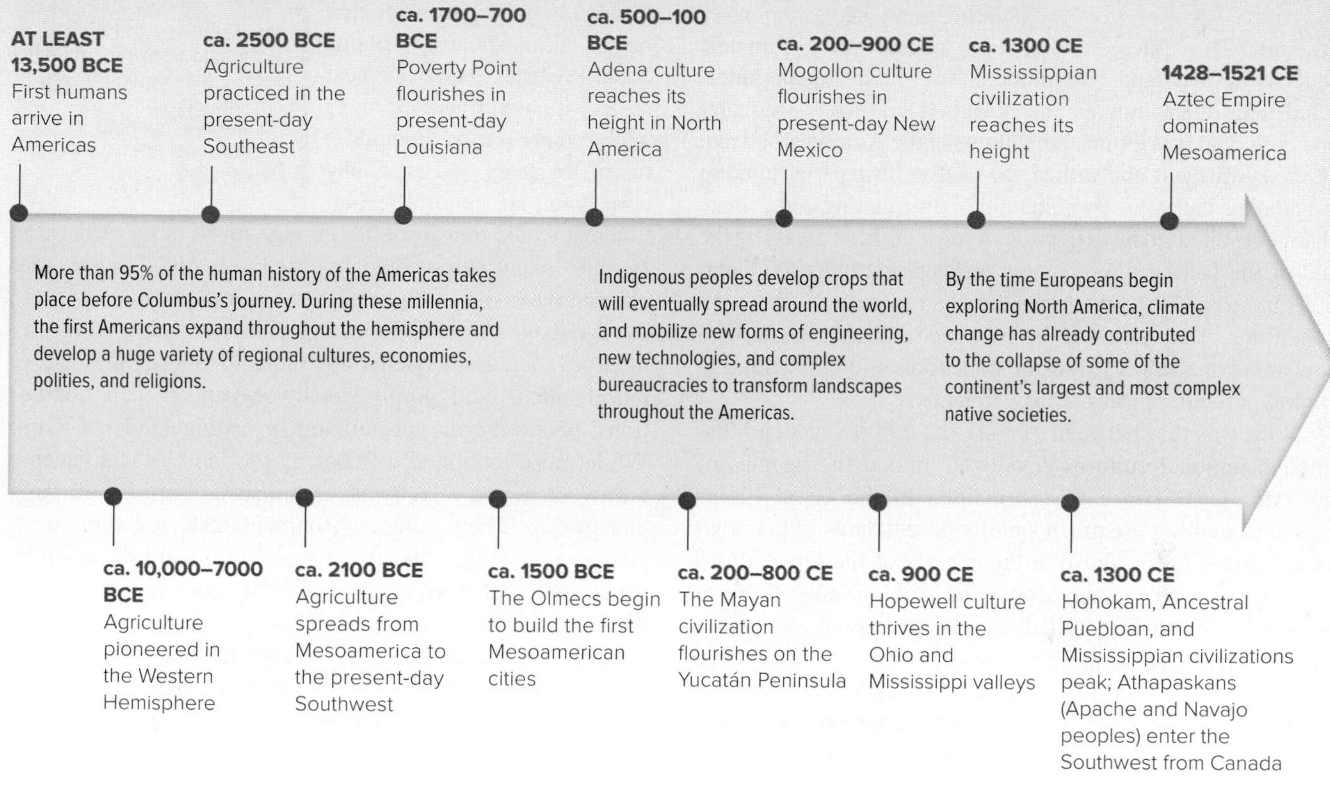
AT LEAST 13,500 BCE
First humans arrive in Americas
ca. 2500 BCE
Agriculture practiced in the present-day Southeast
ca. 1700–700 BCE
Poverty Point flourishes in present-day Louisiana
ca. 500–100 BCE
Adena culture reaches its height in North America
ca. 200–900 CE
Mogollon culture flourishes in present-day New Mexico
ca. 1300 CE
Mississippian civilization reaches its height
1428–1521 CE
Aztec Empire dominates Mesoamerica
More than 95% of the human history of the Americas takes place before Columbus's journey. During these millennia, the first Americans expand throughout the hemisphere and develop a huge variety of regional cultures, economies, polities, and religions.
Indigenous peoples develop crops that will eventually spread around the world, and mobilize new forms of engineering, new technologies, and complex bureaucracies to transform landscapes throughout the Americas.
By the time Europeans begin exploring North America, climate change has already contributed to the collapse of some of the continent's largest and most complex native societies.
ca. 10,000–7000 BCE
Agriculture pioneered in the Western Hemisphere
ca. 2100 BCE
Agriculture spreads from Mesoamerica to the present-day Southwest
ca. 1500 BCE
The Olmecs begin to build the first Mesoamerican cities
ca. 200–800 CE
The Mayan civilization flourishes on the Yucatán Peninsula
ca. 900 CE
Hopewell culture thrives in the Ohio and Mississippi valleys
ca. 1300 CE
Hohokam, Ancestral Puebloan, and Mississippian civilizations peak; Athapaskans (Apache and Navajo peoples) enter the Southwest from Canada

# A CONTINENT OF CULTURES

Archaeological and genetic evidence indicate that the first inhabitants of the Americas arrived from Siberia around 15,500 years ago BP.* (This longstanding theory could soon be overthrown; astonishing new discoveries in Southern California suggest humans have been in North America for more than 130,000 years.) Gradually Asian **nomads** filtered southward, some likely following the Pacific coastline in small boats, others making their way down a narrow, glacier-free corridor along the eastern base of the Rocky Mountains and onto the northern Great Plains. There they found and hunted a stunning array of huge mammals, so-called megafauna. These animals included mammoths that were twice as heavy as elephants, giant bison, sloths that were taller than giraffes, several kinds of camels, and terrifying, 8-foot-long lions. Within a few thousand years the descendants of these Siberians, people whom Columbus would wishfully dub "Indians," had spread throughout the length and breadth of the Americas.

**nomad** a member of a group of people who have no fixed home and who move about, usually seasonally, in pursuit of food, water, and other resources.

This first colonization of the Americas coincided with, and perhaps accelerated, profound changes in the natural world. The last Ice Age literally melted away as warmer global

## Make a Case

The vast majority of human history in the Americas took place before Columbus. Why do you think students learn so little about the hemisphere prior to 1492? Why is it so difficult to integrate the pre- and post-contact history?

* Before the Present, used most commonly by archaeologists when the time spans are in multiple thousands of years. This text will also use CE for Common Era, equivalent to the Christian era or AD; BCE is Before the Common Era, equivalent to BC.

**ecosystem** a community and/or region studied as a system of functioning relationships between organisms and their environments.

temperatures freed the great reservoirs of water once locked in glaciers. A rise in sea levels inundated the Bering Strait, submerging the land bridge and creating new lakes and river systems. The emergence of new **ecosystems**—climates, waterways, and land environments in which humans interacted with other animals and plants—made for ever-greater diversity. The first human inhabitants of the Americas had fed, clothed, warmed, and armed themselves in part by hunting megafauna, and some combination of overhunting and climate change resulted in the extinction of most of these giants by the end of the Ice Age. As glaciers receded and human populations increased, the first Americans had to adapt to changing conditions. They adjusted by hunting smaller animals with new, more specialized kinds of stone tools and by learning to exploit particular places more efficiently.

So it was that between 10,000 and 2,500 years ago distinctive regional cultures developed among the peoples of the Americas. Those who remained in the Great Plains turned to hunting the much smaller descendants of the now-extinct giant bison; those in the deserts of the Great Basin survived on small game, seeds, and edible plants; those in the Pacific Northwest relied mainly on fishing; and those east of the Mississippi, besides fishing and gathering, tracked deer and bear and trapped smaller game animals and birds. Over these same centuries, what once seems to have been an original, common language evolved into regional dialects and eventually into a multitude of distinct languages. Linguistic diversity paced other sorts of divergences, in social organizations, kinship practices, politics, and religion. Technological and cultural unity gave way to striking regional diversity as the first Americans learned how to best exploit their particular environments. Glimpses of these profound changes may be found today in burials, stone tools, and some precious sites of long-term or repeated occupation.

## Cultures of Ancient Mexico

>> To the south, pioneers in **Mesoamerica** began domesticating plants 10,000 years ago. Over the next several thousand years farmers added other crops, including beans, tomatoes, and especially corn, to an agricultural revolution that would transform life through much of the Americas. Because many crops could be dried and stored, agriculture allowed these first farmers to settle in one place.

**Mesoamerica** the area stretching from present-day central Mexico southward through Honduras and Nicaragua, in which pre-Columbian civilizations developed.

By about 1500 BCE farming villages began giving way to larger societies, to richer and more advanced cultures. As the abundant food supply steadily expanded their populations, people began specializing in certain kinds of work. While most continued to labor on the land, others became craftworkers and merchants, architects and artists, warriors and priests. Their built environment reflected this social change as humble villages expanded into skillfully planned urban sites that were centers of trade, government, artistic display, and religious ceremony.

The Olmecs, the first city builders in the Americas, constructed large plazas and pyramidal structures and sculpted enormous heads chiseled from basalt. The Olmec cultural influence gradually spread throughout Mesoamerica, perhaps as a result of the Olmecs' trade with neighboring peoples. By about 100 BCE the Olmecs' example had inspired the flowering of Teotihuacán from a small town in central Mexico into a metropolis of towering pyramids. The city had bustling marketplaces, palaces decorated with mural paintings that housed elite warriors and priests, schools for their children, and sprawling suburbs for commoners. At its height, around 650 CE, Teotihuacán spanned more than 10 square miles and had a population of perhaps a quarter million—larger even than that of Rome at the time.

More impressive still were the achievements of the Mayas, who benefited from their contacts with both the Olmecs and Teotihuacán. In the lowland jungles of Mesoamerica they built cities filled with palaces, bridges, aqueducts, baths, astronomical observatories, and pyramids topped with temples. Their priests developed a written language, their mathematicians discovered the zero, and their astronomers devised a calendar more accurate than any then existing. In its glory, between the third and ninth century CE, the Mayan civilization boasted some 50 urban centers scattered throughout the Yucatán Peninsula, Belize, Guatemala, and Honduras.

^ Aztec merchants, or pochtecas, spoke many languages and traveled on foot great distances throughout Mesoamerica and parts of North America. Pictured at left is Yacatecuhtli, Lord Nose, the patron god of merchants. He carries a symbol of the crossroads, with bare footprints. The merchant on the right carries a cargo of quetzal birds.
©Werner Forman/HIP/The Image Works

But neither the earliest urban centers of the Olmecs nor the glittering city-state of Teotihuacán survived. Even the glories of the Maya had stalled by 900 CE. Like the ancient civilizations of Greece and Rome, they thrived for centuries and then declined. Scholars still debate the reasons for their collapse. Military attack may have brought about their ruin, or perhaps their large populations exhausted local resources.

Mayan grandeur was eventually rivaled in the Valley of Mexico. In the middle of the thirteenth century the Aztecs, a people who had originally lived on Mesoamerica's northern frontiers, swept south and settled in central Mexico. By the end of the fifteenth century they ruled over a vast empire from their capital at Tenochtitlán, an island metropolis of perhaps a quarter of a million people. At its center lay a large plaza bordered by sumptuous palaces and the Great Temple of the Sun. Beyond stood three broad causeways connecting the island to the mainland, many other tall temples adorned with brightly painted carved images of the gods, zoological and botanical gardens, and well-stocked marketplaces. Through Tenochtitlán's canals flowed gold, silver, exotic feathers and jewels, cocoa, and millions of pounds of maize—all trade goods and tribute from the several million other peoples in the region subjugated by the Aztecs.

Unsurpassed in power and wealth, in technological and artistic attainments, theirs was also a highly stratified society. The Aztec ruler, or Chief Speaker, shared governing power with the aristocrats who monopolized all positions of religious, military, and political leadership, while the commoners—merchants, farmers, and craftworkers—performed all manual labor. There were slaves as well, some captives taken in war, others from the ranks of commoners forced by poverty to sell themselves or their children.

## Farmers, Potters, and Builders of the Southwest >>

Recent discoveries suggest that Mesoamerican crops and farming techniques began making their way north to the American Southwest as early as 2100 BCE, though it would be nearly two millennia before regional communities fully adopted sedentary agricultural lifestyles. The most successful full-time farmers in the region were the Mogollon and Hohokam peoples, two cultures that flourished in New Mexico and southern Arizona during the first millennium CE. Both tended to cluster their dwellings near streams, which allowed them to adopt the systems of irrigation as well as the maize cultivation of central Mexico. The Mogollon came to be the master potters of the Southwest. The Hohokam pioneered vast and complex irrigation systems in arid southern Arizona that allowed them to support one of the largest populations in precontact North America.

Their neighbors to the north in what is now known as the Four Corners Region of Arizona, Colorado, New Mexico, and Utah, commonly referred to by the term *Anasazi*, are today more properly known as the Ancestral Pueblo peoples. The Ancestral Puebloans adapted corn, beans, and squash to the relatively high altitude of the Colorado Plateau and soon parlayed their growing surplus and prosperity into societies of considerable complexity. Their most stunning achievements were villages of exquisitely executed masonry buildings—apartment-like structures up to four stories high and containing hundreds of rooms at such places as Mesa Verde (Colorado) and Canyon de Chelly (Arizona). Villages in Chaco Canyon (New Mexico), the largest center of Ancestral Puebloan settlement, were linked to the wider region by hundreds of miles of wide, straight roads.

Besides their impressive dwellings, the Ancestral Puebloans filled their towns with religious shrines, astronomical observatories, and stations for sending signals to other villages. Their craftworkers fashioned delicate woven baskets, beautiful feather and hide sashes, decorated pottery, and turquoise jewelry that they traded throughout the region and beyond. For nearly a thousand years this civilization prospered, reaching its zenith between about 900 and 1100 CE. During those three centuries the population grew to approximately 30,000 spread over 50,000 square miles, a total area larger than present-day California.

## Chiefdoms of the Eastern Woodlands >>

East of the Mississippi, Indian societies prospered in valleys near great rivers (Mississippi, Ohio, Tennessee, and Cumberland), the shores of the Great Lakes, and the coast of the Atlantic. Everywhere the earliest inhabitants depended on a combination of fishing, gathering, and hunting—mainly deer but also bear, raccoon, and a variety of birds. Around 2500 BCE some groups in the temperate, fertile Southeast began growing the gourds and pumpkins first cultivated by Mesoamerican farmers, and later they also adopted the cultivation of maize. Like the ancient farmers of the Southwest, most Eastern Woodland peoples continued to subsist largely on animals, fish, and nuts, all of which were abundant enough to meet their needs and even to expand their numbers.

Indeed, many of the mysterious earthen mounds that would so fascinate Europeans were built by peoples who did not farm. About 1000 BCE residents of a place now known as Poverty Point in northeastern Louisiana fashioned spectacular earthworks—six semicircular rings that rose 9 feet in height and covered more than half a mile in diameter. Although these structures might have been sites for studying the planets and stars, hundreds of other mounds—built about 2,000 years ago by the Adena and the Hopewell cultures of the Ohio and Mississippi valleys—served as the burial places of their leading men and women. Alongside the corpses mourners heaped their richest goods—headdresses of antlers, necklaces of copper, troves of shells and pearls—rare and precious items imported from as far north as Canada, as far west as Wyoming, and as far east as Florida. All these mounds attest powerfully not only to the skill and sheer numbers of their builders but also to the complexity of these ancient societies, their elaborate religious practices, and the wide scope of their trading networks.

# Historian's TOOLBOX

## An Ancient Calendar

**During summer solstice, the spiral is bisected by a single shaft of light. At the winter solstice, as shown here, sunlight shines at the outside edges of the spiral.**

**Why might the Chacoans have used a spiral rather than another image?**

On a blazing hot summer day in 1977, Anna Sofaer climbed up to the top of Fajada Butte in Chaco Canyon, New Mexico, spotted three sandstone slabs resting carefully against a wall, and walked over to investigate. What she saw against the wall astounded her: a spiral glyph, bisected by a pure shaft of light. An artist and amateur archaeologist, Sofaer had keen interest in how indigenous American cultures harnessed light and shadow in their architecture. Knowing that it was nearly the summer solstice, she recognized instantly that she'd discovered an ancient Anasazi calendar. Later research revealed that the device also marked the winter solstice, the summer and winter equinoxes, and the extremes of the moon's 18- to 19-year cycle (the major and minor standstills). These discoveries prompted still more research, and scholars now believe that there are structures throughout Chaco Canyon aligned to solar and lunar events.

### THINKING CRITICALLY

*What practical reasons might there have been to build these sorts of sun and moon calendars? Might there have been cultural, religious, or social purposes to track accurately the movements of the sun and moon?*

*Photo:* ©Charles Walker/TopFoto/The Image Works

Even so, the most magnificent culture of the ancient Eastern Woodlands, the Mississippian, owed much of its prominence to farming. By the twelfth century CE Mississippians had emerged as the premier city-builders north of the Rio Grande, and their towns radiated for hundreds of miles in every direction from the hub of their trading network at Cahokia, a port city of several thousand located directly across from present-day St. Louis at the confluence of the Missouri and the Mississippi Rivers. Cahokia's many broad plazas teemed with farmers hauling their corn, squash, and beans and with craftworkers and merchants plying their wares. But what commanded every eye were the structures surrounding the plazas—more than 100 flat-topped pyramidal mounds crowned by religious temples and elite dwellings.

**Life on the Great Plains** >> Cahokia's size and power depended on consistent agricultural surpluses. Outside the Southwest and the river valleys of the East, agriculture played a smaller role in shaping North American societies. On the Great Plains, for example, some people did cultivate corn, beans, squash, and sunflowers, near reliable rivers and streams. But more typically Plains communities depended on hunting and foraging, migrating to exploit seasonally variable resources. Plains hunters pursued game on foot; the horses that had once roamed the Americas had become extinct after the last Ice Age. Sometimes large groups of people worked together to drive bison over cliffs or to trap them in corrals. The aridity of the plains made it a dynamic and unpredictable place to live. During times of reliable rainfall, bison populations boomed, hunters flocked to the region, and agricultural communities blossomed alongside major rivers. But sometimes centuries passed with lower-than-average precipitation, and families abandoned the plains for eastern river valleys or the foothills of the Rocky Mountains.

**Survival in the Great Basin** >> Some peoples west of the Great Plains also kept to older ways of subsistence. Among them were the Numic-speaking peoples of the Great Basin, which includes present-day Nevada and Utah, eastern California, and western Wyoming and Colorado. Small family groups scoured their stark, arid landscape for the limited supplies of food it yielded, moving with each passing season to make the most of their environment. Men tracked elk and antelope and trapped smaller animals, birds, even toads, rattlesnakes, and insects. But the staples of their diet were edible seeds, nuts, and plants, which women gathered and stored in woven baskets to consume in times of scarcity. Several families occasionally hunted together or wintered in common quarters, but because the desert heat and soil defied farming, these bands usually numbered no more than about 50 people.

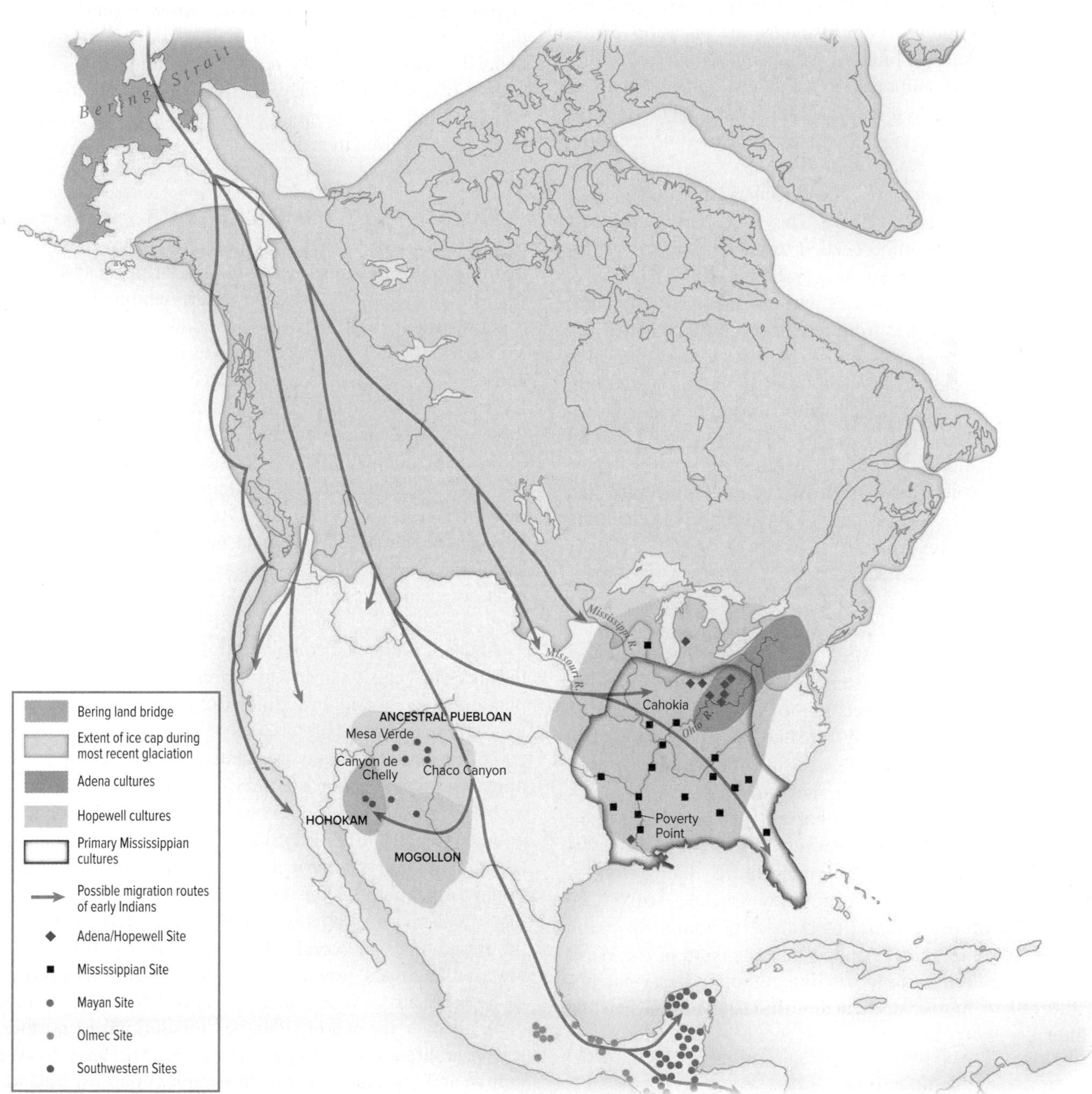

Bering Strait
Mississippi R.
Missouri R.
Ohio R.
Cahokia
Poverty Point
ANCESTRAL PUEBLOAN
Mesa Verde
Canyon de Chelly
Chaco Canyon
HOHOKAM
MOGOLLON
Bering land bridge
Extent of ice cap during most recent glaciation
Adena cultures
Hopewell cultures
Primary Mississippian cultures
Possible migration routes of early Indians
Adena/Hopewell Site
Mississippian Site
Mayan Site
Olmec Site
Southwestern Sites


## MAP 1.1: EARLY PEOPLES OF NORTH AMERICA

Migration routes across the Bering Strait from Asia were taken by peoples whose descendants created the major civilizations of ancient Americans. The influence of Mesoamerica is most striking among the cultures of the Southwest and the Mississippians.
*How would the presence or absence of the ice cap affect the timing of migration over the Bering land bridge?*

**The Plenty of the Pacific Northwest** >> The rugged stretch of coast from the southern banks of present-day British Columbia to northern California has always been an extraordinarily rich natural environment. Its mild climate and abundant rainfall yield forests lush with plants and game; its bays and rivers teem with salmon and halibut, its oceans with whales and porpoises, and its rocky beaches with seals, otters, abalone, mussels, and clams. Agriculture was unnecessary in such a bountiful place. From their villages on the banks of rivers, the shores of bays, and the beaches of low-lying offshore islands, the ancestors of the Nootkans, Makahs, Tlingits, Tshimshians, and Kwakiutls speared or netted salmon, trapped sea mammals, gathered shellfish, and launched canoes. The largest of these craft, from which they harpooned whales, measured 45 feet bow to stern and nearly 6 feet wide.

By the fifteenth century these fecund lands supported a population of perhaps 130,000. They also permitted a culture with the leisure time needed to create works of art as well as an elaborate social and ceremonial life. The peoples of the Northwest built houses and canoes from red cedar; carved bowls and dishes from red alder; crafted paddles and harpoon shafts, bows, and clubs from Pacific yew; and wove baskets from bark and blankets from mountain goat wool. They evolved a society with sharp distinctions among nobles, commoners, and slaves, the last group being mainly women and children captured in raids on other villages. Nonslaves devoted their lives to accumulating and then redistributing their wealth among other villagers in elaborate potlatch ceremonies in order to confirm or enhance their social prestige.

**The Frozen North** >> Most of present-day Canada and Alaska was inhospitable to agriculture. In the farthest northern reaches—a treeless belt of Arctic tundra—temperatures fell below freezing for most of the year. The Subarctic, although densely forested, had only about 100 frost-free days each year. As a result, the peoples of both regions survived by fishing and hunting. The Inuit, or Eskimos, of northern Alaska harvested whales from their umiaks, boats made by stretching walrus skin over a driftwood frame and that could bear more than a ton of weight. In the central Arctic they tracked seals. The inhabitants of the Subarctic, both Algonquian-speaking peoples in the East and Athapaskan speakers of the West, moved from their summer fishing camps to berry patches in the fall to moose and caribou hunting grounds in the winter.

How did native cultures differ region to region, and what accounts for these differences?

# INNOVATIONS AND LIMITATIONS

The first Americans therefore expressed, governed, and supported themselves in a broad variety of ways. And yet they shared certain core characteristics, including the desire and ability to reshape their world. Whether they lived in forests, coastal regions, jungles, or prairies, whether they inhabited high mountains or low deserts, native communities experimented constantly with the resources around them. Over the course of millennia nearly all the Western Hemisphere's peoples found ways to change the natural world in order to improve and enrich their lives.

**America's Agricultural Gifts** >> No innovation proved more crucial to human history than native manipulation of plants. Like all first farmers, agricultural pioneers in the Americas began experimenting accidentally. Modern-day species of corn, for example, probably derive from a Mesoamerican grass known as teosinte. It seems that ancient peoples gathered teosinte to collect its small grains. By selecting the grains that best suited them and bringing them back to their settlements, and by returning the grains to the soil through spillage or waste disposal, they unintentionally began the process of domestic cultivation. Soon these first farmers began deliberately saving seeds from the best plants and sowing them in gardens. In this way over hundreds of generations, American farmers transformed the modest teosinte grass into a staple crop that would give rise to the hemisphere's mightiest civilizations.

Indeed, ever since contact with Europe, the great breakthroughs in Native American farming have sustained peoples around the world. In addition to corn, the first Americans gave humanity scores of varieties of squash, potatoes, beans, and other basic foods. Today plants domesticated by indigenous Americans account for three-fifths of the world's crops, including many that have revolutionized the global diet. For good or ill, a handful of corn species occupies the center of the contemporary American diet. In addition to its traditional forms, corn is consumed in chips, breads, and breakfast cereals; corn syrup sweeteners are added to many of our processed foods and nearly all soft drinks; and corn is fed to almost all animals grown to be consumed, even farmed fish.

Other Native American crops have become integral to diets all over the world. Potatoes revolutionized northern European life in the centuries after contact, helping to avert famine and boost populations in several countries. Ireland's population tripled in the century after the introduction of potatoes. Beans and peanuts became prized in Asia for their protein content. And in Africa, corn, manioc, and other New World crops so improved diets and overall health that the resulting rise in population may have offset the population lost to the Atlantic slave trade.

21


^ Theodore de Bry, *Florida Indians Planting Maize*. De Bry claimed that this image, produced and published in 1591, was based on a colonist's direct observation. Recently, however, scholars have noted that the image likely contains a variety of inaccuracies. Except for the digging stick, the baskets and tools are all European in design. Moreover, the image suggests that men and women shared agricultural labor, whereas in most American societies this work fell primarily to women and children.
©Service Historique de la Marine, Vincennes, France/Bridgeman Images

**Landscapers** >> Plant domestication requires the smallest of changes, changes farmers slowly encourage at the genetic level. But native peoples in the precontact Americas transformed their world on grand scales as well. In the Andes, Peruvian engineers put people to work by the tens of thousands, creating an astonishing patchwork of terraces, dikes, and canals designed to maximize agricultural productivity. Similar public-works projects transformed large parts of central Mexico and the Yucatán. Even today, after several centuries of disuse, overgrowth, and even deliberate destruction, human-shaped landscapes dating from the precontact period still cover thousands of square miles of the Americas.

Recently scholars have begun to find evidence of incredible manipulation of landscapes and environments in the least likely places. The vast Amazon rain forest has long been seen by Westerners as an imposing symbol of untouched nature. But it now seems that much of the Amazon was in fact made by people. Whereas farmers elsewhere in the world domesticated plants for their gardens and fields, farmers in the Amazon cultivated food-bearing trees for thousands of years, cutting down less useful species and replacing them with ones that better suited human needs. All told there are more than 70 different species of domesticated trees throughout the Amazon.

At least one-eighth of the nonflooded rain forest was directly or indirectly created by humans. Likewise, native peoples laboriously improved the soil across as much as a tenth of the Amazon, mixing it with charcoal and a variety of organic materials. These managed soils are more than 10 times as productive as untreated soils in the Amazon. Today farmers in the region still eagerly search for the places where precontact peoples enriched the earth.

Native North Americans likewise transformed their local environments. Sometimes they moved forests. Ancestral Puebloans cut down and transported more than 200,000 trees to construct the floors and the roofs of the monumental buildings in Chaco Canyon. Sometimes they moved rivers. By taming the waters of the Salt and the Gila Rivers in present-day Arizona with the most extensive system of irrigation canals anywhere in precontact North America, the Hohokam were able to support large populations in a desert environment. And sometimes they moved the land itself. Twenty-two million cubic feet of earth were moved to construct just one building in the Mississippian city of Cahokia.

Indians also employed fire to systematically reshape landscapes across the continent. Throughout North America's great eastern and western forests, native peoples periodically set low fires to consume undergrowth and fallen trees. In this way the continent's first inhabitants managed forests and also animals. Burning enriched the soil and encouraged the growth of grasses and bushes prized by game animals such as deer, elk, beaver, rabbit, grouse, and turkey. The systematic use of fire to reshape forests helped hunters in multiple ways: it increased the overall food supply for grazing animals, it attracted those animal species hunters valued most, and, by clearing forests of ground debris, fire made it easier to track, kill, and transport game. Deliberate burns transformed forests in eastern North America to such an extent that bison migrated from their original ranges on the plains and thrived far to the east. Thus, when native hunters from present-day New York to Georgia brought down a buffalo, they were harvesting a resource that they themselves had helped to create.

**The Influence of Geography and Climate** >> No matter how great their ingenuity, the first Americans were constrained by certain natural realities. One of the most important is so basic that it is easy to overlook. Unlike Eurasia, which stretches across the Northern Hemisphere along an east-west axis, the Americas fall along a north-south axis, stretching nearly pole to pole.

^ Fewer large mammal species were available for domestication in the Americas, perhaps because the first wave of humans on the continent contributed to mass extinctions. Native Americans did domesticate dogs, shown here in a watercolor-and-ink sketch of a Mandan dog sled painted by Karl Bodmer in 1834.
©Free Library, Philadelphia, PA, USA/Bridgeman Images

Consequently, the Americas are broken up by tremendous geographic and climactic diversity, making communication and technology transfer far more difficult than it was in the Old World.

Consider the agricultural revolution in Eurasia. Once plants and animals were first domesticated in the Fertile Crescent around 10,000 years ago, they quickly began spreading east and west. Within 1,500 years these innovations had been adopted in Greece and India. A thousand years later the domesticated plants and animals of the Fertile Crescent had reached central Europe, and from there it took perhaps 200 years for them to be embraced in present-day Spain. Eurasia's east-west axis facilitated these transfers. Locations at roughly the same latitude share the same seasonal variation, have days of the same length, and often have similar habitats and rates of precipitation, making it relatively easy for plants and animals to move from one place to the next.

In contrast, the north-south orientation of the Americas erected natural barriers to plant and animal transfer. Mesoamerica and South America, for example, are about as far apart as the Balkans and Mesopotamia. It took roughly 2,000 years for plants and animals domesticated in Mesopotamia to reach the Balkans. But because Mesoamerica and South America are separated by tropical, equatorial lowlands, it took domesticated plants such as corn several thousand years to jump between the two regions. Sometimes the transfer never happened at all before European contact. South American potatoes would have thrived in central Mexico, but the tropics stopped their northward migration. Equatorial jungles also denied Mesoamerican societies the llama and the alpaca, domesticated more than 5,000 years ago in the Andes. One wonders what even greater heights the Olmec, Toltec, Mayan, and Aztec civilizations would have achieved if they had had access to these large creatures as draft animals and reliable sources of protein.

Dramatic variations in climate likewise delayed the transfer of agriculture from Mexico to regions north of the Rio Grande. Archaeologists have discovered evidence of 10,000-year-old domesticated squash in a cave in southern Mexico, an indication that agriculture began in the Americas nearly as early as anywhere else in the world. Yet squash and corn were not cultivated in the present-day American Southwest for another 7,000 years, and the region's peoples did not embrace a fully sedentary, agricultural lifestyle until the start of the Common Era. Major differences in the length of days, the growing season, average temperatures, and rainfall between the Southwest and central Mexico meant that farmers north of the Rio Grande had to experiment for scores of generations before they perfected crops suited to their particular environments. Corn took even longer to become a staple crop in eastern North America, which is why we do not see major urban centers arise there until approximately 1000 CE.

By erecting barriers to communication and the spread of technology, then, the predominantly north-south orientation of the Americas made it more difficult for the hemisphere's inhabitants to build on one another's successes. Had American innovations spread as quickly as innovations in Eurasia, the peoples of the Western Hemisphere would likely have been healthier, more numerous, and more powerful than they were when Europeans first encountered them in 1492.

**Animals and Illness** >> One other profound difference between the Eurasian world and the Americas concerned animals and disease. Most diseases affecting humans originated from domesticated animals, which came inevitably into frequent and close contact with the humans who raised them. As people across Eurasia embraced agriculture and started living with one another and with domesticated animals in crowded villages, towns, and cities, they created ideal environments for the evolution and transmission of infectious disease. For example, measles, tuberculosis, and smallpox all seem to have derived from diseases afflicting cattle.

Eurasians therefore paid a heavy price for living closely with animals. Yet in the long run the continent's terrible illnesses hardened its population. Victims who survived into adulthood enjoyed acquired immunity to the most common diseases: that is, if they had already encountered a particular illness as children, their immune systems would recognize and combat the disease more effectively in the event of reinfection. By the fifteenth century, then, Eurasian bodies had learned to live with a host of deadly communicable diseases.

But Native American bodies had not. With a few important exceptions, including tuberculosis, pneumonia, and possibly herpes and syphilis, human populations in the Western Hemisphere seem to have been relatively free from major communicable pathogens. Insofar as most major diseases emerge from domesticated animals, it is easy enough to see why. Indigenous Americans domesticated turkeys, dogs, Muscovy ducks, and guinea pigs but raised only one large mammal—the llama or alpaca (breeds of the same species).

This scarcity of domestic animals had more to do with available supply than with the interest or ability of their would-be breeders. The extinction of most species of megafauna soon after humans arrived in the Americas deprived the hemisphere of 80 percent of its large mammals. Those that remained, including modern-day bison, elk, deer, and moose, were more or less immune to domestication because of peculiarities in their dispositions, diets, rates of growth, mating habits, and social characteristics. In fact, of the world's 148 species of large mammals, only 14 were successfully domesticated before the twentieth century. Of those 14 only 1—the ancestor to the llama/alpaca—remained in the Americas following the mass extinctions. Eurasia, in contrast, was home to 13—including the 5 most common and adaptable domestic mammals: sheep, goats, horses, cows, and pigs.

With virtually no large mammals to domesticate, Native Americans were spared the nightmarish effects of most of the world's major communicable diseases—until 1492. After that date European colonizers discovered the grim advantage of their millennia-long dance with disease. Old World infections that most colonizers had experienced as children raged through indigenous communities, usually doing the greatest damage to adults whose robust immune systems reacted violently to the novel pathogens. Often native communities came under attack from multiple diseases at the same time. Combined with the wars that attended colonization and the malnutrition, dislocation, and despair that attend wars, disease would kill native peoples by the millions while European colonizers increased and spread over the land. Despite their ingenuity and genius at reshaping plants and environments to their advantage, native peoples in the Americas labored under crucial disadvantages compared to Europe—disadvantages that would contribute to disaster after contact.

 **REVIEW**

How did the native inhabitants of the Americas transform their environments? What natural constraints put them at a disadvantage to Europeans?

# CRISIS AND TRANSFORMATION

With its coastal plains, arid deserts, broad forests, and vast grassy plains, North America has always been a place of tremendous diversity and constant change. Indeed, many of the continent's most dramatic changes took place in the few centuries before European contact. Because of a complex and still poorly understood combination of ecological and social factors, the continent's most impressive civilizations collapsed as suddenly and mysteriously as had those of the Olmecs and the Mayas of Mesoamerica. In the Southwest the Mogollon culture went into eclipse around the twelfth century, the Hohokam and the Ancestral Puebloans by about the fourteenth. In the Eastern Woodlands the story was strikingly similar. Most of the great Mississippian population centers, including the magnificent city of Cahokia, had faded by the fourteenth century.

**Enduring Peoples** >> The survivors of these crises struggled to construct new communities, societies, and political systems. In the Southwest descendants of the Hohokam withdrew to small farming villages that relied on simpler modes of irrigation. Refugees embarked on a massive, coordinated exodus from the Four Corners region and established new, permanent villages in Arizona and New Mexico that the Spaniards would collectively call the Pueblos. The Mogollon have a more mysterious legacy, but some of their number may have helped establish the remarkable trading city of Paquime in present-day Chihuahua. Built around 1300 Paquime contained more than 2,000 rooms and had a sophisticated water and sewage system unlike any other in the Americas. The city included 18 large mounds, all shaped differently from one another, and three ballcourts reminiscent of those found elsewhere in Mexico. Until its demise sometime in the fifteenth century Paquime was the center of a massive trading network, breeding macaws and turkeys for export and channeling prized feathers, turquoise, seashells, and worked copper throughout a huge region.

The dramatic transformations remaking the Southwest involved tremendous suffering. Southwesterners had to rebuild in unfamiliar and oftentimes less productive places. Although some of their new settlements endure even to this day, many failed. Skeletal analysis from an abandoned pueblo on the Rio Grande, for example, indicates that the average life expectancy was only 16.5 years. Moreover, drought and migrations increased conflict over scarce resources. The most successful new settlements were large, containing several hundred people, and constructed in doorless, defensible blocks, or else set on high mesas to ward off enemy attacks. These changes were only compounded by the arrival of Athapaskan-speaking peoples (known to the

Spanish as Apaches and Navajos) in the century or two before contact with Europeans. These hunters and foragers from western Canada and Alaska moved in small bands, were sometimes friendly, sometimes hostile toward different Pueblos, and eventually became key figures in the postcontact Southwest.

In the Eastern Woodlands the great Mississippian chieftainships never again attained the glory of Cahokia, but key traditions endured in the Southeast. In the lower Mississippi valley the Natchez maintained both the temple mound-building tradition and the rigid social distinctions of Mississippian civilization. Below the chief, or "Great Sun," of the Natchez stood a hereditary nobility of lesser "Suns" who demanded respect from the lowly "Stinkards," the common people. Other Muskogean-speakers rejected this rigid and hierarchical social model and gradually embraced a new, more flexible system of independent and relatively **egalitarian** villages that forged confederacies to better cope with outsiders. These groupings would eventually mature into three of the great southeastern Indian confederacies: Creek, Choctaw, and Chickasaw.

**egalitarian** exhibiting or asserting a belief in the equality of humans in a social, political, or economic context.

To the north lived speakers of Iroquoian languages, roughly divided into a southern faction including Cherokees and Tuscaroras, and a northern faction including the powerful Iroquois and Hurons. Like Muskogean peoples to the south, these Iroquoian communities mixed farming with a hunting/gathering economy and lived in semipermanent towns. The distinctive feature of Iroquois and Huron architecture was not the temple mound but rather the longhouse (some stretching up to 100 feet in length). Each sheltered as many as 10 families.

Algonquian speakers were the third major group of Eastern Woodland people. They lived along the Atlantic seaboard and the Great Lakes in communities that were generally smaller than those of people speaking Muskogean or the Iroquoian languages. By the fifteenth century the coastal communities from southern New England to Virginia had adopted agriculture to supplement their diets, but those in the colder northern climates with shorter growing seasons depended entirely on hunting, fishing, and gathering plants such as wild rice.

Cultures of equal and even greater resources persisted and flourished during the fifteenth century in the Caribbean, particularly on the Greater Antilles—the islands of present-day Cuba, Haiti and the Dominican Republic, Jamaica, and Puerto Rico. Although the earliest inhabitants of the ancient Caribbean, the Ciboneys, probably came from the Florida peninsula, it was the Tainos, later emigrants from northern South America, who expanded throughout the Greater Antilles and the Bahamas. Taino chiefs known as *caciques*, along with a small number of noble families, ruled island tribes, controlling the production and distribution of food and tools and exacting tribute from the great mass of commoners, farmers, and fisherfolk. Attending to these elites were the poorest Taino peoples—servants who bedecked their masters and mistresses in brilliant diadems of feathers, fine woven textiles, and gold nose and ear pieces and then shouldered the litters on which the rulers sat and paraded their finery.

## North America on the Eve of Contact >>

By the end of the fifteenth century, 5 to 10 million people lived north of the Rio Grande—with perhaps another million living on the islands of the Caribbean—and they were spread among more than 350 societies speaking nearly as many distinct languages. (The total precontact population for all of the Americas is estimated at between 57 and 112 million.)

These millions lived in remarkably diverse ways. Some peoples relied entirely on farming; others on hunting, fishing, and gathering; still others on a combination of the two. Some, such as the Natchez and the Iroquois, practiced matrilineal forms of kinship, in which women owned land, tools, and even children. Among others, such as the Algonquians, patrilineal kinship prevailed, and all property and prestige descended in the male line. Some societies, like those of the Great Plains and the Great Basin in the West, the Inuit in the Arctic, and the Iroquoians and Algonquians in the East, were roughly egalitarian, whereas others, like many in the Caribbean and the Pacific Northwest, were rigidly divided into nobles and commoners and servants or slaves. Some, such as the Natchez and the Taino, were ruled by powerful chiefs; others, such as the Algonquians and the Pueblos, by councils of village elders or heads of family clans; still others in the Great Basin, the Great Plains, and the Far North looked to the most skillful hunter or the most powerful shaman for direction. Those people who relied on hunting practiced religions that celebrated their kinship with animals and solicited their aid as guardian spirits, whereas predominantly agricultural peoples sought the assistance of their gods to make the rain fall and the crops ripen.

When Europeans first arrived in North America, the continent north of present-day Mexico boasted an ancient and rich history marked by cities, towns, and prosperous farms. At contact it was a land occupied by several million men, women, and children speaking hundreds of languages and characterized by tremendous political, cultural, economic, and religious diversity. This diversity was heightened by the north-south orientation of the Americas rather than the east-west orientation of Eurasia, since the spread of crops and animals in temperate regions was impeded by the tropical zones of the equator. The isolation from European diseases would make Europeans' arrival after 1492 even more devastating. Before 1492, though, the civilizations of North and South America remained populous, dynamic, and diverse.

**REVIEW**

What was life like in the Americas on the eve of European contact?

For most of our nation's short history we have not wanted to remember things this way. European Americans have had a variety of reasons to minimize and belittle the past, the works, even the size of the native populations that ruled North America for 99 percent of its human history. In 1830, for example, President Andrew Jackson delivered an address before Congress in which he tried to answer the many critics of his Indian removal policies. Although "humanity has often wept over the fate of the aborigines of this country," Jackson said, the Indians' fate was as natural and inevitable "as the extinction of one generation to make room for another." He reminded his listeners of the mysterious mounds that had so captivated the founding fathers. "In the monuments and fortresses of an unknown people, spread over the extensive regions of the West, we behold the memorials of a once powerful race, which was exterminated, or has disappeared, to make room for the existing savage tribes." Just as the architects of the mounds supposedly met their end at the hands of these "savage tribes," the president concluded, so, too, must Indians pass away before the descendants of Europe.

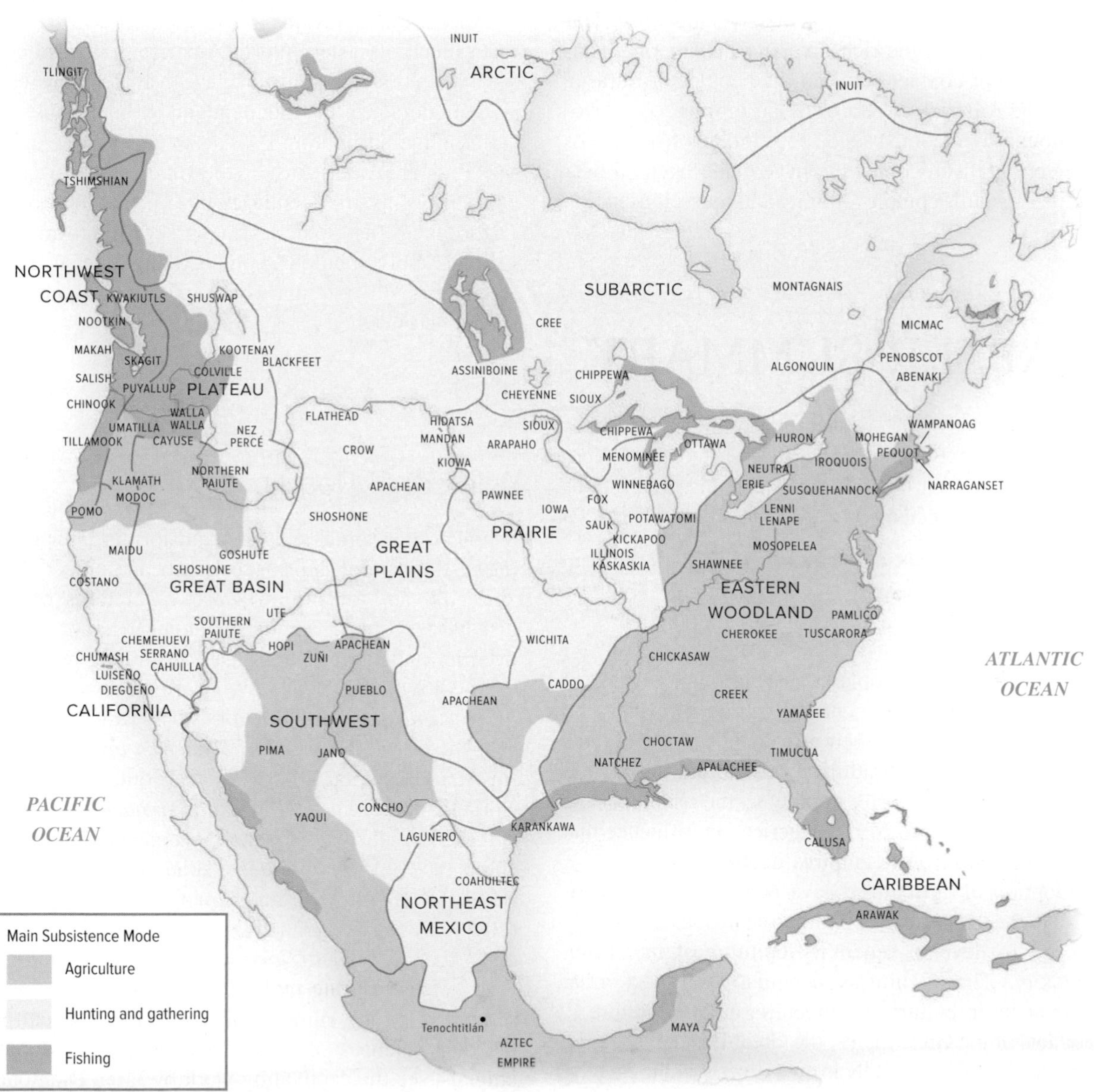
INUIT
ARCTIC
INUIT
TLINGIT
TSHIMSHIAN
NORTHWEST COAST
KWAKIUTLS
SHUSWAP
NOOTKIN
MAKAH
SKAGIT
SALISH
PUYALLUP
CHINOOK
KOOTENAY
BLACKFEET
COLVILLE
PLATEAU
WALLA WALLA
UMATILLA
TILLAMOOK
CAYUSE
NEZ PERCÉ
NORTHERN PAIUTE
KLAMATH
MODOC
POMO
MAIDU
GOSHUTE
SHOSHONE
GREAT BASIN
COSTANO
SOUTHERN PAIUTE
UTE
CHEMEHUEVI
CHUMASH
SERRANO
CAHUILLA
LUISEÑO
DIEGUEÑO
CALIFORNIA
PACIFIC OCEAN
SUBARCTIC
MONTAGNAIS
CREE
MICMAC
ASSINIBOINE
CHIPPEWA
ALGONQUIN
PENOBSCOT
ABENAKI
CHEYENNE
SIOUX
FLATHEAD
HIDATSA
MANDAN
SIOUX
ARAPAHO
CROW
KIOWA
CHIPPEWA
OTTAWA
MENOMINEE
HURON
MOHEGAN
PEQUOT
WAMPANOAG
IROQUOIS
NEUTRAL
ERIE
NARRAGANSET
APACHEAN
PAWNEE
WINNEBAGO
FOX
SUSQUEHANNOCK
SHOSHONE
IOWA
POTAWATOMI
LENNI LENAPE
PRAIRIE
SAUK
KICKAPOO
GREAT PLAINS
ILLINOIS
KASKASKIA
MOSOPELEA
SHAWNEE
EASTERN WOODLAND
PAMLICO
CHEROKEE
TUSCARORA
HOPI
APACHEAN
ZUÑI
WICHITA
CHICKASAW
ATLANTIC OCEAN
CADDO
PUEBLO
APACHEAN
CREEK
SOUTHWEST
YAMASEE
PIMA
JANO
CHOCTAW
NATCHEZ
APALACHEE
TIMUCUA
CONCHO
YAQUI
KARANKAWA
LAGUNERO
CALUSA
COAHUILTEC
NORTHEAST MEXICO
CARIBBEAN
ARAWAK
Main Subsistence Mode
Agriculture
Hunting and gathering
Fishing
Tenochtitlán
AZTEC EMPIRE
MAYA

## MAP 1.2: INDIGENOUS NORTH AMERICA, CA. 1500

Establishing the location of native groups in maps of precontact America is always problematic, since many peoples undertook major migrations in the contact period, boundaries between groups were fluid, and names applied to native communities usually differ from what those communities called themselves before colonization. Nonetheless, this map depicts the rough location of some prominent native peoples and their main modes of subsistence on the eve of contact.

*California is well suited to farming, yet its large precontact population practiced very little agriculture. Why?*

"What good man would prefer a country covered with forests and ranged by a few thousand savages, to our extensive republic, studded with cities, towns, and prosperous farms; embellished with all the improvements which art can devise, or industry execute; occupied by more than twelve millions of happy people, and filled with all the blessings of liberty, civilization, and religion!"

Indeed, stories told about the past have power over both the present and the future. Jackson and many others of his era preferred a national history that contained only a few thousand ranging "savages" to one shaped by millions of indigenous hunters, farmers, builders, and inventors. Yet every generation rewrites its history, and what seems clear from this latest draft is the rich diversity of American cultures on the eve of contact between the peoples of Eurasia, Africa, and the Americas. We are still struggling to find stories big enough to encompass not only Indians from across the continent but also people who have come from all over the world to forge this complex, tragic, and marvelous nation of nations.

# CHAPTER SUMMARY

During the thousands of years after bands of Siberian nomads migrated across the Bering Strait to Alaska, their descendants spread throughout the Americas, creating civilizations that rivaled those of ancient Europe, Asia, and Africa.

- Around 1500 BCE Mesoamerica emerged as the hearth of civilization in the Western Hemisphere, a process started by the Olmecs and brought to its height by the Mayas and Aztecs.
- These Mesoamerican peoples devised complex ways of organizing society, government, and religious worship and built cities remarkable for their art, architecture, and trade.
- Both commerce and migration spread cultural influences throughout the hemisphere, notably to the islands of the Caribbean basin and to North America, an influence that endured long after these empires declined.
- The adoption of agriculture gave peoples in the Southwest and the Eastern Woodlands the resource security necessary to develop sedentary cultures of increasing complexity. These cultures eventually enjoyed great achievements in culture, architecture, and agriculture.
- Inhabitants of the Great Plains, the Great Basin, the Arctic, and the Subarctic evolved their own diverse cultures, relying for subsistence on fishing, hunting, and gathering.
- Peoples of the Pacific Northwest boasted large populations and prosperous economies as well as an elaborate social, ceremonial, and artistic life.
- The native inhabitants of the Americas transformed their environments in a variety of ways, from pioneering crops that would eventually feed the world to landscaping mountains and cultivating jungles.
- Nonetheless, natural constraints would leave Native Americans at a disadvantage compared to Europe. The continent's north-south orientation inhibited the spread of agriculture and technology, and a lack of domesticatable animals compared to Europe left Native Americans with little protection against disease.
- For reasons that remain unclear, many of North America's most impressive early civilizations had collapsed by the end of the fifteenth century. In their wake a diverse array of cultures evolved across the continent.
- In the Southwest, Pueblo Indians were joined by Athapaskan-speakers whom Europeans would later call Apaches and Navajos.
- In much of eastern North America, stratified chiefdoms of the Mississippian era gave way to more egalitarian confederacies of independent villages subsisting on farming and hunting.
- Although Americans in the nineteenth, twentieth, and even twenty-first centuries have been slow to recognize the fact, the societies of precontact America were remarkably populous, complex, and diverse. Their influence would continue to be felt in the centuries after contact.

## Additional Reading

Scholars in several fields are transforming our understanding of the Americas prior to European contact. The magazine *Archaeology* offers clear explanations of the latest discoveries for nonscientific audiences. For an excellent overview, attentive to controversies among researchers, see Charles C. Mann, *1491: New Revelations of the Americas before Columbus* (2005). For North America specifically, see Alice Beck Kehoe, *North America before the European Invasions* (2nd ed., 2016). For the Southwest, see Linda S. Cordell and Maxine E. McBrinn, *Archaeology of the Southwest* (2012). For the Eastern Woodlands, see George R. Milner, *The Moundbuilders: Ancient Peoples of Eastern North America* (2005); and Timothy Pauketat, ed., *Cahokia* (2010). Roger G. Kennedy, *Hidden Cities: The Discovery and Loss of Ancient North American Civilization* (1994), gives a fascinating account of how white Americans responded to the ruins of ancient American cultures. For the consequences of axis alignment and of domesticated animals, see the captivating work by Jared Diamond, *Guns, Germs, and Steel: The Fates of Human Societies* (1998).

For the cultures of precontact Mexico, see Michael D. Coe and Rex Koontz, *Mexico: From the Olmecs to the Aztecs* (7th ed., 2013). For exhaustive surveys of all regional cultures in North America, see William C. Sturtevant, general editor, *Handbook of North American Indians*, 15 volumes to date (1978–2008).

# 2 Old Worlds, New Worlds

## 1400–1600

With sails bellying in a gale, this Dutch ship faced the shallows of a rocky coast. Western European sailors risked much as they crossed the Atlantic in search of fish, silver, gold, and other commodities to trade.



### >> An American Story

## FISHING NETS AND FAR HORIZONS

All the world lay before them. Or so it seemed to mariners from England's seafaring "West Country" coasts, pushing toward unknown lands in the far Atlantic.

The scent of the new land came first—not the sight of it, but the smells, perhaps the scent of fir trees wafted from beyond the horizon, delicious to sailors who had felt nothing but the rolling sea for weeks on end. Straightaway the captain would call for a lead to be thrown overboard to sound the depths. At its end was a hollowed-out socket with a bit of tallow in it, so that some of the sea bottom would stick when the lead was hauled up. A good sailing master could tell where he was by what came up—"oozy sand" or perhaps "soft worms" or "pipplestones" (smooth pebbles) as big as beans.

Through much of the fifteenth century the search for cod had drawn West Country sailors north and west, toward Iceland. In the 1480s and 1490s a few English tried their luck farther west. They returned with little to show for their daring until the coming of an Italian named Giovanni Caboto, called John Cabot by the English. Cabot, who hailed from Venice, obtained the blessing of King Henry VII to hunt for unknown lands. From the port of Bristol his lone ship set out to the west in the spring of 1497.

This time the return voyage brought news of a "new-found" island where the trees were tall enough to make fine masts and the codfish were plentiful. After returning to Bristol, Cabot marched off to London to inform His Majesty, received 10 pounds as his reward, and with the proceeds dressed himself in dashing silks. The multitudes of London flocked after him, wondering over "the Admiral"; then Cabot returned triumphantly to Bristol to undertake a more ambitious search for a northwest passage to Asia. He set sail with five ships in 1498 and was never heard from again.

By the 1550s Cabot's island, now known as Newfoundland, attracted 400 vessels annually, fishermen not only from England but also from France, Portugal, and Spain. The harbor of present-day St. John's, Newfoundland, served as the informal hub of the North Atlantic fishery. Sailors from three kingdoms dropped anchor there to take on supplies in the spring, trade with native peoples, or prepare for the homeward voyage in autumn. There was eager conversation at this meeting place, for these seafarers knew as much as anyone—if not more—about the new world of wonders that was opening to Europeans. They were acquainted with names such as Cristoforo Colombo, the Italian from Genoa whom Cabot might have known as a boy. They listened to Portuguese tales of sailing around the Horn of Africa in pursuit of spices and to stories of Indian empires to the south, rich in gold and silver that Spanish treasure ships were bringing home.

Indeed, Newfoundland was one of the few places in the world where so many ordinary folk of different nations could gather and talk, crammed aboard dank ships moored in St. John's harbor, huddled before blazing fires on its beaches, or crowded into smoky makeshift taverns. When the ships sailed home in autumn, the tales went with them, repeated in the tiniest coastal villages by those pleased to have cheated the sea and death one more time. Eager to fish, talk, trade, and take profits, West Country mariners were almost giddy at the prospect of Europe's expanding horizons.

Most seafarers who fished the waters of Newfoundland's Grand Banks remain unknown today. Yet it is well to begin with these ordinary fisherfolk, for the European discovery of the Americas cannot be looked on simply as the voyages of a few bold explorers. Adventurers such as Christopher Columbus and John Cabot were only the most visible representatives of a much larger expansion of European peoples and culture that began in the 1450s. That expansion arose out of a series of gradual but telling changes in the fabric of European society—changes reflected in the lives of ordinary seafarers as much as in the careers of explorers decked out in silks.

Some of these changes were technological, arising out of advances in the arts of navigating and shipbuilding and the use of gunpowder. Some were economic, involving the development of trade networks such as those linking Bristol with ports in Iceland and Spain. Some were **demographic,** bringing about a rise in Europe's population after a devastating century of plague. Other changes were religious, adding a dimension of devout belief to the political rivalries that fueled discoveries in the Americas. Yet others were political, making it possible for kingdoms to centralize and extend their influence across the ocean. Portugal, Spain, France, and England—all possessing coasts along the Atlantic—led the way in exploration, spurred on by Italian "admirals" such as Caboto and Colombo, Spanish *conquistadores*—"conquerors"—such as Hernán Cortés and Francisco Pizarro, and English sea dogs such as Humphrey Gilbert and Walter Raleigh. Ordinary folk rode these currents, too. The great and the small alike were propelled by forces that were remolding the face of Europe—and were beginning to remold the face of the world. <<

**demographic** factors relating to the characteristics of populations. Demography is the study of populations, looking at such aspects as size, growth, density, and age distribution.

## THEMATIC TIMELINE

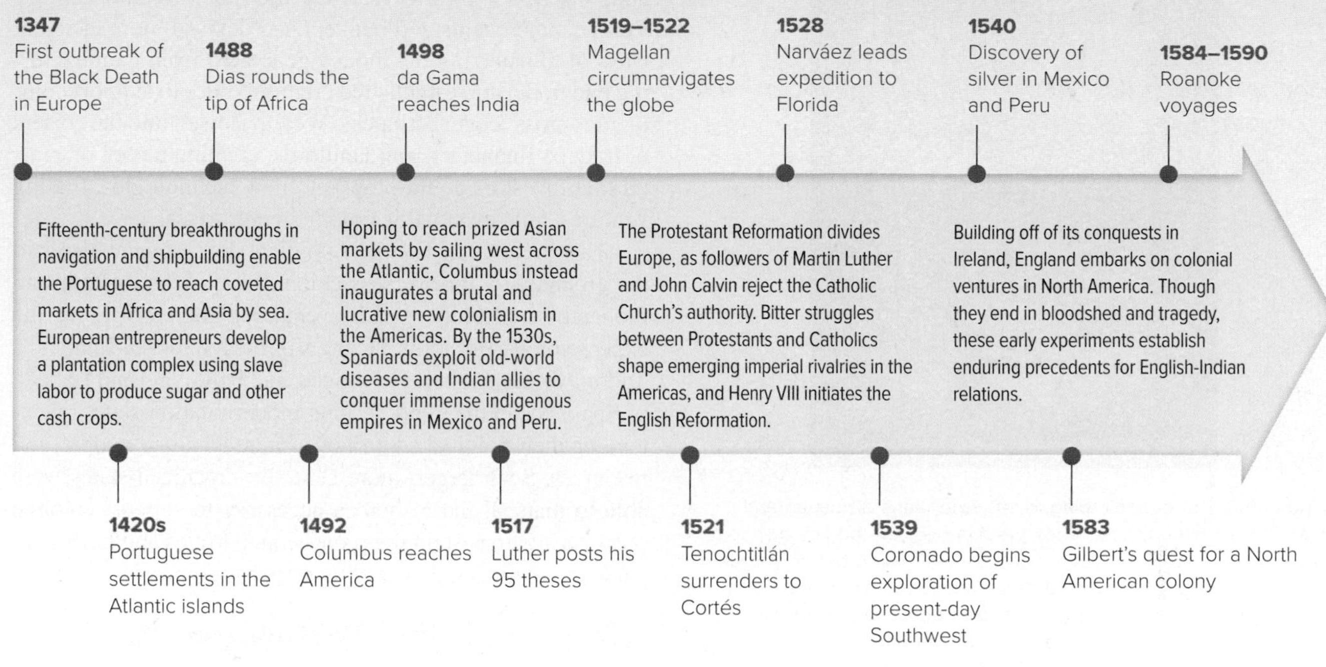
1347
First outbreak of the Black Death in Europe
1488
Dias rounds the tip of Africa
1498
da Gama reaches India
1519–1522
Magellan circumnavigates the globe
1528
Narváez leads expedition to Florida
1540
Discovery of silver in Mexico and Peru
1584–1590
Roanoke voyages
Fifteenth-century breakthroughs in navigation and shipbuilding enable the Portuguese to reach coveted markets in Africa and Asia by sea. European entrepreneurs develop a plantation complex using slave labor to produce sugar and other cash crops.
Hoping to reach prized Asian markets by sailing west across the Atlantic, Columbus instead inaugurates a brutal and lucrative new colonialism in the Americas. By the 1530s, Spaniards exploit old-world diseases and Indian allies to conquer immense indigenous empires in Mexico and Peru.
The Protestant Reformation divides Europe, as followers of Martin Luther and John Calvin reject the Catholic Church's authority. Bitter struggles between Protestants and Catholics shape emerging imperial rivalries in the Americas, and Henry VIII initiates the English Reformation.
Building off of its conquests in Ireland, England embarks on colonial ventures in North America. Though they end in bloodshed and tragedy, these early experiments establish enduring precedents for English-Indian relations.
1420s
Portuguese settlements in the Atlantic islands
1492
Columbus reaches America
1517
Luther posts his 95 theses
1521
Tenochtitlán surrenders to Cortés
1539
Coronado begins exploration of present-day Southwest
1583
Gilbert's quest for a North American colony

# EURASIA AND AFRICA IN THE FIFTEENTH CENTURY

In 1450, the western European kingdoms that would one day dominate much of the world still sat at the fringe of an international economy that revolved around China. By a variety of measures Ming China was the richest, most powerful, and most advanced society in the world. All Eurasia sought Chinese goods, especially spices, ceramics, and silks, and Chinese ships sped these goods to faraway ports. Seven times between 1405 and 1433 China's "treasure fleet"—300 ships manned by 28,000 sailors and commanded by Zheng He (pronounced "Jung Huh")—unfurled its red silk sails off the south China coast and traveled as far as the kingdoms of eastern Africa. The treasure fleet's largest craft were nine-masted junks measuring 400 feet long, sporting multiple decks and luxury cabins. By comparison, Columbus's largest ship in 1492 was a mere 85 feet long, and the crew aboard all three of his ships totaled just 90 men. Political turbulence led Chinese leaders to ground their trading fleet and end the long-distance voyages. But Chinese luxuries, most transported overland, continued to be Eurasia's most sought-after commodities.

The next mightiest powers in the Old World were not European kingdoms but rather huge Islamic empires, especially the Ottomans in the eastern Mediterranean. The Ottomans rose to prominence during the fourteenth and fifteenth centuries, gaining control of critical trade routes and centers of commerce between Asia and Europe. Their greatest triumph came in 1453, when the sultan Mehmet II conquered Constantinople (now Istanbul), the ancient and supposedly impregnable Christian city that straddled Europe and Asia. Mehmet's stunning victory sounded alarms throughout Europe.

**Europe's Place in the World** >> Europe's rulers had good reason for alarm. Distant from Asia's profitable trade and threatened by the Ottomans' military might, most of the continent remained fractious and vulnerable. During the fourteenth and fifteenth centuries 90 percent of Europe's people, widely dispersed in small villages, made their living from the land. But warfare, poor transportation, and low grain yields all created food shortages, and undernourishment produced a population prone to disease. Under

^ The spread of bubonic plague left Europeans dismayed and desperate. While a priest reads prayers over the bodies being buried in a common grave, a man suddenly taken by the plague writhes in agony. In the background, a cart collects more corpses. And in heaven (*upper left*) St. Sebastian, a Christian martyr, intercedes with God to end the suffering.


these circumstances life was, to paraphrase the English philosopher Thomas Hobbes, nasty, brutish, and usually short. One-quarter of all children died in the first year of life. People who reached the age of 40 counted themselves fortunate.

It was also a world of sharp inequalities, where nobles and aristocrats enjoyed several hundred times the income of peasants or craftworkers. It was a world with no strong, centralized political authority, where kings were weak and warrior lords held sway over small towns and tiny fiefdoms. It was a world of violence and sudden death, where homicide, robbery, and rape occurred with brutal frequency. It was a world where security and order of any kind seemed so fragile that most people clung to tradition, and more than a few used witchcraft in an attempt to master the chaotic and unpredictable world around them.

But Europe was changing, in part because of a great calamity. Between the late 1340s and the early 1350s bubonic plague—known as the Black Death—swept away one-quarter of Europe's population. Some urban areas lost 70 percent of their people to the disease. The Black Death disrupted both agriculture and commerce, and provoked a spiritual crisis that resulted in violent, unsanctioned religious movements, scapegoating of marginal groups, even massacres of Jews. Although Europeans seem to have met recurrent outbreaks of the disease with less panic, the sickness continued to disrupt social and economic life.

Yet the sudden drop in population relieved pressure on scarce resources. Survivors of the Black Death found that the relative scarcity of workers and consumers made for higher wages, lower prices, and more land. These changes promoted an overall expansion of trade. In earlier centuries Italian merchants had begun encouraging commerce across Europe and tapping into trade from Africa, the Middle East, and, when able, from Asia. By the late fifteenth century Europe's merchants and bankers had devised more efficient ways of transferring the money generated from manufacturing and trade, and established credit in order to support commerce across longer distances. Wealth flowed into the coffers of traders, financiers, and landlords, creating a pool of capital that investors could plow into new technologies, trading ventures, and, eventually, colonial enterprises.

The direction of Europe's political development also laid the groundwork for overseas colonization. After 1450 strong monarchs in Europe steadily enlarged their power at the expense of warrior lords. Henry VII, the founder of England's Tudor dynasty, Francis I of France, and Ferdinand and Isabella of Spain began the trend, forging modern nation-states by extending their political control over more territory, people, and resources. Such larger, more centrally organized states were able to marshal the resources necessary to support colonial outposts and to sustain the professional armies and navies capable of creating and protecting overseas empires.

## Africa and the Portuguese Wave >>

European expansion began with Africa. For centuries African spices, ivory, and gold had entered the Eurasian market either through ports on the Indian Ocean or through the Sahara Desert and into the Mediterranean Sea. Powerful African kingdoms controlled the routes through which these prized commodities moved, while Islamic expansion in the fifteenth century made competition all the more intense. European merchants yearned to access West African markets directly, by ship. But navigational and shipbuilding technology was not yet up to the challenge of the Atlantic's prevailing currents, which sped ships south along Africa's coast but made the return voyage virtually impossible.

Portugal was the first to solve this problem and tap directly into West African markets, thanks in large part to Prince Henry "the Navigator," as he became known. An ardent Catholic and a man who dreamed of turning back Islam's rising tide, Henry understood that direct commerce with West Africa would allow his kingdom to circumvent the costly trans-Sahara trade. To forward his vision Henry funded exploratory voyages, established a maritime school, and challenged sailors and engineers to conquer the problem of the current. The Portuguese responded by developing the caravel, a lighter, more maneuverable ship that could sail better against contrary winds and in rough seas. More seaworthy than the lumbering galleys of the Middle Ages, caravels combined longer, narrower hulls—a shape built for speed—with triangular lateen sails, which allowed for more flexible steering. The caravel allowed the Portuguese to regularly do what few Europeans had ever done: sail down Africa's west coast and return home. Other advances, including a sturdier version of the Islamic world's astrolabe, enabled Portugal's navigators to calculate their position at sea with unprecedented accuracy.

As the Portuguese pressed southward along the Atlantic rim of sub-Saharan Africa, they began to meet peoples who had never encountered Europeans or even possessed any knowledge of other continents. On catching their first sight of a Portuguese expedition in 1455, villagers on the Senegal River marveled at the strangers' clothing and their white skin. An Italian member of that expedition recounted that some Africans "rubbed me with their spittle to discover whether my whiteness was dye or flesh."

But the Portuguese were wrong to mistake such acts of innocence for economic or political naïveté. Formidable African chiefdoms and states were eager to trade with Europeans but intent on protecting already established commercial networks. Portugal could not simply take what it wanted from West Africa. With few exceptions, it proved impossible for European powers to colonize territory in West Africa before the nineteenth century, because the region's people were too many and too organized. Furthermore, malaria would kill between one-fourth and one-half of all Portuguese unwise enough to try to stay.

To succeed, the newcomers had to seek partners. As the Portuguese built forts and trading houses on the coast, they gave tribute or taxes to local powers in return for trading privileges. The Portuguese offered textiles, especially, but also raw and worked metal goods, currency (in the form of cowry shells), and beads. In return Africans gave up prized commodities such as gold, ivory, and malaguetta pepper. Portuguese traders also expressed interest in another commodity, one that would reshape the wider Atlantic world: slaves.

## Sugar and the Origins of the Atlantic Slave Trade >>

Unfree labor has existed in nearly all human societies. Although the norms, characteristics, and economic importance of slavery have varied widely over time and place, men, women, and children have been held as slaves from before recorded history to the present. (U.S. and international organizations estimate that today there are as many as 27 million people held in some form of labor bondage and that nearly 1 million unfree people are sold across international borders every year.)

By the Middle Ages, elites in Europe had largely abandoned the slave culture of the Roman Empire and relied instead on serfs or peasants for labor. Slaves became more important as status symbols than as workers, and most were young white women. Indeed, the word *slave* comes originally from "Slav"; Slavic girls and women from the Balkans and the coasts of the Black Sea were frequent targets of slave raids.

But European slavery began to change again following the Crusades. In 1099 Christian forces captured Jerusalem from the Seljuk Turks and discovered sugar plantations that the Turks had cultivated in the Holy Land. Crusaders recognized sugar's economic potential. But because sugar required intense work during planting and close tending during the growing season, they found it a difficult commodity to produce. On maturity the crop had to be harvested and processed 24 hours a day to avoid being spoiled. In short, sugar demanded cheap, pliable labor, and the newly arrived crusaders relied in part on slaves.

When Islamic forces under the famed leader Saladin reconquered Jerusalem in the twelfth century, European investors established new plantations on eastern Mediterranean islands. In addition to being labor intensive, though, sugar was a crop that quickly exhausted soils and forced planters to move operations regularly. Plantations spread to new islands, and by the early 1400s sugar was even being grown in Portugal. As production expanded, planters had to work harder than ever to obtain the necessary labor because of the Black Death and because Turkish conquests restricted European access to the traditional slaving grounds of the eastern Mediterranean and the Balkans.

Thus by the fifteenth century the Portuguese were already using slave labor to grow sugar on plantations, but they were seeking new cropland and new sources of slaves. Once again Prince Henry's vision enhanced his kingdom's economic interests. While Portugal's merchants were establishing trading posts along the west coast of Africa, Iberian mariners were discovering or rediscovering islands in the eastern Atlantic: the Canaries, Madeira, and the Azores, islands with rich, volcanic soils ideally suited to sugarcane. By the late 1400s sugar plantations were booming on the Atlantic islands, worked by West African slaves. By 1550 people of African descent accounted for 10 percent of the population of Lisbon, Portugal's capital city.

^ The manufacture of sugar produced large profits but required intense labor under harsh conditions. It also fueled the growth of a new, enlarged slave trade. At this Brazil sugar plantation from around 1640, slaves work at a sugar mill powered by a water wheel at the far right. The sharp distinction in social hierarchy is shown in the lower left, where other slaves transport the wife of the plantation master in a tented hammock suspended from a pole.
©Album/Oronoz/Newscom

Now convinced that they could reach coveted Asian markets by sea, ambitious Portuguese mariners sailed their caravels farther and farther south. In 1488 Bartolomeu Dias rounded the Cape of Good Hope on the southern tip of Africa, sailing far enough up that continent's eastern coast to claim discovery of a sea route to India. Ten years later Vasco da Gama reached India itself, and Portugal's interests ultimately extended to Indochina and China.

Portuguese geographers had long felt certain that travel around Africa was the shortest route to the Orient, but an Italian sailor disagreed. Cristoforo Colombo had spent a decade gaining experience from Portugal's master mariners. He also threw himself into research, devouring Lisbon's books on geography and cartography. Columbus (the Latinized version of his name) became convinced that the fastest route to China lay west, across the uncharted Atlantic Ocean. He appealed to Portugal's king to support an exploratory voyage, but royal geographers scoffed at the idea. They agreed that the world was round but insisted (correctly, as it turns out) that the globe was far larger than Columbus had calculated, making any westward route impractical. Almost a decade of rejection had grayed Columbus's red hair, but—undaunted—he packed up in 1485 and took his audacious idea to Spain.

**REVIEW**

Why did Europeans begin to develop commercial networks in the Atlantic, and how did the Portuguese operate in Africa?

# SPAIN IN THE AMERICAS

He arrived a few years too early. Spain's monarchs, Ferdinand and Isabella, rejected Columbus's offer because they were engaged in a campaign to drive the Muslims out of their last stronghold on the Iberian Peninsula, the Moorish kingdom of Granada. For centuries Arab rulers from Africa had controlled part of present-day Spain and Portugal. But in 1492 Ferdinand and Isabella finally completed what was known as the ***Reconquista,*** their military reconquest of this territory. Flush with victory, the pair listened to Columbus argue that a westward route to Asia would allow Spain to compete with Portugal and generate enough revenue to continue the reconquest, even into the Holy Land itself. Ignoring the advice of their geographers, the monarchs agreed to his proposal.

***Reconquista*** military reconquest of the Iberian Peninsula from Islamic Moors of Africa by European Christian rulers.

Columbus's first voyage across the Atlantic could only have confirmed his conviction that he was destiny's darling. His three ships, no bigger than fishing vessels that sailed to Newfoundland, plied their course over placid seas, south from Seville to the Canary Islands and then due west. On October 11, a little more than two months after leaving Spain, branches, leaves, and flowers floated by their hulls, signals that land lay near. Just after midnight a sailor spied cliffs shining white in the moonlight. On the morning of October 12, the *Niña,* the *Pinta,* and the *Santa Maria* set anchor in a shallow sapphire bay, and their crews knelt on the white coral beach. Columbus christened the place San Salvador (Holy Savior).

**The Spanish Beachhead in the Caribbean** >> Like many men of destiny, Columbus mistook his true destination. At first he confused his actual location, the Bahamas, with an island near Japan. He coasted along Cuba and Hispaniola (today's Haiti and Dominican Republic), expecting at any moment to catch sight of gold-roofed Japanese temples or fleets of Chinese junks. He encountered instead a gentle, generous people who knew nothing of the Great Khan but who welcomed the newcomers profusely. Columbus's journals note that they wore little clothing, but they did wear jewelry—tiny pendants of gold suspended from the nose. He dubbed the Taino people "Indians"—inhabitants of the Indies.

It would take some years before other mariners and geographers understood clearly that these newfound islands and the landmasses beyond them lay between Europe and Asia. One of the earliest geographers to do so was the Florentine Amerigo Vespucci, who first described Columbus's Indies as *Mundus Novus,* a "New World." Rather than dub the new lands "Columbia," a German mapmaker called them "America" in Vespucci's honor. The German's maps proved wildly successful, and the name stuck.

Unlike the kingdoms of West Africa, the Taino chiefdoms lacked the military power to resist European aggression. And Europeans decided that the societies they encountered were better suited to be ruled than partnered with. Moreover, while the newfound islands eventually presented their own threats to European health, they seemed a good deal more inviting than the deadly coast of West Africa. Hints of gold, a seemingly weak and docile population, and a relatively healthy climate all ensured that Columbus's second voyage would be one of colonization rather than commerce. During the 1490s and early 1500s Spanish colonizers imposed a brutal regime on the Tainos, slaughtering native leaders and forcing survivors to toil in mines and fields.

Only a few Spaniards spoke out against the exploitation. Among them was Bartolomé de las Casas, a man who spent several years in the Caribbean, participating in conquests and profiting from native labor. Eventually las Casas renounced his conduct and, as a Dominican friar, became a tireless foe

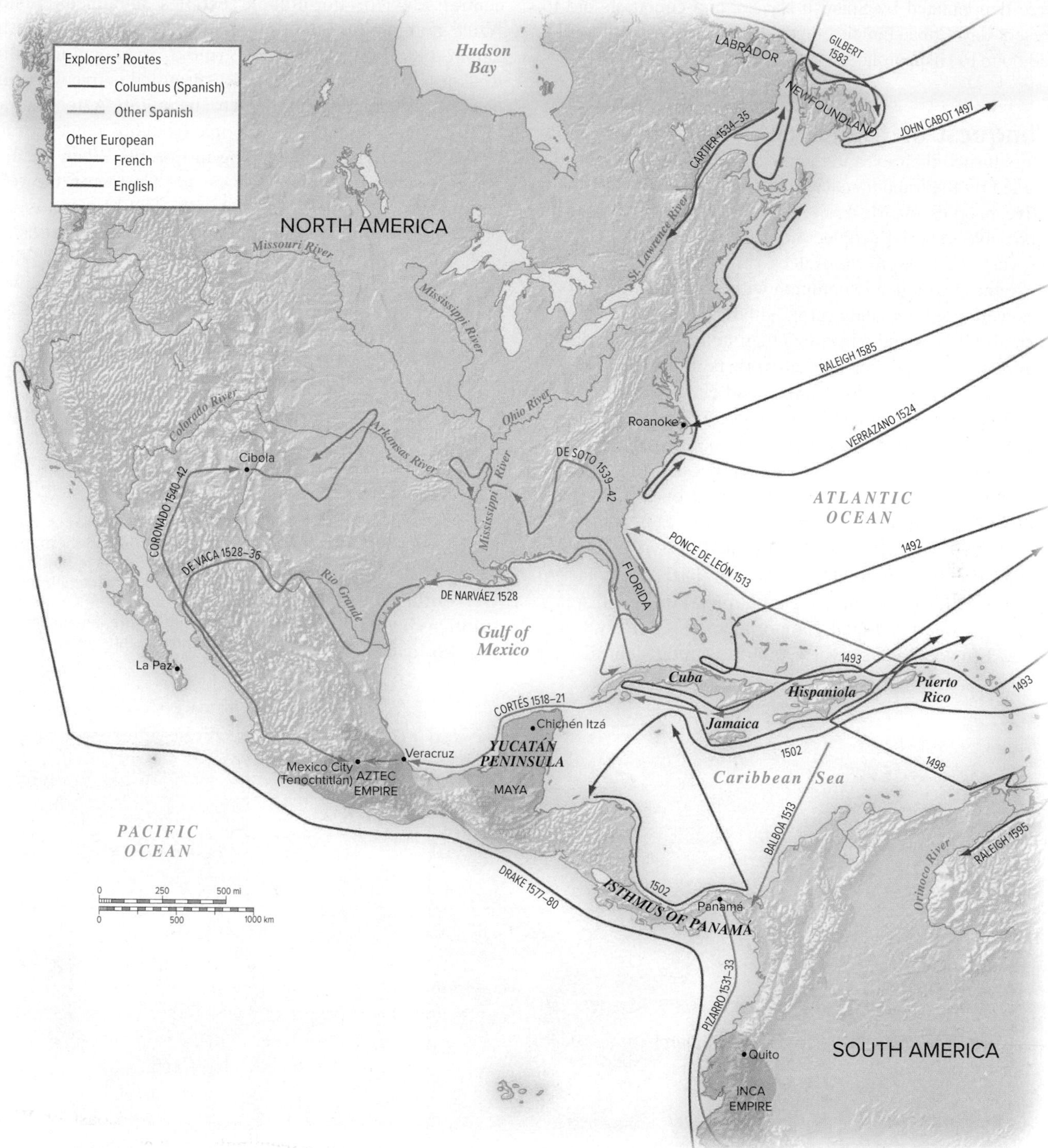

Explorers' Routes
Columbus (Spanish)
Other Spanish
Other European
French
English
Hudson Bay
LABRADOR
GILBERT 1583
NEWFOUNDLAND
JOHN CABOT 1497
CARTIER 1534–35
St. Lawrence River
NORTH AMERICA
Missouri River
Mississippi River
RALEIGH 1585
Colorado River
Ohio River
Roanoke
VERRAZANO 1524
Arkansas River
Cibola
DE SOTO 1539–42
CORONADO 1540–42
ATLANTIC OCEAN
DE VACA 1528–36
PONCE DE LEÓN 1513
1492
Rio Grande
DE NARVÁEZ 1528
FLORIDA
Gulf of Mexico
La Paz
1493
Cuba
Hispaniola
Puerto Rico
CORTÉS 1518–21
Chichén Itzá
Jamaica
Veracruz
YUCATÁN PENINSULA
1502
1498
Mexico City (Tenochtitlán)
AZTEC EMPIRE
MAYA
Caribbean Sea
PACIFIC OCEAN
BALBOA 1513
RALEIGH 1595
Orinoco River
DRAKE 1577–80
1502
ISTHMUS OF PANAMÁ
Panamá
PIZARRO 1531–33
Quito
SOUTH AMERICA
INCA EMPIRE


# MAP 2.1: PRINCIPAL ROUTES OF EUROPEAN EXPLORATION

of Spanish cruelties toward Indians. He railed against the "unjust, cruel, and tyrannical" war waged to force the native peoples into "the hardest, harshest, and most heinous bondage to which men or beasts might ever be bound into." Las Casas's writings, translated throughout Europe and illustrated with gruesome drawings, helped give rise to the "Black Legend" of Spanish atrocities in the Americas.

The warnings had some effect, but not for decades. Within a generation of Columbus's landfall, the Taino population had nearly collapsed from war, overwork, malnutrition, despair, and strange new Eurasian diseases. Ambitious Spaniards began scouring the Caribbean basin, discovering new lands and searching for new populations of Indians to subjugate or enslave in place of the vanishing Tainos. Soon the Bahamas were depopulated by Spanish slavers, and conquests did to present-day Cuba, Jamaica, and Puerto Rico what they first had done to Hispaniola.

## Conquest of the Aztecs

>> Would-be conquistadors turned their eyes to the mainland. In 1519 an expedition led by the impetuous Hernán Cortés made contact with native peoples on Mexico's gulf coast. They spoke of an oppressive imperial people who occupied a fantastic city to the west. These were the Aztecs.

Aztecs had much in common with Spaniards. Both societies were predominantly rural, with most inhabitants living in small villages and engaging in agriculture. In both places merchants and specialized craftworkers clustered in cities, organized themselves into guilds, and clamored for protection from the government. Aztec noble and priestly classes, like those in Europe, took the lead in politics and religion, demanding tribute from the common people. Finally, both societies were robustly expansionist, bent on bringing new lands and peoples under their control.

Yet critical differences between these two peoples shaped the outcome of their meeting. The Aztecs lacked the knowledge of ocean navigation, metal tools and weaponry, and firearms. Equally important, the relatively young Aztec Empire had not yet established total control over central Mexico. Formidable peoples remained outside Aztec domination, and conquered city-states within the empire bitterly resented Aztec rule. Cortés exploited that weakness. Massing an army of disgruntled native warriors, he and his men marched inland to the mighty Aztec capital, Tenochtitlán, home to more people (roughly a quarter million) than any city then existing in Europe. When the emperor Moctezuma's ambassadors met Cortés on the road and attempted to appease him with gold ornaments and other gifts, an Indian witness noted that "the Spaniards . . . picked up the gold and fingered it like monkeys. . . . Their bodies swelled with greed." The newcomers were welcomed into the city as honored guests but soon seized Moctezuma and took him captive. For months Cortés ruled the empire indirectly, but the Aztecs drove the Spanish out after Moctezuma's death.

In the midst of this victory the city encountered another foe—smallpox. Geographically isolated from Eurasia and its complex disease environment, the Aztecs and all other native peoples in the Americas lacked the acquired immunity that gave Europeans a degree of protection against Old World pathogens. The resulting **virgin soil epidemics**—so called because the

**virgin soil epidemics** epidemics in which the populations at risk have had no previous contact with the diseases that strike them and are therefore immunologically almost defenseless.

RITR. DI MOTEZVMA
CAVATO DALL'ORIGINA
VENVTO DAL MESSICO
AL SER. G.D. DI TOSCA

^ Both the Aztecs and the Spanish tried to understand the new in terms of the familiar. Hence an Aztec artist portrayed Cortés as an Indian with strange clothes and a stranger beard, whereas a European artist depicted Moctezuma in the style of a Greco-Roman warrior. The figure speaking to Cortés is Doña Marina (mentioned in Document 1), a Nahua captive who became Cortés's indispensable translator and mother of his first son.
(*Left*) ©The Art Gallery Collection/Alamy; (*right*) Source: Library of Congress, Prints and Photographs Division [LC-USZ62-43530]

*Many* HISTORIES

## How Did Spaniards and Aztecs Remember First Contact?

*The first encounter between the Spaniards under Hernán Cortés and ambassadors of the emperor Moctezuma in 1519 represents a fateful turning point in history. While we have no full contemporary account of that meeting, two remarkable sources present Spanish and Mexican memories of the event written years later. The first selection below was written in the 1560s by one of Cortés's lieutenants, the conquistador Bemal Díaz. The second section comes from a work compiled in the 1540s by the missionary Bernardino de Sahagún, in which indigenous informants recalled Aztec culture, religion, society, and history up to and through the conquest.*

### DOCUMENT 1
### Bernal Díaz

Seeing the big ship with the standards flying they knew that it was there that they must go to speak with the captain; so they went direct to the flagship and going on board asked who was the Tatuan [Tlatoan] which in their language means the chief. Doña Marina who understood the language well, pointed him out. Then the Indians paid many marks of respect to Cortés, according to their usage, and bade him welcome, and said that their lord, a servant of the great Montezuma, had sent them to ask what kind of men we were and of what we were in search. . . . [Cortés] told them that we came to see them and to trade with them and that our arrival in their country should cause them no uneasiness but be looked on by them as fortunate. . . .

[Several days later, one of Montezuma's emissaries] brought with him some clever painters such as they had in Mexico and ordered them to make pictures true to nature of the face and body of Cortés and all his captains, and of the soldiers, ships, sails, and horses, and of Doña Marina and Aguilar, even of the two greyhounds, and the cannon and cannon balls, and all of the army we had brought with us, and he carried the pictures to his master. Cortés ordered our gunners to load the lombards with a great charge of powder so that they should make a great noise when they were fired off. . . . [The emissary] went with all haste and narrated everything to his prince, and showed him the pictures which had been painted. . . .

*Source:* Díaz, Bernal, "The True History of the Conquest of New Spain," excerpted from Schwartz, Stuart B., ed., *Victors and Vanquished: Spanish and Nahua Views of the Conquest of Mexico.* Boston, MA: Bedford/St. Martin, 2000, pp. 85–90.

### DOCUMENT 2
### Fray Bernardino de Sahagún

When they had gotten up into [Cortés's] boat, each of them made the earth-eating gesture before the Captain. Then they addressed him, saying, "May the god attend; his agent Moteucçoma who is in charge in Mexico for him addresses him and says, 'The god is doubly welcome.'"

Then they dressed up the Captain. They put on him the turquoise serpent mask attached to the quetzal-feather head fan, to which were fixed, from which hung the green-stone serpent earplugs. And they put the sleeveless jacket on him, and around his neck they put the plaited green-stone neckband with the golden disk in the middle. On his lower back they tied the back mirror, and also they tied behind him the cloak called a *tzitzilli.* And on his legs they placed the green-stone bands with the golden bells. And they gave him, placing it on his arm, the shield with gold and shells crossing, on whose edge were spread quetzal feathers, with a quetzal banner. And they laid the obsidian sandals before him. . . .

Then the Captain ordered that they be tied up: they put irons on their feet and necks. When this had been done they shot off the cannon. And at this point the messengers truly fainted and swooned; one after another they swayed and fell, losing consciousness. . . . Then [Cortés] let them go.

[Upon returning to Tenochtitlán and reporting to Moteucçoma, he replied] "I will not hear it here. I will hear it at the Coacalco; let them go there." And he gave orders, saying, "Let some captives be covered in chalk [for sacrifice]."

Then the messengers went to the Coacalco, and so did Moteucçoma. There upon the captives died in their presence; they cut open their chests and sprinkled their blood on the messengers. (The reason they did it was that they had gone to very dangerous places and had seen, gazed on the countenances of, and spoken to the gods.) . . .

When this was done, they talked to Moteucçoma, telling him what they had beheld, and they showed him what [the Spaniards'] food was like.

And when he heard what the messengers reported, he was greatly afraid and taken aback, and he was amazed at their food. It especially made him faint when he heard how the guns went off at [the Spaniards'] command, sounding like thunder, causing people to actually swoon, blocking the ears. And when it went off, something like a ball came out from inside, and fire went showering and spitting out. And the smoke that came out had a very foul stench, striking one in the face. And if they shot at a hill, it seemed to crumble and come apart. . . . Their war gear was all iron. They clothed their bodies in iron, they put iron on their heads, their swords were iron, their bows were iron, and their shields were iron.

And the deer that carried them were as tall as the roof. And they wrapped their bodies all over; only their faces could be seen, very white. . . .

And their dogs were huge creatures, with their ears folded over and their jowls dragging. They had burning eyes, eyes like coals, yellow and fiery. . . .

When Moteucçoma heard it, he was greatly afraid; he seemed to faint away, he grew concerned and disturbed.

*Source:* Fray Bernardino de Sahagún, *Florentine The Codex*, excerpted in Schwartz, ed. *Victors and Vanquished*, pp. 91–99.

### THINKING CRITICALLY

*How did the Aztecs and the Spaniards communicate? Why does Díaz pay so little attention to the gifts the emissaries brought Cortés? Why might the painters be absent from the Nahua account? What principles of critical thinking should be kept in mind when reading such documents?*

victims had no previous exposure—took a nightmarish toll. Smallpox claimed millions in central Mexico between 1520 and 1521. This, too, presented Cortés with opportunities. Supported by a massive Indian force, he put Tenochtitlán to siege, killing tens of thousands before the ragged, starving survivors surrendered in August of 1521. The feared Aztec Empire lay in ruins. Conquistadors fanned out from central Mexico, overwhelming new populations and eventually learning of another mighty kingdom to the South. Again relying on political faction, disease, technological advantages, and luck, by 1532 Spaniards under Francisco Pizarro and his brothers had conquered the Inca Empire in South America, which in certain regards outshone even the Aztecs.

**The Columbian Exchange** >> Virgin soil epidemics, which contributed to the collapse of many Indian populations, were only one aspect of a complex web of interactions between the flora and fauna of the Americas on the one hand and those of Eurasia and Africa on the other. Just as germs migrated along with humans, so did plants and animals. These transfers, begun in the decades after Columbus first landed in the Caribbean, are known by historians as the **Columbian exchange,** and they had far-reaching effects on both sides of the Atlantic. Europeans brought a host of American crops home with them, as seen in Chapter 1. They also most likely brought syphilis, an American disease that broke out across Europe in more virulent form than ever before. Europeans brought to the Americas the horses and large dogs that intimidated the Aztecs; they brought oranges, lemons, figs, and bananas from Africa and the Canary Islands. Escaped hogs multiplied so rapidly that they overran some Caribbean islands, as did European rats.

**Columbian exchange** transition of people, plants, insects, and microbes between the two hemispheres, initiated when Columbus reached the Americas in 1492.

The Columbian exchange was not a short-lived event. In a host of different ways it reshaped the globe over the next 500 years as travel, exploration, and colonization brought cultures ever closer. Instead of smallpox, today bird flu from Asia or the West Nile virus threatens populations worldwide. But the exchanges of the sixteenth century were often more extreme, unpredictable, and far-reaching, because of the previous isolation of the two hemispheres.

**The Crown Steps In** >> Proud conquistadors did not long enjoy their mastery in the Americas. Spain's monarchs, who had just tamed an aristocracy at home, were not about to allow a colonial nobility to arise across the Atlantic. The Crown bribed the conquistadors into retirement—or was saved the expense when men such as Francisco Pizarro were assassinated by their own followers. The task of governing Spain's new colonies passed from the conquerors to a small army of officials, soldiers, lawyers, and Catholic bishops, all appointed by the Crown, reporting to the Crown, and loyal to the Crown. Headquartered in urban centers such as Mexico City (formerly Tenochtitlán), an elaborate, centralized bureaucracy administered the Spanish Empire, regulating nearly every aspect of economic and social life.

Few Spaniards besides imperial officials settled in the Americas. By 1600 only about 5 percent of the colonial population was of Spanish descent, the other 95 percent being of Indian, African, or mixed heritage. Even by 1800 only 300,000 Spanish immigrants had come to live in the Americas. Indians often remained on the lands that they had farmed under the Aztecs and the Incas, now paying Spanish overlords their taxes and producing livestock for export. More importantly, Indians paid for the new order through their labor, sometimes as slaves but more often through an evolving administrative system channeling native workers to public and private enterprises throughout the Americas. The Spanish also established sugar plantations in the West Indies; these were worked by black slaves who by 1520 were being imported from Africa in large numbers.

Spain's colonies returned even more spectacular profits by the 1540s—the result of huge discoveries of silver in both Mexico and South America. Silver mining developed into a large-scale capitalist enterprise requiring substantial investment. European investors and Spanish immigrants who had profited from cattle raising and sugar planting poured their capital into equipment and supplies used to mine the silver deposits more efficiently: stamp mills, water-powered crushing equipment, pumps, and mercury. Whole villages of Indians were pressed into service in the mines, joining black slaves and free European workers employed there.

By 1570 the town of Potosí in present-day Bolivia, the site of a veritable mountain of silver, had become larger than any city in either Spain or its American empire, with a population of 120,000. Local farmers who supplied mining centers with food and Spanish merchants in Seville who exported European goods to Potosí profited handsomely. So, too, did the Spanish Crown, which claimed one-fifth of all extracted silver. During the sixteenth century, some 16,000 tons of the precious metal were exported from Spanish America to Europe.

## The Search for North America's Indian Empires

>> Riches and glory radicalized Spanish expectations. Would-be conquistadors embarked on an urgent race to discover and topple the next Aztec or Inca Empire, a race to become the next Cortés or Pizarro. The prevailing mood was captured by the portrait of a Spanish soldier that adorns the frontispiece of a book about the West Indies. He stands with one hand on his sword and the other holding a pair of compasses on top of a globe. Beneath is inscribed the motto "By compasses and the sword/More and more and more and more."

Some of the most ambitious adventurers felt certain that more lands and riches would be found in the North. The Spanish had probed the North American coast up to present-day South Carolina, looking for slaves. But Juan Ponce de León, the conquerer of Puerto Rico, launched the first official expedition to the mainland, which he named Florida in 1513. Everywhere he met armed resistance and was repulsed, because the inhabitants had come to despise Spaniards as slave raiders. Eight years later, he returned, only to be mortally wounded in a battle with Calusa Indians.

Still, the dreams of northern Indian empires persisted. In 1528 Pánfilo de Narváez, a red-bearded veteran from the conquest of Cuba, led a major expedition back to Florida. Ignoring advice from his second-in-command, Alvar Núñez Cabeza de Vaca, Narváez separated from his main force near Tampa Bay and led 300 men on a harrowing march in search of riches. For months Narváez plundered his way through Florida, while the men fell ill or fell victim to Indian archers, whose longbows could bury an arrow six inches into a tree. Disillusioned and desperate, 242 survivors lashed together makeshift rafts and tried to sail along the Gulf Coast to Mexico. Weeks later proud Narváez and most of his men had disappeared at sea, whereas Cabeza de Vaca and a handful of survivors washed up on islands off the Texas coast.

Local Indian groups then turned the tables and made slaves of the Spaniards. After years as prisoners Cabeza de Vaca and three others, including an African slave named Esteban, escaped to make an extraordinary trek across Texas and northern Mexico. Somewhere in present-day Chihuahua they passed through what had been the trading hinterland of Paquime, and Cabeza de Vaca noted an enduring regional commerce in feathers and "green stones"—turquoise. Finally, in July 1536 a shocked party of Spanish slavers stumbled across the four rag-tag castaways and brought them to Mexico City.

The stories the four men told of their ordeal inspired two more massive expeditions to the north. The first, led by Hernán de Soto, scoured the Southeast's agricultural villages searching for gold and taking whatever he wanted: food, clothing, luxury goods, even young women whom he and his men "desired both as servants and for their foul uses. . . ." De Soto's men became the first and last Europeans to glimpse several declining Mississippian chiefdoms, echoes of Cahokia's ancient majesty. Some native communities resisted, inflicting substantial losses on the expedition. Others feigned friendship and sent de Soto to hunt gold in neighboring villages, thus ridding themselves of a great danger and directing it at enemies instead. De Soto's men never found the treasures they sought as they traveled through much of the present-day South (see Map 2.1). But the expedition's cruel and destructive foray did hasten the transformation of the southeastern chiefdoms into decentralized confederacies.

Spanish ambition met a similar fate in the West. In 1539, 29-year-old Francisco Vázquez de Coronado led 300 Spaniards and 1,000 Mexican Indian warriors north into the present-day American Southwest. Coronado was emboldened by tales of cities more wondrous than Tenochtitlán, but his brash confidence began to fail him when instead he found only mud and straw pueblos inhabited by modest farmers. Desperate to turn his hugely expensive expedition to advantage, Coronado sent men in all directions. To the west his scouts were blocked by the vastness of the Grand Canyon. Others traveled east, forcing themselves on the Pueblo peoples of the upper Rio Grande, descendants of the Anasazi. Finally Coronado followed an Indian he dubbed the Turk out onto the Great Plains in search of a rumored kingdom called Quivira. Perhaps the Turk had in mind one of the easternmost Mississippian chiefdoms, but the frustrated conquistador

^ These colorful glass beads, discovered at a site in Georgia in 2006 and after, are valuable evidence helping to pin down where Hernán de Soto traveled during the expedition that set out in 1539. The first beads were found by a high school intern at the dig. This style of bead, fashioned by combining layers of different colored glass, was made only during the years de Soto set out for the Americas.

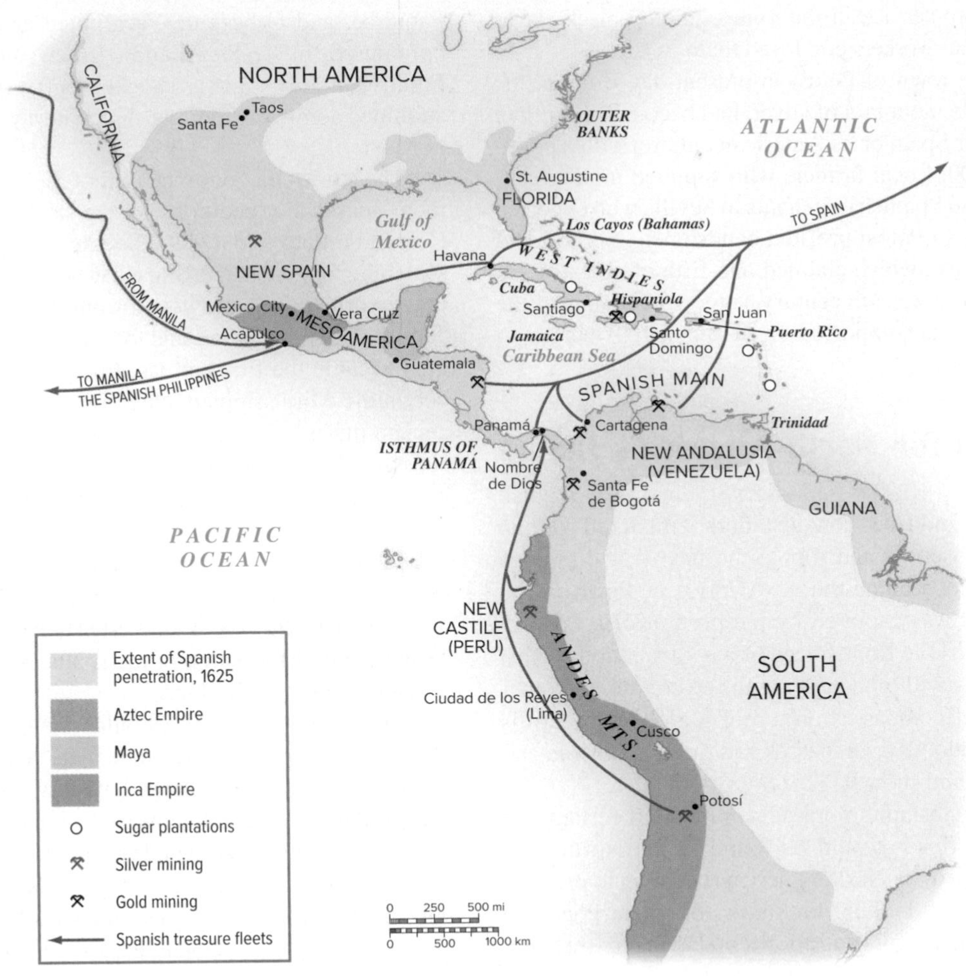

NORTH AMERICA
CALIFORNIA
Taos
Santa Fe
OUTER BANKS
ATLANTIC OCEAN
St. Augustine
FLORIDA
TO SPAIN
Gulf of Mexico
Los Cayos (Bahamas)
Havana
WEST INDIES
NEW SPAIN
FROM MANILA
Mexico City
Vera Cruz
Cuba
Santiago
Hispaniola
San Juan
Puerto Rico
Acapulco
MESOAMERICA
Jamaica
Santo Domingo
Caribbean Sea
Guatemala
TO MANILA
THE SPANISH PHILIPPINES
SPANISH MAIN
Panamá
Cartagena
Trinidad
ISTHMUS OF PANAMÁ
Nombre de Dios
NEW ANDALUSIA (VENEZUELA)
Santa Fe de Bogotá
GUIANA
PACIFIC OCEAN
NEW CASTILE (PERU)
ANDES MTS.
SOUTH AMERICA
Ciudad de los Reyes (Lima)
Cusco
Potosí
Extent of Spanish penetration, 1625
Aztec Empire
Maya
Inca Empire
Sugar plantations
Silver mining
Gold mining
Spanish treasure fleets
0 250 500 mi
0 500 1000 km


## MAP 2.2: SPANISH AMERICA, CA. 1600

By 1600 Spain was extracting large amounts of gold and silver from Mexico and South America, as well as profits from sugar plantations in the Caribbean. Each year, Spanish treasure ships ferried bullion from mines such as the one at Potosí to the Isthmus of Panama, where it was transported by land to the Caribbean coast and from there to Spain. An expedition from Acapulco sailed annually to the Philippines as well, returning with Asian spices and other trade goods.
*For an English adventurer looking to capture Spanish silver, which geographic location would be the best place to pick off Spanish treasure ships?*

became convinced he had been deceived. He had the Turk strangled somewhere in present-day Kansas and in 1542 returned to Mexico, where Crown authorities tried him for inflicting "great cruelties" on Indians.

Such North American expeditions ruined conquistadors such as Coronado and de Soto, but Spain could afford these blunders. It had taken vast wealth from the Americas, conquered the Western Hemisphere's mightiest peoples, and laid claim to the bulk of the New World. Yet for most of the sixteenth century rival European powers took little interest in the Americas. England's fishermen continued to explore the North Sea, Labrador, and Newfoundland. Portugal discovered and laid claim to Brazil. France launched expeditions along North America's eastern shoreline (Giovanni da Verrazano, 1524) and the St. Lawrence River valley (Jacques Cartier, 1534, 1535, and 1541). These efforts proved important in the long run, but for most of the century Spain could treat the Americas as its own.

Spain owed that luxury, in part, to religious upheaval in Europe. During the second decade of the sixteenth century—the same decade in which Cortés laid siege to Tenochtitlán—religious changes of enormous significance began spreading through Europe. That revolution in Christianity, known as the Protestant Reformation, occupied European attention and eventually figured as a crucial force in shaping the history of the Americas.

**REVIEW**

How did the Spanish respond to the discovery of a "new world"?

# RELIGIOUS REFORM DIVIDES EUROPE

During the Middle Ages, the Roman Catholic Church defined what it meant to be a Christian in western Europe. Like other institutions of medieval society, the Catholic Church was a hierarchy. At the top was the pope in Rome, and under him were the descending ranks of other church officials—cardinals, archbishops, bishops. At the bottom of the Catholic hierarchy were parish priests, each serving his own village, as well as monks and nuns living in monasteries and convents. But medieval popes were weak, and their power was felt little in the lives of most Europeans. Like political units of the era, religious institutions of the Middle Ages were local and decentralized.

Between about 1100 and 1500, however, as the monarchs of Europe grew more powerful, so too did the popes. The Catholic Church acquired land throughout Europe, and its swelling bureaucracy added to church income from tithing (taxes contributed by church members) and from fees paid by those appointed to church offices. In the thirteenth century church officials also began to sell "indulgences." For ordinary believers who expected to spend time after death purging their sins in purgatory, the purchase of an indulgence promised to shorten that punishment by drawing on a "treasury of merit" amassed by the good works of Christ and the saints.

By the fifteenth century the Catholic Church and the papacy had become enormously powerful but increasingly indifferent to popular religious concerns. Church officials meddled in secular politics. Popes and bishops flaunted their wealth, while poorly educated parish priests neglected their pastoral duties. At the same time, popular demands for religious assurance grew increasingly intense.

**The Teachings of Martin Luther** >> Into this climate of heightened spirituality stepped Martin Luther, who abandoned studying the law to enter a monastery. Like many of his contemporaries, Luther was consumed by fears over his eternal fate. He was convinced that he was damned, and he could not find any consolation in the Catholic Church. Catholic doctrine taught that a person could be saved by faith in God and by his or her own good works—by leading a virtuous life, observing the sacraments (such as baptism, the Mass, and penance), making pilgrimages to holy places, and praying to Christ and the saints. Because Luther believed that human nature was innately evil, he despaired of being able to lead a life that "merited" salvation. If men and women are so bad, he reasoned, how could they ever win their way to heaven with good works?

Luther finally drew on the Bible to break through his despair. It convinced him that God did not require fallen humankind to earn salvation. Salvation, he concluded, came by faith alone, the "free gift" of God to undeserving sinners. The ability to live a good life could not be the *cause* of salvation but its *consequence:* once men and women believed that they had saving faith, moral behavior was possible. Luther elaborated that idea, known as "justification by faith alone," between 1513 and 1517.

Luther was ordained a priest and then assigned to teach at a university in Wittenberg, Germany. He became increasingly critical, however, of the Catholic Church as an institution. In 1517 he posted on the door of a local church 95 theses attacking the Catholic hierarchy for selling salvation in the form of indulgences.

The novelty of this attack was not Luther's open break with Catholic teaching. Challenges to the church had cropped up throughout the Middle Ages. What was new was the passion and force behind Luther's protest. Using the blunt, earthy Germanic tongue, he expressed the anxieties of many devout laypeople and their outrage at the church hierarchy's neglect. The "gross, ignorant asses and knaves at Rome," he warned, should keep their distance from Germany, or else "jump into the Rhine or the nearest river, and take . . . a cold bath."

The pope and his representatives in Germany at first tried to silence Martin Luther, then excommunicated him. But opposition only pushed Luther toward more radical positions. He asserted that the church and its officials were not infallible; only the Scriptures were without error. Every person, he said, should read and interpret the Bible for himself or herself. In an even more direct assault on church authority, he advanced an idea known as "the priesthood of all believers." Catholic doctrine held that salvation came only through the church and its clergy, a privileged group that possessed special access to God. Luther asserted that every person had the power claimed by priests.

Although Luther had not intended to start a schism within Catholicism, independent Lutheran churches were forming in Germany by the 1520s. During the 1530s Luther's ideas spread throughout Europe, where they were eagerly taken up by other reformers.

**The Contribution of John Calvin** >> Luther's most influential successor was John Calvin, a French lawyer turned theologian. Calvin agreed with Luther that men and women could not merit their salvation. But, whereas Luther's God was a loving deity who extended his mercy to sinful humankind, Calvin conceived of God as awesome, all-knowing and all-powerful—the controlling force in human history that would ultimately triumph over Satan. To bring about that final victory, to usher in his heavenly kingdom, God had selected certain people as his agents, Calvin believed. These people—"the saints," or "the **elect**"—had been "predestined" by God for eternal salvation in heaven.

**elect** in theology, those of the faithful chosen, or "elected" by God for eternal salvation.

Calvin's emphasis on predestination led him to another distinctively Protestant notion—the doctrine of calling. How could a person learn whether he or she belonged to the elect who were saved? Calvin answered: strive to behave like a saint. God expected his elect to serve the good of society by unrelenting work in a "calling," or occupation, in the world. In place of the Catholic belief in the importance of good works, Calvin emphasized the goodness of work itself. Success in attaining discipline and self-control, in bringing order into one's own life and the entire society, revealed that a person might be among the elect.

Calvin fashioned a religion to change the world. Whereas Luther believed that Christians should accept the existing social order, Calvin called on Christians to become activists, reshaping society and government to conform with God's laws laid down in the Bible. He wanted all Europe to become like Geneva, the Swiss city that he had converted into a holy commonwealth in which the elect regulated the behavior and morals of everyone else. And unlike Luther, who wrote primarily for a German audience, Calvin addressed his most important book, *The Institutes of the Christian Religion* (1536), to Christians throughout Europe. Reformers from every country flocked to Geneva to learn more about Calvin's ideas.

^ Though both were Protestant reformers, Luther and John Calvin (shown here) were a study in contrasts. Luther was down-to-earth, friendly, and emotional. Calvin, on the other hand, was cool and logical—a brilliant thinker whose long, angled face and pointed beard shone with the confidence that he was carrying out God's word.
©G. Costa/De Agostini Picture Library/Bridgeman Images

**French Huguenots and the Birth of Spanish Florida** >> The Protestant Reformation shattered the unity of Christendom in western Europe. Spain, Ireland, and Italy remained firmly Catholic. England, Scotland, the Netherlands, Switzerland, and France developed either dominant or substantial Calvinist constituencies. Much of Germany and Scandinavia opted for Lutheranism. As religious groups competed for political power and the loyalties of believers, brutal wars swept sixteenth-century Europe. France experienced some of the worst violence. An influential group of Huguenots (Calvin's French followers) saw in North America a potential refuge from religious persecution. Under Jean Ribault, 150 Huguenots in 1562 established a simple village on Parris Island off present-day South Carolina. That experiment ended in desperation and cannibalism, but two years later Ribault led another, larger group to a site south of present-day Jacksonville, Florida. Here, at Fort Caroline, the Huguenots nurtured a cordial relationship with the local Timucua Indians. It seemed a promising start.

But Spanish authorities in the Caribbean took the Huguenots for a triple threat. First, French pirates had long tried to siphon silver from the Americas by waylaying Spanish galleons as they rode the Gulf Stream up the southeastern coast of North America before turning east toward Spain. With good reason, Spanish administrators feared that Fort Caroline would entrench the threat of piracy. Second, Spain worried that France would take a broader interest in the Americas, perhaps eventually planting colonies in all of North America. Finally, many Spanish Catholics saw Protestantism as a loathsome contagion, to be expunged from Europe and barred from the Americas.

These interlocking concerns prompted Spain to found a permanent colony in Florida under the direction of a focused and unforgiving man named Pedro Menéndez de Avilés. In 1565 Menéndez established a settlement on the coast called St. Augustine (still the United States' oldest continuously occupied non-Indian settlement). Next he and 500 soldiers slogged through the rain and marsh until they found Fort Caroline. In battle and through later executions the attackers killed Ribault and about 500 of his Huguenots. Flush with victory Menéndez established several more outposts on Florida's Atlantic and Gulf coasts and in 1570 even encouraged a short-lived Jesuit mission just miles from where English colonists would establish Jamestown a generation later. As for the Huguenots, the calamity at Fort Caroline dashed hope that the New World would be their haven. Most had to resign themselves to intensifying persecution in France.

**The English Reformation** >> While the Reformation racked northern Europe, King Henry VIII of England labored at a goal more worldly than those of Luther and Calvin. He wanted a son, a male heir to continue the Tudor dynasty. When his wife, Catherine of Aragon, gave birth to

## Make a Case

Do you think religion was only a surface justification or a primary motivation for the religious wars and rivalries of the sixteenth century? What sorts of evidence would help you make a compelling argument either way?

a daughter, Mary, Henry petitioned the pope to have his marriage annulled in the hope that a new wife would give him a son. This move enraged the king of Spain, who also happened to be Catherine's nephew. He persuaded the pope to refuse Henry's request. Defiantly, England's king proceeded with the divorce nonetheless and quickly married his mistress, Anne Boleyn. He then went further, making himself, not the pope, the head of the Church of England. Henry was an audacious but practical man, and he had little interest in promoting reformist doctrine. Apart from discarding the pope, the Church of England remained essentially Catholic in its teachings and rituals.

England's Protestants gained ground during the six-year reign of Henry's son Edward VI but then found themselves persecuted when Edward's Catholic half-sister Mary became queen in 1553. Five years later the situation turned again, when Elizabeth I (Anne Boleyn's daughter) took the throne, proclaiming herself the defender of Protestantism. Elizabeth was no radical Calvinist, however. A vocal minority of her subjects were reformers of that stripe, calling for the English church to purge itself of bishops, elaborate ceremonies, and other Catholic "impurities." Because of the austerity and zeal of such Calvinist radicals, their opponents proclaimed them "Puritans."

Radical Protestants might annoy Elizabeth as she pursued her careful, moderate policies, but radical Catholics frightened her. She had reason to worry that Spain might use English Catholics to undermine her rule. More ominously, Elizabeth's advisers cautioned that Catholic Ireland to the west would be an ideal base from which Spain or France could launch an invasion of England. Beginning in 1565 the queen encouraged a number of her elite subjects to sponsor private ventures for subduing the native Irish and settling loyal English Protestants on their land. As events fell out, this Irish venture proved to be a prelude to England's bolder attempt to found colonies across the Atlantic.

**REVIEW**

What were the major branches of Protestant reform, and how did the religious wars affect the Americas?

# ENGLAND'S ENTRY INTO AMERICA

Among the gentlemen eager to win fame and fortune were Humphrey Gilbert and Walter Raleigh, two adventurers with conquistador appetites for more and more. The pair were like most of the English who went to Ireland, ardent Protestants who viewed the native Catholic inhabitants as superstitious, pagan savages: "They blaspheme, they murder, commit whoredome," complained one Englishman, "hold no wedlocke, ravish, steal. . . ." Thus the English found it easy enough to justify their conquest. They proclaimed it their duty to teach the Irish the discipline of hard work, the rule of law, and the truth of Protestant Christianity. And, while the Irish were learning these civilized, English ways, they would not be allowed to buy land or hold office or serve on juries or give testimony in courts or learn a trade or bear arms.

When the Irish rebelled at that program of "liberation," the English ruthlessly repressed them, slaughtering not only combatants but civilians as well. Most English in Ireland, like most Spaniards in America, believed that native peoples who resisted civilization and proper Christianity should be subdued at any cost. In an insurgent country, no scruples stopped Humphrey Gilbert from planting the path to his camp with the severed heads of Irish rebels.

The struggle to colonize and subdue Ireland would serve as a rough model for later English efforts at expansion. The approach was essentially military, like that of the conquistadors. It also set the ominous precedent that Englishmen could treat "savage" peoples with a level of brutal cruelty that would have been inappropriate in wars between "civilized" Europeans. Finding "neither reputation, or profytt [profit]" in Ireland, Gilbert, Raleigh, and other West Country gentry took their ambition and their Irish education to North America.

### The Ambitions of Gilbert, Raleigh, and Wingina

>> In 1578 Gilbert got his chance for glory when Elizabeth granted him a royal patent—the first English colonial **charter**—to explore, occupy, and govern any territory in America "not actually possessed of any Christian prince or people." The vague, wildly unrealistic charter ignored the Indian possession of North America and made Gilbert proprietor of all the land lying between Florida and Labrador. In many ways his dreams looked backward. Gilbert hoped to set up a kind of medieval kingdom of his own, where loyal tenant farmers would work the lands of manors, paying rent to feudal lords. Yet his vision also looked forward to a utopian society. He planned to encourage England's poor to emigrate by providing them free land and a government "to be chosen by consent of the people."

**charter** document issued by a sovereign ruler, legislature, or other authority creating a public or private corporation.

Elizabeth had high hopes for her haughty champion, but a fierce storm got the better of his ship, and the Atlantic swallowed him before he ever set foot in his American dominions.

Meanwhile, Gilbert's stepbrother Walter Raleigh had been laying the groundwork for a British-American empire. Raleigh enlisted the talents of Richard Hakluyt, a clergyman, to write an eloquent plea for the English settlement of America, titled *A Discourse Concerning Westerne Planting*. North America's temperate and fertile lands, Hakluyt argued, would not only grow profitable crops, they would also make an excellent base from which to harry the Spanish, search for a northwest passage to Asia, and spread Protestantism. Finally, Hakluyt predicted that because the "Spaniardes have executed most outragious and more then Turkishe cruelties in all the west Indies," Indians would greet Englishmen as liberators.

By the summer of 1584 Raleigh had dispatched an exploratory voyage to the Outer Banks of present-day North Carolina. Expedition leaders made friendly contact with a people known as the Roanoke and ruled by a "weroance," or chief, named Wingina. The enthusiastic Hakluyt envisioned a colony that would become the Mexico of England, full of plantations producing sugar and silk and mountains yielding gold. Elizabeth knighted Raleigh and allowed him to name the new land "Virginia," after his virgin queen.

But Raleigh was not the only one with grand plans. Almost certainly Wingina had encountered or at least heard of Europeans before 1584. Like most coastal groups in the region, his people would have obtained prized European tools and commodities through indirect trade or by scouring wrecked ships. Eager to fortify his own and his people's power, Wingina recognized that friendly relations with the English would give him access to their trade and influence. Perhaps he believed he would act as patron to the newcomers. After all, they knew little of the region, spoke no Indian languages, and even lacked the skills necessary to survive in the area without native assistance. In short, Wingina seems to have welcomed the English because he believed that they could be useful and that they could be controlled. It was a tragic if understandable miscalculation—one that Indian leaders would make again and again in colonial America.

<< John White's sensitive watercolor *Indian Elder or Chief* may well be of Wingina. The portrayal includes the copper ornament hanging from his neck, indicating both high social status and the presence of an active trade network, since copper is not found on the island. Just as Raleigh had to gauge his strategy in dealing with the Indians, Wingina had to decide how to treat the strange newcomers from across the Atlantic. ©Bridgeman Images

Raleigh apparently aimed to establish on Roanoke a mining camp and a military garrison. In a stroke of genius he included in the company of 108 men a scientist, Thomas Hariot, to study the country's natural resources, and an artist, John White, to make drawings of the Virginia Indians. *A Briefe and True Reporte of the New Found Land of Virginia* (1588), written by Hariot and illustrated by White, served as one of the principal sources about North America and its Indian inhabitants for more than a century. Far less inspired was Raleigh's choice to lead the expedition—two veterans of the Irish campaigns, Sir Richard Grenville and Ralph Lane. Even his fellow conquistadors in Ireland considered Lane proud and greedy. As for Grenville, he was given to breaking wineglasses between his teeth and then swallowing the shards to show that he could stand the sight of blood, even his own.

The bullying ways of both men quickly alienated the natives of Roanoke. Wingina found the newcomers disrespectful, haughty, and cruel: when a local stole a cup, the English tried to teach everyone a lesson by torching his village and destroying its corn stores. As suspicions and resentments mounted on each side, Wingina tried to regain control of the situation the following summer by meeting with Lane to improve relations. But the meeting was a trap. Lane's men opened fire at the Indian envoys, killed Wingina, and hacked the head from his body. All that averted a massive counterattack was the arrival of England's preeminent privateer, Sir Francis Drake, fresh from freebooting up and down the Caribbean. The settlement's 102 survivors piled onto Drake's ships and put an ocean between themselves and the avenging Roanokes.

## A Second Roanoke—and Croatoan >>

Undaunted, Raleigh organized a second expedition to plant a colony farther north, in Chesapeake Bay. He recruited 119 men, women, and children, members of the English middle class, and granted each person an estate of 500 acres. He also appointed as governor the artist John White, who brought along a suit of armor for ceremonial occasions.

White deplored Lane's treachery toward Wingina and hated the senseless violence that had characterized the entire endeavor. The artist had spent his time on Roanoke closely observing native peoples, their material cultures, and their customs. His sensitive watercolors, especially those featuring women and children, indicate a genuine respect and affection. White believed that under prudent, moral leaders an English colony could indeed coexist peacefully with American Indians.

Despite his best intentions, everything went wrong. In July of 1587 the expedition's pilot insisted on leaving the colonists at Roanoke Island rather than the Chesapeake. Understandably, the Roanokes took no pleasure in seeing the English return. Sensing that the situation on Roanoke could quickly become desperate, the colonists sent White home to fetch reinforcements.

He returned to England in 1588 just as the massive Spanish navy, the Armada, was preparing an assault on England. Elizabeth enlisted every seaworthy ship and able-bodied sailor to stave off invasion. The Armada was defeated, but White was unable to return to Roanoke Island until 1590. There, he found only an empty fort and a few cottages in a clearing. The sole clue to the colony's fate was an inscription carved on a post: CROATOAN. It was the name of a nearby island off Cape Hatteras.

Had the Roanoke colonists fled to Croatoan for safety? Had they moved to the mainland and joined Indian communities? Had they been killed by Wingina's people? The fate of the "lost colony" remains a mystery, though later rumors suggest that the missing colonists merged with native societies in the interior. His dream of a tolerant, cooperative colony dashed, White sailed back to England, leaving behind the little cluster of cottages, which would soon be overgrown with vines, and his suit of armor, which was already "almost eaten through with rust."

**REVIEW**

Why did Elizabeth agree to charter a colony in America, and how successful were the first attempts?

All the world lay before them, or so it had seemed to the young men from England's West Country who dreamed of gold and glory, conquest and colonization. They harbored those dreams even though they lived on the fringe of the civilized world in the fifteenth and sixteenth centuries. For the English on Europe's far western shores, China remained the distant, exotic kingdom of power and wealth, supplying silks and spices and other luxurious goods. Islamic empires stood astride the land routes from Europe to the east. Nations on the western edge of Europe thus took to the seas. Portugal sent slave and gold traders to Africa, as well as merchants to trade with the civilizations of the Indies. Spanish conquerors such as Cortés toppled Indian empires and brought home mountains of silver. But England's West County sea dogs—adventurers who dreamed of becoming conquistadors—met only with frustration. In 1600, more than a century after Columbus's first crossing, not a single English settlement existed in the Americas.

What was left of the freebooting West Country world? Raleigh, his ambition still afire, sailed to South America in quest of a rich city named El Dorado. In 1603, however, Elizabeth's death brought to the English throne her cousin James I, the founder of the Stuart dynasty. The new king arrested the old queen's favorite for treason and imprisoned him for 15 years in the Tower of London. Set free in 1618 at the age of 64, Raleigh returned to South America, his lust for El Dorado undiminished. Along the way he plundered some Spanish silver ships, defying King James's orders. It was a fatal mistake, because England had made peace with Spain. Raleigh lost his head.

James I did not want to harass the king of Spain; he wanted to imitate him. The Stuarts were even more determined than

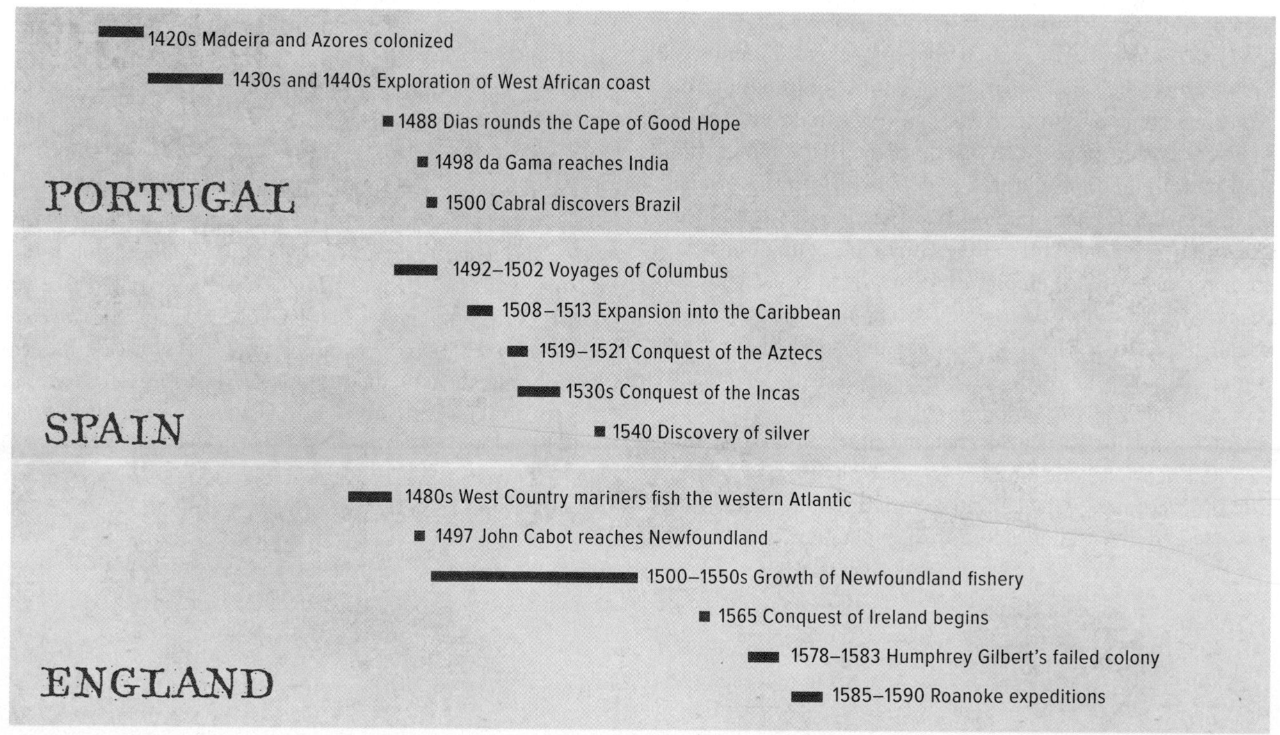

PORTUGAL
1420s Madeira and Azores colonized
1430s and 1440s Exploration of West African coast
1488 Dias rounds the Cape of Good Hope
1498 da Gama reaches India
1500 Cabral discovers Brazil
SPAIN
1492–1502 Voyages of Columbus
1508–1513 Expansion into the Caribbean
1519–1521 Conquest of the Aztecs
1530s Conquest of the Incas
1540 Discovery of silver
ENGLAND
1480s West Country mariners fish the western Atlantic
1497 John Cabot reaches Newfoundland
1500–1550s Growth of Newfoundland fishery
1565 Conquest of Ireland begins
1578–1583 Humphrey Gilbert's failed colony
1585–1590 Roanoke expeditions

the Tudors had been to enlarge the sphere of royal power. There would be no room in America for a warrior nobility of conquistadors, no room for a feudal fiefdom ruled by the likes of Raleigh or Gilbert. Instead, there would be profitable plantations and colonies managed by loyal, efficient bureaucrats. America would strengthen English monarchs, paving their path to greater power, just as the dominions of Mexico and Peru had enlarged the authority of the Spanish Crown. America would be the making of kings and queens.

Or would it? For some Europeans, weary of freebooting conquistadors and sea rovers, the security that Crown rule and centralized states promoted in western Europe would be enough. But others, men and women who were often desperate and sometimes idealistic, would cast their eyes west across the Atlantic and want more.

# CHAPTER SUMMARY

During the late fifteenth century, Europeans and Africans for the first time came into contact with the Americas, where native cultures were numerous and diverse.

- During the fourteenth and early fifteenth centuries, western Europeans were on the fringes of an international economy drawn together by Chinese goods such as spices, ceramics, and silks.
- A combination of technological advances, the rise of new trade networks and techniques, and increased political centralization made Europe's expansion overseas possible.
- Led by Portugal, European expansion began with a push southward along the West African coast, in pursuit of spices, ivory, and gold. As sugar plantations were established in the islands of the eastern Atlantic, a slave trade in Africans became a part of this expansive commerce.
- Spain took the lead in exploring and colonizing the Americas, consolidating a vast and profitable empire of its own in the place of Aztec and Inca Empires. Divisions within Indian empires and the devastating effects of European diseases made Spanish conquest possible.
- The conquistadors who led the Spanish occupation were soon replaced by an elaborate, centralized royal bureaucracy, which regulated most aspects of economic and social life. The discovery of silver provided Spain with immense wealth, while leading to sharply increased mortality among the native population.
- Spanish conquistadors also explored much of the present-day southeastern and southwestern United States. They found no empires, silver mines, or rich empires and were thwarted by the Indian peoples they encountered.
- The Protestant Reformation was inaugurated by Martin Luther in 1517 and carried on by John Calvin, whose more activist theology spread from his headquarters in Geneva outward to England, Scotland, the Netherlands, and the Huguenots in France.
- England, apprehensive of Spain's power, did not turn its attention to exploration and colonization until the 1570s and 1580s. By the time it did, European rivalries were heightened by splits arising out of the Protestant Reformation.
- England's merchants and gentry lent support to colonizing ventures, although early efforts, such as those at Roanoke, failed.

## Additional Reading

For ordinary folk in the era of exploration, see Kenneth R. Andrews, *Trade, Plunder, and Settlement* (1985). For Portugal's initial expansion, see Malyn Newitt, *A History of Portuguese Overseas Expansion, 1400–1668* (2004). David Northrup's *Africa's Discovery of Europe, 1450–1850* (2008) explores West Africa's encounter with Europeans. For sugar and expansion, see Philip D. Curtin, *The Rise and Fall of the Plantation Complex* (2nd ed., 1998). The demographic catastrophe that followed contact is explored in Massimo Livi-Bacci, *Conquest: The Destruction of the American Indios* (2008). For telling comparisons between Iberian and English colonialism in the New World, see John Elliott's magisterial *Empires of the Atlantic World: Britain and Spain in America, 1492–1830* (2007). Charles Mann's *1493: Uncovering the New World Columbus Created* (2011) deftly integrates insights from multiple disciplines about the consequences of contact. Jace Weaver considers native engagement with the Atlantic World generally in *The Red Atlantic* (2014). For Spain in the Caribbean, see David Abulafia, *The Discovery of Mankind* (2008). Miguel Leon-Portilla and Lysander Kemp give us a fascinating glimpse into how Aztecs viewed the Spanish conquest in *The Broken Spears* (2006). For an indispensable narrative of Spain's activities in North America, see David J. Weber, *The Spanish Frontier in North America* (1992). Coronado's sojourn is the subject of the exacting work by Richard Flint, *No Settlement, No Conquest* (2008). For the Southeast, see Daniel S. Murphree, *Constructing Floridians* (2006). For a good introduction to the Reformation in England, see Eamon Duffy, *The Stripping of the Altars* (2nd ed., 2005). For early English attempts at colonization, in both Ireland and the Americas, consult the works of Nicholas Canny, as well as Michael Leroy Oberg, *The Head in Edward Nugent's Hand* (2007).

# 3 Colonization & Conflict in the South

## 1600–1750

This Native American drawing on a canyon wall in present-day Arizona represents the progress of the Spanish into the Southwest. Indians would soon put horses, prominently featured here, to their own uses.



## >> An American Story

## OUTLANDISH STRANGERS

In the year 1617, as Europeans counted time, on a bay they called the Chesapeake, in a land they named Virginia, the mighty weroance Powhatan surveyed his domain. It had all worked according to plan, and Powhatan, leader of the Pamunkeys, had laid his plans carefully. While in his prime, the tall, robust man had drawn some 30 villages along the Virginia coast into a powerful confederacy numbering nearly 9,000 souls. The natives of the Chesapeake, like the peoples who inhabited the length of eastern North America, lived for most of the year in small agricultural

MATOAKA ALS REBECCA FILIA POTENTISS: PRINC: POWHATANI IMP: VIRGINIÆ.

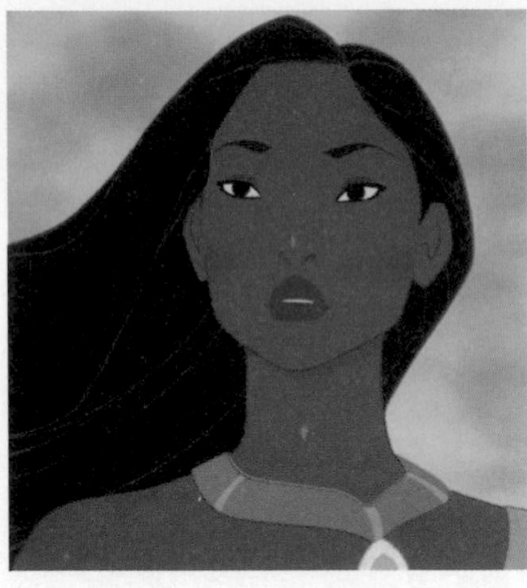

^ Pocahontas, daughter of the mighty weroance Powhatan and wife of English colonist John Rolfe, has long fascinated nonnatives. In an image from 1616, she is represented as a high-status English lady, stripped of all marks of her native culture save her name, Matoaka (Pocahontas was a nickname). The second image, from the 1993 Disney film *Pocahontas*, portrays her as a pretty and innocent child of nature. Now as then, we see in her what we want to.
(*Left*) Source: Library of Congress, Prints and Photographs Division [LC-USZ62-8104]; (*Right*) ©Walt Disney Pictures/Photofest, Inc.

villages. As tribute for his protection and leadership Powhatan collected food, furs, and skins from the villagers. He forged alliances with communities too distant or too powerful for him to dominate. He married the daughters of prominent men, dozens in all, to solidify his network of patronage and power.

After 1607 Powhatan had been forced to take into account yet another group. The English, as this new people called themselves, had come by sea, crammed into three ships. They were 100 men and 4 boys, all clad in heavy, outlandish clothing, many dressed in gaudy colors. The ships had followed a river deep into Powhatan's territory and built a fort on a swampy, mosquito-infested site that they called Jamestown.

Powhatan had not been frightened. He knew of these strangers from across the waters. Even amid the bounty of the Chesapeake they had failed to feed themselves. With bows and arrows, spears and nets, Indian men brought in an abundance of meat and fish. Fields tended by Indian women yielded generous crops of corn, beans, squash, and melon, and edible nuts and fruits grew wild. Still the English had starved, and not just during the first few months of their settlement but for several years afterward. Powhatan could understand why the English had refused to grow food. Cultivating crops was women's work—like building houses; or making clothing, pottery, and baskets; or caring for children. And the English settlement had included no women until two arrived in the fall of 1608. Yet even after more women came, the English had still starved, and they had expected—no, they had demanded—that Powhatan's people feed them.

And yet these hapless folk put on such airs. They boasted about the power of their god—they had only one—and denounced the Indians' "devil-worship" of "false gods." They crowed endlessly about the power of their king, James I, who expected Powhatan to become his vassal. Inconceivable—that Powhatan should willingly bow before this King James, the ruler of so small and savage a race! When the Indians made war, they killed the male warriors of rival communities but adopted their women and children. But when Powhatan's people withheld food or defended their land from these invaders, the English retaliated by murdering Indian women and children. Worse, the English could not even keep order among themselves. Too many of them wanted to lead, and they squabbled constantly.

The temptation to wipe out the helpless, troublesome, arrogant tribe of English—or simply to let them starve to death—had been almost overwhelming. But Powhatan had allowed the English to survive. Like Wingina before him, he had decided that even these barbaric people had their uses. English labor, English trading goods, and, most important, English guns could help quell resistance within his confederacy and subdue his Indian rivals to the west. In 1614 Powhatan had cemented his claim on the English and their weapons with the marriage between his favorite child, Pocahontas, and an ambitious Englishman, John Rolfe.

By 1617 events had vindicated Powhatan's strategy of tolerating the English. His chiefdom flourished, ready to be passed on to his brother. Powhatan's people still outnumbered the English, who seldom starved outright now but continued to fight among themselves and sicken and die. Only one thing had changed in the Chesapeake by 1617: the English were clearing woodland along the rivers and planting tobacco.

That was the doing of Powhatan's son-in-law, Rolfe, a man as strange as the rest of the newcomers, all of them eager to store up wealth and worldly goods. Rolfe had been obsessed with finding a crop that could be grown in Virginia and then sold for gain across the sea. When he succeeded by growing tobacco, other English followed his lead. Odder still, not women but men tended the tobacco fields. Here was more evidence of English inferiority. Men wasted long hours laboring when they might supply their needs with far less effort.

In 1617 Powhatan, ruler of the Pamunkeys, surveyed his domain, and sometime in that year, he died. He had lived long enough to see the tobacco fields lining the riverbanks, straddling the charred stumps of felled trees. But perhaps he went to his grave believing that he had done what Wingina had failed to do: bend the English to his purposes. He died before those stinking tobacco weeds spread over the length of his land and sent his hard-won dominion up in smoke.

Wingina and Powhatan were not the only native leaders who dreamed of turning Europeans to their advantage. Across North America, the fleeting if destructive encounters of the sixteenth century gave way to sustained colonialism in the seventeenth. As Europeans began to colonize the edges of North America in earnest, Indian peoples struggled not only to survive and adapt to new realities but also, when possible, to profit from the rapid changes swirling around them.

Those often dramatic changes reflected upheavals under way all across the globe. The tobacco John Rolfe had begun to cultivate was only one of several plantation **monocultures** that Europeans began to establish in their far-flung colonies. Sugar, already flourishing in the Atlantic islands off the coast of West Africa, was gaining a foothold in the islands of the Caribbean. Rice, long a staple in Asia and grown also in Africa, made its way into South Carolina toward the end of the seventeenth century. Because these crops were grown most efficiently on plantations and required intensive labor, African slavery spread during these years, fueled by an expanding international slave trade. Europeans, Africans, and Indians were all, in different ways, caught up in the wrenching transformations. <<

**monoculture** a single crop grown to the virtual exclusion of all others, either on a farm or more generally within a region.

## THEMATIC TIMELINE

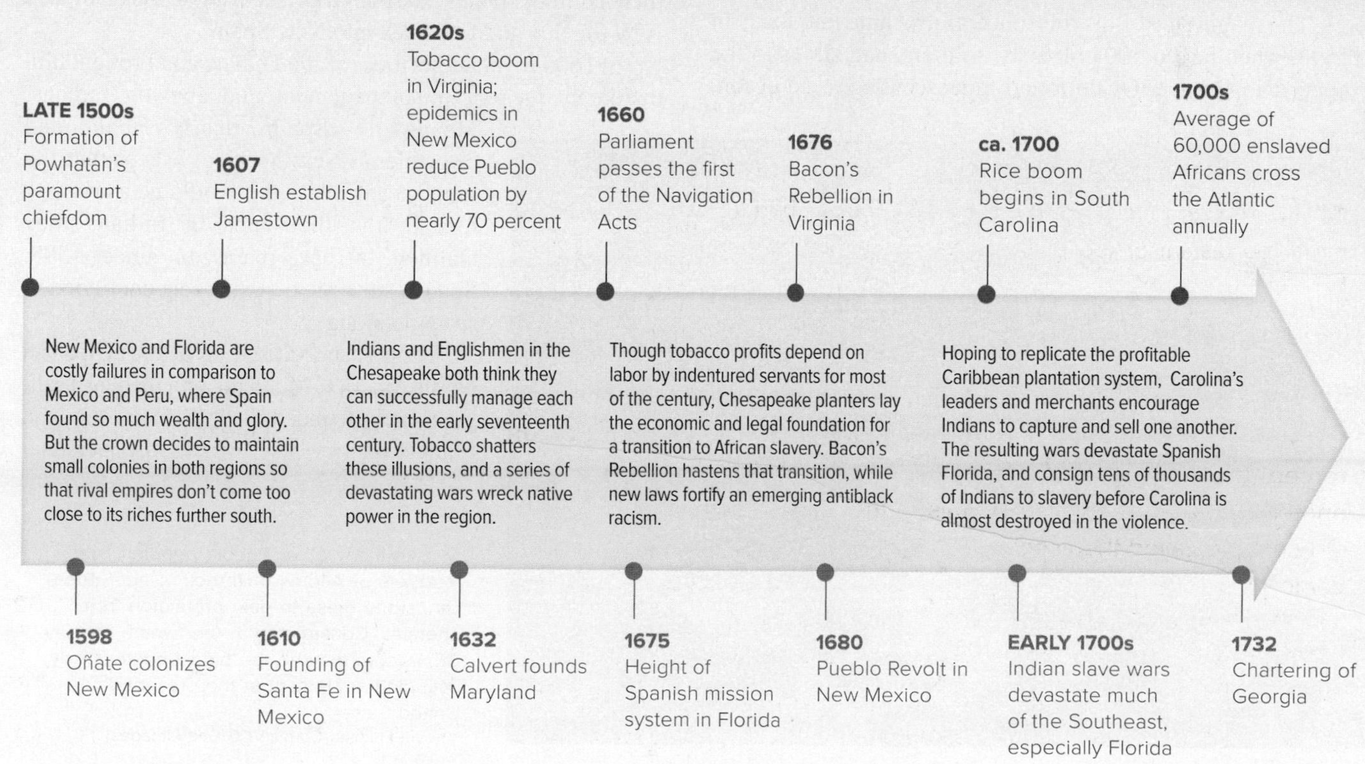

LATE 1500s Formation of Powhatan's paramount chiefdom
1607 English establish Jamestown
1620s Tobacco boom in Virginia; epidemics in New Mexico reduce Pueblo population by nearly 70 percent
1660 Parliament passes the first of the Navigation Acts
1676 Bacon's Rebellion in Virginia
ca. 1700 Rice boom begins in South Carolina
1700s Average of 60,000 enslaved Africans cross the Atlantic annually
New Mexico and Florida are costly failures in comparison to Mexico and Peru, where Spain found so much wealth and glory. But the crown decides to maintain small colonies in both regions so that rival empires don't come too close to its riches further south.
Indians and Englishmen in the Chesapeake both think they can successfully manage each other in the early seventeenth century. Tobacco shatters these illusions, and a series of devastating wars wreck native power in the region.
Though tobacco profits depend on labor by indentured servants for most of the century, Chesapeake planters lay the economic and legal foundation for a transition to African slavery. Bacon's Rebellion hastens that transition, while new laws fortify an emerging antiblack racism.
Hoping to replicate the profitable Caribbean plantation system, Carolina's leaders and merchants encourage Indians to capture and sell one another. The resulting wars devastate Spanish Florida, and consign tens of thousands of Indians to slavery before Carolina is almost destroyed in the violence.
1598 Oñate colonizes New Mexico
1610 Founding of Santa Fe in New Mexico
1632 Calvert founds Maryland
1675 Height of Spanish mission system in Florida
1680 Pueblo Revolt in New Mexico
EARLY 1700s Indian slave wars devastate much of the Southeast, especially Florida
1732 Chartering of Georgia

# SPAIN'S NORTH AMERICAN COLONIES

Long before Powhatan made his fateful choices, Spain had already established lasting colonies north of Mexico. But while France and especially England eventually established large colonial populations on territory suited to European-style agriculture, Spain confined its northern ventures to the ecologically challenging regions of the upper Rio Grande and coastal Florida. Because economic opportunities and good farmland were abundant elsewhere in Spanish America, few Spaniards migrated to distant and difficult northern outposts. Even so, Spain's colonial endeavors had tremendous implications for North America's native peoples and for the geopolitics of the continent as a whole.

**The Founding of a "New" Mexico** >> By the 1590s Coronado's dismal expedition a half century earlier had been all but forgotten. Again, rumors spread in Mexico about great riches in the North. New Spain's viceroy began casting about for a leader to establish a "new" Mexico as magnificent and profitable as its namesake. He chose Juan de Oñate, son of one of New Spain's richest miners and husband to Isabel de Tolosa Cortés Moctezuma, granddaughter of Hernán Cortés and great-granddaughter of Moctezuma. Ignorant of northern geography and overestimating New Mexico's riches, Oñate proposed to sail ships up the Pacific to Pueblo country, so that twice a year he could resupply his would-be colony and export its expected treasures.

The magnitude of his misconceptions came into focus in 1598, when he led 500 colonists, soldiers, and slaves to the upper Rio Grande. Oñate found modest villages, no ocean, and no significant mineral wealth. Even so, he had come with women and children, with livestock and tools, with artisans and tradesmen, with seeds and books and bibles. He had come to stay. Eager to avoid the violence of earlier encounters, Tewa-speaking Pueblos evacuated a village for the newcomers to use. Many native leaders pledged Oñate their allegiance, Pueblo artisans labored on irrigation systems and other public works for the Spaniards, and Indian women (traditionally the builders in Pueblo society) constructed the region's first Catholic Church.

The colonizers mistook this cautious courtesy for subservience. Oñate's oldest nephew, Juan de Zaldívar, was bolder and cruder than most. At Acoma Pueblo, known today as "Sky City" because of its position high atop a majestic mesa, he brazenly seized several sacred turkeys to kill and eat, answering Indian protests with insults. Outraged, Acoma's men fell upon Zaldívar, killing him and several companions. Fueled by grief and rage, Zaldívar's younger brother Vicente laid siege to Acoma Pueblo, killed perhaps 800 of its residents, and made slaves of several hundred more. The savagery of the Acoma siege and similar repressive measures educated all of the region's native communities about the risks of resistance.

But it was easier to instill terror than grow rich. Desperate to salvage their enterprise, Oñate and key followers toiled on long, fruitless expeditions in search of gold, silver, and cities. Vicente de Zaldívar, the headstrong conqueror of Acoma, tried to domesticate bison as had been done with cattle, rather than search for them on the plains. But the bison—"stubborn animals, brave beyond praise"—quickly broke free of the cottonwood coral his men constructed. Most Spaniards turned to the less hazardous pursuit of farming and ranching to support their families. Others despaired of securing a living in arid New Mexico and fled back into New Spain.

In 1606 royal authorities recalled Oñate and brought him up on charges of mismanagement and abusing Indians. Meanwhile Spain nearly abandoned "worthless" New Mexico, except that the Franciscans insisted it would be a crime to forsake the thousands of Indians they claimed to have baptized since 1598. Spain's New Mexican outpost continued to struggle along.

Franciscans became key actors in Spanish North America. Members of a medieval religious order founded by St. Francis of Assisi, Franciscan monks owned no personal

<< Like many other Pueblo peoples, the founders of Acoma built their village atop a sandstone mesa to gain protection from enemies. Constructed in the twelfth century CE, Acoma may be the oldest continuously occupied settlement in the present-day United States.
©Kevin Fleming/Corbis/VCG/Getty Images

**celibate** abstaining from sexual intercourse; also unmarried.

property, remained **celibate**, and survived by begging for alms or accepting donations from wealthy patrons. Franciscans had accompanied Columbus on his second voyage, and they began ministering to the Indians of central Mexico soon after Tenochtitlán fell. By the 1570s Spanish authorities started secularizing central Mexico's missions, transforming them into self-supporting parishes. Franciscans went on to become powerful figures in colonial New Mexico, while Jesuits established several missions in present-day Arizona.

**The Growth of Spanish Florida** >> For strategic reasons the Crown needed the Franciscans even more in Florida than in New Mexico's distant outposts. As long as pirates or rival colonies on the Atlantic seaboard threatened Spanish shipping, the king had to control Florida. Pedro Menéndez de Avilés did much to secure the peninsula in the 1560s when he destroyed France's Fort Caroline and established several posts on the coast (see Chapter 2). By 1600, however, Menéndez was dead and only St. Augustine endured, with a population of perhaps 500. Spanish Florida needed something more to survive.

To extend his influence the king first offered the peninsula's many native peoples trade privileges and regular diplomatic presents. In return, native leaders promised to support the Spanish in war and tax their people on behalf of the king. Once these alliances were in place, Indian communities were made to accept Franciscan missions and a few resident soldiers, a policy critical to molding and monitoring native villages. By 1675, 40 missions were ministering to as many as 26,000 baptized Indians. The bishop of Cuba toured Florida and spoke enthusiastically of converts who embraced "with devotion the mysteries of our holy faith." Florida's mission system and network of Indian alliances convinced Spanish authorities that they could maintain their grip on this crucial peninsula.

**Popé and the Pueblo Revolt** >> As the seventeenth century progressed, New Mexico also seemed to stabilize. Enough Spanish colonists remained to establish a separate town, La Villa Real de la Santa Fe, in 1610. Santa Fe (the second-oldest European town in the United States after St. Augustine) became the hub of Spanish life in New Mexico. Many families settled elsewhere on the Rio Grande, on well-watered lands near Pueblo villages. Economic and political life revolved around a dozen prominent families. By 1675 New Mexico had a diverse colonial population of perhaps 2,500, including Spaniards, Africans, Mexican Indians, mestizos (persons of mixed Spanish-Indian heritage), and mulattoes (of Spanish-African heritage).

This population also included large numbers of Indian captives. Occasionally captives came to Spanish households through war, as after the siege of Acoma. In addition, Spaniards purchased enslaved women and children from other Indians

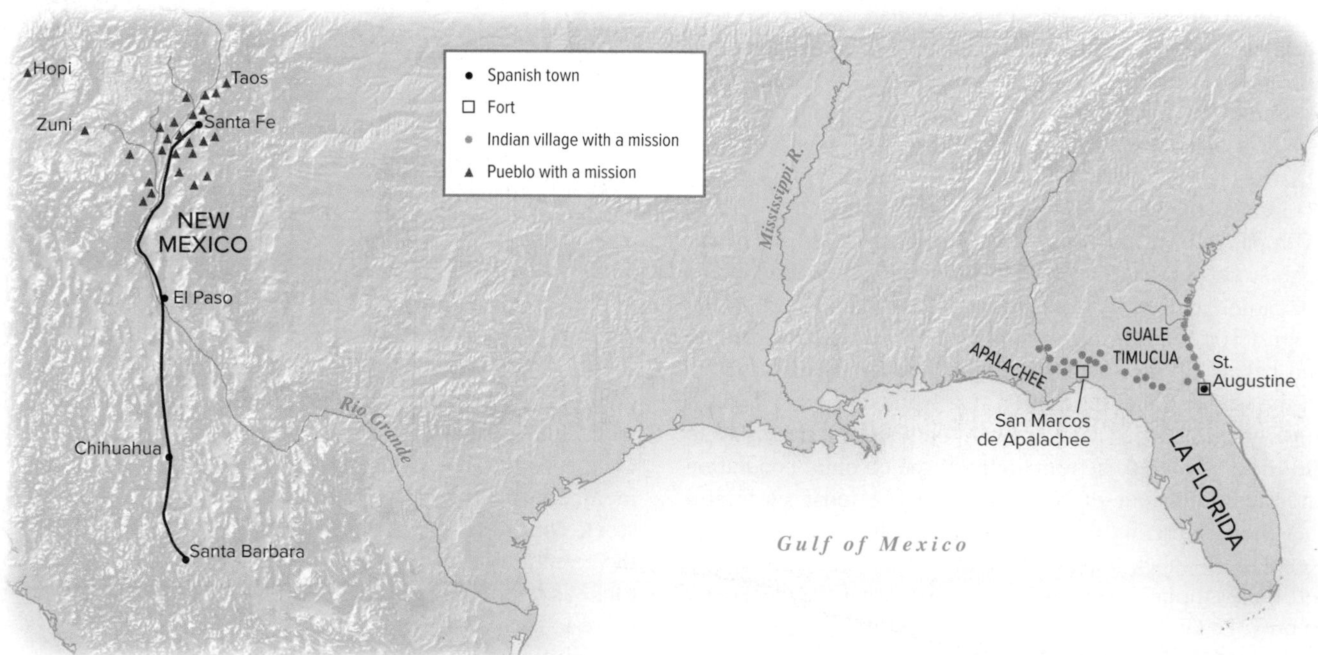

Spanish town
Fort
Indian village with a mission
Pueblo with a mission
Hopi
Taos
Zuni
Santa Fe
NEW MEXICO
El Paso
Chihuahua
Santa Barbara
Rio Grande
Mississippi R.
APALACHEE
GUALE
TIMUCUA
St. Augustine
San Marcos de Apalachee
LA FLORIDA
Gulf of Mexico


## MAP 3.1: SPANISH MISSIONS IN NORTH AMERICA, CA. 1675

From St. Augustine, Spanish missionaries spread into Guale Indian villages in present-day Georgia and westward among the Indians of Timucua and Apalachee Provinces. In New Mexico, missions radiated outward from the Rio Grande, as distant as Hopi villages in the west. *What was the point of origin from which Spanish missions in New Mexico spread?*

and regularly launched slave raids against so-called enemy Indians such as Utes, Apaches, and Navajos. By 1680 half of all New Mexican households included at least one Indian captive. Depending on age, gender, and the master's disposition, such captives could be treated as low-status family members or terrorized and abused as disposable human property.

The colonists also extracted labor from Pueblo Indians. Officially Pueblo households had to surrender three bushels of corn and one processed hide or large cotton blanket each year. Pueblos also sometimes labored on public works, and elite Spaniards often exploited their privileges by insisting on more tribute and labor than legally allowed. Still, the populous Pueblos could have satisfied Spanish demands with little difficulty except for other changes in their world. First and most importantly, colonialism meant epidemics. Beginning in the 1620s smallpox killed 70 percent of the population within a generation. Whereas New Mexico had boasted about 100 native villages at contact, by 1680 only 30 remained inhabited. Infestations of locusts, severe droughts, and crop failures compounded the crisis. A distraught Franciscan reported starving native men, women, and children "lying dead along the roads, in the ravines, and in their hovels." Mounted Utes, Apaches, and Navajos, embittered by New Mexican slaving and barred from their customary trade in the pueblos, launched punishing raids against the most vulnerable Pueblo villages.

In their deepening misery Pueblos turned to religion—their own. Since 1598 the Franciscans had worked tirelessly to suppress the dances, idols, and ceremonies that had long mediated Pueblo relationships with the divine. By the 1670s Pueblo elders were arguing that the calamities of the past decades could be reversed only by rejecting Christianity and returning to the old faith. Franciscans and civil authorities scrambled to extinguish the revival movement, arresting Pueblo leaders, executing 2 and whipping 43 others in front of large crowds.

One of the 43, a prominent Tewa man known to history as Popé, nursed his wounds in Taos and called for a war against the Spaniards to purify the land. Many individuals and some entire villages refused to participate. But on August 10, 1680, Indians from across New Mexico rose up and began killing Spaniards, pursuing astonished survivors all the way to Santa Fe. Within weeks the desperate Spanish governor, wounded by an arrow in the face and a gunshot to the chest, gathered the remainder of the colonial population and fled south out of New Mexico. The most successful Pan-Indian uprising in North American history, the Pueblo Revolt sent shock waves throughout Spanish America and left the Catholic devout agonizing over what they had done to provoke God's wrath.

REVIEW

Where and why did Spain establish colonies in North America, and how did native peoples resist colonization?

# ENGLISH SOCIETY ON THE CHESAPEAKE

By 1700, then, Spain viewed its situation in the Americas very differently than it had 100 years earlier. The Pueblo Revolt had checked its power at the northern reach of its American possessions. Equally disturbing was the progress of Spain's European rivals in the Americas during the seventeenth century. During the sixteenth, both France and England had envied Spain's American conquests and wealth but did little to compete, beyond preying on Spanish ships and fishing for cod. During the seventeenth century, this would change.

In fact, even by 1600 other European kingdoms were beginning to view overseas colonies as essential to a nation's power and prosperity. They did so in part because of an economic model known as **mercantilism**, which guided Europe's commercial expansion for 200 years. The primary objective of mercantilism was to enrich a nation by fostering a favorable balance of trade. Once the value of exports exceeded the cost of imports, its advocates argued, gold and silver would flow into home ports.

**mercantilism** European economic doctrine calling for strict regulation of the economy in order to ensure a balance of exports over imports and increase the amount of gold and silver in a nation's treasury.

If a nation could make do without any imports from other countries, so much the better. It was here that the idea of colonies entered the mercantilist scheme. Colonial producers would supply raw materials that the mother country could not produce, while colonial consumers swelled demand for the finished goods and financial services that the mother country could provide. That logic led England's King James I to approve a private venture to colonize the Chesapeake Bay, a sprawling inlet of the Atlantic Ocean fed by more than 100 rivers and streams.

**The Virginia Company** >> In 1606 the king granted a charter to a number of English merchants, gentlemen, and aristocrats, incorporating them as the Virginia Company of London. The members of the new **joint stock company** sold stock in their venture to English investors, as well as awarding a share to those willing to settle in Virginia at their own expense. With the proceeds from the sale of stock, the company planned to send to Virginia hundreds of poor and unemployed people as well as scores of skilled craftworkers. These laborers were to serve the company for seven years in return for their passage, pooling their efforts to

**joint stock company** business in which capital is held in transferable shares of stock by joint owners. The joint stock company was an innovation that allowed investors to share and spread the risks of overseas investments.

^ This facial reconstruction gives an idea of what one of the few girls at Jamestown might have looked like before the "starving-time" winter of 1609–1610. The reconstruction is based on a skull found at Jamestown by archaeologists, which exhibits cuts and sawing marks around the cranium and facial areas. The evidence suggests that she was killed for food by another desperate colonist.


produce any commodities that would return a profit to stockholders. If gold and silver could not be found, perhaps North America would yield other valuable commodities—furs, pitch, tar, or lumber. In the spring of 1607—nearly a decade after Oñate had launched Spain's colonies in New Mexico—the first expedition dispatched by the Virginia Company founded Jamestown.

Making the first of many mistakes, Jamestown's 104 colonists pitched their fort on a swampy inland peninsula in order to prevent a surprise attack from the Spanish. Weakened by bouts of dysentery, typhoid, and yellow fever, however, they died by the scores.

Even before sickness took its toll, few of Jamestown's colonists had a knack for labor. The gentlemen of the expedition expected to lead rather than to work, while most of the other early settlers were gentlemen's servants and craftworkers who knew nothing about growing crops. Many colonists suffered from malnutrition, which heightened their susceptibility to disease. Though new colonists had arrived since 1607, only 60 inhabitants lived through the winter of 1609–1610, known as the "starving time." Desperate colonists unearthed and ate corpses; one settler even butchered his wife. Others imitated their predecessors on Roanoke, bullying Indians for food. Martial law failed to turn the situation around, and skirmishes with native peoples became more brutal and frequent as rows of tobacco plants steadily invaded tribal lands.

**Reform and a Boom in Tobacco** >> Determined to salvage their investment, Virginia Company managers in 1618 set in place sweeping reforms. To attract more capital and colonists, the company established a "headright" system for granting land to individuals. Those already settled in the colony received 100 acres apiece. New settlers each received 50 acres, and anyone who paid the passage of other immigrants to Virginia—either family members or servants—received 50 acres per "head." The company also abolished martial law, allowing the planters to elect a representative assembly. Along with a governor and an advisory council appointed by the company, the House of Burgesses had the authority to make laws for the colony. It met for the first time in 1619, beginning what would become a strong tradition of representative government in the English colonies.

The new measures met with immediate success. The free and unfree laborers who poured into Virginia during the 1620s made up the first wave of an English migration to the Chesapeake that numbered between 130,000 and 150,000 over the seventeenth century. Drawn from the ranks of ordinary English working people, the immigrants were largely men, outnumbering women by six to one. Most were young, ranging in age from 15 to 24. Because of their youth, most lacked skills or wealth. Some of those who came to the Chesapeake as free immigrants prospered as Virginia's tobacco economy took off. When in the 1620s demand soared and prices peaked in European markets, colonists with an eye for profit planted every inch of their farms in tobacco and reaped windfalls.

Indentured servants accounted for three-quarters of all immigrants to Virginia. For most, the crossing was simply the last of many moves made in the hope of finding work. Although England's population had been rising since the middle of the fifteenth century, the demand for farm laborers was falling because many landowners were converting croplands into pastures for sheep. The search for work pushed young men and women out of their villages, sending them through the countryside and then into the cities. Down and out in London, Bristol, or Liverpool, some decided to make their next move across the Atlantic and signed **indenture**. Pamphlets promoting immigration promised land and quick riches once servants had finished their terms of four to seven years.

**indenture** contract signed between two parties, binding one to serve the other for a specified period of time.

Even the most skeptical immigrants were shocked at what they found. The death rate in Virginia during the 1620s was higher than that of England during times of epidemic disease. The life expectancy for Chesapeake men who reached the age of 20 was a mere 48 years; for women it was lower still. Servants fared worst of all, because malnutrition, overwork, and abuse made them vulnerable to disease. As masters scrambled to make quick profits, they extracted the maximum amount of work before death carried off their laborers. An estimated 40 percent of servants did not survive to the end of their indentured terms.

**War with the Confederacy** >> The expanding cultivation of tobacco also claimed many lives by putting unbearable pressure on Indian land. After Powhatan's death in 1617 leadership of the confederacy passed to Opechancanough, who watched, year after year, as the tobacco mania grew. In March 1622 he coordinated a sweeping attack on white settlements that killed about a quarter of Virginia's colonial population. English retaliation over the next decade cut down an entire generation of young Indian men, drove the remaining Powhatans to the west, and won the colonists hundreds of thousands more acres for tobacco.

News of the ongoing Indian war jolted English investors into determining the true state of their Virginia venture. It came to light that, despite the tobacco boom, the Virginia Company was plunging toward bankruptcy. Nor was that the worst news. Stockholders discovered that more than 3,000 immigrants had not survived the brutal conditions of Chesapeake life. An investigation by James I revealed the grisly truth, prompting the king to dissolve the Virginia Company and take control of the colony himself in 1624. Henceforth Virginia would be governed as a royal colony.

As the tobacco boom broke in the 1630s and 1640s, Virginians began producing more corn and cattle. Nutrition and overall health improved as a result. More and more poor men began surviving their indenture and establishing modest farms of their own. For women who survived servitude, prospects were even brighter. Given the ongoing gender imbalance in the colony, single women stood a good chance of improving their status by marriage. Even so, high mortality rates still fractured families: one out of every four children born in the Chesapeake did not survive to maturity, and among those children who reached their 18th birthday, one-third had lost both parents to death.

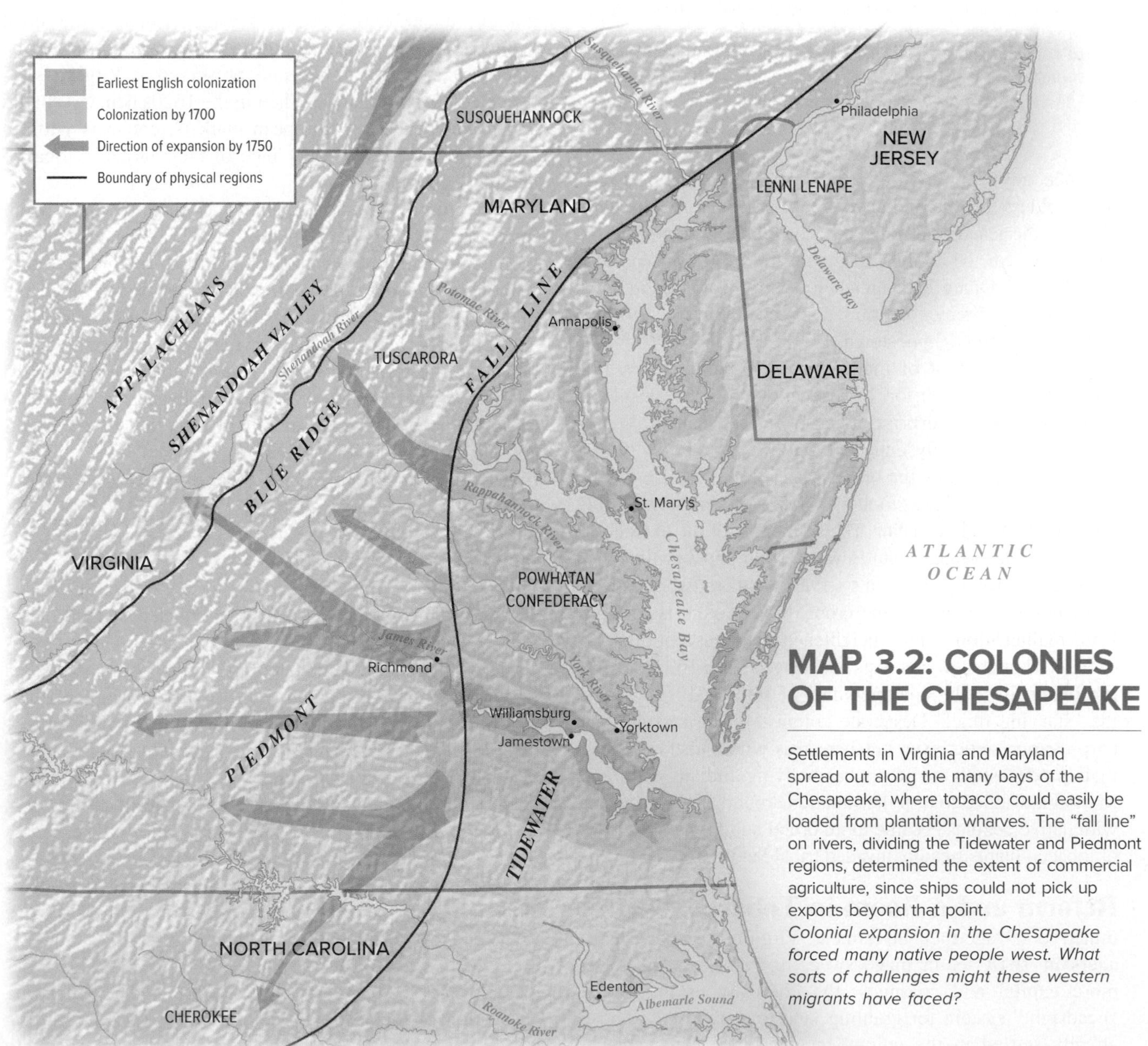

Earliest English colonization
Colonization by 1700
Direction of expansion by 1750
Boundary of physical regions
SUSQUEHANNOCK
Susquehanna River
Philadelphia
NEW JERSEY
LENNI LENAPE
MARYLAND
Delaware Bay
APPALACHIANS
SHENANDOAH VALLEY
Shenandoah River
Potomac River
FALL LINE
Annapolis
TUSCARORA
DELAWARE
BLUE RIDGE
Rappahannock River
St. Mary's
Chesapeake Bay
ATLANTIC OCEAN
VIRGINIA
POWHATAN CONFEDERACY
James River
Richmond
York River
PIEDMONT
Williamsburg
Yorktown
Jamestown
TIDEWATER
NORTH CAROLINA
Edenton
Albemarle Sound
CHEROKEE
Roanoke River


## MAP 3.2: COLONIES OF THE CHESAPEAKE

Settlements in Virginia and Maryland spread out along the many bays of the Chesapeake, where tobacco could easily be loaded from plantation wharves. The "fall line" on rivers, dividing the Tidewater and Piedmont regions, determined the extent of commercial agriculture, since ships could not pick up exports beyond that point.
*Colonial expansion in the Chesapeake forced many native people west. What sorts of challenges might these western migrants have faced?*

By 1650 Virginia could boast about 15,000 colonists, with more arriving every year. But Virginians looking to expand into more northerly bays of the Chesapeake found their way blocked by a newer English colony.

### The Founding of Maryland and the Renewal of Indian Wars >>

Unlike Virginia, established by a private corporation and later converted into a royal colony, Maryland was founded in 1632 by a single aristocratic family, the Calverts. They held absolute authority to dispose of 10 million acres of land, administer justice, and establish a civil government. All these powers they exercised, granting estates, or "manors," to their friends and dividing other holdings into smaller farms for ordinary immigrants. From all these "tenants"—that is, every settler in the colony—the family collected "quitrents" every year, fees for use of the land. The Calverts appointed a governor and a council to oversee their own interests while allowing the largest landowners to dispense local justice in manorial courts and make laws for the entire colony in a representative assembly.

Virginians liked nothing about Maryland. To begin with, the Calvert family was Catholic and had extended complete religious freedom to all Christians, making Maryland a haven for Catholics. Worse still, the Marylanders were a source of economic competition. Two thousand inhabitants had settled on Calvert holdings by 1640, virtually all of them planting tobacco on land coveted by the Virginians.

Another obstacle to Virginia's expansion was the remnant of the Powhatan confederacy. Hounded for corn and supplies (most colonial fields grew tobacco rather than food) and constantly pressured by the expanding plantation economy, Virginia's native peoples became desperate and angry enough to risk yet another war. Aged Opechancanough sent a new generation of Indians into battle in 1644 against the encroaching Virginia planters. Though his warriors killed several hundred English and brought the frontier to a standstill, Opechancanough was eventually captured and summarily shot through the head. The Powhatan confederacy died with him. Virginia's Indians would never again be in a position to go on the offense against the colony. Over the next decades and centuries, many Indians fled the region altogether. But whole communities remained, quietly determined to continue their lives and traditions in their homeland.

### Changes in English Policy in the Chesapeake >>

Throughout the 1630s and 1640s colonial affairs drew little concern from royal officials. England itself had become engulfed first by a political crisis and then by a civil war.

Outraged at the contempt that King Charles I had shown toward Parliament, disaffected elites and radical Puritans overthrew the king and executed him in 1649. When the "republic" of Oliver Cromwell turned out to be something closer to a military dictatorship, most English were happy to see their throne restored in 1660 to Charles II, the son of the beheaded king. The new monarch was determined that not only his subjects at home but also his American colonies abroad would contribute to England's prosperity. His colonial policy was reflected in a series of regulations passed in the 1660s and 1670s known as the Navigation Acts.

The acts severely restricted colonial trade with Britain's imperial rivals. In this sense they were mercantilistic, designed to ensure that England alone would profit from colonial production and trade. Chesapeake planters chafed under the Navigation Acts. They were used to conducting their affairs as they pleased—and they were often pleased to trade with the Dutch. And, adding to the unhappiness, the new restrictions came just as tobacco prices were dropping. In the effort to consolidate its empire England had unintentionally worsened the economic and social difficulties of Chesapeake society.

How did the Chesapeake colonies support the aims of British mercantilism?

## CHESAPEAKE SOCIETY IN CRISIS

By the 1660s overproduction was depressing tobacco prices, and wealthy planters reacted by putting even more prime coastal land into production. Newly freed servants had to either become tenants or try to establish farms to the west in Indian country. Meanwhile, export duties on tobacco paid under the Navigation Acts helped plunge many small planters into crushing debt, and some were forced back into servitude. By 1676 one-quarter of Virginia's free white men remained landless and frustrated.

As the discontent of the poor mounted, so did the worries of big planters. The assembly of the colony lengthened terms of servitude, hoping to limit the number of servants entering the free population. It curbed the political rights of landless men, hoping to stifle opposition by depriving them of the vote. But these measures only set off a spate of mutinies among servants and protests over rising taxes among small planters.

### Bacon's Rebellion and Coode's Rebellion >>

Tensions came to a head in 1676. The immediate spark to rebellion was renewed fighting between desperate Indians and the expanding colonial population. Virginia's royal governor, William Berkeley, favored building forts to guard against Indians, but frontier farmers opposed his plan as expensive and an ineffective way to defend their scattered plantations. When they clamored for an expedition to punish the Indians, Nathaniel Bacon stepped forward to lead it.

Wealthy and well connected, Bacon had arrived recently from England, expecting to receive every favor from the

>> This ceramic pipe from the 1670s was probably used by an indentured servant or tenant farmer living near Jamestown. Its design, featuring an animal carved around the pipe bowl, combined features typical of pipes made by English colonists, Indians, and African Americans. Virginia during this period experienced unstable relations between the expanding English population, the declining Indian population (due to wars and enslavement), and the growing number of enslaved Africans taking a larger role in the colony.
©Virginia Historical Society/Xanterra Corporation

governor—including permission to trade with the Indians from his frontier plantation. But Berkeley and a few select friends already held a monopoly on the Indian trade. When they declined to include Bacon, he took up the cause of his poorer frontier neighbors. Other recent, well-to-do immigrants who resented being excluded from Berkeley's circle of power and patronage also joined the cause.

In the summer of 1676 Bacon marched into Jamestown with a body of armed men and bullied the assembly into approving his expedition to kill Indians. While Bacon carried out that grisly business, slaughtering friendly as well as hostile natives, Berkeley rallied his supporters and declared Bacon a rebel. Bacon retaliated by turning his forces against those led by the governor. Both sides sought allies by offering freedom to servants and slaves willing to join their ranks. Many were willing: for months the followers of Bacon and Berkeley plundered one another's plantations. In September 1676 Bacon reduced Jamestown to a mound of ashes. Only his death from dysentery snuffed out the rebellion.

Political upheaval also shook Maryland, where colonists had long resented the sway of the Calvert family. As proprietors the Calverts and their favorites monopolized political offices, just as Berkeley's circle had in Virginia. Well-to-do planters wanted a share of the Calverts' power. Smaller farmers, like those in Virginia, wanted a less expensive and more representative government. Compounding the tensions were religious differences: the Calverts and their friends were Catholic, but other colonists, including Maryland's most successful planters, were Protestant.

The unrest peaked in July 1689. A former member of the assembly, John Coode, gathered an army, captured the proprietary governor, and then took grievances to authorities in England. There Coode received a sympathetic hearing. The Calverts' charter was revoked and not restored until 1715, by which time the family had become Protestant.

After the rebellions, rich planters in both Chesapeake colonies fought among themselves less and cooperated more. In Virginia older leaders and newer arrivals divided the spoils of political office. In Maryland Protestants and Catholics shared power and privilege. Those arrangements ensured that no future Bacon or Coode would mobilize restless gentlemen against the government. By acting together in legislative assemblies, the planter elite managed to curb the power of royal and proprietary governors for decades.

But the greater unity among the Chesapeake's leading families did little to ease that region's most fundamental problem—the sharp inequality of white society. The gulf between rich and poor planters, which had been etched ever more deeply by the troubled tobacco economy, persisted long after the rebellions of Bacon and Coode. All that saved white society in the Chesapeake from renewed crisis and conflict was the growth of African slavery.

**From Servitude to Slavery** >> Like the tobacco plants that spread across Powhatan's land, a labor system based on African slavery was an on-the-ground innovation. Both early promoters and planters preferred paying for English servants to importing alien African slaves. Black slaves, because they served for life, were more expensive than white workers, who served only for several years. Because neither whites nor blacks lived long, cheaper servant labor was the logical choice. The black population of the Chesapeake remained small for most of the seventeenth century, constituting just 5 percent of all inhabitants in 1675.

Africans had arrived in Virginia by 1619, most likely via the Dutch, who dominated the slave trade until the middle of the eighteenth century. The lives of those newcomers resembled the lot of white servants, with whom they shared harsh work routines and living conditions. White and black bound laborers socialized with one another and formed sexual liaisons. They conspired to steal from their masters and

<< Nathaniel Bacon and his rebels briefly occupied Jamestown and, before being forced to retreat, set the town on fire, including the brick church whose remains survive today. That evening Governor Berkeley watched from the deck of his ship as flames lit up the night sky.
Source: Library of Congress, Prints and Photographs Division [LC-D4-14191]

## Make a Case

Very few European colonists opposed slavery in the seventeenth century. Why did something that seems so obviously wrong now seem so natural and unremarkable then?

H

## Hip Mask from Benin

These images of mudfish alternate with those of Portuguese merchants. What might the mudfish be meant to symbolize? (Use a few key terms to find answers on the web.)
These pieces of inlaid iron represent medicine-filled incisions that were said to have given Idia metaphysical powers.
Object is hollow at the back; may have been used as receptacle for medicines, as well as a pendant for a hip belt.


This exquisite sixteenth-century ivory mask, now in New York's Metropolitan Museum of Art, graced the neck of Benin's king during ceremonial occasions. Its subtlety and precision suggest that it was produced by Benin's famed guild of royal ivory carvers, specifically for royalty. The object communicates a tremendous amount of visual information. The face itself is a portrait of Idia, mother of Benin's great early sixteenth-century leader Esigie. A powerful political figure in her own right, Idia helped secure the throne for her son and remained an influential adviser throughout his reign. On her head and around her neck are miniature faces of Portuguese merchants who brought great wealth to Benin and enriched and empowered its leaders through the slave trade.

### THINKING CRITICALLY

*Why pair the mudfish and the Portuguese? Do you think that the artist conceived of the Portuguese merchants as equals? Would you expect Benin's artistic sophistication to shape how the Portuguese regarded the kingdom?*

*Source:* Metropolitan Museum of Art, www.metmuseum.org/toah/ho/08/sfg/ho_1978.412.323.htm.; *Photo:* ©VCG Wilson/Corbis via Getty Images

ran away together; if caught, they endured similar punishments. There was more common ground: many of the first black settlers did not arrive directly from Africa but came from the Caribbean, where some had learned English and had adopted Christian beliefs. And not all were slaves: some were indentured servants; a handful were free.

A number of changes after 1680 caused planters to invest more heavily in slaves than in servants. First, as death rates in the Chesapeake began to drop, slaves became a more profitable investment. Although they were more expensive to buy than servants, planters could now expect to get many years of work from their bondspeople. Equally important, masters would have title to the children that slaves were now living long enough to have. At the same time, the influx of white servants was falling off just as the pool of available black labor was expanding. When the Royal African Company lost its monopoly on the English slave trade in 1698, other merchants entered the market. The number of Africans sold by British dealers swelled to 20,000 annually.

## Africa and the Atlantic Slave Trade >>

From 1492 to 1820, enslaved African arrivals outnumbered European migrants to the New World by nearly five to one. Put differently, before the twentieth-century, African workers did most of the heavy lifting in the economies of the Americas.

# MAP 3.3: SLAVE TRADE ALONG THE GOLD COAST

Toward the end of the seventeenth century, Chesapeake and Carolina planters began importing increasing numbers of slaves. In Africa, the center of that trade lay along a mountainous region known as the Gold Coast, where more than a hundred European trading posts and forts funneled the trade. Despite the heavy trade, only about 4 percent of the total transatlantic slave trade went to North America. *How many different ethnic groups are shown on the map? Would that number be likely to encourage the slave trade, and if so, how?*

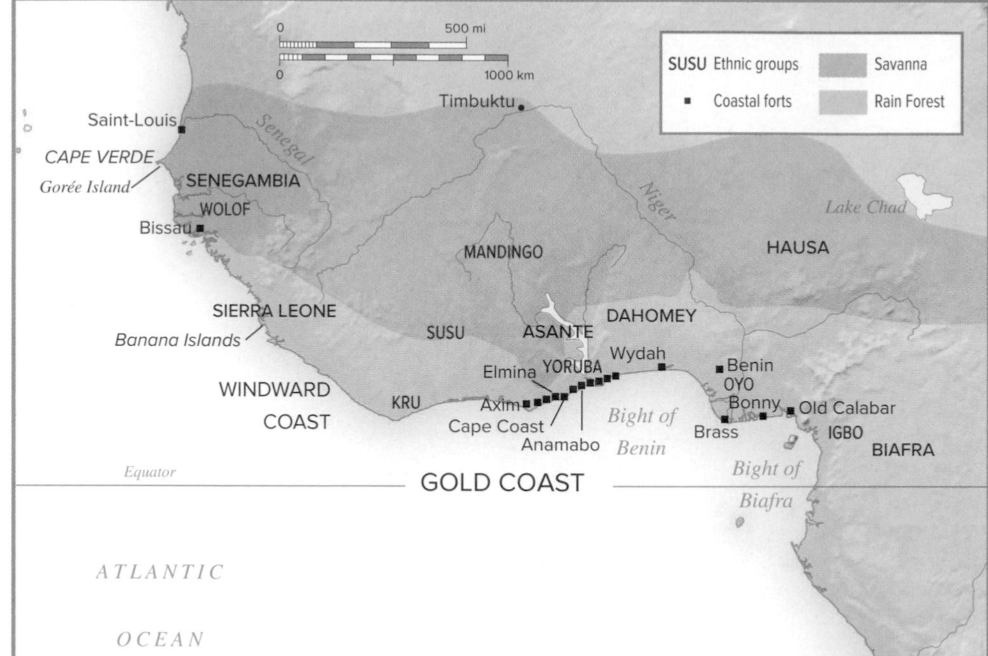

0
500 mi
0
1000 km
SUSU Ethnic groups
Coastal forts
Savanna
Rain Forest
Timbuktu
Saint-Louis
CAPE VERDE
Gorée Island
SENEGAMBIA
WOLOF
Bissau
Senegal
Niger
Lake Chad
HAUSA
MANDINGO
SIERRA LEONE
Banana Islands
SUSU
ASANTE
DAHOMEY
Elmina
YORUBA
Wydah
Benin
OYO
WINDWARD COAST
KRU
Axim
Cape Coast
Anamabo
Bight of Benin
Bonny
Old Calabar
Brass
IGBO
BIAFRA
Bight of Biafra
Equator
GOLD COAST
ATLANTIC OCEAN

^ Katharina, sketched in 1521, was a servant living in the Netherlands. She was probably one of the increasing number of Africans being brought to Europe owing to the growing slave trade.
©Photoservice Electa/Universal Images Group/SuperStock

>> Slaves captured in the African interior were marched out in slave "coffles," a forced march in which captives were linked either by chains or by wooden yoke restraints linking two slaves together as they walked.
©The Granger Collection, New York

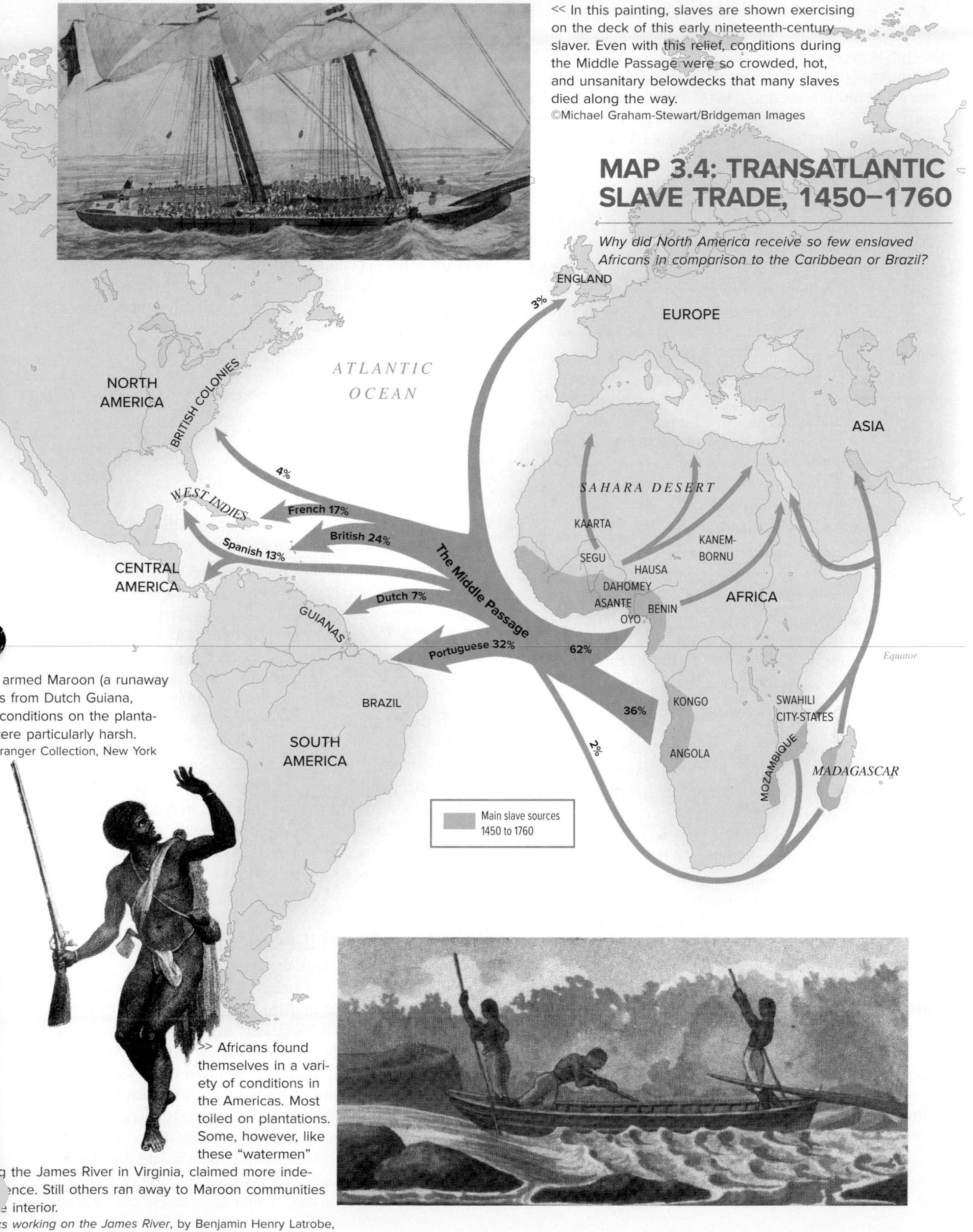

ENGLAND
EUROPE
ASIA
AFRICA
NORTH AMERICA
CENTRAL AMERICA
SOUTH AMERICA
ATLANTIC OCEAN
BRITISH COLONIES
WEST INDIES
GUIANAS
BRAZIL
SAHARA DESERT
KAARTA
SEGU
HAUSA
KANEM-BORNU
DAHOMEY
ASANTE
OYO
BENIN
KONGO
ANGOLA
SWAHILI CITY-STATES
MOZAMBIQUE
MADAGASCAR
Equator
The Middle Passage
3%
4%
French 17%
British 24%
Spanish 13%
Dutch 7%
Portuguese 32%
62%
36%
2%
Main slave sources 1450 to 1760


## MAP 3.4: TRANSATLANTIC SLAVE TRADE, 1450–1760

*Why did North America receive so few enslaved Africans in comparison to the Caribbean or Brazil?*

<< In this painting, slaves are shown exercising on the deck of this early nineteenth-century slaver. Even with this relief, conditions during the Middle Passage were so crowded, hot, and unsanitary belowdecks that many slaves died along the way.
©Michael Graham-Stewart/Bridgeman Images

; armed Maroon (a runaway is from Dutch Guiana, conditions on the planta- vere particularly harsh.
Granger Collection, New York

>> Africans found themselves in a variety of conditions in the Americas. Most toiled on plantations. Some, however, like these "watermen" g the James River in Virginia, claimed more inde- ence. Still others ran away to Maroon communities e interior.
*ks working on the James River*, by Benjamin Henry Latrobe, 8-99. Courtesy of the Library of Virginia

For a century after Columbus's arrival, the traffic in slaves to the Americas had numbered a few thousand annually. But as sugar cultivation steadily prospered after 1600, slave imports rose to 19,000 a year during the seventeenth century and mushroomed to 60,000 a year in the eighteenth century. All told, as many as 21 million people were captured in West and Central Africa between 1700 and 1850: some 9 million among them entered the Americas as slaves, but millions died before or during the Atlantic crossing, and as many as 7 million remained slaves in Africa. Although slavery became indispensable to its economy, British North America played a relatively small role in the Atlantic slave trade. Nine-tenths of all Africans brought to the New World landed in Brazil or the Caribbean islands (see Map 3.4).

The rapid growth of the trade transformed not only the Americas but also Africa. Slavery became more widespread within African society, and slave trading more central to its domestic and international commerce. Most important, the African merchants and political leaders most deeply invested in the slave trade used their profits for political advantage—to build new chiefdoms and states such as Dahomey, Asante, and the Lunda Empire. Their ambitions and the greed of European slave dealers drew an increasingly large number of Africans, particularly people living in the interior, into slavery's web. By the late seventeenth century, Africans being sold into slavery were no longer only those who had put themselves at risk by committing crimes, running into debt, or voicing unpopular political and religious views. The larger number were instead captives taken by soldiers or kidnappers in raids launched specifically to acquire prisoners for the slave trade, or else desperate refugees captured while fleeing war, famine, and disease. During the decades after 1680, captives coming directly from Africa made up more than 80 percent of all new slaves entering the Chesapeake and the rest of mainland North America. Many were shipped from the coast of Africa that Portuguese explorers had first probed, between the Senegal and Niger Rivers. Most of the rest came from Angola, farther south.

Seized by other Africans, captives were yoked together at the neck and marched hundreds of miles through the interior to coastal forts or other outposts along the Atlantic. There, they were penned in hundreds of prisons, in lots of anywhere from 20 or 30 to more than 1,000. They might be forced to wait for slaving vessels in French *captiveries* below the fine houses of traders on the island of Gorée, or herded into "outfactories"on the Banana Islands upstream on the Sierra Leone River, or perhaps marched into the dank underground slaveholds at the English fort at Cape Coast (see Map 3.3). Farther south, captives were held in marshy, fever-ridden lowlands along the Bight of Benin, waiting for a slaver to drop anchor. One African, Ottobah Cugoano, recalled finally being taken aboard ship:

> There was nothing to be heard but the rattling of chains, smacking of whips, and the groans and cries of our fellow-men. Some would not stir from the ground, when they were lashed and beat in the most horrible manner. . . . And when we found ourselves at last taken away, death was more preferable than life, and a plan was concerted amongst us that we might burn and blow up the ship and to perish altogether in the flames.

**Middle Passage** the harrowing ocean journey slaves took from Africa to the Americas.

Worse than the imprisonment was the voyage itself: the so-called **Middle Passage**, a nightmarish journey across the Atlantic that could take anywhere between three weeks and three months, depending on currents, weather, and where ships disembarked and landed. Often several hundred black men, women, and children were packed below decks, squeezed onto platforms built in tiers spaced so close that sitting upright was impossible. It was difficult to know whether the days or the nights were more hellish. Slaves were taken out and forced to exercise for their health for a few hours each day; the rest of the day, the sun beat down and the heat below the decks was "so excessive," one voyager recalled, that the doctors who went below to examine slaves "would faint away, and the candles would not burn." At night, the slaves "were often heard making a howling melancholy kind of noise," noted a doctor aboard another ship. It was because the slaves, while sleeping, had dreamed "they were back in their own country again, amongst their families and friends" and "when they woke up to find themselves in reality on a slave ship they began to bay and shriek." Historians estimate that for every 85 enslaved Africans that set foot in the Americas, 15 died during the Middle Passage.

After the numb, exhausted survivors reached American ports, they faced more challenges to staying alive. The first year in the colonies was the most deadly for new, "unseasoned" slaves. The sickle-cell genetic trait gave them a greater immunity to malaria than Europeans, but slaves were highly susceptible to respiratory infections. One-quarter of all Africans died during their first year in the Chesapeake, and among Carolina and Caribbean slaves, mortality rates were far higher. In addition to the new disease environment, Africans had to adapt to lives without freedom in a wholly unfamiliar country and culture.

## A Changing Chesapeake Society >>

Exchanging a labor system based on servitude for one based on slavery transformed Chesapeake society. Most obviously, the number of Afro-Virginians rose sharply. By 1740, 40 percent of all Virginians were black, and most of those were African-born. Unlike many African men and women who had arrived earlier from the Caribbean, these new inhabitants had little familiarity with English language and culture. This larger, more distinctively African community was also locked into a slave system that was becoming ever more rigid and demeaning. By the late decades of the seventeenth century, new laws made it more difficult for masters to free slaves. Other legislation used racial categories to separate people. Laws prohibited free black settlers from having white servants, and forbade interracial marriages and sexual relationships. The legal code fostered **racism** and white contempt for black Virginians in a variety of other ways. While masters were prohibited from whipping their white servants on the bare back, slaves had no such protection. And "any Negro that shall presume to strike any white" was to receive 30 lashes for that rash act.

**racism** discrimination based on inherited physical differences, which according to racist thought separated humans into a few distinct and unequal groups or "races."

These and other new laws both reflected and encouraged racism among white colonists of all classes. Deepening racism, in turn, made it unlikely that poor white planters, tenants, and servants would ever join with poor black slaves to challenge the privilege of great planters. Instead of identifying with the plight of the slaves, the Chesapeake's poorer white residents considered black Virginians their natural inferiors. They could pride themselves on sharing with wealthy white gentlemen the same skin color and on being their equals in the eyes of the law.

The leaders of the Chesapeake colonies cultivated unity among white inhabitants by improving economic prospects for freed servants and lesser planters. The Virginia assembly made provisions for freed servants to get a better start as independent farmers. It lowered taxes, allowing small planters to keep more of their earnings. New laws also gave most white male Virginians a vote in elections, allowing them an outlet to express their grievances. Economic trends toward the end of the seventeenth century contributed to the greater prosperity of small planters, because tobacco prices rose slightly and then stabilized. As a result of Bacon's savage campaign against the Virginia Indians, new land on the frontier became available. Even the domestic lives of ordinary people became more secure as mortality rates declined and the numbers of men and women in the white population evened out. As a result, virtually all men were now able to marry, and families were fragmented less often by the premature deaths of spouses and parents.

After 1700 the Chesapeake evolved into a more stable society. Gone were the bands of wild, landless, young bachelors one step ahead of the law, the small body of struggling lesser planters one step ahead of ruin, and the great mass of exploited servants one step away from rebellion. Virginia and Maryland became colonies of farming families, most of them small planters who owned between 50 and 200 acres. These families held no slaves, or at most two or three. And they accepted, usually without question, the social and political leadership of their acknowledged "superiors," great planters who styled themselves the "gentry."

REVIEW

Why did slavery replace servitude as the dominant labor system in Virginia and Maryland?

# FROM THE CARIBBEAN TO THE CAROLINAS

During the same decade that the English invaded Powhatan's land, they began to colonize the Caribbean, whose islands extended north and west, like beads on a string, from the Lesser Antilles toward the more substantial lands of Puerto Rico, Hispaniola, Jamaica, and Cuba (see Map 3.5). At their long journey's end English sailors found what seemed a paradise: shores rimmed with white sand beaches that rose sharply to coral terraces, then to broad plateaus or mountain peaks shrouded in rain forests. The earliest arrivals came intending not to colonize but to steal from the Spanish. Even after 1604 when some English settled on the islands, few intended to stay.

Yet the English did establish permanent plantation colonies in the West Indies. Beyond that, their Caribbean settlements became the jumping-off points for a new colony on the North American mainland—South Carolina. Because of the strong West Indian influence, South Carolina developed a social order in some ways distinct from that of the Chesapeake colonies. In other ways, however, the development paralleled Virginia and Maryland's path. In both regions, extreme violence, high mortality, and uncertainty gave way to relative stability only over the course of many decades.

**Paradise Lost** >> The English had traded and battled with the Spanish in the Caribbean since the 1560s. From those island bases English buccaneers conducted an illegal trade with Spanish settlements, sacked the coastal towns, and plundered silver ships bound for Seville. Weakened by decades of warfare, Spain could not hold the West Indies. The Dutch drove a wedge into Caribbean trade routes, and the French and the English began to colonize the islands.

In the 40 years after 1604 some 30,000 immigrants from the British Isles planted crude frontier outposts on St. Kitts, Barbados, Nevis, Montserrat, and Antigua. The settlers—some free, many others indentured servants, and almost all young men—devoted themselves to working as little as possible, drinking as much as possible, and returning to England as soon as possible. They cultivated for export a poor-quality tobacco, which returned just enough profit to maintain straggling settlements of small farms.

Then, nearly overnight, sugar cultivation transformed the Caribbean. In the 1640s Barbados planters learned from the Dutch how to process sugarcane. The Dutch also supplied African slaves to work the cane fields and marketed the sugar for high prices in the Netherlands. Sugar plantations and slave labor rapidly spread to other English and French islands as Europeans developed an insatiable sweet tooth for

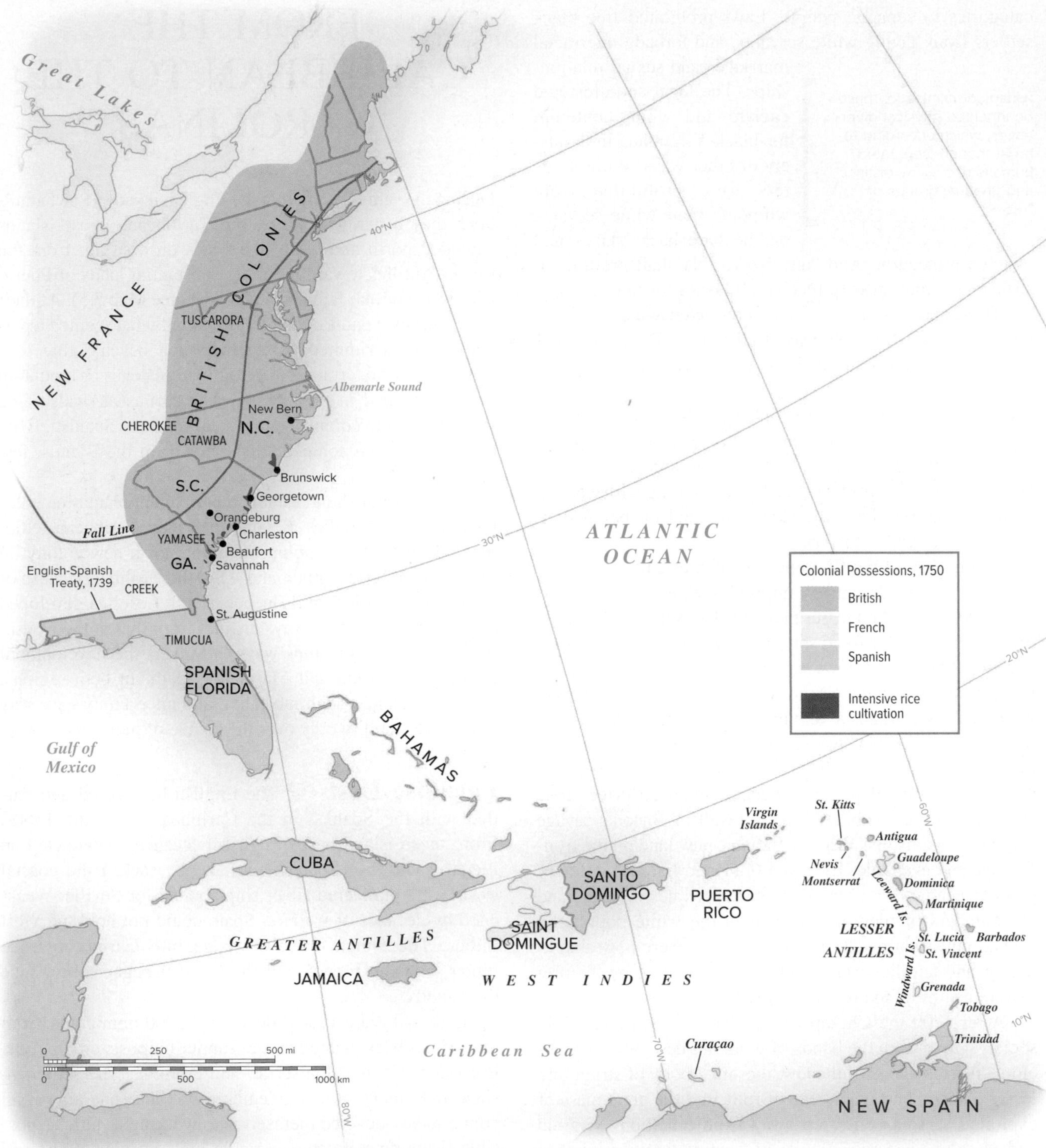
Great Lakes
NEW FRANCE
BRITISH COLONIES
TUSCARORA
Albemarle Sound
New Bern
N.C.
CHEROKEE
CATAWBA
Brunswick
S.C.
Georgetown
Orangeburg
Fall Line
YAMASEE
Charleston
Beaufort
GA.
Savannah
English-Spanish Treaty, 1739
CREEK
St. Augustine
TIMUCUA
SPANISH FLORIDA
Gulf of Mexico
BAHAMAS
ATLANTIC OCEAN
40°N
30°N
20°N
10°N
60°W
70°W
80°W
Colonial Possessions, 1750
British
French
Spanish
Intensive rice cultivation
CUBA
SANTO DOMINGO
PUERTO RICO
SAINT DOMINGUE
GREATER ANTILLES
JAMAICA
WEST INDIES
Virgin Islands
St. Kitts
Antigua
Nevis
Montserrat
Guadeloupe
Dominica
Martinique
Leeward Is.
LESSER ANTILLES
St. Lucia
Barbados
St. Vincent
Windward Is.
Grenada
Tobago
Trinidad
Curaçao
Caribbean Sea
NEW SPAIN
0
250
500 mi
0
500
1000 km

# MAP 3.5: THE CAROLINAS AND THE CARIBBEAN

The map underscores the geographic link between West Indian and Carolina settlements. Emigrants from Barbados dominated politics in early South Carolina, while Carolinians provided foodstuffs, grain, and cattle to the West Indies. As South Carolinians began growing rice, Caribbean slave ships found it an easy sail north and west to unload their cargoes in Charleston.

*The fall line is marked here and on Map 3.2, Colonies of the Chesapeake. What is the fall line? Why is it significant?*

<< With large majorities of their populations enslaved, the sugar-producing islands of the Caribbean were anxious, fearful places of brutal labor and gruesome discipline. But they were also sites of rich social life and cultural development, as this slave dance on the island of St. Vincent suggests.


the once-scarce commodity. Caribbean sugar made more money for England than the total volume of commodities exported by all the mainland American colonies.

Even though its great planters became the richest people in English America, they could not have confused the West Indies with paradise. Throughout the seventeenth century disease took a fearful toll, and island populations grew only because of immigration. In the scramble for land, small farmers were pushed onto tiny plots that barely allowed them to survive.

The desperation of bound laborers posed another threat to British planters. After the Caribbean's conversion to cultivating sugar, African slaves gradually replaced indentured servants in the cane fields. By the beginning of the eighteenth century, resident Africans outnumbered English by four to one. Fear of servant mutinies and slave rebellions frayed the nerves of island masters. They tried to contain the danger by imposing harsh slave codes and inflicting brutal punishments on all laborers. But planters lived under a constant state of siege. One visitor to Barbados observed that whites fortified their homes with parapets from which they could pour scalding water on attacking servants and slaves. During the first century of settlement, seven major slave uprisings shook the English islands.

As more people squeezed onto the islands, some settlers looked for a way out. With all the land in use, the Caribbean no longer offered opportunity to freed servants or even planters' sons. It was then that the West Indies started to shape the history of the American South.

**The Founding of the Carolinas** >> The colonization of the Carolinas began with the schemes of Virginia's royal governor, William Berkeley, and Sir John Colleton, a supporter of Charles I who had been exiled to the Caribbean at the end of England's civil war. Colleton saw that the Caribbean had a surplus of white settlers, and Berkeley knew that Virginians needed room to expand as well. Together the two men set their sights on the area south of Virginia. Along with a number of other aristocrats, they convinced Charles II to make them joint proprietors in 1663 of a place they called the Carolinas, in honor of the king.

A few hardy souls from Virginia had already squatted around Albemarle Sound in the northern part of the Carolina grant. In 1701, the proprietors set off North Carolina as a separate colony. The desolate region proved a disappointment. Lacking good harbors and navigable rivers, the colony had no convenient way of marketing its produce. North Carolina remained a poor colony, its sparse population engaged in general farming and the production of masts, pitch, tar, and turpentine.

The southern portion of the Carolina grant held far more promise, especially in the eyes of one of its proprietors, Sir Anthony Ashley Cooper, Earl of Shaftesbury. In 1669 Cooper sponsored an expedition of a few hundred English and Barbadian immigrants, who planted the first permanent settlement in South Carolina. By 1680 the colonists had established the center of economic, social, and political life at the confluence of the Ashley and Cooper Rivers, naming the site Charles Town (later Charleston) after the king. Like others before him, Cooper hoped to create an ideal society in America. His utopia was a place where a few landed aristocrats and gentlemen would rule with the consent of many smaller property holders. With his personal secretary, the renowned philosopher John Locke, Cooper drew up an intricate scheme of government, the Fundamental Constitutions. The design provided Carolina with a proprietary governor and a hereditary nobility who, as a Council of Lords, would recommend all laws to a Parliament elected by lesser landowners.

The Fundamental Constitutions met the same fate as other lordly dreams for America. Instead of peacefully observing its provisions, most of the Carolinians, migrants from Barbados, plunged into economic and political wrangling. They challenged proprietary rule, protested or ignored laws and regulations imposed on them, and rejected the proprietors' relatively benevolent vision of Indian relations. Instead, the colonists fomented a series of Indian slave wars that nearly destroyed the colony altogether.

## Carolina, Florida, and the Southeastern Slave Wars

>> Taking wealthy Barbados as the model, the colonists intended to grow Carolina's economy around cash crops tended by African slaves. But before they could afford to establish such a regime, the newcomers needed to raise capital through trade with Indians. Colonists gave textiles, metal goods, guns, and alcohol in exchange for hundreds of thousands of deerskins, which they then exported.

But the trade soon came to revolve around a commodity dearer still. As did most peoples throughout history, southeastern Indians sometimes made slaves of their enemies. Carolina's traders vastly expanded this existing slave culture by turning captives into prized commodities. Convinced that local Indians were physically weaker than Africans and more likely to rebel or flee, colonial traders bought slaves from Indian allies and then exported them to other mainland colonies or to the Caribbean. They found eager native partners in this business. Contact with Europe had unleashed phenomenal changes in interior North America. Epidemics ruined one people and gave advantage to another, new commercial opportunities sparked fierce wars over hunting and trading territories, and many thousands of Indian families became displaced and had to rebuild their lives somewhere new. The chaos, conflict, and movement gave enterprising Indians ample opportunity to enslave weak neighbors and stock Carolina's slave pens.

To ensure a steady supply of slaves, Carolinian merchants courted a variety of Indian allies during the late seventeenth and early eighteenth centuries and encouraged them to raid mission Indians in Spanish Florida. By 1700 Florida's Indian peoples were in sharp decline, and Charles Town's slave traders turned to the large and powerful Creek, Choctaw, Chickasaw, and Cherokee confederacies of the interior, encouraging them to raid one another. Before long the slave wars had a momentum all their own, extending as far west as the Mississippi River. Even native peoples who deplored the violence and despised the English felt compelled to participate, lest they too become victims.

The trade became central to Carolina's economy, and colonists high and low sought to profit from it. In 1702 Governor James Moore, one of the colony's chief slave traders, launched an audacious raid against Spanish St. Augustine and Florida's missions, returning with hundreds of Indian captives. His campaign inspired still more raids, and over the next few years Creeks, Yamasees, and Englishmen laid waste to 29 Spanish missions, shattering thousands of lives and destroying Spain's precarious system of Indian alliances. By 1706 Spanish authority was once again confined to St. Augustine and its immediate vicinity. Within another 10 years most of Florida had been depopulated.

It seemed a double victory from Charles Town's perspective. The English had bested a European rival for the Crown and had reaped enormous profits besides. The fragmentary evidence suggests that Carolinians had purchased or captured between 30,000 and 50,000 Indian slaves before 1715. Indeed, before that date South Carolina exported more slaves than it imported from Africa or the Caribbean. But in 1715 Carolina's merchants finally paid a price for the wars that they had cynically fomented for over 40 years.

With Florida virtually exhausted of slaves, the Yamasees grew nervous. Convinced that Carolina would soon turn on them as it had on other onetime allies, the Yamasees struck first. They attacked traders, posts, and plantations on the outskirts of Charles Town, killing hundreds of colonists and dragging scores more to Florida to sell as slaves in St. Augustine. Panicked authorities turned to other Indian peoples in the region but found most had either joined the Yamasees or were too hostile and suspicious to help.

Though Carolina narrowly survived the Yamasee War, it took decades to recover. The destructive regional slave trade virtually came to an end, and animal skins again dominated regional commerce. The powerful southern confederacies grew wary of aligning too closely with any single European power and henceforth sought to play colonies and empires off each other. It was a strategy that would bring them relative peace and prosperity for generations.

## White, Red, and Black: The Search for Order

>> Postwar Carolina invested more and more of its resources in African slaves and in the cultivation of rice, a crop that eventually made South Carolina's planters the richest cohort in mainland North America. Unfortunately,

>> Mulberry Plantation in South Carolina was first carved from coastal swamps in 1714. This painting, done half a century later, shows the Great House visible in the distance, flanked by slave quarters. African slaves skilled in rice cultivation oversaw the arduous task of properly planting and irrigating the crop. *View of Mulberry, House and Street, ca. 1800,* by Thomas Coram. 1968.018.0001. Image Courtesy of the Gibbes Museum of Art/Carolina Art Association

South Carolina's swampy coast, so perfectly suited to growing rice, was less suited for human habitation. Weakened by chronic malaria, settlers died in epic numbers from yellow fever, smallpox, and respiratory infections. The European population grew slowly, through immigration rather than natural increase, and numbered only 10,000 by 1730.

Early South Carolinians had little in common but the harsh conditions of frontier existence. Most colonists lived on isolated plantations; early deaths fragmented families and neighborhoods. Immigration after 1700 further intensified the colony's ethnic and religious diversity, adding Swiss and German Lutherans, Scots-Irish Presbyterians, Welsh Baptists, and Spanish Jews. The colony's only courts were in Charles Town; churches and clergy of any denomination were scarce. On those rare occasions when early Carolinians came together, they gathered at Charles Town to escape the pestilential air of their plantations, to sue one another for debt and haggle over prices, or to fight over religious differences and proprietary politics.

Finally, in 1729, the Crown formally established royal government; by 1730 economic recovery had done much to ease the strife. Even more important in bringing greater political stability, the European colonists of South Carolina came to realize that they must unite if they were to counter the Spanish in Florida and the French and their Indian allies on the Gulf Coast.

The growing African population gave European Carolinians another reason to maintain a united front. During the first decades of settlement, frontier conditions and the scarcity of labor had forced masters to allow enslaved Africans greater freedom within bondage. European and African laborers shared chores on small farms. On stock-raising plantations called "cowpens," African cowboys ranged freely over the countryside. African contributions to the defense of the colony also reinforced racial interdependence and muted European domination. Whenever threats arose—during the Yamasee War, for example—Africans were enlisted in the militia.

European Carolinians depended on African labor even more after turning to rice as their cash crop. In fact, planters began to import slaves in larger numbers partly because of West African skill in rice cultivation. But Europeans harbored deepening fears of the African workers whose labor built planter fortunes. As early as 1708 African men and women had become a majority in the colony, and by 1730 they outnumbered European settlers by two to one. As their colony began to prosper, European Carolinians put into effect strict slave codes like those in the Caribbean that converted their colony into an armed camp and snuffed out the marginal freedoms that African settlers had once enjoyed.

**The Founding of Georgia** >> After 1730 Carolinians could take comfort not only in newfound prosperity and new political harmony but also in the founding of a new colony on their southern border. South Carolinians liked Georgia a great deal more than the Virginians had liked Maryland, because the colony formed a buffer between British North America and Spanish Florida in much the same way that Yamasees had, before the war.

Enhancing the military security of South Carolina was only one reason for the founding of Georgia. More important to General James Oglethorpe and other idealistic English gentlemen was the aim of aiding the "worthy poor" by providing them with land, employment, and a new start. They envisioned a colony of hardworking small farmers who would produce silk and wine, sparing England the need to import those commodities. That dream seemed within reach when George II made Oglethorpe and his friends the trustees of the new colony in 1732, granting them a charter for 21 years. At the end of that time Georgia would revert to royal control.

The trustees did not, as legend has it, empty England's debtors' prisons to populate Georgia. They freed few debtors but from every country in Europe recruited paupers who seemed willing to work hard—and who professed Protestantism. Trustees paid the paupers' passage and provided each with 50 acres of land, tools, and a year's worth of supplies. Settlers who could pay their own way were encouraged to come by being granted larger tracts of land. Much to the trustees' dismay, that generous offer was taken up not only by many hoped-for Protestants but also by several hundred Ashkenazim (German Jews) and Sephardim (Spanish and Portuguese Jews), who established a thriving community in early Savannah.

The trustees were determined to ensure that Georgia became a small farmers' utopia. Rather than selling land, the trustees gave it away, but none of the colony's settlers could own more than 500 acres. The trustees also outlawed slavery and hard liquor in order to cultivate habits of industry and sustain equality among whites. This design for a virtuous and egalitarian utopia was greeted with little enthusiasm by Georgians. They pressed for a free market in land and argued that the colony could never prosper until the trustees revoked their ban on slavery. Because the trustees had provided for no elective assembly, settlers could express their discontent only by moving to South Carolina—which many did during the early decades. As mounting opposition threatened to depopulate the colony, the trustees caved in. They revoked their restrictions on land, slavery, and liquor a few years before the king assumed control of the colony in 1752. Under royal control Georgia continued to develop an ethnically and religiously diverse society, akin to that of South Carolina. Similarly, its economy was based on rice cultivation and the Indian trade.

**REVIEW**

How was the colonization of Carolina both distinct from and parallel to that of the Chesapeake?

Empire . . . utopia . . . independence. . . . For more than a century after the founding of Oñate's colony on the upper Rio Grande in 1598, those dreams inspired newcomers to New Mexico, Florida, the Chesapeake, the English Caribbean, the Carolinas, and Georgia. Each of these regions served as a staging ground where kings and commoners, free and unfree, men and women, Native Americans, Europeans, and Africans played out their hopes. Their acts were as often filled with desperation, for conditions were often unimaginably harsh.

The dream of an expanding empire faltered for the Spanish, who found few riches in the Southwest and eventually found rebellion. The dream of empire failed, too, when James I and Charles I, England's early Stuart kings, found their power checked by Parliament. And the dream foundered fatally for Indians—for Powhatan's successors, who were unable to resist Old World diseases and land-hungry tobacco planters; for the Yamasees; and for the many Indian peoples of Florida who sought to survive, accommodate, or exploit colonialism, but fell to ruin in the end.

English lords had dreamed of establishing feudal utopias in America. But proprietors such as the Calvert family in Maryland and Cooper in the Carolinas found themselves hounded by frontier planters and farmers who sought economic and political power. Georgia's trustees struggled in vain to nurture their dream of a utopia for the poor. The dream of a Spanish Catholic utopia brought by missionaries to the American Southwest dimmed with native resistance and rebellion.

The dream of independence proved the most deceptive of all, especially for the inhabitants of England's colonies. Just a bare majority of the European servant emigrants to the Chesapeake survived to enjoy freedom. The rest were struck down by disease or worn down at the hands of tobacco barons eager for profit. Not only in the Chesapeake but also in the Caribbean and the Carolinas, real independence eluded the English planters. Poorer folk—dependent on richer settlers for land and leadership—deferred to them at church and on election days and depended on them to buy crops or to extend credit. Even the richest planters were dependent on the English and Scottish merchants who supplied them with credit and marketed their crops, as well as on the English officials who made colonial policy.

And everywhere in the American Southeast and Southwest, the lingering dreams of Europeans were realized only through the labor of the least free members of colonial America. That stubborn reality would haunt all Americans who continued to dream of freedom and independence.

# CHAPTER SUMMARY

During the seventeenth century, Spain and England moved to colonize critical regions of southern North America.

- Native peoples everywhere in the American South resisted colonization, despite losses from warfare, disease, and enslavement.
- Spanish colonies in New Mexico and Florida grew slowly and faced a variety of threats. By the late seventeenth century, Spanish New Mexico had been lost to the Pueblo Revolt, and Florida's delicate mission system was under siege from English Carolina and its Indian allies.
- Thriving monocultures were established in all of England's southern colonies—tobacco in the Chesapeake, rice in the Carolinas, and sugar in the Caribbean.
- Despite a period of intense enslavement of native peoples, African slavery emerged as the dominant labor system throughout these regions.
- Instability and conflict characterized both Spanish and English colonies in the South for most of the first century of their existence.

## Additional Reading

David J. Weber's *Spanish Frontier in North America* (1992) remains indispensable. Andrés Reséndez's *The Other Slavery* (2015) brilliantly excavates the history of Indian servitude in Spanish North America, and James Brooks's *Mesa of Sorrows* (2015) uses a single traumatic event to explore violence, identity, and memory in the Southwest. For Spain in the Southeast, see Paul E. Hoffman's *Florida's Frontiers* (2002); and Daniel S. Murphree's *Constructing Floridians* (2006).

For enduring treatments of early Virginia, see Edmund S. Morgan, *American Slavery, American Freedom* (1975); and Kathleen Brown, *Good Wives, Nasty Wenches, and Anxious Patriarchs* (1996). James D. Rice's *Tales from a Revolution* (2012) explores the multiple perspectives of Indians to Bacon's Rebellion. For Indians in the colonial Southeast, see Gregory A. Waselkov, Peter Wood, and Tom Hatley, eds., *Powhatan's Mantle* (2006). For native Virginia, see also Hellen C. Rountree, *Pocahontas, Powhatan, Opechancanough* (2005). Bernard Bailyn's *The Barbarous Years* (2012) paints an unforgivingly brutal portrait of English colonization in North America.

Recent years have seen a surge in scholarship on African slavery in the New World. David Brion Davis provides a magisterial overview in *Inhuman Bondage* (2006). For British North America, see Ira Berlin, *Many Thousands Gone* (1998); and Philip D. Morgan, *Slave Counterpoint* (1998). The classic account of the British Caribbean remains Richard Dunn's *Sugar and Slaves* ([1972] 2000). Vincent Brown's *Reaper's Garden* (2008) examines the brutalities of the Jamaican slave system. Stephanie Smallwood's *Saltwater Slavery* (2007) provides a haunting portrait of the Middle Passage.

The best overview of South Carolina's development remains Robert Weir, *Colonial South Carolina* (1982). The complexities of Carolina's slave wars are explored in Alan Gallay, *The Indian Slave Trade* (2002). For the topic more broadly, see Christina Snyder, *Slavery in Indian Country* (2010).

# 4 Colonization & Conflict in the North

## 1600–1700

New Amsterdam—present-day New York City—had a windmill *(left)* and a gallows *(center)* in 1664, when the English captured the outpost from the Dutch.



### >> An American Story

## BEARS ON FLOATING ISLANDS

They came to her one night while she slept. Into her dreams drifted a small island, and on the island were tall trees and living creatures, one of them wearing the fur of a white rabbit. When she told of her vision, no one took her seriously, not even the shamans and conjurers whose business it was to interpret dreams. No one, that is, until two days later, when the island appeared to all, floating toward shore. On it, as she had seen, were tall trees, and on their branches—bears. Or creatures that looked so much like bears that the men grabbed their weapons and raced to the beach, eager for the good hunt sent by the gods. They were disappointed. The island was not an island at all but a strange wooden ship planted with the trunks of trees. And the bears were not bears at all but a strange sort of men whose bodies were covered with hair. Strangest among them, as she had somehow known, was a man dressed all in white. He commanded great respect among the bearlike men as their "shaman," or priest.

In that way, foretold by the dreams of a young woman, the Micmac Indians in 1869 recounted their people's first encounter with Europeans more than two centuries earlier. Uncannily, the traditions of other northern tribes record similar dreams predicting the European arrival: "large canoes with great white wings like those of a giant bird," filled with pale bearded men bearing "long black tubes."

However Micmacs and other northern Indians first imagined and idealized Europeans, they quickly came to see them as fully human. Traders might bring seemingly wondrous goods, goods that could transform the way labor, commerce, politics, and war functioned in native communities. Yet the traders themselves hardly seemed magical. They could be by turns generous and miserly, brave and frightful, confident and confused, kind and cruel.

Moreover, it soon became clear that these newcomers hailed from different nations, spoke different languages, and often had different goals. English colonists, it seemed, were every day more numerous and wanted nothing so much as land. The French, in contrast, were relatively few and seemed to care for nothing so much as trade—unless it was their Christian God brought with them from across the waters. Strange to say, the Europeans argued over their deity as they did over so many other things. The English, the French, and the Dutch were all rivals, and the Micmacs and others who encountered these new peoples studied them closely and began to make alliances.

Everywhere they went, the newcomers provoked dramatic changes. Thousands of English migrants founded villages and towns throughout the seventeenth century. They not only took up land but also brought animals and plants that changed the way Indians lived. The Dutch, Europe's most powerful commercial nation, planted only a handful of trading settlements along the Hudson River, but they encouraged the Iroquois confederacy to push into rival Indian territories in a quest for furs to trade. Even the French, who claimed to want little more than beaver pelts, brought profound, sometimes cataclysmic changes—changes that would upend the world that natives knew when Europeans were but bears on floating islands. <<

## THEMATIC TIMELINE

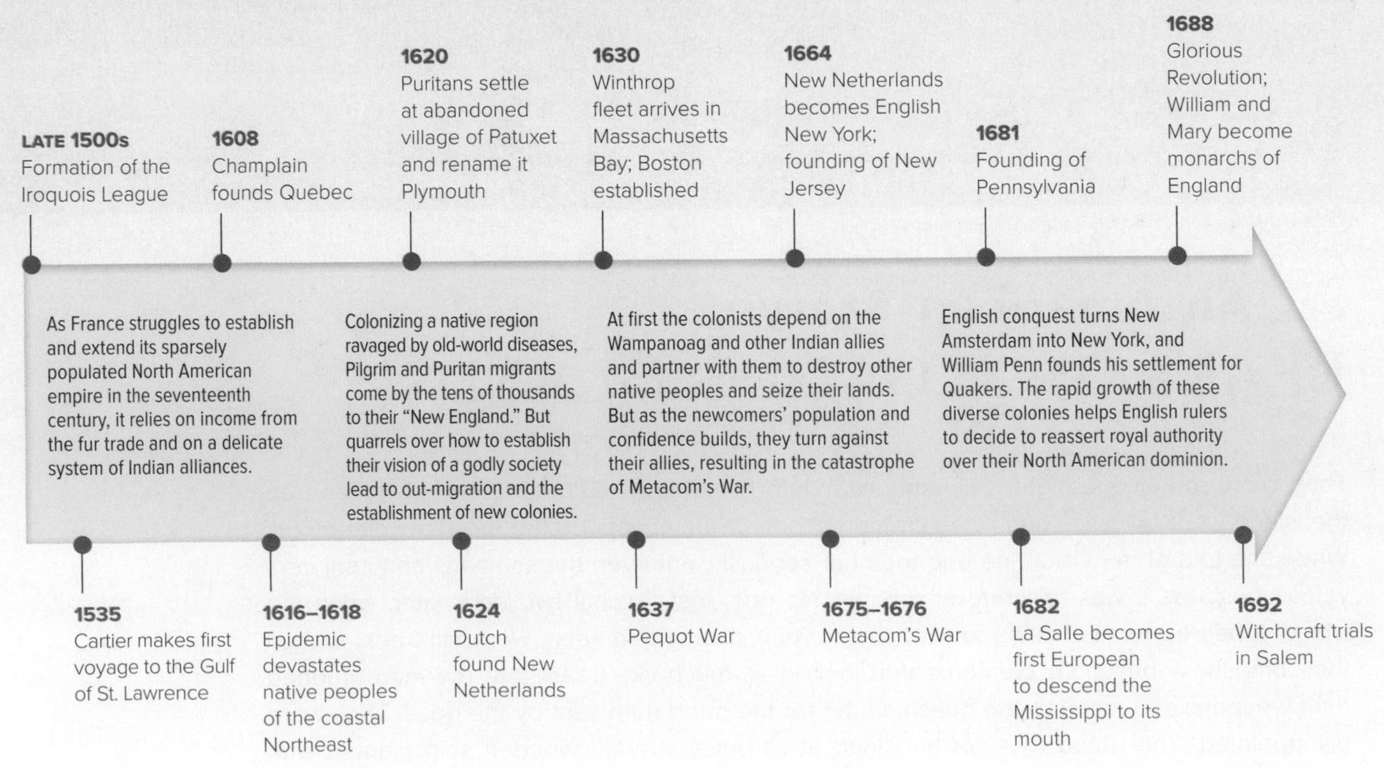

LATE 1500s
Formation of the Iroquois League
1535
Cartier makes first voyage to the Gulf of St. Lawrence
1608
Champlain founds Quebec
1616–1618
Epidemic devastates native peoples of the coastal Northeast
1620
Puritans settle at abandoned village of Patuxet and rename it Plymouth
1624
Dutch found New Netherlands
1630
Winthrop fleet arrives in Massachusetts Bay; Boston established
1637
Pequot War
1664
New Netherlands becomes English New York; founding of New Jersey
1675–1676
Metacom's War
1681
Founding of Pennsylvania
1682
La Salle becomes first European to descend the Mississippi to its mouth
1688
Glorious Revolution; William and Mary become monarchs of England
1692
Witchcraft trials in Salem
As France struggles to establish and extend its sparsely populated North American empire in the seventeenth century, it relies on income from the fur trade and on a delicate system of Indian alliances.
Colonizing a native region ravaged by old-world diseases, Pilgrim and Puritan migrants come by the tens of thousands to their "New England." But quarrels over how to establish their vision of a godly society lead to out-migration and the establishment of new colonies.
At first the colonists depend on the Wampanoag and other Indian allies and partner with them to destroy other native peoples and seize their lands. But as the newcomers' population and confidence builds, they turn against their allies, resulting in the catastrophe of Metacom's War.
English conquest turns New Amsterdam into New York, and William Penn founds his settlement for Quakers. The rapid growth of these diverse colonies helps English rulers to decide to reassert royal authority over their North American dominion.

# FRANCE IN NORTH AMERICA

Jacques Cartier first explored the land the French would call Canada in 1535, sailing through the Gulf of St. Lawrence. But not until 1605 did the French plant a permanent colony, at Port Royal in Acadia (Nova Scotia). Three years later Samuel de Champlain established Quebec farther up the St. Lawrence valley to pursue the fur trade with less competition from rival Europeans. Champlain aligned himself with local Montagnais, Algonquins, and, especially, the mighty Hurons—a confederacy of farmers 20,000 strong whose towns near Georgian Bay straddled a vast trading network.

^ The brief life of Kateri Tekakwitha, a Mohawk woman, reflected the chaotic circumstances set in motion by European fur traders. Her mother was an Algonquin captured by Mohawk raiders, seeking to fill losses brought about by war and disease. Tekakwitha, her Indian name, meant "She who bumps into things," perhaps given to her because at the age of four a smallpox epidemic left her with impaired vision. In the midst of continued conflict, Tekakwitha converted to Christianity after contact with French Jesuit missionaries. They named her Kateri, in honor of St. Catherine of Sienna. She died at the age of 24 and in 2012 was canonized by Pope Benedict XVI. ©Vandeville Eric/ABACA/Newscom

## The Origins of New France >>

The Hurons, Montagnais, and Algonquins had reason to embrace Champlain. Like Europeans elsewhere in North America, the Frenchman came with wondrous textiles, glass, copper, and ironware. At first the Indians treated such things as exotic commodities rather than utilitarian items. But before long, metal tools began transforming native life. The new knives made it far easier to butcher animals; trees could be felled and buildings put up far more easily with iron axes rather than stone; cooking was more efficient with brass kettles that could be placed directly on the fire; flint strike-a-lights eliminated the need to carry hot coals in bounded shells; beads, cloth, needles, and thread allowed for a new level of creative and visual expression; and, because they traveled farther and truer than stone ones, metal arrowheads made hunters and warriors more deadly than ever before.

For native peoples, all exchanges of goods were bound up in complex social relations. Thus the Montagnais, Algonquins, and Hurons insisted Champlain be a friend as well as a merchant. Champlain proved his worth in 1609 when he and his native companions confronted two hundred Mohawk warriors in what is now upstate New York. The Frenchman strode to the front as the battle was about to begin, raised his musket, and shot dead two Mohawk chiefs. Champlain's allies let out a joyous cry, for few if any of the warriors had ever seen a gun fired in combat. They drove the remaining Mohawks from the field. It was not the last time European newcomers would alter the balance of power in North America.

The Montagnais, Algonquins, and Hurons became eager trading partners over the next generation. In return for European goods, they provided tens of thousands of beaver pelts, source of the world's best felt for making hats: sturdy, rain-resistant, and lush. Europeans had long ago trapped their continent's beaver populations to near extinction, so for generations most consumers had to make do with inferior wool hats. Once a steady stream of beaver pelts began coming in from North America, "beavers," as the newly available hats were known, became all the rage. Aristocrats, the merchant elite, military officers, and anyone else with money and social ambition had to have one. As early as the 1610s a beaver sold for ten times as much as a wool hat.

Though some derided New France as nothing more than a *comptoir,* a storehouse for the skins of dead animals, revenue from the pelt trade sustained Champlain's colonial dreams, barely. He struggled to bring more permanent settlers to Canada and, above all, he looked to bind his native allies firmly to the colonial project. To that end Champlain recruited certain French men and boys to live with Indian families, to learn their language and customs.

Along with these *coureurs de bois,* or "runners in the woods," French authorities engaged Jesuits, members of the Society of Jesus, to establish missions among the Indians. The Jesuits were fired with the passions of the **Counter-Reformation** in Europe, a movement by devout Catholics to correct those abuses that had prompted the Protestant Reformation. At first France's Indian allies tolerated Jesuit missionaries but listened to them little. By the 1630s, however, Champlain began insisting that trading partners allow Jesuits to live among them. Conversions increased, cultural changes became more apparent, and internal divisions began to erupt within native communities. These pressures gradually left the Huron confederacy, in particular, fragmented and vulnerable to enemies.

**Counter-Reformation** reform movement within the Roman Catholic Church in response to the Protestant Reformation, seeking to reform and reinvigorate the church.

## New Netherlands, the Iroquois, and the Beaver Wars >>

If Canada was merely a *comptoir,* it was a profitable one, and the rival Dutch noticed. By around 1600 the Netherlands possessed the greatest manufacturing capacity in the world and had become the

<< This undated French engraving depicts something often overlooked or trivialized by European observers: native women's work. Two Iroquois women grind corn into meal while a swaddled infant rests in a backboard. ©The Granger Collection, New York

key economic power in Europe. Because they enjoyed prosperity and religious freedom at home, few Dutch folk had any desire to plant colonies abroad. But they did want to tap into the wealth flowing out of North America, and therefore they laid claim to a number of sites around the Connecticut, Delaware, and Hudson Rivers (the last named for the Englishman Henry Hudson, who first explored it for the Dutch in 1609). Most of New Netherlands's few settlers clustered in the village of New Amsterdam on Manhattan Island at the mouth of the Hudson.

More important for the geopolitics of the continent, the Dutch West India Company established a trading outpost 150 miles upriver known as Fort Orange (present-day Albany). By 1630 the powerful Mohawks came to dominate that fort's commerce. Ever since their encounter with Champlain's musket, the Mohawks and the other four members of the **Iroquois League**—the Oneidas, Onondagas, Cayugas, and Senecas—had suffered from their lack of direct access to European tools and weapons. At Fort Orange, the Iroquois finally found that access. As the beaver population, always fragile, collapsed within Iroquois territory, the league used its new weapons to go on the offensive against its northern enemies. To maintain its trading position, Iroquois warriors began preying upon Huron convoys on their way to Quebec, and then selling the plundered pelts to the Dutch.

**Iroquois League** Indian confederacy consisting of the Mohawks, Oneidas, Onondagas, Cayugas, and Senecas (a sixth nation, the Tuscaroras, would join in 1712). The league exerted enormous influence throughout colonial eastern North America.

Just as this old rivalry revived, a smallpox epidemic plunged the region into catastrophe. Waves of the disease took a nightmarish toll, especially in Indian agricultural communities with densely populated towns. Between 1634 and 1640 the disease killed more than 10,000 Hurons, reducing their total population by half and precipitating a spate of conversions to Christianity that divided the community all the more. The Iroquois likewise suffered greatly but, unlike the Hurons, reacted by waging war in an effort to obtain captives that could formally replace dead kin.

A second transformative event was the dramatic expansion of the region's arms trade. Reluctant at first to deal in guns, the Dutch at Fort Orange relaxed their policy by the late 1630s in order to obtain more furs. Soon the Iroquois had many times more muskets than the Hurons, whom the French had refused to arm so long as they remained unconverted.

Reeling from disease and internal division, the Hurons saw their world collapsing. In 1648 well-armed Iroquois warriors destroyed three Huron towns. The Hurons made the wrenching decision to burn their remaining towns and abandon their lands for good. Perhaps 2,000 became Iroquois, as either war captives or humble refugees. Others merged with neighboring peoples, while thousands more fled and starved or died of exposure in the harsh winter of 1649–1650.

So began the Beaver Wars, a series of conflicts that transformed the colonial north at least as much as the Indian slave wars had the south. Seeking new hunting grounds and new captives to replenish their diminishing population, Iroquois raiders attacked peoples near and far. After the Hurons, they scattered the nearby Petuns, Eries, and Neutrals—peoples who, like the Hurons, were Iroquoian speakers and could be integrated into Iroquois communities with relative ease. Warriors next moved against non-Iroquoian groups, including Delawares and Shawnees in the Ohio valley, and even extended their raids south to the Carolinas. To the north they attacked Algonquians in the Canadian Shield, and Abenakis and others in New England.

The Beaver Wars continued in fits and starts for the rest of the seventeenth century, provoking a massive refugee crisis as families fled their traditional territories and tried to rebuild their lives. The wars also very nearly ruined New France. About 300 Frenchmen were killed or captured, cutting the colony's meager population in half by 1666. French authorities scrambled to find reliable new partners in the fur trade and became less reluctant to trade guns to Indian allies. In the end, the scope of the conflict and the far-flung movement of refugees led the French to take a more expansive view of the continent and their place in it.

>> The Hurons who became infected with smallpox in the 1630s would have experienced fevers, aches, and vomiting before the telltale spots emerged on their skin. Agonizing pustules would have soon covered them from head to toe, as in this modern photograph, and sometimes the pustules merged into oozing sheets that caused large sections of the victims' skin to peel away from their bodies. The disease claimed millions of lives in the Americas after 1492. ©Everett Collection/SuperStock

## The Lure of the Mississippi

>> That expansive view was encouraged by the discovery of the Mississippi River. By the 1660s, French traders, priests, and officers were making inroads among refugee villages in the Western Great Lakes, a region the French referred to as the ***pays d'en haut,*** or "upper country." As they did so, they began exploring the greatest watercourse in North America.

***pays d'en haut*** in the seventeenth century, the lands referred to by the French as the "upper country," the land upriver from Montreal as French fur traders passed into the Great Lakes beyond the southern shores of Lake Ontario.

The Mississippi travels nearly 2,500 miles from its source in present-day Minnesota to the Gulf of Mexico, carrying water from several major rivers and dominating a drainage area larger than the Indian subcontinent in Asia. As the French began exploring in earnest, it dawned on them that the Mississippi valley could be the strategic key to success in North America. French officials courted Indian peoples along the river and its tributaries, employing their hard-won insights into native diplomatic culture along the way. The region's peoples—the Illinois, Shawnees, Quapaws, and others—expressed keen interest in French trade, as well as fear and hatred of their common Iroquois enemies. When René Robert Cavelier, Sieur de La Salle became the first European to descend the river to the Gulf in 1682, he encountered the Natchez, Chickasaws, and others who had not seen Europeans since De Soto and his maniacal march nearly a century and a half before. Other Frenchmen erected trading posts and simple missions, even making contact and tentative alliances with Osages, Arkansas, Ottos, Pawnees, and others west of the great river.

By the early eighteenth century New France had helped broker an uneasy peace between the Iroquois and Indian nations to the west, extended its influence over a vast area, and fortified its colonial core along the St. Lawrence River. In 1700 the colony had scores of simple missions and three modest cities—Quebec, Montreal, and Trois-Rivières—containing a population of about 15,000. Most immigrants to New France eventually returned to Europe, and shortsighted French monarchs insisted that Canada remain Catholic, off limits to France's most obvious emigrants, the Protestant Huguenots. But even with its small colonial population, New France emerged as a powerful player in North America. The French had reason to hope that their strategic and economic alliances with native peoples could help contain the Spanish to the west and limit English expansion from the east.

REVIEW

What caused the Beaver Wars, and how did the French respond?

# THE FOUNDING OF NEW ENGLAND

At first the English regarded the northern part of North America as a place in which only the mad French could see possibility. English fisherfolk who strayed from Newfoundland to the coast of Acadia and New England carried home descriptions of the long, lonely coast, rockbound and rugged. Long winters of numbing cold melted into short summers of steamy heat. There were no minerals to mine, no crops suitable for export, no huge native populations to enslave. The Chesapeake, with its temperate climate and long growing season, seemed a much likelier spot.

But by 1620 worsening conditions at home had instilled in some English men and women the mixture of desperation and idealism needed to settle an uninviting, unknown world. Religious differences among English Protestants became a matter of sharper controversy during the seventeenth century. Along with the religious crisis came mounting political tensions and continuing problems of unemployment and recession. Times were bad—so bad that the anticipation of worse times to come swept English men and women to the shores of New England.

## The Puritan Movement

>> The colonization of New England started with a king who chose his enemies unwisely. James I, shortly after succeeding Elizabeth I in 1603, vowed to purge England of all radical Protestant reformers. The radicals James had in mind were the **Puritans,** most of whom were either Presbyterians or Congregationalists. Although both groups of Puritan reformers embraced Calvin's ideas, they differed on the best form of church organization. Individual **Presbyterian** churches (or congregations) were guided by higher governing bodies of ministers and laypersons. Those in the **Congregationalist** churches, in contrast, believed that each congregation should conduct its own affairs independently, answering to no other authority.

**Puritans** reformers within the Church of England during the sixteenth century, who ultimately formed the Congregationalist and Presbyterian churches. Puritans strove to reform English religion, society, and politics by restricting church membership to the pious and godly and by enlisting the state to enforce a strict moral code.

**Presbyterians** members of a Protestant denomination that originated in sixteenth-century Britain as part of the Puritan movement. Presbyterians embraced Calvinist beliefs and favored a hierarchical church organization in which individual congregations were guided by presbyteries and synods comprising both laymen and ministers.

**Congregationalists** members of a Protestant denomination that originated in sixteenth-century Britain as part of the Puritan movement. Congregationalists held that each individual congregation should conduct its own religious affairs, answering to no higher authority.

Like all Christians, Protestant and Catholic, the Puritans believed that God was all-knowing and all-powerful. And, like all Calvinists, the Puritans emphasized that idea of divine sovereignty known as **predestination**. At the center of their thinking was this belief that God had ordained the outcome of history, including the eternal fate of every human being. The Puritans found comfort in their belief in predestination, because it provided their lives with meaning and purpose. They felt assured that a sovereign God was directing the fate of individuals, nations, and all of creation. The Puritans strove to play their parts in that divine drama of history and to discover in their performances some signs of personal salvation.

**predestination** basis of Calvinist theology and a belief that holds that God has ordained the outcome of all human history before the beginning of time, including the eternal fate of every human being.

The divine plan, as the Puritans understood it, called for reforming both church and society along the lines laid down by John Calvin. It seemed to the Puritans that England's government hampered rather than promoted religious purity and social order. It tolerated drunkenness, theatergoing, gambling, extravagance, public swearing, and Sabbath-breaking. It permitted popular recreations rooted in pagan custom and superstition—sports such as bear baiting and maypole dancing and festivals such as the celebration of Christmas and saints' days.

Even worse, the state had not done enough to purify the English church of the "corruptions" of Roman Catholicism. The Church of England counted as its members everyone in the nation, saint and sinner alike. To the Puritans, belonging to a church was no birthright. They wished to limit membership and the privileges of baptism and communion to godly men and women. The Puritans also deplored the hierarchy of bishops and archbishops in the Church of England, as well as its elaborate ceremonies in which priests wore ornate vestments. Too many Anglican clergy were "dumb dogges" in Puritan eyes, too poorly educated to instruct churchgoers in the truths of Scripture or to deliver a decent sermon.

Because English monarchs refused to take stronger measures to reform church and society, the Puritans became their outspoken critics. Elizabeth I had tolerated this opposition, but James I would not endure it and intended to rid England of these radicals. With some of the Puritans, known as the Separatists, he seemed to succeed.

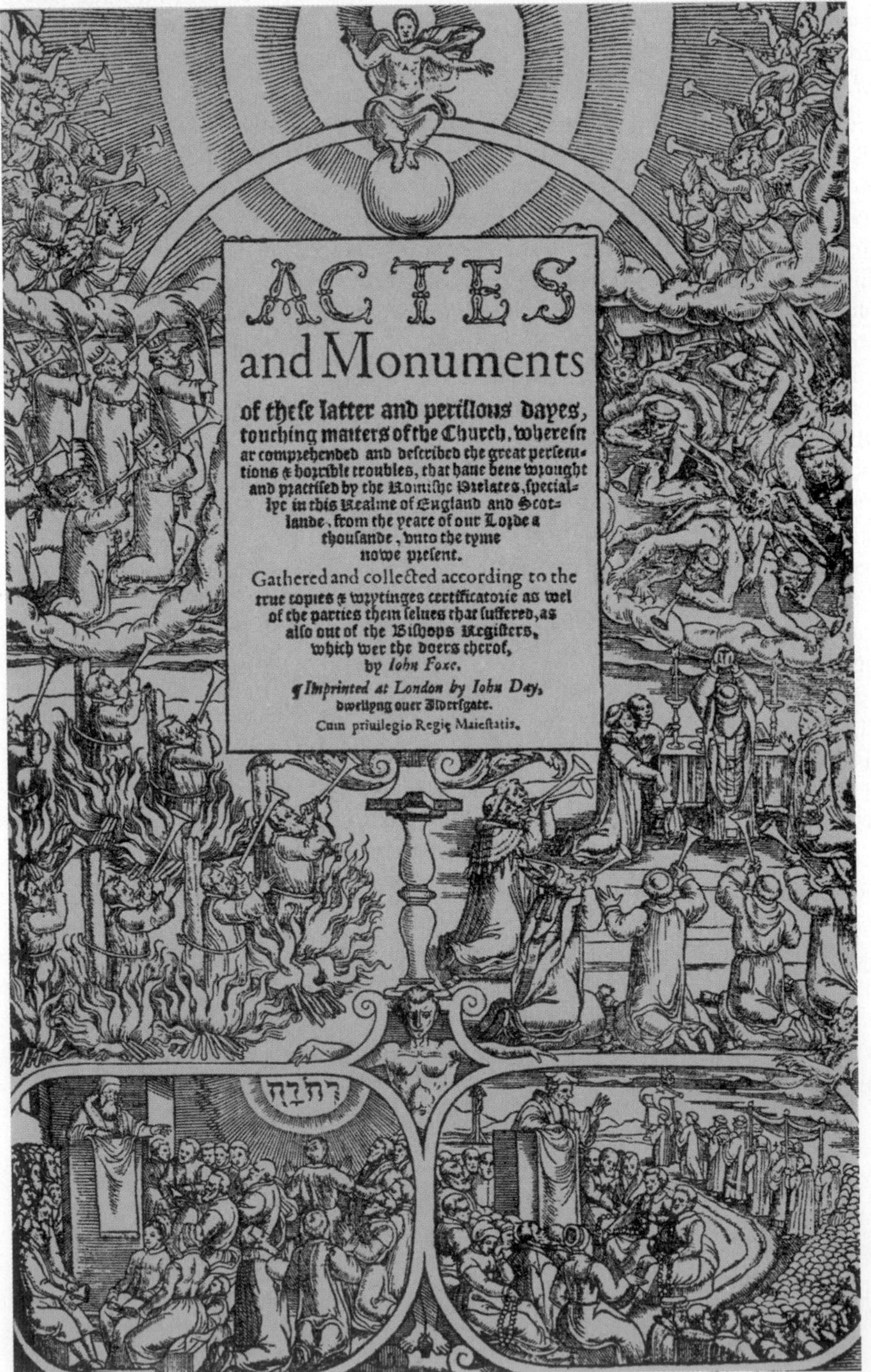

ACTES
and Monuments
of these latter and perillous dayes,
touching matters of the Church, wherein
ar comprehended and described the great persecu-
tions & horrible troubles, that haue bene wrought
and practised by the Romishe Prelates, special-
lye in this Realme of England and Scot-
lande, from the yeare of our Lorde a
thousande, vnto the tyme
nowe present.
Gathered and collected according to the
true copies & wrytinges certificatorie as wel
of the parties them selues that suffered, as
also out of the Bishops Registers,
which wer the doers therof,
by Iohn Foxe.
Imprinted at London by Iohn Day,
dwellyng ouer Aldersgate.
Cum priuilegio Regię Maiestatis.


<< John Foxe's *Actes and Monuments* (1563), a book revered by the Puritan founders of New England, arrayed the forces of righteousness (*left side of the illustration*) against a host of devil-worshiping priests and their sheeplike followers, who superstitiously hold rosary beads (*lower right*). Under the Catholic Queen Mary, Protestants were regarded as heretics, and some were burned at the stake (*middle left*). ©Universal History Archive/UIG/Bridgeman Images

**The Pilgrim Settlement at Plymouth Colony** >> The Separatists were devout Congregationalists who concluded that the Church of England was too corrupt to be reformed. They abandoned Anglican worship and met secretly in small congregations. From their first appearance in England during the 1570s, the Separatists suffered persecution from the government—fines, imprisonment, and, in a few cases, execution. Always a tiny minority within the Puritan movement, the Separatists were people from humble backgrounds: craftworkers and farmers without influence to challenge the state. By 1608 some had become so discouraged that they migrated to Holland, where the Dutch government permitted complete freedom of religion. But when their children began to adopt Dutch customs and other religions, some Separatists decided to move again, this time to Virginia.

It can only be imagined what fate would have befallen the unworldly Separatists had they actually settled in the Chesapeake during the tobacco boom. But a series of mistakes—including an error in charting the course of their ship, the *Mayflower*—brought the little band far to the north, to a region Captain John Smith had earlier dubbed "New England." In November 1620 some 88 Separatist "Pilgrims" set anchor at a place they called Plymouth on the coast of present-day southeastern Massachusetts. They were sick with scurvy, weak from malnutrition, and shaken by a shipboard mutiny, and neither the site nor the season invited settlement. As one of their leaders, William Bradford, later remembered:

> For summer being done, all things stand upon them with a weatherbeaten face, and the whole country, full of woods and thickets represented a savage hue. If they looked behind them, there was the mighty ocean which they had passed and was now as a main bar and gulf to separate them from all the civil parts of the world.

For some, the shock was too great. Dorothy Bradford, William's wife, is said to have fallen overboard from the *Mayflower* as it lay anchored off Plymouth. It is more likely that she jumped to her death.

Few Pilgrims could have foreseen founding the first permanent European settlement in New England, and many did not live long enough to enjoy the distinction. They had arrived too late to plant crops and had failed to bring an adequate supply of food. By the spring of 1621 half the immigrants had died. English merchants who had financed the *Mayflower* voyage failed to send supplies to the struggling settlement. Plymouth might have become another doomed colony except that the Pilgrims received better treatment from native inhabitants than they did from their English backers.

Though they understood it only dimly, the Pilgrims were, in one historian's memorable phrase, the "beneficiaries of catastrophe." Only four years before their arrival coastal New England had been devastated by a massive epidemic, possibly the plague. Losses varied locally, but overall the native coastal population may have been reduced by as much as 90 percent. Abandoned villages lay in ruins up and down the coast, including the village of Patuxet, where the Pilgrims established Plymouth. Years later visitors would still marvel at heaps of unburied human remains dating from the epidemic.

The Wampanoags dominated the lands around Plymouth. Still reeling from loss in 1620 and eager to obtain trade goods and assistance against native enemies, Massasoit, their chief, agreed to help the starving colonists. At first, the peoples communicated through a remarkable Wampanoag named Squanto, who had been kidnapped by English sailors before the epidemic. Taken to Europe, Squanto learned English and returned to America in time to act as a mediator between Massasoit and the newcomers. The Pilgrims accepted Wampanoag hospitality and instruction, and invited native leaders to a feast in honor of their first successful harvest in 1621 (the genesis of the "first Thanksgiving" story).

The Pilgrims set up a government for their colony, the framework of which was the Mayflower Compact, drawn up on board ship before landing. That agreement provided for a governor and several assistants to advise him, all to be elected annually by Plymouth's adult males. In the eyes of English law the Plymouth settlers had no clear basis for their land claims or their government, for they had neither a royal charter nor approval from the Crown. But English authorities, distracted by problems closer to home, left the tiny colony of farmers alone.

**The Puritan Settlement at Massachusetts Bay** >> Among the Crown's distractions were two groups of Puritans more numerous and influential than the Pilgrims. They included both the Presbyterians and the majority of Congregationalists who, unlike the Pilgrim Separatists, still considered the Church of England capable of being reformed. But the 1620s brought these Puritans only fresh discouragements. In 1625 Charles I inherited his father's throne and all his enemies. When Parliament attempted to limit the king's power, Charles simply dissolved it, in 1629, and proceeded to rule without it. When Puritans pressed for reform, the king began to move against them.

This persecution swelled a second wave of Puritan migration that also drew from the ranks of Congregationalists. Unlike the humble Separatists, these emigrants included merchants, landed gentlemen, and lawyers who organized the Massachusetts Bay Company in 1629. Those able Puritan leaders aimed to build a better society in America, an example to the rest of the world. Unlike the Separatists, they had a strong sense of mission and destiny. They were not abandoning the English church, they insisted, but merely regrouping across the Atlantic for another assault on corruption.

Despite the company's Puritan leanings, it somehow obtained a royal charter confirming its title to most of present-day Massachusetts and New Hampshire. Advance parties in 1629 established the town of Salem on the coast well north of Plymouth. In 1630 the company's first governor, a tough-minded and visionary lawyer named John Winthrop, sailed from England with a dozen other company stockholders and a fleet of men and women to establish the town of Boston. The newcomers intended to build a godly "city on a hill" that would serve as an example to the world.

Once established in the Bay Colony, Winthrop and the other stockholders transformed the charter for their trading company into the framework of government for a colony. The company's governor became the colony's chief executive, and the company's other officers became the governor's assistants. The charter provided for annual elections of the governor and his assistants by company stockholders, known as the freemen. But to create a broad base of support for the new government, Winthrop and his assistants expanded the freemanship in 1631 to include every adult male church member.

The governor, his assistants, and the freemen together made up the General Court of the colony, which passed all laws, levied taxes, established courts, and made war and peace. In 1634 the whole body of the freemen stopped meeting and instead each town elected representatives or deputies to the General Court. Ten years later, the deputies formed themselves into the lower house of the Bay Colony legislature, and the assistants formed the upper house. By refashioning a company charter into a civil constitution, Massachusetts Bay Puritans were well on the way to shaping society, church, and state to their liking.

Contrary to expectations, New England proved more hospitable to the English than did the Chesapeake. The character of the migration itself gave New England settlers an advantage, for most arrived in family groups—not as young, single, indentured servants of the sort whose discontents unsettled Virginia society. The heads of New England's first households were typically freemen—farmers, artisans, and merchants. Most were skilled and literate. Since men usually migrated with their wife and children, the ratio of men to women within the population was fairly evenly balanced.

Most of the emigrants, some 21,000, came in a cluster between 1630 and 1642. Thereafter new arrivals tapered off because of the outbreak of the English Civil War. This relatively rapid colonization fostered solidarity, because emigrants shared a common past of persecution and a strong desire to create an ordered society modeled on Scripture.

REVIEW

Who settled the earliest New England colonies, and why?

## Make a Case

Did the Puritans colonize North America mainly to secure freedom of religion, or did they have other motives?

# STABILITY AND ORDER IN EARLY NEW ENGLAND

Puritan emigrants and their descendants thrived in New England's bracing but healthy climate. The first generation of colonists lived to an average age of 70, nearly twice as long as Virginians and 10 years longer than men and women living in England. With 90 percent of all offspring reaching adulthood, the typical family consisted of seven or eight children who came to maturity. Because of low death rates and high birthrates, the number of New Englanders doubled about every 27 years—while the populations of Europe and the Chesapeake barely reproduced themselves. By 1700 New England and the Chesapeake both had populations of approximately 100,000. But New England's population expanded primarily through natural increase, in contrast to the southern colonies that relied upon the arrival of indentured servants and convicts from Europe (slaves from Africa wouldn't become the key driver of southern population growth until the eighteenth century).

Early emigrants to the Bay Colony carved out an arc of villages around Massachusetts Bay. Within a decade settlers pressed into Connecticut, Rhode Island, and New Hampshire. Connecticut and Rhode Island received separate charters from Charles II in the 1660s, guaranteeing their residents the rights to land and government. New Hampshire, at first part of Massachusetts, became a separate colony in 1679, whereas the handful of hardy souls living along the coast of present-day Maine still accepted the Massachusetts Bay Colony's authority.

Early New Englanders established most of their settlements with an eye to stability and order. Unlike the Virginians, who scattered across the Chesapeake to isolated plantations, most New Englanders established tight-knit communities like those they had left behind in England. Each family received a lot for a house along with about 150 acres of land in nearby fields. Farmers left many of their acres uncultivated as a legacy for future generations, for most had only the labor of their own family to work their land. While the Chesapeake abounded with servants, tenant farmers, and slaves, almost every adult male in rural New England owned property. With little hope of prospering through commercial agriculture, New England farmers also had no incentive to import large numbers of servants and slaves or to create large plantations.

Strong family institutions contributed to New England's order and stability. While the early deaths of parents regularly splintered Chesapeake families, two adult generations were often on hand to encourage order within New England households. Husbands and fathers exacted submission from women and strict obedience from children. Land gave New

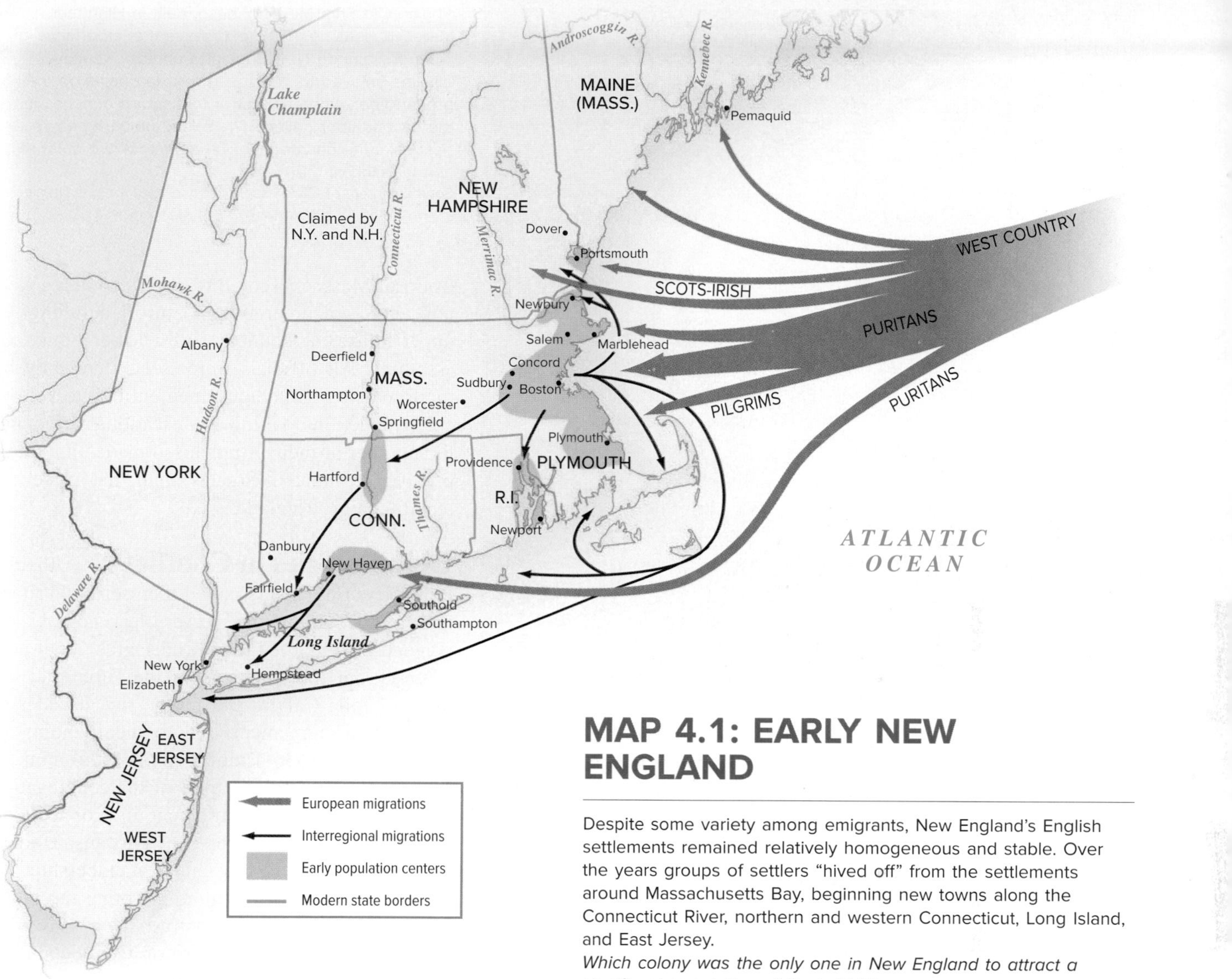

## MAP 4.1: EARLY NEW ENGLAND

Despite some variety among emigrants, New England's English settlements remained relatively homogeneous and stable. Over the years groups of settlers "hived off" from the settlements around Massachusetts Bay, beginning new towns along the Connecticut River, northern and western Connecticut, Long Island, and East Jersey.

*Which colony was the only one in New England to attract a significant population of Scots-Irish?*

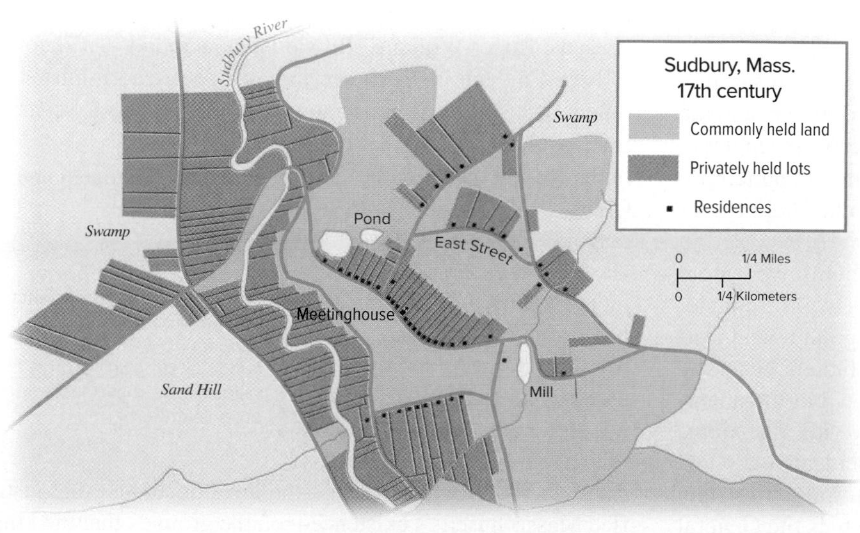

Sudbury River
Swamp
Swamp
Pond
East Street
Meetinghouse
Mill
Sand Hill
Sudbury, Mass.
17th century
Commonly held land
Privately held lots
Residences
0 1/4 Miles
0 1/4 Kilometers


## MAP 4.2: SUDBURY, MASSACHUSETTS

Everyday life in New England centered in small towns such as Sudbury, west of Boston. Families lived in houses clustered around the meetinghouse, in contrast to the decentralized plantations of the south. The privately held farm lots were mixed together as well, so that neighbors worked and lived in close contact with one another.

*How does the pattern of settlement in Sudbury differ from the pattern of settlement in the Chesapeake region?*

<< The Old Ship Meetinghouse, built in Hingham, Massachusetts, in 1681, expresses the importance of hierarchy among New England Puritans. Wealthy families enjoyed the enclosed wooden pews on the ground floor, whereas poorer folk sat on benches in the second-floor gallery. The raised pulpit (*front*) bespeaks the congregation's respect for the authority and learning of the clergy.
Source: Library of Congress, Prints and Photographs Division [HABS MASS,12-HING,5-26]

England's long-lived fathers great authority over even their grown children; sons and daughters relied on paternal legacies of farms in order to marry and establish their own families.

Whereas churches were few and far between in seventeenth-century Virginia, they constituted the center of community life in colonial New England. Individual congregations ran their own affairs and regulated their own membership. Those wishing to join had to convince ministers and church members that they had experienced a genuine spiritual rebirth or "conversion." Most New Englanders sought and won membership. As majority institutions supported by public taxes, churches had the reach and the resources to oversee public morality, often censuring or expelling wayward neighbors. Still, ministers enjoyed less public power in New England than in the old country. New England's ministers did not serve as officers in the civil government, and the Congregational churches owned no property. In contrast, Catholic and Anglican church officials wielded real temporal power in European states, and the churches held extensive tracts of land.

Finally, New Englanders governed themselves more democratically than did their counterparts in England. Communities throughout the region held regular town meetings of all resident white men. The town fathers generally set the meeting's agenda and offered advice, but the unanimous consent of townsmen determined all decisions. Colony governments in early New England also evolved into representative and responsive institutions. Typically the central government of each colony, such as the General Court of Massachusetts Bay, consisted of a governor and a bicameral legislature, including an upper house, or council, and a lower house, or assembly. All officials were elected annually by the freemen—white adult men entitled to vote in colony elections. Voting qualifications varied, but the number of men enfranchised made up a much broader segment of society than that in seventeenth-century England.

**Communities in Conflict** >> Although most New Englanders called themselves Puritans and Congregationalists, the very fervency of their convictions often led them to disagree about how to carry out the teachings of the Bible and the ideas of John Calvin. During the first decades of colonization, such disagreements led to the founding of breakaway colonies. In 1636 Thomas Hooker, the minister of Cambridge, Massachusetts, led part of his congregation to establish the first English settlement in Connecticut. Somewhat more liberal than other Bay Puritans, Hooker favored more lenient standards for church membership. He also opposed the Bay's policy of limiting voting in colony elections to church members. In contrast, New Haven (a separate colony until it became part of Connecticut in 1662) was begun in 1638 by strict Congregationalists who found Massachusetts too liberal.

While Connecticut and New Haven emerged from voluntary migration, enforced exile filled Rhode Island with men and women whose radical ideas unsettled the rest of Massachusetts. Roger Williams, Rhode Island's founder, had come to New England in 1631, serving as a respected minister of Salem. But soon Williams announced that he was a Separatist, like the Pilgrims of Plymouth. He encouraged the Bay Colony to break all ties to the corrupt Church of England. He also urged a more complete **separation of church and state** than most New Englanders were prepared to accept, and later in his career he endorsed full religious toleration. Finally, Williams denounced the Bay's charter—the legal document that justified Massachusetts's existence—on the grounds that the king

**separation of church and state** principle that religious institutions and their representatives should exercise no civil or judicial powers and that civil governments should give no official sanction, privileges, or financial support to any religious denomination or organization.

had no right to grant land that he had not purchased from the Indians. When Williams boldly suggested that Massachusetts actually inform the king of his mistake, angry authorities prepared to deport him. Instead, Williams fled the colony in the dead of winter to live with the Indians. In 1636 he became the founder and first citizen of Providence, later to be part of Rhode Island.

Another charismatic heretic from Massachusetts arrived soon after. Anne Hutchinson, a skilled midwife and the spouse of a wealthy merchant, had come to Boston in 1634. Enthusiasm for her minister, John Cotton, started her on a course of explaining his sermons to gatherings of her neighbors—and then to elaborating ideas of her own. The fact that a woman would do such things made the authorities uneasy; they became positively alarmed when they learned that Hutchinson embraced controversial positions on doctrine. Soon a majority of the Bay's ministers accused the popular Hutchinson of holding heretical views. She in turn denounced her detractors, and the controversy escalated. In 1638 the Bay Colony government expelled Hutchinson and her followers for sedition. She settled briefly in Rhode Island before moving on to Long Island, where she died in an Indian attack.

**Goodwives and Witches** >> If Anne Hutchinson had been a man, her ideas would still have been deemed heretical. However, if she had been a man, she might have found other ways to express her intelligence and magnetism. But life in colonial New England offered women, especially married women, little scope for their talents.

Most adult women were hardworking farm wives who cared for large households of children. Between marriage and middle age, most New England wives were pregnant except when breast-feeding. When they were not nursing or minding children, mothers were producing and preparing much of what was consumed and worn by their families. They planted vegetable gardens and pruned fruit trees, salted beef and pork and pressed cider, milked cows and churned butter, kept bees and tended poultry, cooked and baked, washed and ironed, spun, wove, and sewed. While husbands and sons engaged in farmwork that changed with the seasons, took trips to taverns and mills, and went off to hunt or fish, housebound wives and daughters kept up with a dizzying array of tasks.

Women suffered legal disadvantages as well. In contrast to New Mexico and Florida with their Spanish civil law traditions, English common law and colonial legal codes accorded married women virtually no control over property. Wives could not sue or be sued, they could not make contracts, and they surrendered to their husbands any property that they had possessed before marriage. Divorce was almost impossible to obtain until the late eighteenth century. Only widows and a few single women had the same property rights as men, but they could not vote in colony elections.

The one arena in which women could attain something approaching equal standing with men was the churches. Puritan women could not become ministers, but after the 1660s they made up the majority of church members. In some churches membership enabled them to vote for ministerial candidates and to voice opinions about admitting and disciplining members. Puritan doctrine itself rejected the medieval Catholic suspicion of women as "a necessary evil," seeing them instead as "a necessary good." Even so, the Puritan ideal of the virtuous woman was a chaste, submissive "helpmeet," a wife and mother who served God by serving men.

Communities sometimes responded to assertive women with accusations of witchcraft. Like most early modern Europeans, New Englanders believed in wizards and witches, men and women who were said to acquire supernatural powers by signing a compact with Satan. A total of 344 New Englanders were charged with witchcraft during the first colonial century, with the notorious Salem Village episode of 1692 producing the largest outpouring of accusations and 20 executions. More than three-quarters of all accused witches were women, usually middle-aged and older, and most of those accused were regarded as unduly independent. Before they were charged with witchcraft, many had been suspected of heretical religious beliefs, others of sexual impropriety. Still others had inherited or stood to inherit property.

**The People in the Way** >> Whatever their political battles, doctrinal disputes, and inequalities, New Englanders were all participants in a colonial project that depended on taking land from other people. At the time of first contact, perhaps 100,000 Algonquin men and women lived in the area reaching from the Kennebec River in Maine to Cape Cod. Like the Puritans, they relied on fishing in spring and summer, hunting year-round, and cultivating and harvesting corn and other crops in spring and fall. To an even greater degree than among the colonists, Indian political authority was local. Within each village, a single leader known as the "sachem" or "sagamore" directed economic life, administered justice, and negotiated with other tribes and English settlers. As with New England's town fathers, a sachem's power depended on keeping the trust and consent of his people.

Thus, the newcomers had more in common with their hosts than they cared to admit. But English expansion in the region had to come at someone's expense, and colonists obtained Indian lands in one of three ways. Sometimes they purchased it. Sales varied—they might be free and fair, fraudulent, subtly coerced, or forced through intimidation and violence. Second, colonists eagerly expanded into lands emptied by epidemics. The English often saw God's hand in such events. "Without this remarkable and terrible stroke of God upon the natives," wrote one New Englander after a smallpox epidemic, "[we] would with much more difficulty have found room" to settle.

# Accusations and Defenses in the Salem Witchcraft Trials

*The Salem Witchcraft trials of 1692 set neighbor against neighbor and resulted in the execution of 20 women and men. One of the accused was tavern owner John Proctor, on whom Arthur Miller loosely based the main protagonist in his famous play* The Crucible. *The documents below include testimony of three witnesses against Proctor, and his own remarkable response.*

## DOCUMENT 1
## The Accusations

**Sarah Vibber**

The Deposition of Sarah Vibber agged about 36 years who testifieth and saith that on the 3 june 1692. Jno: proctor. sen'r came to me and did most greviously torment me by pinching pricking and almost presing me to death urging me to drink: drink as Red as blood which I refusing he did tortor me with variety of tortors and immediatly he vanished away also on the same day I saw Jno: proctor most greviously tortor Susannah Shelden by claping his hands on hir throat and almost choaking hir. also severall times sence Jno: proctor sen'r has most greviously tortored me a grat many times with a variety of tortors.

Sara vibber ownid this har testimony to be the truth on har oath before the Jurirars of Inqwest this: 30. of June 1692.

Jurat in Curia

(Reverse) Sarah Vibber

**Ann Putnam**

The Deposistion of Ann putnam Jun'r who testifieth and saith I have often seen the Apperishtion of Jno procktor senr. amongst the wicthes but he did not doe me much hurt tell a little before his examination which was on the 11th of April 1692 and then he sett upon me most greviously and did tortor me most dreadfully also in the time of his examination he afflected me very much: and severall times sence the Apperishtion of John procktor senr, has most greviously tortored me by pinching and allmost choaking me urging me vehemently to writ in his book also on the day of his examination I saw the Apperishtion of Jno: proctor senr goe and afflect and most greviously tortor the bodys of Mistris pope mary walcott Mircy lewes. Abigail williams and Jno: Indian. and he and his wife and Sarah Cloys keept Elizabeth Hubburd speachless all the time of their examination.

*(Mask) Ann Putnam*

Ann Putman owned what is above written upon oath before and unto the Grand inquest on the 30'th Day of June 1692 (Reverse) Ann puttnam ag't John procter.

**Mary Warren**

The deposition of mary warrin aged 20 y'rs ho testifieth I have seen the apparition of John procter sen'r among the wiches and he hath often tortored me by penching me and biting me and Choakeing me and presing me one my Stomack tell the blood came out of my mouth and all so I saw him tortor Mes poap and marcey lues and John Indian a po n the day of his examination and he hath allso t emted me to right in his book and to eat bread which he brought to me which I Refuseing to doe: Jno proctor did most greviously tortor me with variety of torturs all most Redy to kill me.

Mary Warren owned the above written upon her oath before & unto the Grand inquest on the 30'th Day of June 1692

*Source:* Sarah Bibber, Ann Putnam and Mary Warren, "The Accusations."

## DOCUMENT 2
## The Defense

SALEM-PRISON, July 23, 1692. *Mr. Mather, Mr. Allen, Mr. Moody, Mr. Willard, and Mr. Bailey. Reverend Gentlemen.*

The innocency of our Case with the Enmity of our Accusers and our Judges, and Jury, whom nothing but our Innocent Blood will serve their turn, having Condemned us already before our Tryals, being so much incensed and engaged against us by the Devil, makes us bold to Beg and Implore your Favourable Assistance of this our Humble Petition to his Excellency, That if it be possible our Innocent Blood may be spared, which undoubtedly otherwise will be shed, if the Lord doth not mercifully step in. The Magistrates, Ministers, Jewries, and all the People in general, being so much inraged and incensed against us by the Delusion of the Devil, which we can term no other, by reason we know in our own Consciences, we are all Innocent Persons. Here are five Persons who have lately confessed themselves to be Witches, and do accuse some of us, of being along with them at a Sacrament, since we were committed into close Prison, which we know to be Lies. Two of the 5 are (Carriers Sons) Youngmen, who would not confess any thing till they tyed them Neck and Heels till the Blood was ready to come out of their Noses, and 'tis credibly believed and reported this was the occasion of making them confess that they never did, by reason they said one had been a Witch a Month, and another five Weeks, and that their Mother had made them so, who has been confined here this nine Weeks. My son William Procter, when he was examin'd, because he would not confess that he was Guilty, when he was Innocent, they tyed him Neck and Heels till the Blood gushed out at his Nose, and would have kept him so 24 Hours, if one more Merciful than the rest, had not taken pity on him, and caused him to be unbound. These actions are very like the Popish Cruelties. They have already undone us in our Estates, and that will not serve their turns, without our Innocent Bloods. If it cannot be granted that we can have our Trials at Boston, we humbly beg that you would endeavour to have these Magistrates changed, and others in their rooms, begging also and beseeching you would be pleased to be here, if not all, some of you at our Trials, hoping thereby you may be the means of saving the sheeding our Innocent Bloods, desiring your Prayers to the Lord in our behalf, we rest your Poor Afflicted Servants.

*JOHN PROCTER, etc.*

*Source:* John Procter, "The Defense."

### THINKING CRITICALLY

*What patterns do you see in the accusations? What does the language in all four pieces tell you about how members of this community conceived of Satan? How does Proctor try to defend himself? What do you think he was trying to accomplish by comparing the interrogations his son and others faced to "Popish Cruelties"?*

Third and finally, colonists commonly encouraged and participated in regional wars to obtain native lands. This proved easy enough to do, because, like Europeans, the Indians of New England quarreled frequently with neighboring nations. The antagonism among the English, Spanish, Dutch, and French was matched by the hostilities among the Abenakis, Pawtuckets, Massachusetts, Narragansetts, and Wampanoags of the north Atlantic coast. Epidemics only intensified existing rivalries, because they opened up new opportunities for stronger neighbors to press their advantage.

The English began by aligning with Massasoit and his Wampanoags against other coastal peoples in New England. In 1637 colonial forces joined the Narragansetts in a campaign against the formidable Pequots, who controlled coveted territory in Connecticut. The colonists shocked even their Indian allies when they set fire to the main Pequot village, killing hundreds of men, women, and children. Plymouth's William Bradford recalled that "it was a fearful sight to see them thus frying in the fire, and the streams of blood quenching the same, and horrible was the stink and scent thereof; but the victory seemed a sweet sacrifice, and they gave the praise thereof to God, who had wrought so wonderfully for them." Several years later the colonists turned against their former allies, joining forces with the Mohegans to intimidate the Narragansetts into ceding much of their territory. Only a few colonists objected to those ruthless policies, among them Roger Williams. "God Land," he warned one Connecticut leader, "will be . . . as great a God with us English as God Gold was with the Spaniards."

**Metacom's War** >> Throughout these wars, the colonists more or less nurtured their original alliance with Massasoit and his Wampanoags. Indeed, certain colonists tried to bring the two societies closer together. While the impulse to convert was not nearly as strong in New England as in New Spain or New France, a few Englishmen worked tirelessly to bring the word of their God to Indians.

Puritan minister John Eliot began preaching in Algonquian in the 1640s. Over the next two decades he oversaw a project to publish the Scriptures in Algonquian using the Latin alphabet. He also trained scores of native ministers (many of whom became literate) and established seven villages or "praying towns" for Christian Indians. Eliot was not alone. Harvard College defined its mission as "the education of English & Indian youth of this Country" and in 1655 established an Indian college and dormitory on campus. None of these efforts embodied respect for Indian culture or religion. But some New Englanders, at least, wanted to assimilate Indians rather than drive them away.

And yet the colony always grasped for more land. Over time the Puritan-Wampanoag partnership had become a relationship of subordination and suspicion. Rumors of potential native rebellion led colonial authorities to conduct humiliating interrogations and put in place severe rules and restrictions. The colonists' cows and pigs invaded and destroyed Indian fields, provoking innumerable conflicts. When Indians tried to adapt by raising their own cows and pigs, colonial authorities barred them from using common pasture or selling meat in Boston. At the same time, as many as half the dwindling Wampanoags had followed Eliot into the praying towns, threatening tribal unity in a time of mounting crisis.

By 1675 such pressures convinced Massasoit's son and heir, Metacom, whom the English called King Philip, that his nation could be preserved only by chancing war. Complaining that the English were plotting to kill him and other sachems and replace them with Christian Indians more willing to sell land, Metacom organized for war. He rallied many of southern New England's

<< Though no images of Metacom survive from his time, in later years artists frequently portrayed him. This image is based on an engraving by Paul Revere.
Source: Library of Congress, Prints and Photographs Division [LC-USZ62-96234]

remaining native nations, peoples who had likewise suffered from colonization, and together they laid waste to more than two dozen towns in Plymouth Colony. By the spring of 1676, indigenous fighting men from across the region were raiding settlements within 20 miles of Boston. The offensive threatened New England's very existence.

But its momentum could not be sustained. Faced with shortages of food and ammunition, Metacom tried and failed to secure alliances with former enemies, including the Mohegans and the Mohawks. These powerful peoples instead aligned themselves with the English. By early 1676 the tide had turned. Metacom was killed that summer; colonial forces brought his severed head to Boston and his hands to Plymouth as trophies.

In proportion to population, "King Philip's War" inflicted twice the casualties on New England that the United States as a whole would suffer in the American Civil War. But in the end the region's surviving Indians, Christian or not, found themselves consigned to quiet and often desperate lives on the margins of colonial life.

REVIEW

What were the sources of stability and conflict in early New England?

# THE MID-ATLANTIC COLONIES

The inhabitants of the mid-Atlantic colonies—New York, New Jersey, Pennsylvania, and Delaware—enjoyed more secure lives than did most southern colonials. But they lacked the common bonds that lent stability to early New England. Instead, throughout the mid-Atlantic region a variety of ethnic and religious groups vied for wealth from farming and the fur trade and contended bitterly against governments that commanded little popular support.

**English Rule in New York** >> By the 1660s the Dutch experiment on the mid-Atlantic coast was faltering. While Fort Orange continued to secure furs for the Dutch West India Company, the colonial population remained small and fractious. The company made matters worse by appointing corrupt, dictatorial governors who ruled without an elective assembly. It also provided little protection for outlying Dutch settlements; when it did attack neighboring Indian nations, it did so savagely, triggering terrible retaliations. By the time the company went bankrupt in 1654, it had virtually abandoned its American colony.

Taking advantage of the disarray in New Netherlands, Charles II ignored Dutch claims in North America and granted his brother, James, the Duke of York, a proprietary charter there. The charter granted James all of New Netherlands to Delaware Bay as well as Maine, Martha's Vineyard, and Nantucket Island. In 1664 James sent an invading fleet, whose mere arrival caused the Dutch to surrender.

New York's dizzying diversity would make it difficult to govern. The Duke inherited 9,000 or so colonists: Dutch, Belgians, French, English, Portuguese, Swedes, Finns, and Africans—some enslaved, others free. The colony's ethnic diversity ensured a variety of religions. Although the Dutch Reformed church predominated, other early New Netherlanders included Lutherans, **Quakers**, and Catholics. There were Jews as well, refugees from Portuguese Brazil, who were required by law to live in a ghetto in New Amsterdam. The Dutch resented English rule, and only after a generation of intermarriage and acculturation did that resentment fade. James also failed to win friends among New Englanders who had come to Long Island seeking autonomy and cheap land during the 1640s. He grudgingly gave in to their demand for an elective assembly in 1683 but rejected its first act, the Charter of Liberties, which would have guaranteed basic political rights. The chronic political strife discouraged prospective settlers. By 1698 the colony numbered only 18,000 inhabitants, and New York City, the former New Amsterdam, was an overgrown village of a few thousand.

**Quakers** Protestant sect, also known as the Society of Friends, founded in mid-seventeenth-century England. The Quakers believed that the Holy Spirit dwells within each human being, and religious conviction was the source of their egalitarian social practices, which included allowing women to speak in churches and to preach in public gatherings.

**The Founding of New Jersey** >> Confusion attended New Jersey's beginnings. The lands lying west of the Hudson and east of the Delaware River had been part of the Duke of York's proprietary grant. But in 1664 he gave about 5 million of these acres to Lord Berkeley and Sir George Carteret, two of his favorites who were already involved in the proprietary colonies of the Carolinas. New Jersey's new owners guaranteed settlers land, religious freedom, and a representative assembly in exchange for a small quitrent, an annual fee for the use of the land. The proprietors' terms promptly drew Puritan settlers from New Haven, Connecticut. At the same time, unaware that James had already given New Jersey to Berkeley and Carteret, New York's governor Richard Nicolls granted Long Island Puritans land there.

More complications ensued when Berkeley and Carteret decided to divide New Jersey into east and west and sell both halves to Quaker investors—a prospect that outraged New Jersey's Puritans. Although some English Quakers migrated to West Jersey, the investors quickly decided that two Jerseys were less desirable than one Pennsylvania and resold both East and West Jersey to speculators. In the end the Jerseys became a patchwork of religious and ethnic groups. Settlers who shared a common religion or national origin formed communities and established small family farms.

When the Crown finally reunited East and West Jersey as a single royal colony in 1702, New Jersey was overshadowed by settlements not only to the north but now, also, to the south and west.

**Quaker Odysseys** >> Religious and political idealism similar to that of the Puritans inspired the colonization of Pennsylvania, making it an oddity among the mid-Atlantic colonies. The oddity began with an improbable founder, William Penn. Young Penn devoted his early years to disappointing his distinguished father, Sir William Penn, an admiral in the Royal Navy. Several years after being expelled from college, young Penn finally chose a career that may have made the admiral yearn for mere disappointment: he undertook a lifelong commitment to put into practice Quaker teachings. By the 1670s he had emerged as an acknowledged leader of the Society of Friends, as the Quakers formally called themselves.

The Quakers behaved in ways and believed in ideas that most people regarded as odd. They dressed in a deliberately plain and severe manner. They withheld from their social superiors the customary marks of respect, such as bowing, kneeling, and removing their hats. They refused to swear oaths or to make war. They allowed women public roles of religious leadership. That pattern of behavior reflected their egalitarian ideals, the belief that all men and women shared equally in the "light within." Some 40,000 English merchants, artisans, and farmers embraced Quakerism by 1660, and many suffered fines, imprisonment, and corporal punishment.

^ In this painting of a Welsh Quaker meeting, which figure is the most controversial? To modern eyes it may not be obvious, but she stands in the middle of the painting wearing a tall hat, her back to us, as she addresses other members of the meeting. For most seventeenth-century Christians, women were meant to be seen rather than heard in worship services, but Quakers took a more egalitarian view, allowing women as well as men to express the feelings of devotion inspired by an "inner light." Many Quakers from Wales settled in the colony of Pennsylvania. Source: Haverford College Libraries

Since the English upper class had often prized eccentricity among its members, it is not surprising that Penn, despite his Quakerism, remained a favorite of Charles II. More surprising is that the king's favor took the extravagant form of presenting Penn in 1681 with all the land between New Jersey and Maryland. Perhaps the king was repaying Penn for the large sum that his father had lent the Stuarts. Or perhaps the king was hoping to export England's Quakers to an American colony governed by his trusted personal friend.

Penn envisioned that his proprietary colony would provide a refuge for Quakers while producing quitrents for himself. To publicize his colony, he distributed pamphlets praising its attractions throughout the British Isles and Europe. The response was overwhelming: by 1700 its population stood at 21,000. The only early migration of equal magnitude was the Puritan colonization of New England.

**Patterns of Growth** >> Perhaps half of Pennsylvania's settlers arrived as indentured servants, while the families of free farmers and artisans made up the rest. The majority were Quakers from Britain, Holland, and Germany, but the colonists also included Catholics, Lutherans, Baptists, Anglicans, and Presbyterians. In 1682, when Penn purchased and annexed the Three Lower Counties (later the colony of Delaware), his colony included the 1,000 or so Dutch, Swedes, and Finns living there.

Quakers from other colonies—West Jersey, Maryland, and New England—also flocked to the new homeland. Those experienced settlers brought skills and connections that contributed to Pennsylvania's rapid economic growth. Farmers sowed their rich lands into a sea of wheat, which merchants exported to the Caribbean. The center of the colony's trade was Philadelphia, a superb natural harbor situated at the confluence of the Delaware and Schuylkill Rivers.

In contrast to New England's landscape of villages, the Pennsylvania countryside beyond Philadelphia was dotted with dispersed farmsteads. Commercial agriculture required larger farms, which kept settlers at greater distances from one another. As a result, the county rather than the town became the basic unit of local government in Pennsylvania.

Another reason that farmers did not need to cluster their homes within a central village was that they were at peace with the coastal Indians, the Lenni Lenapes (also called Delawares by the English). Thanks to two Quaker beliefs—a commitment to pacifism and the conviction that the Indians rightfully owned their land—peace prevailed between native inhabitants and newcomers. Before Penn sold any land to colonists, he purchased it from the Indians. He also prohibited the sale of alcohol to the tribe, strictly regulated the fur trade, and learned the language of the Lenni Lenapes. "Not a language spoken in Europe," he remarked, "hath words of more sweetness in Accent and Emphasis than theirs."

"Our Wilderness flourishes as a Garden," Penn declared late in 1683, and in fact, his colony lived up to its promises.

New arrivals readily acquired good land on liberal terms, while Penn's Frame of Government instituted a representative assembly and guaranteed all inhabitants the basic English civil liberties and complete freedom of worship.

**Quakers and Politics** >> Even so, Penn's colony suffered constant political strife. Rich investors whom he had rewarded with large tracts of land and trade monopolies dominated the council, which held the sole power to initiate legislation. That power and Penn's own claims as proprietor set the stage for controversy. Members of the representative assembly battled for the right to initiate legislation. Farmers opposed Penn's efforts to collect quitrents. The Three Lower Counties agitated for separation, their inhabitants feeling no loyalty to Penn or Quakerism.

Penn finally bought peace at the price of approving a complete revision of his original Frame of Government. In 1701 the Charter of Privileges, Pennsylvania's new constitution, stripped the council of its legislative power, leaving it only the role of advising the governor. The charter also limited Penn's privileges as proprietor to the ownership of ungranted land and the power to veto legislation. Thereafter an elective unicameral assembly, the only single-house legislature in the colonies, dominated Pennsylvania's government.

As Pennsylvania prospered, Philadelphia became the commercial and cultural center of England's North American empire. Gradually the interior of Pennsylvania filled with emigrants—mainly Germans and Scots-Irish—who harbored no "odd" ideas about Indian rights, and the Lenni Lenapes and other native peoples were bullied into moving farther west. As for William Penn, he returned to England and spent time in a debtors' prison after being defrauded by his unscrupulous colonial agents. He died in 1718, an ocean away from his American utopia.

REVIEW

In what ways were the mid-Atlantic colonies more diverse than the other colonies of the period?

# ADJUSTMENT TO EMPIRE

Whatever Penn's personal disappointments, his colony had enjoyed spectacular growth—as had British North America more generally. And yet by the 1680s England's king had reason to complain. Although North America now abounded in places named in honor of English monarchs, the colonies themselves lacked any strong ties to the English state. Until Parliament passed the first Navigation Acts in 1660, England had not even set in place a coherent policy for regulating colonial trade. And the acts had not produced the desired sense of patriotism in the colonies. While Chesapeake planters grumbled over the customs duties levied on tobacco, New Englanders, the worst of the lot, ignored the Navigation Acts altogether and traded openly with the Dutch. Royally appointed proprietors increasingly met defiance in New York, New Jersey, the Carolinas, and Pennsylvania. If England were to prosper from colonies as Spain's monarchs had, the Crown needed to take matters in hand.

**The Dominion of New England** >> The Crown did so in 1686. At the urging of the new King James II (formerly the Duke of York), the Lords of Trade consolidated the colonies of Connecticut, Plymouth, Massachusetts Bay, Rhode Island, and New Hampshire into a single entity to be ruled by a royal governor and a royally appointed council. By 1688 James had added New York and New Jersey to that domain, called the Dominion of New England. Showing the typical Stuart distaste for representative government, James also abolished all northern colonial assemblies. The king's aim to centralize authority over such a large territory made the Dominion not only a royal dream but also a radical experiment in English colonial administration.

The experiment failed spectacularly. In England, James II revealed himself to be yet another Stuart who tried to dispense with Parliament and who had embraced Catholicism besides. In a quick, bloodless coup d'état known as the Glorious Revolution, Parliament forced James into exile in 1688. In his place it elevated to the throne his daughter, Mary, and her Dutch husband, William of Orange. Mary was a distinctly better sort of Stuart—a staunch Protestant—and she agreed to rule with Parliament.

William and Mary officially dismembered the Dominion of New England and reinstated representative assemblies everywhere in the northern colonies. Connecticut and Rhode Island were restored their old charters, but Massachusetts received a new charter in 1691. Under its terms Massachusetts, Plymouth, and present-day Maine were combined into a single royal colony headed by a governor appointed by the Crown rather than elected by the people. The charter also imposed religious toleration and made property ownership rather than church membership the basis of voting rights.

**Royal Authority in America in 1700** >> William and Mary were more politic than James II, but no less interested in revenue. In 1696 Parliament enlarged the number of customs officials stationed in each colony to enforce the Navigation Acts. To prosecute smugglers, Parliament established colonial vice-admiralty courts, tribunals without juries presided over by royally appointed justices. To keep current on colonial matters, the king appointed a new Board of Trade to replace the old Lords of Trade. The new enforcement procedures generally succeeded in discouraging smuggling and channeling colonial trade through England.

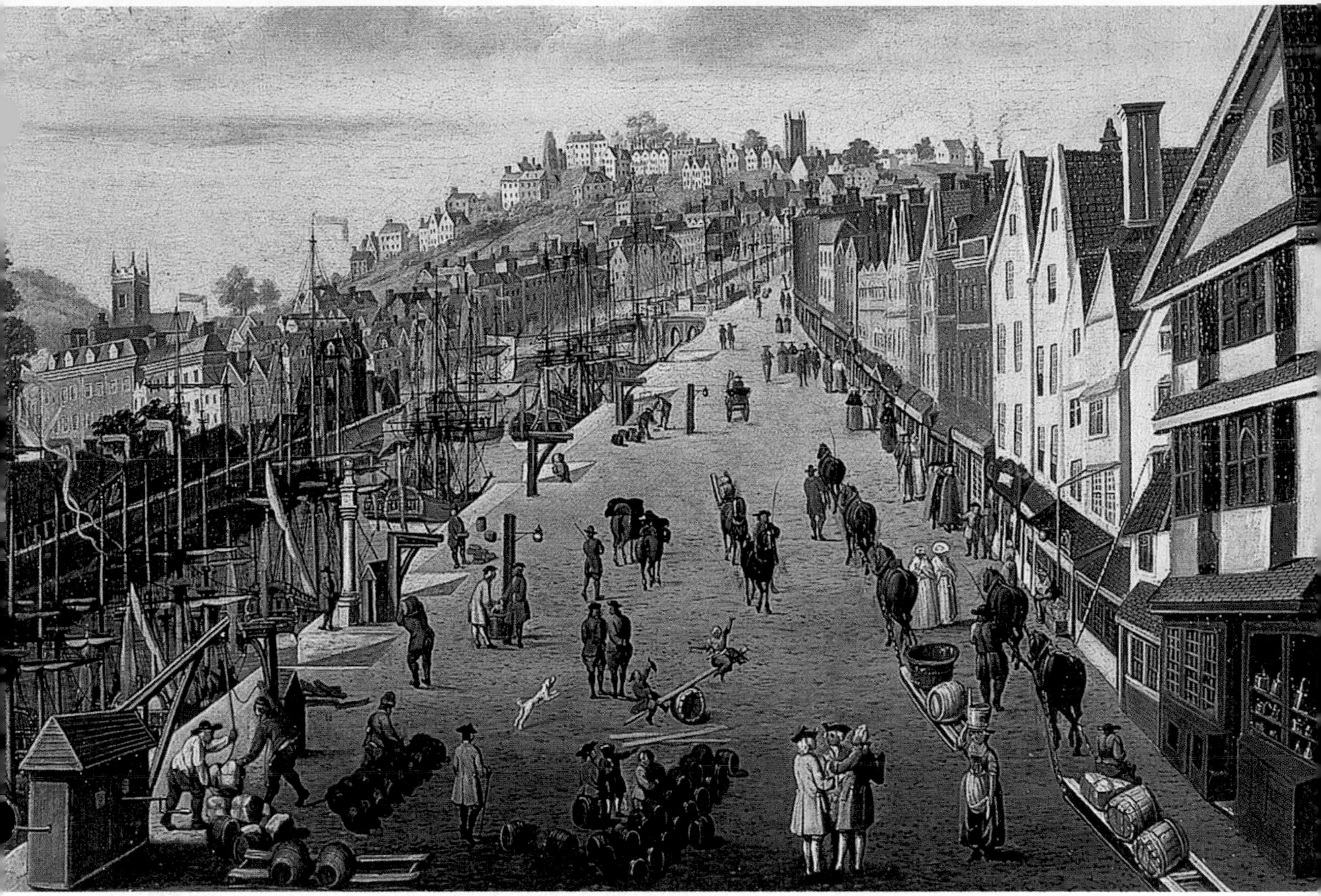

England, in an effort to regulate colonial trade, required all ships bound from America to pass through British ports and pay customs duties. Places such as Plymouth, Liverpool, and Bristol (*shown here*) thrived as a result.


These changes strengthened royal control enough to satisfy England's monarchs for the next half century. By 1700 Virginia, New York, Massachusetts, and New Hampshire all had royal governments. New Jersey, the Carolinas, and Georgia would soon join that list. Royal rule meant that the monarch appointed governors and (everywhere except Massachusetts) also appointed their councils. Royally appointed councils could veto any law passed by a colony's representative assembly, royally appointed governors could veto any law passed by both houses, and the Crown could veto any law passed by both houses and approved by the governor.

Even so, the sway of royal power remained more apparent than real after 1700. The Glorious Revolution asserted once and for all that Parliament's authority—rule by the legislative branch of government—would be supreme in the governing of England. In the colonies, members of representative assemblies grew more skilled at dealing with royal governors and more protective of their rights. They guarded most jealously their strongest lever of power—the right of the lower houses to levy taxes.

The political reality of the assemblies' power reflected a social reality as well. No longer mere outposts along the Atlantic, the colonies of 1700 were becoming more firmly rooted societies. Their laws and traditions were based not only on what they had brought from England but also on the conditions of life in America. That social reality had already blocked Stuart ambitions to shape the future of North America, just as it had thwarted the designs of lordly proprietors and the dreams of religious reformers.

**REVIEW**

How did William and Mary try to increase colonial revenue?

Still, the dream of empire would revive among England's rulers in the middle of the eighteenth century—in part because French kings had never abandoned their own imperial visions. France had long been Europe's largest and most populous kingdom. By the 1660s bureaucratic, financial, and political reforms made it the mightiest military power as well. Eager to expand on the continent, France's ambitious king, Louis XIV, unleashed his titanic war machine against his neighbors four times between 1667 and 1714.

Even after 1714 France, England and, to a lesser extent, Spain waged a kind of cold war for a quarter of a century, jockeying for position and influence. Western European monarchs had come to realize that confrontations in North America's vast and distant interior could affect their wars closer to home. In this global chess game, the British had the advantage of numbers: nearly 400,000 subjects in the colonies in 1720, compared with only about 25,000 French spread along a thin line of fishing stations and fur-trading posts, and a meager 5,000 or so Spaniards in New Mexico, Texas, and Florida. But by a considerable margin, native peoples still represented the majority population in North America. Moreover, they still controlled more than 90 percent of its territory. If events in North America could affect the balance of power in Europe, then French and Spanish administrators could still believe that their Indian alliances might yet help them prevail against each other and, especially, against Britain's booming colonies.

# CHAPTER SUMMARY

While the French colonized Canada, the Protestant Reformation in England spurred the colonization of New England and Pennsylvania.

- During the seventeenth century, the French slowly established a fur trade, agricultural communities, and religious institutions in Canada while building Indian alliances throughout the Mississippi drainage.
- Competition over the fur trade in New France and New Netherlands contributed to a devastating series of wars between Iroquois, Hurons, and dozens of other Indian groups.
- Over the same period, English Puritans planted more populous settlements between Maine and Long Island.
- The migration of family groups and a rough equality of wealth lent stability to early New England society, reinforced by the settlers' shared commitment to Puritanism and a strong tradition of self-government.
- The mid-Atlantic colonies also enjoyed a rapid growth of people and wealth, but political wrangling as well as ethnic and religious diversity made for a higher level of social conflict.
- Whereas New Englanders attempted to subdue native peoples, colonists in the mid-Atlantic enjoyed more harmonious relations with the region's original inhabitants, thanks in part to William Penn's Quaker principles.
- The efforts of the later Stuart kings to centralize England's empire ended with the Glorious Revolution in 1688, which greatly reduced tensions between the colonies and the parent country.

## Additional Reading

For penetrating studies of French and Indian relations, see Allan Greer, *Mohawk Saint* (2005); and Brett Rushforth, *Bonds of Alliance* (2013). Colin G. Calloway's *One Vast Winter Count* (2003) masterfully synthesizes the history of natives and Europeans in early North America west of the Appalachians; and Daniel K. Richter does the same for Eastern North America in *Before the Revolution* (2011). For a history of Dutch America, see Jaap Jacobs, *New Netherland* (2005). *Vermeer's Hat* (2008) by Timothy Brook is a marvelous exploration of the ways furs and other commodities bound together the seventeenth-century world. For important work on Indians in the colonial Northeast, see Jenny Hale Pulsipher, *Subjects unto the Same King* (2008); and Andrew Lipman, *The Saltwater Frontier* (2015). The best and most recent introduction to Puritanism is Coffey and Lim, *The Cambridge Companion to Puritanism* (2008). For Puritanism in New England, read Stephen Foster, *The Long Argument* (1991), and Mark Peterson, *The Price of Redemption* (1997). And to learn more about the diversity of religious and supernatural views in New England, consult Philip Gura, *A Glimpse of Sion's Glory* (1984); and David Hall, *Worlds of Wonder, Days of Judgment* (1989).

For the everyday lives of northern colonists in New England and New York, rely on Virginia Dejohn Anderson's *New England's Generation* (1991); and Joyce Goodfriend's *Before the Melting Pot* (1991). For African slavery in New England, see Wendy Warren, *New England Bound* (2016). For a geographical perspective on British America (including the West Indies and Canada), see Stephen J. Hornsby, *British Atlantic American Frontier* (2005). For the complex interplay among English colonialism, environmental change, and Indian power in the Northeast, see William Cronon's classic *Changes in the Land* (rev. ed., 2003). The event and memory of "King Philip's War" are the subjects of Jill Lepore's *The Name of War* (1998).

# 5 The Mosaic of Eighteenth-Century America

## 1689–1768

A remarkable eighteenth-century painting created on an animal hide portrays the Pawnee surprise attack along the banks of the Platte River in August 1720.

Courtesy Palace of the Governors Photo Archives (NMHM/DCA) neg. 158345

## >> An American Story

## THE TALE OF A TATTOOED TRAVELER

August 13, 1720: Morning sunlight reaches across the junction of the Platte and Loup Rivers in what today is Nebraska. Jean L'Archevêque rises stiffly from where he slept and looks about camp. Spanish soldiers don their wide-brimmed hats, and Pueblo Indian warriors talk softly to one another in the early light. A friar in his habit makes his way around the tents. Don Pedro de Villasur, lieutenant governor of New Mexico and leader of the party, threads his arms through a bright red officer's coat and orders the soldiers to bring in their horses.

Born in 1672 in Bayonne, France, L'Archevêque had followed a tangled path to that spot in Nebraska. Fleeing family bankruptcy, he was only a boy when he boarded ship to the French Caribbean and joined a scheme to colonize coastal Louisiana. Led by the famous French explorer René Robert Cavelier, Sieur de La Salle (the first European to navigate the immense Mississippi), L'Archevêque, and nearly 300 colonists enlisted in the venture had reason for optimism.

But things sometimes go badly for kings and their servants. La Salle and his followers wound up shipwrecked on the coast of present-day Texas and proceeded to starve, sicken, and die. Weakened survivors blamed their leader and in 1687 hatched a plan to be rid of him. Young L'Archevêque seems to have played a part, distracting the great explorer while an accomplice blew his head apart with a musket shot. Jean and the other murderers soon found themselves unhappy guests among Caddo Indians in east Texas. The Caddos tattooed the Frenchmen's faces, carefully inserting a dye made from walnuts into countless tiny cuts. In 1690 Spanish explorers stumbled across L'Archevêque and a companion, ransomed the grateful pair from the Caddos, and sent them off in chains for interrogation in Mexico City, Spain, and then back to Mexico.

L'Archevêque had become a pawn in a high-stakes game. News of La Salle's stillborn colony convinced Spanish officials that they needed to secure their claims on the North American West and stop France from using the region as a base for threatening New Spain and its all too famous silver mines. Crucially, Spain had to reconquer New Mexico. Popé's Pueblo Revolt of 1680 had expelled the Spanish (Chapter 3), but the determined unity of the diverse Pueblo villages collapsed within a dozen years. When Spanish colonists returned in 1692 under Diego de Vargas, they met only fragmented resistance.

In reconquered New Mexico L'Archevêque found his first real home since boyhood. Sent north perhaps because of his facility not only with French but also Indian languages, L'Archevêque prospered in Santa Fe, marrying well and gaining the trust of his neighbors. But eventually the Spanish began hearing complaints from the Plains Apaches about Pawnee raiders armed with French guns. Sensing a threat, in 1719 New Mexico's governor ordered his lieutenant Villasur to take L'Archevêque and a mixed group of Indian and Spanish fighters to confront the French—hence the long trek to the Platte River the following summer, where the men awoke at daybreak on August 13 to do the king's business.

But, again, things sometimes go badly for kings and their servants. Moments after ordering his men to bring in their horses, Villasur heard wild screams as dozens of painted Pawnee warriors rushed his camp. The lieutenant governor was one of the first to die, mouth agape just outside his tent; the well-traveled L'Archevêque fell soon after. Only 13 Spaniards and 40 Pueblo warriors escaped to bring the doleful news to Santa Fe, where for generations residents remembered the ambush as one of the great calamities of their history.

That a merchant's boy from Bayonne, France, could be shipwrecked, recruited to murder, tattooed in Texas, imprisoned in Mexico and Spain, married and made respectable on the upper Rio Grande, and finally shot dead and buried somewhere in Nebraska testifies in a very personal way to the unpredictable changes roiling eighteenth-century North America. As Europeans established colonies and began competing with one another across the continent, native peoples found life changing at astonishing speed. Europeans, with their animals, plants, technologies, diseases, and designs, sparked a fever pitch of transformation. But Europeans could not predict and did not control the process. Despite their grand ambitions, colonial newcomers often found their own plans upended and their lives reordered by the same forces reworking native life. <<

## THEMATIC TIMELINE

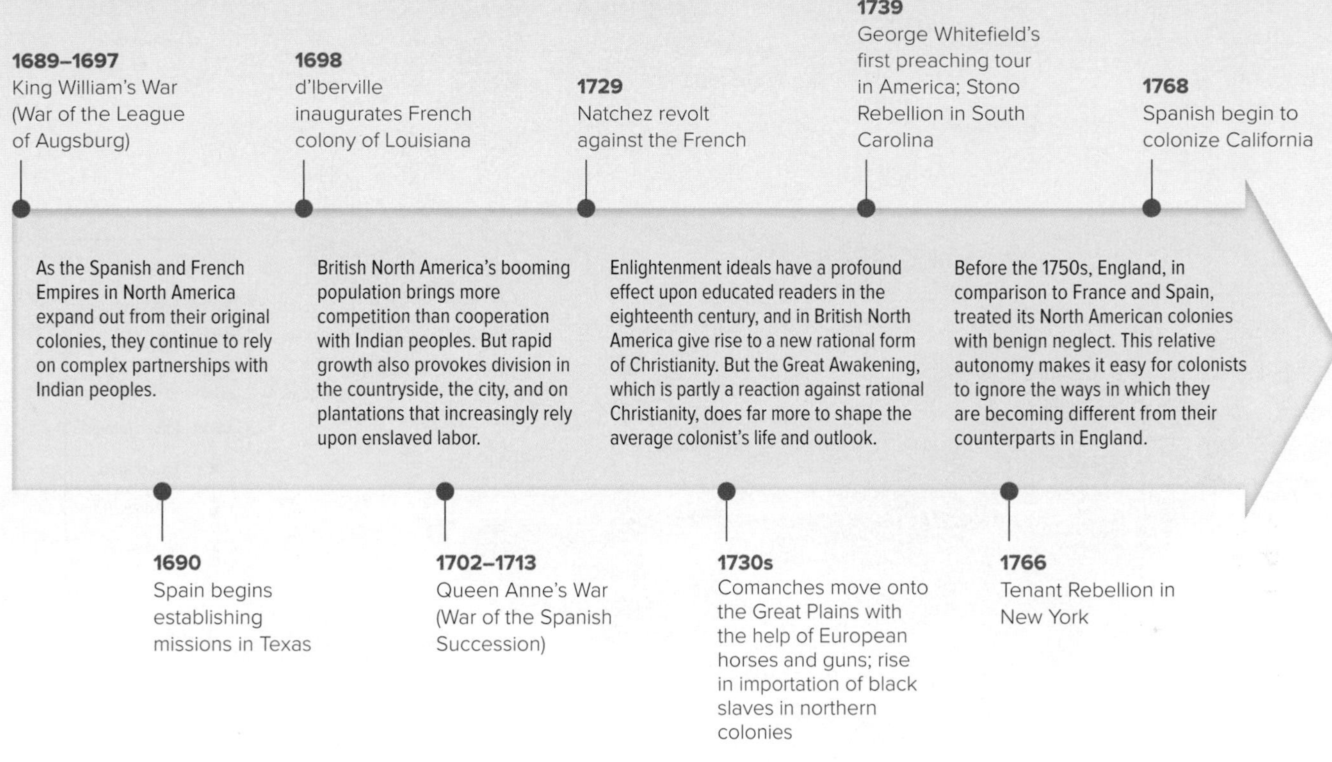
1689–1697
King William's War (War of the League of Augsburg)
1698
d'Iberville inaugurates French colony of Louisiana
1729
Natchez revolt against the French
1739
George Whitefield's first preaching tour in America; Stono Rebellion in South Carolina
1768
Spanish begin to colonize California
As the Spanish and French Empires in North America expand out from their original colonies, they continue to rely on complex partnerships with Indian peoples.
British North America's booming population brings more competition than cooperation with Indian peoples. But rapid growth also provokes division in the countryside, the city, and on plantations that increasingly rely upon enslaved labor.
Enlightenment ideals have a profound effect upon educated readers in the eighteenth century, and in British North America give rise to a new rational form of Christianity. But the Great Awakening, which is partly a reaction against rational Christianity, does far more to shape the average colonist's life and outlook.
Before the 1750s, England, in comparison to France and Spain, treated its North American colonies with benign neglect. This relative autonomy makes it easy for colonists to ignore the ways in which they are becoming different from their counterparts in England.
1690
Spain begins establishing missions in Texas
1702–1713
Queen Anne's War (War of the Spanish Succession)
1730s
Comanches move onto the Great Plains with the help of European horses and guns; rise in importation of black slaves in northern colonies
1766
Tenant Rebellion in New York

# CRISIS AND TRANSFORMATION IN NORTHERN NEW SPAIN

As European rivals laid claim to more and more of North America, nervous Spanish officials stared at their maps. Around the former Aztec Empire, Spain controlled enormous cities, booming towns, and agricultural villages—a region still home to millions despite waves of epidemics. Though drier and less populated, the lands hundreds of miles north boasted remarkable silver mines. To protect these places from French designs, Spain had to start paying more attention to the blank spaces still farther north on their maps—spaces entirely controlled by Indians.

**Defensive Expansion into Texas** >> Nowhere did the French seem more menacing than in Texas, one of the many blank spots on Spanish maps. La Salle's adventure could have turned out differently: before his grisly death, the Frenchman had pledged to invade northern New Spain with an army of thousands of Indians who, he believed, had "a deadly hatred of the Spaniards." Fearful that another French expedition might actually acquire such an army, in 1690 Spain began establishing missions among the native peoples of Texas. By the early 1720s the Spanish had fortified their claim on Texas with ten Franciscan missions, four presidios (military garrisons), and the beginnings of a civilian settlement on the San Antonio River.

Still, missions disappointed Franciscans and natives alike. Missionaries baptized Indians by the thousands and hoped to create orderly, regimented communities where converts could be shielded from outside influence and taught to be industrious and devout. But Indians insisted on coming and going when they pleased. Many sought the food and sanctuary missions offered, only to leave periodically to rendezvous with kin, hunt, and harvest wild plant foods. Their comings and goings confounded the missionaries. Matters were even worse for Franciscans in east Texas, where sedentary and relatively prosperous Caddos had no need of Spanish crops or protection and preferred to trade with the more liberal French in Louisiana.

However successful they were at retaining autonomy, Indians throughout Texas paid a steep price for any benefits they wrung from missions. Those compelled inside by

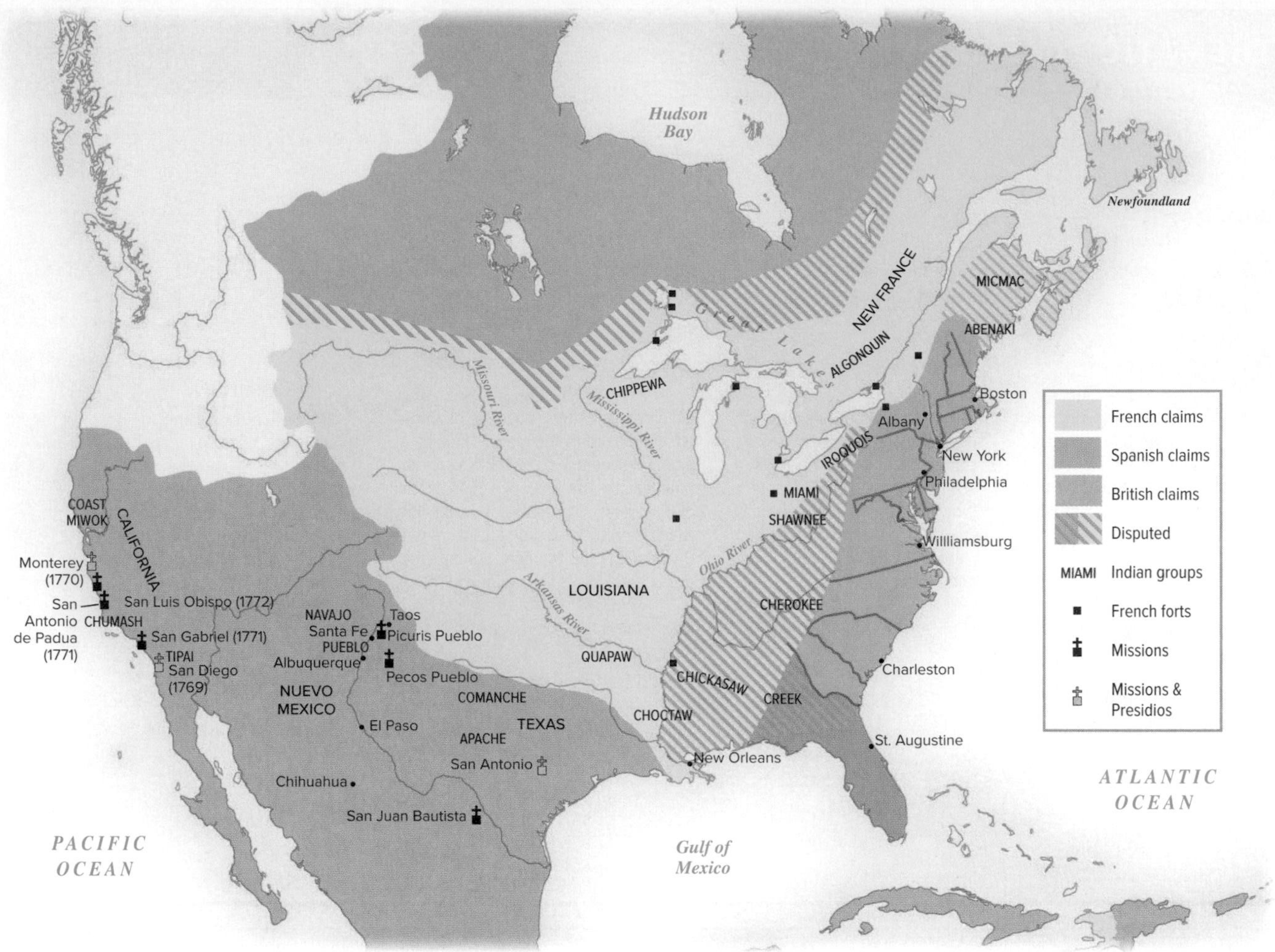

Hudson Bay
Newfoundland
NEW FRANCE
MICMAC
ABENAKI
ALGONQUIN
Great Lakes
CHIPPEWA
Missouri River
Mississippi River
Boston
Albany
IROQUOIS
New York
Philadelphia
MIAMI
SHAWNEE
Ohio River
Williamsburg
COAST MIWOK
CALIFORNIA
Monterey (1770)
San Antonio de Padua (1771)
San Luis Obispo (1772)
CHUMASH
San Gabriel (1771)
TIPAI
San Diego (1769)
NAVAJO
Taos
Santa Fe
Picuris Pueblo
PUEBLO
Albuquerque
Pecos Pueblo
NUEVO MEXICO
COMANCHE
LOUISIANA
Arkansas River
QUAPAW
CHEROKEE
CHICKASAW
CREEK
CHOCTAW
Charleston
El Paso
TEXAS
APACHE
San Antonio
St. Augustine
New Orleans
Chihuahua
San Juan Bautista
PACIFIC OCEAN
Gulf of Mexico
ATLANTIC OCEAN
French claims
Spanish claims
British claims
Disputed
MIAMI Indian groups
French forts
Missions
Missions & Presidios


## MAP 5.1: EUROPEAN TERRITORIAL CLAIMS IN THE EIGHTEENTH CENTURY

The French, English, and Indian nations all jockeyed for power and position across North America during the eighteenth century. The French expanded their fur trade through the interior, while the English at midcentury began to press the barrier of the Appalachians. But native peoples still controlled the vast majority of the continent and often held the balance of power in interimperial struggles. *What geographic advantages did the French enjoy? And the English?*

hunger and insecurity often endured harsh discipline and corporal punishment for disobeying orders. Worse, missions proved ideal vectors for epidemic disease. In the 1730s alone, smallpox killed more than 1,000 mission Indians near San Antonio. Other illnesses became commonplace in what were often filthy, cramped buildings. Children found missions especially dangerous. In eighteenth-century Mission San Antonio, for example, only one in three newborns survived to their third birthday.

Meanwhile, royal administrators encouraged Spanish emigration to Texas—but with little success. In 1731 the province's nonnative population barely amounted to 500 men, women, and children; by 1760 that figure had slightly more than doubled. In 1778 a Franciscan inspector described San Antonio, Texas's major civilian settlement, as "a town so miserable that it resembles a most wretched village." He counted "59 houses of stone and mud, and 79 of wood, but all poorly built." After many decades, Spain's push into Texas had created only a slender archipelago of missions, presidios, and a few towns.

**Crisis and Rebirth in New Mexico** >> Elsewhere the region remained in the hands of unconquered Indians whose regional power only seemed to be expanding. At first Apaches did most to threaten Spain's ambitions in Texas. Their raids thinned Spanish herds, prevented ranching and farming communities from expanding, and threatened missions with destruction. Spaniards responded with merciless slave raids on Apache camps, and the violence escalated.

^ These two Franciscans were regarded as hero-martyrs by their fellow missionaries after Comanches and Wichitas killed them during a 1758 attack on the San Saba mission in Texas.
©DeAgostini/Getty Images

By the 1730s, however, a new force appeared to eclipse even Apaches. They called themselves Numunuu, "the People." Their enemies came to call them Comanches. Emerging from the foothills of the Rockies in the late sixteenth century, Comanches acquired horses, moved permanently onto the plains, and quickly became some of the most formidable equestrian warriors in history. They allied with Indians who could provide them French guns and ammunition from Louisiana and embarked on a program of territorial expansion. By the mid-eighteenth century Comanches drove most Apaches from the plains and took over their rich bison-hunting territories on the southern plains. Without bison Apaches turned more and more to stealing Spanish animals to survive. Spaniards from Santa Fe to San Antonio soon found themselves at war with Apaches and Comanches both; New Mexico often came into conflict with Navajos and Utes as well. Much of northern New Spain became a theater of desolation, abandoned villages up and down the Rio Grande testifying to the limits of Spanish power.

Spaniards accused the "barbarians" of animalistic savagery, but all sides inflicted horrors. Outside the besieged town of Tucson, for example, Lt. Col. Pedro de Allende boasted that he had decapitated a fallen Apache in front of the dead man's comrades and "charged the Apache line single-handed, with the head stuck on his lance." Away from the din of battle a prominent Spaniard noted that his people accuse the Indians of cruelty but added dryly, "I do not know what opinion they would have of us."

By the 1780s nearly everyone had had enough of war. A farsighted Comanche leader named Ecueracapa helped broker peace with Spanish authorities in 1786, after which the new allies cooperated to entice or threaten Utes, Navajos, and even Apaches into peace as well. Northern New Spain gradually entered a period of relative peace, expansion, and economic growth.

Changes were most dramatic in New Mexico, where Spanish subjects opened up new farms and ranches, enlarged their flocks and herds, and devoted new energy to local manufacturing. As New Mexico's non-Indian population grew (20,000 by the close of the eighteenth century), new roads funded by the Crown eased the province's isolation. Increased trade allowed caravans to set out from Santa Fe for Chihuahua City once or even twice a year.

Some of the New Mexicans who profited from the newfound opportunities patronized artists and skilled craftsmen. By the late eighteenth century a distinctive New Mexican culture emerged, marked by new traditions in such crafts as woodworking and weaving, as well as in religious art and practice. A master craftsman known only as the Laguna Santero helped define this movement by training local apprentices in his workshop and making pieces for wealthy patrons. The Laguna Santero, his apprentices, and others he inspired began making exquisite portraits of saints on pine boards (*retablos*), hide paintings, elaborate altar screens for churches, and wooden statues of saints (*bultos*)—all art forms still associated with New Mexican folk culture today.

**Spanish California** >> Spanish California became the empire's last major colonial project in North America. Like the colonies in Texas and Florida, settlement was sparked by anxiety over foreign competition, this time from Russians moving south from Alaska. Though Spaniards first explored the California coast in 1542, not until 1768 did the Crown authorize permanent colonization. A joint expedition of military men and Franciscans, led by the pragmatic Gaspar de Portolá and the physically frail but iron-willed Friar Junípero Serra, braved shipwrecks, scurvy, and earthquakes to establish ramshackle presidios (military garrisons) and missions at San Diego and Monterey.

^ The Ukrainian Louis Choris visited Mission Dolores in 1822 and captured this scene of Ohlone Indians playing games of chance. But the artist's overall impression of Ohlone life at the mission was one of sorrow and despair. "I have never seen one laugh. I have never seen one look one in the face. They look as though they were interested in nothing."
©Private Collection/Bridgeman Images

Recruiting colonists was difficult. In desperation, officials even scoured the orphanages and prisons of New Spain. Those who journeyed north found the sea voyage difficult and sometimes deadly. The backbreaking overland route from northwestern New Spain had to be abandoned after 1781, when an uprising of Yuma Indians shut down the crossing at the Colorado River. Still, the colony enjoyed modest growth. By 1800 California had two more presidios (at San Francisco and Santa Barbara), three Spanish towns (San José, Los Angeles, and Branciforte, near present-day Santa Cruz), and eighteen Franciscan missions, ministering to 13,000 Indian converts.

Like their colleagues in Texas and Florida, Franciscans in California tried to entice Indians into missions with promises of food, shelter, instruction, and protection. All the while Indians saw the world changing around them. In Monterey, for example, imported pigs, sheep, mules, horses, and cows multiplied at astonishing speed. These animals radiated out from the mission and presidio, overgrazing and annihilating native plants. Soon weeds and plants that Spaniards had unwittingly brought with them spread throughout the region. Pollen analysis of the vegetable matter in adobe from the early nineteenth century indicates that by the time the bricks were made, alien weeds had all but displaced native plants. With their lands transformed by overgrazing and invasive plant species, and their populations diminished by epidemics and hampered by falling birthrates, native families around Monterey abandoned their villages and either fled to the interior or surrendered to the discipline and danger of mission life. Indians provided labor and food for California's missions, presidios, and three colonial towns.

By 1800 California was home to only 1,800 Hispanic residents. Despite their relative poverty and isolation, they nurtured distinctive traditions ranging from the profound to the comical. In 1835, for example, an American guest recorded something curious at a wedding in Santa Barbara. Amid the singing, dancing, and celebrating, he watched young women knocking off men's sombreros and breaking cologne-filled eggs on their heads. The men were "bound in gallantry to find out the lady and return the compliment, though it must not be done if the person sees you."

English and American visitors to California wrote frequently about the women they encountered there, though usually kept their observations to the superficial. But the most important differences separating women in California from counterparts in Boston and London had nothing to do with dress, hair, dancing, or wedding customs.

**Women and the Law in New Spain and British North America** >> Women in California and throughout the Spanish world enjoyed a host of legal rights denied to women in English-speaking realms. When parents died, Spanish law ensured that daughters inherited property equally with sons. English law, in contrast, allowed fathers to craft wills however they wished. If an Englishman died without a will ("intestate"), his eldest son inherited all the land and any buildings on it. Daughters and younger brothers received only a share of the remaining personal property.

In marriage Spanish women retained control over their personal property, and ownership of any dowry (sum of money) they brought into the union. They also maintained the right to buy and sell land and to legally represent themselves in court. Married English women had virtually no control over any kind of property, could not write a will, and could initiate no legal action without a husband's consent. These differences in law persisted into widowhood. Spanish widows were legally entitled not only to their original dowries but also to at least one-half of all property they and their deceased husbands had accumulated in marriage. Their English counterparts had no right to their dowries in widowhood—only to control over a third of their dead husband's property. Even this proved temporary; in contrast to Spanish law, English law maintained that this third share would revert to the deceased *husband's* family upon the widow's death.

For the poorest women such legal differences meant little. But for those who did have some property or wealth, it mattered a great deal whether they lived in New Spain or British North America.

 REVIEW

Why did Spain establish colonies in Texas and California, and what role did missions play in anchoring the Spanish presence?

# EIGHTEENTH-CENTURY NEW FRANCE

Like Spain's vast and sprawling territorial claims in North America, France's imperial ambitions were nothing if not grand. French colonial maps laid claim to the heart of the continent, a massive imperial wedge stretching from Newfoundland southwest to the Mississippi delta, then northwest across the Great Plains and into the cold north woods, and east again through Upper Canada to the North Atlantic. (See Map 5.1.)

**Colonial Compromises** >> Despite these grand claims, most eighteenth-century French Americans continued to live along the St. Lawrence River. They dwelt in farming communities up and down the river valley between the towns of Montreal and Quebec, capital of New France. Jesuit missions also lined the river, ministering to native converts. After a brief boost from colonization in the 1660s and 1670s, the French population grew almost totally through natural increase. Fortunately for France the colonists excelled at natural increase—nurturing large, thriving families and doubling their population every generation.

Those determined enough to endure darkness, isolation, and numbing cold in winter and then heat, humidity, and swarming mosquitoes in summer found life in Canada considerably easier than life in France. Colonists lived longer, more often owned land, and enjoyed greater freedoms than peasants at home. By 1760 the valley contained 75,000 French colonists, soldiers, and priests. Many Canadian households also included Indian slaves: mostly women and children who had been captured by other Indians in places as far away as Texas and the Arkansas valley and eventually brought to New France.

To the west and north of New France, in the country known as the *pays d'en haut,* the French venture looked quite different. Here forts and missions rather than farms or towns anchored French ambition. More exactly, the goodwill of Indian peoples provided the anchor. Though certainly willing to use violence, the French in North America recognized that they were too few to secure their interests through force alone. France gained an edge over its rivals in the interior by being useful to Indians, primarily the Algonquian-speaking nations who spread across eastern Canada and the upper Mississippi. French merchants brought coveted European presents and trade goods, while military men, administrators, and Jesuits often mediated in conflicts between native groups. Vastly outnumbered by Indians throughout most of the territory that it claimed in North America, France remained deeply dependent on native peoples.

Dependence meant compromise. The two peoples had radically divergent expectations about warfare, trade, marriage, child rearing, religion, food, beauty, and many other areas of life. Few cultural differences seemed as difficult to bridge as those concerning law. In 1706, for example, men associated with a prominent Ottawa leader known as Le Pesant killed a priest and a French soldier outside Fort Detroit. Enraged French authorities demanded that Le Pesant be surrendered so that he could be tried and, once found guilty, executed for murder. Ottawa leaders countered by offering to replace the dead Frenchmen with Indian slaves. "Raising" the dead this way was a common Ottawa remedy in cases of murder between allies, because it helped avoid a potentially disastrous cycle of blood revenge.

Neither side gave in to the other. Instead, they crafted a novel solution that exemplified the pattern of creative, mutual compromises typical of what one scholar has called the "middle ground" characterizing French-Indian relations in the *pays d'en haut.* Ottawa leaders turned over Le Pesant to French authorities, whereupon this elderly, obese prisoner miraculously "escaped" just before his execution. Clearly the French and their Ottawa allies had come to an understanding. Le Pesant would be surrendered and, once condemned, quietly released. The compromise satisfied both sides more or less and became a model solution to later French-Indian murder cases.

Necessary and inevitable, such compromises nonetheless rankled authorities in Paris. In 1731 one such official bemoaned the fact that after more than a century, colonial administrators in New France had failed to make the "savages" obedient to the Crown. The colony's governor general dashed off a terse reply: "if this has not been done, it is because we have found the task to be an impossible one. Kindly apprise me of any means you should conceive of for securing such obedience."

**France on the Gulf Coast** >> Forced into uncomfortable compromises in the north, authorities in Paris hoped to establish a colony on the Gulf Coast that could be more profitable, and more French. After La Salle's failure in Texas, it fell to Pierre Le Moyne d'Iberville to establish French Louisiana. A veteran sailor and soldier, d'Iberville spent much of the 1690s attacking British settlements in Newfoundland and the North Atlantic. Sent to the Gulf in 1698, he inaugurated the new colony of Louisiana with a post at Biloxi Bay. D'Iberville's successors established settlements at Mobile Bay and, in 1718, the town of New Orleans. Crown officers and entrepreneurs envisioned an agricultural bonanza, expecting Louisiana to have far more in common with the Caribbean's profitable sugar islands than with the maddening *pays d'en haut.*

Nothing went according to plan. Here, too, Indians forced the French into painful concessions. Louisiana came into conflict with the mighty Chickasaws, and in 1729 the Natchez Indians pushed back, killing or capturing some 500 colonists. Underfunded and usually neglected by the crown, Louisiana's officials became notoriously corrupt and arbitrary. The colony was, according to one observer, a place "without religion, without justice, without discipline, without order, and without police."

More to the point, the Gulf Coast was without many colonists, having acquired a reputation among would-be French migrants as unattractive and unhealthy. When colonists were not fighting Indians, they contended with heat, humidity, hurricanes, droughts, and crop failures; with never-ending battles to turn swamps and forests into farmland; and with the scourges of malaria and yellow fever. By 1731 two-thirds of the French who had journeyed to Louisiana had died or fled. Still, like New Mexico, Canada, California, and Texas, colonial Louisiana persevered and slowly become more populous and more prosperous. Nearly 4,000 French men, women, and children called the colony home by 1746. Their fortunes had in large part come to depend on another, even larger group of newcomers: French Louisiana's African slaves.

**Slavery and Colonial Society in French Louisiana** >> Within a year of its founding, New Orleans imported nearly 6,000 slaves—most men, brought directly from Africa. But Louisiana tobacco and, later, indigo proved inferior to the varieties exported from Britain's colonies, and the sudden influx of Africans challenged French control. In 1729 some newly arrived slaves joined forces with the Natchez Indians in their rebellion. The alliance sent waves of panic through the colony, whose population by then had more slaves than free French. The colonists retaliated in a devastating counterattack, enlisting both the Choctaw Indians, rivals of the Natchez, and other enslaved blacks, who were promised freedom in return for their support.

The planters' costly victory persuaded French authorities to stop importing slaves. Nonetheless, blacks continued to make up a majority of all Louisianans, and by the middle of the eighteenth century nearly all were native-born. The vast majority remained enslaved, but their work routines—tending cattle, cutting timber, producing naval stores, manning boats—allowed them relative autonomy of movement. But the greatest prize—freedom—was awarded those black men who served in the French militia, defending the colony from the English and Indians as well as capturing slave runaways. The descendants of these black militiamen would become the core of Louisiana's free black community.

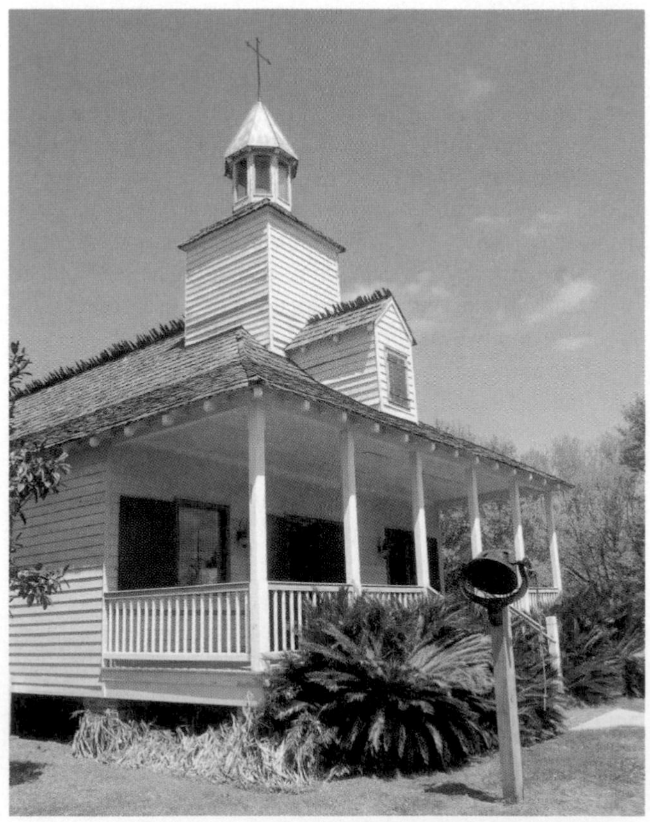

^ La Chapelle des Attakapas, located at the Vermilionville living history museum in Lafayette, Louisiana, is a reproduction in the style of churches built in French Louisiana in the eighteenth century. Note the unusual ridge lines on the roof made of cypress shingles. One side was allowed to project above the top of the ridge line in order to provide greater protection against rain blown by the prevailing winds.
©James West Davidson

**Imperial Rivalries** >> Male subjects throughout French America stood ready to perform militia duty, formally or informally. They had to. Disputes with Indians proved depressingly common. More to the point, European wars frequently spilled over into North America. In 1689 England joined the Netherlands and the League of Augsburg (several German-speaking states) in a war against France. While the main struggle raged in Europe, French and English colonials, joined by their Indian allies, skirmished in what was known as King William's War. Peace returned in 1697, but only until the Anglo-French struggle resumed with Queen Anne's War, from 1702 to 1713.

For a quarter of a century thereafter the two nations waged a kind of cold war, competing for advantage. At stake was not so much control over people or even territory as control over trade. In North America, France and England vied for access to the sugar islands of the Caribbean, a monopoly on supplying manufactured goods to Spanish America, and dominance of the fur trade. The British had the advantage of numbers: nearly 400,000 subjects in the colonies in 1720, the year of Jean L'Archevêque's death, compared with only about 25,000 French. But this is precisely where France's many compromises paid off. So long as the French maintained their network of alliances with powerful native peoples, British colonies had little chance of expanding west of the Appalachian Mountains.

How did Louisiana differ from French Canada?

# FORCES OF DIVISION IN BRITISH NORTH AMERICA

British colonials from Maine to the Carolinas distrusted the French and resented their empire of fish and furs. But the English were preoccupied with their own affairs and, by and large, uninterested in uniting against New France. Indeed, a traveler during the first half of the eighteenth century would have been struck by how hopelessly divided and disunited England's mainland colonies were, split by ethnicity, race, region, wealth, and religion. The British colonies were a diverse and fragmented lot.

**Population Growth** >> One of the largest new groups—250,000 men, women, and children—had come to the colonies from Africa in chains. White arrivals included many English immigrants but also a quarter of a million Scots-Irish, the descendants of seventeenth-century Scots who had regretted settling in northern Ireland; perhaps 135,000 Germans; and a sprinkling of Swiss, Swedes, Highland Scots, and Spanish Jews. Most non-English white immigrants were fleeing lives torn by famine, warfare, and religious persecution. All the voyagers, English and non-English, risked the hazardous Atlantic crossing. Many had paid for passage by signing indentures to work as servants in America.

The immigrants and slaves who arrived in the colonies between 1700 and 1775 swelled a colonial American population that was already growing dramatically from natural increase. The birthrate in eighteenth-century America was triple what it is today. Most women bore between five and eight children, and most children survived to maturity.

This astonishing population explosion exemplified a more general global acceleration of population in the second half of the eighteenth century. China's 150 million inhabitants in 1700 had doubled to more than 313 million by century's end. Europe's total rose from about 118 million to 187 million over the same period. The unprecedented global population explosion had several causes. Europe's climate, for one, had become warmer and drier, allowing for generally better harvests. Health and nutrition improved globally with the worldwide spread of Native American crops. Irish farmers discovered that a single acre planted with the American potato could support an entire family. The tomato added crucial vitamins to the Mediterranean diet, and in China the American sweet potato thrived in hilly regions where rice would not grow.

Dramatic population increase in the British colonies, fed by the importation of slaves, immigration, and natural increase, made it hard for colonials to share any common identity. Far from fostering political unity, almost every aspect of social development set Americans at odds with one another. And that process of division and disunity was reflected in the outpouring of new settlers into the backcountry.

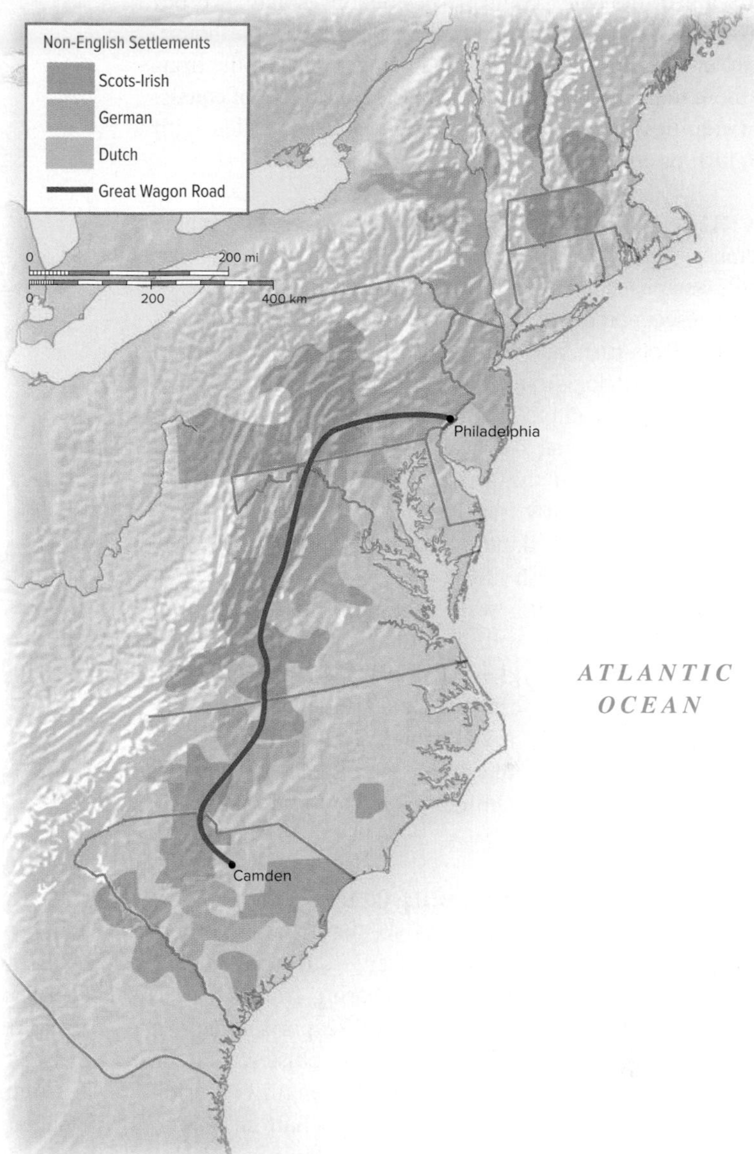
Non-English Settlements
Scots-Irish
German
Dutch
Great Wagon Road
0
200 mi
0
200
400 km
Philadelphia
Camden
ATLANTIC
OCEAN

## MAP 5.2: NON-ENGLISH SETTLEMENTS IN EIGHTEENTH-CENTURY BRITISH NORTH AMERICA

Many non-English settlers spilled into the backcountry: the Scots-Irish and the Germans followed the Great Wagon Road (*red line*) through the western parts of the middle colonies and southern colonies, while the Dutch and other Germans moved up the Hudson River valley.

*In what ways did the concentration of non-English immigrants in the backcountry influence the development of that region?*

## Moving into the Backcountry >>

To immigrants from Europe weary of war or worn by want, the seaboard's established communities must have seemed havens of order and stability. But by the beginning of the eighteenth century, land scarcity pushed both native-born and newly arrived families to look westward. While descendants of old Yankee families created new communities in frontier New England, immigrants from Europe had more luck obtaining land south of New York. By the 1720s German and Scots-Irish immigrants as well as native-born colonists were pouring into western Pennsylvania. Some settled permanently, but others streamed southward into the backcountry of Virginia and the Carolinas, where they encountered native-born southerners pressing westward.

Living in the West could be profoundly isolating. From many farmsteads it was a day's ride to the nearest courthouse, tavern, or church. This forced self-sufficiency made the frontier, more than anywhere else in America, a society of equals. Most families crowded into one-room shacks walled with mud, turf, or crude logs. And everyone worked hard.

## Social Conflict and the Frontier >> 

Ethnic differences heightened sectional tensions between the seaboard's established communities and the frontier. People of English descent predominated along the Atlantic coast, whereas Germans, Scots-Irish, and other white minorities were concentrated in the interior. Many English colonials regarded these new immigrants as culturally inferior and politically subversive. Charles Woodmason, an Anglican missionary in the Carolina backcountry, lamented the arrival of "5 or 6,000 Ignorant, mean, worthless, beggarly Irish Presbyterians, the Scum of the Earth, the Refuse of Mankind," who "delighted in a low, lazy, sluttish, heathenish, hellish life."

German immigrants were generally credited with steadier work habits, as well as higher standards of sexual morality and personal hygiene. But like the clannish Scots-Irish, the Germans preferred to live, trade, and worship among themselves. By 1751 Benjamin Franklin was warning that the Germans would retain their separate language and customs: the Pennsylvania English would be overrun by "the Palatine Boors."

## Eighteenth-Century Seaports >> 

While most Americans on the move flocked to the frontier, others swelled the populations of colonial cities. By present-day standards such cities were small, harboring from 8,000 to 22,000 citizens by 1750. The scale of seaports remained intimate, too: all of New York City was clustered at the southern tip of Manhattan island, and the length of Boston or Charleston could be walked in less than half an hour.

All major colonial cities were seaports, their waterfronts fringed with wharves and shipyards. By the 1750s the grandest and most populous was Philadelphia, which boasted straight, neatly paved streets, flagstone sidewalks, and three-story brick buildings. Older cities such as Boston and New York had a medieval aspect: most of their dwellings and shops were wooden structures with tiny windows and low ceilings, rising no higher than two stories to steeply pitched roofs. The narrow cobblestone streets of Boston and New York also challenged pedestrians, who competed for space with livestock being driven to the butcher, roaming herds of swine and packs of dogs, clattering carts, carriages, and horses.

Commerce, the lifeblood of seaport economies, was managed by merchants who tapped the wealth of surrounding regions. Traders in New York and Philadelphia shipped the Hudson and Delaware valleys' surplus of grain and livestock to the West Indies. Boston's merchants sent fish to the

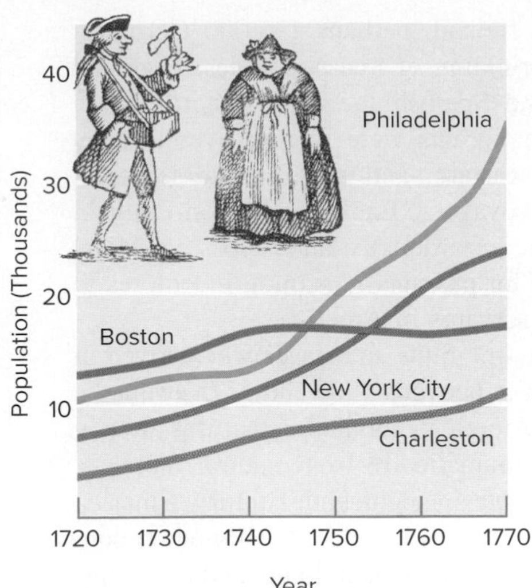

Population (Thousands)
40
30
20
10
Philadelphia
Boston
New York City
Charleston
1720
1730
1740
1750
1760
1770
Year


### ESTIMATED POPULATION OF COLONIAL CITIES, 1720–1770

Although Boston's population remained stable after 1740, it was surpassed owing to the sharp growth of New York City and, especially, Philadelphia.

^ In the mid-eighteenth century, Philadelphia became the largest city in the colonies and the second largest in all the British Empire. Its busy harbor served not only as a commercial hub but also as the disembarkation point for thousands of people.

# *Historian's* TOOLBOX

## The Hadley Chest

MW


**Later owners stripped and refinished this chest, removing the original painted surface that probably featured brilliant blues and reds.**

**The initials "MW" identify the original owner, while the carvings of tulips and oak leaves, a decorative motif fashionable in early America, covered its façade.**

**What sorts of possessions do you think Martha Williams might have kept in these drawers?**

Objects can help historians appreciate complex connections. For example, the first owner of this exuberantly designed cupboard of white oak and pine, Martha Williams, lived in western Massachusetts during the decades around 1700, a time of chronic warfare between the English and their French and Indian allies. Most likely she received the chest as part of her dowry when she married Edward Partridge in 1707, its very solidity assuring this young couple of stability and continuity in a violent and insecure world. Items of similar design have turned up elsewhere in New England, and their first collector dubbed them "Hadley chests," a distinct local craft tradition. This chest and the textiles it probably contained open a window into the sorts of property Anglo-American women retained in marriage and passed down to their descendants. According to historian Laurel Thatcher Ulrich, an artifact such as the Hadley chest "teaches us that material objects were not only markers of wealth but devices for building relationships and lineages over time, and it helps us to understand the cultural framework within which ordinary women became creators as well as custodians of household goods."

### THINKING CRITICALLY

*Why did Martha Williams have her maiden name emblazoned on the cupboard? Might it have something to do with the restrictive English laws about what women could own in marriage? Do you think women in New Spain or New France would have done the same? What might objects such as these tell us about how women viewed property and identity in British North America?*

*Photo:* ©Shelburne Museum, Shelburne, Vermont

Caribbean and Catholic Europe, masts to England, and rum to West Africa. Charlestonians exported indigo to English dyemakers and rice to southern Europe.

No large-scale domestic industry produced goods for a mass market: instead, craft shops filled orders for specific items placed by individual purchasers. Some **artisans** specialized in the maritime trades as shipbuilders, blacksmiths, and sailmakers. Others, such as butchers, millers, and distillers, processed and packed raw materials for export or served the basic needs of their cities.

**artisan** skilled craftworker, such as a blacksmith, a cooper, a miller, or a tailor.

On the lowest rung of a seaport's social hierarchy were free and bound workers. Free laborers were mainly young white men and women—journeyman artisans, sailors, fisherfolk, domestic workers, seamstresses, and prostitutes. The ranks of unfree workers included apprentices and indentured servants doing menial labor in shops and on the docks.

Black men and women made up a substantial part of the bound labor force in colonial seaports, but the character of slavery there changed decisively during the mid-eighteenth century. As wars raging in Europe reduced the supply of white indentured servants, colonial cities imported a larger number of Africans. In the two decades after 1730 one-third of all people arriving in New York harbor were black; by 1760 blacks constituted more than three-quarters of all bound laborers in Philadelphia.

Working women found a number of opportunities in port cities. Young single women from poor families worked in wealthier households as maids, cooks, laundresses, seamstresses, or nurses. The highest-paying occupations for women were midwifery and dressmaking, and both required long apprenticeships and expert skills. But less than 10 percent of women in seaports worked outside their own homes. Most women spent their workday caring for households: seeing to the needs of husbands and children, tending to gardens and domestic animals, and engaged in spinning and weaving—activities crucial to both household and local economies.

While city dwellers—perhaps 1 out of every 20 Americans—endured more ethnic division, poverty, and crime than countryfolk, they had more to do. Plays, balls, and concerts for the wealthiest; taverns, clubs, celebrations, and church services for everyone. Men of every class found diversion in drink and cockfighting. Crowds swarmed to tavern exhibitions of trained dogs or the spectacular waxworks of one John Dyer, featuring "a lively Representation of Margaret, Countess of Herrinburg, who had 365 Children at one Birth."

**REVIEW**

What kinds of divisions led to social tensions and conflicts in British North America?

# SLAVE SOCIETIES IN THE EIGHTEENTH-CENTURY SOUTH

Inequalities and divisions between slave and free in the South dwarfed those among seaport dwellers. By 1775 one out of every five Americans was of African ancestry, and more than 90 percent of all black Americans lived in the South, most along the seaboard.

The character of a slave's life depended to a great extent on whether he or she lived in the Chesapeake or the Lower South. Slaves in the low country of South Carolina and Georgia lived on large plantations with as many as 50 other black workers, about half African-born. They had infrequent contact with whites. "They are as 'twere, a Nation within a Nation," observed Francis LeJau, an Anglican priest in the low country. And their work was arduous, for rice required constant cultivation. Black laborers tended young plants and hoed fields in the sweltering summer heat of the mosquito-infested lowlands. During the winter and early spring, they built dams and canals to regulate the flow of water into the rice fields. But the use of the **task system** rather than gang labor widened the window of freedom within slavery. When a slave had completed his assigned task for the day, one planter explained, "his master feels no right to call upon him."

**task system** way of organizing slave labor. Masters and overseers of rice and indigo plantations generally assigned individual slaves a daily task, and after its completion, slaves could spend the rest of the day engaged in pursuits of their own choosing.

Most Africans and African Americans in the Chesapeake lived on plantations with fewer than 20 fellow slaves. Less densely concentrated than in the low country, Chesapeake slaves also had more contact with whites. Unlike Carolina's absentee owners, who left white overseers and black drivers to run their plantations, Chesapeake masters actively managed their estates and subjected their slaves to closer scrutiny.

**The Slave Family and Community** >> The four decades following 1700 marked the heaviest years of slave importation into the Chesapeake and Carolina regions. The newcomers from Africa had to cope not only with the lingering traumas of capture and the Middle Passage but also with alien landscapes, new languages, and new threats. They also had to adjust to their fellow slaves. The "new Negroes" hailed from a number of diverse West African peoples, each with a separate language or dialect and distinctive cultures and kinship systems. Often they had little in common with one another and even less in common with the American-born black minority. Native-born African Americans enjoyed better health, command of English, and experience in dealing with whites. They were also more likely to enjoy a family life, because their advantages probably made them the preferred partners of black women, who were outnumbered two to one by black men. And, since African-born women waited two or three years before marrying, some African-born men died before they could find a wife.

After the middle of the eighteenth century, a number of changes fostered the growth of black families and the vitality

## Make a Case

We usually think that the main geographic divide in American history was north-south. But what evidence would you use to argue that the east-west divide was more important?

^ *The Old Plantation* affords a rare glimpse of life in the slave quarters. At this festive gathering, both men and women dance to the music of a molo (a stringed instrument similar to a banjo) and drums.
©Art Media/HIP/The Image Works

of slave communities. As slave importations began to taper off, the rate of natural reproduction among blacks started to climb. Gender ratios became more equal. These changes, along with the rise of larger plantations throughout the South, made it easier for black men and women to find partners and start families. Elaborate kinship networks gradually developed, often extending over several plantations in a single neighborhood. And, as the African-born generations were replaced by native-born offspring, earlier sources of tension and division within the slave community disappeared.

Even so, black families remained vulnerable. If a planter fell on hard times, members of black families might be sold off to different buyers to meet his debts. When an owner died, black spouses, parents, and children might be divided among surviving heirs. Even under the best circumstances, fathers might be hired out to other planters for long periods or sent to work in distant quarters. Then, as more slaveholders moved from the coast to the interior, black family life suffered. Between 1755 and 1782, masters on the move resettled fully one-third of all adult African Americans living in tidewater Virginia. Most slaves forced to journey west were men and women in their teens and early 20s, who had to begin again the long process of establishing families and neighborhood networks far from kin and friends.

Black families struggling with terrible uncertainties were sustained by the distinctive African American culture evolving in the slave community. The high percentage of native Africans among the eighteenth-century American black population made it easier for slaves to retain homeland traditions. Christianity won few converts, in part because masters feared that baptizing slaves might make them more rebellious but also because African Americans preferred their traditional religions. Slaves also brought agricultural skills and practices from Africa, as well as folktales, music, and dances.

## Slave Resistance in Eighteenth-Century British North America >>

British North America had no shortage of African Americans who both resisted captivity and developed strategies for survival. Collective attempts at escape were most common among recently arrived Africans. Groups of slaves, often made up of newcomers from the same tribe, fled inland and formed **Maroon communities** of runaways. These efforts rarely succeeded, because the Maroon settlements were too large to go undetected for long.

More-acculturated blacks turned to subtler subversions, employing what one scholar has called "weapons of the weak." Domestics and field hands alike faked illness, feigned stupidity and laziness, broke tools, pilfered from storehouses, hid in the woods for weeks at a time, or simply took off to visit other plantations. Other slaves, usually escaping bondage as solitary individuals, found a new life as craftworkers, dock laborers, or sailors in the relative anonymity of colonial seaports.

Sometimes slaves rebelled openly. Whites in communities with large numbers of blacks lived in gnawing dread of arson, poisoning, and insurrection. Four slave conspiracies were reported in Virginia during the first half of the eighteenth century. In South Carolina more than two decades of abortive uprisings and insurrection scares culminated in the Stono Rebellion of 1739, the largest slave revolt of the colonial period. Nearly 100 African Americans, led by a slave named Jemmy, seized arms from a store in the coastal district of Stono and killed several white neighbors before they were caught and killed by the colonial militia. But throughout the eighteenth century slave rebellions occurred far less frequently on the mainland of North America than in the Caribbean or Brazil. Whites outnumbered blacks in all of Britain's mainland colonies except South Carolina, and only in Georgia did rebels have a haven for a quick escape—Spanish Florida. Faced with those odds, most slaves reasoned that the risks of rebellion outweighed the prospects for success—and most sought families and opportunities for greater personal freedom within the slave system itself.

**Maroon communities** groups of escaped slaves, often newly arrived Africans, who fled to the frontiers of colonial settlements in the American South, the Caribbean, and South America.

**REVIEW**

How did African American culture evolve in the slave community, and what forms did resistance to captivity take?

# ENLIGHTENMENT AND AWAKENING IN AMERICA

Where colonists lived, how well they lived, whether they were male or female, native born or immigrant, slave or free—all these variables fostered distinctive worldviews, differing attitudes and assumptions about the individual's relationship to nature, society, and God. The diversity of colonials' inner lives became even more pronounced during the eighteenth century because of the Enlightenment, an intellectual movement that started in Europe during the seventeenth century.

## The Enlightenment in America >>

The leading figures of the Enlightenment, the *philosophes,* stressed the power of human reason to promote progress by revealing the laws that governed both nature and society. Isaac Newton in England charted the orbits of the planets and devised a theory of gravity, and John Locke applied reason to the construction of political systems. In France, Voltaire wrote essays, novels, and plays criticizing religion, oppressive governments, and censorship.

Like many devotees of the **Enlightenment**, Benjamin Franklin of Philadelphia was most impressed by its emphasis on useful knowledge and experimentation. He pondered air currents and then invented a stove that heated houses more efficiently. He toyed with electricity and then invented lightning rods to protect buildings in thunderstorms. Other amateur colonial scientists constructed simple telescopes, classified animal species native to North America, or sought to explain epidemics in terms of natural causes.

**Enlightenment** intellectual movement that flourished in Europe from the mid-1600s through the eighteenth century and stressed the power of human reason to promote social progress by discovering the laws that governed both nature and society.

American colleges helped promote Enlightenment thinking. Although institutions such as Harvard (founded 1636) and Yale (1701) initially focused on training ministers, by the eighteenth century their graduates included lawyers, merchants, doctors, and scientists. Most offered courses in mathematics and the natural sciences, which taught students algebra and such advanced theories as Copernican astronomy and Newtonian physics.

By the middle of the eighteenth century, Enlightenment ideals had given rise to "rational Christianity," which commanded a small but influential following among Anglicans and liberal Congregationalists in the colonies. Their God was not the Calvinists' awesome deity but a benevolent creator who offered salvation to everyone. They believed that God's greatest gift to humankind was reason, which enabled all human beings to follow the moral teachings of Jesus. Some even embraced deism, which rejected the divinity of Jesus and looked to nature rather than the Bible for proof of God's existence.

Enlightenment philosophy and rational Christianity did little to change the lives of most colonials. Few colonial readers had the interest or the background necessary to tackle the learned writings of Enlightenment *philosophes.* The great majority still explained the workings of the world in terms of divine providence rather than natural law. Church attendance ran highest in the northern colonies, where some 80 percent of the population turned out for public worship on the Sabbath. In the South, because of the greater distances involved and the shortage of clergy, about half of all colonials regularly attended Sunday services.

Still, many ministers grew alarmed over the influence of rational Christianity. They also worried about isolated frontier families abandoning Christianity altogether. Exaggerated as these fears may have been, they gave rise to a major religious revival that swept the colonies during the middle decades of the eighteenth century.

## The First Great Awakening >>

The **Great Awakening**, as the revival came to be called, first appeared in the 1730s among Presbyterians and Congregationalists in the middle colonies and New England. Many ministers in these churches preached an "evangelical" message, emphasizing the need for individuals to experience a "new birth" through religious conversion. Among them was Jonathan Edwards, the pastor of a Congregational church in Northampton, Massachusetts. Edwards's Calvinist preaching combined moving descriptions of God's grace with terrifying portrayals of eternal damnation. "The God that holds you over the pit of hell, much as one holds a spider or some loathsome insect over the fire, abhors you and is dreadfully provoked," he declaimed to one congregation. "There is no other reason to be given, why you have not dropped into hell since you arise in the morning, but that God's hand has held you up."

**Great Awakening** one of the periods of intense religious piety and commitment among Americans that fueled the expansion of Protestant churches.

These local revivals of the 1730s were mere tremors compared to the earthquake of religious enthusiasm that shook the colonies with the arrival in the fall of 1739 of George Whitefield. This handsome (though cross-eyed) "boy preacher" from England electrified crowds from Georgia to New Hampshire during his two-year tour of the colonies. He and his many imitators among colonial ministers turned the church into a theater, enlivening sermons with dramatic gestures, flowing tears, and gruesome depictions of hell. The drama of such performances appealed to people of all classes, ethnic groups, and races. By the time Whitefield sailed back to England in 1741, thousands of awakened souls were joining older churches or forming new ones.

## The Aftermath of the Great Awakening >>

Whitefield also left behind a raging storm of controversy. Many "awakened" church members now openly criticized

^ A sharp critic of the evangelical revivals that swept both sides of the Atlantic, the English artist William Hogarth satirized preaching in the style of George Whitefield. In this detail from an engraving of 1762 titled "Credulity, Superstition, and Fanaticism," the minister plays upon the superstitious beliefs of his congregation by dangling a witch from one hand, a devil from the other. The page before him reads, "I speak as a fool"; the ribbon on the right shows a musical scale of "vociferation" that runs from a "Natural Tone" of speaking all the way up to "Bull Roar." Hogarth did not think critical thinking was incompatible with biblical teachings, for below the engraving he included a bit of scripture: "Believe not every Spirit, but try the Spirits whether they are of God: because many false Prophets are gone out into the World."
©The Stapleton Collection/Bridgeman Images

their ministers as cold, unconverted, and uninspiring. To supply the missing fire some laymen—"and even Women and Common Negroes"—took to "exhorting" any audience willing to listen. The most popular ministers became "itinerants," traveling like Whitefield from one town to another.

Northern churches splintered and bickered over the Great Awakening, but the fires of revivalism spread rapidly to the South and its backcountry. From the mid-1740s until the 1770s, scores of new Presbyterian and Baptist churches formed, sparking controversy. Ardent Presbyterians disrupted Anglican worship by loosing packs of dogs in local chapels. County officials, prodded by resentful Anglican parsons, harassed, fined, and imprisoned Baptist ministers.

And so a diverse lot of Americans found themselves continually at odds with one another: arguing over religion and the Enlightenment, conflicted over racial and ethnic tensions, and divided between coastal and backcountry cultures. Benjamin Franklin, a man who made it his business to know, understood the depth of those divisions better than most. Yet even he harbored hopes for political unity among the fractious colonists. After all, most were English. That much they had in common.

Describe the different outlooks of Enlightenment and evangelical Christians.

# ANGLO-AMERICAN WORLDS OF THE EIGHTEENTH CENTURY

Although most Americans prided themselves on being English, some differences made colonials feel inferior, ashamed of their simplicity when compared with London's sophistication. But they also came to appreciate the greater equality of their society and the more representative character of their governments. If it was good to be English, it was, on balance, better still to be English in America.

**English Economic and Social Development >>** The differences between England and America began with their economies. England's huge financial institutions and corporations, its growing factories and profitable mines, and its tenant-based commercial agriculture stood in sharp contrast to the mostly humble economic activity in British North America. England's more developed economy fostered the growth of cities, especially London, a teeming colossus of 675,000 in 1750. In contrast, 90 percent of all eighteenth-century colonials lived in towns of fewer than 2,000. But in another respect, England's more advanced economy drew the colonies and the parent country together. Americans were so eager to acquire British-made commodities that their per capita consumption of imported manufactures rose 120 percent between 1750 and 1773. People of all classes demanded and indulged in such small luxuries as a tin of tea, a pair of gloves, and a bar of Irish soap.

**Inequality in England and America >>** Then there were people of no means. In England they were legion. London seethed with filth, crime, and desperate poverty. The poor and the unemployed as well as pickpockets and prostitutes crowded into its gin-soaked slums, taverns, and brothels. The contrast between the luxuries enjoyed by a wealthy few Londoners and the misery of the many disquieted colonial observers. Ebenezer Hazard, an American Quaker visiting London, knew for certain he was in "a Sink of Sin."

New wealth and the inherited privileges of England's landed aristocracy made for deepening class divisions. Two percent of England's population owned 70 percent of its land. By right of birth, English aristocrats claimed membership in the House of Lords; by custom, certain powerful gentry families dominated the other branch of Parliament, the House of Commons.

The colonies had their own prominent families but no titled ruling class holding political privilege by hereditary right. And if England's upper classes lived more splendidly, its lower classes were larger and worse off than those in the colonies. Less than a third of England's inhabitants belonged to the "middling sort" of traders, professionals, artisans, and tenant farmers. More than two-thirds struggled for survival at the bottom of society. In contrast, the colonial middle class counted for nearly three-quarters of the white population. With land cheap, labor scarce, and wages for both urban and rural workers 100 percent higher in America than in England, it was much easier for colonials to accumulate savings and farms of their own.

Colonials were both fascinated and repelled by English society. Benjamin Rush, a Philadelphia physician, felt in the House of Lords as if he "walked on sacred ground." He begged his guide for permission to sit on the throne therein and then sat "for a considerable time." Other colonials gushed over the grandeur of aristocratic estates and imported suits of livery for their servants, tea services for their wives, and wallpaper for their drawing rooms.

But colonials recognized that England's ruling classes purchased their luxury and leisure at the cost of the rest of the nation. In his autobiography Benjamin Franklin painted a devastating portrait of the degraded lives of his fellow workers in a London printshop, who drowned their disappointments by drinking throughout the workday, even more excessively on the Sabbath, and then faithfully observing the "St. Monday's" holiday to nurse their hangovers. Like Franklin many colonials regarded the idle among England's rich and poor alike as ominous signs of a degenerate nation.

## Politics in England and America

>> Colonials were also of two minds about England's government. Although they praised the English constitution as the basis of all liberties, they were alarmed by the actual workings of English politics. In theory, England's **balanced constitution** gave every order of society a voice in government. Whereas the Crown represented the monarchy and the House of Lords represented the aristocracy, the House of Commons represented the democracy, the people of England.

**balanced constitution** a constitution intended to give every part of a society some voice in the workings of its government.

^ Coffeehouses such as this establishment in London were favorite gathering places for eighteenth-century Americans visiting Britain. Here merchants and mariners, ministers and students, lobbyists and tourists warmed themselves, read newspapers, and exchanged gossip about commerce, politics, and social life.
©British Museum, London, UK/Bridgeman Images

Americans liked to think that their colonial governments mirrored the ideal English constitution. Most colonies had a royal governor who represented the monarch in America and a bicameral (two-house) legislature made up of a lower house (the assembly) and an upper house (or council). The democratically elected assemblies, like the House of Commons, stood for popular interests, whereas the councils, some of which were elected and others appointed, more roughly approximated the House of Lords.

But these formal similarities masked real differences between English and colonial governments. In any showdown with their assemblies most royal governors had to give way, because they lacked the government offices and contracts that bought loyalty. The colonial legislatures possessed additional leverage, since all of them retained the sole authority to levy taxes.

At the same time, widespread ownership of land meant that more than half the colonies' white adult male population could vote. The larger electorate made it more difficult to buy votes. The colonial electorate was also more watchful. Representatives had to reside in the districts that they served, and a few even received binding instructions from their constituents about how to vote.

Most Americans were as pleased with their inexpensive and representative colonial governments as they were horrified by the conduct of politics in England, where webs of patronage and corruption compromised the entire system. John Dickinson, a young Pennsylvanian training as a lawyer in London, was scandalized by a parliamentary election he witnessed in 1754. The king and his ministers had spent over 100,000 pounds sterling to buy support for their candidates, he wrote his father, and "if a man cannot be brought to vote as he is desired, he is made dead drunk and kept in that state, never heard of by his family and friends, till all is over and he can do no harm."

## The Imperial System before 1760 >>

Few Britons gave the colonists as much thought as the colonists gave them. Those few who thought about America at all believed that colonials resembled the "savage" Indians more than the "civilized" English. As a London acquaintance remarked to Thomas Hancock, it was a pity Mrs. Hancock had to remain in Boston when he could "take her to England and make her happy with Christians."

The same ignorant indifference contributed to England's haphazard administration of its colonies. Aside from passing an occasional law to regulate trade, restrict manufacturing, or direct monetary policy, Parliament made no effort to assert its authority in America. For the colonies this chaotic and inefficient system of colonial administration left them a great deal of freedom. Even England's regulation of trade rested lightly on the shoulders of most Americans. Southern planters were obliged to send their rice, indigo, and tobacco to Britain only, but they enjoyed favorable credit terms and knowledgeable marketing from English merchants. Colonials were prohibited from finishing iron products and exporting hats and textiles, but they had scant interest in developing domestic industries. Americans were required to import all manufactured goods through England, but by doing so, they acquired high-quality goods at low prices. At little sacrifice, most Americans obeyed imperial regulations.

Following this policy of **benign neglect**, the British Empire rumbled along to the satisfaction of most people on both sides of the Atlantic. Economic growth and political **autonomy** kept most white Americans happy being English, despite their misgivings about the motherland. If imperial arrangements had remained as they were in 1754, the empire might have muddled on indefinitely.

**benign neglect** policy of noninterference, also known as "salutary neglect," pursued by the British Empire in governing its American colonies until the end of the Seven Years' War.

**autonomy** condition of being independent or, in the case of a political structure, the right to self-government.

## MAP 5.3: OVERSEAS TRADE NETWORKS

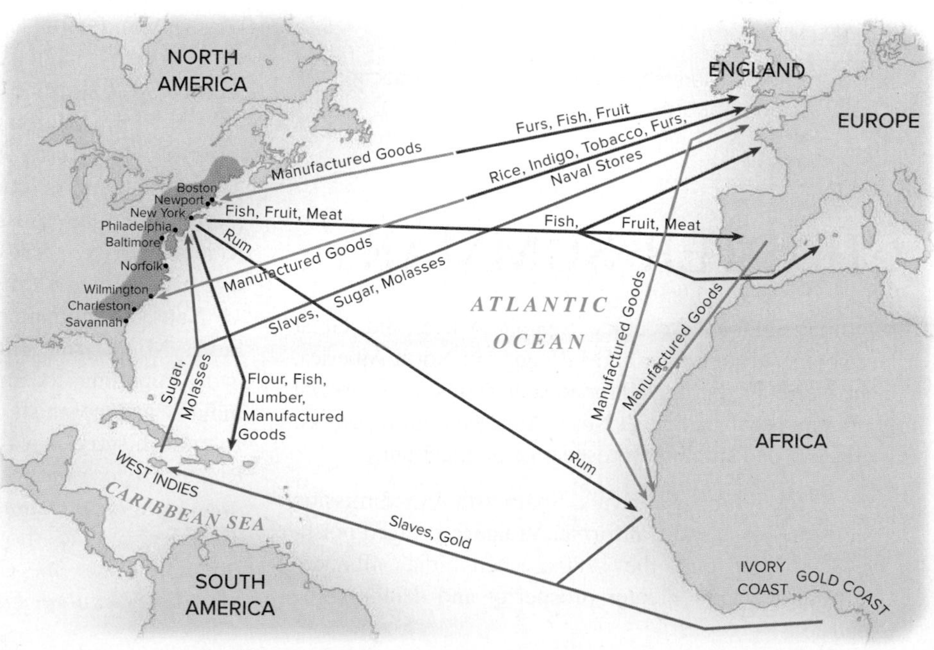
NORTH AMERICA
ENGLAND
EUROPE
AFRICA
SOUTH AMERICA
ATLANTIC OCEAN
WEST INDIES
CARIBBEAN SEA
IVORY COAST
GOLD COAST
Boston
Newport
New York
Philadelphia
Baltimore
Norfolk
Wilmington
Charleston
Savannah
Furs, Fish, Fruit
Rice, Indigo, Tobacco, Furs, Naval Stores
Manufactured Goods
Fish, Fruit, Meat
Fish, Fruit, Meat
Rum
Manufactured Goods
Slaves, Sugar, Molasses
Sugar, Molasses
Flour, Fish, Lumber, Manufactured Goods
Manufactured Goods
Manufactured Goods
Rum
Slaves, Gold

Commercial ties to Spain and Portugal, Africa, and the Caribbean sustained the growth of both seaports and commercial farming regions on the British North American mainland and enabled colonials to purchase an increasing volume of finished goods from England.
*Why was rum sent from America to Africa? What was the most common product sent from England to the colonies?*

But something important seemed to be changing, both within the British world and in the international order as well. For decades, Europe's imperial wars found their way to America almost as an afterthought. Colonial officials, traders, land speculators, and would-be pioneers regularly seized on news of the latest European conflict as an excuse to attack their Spanish or French or British counterparts in the North American borderlands. The interests of kings and queens had to be served, of course. But by and large it was easier to exploit war for local or personal purposes out on the far margins of Europe's empires. Eastern North America's native peoples likewise sought advantage in these interimperial flare-ups. But for them the stakes were higher. When Indian leaders joined in a fight for profit or revenge, or to please one or another colonial ally, they also put their own people at risk.

As all North Americans learned, however, the outcome of their struggles could be determined by men they would never see: well-heeled diplomats sipping drinks around mahogany tables in European capitals. Victories, defeats, territories won or lost—all this could be and often was undone in treaty talks in Paris, Madrid, or London. The message was clear: great imperial struggles began in Europe and ended in Europe. America followed.

Though few recognized it in 1754, this older model was about to be swept away. That year marked the beginning of yet another imperial war, one begun not in Europe but in the American borderlands. Rather than following events, this time Indians proved decisive to the war's origins, course, and outcome. And rather than the conflict ending with a return to the status quo, this time war would produce changes greater than anyone could have anticipated. In waging the war and managing its aftermath, London would pursue policies that made it difficult—and ultimately impossible—for its American subjects to remain within the empire.

What were the similarities, differences, and connections between England and America?

# CHAPTER SUMMARY

During the eighteenth century Spain, France, and Great Britain competed for power and influence in North America, while native peoples struggled for advantage or simple survival amid profound change. British North Americans grew increasingly diverse, darkening the prospect of political unity.

- Spurred on by imperial rivals, Spain established mission systems in Texas and California. Violence ravaged northern New Spain until the 1780s, when Indian alliances finally allowed for greater prosperity and demographic expansion.
- Underpopulated New France had to seek alliances with Indians. French Louisiana failed to develop into a booming plantation colony despite reliance upon African slave labor.
- In British North America differences erupted among English and non-English immigrants and were compounded by backcountry settlement and the growth of seaports.
- The South became more embattled, too, following massive importation of slaves during the first half of the eighteenth century and a rising tide of black resistance to slavery.
- Religious conflict among colonials was intensified by the spread of Enlightenment ideas and the influence of the Great Awakening of the 1730s.
- Despite their many differences a majority of white colonials took pride in their common English ancestry and in belonging to a powerful empire.

## Additional Reading

For early Texas and New Mexico, see Juliana Barr, *Peace Came in the Form of a Woman* (2007); H. Ross Frank, *From Settler to Citizen* (2000); and Omar Valerio-Jiménez, *River of Hope* (2013). On mission-era California, look to Steven Hackel's *Children of Coyote, Missionaries of St. Francis* (2005); and Lisbeth Haas, *Saints and Citizens* (2013). For France in America see *The People of New France* by Allan Greer (2000); and Michael Witgen, *An Infinity of Nations* (2012). Alan Taylor's *American Colonies* (2001) takes a sweeping, continental perspective on North American history during this era. For women's property rights, see Deborah A. Rosen, "Women and Property across Colonial America: A Comparison of Legal Systems in New Mexico and New York," *William and Mary Quarterly* 60, no. 2 (2003): 355–382.

For the demographics of European colonization in British North America, see Bernard Bailyn, *Voyagers to the West* (1986). On the tensions and transformations that came with diverse societies, see John Smolenski, *Friends and Strangers* (2010); and Peter Silver, *Our Savage Neighbors* (2007). Philip Morgan's *Slave Counterpoint* (1998) contrasts slave cultures in the early South. For tensions in American seaports, consult Jill Lepore, *New York Burning* (2005); and Gary Nash's *Urban Crucible* (1979). Thomas Kidd's *The Great Awakening* (2007) is a recent comprehensive history of the religious transformation.

Nancy Shoemaker, *A Strange Likeness* (2004); and James M. Merrell, *Into the American Woods* (1999), are two compelling accounts of perceived differences between Indians and colonists. For a rich synthesis of native and colonial history in eastern North America, see Daniel K. Richter, *Before the Revolution* (2011). Caroline Winterer's *American Enlightenments* (2016) brilliantly recovers the diversity of the movement. On religion, see Patricia Bonomi, *Under the Cope of Heaven* (1986); and George Marsden, *Jonathan Edwards* (2003).

# 6 Imperial Triumph, Imperial Crisis

## 1754–1776

George Washington was only 22 when he led 200 militiamen and a party of Indians to confront French forces in the Ohio Country in the spring of 1754. He came upon a French detachment at Jumonville Glen, shown in this 2007 photo.

*(Jumonville Glen)* Source: Fort Necessity Battlefield, National Park Service; *(George Washington)* ©Peter Newark American Pictures/Bridgeman Images

## >> An American Story

## GEORGE WASHINGTON AND THE HALF-KING

Everyone seemed to want something from the Ohio Country. And when so many rivals—assertive, anxious, and aggressive—assembled in one location, it was a situation made for disaster. Young George Washington, deep in the forests of the Ohio Country, learned this lesson in the spring of 1754.

Rich in game and richer still in agricultural potential, the region north of the Ohio River had been a no-man's land for decades following the Beaver Wars. Though the mighty Iroquois had no interest in occupying the territory, they claimed sovereignty over it into the 1750s by right of conquest. By then, however, Delawares, Shawnees, Mingos, and other native peoples had established villages in the territory. If they looked to the Iroquois it was for advice, not orders. Who, then, could claim dominion over the Ohio Country?

European rivalries compounded these uncertainties. By the 1750s both Britain and France saw the lands as vital to their strategic interests. Pennsylvania traders had wandered the territory for years, their reports drawing the interest of land speculators. Wealthy Virginians and Pennsylvanians envisioned colonies in the Ohio Country—schemes London happily encouraged in hopes of weakening New France. In 1745 the Virginia House of Burgesses granted 300,000 acres of land to a newly formed enterprise called the Ohio Company. For their part, the French in Quebec relied on the Ohio lands as a buffer between their own relatively small settlements and the populous British to the east. Anxious, the French built new forts and shored up their Indian alliances.

The British countered. In 1754 Virginia's governor (a major investor in the Ohio Company) ordered 200 militiamen under 22-year-old Lt. Col. George Washington (another investor) to assert British interests in the Ohio Country. Washington's militia marched west with the help of several Indians under the "Half-King" Tanaghrisson, the Iroquois representative for the Ohio Country. Tanaghrisson had grown up near the important forks of the Ohio River (present-day Pittsburgh) and advised the British to build a "strong house" at this key position. Washington, who was intelligent, able, and disciplined but inexperienced and badly out of his depth, soon discovered how little control he had over the circumstances—or even over his own expedition.

To begin with, the French had beaten the Virginians to the forks of the Ohio, where they erected Fort Duquesne. On hearing of the approaching British militia the French commander there dispatched 35 men under an ensign named Jumonville to advise Washington to withdraw. Following Tanaghrisson's lead the British surprised Jumonville's party and fired on it. Badly wounded along with nearly half of his men, the ensign cried out to stop shooting, that he had come only to talk. Once Washington had gotten control of his force, Jumonville tried to hand him a letter from the French commander. But Tanaghrisson stepped in front of the Frenchman, sank a hatchet into his head, ripped his skull apart, and pulled out his brains. Washington staggered back dumbstruck as Tanaghrisson's Indians set about killing the wounded French soldiers.

This was not how it was supposed to happen. Washington hastily retreated some way, threw up a makeshift structure, aptly named "Fort Necessity," and waited for reinforcements from Virginia. About a month later a formidable French force (led by Jumonville's grieving brother) laid siege and quickly compelled Washington's surrender. The Virginians returned home in defeat, bearing the news that the Shawnees, Delawares, and Mingos had either sided with the French or refused to fight. "The chief part" of his men, Washington wrote in dismay, "are almost naked, and scarcely a man has either Shoes, Stockings or Hat." It was an ignominious beginning to a war that would extend for seven years and spread across the entire globe. <<

## THEMATIC TIMELINE

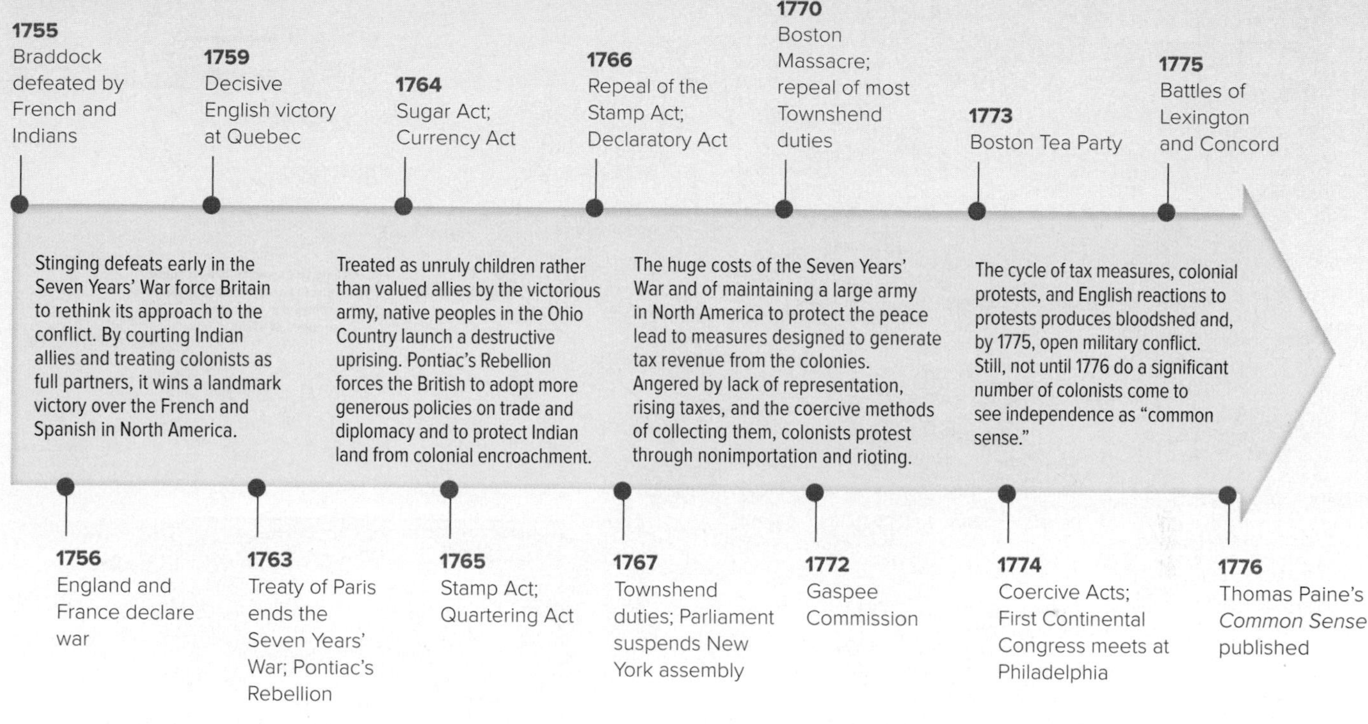

1755
Braddock defeated by French and Indians
1759
Decisive English victory at Quebec
1764
Sugar Act; Currency Act
1766
Repeal of the Stamp Act; Declaratory Act
1770
Boston Massacre; repeal of most Townshend duties
1773
Boston Tea Party
1775
Battles of Lexington and Concord
Stinging defeats early in the Seven Years' War force Britain to rethink its approach to the conflict. By courting Indian allies and treating colonists as full partners, it wins a landmark victory over the French and Spanish in North America.
Treated as unruly children rather than valued allies by the victorious army, native peoples in the Ohio Country launch a destructive uprising. Pontiac's Rebellion forces the British to adopt more generous policies on trade and diplomacy and to protect Indian land from colonial encroachment.
The huge costs of the Seven Years' War and of maintaining a large army in North America to protect the peace lead to measures designed to generate tax revenue from the colonies. Angered by lack of representation, rising taxes, and the coercive methods of collecting them, colonists protest through nonimportation and rioting.
The cycle of tax measures, colonial protests, and English reactions to protests produces bloodshed and, by 1775, open military conflict. Still, not until 1776 do a significant number of colonists come to see independence as "common sense."
1756
England and France declare war
1763
Treaty of Paris ends the Seven Years' War; Pontiac's Rebellion
1765
Stamp Act; Quartering Act
1767
Townshend duties; Parliament suspends New York assembly
1772
Gaspee Commission
1774
Coercive Acts; First Continental Congress meets at Philadelphia
1776
Thomas Paine's *Common Sense* published


# THE SEVEN YEARS' WAR

Britain and France had come to blows in the backcountry before. And Indian peoples had long sought to profit from the imperial rivalry of Europeans and turn it to their own ends. But in the Seven Years' War, bloodshed in the forests of North America for the first time led Europe into war rather than the other way around. And Washington's misadventure set the pattern for the early years of the conflict—years marked by British missteps and British defeats.

**Years of Defeat** >> The surrender at Fort Necessity only stiffened Britain's resolve to control the Ohio Country. London sent two army divisions under the famed General Edward Braddock to wrest the region from France. France countered with the equivalent of eight divisions to Canada. Unfortunately for the English, General Braddock had all but sealed his doom before even marching into the backcountry. Ignoring American advisers who insisted that Indian alliances would be key to victory, Braddock alienated native leaders and refused to acknowledge their claims to land. His divisions pushed into the Ohio Country with fewer than 10 Indian allies and in 1755 were nearly annihilated by their French and Indian adversaries. The defeat was one of the worst in British military history and cost Braddock his reputation as well as his life. It also sent shock waves through the empire, emboldened the French, and convinced many wavering Indian peoples that the French were the ones to support. Raiding parties began striking backcountry settlements from New York to Virginia; terrified refugees fled east.

Britain's war went from bad to worse, because most British colonials found it difficult to cooperate among themselves. At the start of the war representatives from throughout the colonies attended the so-called Albany Congress in the summer of 1754, designed in part to convince the Iroquois not to ally with New France. Benjamin Franklin, who attended, had larger aims. He presented delegates with a plan for colonial cooperation, in which a federal council made up of representatives from each colony would assume responsibility for a united defense. The Albany delegates were alarmed enough by the wavering Iroquois (who also attended) to accept Franklin's idea. But when they presented the proposal to their legislatures at home, each rejected the Albany Plan of Union. "Everyone cries, a union is necessary," Franklin complained, "but when they come to the

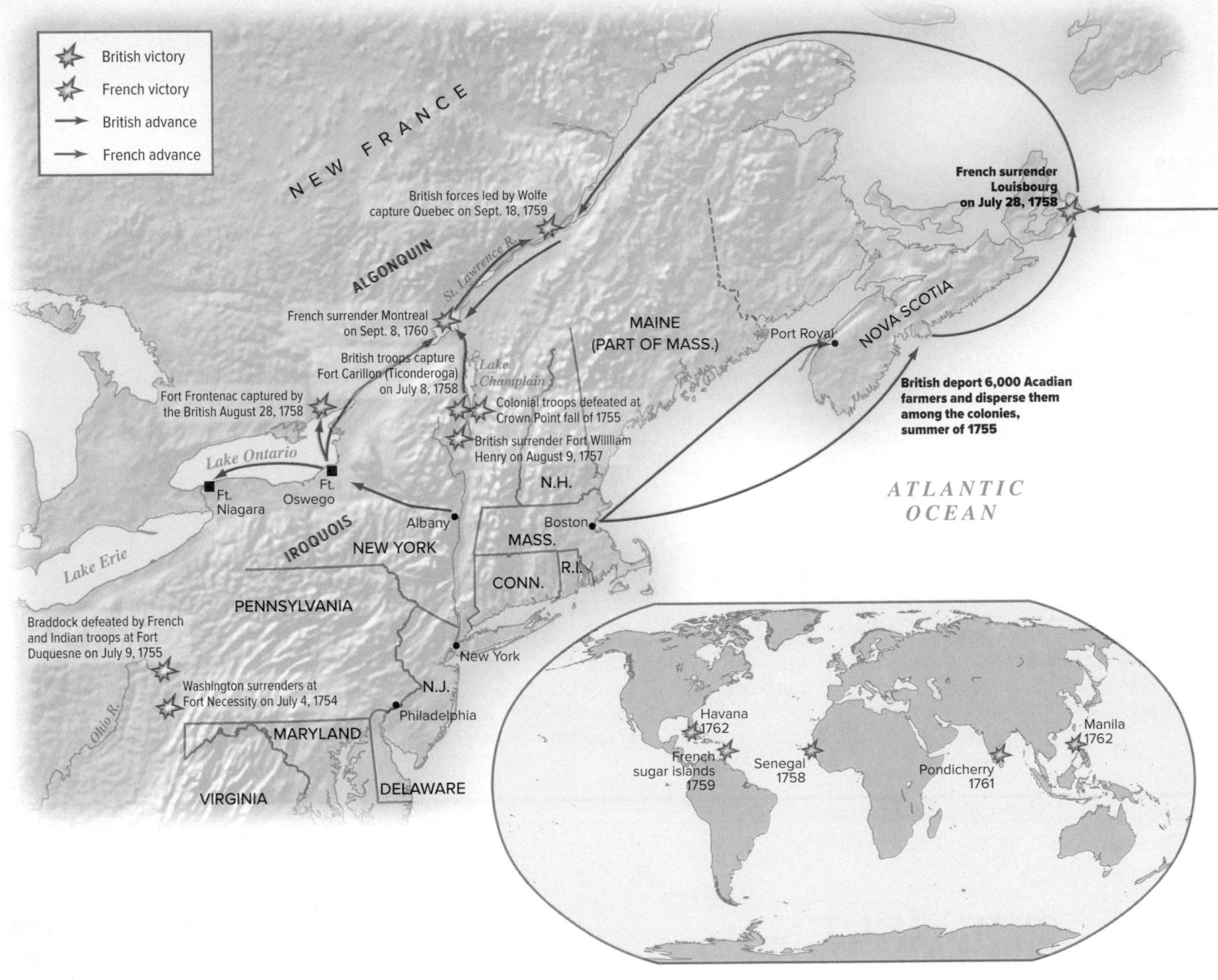

British victory
French victory
British advance
French advance
NEW FRANCE
British forces led by Wolfe capture Quebec on Sept. 18, 1759
French surrender Louisbourg on July 28, 1758
ALGONQUIN
St. Lawrence R.
French surrender Montreal on Sept. 8, 1760
British troops capture Fort Carillon (Ticonderoga) on July 8, 1758
Fort Frontenac captured by the British August 28, 1758
Lake Champlain
Colonial troops defeated at Crown Point fall of 1755
British surrender Fort Willliam Henry on August 9, 1757
MAINE (PART OF MASS.)
Port Royal
NOVA SCOTIA
British deport 6,000 Acadian farmers and disperse them among the colonies, summer of 1755
Lake Ontario
Ft. Niagara
Ft. Oswego
N.H.
ATLANTIC OCEAN
Albany
Boston
IROQUOIS
NEW YORK
MASS.
Lake Erie
R.I.
CONN.
PENNSYLVANIA
Braddock defeated by French and Indian troops at Fort Duquesne on July 9, 1755
New York
Washington surrenders at Fort Necessity on July 4, 1754
N.J.
Ohio R.
Philadelphia
MARYLAND
DELAWARE
VIRGINIA
Havana 1762
French sugar islands 1759
Senegal 1758
Pondicherry 1761
Manila 1762


## MAP 6.1: THE SEVEN YEARS' WAR

After Washington's surrender and Braddock's defeat in the Pennsylvanian backcountry, the British and the French waged their final contest for supremacy in North America in northern New York and Canada. But the rivalry for empire between France and Britain was worldwide, with naval superiority providing the needed edge to Britain. The British navy isolated French forces in India, winning a victory at Pondicherry, while English offensives captured the French sugar islands in the Caribbean and French trading posts along the West African coast. When Spain entered the war on the side of France, British fleets captured both Havana and the strategic port of Manila in the Philippines.

*Which victory sealed the British triumph over New France? Why was the win geographically important?*

manner and form of the union, their weak noodles are perfectly distracted."

London did little to encourage collective self-sacrifice. John Campbell, the Earl of Loudoun, took command of the North American theater in 1756. American soldiers and colonial assemblies alike despised Lord Loudoun. They balked at his efforts to take command over colonial troops and dragged their heels at his high-handed demands for men and supplies. Meanwhile, the French appointed an effective new commanding general of their forces in Canada, Louis Joseph, the Marquis de Montcalm. Montcalm drove southward, capturing key British forts and threatening the security of both New York and New England.

France pressed its advantage in Europe as well, threatening England itself and British holdings throughout the Mediterranean. Meanwhile, the complex system of alliances that was supposed to keep continental Europe at peace began to fail. In August of 1756 Prussia, an English ally, invaded Austria, a French ally. France went to Austria's aid and Prussia suddenly found itself on the defensive, begging London for help. The war was spreading in all directions, none to the advantage of the British Empire.

**A Shift in Policy** >> British fortunes rebounded only when the veteran English politician William Pitt came out of retirement to direct the war. Pitt was an odd character. Subject to bouts of depression and loathed for his opportunism and egotism, he was nonetheless buoyed by a strong sense of destiny—his own and that of England. France seemed to him the greatest obstacle to this British destiny—and Pitt returned to the political fray charged with energy. "I know that I can save this country," he declared confidently, "and that no one else can."

Pitt unveiled an audacious strategy. He would leave the fighting in Europe to the Prussians but fund them with massive infusions of cash. Meanwhile, England would attack France everywhere else—in the Caribbean, in West Africa, and even in their colonies along the Indian Ocean. Most especially, Pitt would attack them in North America. Indeed, he pledged to drive France out of the continent forever. To do so he would treat the colonials as partners and equals. Pitt recalled the Earl of Loudoun, pledged to respect the officers in colonial militias and, crucially, promised that London—not the colonies—would bear the costs of the war.

Last but certainly not least, the new English government acknowledged how important Indians were to the war effort. The new officers Pitt sent listened to colonial Indian agents and go-betweens, subsidized trade, and approved the distribution of presents to key leaders. These conciliatory gestures were well timed, because the Indian peoples of the Ohio Country and the *pays d'en haut* had increasingly come to question the French alliance.

Though French authorities often took Indians more seriously than did their English counterparts, they too struggled with cultural differences. In the aftermath of joint victories, for example, French officers sometimes felt obliged by European military protocol to deny their Indian allies customary war spoils—captives, plunder, and scalps. Disgruntled native warriors generally took them anyway and often refused to fight for France again. Even more to the point, by 1757 Britain's unsurpassed navy had in place a blockade of the St. Lawrence River that cut off supplies to French Canada. Without arms, ammunition, and metal goods, French authorities found it difficult to maintain their Indian alliances.

**Years of Victory** >> The reforms galvanized the colonies and turned the tide of the war. Most British North Americans willingly fought for the empire if they were treated as equals. In July 1758 the British gained control of the St. Lawrence River when the French fortress at Louisbourg fell to the Royal Navy and British and colonial troops. In August a force of New Englanders captured Fort Frontenac, thereby isolating French forts lining the Great Lakes and the Ohio valley. More Indians, seeing the French routed from the interior, switched their allegiance to the English.

The British succeeded even more brilliantly in 1759. In Canada Brigadier General James Wolfe gambled on a daring stratagem and won the fortress city of Quebec from Montcalm. Under the cover of darkness naval squadrons landed Wolfe's men beneath the city's steep bluffs, where they scaled the heights to a plateau known as the Plains of Abraham. A fierce battle ensued, and five days later both Wolfe and Montcalm lay dead, along with 1,400 French soldiers and 600 British and American troops. Quebec had fallen to the British. A year later the French surrender of Montreal finally ended the imperial war in North America, although it continued elsewhere around the world for another two years.

The Treaty of Paris, signed in February 1763, put an end to all French claims in North America and confirmed British title to all French territory east of the Mississippi. Spain had foolishly entered the war on France's side in 1762 and quickly lost Havana to British warships. The treaty restored Cuba to Spain, but at a high price: the Spanish ceded Florida

<< John Campbell (*left*), the Earl of Loudoun, was a Scottish military man and an aristocrat who expected that colonial soldiers would obey his commands. But colonials and their legislatures resisted his efforts to organize and fund the military campaign. "They have assumed to themselves, what they call Rights and Priviledges, totaly unknown in the Mother Country," he complained. William Pitt (*right*) was no less arrogant ("I know that I can save this country," he declared, "and that no one else can".) But Pitt was willing to treat the colonists as equals and pay handsomely for their services.

*(left)* ©Christie's Images/Bridgeman Images; *(right)* Source: Library of Congress, Prints and Photographs Division [LC-DIG-pga-03847]

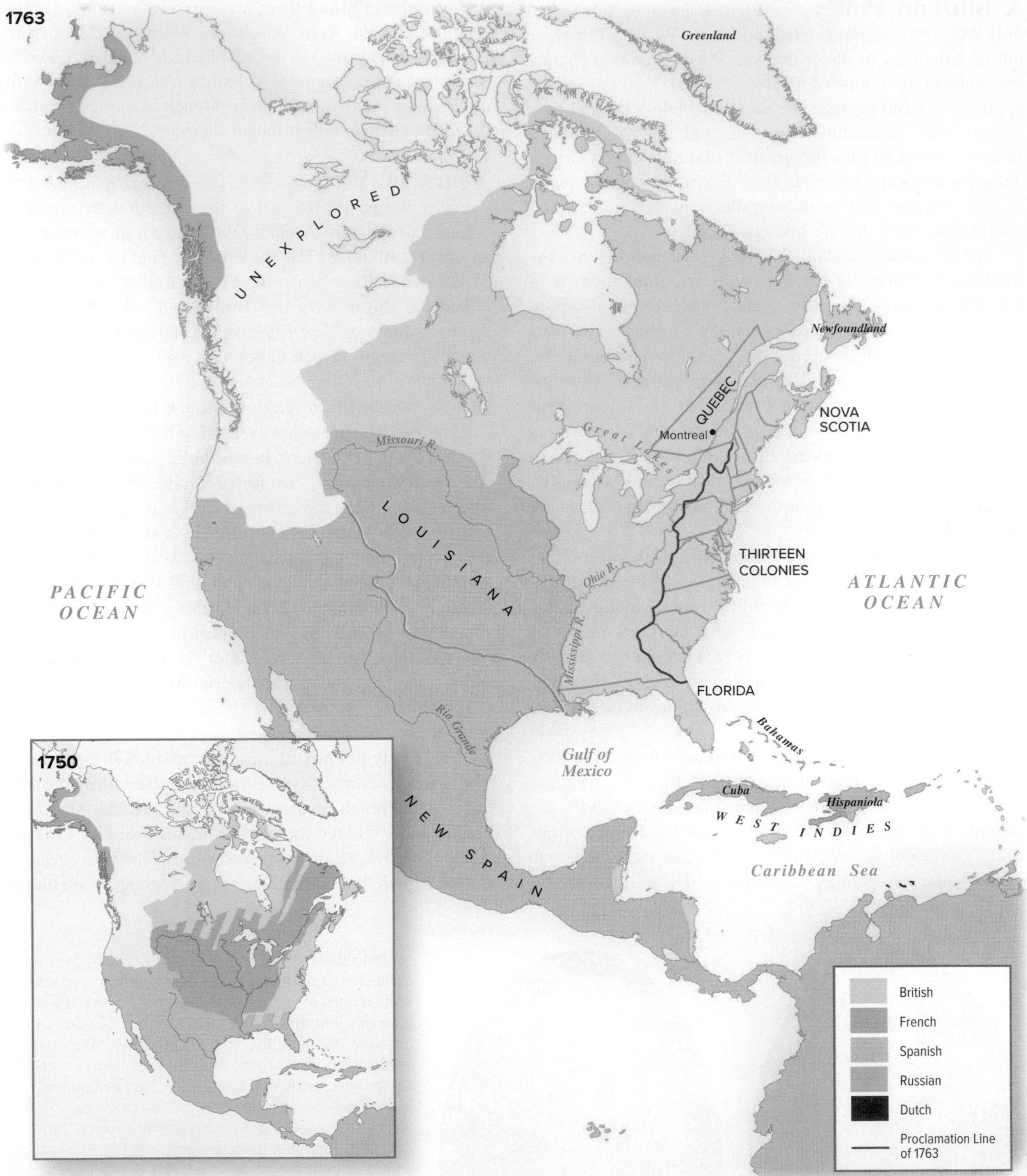

1763
Greenland
UNEXPLORED
Newfoundland
QUEBEC
NOVA SCOTIA
Montreal
Great Lakes
Missouri R.
LOUISIANA
Ohio R.
THIRTEEN COLONIES
PACIFIC OCEAN
ATLANTIC OCEAN
Mississippi R.
FLORIDA
Rio Grande
Bahamas
Gulf of Mexico
Cuba
Hispaniola
WEST INDIES
NEW SPAIN
Caribbean Sea
1750
British
French
Spanish
Russian
Dutch
Proclamation Line of 1763


## MAP 6.2: EUROPEAN CLAIMS IN NORTH AMERICA, 1750 AND 1763

The British victory in the Seven Years' War secured Britain's title to a large portion of the present-day United States and Canada. *What were the major shifts in power among European nations as a result of the Seven Years' War?*

to Britain. It reluctantly took nominal control of France's vast and ill-defined territory of Louisiana, west of the Mississippi, but only to prevent Britain from having it. That territory included the port of New Orleans. In addition to its North America spoils, Britain won several Caribbean islands in the war, as well as Senegal in West Africa.

After generations of inconclusive imperial wars, British North Americans found the victory almost impossibly grand. Towns up and down the Atlantic coast lit up the night with celebratory bonfires and rang with the sounds of clanking tankards and boisterous song. How good it was to be British!

**Postwar Expectations** >> Grand expectations crowded on the heels of these joyful celebrations. The end of the war, Americans assumed, meant the end of high taxes and access to the fertile lands of the Ohio. Just as important, Americans expected to be given more consideration within the British Empire. Now, as one anonymous pamphleteer put it, Americans would "not be thought presumptuous, if they consider[ed] themselves upon an equal footing" with English in the parent country.

Few in England seemed to agree. British statesmen grumbled that colonial assemblies had been tightfisted when it came to supplying the army. British commanders charged that colonial troops had been lily-livered when it came to combat. Differing perspectives on the war and differing expectations of the colonies' place in the empire primed the postwar generation for crisis.

REVIEW

What started the Seven Years' War, and how did Britain emerge victorious?

# THE IMPERIAL CRISIS

It was common sense. Great Britain had waged a costly war to secure its empire in America; now it needed to consolidate those gains. The empire's North American territory had to be protected, its administration tightened, and its colonies made more profitable for the parent nation. Thus Britain would have to leave a standing army of several thousand troops in America after the Seven Years' War. And, of course, armies needed to be paid for; taxes would be unavoidable. That the colonists, who benefited most from the great victory, ought to be the ones to pull out their purses for king and country—well, London thought that, too, was common sense.

**Pontiac's Rebellion** >> British authorities justified the army's continued presence in part by pointing to the various alien peoples that the Crown now had to administer. The army would have to police French colonists in Canada, Spaniards in Florida, and, most especially, dozens of formidable native peoples west of the Appalachians. General Jeffery Amherst, the top British officer in North America, believed Indian troubles could be avoided if military and civil authorities simply projected strength. With the French no longer on the continent, Amherst believed, Britain need not purchase Indian friendship with presents, subsidized trade, and tiresome diplomatic ceremonies. When knowledgeable colonists insisted that Indian relations hinged on such practices, Amherst scoffed. "When men of what race soever behave ill," the general scolded, "they must be punished but not bribed."

Still reeling from the war, Indian peoples reacted to Britain's triumphal attitude and the new westward surge of speculators and colonists with a religious revival that cut across tribal lines. The Delaware holy man Neolin told followers that God, or the Master of Life, believed his native children should "drive [the British] out, make war on them . . . they know me not, and are my enemies. Send them back to the lands I have created for them. . . ."

Pontiac, a charismatic Ottawa chief, embraced Neolin's message of Indian unity and organized attacks against British forts in the summer of 1763. Shawnees, Mingos, Potawatomis, Wyandots, and other Indian peoples in the Ohio Country, working with Pontiac or independently, captured every British fort west of Detroit by early July. Backcountry settlements from Pennsylvania to Virginia came under attack, leaving hundreds of colonials dead and hundreds more fleeing east. Determined to assert British rule, an enraged Amherst sent troops west to attack Indian forces and native villages. He also authorized the commander at Fort Pitt to give Indians blankets from the forts' infirmary, where several men had been stricken with smallpox.

Hatreds mounted on all sides. In western Pennsylvania, where Indian raids had taken an especially grim toll, a number of Scots-Irishmen calling themselves the "Paxton Boys" set out to purge the colony of Indians altogether. In December of 1763 they burst into a small village of Christian Indians, killed six people, and burned the settlement to the ground. Fourteen other inhabitants fled to the town of Lancaster, which gave them protective custody. Leading a mob the Paxton Boys forced their way into the safe house and massacred all 14 men, women, and children with broadswords. Colonists and natives alike were increasingly willing to simplify difference and see all "Indians" or all "whites" as despicable enemies.

Officials in London blamed Pontiac's Rebellion on bad leadership and replaced General Amherst. More important, the crown issued the Proclamation of 1763, which significantly transformed colonial policy. Presents and respectful diplomacy were to resume, and the Crown appointed two Indian superintendents (one in South Carolina and the other in New York) to oversee good relations. Most critically, colonial settlement was to cease west of the Appalachians. A so-called proclamation line reserved all western lands as Indian Territory (see Map 6.2). (Quebec and Florida were exceptions, divided into eastern and western halves, for colonials and Indians.) Restricting westward movement might ease Indian fears, the British hoped, and so stave off future conflicts.

However sensible and just the Proclamation Line might have seemed from the perspective of the Ohio Country or London, most British colonists viewed it as a betrayal by

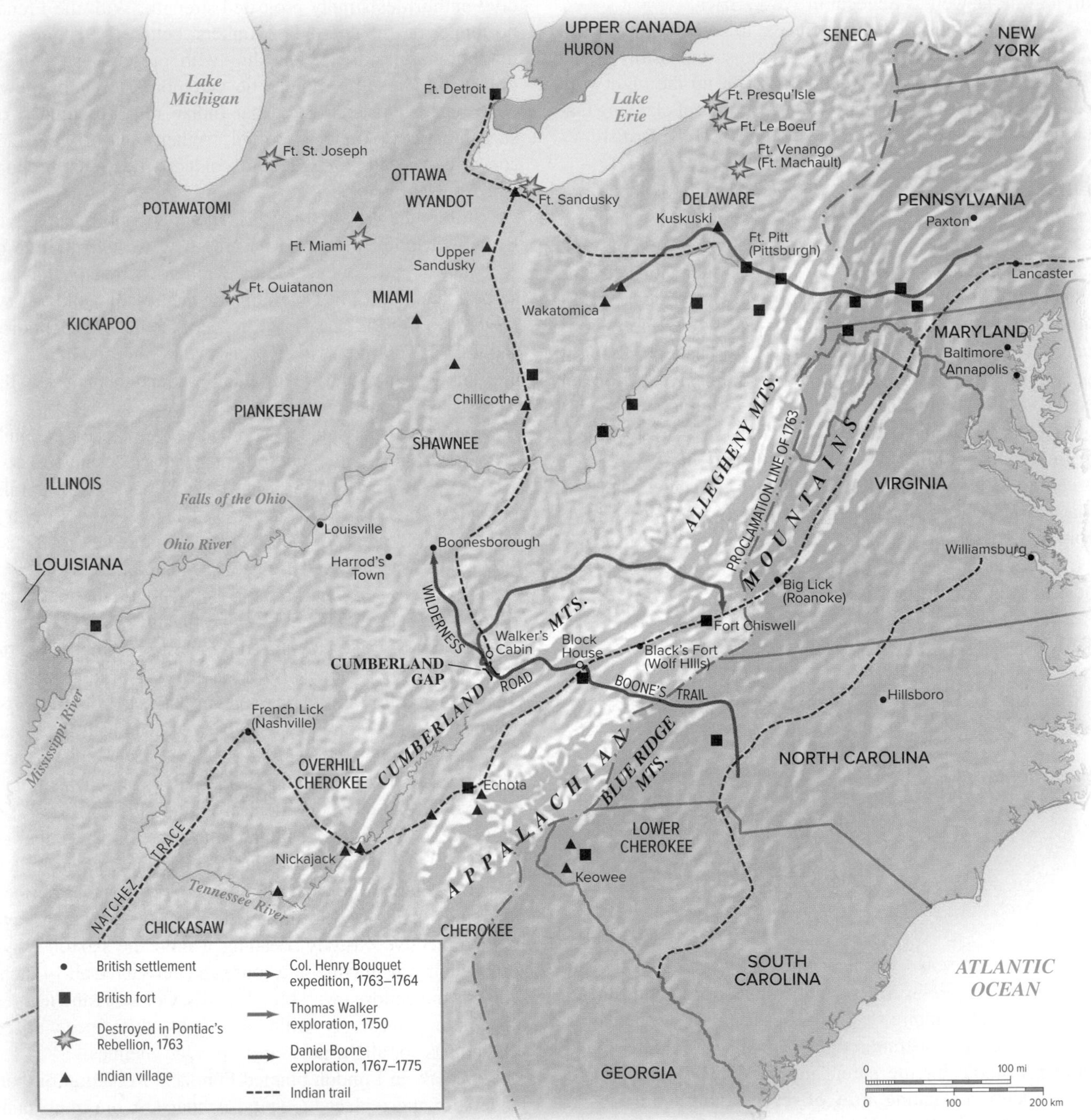

UPPER CANADA
HURON
SENECA
NEW YORK
Lake Michigan
Ft. Detroit
Lake Erie
Ft. Presqu'Isle
Ft. Le Boeuf
Ft. Venango (Ft. Machault)
Ft. St. Joseph
OTTAWA
WYANDOT
Ft. Sandusky
DELAWARE
PENNSYLVANIA
POTAWATOMI
Kuskuski
Paxton
Ft. Miami
Upper Sandusky
Ft. Pitt (Pittsburgh)
Lancaster
Ft. Ouiatanon
MIAMI
Wakatomica
KICKAPOO
MARYLAND
Baltimore
Annapolis
Chillicothe
PIANKESHAW
ALLEGHENY MTS.
PROCLAMATION LINE OF 1763
SHAWNEE
MOUNTAINS
ILLINOIS
VIRGINIA
Falls of the Ohio
Louisville
Ohio River
Boonesborough
Williamsburg
LOUISIANA
Harrod's Town
Big Lick (Roanoke)
WILDERNESS
Fort Chiswell
Walker's Cabin
MTS.
Block House
Black's Fort (Wolf Hills)
CUMBERLAND GAP
ROAD
BOONE'S TRAIL
Hillsboro
Mississippi River
French Lick (Nashville)
CUMBERLAND
BLUE RIDGE MTS.
NORTH CAROLINA
OVERHILL CHEROKEE
Echota
APPALACHIAN
LOWER CHEROKEE
TRACE
Nickajack
Keowee
NATCHEZ
Tennessee River
CHICKASAW
CHEROKEE
British settlement
British fort
Destroyed in Pontiac's Rebellion, 1763
Indian village
Col. Henry Bouquet expedition, 1763–1764
Thomas Walker exploration, 1750
Daniel Boone exploration, 1767–1775
Indian trail
SOUTH CAROLINA
ATLANTIC OCEAN
GEORGIA
0
100 mi
0
100
200 km


## MAP 6.3: THE APPALACHIAN FRONTIER, 1750–1775

Increasingly, land-hungry colonials spilled into the West through the Cumberland Gap, a notch in the chain of mountains stretching the length of the North American interior. A route through the gap was scouted in 1750 by Dr. Thomas Walker and a party of Virginians on behalf of a company of land speculators. In 1763 Indians led by Pontiac seized eight British forts before troops under Colonel Henry Bouquet stopped the offensive. In 1775 Daniel Boone led the first large party of pioneers through the gap to Boonesborough, in present-day Kentucky. *How did efforts to expand American settlement west of the Appalachians help spark conflict between the British and the American colonists?*

their own government. Many wondered why they had fought and sacrificed in the war against France, if all the territory they helped win was set aside for Indians.

## George Grenville's New Measures >>

If Pontiac's Rebellion and the Proclamation of 1763 had been the only postwar disappointments colonists faced, that would have been trouble enough. But George Grenville, the first lord of the treasury, also confronted the dismal financial consequences of the Seven Years' War.

Britain's national debt had doubled in the decade after 1754. Adding to that burden was the drain of supporting troops in the colonies. As matters stood, heavy taxes were already triggering protests among hard-pressed Britons. Americans, in contrast, paid comparatively low taxes to their colonial governments and little in trade duties to the empire. Indeed, Grenville discovered that the colonial customs service paid out four times more in salaries to its collectors than it gathered in duties. Rampant bribery and tax evasion allowed merchants to avoid existing duties on foreign molasses, for example, which New England merchants imported to make rum.

George Grenville reasoned that if Americans could pay out a little under the table to protect an illegal trade, they would willingly pay a little more to go legitimate. Parliament agreed. In April 1764 it passed the Revenue Act, commonly called the Sugar Act. This **tariff** actually lowered the duty on foreign molasses from six to three pence a gallon. This time, however, the tax would be scrupulously collected, ships would be tightly monitored to make sure they complied, and violators would be tried in admiralty courts, far harsher than typical colonial courts.

**tariff** duty on trade, the purpose of which is primarily to regulate the flow of commerce rather than to raise a revenue.

Parliament approved other proposals by Grenville, all designed to improve British finances. The Currency Act of 1764 prohibited the colonies from making their paper money legal tender. That prevented Americans from paying their debts to British traders in currency that had fallen to less than its face value. The Quartering Act of 1765 obliged any colony in which troops were stationed to provide suitable accommodations. That contributed to the cost of keeping British forces in America. Finally, in March 1765 Parliament passed the Stamp Act.

The Stamp Act placed **taxes** on legal documents, customs papers, newspapers, almanacs, college diplomas, playing cards, and dice. After November 1, 1765, all these items had to bear a stamp signifying that their possessor had paid the tax. Violators of the Stamp Act, like those disobeying the Sugar Act, were to be tried without juries in admiralty courts. The English had been paying a similar tax for nearly a century, so Grenville expected few objections. Little did he understand the colonial viewpoint.

**taxes** duty on trade (known as external taxation) or a duty on items circulating within a nation or a colony (known as internal taxation) intended primarily to raise a revenue rather than to regulate the flow of commerce.

^ British grenadier
©Philadelphia History Museum at the Atwater Kent/Courtesy of Historical Society of Pennsylvania Collection/ Bridgeman Images

## The Beginning of Colonial Resistance >>

Like other Britons, colonials in America accepted a maxim laid down by the English philosopher John Locke: property guaranteed liberty. Property, in this view, was not merely real estate, or wealth, or material possessions. It was the source of strength for every individual, providing the freedom to think and act independently. It followed from this close connection between property, power, and liberty that no people should be taxed without consenting—either personally or through elected representatives. The power to tax was the power to destroy, by depriving a person of property. Yet both the Sugar Act and the Stamp Act were taxes passed by members of Parliament, none of whom had been elected by colonials.

Like the English, colonials also prized the right of trial by jury as one of their basic constitutional liberties. Yet both the Sugar Act and the Stamp Act would prosecute offenders in the admiralty courts, not in local courts, thus depriving colonials of the freedom claimed by all other English men and women.

The concern for protecting individual liberties was only one of the convictions shaping the colonies' response to Britain's new policies. Equally important was their deep suspicion of power itself, a preoccupation that colonials shared with a minority of radical English thinkers. These radicals were known by a variety of names: the Country Party, the Commonwealthmen, and the **Opposition**. They drew their inspiration from the ancient tradition of **classical republicanism**, which held that representative government safeguarded liberty more reliably than either monarchy or oligarchy did. Underlying that judgment was the belief that human beings were driven by passion and insatiable ambition. One person (a monarch), or even a few people (an oligarchy), could not be entrusted with governing because they would inevitably become corrupted by power and turn into despots. Even in representative governments, the people were obliged to watch those in power at all times. The price of liberty was eternal vigilance.

**Opposition** diverse group of political thinkers and writers in Great Britain, also known as the Country Party and the Commonwealthmen, who elaborated the tradition of classical republicanism from the late seventeenth century through the eighteenth century.

**classical republicanism** a theory of government that emphasizes that all rulers need to be watched because of a tendency for power to corrupt human nature.

The Opposition believed that the people of England were not watching their rulers closely enough. During the first half of the eighteenth century, they argued, the entire executive branch of England's government—monarchs and their ministers—had been corrupted by their appetite for power. Proof of their ambition could be found in the bloated state bureaucracy, the massive standing army, and the rising taxes. The Opposition warned that a sinister conspiracy originating in the executive branch of government threatened English liberty.

Opposition writers were more or less ignored in England, but colonial leaders revered them. The Opposition's view of politics confirmed colonial anxieties about England, doubts that ran deeper after 1763. Parliament's attempt to tax the colonies and the quartering of a standing army on the frontier smacked of a corrupt plot to enslave the colonies.

Britain's attempt to raise revenue after 1763 was a disaster of timing, not just psychologically but also economically. By then the colonies were in the throes of a recession. The boom produced in America by government spending during the war had collapsed once British subsidies were withdrawn. Colonial response to the Sugar Act reflected these painful postwar trends. New England merchants led the opposition, objecting to the Sugar Act principally on economic grounds.

But with the passage of the Stamp Act, the terms of the imperial debate widened. The new act took money from the pockets of anyone who made a will, filed a deed, traded out of a colonial port, bought a newspaper, consulted an almanac, graduated from college, took a chance at dice, or played cards. More important, the Stamp Act served notice that Parliament claimed the authority to tax the colonies directly.

**Riots and Resolves** >> That unprecedented assertion provoked an unprecedented development: the first display of colonial unity. During the spring and summer of 1765, American assemblies passed resolves denying Parliament's authority to tax the colonies. That right belonged to colonial assemblies alone, they argued, by the law of nature and by the liberties guaranteed in colonial charters and in the British constitution.

Virginia's assembly, the House of Burgesses, took the lead in protesting the Stamp Act, prodded by Patrick Henry. Just 29 years old in 1765, Henry had tried his hand at planting in western Virginia before recognizing his real talent—demagoguery. Blessed with the eloquence of an evangelical preacher, the dashing charm of a southern gentleman, and a mind uncluttered by much learning, Henry parlayed his popularity as a smooth-talking lawyer into a place among the Burgesses. He took his seat just 10 days before introducing the Virginia Resolves against the Stamp Act.

The Burgesses passed Henry's resolutions upholding their exclusive right to tax Virginians. Other assemblies followed suit, affirming that the sole right to tax Americans resided in their elected representatives. In October 1765 delegates from nine colonies convened in New York, where they prepared a joint statement of the American position and petitioned the king and Parliament to repeal both the Sugar Act and the Stamp Act.

Meanwhile, colonial leaders turned to the press to arouse popular opposition to the Stamp Act. Disposed by the writings of the English Opposition to think of politics in conspiratorial terms, they warned that Grenville and the king's other ministers schemed to deprive the colonies of their liberties by unlawfully taxing their property. The Stamp Act was only the first step in a sinister plan to enslave Americans. In response the merchants of Boston, New York, and Philadelphia agreed to stop importing English goods in order to pressure British traders to lobby for repeal. In every colony organizations emerged to ensure that the Stamp Act, if not repealed, would never be enforced.

The new resistance groups, which styled themselves the "Sons of Liberty," consisted of traders, lawyers, and prosperous artisans. With great success, they organized the lower classes of the seaports in opposition to the Stamp Act. The sailors, dockworkers, poor artisans, apprentices, and servants who poured into the streets resembled mobs that had been organized from time to time earlier in the century. Previous riots against houses of prostitution, merchants who hoarded goods, or supporters of smallpox inoculation had not been spontaneous, uncontrolled outbursts. Crowds chose their targets and their tactics carefully and usually carried out the communal will with little personal violence.

## Make a Case

Were colonists right to worry about the dangers of a standing army? If so, does our standing army pose a danger today?

In every colonial city the mobs of 1765 burnt the stamp distributors in effigy, insulted them on the streets, demolished their offices, and attacked their homes. One hot night in August 1765 a mob went further than the Sons of Liberty had planned. They all but leveled the stately mansion of Thomas Hutchinson, the unpopular lieutenant governor of Massachusetts and the brother-in-law of the colony's stamp distributor. The destruction stunned Bostonians, especially the Sons of Liberty, who resisted Britain in the name of protecting private property. Thereafter they took care to keep crowds under tighter control. By the first of November, the day the Stamp Act took effect, most of the stamp distributors had resigned.

## Repeal of the Stamp Act >>

Meanwhile, repeal of the Stamp Act was already under way back in England. The man who came—unintentionally—to America's relief was George III. The young king was a good man, industrious and devoted to the empire, but he was also immature and not particularly bright. Insecurity made him an irksome master, and he ran through ministers rapidly. By the end of 1765 George had replaced Grenville with a new first minister, the Marquis of Rockingham. Opposed to the Stamp Act from the outset, Rockingham secured its repeal in March 1766.

The Stamp Act controversy demonstrated to colonials how similar in political outlook they were to one another and how different they were from the British. Most fundamentally, Americans agreed about the meaning of representation. To counter colonial objections to the Stamp Act, Grenville and his supporters had claimed that Americans were virtually represented, because each member of Parliament stood for the interests of the whole empire. But colonials put little stock in the theory of **virtual representation**. After all, living an ocean away, their interests differed significantly from those of Britons. They insisted on **actual representation**,

**virtual representation** view that representation is not linked to election but rather to common interests. During the imperial crisis, the British argued that Americans were virtually represented in Parliament, even though colonials elected none of its members.

**actual representation** view that the people can be represented only by a person whom they have actually elected to office.

THE REPEAL. Or the Funeral Procession, of MISS AMERIC-STAMP.
1745
Sheffield and Birmingham Warehouse
Goods now Shipp'd for America
Stamps
Leeds

A political cartoon, *The Repeal, or the Funeral Procession of Miss Americ-Stamp,* was published in London on the day the Stamp Act was repealed. The little toddler, the caption explained, "died hard in 1766." The "mourners" are caricatures of officials who supported the act, including George Grenville, "full of Grief and dispair" as he carries the infant's tiny coffin. Meanwhile the ships in the harbor represent the fruits of repeal: the full resumption of trade between merchants in England and America.

emphasizing that elected officials were directly accountable to their constituents.

Americans also agreed that Parliament had no legitimate right to tax the colonies. Colonials conceded Parliament's right to legislate and to regulate trade for the good of the whole empire. But taxation, in their view, was the free gift of the people through their representatives—who were not sitting in Parliament.

Members of Parliament brushed aside colonial petitions and resolves, all but ignoring these constitutional arguments. To make its own authority clear, Parliament accompanied the repeal of the Stamp Act with a Declaratory Act, asserting that it had the power to make laws for the colonies "in all cases whatsoever." In fact, the Declaratory Act clarified nothing. Did Parliament understand the power of legislation to include the power of taxation?

**The Townshend Acts >>** In the summer of 1766 George III—again unintentionally—gave the colonies what should have been an advantage by changing ministers yet again. The king replaced Rockingham with William Pitt, who enjoyed great favor among colonials for his leadership during the Seven Years' War and for his opposition to the Stamp Act. Almost alone among British politicians, Pitt had grasped and approved the colonists' constitutional objections to taxation. During Parliament's debate over repeal of the Stamp Act, Grenville asked sarcastically, "Tell me when the colonies were emancipated?" Pitt immediately shot back, "I desire to know when they were made slaves!"

If the man who believed that Americans were "the sons not the bastards of England" had been well enough to govern, matters between Great Britain and the colonies might have turned out differently. But almost immediately after Pitt took office his health collapsed, and power passed into the hands of Charles Townshend, the chancellor of the exchequer, who wished only to raise more revenue. In 1767 Townshend persuaded Parliament to tax the lead, paint, paper, glass, and tea that Americans imported from Britain. Then he used revenue from these new tariffs to pay the salaries of many royal officials serving in the colonies.

This was a change—and an important one. Previously, governors and other officers such as customs collectors and judges had received their salaries from colonial legislatures. The assemblies lost that crucial leverage when Townshend used the revenues to pay those bureaucrats directly. Royal officials depended less, now, on coming to terms with American legislators. Finally, in order to ensure more effective enforcement of all the duties on imports, Townshend created an American Board of Customs Commissioners, who appointed a small army of new customs collectors. He also established three new vice-admiralty courts in Boston, New York, and Charleston to bring smugglers to justice.

**The Resistance Organizes >>** In Townshend's efforts to centralize the administration of the empire, Americans saw new evidence that they were not being treated like the English. A host of newspapers and pamphlets took up the cry against taxation. The most widely read publication, "A Letter from a Farmer in Pennsylvania," was the work of John Dickinson—who was, in fact, a Philadelphia lawyer. He urged Americans to protest the Townshend duties by consuming fewer imported English luxuries. The virtues of hard work, thrift, and home manufacturing, Dickinson argued, would bring about repeal.

As Dickinson's star rose over Philadelphia, the Townshend Acts also shaped the destiny of another man farther north. Samuel Adams was a leader in the Massachusetts assembly, one whose rise had been unlikely. Adams's earlier ventures as a merchant had ended in bankruptcy; his stint as a tax collector had left all of Boston in the red. But he proved a consummate political organizer and agitator. First his enemies and later his friends claimed that Adams had decided on independence for America as early as 1768. In that year he persuaded the assembly to send to other colonial legislatures a circular letter condemning the Townshend Acts and calling for a united American resistance.

As John Dickinson and Samuel Adams whipped up public outrage, the Sons of Liberty again organized the opposition in the streets. Customs officials, like the stamp distributors before them, became targets of popular hatred. But the customs collectors gave as good as they got. Using the flimsiest excuses, they seized American vessels for violating royal regulations. With cold insolence they shook down American merchants for what amounted to protection money. The racketeering in the customs service brought tensions in Boston to a flash point in June 1768 after officials seized and condemned the *Liberty*, a sloop belonging to one of the city's biggest merchants, John Hancock. Several thousand Bostonians vented their anger in a night of rioting, searching out and roughing up customs officials.

The new secretary of state for the colonies, Lord Hillsborough, responded to the *Liberty* riot by sending two regiments of troops to Boston. In the fall of 1768 the redcoats, like a conquering army, paraded into town under the cover of warships lying off the harbor. In the months that followed, citizens bristled when challenged on the streets by armed soldiers. Even more disturbing to Bostonians was the execution of British military justice on the Common. British soldiers were whipped savagely for breaking military discipline, and desertion was punished by execution.

The *Liberty* riot and the arrival of British troops in Boston

<< John Dickinson of Philadelphia
©North Wind Picture Archives/Alamy

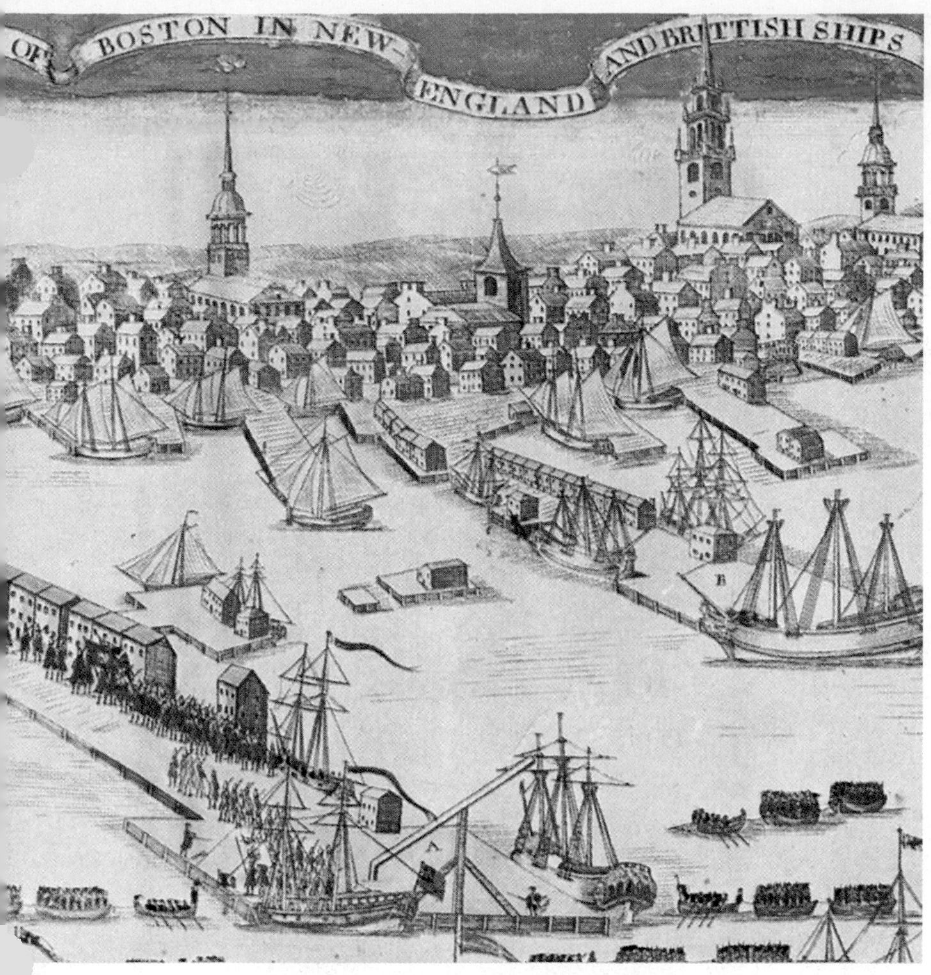
OF BOSTON IN NEW-
ENGLAND
AND BRITTISH SHIPS

^ Like a swarm of angry bees, British troops disembark on one of Boston's long wharves in 1768. American colonials who had cheered the triumphs of British soldiers only a few years earlier now complained bitterly about the presence of a standing army designed to intimidate them.
©Bettmann/Getty Images

pushed colonial assemblies to coordinate their resistance more closely. Most legislatures endorsed the Massachusetts circular letter of protest sent to them by Samuel Adams. They promptly adopted agreements not to import or to consume British goods. The reluctance among some merchants to revive nonimportation in 1767 gave way to greater enthusiasm by 1768, and by early 1769 such agreements were in effect throughout the colonies.

The Stamp Act crisis had also called forth intercolonial cooperation and tactics such as nonimportation. But the protests against the Townshend Acts raised the stakes by creating new institutions to carry forward the resistance. Subscribers to the nonimportation agreements established "committees of inspection" to enforce the ban on trade with Britain. The committees publicly denounced merchants who continued to import, vandalized their warehouses, forced them to stand under the gallows, and sometimes resorted to tar and feathers.

After 1768 the resistance also brought a broader range of colonials into the politics of protest. Artisans, who recognized that nonimportation would spur domestic manufacturing, began to organize as independent political groups. In many towns women took an active part in opposing the Townshend duties. The "Daughters of Liberty" took to heart John Dickinson's advice: they wore homespun clothing instead of English finery, served coffee instead of tea, and boycotted shops selling British goods.

**The International Sons of Liberty** >> The resistance after 1768 grew broader in another sense. Many of its supporters in the colonies felt a new sense of kinship with freedom fighters throughout Europe. Eagerly they read about the doings of men such as Charles Lucas, an Irish newspaper editor and member of the Irish Parliament, and John Wilkes, a London journalist and a leading politician of the Opposition. Both men charged the king's ministers with corrupting the political life of the British Isles. The doings of political rebels even in distant Poland and Turkey engaged colonial sympathies, too. But perhaps the international cause dearest to American lovers of liberty was the fate of Corsica.

For years this tiny island off the coast of Italy had fought for its independence, first from the Italian state of Genoa and then from France, which bought the island in 1768. The leader of the Corsican rebellion, Pascal Paoli, hoped that England would rally to defend Corsica's freedom, if only to keep France from seizing this strategic Mediterranean outpost. But British statesmen had no intention of going to war with France over mere Corsica, and when French troops routed his rebel army, Paoli fled to exile in England in 1769. Adding insult to injury this "greatest man of earth," as he was lionized, began to hobnob with British nobles. He even accepted a pension of 1,000 pounds a year from George III. The moral of the sad story, according to more than one colonial newspaper, was that British corruption pervaded not only the empire but all of Europe. Within a few years Europeans sympathizing with these notions would cross the Atlantic to fight in the American Revolution.

**The Boston Massacre** >> Meanwhile, the situation in Boston deteriorated steadily. British troops found themselves regularly cursed by citizens and occasionally pelted with stones, dirt, and human excrement. The British regulars were particularly unpopular among Boston's laboring classes, because they competed with them for jobs. Off-duty soldiers moonlighted as maritime laborers, and they sold their services at rates cheaper than the wages paid

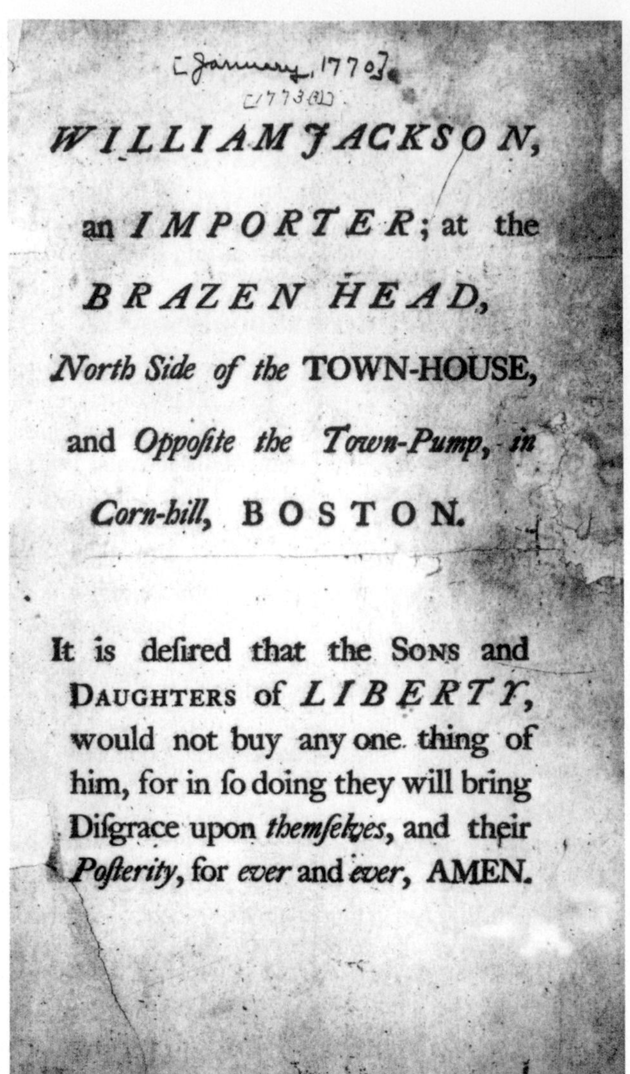

WILLIAM JACKSON,

an IMPORTER; at the

BRAZEN HEAD,

North Side of the TOWN-HOUSE,

and Oppoſite the Town-Pump, in

Corn-hill, BOSTON.

It is deſired that the SONS and DAUGHTERS of LIBERTY, would not buy any one thing of him, for in ſo doing they will bring Diſgrace upon themſelves, and their Poſterity, for ever and ever, AMEN.

^ A nonimportation leaflet from Boston.
©MPI/Getty Images

to locals. By 1769 brawls between British regulars and waterfront workers broke out frequently.

With some 4,000 redcoats enduring daily contact with some 15,000 Bostonians under the sway of Samuel Adams, what happened on the night of March 5, 1770, was nearly inevitable. A crowd gathered around the customshouse for the sport of heckling the 10 soldiers who guarded it. The redcoats panicked and fended off insults and snowballs with live fire, hitting 11 rioters and killing 5. Adams and other propagandists seized on the incident. Labeling the bloodshed the "Boston Massacre," they publicized that "atrocity" throughout the colonies. The radical Boston *Gazette* framed its account in an eye-catching black-bordered edition headed with a drawing of five coffins.

While Townshend's policies spurred the resistance in America, the obvious finally dawned on Parliament. They recognized that Townshend's duties on imported English goods only discouraged sales to colonials and encouraged them to manufacture at home. The argument for repeal was overwhelming, and the way had been cleared by the unexpected death of Townshend. In 1770 his successor, Lord North, convinced Parliament to repeal all the Townshend duties except the one on tea, allowing that tax to stand as a source of revenue and as a symbol of Parliament's authority.

**Resistance Revived** >> Repeal of the Townshend duties took the wind from the sails of American resistance for more than two years. But the controversy between England and the colonies had not been resolved. Colonials still paid taxes on molasses and tea, taxes to which they had not consented. They were still subject to trial in admiralty courts, which operated without juries. They still lived with a standing army in their midst. Beneath the banked fires of protest smoldered the live embers of Americans' political inequality. Any shift in the wind could fan those embers into flames.

The wind did shift, quite literally, on Narragansett Bay in 1772, running aground the *Gaspee*, a British naval schooner

>> While the new political activism of some American women merely amused male leaders of the resistance, it inspired the scorn of some defenders of British authority. When the women of Edenton, North Carolina, renounced imported tea, this British cartoon mocked them. Can you find at least five details in the drawing used by the artist to insult the Americans?
Source: Library of Congress, Prints and Photographs Division [LC-USZ62-12711]

Many HISTORIES

## Who Was to Blame for the Boston Massacre?

*Following the shootings in King Street, Captain Thomas Preston and six of his men stood trial for murder. Two radical patriot lawyers, Josiah Quincy Jr. and future president John Adams, served as defense counsel. Convinced that Boston must prove itself fair and faithful to the rule of law, both lawyers performed brilliantly. The jury acquitted Preston and four of the soldiers, and convicted two others of manslaughter. The depositions from the trial provide some of our best evidence for how soldiers and Bostonians viewed the standoff differently.*

### DOCUMENT 1
### Deposition of Captain Thomas Preston, March 1770

The mob still increased and were more outrageous, striking their clubs or bludgeons one against another, and calling out, come on you rascals, you bloody backs, you lobster scoundrels, fire if you dare, G-d damn you, fire and be damned, we know you dare not, and much more such language was used. At this time I was between the soldiers and the mob, parleying with, and endeavouring all in my power to persuade them to retire peaceably, but to no purpose. They advanced to the points of the bayonets, struck some of them and even the muzzles of the pieces, and seemed to be endeavouring to close with the soldiers. On which some well-behaved persons asked me if the guns were charged. I replied yes. They then asked me if I intended to order the men to fire. I answered no, by no means, observing to them that I was advanced before the muzzles of the men's pieces, and must fall a sacrifice if they fired; that the soldiers were upon the half cock and charged bayonets, and my giving the word fire under those circumstances would prove me to be no officer. While I was thus speaking, one of the soldiers having received a severe blow with a stick, stepped a little on one side and instantly fired, on which turning to and asking him why he fired without orders, I was struck with a club on my arm, which for some time deprived me of the use of it, which blow had it been placed on my head, most probably would have destroyed me. On this a general attack was made on the men by a great number of heavy clubs and snowballs being thrown at them, by which all our lives were in imminent danger, some persons at the same time from behind calling out, damn your bloods—why don't you fire. Instantly three or four of the soldiers fired, one after another, and directly after three more in the same confusion and hurry. The mob then ran away, except three unhappy men who instantly expired, in which number was Mr. Gray at whose rope-walk the prior quarrels took place; one more is since dead, three others are dangerously, and four slightly wounded. The whole of this melancholy affair was transacted in almost 20 minutes. On my asking the soldiers why they fired without orders, they said they heard the word fire and supposed it came from me. This might be the case as many of the mob called out fire, fire, but I assured the men that I gave no such order; that my words were, don't fire, stop your firing. In short, it was scarcely possible for the soldiers to know who said fire, or don't fire, or stop your firing.

"Deposition of Captain Thomas Preston, March 1770."

### DOCUMENT 2
### Deposition of Robert Goddard, March 1770

The Soldiers came up to the Centinel and the Officer told them to place themselves and they formed a half moon. The Captain told the Boys to go home least there should be murder done. They were throwing Snow balls. Did not go off but threw more Snow balls. The Capt. was behind the Soldiers. The Captain told them to fire. One Gun went off. A Sailor or Townsman struck the Captain. He thereupon said damn your bloods fire think I'll be treated in this manner. This Man that struck the Captain came from among the People who were 7 feet off and were round on one wing. I saw no person speak to him. I was so near I should have seen it. After the Capt. said Damn your bloods fire they all fired one after another about 7 or 8 in all, and then the officer bid Prime and load again. He stood behind all the time. Mr. Lee went up to the officer and called the officer by name Capt. Preston, I saw him coming down from the Guard behind the Party. I went to Gaol the next day being sworn for the Grand Jury to see the Captain. Then said pointing to him that's the person who gave the word to fire. He said if you swear that you will ruin me everlastingly. I was so near the officer when he gave the word fire that I could touch him. His face was towards me. He stood in the middle behind the Men. I looked him in the face. He then stood within the circle. When he told 'em to fire he turned about to me. I looked him in the face.

"Deposition of Robert Goddard, March 1770."

### THINKING CRITICALLY

*Preston and Goddard come to different conclusions about the shootings but describe similar details (the snowballs, the man who struck Preston). How might details from these two accounts be reconciled? Do they simply have different perspectives on the same event, or do you think one of the depositions must be misleading? Given the tensions these accounts relate, how likely do you think it was that some kind of violent confrontation would occur?*

in hot pursuit of Rhode Island smugglers. Residents of nearby Providence quickly celebrated the *Gaspee*'s misfortune by burning it down to the waterline. Outraged British officials sent a special commission to look into the matter, intending once again to bypass the established colonial court system. The arrival of the Gaspee Commission reignited the imperial crisis, and in America, once again, resistance flared.

It did so through an ingenious mechanism, the **committees of correspondence**. Established in all the colonies by their assemblies, the committees drew up statements of American rights and grievances, distributed those documents within and among the colonies, and solicited responses from towns and counties. The brainchild of Samuel Adams, the committee structure formed a new communications network, one that fostered an intercolonial agreement on resistance to British measures. The strategy succeeded, and not only among colonies. The committees spread the scope of the resistance from colonial seaports into rural areas, engaging farmers and other country folk in the opposition to Britain.

**committees of correspondence** strategy devised by Samuel Adams in 1772 to rally popular support among American colonials against British imperial policies.

The committees had much to talk about when Parliament passed the Tea Act in 1773. The law was an effort to bail out the bankrupt East India Company by granting that corporation a monopoly on the tea trade to Americans. Because the company could use agents to sell its product directly, cutting out the middlemen, it could offer a lower price than that charged by colonial merchants. Thus, although the Tea Act would hurt American merchants, it promised to make tea cheaper for ordinary Americans. Still, many colonials saw the act as Parliament's attempt to trick them into accepting its authority to tax the colonies. They set out to deny that power once and for all.

In the early winter of 1773 popular leaders in Boston called for the tea cargoes to be returned immediately to England. On the evening of December 16, thousands of Bostonians, as well as farmers from the surrounding countryside, packed into the Old South Meetinghouse. Some members of the audience knew what Samuel Adams planned for the evening's agenda, and they awaited their cue. It came when Adams told the meeting that they could do nothing more to save their country. War whoops rang through the meetinghouse, the crowd spilled onto the streets and out to the waterfront, and the Boston Tea Party commenced. From the throng emerged 50 men dressed as Indians to disguise their identities. The party boarded three vessels docked off Griffin's Wharf, broke open casks containing 90,000 pounds of tea, and brewed a beverage worth 10,000 pounds sterling in Boston harbor.

## The Empire Strikes Back >>

The Boston Tea Party proved to British satisfaction that the colonies aimed at independence. Lord North's assessment was grim: "We are now to dispute whether we have, or have not, any authority in that country." To reassert its authority, Parliament passed the Coercive Acts, dubbed in the colonies the "Intolerable Acts." The first of these came in March 1774, after hearing of the Tea Party, when Parliament passed the Boston Port Bill, closing that harbor to all oceangoing traffic until such time as the king saw fit to reopen it. And George, Parliament announced, would not see fit until colonials paid the East India Company for their losses.

During the next three months Parliament approved three other "intolerable" laws designed to punish Massachusetts. The Massachusetts Government Act handed over the colony's government to royal officials. Even convening town meetings would require royal permission. The Impartial Administration of Justice Act permitted any royal official accused of a crime in Massachusetts to be tried in England or in another colony. The Quartering Act allowed the housing of British troops in uninhabited private homes, outlying buildings, and barns—not only in Massachusetts but in all the colonies.

Many colonials saw the Coercive Acts as proof of a plot to enslave the colonies. In truth, the taxes and duties, laws and regulations of the past decade *were* part of a deliberate design—a plan to centralize the administration of the British Empire that seemed only common sense to British officials. But those efforts by the king's ministers and Parliament to run the colonies more efficiently and profitably were viewed by more and more Americans as a sinister conspiracy against their liberties.

For colonials the study of history confirmed that interpretation, especially their reading of the histories written by the English Opposition. The Opposition's favorite historical subject was the downfall of republics, whether those of ancient Greece and Rome or more recent republican governments in Venice and Denmark. The lesson of their histories was always the same: power overwhelmed liberty, unless the people remained vigilant. The pattern, argued radicals, had been repeated in America over the previous dozen years: costly wars waged; oppressive taxes levied to pay for them; standing armies sent to overawe citizens; corrupt governors, customs collectors, and judges appointed to enrich themselves by enforcing the measures. Everything seemed to fit.

Week after week in the spring of 1774, reports of legislative outrages came across the waters. Shortly after approving the Coercive Acts, Parliament passed the Quebec Act, which established a permanent government in what had been French Canada. Ominously, it included no representative assembly. Equally ominous to Protestant colonials, the Quebec Act officially recognized the Roman Catholic Church and extended the bounds of the province to include all land between the Mississippi and Ohio Rivers. Suddenly New York, Pennsylvania, and Virginia found themselves bordering a British colony whose subjects had no voice in their own government.

With the passage of the Coercive Acts, many more colonials came to believe not only that ambitious men plotted to enslave the colonies but also that those conspirators included almost all British political leaders. At the time of the Stamp Act and again during the agitation against the Townshend Acts, most colonials had confined their suspicions to the king's ministers. By 1774 members of Parliament were also implicated in that conspiracy—and a few radicals were wondering aloud about George III.

As alarm deepened in the wake of the Coercive Acts, one colony after another called for an intercolonial congress—like the one that had met during the Stamp Act crisis—to determine the best way to defend their freedom. But many also remained unsettled about where the logic of their actions seemed to be taking them: toward a denial that they were any longer English.

 **REVIEW**

How did British colonial policy change after the Seven Years' War, and in what ways did colonial Americans resist it?

# TOWARD THE REVOLUTION

By the beginning of September 1774, when 55 delegates to the First Continental Congress gathered in Philadelphia, the news from Massachusetts was grim. The colony verged on anarchy, it was reported, as its inhabitants resisted the enforcement of the Massachusetts Government Act.

In the midst of this atmosphere of crisis, the members of Congress also had to take one another's measure. Many of the delegates had not traveled outside their own colony before. (All but Georgia sent representatives.) Although the delegates encountered a great deal of diversity, they quickly discovered that they esteemed the same traits of character, attributes that they called "civic virtue." These traits included simplicity and self-reliance, industry and thrift, and above all, an unselfish commitment to the public good. Most members of the Congress also shared a common mistrust of England, associating the mother country with vice, extravagance, and corruption. Still, the delegates had some misgivings about those from other colonies. Massachusetts in particular brought with it a reputation—well deserved, considering that Samuel Adams was along—for radical action and a willingness to use force to accomplish its ends.

**The First Continental Congress** >> As the delegates settled down to business, their aim was to reach agreement on three key points: How were they to justify the rights they claimed as American colonials? What were the limits of Parliament's power? And what were the proper tactics for resisting the Coercive Acts? Congress quickly agreed on the first point. The delegates affirmed that the law of nature, the colonial charters, and the British constitution provided the foundations of American liberties. This position was what most colonials had argued since 1765.

On the two other issues, the Congress charted a middle course between the demands of radicals and the reservations of conservatives. Since the time of the Stamp Act, most colonials had insisted that Parliament had no authority to tax the colonies. But later events had demonstrated that Parliament could undermine colonial liberties by legislation as well as by taxation. The suspension of the New York legislature, the Gaspee Commission, and the Coercive Acts all fell into this category. Given those experiences, the delegates adopted a Declaration of Rights and Grievances on October 14, 1774, asserting the right of the colonies to tax and legislate for themselves. The Declaration of Rights thus limited Parliament's power over Americans more strictly than colonials had a decade earlier.

By denying Parliament's power to make laws for the colonies, the Continental Congress blocked efforts of the most conservative delegates to reach an accommodation with England. Their leading advocate, Joseph Galloway of Pennsylvania, proposed a plan of union with Britain similar to the one set forth by the Albany Congress in 1754. Under it, a grand council of the colonies would handle all common concerns, with any laws it passed subject to review and veto by Parliament. For its part, Parliament would have to submit for the grand council's approval any acts it passed affecting America. A majority of delegates judged that Galloway left Parliament too much leeway in legislating for colonials, and they rejected his plan.

Although the Congress denied Parliament the right to impose taxes or to make laws, delegates stopped short of declaring that it had no authority in the colonies. They approved Parliament's regulation of trade, but only because of the interdependent economy of the empire. And although some radical pamphleteers were attacking the king for plotting against American liberties, the Congress acknowledged the continuing allegiance of the colonies to George III. In other words, the delegates called for a return to the situation that had existed in the empire before 1763, with Parliament regulating trade and the colonies exercising all powers of taxation and legislation.

On the question of resistance, the Congress satisfied the desires of its most radical delegates by drawing up the Continental Association, an agreement to cease all trade with Britain until the Coercive Acts were repealed. They agreed that their fellow citizens would immediately stop drinking East India Company tea and that by December 1, 1774, merchants would no longer import goods of any sort from Britain. A ban on the export of American produce to Britain and the West Indies would go into effect a year later, during September 1775—the lag being a concession to southern rice and tobacco planters, who wanted to market crops already planted.

The Continental Association provided for the total cessation of trade, but Samuel Adams and other radicals wanted bolder action. They received help from Paul Revere, a Boston silversmith who had long provided newspapers with lurid engravings showing British abuses. On September 16 Revere galloped into Philadelphia bearing a copy of resolves drawn up by Bostonians and other residents of Suffolk County. The Suffolk Resolves, as they were called, branded the Coercive Acts as unconstitutional and called for civil disobedience to protest them. The Congress endorsed the resolves, as Adams had hoped. But it would not approve another part of the radicals' agenda—preparing for war by authorizing proposals to strengthen and arm colonial militias.

Thus the First Continental Congress steered a middle course. Although determined to bring about repeal of the Coercive Acts, it held firm in resisting any revolutionary course of action. If British officials had responded to its recommendations and restored the status quo of 1763, the war for independence might have been postponed—perhaps indefinitely. However, even though the Congress did not go to the extremes urged by the radicals, its decisions drew colonials farther down the road to independence.

## The Last Days of the British Empire in America >>

Most colonials applauded the achievements of the First Continental Congress. They expected that the Association would bring about a speedy repeal of the Coercive Acts. But fear that the colonies were moving toward a break with Britain led others to denounce the doings of the Congress. Conservatives were convinced that if independence were declared, chaos would ensue. Colonials, they argued, would quarrel over land claims and sectional tensions and religious differences, as they had so often in the recent past. Without Britain to referee such disputes, they feared, the result would be civil war, followed by anarchy.

The man in America with the least liking for the Continental Congress sat in the hottest seat in the colonies, that of the governor of Massachusetts. General Thomas Gage watched as royal authority crumbled in Massachusetts and the rebellion spread to other colonies. In June 1774 a desperate Gage dissolved the Massachusetts legislature, only to see it re-form, on its own, into a Provincial Congress. That new body assumed the government of the colony in October and began arming the militia. Gage then started to fortify Boston and pleaded for more troops—only to find his fortifications damaged by saboteurs and his requests for reinforcements ignored by Britain.

Outside Boston, royal authority fared no better. Farmers in western Massachusetts forcibly closed the county courts, turning out royally appointed justices and establishing their own tribunals. Popularly elected committees of inspection charged with enforcing the Association took over towns everywhere in Massachusetts, not only restricting trade but also regulating every aspect of local life. The committees called on townspeople to display civic virtue by renouncing "effeminate" English luxuries such as tea and fine clothing and "corrupt" leisure activities such as dancing, gambling, and racing. The committees also assigned spies to report on any citizen unfriendly to the resistance. "Enemies of American liberty" risked being roundly condemned in public or beaten and pelted with mud and dung by hooting, raucous mobs.

Throughout the other colonies a similar process was under way. During the winter and early spring of 1775 provincial congresses, county conventions, and local committees of inspection were emerging as revolutionary governments, replacing royal authority at every level. As the spectacle unfolded before General Gage, he concluded that only force could subdue the colonies. It would take more than he had at his command, but reinforcements might be on the way. In February 1775 Parliament had approved an address to the king declaring that the colonies were in rebellion.

## The Fighting Begins >>

As spring came to Boston the city waited. A band of artisans, organized as spies and express riders by Paul Revere, watched General Gage and waited for him to act. On April 14 word from Lord North finally arrived: Gage was to seize the leaders of the Provincial Congress, an action that would behead the rebellion, North said. Gage knew better than to believe North—but he also knew that he had to do something.

On the night of April 18 the sexton of Boston's Christ Church hung two lamps from its steeple. It was a signal that British troops had moved out of Boston and were marching toward the arms and ammunition stored by the Provincial Congress in Concord. As the lamps flashed the signal, Revere and a comrade, William Dawes, rode out to arouse the countryside.

When the news of a British march reached Lexington, its Minuteman militia of about 70 farmers, chilled and sleepy, mustered on the Green at the center of the small rural town. Lexington Green lay directly on the road to Concord. About four in the morning 700 British troops massed on the Green, and their commander, Major John Pitcairn, ordered the Lexington militia to disperse. The townsmen, outnumbered and overawed, began to obey. Then a shot rang out—whether the British or the Americans fired first is unknown—and then two volleys burst from the ranks of the redcoats. With a cheer the British set off for Concord, five miles distant, leaving eight Americans dead on Lexington Green.

By dawn hundreds of Minutemen from nearby towns were surging into Concord. The British entered at about seven in the morning and moved, unopposed, toward their target, a house lying across the bridge that spanned the Concord River. While three companies of British soldiers searched for American guns and ammunition, three others, posted on the bridge, had the misfortune to find those American arms—borne by the rebels and being fired with deadly accuracy. By noon the British were retreating to Boston.

The narrow road from Concord to Boston's outskirts became a corridor of carnage. Pursuing Americans fired on the column of fleeing redcoats from the cover of fences and forests. By the end of April 19 the British had sustained 273 casualties; the Americans, 95. It was only the beginning. By evening of the next day some 20,000 New England militia had converged on Boston for a long siege.

## *Common Sense* >>

The bloodshed at Lexington Green and Concord's North Bridge committed colonials to a course of rebellion—and independence. That was the conclusion drawn by Thomas Paine, who urged other Americans to join the rebels.

Paine himself was hardly an American. He was born in England, first apprenticed as a corsetmaker, appointed later

^ Amos Doolittle engraved this scene of retreating British troops after the skirmishes at Lexington and Concord. As the engraving makes clear, American militia took advantage of the stone fences to provide cover as sharpshooters picked off the retreating redcoats.


a tax collector, and fated finally to become midwife to the age of republican revolutions. Paine came to Philadelphia late in 1774, set up as a journalist, and made the American cause his own. "Where liberty is, there is my country," he declared. In January 1776 he wrote a pamphlet to inform colonials of their identity as a distinct people and their destiny as a nation. *Common Sense* enjoyed tremendous popularity and wide circulation, selling 120,000 copies.

After Lexington and Concord Paine wrote, as the imperial crisis passed "from argument to arms, a new era for politics is struck—a new method of thinking has arisen." That new era of politics for Paine was the age of republicanism. He denounced monarchy as a foolish and dangerous form of government, one that violated the dictates of reason as well as the word of the Bible. By ridicule and remorseless argument, he severed the ties of colonial allegiance to the king. *Common Sense* scorned George III as "the Royal Brute of Britain," who had enslaved the chosen people of the new age—the Americans.

Nor did Paine stop there. He rejected the idea that colonials were or should want to be English. The colonies occupied a huge continent an ocean away from the tiny British Isles—clear proof that nature itself had fashioned America for independence. England lay locked in Europe, doomed to the corruption of an Old World. America had been discovered anew to become an "asylum of liberty."

Many Americans had liked being English, but being English hadn't worked. Perhaps that is another way of saying that over the course of nearly two centuries colonial society and politics had evolved in such a way that for Americans an English identity no longer fit.

The radicals in America viewed this change in identity in terms of age-old conspiracies that repeated themselves throughout history. First, the people of a republic were impoverished by costly wars—as the colonists could appreciate after the Seven Years' War. Then the government burdened the people with taxes to pay for those wars—as in the case of the Sugar Act or the Stamp Act or the Townshend duties. Next, those in power stationed a standing army in the country, pretending to protect the people but actually lending military force to their rulers. The rhetoric of the Opposition about ministerial conspiracies gave such talk a fervid quality that, to some modern ears, may seem an exaggeration.

Take away the rhetoric, however, and the argument makes uncomfortable sense. The British administration began its "backwoods" war with France, intending to limit it to the interior of North America. But the war aims of William Pitt—the leader Americans counted as their friend—grew with every victory, turning the conflict into a world war, driving France out of India and attacking Spain's colonies in the Philippines and Cuba. Peace came only once Britain and the major powers had bankrupted their treasuries. Conspiracy may not have been at the heart of the plan. But wars must be paid for. And so began the effort to regulate and bring order to Britain's "ungrateful" colonies.

In America, colonials were ungrateful precisely because their political institutions made the rights of "freeborn

Britons" more available to ordinary citizens than they were in the nation that had created those liberties. Ironically, perhaps most Americans had succeeded *too* well at becoming English, regarding themselves as political equals entitled to basic constitutional freedoms. The imperial crisis made clear that despite all that the English and Americans shared, they stood fundamentally at odds over the distribution of political power. The call to arms at Lexington and Concord made retreat impossible.

On that point Paine was clear. It was the destiny of Americans to be republicans, not monarchists. It was the destiny of Americans to be independent, not subject to British dominion. It was the destiny of Americans to be American, not English. That, according to Thomas Paine, was common sense.

 **REVIEW**

What course of events had occurred by the mid-1770s to transform nonimportation and political protest into organized rebellion?

# CHAPTER SUMMARY

Following its victory in the Seven Years' War Britain adopted policies designed to administer new territories and boost revenue. But these policies provoked a colonial backlash that led ultimately to the Revolutionary War.

- French and Indian forces did well at first during the Seven Years' War, as British policies alienated colonials and Indians alike.
- But William Pitt's reforms galvanized the colonies, won Britain Indian allies, and triumphed over France throughout the continent.
- Partly in response to Pontiac's Rebellion, Britain moderated its Indian policies and, with the Proclamation of 1763, forbade all colonial settlement west of the Appalachians.
- The new measures passed by Parliament in the early 1760s—the Proclamation of 1763, the Sugar Act, the Stamp Act, the Currency Act, and the Quartering Act—were all designed to generate revenue and bind the colonies more closely to the empire.
- These new measures deflated American expectations that they would be treated equally and violated what they held to be their right to consent to taxation, their right to trial by jury, and their right to freedom from standing armies.
- Although Parliament repealed the Stamp Act in the face of colonial protests, it reasserted its authority to tax Americans by passing the Townshend Acts in 1767.
- The Coercive Acts of 1774 led Americans to conclude that British actions in the past decade were part of a plot to enslave Americans by depriving them of property and liberty.
- At the First Continental Congress, delegates resisted both radical demands to mobilize for war and conservative appeals to reach an accommodation. The Congress denied Parliament any authority in the colonies except the right to regulate trade; it also drew up the Continental Association, an agreement to cease all trade with Britain until the Coercive Acts were repealed.
- When General Thomas Gage sent troops from Boston in April 1775 to seize arms being stored at Concord, the first battle of the Revolution took place. By the start of 1776, Thomas Paine found an eager national audience for the argument that independence was only common sense.

## Additional Reading

Fred Anderson, *Crucible of War* (2000), offers a magisterial account of the Seven Years' War; and Colin Calloway, *A Scratch of the Pen* (2006), explores the implications of British victory for American Indians, while Paul Mapp's *The Elusive West* (2011) brilliantly explains the significance of the far west to inter-imperial competition. *The Stamp Act Crisis* (1953) by Edmund S. Morgan and Helen M. Morgan remains the clearest and most vivid portrayal of that defining moment. For American resistance after the Stamp Act, see Pauline Maier, *From Resistance to Revolution* (1972); and to understand that struggle as lived and recalled by a Boston artisan, read Alfred F. Young's engaging book *The Shoemaker and the Tea Party* (1999). Two key interpretations of the logic of revolutionary resistance in Massachusetts and Virginia are Robert Gross, *The Minutemen and Their World* (1976); and Timothy Breen, *Tobacco Culture* (1985).

Bernard Bailyn, *The Ideological Origins of the American Revolution* (1967), remains the classic study of the English Opposition and republican political thought in America. For a more recent exploration, stressing the longstanding nature of republican thinking in America, see Thomas P. Slaughter, *Independence* (2014). T. H. Breen's *The Marketplace of Revolution* (2004) take a very different perspective, emphasizing the importance of economics and consumer sentiment. For biographies of eighteenth-century Americans who led—or opposed—the resistance to Britain, see Pauline Maier, *The Old Revolutionaries* (1980); Bailyn's *The Ordeal of Thomas Hutchinson* (1974); and two biographies of Thomas Paine (both published in 2006): *Thomas Paine and the Promise of America* by Harvey Kaye; and *Thomas Paine: Enlightenment, Revolution, and the Birth of Modern Nations* (2006) by Craig Nelson.

# 7 The American People and the American Revolution

## 1775–1783

CHARLES TOWN
BOSTON

On June 17, 1775, colonials flocked to the rooftops and upper windows of their Boston homes to witness the British attack on Breed's Hill across the water on nearby Charlestown.



## >> An American Story

## "WILL HE FIGHT?"

From a high place somewhere in the city—Beacon Hill, perhaps, or Copse Hill—General Thomas Gage looked down on Boston. Through a spyglass his gaze traveled over the church belfries and steeples, the roofs of brick and white frame houses. Finally he fixed his sights on a figure far in the distance across the Charles River. The man was perched atop a crude fortification on Breed's Hill, an elevation lying just below Bunker Hill on the Charlestown peninsula. Gage took the measure of his enemy: an older man, past middle age, a sword swinging beneath his homespun coat, a broad-brimmed hat shading his eyes. As he passed the spyglass to his ally, an American loyalist, Gage asked Abijah Willard if he knew the man on the fort. Willard peered across the Charles and identified his own brother-in-law, Colonel William Prescott. A veteran of the Seven Years' War, Prescott was now a leader in the rebel army laying siege to Boston.

"Will he fight?" Gage wondered aloud.

"I cannot answer for his men," Willard replied, "but Prescott will fight you to the gates of hell."

Fight they did on June 17, 1775, both William Prescott and his men. The evening before, three regiments had followed the colonel from Cambridge to Breed's Hill—soldiers drawn from the thousands of militia who had surrounded British-occupied Boston after the bloodshed at Lexington and Concord. Through the night they dug trenches and built up high earthen walls atop the hill. At the first light of day a British warship spotted the new rebel outpost and opened fire. By noon barges were ferrying British troops under Major General William Howe across the half mile of river that separated Boston from Charlestown. The 1,600 raw rebel troops tensed at the sight of scarlet-coated soldiers streaming ashore, glittering bayonets grasped at the ready. The rebels were farmers and artisans, not professional soldiers, and they were frightened out of their wits.

But Prescott and his men held their ground. The British charged Breed's Hill twice, and Howe watched in horror as streams of fire felled his troops. Finally, during the third British frontal assault, the rebels ran out of ammunition and were forced to withdraw. Redcoats poured into the rebel fort, bayoneting its handful of remaining defenders. By nightfall the British had taken Breed's Hill and the rest of the Charlestown peninsula. They had bought a dark triumph at the cost of 228 dead and 800 wounded.

The cost came high in loyalties as well. The fighting on Breed's Hill fed the hatred of Britain that had been building since April. Throughout America preparations for war intensified: militia in every colony mustered; communities stockpiled arms and ammunition. Around Charlestown civilian refugees fled the countryside, abandoning homes and shops set afire by the British shelling of Breed's Hill. "The roads filled with frightened women and children, some in carts with their tattered furniture, others on foot fleeing into the woods," recalled Hannah Winthrop, one of their number.

The bloody, indecisive fight on the Charlestown peninsula known as the Battle of Bunker Hill actually took place on Breed's Hill. And the exchange between Thomas Gage and Abijah Willard that is said to have preceded the battle may not have taken place. But the story has persisted in the folklore of the American Revolution. Whether it really happened or not, the conversation between Gage and Willard raised the question that both sides wanted answered: Were Americans willing to fight for independence from British rule? It was one thing, after all, to oppose the British ministry's policy of taxation. It was another to support a rebellion for which the ultimate price of failure was hanging for treason. And it was another matter entirely for men to wait nervously atop a hill as the seasoned troops of their own "mother country" marched toward them with the intent to kill.

Indeed, the question "Will they fight?" was revolutionary shorthand for a host of other questions concerning how ordinary Americans would react to the tug of loyalties between long-established colonial governments and a long-revered parent nation and monarch. For slaves, the question revolved around their allegiance to masters who spoke of liberty or to their masters' enemies who promised liberation. For those who led the rebels, it was a question of strengthening the resolve of the undecided, coordinating resistance, instilling discipline—translating the will to fight into the ability to do so. And for those who believed the rebellion was a madness whipped up by artful politicians, it was a question of whether to remain silent or risk speaking out, whether to take up arms for the king or flee. All these questions were raised, of necessity, by the act of revolution. But the barrel of a rifle shortened them to a single, pointed question: Will you fight? <<

## THEMATIC TIMELINE

**1775**
Second Continental Congress convenes at Philadelphia; Congress creates the Continental Army; Battle of Bunker Hill

**1776**
Publication of *Common Sense;* British troops evacuate Boston; Declaration of Independence; British occupy New York City, forcing Washington to retreat through New Jersey into Pennsylvania; Washington counterattacks at Battle of Trenton

**1777**
British summer drive to occupy Philadelphia; battles of Brandywine Creek, Germantown; Burgoyne surrenders at Saratoga; Continental Army encamps for winter at Valley Forge

**1778**
France allies with rebel Americans; France and Britain declare war; British shift focus to the South; Savannah falls

**1780**
British occupy Charleston; partisan warfare of Marion, Sumter; rebel victory at King's Mountain, South Carolina; Nathanael Greene takes southern command

**1781**
Engagements at Cowpens, Guilford Courthouse; Cornwallis surrenders at Yorktown

**1783**
Treaty of Paris

The Declaration of Independence announces the American intention to create a new republic. But a significant minority in the colonies are either ambivalent or are outright loyalists who denounce the rebellion.

Washington and his officers work to turn unevenly trained militiamen into disciplined Continental Army soldiers. British and American forces struggle to control major coastal cities—Boston, New York, and Philadelphia—while Washington's army dwindles.

France and Spain secretly aid the rebels; huge shipments of arms and supplies in early 1777 equip the stunning American victory at Saratoga later that year. In 1778 France openly joins the war against Britain, and Spain soon follows.

Forced to fight an international war, Britain concentrates its North American forces in the South. Indians and African Americans are courted by both sides. In 1781, French and American forces defeat the British Army at Yorktown, effectively ending the continental war.

# THE DECISION FOR INDEPENDENCE

The delegates to the Second Continental Congress gathered at Philadelphia on May 10, 1775, just one month after the battles at Lexington and Concord. They had to determine whether independence or reconciliation offered the best way to protect the liberties of their colonies. Yet during the spring and summer of 1775, even strong advocates of independence did not openly seek a separation from Britain. If independence was to be achieved, radicals needed to forge greater agreement among Americans. Moderates and conservatives harbored deep misgivings about independence: they had to be brought along slowly.

**The Second Continental Congress** >> To bring them along, Congress adopted the "Olive Branch Petition" in July 1775, which affirmed American loyalty to George III and asked the king to disavow the policies of his principal ministers. At the same time, Congress issued a declaration denying that the colonies aimed at independence. Yet, less than a month earlier, Congress had authorized the creation of a rebel military force, the **Continental Army**, and had issued paper money to pay for the troops.

**Continental Army** main rebel military force, created by the Second Continental Congress in July 1775 and commanded by George Washington.

A Congress that sued for peace while preparing for war was a puzzle that British politicians did not even try to understand, least of all Lord George Germain. A tough-minded statesman charged with colonial affairs, he was determined to subdue the rebellion by force. George III proved just as stubborn: he refused to receive the Olive Branch Petition. By the end of that year Parliament had shut down all trade with the colonies and had ordered the Royal Navy to seize colonial merchant ships on the high seas. In November 1775 Virginia's royal governor, Lord Dunmore, offered freedom to any slaves who would join the British. During January of the next year he ordered the shelling of Norfolk, Virginia, reducing that town to smoldering rubble.

British belligerence withered the cause of reconciliation within Congress and the colonies. Support for independence gained more momentum from the overwhelming reception of *Common Sense* in January 1776. On June 7 Virginia's Richard Henry Lee offered the motion "that these United Colonies are, and of right ought to be, free and independent States . . . and that all political connection between them and the State of Great Britain is, and ought to be, totally dissolved."

**The Declaration** >> Congress postponed a final vote on Lee's motion until July. Some opposition still lingered among delegates from the middle colonies, and a committee appointed to write a declaration of independence needed time to complete its work. That committee included some of the leading delegates in Congress: John Adams, Benjamin Franklin, Connecticut's Roger Sherman, and New York's Robert Livingston. But the man who did most of the drafting was a young planter and lawyer from western Virginia.

Thomas Jefferson was just 33 years old in the summer of 1776 when he withdrew to his lodgings on the outskirts of Philadelphia, pulled a portable writing desk onto his lap, and wrote the statement that would explain American independence to a "candid world." In the document's brief opening section Jefferson set forth a general justification of revolution that invoked the "self-evident truths" of human equality and "unalienable rights" to "life, liberty, and the pursuit of happiness." These natural rights had been "endowed" to all persons "by their Creator," the Declaration pointed out; thus there was no need to appeal to the narrower claim of the "rights of Englishmen."

While the first part of the Declaration served notice that Americans no longer considered themselves English, its second and longer section denied England any authority in the colonies. In its detailed history of American grievances against the British Empire, the Declaration referred only once to Parliament. Instead, it blamed George III for a "long train of abuses and usurpations" designed to achieve "absolute despotism." Congress adopted the Declaration of Independence on July 4, 1776.

The colonies thus followed the course set by common sense into the storms of independence. To those Britons who took a wide view of their empire, the decision for independence made no sense, and their perplexity is understandable. Since the end of the Seven Years' War Britain had added to its overseas dominion a vast and diverse number of subjects formerly under French rule—Native Americans, French Catholic Canadians, peoples of African descent in the Caribbean. And then there was India: part Hindu, part Muslim, most of it ruled by the East India Company. What better, more efficient way to regulate this sprawling empire than to bring all its parts under the rule of a sovereign Parliament? What other way could the empire endure and prosper—and fend off future challenges from Catholic, monarchical France? British officials took it for granted that colonials could not be granted the same rights as Britons: an

^ This painting, which commemorated the signing of the Declaration of Independence, shows Benjamin Franklin (*seated center*) weighing the consequences of the action he and his colleagues are about to undertake. John Hancock, the president of the Congress, is reported to have remarked, "We must be unanimous; there must be no pulling different ways; we must all hang together." Franklin is said to have rejoined, "Yes, we must indeed all hang together, or most assuredly, we shall all hang separately."

empire firmly based on hierarchy was needed to hold chaos at bay. Most colonial elites agreed with the logic of that position—East India Company officials, Bengal nabobs, Canadian traders and landlords. Only the leading men in Britain's original 13 colonies would not go along.

## American Loyalists >>

But the sentiment for independence was not universal. Those who would not back the rebellion, supporters of the king and Parliament, numbered perhaps one-fifth of the population in 1775. While they proclaimed themselves **"loyalists,"** their rebel opponents dubbed them "Tories." That division made the Revolution a conflict pitting Americans against one another as well as the British.

**loyalists** supporters of the king and Parliament and known to the rebels as "Tories."

Predictably, the king and Parliament commanded the strongest support in colonies that had been wracked by internal strife earlier in the eighteenth century. In New York, New Jersey, and Pennsylvania, tenants who lived on land controlled by proprietors rebelled from time to time over the quitrents they were required to pay their landlords. Tenant riots plagued New Jersey in the 1740s, and New York's Hudson valley manors took up arms in 1757 and more violently in 1766. In the Carolinas, settlers in western counties took matters into their own hands when eastern legislators ignored their needs, serving out vigilante justice in South Carolina and taking over corrupt county courts in North Carolina, in movements known as "the Regulation." These quarrels reignited during the Revolution, with old enemies taking opposite sides. To win support against Carolina's rebels, whose ranks included most wealthy coastal planters, western loyalist leaders played on ordinary settlers' resentments of

Hudson Bay
N
NEWFOUNDLAND
Anticosti I.
St. Pierre and Miquelon (Fr.)
NOVA SCOTIA
Halifax
LOWER CANADA
ME. (MASS.)
L. Superior
UPPER CANADA
N.H.
Boston
MASS.
L. Huron
L. Ontario
NEW YORK
CONN.
L. Michigan
L. Erie
PENNSYLVANIA
N.J.
MD.
DEL.
ATLANTIC OCEAN
VIRGINIA
Bermuda
N.C.
S.C.
SPANISH LOUISIANA
Charleston
GEORGIA
FLORIDA
BAHAMAS
Gulf of Mexico
SPANISH CUBA
Strongly loyalist
Loyalist or neutral Indians
Strongly neutral
Strong support for rebels
Other British territory


## MAP 7.1: PATTERNS OF ALLEGIANCE

Although most New Englanders rallied behind the rebel cause, support for the Revolution was not as widespread in the middle colonies and southern colonies.
*According to the text, what disputes among Americans encouraged loyalism to flourish? Locate these regions on the map.*

privileged easterners. Decades-old grievances also influenced the revolutionary allegiances of former land rioters of New York and New Jersey. If their old landlord opponents opted for the rebel cause, the tenants took up loyalism.

Other influences also fostered allegiance to Britain. Government officials who owed their jobs to the empire, major city merchants who depended on British trade, and Anglicans living outside the South retained strong ties to the parent country. Loyalists were also disproportionately represented among recent emigrants from the British Isles.

Many who took up the king's cause had not lacked sympathy for the resistance. Loyalist leaders such as Joseph Galloway and Daniel Leonard had opposed the Stamp Act in 1765 and disapproved of imperial policy thereafter. It was not until the crisis reached a fever pitch in 1774 that more colonials cast their lot with the king. Worse than British taxation, in their view, was the radicalism of American resistance—the dumping of tea into Boston harbor, the forming of the Association, and the defying of royal authority.

Such acts of defiance touched what was for loyalists the rawest nerve: a deep-seated fear of the divisions and instability of colonial society. Without the British around to maintain order, they warned, differences among Americans would result in civil war. It would take the passage of less than a century for such fears to be borne out by events—the Union divided and the North and South locked in a fratricidal war.

Although a substantial minority, loyalists never became numerous enough anywhere to pose a serious threat to the Revolution. A more formidable threat was posed by the British army. And the greatest threat of all was posed by those very Americans who claimed that they wanted independence. For the question remained: Would they fight?

What were the arguments for and against independence, and how did the advocates for independence prevail?

# THE FIGHTING IN THE NORTH

In the summer of 1775 Americans who wished to remain neutral probably outnumbered either loyalists or rebels. From the standpoint of mere survival, staying neutral made more sense than fighting for independence. Even the most ardent advocates of American rights had reason to harbor doubts, given the odds against the rebel colonists defeating the armed forces of the British Empire.

Perhaps no friend of American liberty saw more clearly how slim the chances of a rebel victory were than George Washington. Yet June of 1775 found him, then 43 years old, attending the deliberations of the Second Continental Congress and dressed—a bit conspicuously—in his officer's uniform. Washington was the most celebrated American veteran of the Seven Years' War who was still young enough to lead a campaign. Better still, as a southerner he could bring his region into what thus far had remained mostly New England's fight. Congress readily appointed him commander in chief of the newly created Continental Army.

**The Two Armies at Bay >>** Thus did Washington find himself, only a month later, looking to bring order to the rebel forces around Boston. He knew he faced a formidable foe, for the king's troops were seasoned professionals. An aristocratic officer corps drilled and disciplined rank-and-file soldiers, men drawn mainly from the bottom of British society, into a savage fighting machine. At the height of the campaign in America, reinforcements brought the number of British troops to 50,000, strengthened by some 30,000 Hessian mercenaries from Germany and the support of half the ships in the British navy, the largest in the world.

Washington was more modest about the army under his command, and he had much to be modest about. At first Congress recruited his fighting force of 16,600 rebel "regulars," the Continental Army, from the ranks of local New England militia bands. Although enlistments swelled briefly during the patriotic enthusiasm of 1775, for the rest of the war Washington's Continentals suffered chronic shortages of men and supplies. Most men preferred to fight instead as members of local militia units, the "irregular" troops who turned out to support the regular army whenever British forces came close to their neighborhoods.

The general reluctance to join the Continental Army created a host of difficulties for its commander and for Congress. Washington could not create an effective fighting force out of militias that mustered occasionally or men who enlisted for short stints in the Continental Army. But his desire for a professional military establishment clashed with the preferences of most republican leaders. They feared standing armies and idealized "citizen-soldiers"—men of selfless civic virtue who would volunteer whenever needed—as the backbone of the common defense.

Only the dwindling number of volunteers gradually overcame republican fears of standing armies. In September 1776 Congress set terms in the Continental Army at a minimum of three years or for the duration of the war and assigned each state to raise a certain number of troops. They offered every man who enlisted in the army a cash bounty and a yearly clothing issue; enlistees for the duration were offered 100 acres of land as well. Still the problem of recruitment persisted. Less than a year later Congress recommended that the states adopt a draft, but Congress had no authority to compel the states to meet their troop quotas.

Even in the summer of 1775, before enlistments fell off, Washington was worried. As his Continentals laid siege to British-occupied Boston, most officers provided no real leadership, and the men under their command shirked their duties. They slipped away from camp at night; they left sentry duty before being relieved; they took potshots at the British; they tolerated filthy conditions in their camps.

**Women and the War** >> While Washington strove to impose discipline on his Continentals, he also attempted, without success, to rid himself of "the Women of the Army." Thousands of poor women, as many as 1 for every 15 soldiers, drifted after the troops. In return for half-rations, they cooked and washed for the men, nursed the wounded, buried the dead, and scavenged the field for clothing and equipment. Necessity mattered more than patriotism, and a great many women attached themselves to the better-supplied British camps. Nonetheless, these women provided indispensable (if often underappreciated) work for Washington's forces, not least by reducing the desertion rate of their male companions.

Other colonial women played more direct roles in the Revolution. Some dressed as men in order to enlist and fight alongside their brothers or husbands. Deborah Sampson of Massachusetts served for nearly a year and a half, protecting her secret even after being shot in battle. Another female soldier, Sally St. Clair, had her gender revealed only when she was killed fighting the British. Still other women achieved fame through their heroic service—women like the daring spy Lydia Darragh, the wartime messenger Deborah Champion, or 25-year-old Margaret Corbin, who was gravely wounded while "manning" cannon after her artillerist husband was shot dead.

Notwithstanding such remarkable stories, the prevailing gender norms of the day meant that the vast majority of colonial women spent the war at the home front. Those with fathers or husbands in the army had to assume responsibility for running farms and businesses, raising children, and protecting their households in wartime. In addition, thousands of women helped to supply the troops by sewing clothing, making blankets, and saving rags and lead weights for bandages and bullets. Others organized relief for the widows and orphans of soldiers, and led protests against merchants who hoarded scarce commodities. Wives and daughters were left to assume the work of husbands and sons while coping with loneliness, anxiety, and grief. Often enough the disruptions, flight, and loss of family members left lasting scars. Two years after she fled before British campaigns into upstate New York, Ann Eliza Bleecker confessed to a friend, "I muse so long on the dead until I am unfit for the company of the living."

**Laying Strategies** >> At the same time that he tried to discipline the Continentals, Washington designed a defensive strategy to compensate for their weakness. To avoid exposing raw rebel troops on "open ground against their Superiors in number and Discipline," he planned to fight the British from strong fortifications. With that aim in mind, in March 1776, Washington barricaded his army on Dorchester Heights, an elevation commanding Boston harbor from the south. That maneuver, which allowed American artillery to fire on enemy warships, confirmed a decision already made by the British to evacuate their entire army from Boston and sail for Halifax, Nova Scotia.

Britain had hoped to reclaim its colonies with a strategy of strangling the resistance in Massachusetts. But by the spring of 1776 they saw clearly that more was required than a show of force against New England. Instead, the situation called for Britain to wage a conventional war in America, capturing major cities and crushing the Continental forces in a decisive battle. Military victory, the British believed, would enable them to restore political control and reestablish imperial authority.

The first target was New York City. General William Howe and Lord George Germain, the British officials now charged with overseeing the war, chose that seaport for its central location and—they hoped—its large loyalist population. Howe's army intended to move from New York City up the Hudson River, meeting with British troops under General Sir Guy Carleton coming south from Canada. Either the British drive would lure Washington into a major engagement, crushing the Continentals or, if unopposed, the British offensive would cut America in two, smothering resistance to the south by isolating New England.

Unfortunately for the British, the strategy was sounder than the men placed in charge of executing it. Concern for preserving manpower addicted General Howe to caution, when daring more would have carried the day. Howe's brother, Admiral Lord Richard Howe, the head of naval operations in America, also stopped short of pressing the British advantage, owing to his personal desire for reconciliation. The reluctance of the Howe brothers to fight became the formula for British frustration in the two years that followed.

**The Campaigns in New York and New Jersey** >> By mid-August of 1776, 32,000 British troops, including 8,000 **Hessians**—the largest expeditionary force of the eighteenth century—faced Washington's army of 23,000, which had marched from Boston to take up positions on Long Island. At dawn on August 22 the Howe brothers launched their offense, pushing the rebel army back across the East River to Manhattan. After lingering on Long Island for a month the Howes again lurched into action, ferrying their forces to Kip's Bay, just a few miles south of Harlem. When the British landed, the handful of rebel defenders at Kip's Bay fled—straight into the towering wrath of Washington, who happened on the scene during the rout. For once the general lost his habitual self-restraint, flogged both officers and men with his riding crop, and came close to being captured himself. But the Howes remained reluctant to hit hard,

**Hessians** German soldiers who fought with the British army during the American Revolution.

occupying New York City but letting Washington's army escape from Manhattan to Westchester County.

Throughout the fall of 1776 General Howe's forces followed as Washington's fled southward across New Jersey. On December 7, the British nipping at their heels, the rebels crossed the Delaware River into Pennsylvania. There Howe stopped, pulling back most of his army to winter in New York City and leaving the Hessians to hold the British line of advance along the New Jersey side of the Delaware River.

Although the retreat through New York and New Jersey had shriveled rebel strength to only 3,000 men, Washington decided that the campaign of 1776 was not over. On a snowy Christmas night, the Continentals floated back across the Delaware, picked their way over roads sleeted with ice, and finally slid into Hessian-held Trenton at eight in the morning. One thousand German soldiers, still recovering from their spirited Christmas celebration and caught completely by surprise, quickly surrendered. Washington's luck held on January 3, 1777, when the Continentals defeated British troops on the outskirts of Princeton, New Jersey.

During the winter of 1776–1777 the British lost more than battles: they alienated the very civilians whose loyalties

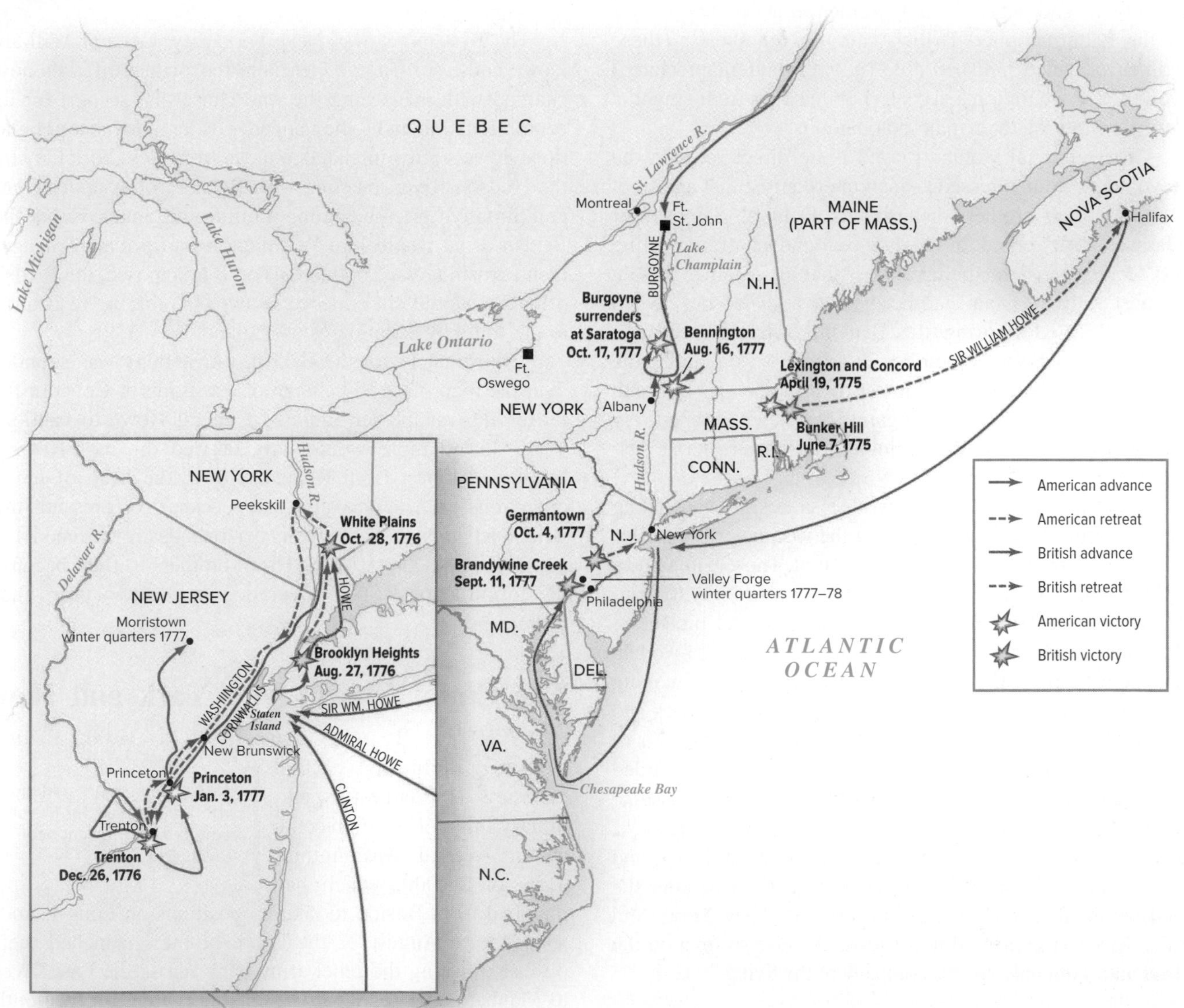

QUEBEC
Lake Michigan
Lake Huron
Lake Ontario
St. Lawrence R.
Montreal
Ft. St. John
Lake Champlain
BURGOYNE
MAINE (PART OF MASS.)
NOVA SCOTIA
Halifax
N.H.
Burgoyne surrenders at Saratoga Oct. 17, 1777
Bennington Aug. 16, 1777
Ft. Oswego
Lexington and Concord April 19, 1775
SIR WILLIAM HOWE
NEW YORK
Albany
MASS.
Bunker Hill June 7, 1775
R.I.
CONN.
Hudson R.
PENNSYLVANIA
Germantown Oct. 4, 1777
N.J.
New York
Brandywine Creek Sept. 11, 1777
Valley Forge winter quarters 1777–78
Philadelphia
MD.
DEL.
ATLANTIC OCEAN
VA.
Chesapeake Bay
N.C.
American advance
American retreat
British advance
British retreat
American victory
British victory
NEW YORK
Peekskill
White Plains Oct. 28, 1776
HOWE
Delaware R.
NEW JERSEY
Morristown winter quarters 1777
Brooklyn Heights Aug. 27, 1776
WASHINGTON
CORNWALLIS
Staten Island
SIR WM. HOWE
ADMIRAL HOWE
New Brunswick
Princeton
Princeton Jan. 3, 1777
CLINTON
Trenton
Trenton Dec. 26, 1776


## MAP 7.2: THE FIGHTING IN THE NORTH, 1775–1777

After the British withdrew from Boston in 1775, they launched an attack on New York City the following year. Washington was forced to retreat northward, then across the Hudson and south into New Jersey and Pennsylvania, before surprising the British at Trenton and Princeton. Burgoyne's surrender at Saratoga in 1777 marked a turning point in the war.

*If General Howe had moved forces toward Albany, could he and General Burgoyne have split rebel New England from the rest of the former colonies? If so, how?*

they had hoped to ensure. In New York City the presence of the main body of the British army brought shortages of food and housing and caused constant friction between soldiers and city dwellers. In the New Jersey countryside still held by the Hessians, the situation was more desperate. Forced to live off the land, the Germans aroused resentment among local farmers by seizing "hay, oats, Indian corn, cattle, and horses, which were never or but very seldom paid for," as one loyalist admitted. The Hessians ransacked and destroyed homes and churches; they kidnapped and raped young women.

**militia** local defense band of civilians comprising men between the ages of 16 and 65 whose military training consisted only of occasional gatherings known as musters.

Many neutrals and loyalists who had had enough of the king's soldiers now took their allegiance elsewhere. Bands of **militia** on Long Island, along the Hudson River, and all over New Jersey rallied to support the Continentals.

**Capturing Philadelphia** >> By the summer of 1777 General Howe had decided to goad the Americans into battle by capturing Philadelphia. In early August the redcoats disembarked on the Maryland shore and headed for Philadelphia. Washington engaged Howe twice—in September at Brandywine Creek and in October in an early dawn attack at Germantown—but both times the rebels were beaten back. He had been unable to prevent the British occupation of Philadelphia.

But in Philadelphia, as in New York, British occupation created hostility as the flood of troops jacked up prices for food, fuel, and housing. Philadelphians complained of redcoats looting their shops, trampling their gardens, and harassing them on the streets.

Even worse, the British march through Maryland and Pennsylvania had outraged civilians, who fled before the army and then returned to find their homes and barns bare, their crops and livestock gone. Everywhere Howe's men went in the middle states, they left in their wake Americans with compelling reasons to support the rebels. Worst of all, just days after Howe marched his occupying army into Philadelphia in the fall of 1777, another British commander in North America surrendered his entire army to rebel forces at Saratoga, New York.

**Disaster for the British at Saratoga** >> The calamity that befell the British at Saratoga was the doing of a glory-mongering general, John "Gentleman Johnny" Burgoyne. After his superior officer, Sir Guy Carleton, bungled a drive into New York in 1776, Burgoyne won approval to command another attack from Canada. The following summer he set out from Quebec with a force of 9,500 redcoats, 2,000 women and children, and a baggage train that included the commander's silver dining service, his dress uniforms, and numerous cases of champagne. As Burgoyne's bloated entourage lumbered southward, General Horatio Gates waited for it several miles below Saratoga at Bemis Heights, with an army more than 12,000 men strong.

On September 19 Gates's rebel scouts, nested high in the trees, spied the glittering bayonets of Burgoyne's approaching force. Benedict Arnold, a brave and brilliant young officer, led 3,000 rebels into battle at a clearing at Freeman's Farm. After several bloody hours, British reinforcements finally pushed the rebels back from a battlefield piled high corpses. Burgoyne regrouped and a few weeks later tried to flee to Canada. But he got no farther than Saratoga, where he was forced to surrender his army to Gates on October 17.

Saratoga shifted the war. Burgoyne's surrender helped convince France that, with the right assistance, the Americans might well reap the fruits of victory.

 REVIEW

What challenges did the Continental Army face between 1775 and 1777?

# THE TURNING POINT

France had been waiting for an opportunity to humble Britain ever since being throttled in the Seven Years' War. Now the French foreign minister, Charles Gravier de Vergennes, took great interest in the drama unfolding across the Atlantic, and patiently worked to turn it to his advantage.

**The American Revolution as a Global War** >> Victory in the Seven Years' War had helped make Britain the mightiest military and commercial power in the world. Vergennes saw that if it lost most of its North American colonies, Britain would be cut back down to size, restoring a more favorable balance of power. Though France was building ships as a furious pace, in 1775 it didn't yet have a navy big enough for outright war. If Vergennes was going to help the rebels he first had to do so quietly.

Initially, French authorities helped by simply looking the other way when rebel smugglers tried to buy guns and ammunition in their ports. The North Americans had no arms industry to speak of, so the rebellion totally depended on foreign imports. Painfully aware of this fact, the Continental Congress dispatched representatives to Europe, led by the resourceful Benjamin Franklin, in order to make arms deals and woo potential allies. Before long Vergennes convinced Spain to cooperate in a massive, covert supply program, jointly providing the Americans huge cash loans, desperately needed supplies, hundreds of tons of gunpowder, tens of thousands of muskets. The victory at Saratoga was won with French muskets, and, with the Navy nearly rebuilt, it helped Vergennes convince his cautious young king that the time had come for a formal alliance with the rebels against Britain.

France signed treaties of commerce, friendship, and alliance with America in early 1778; Congress eagerly approved them in May. Less than a year later Spain joined France, and by 1780 friendless Britain was at war with the Dutch, too.

**Winding Down the War in the North** >> So it was that the Revolution widened into a global war after 1778. Preparing to fight France, Spain, and eventually Holland forced the British to divert resources and men from North America in order to fend off challenges all over the world. In May Sir Henry Clinton replaced William Howe as commander in chief and received orders to withdraw from Philadelphia to New York City.

Only 18 miles outside Philadelphia, at Valley Forge, Washington and his Continentals were assessing their own situation. Some 11,000 rebel soldiers had passed a harrowing winter in that isolated spot, starving for want of food, freezing for lack of clothing, huddling in miserable huts, and hating the British who lay 18 miles away in the warmer quarters of Philadelphia. The army also cursed their fellow citizens, for its misery resulted from congressional disorganization and civilian indifference. Congress lacked both money to pay and maintain the army and an efficient system for dispensing provisions to the troops. Most farmers and merchants preferred to supply the British, who could pay handsomely, than to do business with financially strapped Congress. What little did reach the army often was food too rancid to eat or clothing too rotten to wear. Perhaps 2,500 perished at Valley Forge, the victims of cold, hunger, and disease.

Why did civilians who supported the rebel cause allow the army to suffer? Probably because by the winter of 1777 the Continentals came mainly from social classes that received little consideration at any time. The respectable, propertied farmers and artisans who had laid siege to Boston in 1775 had stopped enlisting. Serving in their stead were single men in their teens and early 20s, some who joined the army out of desperation, others who were drafted, still others who were hired as substitutes for the affluent. The landless sons of farmers, unemployed laborers, drifters, petty criminals, vagrants, indentured servants, slaves, even captured British and Hessian soldiers—all men with no other means and no other choice—were swept into the Continental Army. The social composition of the rebel rank and file had come to resemble that of the British army. It is the great irony of the Revolution: a war to protect liberty and property was waged by those Americans who were poorest and least free.

The beginning of spring in 1778 brought a reprieve. Supplies arrived at Valley Forge, and so did a fellow calling himself Baron von Steuben, a penniless Prussian soldier of fortune. Although Washington's men had shown spirit and resilience ever since Trenton, they still lacked discipline and training. Those defects and more von Steuben began to remedy. Barking orders and spewing curses in German and French, the baron (and his translators) drilled the rebel regiments to march in formation and to handle their bayonets like proper Prussian soldiers. By the summer of 1778 morale had rebounded.

Spoiling for action after their long winter, Washington's army, now numbering nearly 13,500, harassed Clinton's army as it marched overland from Philadelphia to New York. On June 28 at Monmouth Courthouse, a long, confused battle ended in a draw. After both armies retired for the night,

A VIEW IN AMERICA IN 1778

<< A member of the Continental Congress (*center*) refuses to look at the sufferings of cold, poorly clad white soldiers and a wounded African American fallen to the ground. Why would the British have published such a cartoon in 1778? What messages are conveyed? Source: Library of Congress, Prints and Photographs Division [LC-USZ62-46659]

THE ALLIES.— Par nobile Fratrum!
Qui facit per alium, facit per se.

<< While both sides in the Revolution sought Indian allies, the American rebels sensationalized the efforts of British leaders to enlist Native Americans. Stories and images featuring British and Indian cruelty to American victims stirred debate even back in Britain. In this 1780 cartoon printed in London, the prime minister, Lord North, joins with Indians in feasting on a child, an act of cannibalism that revolts even a dog. The archbishop of York approaches, hypocritically promising to make God's ways "known upon Earth" as his porter, professing that "we are hellish good Christians," carries boxes of scalping knives, tomahawks, and crucifixes. This propaganda fueled the hatred of Indians by Americans who expanded westward after the Revolution.

Source: Library of Congress, Prints and Photographs Division [LC-DIG-ppmsca-19864]

Clinton's forces slipped away to safety in New York City. Washington pursued, but he lacked the numbers to launch an all-out assault on New York City.

During the two hard winters that followed, resentments mounted among the rank and file over spoiled food, inadequate clothing, and arrears in pay. The army retaliated with **mutinies**. Between 1779 and 1780, officers managed to quell uprisings in three New England regiments. But in January 1781 both the Pennsylvania and the New Jersey lines mutinied outright and marched on Philadelphia, where Congress had reconvened. Order returned only after Congress promised back pay and provisions and Washington put two ringleaders in front of a firing squad.

**mutiny** refusal of rank-and-file soldiers to follow the commands of their superior officers.

**War in the West** >> The battles between Washington's Continentals and the British made the war in the West seem, by comparison, a sideshow of attacks and counterattacks that settled little. American fighters, such as George Rogers Clark, captured outposts such as Kaskaskia and Vincennes without materially affecting the outcome of the war. Yet the conflict sparked a tremendous upheaval in the West, both from the dislocations of war and from the disease that spread in war's wake.

The disruptions were so widespread because the "War for Independence" had also become a war involving the imperial powers of Britain, France, and Spain. Those European powers and the United States pressed Indian tribes to become allies and attacked them when they did not. Caught in the crossfire, some Indian nations were pushed to the brink of their own civil war, splitting into pro-American or pro-British factions.

Indians understood that the pressures of war always threatened to deprive them of their homelands. "You are drawing so close to us that we can almost hear the noise of your axes felling our Trees," one Shawnee told the Americans. Thousands fled the raids and counter-raids, while whole villages relocated. Hundreds made their way even beyond the Mississippi, to seek shelter in territory claimed by Spain.

The political instability was vastly compounded by a smallpox epidemic that broke out first among American troops besieging Quebec in 1775. The disease soon spread to Washington's troops in New England and then south along the coast; it eventually reached New Orleans and leapt to Mexico City by the autumn of 1779. From New Orleans it spread via fur traders up the Mississippi River and across the central plains, and from New Spain northward as well. By the time the pandemic burned out in 1782, it had felled over 130,000. By contrast, the Revolutionary War caused the deaths of some 8,000 soldiers while fighting in battle and another 13,000 from disease, including the mortality from smallpox.

 **REVIEW**

How did the Revolution become a global war, and what were conditions like for both soldiers and civilians?

# THE STRUGGLE IN THE SOUTH

By the autumn of 1778 the British had come to believe that their most vital aim was to regain their colonies in the mainland South. The Chesapeake and the Carolinas were more profitable to the empire and more strategically important, being so much closer to rich British sugar islands in the West Indies. Inspired by this new "southern strategy," Clinton dispatched forces to the Caribbean and Florida. In addition, the British laid plans for a new offensive drive into the Carolinas and Virginia.

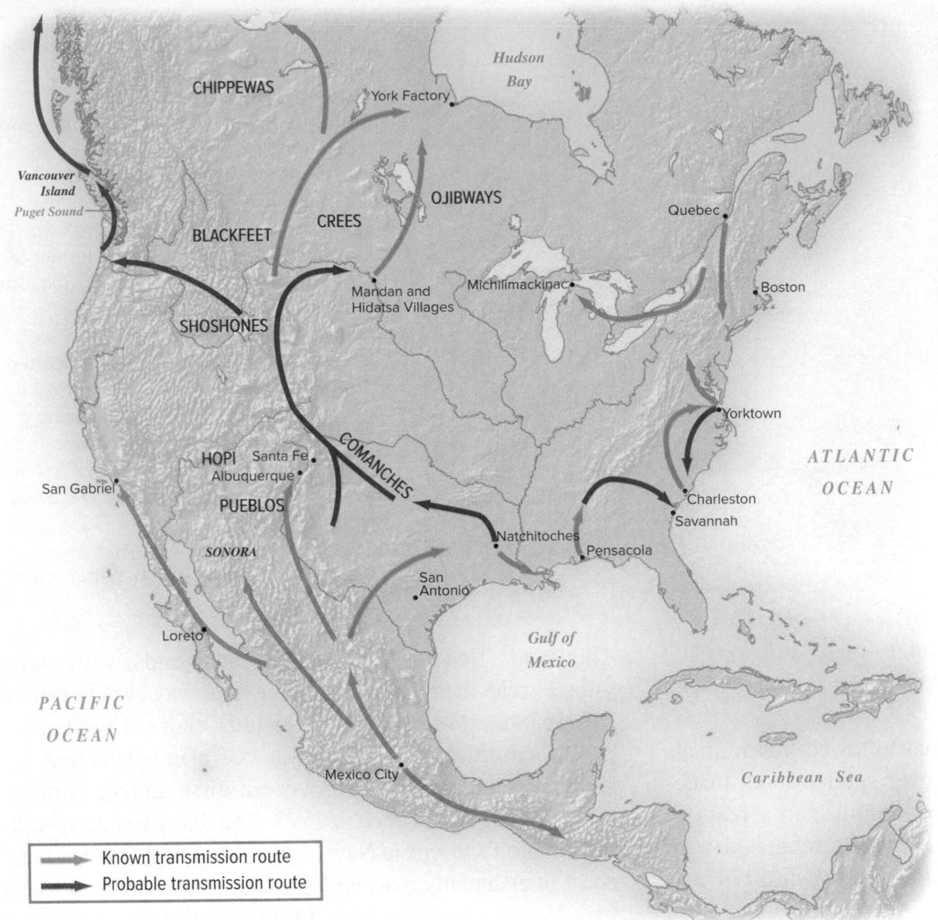

Hudson Bay
CHIPPEWAS
York Factory
Vancouver Island
Puget Sound
OJIBWAYS
CREES
BLACKFEET
Quebec
Boston
Mandan and Hidatsa Villages
Michilimackinac
SHOSHONES
Yorktown
ATLANTIC OCEAN
HOPI
Santa Fe
Albuquerque
COMANCHES
San Gabriel
PUEBLOS
Charleston
Savannah
Natchitoches
Pensacola
SONORA
San Antonio
Loreto
Gulf of Mexico
PACIFIC OCEAN
Mexico City
Caribbean Sea
Known transmission route
Probable transmission route


## MAP 7.3: THE SMALLPOX PANDEMIC, 1775–1782

Smallpox spread across North America beginning late in 1775 as American forces attacked the city of Quebec in Canada. The routes of transmission give only a rough idea of the disease's impact, as it moved down the eastern seaboard and around the Gulf of Mexico, and then penetrated the interior, where the scattered surviving data make the pandemic harder to track. But the ravages of smallpox, combined with the disruptions sparked by the western raids of the Revolutionary War, placed severe stress on Indian peoples all across the continent.

*How can you tell that smallpox was a European disease? Where are the two major points from which the disease first spreads?*

English politicians and generals believed that the war could be won in the South. Loyalists were numerous, they believed, especially in the backcountry, where resentment of the seaboard, a rebel stronghold, would breed readiness among frontier folk to take up arms for the king at the first show of British force. And southern rebels—especially the vulnerable planters along the coast—could not afford to turn their guns away from their slaves. So, at least, the British theorized. All that was needed, they concluded, was for the British army to establish a beachhead in the South and then, in league with loyalists, drive northward, pacifying the population while pressing up the coast.

**The Siege of Charleston** >> The southern strategy worked well for a short time in a small place. In November 1778 Clinton sent 3,500 troops to Savannah, Georgia. The resistance in the tiny colony quickly collapsed, and a large number of loyalists turned out to help the British. Encouraged by that success, the British moved on to South Carolina.

During the last days of 1779 an expedition under Clinton himself set sail from New York City. Landing off the Georgia coast, his troops mucked through the swamps to the peninsula lying between the Ashley and Cooper Rivers. At the tip of that neck of land stood Charleston, and the British began to lay siege. By then an unseasonably warm spring had set in, making the area a heaven for mosquitoes and a hell for human beings. Sweltering and swatting, redcoats weighted down in their woolen uniforms inched their siegeworks toward the city. By early May Clinton's army had closed in, and British shelling was setting fire to houses within the city. On May 12 Charleston surrendered.

Clinton sailed back to New York at the end of June 1780, leaving behind 8,300 redcoats to carry the British offensive northward to Virginia. The man charged with leading that campaign was his ambitious and able subordinate Charles, Lord Cornwallis.

**The Partisan Struggle in the South** >> Cornwallis's task in the Carolinas was complicated by the bitter animosity between rebels and loyalists there. Many Carolinians had taken sides years before Clinton's conquest of Charleston. In the summer and fall of 1775 the supporters of Congress and the new South Carolina revolutionary government mobbed, tortured, and imprisoned supporters of the king in the backcountry. These attacks only hardened loyalist resolve: roving bands seized ammunition, broke their leaders out of jail, and besieged rebel outposts. But within a matter of months, a combined force of rebel militias from the coast and the frontier managed to defeat loyalist forces in the backcountry.

With the fall of Charleston in 1780 the loyalist movement on the frontier returned to life. Out of loyalist vengefulness and rebel desperation issued the brutal civil war that seared the southern backcountry after 1780. Neighbors and even family members fought and killed one another as members of roaming rebel and Tory militias. The intensity of **partisan warfare** in the backcountry produced unprecedented destruction. All of society, observed one minister, "seems to be at an end. Every person keeps close on his own plantation. Robberies and murders are often committed on the public roads. . . . Poverty, want, and hardship appear in almost every countenance."

**partisan warfare** armed clashes among political rivals, typically involving guerrilla fighting and the violent intimidation of civilians by militias.

Cornwallis, when confronted with the chaos, erred fatally. He did nothing to stop his loyalist allies or his own troops from mistreating civilians. A Carolina loyalist admitted that "the lower sort of People, who were in many parts originally attached to the British Government, have suffered so severely . . . that Great Britain has now a hundred enemies, where it had one before."

A growing number of civilians outraged by the king's men cast their lot with the rebels. That upsurge of popular support enabled Francis Marion, the "Swamp Fox," and his band of white and black raiders to cut British lines of communication between Charleston and the interior. It mobilized the "over-the-mountain men," a rebel militia in western Carolina, who claimed victory at the Battle of King's Mountain in October 1780. By the end of 1780 these successes had persuaded most civilians that only the rebels could restore order.

If rebel fortunes prospered in the partisan struggle, they faltered in the conventional warfare being waged at the same time in the South. In August 1780 the Continentals commanded by Horatio Gates lost a major engagement to the British force at Camden, South Carolina. In the fall of 1780 Congress replaced Gates with Washington's candidate for the southern command, Nathanael Greene, an energetic, 38-year-old Rhode Islander and a veteran of the northern campaigns.

**Greene Takes Command** >> Greene bore out Washington's confidence by grasping the military situation in the South. He understood the needs of his 1,400 hungry, ragged, and demoralized troops and instructed von Steuben to lobby Virginia for food and clothing. He understood the importance of the rebel militias and sent Lieutenant Colonel Henry "Light Horse Harry" Lee to assist Marion's raids. He understood the weariness of southern civilians and prevented his men from plundering the countryside.

Above all, Greene understood that his forces could never hold the field against the whole British army. That led him to break the first rule of conventional warfare: he divided his army. In December 1780 he dispatched to western South Carolina a detachment of 600 men under the command of Brigadier General Daniel Morgan of Virginia.

Back at the British camp Cornwallis worried that Morgan and his rebels, if left unchecked, might rally the entire backcountry against the British. However, Cornwallis reckoned that he could not commit his entire army to the pursuit of Morgan's men, for then Greene and his troops might retake Charleston. The only solution, unconventional to be sure, was for Cornwallis to divide his army. That he did, sending Lieutenant Colonel Banastre Tarleton and 1,100 men west after Morgan. Cornwallis had played right into Greene's hands: the rebel troops might be able to defeat a British army split into two pieces. For two weeks Morgan led Tarleton's troops on a breakneck chase across the Carolina countryside. In January 1781 at an open meadow called Cowpens, Morgan routed Tarleton's force.

Now Cornwallis took up the chase. Morgan and Greene joined forces and agreed to keep going north until the British army wore out. Cornwallis finally stopped at Hillsboro, North Carolina, but few local loyalists responded to his call for reinforcements. To ensure that loyalist ranks remained thin, Greene decided to make a show of force near the tiny village of Guilford Courthouse. On a brisk March day the two sides joined battle, each sustaining severe casualties before Greene was forced to retreat. But the high cost of victory convinced Cornwallis that he could not put down the rebellion in the Carolinas.

Although Nathanael Greene's command provided the Continentals with effective leadership in the South, it was the resilience of rebel militias that thwarted the British offensive in the Carolinas. Many Continental Army officers complained about the militia's lack of discipline, its habit of melting away when homesickness set in or harvest approached, and its record of cowardice under fire in conventional engagements. But when set the task of ambushing supply trains and dispatch riders, harrying bands of local loyalists, or making forays against isolated British outposts, the militia came through. Many southern civilians refused to join the British or to provide the redcoats with food and information because they knew that once the British army left their neighborhoods, the rebel militia would always be back. The Continental Army in the South lost many conventional battles, but the militia kept the British from restoring political control over the backcountry.

**African Americans in the Age of Revolution** >> The British also lost in the Carolinas because they did not seek greater support from those southerners who would have fought for liberty with the British: African American slaves.

American forces
American victory
British victory
Major skirmishes of the partisan conflict in the backcountry
VIRGINIA
Richmond
Yorktown
Chesapeake Bay
Roanoke R.
Guilford Courthouse
Mar. 15, 1781
Hillsboro
NORTH CAROLINA
Salisbury
Pee Dee R.
Neuse R.
Kings Mountain
Oct. 7, 1780
Cowpens
Jan. 17, 1781
Cheraw
Cape Fear R.
Winnsboro
Camden
Aug. 16, 1780
ATLANTIC
OCEAN
SOUTH CAROLINA
Savannah R.
Eutaw Springs
Sept. 8, 1781
Charleston
May 12, 1780
GEORGIA
Savannah

## MAP 7.4: THE FIGHTING IN THE SOUTH, 1780–1781

In December 1780 Nathanael Greene made the crucial decision to split his army, sending Daniel Morgan west, where he defeated the pursuing Banastre Tarleton at Cowpens. Meanwhile, Greene regrouped and replenished at Cheraw, keeping Cornwallis off balance with a raid (*dotted line*) toward Charleston and the coast. Then, with Cornwallis in hot pursuit, Greene and Morgan rejoined at Salisbury, retreating into Virginia. Cornwallis was worn down in this vain pursuit and lost three-quarters of the troops he began with before finally abandoning the Carolina campaign.
*What was General Nathanael Greene's risky strategy, according to the text? And how does the map show that strategy?*

Black Americans, virtually all in bondage, made up one-third of the population between Delaware and Georgia. Since the beginning of the resistance to Britain, white southerners had worried that the watchwords of liberty and equality would spread to the slave quarters. Gripped by the fear of slave rebellion, southern revolutionaries began to take precautions. Marylanders disarmed black inhabitants and issued extra guns to the white militia. Charlestonians hanged and then burned the body of Thomas Jeremiah, a free black who was convicted of spreading the word to others that the British "were coming to help the poor Negroes."

Southern whites fully expected the British to turn slave rebelliousness to their strategic advantage. As early as 1775 Virginia's royal governor, Lord Dunmore, confirmed white fears by offering to free any slave who joined the British. When Clinton invaded the South in 1779 he renewed that offer. According to Janet Schaw, an Englishwoman visiting her brother's North Carolina plantation, the neighbors had heard that loyalists were "promising every Negro that would murder his master and family he should have his Master's plantation" and that "the Negroes have got it amongst them and believe it to be true."

But in Britain there was overwhelming opposition to organizing support among African Americans. British leaders dismissed Dunmore's ambitious scheme to raise a black army of 10,000 and another plan to create a sanctuary for black loyalists on the southeastern coast. Turning slaves against masters, they recognized, was not the way to retain the support of white southern loyalists.

Even so, southern fears of insurrection made the rebels reluctant to enlist black Americans as soldiers. At first, Congress barred African Americans from the Continental Army. But as the rebels became more desperate for manpower, policy changed. Northern states actively encouraged black enlistments, and in the Upper South, some states allowed free men of color to join the army or permitted slaves to substitute for their masters.

Slaves themselves sought freedom from whichever side seemed most likely to grant it. Perhaps 10,000 slaves took up Dunmore's offer in 1775 and deserted their masters, and thousands more flocked to Clinton's forces after the fall of Charleston.

For many runaways the hope of liberation proved an illusion. Although some served the British army as laborers, spies, and soldiers, many died of disease in army camps (upward of 27,000 by one estimate) or were sold back into slavery in the West Indies. About 5,000 black soldiers served in the Revolutionary army in the hope of gaining freedom. In addition, the number of runaways to the North soared during the Revolution. In total perhaps 100,000 men and women—nearly a fifth of the total slave population—attempted to escape bondage. Their odysseys to freedom took some to far-flung destinations: loyalist communities in Nova Scotia, a settlement established by the British in Sierra Leone on the West African coast, even the Botany Bay penal colony in Australia.

**REVIEW**

Why did the British fail to achieve their military and political goals in the South?

# Historian's TOOLBOX

## Runaways

**What is implied by the tallying of children ["girls" and "boys"] with slave women?**

**What is the significance of the list specifying occupations for some of the slave men?**

A List of Negroes that went off to Dunmore April 14th 1776

| Women | Ages | Girls | Boys |
|---|---|---|---|
| Planant | 55 | 1 | |
| Nancy | 46 | 4 | |
| Marcy | 30 | 2 | 1 |
| Judey | 28 | 3 | 2 |
| Lucey | 25 | 1 | 5 |
| Keziah | 23 | | 3 |
| Cate | 30 | 2 | 1 |
| Rachell | 25 | | 4 |
| Easter | 27 | | 6 |
| Betsie | 23 | 1 | |
| Jeney | 42 | | |
| Lindah | 27 | 2 | 2 |
| Manda | 25 | | 5 |
| Dynah | 26 | 2 | |
| Lidia | 26 | 2 | 1 |
| Aby | 29 | | 3 |
| Bess | 23 | 1 | |
| Jeney | 30 | | |
| Joice | 16 | | |

| Negro Men | Ages |
|---|---|
| Isaac a Sawyer | 60 |
| Toby Do. | 54 |
| Ned | 44 |
| Peter a house Carpenter | 37 |
| James a Shoemaker | 35 |
| Robin a Sawyer | 25 |
| Bob | 30 |
| Charles | 24 |
| Glascow | 21 |
| Will | 21 |
| Anthony | 19 |
| George | 18 |
| Jacob | 20 |
| Isack | 16 |

Total 87

Entailed.

| | Ages | Girls |
|---|---|---|
| Nell | 25 | 2 |
| Pegg | 18 | |

| | Ages |
|---|---|
| Bristow a Sawyer | 25 |
| Moses a house Carpt. | 25 |

Bill 5

Fee Simple

| Women | Girls | Boys | Men |
|---|---|---|---|
| 21 | 23 | 27 | 16 |

Jno. Willoughby

**How does the number of female runaways compare with that of males? Children with adults?**

*"A List of Negroes That Went Off to Dunmore," dated April 14, 1776, Library of Virginia, Richmond.*
*A list of negroes who went off to Dunmore, Norfolk Co, 3 June 1777.* Courtesy of the Library of Virginia

Americans in earlier centuries were inveterate listmakers, providing present-day historians with a rich trove of evidence. College students recorded the titles of books they read; ministers noted the Bible passages on which they preached; clerks kept count of church members; tax assessors enumerated household members and the rates owed and paid; probate court officers inventoried the possessions of the dead, often down to chipped crockery and broken tools. But the roster of slaves shown above is an extraordinary list, drawn up not on account of their master's death but because these 87 men, women, and children had fled their Virginia plantation, emboldened by Lord Dunmore's promise of freedom. It is impossible to know whether they ran away in small groups, stealing off over a period of several months between 1775 and 1776, or whether they ran away in larger companies within the space of a few days. But we do know that throughout Virginia, as on this plantation, women and children made up a significant percentage of the runaways.

### THINKING CRITICALLY

*For what purposes might the Virginia master have composed this list? Why are slave artisans so well represented among the men on this list? Why were slave women and their children willing to risk escape in such large numbers?*

# THE WORLD TURNED UPSIDE DOWN

Despite his losses in the Carolinas, Cornwallis still believed that he could score a decisive victory against the Continental Army. The theater he chose for that showdown was the Chesapeake. During the spring of 1781 he and his army joined forces along the Virginia coast with the hero of Saratoga, who had newly turned loyalist, Benedict Arnold. Embarrassed by debt and disgusted by Congress's shabby treatment of the Continental Army, Arnold had started exchanging rebel secrets for British money in 1779 before defecting outright in 1780. By June of 1781 Arnold and Cornwallis were fortifying a site on the tip of the peninsula formed by the York and James Rivers, a place called Yorktown.

Meanwhile, Washington and his French ally, the comte de Rochambeau, met in Connecticut to plan a major attack. Rochambeau urged a coordinated land-sea assault on the Virginia coast. Washington insisted instead on a full-scale offensive against New York City. Just when the rebel commander was about to have his way, word arrived that a French fleet under the comte de Grasse was sailing for the Chesapeake to blockade Cornwallis by sea. Washington's Continentals headed south.

**Surrender at Yorktown** >> By the end of September, 7,800 Frenchmen, 5,700 Continentals, and 3,200 militia had sandwiched Yorktown between the devil of an allied army and the deep blue sea of French warships. "If you cannot relieve me very soon," Cornwallis wrote to Clinton, "you must expect to hear the worst." The British navy did arrive—but seven days *after* Cornwallis surrendered his 9,000-man army to the rebels on October 19, 1781.

It need not have ended at Yorktown, but timing made all the difference. At the end of 1781 and early in 1782 the British army received setbacks in the other theaters of the war: India, the West Indies, and Florida. The French and the Spanish were everywhere in Europe as well,

Reddition de l'Armée Angloises Commandée par Mylord Comte de Cornwallis aux Armees Combinées des Etats unis de l'Amerique et de France aux ordres des Generaux Washington et de Rochambeau a Yorck touwn et Glocester dans la Virginie. le 19 Octobre 1781. Il s'est trouvés dans ses deux postes 6000 hommes de troupes reglées Angloises ou Hessoises et 22 Drapeaux 1500 Matelots 160 Canons de tout Calibre dont 75 de Fonte 8 Mortiers 40 Batimens dont un Vaisseau de 50 Canons qui a été Brulé 20 Coulés Bas; Ce jour a jamais memorables pour les Etats unis en ce qu'il assura definitivement leurs indépendances
A. Yorck Touwn
B. Glocester
C. Armées Angloise sortant de la place
D. Les Armes des ennemis posée en Faisceaux
E. Armée Francoise
F. Armée Americaine
G. Armée naval de France aux Ordres du Comte de Grace
H. Baye de Chesapeack
I. Riviere d'Yorck
^ The British surrender. Unlike some illustrations, this French engraving shows the key role played by French naval forces under the command of Admiral de Grasse. The normally dignified Washington understood well that the French navy would prove crucial in trapping Cornwallis, but when he received word that the French had appeared in Chesapeake Bay, he waved a handkerchief in one hand and his hat in the other, calling out "de Grasse!" to a comrade with "the greatest joy."
Source: Library of Congress, Geography and Map Division [G3884.Y6S3 1781 .M6 Vault]

gathering in the English Channel, planning a major offensive against Gibraltar. The cost of the fighting was already enormous. British leaders recognized that the rest of the empire was at stake and set about cutting their losses in America.

The Treaty of Paris, signed on September 3, 1783, was a diplomatic triumph for the American negotiators: Benjamin Franklin, John Adams, and John Jay. They dangled before Britain the possibility that a generous settlement might weaken American ties to France. The British jumped at the bait. They recognized the independence of the United States and agreed to ample boundaries for the new nation: the Mississippi River on the west, the 31st parallel on the south, and the present border of Canada on the north. American negotiators then persuaded a skeptical France to approve the treaty by arguing that, as allies, they were bound to present a united front to the British. When the French finally persuaded Spain, the third member of the alliance, to reduce its demands on Britain for territorial concessions, the treaty became an accomplished fact. The Spanish settled for Florida and Minorca, an island in the Mediterranean.

Those present at Yorktown on that clear autumn afternoon in 1781 watched as the British second-in-command to Cornwallis (who had sent word that he was "indisposed") surrendered his superior's sword. He offered the sword first, in a face-saving gesture, to the French commander Rochambeau, who politely refused and pointed to Washington. But the American commander in chief, out of a mixture of military protocol, nationalistic pride, and perhaps even wit, pointed to his second-in-command, Benjamin Lincoln.

**REVIEW**

How did the United States manage to prevail in the war and in the treaty negotiations?

Some witnesses recalled that British musicians arrayed on the Yorktown green played "The World Turned Upside Down." Their recollections may have been faulty, but the story has persisted as part of the folklore of the American Revolution. The world had, it seemed, turned upside down with the coming of American independence. The colonial rebels shocked the British with their answer to the question "Would they fight?"

The answer had been yes—but on their own terms. By 1777 most propertied Americans avoided fighting in the Continental Army. Yet whenever the war reached their homes, farms, and businesses, many Americans gave their allegiance to the new nation by turning out with rifles or supplying homespun clothing, food, or ammunition. They rallied around Washington in New Jersey, Gates in upstate New York, Greene in the Carolinas. Middle-class American men fought, some from idealism, others out of self-interest, but always on their own terms, as members of the militia. These citizen-soldiers turned the world upside down by defeating professional armies.

Of course, the militia did not bear the brunt of the fighting. That responsibility fell to the Continental Army, which by 1777 drew its strength from the poorest ranks of American society. Yet even the Continentals, for all their desperation, managed to fight on their own terms. Some asserted their rights by raising mutinies, until Congress redressed their grievances. All of them, as the Baron von Steuben observed, behaved differently than European soldiers did. Americans followed orders only if the logic of commands was explained to them. The Continentals, held in contempt by most Americans, turned the world upside down by sensing their power and asserting their measure of personal independence.

Americans of African descent dared as much and more in their quests for liberty. Whether they chose to escape slavery by fighting for the British or the Continentals or by striking out on their own as runaways, their defiance, too, turned the world upside down. Among the tens of thousands of slaves who would not be mastered was one Henry Washington, a native of Africa who had become the slave of George Washington in 1763. But Henry Washington made his own declaration of independence in 1776, slipping behind British lines and serving as a corporal in a black unit. Thereafter, like thousands of former slaves, he sought to build a new life elsewhere in the Atlantic world, settling first in Nova Scotia and finally in Sierra Leone. By 1800 he headed a community of former slaves who were exiled to the outskirts of that colony for their determined efforts to win republican self-government from Sierra Leone's white British rulers. Like Thomas Paine, Henry Washington believed that freedom was his only country.

In all those ways a revolutionary generation turned the world upside down. They were a diverse lot—descended from Indians, Europeans, and Africans, driven by desperation or idealism or greed—but joined, even if they did not recognize it, by their common struggle to break free from the rule of monarchs or masters. What now awaited them in the world of the new United States?

# Make a Case

Would the American colonies have won their independence without the military assistance of France? What is the evidence for your position?

# CHAPTER SUMMARY

The American Revolution brought independence to Britain's former colonies after an armed struggle that began in 1775 and concluded with the Treaty of Paris in 1783.

- When the Second Continental Congress convened in the spring of 1775, many of the delegates still hoped for reconciliation—even as they approved the creation of the Continental Army.
- The Second Continental Congress adopted the Declaration of Independence on July 4, 1776, hoping that they could count on a majority of Americans to support the Revolution.
- The British scored a string of victories in the North throughout 1776 and 1777, capturing both New York and Philadelphia.
- The British suffered a disastrous defeat at the Battle of Saratoga in October 1777, which helped convince France to openly ally with the American rebels soon thereafter.
- By 1780 Britain aimed to win the war by claiming the South and captured both Savannah, Georgia, and Charleston, South Carolina.
- The Continental Army in the South, led by Nathanael Greene, foiled the British strategy. Cornwallis surrendered after French and American forces triumphed at the Battle of Yorktown in 1781.
- Except for the first year of fighting, the rank and file of the Continental Army was drawn from the poorest Americans. Women played critical support roles for the army, and on occasion took up arms. African Americans, enlisted by both sides, struggled for a freedom that elite rebels invoked only in the abstract.

## Additional Reading

The outstanding military histories of the American Revolution include Don Higginbotham, *The War for American Independence* (1971); and Robert Middlekauff, *The Glorious Cause, 1763 to 1789* (1982). Both provide a wealth of detail about battles, contending armies, and the role of militias and civilian populations in the fighting. For a compelling treatment of the lives of soldiers in the Continental Army, read Caroline Cox, *A Proper Sense of Honor* (2004); and to become better acquainted with their commander in chief, turn to *Washington's Revolution* (2015) by Robert Middlekauff. For rich new work on the West and the South during the Revolutionary era, see Claudio Saunt, *West of the Revolution* (2014), and Kathleen DuVal, *Independence Lost* (2015). Colin Calloway's *The American Revolution in Indian Country* (1995) explores how native people shaped and were shaped by the Revolution.

Jonathan Dull's *A Diplomatic History of the American Revolution* (1985) remains the standard work on the topic. The international alliance with France and Spain come in for lively chronicling by Larrie D. Ferreiro in *Brothers at Arms* (2016). Impressive interpretations of the war's impact on American society include Charles Royster, *A Revolutionary People at War* (1979); and John Shy, *A People Numerous and Armed* (rev. ed., 1990). Douglas R. Egerton, *Death or Liberty* (2009), offers a thoughtful history of African Americans during this era; and Cassandra Pybus, *Epic Journeys of Freedom* (2006), recounts the experiences of runaway slaves who seized on the wartime crisis to gain liberty. For the varied roles that women played in the Revolutionary era, see Carol Berkin, *Revolutionary Mothers* (2005); and Ellen Hartigan-O'Connor, *The Ties That Buy* (2009).

# 8 Crisis and Constitution

## 1776–1789

South Carolina's low country supplies the background for this portrait of a wealthy Charleston couple, John Purves and his wife, Anne Pritchard Purves. John saw military service in both the state militia and the Continental Army; Anne, with her classically draped dress, evokes the goddess of Liberty. What do you make of the expressions on the couple's faces?



## >> An American Story
## "THESE UNITED STATES"

"I am not a Virginian, but an American," Patrick Henry declared in the Virginia House of Burgesses. Most likely he was lying. Certainly no one listening took him seriously, for the newly independent colonists did not identify themselves as members of a nation. They would have said, as did Thomas Jefferson, "Virginia, Sir, is my country." Or as John Adams wrote to another native son, "Massachusetts is our country." Jefferson and Adams were men of wide political vision and experience: both were leaders in the Continental Congress and more inclined than most to think nationally. But like other members of the revolutionary generation, they identified deeply with their home states and even more deeply with their home counties and towns.

It followed that allegiance to the states, not the Union, determined the shape of the first republican political experiments.

For a decade after independence the revolutionaries were less committed to creating an American nation than to organizing 13 separate state republics. The Declaration of Independence referred explicitly not to the United States but to these United States. It envisioned not one republic so much as a federation of 13.

Only when peace was restored during the decade of the 1780s were Americans forced to face some unanswered questions raised by their revolution. The Declaration proclaimed that these "free and independent states" had "full power to levy war, conclude peace, contract alliances, establish commerce." Did that mean that New Jersey could sign a trade agreement with France, excluding the other states? If the United States were to be more than a loose federation, how could it assert power on a national scale? Similarly, American borderlands to the west presented problems. If these territories were settled by Americans, would they eventually join the United States? Go their own ways as independent nations? Become new colonies of Spain or England?

Such problems were more than political; they were rooted in social realities. For a political union to succeed, the inhabitants of 13 separate states had to start thinking of themselves as Americans. When it came right down to it, what united a Vermont farmer working his rocky fields and a South Carolina gentleman presiding over a vast rice plantation? What bonds existed between a Kentuckian rafting the Ohio River and a Salem merchant sailing to China for porcelain?

And in a society in which all citizens were said to be "created equal," social inequalities had to be confronted. How could women participate in the Revolution's bid for freedom if they were not free to vote or to hold property? How would free or enslaved African Americans live in a republic based on equality? How could black Americans feel a bond with white Americans when so often the only existing bonds had been forged with chains?

To such questions there were no final answers in 1781. There was ferment, excitement, and experimentation as 13 states each sought to create their governments anew; as Americans—or rather, Virginians and New Yorkers and Georgians and citizens of other countries—began to imagine how the revolutionary virtue of equality might transform their societies. But as the decade progressed, the sense of crisis deepened. <<

## THEMATIC TIMELINE

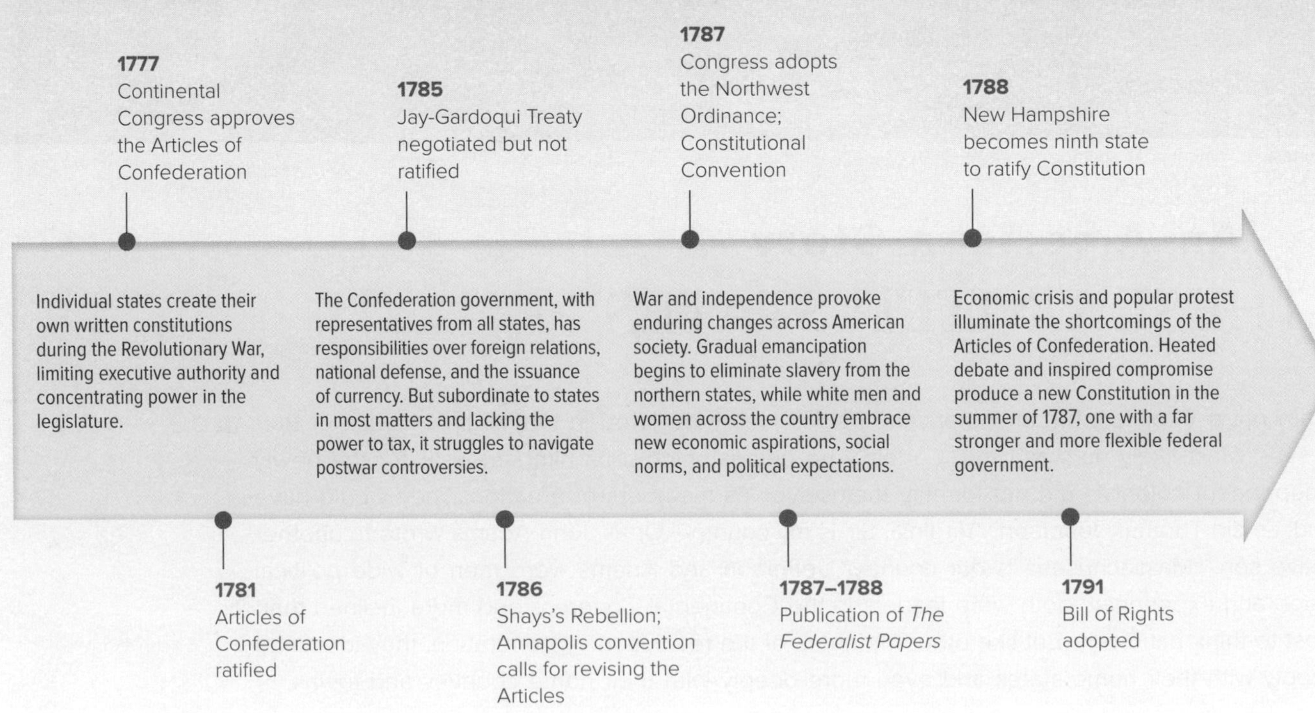

1777
Continental Congress approves the Articles of Confederation
1785
Jay-Gardoqui Treaty negotiated but not ratified
1787
Congress adopts the Northwest Ordinance; Constitutional Convention
1788
New Hampshire becomes ninth state to ratify Constitution
Individual states create their own written constitutions during the Revolutionary War, limiting executive authority and concentrating power in the legislature.
The Confederation government, with representatives from all states, has responsibilities over foreign relations, national defense, and the issuance of currency. But subordinate to states in most matters and lacking the power to tax, it struggles to navigate postwar controversies.
War and independence provoke enduring changes across American society. Gradual emancipation begins to eliminate slavery from the northern states, while white men and women across the country embrace new economic aspirations, social norms, and political expectations.
Economic crisis and popular protest illuminate the shortcomings of the Articles of Confederation. Heated debate and inspired compromise produce a new Constitution in the summer of 1787, one with a far stronger and more flexible federal government.
1781
Articles of Confederation ratified
1786
Shays's Rebellion; Annapolis convention calls for revising the Articles
1787–1788
Publication of *The Federalist Papers*
1791
Bill of Rights adopted

# REPUBLICAN EXPERIMENTS

After independence was declared in July 1776, many of America's best political minds turned to draw up **constitutions** for their individual states. In truth, the state constitutions were crucial republican experiments, the first efforts at establishing a government of and by the people. All the revolutionaries agreed that the people—not a king or a few privileged aristocrats—should rule. Yet they were equally certain that republican governments were best suited to small territories. They believed that the new United States was too sprawling and its people too diverse to be safely consolidated into a single national republic. They feared, too, that the government of a large republic would inevitably grow indifferent to popular concerns, being distant from many of its citizens. Without being under the watchful eye of the people, representatives would become less accountable to the electorate and turn tyrannical. A federation of small state republics, they reasoned, would stand a far better chance of enduring.

**constitution** framework of government establishing the contract between rulers and ruled.

**The State Constitutions** >> The new state constitutions retained the basic form of their old colonial governments, most providing for a governor and a bicameral legislature. But most states dramatically changed the balance of power among the different branches of government.

From the republican perspective in 1776, the greatest problem of any government lay in curbing executive power. What had driven Americans into rebellion was the abuse of authority by the king and his appointed officials. To ensure that the executive could never again threaten popular liberty, the new states either accorded almost no power to their governors or abolished that office. The governors had no authority to convene or dissolve the legislature. They could not veto the legislatures' laws, grant land, or erect courts. Most important, governors had few powers to appoint other state officials. All these limits were designed to deprive the executive of any patronage or other form of influence over the legislature.

What the state governors lost, the legislatures gained. To ensure that those powerful legislatures truly represented the will of the people, the new state constitutions called for annual elections and required candidates for the legislature to live in the district they represented. Many states even asserted the right of voters to instruct the men elected to office how to vote on specific issues. Although no state granted universal manhood suffrage, most reduced the amount of property required of qualified voters. Finally, state supreme courts were also either elected by the legislatures or appointed by an elected governor.

With all power vested in popular assemblies, a majority of voters within a state could do whatever they wanted, unchecked by governors or courts—which opened the door for legislatures to turn as tyrannical as governors. But the revolutionaries brushed that prospect aside: republican theory assured them that the people possessed a generous share of civic virtue, the capacity for selfless pursuit of the general welfare.

In an equally momentous change, the revolutionaries insisted on written state constitutions. Whenever government appeared to exceed the limits of its authority, Americans wanted to have at hand the written contract between rulers and ruled. When eighteenth-century Englishmen used the word *constitution*, they meant the existing arrangement of government—not an actual document but a collection of parliamentary laws, customs, and precedents. But Americans believed that a constitution should be a written code that stood apart from and above government, a yardstick against which the people measured the performance of their rulers. After all, they reasoned, if Britain's constitution had been written down, available for all to consult, would American rights have been violated?

^ Americans responded to independence with rituals of "killing the king," as did this New York crowd in 1776, which is pulling down a statue of George III. Americans also expressed their mistrust of monarchs by establishing state governments with weak executive branches.

Source: Library of Congress, Prints and Photographs Division [LC-DIG-pga-02158]

**From Congress to Confederation** >> While Americans lavished attention on their state constitutions, the national government nearly languished during the decade after 1776. With the coming of independence the Second Continental Congress conducted the common business of the federated states. It created and maintained the Continental Army, issued currency, and negotiated with foreign powers.

Although Congress acted as a central government by common consent, it lacked any legal basis for its authority. To redress that need, in July 1776 Congress appointed a committee to draft a constitution for a national government. The urgent business of waging the war made for delay, but Congress approved the first national constitution in November 1777. It took four more years—until February 1781—for all of the states to ratify these Articles of Confederation.

The Articles of Confederation provided for a government by a national legislature—essentially a continuation of the Second Continental Congress. That body had the authority to declare war and make peace, conduct diplomacy, regulate Indian affairs, appoint military and naval officers, and requisition men from the states. In affairs of finance it could coin money and issue paper currency. Extensive as these responsibilities were, Congress could not levy taxes or even regulate trade. The crucial power of the purse rested entirely with the states, as did the final power to make and execute laws. Even worse, the national government had no distinct executive branch. Congressional committees, constantly changing in their membership, not only had to make laws but had to administer and enforce them as well.

Those weaknesses appear more evident in hindsight. For Congress in 1777 it was no easy task to frame a new government in the midst of a war. And most American leaders in the 1770s had given little thought to federalism, the means by which political power could be divided among the states and the national government. In any case, creating a strong national government would have antagonized many Americans, who after all had just rebelled against the distant, centralized authority of Britain's king and Parliament.

Guided by republican political theory and by their colonial experience, American revolutionaries created a loose confederation of 13 independent state republics under a nearly powerless national government. They succeeded so well that the United States almost failed to survive its first decade of independence. The problem was that lessons from the colonial past were not always useful guides to postwar realities. Only when events forced Americans to think nationally did they begin to consider the possibility of reinventing "these United States"—this time under the yoke of a truly federal republic.

**REVIEW**

What political concerns shaped the first constitutions?

# THE TEMPTATIONS OF PEACE

The surrender of Cornwallis at Yorktown in 1781 marked the end of military crisis in America. But as the threat from Britain receded, so did the source of American unity. The many differences among Americans, most of which lay submerged during the struggle for independence, surfaced in full force. Those domestic divisions, combined with challenges to the new nation from Britain and Spain, created conflicts that neither the states nor the national government proved equal to handling.

**The Temptations of the West** >> The greatest opportunities and the greatest problems for postwar Americans awaited in the rapidly expanding West. With the boundary of the new United States now set at the Mississippi

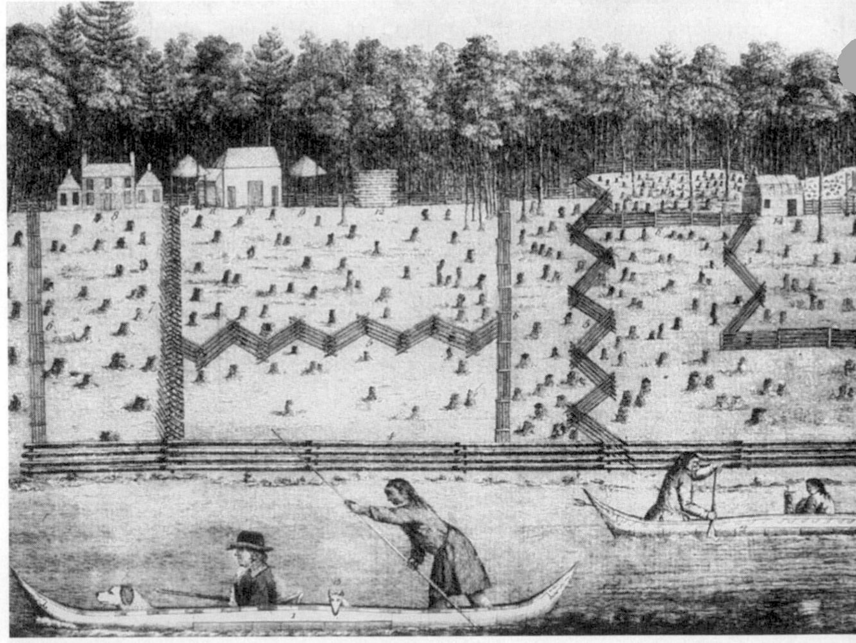

^ As the stumps dotting the landscape indicate, western farmers first sought to "improve" their acreage by felling trees. But their dwellings were far less substantial than those depicted in this idealized sketch of an "American New Cleared Farm." And although some Indians guided parties of whites into the West, as shown in the foreground, more often they resisted white encroachment. For that reason dogs, here perched placidly in canoes, were trained to alert their white masters to the approach of Indians.
Source: Library of Congress, Prints and Photographs Division [LC-USZ62-2766]

River, more whites spilled across the Appalachians, planting farmsteads and towns throughout Ohio, Kentucky, and Tennessee. By 1790 places that had been almost uninhabited by whites in 1760 held more than 2.25 million, one-third of the nation's population.

After the Revolution, as before, western settlement fostered intense conflict. American claims that its territory stretched all the way to the Mississippi were by no means taken for granted by European and Indian powers. The West also confronted Americans with questions about their own national identity: Would the newly settled territories enter the nation as states on an equal footing with the original 13 states? Would they be ruled as dependent colonies? The fate of the West, in other words, constituted a crucial test of whether "these" United States could grow and still remain united.

## Foreign Intrigues >>

Both the British from their base in Canada and the Spanish in Florida and Louisiana hoped to chisel away at American borders. Their considerable success in the 1780s exposed the weakness of Confederation diplomacy.

Before the ink was dry on the Treaty of Paris, Britain's ministers were secretly instructing Canadians to maintain their forts and trading posts inside the United States' northwestern frontier. They reckoned—correctly—that with the Continental Army disbanded, the Confederation could not force the British to withdraw.

The British also made mischief along the Confederation's northern borders, mainly with Vermont. For decades Ethan Allen and his Green Mountain Boys had waged a war of nerves with neighboring New York, which claimed Vermont as part of its territory. After the Revolution the British tried to woo Vermont into their empire as a province of Canada, a flirtation that pressured Congress into granting Vermont statehood in 1791.

The loyalty of the southwestern frontier was even less certain. By 1790 more than 100,000 settlers had poured through the Cumberland Gap to reach Kentucky and Tennessee. But the commercial possibilities of the region depended entirely on access to the Mississippi and the port of New Orleans, since it was far too costly to ship southwestern produce over the rough trails east across the Appalachians. And the Mississippi route was still dominated by the Spanish, who controlled Louisiana as well as forts along western Mississippi shores as far north as St. Louis. The Spanish, seeing their opportunity, closed the Mississippi to American navigation in 1784. That action prompted serious talk among southwesterners about seceding from the United States and joining Spain's empire.

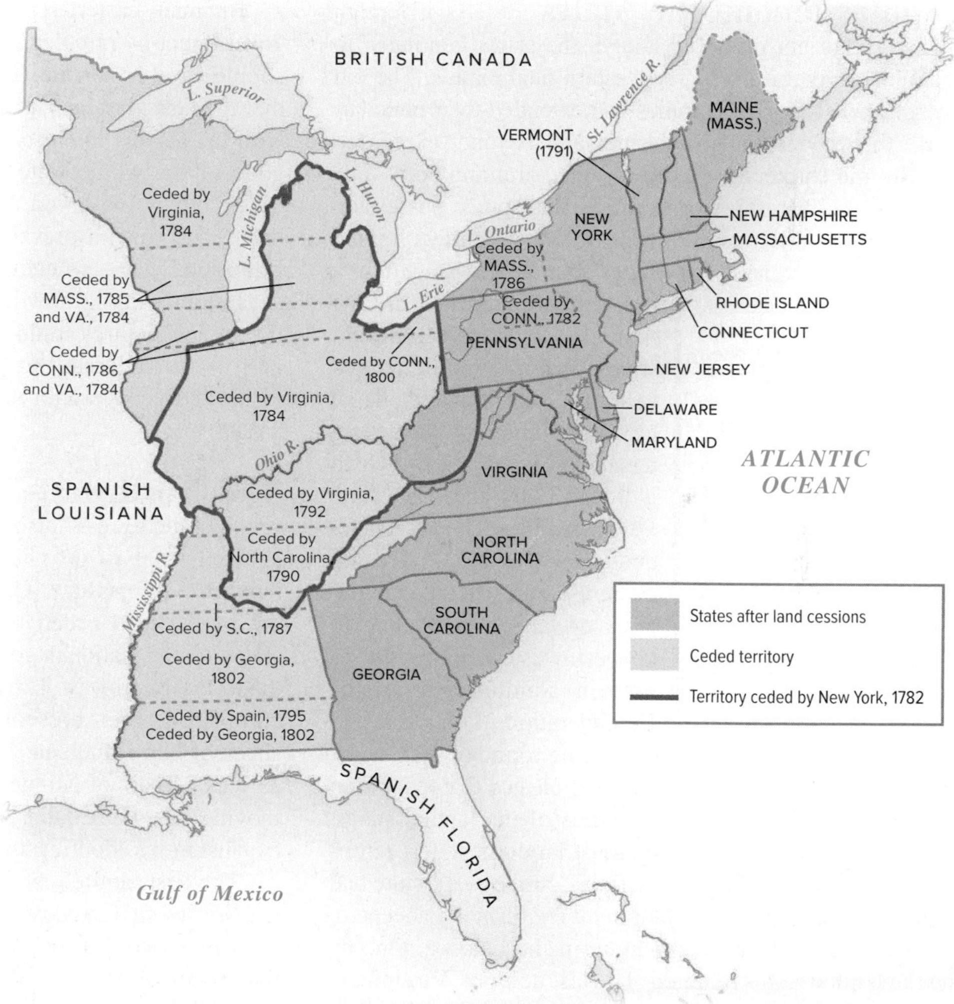

BRITISH CANADA
L. Superior
L. Michigan
L. Huron
L. Ontario
L. Erie
St. Lawrence R.
Ohio R.
Mississippi R.
MAINE (MASS.)
VERMONT (1791)
NEW YORK
NEW HAMPSHIRE
MASSACHUSETTS
RHODE ISLAND
CONNECTICUT
NEW JERSEY
DELAWARE
MARYLAND
PENNSYLVANIA
VIRGINIA
NORTH CAROLINA
SOUTH CAROLINA
GEORGIA
Ceded by Virginia, 1784
Ceded by MASS., 1785 and VA., 1784
Ceded by CONN., 1786 and VA., 1784
Ceded by MASS., 1786
Ceded by CONN., 1782
Ceded by CONN., 1800
Ceded by Virginia, 1784
Ceded by Virginia, 1792
Ceded by North Carolina, 1790
Ceded by S.C., 1787
Ceded by Georgia, 1802
Ceded by Spain, 1795
Ceded by Georgia, 1802
SPANISH LOUISIANA
SPANISH FLORIDA
ATLANTIC OCEAN
Gulf of Mexico
States after land cessions
Ceded territory
Territory ceded by New York, 1782


## MAP 8.1: WESTERN LAND CLAIMS, 1782–1802

The Confederation's settlement of conflicting western land claims was an achievement essential to the consolidation of political union. Some states asserted that their original charters extended their western borders to the Mississippi River. A few states, such as Virginia, claimed western borders on the Pacific Ocean.

*Which states claimed western lands that they eventually ceded to the Confederation?*

The Spanish also tried to strengthen their hold on North America by making common cause with the Indians. Of particular concern to both groups was protecting Spanish Florida from the encroachment of American settlers filtering south from Georgia. Florida's governor complained that those backwoods folk were "distinguished from savages only in their color, language, and the superiority of their depraved cunning and untrustworthiness." So Spanish colonial officials responded eagerly to the overtures of Alexander McGillivray, a young Indian leader whose mother was of French-Creek descent and whose father was a Scots trader. His efforts brought about a treaty of alliance between the Creeks and the Spanish in 1784, quickly followed by similar alliances with the Choctaws and the Chickasaws.

## Disputes among the States >>

As if foreign intrigues were not divisive enough, the states continued to argue among themselves over western land claims. The old royal charters for some colonies had extended their boundaries all the way to the Mississippi and beyond. (See Map 8.1.) But the charters were often vague, granting both Massachusetts and Virginia, for example, undisputed possession of present-day Wisconsin. In contrast, other charters limited state boundaries to within a few hundred miles of the Atlantic coast. **"Landed" states** such as Virginia wanted to secure control over the large territory granted by their charters. **"Landless" states** (which included Maryland, Delaware, Pennsylvania, Rhode Island, and New Jersey) called on Congress to restrict the boundaries of landed states and to convert western lands into a domain administered by the Confederation.

**landed states and landless states** some of the 13 colonies that became the United States had originally been granted land whose western boundaries were vague or overlapped the land granted to other colonies. During the Confederation period, the so-called "landless" states had boundaries that were firmly drawn on all sides, such as Maryland and New Jersey. "Landed" states possessed grants whose western boundaries were not fixed.

The landless states lost the opening round of the contest over ownership of the West. The Articles of Confederation acknowledged the old charter claims of the landed states. Then Maryland, one of the smallest landless states, retaliated by refusing to ratify the Articles. Since every state had to approve the Articles before they were formally accepted, the fate of the United States hung in the balance. One by one the landed states relented. The last holdout, Virginia, in January 1781 ceded its charter rights to land north of the Ohio River.

## The More Democratic West >>

An even greater source of contention concerned the sort of men westerners elected to political office. The state legislatures of the 1780s were both larger and more democratic in their membership than the old colonial assemblies were. Before the Revolution no more than a fifth of the men serving in the assemblies were middle-class farmers or artisans; government was almost exclusively the domain of the wealthiest merchants, lawyers, and planters. After the Revolution twice as many state legislators were men of moderate wealth. The shift was more marked in the North, where middle-class men predominated among representatives. But in every state some men of modest means, humble background, and little formal education attained political power.

State legislatures became more democratic in membership mainly because as backcountry districts grew, so did the number of their representatives. Since western districts tended to be less developed economically and culturally, their leading men were less rich and cultivated than the seaboard elite.

But many eastern republican gentlemen, while endorsing government by popular consent, doubted whether ordinary people were fit to rule. The problem, they contended, was that the new western legislators concerned themselves only with the narrow interests of their constituents, not with the good of the whole state. As Ezra Stiles, the president of Yale College, observed, the new breed of politicians were those with "the all-prevailing popular talent of coaxing and flattering," who "whenever a bill is read in the legislature . . . instantly thinks how it will affect his constituents." And if state legislatures could not rise above petty bickering and narrow self-interest, how long would it be before civic virtue and a concern for the general welfare simply withered away?

## The Northwest Territory >>

Such fears of "democratic excess" also influenced policy when Congress debated what to do with the **Northwest Territory**. Carved out of the land ceded by the states to the national government, the Northwest Territory comprised the present-day states of Ohio, Indiana, Illinois, Michigan, and Wisconsin, as well as part of Minnesota. With so many white settlers moving into these lands, Congress dealt with the issue of expansion by adopting three ordinances.

**Northwest Territory** present-day states of Ohio, Indiana, Illinois, Michigan, Wisconsin, and part of Minnesota.

The first, drafted by Thomas Jefferson in 1784, divided the Northwest Territory into 10 states, each to be admitted to the Union on equal terms as soon as its population equaled that in any of the existing states. In the meantime, Jefferson provided for democratic self-government of the territory by all free adult males. A second ordinance of 1785 set up an efficient mechanism for dividing and selling public lands. The Northwest Territory was surveyed into townships of six miles square. Each township then was divided into 36 lots of one square mile, or 640 acres.

Congress waited in vain for buyers to flock to the land offices it established. The cost of even a single lot—$640—was

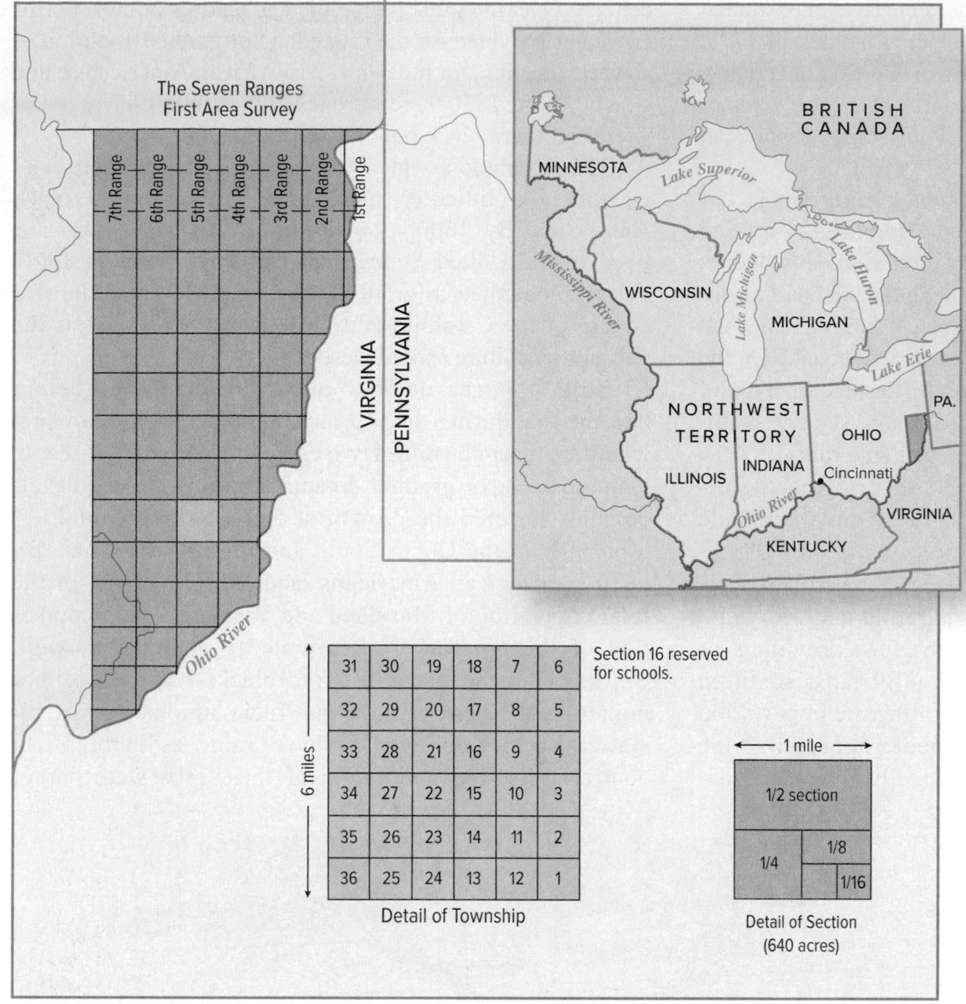
The Seven Ranges
First Area Survey
7th Range
6th Range
5th Range
4th Range
3rd Range
2nd Range
1st Range
VIRGINIA
PENNSYLVANIA
Ohio River
BRITISH
CANADA
MINNESOTA
Lake Superior
WISCONSIN
Mississippi River
Lake Michigan
Lake Huron
MICHIGAN
Lake Erie
PA.
NORTHWEST
TERRITORY
OHIO
INDIANA
ILLINOIS
Cincinnati
Ohio River
VIRGINIA
KENTUCKY
Section 16 reserved for schools.
6 miles
1 mile
1/2 section
1/4
1/8
1/16
Detail of Township
Detail of Section (640 acres)

| 31 | 30 | 19 | 18 | 7 | 6 |
|---|---|---|---|---|---|
| 32 | 29 | 20 | 17 | 8 | 5 |
| 33 | 28 | 21 | 16 | 9 | 4 |
| 34 | 27 | 22 | 15 | 10 | 3 |
| 35 | 26 | 23 | 14 | 11 | 2 |
| 36 | 25 | 24 | 13 | 12 | 1 |

## MAP 8.2: THE ORDINANCE OF 1785

Surveyors entered the Northwest Territory in September 1785, imposing on the land regular grids of six square miles to define new townships, as shown on this range map of a portion of Ohio. Farmers purchased blocks of land within townships, each one mile square, from the federal government or from land speculators.

too steep for most farmers. Disappointed by the shortage of buyers and desperate for money, Congress finally accepted a proposition submitted by a private company of land speculators that offered to buy some 6 million acres in present-day southeastern Ohio. That several members of Congress numbered among the company's stockholders no doubt added to enthusiasm for the deal.

The transaction concluded, Congress calmed the speculators' worries that incoming settlers might enjoy too much self-government by scrapping Jefferson's democratic design and substituting the Northwest Ordinance of 1787. That ordinance provided for a period in which Congress held sway in the territory through its appointees—a governor, a secretary, and three judges. When the population reached 5,000 free adult males a legislature was to be established, although its laws required the governor's approval. A representative could sit in Congress but had no vote. When the population reached 60,000 the inhabitants might apply for statehood, and the whole Northwest Territory was to be divided into not less than three or more than five states. The ordinance outlawed slavery throughout the region, but it provided for the return of fugitive slaves to the South. It also guaranteed basic rights—freedom of religion and trial by jury—and provided for the support of public education.

With the Northwest Ordinance in place, Congress had succeeded in extending republican government to the West and incorporating the frontier into the new nation. The Republic now had an orderly way to expand its federation of states in a way that minimized the tensions between the genteel East and the democratic West that had plagued the colonies and the Confederation throughout much of the eighteenth century. Yet ironically, the new ordinance served to heighten tensions in a different way. By limiting the spread of slavery in the northern states, Congress deepened the critical social and economic differences between the North and South, evident already in the 1780s.

The consequences of the new territorial system were also significant for hundreds of thousands of the continent's other inhabitants. In the short term the ordinance ignored completely the rights of the Shawnee, Chippewa, and other Indian peoples who lived in the region. In the long term the system "laid the blueprint," as one historian noted, for bringing new lands into the United States. The ordinance thus accelerated the pressures on Indian lands and aggravated the social and geographic dislocations already set in motion by disease and the western conflicts of the Revolutionary War.

**Slavery and Sectionalism** >> When white Americans declared their independence, they owned nearly half a million black Americans. African Americans of the revolutionary generation, most of them enslaved, constituted 20 percent of the total population of the colonies in 1775, and nearly 90 percent of them lived in the South. Yet few political leaders directly confronted the issue of whether slavery should be permitted to exist in a truly republican society.

When political discussion did stray toward the subject of slavery, southerners—especially ardent republicans—bristled defensively. Theirs was a difficult position, riddled with contradictions. On the one hand, they had condemned parliamentary taxation as tantamount to political "slavery" and had rebelled, declaring that all men were "created equal." On the other hand, enslaved African Americans formed the basis of the South's plantation economy. To surrender slavery, southerners believed, would be to usher in economic ruin.

Some planters in the Upper South resolved the dilemma by freeing their slaves. Such decisions were made easier by changing economic conditions in the Chesapeake. As planters shifted from tobacco toward wheat, a crop demanding much less labor, Virginia and Maryland liberalized their manumission statutes, laws providing for freeing slaves. Between 1776 and 1789 most southern states also joined the North in prohibiting the importation of slaves, and a few antislavery societies appeared in the Upper South. But no southern state legally abolished slavery. Masters defended their right to hold human property in the name of republicanism.

Eighteenth-century republicans regarded property as crucial, because it provided a man and his family with security, status, and wealth. More important, it provided a measure of independence: to be able to act freely, without fear or favor of others. People without property were dangerous, republicans believed, because the poor could never be politically independent. Southern defenders of slavery thus argued that free, propertyless black people would pose a political threat to the liberty of propertied white citizens. Subordinating the human rights of blacks to the property rights of whites, southern republicans reached the paradoxical conclusion that their freedom depended on keeping African Americans in bondage.

The North followed a different course. Because its economy depended far less on slave labor, black emancipation did not run counter to powerful economic interests. Antislavery societies, the first founded by the Quakers in 1775, spread throughout the northern states during the next quarter century. Over the same period the legislatures of most northern states provided for the immediate or gradual abolition of slavery. Freedom for most northern African Americans came slowly, but by 1830 there were fewer than 3,000 slaves out of a total northern black population of 125,000.

The Revolution, which had been fought for liberty and equality, did little to change the status of most black Americans. By 1800 more enslaved African Americans lived in the United States than had lived there in 1776. Slavery continued to grow in the Lower South as the rice culture of the Carolinas and Georgia expanded and as the new cotton culture spread westward.

Still, a larger number of slaves than ever before became free during the war and in the decades following, whether through military service, successful escape, manumission, or gradual emancipation. All these developments fostered the growth of free black communities, especially in the Upper South and in northern cities. By 1810 free African Americans made up 10 percent of the total population of Maryland and Virginia. The composition of the postwar free community changed as well. Before independence most free blacks had been either mulattoes—the offspring of interracial unions—or former slaves too sick or aged to have value as laborers. In contrast, the free population of the 1780s were darker

^ In 1787 in Philadelphia, the year delegates to the Constitutional Convention met, Richard Allen and Absalom Jones founded Bethel African Methodist Episcopal Church. The first church was a former blacksmith's shop that the members hauled to a site they purchased on Sixth Street. By the time this illustration was created in 1829, a more spacious building had replaced the first church.
©The Library Company of Philadelphia/Bridgeman Images

skinned, younger, and healthier. This group injected new vitality into black communal life, organizing independent schools, churches, and mutual benefit societies for the growing number of "free people of color."

**peculiar institution** euphemism for slavery, perhaps revealing in its use. *Peculiar* also suggests the contradiction with the ideals of the Declaration of Independence that "all men are created equal."

After the Revolution slavery ceased to be a national institution. It became the **"peculiar institution"** of a single region, the American South.

### Wartime Economic Disruption >> 

With the outbreak of the Revolution, Americans had suffered an immediate loss of the manufactured goods, markets, and credit that Britain had formerly supplied. Matters did not improve with the coming of peace. France and Britain flooded the new states with their manufactures, and postwar Americans, eager for luxuries, indulged in a most unrepublican spending spree. The flurry of buying left some American merchants and consumers as deeply in debt as their governments. When loans from private citizens and foreign creditors such as France had proved insufficient to finance the fighting, both Congress and the states had printed paper money—a whopping total of $400 million. The paper currency was backed only by the government's promise to redeem the bills with money from future taxes, since legislatures balked at the unpopular alternative of levying taxes during the war. For the bills to be redeemed the United States had to survive, so by the end of 1776, when Continental forces sustained a series of defeats, paper money started to depreciate dramatically. By 1781 it was virtually without value, and Americans coined the expression "not worth a Continental."

The printing of paper money, combined with a wartime shortage of goods, triggered an inflationary spiral of scarcer and scarcer goods costing more and more worthless dollars. In this spiral, creditors were gouged by debtors, who paid them back with depreciated currency. At the same time, soaring prices for food and manufactured goods eroded the buying power of wage earners and small farmers. And the end of the war brought on demands for prompt repayment from the new nation's foreign creditors as well as from soldiers seeking back pay and pensions.

Congress could do nothing. With no power to regulate trade, it could neither dam the stream of imported goods rushing into the states nor stanch the flow of gold and silver to Europe to pay for these items. With no power to prohibit the states from issuing paper money, it could not halt depreciation. With no power to regulate wages or prices, it could not curb inflation. With no power to tax, it could not reduce the public debt. Efforts to grant Congress greater powers met with determined resistance from the states.

Within states, too, economic problems aroused discord. Some major merchants and large commercial farmers had profited handsomely during the war by selling supplies to the American, British, and French armies at high prices. Eager to protect their windfall, they lobbied state legislatures for an end to inflationary monetary policies. That meant passing high taxes to pay wartime debts, a paper currency that was backed by gold and silver, and an active policy to encourage foreign trade.

Less affluent men fought back, pressing legislatures for programs that met their needs. Western farmers, often in debt, urged the states to print more paper money and to pass laws lowering taxes and postponing the foreclosure of mortgages. Artisans opposed merchants by calling for protection from low-priced foreign imports that competed with the goods they produced. They set themselves against farmers as well by demanding price regulation of the farm products they consumed. In the continuing struggle the state legislatures became the battleground of competing economic factions.

As the 1780s wore on, conflicts mounted. As long as the individual states remained sovereign, the Confederation was crippled—unable to conduct foreign affairs effectively, unable to set coherent economic policy, unable to deal with discontent in the West. Equally dismaying was the discovery that many Americans, instead of being selflessly concerned for the public good, selfishly pursued their private interests.

 **REVIEW**

What challenges did the West pose for the new republic?

# REPUBLICAN SOCIETY

The war for independence transformed not only America's government and economy but also its society and culture. Inspired by the Declaration's ideal of equality, some Americans rejected the subordinate position assigned to them under the old colonial order. Westerners, newly wealthy entrepreneurs, urban artisans, and women all claimed greater freedom, power, and recognition. The authority of the traditional leaders of government, society, and the family came under a new scrutiny; the impulse to defer to social superiors became less automatic. The new assertiveness demonstrated how deeply egalitarian assumptions were taking root in American culture.

### The New Men of the Revolution >> 

The Revolution gave rise to a new sense of social identity and a new set of ambitions among several groups of men who had once accepted a humbler status. The war also offered opportunities to aspiring entrepreneurs everywhere, and often they were not the same men who had prospered before the war. At a stroke, independence swept away the prominence of loyalists, whose ranks included an especially high number of government officials, large landowners, and major merchants. And while loyalists found their properties confiscated by revolutionary governments, other Americans grew rich. Many northern merchants gained newfound wealth from military contracts or from privateering (sending privately owned armed vessels to attack enemy shipping). Commercial farmers in the mid-Atlantic states prospered from the high food prices caused by wartime scarcity and army demand.

The Revolution effected no dramatic redistribution of wealth. Indeed, the gap between rich and poor increased during the 1780s. But the Revolution's republican ideals of equality and experience emboldened city artisans to demand a more prominent role in politics. Calls for men of their own kind to represent them in government came as a rude shock to such gentlemen as South Carolina's William Henry Drayton, who balked at sharing power with men "who were never in a way to study" anything except "how to cut up a beast in the market to best advantage, to cobble an old shoe in the neatest manner, or to build a necessary house." The journeymen who worked for master craftsmen also exhibited a new sense of independence, forming new organizations to secure higher wages.

But the greatest gains came to those men newly enriched by the war and by the opportunities of independence. Representative of this aspiring group was William Cooper, a Pennsylvania Quaker who did not support the Revolution but in its aftermath strove to transform himself from a wheelwright into a gentleman. He hoped to effect that change through another: the transformation of thousands of acres of hilly, heavily forested land around Otsego Lake in upstate New York into wheat-producing farms clustered around a market village called Cooperstown. Yankee emigrants fleeing the shrinking farms of long-settled New England made Cooper's vision a reality and made him the leading land developer of the 1790s. But the influx of white settlement radically altered the environment of what had once been part of Iroquois territory. Farmers killed off panthers, bears, and wolves to protect their livestock. Grain farming leeched nutrients from the thin topsoil, forcing farmers to clear more trees, and as the forest barrier fell, weeds and insects invaded. By the beginning of the nineteenth century, the children of many small farmers were migrating to western New York and northern Ohio.

Similar scenarios played out on frontiers throughout the new United States. And everywhere, too, men like William Cooper demanded and received social recognition and political influence. Even though some, like Cooper, never lost the crude manners that betrayed humble origins, they styled themselves as the "aristocracy of merit" enshrined by republican ideals.

**The New Women of the Revolution** >> Not long after the fighting with Britain had broken out, Margaret Livingston of New York wrote to her sister Catherine, "You know that our Sex are doomed to be obedient in every stage of life so that we shant be great gainers by this contest." By war's end, however, Eliza Wilkinson from rural South Carolina was complaining boldly to a woman friend: "The men say we have no business with political matters . . . it's not our sphere . . . [But] I won't have it thought that because we are the weaker Sex (as to bodily strength my dear) we are Capable of nothing more, than minding the Dairy . . . surely we may have enough sense to give our Opinions."

What separated Margaret Livingston's resignation from Eliza Wilkinson's confidence was the Revolution. Wilkinson had managed her parents' plantation during the war and defended it from British marauders. Other women discovered similar reserves of skill and resourcefulness. When soldiers returned home, some were surprised to find their wives and daughters, who had been running family farms and businesses, less submissive and more self-confident.

But American men had not fought a revolution for the equality of American women. In fact, male revolutionaries gave no thought to the role of women in the new nation, assuming that those of the "weaker sex" were incapable of making informed and independent political decisions. Most women of the revolutionary generation agreed that the proper female domain was the home, not the public arena of politics. Still, the currents of the Revolution occasionally left gaps that allowed women to display their political interests. When a loosely worded provision in the New Jersey state constitution gave the vote to "all free inhabitants" owning a specified amount of property, white widows and single women went to the polls. Only in 1807 did the state legislature close the loophole.

**Mary Wollstonecraft's Vindication** >> In the wake of the Revolution there also appeared in England a book that would become a classic text of modern feminism, Mary Wollstonecraft's *A Vindication of the Rights of Woman* (1792). Attracting a wide, if not widely approving, readership in America as well, it called not only for laws to guarantee women civil and political equality but also for educational reforms to ensure their social and economic equality.

Wollstonecraft dashed off *Vindication* in six short months. She charged that men deliberately conspired to keep women in "a state of perpetual childhood" by giving them inferior, frivolous educations. That encouraged young girls to fixate on fashion and flirtation and made them "only anxious to inspire love, when they ought to cherish a nobler ambition, and by their abilities and virtues exact respect." Girls, she proposed, should receive the same education as boys, including training that would prepare them for careers in medicine, politics, and business. No woman should have to pin her hopes for financial security on making a good marriage, Wollstonecraft argued. On the contrary,

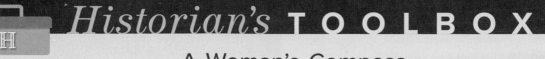

## A Woman's Compass

**A woman drinking spirits as her baby tumbles from her lap.**

**A woman crying, pointing to letters on a table. Was she jilted by a lover? Other possibilities?**

How bleſt the Maid whoſe boſom no headſtrong paſsion knows,
Her days in Joy ſhe Paſses, her nights in soft repose.
KEEP
WITHIN
COMPASS
SURE. TO AVOID MANY TROUBLES, WHICH OTHERS ENDURE: KEEP WITHIN COMPASS AND YOU SHALL BE
A Virtuous Woman is a Crown to her Husband.
ENTER NOT INTO THE WAY OF THE WICKED, AND GO NOT IN THE PATH OF EVIL MEN.

**A woman at hard labor in prison.**

**A woman being apprehended by the authorities. For prostitution? Drunkenness? Debt?**

Courtesy of Winterthur Museum

Could there be any more eloquent testimony to the anxieties aroused by the newly confident (and sometimes outspoken) women of postrevolutionary America? Much like jokes, idealized images (for example, the smiling woman within the compass) can point historians toward areas of tension and conflict in the past. In this illustration, the four scenes displayed outside the compass send even clearer signals. Published sometime between 1785 and 1805 and titled "Keep Within Compass," the illustration celebrates domesticity and wifely devotion while also warning women tempted to stray from that straight and narrow path. It promises a contented and prosperous life—lovely home, thriving garden, elegant silk dress, killer hat, and even a pet squirrel—to the woman "whose bosom no passion knows." But woe betide her erring sisters who strayed from the path of virtue, disgracing themselves as well as the men in their lives! Those twin themes proved equally popular in American novels published during the decades around 1800.

### THINKING CRITICALLY

*Is the kind of virtue promoted by the illustration similar to or different from the republican understanding of virtue? What accounts for the concern about the virtue of women in the decades around 1800? Why did the virtue of women loom so large, since they had few legal or political rights?*

"Keep Within Compass," illustration, ca. 1785–1805, Winterthur Museum.

well-educated and resourceful women capable of supporting themselves would make the best wives and mothers, assets to the family and the nation.

*Vindication* might have been written in gunpowder rather than ink, given the reaction it aroused on both sides of the Atlantic. Even so, Wollstonecraft won many defenders among both men and women, who sometimes publicly and more often privately expressed their agreement with her views. Among them was the Philadelphia Quaker Elizabeth Drinker, who confided to her diary that "in very many of her sentiments, she . . . speaks my mind."

^ A devoted mother with her daughter from the 1790s: but note the generation gap. While the mother holds fancy needlework in her lap, her daughter looks up from an opened book. Many women—especially younger women—in the decades around 1800 chose to include books in their portraits, indicating that literacy and education were becoming essential to their identity and self-esteem.
Courtesy of Winterthur Museum

## Seduction Literature and the Virtue of Women >>

The decades around 1800 also witnessed a heightened concern for the chastity of women. Books, magazines, and newspapers on both sides of the Atlantic overflowed with cautionary tales of young white women who were seduced or coerced into surrendering their virginity by unscrupulous "rakes," only to be abandoned by these faithless lovers, disowned by their families for becoming pregnant out of wedlock, and finally reduced to beggary or prostitution.

"Seduction literature" sent the unmistakable message that young women must preserve their sexual purity. Women were equipped with greater self-control by nature, authors advised, and they were obliged to inspire the same restraint in their suitors, because men were naturally passionate and impulsive. Depicting women as the guardians of sexual virtue marked a major shift in cultural attitudes, because for centuries before, most male writers had insisted that women were the more dangerous sex, their insatiable lust and deceitful ways luring men into sin.

## Republican Motherhood and Education for Women >>

In the new republic, the new image of women as the upholders of private virtue met with an enthusiastic reception, especially among those who believed that wives and mothers had an obligation to encourage republican virtue in their husbands and children. That view, known as **"republican motherhood,"** inspired many educational reformers in the revolutionary generation. Philadelphian Benjamin Rush argued that only educated and independent-minded women could raise the informed and self-reliant citizens that a republican government required, while New Englander Judith Sargent Murray urged the cultivation of women's minds to encourage self-respect. Their efforts contributed to the most dramatic change in the lives of women after the war—the spread of female literacy.

**republican motherhood** redefinition of the role of women promoted by many American reformers in the 1780s and 1790s, who believed that the success of republican government depended on educated and independent-minded mothers who would raise children to become informed and self-reliant citizens.

Between 1780 and 1830 the number of American colleges and secondary academies rose dramatically, and some of these new institutions were devoted to educating women. Not only did the number of schools for women increase, but these schools also offered a solid academic curriculum. By 1850—for the first time in American history—there were as many literate women as there were men.

The Revolution also prompted some states to reform their marriage laws, making divorce somewhat easier, although it remained extremely rare. But although women won greater freedom to divorce, married women still could not sue or be sued, make wills or contracts, or buy and sell property. Any wages they earned went to their husbands; so did all personal property that wives brought into a marriage; so did the rents and profits of any real estate they owned. Despite the high ideals of republican motherhood, most women remained confined to the "domestic sphere" of the home and deprived of the most basic legal and political rights.

## The Attack on Aristocracy >>

Why wasn't the American Revolution more revolutionary? Independence secured the full political equality of white men who owned property, but women were still deprived of political rights, and African Americans of human rights. Why did the revolutionaries stop short of extending equality to the most unequal groups in American society—and with so little sense that they were being inconsistent?

In part, the lack of concern was rooted in republican ideas themselves. Republican ideology viewed property as the key to independence and power. Lacking property, women and black Americans were easily consigned to the custody of husbands and masters. Then, too, prejudice played its part: the perception of women and blacks as naturally inferior beings.

But revolutionary leaders also failed to press for greater equality because they conceived their crusade in terms of eliminating the evils of a European past dominated by kings and aristocrats. They believed that the great obstacle to equality was monarchy—kings and queens who bestowed hereditary honors and political office on favored individuals and granted legal privileges and monopolies to favored churches and businesses. These artificial inequalities posed the real threat to liberty, most republicans concluded. In other words, the men of the Revolution were intent on attaining equality by leveling off the top of society. It did not occur to most republicans that the cause of equality could also be served by raising up the bottom—by attacking the laws and prejudices that kept African Americans enslaved and women dependent.

The most significant reform of the republican campaign against artificial privilege was the dismantling of state-supported churches. Most states had a religious establishment. In New York and the South, it was the Anglican Church; in New England, the Congregational Church. Since the 1740s, dissenters who did not worship at state churches had protested laws that taxed all citizens to support the clergy of established denominations. After the Revolution, as more dissenters became voters, state legislators gradually abolished state support for Anglican and Congregational churches.

Not only in religious life but in all aspects of their culture, Americans rejected inequalities associated with a monarchical past. In that spirit reformers attacked the Society of Cincinnati, a group organized by former officers of the Continental Army in 1783. The society, which was merely a social club for veterans, was forced to disband for its policy of passing on its membership rights to eldest sons. In this way, critics charged, the Society of Cincinnati was creating artificial distinctions and perpetuating a hereditary warrior nobility.

Today many of the republican efforts at reform seem misdirected. While only a handful of revolutionaries worked for the education of women and the emancipation of slaves, enormous zeal went into fighting threats from a monarchical past that had never existed in America. Yet the threat from kings and aristocrats was real to the revolutionaries—and indeed remained real in many parts of Europe. Their determination to sweep away every shred of formal privilege ensured that these forms of inequality never took root in America.

How did the Revolution alter American society?

# FROM CONFEDERATION TO CONSTITUTION

While Americans from many walks of life sought to realize the republican commitment to equality, Congress wrestled with the problem of preserving the nation itself. With the new republic slowly rending itself to pieces, some political leaders concluded that neither the Confederation nor the state legislatures were able to remedy the basic difficulties facing the nation. But how could the states be convinced to surrender their sovereign powers? The answer came in the wake of two events—one foreign, one domestic—that lent momentum to the cause of strengthening the central government.

**The Jay-Gardoqui Treaty** >> The international episode that threatened to leave the Confederation in shambles was a debate over a proposed treaty with Spain. In 1785 southwesterners still could not legally navigate the Mississippi and still were threatening to secede from the union and annex their territory to Spain's American empire. To shore up southwestern loyalties, Congress instructed its secretary of foreign affairs, John Jay, to negotiate an agreement with Spain preserving American rights to navigate on the Mississippi River. But the Spanish emissary, Don Diego de Gardoqui, sweet-talked Jay into accepting a treaty by which the United States would give up all rights to the Mississippi for 25 years. In return Spain agreed to grant trading privileges to American merchants.

Jay, a New Yorker, knew more than a few northern merchants who were eager to open new markets. But when the proposed treaty became public knowledge, southwesterners denounced it as nothing short of betrayal. The treaty was never ratified, but the hostility stirred up during the debate revealed the strength of sectional feelings. Only a decade later, when the Senate ratified a treaty negotiated with Spain by Thomas Pinckney in 1796, did Americans gain full access to the Mississippi.

**Shays's Rebellion** >> On the heels of this humiliation by Spain came an internal conflict that challenged the notion that individual states could maintain order in their own territories. The trouble erupted in western Massachusetts, where many small farmers were close to ruin. Yet they still had to pay mortgages on their farms, still had other debts, and were perpetually short of money. In 1786 the lower house of the Massachusetts legislature obliged the farmers with a package of relief measures. But creditors in eastern Massachusetts, determined to safeguard their own investments, persuaded the upper house to defeat the measures.

<< These portraits provide a sharp contrast between opponents during Shays's Rebellion. A crude woodcut from a popular almanac represents Daniel Shays. The son of two Irish immigrants, Shays worked as a hired farmhand growing up. An officer in the Continental Army during the Revolution, he was presented with a ceremonial sword by General Lafayette, which he was forced to sell to make ends meet after the war. Governor of Massachusetts James Bowdoin was a merchant who pushed to collect unpaid taxes. His portrait, unlike Shays's, was painted by a respected artist, and the sheen of his satin clothing reflects his inability to sympathize with the poor farmers led by Shays.
*Shays:* ©Hi-Story/Alamy; *Bowdoin:* Source: Bowdoin College Museum of Art, Brunswick, Maine

In the summer of 1786 western farmers responded, demanding that the upper house of the legislature be abolished and that the relief measures go into effect. That autumn 2,000 farmers rose in armed rebellion, led by Captain Daniel Shays, a veteran of the Revolution. They closed the county courts to halt creditors from foreclosing on their farms and marched on the federal arsenal at Springfield. The state militia quelled the uprising by February 1787, but the insurrection left many in Massachusetts and the rest of the country thoroughly shaken.

Daniel Shays's rebels were no impoverished rabble. They were reputable members of western communities who wanted their property protected and believed that government existed to provide that protection. The Massachusetts state legislature had been unable to safeguard the property of farmers from the inroads of recession or to protect the property of creditors from the armed debtors who closed the courts. It had failed, in other words, to fulfill the most basic aim of republican government.

Other states with discontented debtors feared what the example of western Massachusetts might mean for the future of the Confederation itself. But by 1786 Shays's Rebellion supplied only the sharpest jolt to a movement for reform that was already under way. Even before the rebellion, a group of Virginians had proposed a meeting of the states to adopt a uniform system of commercial regulations. Once assembled at Annapolis in September 1786, the delegates from five states agreed to a more ambitious undertaking. They called for a second, broader meeting in Philadelphia, which Congress approved, for the "express purpose of revising the Articles of Confederation."

**Framing a Federal Constitution** >> It was the wettest spring anyone could remember. The 55 men who traveled over muddy roads to Philadelphia in May 1787 arrived drenched and bespattered. Fortunately, most of the travelers were men in their 30s and 40s, young enough to survive a good soaking. Since most were gentlemen of some means—planters, merchants, and lawyers with powdered wigs and prosperous paunches—they could recover from the rigors of their journey in the best accommodations offered by America's largest city.

The delegates came from all the states except Rhode Island. The rest of New England supplied shrewd backroom politicians—Roger Sherman and Oliver Ellsworth from Connecticut and Rufus King and Elbridge Gerry, Massachusetts men who had learned a trick or two from Sam Adams. The middle states marshaled much of the intellectual might: two Philadelphia lawyers, John Dickinson and James Wilson; one Philadelphia financier, Robert Morris; and the aristocratic Gouverneur Morris. From New York there was Alexander Hamilton, the mercurial and ambitious young protégé of Washington. South Carolina provided fiery orators Charles Pinckney and John Rutledge.

It was "an assembly of the demigods," gushed Thomas Jefferson, who, along with John Adams, was serving as a diplomat in Europe when the convention met. In fact, the only delegate who looked even remotely divine was the convention's presiding deity. Towering a full half foot taller than most of his colleagues, George Washington displayed his usual self-possession from a chair elevated on the speaker's platform where the delegates met, in the Pennsylvania State House. At first glance, the delegate of least commanding presence was Washington's fellow Virginian, James Madison. Short and slightly built, the 36-year-old Madison had no profession except hypochondria. But he was an astute politician and a brilliant political thinker who, more than anyone else, shaped the framing of the federal Constitution.

The delegates from 12 different states had two things in common: they were all men of considerable political experience, and they all recognized the need for a stronger national union. So when the Virginia delegation introduced Madison's outline for a new central government, the convention was ready to listen.

**The Virginia and New Jersey Plans** >> What Madison had in mind was a truly national republic, not a confederation of independent states. His "Virginia Plan" proposed a central government with three branches: legislative, executive, and judicial. Furthermore, the legislative branch, Congress, would possess the power to veto all state legislation. In place of the Confederation's single assembly, Madison substituted a bicameral legislature, with a lower house elected directly by the people and an upper house chosen by the lower from nominations made by state legislatures. Representatives to both houses would be apportioned according to population—a change from practice under the Articles, in which each state had a single vote in Congress. Madison also revised the structure of government that had existed under the Articles by adding an executive, who would be elected by Congress, and an independent federal judiciary.

After two weeks of debate over the Virginia Plan, William Paterson, a lawyer from New Jersey, presented a less radical counterproposal. While his "New Jersey Plan" increased Congress's power to tax and to regulate trade, it kept the national government as a unicameral assembly, with each state receiving one vote in Congress under the policy of equal representation. The delegates took just four days to reject Paterson's plan. Most endorsed Madison's design for a stronger central government.

Even so, the issue of apportioning representation continued to divide the delegates. While smaller states pressed for each state's having an equal vote in Congress, larger states backed Madison's provision for basing representation on population. Underlying the dispute over representation was an even deeper rivalry between southern and northern states. While northern and southern populations were nearly equal in the 1780s and the South's population was growing more rapidly, the northern states were more numerous. Giving the states equal votes would put the South at a disadvantage. Southerners feared being outvoted in Congress by the northern states and felt that only proportional representation would protect the interests of their section.

That division turned into a deadlock as the wet spring burned off into a blazing summer. The stifling heat was made even worse because the windows remained shut, to keep any news of the proceedings from drifting out onto the Philadelphia streets.

**The Deadlock Broken** >> Finally, as the heat wave broke, so did the political stalemate. On July 2 a committee headed by Benjamin Franklin suggested a compromise. States would be equally represented in the upper house of Congress, each state legislature appointing two senators to six-year terms. That satisfied the smaller states. In the lower house of Congress, which alone could initiate money bills, representation was to be apportioned according to population. Every 30,000 inhabitants would entitle a state to send one representative for a two-year term. A slave was to count as three-fifths of a free person in the calculation of population, and the slave trade was to continue until 1808. That satisfied the larger states and the South.

By the end of August the convention was prepared to approve the final draft of the Constitution. The delegates agreed that the executive, now called the president, would be chosen every four years. Direct election seemed out of the question—after all, how could citizens in South Carolina know anything about a presidential candidate who happened to live in distant Massachusetts, or vice versa? But if each state chose presidential electors, either by popular election or by having the state legislature name them, those eminent men would likely have been involved in national politics, have known the candidates personally, and be prepared to vote wisely. Thus the Electoral College was established, with each state's total number of senators and representatives determining its share of electoral votes.

An array of other powers ensured that the executive would remain independent and strong: the president would have command over the armed forces, authority to conduct diplomatic relations, responsibility to nominate judges and officials in the executive branch, and the power to veto congressional legislation. Just as the executive branch was made independent, so, too, the federal judiciary was separated from the other two branches of government. Madison believed that this clear **separation of powers** was essential to a balanced republican government.

**separation of powers** principle that each branch of government—the legislature (Congress), the executive (the president), and the judiciary (the Supreme Court)—should wield distinct powers independent from interference or infringement by other branches of government.

Madison's only real defeat came when the convention refused to give Congress veto power over state legislation. Still, the new bicameral national legislature enjoyed much broader authority than Congress had under the Confederation, including the power to tax and to regulate commerce. The Constitution also limited the powers of state legislatures, prohibiting them from levying duties on trade, coining money or issuing paper currency, and conducting foreign relations. The Constitution and the acts passed by Congress were declared the supreme law of the land, taking precedence over any legislation passed by the states. And changing the Constitution would not be easy. Amendments could be proposed only by a two-thirds vote of both houses of Congress or in a convention requested by two-thirds of the state legislatures. Ratification of amendments required approval by three-quarters of the states.

On September 17, 1787, 39 of the 42 delegates remaining in Philadelphia signed the Constitution. Charged only with revising the Articles, the delegates had instead written a completely new frame of government. And to speed up ratification, the convention decided that the Constitution

## Make a Case

Why did the founding fathers feel the need for an Electoral College? Do you think that the Electoral College still serves a useful purpose today?

would go into effect after only nine states had approved it. They further declared that the people themselves—not the state legislatures—would pass judgment on the Constitution in special ratifying conventions. To serve final notice that the new central government was a republic of the people and not merely another confederation of states, Gouverneur Morris of Pennsylvania hit on a happy turn of phrase to introduce the Constitution. "We the People," the document begins, "in order to form a more perfect union . . ."

**Ratification** >> With grave misgivings on the part of many, the states called for conventions to decide whether to ratify the new Constitution. Those with the gravest misgiving—the Anti-Federalists, as they came to be called—voiced familiar republican fears. Older and less cosmopolitan than their **Federalist** opponents, the Anti-Federalists drew on their memories of the struggle with England to frame their criticisms of the Constitution. Expanding the power of the central government at the expense of the states, they warned, would lead to corrupt and arbitrary rule by new aristocrats. Extending a republic over a large territory, they cautioned, would separate national legislators from the interests and close oversight of their constituents.

**Federalist** proponent of the draft constitution and the establishment of a strong national government.

Madison responded to these objections in *The Federalist Papers,* a series of 85 essays written with Alexander Hamilton and John Jay during the winter of 1787–1788. He countered Anti-Federalist concerns over the centralization of power by pointing out that each separate branch of the national government would keep the others within the limits of their legal authority. That mechanism of **checks and balances** would prevent the executive from oppressing the people while preventing the people from oppressing themselves.

**checks and balances** mechanism by which each branch of government—executive, legislative, and judicial—keeps the others within the bounds of their constitutional authority.

To answer Anti-Federalist objections to a national republic, Madison drew on the ideas of an English philosopher, David Hume. In his famous 10th essay in *The Federalist Papers*, Madison argued that in a great republic "the Society becomes broken into a greater variety of interests, of pursuits, of passions, which check each other." The larger the territory, the more likely it was to contain multiple political interests and parties, so that no single faction could dominate. Instead, each would cancel out the others.

The one Anti-Federalist criticism Madison could not get around was the absence of a national bill of rights. Opponents insisted on an explicit statement of rights to prevent

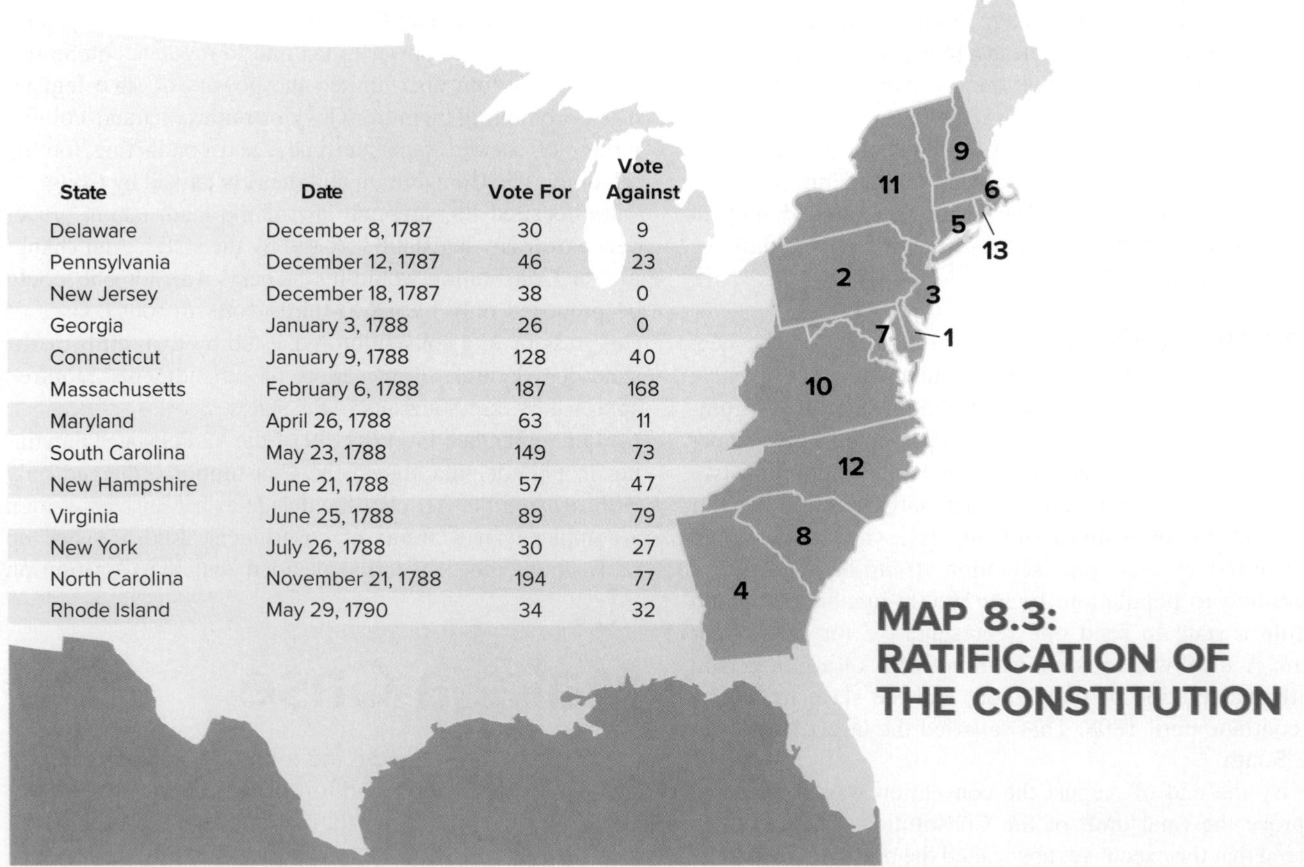

| State | Date | Vote For | Vote Against |
|---|---|---|---|
| Delaware | December 8, 1787 | 30 | 9 |
| Pennsylvania | December 12, 1787 | 46 | 23 |
| New Jersey | December 18, 1787 | 38 | 0 |
| Georgia | January 3, 1788 | 26 | 0 |
| Connecticut | January 9, 1788 | 128 | 40 |
| Massachusetts | February 6, 1788 | 187 | 168 |
| Maryland | April 26, 1788 | 63 | 11 |
| South Carolina | May 23, 1788 | 149 | 73 |
| New Hampshire | June 21, 1788 | 57 | 47 |
| Virginia | June 25, 1788 | 89 | 79 |
| New York | July 26, 1788 | 30 | 27 |
| North Carolina | November 21, 1788 | 194 | 77 |
| Rhode Island | May 29, 1790 | 34 | 32 |

9
11
6
5
13
2
3
7
1
10
12
8
4

**MAP 8.3: RATIFICATION OF THE CONSTITUTION**

the freedoms of individuals and minorities from being violated by the federal government. Madison finally promised to place a bill of rights before Congress immediately after the Constitution was ratified.

Throughout the early months of 1788 Anti-Federalists continued their opposition. But they lacked the articulate and influential leadership that rallied behind the Constitution and commanded greater access to the public press. In the end, too, Anti-Federalist fears of centralized power proved less compelling than Federalist prophecies of the chaos that would follow if the Constitution were not adopted.

By the end of July 1788 all but two states had voted in favor of ratification. The last holdout, Rhode Island, finally came aboard in May 1790, after Madison had carried through on his pledge to submit a Bill of Rights to the new Congress. Indeed, these 10 amendments—ratified by enough states to become part of the Constitution by the end of 1791—proved to be the Anti-Federalists' most impressive legacy. The Bill of Rights set the most basic terms for defining personal liberty in the United States. Among the rights guaranteed were freedom of religion, the press, and speech, as well as the right to assemble and petition and the right to bear arms. The amendments also established clear procedural safeguards, including the right to a trial by jury and protection against illegal searches and seizures. They prohibited excessive bail, cruel and unusual punishment, and the quartering of troops in private homes.

REVIEW

What short-term crises precipitated the Constitutional Convention, and what were the main points of debate at that meeting?

Within the life span of a single generation, Americans had declared their independence twice. In many ways the political freedom claimed from Britain in 1776 was less remarkable than the intellectual freedom from the Old World that Americans achieved by agreeing to the Constitution. The Constitution represented a triumph of the imagination—a challenge to many beliefs long cherished by western Europe's republican thinkers.

Revolutionary ideals had been deeply influenced by the conflicts of British politics, in particular the Opposition's warnings about the dangers of executive power. Those concerns at first committed the revolutionaries to making legislatures supreme. In the end, though, Americans ratified a constitution that provided for an independent executive and a balanced government. The Opposition's fears of distant, centralized power had at first prompted the revolutionaries to embrace state sovereignty. But in the Constitution, Americans established a national government with authority independent of the states. Finally, the common sense among all of western Europe's republican theorists—that large national republics were an impossibility—was rejected by Americans, making the United States an impossibility that still endures.

What, then, became of the last tenet of the old republican creed—the belief that civic virtue would sustain popular liberty? The hard lessons of the war and the crises of the 1780s withered confidence in the capacity of Americans to sacrifice their private interests for the public welfare. Many came to share Washington's sober view that "the few . . . who act upon Principles of disinterestedness are, comparatively speaking, no more than a drop in the Ocean." The Constitution reflected the new recognition that interest rather than virtue shaped the behavior of most people most of the time and that the clash of diverse interest groups would remain a constant of public life.

Yet Madison and many other Federalists did not believe that the competition between private interests would somehow result in policies fostering public welfare. That goal would be met instead by the new national government acting as "a disinterested and dispassionate umpire in disputes between different passions and interests in the State." The Federalists looked to the national government to fulfill that role, because they trusted that a large republic, with its millions of citizens, would yield more of that scarce resource: disinterested gentlemen dedicated to serving the public good. Such gentlemen, in Madison's words, "whose enlightened views and virtuous sentiments render them superior to local prejudices," would fill the small number of national offices.

Not all the old revolutionaries agreed. Anti-Federalists drawn from the ranks of ordinary Americans still believed that common people were more virtuous and gentlemen more interested than the Federalists allowed. "These lawyers and men of learning, and moneyed men, that talk so finely," complained one Anti-Federalist, would "get all the power and all of the money into their own hands, and then they will swallow up all us little folks." Instead of being dominated by enlightened gentlemen, the national government should be composed of representatives from every social class and occupational group.

The narrow majorities by which the Constitution was ratified reflected the continuing influence of such sentiments, as well as fear that the states were surrendering too much power. That fear made Patrick Henry so ardent an Anti-Federalist that he refused to attend the Constitutional Convention in 1787, saying that he "smelt a rat." "I am not a Virginian, but an American," Henry had once declared. Most likely he was lying. Or perhaps Patrick Henry, a southerner and a slaveholder, could see his way clear to being an "American" only as long as sovereignty remained firmly in the hands of the individual states. Henry's convictions, 70 years hence, would rise again to haunt the Union.

# CHAPTER SUMMARY

Leading Americans would give more thought to federalism, the organization of a United States, as the events of the postrevolutionary period revealed the weaknesses of the state and national governments.

- For a decade after independence the revolutionaries were less committed to creating a single national republic than to organizing 13 separate state republics, each dominated by popularly elected legislatures.
- The Articles of Confederation provided for a government by a national legislature but left the crucial power of the purse, as well as all final power to make and execute laws, entirely to the states.
- Many conflicts in the new republic were occasioned by westward expansion, which created both international difficulties with Britain and Spain and internal tensions over the democratization of state legislatures.
- In the wake of the Revolution, ordinary Americans struggled to define republican society: workers began to organize; and some women claimed a right to greater political, legal, and educational opportunities.
- In the mid-1780s the political crisis of the Confederation came to a head, prompted by the controversy over the Jay-Gardoqui Treaty and Shays's Rebellion.
- The Constitutional Convention of 1787 produced an entirely new frame of government that established a truly national republic and provided for a separation of powers among a judiciary, a bicameral legislature, and a strong executive.
- The Anti-Federalists, opponents of the Constitution, softened their objections when promised a Bill of Rights after ratification, which was incorporated into the Constitution by 1791.

## Additional Reading

The work of Gordon Wood is indispensable for understanding the transformation of American politics and culture during the 1780s and thereafter; see especially *The Creation of the American Republic* (1969) and *The Radicalism of the American Revolution* (1992). Woody Holton's *Unruly Americans* (2007) emphasizes struggles over economic policy and democracy. For a marvelous synthesis of current research on the revolution and early republic, see the essays in Andrew Shankman, ed., *The World of the American Revolutionary Republic* (2014). For arguments over the Constitution, in and out of Congress, see Max Edling, *A Revolution in Favor of Government* (2008); Pauline Maier, *Ratification: The People Debate the Constitution* (2011); and Michael J. Klarman, *The Framers' Coup* (2016). To appreciate the Anti-Federalist argument, read Saul Cornell, *The Other Founders* (1999); and the classic writings of Cecilia Kenyon, collected in *Men of Little Faith* (2003).

Carroll Smith-Rosenberg's *This Violent Empire* (2010) argues that exclusion of "others" (especially Indians, African Americans, women, and the poor) was indispensable to early American nationalism. To explore the meaning of republicanism for American women, see two fine studies by Linda Kerber, *Women of the Republic* (1980) and *No Constitutional Right to Be Ladies* (1998); as well as Rosemarie Zagarri's superb biography of Mercy Otis Warren, *A Woman's Dilemma* (2nd ed., 2014). For a vivid sense of how the 1780s transformed local society and politics in one Massachusetts county, read John Brooke, *The Heart of the Commonwealth* (1991); and for a fascinating tale of how the Revolution made one ordinary man's life extraordinary, enjoy Alan Taylor, *William Cooper's Town* (1995). The best accounts of how the Revolution's legacy affected the lives of African Americans in the North include Shane White, *Somewhat More Independent* (1991); and Joan Pope Melish, *Disowning Slavery* (1998).

# 9 The Early Republic

## 1789–1824

TAMMANY HALL

Fourth of July parades helped citizens define the identity of their young republic. This New York parade was led by the Tammany Society, which rejected the aristocratic leanings of the Federalist Party. The society was named to honor a Delaware Indian chief; its members often marched wearing Indian-style garb, as seen here. But by 1812 the patriotic associations of Indian dress (recall the Boston Tea Party disguises) were becoming less popular due to increased clashes with Indians on the frontier.



## >> An American Story

## "I FELT MYSELF MAD WITH PASSION"

One spring evening in 1794 General John Neville was riding home from Pittsburgh with his wife and granddaughter. As they went up a hill, his wife's saddle started to slip, so Neville dismounted. As he adjusted the strap, he heard the clip-clop of an approaching horse. A rider galloped up and in a gruff voice asked, "Are you Neville the excise officer?" "Yes," Neville replied, without turning around.

"Then I must give you a whipping!" cried the rider and leapt from his horse. He grabbed Neville by the hair and lunged at his throat. Breaking free, Neville finally managed to knock the man down: he recognized his attacker as Jacob Long, a local farmer. After Long fled, Neville resumed his journey, badly shaken.

AN EXCISEMAN.

In this antigovernment cartoon, a devil's imp with horns and barbed tail offers to escort a tax collector—the Exciseman—to his master. Like the Stamp Act riots of the Revolutionary period, protesters in western Pennsylvania against the excise tax ritually hanged tax collectors in effigy (*left*).



John Neville was not accustomed to such treatment. As one of the wealthiest men in the area, he expected respect from those of lower social rank. And he had received it—until becoming embroiled in a controversy over the new "whiskey tax" on distilled spirits. In a frontier district like western Pennsylvania, farmers regularly distilled their grain into whiskey for barter and sale. Not surprisingly, the **excise tax,** passed by Congress in 1791, was notoriously unpopular. Still, Neville had accepted an appointment to be one of the tax's regional inspectors. For three years he had endured threats as he enforced the law, but this roadside assault showed that popular hostility was rising.

**excise tax** a tax placed on a commodity produced or sold within a country, usually a luxury item or nonessential.

As spring turned to summer the grain ripened, and so did the people's anger. In mid-July a federal marshal arrived to serve summonses to a number of farmer-distillers who had not paid taxes. One, William Miller, squinted at the paper and was amazed to find the government ordering him to appear in court—hundreds of miles away in Philadelphia—in little more than a month. Even worse, the papers claimed he owed $250. And there, next to this unknown federal marshal, stood the unyielding John Neville.

"I felt myself mad with passion," recalled Miller. "I thought $250 would ruin me; and . . . I felt my blood boil at seeing General Neville along to pilot the sheriff to my very door." Word of the marshal's presence brought 30 or 40 laborers swarming from a nearby field. Armed with muskets and pitchforks, they forced Neville and the marshal to beat a hasty retreat.

Next morning the local militia company marched to Neville's estate. A battle ensued, and the general, aided by his slaves, beat back the attackers. A larger group, numbering 500 to 700, returned the following day to find Neville fled and his home garrisoned by a group of soldiers from nearby Fort Pitt. The mob burned down most of the outbuildings and, after the soldiers surrendered, torched Neville's elegantly furnished home.

Throughout the region that summer, marauding bands roamed the countryside, burning homes and attacking tax collectors. While the greatest unrest flared in western Pennsylvania, farmers in the western districts of several other states also defied federal officials and refused to pay the tax, thus launching a full-scale "Whiskey Rebellion" in the summer of 1794.

Alexander Hamilton, a principal architect of the strong federal government established by the Constitution, knew a challenge to authority when he saw one: "Shall there be a government, or no government?" So did an alarmed George Washington, now president and commander in chief of the new republic, who led an army of 13,000 men—larger than the one he had commanded at Yorktown against the British—into the Pennsylvania countryside.

That show of force cowed the Pennsylvania protesters, snuffing out the Whiskey Rebellion. But the riots and rebellion deepened fears for the future of the new republic. As Benjamin Franklin had remarked in 1788, Americans were skilled at overthrowing governments, but only time would tell whether they were any good at sustaining them. By 1794 Franklin's warning seemed prophetic.

Federalists such as Washington and Hamilton—supporters of a powerful national government—had high hopes for their newly created republic. Stretching over some 840,000 square miles in 1789, it was approximately four times the size of France, five times the size of Spain, ten times the size of Great Britain. Yet the founders of the republic knew how risky it was to unite such a vast territory. Yankee merchants living along Boston wharves had economic interests and cultural traditions distinct from those of backcountry farmers who raised hogs, tended a few acres of corn, and distilled whiskey. Even among farmers, there was a world of difference between a South Carolina planter who shipped tons of rice to European markets and a New Hampshire family whose stony fields yielded barely enough to survive. Could the new government established by the Constitution provide a framework strong enough to unite such a socially diverse nation? Within a decade national political leaders split into two sharply opposed political parties, drawing ordinary men and women into civic life.

Social and political divisions within the nation were sharpened by currents of global change, both across the Atlantic and westward across the continent. After 1789 an increasingly bloody revolution in France sharpened old rivalries, and as Europe plunged into war, Americans were torn in their loyalties. Britain also determined to make Americans fight for their independence once again, while in the West, Spain and later France pressured white settlers beyond the Appalachians. Indian nations, buffeted by disease and dislocation, sought to unite in a confederacy west of the Appalachian Mountains.

In short, the early republic was a fragile creation, buffeted by changes beyond its borders and struggling to create a stable government at home. During the nation's first three decades its survival depended on balancing the interests of a socially and economically diverse population. <<

## THEMATIC TIMELINE

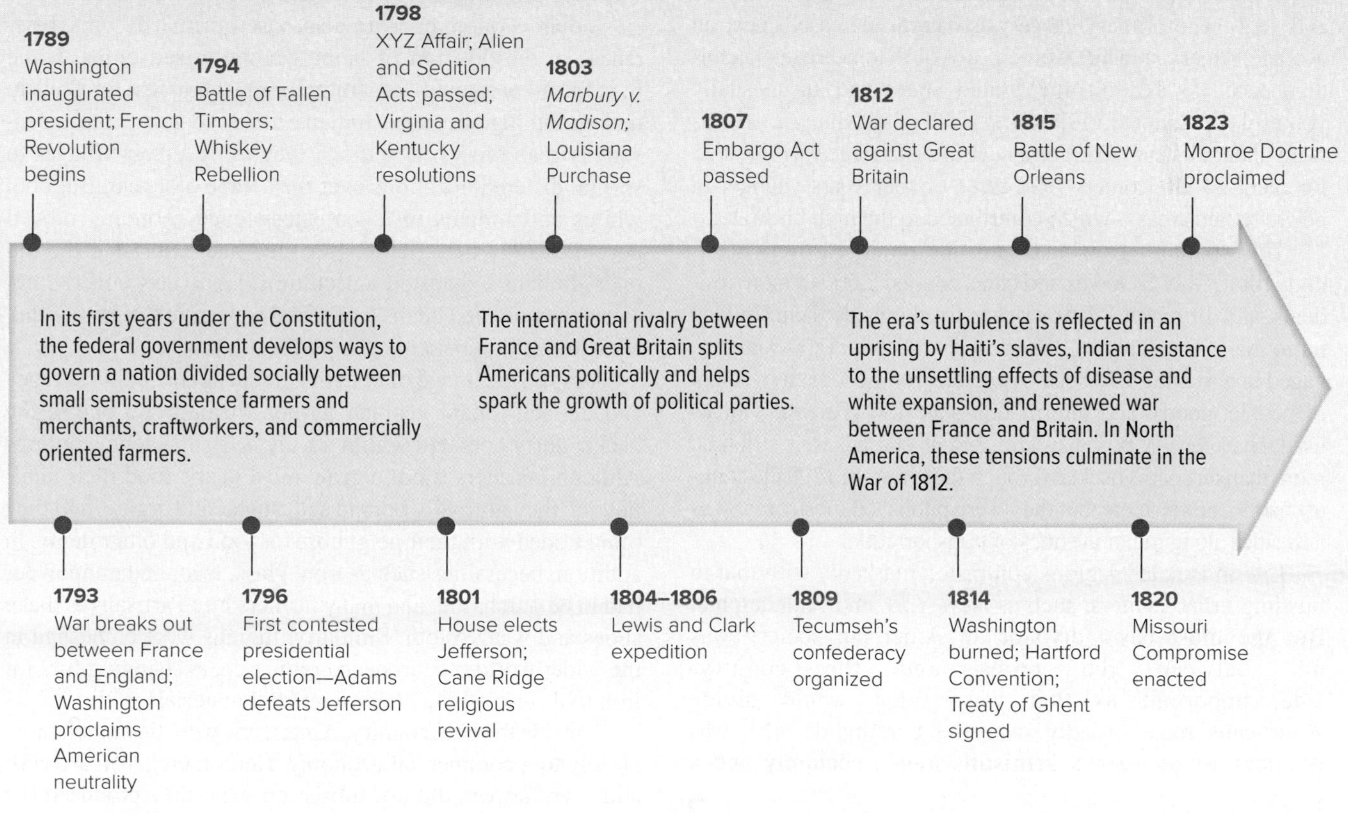

1789
Washington inaugurated president; French Revolution begins
1794
Battle of Fallen Timbers; Whiskey Rebellion
1798
XYZ Affair; Alien and Sedition Acts passed; Virginia and Kentucky resolutions
1803
*Marbury v. Madison;* Louisiana Purchase
1807
Embargo Act passed
1812
War declared against Great Britain
1815
Battle of New Orleans
1823
Monroe Doctrine proclaimed
In its first years under the Constitution, the federal government develops ways to govern a nation divided socially between small semisubsistence farmers and merchants, craftworkers, and commercially oriented farmers.
The international rivalry between France and Great Britain splits Americans politically and helps spark the growth of political parties.
The era's turbulence is reflected in an uprising by Haiti's slaves, Indian resistance to the unsettling effects of disease and white expansion, and renewed war between France and Britain. In North America, these tensions culminate in the War of 1812.
1793
War breaks out between France and England; Washington proclaims American neutrality
1796
First contested presidential election—Adams defeats Jefferson
1801
House elects Jefferson; Cane Ridge religious revival
1804–1806
Lewis and Clark expedition
1809
Tecumseh's confederacy organized
1814
Washington burned; Hartford Convention; Treaty of Ghent signed
1820
Missouri Compromise enacted

# 1789: A SOCIAL PORTRAIT

When the Constitution went into effect, the United States stretched from the Atlantic Ocean to the Mississippi River. The first federal census, compiled in 1790, counted approximately 4 million people, divided about evenly between the northern and southern states. Only about 100,000 settlers lived beyond the Appalachians in the Tennessee and Kentucky territories, which were soon to become states.

Within the Republic's boundaries were two major groups that lacked effective political influence: African Americans and Indians. In 1790 black Americans numbered 750,000, almost one-fifth the total population. More than 90 percent lived in the southern states from Maryland to Georgia; most were slaves who worked on tobacco and rice plantations, but there were free blacks as well. The census did not count the number of Indians living east of the Mississippi. North of the Ohio, the powerful Miami Confederacy discouraged settlement, while to the south, five strong, well-organized tribes—the Creeks, Cherokees, Chickasaws, Choctaws, and Seminoles—dominated the region from the Appalachians to the Mississippi River.

That composition would change as the white population continued to double about every 22 years. Immigration contributed only a small part to this astonishing growth. On average, fewer than 10,000 Europeans arrived annually between 1790 and 1820. The primary cause was natural increase, since, on average, American white women gave birth to nearly eight children each. As a result, the United States had an unusually youthful population: in 1790 almost half of all white Americans were under 16 years old. The age at first marriage was about 25 for men, 24 for women—and three or four years younger in newly settled areas—which contributed to the high birthrate.

This youthful, growing population remained overwhelmingly rural. Only 24 towns and cities boasted 2,500 or more residents, and 19 out of 20 Americans lived outside them. In fact, more than 80 percent of American families in 1800 were engaged in agriculture. In such a rural environment the movement of people, goods, and information was slow. Few individuals used the expensive postal system, and most roads were still little more than dirt paths hacked through the forest. In 1790 the country had 92 newspapers, but they were published mostly in towns and cities along major avenues of transportation.

Life in isolated regions contrasted markedly with that in bustling urban centers, such as New York and Philadelphia. But the most basic division in American society was not between the cities and the countryside, important as that was. What would divide Americans most broadly over the coming decades was the contrast between a **semisubsistence economy** and a **commercial economy.** Semisubsistence farmers lived on the produce of their own land and labor. Americans in the commercial economy were tied more closely to the larger markets of a far-flung world.

**semisubsistence economy** economy in which individuals and families produce most of what they need to live on.

**commercial economy** economy in which individuals are involved in a network of markets and commercial transactions. Such economies are often urban, where goods and services are exchanged for money and credit; agricultural areas are also commercial when crops and livestock are sold in markets rather than consumed by those who grew or raised them.

## Semisubsistence and Commercial Economies

>> Most rural white Americans in the interior of the northern states and the backcountry of the South lived off the produce of their own land. Wealth in those areas, although not distributed equally, was spread fairly broadly. And subsistence remained the goal of most white families. "The great effort was for every farmer to produce anything he required within his own family," one European visitor noted. In such an economy women played a key role. Wives and daughters had to be skilled in making such articles as candles, soap, clothing, and hats, since the cost of buying them was steep.

With labor scarce and expensive, farmers also depended on their neighbors to help clear fields, build homes, and harvest crops. If a farm family produced a small surplus, it usually exchanged it locally rather than selling it for cash in a distant market. In this barter economy, money was seldom seen and was used primarily to pay taxes and purchase imported goods.

Indian economies were also based primarily on subsistence. In the division of labor women raised crops, while men fished or hunted—not only for meat but also for skins to make clothing. Because Indians followed game more seasonally than did white settlers, they moved their villages to several different locations over the course of a year. But both whites and Indians in a semisubsistence economy moved periodically to new fields after they had exhausted the old ones. Indians exhausted agricultural lands less quickly, because they planted beans, corn, and squash in the same field, a technique that better conserved soil nutrients.

Despite the image of both the independent "noble savage" and the self-reliant yeoman farmer, virtually no one in the backcountry operated within a truly self-sufficient economy. Although farmers tried to grow most of the food their families ate, they normally bought salt, sugar, and coffee, and they often traded with their neighbors for food and other items. In addition, necessities such as iron, glass, lead, and gunpowder had to be purchased, and many farmers hired artisans to make shoes and weave cloth. Similarly, Indians were enmeshed in the wider world of European commerce, exchanging furs for iron tools or clothing and ornamental materials.

Outside the backcountry, Americans were tied much more closely to a commercial economy. Here, merchants, artisans, and even farmers did not subsist on what they produced but instead sold goods or services in a wider market and lived on their earnings. Cities and towns, of course, played a key part

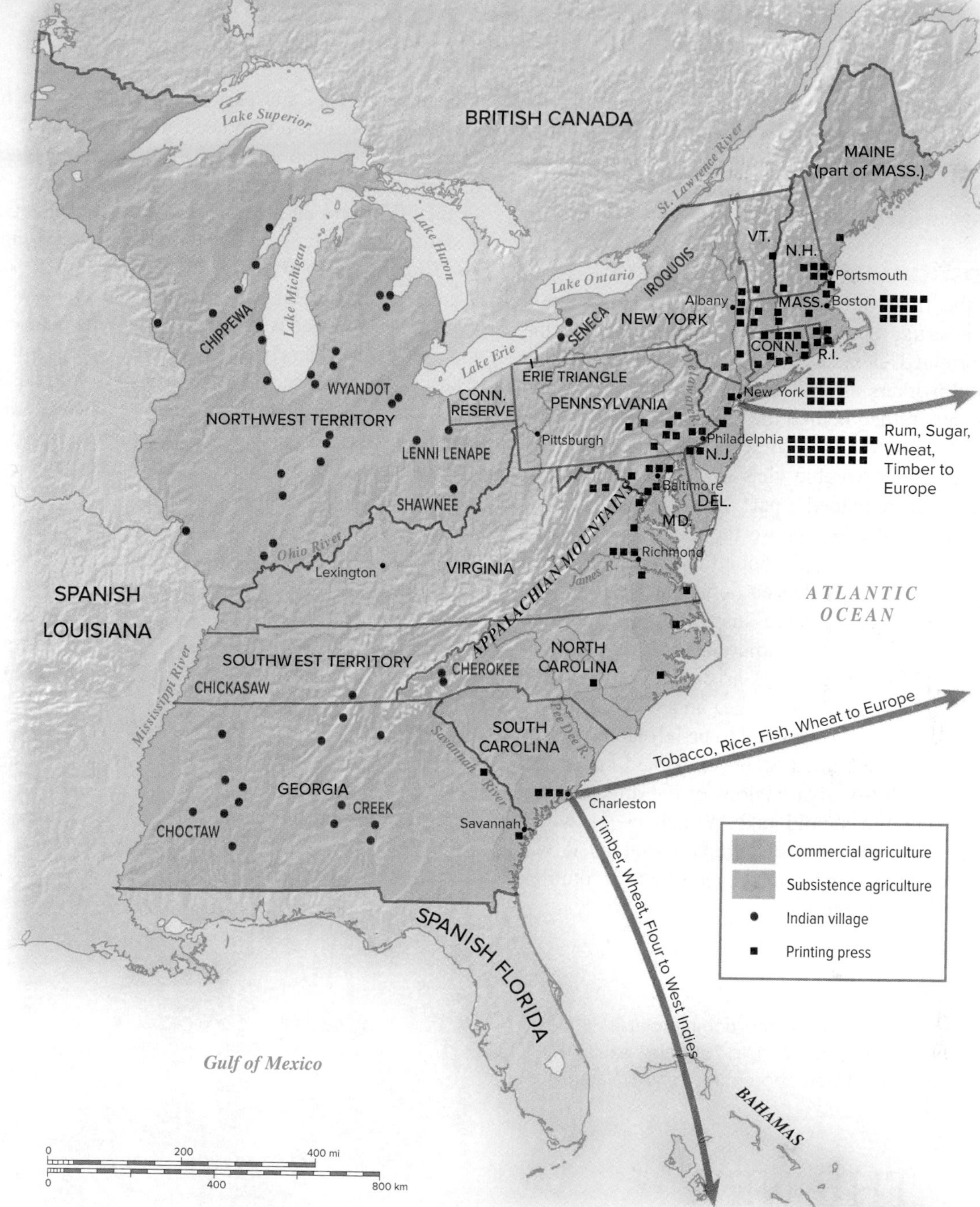
BRITISH CANADA
Lake Superior
MAINE
(part of MASS.)
St. Lawrence River
Lake Michigan
Lake Huron
VT.
N.H.
Portsmouth
Lake Ontario
IROQUOIS
Albany
MASS.
Boston
NEW YORK
SENECA
CHIPPEWA
CONN.
R.I.
Lake Erie
ERIE TRIANGLE
New York
WYANDOT
CONN.
RESERVE
PENNSYLVANIA
NORTHWEST TERRITORY
Pittsburgh
Philadelphia
Rum, Sugar,
Wheat,
Timber to
Europe
N.J.
LENNI LENAPE
Baltimore
SHAWNEE
DEL.
MD.
Ohio River
Richmond
Lexington
VIRGINIA
APPALACHIAN MOUNTAINS
James R.
SPANISH
LOUISIANA
ATLANTIC
OCEAN
Mississippi River
SOUTHWEST TERRITORY
NORTH
CAROLINA
CHEROKEE
CHICKASAW
SOUTH
CAROLINA
Pee Dee R.
Tobacco, Rice, Fish, Wheat to Europe
Savannah River
GEORGIA
CREEK
Charleston
CHOCTAW
Savannah
Timber, Wheat, Flour to West Indies
Commercial agriculture
Subsistence agriculture
Indian village
Printing press
SPANISH FLORIDA
Gulf of Mexico
BAHAMAS
0
200
400 mi
0
400
800 km

## MAP 9.1: SEMISUBSISTENCE AND COMMERCIAL AMERICA, 1790

To prosper, a commercial economy demanded relatively cheap transportation to move goods. Thus in 1790 American commerce was confined largely to settled areas along the coast and to navigable rivers below the fall line. Because commerce depended on an efficient flow of information and goods, newspapers flourished in these areas.
*What was the geographic boundary for the western border of commercial agriculture in the early republic?*

in the commercial economy. But so did the agricultural regions near the seaboard and along navigable rivers.

For commerce to flourish, goods had to move from producers to market cheaply enough to reap profits. Water offered the only cost-effective transportation over any distance; indeed, it cost as much to ship goods a mere 30 miles over primitive roads as to ship by boat 3,000 miles across the Atlantic to London. Cost-effective transportation was available to the planters of the Tidewater South, and city merchants used their access to the sea to establish trading ties to the West Indies and Europe. But urban artisans and workers were also linked to this market economy, as were many farm families in the Hudson valley, southeastern Pennsylvania, and southern New England.

In commercial economies, wealth was less equally distributed. By 1790 the richest 10 percent of Americans living in cities and in the plantation districts of the Tidewater South owned about 50 percent of the wealth. In the backcountry the top 10 percent was likely to own 25 to 35 percent of the wealth.

**The Constitution and Commerce** >> In many ways the fight over ratification of the Constitution represented a struggle between the commercial- and the subsistence-oriented elements of American society. Urban merchants and workers as well as commercial farmers and planters generally rallied behind the Constitution. They took a broader, more cosmopolitan view of the nation's future, and they had a more favorable view of government power.

Americans who remained a part of the semisubsistence **barter economy** tended to oppose the Constitution. More provincial in outlook, they feared concentrated power, were suspicious of cities and commercial institutions, opposed aristocracy and special privilege, and in general just wanted to be left alone.

**barter economy** networks of trade based on the mutual exchange of goods and services with little or no use of coin or currency.

And so in 1789 the United States embarked on its new national course, with two rival visions of the direction that the fledgling Republic should take. Which vision would prevail—a question that was as much social as it was political—increasingly divided the generation of revolutionary leaders in the early republic.

 REVIEW

Describe the semisubsistence and commercial economies of the United States in 1789, and explain their differing visions of how the country should develop.

# THE NEW GOVERNMENT

Whatever the Republic was to become, Americans agreed that George Washington personified it. When the first Electoral College cast its votes, Washington was unanimously elected, the only president in history so honored. John Adams became vice president. Loyalty to the new republic, with its untried form of government and diversity of peoples and interests, rested to a great degree on the trust and respect Americans gave Washington.

**Washington Organizes the Government** >> George Washington realized that as the first occupant of the executive office, everything he did was fraught with significance. "I walk on untrodden ground," he commented. "There is scarcely any part of my conduct which may not hereafter be drawn into precedent."

The Constitution made no mention of a cabinet. Yet the drafters of the Constitution, aware of the experience of the Continental Congress under the Articles of Confederation, clearly assumed that the president would have some system of advisers. Congress authorized the creation of four departments—War, Treasury, State, and Attorney General—whose heads were to be appointed with the consent of the Senate. Washington's most important choices were Alexander Hamilton as secretary of the treasury and Thomas Jefferson to head the State Department. Washington gradually excluded Adams from cabinet discussions, and any meaningful role for the vice president, whose duties were largely undefined by the Constitution, soon disappeared.

The Constitution created a federal Supreme Court but beyond that was silent about the court system. The Judiciary

As Washington traveled from his plantation at Mount Vernon to New York, to be inaugurated as president, he was treated nearly as a god. At Trenton, where he had won a victory after his famous crossing of the Delaware River, maidens scattered flowers in his path as he proceeded through an archway festooned with flowers and evergreens. Philadelphia went one better and dangled a boy above him, to lower a crown of laurel onto Washington's head. The general was so mortified by the attention that he snuck out of town the next morning an hour before a cavalry guard arrived to escort him.
Source: Library of Congress, Prints and Photographs Division [LC-USZC2-3163]

Act of 1789 set the size of the Supreme Court at 6 members; it also established 13 federal district courts and 3 circuit courts of appeal. Supreme Court justices spent much of their time serving on these circuit courts, a distasteful duty whose long hours "riding the circuit" caused one justice to grumble that Congress had made him a "traveling postboy." The Judiciary Act made it clear that federal courts had the right to review decisions of the state courts and specified cases over which the Supreme Court would have original jurisdiction. Washington appointed John Jay of New York, a staunch Federalist, as the first chief justice.

**Hamilton's Financial Program** >> When Congress called on Alexander Hamilton to prepare a report on the nation's finances, the new secretary of the treasury undertook the assignment eagerly. A brilliant thinker and an ambitious politician, he did not intend to be a minor figure in the new administration. Convinced that human nature was fundamentally selfish, Hamilton was determined to link the interests of the wealthy with those of the new government. He also intended to use federal power to encourage manufacturing and commerce in order to make the United States economically strong and independent of Europe.

Neither goal could be achieved until the federal government solved its two most pressing financial problems: revenue and credit. Without revenue it could not be effective. Without credit—the faith of merchants and other nations that the government would repay its debts—it would lack the ability to borrow. Hamilton proposed that all $52 million of the federal debt, much of it generated by the Revolutionary War, be paid in full (or funded). He also recommended that the federal government assume responsibility for the remaining $25 million in debts that individual states owed—a policy of "assumption." He intended with these twin policies to put the new federal government on a sound financial footing and enhance its power by increasing its need for revenue and making the wealthy look to the national government, not the states. Hamilton also proposed a series of excise taxes, including a controversial 25 percent levy on whiskey, to help meet government expenses.

After heated debate Congress deadlocked over funding and assumption. Finally, at a dinner with Hamilton, Thomas Jefferson and James Madison of Virginia agreed to support his proposal if, after 10 years in Philadelphia, the permanent seat of government would be located in the South, on the Potomac River between Virginia and Maryland. Aided by this understanding, funding and assumption passed Congress. In 1791 Congress also approved a 20-year charter for the first Bank of the United States. The bank would hold government deposits and issue banknotes that would be received in payment of all debts owed the federal government. Congress proved less receptive to the rest of Hamilton's program, although a limited tariff to encourage manufacturing and several excise taxes, including the one on whiskey, won approval.

The passage of Hamilton's program caused a permanent rupture among supporters of the Constitution. Madison, who had collaborated closely with Hamilton in the 1780s, broke with his former ally over funding and assumption. Jefferson finally went over to the opposition when Hamilton announced plans for a national bank. Eventually the two warring factions organized themselves into political parties: the Republicans, led by Jefferson and Madison, and the Federalists, led by Hamilton and Adams.[1] But the division emerged slowly over several years.

Hamilton's program promoted the commercial sector at the expense of semisubsistence farmers. Thus it rekindled many of the concerns that had surfaced during the struggle over ratification of the Constitution. The ideology of the Revolution had stressed that republics inevitably contained groups who sought power in order to destroy popular liberties and overthrow the republic. To some Americans, Hamilton's program seemed a clear threat to establish a privileged and powerful financial aristocracy—perhaps even a monarchy.

Who, after all, would benefit from the funding proposal? During and after the Revolution, the value of notes issued by the Continental Congress dropped sharply. Speculators had bought up most of these notes for a fraction of their face value from small farmers and workers. If the government finally paid back the debt, speculators would profit accordingly. Equally disturbing, members of Congress had been purchasing the notes before the adoption of Hamilton's program. Nearly half the members of the House owned U.S. securities, a dangerous mimicking of Britain, where the Bank of England's loans to many members of Parliament gave the bank great political influence.

Fears were heightened, because Americans had little experience with banks: only three existed in the country when

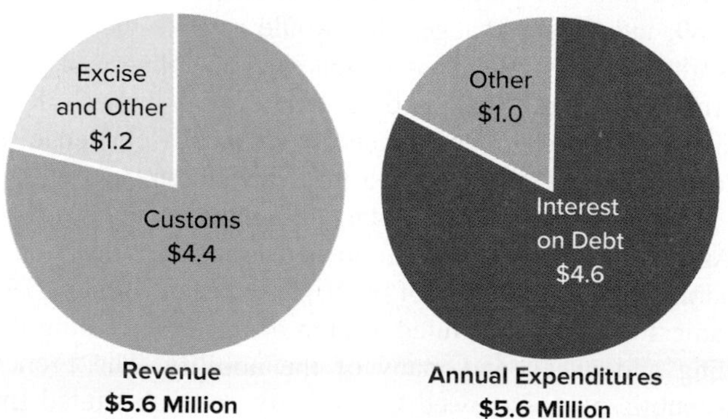

Excise and Other $1.2
Customs $4.4
Revenue $5.6 Million
Other $1.0
Interest on Debt $4.6
Annual Expenditures $5.6 Million


## HAMILTON'S FINANCIAL SYSTEM

Under Hamilton's financial system, more than 80 percent of federal revenues went to pay the interest on the national debt of over $75 million. Note that most of the revenue came from tariff duties (customs).

[1] The Republican Party of the 1790s, sometimes referred to as the Jeffersonian Republicans, is not to be confused with the modern-day Republican Party, which originated in the 1850s.

the Bank of the United States was chartered. One member of Congress expressed a common attitude when he said that he would no more be caught entering a bank than a house of prostitution. Then, too, banks and commerce were a part of the urban environment that rural Americans so distrusted. Although Hamilton's opponents admitted that a certain amount of commerce was necessary, they believed that it should remain subordinate. Hamilton's program, in contrast, encouraged manufacturing and urbanization, developments that history suggested were incompatible with liberty and equality.

After Congress approved the bank bill, Washington hesitated to sign it. When he consulted his cabinet, Jefferson stressed that the Constitution did not specifically authorize Congress to charter a bank. Both he and Madison upheld the idea of strict construction—that the Constitution should be interpreted narrowly and the federal government restricted to powers expressly delegated to it. Otherwise, the federal government would be the judge of its own powers, and there would be no safeguard against the abuse of power.

Hamilton countered that the Constitution contained implied as well as enumerated powers. He particularly emphasized the clause that permitted Congress to make all laws "necessary and proper" to carry out its duties. A bank would be useful in carrying out the enumerated powers of regulating commerce and maintaining the public credit; Congress thus had a right to decide whether to establish one. In the end Washington accepted Hamilton's arguments and signed the bill.

Economically Hamilton's program was a success. The government's credit was restored, and the national bank ended the inflation of the previous two decades and created a sound currency. In addition, Hamilton's theory of implied powers and broad construction gave the nation the flexibility necessary to respond to unanticipated crises.

^ Alexander Hamilton took a leading role both in the Washington administration and in the formation of the Republic's first political parties. In the popular modern musical *Hamilton*, Lin-Manuel Miranda played the title character. The drama, played out through rap singing, made much of Hamilton's illegitimate parentage and upwardly mobile aspirations. The real Hamilton, however, was less democratically inclined.

*Hamilton portrait:* Source: Courtesy National Gallery of Art, Washington; *musical:* ©Theo Wargo/Getty Images

## The Emergence of Political Parties >>

Members of the revolutionary generation fervently hoped that political parties would not take root in the United States. "If I could not go to heaven but with a party, I would not go at all," remarked Jefferson. Influenced by radical English republican thought, American critics condemned parties as narrow interest groups that placed selfishness and party loyalty above a concern for the public good. Despite Americans' distrust of such institutions, however, the United States became the first nation to establish truly popular parties.

Social conditions encouraged the rise of parties. Because property ownership was widespread, the nation had a broad **suffrage.** During the American Revolution legislatures lowered property requirements in many states, increasing the number of voters still further. If party members hoped to hold office, they had to offer a program attractive to the broader voting public. When parties acted as representatives of economic and social interest groups, they became one means by which a large electorate could make its feelings known. In addition, the United States had the highest literacy rate in the world and the largest number of newspapers, further encouraging political interest and participation. Finally, the fact that well-known patriots of the Revolution headed both the Federalists and the Republicans helped defuse the charge that either party was hostile to the Revolution or the Constitution.

**suffrage** right to vote.

## Americans and the French Revolution >>

While domestic issues first split the supporters of the Constitution, it was a crisis in Europe that pushed the nation toward political parties. Revolution erupted in France in 1789, unleashing changes that would remake the western world. France's rising population and the collapse of government finances (due in no small part to Vergennes's decision to aid the American rebels) sparked a challenge to royal authority that became a mass revolution.

Most Americans rejoiced to learn that the new National Assembly in France had abolished feudal privileges and adopted the Declaration of the Rights of Man. But by 1793 radical elements instituted a reign of terror, executing the king and queen and many of the nobility. The French Republic even outlawed Christianity and substituted the worship of Reason. And in 1793 republican France and monarchical England went to war. Americans were deeply divided over which power to support.

Hamilton and his allies viewed the French Revolution as sheer anarchy. French radicals seemed to be destroying the very institutions that held civilization together: the church, social classes, property, law and order. The United States, Hamilton argued, should renounce the 1778 treaty of alliance with France and side with Britain. Jefferson and his followers supported the treaty and regarded France as a sister republic. They believed that despite deplorable excesses, its revolution was spreading the doctrine of liberty. But regardless of party, nearly all American politicians deplored the closest manifestation of the French Revolution, on the Caribbean island colony of Saint Domingue.

In 1790 Saint Domingue was the richest colony in the world, producing 40 percent of the world's sugar and 60 percent of its coffee. It was the United States' second most important trading partner, after Great Britain. While only 30,000 white colonists lived in the colony, their riches came from the toil of half a million slaves. (That number was more than two-thirds as many slaves as were living in the United States at the time.)

In 1791, amid rising disputes on the island about whether and how the French Revolution would transform race relations in the colonies, slaves rebelled against their masters. Within months, thousands of whites and blacks were dead, the colony's main city had been burned to the ground, and former slaves controlled a third of the island. Tens of thousands of white French refugees fled to the United States. Forced by the turmoil to live up to its radical commitments, in 1794 the French National Convention abolished slavery throughout its colonies, and granted all men citizenship "without distinction of color." White Americans, especially in the South, regarded these developments with horror and worried deeply that the example could inspire their own slaves.

**Washington's Neutral Course** >> Washington had compassion for French refugees and extended limited financial aid. But he was convinced that in order to prosper, the United States had to remain independent of European quarrels and wars. Thus he issued a proclamation of American neutrality and tempered Jefferson's efforts to support France.

Under international law, neutrals could trade with belligerents—nations at war—as long as the trade had existed before the outbreak of hostilities and did not involve war supplies. But both France and Great Britain refused to respect the rights of neutrals in the midst of their desperate struggle. They began intercepting American ships and confiscating cargoes. In addition, Britain, which badly needed manpower to maintain its powerful navy, impressed into service American sailors it suspected of being British subjects. Britain also continued to maintain the western forts it had promised to evacuate in 1783, and it closed the West Indies, a traditional source of trade, to American ships.

Recognizing that the United States was not strong enough to challenge Britain militarily, Washington sent John Jay to negotiate the differences between the two countries. Although Jay did persuade the British to withdraw their troops from the Northwest, he could gain no other concessions. Disappointed, Washington nonetheless submitted Jay's Treaty to the Senate. After a bitter debate, the Senate narrowly ratified it in June 1795.

**The Federalists and the Republicans Organize** >> Thus events in Europe contributed directly to the rise of parties in the United States by stimulating fears over the course of American development. By the mid-1790s both sides were organizing on a national basis. Hamilton took the lead in coordinating the Federalist Party, which grew out of the voting bloc in Congress that had enacted his economic program. Increasingly, Washington drew closer to Federalist advisers and policies and became the symbol of the Federalist Party, although he clung to the vision of a **nonpartisan** administration—one that stood above any party.

**nonpartisan** avoiding any ties to a political party.

The guiding genius of the opposition movement was Hamilton's onetime colleague James Madison. Jefferson, who resigned as secretary of state at the end of 1793, became the symbolic head of the Republican Party, much as Washington reluctantly headed the Federalists. But it was Madison who orchestrated the Republican strategy and lined up their voting bloc in the House. The disputes over Jay's Treaty and over the whiskey tax in 1794 and 1795 gave the Republicans popular issues, and they began organizing on the state and local levels. Republican leaders had to be careful to distinguish between opposing the administration and opposing the Constitution. And they had to overcome the ingrained idea that an opposition party was seditious.

As more and more members of Congress allied themselves with one faction or the other, voting became increasingly partisan. By 1796 even minor matters were decided by partisan votes. Gradually, party organization extended all the way from the national level to local communities.

**The 1796 Election** >> As long as Washington remained head of the Federalists, they enjoyed a huge advantage. But in 1796 the weary president, stung by the abuse heaped on him by the opposition press, announced that he would not accept a third term. In doing so he set a two-term precedent that future presidents followed until Franklin Roosevelt. In his Farewell Address, Washington warned against the dangers of parties and urged a return to the earlier nonpartisan system. That vision, however, had become obsolete: parties were an effective way of expressing the interests of different social and economic groups within the nation. When the Republicans chose Thomas Jefferson to oppose John Adams, the possibility of a constitutional system without parties ended.

The framers of the Constitution did not anticipate that political parties would run competing candidates for both the presidency and the vice presidency. Thus they provided that, of the candidates running for president, the one with the most electoral votes would win and the one with the second highest number would become vice president. But Hamilton strongly disliked both Adams and Jefferson. Ever the intriguer, he tried to manipulate the electoral vote so that the Federalist vice presidential candidate, Thomas Pinckney of South Carolina, would be elected president. In the ensuing confusion Adams won with 71 electoral votes, and his rival, Jefferson, gained the vice presidency with 68 votes.

### Federalist and Republican Ideologies >>

The fault line between Federalists and Republicans reflected basic divisions in American life. Geographically, the Federalists were strongest in New England, with its commercial ties to Great Britain and its powerful tradition of hierarchy and order. Farther south, the party became progressively weaker. Of the southernmost states, the Federalists enjoyed significant strength only in aristocratic South Carolina. The Republicans won solid support in semisubsistence areas such as the West, where farmers were only weakly involved with commerce. The middle states were closely contested, although the most cosmopolitan and commercially oriented elements remained the core of Federalist strength.

In other ways, each party looked both forward and backward: toward certain traditions of the past as well as toward newer social currents that would shape America in the nineteenth century.

Most Federalists viewed themselves as a kind of natural aristocracy making a last desperate stand against the excesses of democracy. They clung to the notion that the upper class should rule over its social and economic inferiors. In supporting the established social order, most Federalists opposed unbridled individualism. In their view, government should regulate individual behavior for the good of society and protect property from the violent and unruly.

Yet the Federalists were remarkably forward-looking in their economic ideas. They sensed that the United States would become a major economic and military power only by government encouragement of economic development.

The Republicans, in contrast, looked backward to the traditional revolutionary fear that government power threatened liberty. The Treasury, they warned, was corrupting Congress, the army would enslave the people, and interpreting the Constitution broadly would make the federal government all-powerful. Nor did Republican economic ideals anticipate future American development. For the followers of Madison and Jefferson, agriculture—not commerce or manufacturing—was the foundation of American liberty and virtue. Republicans also failed to appreciate the role of financial institutions in promoting economic growth, condemning speculators, bank directors, and holders of the public debt.

Yet the Jeffersonians were more farsighted in matters of equality and personal liberty. Their faith in white men, regardless of station or status, put them in tune with the emerging egalitarian temper of society. They embraced the virtues of individualism, hoping to reduce government to the bare essentials. And they looked to the West—the land of small farms and a more equal society—as the means to preserve opportunity and American values.

REVIEW

What fostered the intense political loyalties of the 1790s?

## THE PRESIDENCY OF JOHN ADAMS

As president, John Adams became the head of the Federalists, although in many ways he was out of step with his party. Unlike Hamilton, Adams felt no pressing need to aid the wealthy, nor was he fully committed to Hamilton's commercial-industrial vision. As a revolutionary leader who in the 1780s had served as American minister to England, Adams also opposed any alliance with Britain.

Increasingly, Adams and Hamilton clashed over policies and party leadership. Part of the problem stemmed from personalities. Adams was so thin-skinned that it was difficult for anyone to get along with him, and Hamilton's intrigues in the 1796 election had not improved relations between the two men. Although Hamilton had resigned from the Treasury Department in 1795, key members of Adams's cabinet regularly turned to the former secretary for advice. Indeed, they opposed Adams so often that the frustrated president sometimes dealt with them, according to Jefferson, "by dashing and trampling his wig on the floor."

### The Naval War with France >>

Adams began his term trying to balance relations with both Great Britain and France. Because the terms of Jay's Treaty were so favorable to the British, the French in retaliation set their navy and privateers to raiding American shipping. To resolve the conflict Adams dispatched three envoys to France in 1797, but the French foreign minister demanded a bribe before negotiations could even begin. The American representatives refused, and when news of these discussions became public, it became known as the XYZ Affair.

In the public's outrage over French bribery, Federalist leaders saw a chance to retain power by going to war. In 1798 Congress repudiated the French alliance of 1778 and enlarged the army and navy. But Adams feared he would become a scapegoat if his policies failed, and he distrusted standing armies. So an unofficial naval war broke out between the United States and France as ships in each navy raided the fleets of the other, while Britain continued to impress American sailors and seize ships suspected of trading with France.

### Suppression at Home >>

Meanwhile, Federalist leaders attempted to suppress disloyalty at home. In the summer of 1798 Congress passed several measures known together as the Alien and Sedition Acts. The Alien Act authorized the president to arrest and deport aliens suspected of "treasonable" leanings. Although never used, the act directly threatened immigrants who had not yet become citizens, many of whom were prominent Jeffersonians. To limit the number of immigrant voters—again, most of them Republicans—Congress increased the period of residence required to become a **naturalized** citizen from 5 to 14 years.

**naturalization** act of granting full citizenship to someone born outside the country.

But the more controversial law was the Sedition Act, which established heavy fines and even imprisonment for writing, speaking, or publishing anything of "a false, scandalous and malicious" nature against the government or any officer of the government. Because of the partisan way it was enforced, the Sedition Act quickly became a symbol of tyranny. Federalists convicted and imprisoned a number of prominent Republican editors, and several Republican papers ceased publication. In all, 25 people were arrested under the law and 10 convicted and imprisoned.

Previously, most Americans had agreed that newspapers should not be restrained before publication but that they could be punished afterward for sedition. Jefferson and others now argued that the American government was uniquely based on the free expression of public opinion, and thus criticism of the government was not a sign of criminal intent. Only overtly seditious acts, not opinions, should be subject to prosecution. The courts eventually endorsed this view, adopting a new, more absolute view of freedom of speech guaranteed by the First Amendment.

## Virginia and Kentucky Resolutions >>

The Republican-controlled legislatures of Virginia and Kentucky each responded to the crisis of 1798 by passing a set of resolutions. Madison secretly wrote those for Virginia, and Jefferson those for Kentucky. These resolutions proclaimed that the Constitution was a compact among sovereign states that delegated strictly limited powers to the federal government. When the government exceeded those limits and threatened the liberties of citizens, states had the right to interpose their authority. In the 1830s the two resolutions would serve as the precedent for state efforts to nullify federal laws.

But Jefferson and Madison were not ready to rend a union that had so recently been forged. The two men intended for the Virginia and Kentucky resolutions only to rally public opinion to the Republican cause. They opposed any effort to resist federal authority by force.

## The Election of 1800 >>

With a naval war raging on the high seas and the Alien and Sedition Acts sparking debate at home, Adams shocked his party by negotiating a peace treaty with France. It was a courageous act, because Adams not only split his party in two but also ruined his own chances for reelection by driving Hamilton's pro-British wing of the party into open opposition. But the nation benefited, as peace returned.

With the Federalist Party split, Republican prospects in 1800 were bright. Again the party chose Jefferson to run against Adams, along with Aaron Burr for vice president. Sweeping to victory the Republicans won the presidency, as well as control of both houses of Congress for the first time. Yet for almost a week the election remained deadlocked, because Jefferson and Burr received an equal number of votes and Burr refused to step aside. Finally the Federalists decided that Jefferson represented the lesser of two evils and allowed his election on the 36th ballot. In 1804 the Twelfth Amendment corrected the problem of a tie, specifying that electors were to vote separately for president and vice president.

## John Marshall and Judicial Review >>

Having lost both the presidency and the control of Congress in 1800, the Federalists expanded the size of the federal court system, the one branch of the federal government that

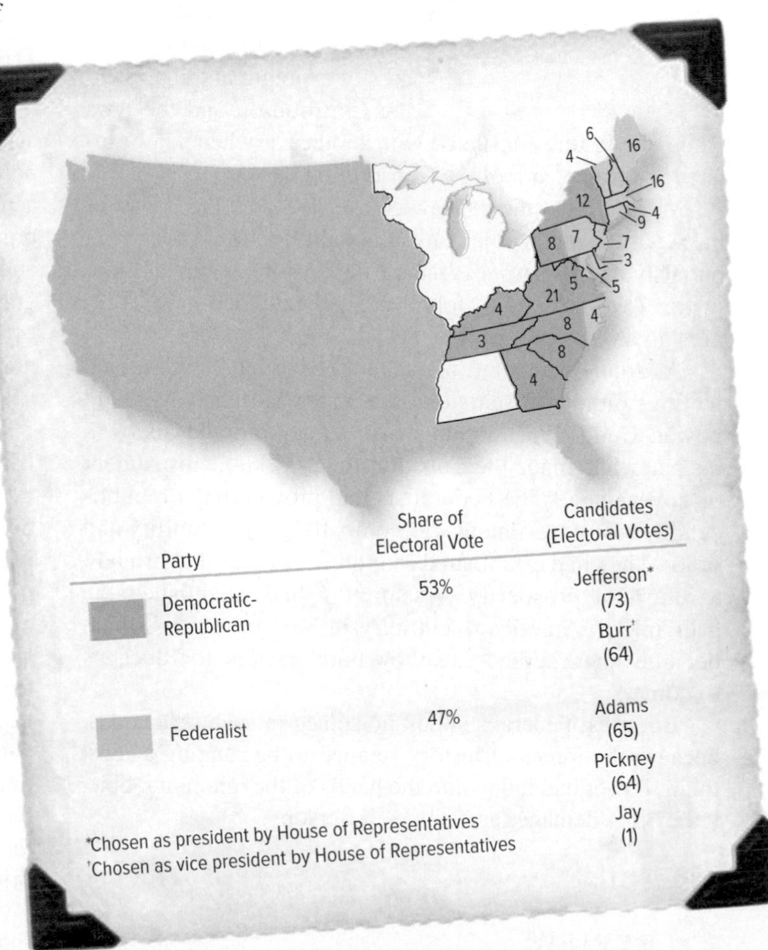

Party
Share of Electoral Vote
Candidates (Electoral Votes)
Democratic-Republican
53%
Jefferson* (73)
Burr† (64)
Federalist
47%
Adams (65)
Pickney (64)
Jay (1)
*Chosen as president by House of Representatives
†Chosen as vice president by House of Representatives


**MAP 9.2: ELECTION OF 1800**

they still controlled. The Judiciary Act of 1801 created 6 circuit courts and 16 new judgeships. Federalists justified these "midnight appointments" on the grounds that the expanding nation required a larger judiciary.

Among Adams's last-minute appointments was that of William Marbury as justice of the peace for the District of Columbia. When James Madison assumed the office of secretary of state under the new administration, he found a batch of undelivered commissions, including Marbury's. Wishing to appoint loyal Republicans to these posts, Jefferson instructed Madison not to hand over the commissions, whereupon Marbury sued. The case of *Marbury v. Madison* went directly to the Supreme Court in 1803.

Chief Justice John Marshall, a Federalist and one of Adams's late-term appointments, actually ruled in favor of Madison—but in a way that strengthened the power of the federal courts. Marshall affirmed the right of the Supreme Court to review statutes and interpret the meaning of the Constitution. "It is emphatically the province of and duty of the judicial department to say what the law is," he wrote in upholding the doctrine of **judicial review.** In Marshall's view, the Court "must of necessity expound and interpret" the Constitution and the laws when one statute conflicted with another or when a law violated the framework of the Constitution.

**judicial review** doctrine set out by Chief Justice John Marshall in *Marbury v. Madison*, that the judicial branch of the federal government possesses the power to determine whether the laws of Congress or the actions of the executive branch violate the Constitution.

Marshall and his colleagues later asserted the power of the Court to review the constitutionality not only of federal but also of state laws. In fact, during his long tenure as chief justice (over 30 years), John Marshall extended judicial review to all acts of government.

As John Adams left office, he looked back with mixed feelings on the 12 years that the Federalist Party had held power. Under Washington's firm leadership and his own, his party had made the Constitution a workable instrument of government. The Federalists had proved that a republican form of government was compatible with stability and order. They had established economic policies that brought a return of prosperity. Washington had established the principle of American neutrality in foreign affairs, which became an accepted ideal by both parties for decades to come.

But most Federalists took no solace in such reflections, because the forces of history seemed to be running against them. Power had fallen into the hands of the ignorant rabble, led by that demagogue Thomas Jefferson.

Why did John Adams lose the election of 1800?

# THE POLITICAL CULTURE OF THE EARLY REPUBLIC

Neither Federalists nor Republicans could accept the novel idea that political parties might peacefully resolve differences among competing social, geographic, and economic interests. Instead, each party regarded its opponents as a dangerous faction of ambitious men striving to increase their wealth and power at the expense of republican liberty.

What resulted was a political culture marked by verbal and, at times, physical violence. Republicans accused Washington and Hamilton of being British agents and monarchists; Federalists denounced Jefferson as an atheist and his partisans as a pack of "blood-drinking cannibals." The leading Republican newspaper editor in Philadelphia plunged into a street brawl with his Federalist rival; two members of Congress slugged it out on the floor of the House of Representatives. Mobs threatened the leaders of both parties, and at the height of the crisis of 1798–1799, Adams smuggled guns into his home for protection.

## Popular Participation in Political Festivals

>> The deepening divisions among national leaders also encouraged ordinary Americans to take an interest in politics. Beginning in the 1790s and for decades thereafter, activists in cities and villages everywhere in the new republic organized grand festivals to celebrate American patriotism and the glories of the Republicans or the Federalists. That grassroots movement democratized the conduct of politics by educating men and women, white and black, voters and nonvoters alike, about the issues of the day. In doing so, such activities encouraged strong partisan loyalties.

Holidays such as the Fourth of July and Washington's Birthday became prime occasions for local party leaders to rally their fellow citizens. They hosted celebrations that began with parades in which marchers, hoisting banners to identify their particular trade, militia company, or social club, processed through the main street to a church, meeting hall, or public square. There the assembled throng of marchers and onlookers sang patriotic songs, recited prayers, and listened to the reading of the Declaration of Independence, all capped by a rousing sermon or political oration. Then the party started: in the North, taverns and hotels hosted community banquets; in the South, the crowds flocked to outdoor barbecues. Everywhere, the feasts ended with many toasts to the glories of republican liberty and, of course, to the superiority of Federalists or Republicans.

These local celebrations not only made an impact on those who were able to attend the festivities but also reached a wider audience through newspaper accounts. During the 1790s and beyond, the number of local or regional newspapers in the new republic mushroomed, but their coverage was far from objective. Most editors were either staunch Federalists or ardent Republicans who could be counted on to publish glowing accounts of the festivities sponsored by their party and to instruct a much wider audience about party policies and values.

^ This artist of the early Republic used watercolor and ink to draw a scene on silk cloth. Young women were no longer being educated merely in the polite arts of dancing, sewing, and embroidery. An increasing number were taking such academic subjects as algebra, history, and geography (note the young woman making measurements on the globe).
Detail of *Miniature Panorama: Scenes from a Seminary for Young Ladies,* c.1810–20, Saint Louis Art Museum 89:1976

## African American Celebrations >>

African Americans, too, were drawn to political festivals, but they discovered that party organizers were determined to keep them away. In the years after 1800, bullies often drove black men and women from Fourth of July celebrations with taunts, threats, and assaults. James Forten, a leading citizen of Philadelphia's African American community, complained that because of the hostility of drunken whites, "black people, upon certain days of public jubilee, dare not to be seen" on the streets after noon.

The growing free black population of northern cities countered that opposition by organizing celebrations to express their own political convictions. They established annual holidays to celebrate the abolition of the slave trade in Britain and the United States as well as the successful slave revolt in the Caribbean that resulted in the founding of Haiti in 1804. Those acts of defiance—the spectacle of blacks marching down the main streets with banners flying and bands of music playing, and of black audiences cheering orators who publicly condemned slavery—only inflamed racial hatred and opposition among many whites.

But African Americans continued to press for full citizenship by persuading sympathetic white printers to publish poetry, slave narratives, and pamphlets composed by black authors. The strategy of those writings was to refute racist notions by drawing attention to the intelligence, virtue, and patriotism of black American women and men, both free and enslaved. Typical was the autobiography of Venture Smith, the first slave narrative published in the United States (1798), which followed his captivity as a young boy in West Africa through his lifelong struggle in New England to purchase his own freedom and that of his wife and children. Hardworking and thrifty, resourceful and determined to better himself and his family, Venture Smith's story invited white readers to conclude that he was as true a republican and a self-made man as Benjamin Franklin.

## White Women's Civic Participation >>

The new republic's political festivals and partisan newspapers aimed to woo the loyalty of white adult males who held enough property to vote. But they also sought the support of white women, some of whom joined in the crowds and even took part in the parades. In one New Jersey village the folks lining the parade route cheered as "16 young ladies uniformed in white with garlands in their hats" marched past, playing a patriotic anthem on their flutes. Federalists and Republicans alike encouraged women's involvement on those occasions, hoping that displays of approval from "the American fair" would encourage husbands and male admirers to support their parties.

Many women seized on such opportunities for greater civic involvement. True, the law excluded most from taking direct part in voting and governing, but those prohibitions did not prevent women from taking an active interest in politics and voicing their opinions. In *The Coquette,* Hannah Webster Foster's best-selling novel of the 1790s, when a female guest "simpered" that their sex should not meddle with politics, her hostess shot back, "Why then should the love of our country be a masculine passion only? Why should government, which involves the peace and order of society, of which we are a part, be wholly excluded from our observation?"

REVIEW

In what ways did politics become more participatory during the 1790s?

# *Many* HISTORIES

## Can This Marriage Be Saved?

*Proponents of providing women with greater educational opportunities—here identified as "The Female Advocate"—often held ideals of marriage that differed dramatically from those embraced by conservative Americans such as Samuel Jennings, a Methodist minister and the founder of a medical college in Baltimore.*

### DOCUMENT 1
### "The Female Advocate" on the Virtues of an Educated Wife

How greatly doth a man of science [knowledge] misjudge in choosing a companion for life, if he selects one from the class of ignorant and untaught, that he may, by this mean, the more securely retain his favorite supremacy. Is it not a total blindness to the ideas of refined happiness, arising from a reciprocity of sentiments and the exchange of rational felicity, as well as an illiberal prejudice, thus to conduct? Shall a woman be kept ignorant, to render her more docile in the management of domestic concerns? How illy capable is such a person of being a companion for a man of refinement? How miserably capable of augmenting his social joys, or managing prudently the concerns of a family, or educating his children? Is it not of the utmost consequence, that the tender mind of the youth receive an early direction for future usefulness? And is it not equally true, that the first direction of a child necessarily becomes the immediate and peculiar province of the woman? And may I not add, is not a woman of capacious and well stored mind, a better wife, a better widow, a better mother, and a better neighbor; and shall I add, a better friend in every respect. . . .

When women, no longer the humble dependent, or the obsequious slave, but the companion and friend, is party to an attachment founded on mutual esteem, then, and not till then, does man assume his intended rank in the scale of creation. . . .

Suppose one who has from her youth been indoctrinated and habituated to sentiments of female inferiority, one who has never been suffered to have an opinion of her own, but on the reverse, has been taught, and accustomed to rely, and implicitly believe, right or wrong, on her parents, guardians, or husband. What will be the consequence of this, in a situation when deprived of the counsel of either or all of them, she is necessitated to act for herself, or be exposed to the fraudulence of an unfriendly world? Perhaps she is left a widow with a large property and a flock of small dependent children? But where have they to look for protection, or on whom to rely, but on their insufficient, helpless mother? How poorly capable is she to fill the vacancy, and act to her tender babes and orphans, in their bereaved situation, as is absolutely necessary, both father and mother? How incapable also is she of assisting in the settlement and adjustment of the estate; how liable to fraud, and how probable to be injured by unreal or exaggerated debts.

*Source:* "The Female Advocate' on the Virtues of an Educated Wife," from *The Female Advocate*, Written by a Lady. New Haven, CT: Thomas Green and Son, 1801.

### DOCUMENT 2
### Samuel K. Jennings on the Virtues of a Submissive Wife

As it is your great wish and interest, to enjoy much of your husband's company and conversation, it will be important to acquaint yourself with his temper, his inclination, and his manner, that you may render your house, your person, and your disposition quite agreeable to him. . . .

Your choice in forming the connexion [marriage], was at best a passive one. Could you have acted the part of a courtier and made choice of a man whose disposition might have corresponded precisely with yours, there would have been less to do afterwards. But under present circumstances, it is your interest to adapt yourself to your husband, whatever may be his peculiarities.

Again, nature has made man the stronger, the consent of mankind has given him superiority over his wife, his inclination is, to claim his natural and acquired rights. He of course expects from you a degree of condescension, and he feels himself the more confident of the propriety of his claim, when he is formed, that St. Paul adds to his authority its support. "Wives submit to your own husbands, as unto the Lord, for the husband is the head of his wife."

In obedience then to this precept of the gospel, to the laws of custom and of nature, you ought to cultivate a cheerful and happy submission. . . .

Do not suppose, that my plan implies that the husband has nothing to do. So far from this he is bound "To love and cherish his wife, as his own flesh." But I repeat, this obligation seems, in a great degree, to rest on the condition of a loving and cheerful submission on the part of the wife. Here again perhaps you object and say, "Why not the husband, first shew a little condescension as well as the wife?" I answer for these plain reasons. It is not his disposition; it is not the custom but with the henpecked; it is not his duty; it is not implied in the marriage contract; it is not required by law or the gospel.

*Source:* Jennings, Samuel K., "On the Virtues of a Submissive Wife," *The Married Lady's Companion, or Poor Man's Friend*. New York, NY: Lorenzo Dow, 1808.

#### THINKING CRITICALLY

*How did "The Female Advocate" advise men to choose their wives? How to behave as husbands? Why did she believe that her advice served the best interests of men? On what grounds did Samuel Jennings argue that women should submit to their husbands?*

# JEFFERSON IN POWER

The growing political engagement of ordinary white Americans played an important role in electing Thomas Jefferson to the presidency. He later referred to his election as "the Revolution of 1800," asserting that it "was as real a revolution in the principles of our government as that of 1776 was in its form." That claim exaggerates: Jefferson's presidency did little to enhance political rights or social opportunities of white women or African Americans. Even so, during the following two decades Republicans did set the United States on a more democratic course. And in their dealings with Britain and France, as well as with the Indian tribes of the West, Republican administrations defined, for better and worse, a fuller sense of American nationality.

**The New Capital City** >> Thomas Jefferson was the first president to be inaugurated in the new capital, Washington, D.C. In 1791 George Washington had commissioned Pierre Charles L'Enfant, a French architect and engineer who had served in the American Revolution, to draw up plans for the new seat of government. L'Enfant designed a city with broad avenues, statues and fountains, parks and plazas, and a central mall. Because the Federalists believed that government was the paramount power in a nation, they had intended that the city would be a new Rome—a cultural, intellectual, and commercial center of the Republic.

The new city fell far short of this grandiose dream. It was located in a swampy river bottom near the head of the Potomac, and the surrounding hills rendered the spot oppressively hot and muggy during the summer. The streets were filled with tree stumps and became seas of mud after a rain. Much of the District was wooded, and virtually all of it remained unoccupied. When the government moved to its new residence in 1800, the Senate chamber, where Jefferson took the oath of office, was the only part of the Capitol that had been completed.

This isolated and unimpressive capital city reflected the new president's attitude toward government. Distrustful of centralized power of any kind, Jefferson deliberately set out to remake the national government into one of limited scope that touched few people's daily lives. The states rather than the federal government were "the most competent administrators for our domestic concerns," he asserted in his inaugural address. Ever the individualist, he recommended a government that left people "free to regulate their own pursuits of industry and improvement."

**Jefferson's Philosophy** >> Jefferson was a product of the Enlightenment, with its faith in the power of human reason to improve society and decipher the universe. He considered "the will of the majority" to be "the only sure guardian of the rights of man," which he defined as "life, liberty, and the pursuit of happiness." Although he conceded that the masses might err, he was confident they would soon return to correct principles. His faith in human virtue exceeded that of most of the founding generation, yet in good republican fashion, he feared those in power, even if they had been elected by the people. Government seemed to Jefferson a necessary evil at best.

To Jefferson agriculture was a morally superior way of life. "Those who labour in the earth are the chosen people of God, if ever he had a chosen people," he wrote in *Notes on the State of Virginia* (1787). Jefferson praised rural life for nourishing the honesty, independence, and virtue so essential in a republic.

Although Jefferson asserted that "the tree of liberty must be refreshed from time to time by the blood of patriots and tyrants," he was no radical. Although he wanted to give the vote to a greater number of Americans, he embraced the traditional republican idea that voters should own property. Republican theorists had long argued that property owners were more economically independent and therefore less likely to be bribed or swayed by demagogues. One of the largest slaveholders in the country, he increasingly muffled his once-bold condemnation of slavery, and in the last years of his life he reproached critics of the institution who sought to prevent it from expanding westward.

Slaveholding aristocrat and apostle of democracy, lofty theorist and pragmatic politician, Jefferson was a complex, at times contradictory, personality. But like most politicians he was flexible in his

>> Befitting his democratic sympathies Jefferson as president was deliberately more informal than his Federalist predecessors, Washington and Adams. But personal habits amplified that informality. The new president was awkward, loose-jointed, reserved, and ill at ease in public. Testifying before a congressional committee, he casually lounged in a chair and spoke in a rambling, nonstop manner. "Yet he scattered information wherever he went," conceded Senator William Maclay of Pennsylvania, "and some even brilliant sentiments sparkled from him."
©Bettmann/Getty Images

approach to problems and tried to balance means and ends. And like most leaders he quickly discovered that he confronted very different problems in power than he had in opposition.

**Jefferson's Economic Policies** >> The new president quickly proceeded to cut spending and to reduce the size of the government. He also abolished the internal taxes enacted by the Federalists, including the controversial excise on whiskey, and thus was able to get rid of all tax collectors and inspectors. Land sales and tariff duties would supply the funds needed to run the scaled-down government.

The most serious spending cuts were made in the military branches. Jefferson slashed the army budget in half, decreasing the army to 3,000 men. In a national emergency, he reasoned, the militia could defend the country. Jefferson reduced the navy even more, halting work on powerful frigates authorized during the naval war with France.

By such steps Jefferson made significant progress toward paying off Hamilton's national debt. Still, he did not entirely dismantle the Federalists' economic program. Funding and assumption could not be reversed—the nation's honor was pledged to paying these debts, and Jefferson understood the importance of maintaining the nation's credit. More surprising, Jefferson argued that the national bank should be left to run its course until 1811, when its charter would expire. In reality, he expanded the bank's operations and, in words reminiscent of Hamilton, advocated tying banks and members of the business class to the government by rewarding those who supported the Republican Party. In effect, practical politics had triumphed over agrarian economics.

How does Jefferson compare to the Federalist presidents who preceded him?

# WHITES AND INDIANS IN THE WEST

For all his pragmatism Jefferson still viewed the lands stretching from the Appalachians to the Pacific through the perspective of his agrarian ideals. America's vast spaces provided enough land to last for a thousand generations, he predicted in his inaugural address, enough to transform the United States into "an empire of liberty."

**The Miami Confederacy Resists** >> That optimistic vision contrasted sharply with the views of most Federalists, who feared the West as a threat to social order and stability. In the 1790s they had good reason to fear. British troops refused to leave their forts in the Northwest, and Indian nations still controlled most of the region. Recognizing that fact, the United States conceded that Indian nations had the right to negotiate as sovereign powers. North of the Ohio, leaders of the Miami Confederacy, composed of eight tribes, stoutly refused to sell their homelands without "the united voice of the confederacy."

In response the Washington administration sent 1,500 soldiers in 1790 under General Josiah Harmar to force the Indians to leave by burning their homes and fields. The Miami Confederacy, led by Blue Jacket and Little Turtle, roundly defeated the whites. Harmar was court-martialed, the nation embarrassed, and a second expedition organized the following year under General Arthur St. Clair. This force of over 2,000 was again routed by Little Turtle, whose warriors killed 600 and wounded another 300. The defeat was the worst in the history of Indian wars undertaken by the United States. (In contrast, Custer's defeat in 1876 counted 264 fatalities.)

President Washington dispatched yet another army of 2,000 to the Ohio valley, commanded by "Mad Anthony" Wayne, an accomplished general. At the Battle of Fallen Timbers in August 1794, Wayne won a decisive victory, breaking the Indians' hold on the Northwest. In the Treaty of Greenville (1795), the tribes **ceded** the southern two-thirds of the area between Lake Erie and the Ohio River, opening it up to white families. Federalists were still not eager to see the land settled. Although they allowed the sale of federal land, they kept the price high, with a required purchase of at least 640 acres—more than four times the size of most American farms.

**cede** to give up possession of.

Once in power, Jefferson and the Republicans encouraged settlement by reducing the minimum tract that buyers could purchase (to 320 acres) and by offering land on credit. Sales boomed. By 1820 more than 2 million whites lived in a region they had first entered only 50 years earlier. From Jefferson's perspective, western expansion was a blessing economically, socially, and even politically, because most of the new westerners were Republican.

**Napoleon, Haiti, and Louisiana** >> Jefferson's "empire of liberty" for whites required more than dispossessing Indian families of their lands; it required delicate diplomacy with the European powers in North America. This task was greatly complicated in 1802 when, under pressure from revolutionary France's audacious leader Napoleon Bonaparte, Spain surrendered the sprawling Louisiana territory to the French. Knowing better than anyone that the agriculture of the western United States had to flow out the Mississippi to reach world markets, Jefferson turned grave when he heard the news. "There is on the globe one single spot, the possessor of which is our natural and habitual enemy," he told his envoy in France. "It is New Orleans."

Napoleon dreamed of re-creating France's North American empire by reoccupying Louisiana and eventually reconquering Canada. But first he had to subdue rebellious Saint Domingue and recapture the immense profits from plantation sugar and coffee. Since the stunning slave rebellion in 1791, insurgents on the island had fought a complex series of wars and gained de facto independence under a brilliant leader, the former slave Toussaint Louverture.

Napoleon sent a massive, veteran army to reconquer the colony and re-enslave its people. He captured Louverture and shipped him off to die in a frigid prison. But the campaign turned into a nightmare for Napoleon's men. Yellow fever and black men with guns devastated the French forces, which in turn resorted to mass killings and other atrocities. By 1804 the French withdrew, leaving the victorious rebels to declare their independent Republic of Haiti. By that time Napoleon was long sick of his rash adventure. "Damn sugar, damn coffee, damn colonies!" he exclaimed angrily.

Jefferson feared and despised the Haitian rebels, but ironically his goals depended on their success. Napoleon realized that without Saint Domingue, his vision of a North American empire was unworkable, so in April 1803 he offered to sell the entire Louisiana territory to the United States. James Monroe and Robert Livingston, the stunned U.S. envoys who had traveled to France in hopes of buying just the city of New Orleans, debated whether to exceed their instructions. Pressed for an immediate answer, the pair took a deep breath and agreed to buy Louisiana for about $15 million. In one fell swoop the American negotiators had doubled the country's nominal size by adding some 830,000 square miles.

Even before the Louisiana Purchase was completed, Congress secretly funded an expedition up the Missouri River to the Pacific. Leading that party were Meriwether Lewis, Jefferson's personal secretary, and William Clark, a younger brother of George Rogers Clark. Jefferson

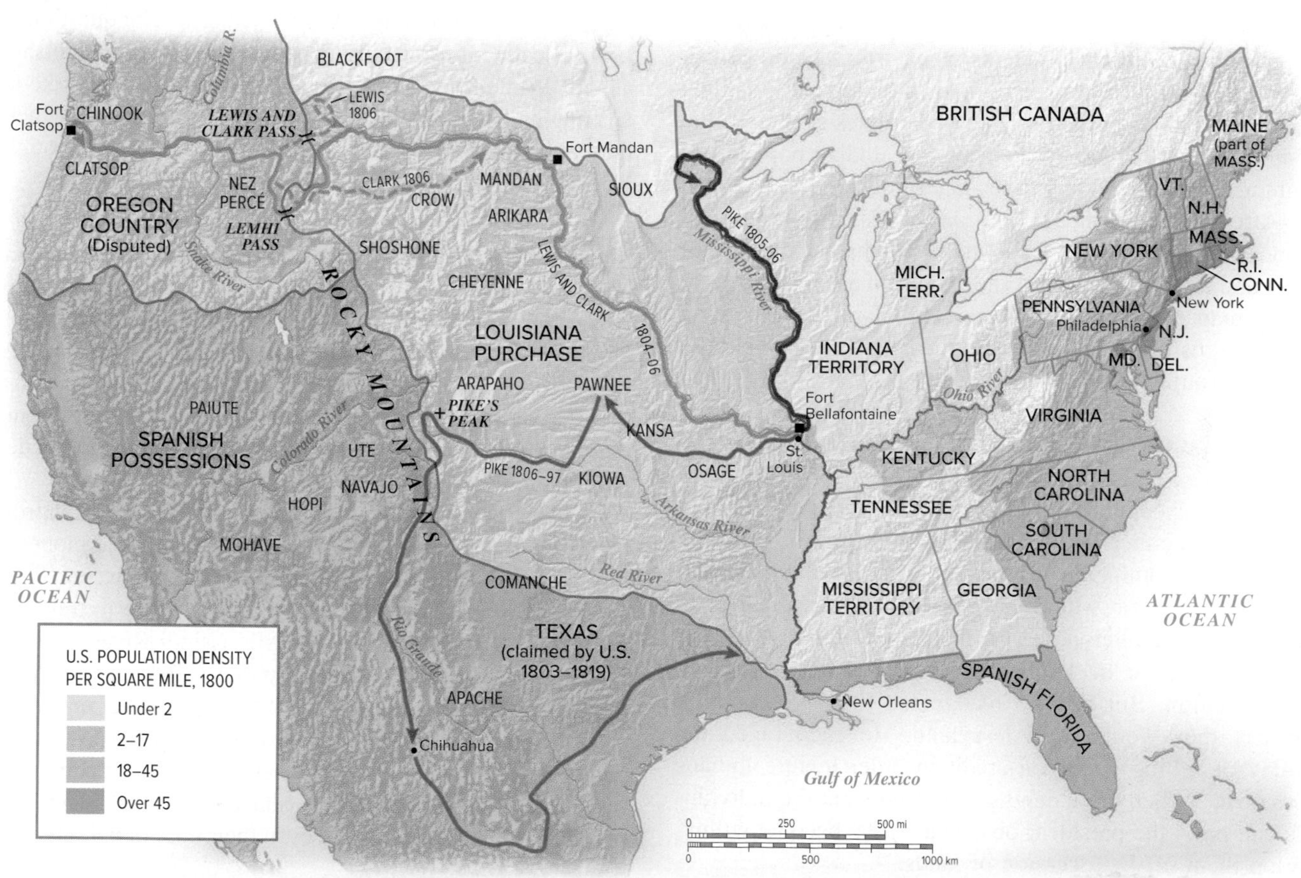

BLACKFOOT
Columbia R.
LEWIS 1806
Fort Clatsop
CHINOOK
LEWIS AND CLARK PASS
Fort Mandan
BRITISH CANADA
MAINE (part of MASS.)
CLATSOP
NEZ PERCÉ
CLARK 1806
MANDAN
CROW
SIOUX
VT.
N.H.
MASS.
OREGON COUNTRY (Disputed)
LEMHI PASS
ARIKARA
PIKE 1805-06
Mississippi River
NEW YORK
R.I.
CONN.
Snake River
SHOSHONE
LEWIS AND CLARK
MICH. TERR.
New York
ROCKY MOUNTAINS
CHEYENNE
PENNSYLVANIA
Philadelphia
N.J.
LOUISIANA PURCHASE
1804–06
INDIANA TERRITORY
OHIO
MD.
DEL.
ARAPAHO
PAWNEE
PAIUTE
PIKE'S PEAK
Colorado River
Fort Bellafontaine
Ohio River
VIRGINIA
SPANISH POSSESSIONS
UTE
KANSA
St. Louis
KENTUCKY
PIKE 1806–07
KIOWA
OSAGE
NORTH CAROLINA
NAVAJO
HOPI
TENNESSEE
Arkansas River
MOHAVE
SOUTH CAROLINA
PACIFIC OCEAN
COMANCHE
Red River
MISSISSIPPI TERRITORY
GEORGIA
ATLANTIC OCEAN
Rio Grande
TEXAS (claimed by U.S. 1803–1819)
U.S. POPULATION DENSITY PER SQUARE MILE, 1800
Under 2
2–17
18–45
Over 45
SPANISH FLORIDA
APACHE
New Orleans
Chihuahua
Gulf of Mexico
0
250
500 mi
0
500
1000 km


## MAP 9.3: EXPLORATION AND EXPANSION: THE LOUISIANA PURCHASE

The vast, largely uncharted Louisiana Purchase lay well beyond the most densely populated areas of the United States. The Lewis and Clark expedition, along with Lieutenant Zebulon Pike's exploration of the upper Mississippi River and the Southwest, opened the way for westward expansion.

*What territory did the Lewis and Clark expedition traverse in addition to the Louisiana Purchase? What territory did the Pike expedition traverse?*

instructed them to make detailed observations of the territory's geography, climate and wildlife. They were also to investigate the practicability of an overland route to the Pacific and engage in diplomacy with the Indians along the way. By pushing onward to the Pacific Lewis and Clark would strengthen the American title to Oregon, which several nations claimed but none effectively occupied.

In the spring of 1804 the "Corps of Discovery" left St. Louis and headed up the Missouri River with 48 men. They laboriously hauled their boats upstream to present-day North Dakota, where they spent the winter with the Mandan Indians. The next spring, the expedition pushed on through the rugged mountains and then floated down first the Snake and then the Columbia River to the Pacific.

The country Lewis and Clark traversed had been shaken by momentous changes over the previous decades. Trade goods circulated in greater quantities than ever before, across the plains and through the mountains. Horses and guns in particular upset older Indian ways, making tribes more mobile and more dangerous. Lewis and Clark spotted Spanish horse gear from Mexico in villages along the upper Missouri River, guns from French traders to the northeast, and British teapots along the Columbia River. Most disruptive, smallpox had made its way along the same trade routes ever since the pandemic of the 1780s (see Chapter 7). Indian populations plummeted, forcing many tribes to resettle.

After a bleak winter in Oregon the expedition returned home over the Rockies in 1806. It brought back thousands of plant and animal specimens and produced a remarkably accurate map of its journey. Lewis and Clark had crossed a continent disrupted by change. In the century to come those changes would only accelerate.

## Make a Case

Was there any strategy that Indian nations between the Appalachians and the Mississippi could have adopted to halt white expansion? Would a Pan-Indian union have held the possibility of success?



**Pressure on Indian Lands and Culture >>** East of the Mississippi, white settlers continued to flood into the backcountry. Jefferson endorsed the policy that Indian tribes either would have to assimilate into American culture by becoming farmers and abandoning their seminomadic hunting or would have to move west. Jefferson defended these alternatives as in the best interests of the Indians, because he believed that otherwise they faced extermination. But he also recognized that by becoming farmers they would need less land. He encouraged the policy of selling goods on credit in order to lure Indians into debt. "When these debts get beyond what the individuals can pay," the president observed, "they become willing to lop them off by a cession of lands."

Between 1800 and 1810, whites pressed Indians into ceding more than 100 million acres in the Ohio River valley. The loss of so much land devastated Indian cultures and transformed their environment by reducing hunting grounds and making game and food scarce. "Stop your people from killing our game," the Shawnees complained in 1802 to federal Indian agents. "They would be angry if we were to kill a cow or hog of theirs, the little game that remains is very dear to us." Tribes also became dependent on white trade to obtain blankets, guns, metal utensils, alcohol, and decorative beads. To pay for these goods with furs Indians often overtrapped, which forced them to invade the lands of neighboring tribes, provoking wars.

The strain produced by white expansion led to alcoholism, growing violence among tribe members, family disintegration, and the collapse of the clan system designed to regulate relations among different villages. The question of how to deal with white culture became a matter of anguished debate. While some Native Americans attempted to take up farming and accommodate to white ways, for most of them the course of assimilation proved unappealing and fraught with risk.

**White Frontier Society >>** Whites faced their own problems on the frontier. In the first wave of settlement came backwoods families who cleared a few acres of forest by girdling the trees, removing the brush, and planting corn between the dead trunks. Such settlers were mostly squatters without legal title to their land. As a region filled up, these pioneers usually sold their improvements and headed west again.

Taking their place, typically, were young single men from the East, who married and started families. These pioneers, too, engaged in semisubsistence agriculture, except those lucky few whose prime locations allowed them to transport their crops down the Ohio and Mississippi Rivers to New Orleans for shipment to distant markets. But many frontier families struggled, moving several times but never managing to rise from the ranks of squatters or tenant farmers to become independent landowners. Fledgling western communities lacked schools, churches, and courts, and inhabitants often lived miles distant from even their nearest neighbors.

**The Beginnings of the Second Great Awakening >>** This hardscrabble frontier proved the perfect tinder for sparking a series of dramatic religious revivals in the decades surrounding 1800. What lit the fire were missionary efforts by major Protestant churches—particularly the Baptists and the Methodists—who sent their ministers to travel the countryside on horseback and to preach wherever they could gather a crowd. Often those

^ Tents ringed the central area of a camp meeting where benches faced the preachers' platform. What does this illustration of an 1837 camp meeting suggest about gender relations and religious experience?



religious meetings took place outdoors and drew eager hearers from as far as 100 miles away, who camped for several days in makeshift tents to listen to sermons and to share in praying and singing hymns.

Thus was born a new form of Protestant worship, the camp meeting, which drew national notice after a mammoth gathering at Cane Ridge, Kentucky, in August 1801. At a time when the largest city in the state had only 2,000 people, more than 10,000 men, women, and children, white and black, flocked there to hear dozens of ministers preaching the gospel. Many in the crowd were overwhelmed by powerful religious feelings, some shrieking and shaking over guilt for their sins, others laughing and dancing from their high hopes of eternal salvation.

Some Protestant ministers denounced the "revival" at Cane Ridge and elsewhere as yet another instance of the ignorance and savagery of westerners. Other ministers were optimistic: they saw frontier camp meetings as the first sign of a Protestant Christian renewal that would sweep the new republic. Their hopes set the stage for what would come to be called the Second Great Awakening, a wave of religious revivals that swept throughout the nation after 1800 (see Chapter 12).

**The Prophet, Tecumseh, and the Pan-Indian Movement** >> Native peoples also turned to religion to meet the challenges of the early national frontier. Indeed, in traditional Indian religions they found the resource to revitalize their cultures by severing all ties with the white world. During the 1790s a revival led by Handsome Lake took hold among the Iroquois, following the loss of most of the Iroquois lands and the collapse of their military power in western New York. Later Lalawethika, also known as the Prophet, sparked a religious renewal among the Shawnees. The Prophet's early life was bleak: he was a poor hunter and as a child had accidentally blinded himself in the right eye with an arrow; the ridicule of his fellow tribe members drove him to alcoholism. Suddenly, in April 1805 he lapsed into a trance so deep that he was given up for dead. When he revived he spoke of being reborn. From this vision and others he outlined a new creed for the Shawnees.

Taking a new name—Tenskwatawa (Open Door)—he urged the Shawnees to renounce whiskey and white goods and return to their old ways of hunting with bows and arrows, eating customary foods such as corn and beans, and wearing traditional garb. The Shawnees could revitalize their culture, the Prophet insisted, by condemning intertribal violence, embracing monogamous marriage, and rejecting the idea of private instead of communal property. Except for guns, which could be used in self-defense, his followers were to discard all items made by whites. Intermarriage with white settlers was forbidden.

Setting up headquarters in 1808 at the newly built village of Prophetstown in Indiana, Tenskwatawa led a wider revival among the tribes of the Northwest. Just as thousands of white settlers traveled to Methodist or Baptist camp meetings in the woods, where preachers denounced the evils of liquor and called for a return to a pure way of life, so thousands of Indians from northern tribes traveled to the Prophet's village for inspiration. Many were concerned about the threatened loss of Indian lands.

Whereas Tenskwatawa's strategy of revitalization was primarily religious, his older brother

<< Where the Prophet centered his attempts at Indian unity on religious renewal, his brother Tecumseh, pictured here, took a political approach to the Indian revitalization movement. Advocating political unity in order to preserve Indian lands and cultures, Tecumseh was the dominant figure among Indians east of the Mississippi until he died fighting alongside the British in the War of 1812.

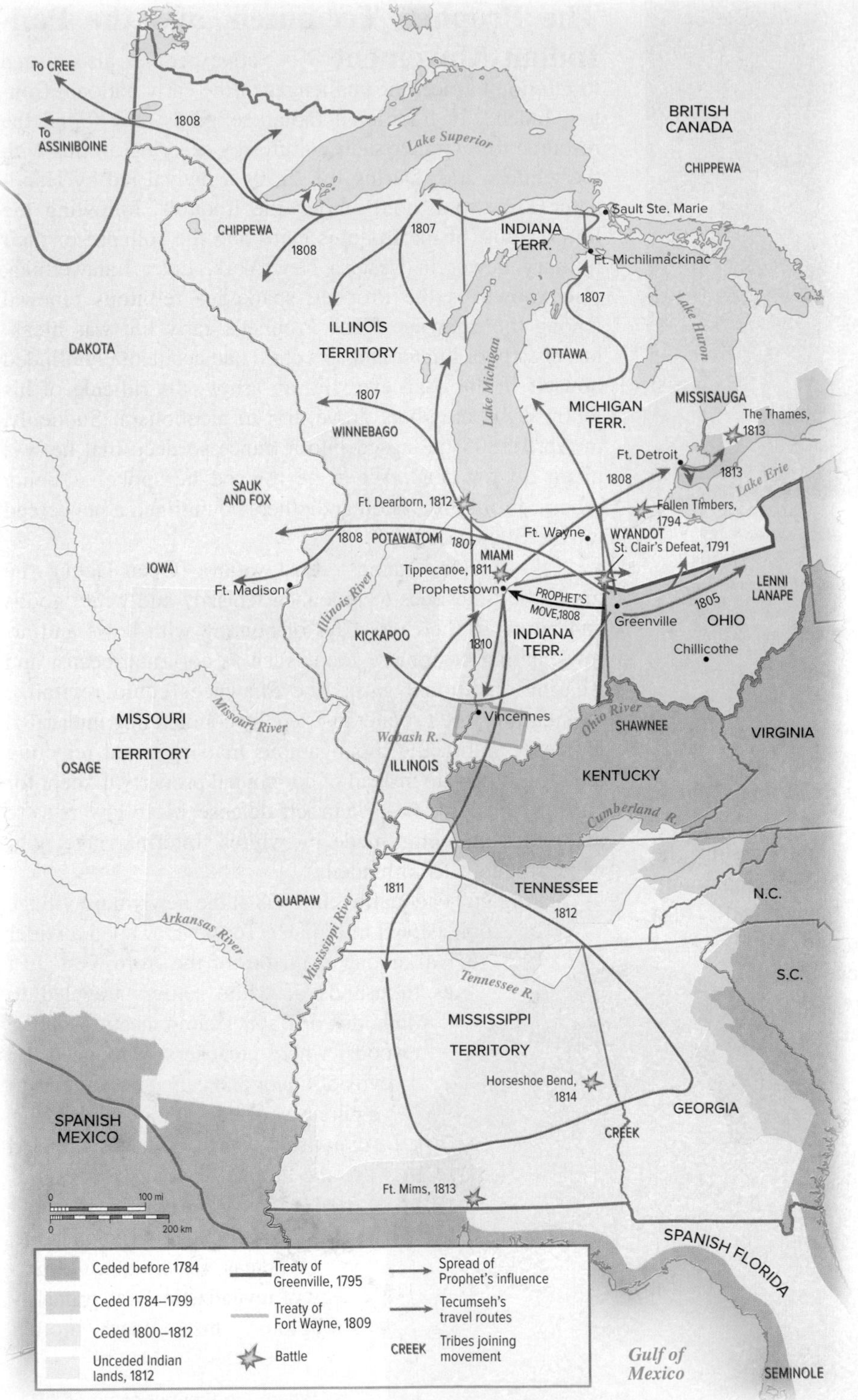

## MAP 9.4: THE INDIAN RESPONSE TO WHITE ENCROACHMENT

With land cessions and white western migration placing increased pressure on Indian cultures after 1790, news of the Prophet's revival fell on eager ears. It spread especially quickly northward along the shores of Lake Michigan and westward along Lake Superior and the interior of Wisconsin. Following the Battle of Tippecanoe, Tecumseh eclipsed the Prophet as the major leader of Indian resistance, but his trips south to forge political alliances met with less success.

*How far south did Tecumseh travel in his attempt to unite Indian resistance?*

Tecumseh turned to political and military solutions. William Henry Harrison described Tecumseh as "one of those uncommon geniuses which spring up occasionally to produce revolutions and overturn the established order of things." Tall and athletic, an accomplished hunter and warrior, Tecumseh traveled throughout the Northwest, urging tribes to forget ancient rivalries and unite to protect their lands. Just as Indian nations in the past had adopted the strategy of uniting in a confederacy, Tecumseh's alliance brought together the Wyandot, Chippewa, Sauk and Fox, Winnebago, Potawatomi, and other tribes on an even larger scale.

But the campaign for Pan-Indian unity ran into serious obstacles. Often, Tecumseh was asking tribes to unite with their traditional enemies in a common cause. When he headed south in 1811 he encountered greater resistance. Compared with northern tribes, most southern tribes were more prosperous, were more acculturated, and felt less immediate pressure on their land from whites. His southern mission ended largely in failure.

To compound Tecumseh's problems, while he was away a force of Americans under Governor Harrison defeated the Prophet's forces at the Battle of Tippecanoe in November 1811 and destroyed Prophetstown. As a result Tecumseh became convinced that the best way to contain white expansion was to play off the Americans against the British, who still held forts in the Great Lakes region. Indeed, by 1811 the United States and Great Britain were on the brink of war.

### REVIEW

How did Jefferson's presidency shape the settlement of the West?

# THE SECOND WAR FOR AMERICAN INDEPENDENCE

As Tecumseh worked to achieve a Pan-Indian alliance, Jefferson encountered his own difficulties in trying to achieve American political unity. The president hoped to woo all but the most extreme Federalists into the Republican camp. His reelection in 1804 showed how much progress he had made, as he defeated Federalist Charles Cotesworth Pinckney and carried 15 of 17 states. With the Republicans controlling three-quarters of the seats in Congress, one-party rule seemed at hand.

But events across the Atlantic complicated the efforts to unite Americans. Only two weeks after Napoleon agreed to sell Louisiana to the United States, war broke out between France and Great Britain. As in the 1790s the United States found itself caught between the world's two greatest powers. Jefferson insisted that the nation should remain neutral in a European war. But the policies he proposed to maintain neutrality sparked sharp divisions in American society and momentarily revived the two-party system.

In the past Jefferson had not shrunk from the use of force in dealing with foreign nations—most notably the Barbary States of North Africa—Algiers, Morocco, Tripoli, and Tunis. During the seventeenth and eighteenth centuries their corsairs plundered the cargo of enemy ships and enslaved the crews. European nations found it convenient to pay tributes to the Barbary States so their ships could sail unmolested. But both Jefferson and John Adams disliked that idea. The "policy of Christendom" of paying tribute, complained Adams, "has made Cowards of all their Sailors before the Standard of Mahomet [Mohammed]."

By the time John Adams became president he had subdued his outrage and agreed to tributes. But when Tripoli increased its demands in 1801 President Jefferson sent a squadron of American ships to force a settlement. In 1803 Tripoli captured the USS *Philadelphia.* Only the following year did Lieutenant Stephen Decatur repair the situation by sneaking into Tripoli's harbor and burning the vessel. The American blockade that followed forced Tripoli to give up its demands for tribute. Even so, the United States continued paying tribute to the other Barbary States until 1816.

**The Embargo** >> Jefferson was willing to fight the Barbary States, but he drew back from declaring war against Britain or France. Between 1803 and 1807 Britain seized more than 500 American ships; France more than 300. The British navy also impressed into service thousands of

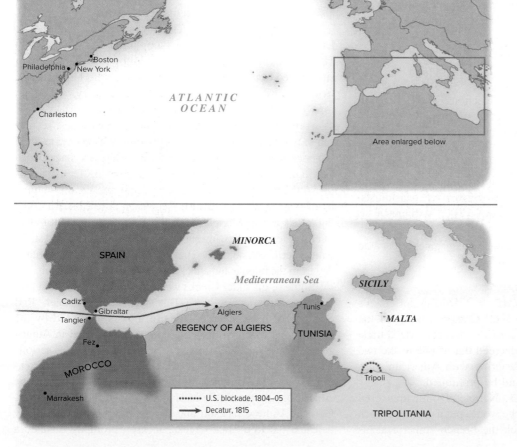

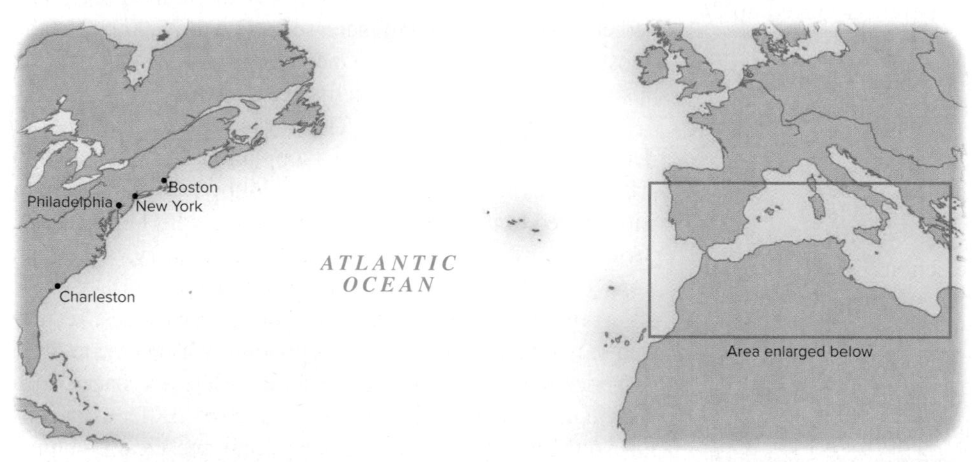

Boston
Philadelphia
New York
Charleston
ATLANTIC OCEAN
Area enlarged below
SPAIN
MINORCA
Mediterranean Sea
SICILY
MALTA
Cadiz
Gibraltar
Tangier
Algiers
Tunis
REGENCY OF ALGIERS
TUNISIA
Fez
MOROCCO
Marrakesh
Tripoli
TRIPOLITANIA
U.S. blockade, 1804–05
Decatur, 1815


## MAP 9.5: THE UNITED STATES AND THE BARBARY STATES, 1801—1815

The young United States, like many European powers, found its trading vessels challenged by the Barbary States of Morocco, Algiers, Tunis, and Tripoli. When the pasha of Tripoli declared war on the United States in 1801, Jefferson dispatched a force that blockaded Tripoli to bring the war to an end in 1805. Tribute paid to the other Barbary States continued until 1816, after a new naval force, led by Captain Stephen Decatur, forced the ruler of Algiers to end the practice. *What cultural factors made Jefferson and Adams reluctant to pay tribute to the Barbary States?*

sailors, some who were deserters from England's fleet but others who were native-born Americans. Despite such harrassment, Jefferson pursued a program of "peaceable coercion" designed to protect neutral rights without war. His proposed **embargo** not only prohibited American ships from trading with foreign ports but also stopped the export of all American goods. The president was confident that American exports were so essential to the two belligerents that they would quickly agree to respect American neutral rights. In December 1807 Congress passed the Embargo Act.

**embargo** government act prohibiting trade with a foreign country or countries, usually to exert economic pressure.

Jefferson had seriously miscalculated. France did not depend on American trade and so managed well enough, while British ships quickly took over the carrying trade as American vessels lay idle. Under the embargo, both American imports and exports plunged. As the center of American shipping, New England port cities protested the loudest, and their merchants smuggled behind officials' backs.

## Madison and the Young Republicans >>

Following Washington's example Jefferson did not seek a third term. A caucus of Republican members of Congress selected James Madison to run against Federalist Charles Cotesworth Pinckney. Madison triumphed easily, although in discontented New England, the Federalists picked up 24 seats in Congress.

Few men have assumed the presidency with more experience than James Madison, yet his tenure as president proved disappointing. Despite his intellectual brilliance, he lacked the force of leadership and the inner strength to impose his will on less capable men.

With a president reluctant to fight for what he wanted, leadership passed to Congress. The elections of 1810 swept in a new generation of Republicans, led by the magnetic 34-year-old Henry Clay of Kentucky, who gained the rare distinction of being elected Speaker in his first term. These younger Republicans were more nationalistic than the generation led by Jefferson and Madison. They sought an ambitious program of economic development and were aggressive expansionists, especially those from frontier districts. Their willingness to go to war earned them the name of War Hawks. Though they numbered fewer than 30 in Congress, they quickly became the driving force in the Republican Party.

## The Decision for War >>

During Jefferson's final week in office in early 1809 Congress repealed the Embargo Act. The following year Congress authorized trade with France and England but decreed that if one of the two belligerents agreed to stop interfering with American shipping, trade with the other would be prohibited.

Given these circumstances, Napoleon outmaneuvered the British by announcing that he would put aside the French trade regulations. Madison took the French emperor at his word and reimposed a ban on trade with England. French raiders continued to seize American ships, but American anger focused on the British, who then seized many more ships and continued to impress American sailors. Finally, on June 16, 1812, the British ministry suspended the searches and seizures of American ships.

The concession came too late. Two days earlier, unaware of the change in policy, Congress granted Madison's request for a declaration of war against Britain. The vote was mostly along party lines, with every Federalist voting against war. By contrast, members of Congress from the South and the West clamored most strongly for war. Their constituents were consumed with a desire to seize additional territory in Canada or in Florida (owned by Britain's ally Spain). In addition, they accused the British of stirring up hostility among the Indian tribes.

Perhaps most important, the War Hawks were convinced that Britain had never truly accepted the verdict of the American Revolution. To them, American independence—and with it republicanism—hung in the balance. For Americans hungering to be accepted in the community of nations, nothing rankled more than still being treated by the British as colonials.

With Britain preoccupied by Napoleon, the War Hawks expected an easy victory. In truth, the United States was totally unprepared for war. Crippled by Jefferson's cutbacks, the navy was unable to lift the British blockade of the American coast, which bottled up the country's merchant marine and most of its navy. As for the U.S. Army, it was small and poorly led. When Congress moved to increase its size to 75,000, even the most hawkish states failed to meet their quotas. Congress was also reluctant to levy taxes to finance the war.

A three-pronged American invasion of Canada from Detroit, Niagara, and Lake Champlain failed dismally in 1812. Americans fared better the following year, as both sides raced to build a navy on the strategically located Lake Erie. Led by Commander Oliver Hazard Perry, American forces won a decisive victory at Put-In Bay in 1813.

As the United States struggled to organize its forces, Tecumseh sensed that his long-awaited opportunity had come to drive Americans out of the western territories. "Here is a chance, such as will never occur again," he told a war council, "for us Indians of North America to form ourselves into one great combination." Allying with the British, Tecumseh traveled south in the fall to talk again with his Creek allies. To coordinate an Indian offensive for the following summer, he left a bundle of red sticks with eager Creek soldiers. They were to remove one stick each day from the bundle and attack when the sticks had run out.

Some of the older Creeks were more acculturated and preferred an American alliance. But about 2,000 younger "Red Stick" Creeks launched a series of attacks, climaxed by the destruction of Fort Mims along the Alabama River in August 1813. Once again, the Indians' lack of unity was a serious handicap, as warriors from the Cherokee, Choctaw, and Chickasaw tribes, traditional Creek enemies, allied with the Americans. At the Battle of Horseshoe Bend in March 1814, General Andrew Jackson and his Tennessee militia soundly defeated the Red Stick Creeks. Jackson promptly dictated a

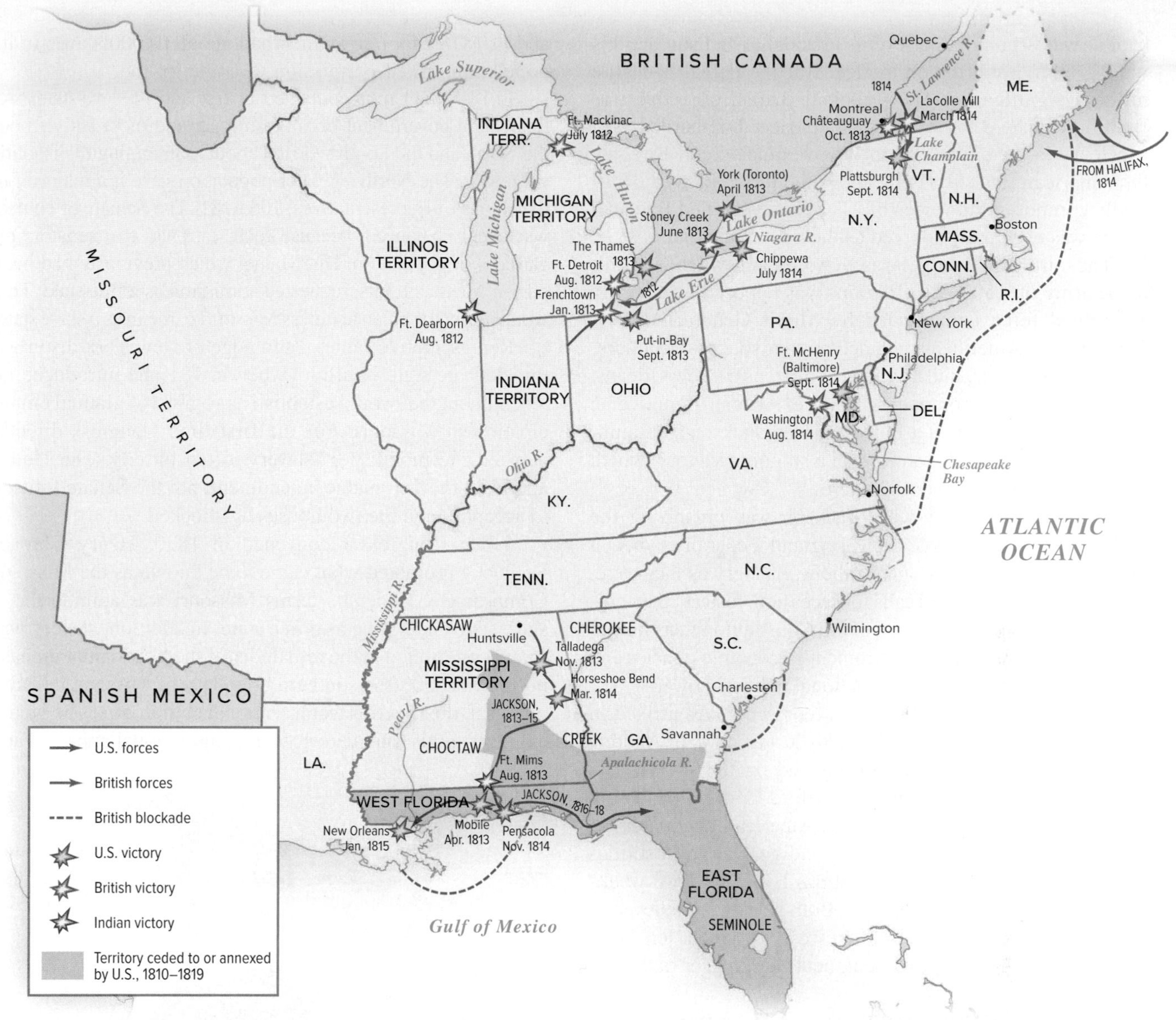

BRITISH CANADA
Quebec
St. Lawrence R.
ME.
1814
Montreal
Châteauguay
Oct. 1813
LaColle Mill
March 1814
Lake Champlain
Plattsburgh
Sept. 1814
VT.
N.H.
FROM HALIFAX, 1814
Lake Superior
INDIANA TERR.
Ft. Mackinac
July 1812
Lake Huron
Lake Michigan
MICHIGAN TERRITORY
York (Toronto)
April 1813
Stoney Creek
June 1813
Lake Ontario
Niagara R.
Chippewa
July 1814
N.Y.
MASS.
Boston
CONN.
R.I.
ILLINOIS TERRITORY
The Thames
1813
Ft. Detroit
Aug. 1812
Frenchtown
Jan. 1813
1812
Lake Erie
Put-in-Bay
Sept. 1813
PA.
New York
Ft. Dearborn
Aug. 1812
MISSOURI TERRITORY
Ft. McHenry
(Baltimore)
Sept. 1814
Philadelphia
N.J.
INDIANA TERRITORY
OHIO
Washington
Aug. 1814
MD.
DEL.
VA.
Chesapeake Bay
Ohio R.
KY.
Norfolk
ATLANTIC OCEAN
TENN.
N.C.
Mississippi R.
CHICKASAW
Huntsville
CHEROKEE
Talladega
Nov. 1813
Wilmington
S.C.
MISSISSIPPI TERRITORY
Horseshoe Bend
Mar. 1814
Charleston
SPANISH MEXICO
JACKSON, 1813–15
Pearl R.
CREEK
GA.
Savannah
CHOCTAW
LA.
Ft. Mims
Aug. 1813
Apalachicola R.
WEST FLORIDA
JACKSON, 1816–18
New Orleans
Jan. 1815
Mobile
Apr. 1813
Pensacola
Nov. 1814
EAST FLORIDA
SEMINOLE
Gulf of Mexico
U.S. forces
British forces
British blockade
U.S. victory
British victory
Indian victory
Territory ceded to or annexed by U.S., 1810–1819


## MAP 9.6: THE WAR OF 1812

After the American victory on Lake Erie and the defeat of the western Indians at the Battle of the Thames, the British adopted a three-pronged strategy to invade the United States, climaxing with an attempt on New Orleans. But they met their match in Andrew Jackson, whose troops marched to New Orleans after fighting a series of battles against the Creeks and forcing them to cede a massive tract of land. *Why did so much of the fighting in the War of 1812 take place on the northern borders of the United States?*

peace treaty under which the Creeks ceded 22 million acres of land in the Mississippi Territory. They and the other southern tribes still retained significant landholdings, but Indian military power had been broken in the South, east of the Mississippi.

Farther north, in October 1813, American forces under General William Henry Harrison defeated the British and their Indian allies at the Battle of the Thames. In the midst of heavy fighting Tecumseh was killed. With him died any hope of a Pan-Indian movement.

**The British Invasion** >> As long as the war against Napoleon continued, the British were unwilling to divert army units to North America. But in 1814 Napoleon was at last defeated. Free to concentrate on America, the British devised a coordinated strategy to invade the United States in the northern, central, and southern parts of the country. The main army headed south from Montreal but was checked when Americans destroyed the British fleet on Lake Champlain.

Meanwhile, a smaller British force captured Washington and burned several public buildings, including the Capitol and the president's home. To cover the scars of this destruction, the executive mansion was painted with whitewash and became known as the White House. The burning of the capital was a humiliating event: President Madison and his wife, Dolley, were forced to flee. But the defeat had little military significance. The principal British objective was Baltimore, where for 25 hours their fleet bombarded Fort McHenry in the city's harbor. When Francis Scott Key saw the American flag still flying above the fort at dawn, he hurriedly composed the verses of "The Star Spangled Banner," which was eventually adopted as the national anthem.

The third British target was New Orleans, where a formidable army of 7,500 British troops was opposed by a hastily assembled force commanded by Major General Andrew Jackson. The Americans included regular soldiers; frontiersmen from Kentucky and Tennessee; citizens of New Orleans, including several companies of free African Americans; Choctaw Indians; and a group of pirates. Jackson's outnumbered and ill-equipped forces won a stunning victory, which made the general an overnight hero.

In December 1814, while Jackson was organizing the defense of New Orleans, New England Federalists met in Hartford to map strategy against the war. Angry as they were, the delegates still rejected calls for secession. Instead, they proposed a series of amendments to the Constitution that showed their displeasure with the government's economic policies and their resentment of the South's national political power.

To the convention's dismay its representatives arrived in Washington to present their demands just as news of Andrew Jackson's victory was being trumpeted on the streets. The celebrations badly undercut the Hartford Convention, as did news from across the Atlantic that American negotiators in Ghent, Belgium, had signed a treaty ending the war. Hostilities had ceased, technically, on Christmas Eve 1814, two weeks before the Battle of New Orleans. Both sides were relieved to end the conflict, even though the Treaty of Ghent left unresolved the issues of impressment, neutral rights, or trade.

**America Turns Inward** >> The return of peace hard on the heels of Jackson's victory sparked a new confidence in many Americans. The new nationalism sounded the death knell of the Federalist Party, for even talk of secession at the Hartford Convention had tainted the party with disunion and treason. In the 1816 election Madison's secretary of state, James Monroe, resoundingly defeated Federalist Rufus King of New York. Four years later Monroe ran for reelection unopposed.

**Monroe's Presidency** >> The major domestic challenge that Monroe faced was the renewal of sectional rivalries in 1819, when the Missouri Territory applied for admission as a slave state. Before the controversy over Missouri erupted, slavery had not been a major issue in American politics. Congress had debated the institution when it prohibited the African slave trade in 1808, the earliest year this step could be taken under the Constitution. But lacking any specific federal legislation to stop it, slavery had crossed the Mississippi River into the Louisiana Purchase. Louisiana entered the Union in 1812 as a slave state, and in 1818 Missouri, which had about 10,000 slaves in its population, asked permission to come in, too.

In 1818 the Union contained 11 free and 11 slave states. As the federal government became stronger and more active, both the North and the South worried about maintaining their political power. The North's greater population gave it a majority in the House of Representatives, 105 to 81. The Senate, of course, was evenly balanced, because each state had two senators regardless of population. But Maine, which previously had been part of Massachusetts, requested admission as a free state. That would upset the balance unless Missouri came in as a slave state.

Representative James Tallmadge of New York disturbed this delicate state of affairs when in 1819 he introduced an amendment that would establish a program of gradual emancipation in Missouri. For the first time Congress directly debated the morality of slavery, often bitterly. The House approved the Tallmadge amendment, but the Senate refused to accept it, and the two houses deadlocked.

When Congress reconvened in 1820, Henry Clay of Kentucky promoted what came to be known as the Missouri Compromise. Under its terms Missouri was admitted as a slave state and Maine as a free state. In addition, slavery was forever prohibited in the remainder of the Louisiana Purchase north of 36°30′ (the southern boundary of Missouri). Clay's proposal, the first of several sectional compromises he would engineer in his long career, won congressional approval and

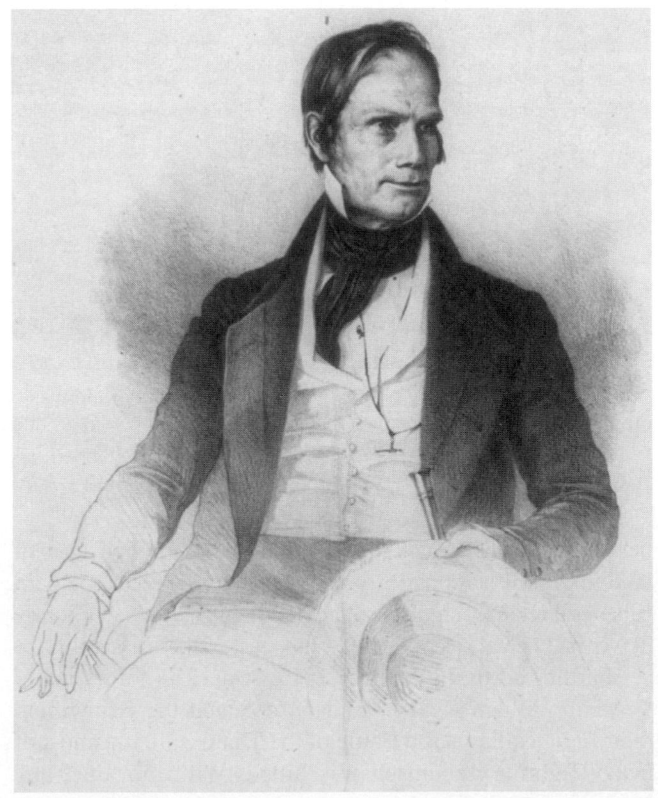

^ Young Henry Clay of Kentucky promoted the Missouri Compromise.
Source: Library of Congress, Prints and Photographs Division [LC-USZ62-63409]

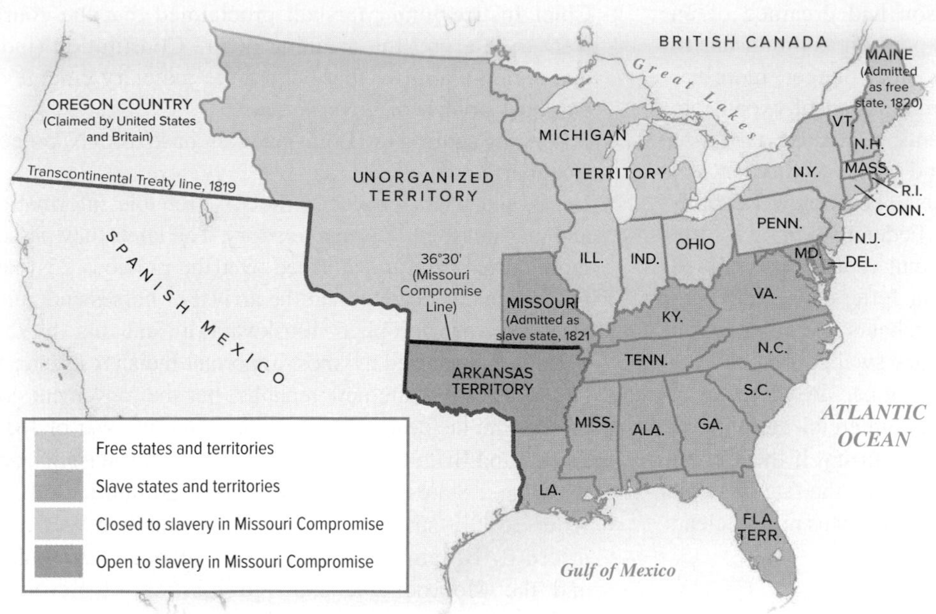
BRITISH CANADA
Great Lakes
MAINE (Admitted as free state, 1820)
OREGON COUNTRY (Claimed by United States and Britain)
Transcontinental Treaty line, 1819
UNORGANIZED TERRITORY
MICHIGAN TERRITORY
VT.
N.H.
MASS.
R.I.
CONN.
N.Y.
PENN.
N.J.
DEL.
MD.
OHIO
IND.
ILL.
VA.
KY.
36°30' (Missouri Compromise Line)
MISSOURI (Admitted as slave state, 1821)
SPANISH MEXICO
TENN.
N.C.
S.C.
ARKANSAS TERRITORY
MISS.
ALA.
GA.
ATLANTIC OCEAN
LA.
FLA. TERR.
Gulf of Mexico
Free states and territories
Slave states and territories
Closed to slavery in Missouri Compromise
Open to slavery in Missouri Compromise

## MAP 9.7: THE MISSOURI COMPROMISE AND THE UNION'S BOUNDARIES IN 1820

Monroe signed the measure, ending the crisis. But southern fears for the security of slavery and northern fears about its spread remained. Monroe's greatest achievements were diplomatic, accomplished largely by his talented secretary of state, John Quincy Adams, the son of President John Adams. An experienced diplomat, Adams thought of the Republic in continental terms and was intent on promoting expansion to the Pacific. Such a vision required dealing with Spain, which had never recognized the legality of the Louisiana Purchase. In addition, between 1810 and 1813 the United States had occupied and unilaterally annexed Spanish West Florida.

But Spain was preoccupied with events farther south in the Americas. In the first quarter of the nineteenth century its colonies one after another revolted and established themselves as independent nations. These revolutions increased the pressure on the Spanish minister to America, Luis de Onís, to come to terms with the United States. So, too, did Andrew Jackson, who marched into East Florida and captured several Spanish forts in 1818. Jackson had exceeded his instructions, but Adams understood the additional pressure this aggression put on Onís and refused to disavow it.

Fearful that the United States might next invade Texas or other Spanish territory, Spain agreed to the Transcontinental Treaty in February 1819. Its terms set the boundary between American and Spanish territory all the way to the Pacific. Spain not only gave up its claims to the Pacific Northwest but also ceded Florida. In order to obtain the line to the Pacific, the United States abandoned its contention that Texas was part of the Louisiana Purchase.

More important, the United States also came to terms with Great Britain. Following the War of 1812 the British abandoned their connections with the western Indian tribes and no longer attempted to block American expansion to the Rocky Mountains. In a growing spirit of cooperation the countries agreed in 1818 to the 49th parallel as the northern boundary of the Louisiana Purchase and also to joint control of the Oregon Territory for 10 years, subject to renewal.

In his annual message to Congress, on December 2, 1823, Monroe also announced that the United States would not interfere with already established European colonies in the Western Hemisphere. But any intervention in the new republics of Latin America, he warned, would be considered a hostile act: "The American continents . . . are henceforth not to be considered as subjects for future colonization by any European powers." The essence of this policy was the concept of two worlds, one old and one new, each refraining from interfering in the other's affairs. American public opinion hailed Monroe's statement and then promptly forgot it. Only years later would it be referred to as the Monroe Doctrine.

**REVIEW**

What were the causes of the War of 1812?

The three decades after 1789 demonstrated how profoundly events in the wider world could affect life within the United States, shaping its politics, its boundaries, its economy—its future.

The French Revolution contributed to splintering the once-united leaders of the American Revolution into two rival parties. The wars that followed, between France and England, deepened the divisions between Federalists and Republicans and prompted both parties to mobilize the political loyalties of ordinary white American men and women. Napoleon's ambitions to conquer Europe handed Jefferson the Louisiana Territory, while British efforts to reclaim its American empire tempted some New Englanders to secede from the Union and encouraged Tecumseh's hopes of mounting a Pan-Indian resistance on the frontier. The Haitian Revolution in the Caribbean prompted free blacks in northern cities to protest racial inequalities and slavery within the United States.

But by the 1820s most white Americans paid less attention to events abroad than to expanding across the vast

North American continent. Jefferson had dreamed of an "empire of liberty," delighting in expansion as the means to preserve a nation of small farmers. But younger, more nationalistic Republicans had a different vision of expansion. They spoke of internal improvements, protective tariffs to foster American industries, roads and canals to link farmers with towns, cities, and wider markets. These new Republicans were not aristocratic, like the Federalists of old. Still, their dream of a national, commercial republic resembled Franklin's and Hamilton's more than Jefferson's. They had seen how handsomely American merchants and commercial farmers profited when European wars swelled demand for American wheat and cotton. They looked to profit from speculation in land, the growth of commercial agriculture, and new methods of industrial manufacturing. If they represented the rising generation, what would be the fate of semi-subsistence farm communities? The answer was not yet clear.

# CHAPTER SUMMARY

Basic social divisions between the commercial and semi-subsistence regions shaped the politics of the new United States. Between 1789 and the 1820s the first parties emerged and, along with them, a more popular and participatory political culture. Over the same decades Indian confederacies mounted a sustained resistance to westward expansion, while events in Europe deepened divisions among Federalists and Republicans and threatened the very existence of the fledgling American republic.

- The first party to organize in the 1790s was the Federalists, led by Alexander Hamilton and George Washington.
- Divisions over Hamilton's policies as secretary of the treasury resulted in the formation of the Republicans, led by James Madison and Thomas Jefferson.
- The commercially minded Federalists believed in order and hierarchy, supported loose construction of the Constitution, and wanted a powerful central government to promote economic growth.
- The Republican Party, with its sympathy for agrarian ideals, endorsed strict construction of the Constitution, wanted a less active federal government, and harbored a strong fear of aristocracy.
- The French Revolution, the XYZ Affair, the naval war, and the Alien and Sedition Acts also deepened the partisan division between Federalists and Republicans during the 1790s. The Federalists' controversial domestic and foreign policies, internal divisions, and hostility to the masses eventually led to their downfall.
- Before becoming president, Jefferson advocated the principles of agrarianism, limited government, and strict construction of the Constitution. But once in power, he failed to dismantle Hamilton's economic program and promoted western expansion by acquiring Louisiana from France.
- Chief Justice John Marshall proclaimed that the courts were to interpret the meaning of the Constitution (judicial review), a move that helped the judiciary emerge as an equal branch of government.
- Jefferson acquired the Louisiana Purchase from Napoleon Bonaparte.
- Lewis and Clark produced the first reliable information and maps of the Louisiana territory. The lands they passed through had been transformed over the previous 25 years by disease, dislocation, and the arrival of horses and guns.
- The Shawnee prophet Tenskwatawa and his brother Tecumseh organized the most important Indian resistance to the expansion of the new republic, but the movement collapsed with the death of Tecumseh during the War of 1812.
- France and Britain both interfered with neutral rights, and the United States went to war against Britain in 1812.
- After 1815 a surge in American nationalism was reinforced by Britain's recognition of American sovereignty and the Monroe Doctrine's prohibition of European intervention in the Western Hemisphere. But the Missouri crisis foreshadowed growing sectional rivalries.

## Additional Reading

Two good overviews of early national politics are Stanley Elkins and Eric McKitrick's *The Age of Federalism* (1993); and James Roger Sharp, *American Politics in the Early Republic* (1993). Another approach to understanding the politics of this period is to read about the lives of leading political figures: among the best are Joseph Ellis's biographies of John Adams (*Passionate Sage,* 1993) and Thomas Jefferson (*American Sphinx,* rev. ed., 1998); and two biographies of Alexander Hamilton, one by Ron Chernow (the basis for the musical, *Hamilton*) and one by Gerald Stourzh. For excellent work on the early republic in international context, see David Armitage, *The Declaration of Independence: A Global History* (2007); Eliga Gould, *Among the Powers of the Earth* (2012); and Janet Polasky, *Revolutions without Borders* (2015). For Haiti and the early American republic, see Ashli White, *Encountering Revolution* (2010); and James Alexander Dun, *Dangerous Neighbors* (2016).

To become better acquainted with the popular political culture of the early republic, consult *Beyond the Founders* (2004), a superb collection of essays edited by Jeffrey Pasley, Andrew W. Robertson, and David Waldstreicher. For an engaging narrative about the political influence exerted by white women, see Catherine Allgor, *Parlor Politics* (2000); and for rich descriptions of the social and political interactions among whites, African Americans, and Indians in the new republic, see Joshua Rothman, *Notorious in the Neighborhood* (2003); and John Wood Sweet, *Bodies Politic* (2003). To gain a fuller understanding of the lives of Indians, slaves, and whites in the west, rely on Leonard Sadosky, *Revolutionary Negotiations* (2009); Stephen Aron, *American Confluence* (2006); and Adam Rothman, *Slave Country* (2005).

# 10 The Opening of America

## 1815–1850

Peddlers like the man in this photograph helped spread the market economy to every corner of the United States. Early in his career, clock-maker and businessman Chauncey Jerome had peddled his clocks from farmhouse to farmhouse.

Source: Library of Congress, Prints and Photographs Division [LC-USZC4-4161]

### >> An American Story

## FROM BOOM TO BUST WITH ONE-DAY CLOCKS

In the years before the Civil War, the name of Chauncey Jerome could be found traced in neat, sharp letters in a thousand different places across the globe: everywhere from the fireplace mantels of southern planters to the log cabins of Illinois farmers, and even in Chinese trading houses. For Chauncey Jerome was a New England clock-maker whose clever and inexpensive machines had conquered the markets of the world.

As a boy Jerome had apprenticed himself to a carpenter, but after serving in the War of 1812 he decided to try clock-making. For years he eked out a living peddling his products from farmhouse to farmhouse, until 1824, when his career took off thanks to a "very showy" bronze looking-glass clock. Between 1827 and 1837 Jerome's factory produced more clocks than any other in the country. But when the Panic of 1837 struck, Jerome had to scramble to avoid financial ruin.

Looking for a new opportunity, he set out to produce an inexpensive brass "one-day" clock—so called because its winding mechanism kept it running that long. Traditionally, the works of these clocks were made of wood, and the wheels and teeth had to be painstakingly cut by hand. Jerome's brass version proved more accurate as well as cheaper. Costs came down further when he began to use interchangeable parts and combined his operations for making cases and movements within a single factory in New Haven, Connecticut. By systematically organizing the production process, Jerome brought the price of a good clock within the reach of ordinary people. So popular were the new models that desperate competitors began attaching Jerome labels to their own inferior imitations.

Disaster loomed again in 1855 when Jerome took on several unreliable partners. Within a few years his business faltered, then failed. At the age of 62 the once-prominent business leader found himself working again in a clock factory as an ordinary mechanic. He lived his last years in poverty.

Chauncey Jerome's life spanned the transition from the master-apprentice system of production to the beginnings of mechanization and the rise of the factory system. By 1850 the notion of independent American farmers living mainly on what they themselves produced had become a dream of the past. In its place stood a commercial republic in which a full-blown national market encompassed most settled areas of the country.

The concept of the market is crucial here. Americans tied themselves to one another eagerly, even aggressively, through the mechanism of the free market. They sold cotton or wheat and bought manufactured cloth or brass one-day clocks. They borrowed money not merely to buy a house or farm but also to speculate and profit. They relied, even in many rural villages, on cash and paper money instead of bartering for goods and services. American life moved from less to more specialized forms of labor. It moved from subsistence-oriented to commercially oriented outlooks and from face-to-face local dealings to impersonal, distant transactions. It shifted from the mechanically simple to the technologically complex and from less dense patterns of settlement on farms to more complex arrangements in cities and towns. Such were the changes Chauncey Jerome witnessed—indeed, changes he helped to bring about himself, with his clocks that divided the working days of Americans into more disciplined, orderly segments.

As these changes took place, Jerome sensed that society had taken on a different tone—that the marketplace and its ethos had become dominant. "It is all money and business, business and money which make the man now-a-days," he complained. "Success is every thing." The United States, according to one foreign traveler, had become "one gigantic workshop, over the entrance of which there is the blazing inscription 'No admission here except on business.'" <<

THEMATIC TIMELINE

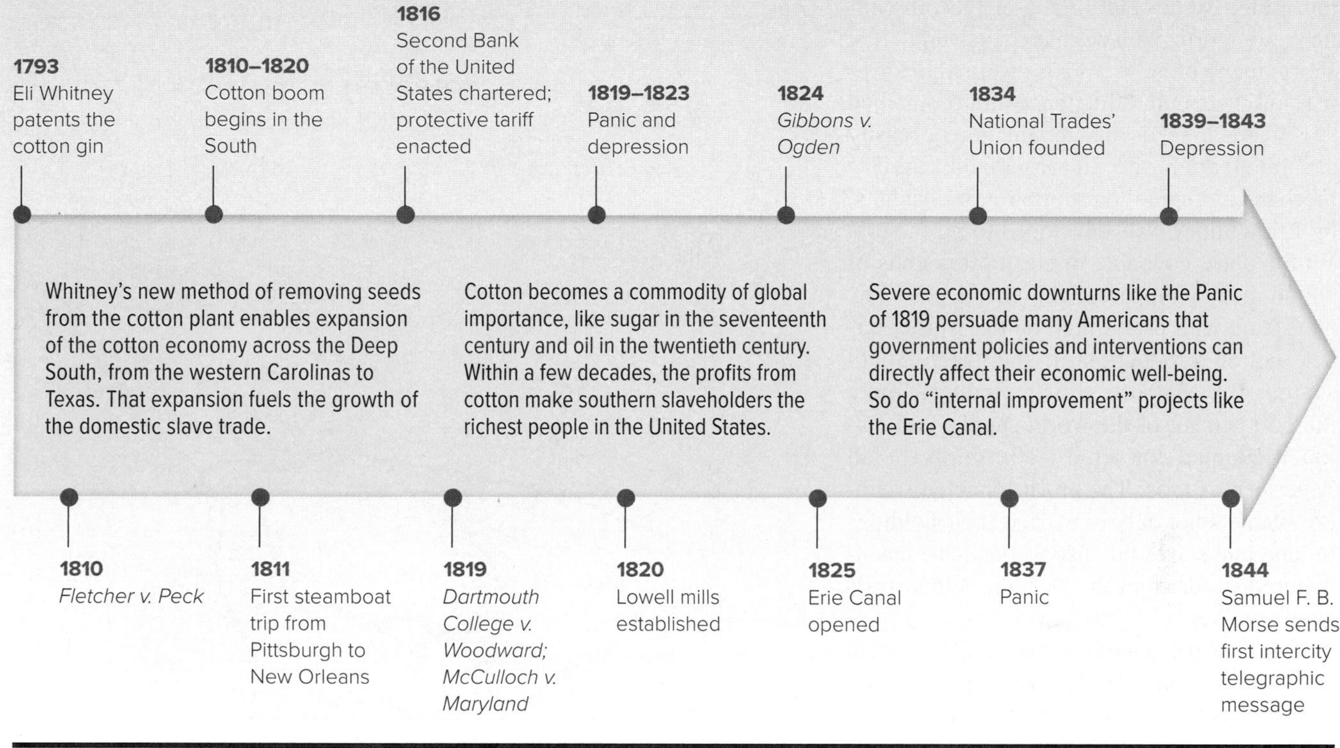

1793
Eli Whitney patents the cotton gin
1810–1820
Cotton boom begins in the South
1816
Second Bank of the United States chartered; protective tariff enacted
1819–1823
Panic and depression
1824
Gibbons v. Ogden
1834
National Trades' Union founded
1839–1843
Depression
Whitney's new method of removing seeds from the cotton plant enables expansion of the cotton economy across the Deep South, from the western Carolinas to Texas. That expansion fuels the growth of the domestic slave trade.
Cotton becomes a commodity of global importance, like sugar in the seventeenth century and oil in the twentieth century. Within a few decades, the profits from cotton make southern slaveholders the richest people in the United States.
Severe economic downturns like the Panic of 1819 persuade many Americans that government policies and interventions can directly affect their economic well-being. So do "internal improvement" projects like the Erie Canal.
1810
Fletcher v. Peck
1811
First steamboat trip from Pittsburgh to New Orleans
1819
Dartmouth College v. Woodward; McCulloch v. Maryland
1820
Lowell mills established
1825
Erie Canal opened
1837
Panic
1844
Samuel F. B. Morse sends first intercity telegraphic message


# THE NATIONAL MARKET ECONOMY

The national market economy began to develop following the War of 1812. As the United States entered a period of unprecedented economic expansion, the economy became varied enough to grow without relying on international trade. Before the war, if European nations suddenly stopped purchasing American commodities such as tobacco and timber, the domestic economy faltered. Since so many Americans remained rural and primarily self-sufficient, they could not absorb any increase in goods produced by American manufacturers.

But the War of 1812 marked an important turning point in the creation and expansion of a domestic market. First the embargo and then the war itself stimulated manufacturing, particularly in textiles. In addition, war had also bottled up capital in Europe. When peace was restored, this capital flowed into the United States to take advantage of new investment opportunities. Finally, the war experience led the federal government to adopt policies designed to spur economic expansion.

**The New Nationalism** >> After the war with Britain, leadership passed to a new generation of the Republic—younger men such as Henry Clay, John C. Calhoun, and John Quincy Adams. Each was an ardent nationalist eager to use federal power to promote development. Increasingly dominant within the Republican Party, they advocated the "New Nationalism," a set of economic policies designed to help all regions prosper and bind the nation more tightly together.

Even James Madison saw the need for increased federal activity, given the problems the government experienced during the war. The national bank had closed its doors in 1811 when its charter expired, and the result had been financial chaos. With Madison's approval Congress in 1816 chartered the Second Bank of the United States for a period of 20 years. Madison also agreed to a mildly protective tariff to aid young American industries by raising the price of competing foreign goods. Finally, Madison supported federal aid for internal improvements such as roads, canals, and bridges, since the war had demonstrated how cumbersome it was to move troops or supplies overland.

**The Cotton Trade and the Domestic Slave Trade** >> The most important spur to American economic development after 1815 was the growing cotton trade. By the end of the eighteenth century, southern planters had discovered that short-fiber cotton would grow in the lower part of the South. But the cotton contained sticky green seeds that could not be easily separated from the lint by hand, until a mechanical engine, or "cotton gin," patented by Eli Whitney, was developed to do the job. With a slave now able to clean 50 pounds of cotton a day (compared with only 1 pound by hand) and with prices high on the world market, cotton production in the Deep South soared. By 1840 the South produced more than 60 percent of the world supply, and cotton accounted for almost two-thirds of all American exports. The profits enabled southern planters not only to expand their holdings in land and slaves but also to purchase manufactured goods from the North and foodstuffs from the West.

Most of the South's exported cotton went to Britain, feeding the steady demands of its booming textile industry. Cotton also transformed the economy of the northern states. Northern factories made money by turning raw cotton into cloth, while northern merchants reaped profits from shipping cotton abroad and selling textiles and other finished goods to southern planters. Bankers and financiers everywhere in the United States extended credit to planters and slave traders. With the end of the international slave trade in 1808, a domestic commerce in slaves flourished, one that enriched both the slaveowners and the entrepreneurs who engaged in that business. As planters in the Upper South shifted to wheat production, which required less labor year-round than tobacco, they sold one million slaves into the Deep South. That forced migration marked a second Middle Passage for African Americans.

Like sugar in the eighteenth century or petroleum in the twentieth, cotton was a commodity of global significance in the nineteenth century. It served as an engine of capitalism and the Industrial Revolution on both sides of the Atlantic. As one Manhattan businessman observed in 1835, "Cotton has enriched all through whose hands it has passed."

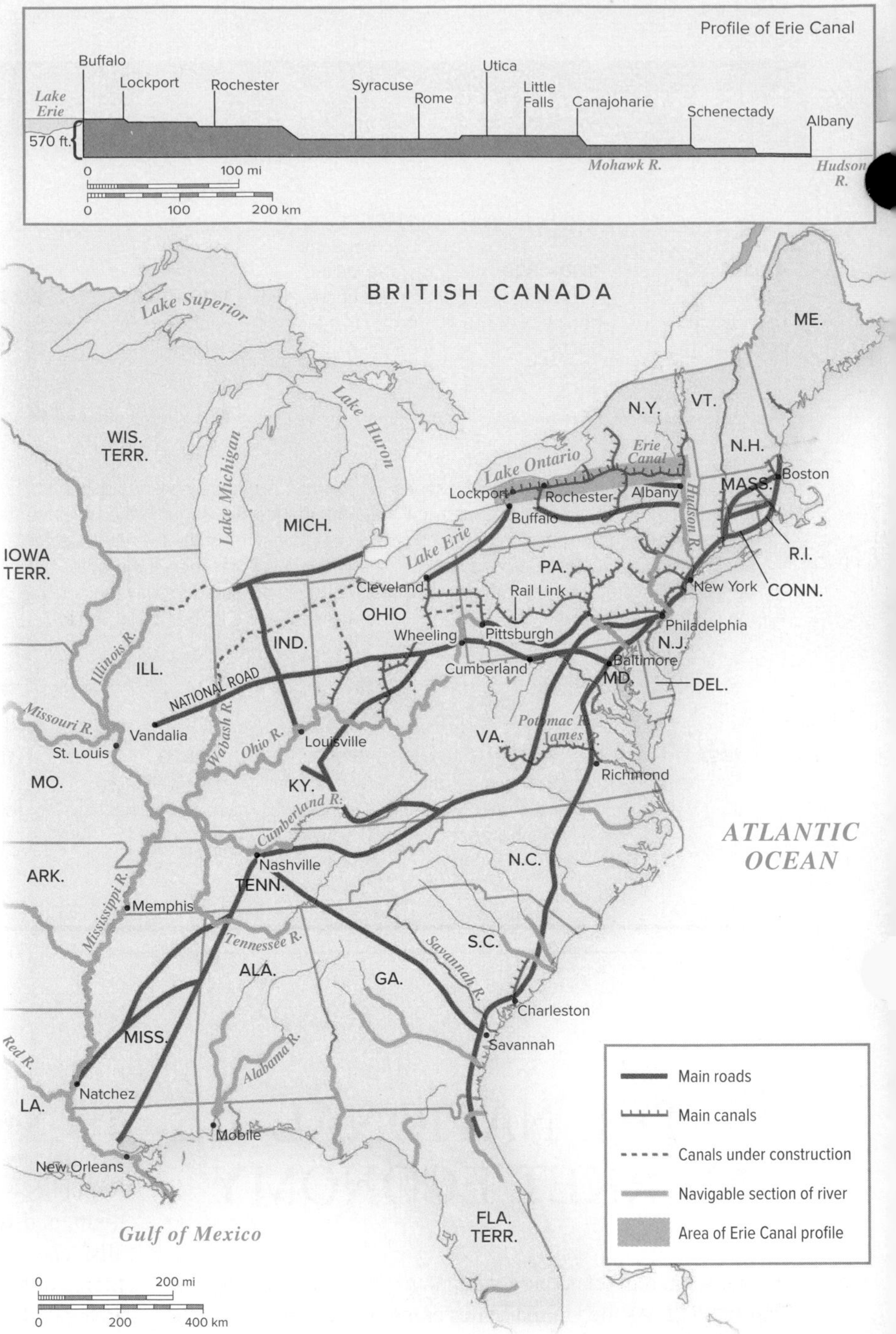

## MAP 10.1: THE TRANSPORTATION NETWORK OF A MARKET ECONOMY, 1840

Canals played their most important role in the Northeast, where they linked eastern cities to western rivers and the Great Lakes. Steamboats were most crucial in the extensive river systems of the South and the West.

*What accounts for the concentration of canals in the northern states?*

# Make a Case

Which Americans benefited the most from the national market economy?

<< New York's Erie Canal transformed many inland settlements into commercial centers. This canal boat is named after the first inland boomtown in America, Rochester.



## The Transportation Revolution

>> For a market economy to become truly national, a transportation network linking various parts of the nation was essential. The economy had not become self-sustaining earlier partly because the only way to transport goods cheaply was by water. Thus trade was limited largely to coastal and international markets, for even on rivers, bulky goods moved easily in only one direction: downstream.

After 1815 all that changed. From 1825 to 1855—the span of a single generation—the cost of transportation on land fell 95 percent, while its speed increased fivefold. As a result, new regions were drawn quickly into the market.

Canals attracted considerable investment capital, especially after the success of the Erie Canal. Built between 1818 and 1825 the canal stretched 364 miles from Albany on the Hudson River to Buffalo on Lake Erie. Its construction by the state was an act of faith, for in 1816 the United States had only 100 miles of canals, none longer than 28 miles. But within a few years of opening, the Erie Canal paid for itself. It reduced the cost of shipping a ton of goods from Buffalo to New York City from more than 19 cents a mile to less than 3 cents. Where the canal's busy traffic passed, settlers flocked, and towns such as Rochester and Lockport sprang up and thrived by moving goods and serving markets. The steady flow of goods eastward gave New York City the dominant position in the scramble for control of western trade.

New York's commercial rivals, like Philadelphia and Baltimore, were soon frantically trying to build their own canals to the West. Western states such as Ohio and Indiana, convinced that their prosperity depended on cheap transportation, constructed canals to link interior regions with the Great Lakes. By 1840 the nation had completed more than 3,300 miles of canals at a cost of about $125 million. Almost half of that amount came from state governments.

Because of its vast expanse, the United States depended particularly on river transportation. But shipping goods downstream from Pittsburgh to New Orleans took 6 weeks, and the return journey required 17 weeks or more. Steamboats reduced the time of an upstream trip from New Orleans to Louisville from 90 to 8 days while cutting costs by 90 percent.

Robert Fulton in 1807 demonstrated the commercial possibilities of propelling a boat with steam when his ship, the *Clermont,* traveled from New York City to Albany on the Hudson River. But steamboats had the greatest effect on transportation on western rivers, where the flat-bottomed boats could haul heavy loads even in low water.

The first significant railroads appeared in the 1830s, largely as feeder lines to canals. Soon enough, cities and towns saw that their future depended on having good rail links. The country had only 13 miles of track in 1830, but 10 years later railroad and canal mileage were almost exactly equal (3,325 miles). By 1850, the nation had a total of 8,879 miles. Railroad rates were usually higher, but railroads were twice as fast as steamboats, offered more direct routes, and could operate year-round. Although railroads increasingly dominated the transportation system after 1850, canals and steamboats were initially the key to creating a national market.

## Revolution in Communications

>> What rail and steam engines did for transportation, Samuel F. B. Morse's telegraph did for communications. Morse in 1837 patented a device that sent electrical pulses over a wire, and before long, telegraph lines fanned out in all directions, linking various parts of the country in instantaneous communication. The new form of communication sped business information, helped link the transportation network, and enabled newspapers to provide readers with up-to-date news.

Indeed, the invention of the telegraph and the perfection of a power press in 1847 by Robert Hoe and his son Richard revolutionized journalism. The mechanical press sharply increased the speed with which sheets could be printed over the old hand method and brought newspapers within economic reach of ordinary families. Hoe's press had a similar impact on book publishing, since thousands of copies could be printed at affordable prices.

## The Postal System >> 
A national market economy depended on mass communications to transmit commercial information and bring into contact producers and sellers separated by great distances. Although postage was relatively expensive, the American postal system subsidized the distribution of newspapers and helped spread other forms of commercial information. Indeed, in the years before the Civil War, the postal system employed more laborers than did any other enterprise in the country. Although the system's primary purpose was to promote commerce, the system had a profound social impact by accustoming people to long-range and even impersonal communication.

When traveling in the United States in 1831, the French commentator Alexis de Tocqueville was amazed at the scope of the postal system. "There is an astonishing circulation of letters and newspapers among these savage woods," he reported from the Michigan frontier. Although the British and French post offices handled a greater volume of mail, the American system was much more extensive.

^ Supreme Court Chief Justice John Marshall wrote the opinion striking down a steamboat monopoly granted by the state of New York. In doing so, Marshall gave the federal government the right to regulate interstate commerce "to its utmost extent." *(Inset):* ©Hulton Archive/Getty Images; Source: Library of Congress, Prints and Photographs Division [LC-USZC2-3031]

## Agriculture in the Market Economy >>
The new forms of transportation had a remarkable effect on farm families: they became linked ever more tightly to a national market system. Given cheap transportation, farmers increased their output in order to sell the surplus at distant markets. In this shift toward commercial agriculture, farmers began cultivating more acres, working longer hours, and adopting scientific farming methods, including crop rotation and the use of manures as fertilizer. Instead of bartering goods with neighbors, they more often paid cash or depended on banks to extend them credit. Instead of marketing crops themselves, they began to rely on regional merchants. Like southern planters, western wheat farmers increasingly sold in a world market.

As transportation and market networks connected more areas of the nation, they encouraged regional specialization. The South increasingly concentrated on staple crops for export, and the West grew foodstuffs, particularly grain. Eastern farmers, unable to compete with the wheat yields of western farms, shifted to producing fruits, vegetables, and dairy products for rapidly growing urban areas. The cities of the East no longer looked primarily to the sea for their trade; they looked to southern and western markets. That, indeed, was a revolution in markets.

## John Marshall and the Promotion of Enterprise >>
A national market system also needed a climate favorable to investment. Under the leadership of Chief Justice John Marshall, the Supreme Court became the branch of the federal government most aggressive in protecting the new forms of business central to the growing market economy.

Marshall, who presided over the Court from 1801 to 1835, convinced his colleagues to uphold the sanctity of private property and the power of the federal government to promote economic growth. In the case of *McCulloch v. Maryland* (1819) the Court upheld the constitutionality of the Second Bank of the United States. Just as Alexander Hamilton had argued in the debate over the first national bank, Marshall emphasized that the Constitution gave Congress the power to make all "necessary and proper" laws to carry out its delegated powers. If Congress believed that a bank would help it meet its responsibilities, such as maintaining the public credit and regulating the currency, then the bank was constitutional. By upholding Hamilton's doctrine of implied powers, Marshall enlarged federal power to an extraordinary degree.

He also encouraged a more freewheeling commerce in *Gibbons v. Ogden* (1824), which gave Marshall a chance to define the greatest power of the federal government in peacetime, the right to regulate interstate commerce. In striking down a steamboat monopoly granted by the state of New York, the chief justice gave the term *commerce* the broadest possible definition, declaring that it covered all commercial dealings and that Congress's power over interstate commerce could be "exercised to its utmost extent." The result was increased business competition throughout society.

At the heart of most commercial agreements were private contracts, made between individuals or companies. Marshall took an active role in defining contract law, which was then in its infancy. The case of *Fletcher v. Peck* (1810) showed how far he was willing to go to protect private property. The justices unanimously declared unconstitutional a Georgia law that struck down a land grant to a group of speculators that had bribed the legislature to get it. A grant was a contract, Marshall declared, and since the Constitution forbade states to impair "the obligation of contracts," the legislature could not interfere with the grant once it had been made. Although the framers of the Constitution probably meant contracts to refer only to agreements between private parties, Marshall made no distinction between public and private agreements, thereby greatly expanding the meaning of the contract clause.

The most celebrated decision Marshall wrote on the contract clause was in *Dartmouth College v. Woodward,* decided in 1819. This case arose out of the attempt by New Hampshire to alter the college's charter of 1769. The Court overturned the state law on the grounds that state charters were also contracts and could not be altered by later legislatures. By this ruling Marshall intended to protect **corporations**, which conducted business under charters granted by individual states.

**corporation** business entity that has been granted a charter granting it legal rights, privileges, and liabilities distinct from the individual members that are a part of it.

Thus the Marshall Court sought to encourage economic risk-taking by protecting property and contracts, by limiting state interference, and by creating a climate of business confidence.

**REVIEW**

Describe the workings of the national market economy and the ways in which it was shaped by the revolutions in transportation and communications.

# A RESTLESS TEMPER

Between 1815 and 1850 the nation reverberated with explosive energy. Americans ate so quickly that one disgruntled European insisted food was "pitch-forked down." An emphasis on speed affected nearly every aspect of American life. Steamboat captains risked boiler explosions for the honor of having the fastest boat on the river, prompting the visiting English novelist Charles Dickens to comment that traveling under these conditions seemed like taking up "lodgings on the first floor of a

^ This traffic jam in New York City conveys the rapid pace and impatient quality of American life in the first half of the nineteenth century. "In the streets all is hurry and bustle," one European visitor to the city reported. "Carts, instead of being drawn by horses at a walking pace, are often met at a gallop, and always in a brisk trot. . . . The whole population seen in the streets seem to enjoy this bustle and add to it by their own rapid pace, as if they were all going to some place of appointment, and were hurrying on under the apprehension of being too late."
Source: Library of Congress, Prints and Photographs Division [LC-USZC4-2722]

[gun]powder mill." American technology emphasized speed over longevity. Unlike European railroads American railroads were lightweight, were hastily constructed, and paid little heed to the safety or comfort of passengers.

**Population Growth** >> If the economic hallmark of this new order was the growth of a national market, there were social factors that also contributed to American restlessness. The American population continued to double about every 22 years—more than twice the rate of Great Britain. The census, which stood at fewer than 4 million in 1790, surpassed 23 million in 1850. Although the birthrate peaked in 1800, it declined only slowly before 1840.

From 1790 to 1820 natural increase accounted for virtually all of the country's population growth. But immigration, which had been disrupted by the Napoleonic Wars in Europe, revived after 1815. In the 1830s some 600,000 immigrants arrived, more than double the number in the quarter century after 1790.

**The Restless Movement West** >> The vast areas of land opened for settlement absorbed much of the burgeoning population. As settlers streamed west, speculation in western lands reached frenzied proportions. Whereas only 68,000 acres of the public domain had been sold during the year 1800, sales peaked in 1818, at a staggering 3.5 million acres.

The Panic of 1819 sent sales and prices crashing, and in the depression that followed many farmers lost their farms. Congress reacted by abolishing credit sales of federal land and demanding payment in cash, but it tempered this policy by lowering the price of the cheapest lands to $1.25 an acre and reducing the minimum tract to 80 acres.

Even so, speculators purchased most of the public lands sold, since there was no limit on the amount of acreage an individual or a land company could buy. These land speculators played a leading role in settlement of the West. To hasten sales they usually sold land partially on credit—a vital aid to poorer farmers. They also provided loans to purchase needed tools and supplies. Many farmers became speculators themselves, buying up property in the neighborhood and selling it to latecomers at a tidy profit.

Given such rapid settlement, geographic mobility became one of the most striking characteristics of the American people. The 1850 census revealed that nearly half of all native-born free Americans lived outside the state where they had been born. The typical American "has no root in the soil," visiting Frenchman Michel Chevalier observed, but "is always in the mood to move on, always ready to start in the first steamer that comes along from the place where he had just now landed."

It was the search for opportunity, more than anything else, that accounted for such restlessness. In 1851 a new

^ St. Louis, a major urban center that developed in the West, depended on the steamboat to sustain its commerce, as this 1859 illustration makes clear.

Source: Library of Congress, Prints and Photographs Division [LC-USZC4-3168]

railroad line bypassed the village of Auburn, Illinois. Despite the village's handsome location, residents quickly abandoned it in order to live in the new town that sprang up around the depot, even though that land was swampier. A neighboring farmer purchased the old village and plowed up the streets, and Auburn reverted to a cornfield.

**Urbanization** >> Even with the growth of a national market, the United States remained a rural nation. Nevertheless, the four decades after 1820 witnessed the fastest rate of urbanization in American history. As a result the ratio of farmers to city dwellers steadily dropped, from 15 to 1 in 1800 to 5.5 to 1 in 1850. Improved transportation, the declining productivity of many eastern farms, the beginnings of industrialization, and the influx of immigrants all stimulated the growth of cities.

The most urbanized area of the country was the Northeast, where in 1860 more than a third of the population lived in cities.[1] Important urban centers such as St. Louis and Cincinnati arose in the West. The South, with only 10 percent of its population living in cities, was the least urbanized region.

 REVIEW

What were the effects of population growth and movement in the United States during the first half of the nineteenth century?

# THE RISE OF FACTORIES

It was an isolated life, growing up in rural, hilly Vermont. But stories of the textile factories that had sprung up in Lowell and other towns in Massachusetts reached even small villages, such as Barnard. Fifteen-year-old Mary Paul was working there as a domestic servant when, in 1845, two friends helped her find her first job at the Lowell mills. "I am in need of clothes which I cannot get about here," she explained to her farm-bound father. After four years she returned home, but now found "countryfied" life too confining, and before long she left her rural hometown—this time for good.

Mary Paul was one of thousands of rural Americans whose lives were fundamentally altered by the economic transformations of the young republic. The changes in her lifestyle and her working habits demonstrated that the new factories and industries needed more than technological innovation to run smoothly. Equally crucial, labor needed to be reorganized.

**Technological Advances** >> Before 1815 manufacturing had been done in homes or shops by skilled artisans. As master craftworkers they imparted the knowledge of their trades to apprentices and **journeymen.** In addition, women often worked in their homes part-time under the putting-out system, making finished articles from raw material supplied by merchant capitalists. After 1815 this older form of manufacturing began to give way to factories with machinery tended by unskilled or semiskilled laborers.

**journeyman** person who has served an apprenticeship in a trade or craft and who is a qualified worker employed by another person.

From England came many of the earliest technological innovations. But Americans often improved on the British machines. "Everything new is quickly introduced here," one visitor commented in 1820. "There is no clinging to old ways; the moment an American hears the word 'invention' he pricks up his ears." From 1790 to 1860 the United States Patent Office granted more patents than England and France combined.

The first machines required highly skilled workers both to build and to repair them. Eli Whitney had a better idea. Having won a contract to produce 10,000 rifles for the government, he developed machinery that would mass-produce parts that were interchangeable from rifle to rifle. Such parts had to be manufactured to rigid specifications, but once the process was perfected, these parts allowed a worker to assemble a rifle quickly with only a few tools. Simeon North applied the same principle to the production of clocks, and Chauncey Jerome followed North's example and soon surpassed him.

**Textile Factories** >> The factory system originated in the Northeast, where capital, water power, and transportation facilities were available. As in England, the production of cloth was the first manufacturing process to use the new technology on a large scale. Eventually all the processes of manufacturing fabrics were brought together in a single location, and machines did virtually all the work.

In 1820 a group of wealthy Boston merchants known as the Boston Associates set up operations at Lowell, Massachusetts, which soon became the nation's most famous center of textile manufacturing. Its founders intended to avoid the misery that surrounded English factories by combining **paternalism** with high profits. Instead of relying primarily on child labor or a permanent working class, the Lowell mills employed daughters of New England farm

**paternalism** attitude or policy of treating individuals or groups in a fatherly manner, by providing for their needs without granting them rights or responsibilities.

[1] The Northeast included New England and the mid-Atlantic states (New York, Pennsylvania, and New Jersey). The South comprised the slave states plus the District of Columbia.

>> These mill workers in Lowell, Massachusetts, wear dresses made from textiles like the ones they helped produce, each pattern slightly different.
Source: Cornell University Library

families. Female workers lived in company boardinghouses under the watchful eye of a matron. To its many visitors, Lowell presented an impressive sight, with huge factories and well-kept houses. Female workers were encouraged to attend lectures and use the library; they even published their own magazine, the *Lowell Offering*.

The reality of factory life, however, involved strict work rules and long hours of tedious, repetitive work. At Lowell, for example, workers could be fined for lateness or misconduct, such as talking on the job, and the women's morals in the boardinghouses were strictly guarded. Work typically began at 7 a.m. (earlier in the summer) and continued until 7 at night, six days a week. With only 30 minutes for the noon meal, many workers had to run to the boardinghouse and back to avoid being late. Winter was the "lighting up" season, when work began before daylight and ended after dark. The only light after sunset came from whale oil lamps that filled the long rooms with smoke.

Although the labor was hard the female operators earned from $2.40 to $3.20 a week, wages considered good by the standards of the time. (Domestic servants and seamstresses were paid less than $1.00 a week.) The average "mill girl" was between 16 and 30 years old. Most were not working to support their families back home on the farm; instead, they wanted to accumulate some money for perhaps the first time in their lives and sample some of life's pleasures. "I must . . . have something of my own before many more years have passed," Sally Rice wrote in rejecting her parents' request that she return home to Somerset, Vermont. "And where is that something coming from if I go home and earn nothing?"

Like Rice, few women in the mills intended to work permanently. The majority stayed no more than five years before getting married. The sense of sisterhood that united women in the boardinghouses made it easier for farm daughters to adjust to the stress and regimen the factory imposed on them.

As competition in the textile industry intensified, factory managers tried to raise productivity. In the mid-1830s the mills began to increase the workloads and speed up the machinery. Even these changes failed to maintain previous profits, and on several occasions factories cut wages. The ever-quickening pace of work finally provoked resistance among the women in the mills. Several times in the 1830s wage cuts sparked strikes in which a minority of workers walked out. In the 1840s workers' protests focused on the demand for a 10-hour day.

As the mills expanded, a smaller proportion of the workers lived in company boardinghouses, and moral regulations were relaxed. But the greatest change was a shift in the workforce from native-born females to Irish immigrants, including men and children. The Irish, who made up only 8 percent of the Lowell workforce in 1845, amounted to almost half by 1860. Desperately poor and eager for any work, they did not view their situation as temporary. Wages continued to decline, and a permanent working class took shape.

**Lowell and the Environment** >> Lowell was a city built on water power. Early settlers had used the power of the Merrimack River to run mills, but never on the scale of the textile factories. As the market spread, Americans came to link progress with the fullest use of the environment's natural resources.

By 1836 Lowell had seven canals, with a supporting network of locks and dams, to govern the Merrimack's flow and distribute water to the city's 26 mills. As more and more mills were built, at both Lowell and other sites, the Boston Associates erected dams at several points along the river to store water and divert it into power canals for factories. At Lawrence they constructed the largest dam in the world at the time, a 32-foot-high granite structure that spanned 1,600 feet across the river. But even dammed, the Merrimack's waters proved insufficient. So the Associates gained control of over 100 square miles of New Hampshire lakes that fed the river system. Damming these lakes provided a regular flow of water, especially in the drier summer months.

By regulating the river's waters, the Associates made the Merrimack valley the nation's greatest industrial center in the first half of the nineteenth century. But not all who lived there benefited. By raising water levels the dams flooded farmlands, blocked the transportation of logs downstream, and damaged mills upstream by reducing the current. The dams also devastated the fish population by preventing upstream spawning, while factories routinely dumped their wastes into the river to be carried downstream, eventually contaminating water supplies. Epidemics of typhoid, cholera, and dysentery increased, so that by midcentury Lowell had a reputation as a particularly unhealthy city.

## MAP 10.2: DEVELOPMENT OF THE LOWELL MILLS

As more mills were built at Lowell the demand increased for water to power them. By 1859 the mills drew water from lakes 80 to 100 miles upstream, including Winnipesaukee, Squam, and Newfound. The map at left shows the affected watersheds. In the city of Lowell (*right*), a system of canals was enlarged over several decades. The photograph shows Pawtucket Canal as it has been preserved at Lowell National Historical Park. Rail links tied Lowell and Boston together.

*How did the mills at Lowell, Massachusetts, affect both farmers and mills in New Hampshire?*

Source: Photo by Jonathan Parker/Lowell National Historic Park/National Park Service

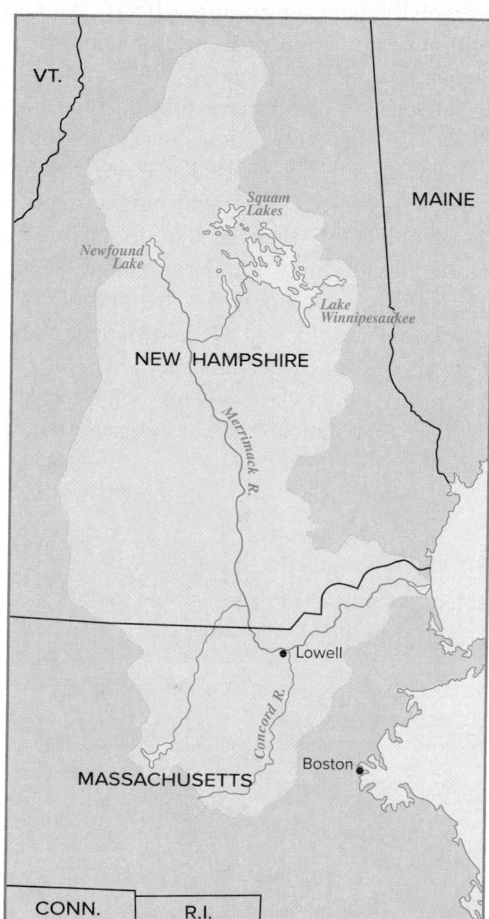
VT.
MAINE
Squam Lakes
Newfound Lake
Lake Winnipesaukee
NEW HAMPSHIRE
Merrimack R.
Lowell
Concord R.
Boston
MASSACHUSETTS
CONN.
R.I.

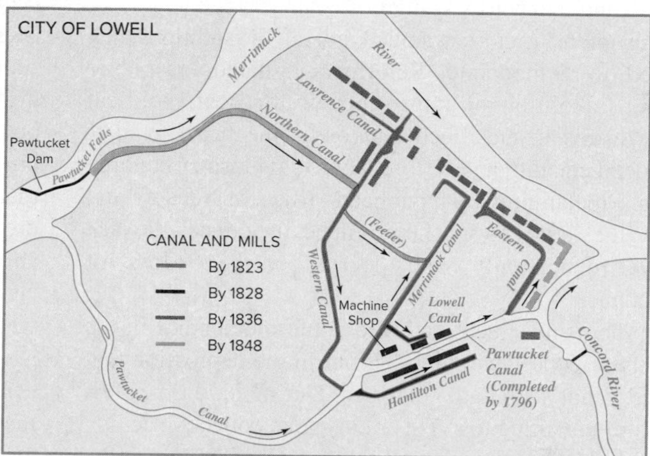
CITY OF LOWELL
Merrimack
River
Lawrence Canal
Northern Canal
Pawtucket Dam
Pawtucket Falls
CANAL AND MILLS
By 1823
By 1828
By 1836
By 1848
(Feeder)
Eastern Canal
Merrimack Canal
Western Canal
Machine Shop
Lowell Canal
Pawtucket Canal (Completed by 1796)
Hamilton Canal
Pawtucket Canal
Concord River

**Industrial Work** >> The creation of an industrial labor force that was accustomed to working in factories did not occur easily. Previously, artisans had worked within the home. Apprentices were considered part of the family, and masters were responsible not only for teaching their apprentices a trade but also for providing them some education and for supervising their moral behavior. Journeymen knew that if they perfected their skill, they could become respected master artisans with their own shops. And skilled artisans worked not by the clock, at a steady pace, but rather in bursts of intense labor alternating with greater leisure.

The factory changed that. Factory goods were not as finished or elegant as those done by hand, and pride in artisanship gave way to rates of productivity. At the same time, workers were required to discard old habits, because industrialism demanded a worker who was sober, dependable, and self-disciplined. Absenteeism, lateness, and drunkenness hurt productivity and disrupted the regular factory routine. Thus industrialization not only produced a fundamental change in the way work was organized but also transformed the very nature of work.

With the loss of personal freedom also came the loss of standing in the community. The master-apprentice relationship gave way to factories' sharp separation of workers from management. Few workers rose through the ranks to supervisory positions, and even fewer could set up their own businesses, as many artisans dreamed. Even well-paid workers sensed their decline in status.

**The Labor Movement** >> In this newly emerging economic order workers sometimes organized to protect their rights and traditional ways of life. Craftworkers such as carpenters, printers, and tailors formed unions, and in 1834 individual unions came together in the National Trades' Union.

Union leaders argued that labor was degraded in America: workers endured long hours, low pay, and low status. Unlike most American social thinkers of the day, they accepted the idea of conflict between different classes. They did not believe that the interests of workers and employers could be reconciled, and they blamed the plight of labor on monopolies, especially banking and paper money, and on machines and the factory system.

If the unions' rhetoric sounded radical, the solutions they proposed were moderate. Reformers agitated for public education, abolition of imprisonment for debt, political action by workers, and effective unions as the means to guarantee social equality and restore labor to its former honored position. Proclaiming the republican virtues of freedom and equality, they attacked special privilege, denounced the lack of equal opportunity, and decried workers' loss of independence.

The labor movement gathered some momentum in the decade before the Panic of 1837, but in the depression that followed, labor's strength collapsed. During hard times few workers were willing to strike or engage in collective action. Nor did skilled craftworkers, who spearheaded the union movement, feel a particularly strong bond with semiskilled factory workers and unskilled laborers. More than a decade of agitation did finally win the 10-hour day for some workers by the 1850s, and the courts also recognized workers' right to strike, but these gains had little immediate impact.

Workers were united in resenting the industrial system and their loss of status, but they were divided by ethnic and racial antagonisms, gender, conflicting religious perspectives, occupational differences, party loyalties, and disagreements over tactics. For them, the factory and industrialism were not agents of opportunity but reminders of their loss of independence and a measure of control over their lives.

## Sam Patch and a Worker's "Art" >>

Some fought against the loss of independence in unusual ways. The waterfalls that served as a magnet for capitalists building mills also attracted their workers. Such cascades were places to visit during off-hours to picnic, swim, fish, or laze about. And for those with nerve, the falls provided a place to show off skills in a different way. Every mill town had its waterfall jumpers, with their own techniques to survive the plunge (knees bent, chest thrust forward). No jumper won more fame than Sam Patch, a young man who had begun working at the Pawtucket mills at the age of seven.

Patch gained wider attention when he jumped at Passaic Falls, New Jersey, where a mill owner was opening a private park that charged admission, in order to keep away "the lazy, idle, rascally" and lower-class riffraff. Workers who resented this undemocratic practice rejoiced when Patch spoiled the park's opening by leaping 70 feet into the foaming water. Thousands of ordinary folk cheered him from outside the park. Eventually Patch's daring led him to the biggest challenge of all: Niagara Falls. Twice he leapt more than 80 feet into the cascade's churning waters. But he drowned a month later when he dared Genesee Falls in another mill town along the Erie Canal—Rochester, New York. Still, his fame persisted for decades. Leaping waterfalls was "an art which I have knowledge of and courage to perform," he once declared defiantly. In a market economy where skilled "arts" were being replaced by machine labor, Sam Patch's acts were a defiant protest against the changing times.

 **REVIEW**

What factors contributed to the beginnings of industrialization in the United States?

^ Waterfalls at mill towns, like this one in Pawtucket, Rhode Island, were places to swim, fish, and relax, as the people are doing in the foreground. Jumpers like Sam Patch leaped off the Pawtucket bridge and also off the roof of a nearby building into the foamy froth.
©Bettmann/Getty Images

# SOCIAL STRUCTURES OF THE MARKET SOCIETY

Thousands of miles beyond Lowell's factory gates a different class of Americans roamed who at first appeared unconnected to the bustle of urban markets. These were the legendary mountain men, who flourished from the mid-1820s through the mid-1840s. Traveling across the Great Plains, along upland streams, and over the passes of the Rockies, outdoorsmen such as Jim Bridger, Jedediah Smith, and James Walker wore buckskin hunting shirts, let their hair grow to their shoulders, and stuck pistols and tomahawks in their belts. Wild and exotic, the mountain men became romantic symbols of the American quest for individual freedom.

Yet these wanderers, too, were tied to the emerging market society. The mountain men hunted beaver pelts and shipped them east, to be turned into fancy hats for gentlemen. The fur trade was not a sporting event but a business, dominated by organizations such as John Jacob Astor's American Fur Company, and the trapper was the agent of an economic structure that stretched from the mountains to eastern cities and even to Europe. Most of these men went into the wilderness not to flee civilization but to make money. Of those who survived the fur trade, most returned and took up respectable new careers as shopkeepers, traders, ranchers, politicians, and even bankers. They, like farmers, were expectant capitalists for whom the West was a land of opportunity.

The revolution in markets, in other words, affected Americans from all walks of life: mountain men as well as merchants, laborers as well as farmers. Equally critical, it restructured American society as a whole.

**Economic Specialization** >> To begin with, the spread of the market produced greater specialization. Transportation networks made it possible for farmers to concentrate on producing certain crops, while factories could focus on making a single item such as cloth or shoes. Within factories, the division of labor meant that the process of manufacturing an item became more specialized, broken down into less-skilled tasks.

This process evolved at different rates. Textiles and milling were completely mechanized, while other sectors of the economy, such as shoes and men's clothing, depended little on machinery. Moreover, large factories were the exception rather than the rule. Still, the tendency was toward more technology, greater efficiency, and increasing specialization.

Specialization had consequences at home as well as in the workplace. The average eighteenth-century American woman produced items such as thread, cloth, clothing, and

<< Indians and fur traders mixed at Fort Laramie, Wyoming, maintained by the government as a way station for the burgeoning fur trade of the 1830s. The scene looks exotic, but the fur trade was a serious and extensive business that stretched from the Rocky Mountains to eastern cities and to Europe beyond.

candles in the home for family use. As factories spread, however, household manufacturing all but disappeared, and women lost many of the economic functions they had previously performed in the family unit. Again, textiles are a striking example. Between 1815 and 1860 the price of cotton cloth fell from 18 cents to 2 cents a yard, and because it was also smoother and more brightly colored than homespun, most women purchased cloth rather than making it themselves. Similarly, the development of ready-made men's clothing reduced the amount of sewing women did, especially in urban centers.

**Materialism** >> European visitors were struck during these years by how much Americans were preoccupied with material goods. The new generation did not invent materialism, but the spread of the market after 1815 made it much more evident. "I know of no country, indeed," Tocqueville commented, "where the love of money has taken stronger hold on the affections of men."

In a nation that had no legally recognized aristocracy, no established church, and class lines that were only informally drawn, wealth became the most obvious symbol of status. Materialism reflected more than a desire for goods and physical comfort. It represented a quest for respect and recognition. The esteem of the founding generation for intellectual achievement was mostly lost in the scramble for wealth that seemed to consume the new generation.

**Wealth and the Emerging Middle Class** >> In the years after 1815 a new middle class took shape in American society. A small class of shopkeepers, professionals, and master artisans had existed earlier, but the creation of a national market economy greatly expanded its size and influence. As specialization increased, office work and selling were more often physically separated from the production and handling of merchandise. Businesspeople, professionals, storekeepers, clerks, office workers, and supervisors began to think of themselves as a distinct social group. Members of the growing middle class had access to more education and enjoyed greater social mobility. They were paid not only more but differently. A manual worker might earn $300 a year, paid as wages computed on an hourly basis. Professionals received a yearly salary and might make $1,000 a year or more.

Middle-class neighborhoods, segregated along income and occupational lines, also began to develop in towns and cities. In larger cities improved transportation enabled middle-class residents to move to surrounding suburbs and commute to work. Leisure also became segregated, as separate working-class and middle-class social organizations and institutions emerged.

As middle-class Americans accumulated greater wealth, they were able to consume more. Thus material goods became emblems of success and status—as clock-maker Chauncey Jerome sadly discovered when his business failed and his wealth vanished. Indeed, this materialistic ethos was most apparent in the middle class, as they strove to set themselves apart from other groups in society.

Furthermore, as American society became more specialized after 1815, greater extremes of wealth appeared. As the new markets created fortunes for the few, the factory system lowered the wages of workers by dividing labor into smaller, less skilled tasks. At the upper end of the social scale, wealth was most highly concentrated in large eastern cities and in the cotton kingdom of the South. Still, throughout the nation the tendency was for the rich to get richer and own a larger share of the community's total wealth. By 1860, 5 percent of American families owned more than 50 percent of the nation's wealth. In villages where the market revolution had not penetrated, wealth tended to be less concentrated.

In a market society, the rich were able to build up their assets, because those with capital were in a position to increase it dramatically by taking advantage of new investment opportunities. Although a few men, such as Cornelius Vanderbilt and John Jacob Astor, vaulted from the bottom ranks of society to the top, most of the nation's richest individuals came from wealthy families.

**Social Mobility** >> The existence of great fortunes is not necessarily inconsistent with the idea of **social mobility** or property accumulation. Although the gap between the rich and the poor widened after 1820, even the incomes of most poor Americans rose, because the total amount of wealth produced in America had become much larger. From about 1825 to 1860 the average per-capita income almost doubled, to $300. Voicing the popular belief, a New York judge proclaimed, "In this favored land of liberty, the road to advancement is open to all."

[ **social mobility** movement of individuals from one social class to another.

Social mobility existed in these years, but not as much as contemporaries boasted. Most laborers—or more often their sons—did manage to move up the social ladder, but only a rung or two. Few unskilled workers rose higher than to a semiskilled occupation. Even the children of skilled workers normally did not escape the laboring classes to enter the middle-class ranks of clerks, managers, or lawyers. For most workers, improved status came in the form of a savings account or home ownership, which gave them some security during economic downswings and in old age.

**A New Sensitivity to Time** >> It was no accident that Chauncey Jerome's clocks spread throughout the nation along with the market economy. The new methods of doing business involved a new and stricter sense of time. Factory life necessitated a more regimented schedule, where work began at the sound of a bell, workers kept machines going at a constant pace, and the day was divided into hours and even minutes.

## The Market and Equality: She Said, He Said

*Frances Wright, a Scotswoman who would later make her career in America as an advocate of slaves, workers, and women, made her first trip in 1819 at the age of 23 and found much to celebrate. Alexis de Tocqueville, 25 when he arrived in the United States in 1831, agreed that white Americans were the freest people in the world, but he described their pursuit of equality as elusive and paradoxical.*

### DOCUMENT 1
### Equality Secures Liberty: Frances Wright

The universal spread of useful and practical knowledge, the exercise of great political rights, the ease and, comparatively, the equality of condition give to this people [Americans] a quality peculiar to themselves. Every hand is occupied, and every head is thinking, not only of the active business of human life (which usually sits lighter upon this people than many others), but of matters touching the general weal of a vast empire. Each man being one of a sovereign people is not only a politician but a legislator—a partner, in short, in the grand concern of the state . . . one engaged in narrowly inspecting its operations, balancing its accounts, guarding its authority, and judging of its interests. A people so engaged are not those with whom a lounger might find it agreeable to associate: he seeks amusement, and he finds business. . . .

It is not very apparent that public virtue is peculiarly requisite for the preservation of political equality; envy might suffice for this: You shall not be greater than I. Political equality is, perhaps, yet more indispensable to preserve public virtue than public virtue to preserve it; wherever an exclusive principle is admitted, baleful passions are excited. Divide a community into classes, and insolence is entailed upon the higher, servility or envy, and often both united, upon the lower. . . .

In all republics, ancient or modern, there has been a leaven of aristocracy. America fortunately had, in her first youth, virtue sufficient to repel the introduction of hereditary honors. . . .

Liberty is here secure, because it is equally the portion of all. The state is liable to no convulsions, because there is nowhere any usurpations to maintain, while every individual has an equal sovereignty to lose.* No king will voluntarily lay down his scepter, and in a democracy all men are kings.

*Source:* Wright, Frances, "Equality Secures Liberty," *Views of Society and Manners in America.* London, England: E. Bliss and E. White, 1821.

*"A grievous exception to this rule is found in the black slavery of the commonwealths of the South."

### DOCUMENT 2
### Equality Promotes Anxiety: Alexis de Tocqueville

In America I saw the freest and most enlightened men, placed in the happiest circumstances which the world affords; it seemed to me as if a cloud habitually hung upon their brow, and I thought them serious and almost sad even in their pleasures.

It is strange to see with what feverish ardor the Americans pursue their own welfare; and to watch the vague dread that constantly torments them lest they should not have chosen the shortest path which may lead to it.

A native of the United States clings to this world's goods as if he were certain never to die; and he is so hasty in grasping at all within his reach, that one would suppose he was constantly afraid of not living long enough to enjoy them. He clutches everything, he holds nothing fast, but soon loosens his grasp to pursue fresh gratifications.

In the United States a man builds a house to spend his latter years in it, and he sells it before the roof is on; he plants a garden, and lets it [rents it] just as the trees are coming into bearing; he brings a field into tillage, and leaves other men to gather the crops; he embraces a profession, and gives it up; he settles in a place, which he soon afterward leaves, to carry his changeable longings elsewhere. If his private affairs leave him any leisure, he instantly plunges into the vortex of politics; and if at the end of a year of unremitting labor he finds he has a few days' vacation, his eager curiosity whirls him over the vast extent of the United States, and he will travel fifteen hundred miles in a few days, to shake off his happiness. Death at length overtakes him, but it is before he is weary of his bootless chase of that complete felicity which is for ever on the wing.

At first sight there is something surprising in this strange unrest of so many happy men, restless in the midst of abundance. The spectacle itself is, however, as old as the world; the novelty is to see a whole people furnish an exemplification of it. . . .

The equality of conditions leads by a still straighter road to several of the effects which I have here described. When all the privileges of birth and fortune are abolished, when all professions are accessible to all, and a man's own energies may place him at the top of any one of them, an easy and unbounded career seems open to his ambition, and he will readily persuade himself that he is born to no vulgar destinies. But this is an erroneous notion, which is corrected by daily experience. The same equality which allows every citizen to conceive these lofty hopes, renders all the citizens less able to realize them; it circumscribes their powers on every side, while it gives freer scope to their desires. Not only are they themselves powerless, but they are met at every step by immense obstacles, which they did not at first perceive. They have swept away the privileges of some of their fellow-creatures which stood in their way: but they have opened the door to universal competition. . . .

Among democratic nations men easily attain a certain equality of conditions; they can never attain the equality they desire. It perpetually retires from before them, yet without hiding itself from their sight, and in retiring draws them on. At every moment they think they are about to grasp it; it escapes at every moment from their hold.

*Source:* de Tocqueville, Alexis, "Equality Promotes Anxiety," *Democracy in America.* 1840.

### THINKING CRITICALLY

*What did Frances Wright admire about Americans? How does she think political equality will help preserve public virtue? How did Alexis de Tocqueville account for the restless ambition of Americans? According to Tocqueville, what was the paradox of pursuing equality?*

Clocks began to invade private as well as public space. With mass production ordinary families could now afford clocks, and even farmers became more sensitive to time as they were integrated into the market.

### REVIEW

What was the effect of the new market economy on social structure and values in the United States during the first half of the nineteenth century?

# PROSPERITY AND ANXIETY

As Americans watched their nation's frontiers expand and its market economy grow, many began to view history in terms of continuous improvement. The path of commerce, however, was not steadily upward. Rather, it advanced in a series of wrenching **boom-and-bust cycles**: accelerating growth, followed by a crash, and then depression.

**boom-and-bust cycle** period of expansion and recession or depression that an economy goes through. Also referred to as *business cycle.*

The country remained extraordinarily prosperous from 1815 until 1819, only to sink into a depression that lasted from 1819 to 1823. During the next cycle the economy expanded slowly during the 1820s, followed by frenzied speculation in the 1830s. Then came the inevitable contraction in 1837, and the country suffered an even more severe depression from 1839 to 1843. The third cycle followed the same pattern: gradual economic growth during the 1840s, frantic expansion in the 1850s, and a third depression, which began in 1857 and lasted until the Civil War. In each of these "panics" thousands of workers were thrown out of work, overextended farmers lost their farms, and many businesses closed their doors.

In such an environment, prosperity and personal success seemed all too fleeting. Because Americans believed the good times would not last—that the bubble would burst and another "panic" set in—their optimism was often tinged by insecurity and anxiety. They knew too many individuals like Chauncey Jerome, who had been rich and then lost all their wealth in a downturn.

**The Panic of 1819** >> The initial shock of this boom-and-bust psychology came with the Panic of 1819, the first major depression in the nation's history. From 1815 to 1818 cotton had commanded truly fabulous prices on the Liverpool market. In this heady prosperity the federal government extended liberal credit for land purchases, and the new national bank encouraged merchants and farmers to borrow in order to catch the rising tide.

But in 1819 the price of cotton collapsed and took the rest of the economy with it.

"I leave this great people prosperous and happy"—Manager's last kick
6 CENTS
"Better Currency"
Hickory Leaf.
HUMBUG GLORY BANK
SIX CENTS in mint drops or Glory at cost
Cunning Reuben Cash'r
Honest Amos Pres't
"In seven months from this time bank rags shall be abolished—Globe of 1834.
6
6

<< This mock banknote illustrates the anxieties often felt in times of "bust," when the value of currencies plummeted and it was difficult to tell whether the banks that issued paper money were solvent. Source: Library of Congress, Prints and Photographs Division [LC-USZ62-89594]

Once the inflationary bubble burst, land values, which had been driven to new heights by the speculative fever, plummeted 50 to 75 percent almost overnight. As the economy went slack, so did the demand for western foodstuffs and eastern manufactured goods and services, pushing the nation into a severe depression. Because the market economy had spread to new areas, the downturn affected not only city folk but rural Americans as well. New cotton planters in the Southwest, who were most vulnerable to the ups and downs of the world market, were especially hard hit.

In what ways did the new market economy shape the hopes and fears of Americans during the first half of the nineteenth century?

As depression spread in the years following 1819, most Americans could not guess that the ups and downs of the boom-and-bust cycle would continue through the next three decades, their swings made sharper by the growing networks of the market economy both nationally and internationally. But the interconnections between buyers and sellers did feed both prosperity and panic. Farmers and factories specialized in order to sell goods to distant buyers. Canals and railroads widened the network, speeding products, information, and profits. And as markets tied distant lands more tightly together, international events contributed to the business cycles.

It was the Liverpool market in England, in fact, that bid the price of American cotton to its high at over 32 cents. Then in 1816 and 1817 English textile manufacturers, looking for cheaper cotton, began to import more cotton from India, plummeting the price of New Orleans cotton to 14 cents. Broader changes also hurt American markets. The French and the British had been at war with each other for decades—more than 100 years, if the imperial wars of the seventeenth and eighteenth centuries were counted. In 1814 and 1815 the major powers of Europe hammered out a peace at the Congress of Vienna, one that lasted, with only minor interruptions, until the coming of World War I in 1914. When Europe had been at war, American farmers had found a ready market abroad. With thousands of European soldiers returning to their usual work as farmers, demand for American goods dropped.

The stresses of the Panic of 1819 shook the political system at home, too. As the depression deepened and hardship spread, Americans viewed government policies as at least partly to blame. The postwar nationalism, after all, had been based on the belief that government should stimulate economic development through a national bank and protective tariff, by improving transportation, and by opening up new lands. As Americans struggled to make sense of their new economic order, they looked to take more direct control of the government that was so actively shaping their lives. During the 1820s the popular response to the market and the Panic of 1819 produced a strikingly new kind of politics in the Republic.

# CHAPTER SUMMARY

By uniting the country in a single market, the new market economy transformed the United States during the quarter century after 1815.

- The federal government promoted the creation of a market through a protective tariff, a national bank, and internal improvements.
- The development of new forms of transportation, including canals, steamboats, and eventually railroads, allowed goods to be transported cheaply on land.
- The Supreme Court adopted a pro-business stance that encouraged investment and risk-taking.
- Economic expansion generated greater national wealth, but it also brought social and intellectual change.
    - Americans pursued opportunity, embraced a new concept of progress, viewed change as normal, developed a strong materialist ethic, and considered wealth the primary means to determine status.
    - Entrepreneurs reorganized their operations to increase production and sell in a wider market.
- The earliest factories were built to serve the textile industry, and the first laborers in them were young women from rural families.
    - Factory work imposed on workers a new discipline based on time and strict routine.
    - Workers' declining status led them to form unions and resort to strikes, but the depression that began in 1837 destroyed these organizations.
- The new market economy distributed wealth much more unevenly and left Americans feeling alternatively buoyant and anxious about their social and economic status.
- Social mobility existed, but it was more limited than popular belief claimed.
- The economy lurched up and down in a boom-and-bust cycle.
- In hard times Americans looked to the government to relieve economic distress.

## Additional Reading

The best study of early-nineteenth-century U.S. history is Daniel Walker Howe, *What Hath God Wrought* (2009). For a provocative overview of the economic changes during this period and their impact on society and culture, consult Charles Sellers, *The Market Revolution* (1991); and Jessica Lepler, *The Many Panics of 1837* (2013). Then dip into two fine anthologies of essays: Melvin Stokes and Stephen Conway, eds., *The Market Revolution in America* (1996); and Scott C. Martin, ed., *Cultural Change and the Market Revolution in America, 1789–1860* (2005). The best recent book on the transportation revolution is John Larson, *Internal Improvements* (2001); and for a fascinating study of the role played by the postal system in linking Americans, see Richard John, *Spreading the News* (1995). There are many fine studies of urban social classes during the first half of the nineteenth century, and among the best are Sean Wilentz, *Chants Democratic* (1984), which traces the formation of New York City's working class; and Stuart Blumin, *The Emergence of the Middle Class* (1989). To understand the market economy's effect on rural society, read John Mack Faragher's vivid account of the transformation of a farming community in frontier Illinois, *Sugar Creek* (1986); and Robert Shalhope, *A Tale of New England* (2003), which traces the fortunes of a Vermont farmer and his family.

There is also no shortage of excellent books exploring the relationship between the market revolution and American culture during the first half of the nineteenth century. Begin with Karen Halttunen's classic study of middle-class culture, *Confidence Men and Painted Women* (1982); and a more recent study, Thomas Augst, *The Clerk's Tale* (2003); and then turn to Paul Johnson's lively exploration of working-class culture, *Sam Patch, the Famous Jumper* (2003). To celebrate any occasion, treat yourself to Stephen Nissenbaum, *The Battle for Christmas* (1996). And to console yourself in between celebrations, turn to Scott Sandage, *Born Losers: A History of Failure in America* (2005).

# 11 The Rise of Democracy

## 1824–1840

"The Will of the People/The Supreme Law" reads the banner at this county election. Beneath the banner a candidate offers his ticket hopefully to one voter. But in the rough-and-tumble of the era's new democratic politics, a shiny top hat, ruffled shirt, or aristocratic manner did not win converts—as both Powhatan Ellis and Franklin Plummer learned to their dismay.

George Caleb Bingham, *The County Election*, 1852, Saint Louis Art Museum, 44:2001

## >> An American Story

## "WANTED: CURLING TONGS, COLOGNE, AND SILK-STOCKINGS . . ."

The notice, printed in a local newspaper, made the rounds in the rural Pearl River district of Mississippi.

A traveler, the advertisement announced, had lost a suitcase while fording the Tallahala River. The contents included "6 ruffled shirts, 6 cambric handkerchiefs, 1 hair-brush, 1 toothbrush, 1 nail-brush . . ."

As the list went on, the popular reaction would inevitably shift from amusement to disdain: "1 pair curling tongs . . . 1 bottle Cologne, 1 [bottle] rose-water, 4 pairs silk stockings, and 2 pairs kid gloves." The howls of derision that filled the air could only have increased on learning that anyone finding said trunk was requested to contact the owner—Mr. Powhatan Ellis of Natchez.

ELECTIONEERING IN MISSISSIPPI.

^ Franklin Plummer campaigning.
Source: Courtesy of the Cornell University Library, "Making of America" Digital Collection

Powhatan Ellis was no ordinary backcountry traveler. Born into a genteel Virginia family, Ellis had moved in 1816 to the raw Southwest to enlarge his fortune. With his cultivated tastes and careful dress, he upheld the tradition of the gentleman politician. In Virginia he would have commanded respect: indeed, in Mississippi he had been appointed district judge and U.S. senator. But for the voters along the Pearl River the advertisement for his trunk of ruffled shirts, hair oils, and fancy "skunkwater" proved to be the political kiss of death. His opponents branded him an aristocrat and a dandy, and his support among the piney-woods farmers evaporated faster than a morning mist along Old Muddy on a sweltering summer's day.

No one was more satisfied with this outcome than the resourceful Franklin E. Plummer, one of Ellis's political enemies. For in truth, although the unfortunate Powhatan Ellis had lost a trunk fording a stream, he had not placed the advertisement trying to locate it. That was the handiwork of Plummer, who well understood the new playing field of American politics in the 1820s. Born in New England Plummer had made his way as a young man to the new state of Mississippi, where he set himself up as an attorney, complete with a law library of three books, and was quickly elected to the legislature.

Plummer's ambition soon extended beyond the state capital, and in 1830 he announced his candidacy for Congress. In his campaign he portrayed himself as the champion of the people battling the aristocrats of Natchez. Contrasting his humble background with that of his wealthy opponent, Plummer proclaimed: "We are taught that the highway to office, distinction and honor, is as free to the meritorious poor man, as to the rich; to the man who has risen from obscurity by his own individual exertions, as to him who has inherited a high and elevated standing in society, founded on the patrimony of his ancestors." Taking as his slogan "Plummer for the People, and the People for Plummer," he was easily elected.

As long as Plummer maintained his image as one of the people, he remained invincible. But when he was a candidate for the U.S. Senate, his touch deserted him. Borrowing money from a Natchez bank, he purchased a stylish coach, put his servant in a uniform, and campaigned across the state. Aghast at such aristocratic pretensions, his followers promptly abandoned him. He died in 1852 in obscurity and poverty. Ah, Plummer! Even the trustiest tribune of the people may succumb to the temptations of power and commerce. In fact, Franklin Plummer was being pulled two ways by the forces transforming American society. The growth of commerce opened up opportunities for more and more Americans during the quarter century after 1815. Through his connections with bankers and the well-to-do, Plummer saw the opportunity to accumulate wealth and to gain status and respect.

Yet at the same time that new markets were producing a more

**stratified** layered; in this case, according to class or social station.

**stratified,** unequal society, the nation's politics were becoming more democratic. The new political system that developed after 1820 differed from that of the early republic. Just as national markets linked the regions of America economically, the new system of national politics with its mass electioneering techniques involved more voters than ever before. Plummer's world reflected that more egalitarian **political culture**. But the relationship between the new equalities of politics and the new opportunities of the market was an uneasy one. <<

**political culture** patterns, habits, institutions, and traits associated with a political system.

## THEMATIC TIMELINE

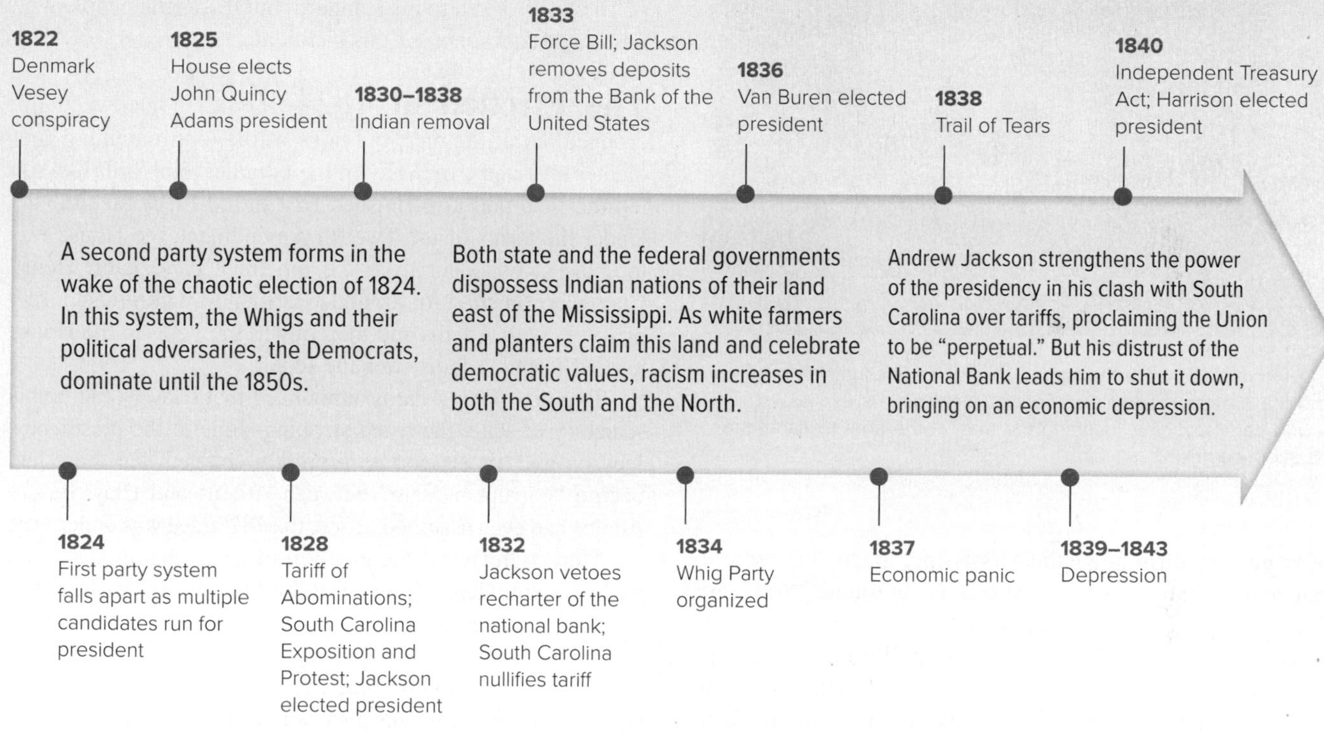

1822
Denmark Vesey conspiracy
1825
House elects John Quincy Adams president
1830–1838
Indian removal
1833
Force Bill; Jackson removes deposits from the Bank of the United States
1836
Van Buren elected president
1838
Trail of Tears
1840
Independent Treasury Act; Harrison elected president
A second party system forms in the wake of the chaotic election of 1824. In this system, the Whigs and their political adversaries, the Democrats, dominate until the 1850s.
Both state and the federal governments dispossess Indian nations of their land east of the Mississippi. As white farmers and planters claim this land and celebrate democratic values, racism increases in both the South and the North.
Andrew Jackson strengthens the power of the presidency in his clash with South Carolina over tariffs, proclaiming the Union to be "perpetual." But his distrust of the National Bank leads him to shut it down, bringing on an economic depression.
1824
First party system falls apart as multiple candidates run for president
1828
Tariff of Abominations; South Carolina Exposition and Protest; Jackson elected president
1832
Jackson vetoes recharter of the national bank; South Carolina nullifies tariff
1834
Whig Party organized
1837
Economic panic
1839–1843
Depression


# EQUALITY, OPPORTUNITY, AND THE NEW POLITICAL CULTURE OF DEMOCRACY

Middle- and upper-class Europeans who visited the United States during these decades were especially sensitive to the egalitarian quality of American life. To begin with, they discovered that only one class of seats was available on stagecoaches and railcars. These were filled according to the rough-and-ready rule of first come, first served. In steamboat dining rooms or at country taverns, everyone ate at a common table, sharing food from the same serving plates. As one upper-class gentleman complained: "The rich and the poor, the educated and the ignorant, the polite and the vulgar, all herd on the cabin floor, feed at the same table, sit in each others laps, as it were." Indeed, the democratic "manners" of Americans seemed positively shocking. In Europe social inferiors would speak only if spoken to. But Americans felt free to strike up a conversation or to shake hands with anyone, including total strangers.

Americans were proud of such democratic behavior, which they viewed as a valued heritage of the Revolution. The keelboaters who carried the future King Louis-Philippe

^ Oyster houses were the sports bars of antebellum America, and the preferred sport was politics. Newspapers expressed strong party loyalties, inspiring the man at the right to harangue his skeptical friend.


of France on a trip down the Mississippi made their republican feelings plain when the keelboat ran aground. "You kings down there!" bellowed the captain. "Show yourselves and do a man's work, and help us three-spots pull off this bar!" The ideology of the Revolution made it clear that, in the American deck of cards at least, "three-spots" counted as much as jacks, kings, and queens. Kings were not allowed to forget that—and neither was Franklin Plummer.

By equality, Americans did not mean equality of wealth or property. "I know of no country where profounder contempt is expressed for the theory of permanent equality of property," Alexis de Tocqueville wrote. Nor did equality mean that all citizens had equal talent or capacity. In the end, what Americans upheld was equality of opportunity, not equality of condition. "True republicanism requires that every man shall have an equal chance—that every man shall be free to become as unequal as he can," one American commented. In an economy that could go bust as well as boom, Americans agreed that one primary objective of government was to safeguard opportunity. Thus the new politics of democracy walked hand in hand with the new opportunities of the market.

The stately James Monroe, with his powdered hair and buckled shoes and breeches, was not part of the new politics. But in 1824 as he neared the end of his second term, a host of new leaders in the Republican Party looked to succeed him. The Republican congressional caucus finally settled on William H. Crawford of Georgia as the party's presidential nominee. Condemning "King Caucus" as undemocratic, three other Republicans, all ardent nationalists, refused to withdraw from the race: Secretary of State John Quincy Adams; John C. Calhoun, Monroe's secretary of war; and Henry Clay, the Speaker of the House.

None of these men bargained on the sudden emergence of another Republican candidate, Andrew Jackson, the hero of the Battle of New Orleans. Because of his limited experience, no one took Jackson's candidacy seriously at first, including Jackson himself. But soon the general's supporters and rivals began receiving reports of his popularity. Savvy politicians flocked to his standard, but it was the people who first made Jackson a serious candidate.

**The Election of 1824** >> Calhoun eventually dropped out of the race, but none of the four remaining candidates received a majority of the popular vote. Still, Jackson led the field and also finished first in the Electoral College. Under the terms of the Twelfth Amendment, the House was to select a president from the top three candidates. Henry Clay, who finished fourth and was therefore eliminated, met privately with Adams and then rallied the votes in the House needed to put Adams over the top.

Two days later Adams announced that Clay would be his secretary of state, the usual stepping-stone to the presidency. Jackson and his supporters promptly charged that there had been a "corrupt bargain" between Adams and Clay. Before Adams had even assumed office, the 1828 race was under way.

More significant, the election of 1824 shattered the old party system. Henry Clay and John Quincy Adams began to organize a new party, known as the National Republicans to distinguish it from Jefferson's old party. For the next decade the political system continued to evolve. By the mid-1830s the National Republicans gave way to the Whigs, a political party that also drew members from another party that flourished briefly, the Anti-Masons.[1] The Democrats as the other major party came together under the leadership of Andrew Jackson. Once established, this second party system dominated the nation's politics until the 1850s.

**Social Sources of the New Politics** >> Why was it that a new style and new system of politics emerged in the 1820s? Part of the answer lay in the Panic of 1819. During the depression that followed, many Americans became convinced that government policy had aggravated, if not actually produced, hard times. Consequently, they decided that the government had a responsibility to relieve distress and promote prosperity.

[1] The Anti-Masons had led a campaign against the Freemasons or Masons, a fraternal order whose members shared the Enlightenment belief in the power of reason but whose secret meetings and rituals seemed aristocratic and undemocratic to many Americans.

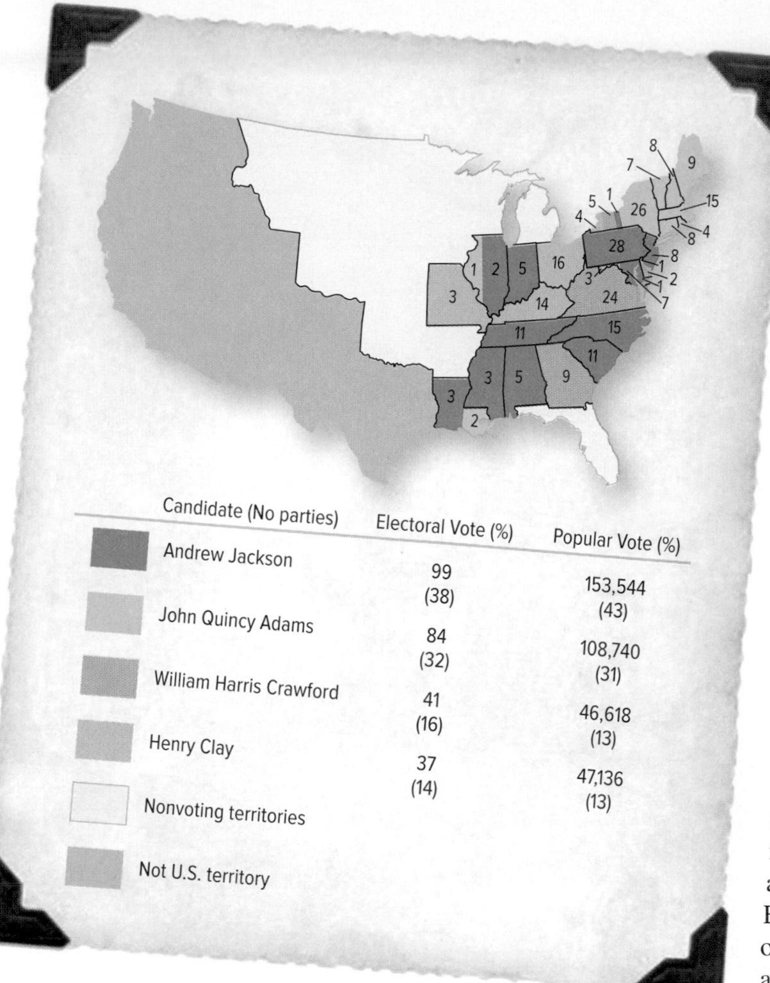
Candidate (No parties)
Electoral Vote (%)
Popular Vote (%)
Andrew Jackson
99 (38)
153,544 (43)
John Quincy Adams
84 (32)
108,740 (31)
William Harris Crawford
41 (16)
46,618 (13)
Henry Clay
37 (14)
47,136 (13)
Nonvoting territories
Not U.S. territory

## MAP 11.1: ELECTION OF 1824

The connection made between government policy and economic well-being stimulated rising popular interest in politics during the 1820s. Agitation mounted, especially at the state level, for government to enact debtor relief and provide other forms of assistance. Elections became the means through which the majority expressed its policy preferences, by voting for candidates pledged to specific programs. The older idea that representatives should be independent, voting their best judgment, gave way to the notion that representatives were to carry out the will of the people, as expressed in the results of elections.

# Make a Case

Explain how American politics were or were not democratized between the American Revolution and the 1830s.

With more citizens championing the "will of the people," pressure mounted to open up the political process. Most states eliminated property qualifications for voting in favor of white manhood suffrage, under which all adult white males were allowed to vote (see Map 11.3). Similarly, property requirements for officeholders were reduced or dropped.

Presidential elections became more democratic as well. By 1832 South Carolina was the only state where the legislature rather than the voters still chose presidential electors. Parties began to hold conventions as a more democratic method of nominating candidates and approving a platform. And because a presidential candidate had to carry a number of states in different sections of the country, the backing of a national party, with effective state and local organizations, became essential.

The democratic winds of change affected European societies and eventually other areas of the world as well. In no other major country, however, were these reforms achieved as early and with as little resistance as in the United States. Suffrage provides a good example. In Britain, in response to growing demonstrations and the cautionary example of the French monarchy's overthrow in 1830, Parliament approved the Reform Bill of 1832, which enfranchised a number of property holders and gave Britain the broadest electorate in Europe. Yet in fact, only about 15 percent of the adult males in Britain enjoyed the right of suffrage after the bill's passage. Even Britain's second Reform Act (1867) enfranchised only about one-third of the adult males. Likewise, virtually all the Latin American republics established in the 1820s and 1830s imposed property requirements on voting or forbade certain occupational groups, such as servants and peasants, to vote.

As the new reforms went into effect in the United States, voter turnout soared. Whereas in the 1824 presidential election only 27 percent of eligible voters had bothered to go to the polls, in 1840, 78 percent cast ballots, probably the highest turnout in American history.

All these developments favored the emergence of a new type of politician: one whose life was devoted to party service and whose living often depended on public office. As the number of state internal improvement projects increased during the 1820s, so did the number of government jobs that could support party workers. No longer was politics primarily the province of the wealthy, who spent only part of their time on public affairs. Instead, political leaders were more likely to come from the middle ranks of society, especially outside the South. As Franklin Plummer demonstrated, a successful politician now had to mingle with the masses and voice their feelings—requirements that put the wealthy elite at a disadvantage.

Politics became mass entertainment, with campaign hoopla frequently overshadowing issues. Parades, massive rallies, and barbecues were used to rouse voters, and treating to drinks became an almost universal campaign tactic. ("The way to men's hearts is down their throats," quipped one

^ Democratic reforms of the 1820s and 1830s brought a new sort of politician to prominence, one whose life was devoted to party service and whose living often depended on public office. This cartoon from 1834 shows the downside of the new situation. Andrew Jackson sports the wings, horns, and tail of a devil as he dangles the rewards of various political offices above a clamoring group of eager job-seekers.
©The Granger Collection, New York

Kentucky vote-getter.) Although politicians talked often about principles, political parties were pragmatic organizations, intent on gaining and holding power.

The Jacksonian era has been called the Age of the Common Man, but such democratic tendencies had distinct limits. Women and slaves were not allowed to vote, nor could free African Americans (except in a few states) or Indians. Nor did the parties always deal effectively with (or even address) basic problems in society. Despite such limitations, however, popular political parties provided an essential mechanism for peacefully resolving differences among competing interest groups, regions, and social classes.

**REVIEW**

In what ways did the political culture of the 1820s and 1830s differ from that of the 1780s and 1790s?

# JACKSON'S RISE TO POWER

When he assumed the presidency in 1825, John Quincy Adams might have worked to create a mass-based party. On the state level, the new democratic style of politics was already making headway. But Adams, a talented diplomat and a great secretary of state, had hardly a political bone in his body. Cold and tactless, he could build no popular support for the ambitious and often farsighted programs he proposed. His proposals that government promote not only manufacturing and agriculture but also the arts, literature, and science left his opponents aghast.

Nor would Adams take any steps to gain reelection. Henry Clay finally undertook to organize the National Republicans, but with a reluctant candidate he labored under serious

^ Jackson's stubborn determination shines through in this portrait painted in 1835. "His passions are terrible," Jefferson noted. "When I was President of the Senate, he was Senator, and he could never speak on account of the rashness of his feelings. I have seen him attempt it repeatedly, and as often choke with rage."
©Collection of the New-York Historical Society, USA/Bridgeman Images

handicaps. The new style of politics came into its own nationally only when Andrew Jackson swept to power at the head of a new party, the Democrats. During the campaign, he remained vague about his position on many issues, and the 1828 race descended into a series of personal attacks, splattering mud on all involved. But Jackson emerged victorious, with enormous majorities behind him in the South.

**President of the People** >> The election of 1828 marked the beginning of politics as Americans have practiced it ever since, with two disciplined national parties actively competing for votes, emphasizing personalities over issues, and resorting to mass electioneering techniques. Yet in terms of public policy, the meaning of the election was anything but clear. The people had voted for Jackson as a national hero without any real sense of what he would do with his newly won power.

The first president from west of the Appalachians, Jackson was a man of action, and though he had a quick mind, he had little use for learning. His troops had nicknamed him Old Hickory out of respect for his toughness, but that strength sometimes became arrogance, and he could be vindictive and a bully. Over the course of his turbulent career he had fought several duels, one of which left a bullet embedded for the rest of his life within inches of his heart. For all his flaws, however, Jackson was a shrewd politician. He knew how to manipulate men and could be affable or abusive as the occasion demanded. He also displayed a keen sense of public opinion, reading the shifting national mood better than any of his contemporaries.

**spoils system** practice of rewarding loyal party members with jobs in government.

As the nation's chief executive Jackson defended the **spoils system,** under which government jobs were awarded to political supporters. Replacing officials regularly was a democratic reform, he insisted: the practice would guard against insensitive bureaucrats who presumed that they held their positions by right. The cabinet, he believed, existed more to carry out his will than to offer counsel. Throughout his term he insisted on his way—and usually got it.

**The Political Agenda in the Market Economy** >> Jackson took office at a time when the market economy was expanding throughout America and the nation's population was spreading geographically. The three major problems his administration faced were directly caused by the resulting growing pains.

First, the demand for new lands put continuing pressure on Indians, whose valuable cornfields and hunting grounds could produce marketable commodities such as cotton and wheat. Second, as the economies of the North, South, and West became more specialized, their rival interests forced a confrontation over the tariff. And finally, the booming economy focused attention on the role of credit and banking in society and on the new commercial attitudes that were a central part of the developing market economy. The president attacked all three issues in his characteristically combative style.

REVIEW

What were the most pressing problems faced by President Andrew Jackson?

# DEMOCRACY AND RACE

As a planter Jackson benefited from the international demand for cotton that was drawing new lands into the market. He had gone off to the Tennessee frontier in 1788, a rowdy, ambitious young man who could afford to purchase only one slave. Caught up in the speculative mania of the frontier, he became a prominent land speculator, established himself as a planter, and, by the time he became president, owned nearly 100 slaves. His popularity derived not only from defeating the British but also from opening extensive tracts of valuable Indian lands to white settlement.

Even so, in 1820 an estimated 125,000 Indians remained east of the Mississippi River. In the Southwest the Choctaws, Creeks, Cherokees, Chickasaws, and Seminoles retained millions of acres of prime agricultural land in the heart of the cotton kingdom. Led by Georgia, southern states demanded that the federal government clear these titles.

As white pressure for removal intensified, a shift in the attitude toward Indians and toward race in general occurred. In the past whites most often had attributed cultural differences among whites, blacks, and Indians to the environment.

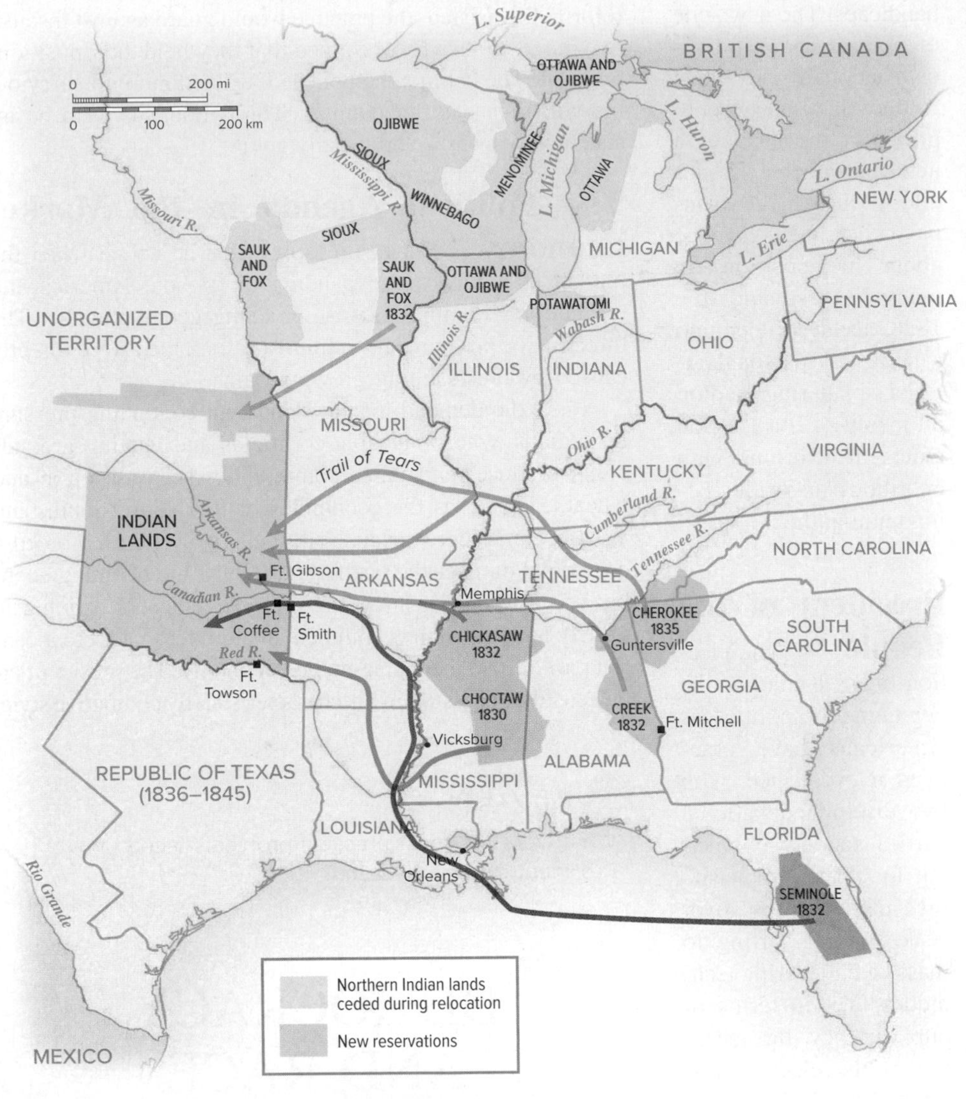

L. Superior
BRITISH CANADA
0 200 mi
0 100 200 km
OTTAWA AND OJIBWE
OJIBWE
SIOUX
Mississippi R.
MENOMINEE
L. Michigan
OTTAWA
L. Huron
L. Ontario
NEW YORK
Missouri R.
WINNEBAGO
SIOUX
MICHIGAN
L. Erie
SAUK AND FOX
SAUK AND FOX 1832
OTTAWA AND OJIBWE
POTAWATOMI
Wabash R.
PENNSYLVANIA
UNORGANIZED TERRITORY
Illinois R.
OHIO
ILLINOIS
INDIANA
MISSOURI
Ohio R.
VIRGINIA
Trail of Tears
KENTUCKY
INDIAN LANDS
Arkansas R.
Cumberland R.
Tennessee R.
NORTH CAROLINA
Ft. Gibson
ARKANSAS
TENNESSEE
Canadian R.
Memphis
Ft. Coffee
Ft. Smith
CHEROKEE 1835
Guntersville
SOUTH CAROLINA
CHICKASAW 1832
Red R.
Ft. Towson
CHOCTAW 1830
GEORGIA
CREEK 1832
Ft. Mitchell
Vicksburg
ALABAMA
REPUBLIC OF TEXAS (1836–1845)
MISSISSIPPI
LOUISIANA
FLORIDA
New Orleans
Rio Grande
SEMINOLE 1832
Northern Indian lands ceded during relocation
New reservations
MEXICO


## MAP 11.2: INDIAN REMOVAL

During Jackson's presidency the federal government concluded nearly 70 treaties with Indian tribes in the Old Northwest as well as in the South. Under their terms, the United States acquired approximately 100 million acres of Indian land.

*Which Indian nation was the latest to be removed to western lands? Why?*

Increasingly after 1815 the dominant white culture stressed "innate" racial differences that could never be erased. A growing number of Americans began to argue that the Indian was a permanently inferior savage who blocked progress.

**Accommodate or Resist?** >> The clamor among southern whites for removal placed the southwestern tribes in a difficult situation. Understandably, they rejected the idea of abandoning their lands. They diverged, however, over how to respond. Among the Cherokees, mixed-bloods led by John Ross argued that a program of accommodation—of adopting white ways—would best stave off removal. After a bitter struggle Ross prevailed, and in 1827 the Cherokees adopted a written constitution modeled after that of the United States. They also enacted the death penalty for any member who sold tribal lands to whites without consent of the governing general council. Developing their own alphabet, they published a bilingual newspaper, the *Cherokee Phoenix*.

The division between traditionalists and those favoring accommodation reflected the fact that Indians too had been drawn into a web of market relationships. As more Cherokee families began to sell their surplus crops, they ceased to share property communally as in the past. Cherokee society became more stratified and unequal, just as white society had, and economic elites dominated the tribal government. Nor were the Cherokees untouched by the cotton boom. Some tribal leaders, particularly half-bloods who could deal easily with white culture, became wealthy planters who owned many black slaves and thousands of acres of cotton land. Largely of mixed ancestry, slaveholders were the driving force behind acculturation.

As cotton cultivation expanded among the Cherokees, slavery became harsher and a primary means of determining status, just as in southern white society. The general council passed several laws forbidding intermarriage with blacks and excluding blacks and mulattoes from voting or holding office. Ironically, at the same time that white racial attitudes toward Indians were deteriorating, the Cherokees' view of African Americans drew closer to that of white society.

**Trail of Tears** >> As western land fever increased and racial attitudes hardened, Jackson prodded Congress to provide funds for Indian removal. At the same time, the Georgia legislature declared Cherokee laws null and void and decreed that tribal members would be tried in state courts. In 1830 Congress finally passed a removal bill, which would forcibly move Indians from their homelands to lands beyond the Mississippi River.

>> Is this a southern belle whose father owned a cotton plantation? Perhaps, but the young woman is a Chickasaw Indian. Her elegant hair and fashionable dress suggest the complexity of cultural relations in the Old Southwest, where some Indians had acculturated to white ways, owning plantations and even slaves. This woman was among the thousands of Indians removed to territory west of the Mississippi during the first half of the nineteenth century. Source: National Museum of the American Indian, Smithsonian Institution (P00452)

But the Cherokees brought suit in federal court against Georgia's actions. In 1832 in the case of *Worcester v. Georgia,* the Supreme Court, in an opinion written by Chief Justice John Marshall, ruled that Georgia had no right to extend its laws over Cherokee territory. Pronouncing Marshall's decision "stillborn," Jackson ignored the Court's edict and went ahead with plans for removal.

Although Jackson assured Indians that they could be removed only voluntarily, he paid no heed when state governments harassed tribes into surrendering lands. Under the threat of coercion, the Choctaws, Chickasaws, and Creeks reluctantly agreed to move to tracts in present-day Oklahoma. In the process land-hungry schemers cheated tribal members out of as much as 90 percent of their land allotments.

The Cherokees held out longest, but to no avail. In order to deal with more pliant leaders of the tribe, Georgia authorities kidnapped Chief John Ross, who had led the resistance to relocation, and threw him into jail. Ross was finally released but not allowed to negotiate the 1835 treaty, which stipulated that the Cherokees leave their lands no later than 1838. When that time came, most refused to leave. In response, President Martin Van Buren had the U.S. Army round up resistant members and force them, at bayonet point, to join the westward march. Of the 15,000 who traveled this Trail of Tears, approximately one-quarter died along the way of exposure, disease, and exhaustion.

Some Indians chose resistance. In the Old Northwest a group of the Sauk and Fox led by Black Hawk recrossed the Mississippi into Illinois in 1832 and were crushed by federal troops and the militia. More successful was the resistance of a minority of Seminoles led by Osceola. Despite Osceola's death the Seminoles held out until 1842 in the Florida Everglades before being subdued and removed. In the end, only a small number of southern tribe members were able to escape removal.

In his Farewell Address in 1837, Jackson defended his policy by piously asserting that the eastern tribes had been finally "placed beyond the reach of injury or oppression, and that [the] paternal care of the General Government will hereafter watch over them and protect them." Indians, however, knew the bitter truth of the matter. Without effective political power, they were at the mercy of the pressures of the marketplace and the hardening racial attitudes of white Americans.

**Free Blacks in the North** >> Unlike with Indian removal, the rising discrimination against free African Americans did not depend directly on presidential action. Still, Jackson's Democratic Party, which was in the vanguard of promoting white equality, was also the most strongly proslavery and the most hostile to black rights. The intensifying racism that accompanied the emergence of democracy in American life bore down with particular force on free African Americans.

Before the Civil War, the free black population remained small: about 171,000 in 1840. Although those numbers amounted to less than 2 percent of the North's population, most states enacted laws to keep African Americans in an inferior position. (For a discussion of free African Americans in the South, see Chapter 13.)

Most black northerners lacked meaningful political rights. Black men could vote on equal terms with whites in only five New England states. New York imposed a property requirement only on black voters, which disenfranchised the vast majority. Moreover, in New Jersey, Pennsylvania, and Connecticut, African American men lost the right to vote after having previously enjoyed that privilege.

Blacks in the North were also denied basic civil rights that whites enjoyed. Five states forbade them to testify against whites, and either law or custom kept African Americans from juries everywhere except in Massachusetts. In addition, several western states passed black exclusion laws prohibiting free African Americans from emigrating to their state. These laws were seldom enforced, but they were available to harass the free black population.

Segregation, or the physical separation of the races, was widely practiced in the free states. African Americans were excluded from public transportation or assigned to separate sections. Throughout the North they could not go into most hotels and restaurants, and if permitted to enter theaters and lecture halls, they sat in the corners and balconies. In white churches they sat in separate pews and took communion after white members. In virtually every community black children were excluded from the public schools or forced to attend overcrowded and poorly funded separate schools. Commented one English visitor: "We see, in effect, two nations—one white and another black—growing up together . . . but never mingling on a principle of equality."

Discrimination pushed African American males into the lowest-paying and most unskilled jobs: servants, sailors,

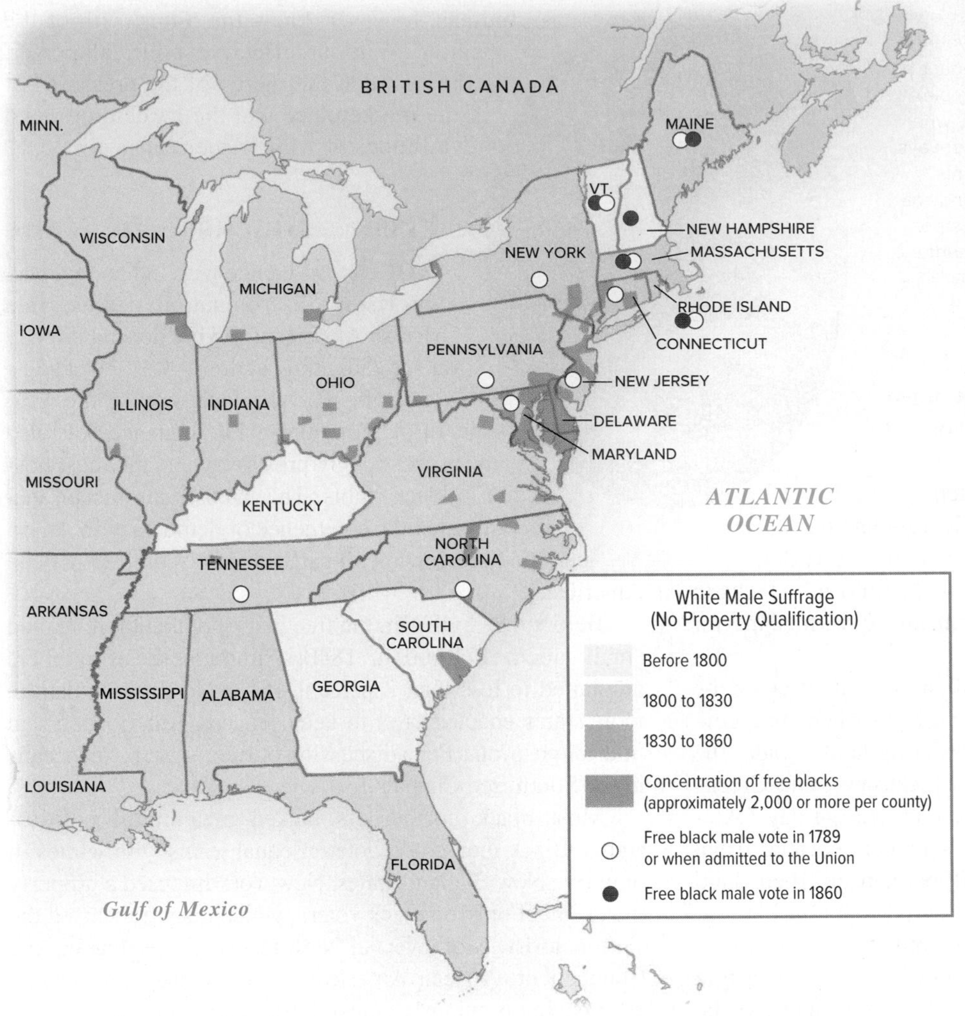
BRITISH CANADA
MINN.
MAINE
VT.
NEW HAMPSHIRE
MASSACHUSETTS
WISCONSIN
NEW YORK
MICHIGAN
RHODE ISLAND
IOWA
CONNECTICUT
PENNSYLVANIA
OHIO
NEW JERSEY
ILLINOIS
INDIANA
DELAWARE
MARYLAND
MISSOURI
VIRGINIA
KENTUCKY
ATLANTIC OCEAN
NORTH CAROLINA
TENNESSEE
ARKANSAS
SOUTH CAROLINA
MISSISSIPPI
ALABAMA
GEORGIA
LOUISIANA
FLORIDA
Gulf of Mexico
White Male Suffrage (No Property Qualification)
Before 1800
1800 to 1830
1830 to 1860
Concentration of free blacks (approximately 2,000 or more per county)
Free black male vote in 1789 or when admitted to the Union
Free black male vote in 1860

## MAP 11.3: THE SPREAD OF WHITE MANHOOD SUFFRAGE

White manhood suffrage became the norm during the Jacksonian era, but in a number of states free black males who had been voting by law or by custom lost the right to vote. After 1821 a $250 property requirement disenfranchised about 90 percent of adult black males in New York.
*What prompted the disenfranchisement of free blacks?*

waiters, and common laborers. African American women normally continued working after marriage, mostly as servants, cooks, laundresses, and seamstresses, since their wages were critical to the family's survival. Blacks were willing strikebreakers, because white workers, fearing economic competition and loss of status, were overtly hostile and excluded them from trade unions. A number of antiblack riots erupted in northern cities during these years. Driven into abject poverty, free blacks in the North suffered from inadequate diet, were more susceptible to disease, and in 1850 had a life expectancy 8 to 10 years shorter than that of whites.

**The African American Community** >> Free blacks had long suffered from such oppression and injustice. Between the Revolution and the War of 1812, they had responded by founding schools, churches, and mutual aid societies to sustain their communities. Some, like Paul Cuffe, sought to escape white prejudice entirely by establishing settlements of free blacks in West Africa. The Quaker son of a West African father and a Wampanoag Indian mother, Cuffe became a sea captain, and in 1816 his merchant ship brought 38 free black New Englanders to settle in West Africa. Cuffe's venture drew white sympathizers who formed the American Colonization Society (ACS) and founded Liberia in West Africa in 1821–1822. Several state legislatures in the North and the Upper South as well as all the major Protestant churches endorsed ACS plans to encourage free black emigration, but its members were an unlikely and unstable coalition. Some opposed slavery and hoped that colonization would encourage manumissions and gradual emancipation, while others believed that ridding the nation of free blacks would secure the future of slavery.

Even as white support for colonization swelled during the 1820s, black enthusiasm for emigration diminished. Many African American leaders in the North were turning to more-confrontational tactics: they advocated resistance to slavery and condemned racism and inequality. Among the most outspoken of this new, more militant generation was David Walker (see Document 2 in Many Histories).

**Racism Strikes a Deeper Root** >> What prompted greater militancy among African Americans after the 1820s was also the growth of an increasingly virulent racism among whites. Ironically, the success of efforts to promote education, religious piety, and temperance within the free black community threatened many lower-class whites and intensified their resentment of African Americans. That animosity found vent in race riots, which erupted in Pittsburgh, Boston, Cincinnati, and New Haven.

The depth of racism in the culture could be seen in the rise of the minstrel show, the most popular form of entertainment in Jacksonian America. Originating in the 1830s and 1840s, these shows played to packed houses in cities and

# African Colonization: Hoping for the Best and Suspecting the Worst

*Henry Clay owned 50 slaves who worked his Kentucky plantation, but he was a lifelong advocate of gradual emancipation and a founder of the American Colonization Society in 1816. He explained his support in 1827. David Walker, a militant leader of the northern free black community, singled out Clay and other colonizationists for sharp criticism.*

## DOCUMENT 1
### In Favor of Colonization: Henry Clay

Numbers of the free African race among us are willing to go to Africa. . . . Why should they not go! Here they are in the lowest state of social gradation; aliens—political, moral, social aliens—strangers though natives. There they would be in the midst of their friends, and their kindred, at home, though born in a foreign land, and elevated above the natives of the country, as much as they are degraded here below the other classes of the community. . . .

What is the true nature of the evil of the existence of a portion of the African race in our population? It is not that there are some, but that there are so many among us of a different caste, of a different physical, if not moral, constitution, who never can amalgate with the great body of our population. Here . . . the African part of our population bears so large a proportion to the residue, of European origin, as to create the most lively apprehension, especially in some quarters of the Union. Any project, therefore, by which, in a material degree, the dangerous element in the general mass can be diminished or rendered stationary, deserves deliberate consideration.

The Colonization Society has never imagined it to be practicable . . . to transport the whole of the African race within the limits of the United States. Nor is that necessary to accomplish the desirable objects of domestic tranquility, and render us one homogeneous people. Let us suppose . . . that the whole population at present of the United States, is twelve millions of which ten may be estimated of the Anglo-Saxon and two of the African race. If there could be annually transported from the United States an amount of the African portion equal to the annual increase of the whole of that caste, while the European race should be left to multiply, we should find at the termination of the period . . . that the relative proportion would be as twenty to two. And if the process were continued, during the second term of duplication, the proportion would be forty to two—one which would eradicate every cause of alarm or solicitude from the breasts of the most timid.

*Source:* Clay, Henry, "Speech at the Annual Meeting of the American Colonization Society, Washington, January 30, 1827," in *The Works of Henry Clay*, Colton, Calvin ed. New York, NY: G. P. Putnam's and Sons, 1904.

## DOCUMENT 2
### Against Colonization: David Walker

Here is demonstrative proof, of a plan got up, by a gang of slaveholders to select the free people of colour from among the slaves, that our more miserable brethren may be the better secured in ignorance and wretchedness, to work their farms and dig their mines, and thus go on enriching the Christians with their blood and groans. What our brethren could have been thinking about, who have left their native land and home and gone away to Africa I am unable to say. This country is as much ours as it is the whites, whether they will admit it or not they will see and believe it by and by. They tell us about prejudice—what have we to do with it? Their prejudices will be obliged to fall like lightning to the ground, in succeeding generations: not, however, with the will and consent of all the whites, for some will be obliged to hold on to the old adage, viz: the blacks are not men, but were made to be an inheritance to us and our children for ever!!!!!! I hope the residue of the coloured people, will stand still and see the salvation of God and the miracle which he will work for our delivery from wretchedness under the Christians!!!!!! . . .

I shall give an extract from the letter of that truly Reverend Divine, (Bishop [Richard] Allen) of Philadelphia, respecting this trick . . . he says, "Dear Sir, I have been for several years trying to reconcile my mind to the Colonizing of Africans in Liberia, but there have always been and there still remain great and insurmountable objections against the scheme. . . . Can we not discern the project of sending the free people of colour away from their country? Is it not for the interest of the slaveholders to select the free people of colour out of the different states, and send them to Liberia? Will it not make their slaves uneasy to see free men of colour enjoying liberty? It is against the law in some of the Southern States, that a person of colour should receive an education, under a severe penalty. . . . See the thousands of foreigners emigrating to America every year: and if there be ground sufficient for them to cultivate, and bread for them to eat, why would they wish to send the *first tillers* of the land away? Africans have made fortunes for thousands, who are yet unwilling to part with their services;

but the free must be sent away, and those who remain must be *slaves*. I have no doubt that there are many good men who do not see as I do, and who are for sending us to Liberia; but they have not duly considered the subject—they are not men of colour. This land which we have watered with our *tears* and *our blood* is now our *mother country*, and we are well satisfied to stay where wisdom abounds and the gospel is free."

*Source:* David Walker, *Appeal to the Coloured Citizens of the World* (1829).

### THINKING CRITICALLY

*What were Henry Clay's concerns about free African Americans? Why did he regard colonization as a viable solution to the problems he believed African Americans posed to the United States? What did David Walker and Richard Allen believe to be the true intentions of the colonizationists? Do you believe that they accurately assessed those motives?*

*Source:* Clay, Henry. "Speech at the Annual Meeting of the American Colonization Society, Washington, January 30, 1827," in *The Works of Henry Clay*, Colton, Calvin ed. New York, NY: G. P. Putnam's and Sons, 1904.

towns throughout the nation. They featured white actors performing in blackface, whose skits dealt in the broadest of racial stereotypes, ridiculing blacks as physically different and portraying them as buffoons.

The confident air of this African American, displayed in a daguerreotype (an early photographic process), suggests the dignity free blacks maintained in the face of unrelenting hostility and discrimination.
Source: Courtesy of the J. Paul Getty Museum, Los Angeles, 84.XT.441.3

Minstrelsy's greatest success came in northern cities. Its basic message was that African Americans could not cope with freedom and therefore did not belong in the North. Slaves were portrayed as happy and contented, whereas free blacks were caricatured either as strutting dandies or as helpless ignoramuses. Drawing its patrons from workers, Irish immigrants, and other poor whites, minstrelsy assured these white champions of democracy that they remained superior.

The unsettling economic, social, and political changes of the Jacksonian era heightened white Americans' fear of failure, which stimulated racism. The popular yet unrealistic expectation was that any white man might become rich. Yet in fact, 20 percent or more of white adult males of this era never accumulated any property. Their lack of success prompted them to relieve personal tensions through increased hostility toward their black neighbors. The power of racism in Jacksonian America stemmed at least in part from the fact that equality remained part of the nation's creed while it steadily receded as a social reality.

### REVIEW

In what ways did Indians and free African Americans attempt to protect their communities in Jacksonian America?

## THE NULLIFICATION CRISIS

Indian removal and antiblack discrimination provided one answer to the question of who would be given equality of opportunity in America's new democracy: Indians and African Americans would not. The issue of nullification raised a different, equally pressing question. As the North, South, and

West increasingly specialized economically in response to the market revolution, how would a democratic system of government help various regions or interest groups to accommodate their differences?

## The Growing Crisis in South Carolina >>

South Carolina had been particularly hard-hit by the depression of 1819. When prosperity returned to the rest of the nation, many of the state's cotton planters still suffered. With lands exhausted from years of cultivation, they could not compete with the fabulous yields of frontier planters in Alabama and Mississippi.

Under these difficult conditions, South Carolinians increasingly blamed federal tariffs for their miseries. When Congress raised the duty rates in 1824, they attacked the tariff as an unfair tax. After all, they sold their cotton on the open market for a price that went up and down, without any tariff protection. But tariffs artificially raised the price of finished goods southerners imported from abroad (including cotton textiles) in order to benefit New England merchants. Other southern states opposed the 1824 tariff as well, though none so vehemently.

The one southern state in which black inhabitants outnumbered whites, South Carolina had also been growing more sensitive about the institution of slavery. In 1822 Denmark Vesey, a daring and resourceful free black carpenter in Charleston, secretly organized a plan to seize control of the city and raise the standard of black liberty. At the last moment, white officials thwarted the conspiracy and executed Vesey and his chief lieutenants; nevertheless, white South Carolinians were convinced that other conspirators still lurked in their midst. As an additional measure of security,

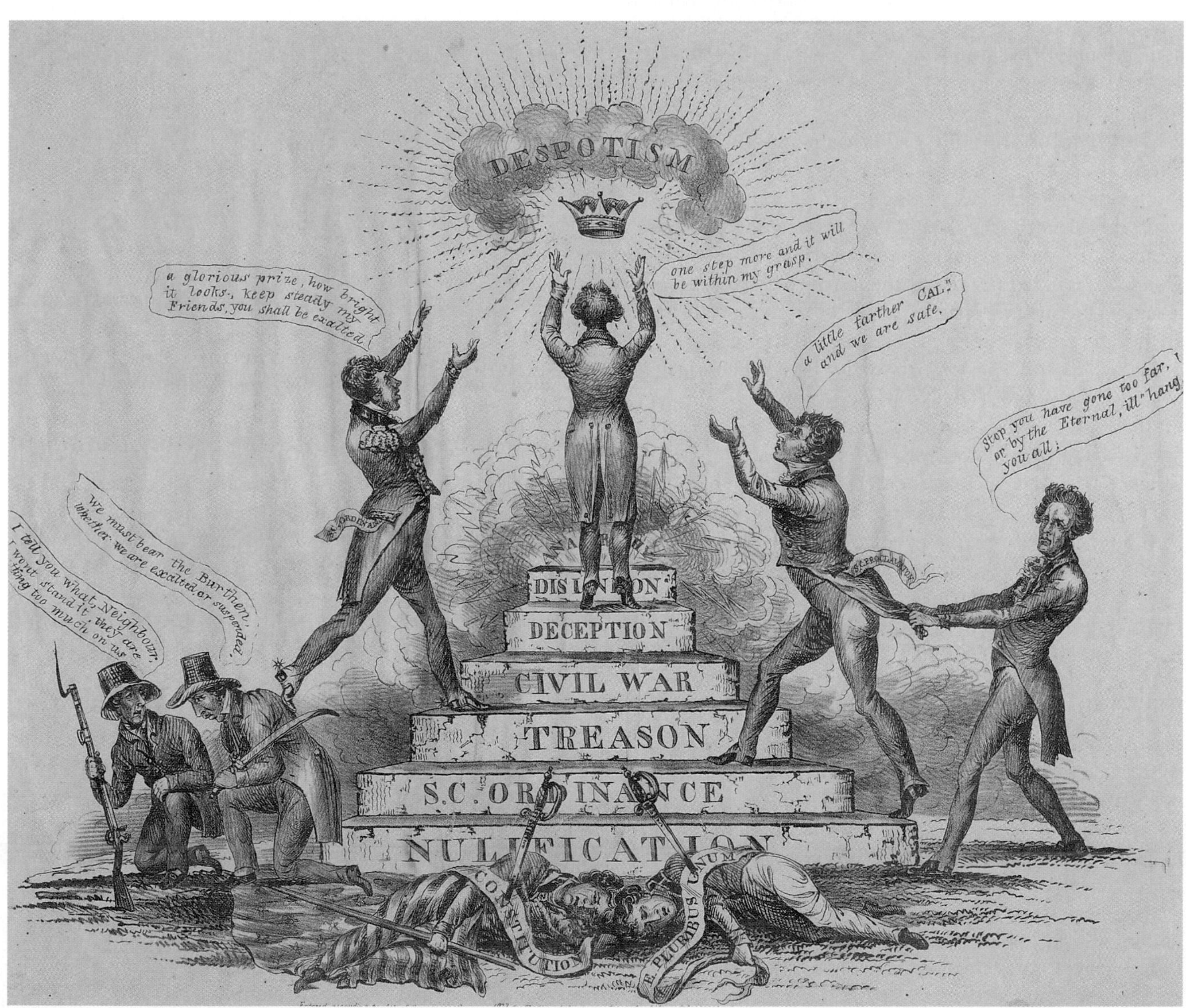
DESPOTISM
a glorious prize, how bright it looks, keep steady my Friends, you shall be exalted.
one step more and it will be within my grasp.
a little farther CAL." and we are safe.
Stop you have gone too far, or by the Eternal, ill" hang you all:
We must bear the Burthen, whether we are exalted or suspended.
I tell you what, Neighbour, I wont stand it, they are taking too much on us
DECEPTION
CIVIL WAR
TREASON
S.C. ORDINANCE
CONSTITUTION
E. PLURIBUS

^ This political cartoon of 1833 warns that Calhoun's doctrine of nullification was only the first step in a path toward "Despotism," with Calhoun reaching for its crown. At right, Andrew Jackson tries to restrain one of Calhoun's followers, declaring "Stop, you have gone too far, or by the Eternal, I'll hang you all." Which aspects of this progression toward despotism seem exaggerated? Which seem prescient?

they began to push for stronger constitutional protection of slavery. After all, the constitutional doctrine of broad construction and implied powers had already been used to justify higher protective tariffs. What was to prevent it from being used to end slavery?

When Congress, over the protests of the state's representatives, raised the duty rates still higher in 1828 with the so-called Tariff of Abominations, South Carolina's legislature published the *South Carolina Exposition and Protest,* which outlined for the first time the theory of nullification. Only later was it revealed that its author was Jackson's own vice president, John C. Calhoun.

Calhoun was the most impressive intellect of his political generation. During the 1820s the South Carolina leader made a slow but steady journey away from nationalism toward an extreme states' rights position that advocates states having more power than the federal government. When he was elected Jackson's vice president, South Carolinians assumed that tariff reform would be quickly forthcoming. But Jackson and Calhoun soon quarreled, and Calhoun lost all influence in the administration.

In his theory of nullification Calhoun argued that the Union was a compact between sovereign states. Thus the people of each state, acting in special conventions, had the right to nullify any federal law that exceeded the powers granted to Congress under the Constitution. In response, Congress could either repeal the law or propose a constitutional amendment expressly giving it the power in question. If the amendment was ratified, the nullifying state could either accept the decision or exercise its ultimate right as a sovereign state and secede from the Union.

In 1830 Senator Daniel Webster of Massachusetts responded that the Union was not a compact of sovereign states. The people, and not the states, he argued, had created the Constitution. "It is the people's constitution, the people's government, made for the people, made by the people, and answerable to the people." Webster also insisted that the federal government did not merely act as the agent of the states but had sovereign powers in those areas where it had been delegated responsibility.

**The Nullifiers Nullified** >> When Congress passed another tariff in 1832 that failed to give the state any relief, South Carolina's legislature called for the election of delegates to a popular convention, which overwhelmingly adopted an ordinance in November that declared the tariffs of 1828 and 1832 "null, void, and no law, nor binding upon this state, its officers or citizens" after February 1, 1833.

Jackson, who had spent much of his life defending the nation, was not about to tolerate any defiance of his authority or the federal government's. In his Proclamation on Nullification, issued in December 1832, he insisted that the Union was perpetual and that under the Constitution, no state had the right to secede. To reinforce his announced determination to enforce the tariff laws, Congress passed the Force Bill, reaffirming the president's military powers.

Yet Jackson was also a skillful politician. At the same time that he threatened South Carolina, he urged Congress to reduce the tariff rates. With no other state willing to follow South Carolina's lead, Calhoun reluctantly agreed to a compromise tariff in 1833. South Carolina's convention repealed the nullifying ordinance, and the crisis passed.

Calhoun's doctrine had proved too radical for the rest of the South. Even so, the controversy convinced many southerners that they were becoming a permanent minority. "We are divided into slave-holding and non-slave-holding states," concluded nullifier William Harper, "and this is the broad and marked distinction that must separate us at last." As that feeling of isolation grew, it was not nullification but the threat of secession that ultimately became the South's primary weapon.

What were the issues being contested in the debate over nullification?

# THE BANK WAR

Jackson understood well the political ties that bound the nation. He grasped much less firmly the economic and financial connections that linked regions of the country through banks and national markets. His clash with the Second Bank of the United States led to the greatest crisis of his presidency.

**The National Bank and the Panic of 1819** >> Chartered by Congress in 1816 for a 20-year period, the Second Bank of the United States suffered from woeful mismanagement. At first it helped fuel the speculative pressures in the economy. Then it turned about-face and sharply contracted credit by calling in loans when the depression hit in 1819. Critics viewed the Bank's policies not as a consequence but as the cause of the financial downswing. To many Americans, the Bank had already become a monster.

The psychological effects of the Panic of 1819 were almost as momentous as the economic. The shock of the depression made the 1820s a time of soul-searching, during which many uneasy farmers and workers came to view the hard times as punishment for having lost sight of the old virtues of simplicity, frugality, and hard work. For these Americans, banks were a symbol of the commercialization of American society and the rapid passing of a simpler way of life.

In 1823 Nicholas Biddle, a rich 37-year-old Philadelphia businessman, became president of the national bank. Biddle was intelligent and thoroughly familiar with the banking system, but he was also impossibly arrogant and politically dense. He set out to use the bank to regulate the amount of credit available in the economy, and thereby provide the nation with a sound currency.

The government regularly deposited its revenues in the national bank. These revenues were paid largely in banknotes (paper money) issued by state-chartered banks. If Biddle believed that a state bank had issued more notes than was safe, he presented them to that bank and demanded they be redeemed in **specie** (gold or silver). Because banks did not have enough specie reserves to back all the paper money they issued, the only way a state bank could continue to redeem its notes was to call in its loans and reduce the amount of its notes in circulation. This action had the effect of lessening the amount of credit in the economy. But if Biddle felt that a bank's credit policies were reasonable, he simply returned the state banknotes to circulation without presenting them for redemption.

**specie** coined money of gold or silver; also referred to as hard money or hard currency. In contrast, banknotes, or notes, are paper money or paper currency.

Under Biddle's direction the Bank became a financial colossus with enormous power over state banks and over the economy. Yet Biddle used this power responsibly to provide the United States a sound paper currency, which the expanding economy needed.

Although the Bank had strong support in the business community, workers complained that they were often paid in **depreciated** state banknotes that could be redeemed for only a portion of their face value, a practice that cheated them of their full wages. They called for a "hard money" currency of only gold and silver. Hard-money advocates viewed bankers and financiers as profiteers who manipulated the paper money system to enrich themselves at the expense of honest, hardworking farmers and laborers.

**depreciated** decreased in value owing to market conditions.

## The Bank Destroyed >>

Jackson's own experiences left him with a deep distrust of banks and paper money. In 1804 his Tennessee land speculations had brought him to the brink of bankruptcy, from which it had taken years of painful struggle to free himself. Reflecting on his personal situation, he became convinced that banks and paper money threatened to corrupt the Republic.

As president, Jackson periodically called for reform of the banking system, but Biddle refused even to consider curbing the Bank's powers. Already distracted by the nullification controversy, Jackson warned Biddle not to inject the bank issue into the 1832 campaign. When Biddle went ahead and applied for a renewal of the Bank's charter in 1832, four years early, Jackson was furious. "The Bank is trying to kill me," he stormed, "but I will kill it."

Despite the president's opposition, Congress passed a recharter bill in the summer of 1832. Immediately, Jackson vetoed it as unconstitutional (rejecting Marshall's earlier ruling in *McCulloch v. Maryland*). Condemning the Bank as an agent of special privilege, the president pledged to protect "the humble members of society—the farmer, mechanics, and laborers" against "the advancement of the few at the expense of the many."

When Congress failed to override Jackson's veto, the Bank became a central issue of the 1832 campaign. Jackson's opponent was Henry Clay, a National Republican who eagerly accepted the financial support of Biddle and his bank. Clay went down to defeat, and, once reelected, Jackson was determined to move boldly. He believed that as a private corporation the Bank wielded a dangerous influence over government policy and the economy, and he was justly incensed over its interference in the election.

To cripple the Bank, the president simply ordered all the government's federal deposits withdrawn. Since such an act clearly violated federal law, Jackson was forced to transfer one secretary of the treasury and fire another before he finally found an ally, Roger Taney, willing to take the job and carry out the edict. Taney (pronounced "Taw-ney") gradually withdrew the government's funds while depositing new revenues in selected state banks.

Biddle fought back by deliberately precipitating a brief financial panic in 1833, but Jackson refused to budge. Eventually Biddle had to relent, and Jackson's victory was complete. When the Bank's charter expired in 1836, no national banking system replaced it.

## Jackson's Impact on the Presidency >>

Jackson approached the end of his administration in triumph. Indian removal was well on its way to completion, the nullifiers had been confounded, and the "Monster Bank" had been destroyed. In the process Jackson immeasurably enlarged the power of the presidency. "The President is the direct representative of the American people," he lectured the Senate when it opposed him. "He was elected by the people, and is responsible to them." With this declaration Jackson redefined the character of the presidential office and its relationship to the people.

Jackson also converted the veto into an effective presidential power. During his two terms in office he vetoed 12 bills, compared with only 9 for all previous presidents combined. Moreover, where his predecessors had vetoed bills only on strict constitutional grounds, Jackson felt free to block laws simply because he thought them bad policy. The threat of such action became an effective way to shape pending legislation to his liking, a tactic that fundamentally strengthened the power of the president over Congress. The development of the modern presidency began with Andrew Jackson.

## "Van Ruin's" Depression >>

With the controls of the national bank removed, state banks rapidly expanded their activities, including the printing of more money. As the currency expanded, so did the number of banks: from 329 in 1829 to 788 in 1837. A spiraling **inflation** set in as prices rose 50 percent after 1830 and interest rates by half as much.

**inflation** increase in the overall price of goods and services over an extended period of time; or a similar decrease over time of the purchasing power of money.

GLORY
JULY 4th 1837
61st ANNIVERSARY
OF OUR INDEPENDENCE
CUSTOM HOUSE
All Bonds must be paid in Specie
MECHANICS BANK
No Specie payments made here
SHAVING
STREET HOTEL
BOTTLE
SHYLOCK GRASPALL
LICENSED PAWNBROKER
R STORE
GIN
MONEY
GRAND SCHEME
SPECIE
SOVEREIGNS
OLD RAGS

^ This Whig cartoon blames the Democratic Party for the depression that began during Van Buren's administration. Barefoot workers go unemployed, and women and children beg and sleep in the streets. Depositors clamor for their money from a bank that has suspended specie payments, while the pawnbroker and liquor store do a thriving business.


As prices soared so did speculative fever. By 1836 land sales, which had been only $2.6 million four years earlier, approached $25 million. Almost all these lands were bought entirely on credit with banknotes. In July 1836 Jackson issued the Specie Circular, which decreed that the government would accept only specie for the purchase of public land. Land sales plummeted, but the speculative pressures in the economy were already too great.

During Jackson's second term, his opponents had gradually come together in a new party, the Whigs. Led by Henry Clay, they charged that "King Andrew I" had dangerously concentrated power in the presidency. The Whigs also embraced Clay's "American System," designed to spur national economic development through a protective tariff, a national bank, and federal aid for internal improvements. In 1836 the Democrats nominated Martin Van Buren, who triumphed over three Whig sectional candidates.

Van Buren had less than two months in office to savor his triumph before the speculative mania collapsed, and with it the economy. After a brief recovery, the bottom fell out of the international cotton market in 1839, and the country entered a serious depression. It was not until 1843 that the economy revived.

Public opinion identified hard times with the policies of the Democratic Party. Since he continued to oppose a new national bank, Van Buren instead persuaded Congress in 1840 to create an Independent Treasury to hold the government's funds. Its offices were forbidden to accept paper currency, issue any banknotes, or make any loans. The government's money would be safe, as Van Buren intended, but it would also remain unavailable to banks to make loans and stimulate the economy. Whigs, in contrast, hoped to encourage manufacturing and revive the economy by passing a protective tariff, continuing state internal improvement projects, protecting corporations, and expanding the banking and credit system.

As the depression deepened, thousands of workers were unemployed, and countless businesses failed. Nationally, wages fell 30 to 50 percent. "Business of all kinds is completely at a stand," wrote New York business and civic leader Philip Hone in 1840, "and the whole body politic sick and infirm, and calling aloud for a remedy."

**The Whigs Triumph** >> For the 1840 presidential campaign the Whigs turned to William Henry Harrison, who had defeated the Shawnee Indians at Tippecanoe, to oppose Van Buren. In the midst of the worst depression of the century, Whigs employed the democratic electioneering techniques that Jackson's supporters had perfected. They hailed Harrison as a man of the people while painting Van Buren as a dandy and an aristocrat who wore a corset, ate off gold plates with silver spoons, and used cologne. Whig rallies featured hard cider and log cabins to reinforce Harrison's image as a man of the people. Ironically, Harrison had been born into one of Virginia's most aristocratic families and was living in a 16-room mansion in Ohio. But the Whig campaign, by casting the election as a contest between aristocracy and democracy, was perfectly attuned to the prevailing national spirit.

In the campaign of 1840 Whigs also prominently involved women, urging them to become politically informed in order to morally instruct their husbands. Women attended Whig rallies, conducted meetings, made speeches, and wrote campaign pamphlets, activities previously performed solely by men. Democrats were uneasy about this innovation, yet had no choice but to follow suit. Within a few years the presence of women at party rallies was commonplace.

The election produced a record turnout, with nearly four-fifths of the eligible voters going to the polls. Although the popular vote was fairly close (Harrison led by about 150,000 votes out of 2.4 million cast), in the Electoral College he won an easy victory, 234 to 60.

The "log cabin" campaign marked the final transition from the deferential politics of the Federalist era to the egalitarian politics that had emerged in the wake of the Panic of 1819. As the *Democratic Review* conceded after the Whigs' victory in 1840, "We have taught them how to conquer us."

**REVIEW**

Why did Jackson oppose the Second Bank of the United States?

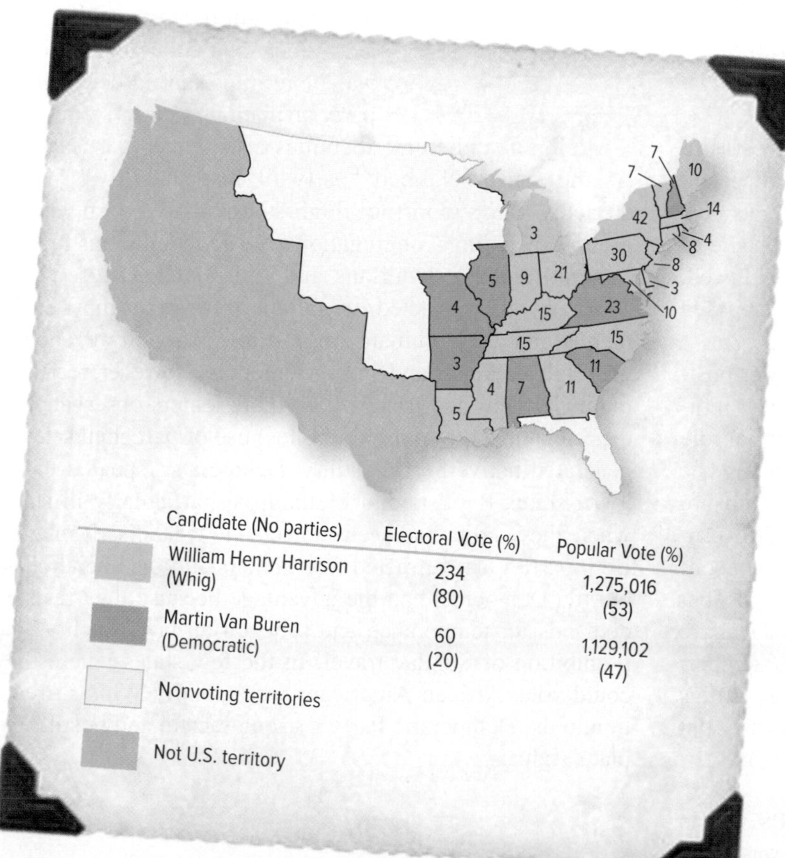

Candidate (No parties)
Electoral Vote (%)
Popular Vote (%)
William Henry Harrison (Whig)
234 (80)
1,275,016 (53)
Martin Van Buren (Democratic)
60 (20)
1,129,102 (47)
Nonvoting territories
Not U.S. territory


MAP 11.4: ELECTION OF 1840

# THE JACKSONIAN PARTY SYSTEM

It is easy, given the hoopla of democratic campaigning, to be distracted from the central fact that the new political system was directly shaped by the social and economic strains of an expanding nation. Whigs and Democrats held different attitudes toward the changes brought about by the market, banks, and commerce.

**Democrats, Whigs, and the Market** >> The Democrats tended to view society as a continuing conflict between "the people"—farmers, planters, and workers—and a set of greedy aristocrats. They charged that this "paper money aristocracy" of bankers, stock jobbers, and investors manipulated the banking system for their own profit. For Democrats, the Bank War became a battle to restore the old Jeffersonian Republic with its values of simplicity, frugality, hard work, and independence.

Jackson understood the dangers private banks posed to a democratic society. Yet Democrats, in effect, wanted the rewards and goods that the market offered without sacrificing the features of a simple agrarian republic. They wanted the wealth that the market produced without the competitive society, the complex dealings, the dominance of urban centers, and the loss of independence that came with it.

Whigs were more comfortable with the market. They envisioned no conflict between farmers and mechanics on the one hand and businesspeople and bankers on the other. The government's responsibility was to provide a well-regulated economy that guaranteed opportunity for citizens of ability. In such an economy, banks and corporations were not only useful but necessary.

^ Whigs drew strongly from the business and commercial classes who were eager to improve themselves. This daguerreotype is said to be of the merchant Cyrus Field, a Whig with a strong commercial vision who partnered with other entrepreneurs to lay a telegraph cable across the Atlantic.
Source: Library of Congress, Prints and Photographs Division [LC-USZ62-27741]

Whigs and Democrats also disagreed over how active government should be. Despite Andrew Jackson's inclination to be a strong president, Democrats as a rule believed in limited government. Government's role in the economy was to promote competition by destroying monopolies and special privileges. In keeping with this philosophy, Democrats also rejected the idea that moral beliefs were the proper sphere of government action. Religion and politics, they believed, should be kept clearly separate, and they generally opposed humanitarian legislation.

The Whigs, in contrast, viewed government power positively. They believed that it should be used to protect individual rights and public liberty, and that it had a special role where individual effort was ineffective. By regulating the economy and competition, the government could ensure equal opportunity. Indeed, for Whigs the concept of government promoting the general welfare went beyond the economy. Northern Whigs in particular also believed that government power should be used to foster the moral welfare of the country. They were much more likely to favor temperance or antislavery legislation and aid to education. Whigs portrayed themselves not only as the party of prosperity but also as the party of respectability and proper behavior.

**The Social Bases of the Two Parties** >> In some ways the social makeup of the two parties was similar. To be competitive Whigs and Democrats both had to have significant support among farmers, the largest group in society, and workers. Neither party could carry an election by appealing exclusively to the rich or the poor.

The Whigs, however, enjoyed disproportionate strength among the business and commercial classes, especially following the Bank War. Whigs appealed to planters who needed credit to finance their cotton and rice trade in the world market, to farmers who were eager to sell their surpluses, and to workers who wished to improve their social position. Democrats attracted farmers isolated from the market or uncomfortable with it, workers alienated from the emerging industrial system, and rising entrepreneurs who wanted to break monopolies and open the economy to newcomers like themselves. The Whigs were strongest in the towns, cities, and rural areas that were fully integrated into the market economy, whereas Democrats dominated areas of semisubsistence farming that were more isolated and languishing economically. Attitude toward the market, rather than economic position, was more important in determining party affiliation.

Religion and ethnic identities also shaped partisanship. As the self-proclaimed "party of respectability," Whigs attracted the support of high-status native-born church groups, including Congregationalists and Unitarians in New England and Presbyterians and Episcopalians elsewhere. The party also attracted immigrant groups that most easily merged into the dominant Anglo-Protestant culture, such as the English, Welsh, and Scots. Democrats, however, recruited more Germans and Irish, whose more lenient observance of the Sabbath and (among Catholics) use of parochial schools generated native-born hostility. Democrats appealed to the lower-status Baptists and Methodists, particularly in states where they earlier had been subjected to legal disadvantages. Both parties also attracted freethinkers and the unchurched, but the Democrats had the advantage because they resisted demands for temperance and sabbatarian laws, such as the prohibition of Sunday travel. In the few states where they could vote, African Americans were solidly Whig in reaction to the Democratic Party's strong racism and hostility to black rights.

 **REVIEW**

What were the major differences between the Whigs and the Democrats?

In the Americas as well as in Europe, the rise of democratic governance and the spread of market economies evolved roughly in tandem over the same half century. Andrew Jackson's triumph was only the latest in a series of upheavals stretching back to the American and French Revolutions of the eighteenth century. Latin America, too, experienced democratic revolutions. From 1808 to 1821 Spain's American provinces declared their independence one by one, taking inspiration from the writings of Jefferson and Thomas Paine as well as the French *Declaration of the Rights of Man.* Democracy did not always root itself in the aftermath of these revolutions, but democratic ideology remained a powerful social catalyst.

In the United States the parallel growth of national markets and democratic institutions exhibited a similarly checkered history. If Jackson championed the cause of the "common people," he also led the movement to displace Indians from their lands. A poor white American might vote for "Old Hickory" at the same time that he took comfort that African Americans could never rise as high as he in an increasingly racist society. Furthermore, the advance of markets created social strains, including the increasing impoverishment of the labor force in the North and the growing gap in society between the richest and the poorest.

Still, Americans had evolved a system of democratic politics to deal with the conflicts that the new order produced. The new national parties, like the new markets, had become essential structures uniting the American nation. They advanced an ideology of equality and opportunity, competed vigorously with one another, and mobilized large numbers of ordinary Americans in the political process. Along with the market, democracy had become an integral part of American life.

# CHAPTER SUMMARY

Beginning in the 1820s the United States experienced a democratic revolution that was identified with Andrew Jackson.

- The rise of democracy was stimulated by the Panic of 1819, which caused Americans to look toward both politicians and the government to address their needs.
- The new political culture of democracy included the use of conventions to make nominations, the celebration of the wisdom of the people, the adoption of white manhood suffrage, and the acceptance of political parties as essential for the working of the constitutional system.
- The new politics had distinct limits, however. Women were not given the vote, and racism intensified.
  - The eastern Indian tribes were forced to move to new lands west of the Mississippi River.
  - Free African Americans found themselves subject to increasingly harsh discrimination and exclusion.
- In politics Andrew Jackson came to personify the new democratic culture. Through his forceful leadership he significantly expanded the powers of the presidency.
  - Jackson threatened to use force against South Carolina when it tried to nullify the federal tariff using John C. Calhoun's theory of nullification—that is, that a state convention could nullify a federal law.
  - In response nationalists advanced the idea of the perpetual Union. The compromise of 1833, which gradually lowered the tariff, ended the crisis.
  - Jackson vetoed a bill to recharter the Second Bank of the United States and destroyed it by removing its federal deposits.
  - Under President Martin Van Buren, the nation entered a severe depression.
- Capitalizing on hard times and employing the democratic techniques pioneered by the Democrats, the Whigs gained national power in 1840.
- By 1840 the two parties had developed different ideologies.
  - The Whigs were more comfortable with the mechanisms of the market and linked commerce with progress.
  - The Democrats were uneasy about the market and favored limited government.

## Additional Reading

The most comprehensive reinterpretation of antebellum political history from Jackson to Lincoln is Sean Wilentz, *The Rise of Democracy* (2005). For a broader perspective on the evolution of American political culture throughout the nineteenth century, see Glenn Altschuler and Stuart Blumin, *Rude Republic* (2000). A good interpretation of Jacksonian politics is Harry Watson, *Liberty and Power* (1990); and important discussions of party ideologies include Marvin Meyers, *The Jacksonian Persuasion* (1957); Daniel Walker Howe, *The Political Culture of American Whigs* (1979); and Lawrence Frederick Kohl, *The Politics of Individualism* (1988). For the history of the Whig Party, the book to read is Michael Holt, *The Rise and Fall of the American Whig Party* (1999). Two important books treat broader themes: Brian Balough's *A Government Out of Sight* (2008) explores the ways in which citizens experienced the authority of the national government, while Ronald P. Formisano's *For the People* (2012) traces the rise of populist movements.

The best account of the nullification crisis is still William Freehling, *Prelude to the Civil War* (1966); and Robert Remini offers a succinct analysis of the banking controversy in *Andrew Jackson and the Bank War* (1967). Paul Goodman, *Towards a Christian Republic* (1988), is the most valuable study of Anti-Masonry. On Indian removal in the South, see John Ehle, *The Trail of Tears* (1997); and Robert Remini, *Andrew Jackson and His Indian Wars* (2001).

# 12 Afire with Faith

## 1820–1850

Bursting with energy and enthusiasm, Methodists head toward a camp meeting in 1819, during the Second Great Awakening.

Source: Library of Congress, Prints and Photographs Division [LC-DIG-pga-05966]

### >> An American Story

## THE BEECHERS AND THE KINGDOM OF GOD

In 1826 the Reverend Lyman Beecher was probably the most celebrated minister of the Republic, and the pulpit of Hanover Street Church was his to command. Beecher looked and spoke like a pious farmer, but every Sunday he was transformed when he mounted the pulpit of Boston's most imposing church. From there he would blaze forth denunciations of dancing, drinking, dueling, and "infidelity," all the while punctuating his sermon with pump-handle strokes of the right hand.

Nor were Beecher's ambitions small. His goal was nothing less than to bring the kingdom of Christ to the nation and the world. Like many ministers Beecher had studied the intriguing final book of the New Testament, the Revelation to John. The Revelation foretold in the latter days of Earth a glorious millennium—a thousand years of peace and triumph—when the saints would rule and evil would be banished from the world. Beecher was convinced that the long-awaited millennium might well begin in the United States.

^ Lyman Beecher (*center*) with his family in 1855. Five of his six sons, all of whom were ministers, stand in back. In front, daughters Catharine (holding his arm to steady it for the long photographic exposure) and Isabella are on the left; Harriet, the author of *Uncle Tom's Cabin*, is at the far right. ©Corbis via Getty Images

To usher in the kingdom of God, entire communities and even nations would have to be swept with the fire of **millennialism**. Toward that end Beecher joined other Protestant ministers in supporting a host of religious reforms and missionary efforts. By 1820 they had formed voluntary organizations devoted to a wide range of activities: blanketing the United States with religious tracts and bibles, educating young men for the ministry, sending missionaries to every corner of the globe, promoting Sunday schools for children, ministering to sailors and the poor, reforming drunkards, and stopping business on the Sabbath. To Beecher the organizations constituting this loosely united "Benevolent Empire" were signs of the coming kingdom.

**millennialism** belief in the thousand-year reign of Christ predicted in the New Testament's final book, the Revelation to John.

As the new pastor at Hanover Street, Beecher also directed his righteous artillery on a host of evils that seemed to be obstructing God's kingdom. With scorn he attacked Unitarians, whose liberal, rational creed rejected the divinity of Jesus. In Boston, Unitarians were mainly upper class and cultured. But he also denounced what he viewed as sinful pastimes of the lower class: playing cards, gambling, and drinking. And he denounced Roman Catholic priests and nuns as superstitious, devious agents of "Antichrist."

Beecher's efforts at "moral reform" antagonized many immigrants and other working people who enjoyed liquor or lotteries. In disdain they referred to Hanover Street Church, with its imposing stone tower, as Beecher's "stone jug." After all, it was there that its pastor drank most deeply of his religious spirits. In 1830 a blaze broke out in the basement of his church, and some of the locals had their revenge. Firefighters stood by and made jokes about "Old Beecher" and hellfire as flames cracked the stone tower from top to bottom and the splendid structure burned into ruins.

Any fire, real or spiritual, is unpredictable as it spreads from one scrap of tinder to the next. That proved to be the case with reform movements of the 1820s and 1830s as, in subsequent decades, they moved in diverging, sometimes contradictory, ways. What did it mean, after all, to make a heaven on earth?

Lyman Beecher embodied the spirit of antebellum (pre–Civil War) evangelical Protestantism. At the core of evangelicalism was the conviction that divine grace brought about a new birth, one that enabled belief in Jesus Christ. That conviction also committed the individual convert to reforming his or her own vices as well as the faults of others. But evangelicalism was changing over the course of Beecher's lifetime, and, as it changed, so did its influence on Christian believers. Early-nineteenth-century evangelical leaders such as Beecher sought to convert individuals through revivals and then to turn their energies toward reforming others through the voluntary associations of the Benevolent Empire. Their conservative aim, as he expressed it, was to restore America to "the moral government of God."

But the next generation of evangelical leaders—including Beecher's own children—sought not merely to convert individuals to Christianity but also to reform the most fundamental institutions structuring American society: slavery, the family, and the political and legal subordination of women. By the 1840s they were joined by many other believers in faiths both secular and religious—Unitarians and transcendentalists, Shakers and socialists. All were afire with the faith that they could radically remake the United States. <<

## THEMATIC TIMELINE

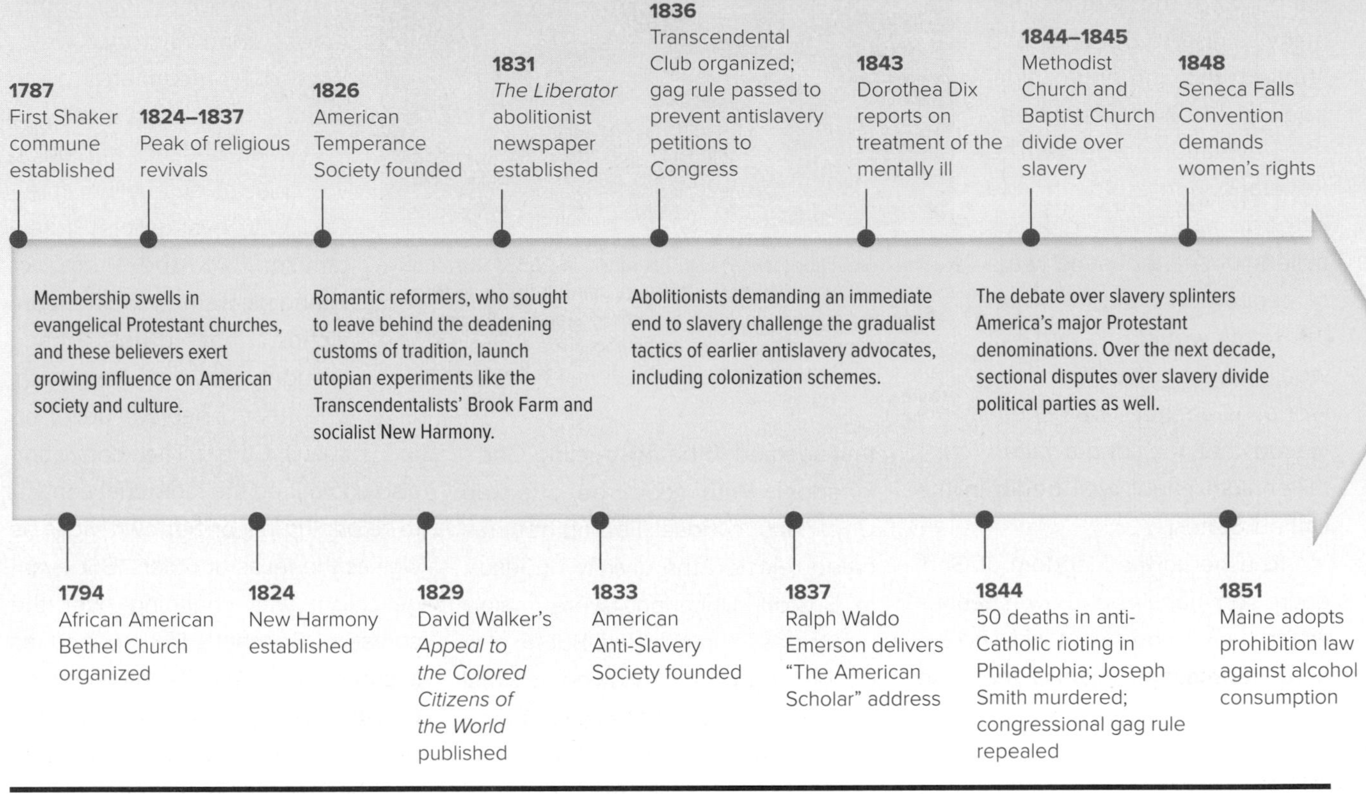
1787
First Shaker commune established
1824–1837
Peak of religious revivals
1826
American Temperance Society founded
1831
The Liberator abolitionist newspaper established
1836
Transcendental Club organized; gag rule passed to prevent antislavery petitions to Congress
1843
Dorothea Dix reports on treatment of the mentally ill
1844–1845
Methodist Church and Baptist Church divide over slavery
1848
Seneca Falls Convention demands women's rights
Membership swells in evangelical Protestant churches, and these believers exert growing influence on American society and culture.
Romantic reformers, who sought to leave behind the deadening customs of tradition, launch utopian experiments like the Transcendentalists' Brook Farm and socialist New Harmony.
Abolitionists demanding an immediate end to slavery challenge the gradualist tactics of earlier antislavery advocates, including colonization schemes.
The debate over slavery splinters America's major Protestant denominations. Over the next decade, sectional disputes over slavery divide political parties as well.
1794
African American Bethel Church organized
1824
New Harmony established
1829
David Walker's Appeal to the Colored Citizens of the World published
1833
American Anti-Slavery Society founded
1837
Ralph Waldo Emerson delivers "The American Scholar" address
1844
50 deaths in anti-Catholic rioting in Philadelphia; Joseph Smith murdered; congressional gag rule repealed
1851
Maine adopts prohibition law against alcohol consumption

# THE TRANSFORMATION OF AMERICAN EVANGELICALISM

Before about 1800, most American **evangelicals** embraced the doctrines of Calvinism (see Chapter 2). They believed that God had determined which individuals were destined to be damned or saved and that no human effort could alter those eternal fates. But by the beginning of the nineteenth century, such propositions seemed increasingly unreasonable to the American heirs of a revolution that celebrated human equality, free will, and reason. As a result, a growing number of evangelicals moved toward an outlook that, although not denying the sinfulness of human nature and the necessity of divine grace for salvation, granted more power to free will and human effort. That more democratic belief—that all men and women might choose and win salvation, that each individual should take an active responsibility for redemption—came to characterize the religious views of most evangelicals among the ranks of Congregationalists, Presbyterians, Baptists, and Methodists over the course of the Second Great Awakening. In turn, their more optimistic assessment of human potential fostered revivals and ambitious programs for reforming individuals and society.

**evangelicals** Christian believers who work actively to spread the "good news," or gospel of Jesus as recounted in the New Testament of the Bible.

## Charles Grandison Finney and Modern Revivalism >>

The man who embodied this transformed evangelicalism was Charles Grandison Finney, the founder of modern revivalism. In 1821, as a young man, Finney experienced a soul-shattering conversion that led him to give up his law practice to become an itinerant minister. Eventually he was ordained in the Presbyterian Church, although he lacked any formal theological training. He first attracted national attention when in the mid-1820s and early 1830s he conducted a series of spectacular

CENTRAL PART OF BUFFALO STREET, ROCHESTER, N. Y.
The view shows the central part of the city, near the junction of State and Exchange streets, with Buffalo street. The spire of the Court House is seen on the right; part of the Methodist church, and other public buildings, on the left.

^ In the winter of 1830–1831, Charles Finney preached frequently in Rochester, the nation's first inland boomtown.
©The Granger Collection, New York

revivals in the booming port cities along the new Erie Canal.

Like George Whitefield before him, Finney had an entrancing voice that carried great distances. His success also resulted from popularizing special techniques—"the new measures" that had been developed during the frontier revivals of the Second Great Awakening (Chapter 9). Finney held "protracted meetings" night after night to build up excitement. Speaking boldly and bluntly, he prayed for sinners by name, encouraged women to testify in public gatherings, and placed those struggling with conversion on the "anxious bench" at the front of the church. Whereas the leaders of the first Great Awakening (Chapter 5) had regarded revivals as god-sent outpourings of grace, Finney viewed them as the consequence of human agency. Like most other antebellum evangelical revivalists, Finney endorsed free will and preached that all men and women who wanted to could be saved.

With salvation within reach of every individual, what might be in store for society at large? "If the church would do her duty," Finney confidently predicted, "the millennium may come in this country in three years."

**The Appeal of Evangelicalism** >> The revivals of the Second Great Awakening drew converts from every segment of American society. Men, women, and children; whites, African Americans, and Indians; northerners and southerners; slave and free—all joined evangelical churches in unprecedented numbers during the opening decades of the nineteenth century. Evangelicalism proved a potent and protean faith, one that could be adapted to answer both the spiritual strivings and needs and the temporal anxieties and sufferings of diverse groups.

In the North middle-class white men under intense pressure from the market economy—lawyers, merchants, and manufacturers—found comfort in evangelicalism's celebration of human ability. It provided them the assurance that they could contend with the many economic uncertainties in their lives. The emerging urban working class, struggling to stay afloat in the face of industrialization, found in evangelicalism's moral code a discipline centered on self-control and self-improvement. Rural southerners—planters and farmers alike—found their mastery over wives, children, and blacks confirmed by evangelical teachings. And white men of all classes, in North and South, found that church membership and the reputation it conferred for sobriety, honesty, and respectability often helped them to get ahead in a rootless, competitive society.

Blacks, both free and enslaved, also joined antebellum churches in impressive numbers, even as they continued to forge a distinctive and liberating faith by infusing evangelicalism with African religious traditions. Increasing racial tensions led to the formation of more black Methodist and Baptist churches in northern and southern cities. The most important was the African Methodist Episcopal (AME) Church, organized at Philadelphia in 1816. Richard Allen, a former Delaware slave who had bought his freedom, became that denomination's first bishop. But as reformers challenged the institution of slavery more openly, many southern white communities, especially in the Deep South, suppressed independent black churches after 1820. Black evangelical churches continued to grow in the North, however, and to serve as organizing centers for the swelling African American opposition to slavery. By 1856 the AME Church boasted some 20,000 members.

**Women, Marriage, and Conversion** >> Despite the prominence of men as both clerical and lay leaders in the Second Great Awakening, it was women—black and white, northern and southern—whose presence dominated antebellum revivals and churches. In most revivals female converts outnumbered males by about three to two. Usually the first convert in a family was a woman, and many men who converted were related to women who had come forward earlier.

Women played an important role in the Awakening partly because of changes in their own social universe. Instead of parents arranging the marriages of their children, couples were beginning to wed more often on the basis of affection. Under such conditions a woman's prospects for marriage became less certain, and in older areas such as New England and the coastal South the migration of so many young men to the West compounded this uncertainty. Yet marriage was deemed important for a woman's happiness, and it remained essential for her economic security.

The unpredictability of these social circumstances drew young women toward religion, especially those between the ages of 12 and 25. Joining a church heightened a young woman's feeling of initiative and gave her a sense of purpose. By establishing respectability and widening her social circle of friends, church membership also enhanced her chances of marriage. And before and after marriage, it opened opportunities to participate in benevolent and reform associations that took women outside the domestic circle and into a realm of public activism.

**The Significance of the Second Great Awakening** >> As a result of the Second Great Awakening, the dominant form of Christianity in America became evangelical Protestantism. Membership in the major Protestant churches—Congregational, Presbyterian, Baptist, and Methodist—soared during the first half of the nineteenth century. By 1840 about half the adult population was connected to some church, with the Methodists emerging as the largest Protestant denomination in both the North and the South. Observers such as French visitor Alexis de Tocqueville noted the striking contrast with Europe, where adherence to Christianity was declining sharply over the same decades.

Not only their sheer numbers but also their institutional presence made evangelicals a formidable force. Their organizations to distribute tracts and bibles, organize Sunday schools and staff missions, encourage temperance and promote Sabbath observance all operated at a national level; the only other institutions able to make such a claim were the Second Bank of the United States and the post office. Evangelical publications dominated the markets for both religious periodicals and books.

Few were more aware of the scope of evangelicalism's sway than the Reverend Lyman Beecher. Earlier in his career Beecher had lamented the collapse of state-supported Congregationalist religious establishments throughout New England. But looking back in later years, he realized that the churches did not need government support to figure as powerful forces in the United States. To his delight Beecher concluded that evangelicals had, in fact, gained "deeper influence" since disestablishment "by voluntary efforts, societies, missions, and revivals."

 REVIEW

How did evangelical Protestants change their doctrines to appeal to new social conditions in the early decades of the nineteenth century?

# REVIVALISM AND THE SOCIAL ORDER

How right Beecher was. The revivals of the Second Great Awakening sparked profound and lasting consequences. Its effects went well beyond the churching of hundreds of thousands of American men, women, and children and the spectacular growth of evangelical Protestant denominations. Religious commitment fundamentally reshaped antebellum society, because, to keep the fervor afire, Beecher, Finney, and their fellow revivalists channeled the energies of converts into a host of benevolent organizations and reform societies. But zealous evangelicals did a great deal more than teach Sunday school at home and dispatch missionaries abroad. As early as the 1820s and 1830s their activism was already affecting three aspects of American culture: drinking habits, ideals of women and the family, and Protestant attitudes toward a growing number of Roman Catholics.

**The Temperance Movement** >> The temperance campaign, a reform dear to the heart of Lyman Beecher and other evangelical clergy, effected a sweeping change in the personal habits of a large number of Americans.

Until the middle of the eighteenth century, most colonials (and Europeans) considered spirits an essential supplement to their diet. But alcohol consumption soared after the Revolution, so that by 1825 the average American over the age of 15 consumed over five gallons of distilled liquors a year, the highest level in American history and nearly triple present-day levels.

## Historian's TOOLBOX

### The Printer's Angel

Printing press, other printers
What is indicated by these mosques and minarets?
A girl in the United States—What is conveyed by her reading a scroll similar to the one in the angel's hands?

The American Tract Society (ATS), one of the many evangelical Protestant voluntary associations founded in the early nineteenth century, celebrated its mission with this illustration. An allegorical rendering of the power of print to convert the world, it shows an angel delivering a scroll, presumably God's word inscribed in the Bible, to a printer's outstretched hands. Although other voluntary associations printed bibles, the ATS produced millions of tracts, small booklets narrating experiences of religious conversion or inculcating moral lessons. Children in the United States, especially those attending Sunday schools, were among the ATS's target audiences: tracts aimed at boys and girls were often illustrated with woodcuts and covered in brightly colored paper. By 1850 millions of copies of children's tracts had flown off the ATS presses, along with millions more for children and adults translated into several languages. As the mother and son shown in the lower right-hand corner indicate, the ATS shared the aim of other Protestant voluntary associations to hasten the millennium by persuading Jews and Muslims, pagans and Roman Catholics, to embrace the beliefs of evangelical Protestants.

#### THINKING CRITICALLY

*What message is conveyed by positioning a Protestant church and a Muslim mosque on opposite sides of the illustration? Why are a woman and a boy—but no adult men—the recipients of tracts in the lower-right scene? Does the image of an angel in the center recall any biblical scene often depicted by Roman Catholic artists? Why would the Protestant illustrator wish to evoke that association?*



Led largely by clergy, the temperance movement at first focused on drunkenness and did not oppose moderate drinking. But in 1826 the American Temperance Society was founded, taking voluntary abstinence as its goal. As the movement gained momentum, annual per-capita consumption of alcohol dropped sharply. By 1845 it had fallen below two gallons a year.

The temperance movement lasted longer and attracted many more supporters than other reforms did. Its success came partly for social reasons. Democracy necessitated sober voters; factories required sober workers. In addition, temperance attracted the upwardly mobile—professionals, small businesspeople, and skilled artisans eager to improve their social standing. Finally, temperance advocates stressed the suffering that men inflicted on women and children, and thus the movement appealed to women as a means to defend the home and carry out their domestic mission.

**Ideals of Women and the Family** >> Evangelicals also contributed substantially to a new ideal of womanhood. The ideal was promoted by the clergy and female authors in sermons, advice manuals, magazine articles, and novels during the first half of the nineteenth century. Called the "cult of **domesticity**" or "true womanhood" or "evangelical womanhood," that ideal cast wives and mothers as the "angels" of their households.

**domesticity** devotion to home life, and a woman's place at the center of that life.

Women were singularly suited to serve as dispensers of love, comfort, and moral instruction to husbands and children. The premise of that new ideal was that men and women, by their very nature, inhabited separate spheres. The rough-and-tumble world of business and politics was the proper province of husbands and fathers, while women

## Consumption of spirits in gallons

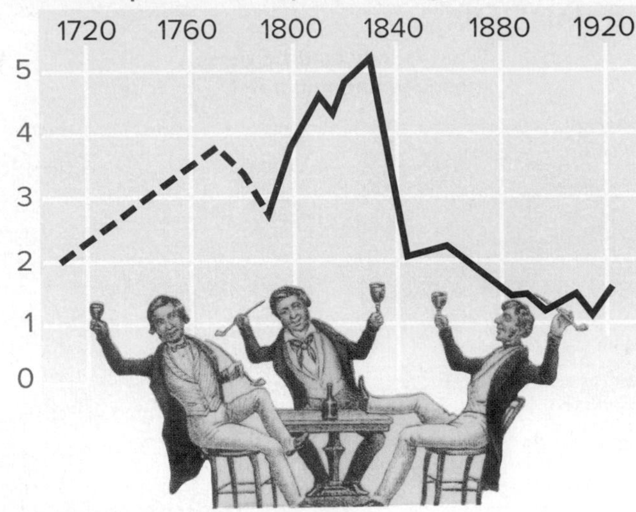
1720
1760
1800
1840
1880
1920
5
4
3
2
1
0

^ Beginning in 1790 per capita levels of drinking steadily rose until 1830, when the temperance movement produced a sharp decline over the next two decades. *What is the range between the highest and lowest years of consumption of spirits, in gallons per capita? Can you research the present average in the United States?*
Source: Library of Congress, Prints and Photographs Division [LC-DIG-ppmsca-32720]

ruled the domestic sphere of home and family. "Love is our life our reality, business yours," Mollie Clark told one suitor.

This new ideal also held that women were by nature morally stronger and more religious than men. That view reversed the negative medieval and early modern views of women as the sinful daughters of the temptress Eve, more passionate by nature and thus less morally restrained and spiritually inclined than men. But the new ideal also held antebellum women to a higher standard of sexual purity. A man's sexual infidelity, although hardly condoned, brought no lasting shame. But a woman who engaged in sexual relations before marriage or was unfaithful afterward was threatened with everlasting disgrace. Under this new double standard women were to be pure, passionless, and passive: they were to submerge their identities in those of their husbands.

Spokespersons for the new ideal of womanhood and the notion of separate spheres directed their message mainly at elite and middle-class women. And that message found an impressionable audience among wives and daughters in the urbanizing Northeast. There the separation of the workplace from the home was most complete. As a result of industrialization, many men worked outside the home, while the rise of factories also led to a decline in part-time work such as spinning, which women had once performed to supplement family income. Home manufacturing was no longer essential, because, except on the frontier, families could easily purchase the articles that women previously had made, such as cloth, soap, and candles. This growing separation of the household from the workplace in the Northeast made it that much easier for the home to be idealized as a place of "domesticity," a haven away from the competitive, workaday world, with the mother firmly at its center.

The celebration of domesticity was not unique to the United States. Indeed, this redefinition of women's roles was more sweeping in Europe, because previously middle-class women had left the task of child-raising largely to hired nurses and governesses. By midcentury these mothers devoted much more time to domestic duties, including rearing the children. Family size also declined, both in France and in England. The middle class was most numerous in England; indeed, the importance of the middle class in Britain during Queen Victoria's reign (1837–1901) gave these ideals the label **Victorianism**.

As elite and middle-class homes came to be seen as havens of moral virtue, those domestic settings developed a new structure and new set of attitudes closer in spirit to those of the modern family. The pressures to achieve success led middle-class young adults to delay marriage, since a husband was expected to have the financial means to support his wife. Smaller family size resulted, since wives, especially those among the urban middle class, began to use birth control to space children farther apart and to minimize the risks of pregnancy. In addition, it has been estimated that before 1860 one abortion was performed for every five or six live births. With smaller

**Victorianism** constellation of middle-class values attributed to the proper virtues of Britain's Queen.

^ Piecework quilts such as this one became affordable to produce only when cheap manufactured cloth was available. Just as the Industrial Revolution encouraged a cult of domesticity to shelter families from the harsh industrial workplace, so, too, did factory-made cloth encourage the making of piecework quilts.
From the Collections of Old Sturbridge Village, Sturbridge, MA (26.23.95)

families, parents could tend more carefully to their children's success. Increasingly, middle-class families took on the expense of additional education to prepare their sons for a career in business. They also frequently equalized inheritances rather than favoring the eldest son or favoring sons over daughters.

## Expanding Public Roles for Women >>

Most women in the United States did not have time to make domesticity the center of their lives. Farmers' wives and enslaved women had to work constantly, whereas lower-class families could not get by without the wages of female members. Still, some elite and middle-class women tried to live up to the new ideals, though many found the effort confining. "The great trial is that I have nothing to do," one complained. "Here I am with abundant leisure and capable, I believe, of accomplishing some good, and yet with no object on which to expend my energies."

In response to those frustrations Lyman Beecher's eldest daughter, Catharine (who never married), made a career out of assuring women that the proper care of household and children was their sex's crucial responsibility. Like the earlier advocates of "republican motherhood," Catharine Beecher supported women's education and argued that women exercised power as moral guardians of the nation's future. She also wrote several books on efficient home management.

But many women yearned to exert moral authority outside the confines of their households. Ironically, the new host of benevolent and reform societies offered them just that opportunity. Devout wives and daughters, particularly those from middle-class families, flocked to these voluntary associations, many of which had separate women's chapters. By serving in such organizations, they gained the practical experiences of holding office on governing boards, conducting meetings, drafting policy statements, organizing reform programs, and raising money.

Evangelicalism thus enabled women to enter public life and to make their voices heard in ways that were socially acceptable. After all, evangelical teachings affirmed that they were the superior sex in piety and morality, a point often invoked by those very women who devoted much of their time to benevolence and reform. They justified such public activism as merely the logical extension of their private responsibility to act as spiritual guides to their families.

## Protestants and Catholics >>

Women's piety and spiritual influence were surely on the mind of Isaac Bird one Saturday morning in the autumn of 1819. A devout evangelical preparing for the ministry, he had wandered into a Roman Catholic church in Boston and now watched with rapt attention a ritual, conducted entirely in Latin, in which two women "took the veil" and became nuns. Bird often visited Boston on his vacations to proselytize its poorest inhabitants. Many were Catholics, as he noted, some of them recent Irish and German immigrants and others African American. It troubled Bird, this gathering presence of devout Catholics.

Protestants had a long history of animosity toward Roman Catholics, especially in New England. But before the beginning of the nineteenth century, the number of Catholics had been small: by 1815 there were only 150,000 scattered throughout the United States, and they often had little access to priests or public worship.

That had begun to change by 1820. French Canadian Catholic immigrants were filtering into New England in growing numbers, and there began what would become during the 1840s and 1850s an influx of Catholic immigrants from the British Isles and German-speaking countries. By 1830 the Catholic population had jumped to 300,000, and by 1850 it accounted for 8 percent of the U.S. population—the same proportion as Presbyterians. As these newcomers settled in eastern cities and on western frontiers, there were an increasing number of priests, nuns, and churches to minister to their spiritual needs.

The differences between Roman Catholicism and Protestantism—especially evangelicalism—were substantial. Where evangelicals stressed the inward transformation of conversion as essential to salvation, Catholics emphasized the importance of outward religious observances, such as faithfully attending mass and receiving the sacraments. Where evangelicals insisted that individuals read the Bible to discover God's will, Catholics urged their faithful to heed church teachings and traditions. Where Catholics believed that human suffering could be a penance paving the way toward redemption, evangelicals regarded it as an evil to be alleviated. Where evangelicals looked toward an imminent millennium, Catholics harbored no such expectation and played almost no role in antebellum benevolent and reform movements.

To Protestants many elements of Catholicism seemed superstitious and even subversive. They rejected the Catholic doctrine of transubstantiation, which held that the bread and wine consecrated by the priest during mass literally turned into the body and blood of Jesus Christ. They condemned as idolatry the Catholic veneration of the Virgin Mary and the saints. They regarded Catholic nuns and convents as threats to the new ideals of womanhood and domesticity. They found it amiss that Catholic laymen had no role in governing their own parishes and dioceses, entrusting that responsibility entirely to priests and bishops.

But the worst fears of Protestants fastened on what they saw as the political dangers posed by Catholics, especially immigrants. Alarmed as Irish and German settlers poured into the West, Lyman Beecher warned that "the world has never witnessed such a rush of dark-minded population from one country to another, as is now leaving Europe and dashing upon our shores." Beecher foresaw a sinister plot hatched by the pope to snuff out American liberty. For what else would follow in a nation overwhelmed by Catholicism, "a religion which never prospered but in alliance with despotic government, has always been and still is the inflexible

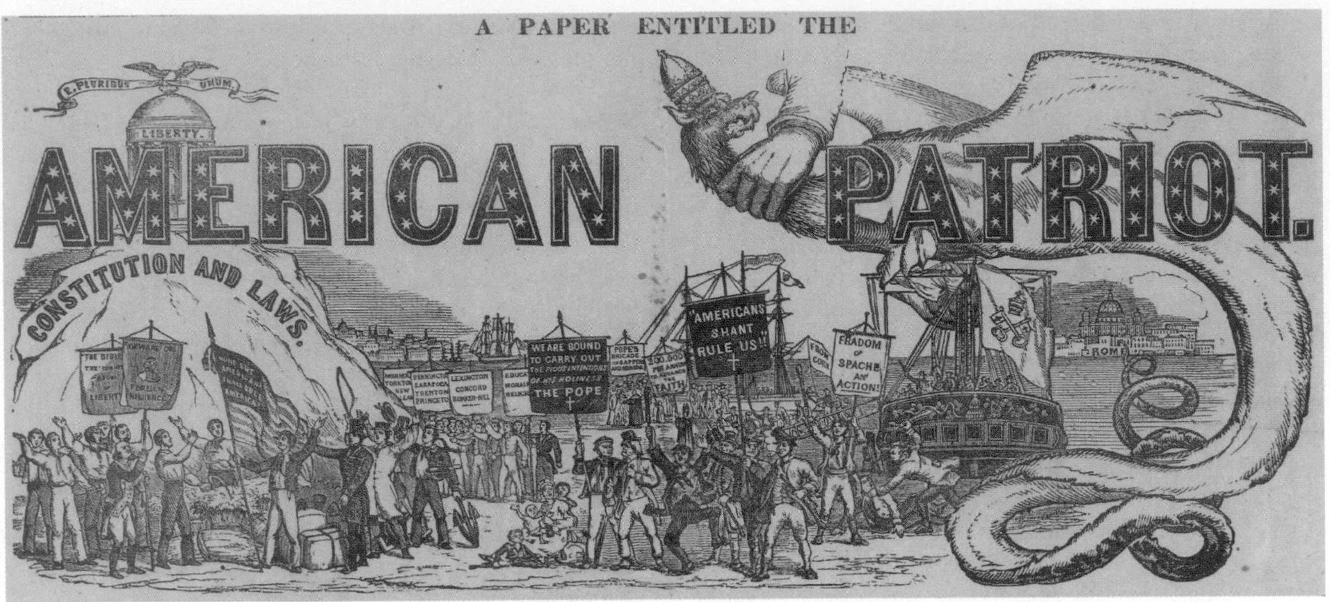
A PAPER ENTITLED THE
AMERICAN PATRIOT.
E PLURIBUS UNUM
LIBERTY.
CONSTITUTION AND LAWS.
WE ARE BOUND TO CARRY OUT
THE POPE
AMERICANS SHANT RULE US!!
FRADOM OF SPACHE AN' ACTION!
ROME

^ This 1852 nativist cartoon warns Americans of the supposed dangers posed by the arrival of immigrants from Germany and Ireland. On the left, native Americans proclaim the virtues of "Constitution and Laws," while a horde of newcomers illustrates the threats. One banner reads "We are bound to carry out the pious intentions of his holiness the Pope." Why is another banner proclaiming "Fradom of Spache and Action!" spelled the way it is?
Source: Library of Congress, Prints and Photographs Division [LC-DIG-ppmsca-07575]

enemy of liberty of conscience and free enquiry, and at this moment is the mainstay of the battle against republican institutions?"

It was all the more appalling to evangelicals, then, that some Protestants found Catholic teachings appealing: so attractive that some 57,000 converted to Catholicism in the 30 years after 1830. In response to those defections many Protestants, believing that converts were drawn by the artistic beauties of Catholic worship, began to include in their churches recognizably Catholic elements such as the symbol of the cross, the use of candles and flowers, organ and choir music, stained glass windows, and Gothic architecture.

Other Protestants attacked Catholicism directly. Writing under the name "Maria Monk," a team of evangelical ministers produced a lurid account of life in a convent, replete with sex orgies involving priests and nuns and a cellar planted with dead babies. Published in 1836 this publication outsold every book except *Uncle Tom's Cabin* in the years before the Civil War. And with anti-Catholic sentiment running so high, predictably, there was violence. In 1834 a mob in Charlestown, Massachusetts, burned a convent to the ground. The sisters and their students escaped injury but, during the summer of 1844 in Philadelphia, two separate outbreaks of anti-Catholic violence left 14 people dead, as well as two churches and three dozen homes in smoldering ruins.

Most antebellum Protestants condemned violence against Catholics. But anti-Catholicism had emerged as a defining feature of American Protestant identity, and the alienation of the two groups ran deep, enduring far into the twentieth century.

**REVIEW**

In what ways did the revivals of the Second Great Awakening reshape American society and culture?

# VISIONARIES

Increasingly hostile to Roman Catholics, evangelicals also stood at odds with other groups in antebellum America who envisioned new ways of improving individuals and society. Although they often expressed optimism about the prospects for human betterment, these other reformers—Unitarians and Transcendentalists, socialists and communitarians—otherwise had little in common with evangelicals.

**The Unitarian Contribution** >> During the opening decades of the nineteenth century, the religious division among Americans that produced the fiercest debates pitted evangelicals against deists, Unitarians, and other rational Christians. A majority only in eastern Massachusetts, Unitarians denied the divinity of Jesus while affirming the ability and responsibility of humankind to follow his moral teachings. Disdainful of the emotionalism of revivals, they were also inclined to interpret the Bible broadly rather than literally. To most Americans such views were so suspect that the presidents who adhered to Unitarianism—John Adams, Thomas Jefferson, and John Quincy Adams—did not wish to publicize their beliefs.

^ In the summer of 1858, members of the cultural Saturday Club of Boston made an excursion to the Adirondacks to observe nature. In *Philosopher's Camp*, painted by William J. Stillman, who organized the expedition, a group on the left dissects a fish under the supervision of the famous scientist Louis Agassiz. Alone at the center of the painting stands Ralph Waldo Emerson, in a contemplative mood. ©Concord Free Public Library

Despite their many differences, Unitarians shared with evangelicals an esteem for the power of human free will and a commitment to the goal of social betterment. Small though their numbers were, Unitarians made large contributions to the cause of reform. One, Boston schoolteacher Dorothea Dix, took the lead in creating state-supported asylums to treat the mentally ill, who were often chained, beaten, and kept in cages. Samuel Gridley Howe promoted education for the blind and deaf, and Horace Mann strove to give greater access to public schooling to children of poor and working-class families.

## From Unitarianism to Transcendentalism >>

A new philosophic outlook—transcendentalism—blossomed in the mid-1830s, when a number of Unitarian clergy such as George Ripley and Ralph Waldo Emerson resigned their pulpits, loudly protesting the church's teachings as dry, bloodless, and self-satisfied. The new "Transcendentalist Club" attracted a small following among other discontented Boston intellectuals, including Margaret Fuller, Bronson Alcott, and Orestes Brownson.

**transcendentalism** a philosophical and religious movement that embraced intuition, emotion, and the divine spark within the individual as the path to transcend, or move beyond, the material world.

**Transcendentalism** emphasized feeling over reason, seeking a spiritual communion with nature. In following this course transcendentalists mirrored the beliefs of Romanticism, a European movement that arose as a reaction to the Enlightenment. As the name suggested, transcendentalists sought to go beyond or to rise above—specifically above reason and beyond the material world. As part of creation, every human being contained a spark of divinity, Emerson avowed. Transcendentalists also shared in Romanticism's glorification of the individual. "Trust thyself. Every heart vibrates to that iron string," Emerson advised. If freed from the constraints of traditional authority, the individual possessed infinite potential. Like the devout at Finney's revivals, who sought to improve themselves and society, listeners who flocked to Emerson's lectures were infused with the spirit of optimistic reform.

In extolling nature, other American writers worried that the advance of civilization, with its market economy and crowded urban centers, might destroy the natural simplicity of the land. In 1845 Henry David Thoreau built a cabin on the edge of Walden Pond in Concord, living by himself for 16 months to demonstrate the advantages of self-reliance. His experiences became the basis for *Walden* (1854), which eloquently denounced Americans' frantic competition for material goods and wealth. Only in nature, Thoreau argued, could one find true independence, liberty, equality, and happiness. Voicing the anti-institutional impulse of Romanticism, he took individualism to its antisocial extreme.

In contrast to Thoreau, who prized isolation, Walt Whitman embraced American society in its infinite variety. A journalist and laborer in the New York City area, Whitman was inspired by the common people, whose "manners, speech, dress, friendships . . . are unrhymed poetry." In taking their measure in *Leaves of Grass* (1855), he pioneered a new, modern form of poetry, unconcerned with meter and rhyme and filled with frank imagery and sexual references.

^ Dancing was an integral part of the Shakers' religion, as this picture of a service at Lebanon, New York, indicates. In worshiping, men and women formed separate lines with their hands held out and moved back and forth in rhythm while singing religious songs. One Shaker hymn proclaimed, "With ev'ry gift I will unite, / And join in sweet devotion / To worship God is my delight, / With hands and feet in motion." Note the presence of African Americans in the community.
Source: "Shakers near Lebanon," The New York Public Library (ps_prn_cd16_235)

**Utopian Communities** >> Evangelicals, Unitarians, and writers such as Thoreau and Whitman focused their attention on how individuals might be saved, improved, fulfilled. But some antebellum believers, both secular and religious, sought to remake society at large by forming communities intended as examples to the rest of the world.

Even some transcendental individualists attempted a utopian venture. During the early 1840s Emerson's friend George Ripley organized Brook Farm, a community near Boston where members could live "a more wholesome and simple life than can be led amid the pressure of our competitive institutions." But predictably, these Romantic individualists could not sustain the group cooperation essential for success.

Some secular thinkers shared the transcendentalists' view that competition, inequality, and acquisitiveness were corrupting American society. Among those critics were socialists, and their goal was to defend the interests of American workers from the ravages of industrialization. The most influential was Robert Dale Owen, the unlikely founder of America's first socialist community. A Welsh industrialist who had made a fortune manufacturing textiles, Owen then turned to realizing his vision of a just society—one in which property was held in common and work equally shared. Such a benign social environment, he believed, would foster tolerant, rational human beings capable of self-government. What better place than America to make this dream come true?

Initially, Owen received a warm reception. John Quincy Adams not only attended both lectures that Owen delivered at the Capitol but also displayed a model of his proposed community in the White House. A few months later about 900 volunteers flocked to Owen's community at New Harmony, Indiana. But alas, most lacked the skills and commitment to make it a success, and bitter factions soon split the settlement. Owen made matters worse by announcing that he rejected both the authenticity of the Bible and the institution of marriage. New Harmony dissolved in 1827, but Owen's principles inspired nearly 20 other short-lived experiments.

The United States was a poor proving-ground for socialist experiments. Wages were too high and land too cheap for such communities to interest most Americans. And individualism was too strong to foster a commitment to cooperative action. Communities founded by believers in religious rather than secular faiths proved far more enduring. Their common spiritual convictions muted individualism, and their charismatic leaders held divisions at bay.

Among the most successful of these religiously based communal groups were the Shakers. Ann Lee, the illiterate daughter of an English blacksmith, believed that God had a dual nature, part male and part female, and that her own life would reveal the feminine side of the divinity, just as Christ had revealed the masculine. In 1774 she led a small band of followers to America. Her followers sometimes shook in the fervent public demonstration of their faith—hence the name Shakers.

As the Second Great Awakening crested, recruits from revivals swelled Shaker ranks, and their new disciples founded about 20 villages. Members held the community's property in common, worked hard, and lived simply. Convinced that the end of the world was at hand so there was no need to perpetuate the human race, Shakers practiced celibacy. Men and women normally worked apart, ate at separate tables in silence, entered separate doorways, and had separate living quarters. Elders typically assigned tasks by gender, with women performing household chores and men laboring in the fields, but leadership of the church was split equally between men and women. Lacking any natural increase, membership began to decline after 1850, from a peak of about 6,000 members.

**The Mormon Experience** >> The most spectacularly successful antebellum religious community—one that mushroomed into a denomination whose followers now number in the millions around the world—was the Church of Jesus Christ of Latter-day Saints. The Mormons, as they are generally known, took their rise from the visions of a young man named Joseph Smith in Palmyra, in western New York, where the religious fires of revivalism often flared. The son of a poor farmer, Smith was robust, charming, almost hypnotic in his appeal. In 1827, at the age of only 22, he announced that he had discovered and translated a set of golden tablets on which was written the Book of Mormon. The tablets told the story of a band of Hebrews who in biblical times journeyed to America, splitting into two groups, the Nephites and Lamanites. The Nephites established a Christian civilization, only to be exterminated by the Lamanites, whose descendants were said to be the Indians of the Americas. Seeking to reestablish the true church, Smith gathered a group of devoted followers.

Like nineteenth-century evangelicalism, Mormonism proclaimed that salvation was available to all. Mormon culture also upheld the middle-class values of hard work, thrift, and self-control. It partook of the optimistic, materialist attitudes of American society. And by teaching that Christ would return to rule the earth, it shared in the hope of a coming millennial kingdom.

Yet Mormonism was less an outgrowth of evangelicalism than of the primitive gospel movement, which sought to reestablish the ancient church. In restoring what Smith called "the ancient order of things," he created a **theocracy** uniting church and state, reestablished biblical priesthoods and titles, and adopted temple rituals.

**theocracy** system of government by priests or clergy claiming divine inspiration or guidance.

Like Roman Catholics, the Mormons drew bitter opposition—and armed attacks. Smith's unorthodox teachings provoked persecution wherever Smith and his followers went, first to Ohio and then to Missouri. Mob violence finally hounded him out of Missouri in 1839. Smith then established a new holy city, which he named Nauvoo, located on the Mississippi River in Illinois.

Reinforced by a steady stream of converts from Britain, Nauvoo became the largest city in Illinois, with a population of 10,000 by the mid-1840s. There Smith introduced the most distinctive features of Mormon theology, including baptism for the dead, eternal marriage, and polygamy, or plural marriage. As a result, Mormonism increasingly diverged from traditional Christianity and became a distinct new religion. To bolster his authority as a prophet, Smith established a theocratic political order under which church leaders controlled political offices and governed the community, with Smith as mayor.

Neighboring residents, alarmed by the Mormons' growing political power and reports that church leaders were practicing polygamy, demanded that Nauvoo's charter be revoked and the church suppressed. In 1844, while in jail for destroying the printing press of dissident Mormons in Nauvoo, Smith was murdered by an anti-Mormon mob. In 1846 the Mormons abandoned Nauvoo, and the following year Brigham Young, Smith's successor, led them westward to Utah.

 **REVIEW**

In what ways did transcendentalism shape the themes of writers of the American Renaissance? Who were the major communitarian reformers of the era?

# ABOLITIONISM AND WOMEN'S RIGHTS

Among the most transformative events of American history was the rise of a militant antislavery movement known as abolitionism. Beginning in the 1830s, growing numbers of white Americans came to believe that the end of slavery should come immediately. What were the influences that propelled antislavery advocates away from the support for gradualism and colonization that had prevailed during earlier decades (see Chapter 11)?

**The Origins of the Abolitionist Movement** >> First was the example of Britain, once the world's leading purchaser and transporter of slaves. Parliament had outlawed the slave trade in 1808 and pressed other European nations to do the same. Thereafter a growing number of activists called for an immediate end to slavery in all of Britain's Caribbean colonies, and in 1833, bowing to overwhelming public pressure, Parliament emancipated nearly 800,000 slaves. Close connections existed between reformers on both sides of the Atlantic, and the British example inspired some Americans to call for an immediate end to slavery.

Even more important was the activism of African Americans. A turning point in their agitation against slavery came in 1829 with the publication of *Appeal to the Colored*

*Citizens of the World*. Its author, David Walker (ca. 1796–1830), born free in North Carolina, had settled in Boston a few years earlier, running a small used-clothing business and working as a community activist and an agent for the first black newspaper in the United States, *Freedom's Journal*. Walker's impassioned argument that America belonged as much to blacks as to whites ended what little support colonization still commanded in the free black community. Going beyond earlier calls for "uplift" through education, he called upon both free and enslaved African Americans to unite and combat white oppression. And woe unto white Americans, Walker warned, if blacks had to fight in order to attain freedom and equality. Whites should instead "throw away your fears and prejudices" and "treat us like men."

Walker's militancy contrasted sharply with the more conservative strategies of earlier antislavery advocates. But shortly after Walker's death, a white New Englander, William Lloyd Garrison, took up his message. In 1829 Garrison was beginning his career as a reformer, working in Baltimore with Benjamin Lundy, a Quaker who edited an antislavery newspaper calling for a gradual end to slavery through colonization. But the better acquainted Garrison became with Baltimore's free blacks, the more he realized that most regarded colonization as a southern strategy to secure slavery's future and promote racism.

Under their influence, Garrison soon developed views far more radical than Lundy's. Returning to Boston and enlisting help from the free black community there, he published the first issue of *The Liberator* on January 1, 1831. Both black and female writers found their contributions welcomed in its pages. Like Walker's *Appeal*, Garrison's *Liberator* repudiated gradual emancipation, embraced immediatism, and denounced colonization. Like Walker, too, Garrison upheld the principle of racial equality and—going farther than British abolitionists—opposed any compensation for slaveholders in the event of emancipation. Southerners ought to be convinced by "moral suasion," Garrison claimed, to renounce slavery as a sin. Garrison diverged from Walker only in embracing a thoroughgoing pacifism.

To Garrison and other abolitionists, slavery was a moral, not an economic, question. The institution seemed a contradiction of the principle of the American Revolution that all human beings had been created with natural rights. Abolitionists condemned slavery because of the breakup of marriages and families by sale, the harsh punishment of the lash, the slaves' lack of access to education, and the sexual abuse of black women. Most of all, they denounced slavery as outrageously contrary to Christian teaching. As one Ohio antislavery paper declared: "We believe slavery to be a sin, always, everywhere, and only, sin—sin itself." So persistent were the abolitionists in their religious objections that they forced the churches to face the question of slavery head-on. In the 1840s the Methodist Church and the Baptist Church each split into northern and southern organizations over the issue.

**The Spread of Abolitionism** >> By 1832 Garrison had joined with other northern reformers to found a national abolitionist organization, the American Anti-Slavery Society. It coordinated a loosely affiliated network of state and local societies. During the years before the Civil War, perhaps 200,000 northerners belonged to an abolitionist society, or about the same proportion of the U.S. population—about 2 percent—who today belong to the National Rifle Association.

Abolitionists were concentrated in the East, especially in New England, and in areas that had been settled by New Englanders, such as western New York and northern Ohio. The movement was not strong in cities or among businesspeople and workers. Most abolitionists were young, being generally in their 20s and 30s when the movement began, and had grown up in rural areas and small towns in middle-class families. Intensely religious, many had been profoundly affected by the revivals of the Second Great Awakening.

<< Black abolitionist Frederick Douglass (*second from left at the podium*) was only 1 of nearly 50 runaway slaves who appeared at an abolitionist convention held in August 1850 in Cazenovia, New York. The question of whether women should be allowed to take active roles in the movement fractured antislavery advocates and sparked women reformers to speak out more strongly for women's rights.

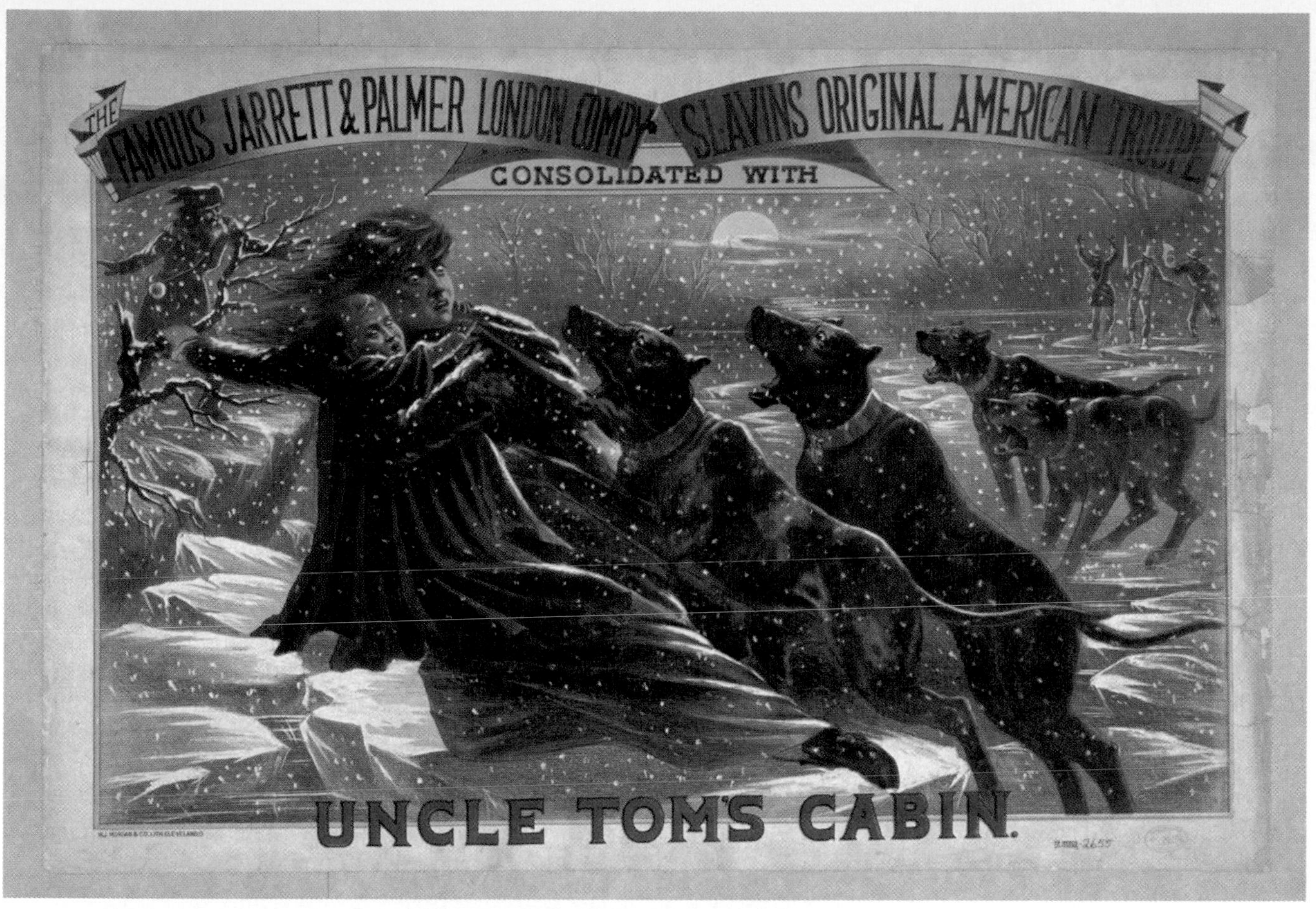
THE FAMOUS JARRETT & PALMER LONDON COMP'Y
SLAVINS ORIGINAL AMERICAN TROUPE
CONSOLIDATED WITH
UNCLE TOM'S CABIN.

^ In this playbill advertising a dramatic production of *Uncle Tom's Cabin*, vicious bloodhounds pursue the light-skinned runaway slave Eliza, who clutches her child as she frantically leaps to safety across the ice-choked Ohio River.
Source: Library of Congress, Prints and Photographs Division [LC-USZC4-1298]

Free African Americans, who made up the majority of subscribers to Garrison's *Liberator*, provided important support and leadership for the movement. Frederick Douglass assumed the greatest prominence. Having escaped from slavery in Maryland, he became an eloquent critic of its evils. Many other important black abolitionists were, like Douglass, runaway slaves who had escaped to freedom. Books and speeches recounting the heroic struggles of Solomon Northrup and William Wells Brown, Sojourner Truth and Harriet Jacobs dramatized the abolitionist message and riveted the attention of audiences both white and black. Aided by many other African Americans, these men and women battled against racial discrimination in the North as well as slavery in the South.

The Underground Railroad, a network of antislavery sympathizers to convey runaway slaves to Canada and freedom, also developed in the North. Although not as extensive or as tightly organized as contemporaries claimed, it hid fugitives and transported them northward from one station to the next. Free African Americans, who were more readily trusted by wary slaves, played a leading role in the Underground Railroad. One of its most famous conductors was Harriet Tubman, an escaped slave who repeatedly returned to the South and eventually escorted more than 200 slaves to freedom.

**Opponents and Divisions** >> The drive for immediate abolition faced massive obstacles within American society. With slavery increasingly important to their region's economy, southerners forced opponents of slavery to flee north. In the North, where racism was equally entrenched, abolitionism provoked bitter resistance.

On occasion northern resistance turned violent. A Boston mob seized Garrison in 1835 and paraded him with a rope around his body until he was rescued. And in 1837 in Alton, Illinois, Elijah Lovejoy was murdered when he tried to protect his printing press from an angry crowd. The leaders of these mobs were not from the bottom of society but, as one of their victims noted, were "gentlemen of property and standing" who were reacting to the threat that abolitionists posed to their prosperity.

The antislavery cause was also hindered by divisions among reformers. Lyman Beecher conceived of sin in terms of individual immorality, not unjust social institutions. But to the abolitionists, America could never become a godly nation until slavery was abolished. Among them was Beecher's daughter, Harriet Beecher Stowe, who in the 1850s wrote the most successful piece of antislavery literature in the nation's history, *Uncle Tom's Cabin*. The abolitionists themselves also splintered, shaken by the opposition they encountered and unable to agree on the most effective response. More conservative reformers wanted to work within established institutions, using the churches and political action to end slavery. But for Garrison and his followers, the mob violence demonstrated that slavery was only part of a deeper national disease, whose cure required the overthrow of American institutions and values.

By the end of the decade Garrison had worked out a program for the total reform of society. He embraced perfectionism—the belief that human beings could lead sinless lives—and pacifism, urged members to leave the churches, and called for an end to all government. Condemning the Constitution as proslavery—"a covenant with death and an agreement with hell"—he publicly burned a copy one July 4th. This platform was radical enough on all counts, but the final straw for Garrison's opponents was his endorsement of women's rights as an inseparable part of abolitionism.

**The Women's Rights Movement** >> American women were kept out of most jobs, denied political rights, and given only limited access to education beyond the elementary grades. When a woman married, her husband became the legal representative of the marriage and gained complete control of her property. If a marriage ended in divorce, the husband was awarded custody of the children. Any unmarried woman was made the ward of a male relative.

When abolitionists divided over the issue of female participation in their societies, women in their ranks found a good deal to identify with in the situation of slaves. While white women were not literally owned by their husbands nor routinely subjected to physical abuse, their freedoms were severely constrained. Sarah and Angelina Grimké, daughters of a slaveholding South Carolina planter, took up the cause of women's rights after they were criticized for speaking against slavery to audiences that included men as well as women. Sarah responded with *Letters on the Condition of Women and the Equality of the Sexes* (1838), arguing that women deserved the same rights as men.

Two abolitionists, Elizabeth Cady Stanton and Lucretia Mott, launched the women's rights movement after they were forced to sit behind a curtain, separated from the male participants, at a world antislavery convention in London. In 1848 Stanton and Mott organized a conference in Seneca Falls, New York, that attracted about a hundred supporters. The meeting issued a Declaration of Sentiments, modeled after the Declaration of Independence, that began, "All men and women are created equal."

The Seneca Falls Convention called for educational and professional opportunities for women, laws giving them control of their property, recognition of legal equality, and repeal of laws awarding the father custody of the children in divorce. The most controversial proposal, and the only resolution that did not pass unanimously, was one demanding the right to vote. The Seneca Falls Convention set forth the arguments and the program for the women's rights movement for the remainder of the century.

In response, several states gave women greater control over their property, and a few made divorce easier or granted women the right to sue in courts. But disappointments and defeats outweighed these early victories. Still, many of the important leaders in the crusade for women's rights after the Civil War had already taken their places at the forefront of the movement. They included Stanton, Susan B. Anthony, Lucy Stone, and—as Lyman Beecher by now must have expected—one of his daughters, Isabella Beecher Hooker.

**The Schism of 1840** >> It was Garrison's position on women's rights that finally split antislavery ranks already divided over other aspects of his growing radicalism. The showdown came in 1840 at the national meeting of the American Anti-Slavery Society, when delegates debated whether women could hold office in the organization. By packing the convention, Garrison carried the day. His opponents resigned to found the rival American and Foreign Anti-Slavery Society.

The schism of 1840 lessened the influence of abolitionism as a reform movement. Although abolitionism heightened moral concern about slavery, it failed to convert the North to its program, and its supporters remained a tiny minority. Despite the considerable courage of its leaders, the movement lacked a realistic, long-range plan for eliminating such a deeply entrenched institution.

 **REVIEW**

What helped to spark the growth of the abolitionist movement? What factors caused the movement to splinter?

# REFORM SHAKES THE PARTY SYSTEM

The crusading idealism of reformers inevitably collided with the hard reality that society could not be perfected by converting individuals. A growing number of frustrated reformers were abandoning the principle of voluntary persuasion and looking to government coercion to achieve their goals.

**The Turn toward Politics** >> Politicians did not particularly welcome the new interest. Because the Whig and Democratic Parties both drew on evangelical and nonevangelical voters, heated moral debates over the harmful effects of drink or the evils of slavery threatened to detach regular party members from their old loyalties and disrupt each party's unity. The strong opposition of German and Irish immigrants to temperance stimulated antiforeign

^ Elizabeth Cady Stanton, one of the instigators and guiding spirits at the Seneca Falls Convention, photographed with two of her children about that time.
Source: Library of Congress, Prints and Photographs Division [LC-USZ62-50821]

sentiment among reformers and further divided both party coalitions, particularly the Democrats.

Because women could not vote, they felt excluded when the temperance and abolitionist movements turned to electoral action to accomplish their goals. By the 1840s female reformers increasingly demanded the right to vote as the means to change society. Nor were men blind to what was at stake: one reason they so strongly resisted female suffrage was that it would give women real power.

The political parties could resist the women's suffrage movement because most of its advocates lacked the right to vote. Less easily put off were temperance reformers. Although drinking had significantly declined in American society by 1840, it had hardly been eliminated. In response, temperance advocates proposed state laws that would outlaw the manufacture and sale of alcoholic beverages. Their first major triumph came in 1851. The Maine Law, as it was known, authorized search and seizure of private property in that state and provided stiff penalties for selling liquor. In the next few years a number of states enacted similar laws, although most were struck down by the courts or later repealed. Prohibition remained a controversial political issue throughout the century.

Although prohibition was temporarily defeated, the issue badly disrupted the Whig and Democratic Parties. It greatly increased party switching and brought to the polls a large number of new voters, including many "wets" who now looked to the Democrats to preserve their right to drink. By dissolving the ties between so many voters and their parties, the temperance issue played a major role in the eventual collapse of the Jacksonian party system in the 1850s.

**Abolitionism and the Party System** >> Slavery proved even more divisive. In 1835 abolitionists distributed more than a million pamphlets, mostly in the South, through the post office. Former senator Robert Hayne led a Charleston mob that burned sacks of U.S. mail containing abolitionist literature, and postmasters in other southern cities refused to deliver the material. Andrew Jackson's administration allowed southern states to censor the mail, leading abolitionists to protest that their civil rights had been violated. In reaction, the number of antislavery societies in the North nearly tripled.

With access to the mails impaired, abolitionists began flooding Congress with petitions against slavery. Asserting that Congress had no power over the institution, angry southern representatives demanded action, and the House in response adopted the so-called gag rule in 1836. It automatically tabled without consideration any petition dealing with slavery. But southern leaders had made a tactical blunder. The gag rule allowed abolitionists not only to attack slavery but also to speak out as defenders of white civil liberties. The appeal of the antislavery movement was broadened, and in 1844 the House finally repealed the controversial rule.

Many abolitionists outside Garrison's circle began to feel that an antislavery third party offered a more effective means of attacking slavery. In 1840 these political abolitionists founded the Liberty Party and nominated for president James Birney, a former slaveholder who had converted to abolitionism. Birney received only 7,000 votes, but the Liberty Party was the seed from which a stronger antislavery political movement would grow. From 1840 onward, abolitionism's importance would be in the political arena rather than as a voluntary reform organization.

 **REVIEW**

How did reform movements create instability in the political system?

## Make a Case

In what ways did the status of women improve in the United States between the American Revolution and the Civil War?

The ferment of reform during the decades from 1820 to 1850 reflected a multitude of attempts to deal with transformations working through not just the United States but also Europe. Abolition was potentially the most dangerous of the trans-Atlantic reforms, because slavery was so deeply and profitably intertwined with the industrial system. Slave labor produced cotton for the textile factories of New England, Great Britain, and Europe. Plantation economies supplied the sugar, rice, tea, and coffee that were a part of European and American diets. Revolutionary France had abolished slavery in 1794, but Napoleon reinstated it, along with the slave trade. Great Britain outlawed the trade in 1808 (as did the United States) and then freed nearly 800,000 slaves in its colonies in 1834.

Any move for emancipation in the United States seemed out of the question, and as late as 1840 abolition lacked the power to threaten the political system. But the growing northern concern about slavery highlighted differences between the two sections. Despite the strength of evangelicalism in the South, the reform impulse spawned by the revivals found little support there, since reform movements were discredited by their association with abolitionism. The party system confronted the difficult challenge of holding together sections that, although sharing much, were also diverging in important ways. To the residents of both sections, the South increasingly appeared to be a unique society with its own distinctive way of life.

# CHAPTER SUMMARY

The Jacksonian era produced the greatest number of significant reform movements in American history.

- The Second Great Awakening, which preached the doctrine of salvation available to all and the coming of the millennium, encouraged revivals and reform.
- Revivals drew converts from every segment of American society and spoke to their spiritual needs.
- Women were most prominent among revival converts.
- The Second Great Awakening made evangelicals the dominant religious subculture in the United States.
- Benevolent and reform societies decisively changed drinking habits and the ideals of womanhood and the family.
- Catholic immigration grew rapidly between 1820 and 1850, and evangelical religious fervor fueled anti-Catholicism.
- Unitarianism and transcendentalism, which emphasized the unlimited potential of each individual, also strengthened reform.
- Utopian communities sought to establish a model society for the rest of the world to follow.
- Mormons developed a following and drew persecution.
- Abolitionism precipitated both strong support and violent opposition, and the movement split in 1840.
- Temperance, abolition, and women's rights movements turned to political action to accomplish their goals.
- Although it survived, the party system was seriously weakened by these reform movements.

## Additional Reading

Good introductions to antebellum evangelical religion and reform include Robert Abzug, *Cosmos Crumbling* (1994); and Charles Hambrick-Stowe, *Charles G. Finney and the Spirit of American Evangelicalism* (1996). For suggestive analyses of the relationship between antebellum evangelicalism and the sweeping changes in economic and political life, consult Richard Carwardine, *Evangelicals and Politics in Antebellum America* (1997); Candy Gunther Brown, *The Word in the World* (2004); and Paul Johnson and Sean Wilentz, *The Kingdom of Matthias* (1994). On antislavery activism, consult Patrick Rael, *Eighty-Eight Years* (2015); Manisha Sinha, *The Slave's Cause* (2016); and Eric Foner, *Gateway to Freedom* (2015). The best studies of the role of women in evangelical churches and reform societies are Anne Boylan, *The Origins of Women's Activism* (1988); Lori Ginzberg, *Women and the Work of Benevolence* (1990); and Nancy Hewitt, *Women's Activism and Social Change* (1984). To understand the link between reformist activism and the early women's rights movement, begin with Lori Ginzberg, *Untidy Origins* (2005); and Nancy Isenberg, *Sex and Citizenship in the United States* (1998).

Despite the dominant influence of evangelical Protestants, both Roman Catholics and Mormons attracted a growing number of adherents during the antebellum period. For a fascinating account of the origins and rise of Mormonism, see John Brooke, *The Refiner's Fire* (1996); and for a compelling account of how American Protestants responded to the growth of Roman Catholicism after the 1830s, see Ryan Smith, *Gothic Arches, Latin Crosses* (2006). To explore the reasons why a small but influential minority of nineteenth-century Americans rejected all forms of Christianity in favor of agnosticism or atheism, rely on James Turner, *Without God, Without Creed* (1985). On Transcendentalism, explore David S. Reynolds, *Beneath the American Renaissance;* and Megan Marshall's biography *Margaret Fuller: A New American Life* (2013).

# 13 The Old South

## 1820–1860

A nurse and child, about 1850. Because it took minutes to expose a daguerreotype print, the nurse is holding one of the child's hands still. Although the South encompassed a wide variety of subregions, classes of people, crops, and climates, its "peculiar institution," slavery, came to deeply shape its identity in the decades before the Civil War. As this portrait indicates, relations between the free and enslaved were closely, and often ambiguously, intertwined. What ambiguities are suggested by the daguerreotype?



### >> An American Story

## WHERE IS THE REAL SOUTH?

The impeccably dressed Colonel Daniel Jordan, master of 261 slaves at Laurel Hill, strolls down his oak-lined lawn to the dock along the Waccamaw River, a day's journey north of Charleston, to board the steamship *Nina*. On Fridays it is Colonel Jordan's custom to visit the exclusive Hot and Hot Fish Club, founded by his fellow low-country planters, to play a game of lawn bowling or billiards and be waited on by black servants in livery as he sips an iced mint julep. For Colonel Jordan, this is the South.

Several hundred miles to the west another steamboat, the *Fashion*, makes its way along the Alabama River. One of the passengers is upset by the boat's slow pace. A very different sort of planter, he has been away from his lands in the Red River country of Texas and is eager to get back. "Time's money, time's money!" he mutters. "Time's worth more'n money to me now; a hundred percent more, 'cause I left my niggers all alone; not a damn white man within four mile on 'em." When asked what they are doing, since the cotton crop has already been picked, he says, "I set 'em to clairin', but they ain't doin' a damn thing. . . . But I'll make it up, I'll make it up when I get thar, now you'd better believe." For this Red River planter, time is money and cotton is his world—indeed, cotton is what the South is all about. "I am a cotton man, I am, and I don't car who knows it," he proclaims. "I know cotton, I do. I'm dam' if I know anythin' but cotton."

At the other end of the South the slave Sam Williams works in the intense heat of Buffalo Forge, an iron-making factory in the Shenandoah Valley. As a refiner, Williams heats pig iron in white-hot coals, then slings the ball of glowing metal onto an anvil, where he pounds it with huge, water-powered hammers to remove the impurities. Ambitious and hardworking, he earns extra money (at the same rate paid to whites) for any iron he produces beyond his weekly quota. His wife, Nancy, in charge of the dairy, earns extra money, too. Their savings at the local bank total more than $150. The income helps them keep their family intact in an unstable environment: they know that their owner is unlikely to sell away slaves who work so hard. For Sam and Nancy Williams, family ties, worship at the local Baptist church, and socializing with their fellow slaves are what make life important.

In the swampy bayous of the Deep South, only a few miles from the Mississippi delta, Octave Johnson hears the dogs coming. For over a year Johnson has been a runaway slave. He fled from a Louisiana plantation when the overseer threatened to whip him for staying in bed. To survive, he hides in the swamps behind the plantation—stealing turkeys, chickens, and pigs and trading with other slaves. As uncertain as this life is, nearly 30 other slaves have joined him over the past year. When the pack of hounds bursts in on Johnson and his comrades, they do not flee but kill as many dogs as possible. Then they plunge into the bayou, and as the hounds follow, alligators make short work of another six. ("Alligators [prefer] dog flesh to personal flesh," he explains later.) For Octave Johnson the real South is a matter of weighing one's prospects between the uncertainties of alligators and the overseer's whip—and deciding when to say no.

Ferdinand Steel and his family are not slaves, forced by an overseer to get up at five in the morning. They rise because the land demands it. Steel, a white southerner in his 20s, owns 170 acres of land in Carroll County, Mississippi. His life is one of continuous hard work, caring for the animals and tending the crops. His mother, Eliza, and sister, Julia, have plenty to keep them busy: making soap, fashioning dippers out of gourds, sewing.

The Steel family grows cotton, too, but not with the single-minded devotion of the planter aboard the *Fashion*. Steel's total crop amounts to only five or six bales. His profit is never enough for him to consider buying even one slave—but the cotton means cash, and cash means that he can buy things he needs in town. Though fiercely independent, Steel and his scattered neighbors help one another raise houses, clear fields, shuck corn, and quilt. They depend on one another and are bound together by blood, religion, obligation, and honor. For small farmers such as Ferdinand Steel, these ties constitute the real South.

The portraits could go on: different people, different Souths, all of them real. Such contrasts make clear the difficulty of trying to define a regional identity. In 1860 the South included 15 slave states plus the District of Columbia. It was a land of great social and geographic diversity.

Yet despite those many differences, the region was united by ties so strong, they eventually outpulled those of the nation itself. At the heart of this unity was an agricultural system that took advantage of the region's warm climate and long growing season. Most important, this rural agricultural economy was based on the institution of slavery, which had far-reaching effects on all aspects of southern society. It shaped not only the culture of the slaves themselves but also the lives of their masters and mistresses, and even of farm families and herders in the hills and backwoods, who saw few slaves from day to day. To understand the Old South, then, we must understand how the southern agricultural economy and the institution of slavery affected the social class structure of both white and black southerners. <<

## THEMATIC TIMELINE

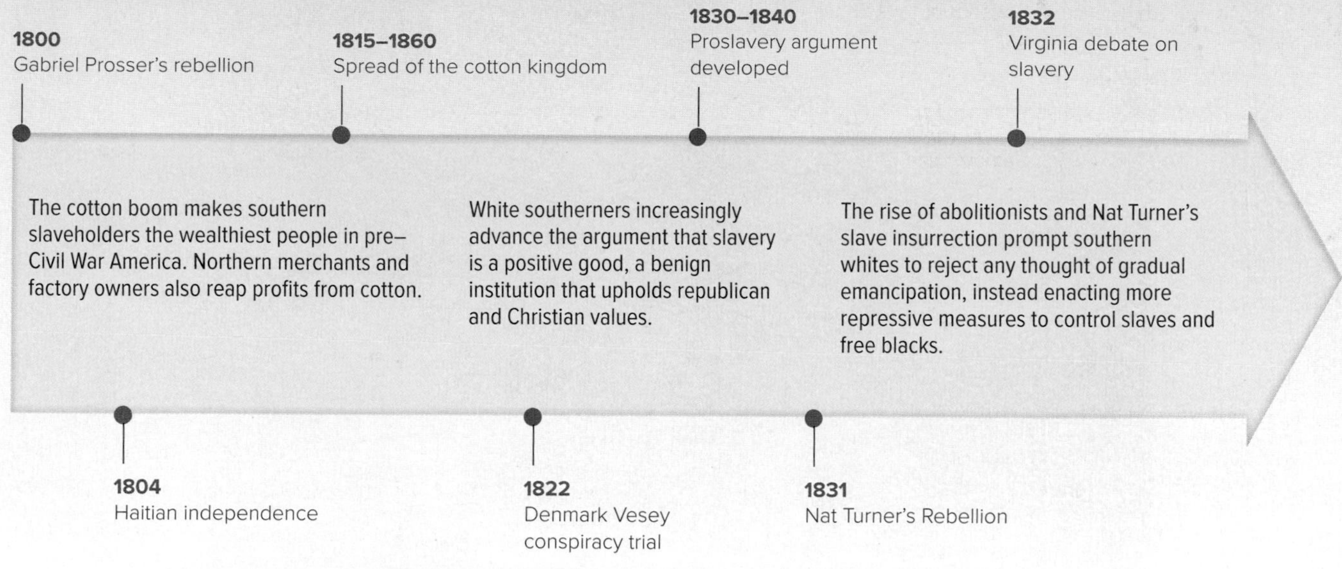
1800
Gabriel Prosser's rebellion
1815–1860
Spread of the cotton kingdom
1830–1840
Proslavery argument developed
1832
Virginia debate on slavery
The cotton boom makes southern slaveholders the wealthiest people in pre–Civil War America. Northern merchants and factory owners also reap profits from cotton.
White southerners increasingly advance the argument that slavery is a positive good, a benign institution that upholds republican and Christian values.
The rise of abolitionists and Nat Turner's slave insurrection prompt southern whites to reject any thought of gradual emancipation, instead enacting more repressive measures to control slaves and free blacks.
1804
Haitian independence
1822
Denmark Vesey conspiracy trial
1831
Nat Turner's Rebellion

# THE SOCIAL STRUCTURE OF THE COTTON KINGDOM

The spread of cotton stimulated the nation's remarkable economic growth after the War of 1812. Demand spurred by the textile industry sent the price of cotton soaring on the international market, and white southerners scrambled into the fresh lands of the Southwest to reap the profits to be made in the cotton sweepstakes.

**The Cotton Environment** >> This new cultivation dramatically transformed the South's landscape, turning countless acres of vines, brush, and trees into open fields. Cotton also imposed a demanding work discipline on slaves, who cultivated hundreds of acres, as well as white farming families, who tended many fewer. Typically they planted the newly cleared land in corn for a year, just long enough for tree stumps to decompose. In the next spring season, a heavy plow pulled by oxen or mules cleaved the fields into deep furrows, followed by workers who pitched cottonseed between the ridges. Then began the battle to protect the sprouting plants from weather, insects, and fungi. It was crucial to thin the excess cotton shoots in the spring and to yank out summer weeds.

But the greatest and most ingenious efforts went into defeating the dreaded army worm, for infestations of those caterpillars could strip an entire district of cotton. During a summer in the 1850s slaves on one plantation dug a deep trench between the cotton fields hoping to halt the pest's progress. Into it the army worms tumbled, "in untold millions," one observer reported, until the trench's bottom "for nearly a mile in extent, was a foot or two deep in [a] living mass of animal life." Then the slaves hitched a team of oxen to a heavy log and, as they pulled it through the ditch, "it seemed to float on a crushed mass" of worms.

**The Boom Country Economy** >> The difficulties of cultivation did little to discourage white southerners' enthusiasm for cotton. Letters, newspapers, and word of mouth all brought tales of the Black Belt region of Alabama, where the dark, rich soil was particularly suited to growing cotton, and of the tremendous yields from the soils along the Mississippi River's broad reaches. "The Alabama Feaver rages here with great violence and has carried off vast numbers of our Citizens," a North Carolinian wrote in 1817. In the 1830s, immigrants still poured in "with a ceaseless tide," but by the 1840s residents were leaving Alabama and Mississippi for even fresher cotton lands along the Red River and up into Texas. By the eve of the Civil War nearly a third of the total cotton crop came from west of the Mississippi River. As Senator James Henry Hammond of South Carolina boasted in 1858, cotton was king in the Old South: its primary export and the major source of southern wealth.

As cotton transformed the boom country of the Deep South, agriculture in the **Upper South** also adjusted. Scientific agricultural

**Upper South** the border states (Delaware, Maryland, Kentucky, and Missouri) and Virginia, North Carolina, Tennessee, and Arkansas.

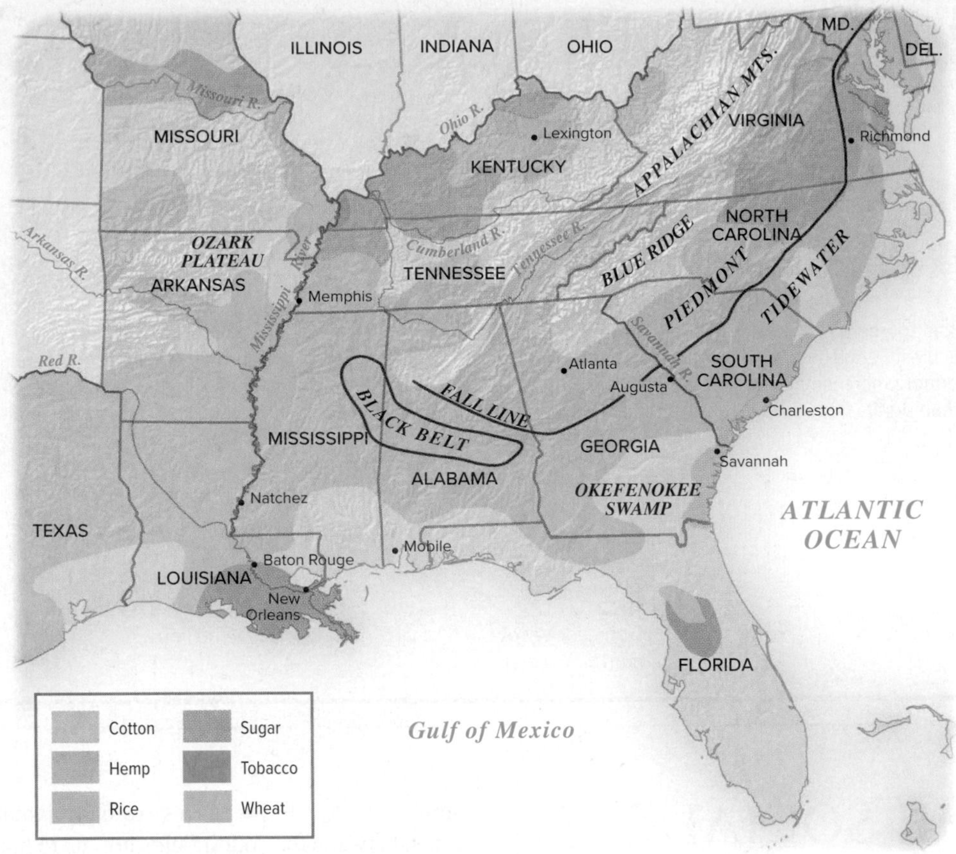
ILLINOIS
INDIANA
OHIO
MD.
DEL.
Missouri R.
Ohio R.
Lexington
APPALACHIAN MTS.
VIRGINIA
Richmond
MISSOURI
KENTUCKY
NORTH CAROLINA
BLUE RIDGE
Arkansas R.
OZARK PLATEAU
ARKANSAS
Mississippi River
Cumberland R.
Tennessee R.
TENNESSEE
PIEDMONT
TIDEWATER
Memphis
Red R.
Savannah R.
Atlanta
Augusta
SOUTH CAROLINA
Charleston
BLACK BELT
FALL LINE
MISSISSIPPI
GEORGIA
Savannah
ALABAMA
OKEFENOKEE SWAMP
Natchez
ATLANTIC OCEAN
TEXAS
Mobile
Baton Rouge
LOUISIANA
New Orleans
FLORIDA
Cotton
Sugar
Hemp
Tobacco
Rice
Wheat
Gulf of Mexico

## MAP 13.1: COTTON AND OTHER CROPS OF THE SOUTH

By 1860 the cotton kingdom extended across the Lower South into the Texas prairie and up the Mississippi River valley. Tobacco and hemp were the staple crops of the Upper South, where they competed with corn and wheat. Rice production was concentrated in the swampy coastal region of South Carolina and Georgia as well as the lower tip of Louisiana. The sugar district was in southern Louisiana. *Why was rice growing concentrated in coastal regions? Which staple crop predominated in the South, according to the map?*

practices reversed the decline in tobacco, which had begun in the 1790s. More important, farmers in the Upper South made wheat and corn their major crops. Because the new crops required less labor, slaveholders in the Upper South sold their surplus slaves to planters in the **Deep South**. There, eager buyers paid as much as $1,500 in the late 1850s for a prime field hand.

**Deep South** South Carolina, Georgia, Florida, Alabama, Mississippi, Louisiana, and Texas.

Southern prosperity, however, masked problems in the economy. Much of the South's new wealth was created as people migrated into more-fertile western lands. The amount of prime farmland was limited and, once settled, the South could not sustain its rate of expansion. Furthermore, the single-crop agriculture practiced by southern farmers (especially in tobacco and corn) rapidly wore out the soil. Wheat production in the Upper South helped to restore soils, but because farmers now plowed fields rather than using the hoe, soil erosion increased. In addition, relying on a single crop increased toxins and parasites in the soil, making southern agriculture more vulnerable than diversified agriculture.

Perhaps the most striking environmental consequence of the expansion of southern society was the increase in disease. Europeans brought epidemic diseases such as malaria, yellow fever, and cholera to the area. And the clearing of land—which increased runoff, precipitated floods, and produced pools of stagnant water—encouraged their spread, especially in the Lower South.

**The Rural South** >> The Old South, then, was expanding, dynamic, and booming. But the region remained overwhelmingly rural, with 84 percent of its labor force engaged in farming in 1860, compared with 40 percent in the North. Conversely, the South produced only 9 percent of the nation's manufactured goods. Efforts to diversify the South's economy made little headway in the face of the high profits from cotton. With so little industry, few cities developed in the South. North Carolina, Florida, Alabama,

Mississippi, Arkansas, and Texas did not contain a single city with a population of 10,000.

As a rural society the South showed far less interest in education. Most wealthy planters opposed a state-supported school system, because they hired tutors or sent their children to private academies. Georgia in 1860 had only one county with a free school system, and Mississippi had no public schools outside its few cities. The 1850 census showed that among native-born white citizens, 20 percent were unable to read and write. In the middle states the figure was 3 percent; in New England, only 0.4 percent.

**Distribution of Slavery** >> Even more than agrarian ways, slavery set the South apart. Whereas in 1776 slavery had been a national institution, by 1820 it was confined to the states south of Pennsylvania and the Ohio River. The South's "peculiar institution" bound white and black southerners together in a multitude of ways.

Slaves were not evenly distributed throughout the region. More than half lived in the Deep South, where African Americans outnumbered white southerners in both South Carolina and Mississippi by the 1850s. Elsewhere in the Deep South, the black population exceeded 40 percent in all states except Texas. In the Upper South, in contrast, whites greatly outnumbered blacks. Only in Virginia and North Carolina did the slave population top 30 percent.

Geography determined some of this distribution. In areas of fertile soil, flat or rolling countryside, and good transportation, slavery and the plantation system dominated. In the pine barrens, areas isolated by lack of transportation, and hilly and mountainous regions, small family farms and few slaves were the rule.

Almost all enslaved African Americans, male and female, worked in agricultural pursuits, with only about 10 percent living in cities and towns. On large plantations a few slaves were domestic servants, and others were skilled

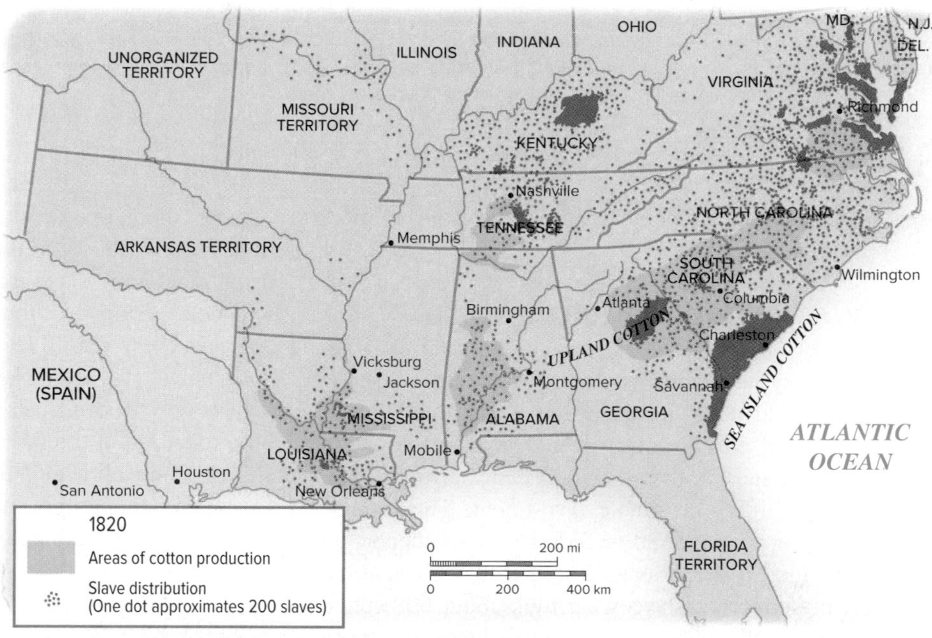
UNORGANIZED TERRITORY
MISSOURI TERRITORY
ILLINOIS
INDIANA
OHIO
MD.
N.J.
DEL.
VIRGINIA
Richmond
KENTUCKY
Nashville
TENNESSEE
NORTH CAROLINA
Memphis
ARKANSAS TERRITORY
SOUTH CAROLINA
Wilmington
Columbia
Atlanta
Birmingham
UPLAND COTTON
Charleston
SEA ISLAND COTTON
MEXICO (SPAIN)
Vicksburg
Jackson
Montgomery
Savannah
MISSISSIPPI
ALABAMA
GEORGIA
ATLANTIC OCEAN
LOUISIANA
Mobile
Houston
San Antonio
New Orleans
1820
Areas of cotton production
Slave distribution
(One dot approximates 200 slaves)
0 200 mi
0 200 400 km
FLORIDA TERRITORY

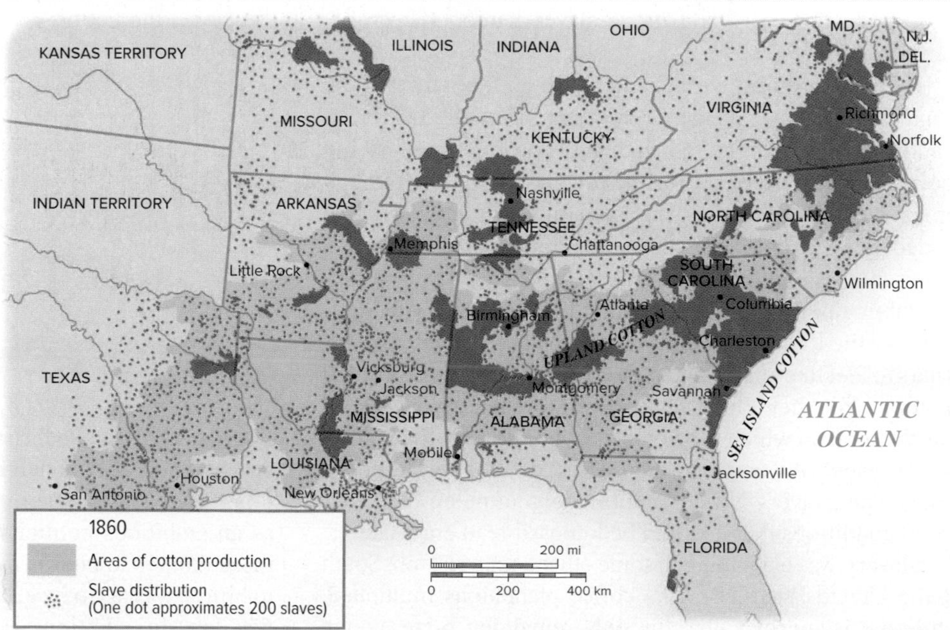
KANSAS TERRITORY
ILLINOIS
INDIANA
OHIO
MD.
N.J.
DEL.
MISSOURI
VIRGINIA
Richmond
Norfolk
KENTUCKY
INDIAN TERRITORY
ARKANSAS
Nashville
TENNESSEE
NORTH CAROLINA
Memphis
Chattanooga
Little Rock
SOUTH CAROLINA
Wilmington
Columbia
Birmingham
Atlanta
UPLAND COTTON
Charleston
Vicksburg
Jackson
Montgomery
Savannah
TEXAS
MISSISSIPPI
ALABAMA
GEORGIA
SEA ISLAND COTTON
ATLANTIC OCEAN
Mobile
LOUISIANA
Houston
San Antonio
New Orleans
Jacksonville
1860
Areas of cotton production
Slave distribution
(One dot approximates 200 slaves)
0 200 mi
0 200 400 km
FLORIDA

## MAP 13.2: THE SPREAD OF SLAVERY, 1820–1860

Between 1820 and 1860 the slave population of the South shifted south and westward, concentrating especially heavily in coastal South Carolina and Georgia, in the Black Belt of central Alabama and Mississippi (so named because of its dark, rich soil), and in the Mississippi valley.

*Comparing this map with Map 13.1, was a heavy concentration of slaves associated with only some of the South's staple crops? What factors contributed to a heavy concentration of slaves?*

^ In this romanticized Currier and Ives print of a cotton plantation, field hands are waist-deep in cotton while other slaves haul the picked cotton to be ginned and then pressed into bales. Mounted on a horse, an overseer rides through the field supervising the work, while the owner and his wife look on. Picking began as early as August and continued in some areas until late January. Because the bolls ripened at different times, a field had to be picked several times.
©Bridgeman Images

artisans—blacksmiths, carpenters, or bricklayers—but most toiled in the fields.

**Slavery as a Labor System** >> Slavery was, first and foremost, a system to manage and control labor. The plantation system, with its extensive estates and large labor forces, could never have developed without slavery. Slaves represented an enormous capital investment, worth more than all the land in the Old South. Furthermore, slavery remained a highly profitable investment. The average slaveowner spent perhaps $30 to $35 a year to support an adult slave; some expended as little as half that. Even at the higher cost of support, a slaveowner took about 60 percent of the annual wealth produced by a slave's labor. For those who pinched pennies and drove slaves harder, the profits were even greater.

By concentrating wealth and power in the hands of the planter class, slavery shaped the tone of southern society. Planters were not aristocrats in the European sense of having special legal privileges or formal titles of rank. Still, the system encouraged southern planters to think of themselves as a landed gentry upholding the aristocratic values of pride, honor, family, and hospitality.

Public opinion in Europe and in the North grew increasingly hostile to the peculiar institution, causing white southerners to feel like an isolated minority defending an embattled position. Yet they clung tenaciously to slavery, because it was the base on which the South's economic growth and way of life rested. As one Georgian observed on the eve of the Civil War, slavery was "so intimately mingled with our social conditions that it would be impossible to eradicate it."

Slavery was expanding in some other countries, too. South of the United States, Brazil's coffee plantations multiplied, while the island of Cuba, the only remaining prize among Spain's colonial possessions, led the world in sugar production. Forced labor was the key to raising both crops, and a thriving Atlantic slave trade—in direct violation of treaties intended to stop it—brought tens of thousands of enslaved Africans every year to Havana and Rio de Janeiro. American investors, mainly from New England and New York, profited handsomely from Cuba's booming economy. They came to hold one-third of the island's wealth as well as thousands of slaves, some of whom they exported for resale to Texas. Despite mounting opposition among some in the West, slavery was far from a dying institution in the Americas.

 REVIEW

How did the cotton economy shape the South's environment and labor system?

# CLASS STRUCTURE OF THE WHITE SOUTH

Once a year around Christmastime, James Henry Hammond gave a dinner for his neighbors at his South Carolina plantation, Silver Bluff. The richest man for miles around as well as an ambitious politician, the aristocratic Hammond used these dinners to put his neighbors under personal obligation to him as well as to receive the honor and respect he believed his due. In addition, Hammond hired his neighbors to perform various tasks and allowed them to use his grist mill and gin their cotton. His less affluent neighbors recognized Hammond's social rank, but they, too, displayed a strong personal pride. When the master of Silver Bluff once complained how inconvenient it was to provide these services, only three of his neighbors came to his Christmas dinner that year, a snub that enraged him. As Hammond's experience demonstrated, class relations among whites in the Old South were a complex blend of privilege, patronage, and equality.

**The Slaveowners** >> In 1860 the region's 15 states had a population of 12 million, of which roughly two-thirds were white, one-third were black slaves, and about 2 percent were free African Americans. Of the 8 million white southerners, only about a quarter either owned slaves or were members of slaveowning families. Moreover, most slaveowners owned only a few slaves. If one uses the census definition of a planter as a person who owned 20 or more slaves, only about 1 out of every 30 white southerners belonged to families of the planter class. A planter of consequence, however, needed to own at least 50 slaves, and there were only about 10,000 such families—less than 1 percent of the white population. This privileged group made up the aristocracy at the top of the southern class structure. Owners of large numbers of slaves were very rare; only about 2,000 southerners, such as Colonel Daniel Jordan, owned 100 or more slaves. Although limited in size, the planter class nevertheless owned more than half of all slaves and controlled more than 90 percent of the region's total wealth.

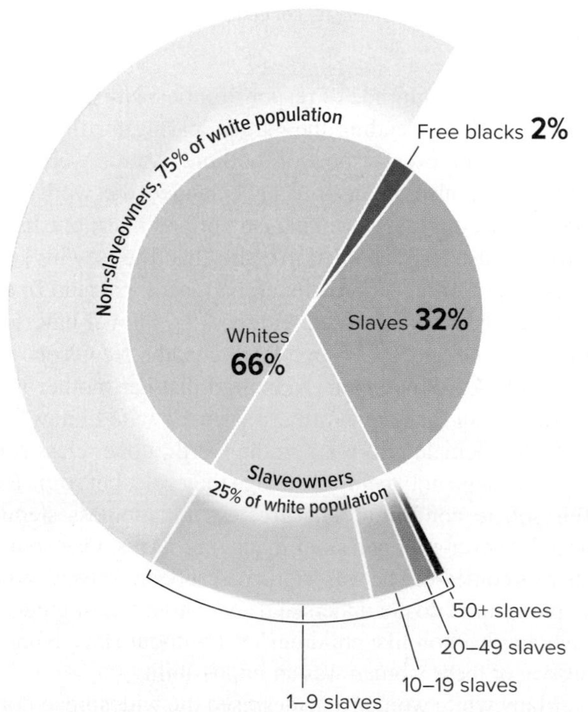
Non-slaveowners, 75% of white population
Free blacks 2%
Whites 66%
Slaves 32%
Slaveowners
25% of white population
50+ slaves
20–49 slaves
10–19 slaves
1–9 slaves

SOUTHERN POPULATION, 1860

**Tidewater and Frontier** >> Southern planters shared a commitment to preserve slavery as the source of their wealth and stature. Yet in other ways they were a diverse group. On the one hand, the tobacco and rice planters of the Atlantic Tidewater were part of a settled region and a culture that reached back 150 to 200 years. States such as Mississippi and Arkansas, in contrast, had rawer and more-volatile societies, since most non-Indian residents had flooded into the region after 1815.

It was along the Tidewater, especially the bays of the Chesapeake and the South Carolina coast, that the legendary "Old South" was born. Here, masters erected substantial homes, some—especially between Charleston and Columbia—the classic white-pillared mansions in the Greek Revival style. An Irish visitor observed that in Maryland and Virginia the great planters lived in "a style which approaches nearer to that of the English country gentleman than what is to be met with anywhere else on the continent." As in England, the local gentry often served as justices of the peace, and the Episcopal Church remained the socially accepted road to heaven. Here, too, family names continued to be important in politics.

While the newer regions of the South boasted of planters with cultivated manners, as a group the cotton lords were a different breed. Whatever their background, these entrepreneurs had moved west for the reason so many other white Americans had: to make their fortunes. By and large the cotton gentry were men of ordinary backgrounds who had risen through hard work, aggressive business tactics, and good luck. For them the cotton boom and the exploitation of enslaved men and women offered the chance to move up in a new society that lacked an entrenched elite.

"Time's money, time's money." For men like the impatient Texan, time was indeed money, slaves were capital, and cotton by the bale signified cash in hand. This business orientation was especially apparent in the cotton kingdom, where planters sought to maximize their profits and constantly reinvested their returns in land and slaves. And while most planters ranked among the richest citizens in America, the homes of the newer cotton gentry were often simple one- or two-story unpainted wooden frame houses. Some were even log cabins. "If you wish to see people worth millions living as [if] they were not worth hundreds," advised one southwestern planter in 1839, "come to the land of cotton and negroes." Practical men, few of the new cotton lords had absorbed the culture and learning of the traditional country gentleman.

**The Master at Home** >> Whether supervising a Tidewater plantation or creating a cotton estate on the Texas frontier, the master had to coordinate a complex agricultural operation. He gave daily instructions concerning the work to be done, settled disputes between slaves and the overseer, and generally handed out rewards and penalties. In addition, the owner made the critical decisions for planting, harvesting, and marketing the crops as well as for investments and expenditures.

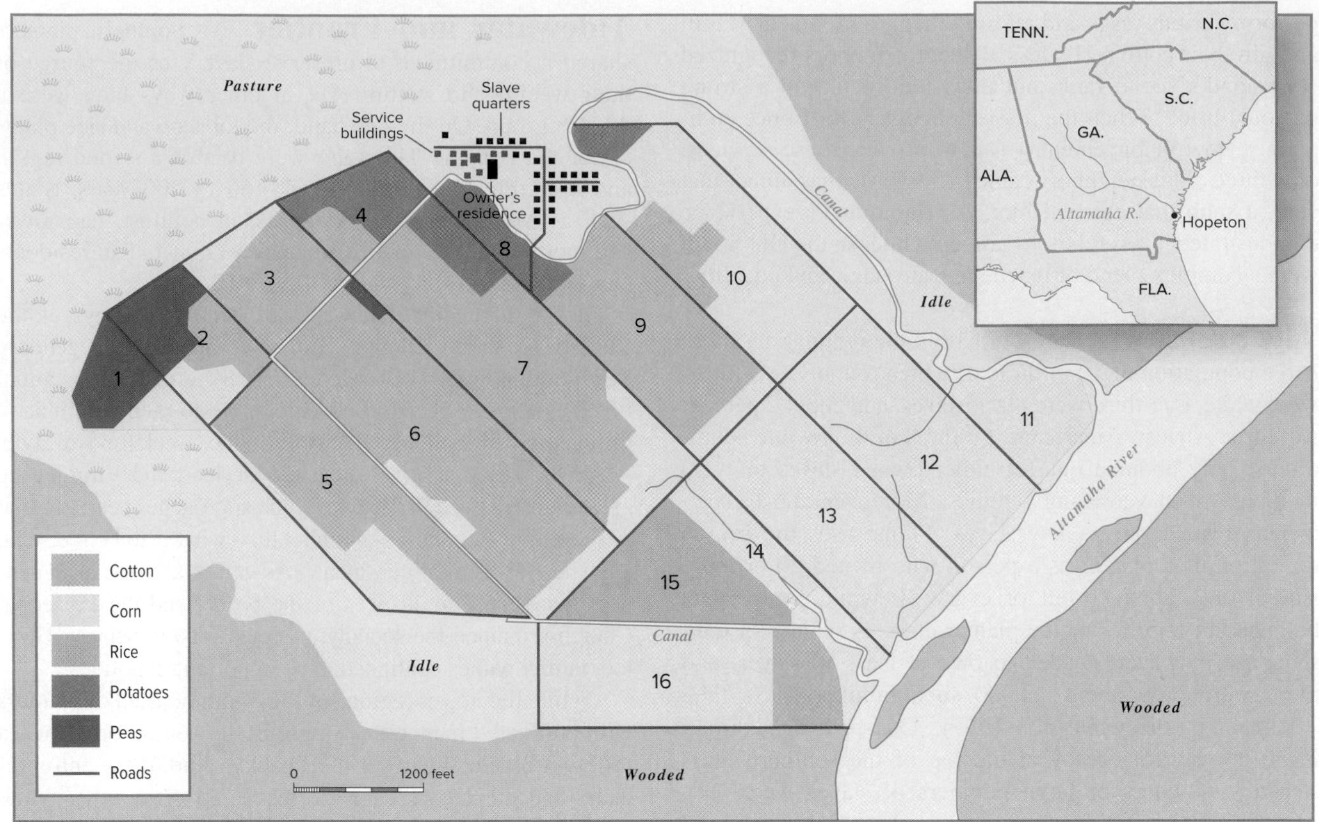
TENN.
N.C.
S.C.
GA.
ALA.
Altamaha R.
Hopeton
FLA.
Pasture
Slave quarters
Service buildings
Owner's residence
Canal
Idle
Altamaha River
Wooded
Canal
Idle
Wooded
1
2
3
4
5
6
7
8
9
10
11
12
13
14
15
16
Cotton
Corn
Rice
Potatoes
Peas
Roads
0
1200 feet

## MAP 13.3: A PLANTATION LAYOUT, HOPETON, GEORGIA

Often covering a thousand acres or more, a plantation was laid out like a small village and contained several fields and usually extensive uncleared woods. Somewhere near the master's "big house" were the quarters—slave cabins clustered along one or more streets. Service buildings might include a smokehouse, stables, a gin house (for cotton) or a rice mill, and an overseer's dwelling. Like most large plantations, Hopeton produced a considerable amount of foodstuffs, but it grew both rice and cotton as staples. Most plantations concentrated on a single cash crop.

In performing his duties the plantation owner was supposed to be the "master" of his crops, his family, and his slaves. Defenders of slavery often held up this paternalistic ideal—the care and guidance of dependent "children"—and maintained that slavery promoted a genuine bond of affection between the caring master and his loyal slaves. In real life, however, the forces of the market made this paternalistic ideal less evident. Even in the Tidewater, planters focused on profits. Indeed, some of the most brutal forms of slavery existed on rice plantations. Except for a few domestic servants, owners of large plantations had little contact with their slaves. Nor could paternalism mask the reality that slavery everywhere rested on violence, racism, and exploitation.

**The Plantation Mistress** >> Upper-class white women in the South, like those in the North, grew up with the ideal of domesticity, reinforced by the notion of a paternalistic master who was lord of the plantation. But the plantation mistress soon discovered that the daily demands placed on her made that ideal hard to fulfill.

In her youth a genteel lady enjoyed a certain amount of leisure. But once married and the mistress of a plantation, she encountered a multitude of responsibilities. Nursing the sick, making clothing, tending the garden, caring for the poultry, and overseeing every aspect of food preparation were all her domain. She also supervised and planned the work of the domestic servants. After taking care of breakfast, one harried Carolina mistress recounted that she "had the [sewing] work cut out, gave orders about dinner, had the horse feed fixed in hot water, had the box filled with cork: . . . now I have to cut out the flannel jackets." Sarah Williams, the New York bride of a North Carolina planter, admitted that her mother-in-law "works harder than any Northern farmer's wife I know."

Unlike female reformers in the North, upper-class southern women did not openly challenge their role, but some found their sphere confining. The greatest unhappiness stemmed from the never-ending task of managing slaves. One southern mistress confessed she was frightened at being "always among people whom I do not understand and whom I must guide, and teach and lead on like children." Yet without slave labor, the lifestyle of these women was an impossibility.

Many white women also despised the widespread double standard for sexual behavior. A man who fathered illegitimate children by slave women suffered no social or legal

^ Sarah Pierce Vick, the mistress of a plantation near Vicksburg, Mississippi, pauses to speak to one of her slaves, who may be holding feed for her horse. A plantation mistress had many duties and, while enjoying the comforts brought by wealth and status, often found her life more difficult than she had anticipated before marriage.


penalties, even in the case of rape (southern law did not recognize such a crime against slave women), whereas a white woman guilty of adultery lost all social respectability. One planter's wife spoke of "violations of the moral law that made mulattoes as common as blackberries," and another recalled, "I saw slavery . . . teemed with injustice and shame to all womankind and I hated it."

Some white women drew a parallel between their situation and that of the slaves. Both were subject to male dominance, and independent-minded women found the subordination of marriage difficult. Susan Dabney Smedes, in her recollection of growing up on an Alabama plantation, recalled that "it was a saying that the mistress of a plantation was the most complete slave on it."

Still, plantation mistresses were unwilling to forgo the material comforts that slavery made possible. Moreover, racism was so pervasive within American society that the few white southern women who privately criticized the institution displayed little empathy for the plight of slaves themselves, including black women. Whatever the burdens of the plantation mistress, they were hardly akin to the bondage of slavery itself.

**Yeoman Farmers >>** In terms of numbers, yeoman farm families were the backbone of southern society, accounting for well over half the southern white population. These farmers owned no slaves and farmed the traditional 80 to 160 acres, like northern farmers. About 80 percent owned their own land. They settled almost everywhere in the South, except in the rice and sugar districts and valuable river bottomlands of the Deep South, which were monopolized by large slaveowners. Like Ferdinand Steel, most were semisubsistence farmers who raised primarily corn and hogs, along with perhaps a few bales of cotton or some tobacco, which they sold to obtain the cash needed to buy items like sugar, coffee, and salt. Yeoman farmers lacked the wealth of planters, but they had a pride and dignity that earned them the respect of their richer neighbors.

While southern farmers led more isolated lives than did their northern counterparts, their social activities were not very different. Religion played an important role at camp meetings held in late summer, after the crops were laid by and before harvest time. As in the North, neighbors also met to exchange labor and tools. The men rolled logs to clear fields of dead trees, women met for quilting bees, and adults and children alike would gather to shuck corn. Court sessions, militia musters, political rallies—these, too, were occasions that brought rural folk together.

Since yeoman farmers lacked cheap slave labor, good transportation, and access to credit, they could not compete with planters in the production of staples. In the North urban centers became a market for small farmers to sell their staple crops, but in the South the lack of towns limited this

A FAMILY GROUP IN THE INTERIOR OF THE STATE OF GEORGIA.

>> A majority of white southerners were members of non-slaveholding yeoman farm families. Ruggedly independent, these families depended on their own labor and often lived under primitive conditions. Basil Hall, an Englishman traveling through the South in 1827 and 1828, sketched members of this Georgia family with the aid of a camera lucida, an optical device that projected an image from real life onto paper, where it could be traced with accuracy.
Source: William L. Clements Library, University of Michigan

internal market. Thus, although southern yeoman farmers were not poor, they suffered from a chronic lack of money and the absence of conveniences that northern farm families enjoyed. Josiah Hinds, who hacked a farm out of the isolated woods of northern Mississippi, worried that his children were growing up "wild." He complained that "education is but little prized by my neighbours," who were satisfied "if the corn and cotton grows to perfection . . . [and] brings a fare price, and hog meat is at hand to boil with the greens."

In some ways, then, the worlds of the yeoman farmers and the upper-class planters were not only different but also in conflict. Still, a hostility between the two classes did not emerge. Yeoman farmers admired planters and hoped that one day they would join the gentry. Furthermore, they accepted slavery as a means of controlling African Americans as members of an inferior social caste based on race. "Now suppose they was free," one poor farmer told Frederick Law Olmsted, a northern visitor. "You see they'd all think themselves as good as we." Racism and fear of black people were sufficient to keep non-slaveholders loyal to southern institutions.

**Poor Whites** >> The poorest white southerners were confined to land that no one else wanted. They lived in rough, windowless log cabins located in the remotest areas and were often squatters without title to the land they were on. The men spent their time hunting and fishing, while women did the domestic work, including what farming they could manage. Circumstances made their poverty difficult to escape. Largely illiterate, they suffered from malnutrition stemming from a monotonous diet of corn, pork, and whiskey, and they were afflicted with malaria and hookworm, diseases that sapped their energy. Other white southerners referred to them scornfully as crackers, white trash, sandhillers, and clay-eaters.

The number of poor whites in the Old South is difficult to estimate. There may have been as few as 100,000 or as many as a million; probably they numbered about 500,000, or a little more than 5 percent of the white population.

Because poor whites traded with slaves, exchanging whiskey for stolen goods, contemptuous planters often bought them out simply to rid the neighborhood of them. For their part, poor whites keenly resented planters, but their hostility toward African Americans was even stronger. Poor whites refused to perform any work commonly done by slaves and vehemently opposed ending slavery. Emancipation would remove one of the few symbols of their status—that they were, at least, free.

What was the relationship between the South's great planters and yeoman farmers? Between planters and poor whites?

# THE PECULIAR INSTITUTION

Slaves were not free. That overwhelming fact must be understood before anything is said about the kindness or the cruelty individual slaves experienced; before any consideration of healthy or unhealthy living conditions; before any discussion of how slave families coped with hardship, rejoiced in shared pleasures, or worshiped in prayer. The lives of slaves were affected day in and day out, in big ways and small, by the basic reality that slaves were not their own masters. The master determined a slave's workload, whether a slave could visit a nearby plantation, and whether a slave family remained intact. Whatever slaves wanted to do, they always had to consider the response of their masters.

When power is distributed as unequally as it was between masters and slaves, every action on the part of the enslaved involved a certain calculation, conscious or unconscious. The enslaved had to consider the consequences of every act, of every expression or gesture. In that sense, the line between freedom and slavery penetrated every corner of a slave's life, and it was an absolute and overwhelming distinction.

One other stark fact reinforced the sharp line between freedom and slavery: slaves were distinguished on the basis of color. While the peculiar institution was an economic system of labor, it was also a **caste system** based on race. The color line of slavery made it easier to defend the institution and win the support of yeoman farmers and poor white southerners, even though in many ways the system held them back. Hence slavery must be understood on many levels: not only as an economic system but also as a racial and cultural one, in terms of not only its outward conditions of life and labor but also the inner demands it made on the soul.

**caste system** system of social stratification separating individuals by various distinctions, among them heredity, rank, profession, wealth, and race.

**Work and Discipline** >> The conditions slaves encountered varied widely, depending on the size of the farm or plantation, the crop being grown, the personality of the master, and whether he was an absentee owner. On small farms, slaves worked in the fields alongside their owners and had much closer contact with whites. On plantations,

## Make a Case

What role did race play in maintaining the institution of slavery? Could a system of white or Indian slavery have existed as easily?

in contrast, most slaves dealt primarily with the overseer, who was paid by the size of the harvest he brought in and was therefore often harsh in his approach.

House servants and the drivers, who supervised the field hands, received the highest status, and skilled artisans such as carpenters and blacksmiths were also given special recognition. The hardest work was done by the field hands, both men and women.

Some planters organized their slaves in the gang system, in which a white overseer or a black driver supervised gangs of 20 to 25 adults. Although this approach could extract long hours of reasonably hard labor, the slaves had to be constantly supervised, and shirking was difficult to detect. Other planters preferred the task system, under which each slave was given a specific daily assignment to complete, after which he or she was finished for the day. This system allowed slaves to work at their own pace, gave them an incentive to work carefully, and freed overseers from having to closely supervise the work. But slaves resisted vigorously if masters tried to increase the workload. The task system was most common in the rice fields, whereas the gang system predominated in the cotton districts. Many planters used a combination of the two systems.

During cultivation and harvest, slaves were in the field 15 to 16 hours a day, eating a noonday meal there and resting before resuming labor. Work was uncommon on Sundays, and frequently only a half day was required on Saturdays. Even so, the routine was taxing. "I am never caught in bed after day light nor is any body else on the place," an Arkansas cotton planter reported, "and we continue in the cotton fields when we can have fair weather till it is so dark we can't see to work."

Often masters rewarded hardworking slaves, but the threat of punishment was always present. Slaves could be denied passes; their food allowance could be reduced; and if all else failed, they could be sold. The most common instrument of punishment was the whip. The frequency of its use varied from plantation to plantation, but few slaves escaped the lash entirely. "We have to rely more and more on the power of fear," planter James Henry Hammond acknowledged. "We are determined to continue masters, and to do so we have to draw the rein tighter and tighter day by day to be assured that we hold them in complete check."

**Slave Maintenance** >> Planters generally bought rough, cheap cloth for slave clothing and each year gave adults at most only a couple of outfits and a pair of shoes. Some planters provided well-built housing, but more commonly slaves lived in cramped, poorly built cabins that were leaky in wet weather, drafty in cold, and furnished with only a few crude chairs or benches and a table, perhaps a mattress filled with corn husks or straw, and a few pots and dishes. To keep medical expenses down, slaveowners treated sick slaves and called in a doctor only for serious cases. On average a slaveowner spent less than a dollar a year on medical care for each slave.

Nevertheless, the United States was the only slave society in the Americas where the slave population increased naturally—indeed, at about the same rate as the white population. Even so, infant mortality among slaves was more than double that of the white population; for every 1,000 live births among southern slaves, more than 200 died before the age of 5. For those who survived infancy, enslaved African Americans had a life expectancy about 8 years less than that of white Americans. As late as 1860 fewer than two-thirds of slave children survived to the age of 10.

**Resistance** >> Given the wide gulf between freedom and slavery, it was only natural that slaves resisted the bondage imposed on them. The most radical form of resistance was rebellion, which occurred repeatedly in slave societies in the Americas. In Latin America and the Caribbean slave revolts were relatively frequent, involving hundreds and even thousands of slaves and pitched battles in which large numbers were killed. None of these revolts were as successful or consequential as the massive slave uprising that began in Saint Domingue in 1791 and eventually resulted in Haitian independence in 1804. But rebellion and fear of rebellion nonetheless had profound effects on slave regimes throughout the hemisphere.

The rich British colony of Jamaica, for instance, averaged one significant revolt every year from 1731 to 1822. A series of slave revolts shook the island of Cuba in 1812. In 1823 thousands rose up in British Guiana. Revolts erupted across the Caribbean in the 1830s, including one in Jamaica involving more than 20,000 slaves. These and similar uprisings were all savagely suppressed. And in Brazil, which had the largest number of slaves outside the United States, the government took 50 years to bring under control a colony of some 20,000 fugitive slaves who had sought refuge in the mountains.

These slave uprisings were often big news in the United States, and the success of the Haitian Revolution haunted slaveowners' dreams. Rumors of planned revolts, real or imagined, kept slaveholding society in a constant state of anxiety in the American South. But in reality slave revolts were relatively rare in the United States. In most places in the Old South whites outnumbered blacks, a majority of slaves were native-born, and many bondspeople developed strong family and communal ties. Local, state, and even federal authorities stood at the ready to suppress rebellions. Slaves recognized the odds against them, and many potential leaders became fugitives instead.

Early in the nineteenth century several well-organized uprisings were barely thwarted. In 1800 Gabriel Prosser, a slave blacksmith, recruited perhaps a couple hundred slaves to march on Richmond and capture the governor. But a few conspirators betrayed the plot, and Prosser and other leaders were captured and executed. Denmark Vesey's conspiracy in Charleston in 1822 met a similar fate.

The most famous slave revolt, led by a literate slave preacher named Nat Turner, was spontaneous. Turner, who lived on a farm in southeastern Virginia, was given unusual privileges by his master, whom he described as a kind and trusting man. A religious mystic, Turner became convinced that God had selected him to punish white people through "terror and devastation." One night in 1831 following an

^ Slaves resisted their masters by fleeing to nearby swamps or forests. Masters often used specially trained dogs to track them. Those shown here were imported from Cuba, and Zachary Taylor, who was elected president of the United States in 1848, was among the planters who imported them.



eclipse of the sun, he and six other slaves stole out and murdered Turner's master and family. Recruiting some 70 slaves as they went, Turner's band killed 57 white men, women, and children. But the revolt was crushed within 48 hours, and Turner was eventually captured, tried, and executed. Even so, the uprising left white southerners uneasy. Turner had seemed a model slave, yet who could read a slave's true emotions behind the mask of obedience?

Few slaves followed Turner's violent example. But there were subtle ways of resisting a master's authority. Most dramatically, slaves could run away. With the odds stacked heavily against them, few runaways escaped safely to freedom except from the border states. More frequently, slaves fled to nearby woods or swamps. Some runaways stayed out only a few days; others, like Octave Johnson, held out for months.

Many slaves resisted by abusing their masters' property. They mishandled animals, broke tools and machinery, misplaced items, and worked carelessly in the fields. Slaves also sought to trick the master by feigning illness or injury and by hiding rocks in the cotton they picked. Slaves complained directly to the owner about an overseer's mistreatment, thereby attempting to drive a wedge between the two.

The most common form of resistance was theft. Slaves raided the master's smokehouse, secretly slaughtered his stock, and killed his poultry. Slaves often distinguished between "stealing" from one another and merely "taking" from white masters. "Dey always done tell us it was wrong to lie and steal," recalled Josephine Howard, a former slave in Texas, "but why did the white folks steal my mammy and her mammy? They lives . . . over in Africy. . . . That's the sinfulles' stealin' there is."

Slaves learned to outwit their masters, one former bondsman testified, by wearing an "impenetrable mask" around whites: "How much of joy, of sorrow, of misery and anguish have they hidden from their tormentors." Frederick Douglass, the most famous fugitive slave, explained that "as the master studies to keep the slave ignorant, the slave is cunning enough to make the master think he succeeds."

**REVIEW**

In what ways did slaves resist their oppression?

# SLAVE CULTURE

Trapped in bondage, slaves could at least forge a culture of their own by combining strands from their African past with customs that evolved from their life in America. This slave culture was most distinct on big plantations, where the large slave population lived farther from white scrutiny.

**The Slave Family** >> Maintaining a sense of family was one of the most remarkable achievements of African Americans in bondage, given the obstacles they faced. Southern law did not recognize slave marriages as legally binding, nor did it allow slave parents complete authority over their children. Black women faced the possibility of rape by the master or overseer without legal recourse, and husbands, wives, and children had to live with the fear of being sold and separated. From 1820 to 1860 more than 2 million slaves were sold in the interstate slave trade. Perhaps 600,000 husbands and wives were separated by such sales.

Still, family ties remained strong, as slave culture demonstrated. The marriage ceremony among slaves varied from a formal religious service to jumping over the broomstick in front of the slave community to nothing more than the master's giving verbal approval. Whatever the ceremony, slaves viewed the ritual as a public affirmation of the couple's commitment to their new duties and responsibilities. Rather than adopting white norms, slaves developed their own moral code concerning sexual relations and marriage. Although young slaves often engaged in premarital sex, they were expected to choose a partner and become part of a stable family. It has been estimated that at least one in five slave women had one or more children before marriage, but most of these mothers eventually married. "The negroes had their own ideas of morality, and they held them very strictly," the daughter of a Georgia planter recalled. "They did not consider it wrong for a girl to have a child before she married, but afterwards were very strict upon anything like infidelity on her part."

The traditional nuclear family of father, mother, and children was the rule, not the exception, among slaves. Women did the indoor work such as cooking, washing, and sewing, and men performed outdoor chores, such as gathering firewood, hauling water, and tending the animals and garden plots. The men also hunted and fished to supplement the spare weekly rations. "My old daddy . . . caught rabbits, coons an' possums," recalled Louisa Adams of North Carolina. "He would work all day and hunt at night."

>> Students of this painting by Christian Friedrich Mayr speculate that the participants in this Kitchen Ball at White Sulphur Springs included both free blacks and slaves who had accompanied their masters to this resort in present-day West Virginia (then part of Virginia).
©De Agostini Picture Library/Bridgeman Images

**Songs and Stories of Protest and Celebration** >> In the songs they sang, slaves expressed some of their deepest feelings about life. "The songs of the slave represent the sorrows of his heart," commented Frederick Douglass. Surely there was bitterness as well as sorrow when slaves sang:

> We raise the wheat
> They give us the corn
> We bake the bread
> They give us the crust
> We sift the meal
> They give us the husk
> We peel the meat
> They give us the skin
> And that's the way
> They take us in

Yet songs were also central to the celebrations held in the slave quarters: for marriages, Christmas revels, and after harvest time. And a slave on the way to the fields might sing, "Saturday night and Sunday too/ Young gals on my mind."

Slaves expressed themselves through stories as well as song. Most often these folktales used animals as symbolic models for the predicaments in which slaves found themselves. In the best known of these, the cunning Brer Rabbit was a weak fellow who used his wits to defeat larger animals, such as Brer Fox and Brer Bear. Such stories, whether direct or symbolic, taught the young how to survive in a hostile world.

**The Lord Calls Us Home** >> Religion stood at the center of slave culture. Slaveowners encouraged a carefully controlled form of religion among slaves. "Church was what they called it," one former slave protested, "but all that preacher talked about was for us slaves to obey our masters and not to lie and steal. Nothing about Jesus was ever said and the overseer stood there to see that the preacher talked as he wanted him to talk." In response, some slaves rejected all religion.

Most, however, sought a Christianity beyond the control of the master. On many plantations they met secretly at night, when they would break into rhythmic singing and dancing, modeled on the ring shout of African religion, in which worshipers would move in a circle, stamping feet and clapping in rhythm. Even in regular services, observers noted the greater emotion of black worshipers. "The way in which we worshiped is almost indescribable," one slave preacher recalled. "The singing was accompanied by a certain ecstasy of motion, clapping of hands, tossing of heads, which would continue without cessation about half an hour." In an environment where slaves, for most of the day, were prevented from expressing their deepest feelings, such meetings provided a satisfying emotional release.

Although secret religious meetings were important, the religious experience of most enslaved African Americans occurred mainly within the regular white-controlled churches of the South. Perhaps a million slaves were included in the southern churches before the Civil War, especially in the Methodist and Baptist Churches. Indeed, in some areas, slaves were a majority in local congregations. As a result most slaves worshiped together with their masters rather than in separate services. At one point during the regular service ministers delivered a special message to the slaves, but they also heard the same sermon as the whites, with its emphasis on faith and salvation. The churches were also the one institution in the South where blacks were accorded a measure of equality. Black members were held to the same standards of conduct as whites, were subject to the same church discipline, and were allowed to testify in court against whites.

Religion also provided slaves with values to guide them through their lives and give them a sense of self-worth. Slaves learned that God one day would raise the poor and downtrodden to honor and glory. Just as certainly, on the final Day of Judgment, masters would be punished for their sins. "This is one reason why I believe in hell," a former slave declared. "I don't believe a just God is going to take no such man as my former master into His Kingdom."

Again, song played a central role. Slaves sang religious "spirituals" at work and at play as well as in religious services. Seemingly meek and otherworldly, the songs often contained a hidden element of protest. Frederick Douglass disclosed that when slaves sang longingly of "Canaan, sweet Canaan," they were thinking not only of the Bible's Promised Land but of the North and freedom.

Religion, then, served not only to comfort slaves after days of toil and sorrow. It also strengthened the sense of togetherness and common purpose and held out the promise of eventual freedom in this world and the next. Having faith that "some of these days my time will come" was one of the most important ways that slaves coped with bondage and resisted its pressure to rob them of their self-esteem.

**The Slave Community** >> While slaves managed to preserve a culture of their own, they found it impossible to escape fully from white control. In terms of social hierarchy, the prestige of a slave driver rested ultimately on the authority of the white master, and skilled slaves and house servants often felt superior to other slaves, an attitude masters promoted. Light-skinned slaves sometimes deemed their color a badge of superiority. Fanny Kemble recorded that one woman begged to be relieved of field labor, which she considered degrading, "on 'account of her color.'"

Despite these divisions the realities of slavery and white racism inevitably drove black people closer together in a common bond and forced them to depend on one another to survive. Excluded from the individualistic society of whites, slaves out of necessity created a community of their own.

**Free Black Southerners** >> Of the 4 million African Americans living in the South in 1860, only 260,000—about 7 percent—were free. More than 85 percent of them lived in the Upper South. Free black southerners were also much more urban than either the southern white or slave populations. In 1860 almost a third of the free African Americans in the Upper South and more than half in the Lower South lived in the few towns and cities. As a rule, free African Americans were more literate than slaves, and they were disproportionately female and much more likely to be of mixed ancestry.

Most free black southerners lived in rural areas, although usually not near plantations. Most eked out a living farming or in low-paying unskilled jobs, but some did well enough to own slaves themselves. In 1830 about 3,600 did, although commonly their "property" was their wives or children, purchased because they could not be emancipated under state laws. A few, however, were full-blown slaveowners.

The boundary sometimes blurred between free and enslaved African Americans. Sally Thomas of Nashville was technically a slave, but in the 1830s and 1840s her owner allowed her to ply her trade as a laundress and keep some of her wages. (She used $350 of these savings to purchase the freedom of one of her sons.) The boundary stretched especially for African Americans working along rivers and the seashore in the fishing trades, as pilots or seamen, or as "watermen" ferrying supplies and stores in small boats. Under such conditions, laborers preserved more freedom and initiative than most agricultural workers.

^ Slave or free? In 1863 artist Eastman Johnson sketched this confident black man, whose high boots, high-buttoned shirt, and jacket suggest he might have driven a carriage or perhaps was a freedman who worked in the army during the Civil War. We don't know the man's identity, but we do know that some slaves had jobs that allowed them to travel unsupervised.
Source: National Gallery of Art, Washington

Along Albemarle Sound in North Carolina, free blacks and slaves flocked from miles around to "fisherman's courts," a kind of annual hiring fair. Amid drinking, carousing, cockfighting, and boxing, men who ran commercial fishing operations signed up workers. The crews would then go down to the shore in late February or early March to net vast schools of fish, working around the clock. A single team might haul 100,000 herring onto the beach in four to seven hours. Women and children then headed, gutted, cleaned, and salted the fish. A good "cutter" might head tens of thousands of herring a day. In such settings African Americans, both free and slave, could share news with folk they did not regularly see.

Following Nat Turner's Rebellion of 1831, southern legislatures increased the restrictions placed on free African Americans. They were forbidden to enter a different state; had to carry their free papers; could not assemble when they wished; were subject to a nightly curfew; often had to post a bond and be licensed to work; and could not vote, hold office, or testify in court against white people.

Free African Americans occupied an uncertain position in southern society, well above black slaves but distinctly beneath even poorer white southerners. They were victims of a society that had no place for them.

 **REVIEW**

In what ways did the culture and communities created by blacks help to sustain them in slavery?

# SOUTHERN SOCIETY AND THE DEFENSE OF SLAVERY

While the South was a remarkably diverse region, it was united above all by the institution of slavery. As the South's economy became more dependent on slave-produced staples, slavery became more central to the life of the South, to its culture—to its very identity.

**The Virginia Debate of 1832** >> During the Revolution the leading critics of slavery were southerners—Jefferson, Washington, Madison, and Patrick Henry among them. But beginning in the 1820s, in the wake of the controversy over admitting Missouri as a slave state, southern leaders became more aggressive in defending slavery. The turning point occurred in the early 1830s, when the South found itself increasingly under attack. It was in 1831 that William Lloyd Garrison began publishing his abolitionist newspaper, *The Liberator*. That was also the year Nat Turner led his revolt, which frightened so many white southerners.

In response to the Turner insurrection, a number of Virginia's western counties, where there were few slaves, petitioned the legislature in 1832 to adopt a program for gradual emancipation. In the end, however, the legislature refused. The debate represented the last significant attempt of white southerners to take action against slavery. Instead, during the 1830s and 1840s southern leaders defended slavery as a good, not just for white but for black people. As John C. Calhoun proclaimed in 1837, "I hold that in the present state of civilization, where two races . . . are brought together, the relation now existing in the slaveholding states between the two is, instead of an evil, a good—a positive good."

**The Proslavery Argument** >> White southern leaders justified slavery in a variety of ways. Ministers argued that none of the biblical prophets or Christ himself had ever condemned slavery. Defenders of the institution pointed out that classical Greece and Rome also depended on slavery. They even cited John Locke, that giant of the

# Historian's TOOLBOX

## George Washington, Slaveholder

This image is a lithograph of a painting. What's a lithograph? (Well worth it to Google "lithograph")

A young neighbor, perhaps Washington's overseer or a yeoman or tenant farmer

Washington's two step-grandchildren

Washington himself. Why so formally dressed for the hay field?

Advocates of the proslavery argument made strategic use of stories and images portraying George Washington as the master of Mount Vernon, his plantation—without mentioning that, upon his death, his will freed all his slaves. This lithograph from 1853 conveyed a proslavery message that found its way into thousands of southern parlors and libraries before the Civil War. (Historians of technology tell us that lithography, a process for reproducing images drawn on stone plates, came into widespread use in the early nineteenth century, allowing for the cheap mass production of images as well as print.) Such stories and pictures portrayed Washington as a benevolent patriarch—a father to his slaves as well as to his country—and depicted slavery as a benevolent institution. At the center of this scene, a group of hale, neatly outfitted black men refresh themselves with water brought by a slave woman, demurely dressed right up to her head covering. Judging by the riding crop in his hand and the horse behind Washington, he has just dismounted, perhaps to give some instructions to his overseer, a young man who holds not a whip but a rake—to help the slaves with the hay gathering.

### THINKING CRITICALLY

*What is the significance of placing whites in the foreground of the painting? What point was the artist making by drawing Washington's two step-grandchildren happily at play in the left corner? What was the artist implying by portraying Washington and the young man (who is plainly of lesser status) talking with easy familiarity?*

*Credit:* Claude Regnier after Junius Brutus Stearns, *Life of George Washington: The Farmer* (lithograph, 1853) LIBRARY OF CONGRESS;
(*Photo*) Source: Library of Congress, Prints and Photographs Division [LC-DIG-pga02419]

Enlightenment, who had recognized slavery in the constitution he drafted for the colony of Carolina. African Americans belonged to an intellectually and emotionally inferior race, slavery's defenders argued, and therefore lacked the ability to care for themselves.

Proslavery writers sometimes argued that slaves in the South lived better than factory workers in the North. Masters cared for slaves for life, whereas northern workers had no claim on their employer when they were unemployed, old, or no longer able to work. In advancing this argument, white southerners exaggerated the material comforts of slavery and minimized the average worker's living conditions—to say nothing, of course, about the incalculable psychological value of freedom. Still, to many white southerners, slavery seemed a more humane system of labor relations.

Defenders of slavery did not really expect to convert northerners. Their target was more often slaveowners themselves. As Duff Green, a southern editor, explained, "We must satisfy the consciences, we must allay the fears of our own people. We must satisfy them that slavery is of itself right—that it is not a sin against God—that it is not an evil, moral or political. In this way only," he went on, "can we prepare our own people to defend their institutions."

**Closing Ranks** >> Not all white southerners could quell their doubts. Still, in the decades before the Civil War, few outside the border states contended that slavery was wrong. And white southerners who did oppose slavery found themselves harassed, assaulted, and driven into exile. Southern mobs destroyed the presses of antislavery papers. Southern mails were forcibly closed to abolitionist propaganda. Southerners such as James Birney and Sarah and Angelina Grimké had to leave their native region to carry on the fight against slavery from the free states.

Increasingly, too, slavery entered the national political debate. Before 1836 Andrew Jackson's popularity in the South blocked the formation of a competitive two-party system. The rise of the abolitionist movement in the 1830s, however, left many southerners uneasy, and when the Democrats nominated the northerner Martin Van Buren in 1836, southern Whigs charged that Van Buren could not be counted on to meet the abolitionist threat to slavery. The Whigs made impressive gains in the South in 1836, carrying several states and significantly narrowing the margin between the two parties.

During the Jacksonian era, most southern political battles did not revolve around slavery. Still, southern politicians in both parties had to be careful about being the least bit critical of slavery or southern institutions. They knew quite well that, even if their constituents were not so fanatical as John Calhoun in the defense of the peculiar institution, southern voters overwhelmingly supported slavery.

 **REVIEW**

How did white southerners defend slavery as a positive good?

As the past several chapters have made clear, two remarkable transformations were sweeping the world in the first half of the nineteenth century. The first was a series of political upheavals leading to increased democratic participation in many nation-states. The second, the Industrial Revolution, applied machine labor and technological innovation to commercial and agricultural economies.

Although it is common to identify the Industrial Revolution with New England's factories and the North's cities, that revolution transformed the rural South, too. Cotton could not have become king without the demand created by textile factories or without the ability to "gin" the seeds out of cotton by Eli Whitney's invention. Nor could cotton production flourish without industrial advances in transportation, which allowed raw materials to be shipped worldwide. As for democratic change, the suffrage was extended in Britain by the Reform Bill of 1832, and popular uprisings spread across Europe in 1830 and 1848. In the United States, white southerners and northerners participated in the democratic reforms of the 1820s and 1830s.

The Industrial Revolution and democratic revolution thus transformed the South as well as the North, though in different ways. Increasingly, slavery became the focus of disputes between the two sections. The Industrial Revolution's demand for cotton increased the demand for slave labor and the profits to be gained from it. Yet the spread of democratic ideology worldwide increased pressure to abolish slavery. France and Britain had already done so. In eastern Europe the near-slavery of feudal serfdom was being eliminated as well: in 1848 within the Hapsburg Empire; in 1861 in Russia; in 1864 in Romania.

By the mid-1840s the contradictory pressures of the Industrial Revolution and democratic revolution were beginning to sharpen, as the United States embarked on a new program of westward expansion that thrust the slavery issue into the center of politics. Americans were forced to debate how much of the newly won territory should be open to slavery; in doing so, some citizens began to question whether the Union could permanently endure, half slave and half free.

# CHAPTER SUMMARY

The Old South was a complex, biracial society that increasingly diverged from the rest of the United States in the years before 1860.

- Southerners placed heavy emphasis on agriculture and upheld the superiority of the rural way of life. Few cities and towns developed.
- Southern commercial agriculture produced staple crops for sale in northern and European markets: tobacco, sugar, rice, and, above all, cotton.
- As southern agriculture expanded into the fresh lands of the Deep South, the slave population moved steadily westward and southward.
- Slavery played a major role in shaping the class structure of the Old South.
- Ownership of slaves brought privilege and status, and the largest slaveowners were extraordinarily wealthy.
- Planters on the older eastern seaboard enjoyed a more refined lifestyle than did those on the new cotton frontier.
- Most slaveowners owned only a few slaves, and the majority of southern whites were non-slaveowning yeoman farmers. Slavery hurt non-slaveholding whites economically, but class tensions were muted in the Old South because of racial fears.

- The institution of slavery was both a labor system and a social system, regulating relations between the races.
- Slaves resisted bondage in many ways, ranging from the subtle to the overt. Slave revolts, however, were rare, although they were far more frequent in the Caribbean and Latin America.
- Slaves developed their own culture, in which the family, religion, and songs played key roles in helping them cope with the pressures of bondage.
- As slavery increasingly came under attack, white southerners rallied to protect their peculiar institution. They developed a set of arguments defending slavery as a positive good.
- Many Americans, in both the North and the South, shared the same values: personal independence, social egalitarianism, evangelical Protestantism. But beginning in the mid-1840s with renewed westward expansion, the slavery issue increased sectional tensions.

## Additional Reading

The reports of Frederick Law Olmsted, who traveled through the South in the 1850s, make a fascinating jumping-off point for a first look at the region. Much of Olmsted's material is conveniently collected in Lawrence Powell, ed., *The Cotton Kingdom* (1984). A contrasting approach to traveling about is to stay at one plantation, as Erskine Clarke does in his brilliant *Dwelling Place: A Plantation Epic* (2005). For a global perspective on the Cotton South, see Sven Beckert, *Empire of Cotton* (2014).

Frank Owsley's *Plain Folk of the Old South* (1949), about southern yeoman farmers, is still useful; it can be supplemented by Samuel C. Hyde Jr., ed., *Plain Folk of the South Revisited* (1997). The lives of upper-class southern white women and their servants are analyzed in Elizabeth Fox-Genovese, *Within the Plantation Household* (1988); and Victoria E. Bynum, *Unruly Women* (1992). Stephanie McCurry, *Masters of Small Worlds* (1995), treats white and black women of lower status.

The best exploration of slavery as a labor system remains Kenneth M. Stampp, *The Peculiar Institution* (1956). For a perceptive treatment of slave culture, see Eugene D. Genovese, *Roll, Jordan, Roll* (1974). John Hope Franklin and Loren Schweninger, *Runaway Slaves* (1999), detail an important aspect of slave resistance. Walter Johnson, *Soul by Soul: Life Inside the Antebellum Slave Market* (1999), provides a concrete and chilling view of the trade that helped sustain the "peculiar institution"; his more recent *River of Dark Dreams* (2013) vividly portrays slavery in the Cotton South. Ira Berlin, *Slaves Without Masters* (1974), is an excellent account of free black southerners. For the evolution of the proslavery argument, see Lacy K. Ford, *Deliver Us From Evil* (2009).

# 14 Western Expansion and the Rise of the Slavery Issue

## 1820–1850

The Hidatsa Indians retreated to these well-insulated earth lodges in the forested and more-sheltered river bottoms to escape the winter storms of the Great Plains. Swiss artist Karl Bodmer painted this scene after a visit in 1833–1834. In the foreground at left two men play a traditional hoop and pole game (the hoop quite small), as spectators watch.

©The Stapleton Collection/Bridgeman Images

### >> An American Story

## STRANGERS ON THE GREAT PLAINS

At first the Crows, Arapahos, and other Indians of the Great Plains paid little attention to the newcomers moving out from the forests far to the east. For as long as they could remember, these peoples had called the plains their own. But the new arrivals were not to be taken lightly. Armed with superior weapons and bringing with them a great many women and children, they seemed to have an unlimited appetite for land. They attacked the villages of the Plains Indians, massacred women and children, and forced defeated tribes to live on reservations.

The invaders who established this dominance were *not* the strange "white men," who also came from the forest. During the 1830s and early 1840s whites were still few in number. The more dangerous people—the ones who truly worried the Plains tribes—were the Sioux.

Westward expansion is usually told as a one-dimensional tale, centering on the wagon trains pressing on toward the Pacific. But frontiers are the transition zones between different cultures or environments, and during the nineteenth century frontiers in the West were constantly shifting. They moved not only east to west, as with the European and the Sioux migrations, but also south to north, as Spanish culture diffused, and west to east, as Asian immigrants came to California.

Furthermore, frontiers marked not only human but also animal boundaries. Horses, cattle, and pigs—species imported from Europe—moved across the continent, often in advance of European settlers. These animals transformed the way Indian peoples lived. Frontiers could also be technological, as in the case of trade goods and firearms. Moreover, disease moved across the continent with disastrous consequences for natives who had not acquired immunity to European microorganisms.

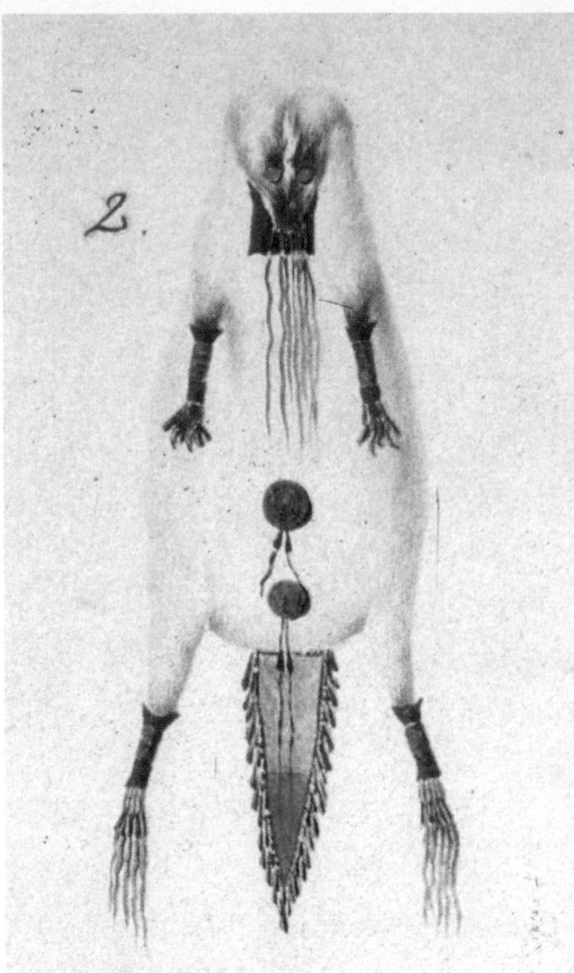
2.

Pouch made from a white skunk skin. The Indian who fashioned the pouch obtained the skin, as well as the decorative beads, from a white trapper. The pouch may have held tobacco or other trade items; or it may have been a medicine pouch.


Three frontiers revolutionized the lives of the Sioux: those of the horse, the gun, and disease. The horse frontier spread ahead of European settlement from the southwest, where horses had first been imported by the Spanish. The Spanish, however—unlike English and French traders—generally refused to sell firearms to Indians, so the gun frontier moved in the opposite direction, from northeast to southwest. The two waves met and crossed along the upper Missouri during the first half of the eighteenth century. For the tribes that possessed them, horses provided greater mobility, both for hunting bison and for fighting. Guns, too, conferred obvious advantages, and the arrival of these new elements inaugurated an extremely unsettled era for Plains Indian cultures.

The Sioux first moved onto the Minnesota prairie during the early 1700s to hunt beaver, whose pelts could be exchanged with European traders for manufactured goods. Having obtained guns in exchange for furs, the Sioux drove the Omahas, Otos, Cheyennes, and Missouris (who had not yet acquired guns) south and west. But by the 1770s their advantage in firepower had disappeared, and any further advance was blocked by powerful tribes such as the Mandans and Arikaras. These peoples were primarily horticultural, raising corn, beans, and squash and living in well-fortified towns. They also owned more horses than the Sioux; thus it was easier for them to resist attacks.

But the third frontier, disease, threw the balance of power toward the Sioux after 1779. That year, a continental smallpox pandemic struck the plains via New Mexico. The horticultural tribes were hit especially hard because they lived in densely populated villages, where the epidemic spread more easily. By the time Lewis and Clark came through in 1804, the Sioux firmly controlled the upper Missouri as far as the Yellowstone River. From an estimated 5,000 in 1804 they grew to 25,000 in the 1850s. Indeed, the Sioux became the largest nation on the plains and was the only nation whose high birthrate approximated that of whites.

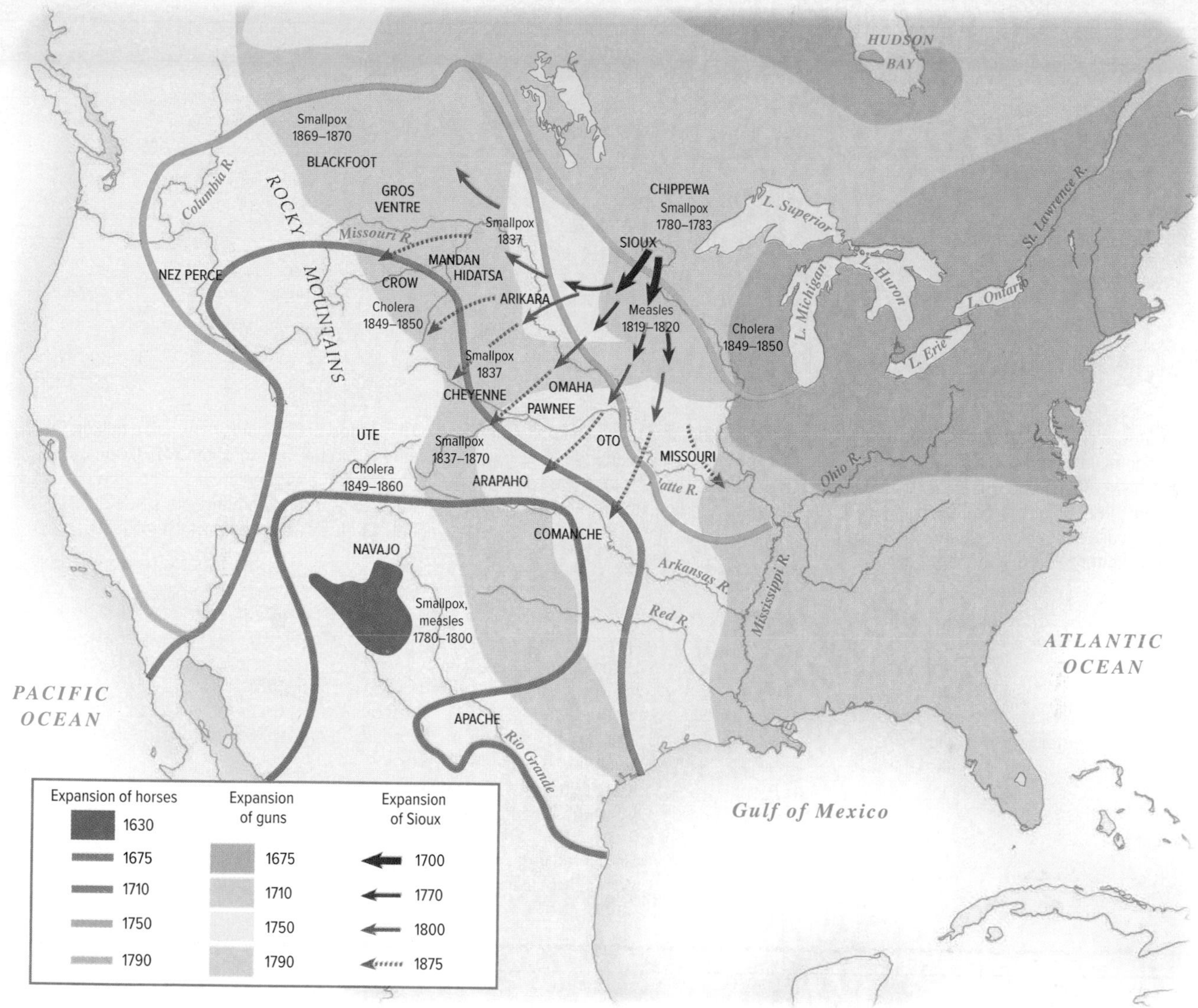
HUDSON BAY
Smallpox 1869–1870
BLACKFOOT
GROS VENTRE
CHIPPEWA
Smallpox 1780–1783
L. Superior
St. Lawrence R.
Columbia R.
ROCKY MOUNTAINS
Missouri R.
Smallpox 1837
SIOUX
MANDAN
HIDATSA
NEZ PERCE
CROW
ARIKARA
L. Michigan
L. Huron
L. Ontario
Cholera 1849–1850
Measles 1819–1820
Cholera 1849–1850
L. Erie
Smallpox 1837
CHEYENNE
OMAHA
PAWNEE
UTE
Smallpox 1837–1870
OTO
MISSOURI
Platte R.
Ohio R.
Cholera 1849–1860
ARAPAHO
COMANCHE
NAVAJO
Arkansas R.
Mississippi R.
Red R.
Smallpox, measles 1780–1800
ATLANTIC OCEAN
PACIFIC OCEAN
APACHE
Rio Grande
Gulf of Mexico
Expansion of horses
1630
1675
1710
1750
1790
Expansion of guns
1675
1710
1750
1790
Expansion of Sioux
1700
1770
1800
1875

## MAP 14.1: SIOUX EXPANSION AND THE HORSE AND GUN FRONTIERS

In 1710 the horse and gun frontiers had not yet crossed, but by 1750 the two waves began to overlap. The Sioux pushed west during the early eighteenth century thanks in part to firearms; they were checked from further expansion until the 1770s, when smallpox epidemics again turned the balance in their favor.

*Why did smallpox prove more dangerous to Mandans, Arikaras, and Hidatsas than to Sioux communities?*

These shifting frontiers of animals, disease, firearms, and trade goods disrupted the political and cultural life of the Great Plains. And as white Americans moved westward, their own frontier lines produced similar disruptions, not only between white settlers and Indians but also between Anglo-American and Hispanic cultures. The relations between Indian peoples and the diverse inhabitants of Mexico were also in flux, as many tribes across the plains began attacking Mexico during the 1830s. There would even be a frontier moving west to east, as thousands of Chinese were drawn, along with other immigrants, to gold fields discovered after 1848. Ironically, perhaps the greatest instability created by the moving frontiers occurred within the United States. As the political system incorporated the new territories, the North and South fiercely debated whether they should become slave or free. Just as the Sioux's cultural identity was brought into question by moving frontiers, so, too, was the identity of the American Republic. <<

## THEMATIC TIMELINE

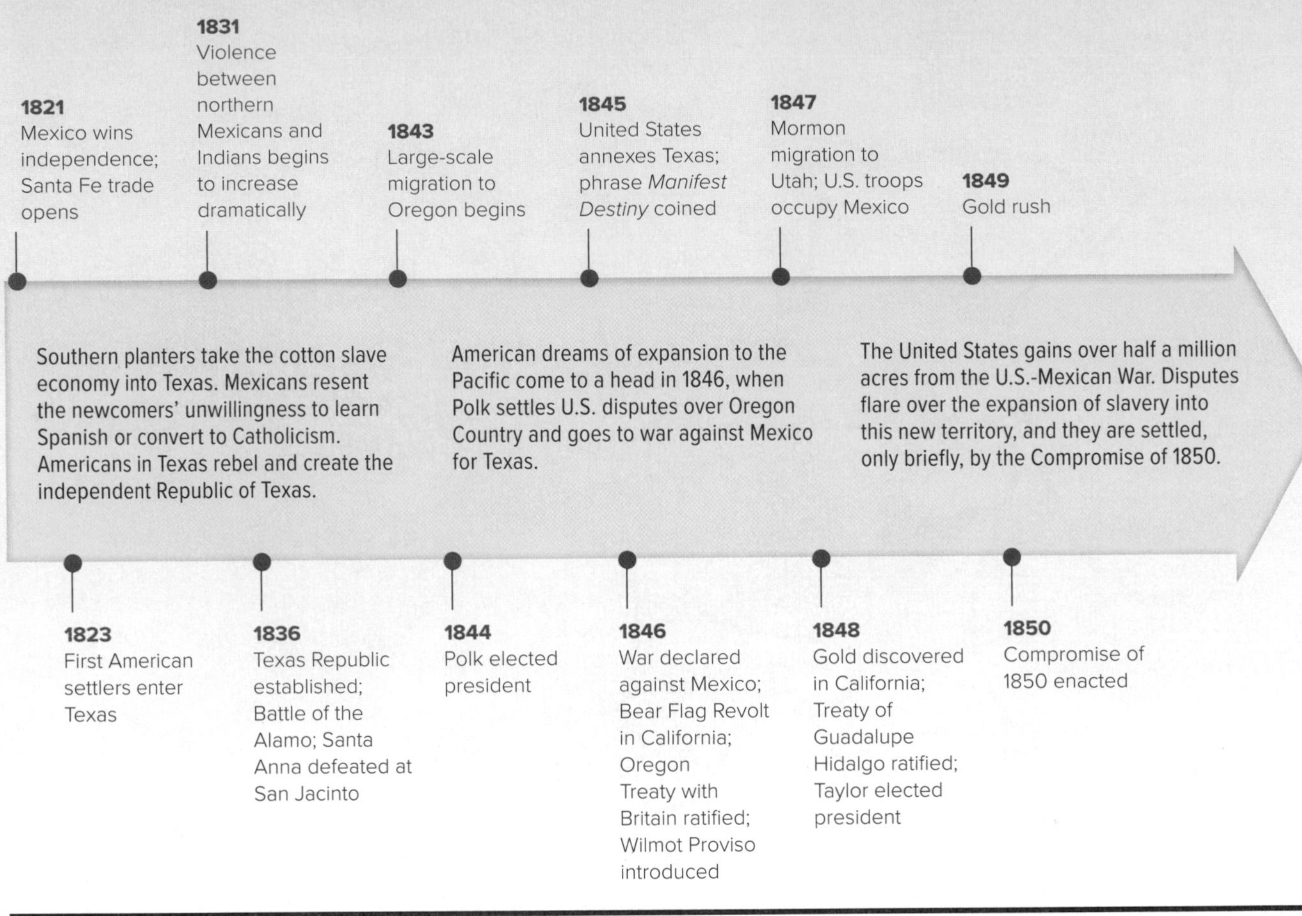
1821
Mexico wins independence; Santa Fe trade opens
1831
Violence between northern Mexicans and Indians begins to increase dramatically
1843
Large-scale migration to Oregon begins
1845
United States annexes Texas; phrase Manifest Destiny coined
1847
Mormon migration to Utah; U.S. troops occupy Mexico
1849
Gold rush
Southern planters take the cotton slave economy into Texas. Mexicans resent the newcomers' unwillingness to learn Spanish or convert to Catholicism. Americans in Texas rebel and create the independent Republic of Texas.
American dreams of expansion to the Pacific come to a head in 1846, when Polk settles U.S. disputes over Oregon Country and goes to war against Mexico for Texas.
The United States gains over half a million acres from the U.S.-Mexican War. Disputes flare over the expansion of slavery into this new territory, and they are settled, only briefly, by the Compromise of 1850.
1823
First American settlers enter Texas
1836
Texas Republic established; Battle of the Alamo; Santa Anna defeated at San Jacinto
1844
Polk elected president
1846
War declared against Mexico; Bear Flag Revolt in California; Oregon Treaty with Britain ratified; Wilmot Proviso introduced
1848
Gold discovered in California; Treaty of Guadalupe Hidalgo ratified; Taylor elected president
1850
Compromise of 1850 enacted

# MANIFEST (AND NOT SO MANIFEST) DESTINY

"Make way . . . for the young American Buffalo—he has not yet got land enough," roared one U.S. politician in 1844. In the space of a few years, the United States acquired Texas, California, the lower half of the Oregon Territory, and the lands between the Rockies and California: nearly 1.5 million square miles in all. John L. O'Sullivan, a prominent Democratic editor in New York, struck a responsive chord when he declared that it had become the United States' "**manifest destiny** to overspread the continent allotted by Providence for the free development of our yearly multiplying millions." The cry of "Manifest Destiny" soon echoed in other editorial pages and in the halls of Congress.

**Manifest Destiny** mid-nineteenth-century political doctrine that argued the benefits of democracy would spread along with territorial expansion. Yet Manifest Destiny was also racist in its assumption of the inferiority of other peoples and cultures; and it encompassed a purely economic desire to expand the nation's commerce and power.

### The Roots of the Doctrine

>> Many Americans had long believed that their country had a special, even divine, mission, which could be traced back to the Puritans' attempt to build a "city on a hill." Manifest Destiny also contained a political component, inherited from the ideology of the Revolution. In the mid-nineteenth century Americans spoke of extending democracy, with widespread suffrage among white males, no king or aristocracy, and no established church, "over the whole North American continent."

Americans believed that their social and economic system, too, should spread around the globe. They pointed to its broad ownership of land, individualism, and free play of economic opportunity as superior features of American life. More important, Manifest Destiny was about power,

^ The idea that the United States could expand to become a continental republic seemed far-fetched to most Americans of the early Republic. But the coming of the telegraph, whose wires allowed for instant communication over long distances, helped convince many that expansion to the Pacific might indeed be the nation's "Manifest Destiny."


especially economic power. American business interests recognized the value of the fine harbors along the Pacific coast, which promised a lucrative trade with Asia, and they hoped to make those harbors American.

However, underlying the doctrine of Manifest Destiny was widespread racism. The same belief in racial superiority that had been used to justify Indian removal under Jackson, to uphold slavery in the South, and to excuse segregation in the North also proved useful in defending expansion westward. The United States had a duty to regenerate the backward peoples of America, declared politicians and propagandists. Their reference was not so much to Indians: the forced expulsion of assimilated Cherokees during Indian removal made clear what most American policy makers thought about Indian "regeneration." By the 1840s it was rather the Mexicans who had caught the attention of Manifest Destiny's prophets of progress. The Mexican race "must amalgamate and be lost, in the superior vigor of the Anglo-Saxon race," proclaimed O'Sullivan's *Democratic Review*, "or they must utterly perish."

Before 1845 most Americans assumed that expansion would be achieved without international war. American settlement would expand westward, and when the time was right, neighboring provinces would fall, like ripe fruit, into American hands: Texas, New Mexico, Oregon, and California. With time, American expansionists became less willing to wait patiently for the fruit to fall.

## The Mexican Borderlands

>> The heart of Spain's American empire was Mexico City, where spacious boulevards spread out through the center of the city, and the University of Mexico, the oldest university in North America, had been accepting students since 1553, a full 85 years earlier than Harvard. From the Mexican point of view, the frontier was 1,000 miles to the north, a four-week journey to the Republic of Texas, another two weeks to Nuevo Mexico, and three months by land and sea to the missions of Alta California. Being isolated, these Mexican provinces developed with little metropolitan supervision.

California's settlements were anchored by four coastal **presidios**, or forts, at San Diego, Santa Barbara, Monterey, and San Francisco. Between them lay 21 Catholic missions run by a handful of Franciscans (only 36 in 1821). The missions controlled enormous tracts of land on which grazed gigantic herds of cattle, sheep, and horses. These animals and irrigated fields were tended by about 20,000 Indians, who in certain ways lived and worked like slaves.

[ **presidio** Spanish military garrison.

When Mexico won its independence from Spain in 1821, little changed in California at first. But in 1833 the Mexican Congress stripped the Catholic Church of its vast landholdings. These lands were turned over to Mexican cattle ranchers, usually in massive grants of 50,000 acres or more. The new *rancheros* ruled their estates much as great planters of the Old South. Labor was provided by Indians, who again were forced to work for little more than room and board. Indeed, the mortality rate of Indian workers was twice that of southern slaves and four times that of nonnative Californians. By the 1830s the Mexican population of California stood at

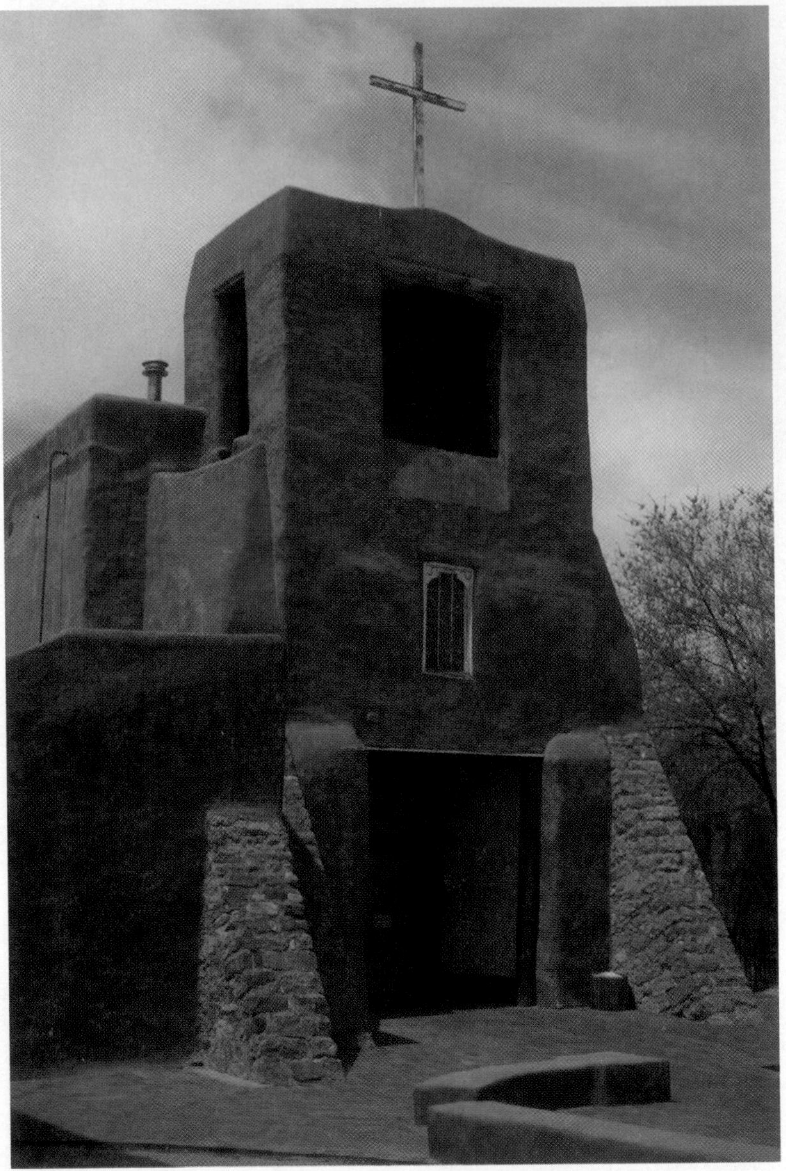

^ Throughout the Spanish and Mexican periods, town life in what are now California, New Mexico, and Texas revolved around central plazas and their churches. One of the first structures built in Santa Fe, the Mission Church of San Miguel (est. ca. 1610), is today the oldest church building in the present-day United States. ©Andre Jenny/Alamy

approximately 4,000. During the 1820s and 1830s Yankee traders set up shop in California in order to buy cattle hides for the growing shoe industry at Lynn, Massachusetts, and elsewhere. Still, in 1845 the American population amounted to only 700.

Spanish settlement of New Mexico was denser than that of California: the province had about 44,000 Spanish-speaking inhabitants in 1827. But as in California, great landowning families dominated, grazing large herds of sheep along the upper Rio Grande valley between El Paso and Taos. A few individuals controlled most of the wealth, while their workers eked out meager livings. Spain had long outlawed any commerce with Americans, but that all changed with Mexican independence. Caravans from the United States began making the long journey along the Santa Fe Trail starting in 1821. Although this trade flourished over the next two decades, developments in the third Mexican borderland, neighboring Texas, would all but wreck relations between Mexico and the United States.

**The Texas Rebellion** >> At first the new government in Mexico encouraged American emigration to Texas, where only about 3,000 Mexicans, mostly ranchers, lived. In 1821 Moses Austin, an American, received a grant from the Spanish government to establish a colony. After his death his son Stephen took over the project, laying out the little town of San Felipe de Austin along the Brazos River and offering large grants of land at almost no cost. By 1824 the colony's population exceeded 2,000. Stephen Austin was only the first of a new wave of American land agents, or *empresarios*, who obtained permission from Mexican authorities to settle families in Texas. Ninety percent of the new arrivals came from the South. Many, intending to grow cotton, brought slaves.

Tensions between Mexicans and American immigrants grew with the Texas economy. Most settlers from the States were Protestant. Although the Mexican government passed no laws mandating Catholicism, it did officially bar Protestant churches. In 1829 Mexico abolished slavery, only to discover, to its chagrin, that Texas slaveholders evaded the law. In the early 1830s the Mexican government began to have second thoughts about American settlement and passed laws prohibiting any new immigration. Austin likened the new anti-immigration laws to "trying to stop the Mississippi with a dam of straw." It was an apt metaphor: between 1830 and 1833, illegal American immigrants and their slaves flooded into Mexican Texas, nearly doubling its colonial population.

Admitting that the new regulations had served only to inflame the American immigrants, Mexico repealed them in 1833. But by then colonial ill-will had soared. By mid-decade the American white population of 40,000 was nearly 10 times the number of **Tejanos**. Once again Mexico's government talked of abolishing slavery in Texas. Even more disturbing to the American newcomers, in 1834 President Antonio López de Santa Anna and his allies in the Mexican Congress passed legislation that took power away from the states and concentrated it in Mexico City. Texans had been struggling for more autonomy, not less. When Santa Anna brutally suppressed an uprising against the central government in the state of Zacatecas, Texans grew more nervous. Finally, when

**Tejano** Spanish-speaking Texan

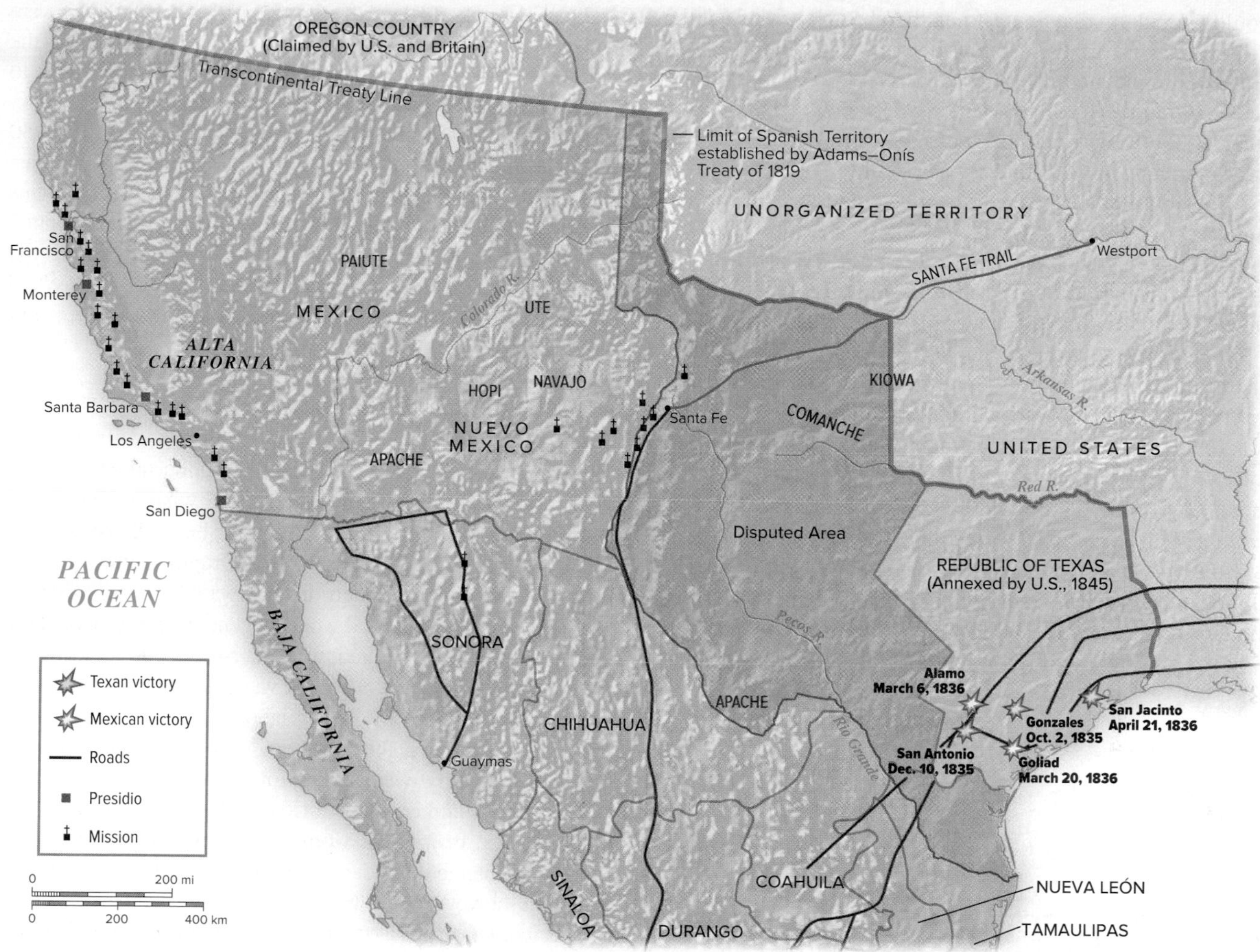
OREGON COUNTRY
(Claimed by U.S. and Britain)
Transcontinental Treaty Line
Limit of Spanish Territory established by Adams–Onís Treaty of 1819
UNORGANIZED TERRITORY
SANTA FE TRAIL
Westport
San Francisco
Monterey
PAIUTE
MEXICO
UTE
Colorado R.
ALTA CALIFORNIA
HOPI
NAVAJO
KIOWA
Arkansas R.
Santa Barbara
Los Angeles
NUEVO MEXICO
Santa Fe
COMANCHE
UNITED STATES
APACHE
Red R.
San Diego
Disputed Area
PACIFIC OCEAN
REPUBLIC OF TEXAS
(Annexed by U.S., 1845)
Pecos R.
SONORA
BAJA CALIFORNIA
Alamo
March 6, 1836
San Jacinto
April 21, 1836
Gonzales
Oct. 2, 1835
APACHE
CHIHUAHUA
San Antonio
Dec. 10, 1835
Goliad
March 20, 1836
Rio Grande
Guaymas
Texan victory
Mexican victory
Roads
Presidio
Mission
0
200 mi
0
200
400 km
SINALOA
COAHUILA
NUEVA LEÓN
DURANGO
TAMAULIPAS

## MAP 14.2: MEXICAN BORDERLANDS, 1821–1845

*What factors explain the concentration of U.S. immigrants in east Texas?*

conflicts over taxes led Santa Anna to march soldiers north and enforce his new regime, a ragtag Texas army drove back the advance party and then captured Mexican troops in nearby San Antonio. A full-scale rebellion was under way.

**The Texas Republic** >> As Santa Anna massed his forces, a provisional government on March 2, 1836, proclaimed Texan independence. The document was signed by a number of prominent Tejanos whose families had been in Texas for generations. The constitution of the new Republic of Texas borrowed heavily from the U.S. Constitution, except that it explicitly prohibited the new Texas Congress from interfering with slavery. Meanwhile, Santa Anna's troops overran a Texan garrison at an old mission in San Antonio, known as the Alamo, and killed all its 187 defenders—including the famous backwoodsman and U.S. congressman, Davy Crockett. The Mexicans, however, paid dearly for the victory, losing more than 1,500 men. The massacre of another force at Goliad after it surrendered further inflamed American resistance.

But anger was one thing; organized resistance another. The commander of the Texas forces was Sam Houston, a former governor of Tennessee. Houston's intellectual ability and talent as a stump speaker thrust him to the forefront of the Texas independence movement. Houston knew his army needed seasoning, so he retreated steadily eastward, buying time in order to forge a disciplined fighting force. By late April he was ready. Reinforced by eager volunteers from the United States, Houston's men surprised the Mexican army camped along the San Jacinto River. Shouting "Remember the Alamo!" they took only 15 minutes to overwhelm the Mexicans (who had been enjoying an afternoon siesta) and capture Santa Anna.

Threatened with execution, the Mexican commander signed treaties recognizing Texan independence and ordering his remaining troops south of the Rio Grande. Texans would later claim that Santa Anna thereby acknowledged the Rio Grande as Texas's southern boundary. The Mexican Congress repudiated the agreement, especially the claim to the Rio Grande. Houston assumed office in October 1836 as president of the new republic, determined to bring Texas into the American Union as quickly as possible.

Houston assumed that the United States would quickly annex such a vast and inviting territory. But Andrew Jackson worried that any such move would revive sectional tensions and hurt Martin Van Buren's chances in the 1836 presidential election. Only on his last day in office did he extend formal diplomatic recognition to the Texas Republic. Van Buren, distracted by the economic panic that broke out shortly after he entered office, took no action during his term.

Rebuffed, the Texans went their own way. In the 10 years following independence, the Lone Star Republic attracted more than 100,000 immigrants by offering free land to settlers. Mexico refused to recognize Texan independence, and the vast majority of its citizens still wished to join the United States, where most of them had been born. There matters stood when the Whigs and William Henry Harrison won the presidency in 1840.

How did Mexico lose Texas?

# THE TREK WEST

As thousands of white Americans were moving into Texas, and increasingly bringing slaves with them, a much smaller trickle headed toward the Oregon country. Since 1818 the United States and Great Britain had occupied that territory jointly, as far north as latitude 54°4′. Although white settlement remained sparse, by 1836 American settlers outnumbered the British in the Willamette valley.

Pushed by the Panic of 1837 and six years of depression and pulled by tales of Oregon's lush, fertile valleys and the healthy, frost-free climate along California's Sacramento River, many American farmers struck out for the West Coast. Missouri was "cleaned" out of money, worried farmer Daniel Waldo, and his wife was even more adamant about heading west: "If you want to stay here another summer and shake your liver out with the fever and ague, you can do it," she announced to her husband, "but in the spring I am going to take the children and go to Oregon, Indians or no Indians." The wagon trains began rolling west.

**The Overland Trail >>** Only a few hundred emigrants reached the West in 1841 and 1842, but by 1844 thousands were following the Overland Trail across the mountains to Oregon. The migration was primarily a family enterprise, and many couples had only recently married. Most adults were between 20 and 50, since the hard journey discouraged the elderly. Furthermore, a family of four needed about $600 to outfit their journey, an amount that excluded the poor.

The trip lasted about 6 months. Caravans of 20 to 30 wagons were common the first few years, but after 1845 parties traveled in smaller trains of 8 to 10 wagons. Breakdowns were frequent, and increasing traffic meant that migrants' cattle, horses, and mules quickly devoured grass along the trail. Scarcity made disagreements more likely, and created desperate problems for Indian peoples trying to keep their own herds alive in winter.

**Women on the Overland Trail >>** The journey west often placed a special strain on women. Few wives were as eager as Dan Waldo's to undertake the move. "Poor Ma said only this morning, 'Oh I wish we never had started,'" one daughter reported, "and she looks so sorrowful and dejected." In one study of Oregon-bound parties, three-fourths of the women did not want to head west.

At first, parties divided work by gender, as had been done back home. Women cooked, washed, sewed, and took care of the children, while men drove the wagons, cared for the stock, stood guard, and did the heavy labor. Necessity placed new demands on women, however, and eventually altered their roles. Within a few weeks, they found themselves helping to repair wagons and construct bridges. When men became exhausted, sick, or injured, women stood guard and drove the oxen. The change in work assignments proceeded only in one direction, however, for few men undertook "women's work."

As women strove to maintain a semblance of home on the trail, many experienced a profound sense of loss. Trains often worked or traveled on the Sabbath, which back home had long been a day for worship and rest and an emblem of women's moral authority. Women also felt the lack of close companions to whom they could turn for comfort. One woman, whose husband separated their wagon from the train after a dispute, sadly watched the other wagons pull away: "I felt that indeed I had left all my friends to journey over the dreaded plains without one female acquaintance even for a companion—of course I wept and grieved about it but to no purpose."

**Indians and the Trail Experience >>** The peoples whose lands were crossed by white wagon trains reacted in a number of ways to the westward tide. The Sioux, who had long traded with whites, regularly visited overlanders to swap for blankets, clothes, cows, rifles, and knives. But the European migrants took a heavy toll on the Plains Indians' way of life: emigrant parties scared off game and reduced buffalo herds, overgrazed the grass, and depleted the supply of wood. Having petitioned unsuccessfully in 1846 for government compensation, some Sioux decided to demand payment from the wagon trains crossing their lands. Whether parties paid or not depended on the relative strength of the two groups, but whites complained bitterly of what seemed to them outright robbery.

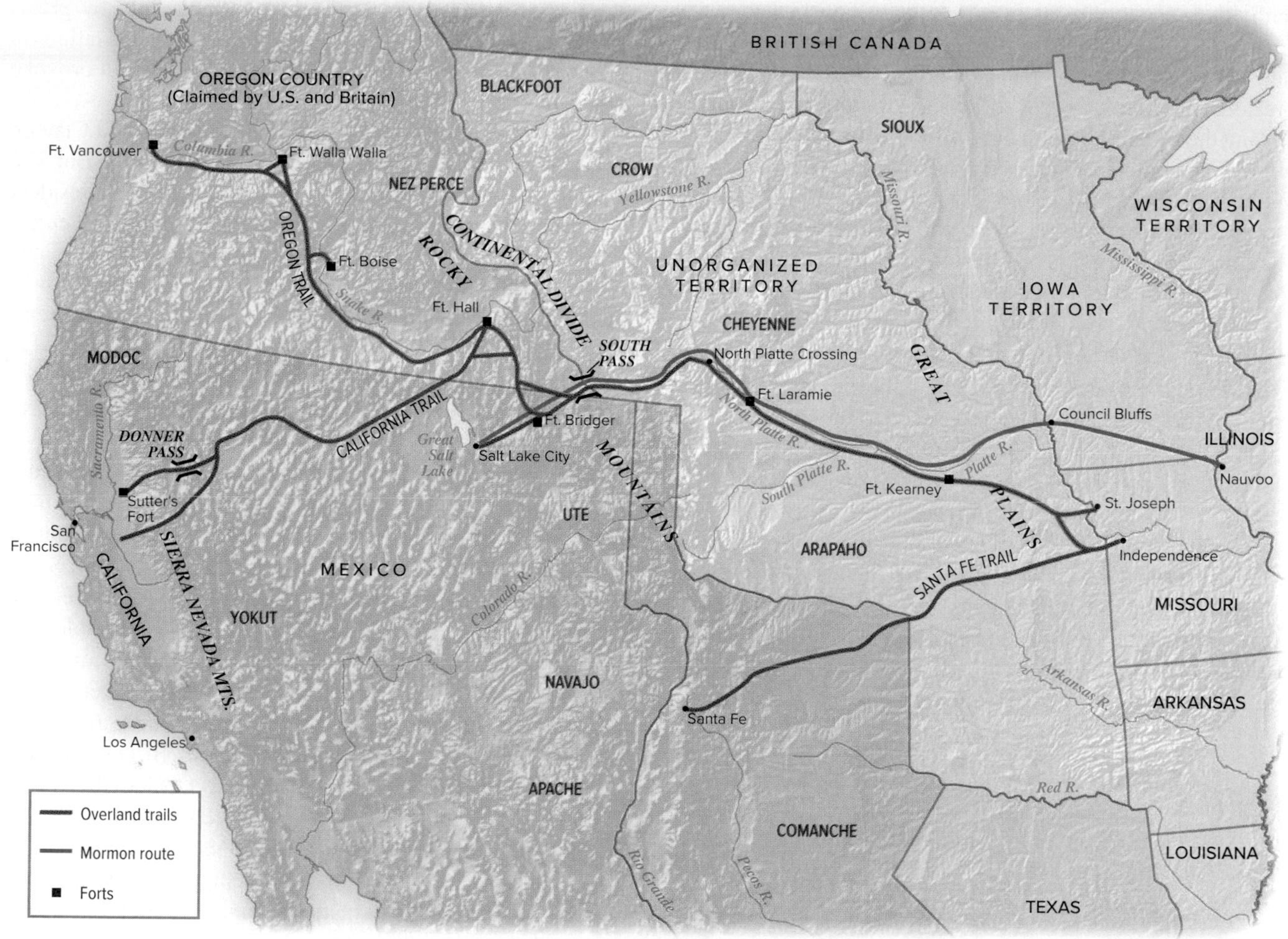

## MAP 14.3: THE OVERLAND TRAIL

Beginning at several different points, the Overland Trail followed the Platte and Sweetwater Rivers across the plains to South Pass, where it crossed the Continental Divide. The trail split near Fort Hall. Between 1840 and 1860 more than a quarter of a million emigrants made the trek. *What would have been the most important considerations when planning an overland route across the West?*

Their fears aroused by sensational stories, overland parties were wary of Indians, but this menace was greatly exaggerated, especially on the plains. Few wagon trains were attacked by Indians, and less than 4 percent of deaths on the trail were caused by Native Americans. In truth, emigrants more often killed Indians. For overlanders the most aggravating problem posed by native peoples was theft of stock. Many parties received valuable assistance from Indians, who acted as guides, directed them to grass and water, and transported animals and wagons across rivers.

**REVIEW**

What motivated Americans to migrate on overland trails, and how did the experiences of women and men differ on the journey?

# THE POLITICAL ORIGINS OF EXPANSION

President William Henry Harrison came into office determined to undo some of Jackson's and Van Buren's key economic policies and eliminate the spoils system in government service. But the old Indian fighter had run out of time. He came down with pneumonia and died only one month after his inauguration.

For the first time in the nation's history, a vice president succeeded to the nation's highest office on the death of the president. John Tyler of Virginia had once been a Democrat and a strong supporter of states' rights. But after he quarreled with Jackson during the nullification controversy (see Chapter 11), Democrats refused to have anything to do with him, so Tyler joined the Whigs, who nominated him for vice president in 1840 in order to balance the ticket sectionally. During the rollicking campaign that followed, the Whigs sang all too accurately: "And we'll vote for Tyler, therefore,/ Without a why or wherefore." Indeed, once in office, Tyler repeatedly vetoed bills passed by his mentor Senator Henry Clay and his own party. Disgusted, the Whigs in Congress formally expelled their president from the party.

**Tyler's Texas Ploy** >> Although shunned by most Whigs and Democrats, Tyler still believed that he might win another four years in the White House if only he latched onto the right popular issue. That issue, he came to believe, was the annexation of Texas. In April 1844 the president sent to the Senate for ratification a treaty he had secretly negotiated to bring Texas into the Union. He also decided to run for president as an independent.

Meanwhile, the frontrunners for the Whig and Democratic presidential nominations were Clay and Van Buren. Although rivals, they were both moderates who feared that the slavery issue would be injected into the campaign if Texas was annexed as a slave state. Apparently by prearrangement, both men issued letters opposing annexation on the grounds that it threatened the Union and would provoke war with Mexico.

As expected, the Whigs unanimously nominated Clay on a platform that ignored the expansion issue entirely. But Van Buren's Democratic opponents viewed the former president as an ineffective leader who had stumbled through a depression and in 1840 gone down in ignominious defeat. They persuaded the convention to adopt a rule requiring a two-thirds vote to nominate a candidate. That blocked Van Buren's nomination. On the ninth ballot the delegates finally turned to James K. Polk of Tennessee, who favored annexation, as well as the "reoccupation" of Oregon, all the way to its northernmost boundary at 54°40′.

Angered by the convention's outcome, Van Buren's supporters in the Senate joined the Whigs in decisively defeating Tyler's treaty of annexation. Tyler eventually withdrew from the race, but the Texas issue would not go away. Seeking to shore up his support in the South, Clay announced that he would be glad to see Texas annexed if it would not lead to war. And in the North, a few antislavery Whigs turned to James G. Birney, running on the Liberty Party ticket.

In the end, Polk squeaked through by about 38,000 votes out of nearly 3 million cast. If just half of Birney's 15,000 ballots in New York had gone to Clay, he would have carried the state and been narrowly elected president by the Electoral College. Indignant Whigs charged that by refusing to support Clay, political abolitionists had made the annexation of Texas, and hence the addition of slave territory to the Union, inevitable. And indeed, in the new atmosphere following Polk's victory, Congress approved a joint resolution annexing Texas. On March 3, 1845, his last day in office, Tyler invited Texas to enter the Union.

| Candidate (Party) | Electoral Vote (%) | Popular Vote (%) |
|---|---|---|
| James K. Polk (Democratic) | 170 (61) | 1,338,464 (50) |
| Henry Clay (Whig) | 105 (39) | 1,300,097 (48) |
| James Birney (Liberty) | – | 62,300 (2) |
| Nonvoting territories | | |
| Not U.S. territory | | |

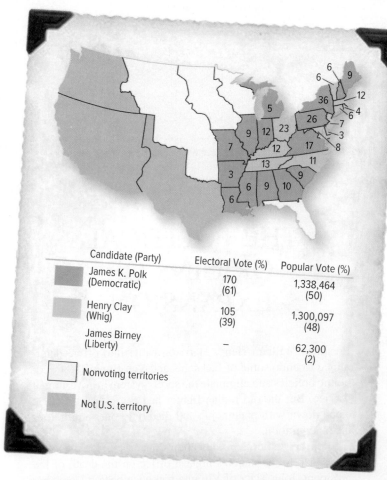

**MAP 14.4: ELECTION OF 1844**

**To the Pacific** >> Humorless, calculating, and often deceitful, President Polk pursued his objectives with dogged determination. Embracing a continental vision of the United States, he not only endorsed Tyler's offer of annexation but looked beyond, hoping to gain the three best harbors on the Pacific: Puget Sound, San Francisco, and San Diego. That meant wresting Oregon from Britain and California from Mexico.

Claiming that American title to all of Oregon was "clear and unquestionable," Polk convinced Congress to terminate the joint occupation. His blustering, which was intended to put pressure on Great Britain, gained weight by the fact that American settlers in Oregon outnumbered the British 5,000 to 750. However, Polk hardly wanted war with a nation as powerful as Great Britain. So when the British offered, in June 1846, to divide the Oregon Territory along the 49th parallel, he readily agreed (see Map 14.6). The arrangement gave the United States Puget Sound, which had been the president's objective all along.

## Provoking a War

>> The Oregon settlement left Polk free to deal with Mexico. In 1845 Congress had admitted Texas to the Union as a slave state, but Mexico had never formally recognized Texas's independence. Mexico insisted, moreover, that Texas's southern boundary was the Nueces River, not the Rio Grande, 130 miles to the south, as claimed by Texas (see Map 14.5). In reality Texas had never controlled the disputed region; the Nueces had always been Texas's boundary when it was a Mexican province; and if taken literally, the Rio Grande border incorporated most of New Mexico, including Santa Fe, Albuquerque, Taos, and other major towns. Few Texans had ever even been to these places. Indeed, the one time Texas tried to exert authority in the region, New Mexicans had to ride out onto the plains to save the lost and starving expedition. Nonetheless, Polk was already looking toward the Pacific and he supported the Rio Grande boundary.

As soon as Texas entered the Union, Mexico broke off diplomatic relations with the United States, and Polk sent American troops under General Zachary Taylor into the newly acquired state. At the same time, knowing that the unstable Mexican government desperately needed money, he attempted to buy territory to the Pacific. Sending John Slidell of Louisiana to Mexico as his special minister, Polk was prepared to offer up to $32 million in return for clear title to the Rio Grande boundary, the remaining part of New Mexico, and California. But the Mexican public overwhelmingly opposed ceding any more territory to the land-hungry "Yankees," and the government refused to receive the proposal. "Depend upon it," reported Slidell, as he departed from Mexico in March 1846, "we can never get along well with them, until we have given them a good drubbing."

Blocked on the diplomatic front, Polk ordered Taylor, who had already crossed the Nueces with 4,000 troops, to proceed south to the Rio Grande. From the Mexican standpoint, the Americans had invaded their country and occupied their territory. For his part Polk hoped that, since he could not buy the territory he wanted, at least Taylor's position on the Rio Grande would provoke the Mexican army into starting a war.

By May 9 Polk and his cabinet had lost patience with the plan and decided to submit a war message to Congress without Mexican provocation. But on that day word arrived that two weeks earlier Mexican forces had crossed the Rio Grande and attacked some of Taylor's troops, killing 11 Americans. The president quickly rewrote his war message, placing the entire blame for the war on Mexico. "Mexico has passed the boundary of the United States, has invaded our territory, and shed American blood upon American soil," he told Congress on May 11. "War exists, and notwithstanding all our efforts to avoid it, exists by the act of Mexico herself." The administration sent a bill to Congress calling for volunteers and requesting money to supply American troops.

## Indians and Mexicans

>> In battle, Mexican forces often outnumbered their American enemies. Even so, Mexico suffered from critical disadvantages in the U.S.-Mexican War. Chronic instability in its central government left the nation divided against itself in its moment of crisis. An empty national treasury fueled this instability and made it difficult to mobilize an effective response to the American invasion. Mexico was also at a disadvantage in terms of military technology. While Mexican forces relied on bulky, fixed cannons, the U.S. Army employed new light artillery that could be repositioned quickly as battles progressed. Light artillery tipped the balance in several crucial engagements.

Finally, much of Mexico had to fight two wars at once. While Mexico enjoyed formal diplomatic title to most of the present-day American West, Indians still controlled the vast majority of that territory, and Mexico had seen its relations with these Indians collapse in the 15 years before the U.S. invasion. During the late eighteenth century Comanches, Navajos, Utes, and several different tribes of Apaches had made peace with Spanish authorities, ending decades of destructive war. Spaniards provided Indian leaders with gifts, guaranteed fair trade, and even handed out rations to minimize the animal thefts that could spark conflict.

This expensive and delicate system began to falter once Mexico achieved independence in 1821. Lacking the finances, the political unity, the stability, and the diplomatic resources of Spain, Mexican authorities watched the peace with northern Indians slip away. By the early 1830s native men were traveling hundreds of miles to raid Mexican ranches, haciendas, and towns, killing or capturing the people they found there, and stealing or destroying animals and other property. Whenever they were able, Mexicans did the same things to their Indian enemies. American markets helped drive the increasing violence, as Indian or white traders from the United States eagerly purchased horses and mules stolen from Mexico. These traders supplied Indian raiders with arms and ammunition in return. By the eve of the U.S. invasion of Mexico, the violence encompassed all or parts of nine Mexican states and had claimed thousands of Mexican and Indian lives.

Thus, when American troops invaded northern Mexico, they were literally marching in the footsteps of Navajos, Kiowas, Comanches, and Apaches, traversing territory that had already endured more than a decade of war. As Indian peoples pursued their own political, strategic, and economic goals, they made it far easier for the United States to achieve its objectives. Too few northern Mexicans were willing or able to resist the U.S. conquest—impoverished, divided, and exhausted as they were by ongoing Indian raids.

## Opposition to the War

>> The war with Mexico posed a dilemma for Whigs. They were convinced (correctly) that Polk had provoked the conflict in order to acquire more territory from Mexico, and many northern Whigs accused the president of seeking to extend slavery. But they remembered, too, that the Federalist Party had doomed itself to extinction by opposing the War of 1812. Throughout the conflict, they strenuously attacked the conduct of "Mr. Polk's War." But they could not bring themselves to cut off funding for it.

# In What Country Did the U.S.-Mexican War Begin?

*When President Polk insisted that Mexico had "shed American blood upon American soil," his critics demanded proof. Everyone acknowledged that the initial clash occurred just north of the Rio Grande. But did the boundary of Texas (and hence the boundary of the United States) extend to the Rio Grande, as Polk insisted, or only to the Nueces River, as had been internationally recognized before the Texas rebellion? Nearly all Mexicans believed that the fighting happened in Mexico, and some prominent Americans agreed. Among their number was a freshman member of Congress, Abraham Lincoln, whose "spot resolutions" took Polk to task. The dispute was motivated partly by politics: Lincoln, a Whig, happily criticized the Democratic Polk. Still, Lincoln's resolutions reflected genuine doubts about the war's legitimacy.*

## DOCUMENT 1
### The War Began in the United States: President James K. Polk

The existing state of the relations between the United States and Mexico renders it proper that I should bring the subject to the consideration of Congress. . . . An envoy of the United States repaired to Mexico with full powers to adjust every existing difference. But though present on Mexican soil by agreement between the two Governments, invested with full powers, and bearing evidence of the most friendly dispositions, his mission has been unavailing. The Mexican Government not only refused to receive him or listen to his propositions, but after a long-continued series of menaces have at last invaded our territory and shed the blood of our fellow-citizens on our own soil. . . . In my message at the commencement of the present session I informed you that upon the earnest appeal both of the Congress and convention of Texas I had ordered an efficient military force to take a position "between the Nueces and Del Norte." This had become necessary to meet a threatened invasion of Texas by the Mexican forces, for which extensive military preparations had been made. The invasion was threatened solely because Texas had determined, in accordance with a solemn resolution of the Congress of the United States, to annex herself to our Union, and under these circumstances it was plainly our duty to extend our protection over her citizens and soil. . . . Meantime Texas, by the final act of our Congress, had become an integral part of our Union. The Congress of Texas, by its act of December 19, 1836, had declared the Rio del Norte to be the boundary of that Republic. Its jurisdiction had been extended and exercised beyond the Nueces. The country between that river and the Del Norte had been represented in the Congress and in the convention of Texas, had thus taken part in the act of annexation itself, and is now included within one of our Congressional districts. Our own Congress had, moreover, with great unanimity, by the act approved December 31, 1845, recognized the country beyond the Nueces as a part of our territory by including it within our own revenue system, and a revenue officer to reside within that district had been appointed by and with the advice and consent of the Senate. It became, therefore, of urgent necessity to provide for the defense of that portion of our country. . . . But no open act of hostility was committed until the 24th of April. On that day General [Mariano] Arista, who had succeeded to the command of the Mexican forces, communicated to General Taylor that "he considered hostilities commenced and should prosecute them." A party of dragoons of 63 men and officers were on the same day dispatched from the American camp up the Rio del Norte, on its left bank, to ascertain whether the Mexican troops had crossed or were preparing to cross the river, "became engaged with a large body of these troops, and after a short affair, in which some 16 were killed and wounded, appear to have been surrounded and compelled to surrender."

*Source:* Polk, James K., "Message to Congress, Washington, May 11, 1846," in *A Compilation of the Messages and Papers of the Presidents, Vol. 4*, Richardson, James D., ed. New York, NY: Bureau of National Literature and Art, 1908, pp. 437–443.

## DOCUMENT 2
### The "Spot" Was beyond the U.S. Borders: Representative Abraham Lincoln

Whereas the President of the United States, in his message of May 11, 1846, has declared that "the Mexican Government not only refused to receive him, [the envoy of the United States,] or listen to his propositions, but, after a long-continued series of menaces, has at last invaded *our territory* and shed the blood of our fellow-citizens on our *own soil*:"

And again, in his message of December 8, 1846, that "we had ample cause of war against Mexico long before the breaking out of hostilities; but even then we forbore to take redress into our own hands until Mexico herself became the aggressor, by invading *our soil* in hostile array, and shedding the blood of our citizens:"

And yet again, in his message of December 7, 1847, that "the Mexican Government refused even to hear the terms of adjustment which he [our minister of peace] was authorized to propose, and finally, under wholly unjustifiable pretexts, involved the two countries in war, by invading the territory of the State of Texas, striking the first blow, and shedding the blood of our citizens on *our own soil*." And whereas this House is desirous to obtain a full knowledge of all the facts which go to establish whether the particular spot on which the blood of our citizens was so shed was or was not at that time *our own soil*: Therefore, *Resolved By the House of*

*Representatives*, That the President of the United States be respectfully requested to inform this House—

1st. Whether the spot on which the blood of our citizens was shed, as in his messages declared, was or was not within the territory of Spain, at least after the treaty of 1819, until the Mexican revolution.

2d. Whether that spot is or is not within the territory which was wrested from Spain by the revolutionary Government of Mexico.

3d. Whether that spot is or is not within a settlement of people, which settlement has existed ever since long before the Texas revolution, and until its inhabitants fled before the approach of the United States army.

4th. Whether that settlement is or is not isolated from any and all other settlements by the Gulf and the Rio Grande on the south and west, and by wide uninhabited regions on the north and east.

5th. Whether the people of that settlement, or a majority of them, or any of them, have ever submitted themselves to the government or laws of Texas or the United States, by consent or compulsion, either by accepting office, or voting at elections, or paying tax, or serving on juries, or having process served upon them, or in any other way.

6th. Whether the people of that settlement did or did not flee from the approach of the United States army, leaving unprotected their homes and their growing crops, *before* the blood was shed, as in the messages stated; and whether the first blood, so shed, was or was not shed within the enclosure of one of the people who had thus fled from it.

7th. Whether our *citizens*, whose blood was shed, as in his message declared, were or were not, at that time, armed officers and soldiers, sent into that settlement by the military order of the President, through the Secretary of War.

8th. Whether the military force of the United States was or was not sent into that settlement after General Taylor had more than once intimated to the War Department that, in his opinion, no such movement was necessary to the defence or protection of Texas.

Resolutions introduced into the House of Representatives Dec. 22, 1847.

*Source:* "The 'Spot' Was Beyond the U.S. Borders: Representative Abraham Lincoln," December 22, 1847.

### THINKING CRITICALLY

*How does Polk justify Taylor's presence on the Rio Grande? How does Lincoln critique Taylor's presence on the Rio Grande? Do they disagree over facts, or over which facts matter? What more information would you need to decide who makes the more persuasive case?*

Prowar sentiment remained strongest in the Old Southwest and most of the Old Northwest. It was much weaker in the East, where antislavery "Conscience Whigs" were prominent. "If I were a Mexican," Senator Thomas Corwin of Ohio affirmed in the Senate, "I would tell you, . . . 'we will greet you with bloody hands and welcome you to hospitable graves.'" With their party deeply divided over the issue of the expansion of slavery, Whigs opposed the acquisition of any territory from Mexico.

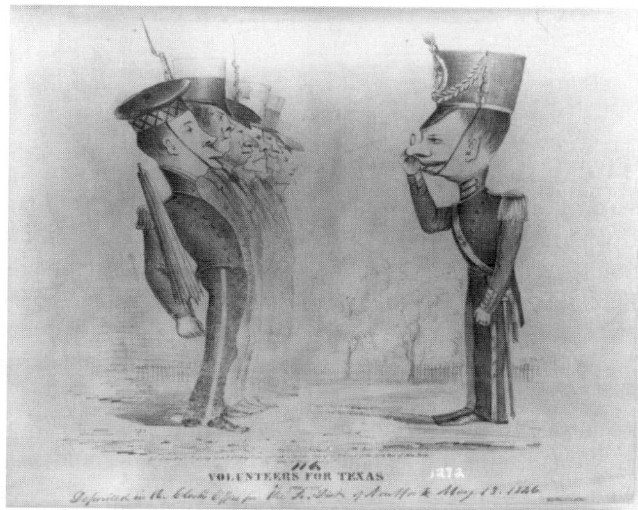
VOLUNTEERS FOR TEXAS

^ The U.S.-Mexican War was a divisive issue even at the outset, when this cartoon was published mocking early recruits. Note that one soldier holds a parasol instead of a rifle and that his prissy commander squints through a monocle.
Source: Library of Congress, Prints and Photographs Division [LC-USZ62-1272]

**Victory and Its Price** >> Even before any word of hostilities arrived in California, a group of impetuous American settlers around Sacramento launched the "Bear Flag Revolt." In June 1846 they proclaimed California an independent republic. While Mexican Californians under former governor Pio Pico organized a determined resistance, by the following January California was safely in American hands.

Meanwhile, Taylor moved south from the Rio Grande and won several battles. At each town conquered or surrendered, he read statements provided in advance by President Polk and the War Department, promising to respect private property and protect the long-suffering residents from Indian attack. Taylor's campaign culminated in a narrow victory over General Antonio López de Santa Anna at Buena Vista in southern Coahuila. Polk had gained the territory he sought to reach the Pacific and wanted an end to the war. But Mexico refused to surrender, so the president ordered an invasion into the heart of the country.

After an American army led by General Winfield Scott captured Mexico City in September 1847, Mexico agreed to terms. The two nations ratified the Treaty of Guadalupe Hidalgo in 1848. The treaty transferred half of Mexico's territory—more than half a million square miles, including Texas—to the United States. In return the United States assumed all the outstanding claims that U.S. citizens had filed against Mexico and gave the Mexicans $15 million.

The war had cost the United States $97 million and 13,000 American lives, mostly as a result of disease. Yet the real cost was even higher. By bringing vast new territories

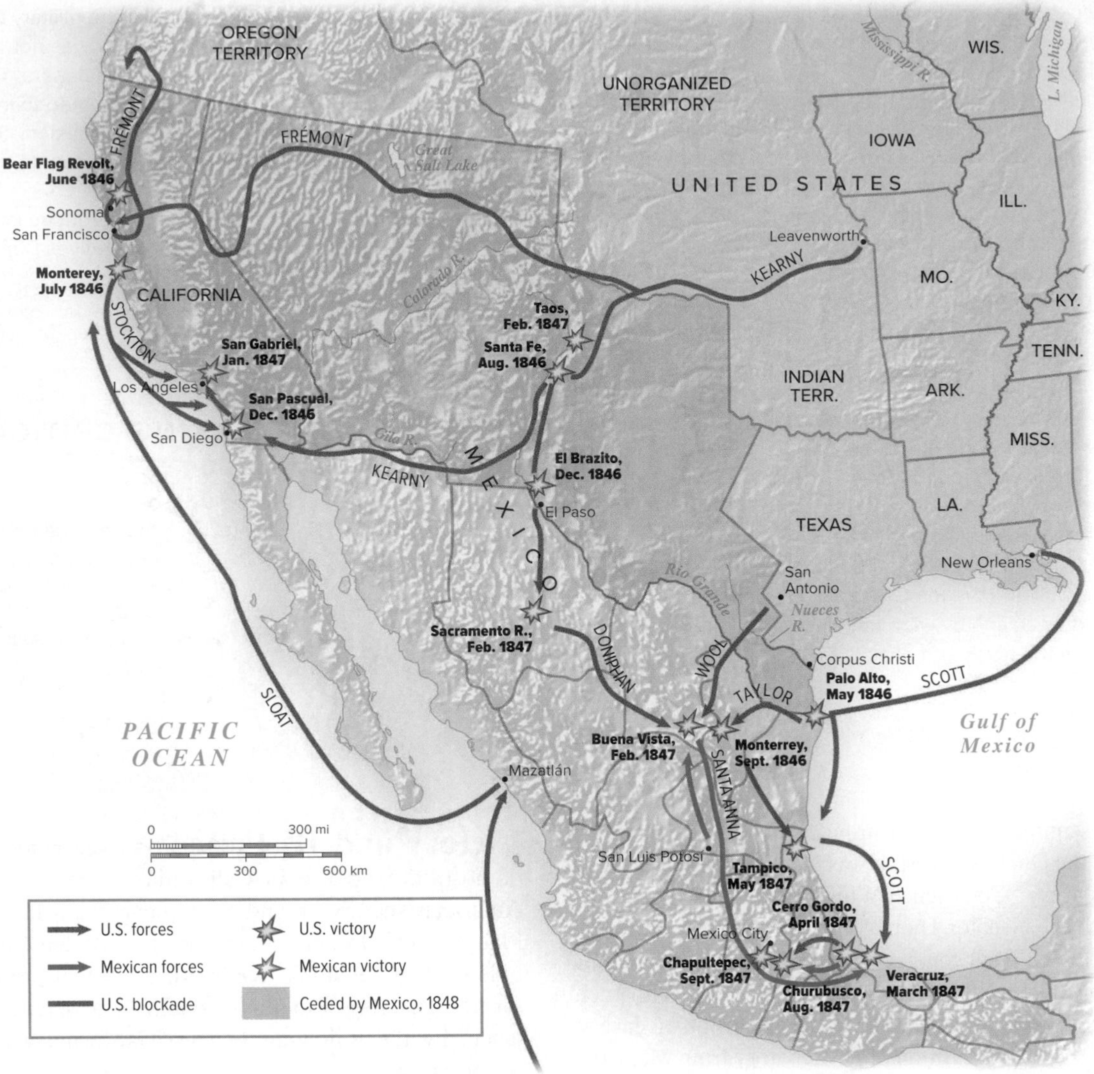

## MAP 14.5: THE U.S.–MEXICAN WAR

*How would the climate of the lands conquered by the United States be likely to affect the issue of slavery?*

into the Union, the war forced the explosive slavery issue to the center of national politics and threatened to upset the balance of power between North and South. Ralph Waldo Emerson had been prophetic: "The United States will conquer Mexico," he wrote when the war began, "but it will be as the man who swallows the arsenic which brings him down in turn. Mexico will poison us."

# Make a Case

What did the United States gain and what did it lose in the U.S.-Mexican War? Was the war justified?

**The Rise of the Slavery Issue** >> From the start, the movement to annex Texas, where slavery flourished, increased suspicions between the North and the South. And President Polk did nothing to ease this problem. Polk was a politician to his bones: constantly maneuvering, promising one thing, doing another, making a pledge, taking it back—using any means to accomplish his ends.

Discontent over his double-dealing finally erupted in August 1846, when Polk requested $2 million from Congress, as he vaguely explained, to "facilitate negotiations" with Mexico. It was widely understood that the money was to be used to bribe the Mexican government to cede territory to the United States. On August 8, David Wilmot, an obscure Pennsylvania congressman, startled Democratic leaders by introducing an amendment to the bill that barred slavery from any territory acquired from Mexico. The Wilmot

Proviso, as the amendment became known, passed the northern-controlled House of Representatives several times, only to be rejected in the Senate, where the South had more power. As such, it revealed mounting sectional tensions.

Wilmot himself was hardly an abolitionist. Indeed, he hoped to keep not only slaves but all black people out of the territories. Denying any "morbid sympathy for the slave," he declared, "I would preserve for white free labor a fair country ... where the sons of toil, of my own race and color, can live without the disgrace which association with negro slavery brings upon free labor." The Wilmot Proviso aimed not to destroy slavery in the South but to confine it to states where it already existed. Still, abolitionists had long contended that southern slaveholders—the "Slave Power"—were plotting to extend their sway over the rest of the country. The political maneuverings of slaveholders such as Tyler, and especially Polk, convinced growing numbers of northerners that the Slave Power did indeed exist.

The status of slavery in the territories became more than an abstract question once peace returned. The United States gained title to an immense territory, including all of what would become the states of California, Nevada, and Utah, nearly all of New Mexico, most of Arizona and Colorado, and parts of Wyoming, Kansas, and Oklahoma. With the United States in control of the Pacific coast from San Diego to Puget Sound, Polk's continental vision had become a reality. But slavery would once again dominate national politics.

What factors best explain the cause and the outcome of the U.S.-Mexican War?

# NEW SOCIETIES IN THE WEST

As Hispanic, Asian, Anglo-American, and dozens of different native cultures interacted, the patterns of development along the frontier varied widely. Some newcomers re-created the farm economies and small towns of the Anglo-American East; others continued the cattle-ranching life of the Hispanic West. In California the new settlements were overwhelmingly shaped by the rush for gold after 1848. And in the Great Basin around Salt Lake, the Mormons established a society whose sense of religious mission was as strong as that of the Puritans.

**Farming in the West** >> The overlanders expected to replicate the societies they had left behind. When a wagon train arrived at its destination, members had usually exhausted their resources and thus quickly scattered in search of employment or a good farm site. "Friday, October 27.—Arrived at Oregon City at the falls of the Willamette," read one pioneer diary. "Saturday, October 28.—Went to work."

In a process repeated over and over, settlers in a new area set up the machinery of government. Although violence was common on the frontier, farming communities tended to resolve problems by traditional means. Churches took time to establish, because ministers were hard to recruit and congregations were often not large enough to support a church. As the population grew, however, a more conventional society evolved. Towns and a middle class developed, the proportion of women increased, schools were established, and the residents became less mobile.

Although opportunity was greater on the frontier and early arrivals had a special advantage, more and more the agricultural frontier of the West resembled the older society of the East. With the development of markets and transportation, wealth became concentrated, some families fell to the lower rungs of society, and those who were less successful left, seeking yet another fresh start.

**The Gold Rush** >> In January 1848, while constructing a sawmill along the American River, James Marshall noticed gold flecks in the millrace. More discoveries followed, and when the news reached the East, it spread like wildfire. The following spring some 55,000 emigrants jammed the Overland Trail as "forty-niners" on the way to California. Another 25,000 traveled by boat. In only two years, from 1848 to the end of 1849, California's population jumped from 14,000 to 100,000. By 1860 it stood at 380,000.

Among those who joined the rush was William Swain, a 27-year-old farmer in western New York. Bidding good-bye to his wife and daughter in 1849, he set off for the gold fields to make his fortune. On his arrival he entered a partnership and staked a claim along the Feather River, but months of backbreaking work in icy waters led only to the discovery that his claim was "worth nothing." He sold out and joined another company, but early rains soon forced a halt to the work. In October 1850, after less than a year in the diggings, Swain returned home, only a few hundred dollars richer. He counted himself one of the vast majority of miners who had seen "their bright daydreams of golden wealth vanish like the dreams of night."

Predictably, "mining" the miners offered a more reliable road to prosperity than digging for gold. Perhaps half the inhabitants of a mining town were shopkeepers, businesspeople, and professionals who provided services for prospectors. Also conspicuous were gamblers, card sharks, and other outcasts, all bent on separating the miner from his riches.

More than 80 percent of the prospectors who poured into the gold country were Americans, including free blacks. Mexicans, Australians, Argentinians, Hawaiians, Chinese, French, English, and Irish also came. Observers praised the diggings' democratic spirit. Yet such assertions overlooked strongly held nativist prejudices: when frustrated by a lack of success, American miners directed their hostility toward foreigners. The miners ruthlessly exterminated the Indians in

^ San Francisco in 1850. In this daguerreotype, the masts of hundreds of sailing ships along the wharves appear like a forest, hemming in the chaos and overcrowding of a city thrown up over a space of months.
Source: Library of Congress, Prints and Photographs Division [LC-USZC4-7421]

the area, sometimes hunting them for sport. Mob violence drove Mexicans out of nearly every camp, and the Chinese were confined to claims abandoned by Americans as unprofitable. The state eventually enacted a foreign miners' tax that fell largely on the Chinese. Free African Americans felt the sting of discrimination as well, both in the camps and in state law. White American miners proclaimed that "colored men were not privileged to work in a country intended only for American citizens."

Only about 5 percent of gold rush emigrants were women or children; given this relative scarcity, men were willing to pay top dollar for women's domestic skills. Women supported themselves by cooking, sewing, and washing, as well as by running hotels and boardinghouses. "A smart woman can do very well in this country," one woman informed a friend in the East. "It is the only country I ever was in where a woman received anything like a just compensation for work." Women went to the mining frontier to be with their husbands, to make money, or to find adventure. But the class most frequently seen in the diggings was prostitutes, who numbered perhaps 20 percent of female Californians in 1850.

Before long the most easily worked claims had been played out, and large corporations moved in heavy equipment to get at hidden ore. Such techniques caused lasting environmental damage. Abandoned prospect holes and diggings pockmarked the gold fields and created piles of debris that heavy rains would wash down the valley, choking streams and ruining lands below. Excavation of hillsides, construction of dams to divert rivers, and the destruction of the forest cover to meet the heavy demand for lumber and firewood caused serious erosion of the soil and spring floods.

**Instant City: San Francisco** >> When the United States assumed control of California, San Francisco had a population of perhaps 200. But thousands of emigrants took the water route west, passing through San Francisco's harbor on their way to the diggings. By 1856 the city's population had jumped to an astonishing 50,000. In a mere 8 years the city had attained the size New York had taken 190 years to reach.

San Francisco developed in helter-skelter fashion. Residents lived in tents or poorly constructed, half-finished buildings. Land prices soared, speculation was rampant, and commercial forces dominated. To enlarge the commercial district, hills began to be leveled, with the dirt used to fill in the bay (thereby creating more usable land). Since the city government took virtually no role in directing development, almost no land was reserved for public use. Property owners defeated a proposal to widen the streets, prompting the city's leading newspaper to complain, "To sell a few more feet of lots, the streets were compressed like a cheese, into half their width."

**The Migration from China** >> The gold rush that swelled San Francisco's streets was a global phenomenon. Americans predominated in the mining population, but Latin Americans, Europeans, Australians, and Chinese flocked to California. An amazing assortment of languages could be heard on the city's streets: indeed, in 1860 San Francisco was 50 percent foreign-born.

The most distinctive ethnic group was the Chinese. They had come to Gum San, the land of the golden mountain. Those who arrived in California overwhelmingly hailed from the area of southern China around Canton (Guangdong)—and not by accident. Although other provinces also suffered from economic distress, population pressures, social unrest, and political upheaval, Canton had a large European presence, since it was the only port open to outsiders. That situation changed after the first Opium War (1839–1842), when Britain forced China to open other ports to trade. For Cantonese the sudden loss of their trade monopoly produced widespread economic hardship. At the same time, a series of religious and political revolts in the region led to fighting that devastated the countryside. Many residents concluded that emigration was the only way to survive, and Western ships in the harbors of Canton and nearby Hong Kong (a British possession since 1842) made it easier to migrate to California rather than to Southeast Asia.

Between 1849 and 1854 some 45,000 Chinese flocked to California. Like other gold seekers, Chinese immigrants were overwhelmingly young and male, and they wanted only to accumulate savings and return home to their families. (Indeed, only 16 Chinese women arrived before 1854.) Generally poor, Chinese immigrants arrived already in debt, having borrowed the price of their steamship ticket; they fell further into debt to Chinese merchants in San Francisco, who loaned them money to purchase needed supplies.

When the Chinese were harassed in the mines, many opened laundries in San Francisco and elsewhere, since little capital was required—soap, scrub board, iron, and ironing board. Other Chinese around San Francisco set up restaurants or worked in the fishing industry. In these early years they found Americans less hostile, as long as they stayed away from the gold fields. As immigration and the competition for jobs increased, however, anti-Chinese sentiment intensified.

Gradually, San Francisco took on the trappings of an orderly community. The city government established a public school system, erected streetlights, created a municipal water system, and halted further filling-in of the bay. Industry was confined to the area south of the city; several new working-class neighborhoods grew up near the downtown section. Fashionable neighborhoods sprouted on several hills, as high rents drove many residents from the developing commercial center, and churches and families became more common. By 1856 the ramshackle city of the gold rush had been replaced by an orderly metropolis whose stone and brick buildings gave it a sense of permanence.

**California Genocide** >> Eager to possess native land, resources, and even Indian slaves; determined to avenge Indian thefts or attacks (real or imagined); or anxious about imagined Indian conspiracies, many white Californians attempted to exterminate the state's indigenous population.

In 1859 California's governor hired notorious Indian killer Walter S. Jarboe to kill or capture any Yuki Indians found outside their newly established reservation, in northwestern California. After four months Jarboe boasted that he and his men had killed or captured nearly 500 Yuki. "However cruel it may be," Jarboe candidly explained, "nothing short of extermination will suffice to rid the Country of them." Some white Californians protested Jarboe's "deliberate, cowardly, brutal massacre of defenseless men, women, and children." But others celebrated, and the state legislature reimbursed Jarboe and men like him for their expenses. Washington encouraged extermination by rejecting treaties that might have provided

>> With their distinctive clothing and bamboo hats, Chinese miners could be seen throughout the diggings. Chinese immigration reached a peak in 1852, when 20,000 arrived in California. In the heyday of the mining camp, perhaps 20 percent of the miners were Chinese. Confronted with intense hostility from other miners, they worked abandoned claims and unpromising sites with primitive and less expensive equipment.
©Archive Photos/Getty Images

Indians some land and security, ignoring the pleas of dismayed federal Indian agents. The federal government reimbursed California nearly $1.5 million for the costs of its ongoing Indian campaigns. Survivors lived to see the seizure of their historic territories, the destruction of the animals they relied upon, profound ecological transformation through overgrazing and hydraulic mining, and the dissolution of families through kidnapping and enslavement. In 1850 the California legislature passed the "Act for the Government and Protection of Indians." The measure legalized the seizure and forced labor of Indian children, as well as the capture of native men and women for loitering, begging, or leading "an immoral or profligate course of life." People seized on these counts were leased out to the highest bidder, for a four-month term of forced labor. By the late 1850s white observers reported Indian villages comprised almost totally of adults, most of the children "doubtless having been stolen and sold."

Though population estimates are imprecise, few historians doubt that California's Indians experienced a demographic, social, and spiritual catastrophe in the mid-nineteenth century. In the 20 years following the U.S.-Mexican War, homicide, displacement, captivity, forced labor, malnutrition, disease, and social trauma reduced the state's native population from perhaps 150,000 to some 30,000. That said, men like Jarboe and their patrons in state and national government failed to "exterminate" California's Indians. Native men, women, and children employed a host of tactics to protect their families and preserve their cultures and values. Today hundreds of thousands of Californians self-identify as Native American, many of them descended from survivors of the California genocide.

## The Mormons in Utah >>

The makeshift, often chaotic society spawned by the gold rush was a product of largely uncontrolled economic forces. In contrast, the society evolving in the Great Basin of Utah exhibited an entirely different but equally remarkable growth. Salt Lake City became the center of a religious kingdom established by the Church of Jesus Christ of Latter-day Saints, also known as the Mormon Church.

After founder Joseph Smith's death in 1844, the Mormon Church was led by Brigham Young, who lacked Smith's religious mysticism but was a brilliant organizer. Young decided to move his followers to the Great Basin, an isolated area a thousand miles from the settled parts of the United States. In 1847 the first thousand settlers arrived, the vanguard of thousands more who extended Mormon settlement throughout the valley of the Great Salt Lake and the West. Church officials also held the government positions, and Young had supreme power in legislative, executive, and judicial matters as well as religious affairs. In 1849 the state of Deseret was officially established, with Brigham Young as governor. It applied for admission to the Union.

The most controversial church teaching was the doctrine of polygamy, or plural marriage, which Young sanctioned publicly in 1852. Visitors reported with surprise that few Mormon wives seemed to rebel against the practice. Some plural wives developed close friendships; indeed, in one sample almost a third of plural marriages included at least two sisters. Moreover, because polygamy distinguished Mormonism from other religions, plural wives saw it as an expression of their religious faith. "I want to be assured of *position in God's estimation*," one such wife explained. "If polygamy is the Lord's order, we must carry it out."

The Mormons connected control of water to their sense of mission and respect for hierarchy. Mormon settlements spread throughout the arid Salt Lake Valley, all connected to

FLOUR

CROSSING THE PLAINS WITH A HAND-CART.

^ In 1847 about a thousand Mormons trekked across the Great Plains to the Great Salt Lake. Thousands more soon followed, many of them hauling their belongings using only handcarts. ©North Wind Picture Archives/Alamy and dependent upon a centralized system of dams, aqueducts, and ditches. By 1850 there were more than 16,000 irrigated acres in what would eventually become the state of Utah.

Manipulation of water reinforced the Mormons' sense of hierarchy and group discipline. In a radical departure from American ideals, church leaders insisted that water belonged to the community, not individuals, and vested this authority in the hands of the local bishop. Control of scarce water resources reinforced the power of the church hierarchy over not just the faithful but dissidents as well. Community needs, as interpreted by church leaders, took precedence over individual rights. Thus irrigation did more than make the desert bloom. By checking the Jeffersonian ideal of an independent, self-sufficient farmer, it also made possible a centralized, well-regulated society under the firm control of the Mormon Church.

**Mexican American Rights and Property** >> At the conclusion of the U.S.-Mexican War, some 100,000 Mexican citizens suddenly found themselves living inside the newly expanded United States. The Treaty of Guadalupe Hidalgo guaranteed them "the free enjoyment of their liberty and property." Mexican negotiators understood how critical that was: without land, their former citizens would enjoy neither economic security nor political influence in their new country. But the treaty said little about how Mexican Americans would prove their ownership of land. They rarely had the sort of documentation that American courts expected. Differences in legal culture, combined with racism and pervasive fraud, led to the dispossession and impoverishment of most Spanish-speaking property holders in the Southwest.

California's Land Act of 1851 required everyone with Spanish- or Mexican-era claims to document them within two years. Hundreds failed to file claims in the time allotted, and by the terms of the Land Act all their territories passed into the public domain. The board eventually confirmed three-quarters of the claims it did receive. But resolution often took years and proved to be enormously expensive. Property owners had to mortgage their lands to pay legal fees, and in the end the great majority lost everything. Claimants in New Mexico likewise lost vast tracts of lands to Anglo ranchers and, especially, to lawyers. The lengthy and expensive review process left Mexican and Pueblo Indian claimants holding only about 6 percent of the lands they had possessed before the U.S. invasion.

Tejanos faced similar pressures. Stigmatized and despised by whites as racial inferiors, they were the poorest group in free society. One response to this dislocation, an option commonly taken by persecuted minorities, was social banditry. An example was the folk hero Juan Cortina. A member of a displaced landed family in southern Texas, Cortina was driven into resistance in the 1850s by American harassment. He began stealing from wealthy Anglos to aid poor Mexicans, proclaiming, "To me is entrusted the breaking of the chains of your slavery." Cortina continued to raid Texas border settlements until finally he was imprisoned by Mexican authorities. While failing to produce any lasting change, Cortina demonstrated the depth of frustration and resentment among Hispanics over their abuse at the hands of the new Anglo majority.

 **REVIEW**

Who were the winners and the losers in the gold rush? Why?

# ESCAPE FROM CRISIS

With the return of peace, Congress confronted the problem of whether to allow slavery in the newly acquired territories. David Wilmot, in his controversial proviso, had already proposed outlawing slavery throughout the Mexican cession. John C. Calhoun, representing the extreme southern position, countered that slavery was legal in all territories. The federal government had acted as the agent of all the states in acquiring the land, Calhoun argued, and southerners had a right to take their property there, including slaves. Only when the residents of a territory drafted a state constitution could they decide the question of slavery.

Two moderate positions softened these extremes. One proposed extending the Missouri Compromise line of 36°30′ to the Pacific, which would have continued the earlier policy of dividing the national domain between the North and the South. The other proposal, championed by Senator Lewis Cass of Michigan and Senator Stephen A. Douglas of Illinois, was to allow the people of the territory rather than Congress to decide the status of slavery. This solution, which became known as *popular sovereignty*, was tactically ambiguous, since its supporters refused to specify whether the residents could make this decision at any time or only when drafting a state constitution, as Calhoun insisted.

When Congress organized the Oregon Territory in 1848, it prohibited slavery there, since even southerners admitted that the region was too far north to grow the South's staple crops. But this seemingly straightforward decision made it impossible to apply the Missouri Compromise line to the other territories. With Oregon already firmly committed to outlawing slavery, the greater part of the remaining land split by the Compromise line would be open to slavery. That included New Mexico, Arizona, and southern California. Northern members of Congress balked at that solution, especially since supporters of the Wilmot Proviso had wanted slavery barred from *all* territories acquired from Mexico. Almost inadvertently, one of the two moderate solutions had been discarded by the summer of 1848.

**A Two-Faced Campaign** >> In the election of 1848 both major parties tried to avoid the slavery issue. The Democrats nominated Lewis Cass, a supporter of popular sovereignty, while the Whigs bypassed all their prominent leaders and selected General Zachary Taylor, who had taken no position on any public issue and who remained silent throughout the campaign. The Whigs adopted no platform and planned instead to emphasize the general's war record.

But the slavery question would not go away. A new antislavery coalition, the **Free Soil Party**, brought together northern Democrats who had rallied to the Wilmot Proviso; Conscience Whigs, who disavowed Taylor's nomination because he was a slaveholder; and political abolitionists in the Liberty Party. To gain more votes, the Free Soil platform focused on the dangers of extending slavery rather than on the evil of slavery itself. Ironically, the party nominated Martin Van Buren—the man who for years had struggled to keep the slavery issue out of national politics.

**Free Soil Party** antislavery party formed in 1848 by northern Democrats disillusioned with southern Democratic support for slavery.

Both the Whigs and the Democrats ran different campaigns in the North and the South. To southern audiences, each party promised it would protect slavery in the territories; to northern voters, each claimed it would keep the territories free. In this two-faced, sectional campaign, the Whigs won their second national victory. Taylor held on to the core of Whig voters in both sections. But in the South, where the contest pitted a southern slaveholder against two northerners, Taylor won many more votes than Clay had in 1844. As one southern Democrat complained, "We have lost hundreds of votes, solely on the ground that General Cass was a Northerner and General Taylor a Southern man." Furthermore, Van Buren polled five times as many votes as the Liberty Party had four years earlier. Increasingly, the two national political parties were being pulled apart along sectional lines.

^ Nicknamed "Old Rough and Ready," General Zachary Taylor was indifferent to fancy dress uniforms and blunt in speech and manner. But Whig party leaders managed to keep the war hero from saying much during the election campaign of 1848. A slaveholder from Louisiana, many southern voters assumed Taylor would wish to extend slavery into the newly annexed territories. They were in for a surprise.


## The Compromise of 1850 >>

Once he became president Taylor could no longer remain silent. The territories gained from Mexico had to be organized; furthermore, by 1849 California had gained enough residents to be admitted as a state. In the Senate the balance of power between North and South stood at 15 states each. California's admission would break the sectional balance.

Called "Old Rough and Ready" by his troops, Taylor was a forthright man of action, but politically inexperienced and prone to oversimplify complex problems. Since even Calhoun admitted that entering states had the right to ban slavery, Taylor naively proposed that the way to end the sectional crisis was to skip the territorial stage and admit the new lands directly as states. He suggested that the entire Mexican cession be split into two huge states, New Mexico and California. Even more shocking to southern Whigs, he proposed to apply the Wilmot Proviso to the entire area, since he believed slavery would never flourish there. When Congress convened in December 1849, Taylor recommended that California and New Mexico be admitted as free states. The president's plan touched off the most serious sectional crisis the Union had yet confronted.

Into this turmoil stepped Henry Clay, now 73 years old and nearing the end of his career. A savvy card player all his life, Clay loved the bargaining, the wheeling and dealing, the late-night trade-offs eased along by a bottle of bourbon that were part of politics. Clay sought a grand compromise to end all disputes between the North and the South and save the Union. Already, Mississippi had summoned a southern convention to meet at Nashville to discuss the crisis, and extremists spoke openly about secession.

Clay's compromise, submitted in January 1850, addressed all the major controversies between the two sections. California, he proposed, should be admitted as a free state, which represented the clear wishes of most settlers there. The rest of the Mexican cession would be organized as two territories, New Mexico and Utah, under the doctrine of **popular sovereignty**. Thus slavery would not be prohibited in these regions. Clay also proposed that Congress abolish the slave trade but not slavery itself in the District of Columbia and that a new, more rigorous fugitive slave law be passed to enable southerners to reclaim runaway slaves. To reinforce the idea that both North and South were yielding ground, Clay combined those provisions

**popular sovereignty** doctrine, devised by Senator Stephen A. Douglas of Illinois, that a territory could decide by vote whether or not to permit slavery within its boundaries.

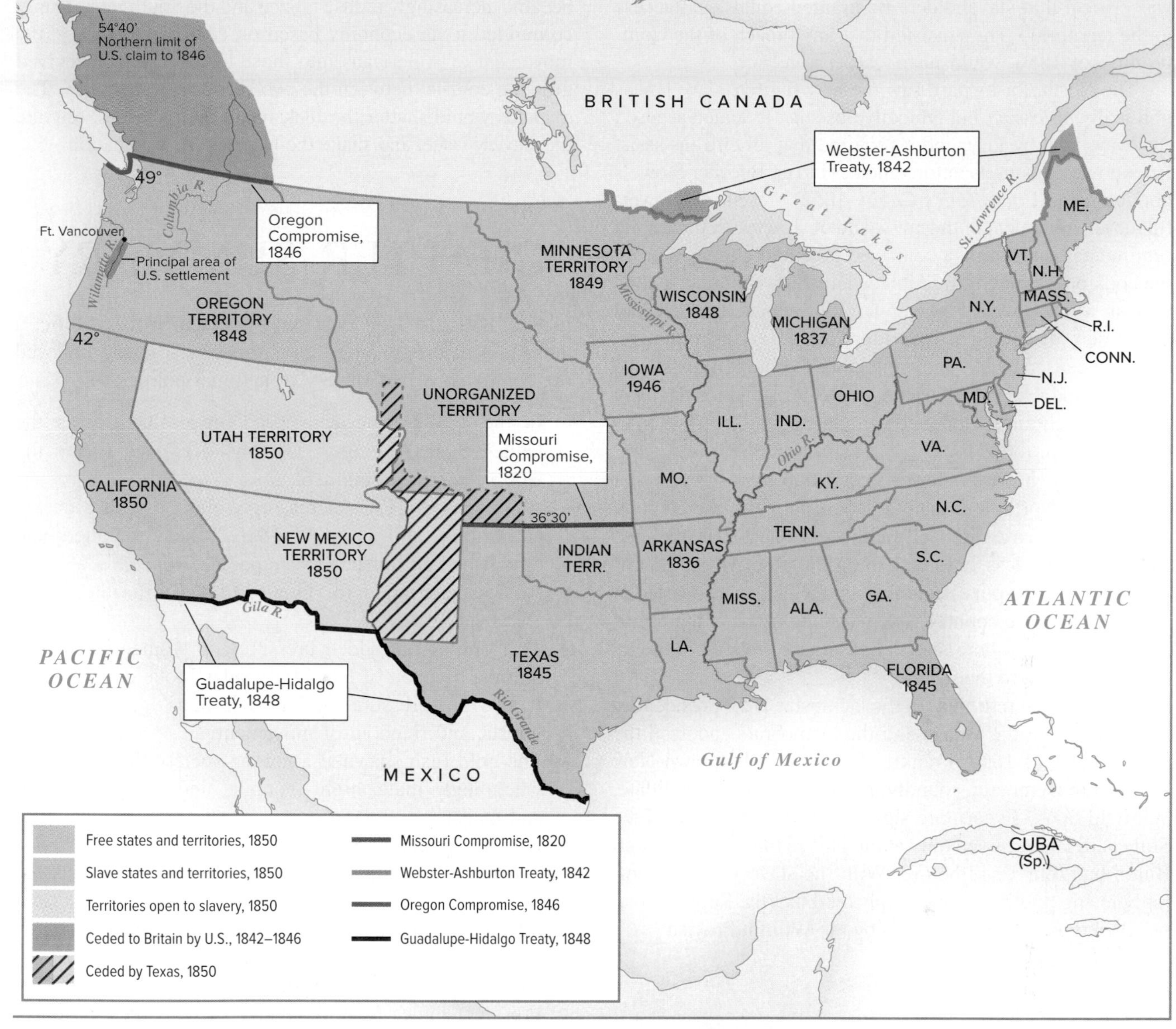

54°40'
Northern limit of
U.S. claim to 1846
BRITISH CANADA
Webster-Ashburton
Treaty, 1842
49°
Columbia R.
Oregon
Compromise,
1846
Great Lakes
St. Lawrence R.
ME.
Ft. Vancouver
Willamette R.
Principal area of
U.S. settlement
MINNESOTA
TERRITORY
1849
Mississippi R.
VT.
N.H.
MASS.
N.Y.
R.I.
CONN.
WISCONSIN
1848
MICHIGAN
1837
OREGON
TERRITORY
1848
42°
PA.
N.J.
DEL.
MD.
IOWA
1946
OHIO
UNORGANIZED
TERRITORY
ILL.
IND.
UTAH TERRITORY
1850
Missouri
Compromise,
1820
Ohio R.
VA.
CALIFORNIA
1850
MO.
KY.
N.C.
36°30'
TENN.
NEW MEXICO
TERRITORY
1850
INDIAN
TERR.
ARKANSAS
1836
S.C.
Gila R.
MISS.
ALA.
GA.
ATLANTIC
OCEAN
PACIFIC
OCEAN
LA.
TEXAS
1845
FLORIDA
1845
Guadalupe-Hidalgo
Treaty, 1848
Rio Grande
Gulf of Mexico
MEXICO
Free states and territories, 1850
Slave states and territories, 1850
Territories open to slavery, 1850
Ceded to Britain by U.S., 1842–1846
Ceded by Texas, 1850
Missouri Compromise, 1820
Webster-Ashburton Treaty, 1842
Oregon Compromise, 1846
Guadalupe-Hidalgo Treaty, 1848
CUBA
(Sp.)


## MAP 14.6: TERRITORIAL GROWTH AND THE COMPROMISE OF 1850

*Why weren't slavery's champions in the 1850s content with the limits established in the Missouri Compromise?*

that dealt with the Mexican cession (and several others adjusting the Texas–New Mexico border) into a larger package known as the Omnibus Bill. With the stakes so high, the Senate debated the bill for six months—and then rejected it.

With Clay exhausted and his strategy in shambles, Democrat Stephen A. Douglas assumed leadership of the pro-compromise forces. The sudden death in July of President Taylor, who had threatened to veto Clay's plan, aided the compromise movement. One by one Douglas submitted the individual measures for a vote. Northern representatives provided the necessary votes to admit California and abolish the slave trade in the District of Columbia, while southern representatives supplied the edge needed to organize the Utah and New Mexico territories and pass the new fugitive slave law. On the face of it everyone had compromised. But in truth only 61 members of Congress, a mere 21 percent of the membership, had not voted against some part of Clay's compromise.

By September 17 all the separate parts of the Compromise of 1850 had passed and been signed into law by the new president, Millard Fillmore. The Union, it seemed, was safe.

**Away from the Brink** >> The general public rallied to the Compromise of 1850. Still, most southerners felt that a firm line had been drawn. With California's admission, they were now outnumbered in the Senate, so it was critical that slaveholders be granted equal legal access to the territories. They insisted that any breach of the Compromise of 1850 would justify secession.

The North, for its part, saw the new fugitive slave law as politically necessary but ethically obscene. It denied accused runaways trial by jury, and it required that all citizens assist federal marshals in its enforcement. Harriet Beecher Stowe's popular novel *Uncle Tom's Cabin* (1852) presented a powerful moral indictment of the law—and of slavery itself. Despite sentimental characters, a contrived plot, and clumsy dialect, the book profoundly moved its readers. Stowe dramatized the ways in which slavery broke up families, violated the chastity of women, discouraged individual ambition and initiative, and even caused blacks and white alike to doubt the existence of a just God. Her novel reached a greater audience than any previous abolitionist work and stimulated moral opposition to the institution.

In reality, however, fewer than 1,000 slaves a year ran away to the North, and many of those failed in the attempt. Despite some cases of well-publicized resistance, the free states more or less enforced the 1850 fugitive slave law. Stephen Douglas spoke accurately enough when he boasted in 1851, "The whole country is acquiescing in the compromise measures—everywhere, North and South. Nobody proposes to repeal or disturb them."

And so calm returned. In the lackluster 1852 presidential campaign, both the Whigs and the Democrats endorsed the Compromise of 1850. Franklin Pierce, a little-known New Hampshire Democrat, soundly defeated the Whig candidate, Winfield Scott. Even more significant, the antislavery Free Soil candidate received only about half as many votes as Van Buren had four years before. With the slavery issue seemingly losing political force, it appeared that the Republic had weathered the storm unleashed by the Wilmot Proviso.

**REVIEW**

What was the crisis of 1850, and how was it averted?

The moving frontier had worked many changes during the 1830s and 1840s, and many more upheavals awaited the decade ahead. From a continental point of view, political relations among the United States, Mexico, and the Indian peoples had shifted significantly. Indian attacks on Mexico in the 1820s and 1830s had weakened Mexico's ability to repel an invasion by the United States. And with the Treaty of Guadalupe Hidalgo, the United States gained over half a million square miles, as its frontier leaped from the Mississippi valley to the Pacific Ocean.

In between remained territory still unorganized and still controlled by formidable Indian peoples. And as the North became increasingly industrialized and the South more firmly committed to an economy based on cotton and slavery, the movement of Americans into those territories soon revived growing conflict between the two sections over slavery. The disputes would shatter the Jacksonian party system, reignite the slavery issue, and shake the Union to its foundation.

# CHAPTER SUMMARY

In the 1840s the United States expanded to the Pacific, a development that required an aggressive war and renewed the controversy over slavery in national politics.

- In the 1840s Americans proclaimed that it was the United States' Manifest Destiny to expand across the North American continent.
- Americans in Texas increasingly clashed with Mexican authorities, and in 1835–1836 Texans revolted and established an independent republic.
- Americans headed for Oregon and California on the Overland Trail.
- The journey put added pressures on women as the traditional division of labor by gender broke down.
- It also put pressure on Plains Indians' grazing lands, forests, and freedom of movement.
- The gold rush spawned a unique society that was overwhelmingly male, highly mobile, and strongly nativist and racist.
- Led by Brigham Young, the Mormons established a tightly organized, centrally controlled society in the Great Salt Lake basin.
- Throughout the Southwest, Hispanic residents suffered at the hands of the new Anglo majority, as did the Chinese immigrants in California.
- President James K. Polk entered office with a vision of the United States as a continental nation. He upheld President John Tyler's annexation of Texas and agreed to divide the Oregon country with Britain.
- Polk instigated a war with Mexico in order to obtain that country's northern territories. Impoverished and distracted by ongoing wars with Indians, Mexico ended up surrendering more than half a million square miles of territory.
- The U.S.-Mexican War reinjected the slavery issue into American national politics.
- The Wilmot Proviso sought to prohibit slavery from any territory acquired from Mexico. The struggle over the proviso eventually disrupted both major parties.
- Congress momentarily stilled the sectional crisis with the Compromise of 1850.

## Additional Reading

For the Sioux, see Richard White, "The Winning of the West: The Expansion of the Western Sioux in the Eighteenth and Nineteenth Centuries," *Journal of American History* (1978), pp. 319–343; and Jeffery Ostler, *The Lakotas and the Black Hills* (2011). For the traumas and challenges facing one Plains Indian community, see Elizabeth Fenn's haunting *Encounters at the Heart of the World* (2015). Western trading families are the focus of Anne Hyde's sweeping *Empires, Nations, and Families* (2002). David J. Weber, *The Mexican Frontier, 1821–1846* (1982), is a superb study of the Southwest prior to American control. For a transnational interpretation of the Texas Rebellion, see Andrés Reséndez, *Changing National Identities at the Frontier* (2005). For the Overland Trail, see John Mack Faragher, *Women and Men on the Overland Trail* (2001). *Mormonism: A Very Short Introduction* (2008), by Richard Bushman, is an elegant primer. For California's missions, see Steven W. Hackel's *Children of Coyote, Missionaries of St. Francis* (2005). Susan Lee Johnson's *Roaring Camp* (2001) explores social interaction during the California gold rush. For the environmental consequences of mining, see Andrew Isenberg's *Mining California* (2005).

The fullest treatment of American life in this period is Daniel Walker Howe's magisterial *What Hath God Wrought* (2007). Thomas R. Hietala examines the social roots of expansionism in *Manifest Design* (rev. ed., 2002). For Indians and the geopolitics of the era, see Brian DeLay, *War of a Thousand Deserts: Indian Raids and the U.S.-Mexican War* (2008). Andrew Torget's *Seeds of Empire* (2015) excavates the centrality of cotton to turning points in Texas's nineteenth-century history. The best discussion of Polk's handling of the Oregon and Texas issues remains David M. Pletcher, *The Diplomacy of Annexation* (1973). Amy Greenberg's *A Wicked War* (2012) is a marvelous study of American politics and the war in Mexico. Michael F. Holt powerfully analyzes the Whig Party's difficulties in *The Rise and Fall of the American Whig Party* (1999). For the California Indian genocide, see Brendan C. Lindsay, *Murder State* (2012); and Benjamin Madley, *An American Genocide* (2016). Howard Lamar's classic account *The Far Southwest* (1966) explores political and economic power in the territories after conquest. Holman Hamilton, *Prologue to Conflict* (new ed., 2005), is an excellent study of the Compromise of 1850.

# 15 The Union Broken

## 1850–1861

As Kansas became a battleground over whether slavery would expand into the new territories, pro- and antislavery factions clashed. This drawing depicts "border ruffians" from Missouri destroying the Free State Hotel. What evidence from the opening narrative suggests that the artist took liberties with this illustration? Does the drawing betray northern or southern sympathies? Why?



## >> An American Story

## THE SACKING OF A KANSAS TOWN

Into town they rode, several hundred strong, unshaven, rough-talking men, "armed . . . to the teeth with rifles and revolvers, cutlasses and bowie-knives." At the head of the procession flapped an American flag, alongside another featuring a crouching tiger emblazoned on black and white stripes; these were followed by banners proclaiming "Southern Rights" and "The Superiority of the White Race." At the rear rolled five artillery pieces. Watching intently from his office window, Josiah Miller, the editor of the *Kansas Free State*, predicted, "Well, boys, we're in for it."

Lawrence, Kansas, had been founded by the New England Emigrant Aid Company, a Yankee association that recruited settlers in an effort to keep Kansas Territory from becoming a slave state. Accepting Senator Stephen Douglas's idea that the people should decide the status of slavery, the town's residents intended to see to it that under this doctrine of "popular sovereignty" Kansas entered the Union as a free state. Emigrants from the neighboring slave state of Missouri were equally determined that no "abolition tyrants" would control the territory. Conflict erupted in Kansas almost immediately.

The federal government seemed to back the proslavery forces. In the spring of 1856 a U.S. district court indicted several of Lawrence's leading citizens for treason, and federal marshal Israel Donaldson led a posse, swelled by eager volunteers from across the Missouri border, to Lawrence on May 20 to make the arrests.

Meanwhile, Lawrence's "committee of safety" had agreed on a policy of nonresistance. Donaldson arrested two men without incident and, finding no one else on his list, dismissed his posse. But Sheriff Samuel Jones, who on his previous visit to Lawrence had been shot, had a score to settle. The irate sheriff took over the band and led the cheering, thoroughly liquored "army" into town at three o'clock in the afternoon. Ignoring the pleas of some leaders, the mob smashed the presses of Miller's *Kansas Free State* as well as that of the *Herald of Freedom*. Then the horde unsuccessfully tried to blow up the now-deserted Free State Hotel, which more closely resembled a fort, before finally putting it to the torch. When the mob rode off, it left the residents of Lawrence unharmed but thoroughly terrified.

Retaliation by free-state partisans was not long in coming. Hurrying north along a different road to Lawrence, an older man with a grim face and steely eyes heard the news that the town had been attacked. "Old Man Brown," as everyone called him, was on his way with several of his sons to provide reinforcements. A severe, God-fearing Calvinist and staunch abolitionist, John Brown had once remarked to a friend that he believed "God had raised him up on purpose to break the jaws of the wicked."

Brooding over the failure of the free-staters to resist the "slave hounds" from Missouri, Brown headed toward Pottawatomie Creek in Franklin County, Kansas, on the night of May 24, with half a dozen others, including his sons. Announcing that they were the "Northern Army" come to serve justice, they burst into the cabin of James Doyle, a proslavery man from Tennessee, with cutlasses drawn. As Brown marched off Doyle and his three sons, Doyle's terrified wife, Mahala, begged him to spare her youngest, and the old man relented. The others were led no more than 100 yards down the road before Owen and Salmon Brown hacked them to death with broadswords. Old Man Brown then walked up to James Doyle's body and put a bullet through his forehead. Before the night was done, two more cabins had been visited and two more proslavery settlers brutally executed. Not one of the five murdered men owned a single slave or had any connection with the raid on Lawrence.

Brown's action precipitated a new wave of fighting in Kansas and controversy throughout the nation. "Everybody here feels as if we are upon a volcano," remarked one congressman in Washington.

Indeed, that smoldering volcano did finally erupt in the spring of 1861, showering civil war, death, and destruction across the land. Popular sovereignty, the last remaining moderate solution to the controversy over the expansion of slavery, had failed dismally. The violence and disorder in Kansas provided a stark reply to Stephen Douglas's proposition: What could be more peaceable, more fair than the notion of popular sovereignty? <<

**Startling News!**

**OUR BORDER IN DANGER!!**

**Missouri to be Invaded!**

We have authority which will not admit of doubt, for stating that Lane, with 3000 lawless abolitionists, and 10 pieces of artillery, is about to march into Missouri, and sack the border towns of Lexington, Independence, Westport, and New Santa Fe. This is no idle rumor; and there can be no doubt of it. These desperadoes swear t hey wil carry everything before them, and spare nothing.

^ A proslavery newspaper—Missouri was never invaded.

## THEMATIC TIMELINE

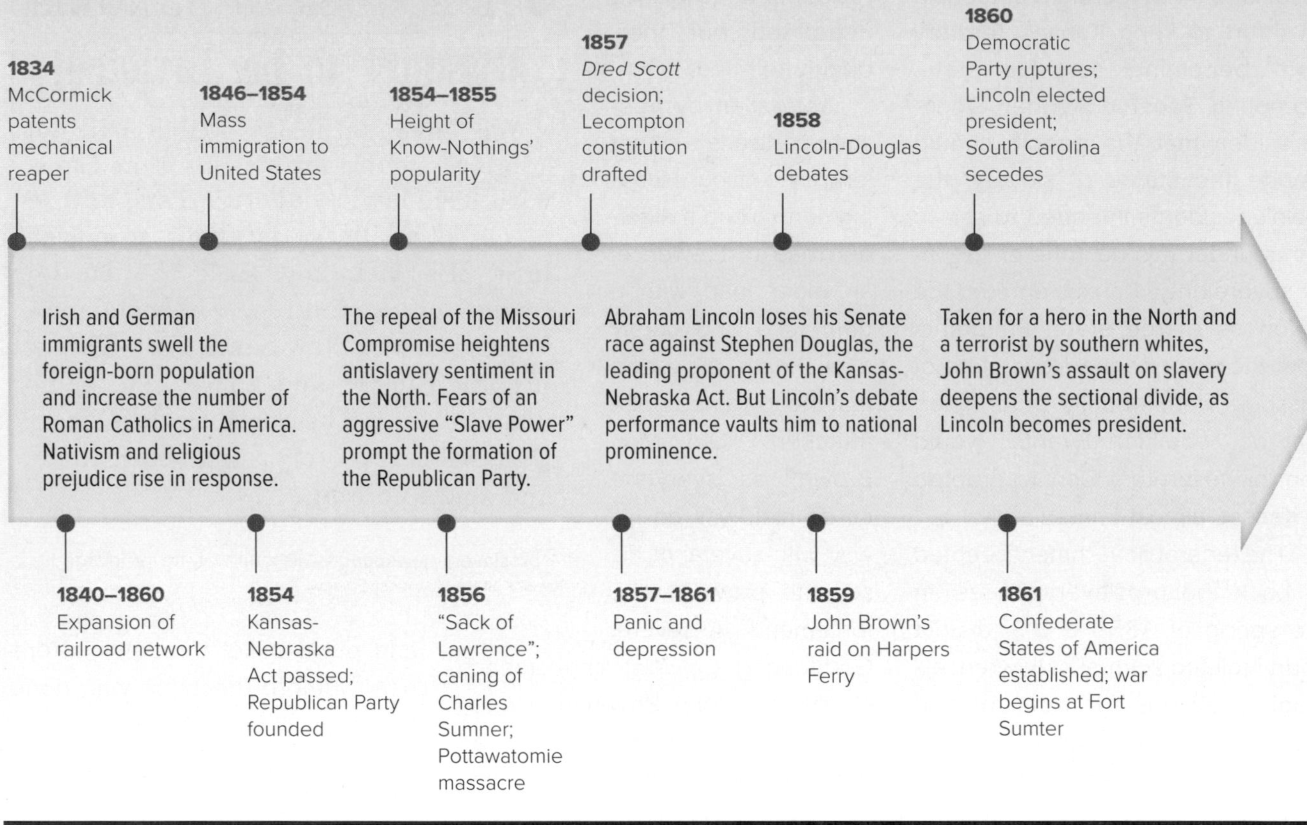
1834
McCormick patents mechanical reaper
1846–1854
Mass immigration to United States
1854–1855
Height of Know-Nothings' popularity
1857
*Dred Scott* decision; Lecompton constitution drafted
1858
Lincoln-Douglas debates
1860
Democratic Party ruptures; Lincoln elected president; South Carolina secedes
Irish and German immigrants swell the foreign-born population and increase the number of Roman Catholics in America. Nativism and religious prejudice rise in response.
The repeal of the Missouri Compromise heightens antislavery sentiment in the North. Fears of an aggressive "Slave Power" prompt the formation of the Republican Party.
Abraham Lincoln loses his Senate race against Stephen Douglas, the leading proponent of the Kansas-Nebraska Act. But Lincoln's debate performance vaults him to national prominence.
Taken for a hero in the North and a terrorist by southern whites, John Brown's assault on slavery deepens the sectional divide, as Lincoln becomes president.
1840–1860
Expansion of railroad network
1854
Kansas-Nebraska Act passed; Republican Party founded
1856
"Sack of Lawrence"; caning of Charles Sumner; Pottawatomie massacre
1857–1861
Panic and depression
1859
John Brown's raid on Harpers Ferry
1861
Confederate States of America established; war begins at Fort Sumter

# SECTIONAL CHANGES IN AMERICAN SOCIETY

The road to war was not straight or short. Six years elapsed between the Compromise of 1850 and the crisis in "Bleeding Kansas." Another four would pass before the first shot was fired. And the process of separation involved more than popular fears, ineffective politicians, and an unwillingness to compromise. As we have seen, Americans were bound together by a growing transportation network, by national markets, and by a national political system. Increasingly, however, the changes occurring in American society heightened sectional tensions. As the North continued to industrialize, its society came into conflict with that of the South. The coming of civil war, in other words, involved social and economic changes as well as political ones.

**The Growth of a Railroad Economy** >> By the time the Compromise of 1850 produced a lull in the tensions between North and South, the American economy had left behind the depression of the early 1840s and was booming again. Its basic structure, however, was changing. Cotton remained the nation's major export, but it was no longer the driving force for American economic growth. After 1839 this role was taken over by the construction of a vast railroad network covering the eastern half of the continent. By 1850 the United States possessed more than 9,000 miles of track; 10 years later it had over 30,000 miles, more than the rest of the world combined. Much of the new construction during the 1850s occurred west of the Appalachian Mountains—over 2,000 miles in Ohio and Illinois alone.

Because western railroads ran through less settled areas, they depended especially on public aid. State and local governments made loans to rail companies and sometimes exempted them temporarily from taxes. Federal land grants were crucial, too. By mortgaging or selling the land to farmers, the railroad raised construction capital and also stimulated settlement, which increased its business and profits. By 1860 Congress had allotted about 28 million acres of federal land to 40 different companies.

The effect of the new lines rippled through the economy. Nearby farmers began to specialize in cash crops and market them in distant locations. For example, before the railroad

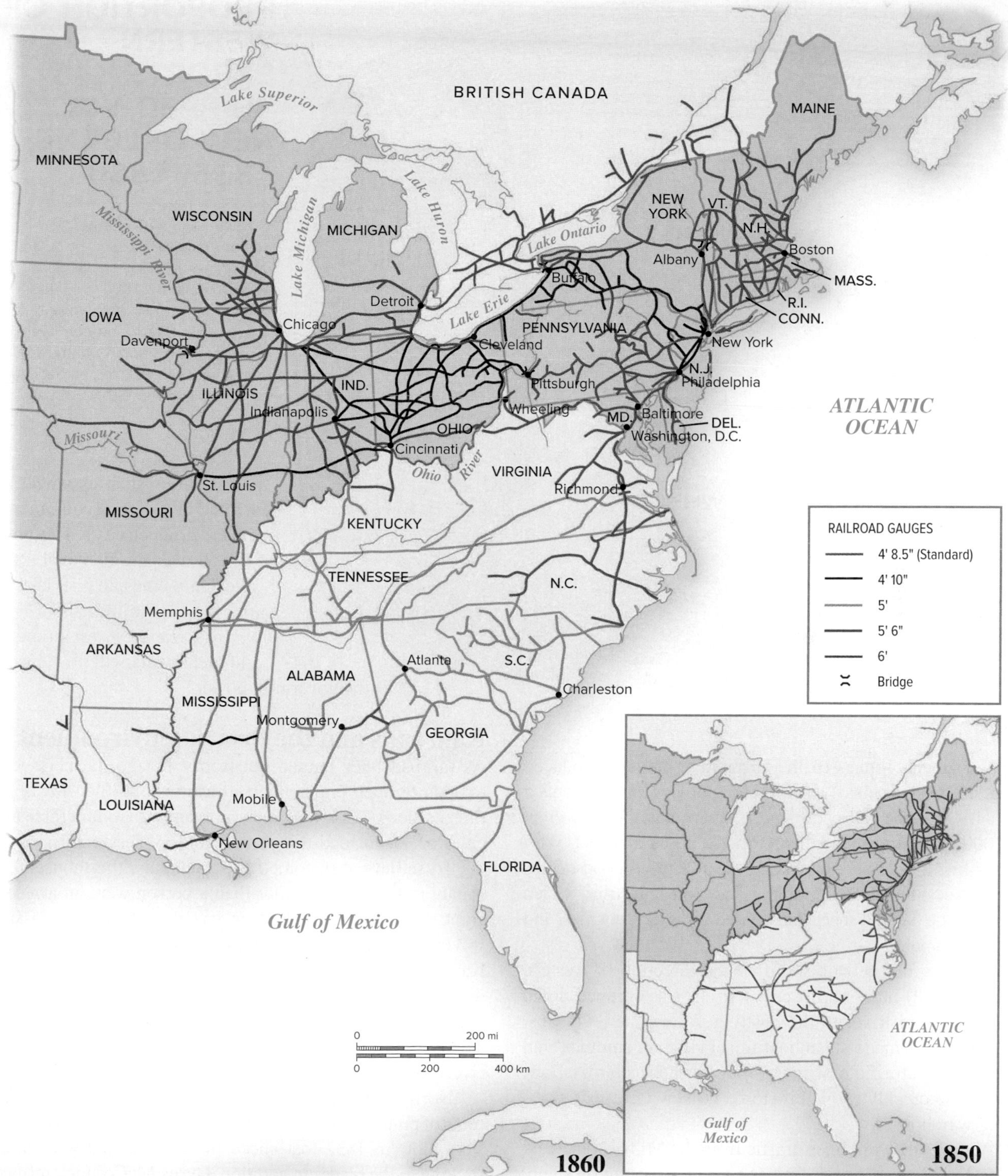
BRITISH CANADA
MINNESOTA
WISCONSIN
MICHIGAN
IOWA
ILLINOIS
IND.
OHIO
PENNSYLVANIA
NEW YORK
VT.
N.H.
MAINE
MASS.
R.I.
CONN.
N.J.
DEL.
MD.
MISSOURI
KENTUCKY
VIRGINIA
TENNESSEE
N.C.
S.C.
ARKANSAS
MISSISSIPPI
ALABAMA
GEORGIA
TEXAS
LOUISIANA
FLORIDA
Lake Superior
Lake Michigan
Lake Huron
Lake Ontario
Lake Erie
Mississippi River
Missouri R.
Ohio River
Chicago
Detroit
Davenport
Indianapolis
Cincinnati
St. Louis
Cleveland
Pittsburgh
Wheeling
Buffalo
Albany
Boston
New York
Philadelphia
Baltimore
Washington, D.C.
Richmond
Memphis
Atlanta
Charleston
Montgomery
Mobile
New Orleans
ATLANTIC OCEAN
Gulf of Mexico
RAILROAD GAUGES
4' 8.5" (Standard)
4' 10"
5'
5' 6"
6'
Bridge
0
200 mi
0
200
400 km
1860
ATLANTIC OCEAN
Gulf of Mexico
1850

## MAP 15.1: GROWTH OF THE RAILROAD NETWORK, 1850–1860

Although many miles of railroad track were laid during the 1850s, total track mileage is misleading because the United States lacked a fully integrated rail network in 1860. A few trunk-line roads had combined smaller lines, making it easier to ship goods. The Pennsylvania Railroad, for example, linked Philadelphia and Pittsburgh. But the existence of five major track gauges (or widths) meant that passengers and freight often had to be transferred from one line to the next. And north-south traffic was further hindered by the lack of bridges over the Ohio River. *How many times, according to the map, did freight have to be moved to a different railroad car between Chicago and New York City? Between St. Louis and New Orleans?*

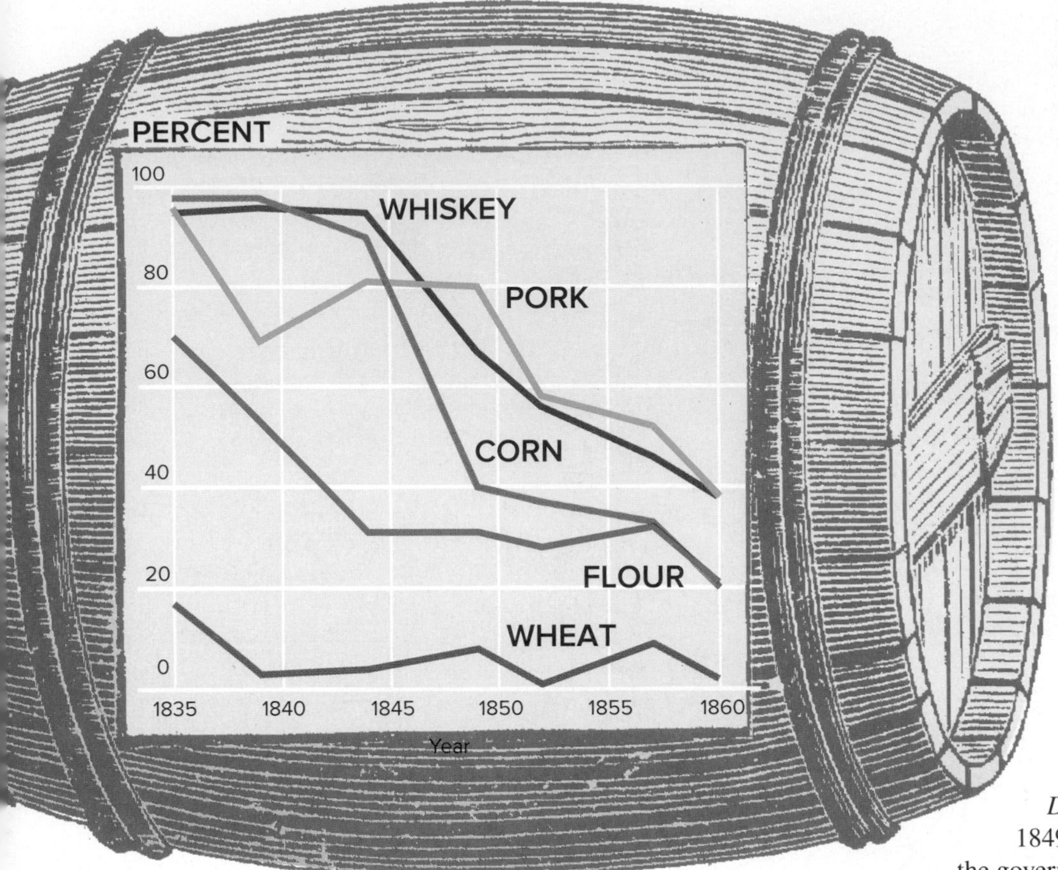
PERCENT
100
80
60
40
20
0
WHISKEY
PORK
CORN
FLOUR
WHEAT
1835
1840
1845
1850
1855
1860
Year

## PROPORTION OF WESTERN EXPORTS SHIPPED VIA NEW ORLEANS, 1835–1860

In 1835 nearly 100 percent of western exports of corn, pork, and whiskey were being shipped via New Orleans. By 1860 only about 40 percent of pork and whiskey and 20 percent of flour and corn were. The change in shipping patterns weakened the political ties between the South and the old Northwest.

reached Athens, Tennessee, the surrounding counties produced about 25,000 bushels of wheat, selling at less than 50 cents a bushel. Once the railroad came, farmers near Athens grew 400,000 bushels and sold their crop at a dollar a bushel. With the profits, the farmers purchased manufactured goods. Railroads also stimulated the mining and iron industries, which provided the bar and sheet iron needed for tracks, engines, and other equipment.

The new rail networks shifted the direction of western trade. In 1840 most northwestern grain was shipped down the Mississippi River to the bustling port of New Orleans. But low water made steamboat travel risky in summer, and ice shut down traffic in winter. Products such as lard, tallow, and cheese quickly spoiled if stored in New Orleans's sweltering warehouses.

With the new rail lines, traffic from the Midwest increasingly flowed west to east. Chicago became the region's hub, connecting the farms of the upper Midwest to New York and other eastern cities. The South's overall share of western trade dropped dramatically. The old political alliance between South and the old Northwest, based on shared economic interests, was weakened by the new patterns of commerce.

The growing rail network was not the only factor that led farmers in the Northeast and Midwest to become more commercially oriented. Another was the sharp rise in international demand for grain. Farmers responded by specializing in cash crops such as wheat and corn and investing in equipment to increase productivity. "The power of cotton over the financial affairs of the Union has in the last few years rapidly diminished," the *Democratic Review* remarked in 1849, "and breadstuffs will now become the governing power."

## Railroads and the Prairie Environment >>

As railroad lines fanned out from Chicago, farmers began to acquire open prairie land in Illinois and then Iowa, putting its deep black soil into production. Commercial agriculture transformed this remarkable treeless environment.

To settlers accustomed to woodlands, the thousands of square miles of grass taller than a person were an awesome sight. In 1838 Edmund Flagg gazed on "the tall grasstops waving in . . . billowy beauty in the breeze; the narrow pathway winding off like a serpent over the rolling surface, disappearing and reappearing till lost in the luxuriant herbage." Tallgrass prairies had their perils, too: year-round, storms sent travelers searching for the shelter of trees along river valleys, and stinging insects were thick in the summer.

Normal plows could not penetrate the densely tangled roots of prairie grass, until John Deere invented a sharp-cutting steel plow in 1837 that sliced through the sod without soil sticking to the blade. In addition, Cyrus McCormick refined a mechanical reaper that harvested 14 times more wheat with the same amount of labor. By the 1850s McCormick was selling 1,000 reapers a year and could not keep up with demand, and Deere turned out 10,000 plows annually.

The new commercial farming transformed the landscape and the environment. Indians had grown corn in the region for years, but never in fields as large as those of white farmers, whose surpluses were shipped east. Prairie farmers also introduced new crops that were not part of the earlier ecological system, notably wheat, along with fruits and vegetables. Native grasses were replaced by a small number of plants cultivated as commodities. Domesticated grasses replaced native grasses in pastures for making hay.

Western farmers altered the landscape by reducing the annual fires, often set by Indians, that had kept the prairie free from trees. In the fires' absence, trees reappeared on land not in cultivation and, if undisturbed, eventually formed woodlots. The earlier unbroken landscape gave way to independent farms, each fenced in the precise checkerboard pattern established by the Northwest Ordinance. It was an artificial ecosystem of animals, woodlots, and crops whose large, uniform layout made western farms more efficient than the more irregular farms in the East.

**Railroads and the Urban Environment** >> Railroads transformed the urban environment as well. Communities soon recognized that their economic survival depended on creating rail links to the countryside and to major urban markets. Large cities feared they would be left behind in the struggle to be the dominant city in the region, and smaller communities saw their very survival at stake in the battle for rail connections.

Communities that obtained rail links found the new technology difficult to adjust to. Merchants in Jacksonville, Illinois, complained about the noise, dirt, and billowing smoke produced by the new locomotives passing through their business district. "The public square was filled with teams [of horses]," one resident recalled, "and whenever the engine steamed into the square making all the noise possible, there was such a stampede." After a few years the tracks were relocated to the outskirts of town. Increasingly, communities kept railroads away from fashionable neighborhoods and shopping areas. As the tracks became a physical marker of social and economic divisions in the town, the notion of living "on the wrong side of the tracks" became a way of defining the urban landscape.

**Rising Industrialization** >> The expansion of commercial agriculture, along with the shift from water power to steam, spurred the growth of industry. Out of the 10 leading American industries, 8 processed raw materials produced by agriculture, including flour milling and the manufacture of textiles, shoes, and woolens. (The only exceptions were iron and machinery.)

Most important, the factory system of organizing labor and the technology of interchangeable parts spread to other areas of the economy during the 1850s. Isaac Singer began using interchangeable parts in 1851 to mass-produce sewing machines, which made possible the ready-made clothing industry, while workers who assembled farm implements performed a single step in the process over and over again. By 1860 the United States had nearly a billion dollars invested in manufacturing, almost twice as much as in 1849. And for the first time, less than half the workers in the North were employed in agriculture.

**Immigration** >> The surge of industry depended on a large factory labor force. Natural increase helped swell the nation's population to more than 30 million by 1860, but only in part, since the birthrate had begun to decline. It was the beginning of mass emigration to America during the mid-1840s that kept population growth soaring.

In the 20 years from 1820 to 1840, about 700,000 newcomers had entered the United States. That figure jumped to 1.7 million in the 1840s, then to 2.6 million in the 1850s. Though even greater numbers arrived after the Civil War, as a percentage of the nation's total population, the wave from 1845 to 1854 was the largest influx of immigrants in American history. The great majority of newcomers were in the prime of life, between 10 and 40 years old. Certainly the booming economy and the lure of freedom drew immigrants, but they were also pushed by deteriorating conditions in Europe. In Ireland a potato blight beginning in 1845 created a *Gorta Mór*—"Great Famine"—leaving potatoes rotting in the fields. The blight may well have spread from the United States and Canada, and it also infected Europe generally. But Ireland suffered more, because nearly a third of its population depended almost entirely on the potato for food. "They are all gone—clean gone," wrote a priest in the Irish town of Galway. "If travelling by night, you would know when a potato field was near by the smell." Out of Ireland's population of 9 million, as many as a million people perished, while a million and a half more emigrated, two-thirds to the United States.

The Irish tended to be poorer than other immigrant groups of the mid-nineteenth century. Although the Protestant Scots-Irish continued to emigrate, as so many had during the eighteenth century, the decided majority of the Irish who came after 1845 were Catholic. Because they were poor and unskilled, the Irish congregated in the cities, where the women performed domestic service and took factory jobs and the men did manual labor.

Germans and Scandinavians also had economic reasons for leaving Europe. They included small farmers whose lands had become marginal or who had been displaced by landlords, and skilled workers thrown out of work by industrialization. Some fled political and social oppression and came to live under the free institutions of the United States. Since arriving in America, wrote a Swede who settled in Iowa in 1850, "I have not been compelled to pay a penny for the privilege of living. Neither is my cap worn out from lifting it in the presence of gentlemen."

Unprecedented unrest and upheaval prevailed in Europe in 1848, the so-called year of revolutions. The famine that had driven so many Irish out of their country was part of a larger food shortage caused by a series of poor harvests. In this situation, middle-class reformers, who wanted civil liberty and a more representative government, joined forces with lower-class workers to overthrow several regimes. France, Austria, Hungary, Italy, and Prussia all witnessed popular uprisings. Yet though these revolts gained

^ German immigrants enjoyed gathering for music and conversation in beer gardens. One of the most elegant and spacious of its day was New York City's German Winter-Garden in the Bowery neighborhood. "There are immense buildings," wrote one American, "fitted up in imitation of a garden. . . . Germans carry their families there to spend a day, or an evening."


temporary success, they were all quashed by the forces of the old order. Liberal hopes for a more open, democratic society suffered a severe setback.

In the aftermath of this failure a number of hard-pressed German workers and farmers as well as disillusioned radicals and reformers emigrated to the United States, the symbol of democratic liberalism in the world. They were joined by the first significant migration from Asia, as thousands of Chinese joined the gold rush to California and other strikes. This migration was part of a century-long phenomenon that brought approximately 50 million Europeans, largely from rural areas, to the Western Hemisphere.

Although many Germans and Scandinavians arrived in modest straits, few were truly impoverished, and many could afford to buy a farm or start a business. Unlike the Irish, Germans tended to emigrate as families, and wherever they settled, they formed social, religious, and cultural organizations to maintain their language and customs. Whereas the Scandinavian, Dutch, and English immigrants were Protestant, half or more of the Germans were Catholic.

Factories came more and more to depend on immigrant labor, including children, since newcomers would work for lower wages and were less likely to protest harsh working conditions. The shift to an immigrant workforce could be seen most clearly in the textile industry, where by 1860 over half the workers in New England mills were foreign-born.

The sizable foreign-born population in many American cities severely strained urban resources. Immigrants who could barely make ends meet were forced to live in overcrowded, unheated tenement houses, damp cellars, and even shacks. Urban slums became notorious for crime and drinking, which took a heavy toll on families and the poor. In the eyes of many native-born Americans, immigrants were to blame for driving down factory wages and pushing American workers out of jobs. Overshadowing these complaints was a fear that America might not be able to **assimilate** the new groups, with their unfamiliar languages and customs. These fears precipitated an outburst of political **nativism** in the mid-1850s.

**assimilate** to absorb a culturally distinct group into the dominant culture.

**nativism** outlook championing the supremacy of "native" cultural traits and political rights over those of immigrants from different backgrounds.

## Southern Complaints >>

With British and northern factories buying cotton in large quantities, southern planters prospered in the 1850s. But instead of investing in machinery as northern commercial farmers had, white southerners invested in slaves. During the 1850s, the price of prime field hands reached record levels.

Despite southern prosperity the section's leaders repeatedly complained that the North had used its power over

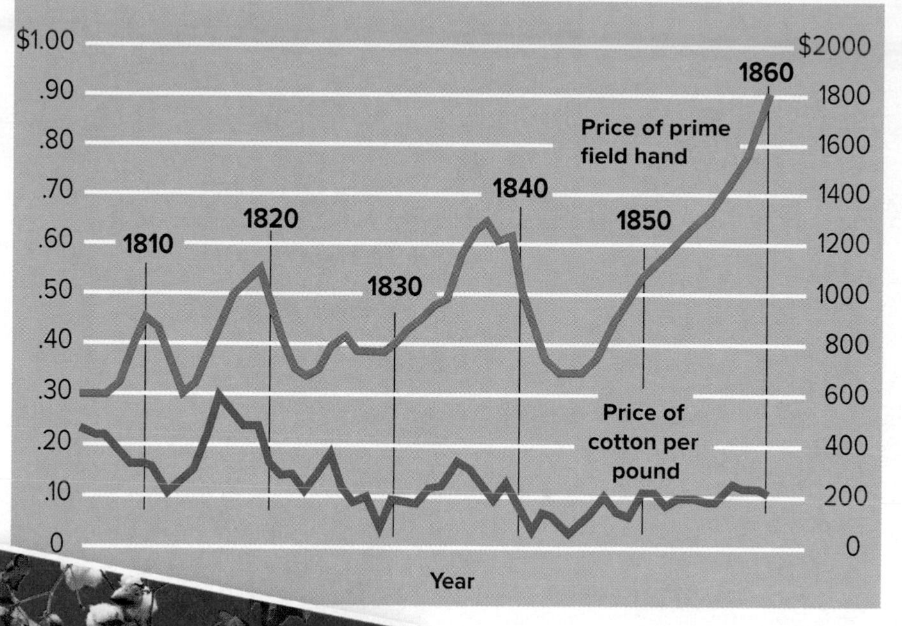
$1.00
.90
.80
.70
.60
.50
.40
.30
.20
.10
0
$2000
1800
1600
1400
1200
1000
800
600
400
200
0
1810
1820
1830
1840
1850
1860
Price of prime field hand
Price of cotton per pound
Year

## PRICES OF COTTON AND SLAVES

From 1815 to 1850 cotton and slave prices generally rose and fell together, as southerners plowed their profits from growing cotton into buying more land and slaves. During the 1850s, however, the booming southern economy and bumper cotton crops drove the price of slaves steeply upward compared to cotton prices, squeezing slaveowners' profit margins and heightening southern anxieties about the future. ©Pixtal/agefotostock RF

banking and commerce to convert the South into a colony. Storage and shipping charges, insurance, port fees, and commissions, which added some 20 percent to the cost of cotton and other commodities, went into the pockets of northern merchants, shippers, and bankers. The idea that the South was a colony of the North was inaccurate, but white southerners found it a convincing explanation of the North's growing wealth. More important, it reinforced their resistance to federal aid for economic development, which they were convinced would enrich the North at southern expense. This attitude further weakened the South's political alliance with the West, which needed federal aid for transportation.

White southerners also feared that the new tide of immigration would shift the sectional balance of power. Most immigrants shunned the South, not wanting to compete with cheap slave labor. The lack of industry and the limited demand for skilled labor also shunted immigrants northward. As a result, the North surged even further ahead of the South in population, thereby strengthening its control of the House of Representatives and heightening southern concern that the North would rapidly settle the western territories.

**REVIEW**

How did the new railroads affect urban and prairie environments? How did they increase sectional tensions?

# THE POLITICAL REALIGNMENT OF THE 1850s

When Franklin Pierce (he pronounced it "Purse") assumed the presidency in 1853, he was only 48 years old, the youngest man yet to be elected president. He was also a supporter of the "Young America" movement of the Democratic Party, which enthusiastically looked to spread democracy around the globe and annex additional territory to the United States.

The believers in Young America felt it idle to argue about slavery when the nation could be developing new resources. In 1853 Pierce did manage to conclude the Gadsden Purchase, thereby gaining control of about 45,000 square miles of Mexican desert, which contained the most practical southern route for a transcontinental railroad. He had no success with his major goal, acquiring Cuba, the rich sugar-producing island where slavery had once been important. In any case, he soon had his hands full with the proposals of another Democrat of the Young America stamp, Senator Stephen A. Douglas of Illinois.

**The Kansas-Nebraska Act** >> Known as the Little Giant, Douglas was ambitious, bursting with energy, and impatient to get things done. As chairman of the Senate's Committee on Territories, he hoped to organize federal lands west of Missouri as part of his program for economic development. And as a citizen of Illinois, he wanted Chicago selected as the eastern terminus of the proposed transcontinental railroad. To do so, the rest of the Louisiana Purchase would have to be organized into territories, since any northern rail route would run through that region.

Under the terms of the Missouri Compromise of 1820, slavery was prohibited in this portion of the Louisiana Purchase. Stephen Douglas had tried once to organize the area while keeping a ban on slavery—only to have his bill voted down by southern opposition in the Senate. In January 1854 he reintroduced the measure. This time, to obtain southern support, he omitted the prohibition on slavery that had been in effect for 34 years.

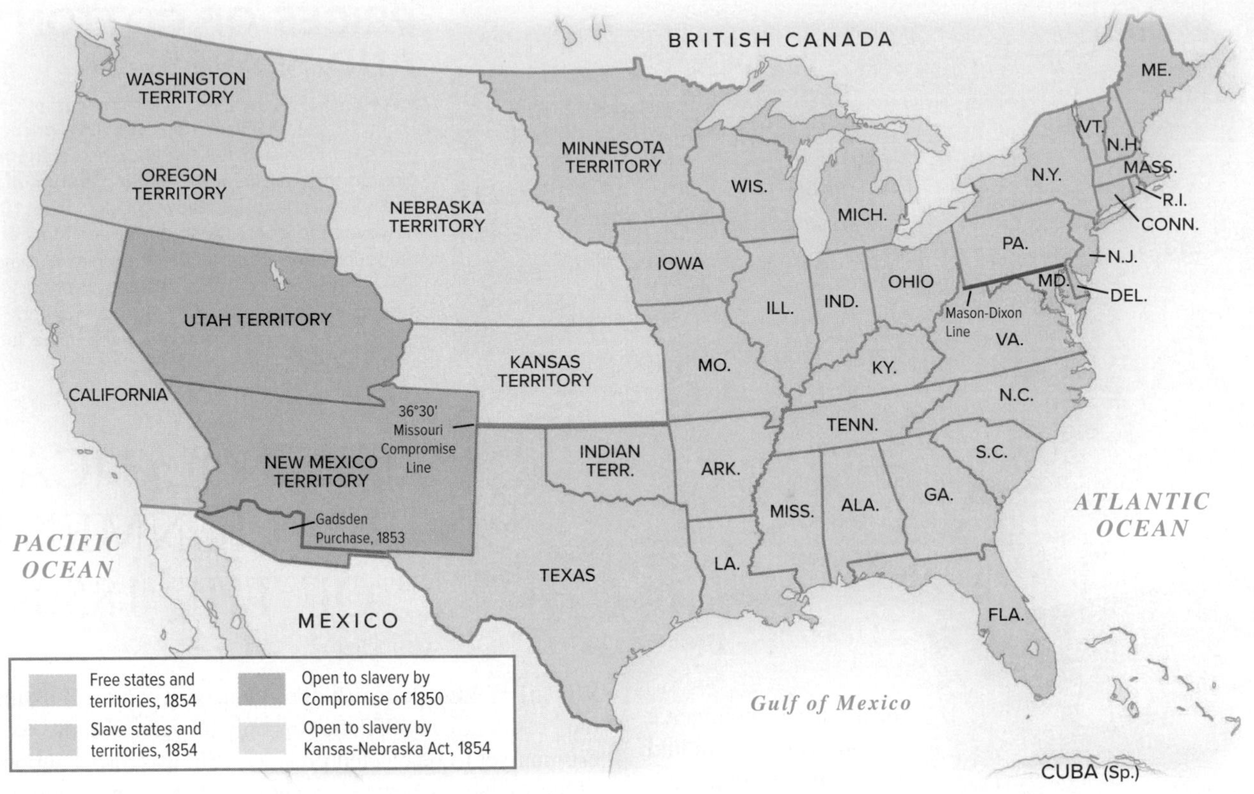
BRITISH CANADA
WASHINGTON TERRITORY
OREGON TERRITORY
MINNESOTA TERRITORY
NEBRASKA TERRITORY
UTAH TERRITORY
CALIFORNIA
KANSAS TERRITORY
36°30' Missouri Compromise Line
NEW MEXICO TERRITORY
Gadsden Purchase, 1853
INDIAN TERR.
TEXAS
MEXICO
PACIFIC OCEAN
ME.
VT.
N.H.
MASS.
R.I.
CONN.
N.Y.
N.J.
PA.
DEL.
MD.
Mason-Dixon Line
VA.
WIS.
MICH.
IOWA
ILL.
IND.
OHIO
MO.
KY.
N.C.
TENN.
S.C.
ARK.
MISS.
ALA.
GA.
LA.
FLA.
ATLANTIC OCEAN
Gulf of Mexico
CUBA (Sp.)
Free states and territories, 1854
Slave states and territories, 1854
Open to slavery by Compromise of 1850
Open to slavery by Kansas-Nebraska Act, 1854

## MAP 15.2: THE KANSAS-NEBRASKA ACT

When the Kansas-Nebraska Act of 1854 opened the remaining portion of the Louisiana Purchase to slavery under the doctrine of popular sovereignty, conflict between the two sections focused on control of Kansas, directly west of the slave state of Missouri.
*Which part of the map indicates the unorganized portion of the Louisiana Purchase? How did the doctrine of popular sovereignty effectively repeal the Missouri Compromise?*

The bill created two territories: Kansas, directly west of Missouri, and a much larger Nebraska Territory, located west of Iowa and the Minnesota Territory. The Missouri Compromise was explicitly repealed. Instead, Douglas's doctrine of popular sovereignty was to determine the status of slavery in both territories, though it was left unclear whether residents of Kansas and Nebraska could prohibit slavery at any time or only at the time of statehood, as southerners insisted. It was widely assumed that Kansas would be a slave state and Nebraska a free state.

The Kansas-Nebraska Act outraged northern Democrats, Whigs, and Free Soilers alike. Critics rejected Douglas's contention that popular sovereignty would keep the territories free. The bill, they charged, was meant to give slaveholders—the "Slave Power"—territory previously consecrated to freedom. Most northern opponents of the bill focused on the expansion of slavery and the political threat of a Slave Power rather than the moral evil of slavery. Indignation swept the North, but the Senate passed the bill easily. The real fight came in the House, where the North held a large majority. President Pierce put intense pressure on his fellow northern Democrats to come along, and finally the bill passed by a narrow margin, 113 to 100. Pierce signed it on May 30, 1854.

**The Collapse of the Second American Party System >>** The furor over the Kansas-Nebraska Act laid bare the underlying tensions that had developed between the North and the South. These tensions put mounting pressure on the political parties, and in the 1850s the Jacksonian party system collapsed. Voters who had been loyal to one party for years, even decades, began switching allegiances. By the time the process of realignment was completed, a new party system had emerged, divided this time along clearly sectional lines.

In part, the old party system decayed because new problems had replaced the traditional economic issues of both Whigs and Democrats. The Whigs alienated many of their traditional Protestant supporters by openly seeking the support of Catholics and recent immigrants. Then, too, the growing agitation for the prohibition of alcohol divided both parties, especially the Whigs. Finally, both the Whigs and the Democrats were increasingly perceived as little more than corrupt engines of plunder. Many voters became disillusioned.

Thus the party system was already weak when the Kansas-Nebraska Act divided the two major parties along sectional lines. In such an unstable atmosphere, independent parties flourished. Antislavery veterans, who had earlier sparked the Liberty and Free Soil parties, united with Whigs and anti-Nebraska Democrats in the new antislavery Republican Party. Their calculations were derailed, however, when another new party capitalized on fears aroused by the recent flood of immigrants.

**The Know-Nothings** >> In 1854 the American Party, a secret nativist organization whose members were called Know-Nothings, suddenly emerged as a potent political force. (Its members, sworn to secrecy, had been instructed to answer inquiries by replying, "I know nothing.") Taking as their slogan "Americans should rule America," Know-Nothings denounced illegal voting by immigrants, the rising crime and disorder in urban areas, and immigrants' heavy drinking. They were also strongly anti-Catholic and were convinced that the church's "undemocratic" hierarchy of bishops and archbishops was conspiring to undermine American democracy. Know-Nothings advocated lengthening the residency period for naturalization and ousting from office corrupt politicians who openly bid for foreign and Catholic votes.

The Know-Nothings won a series of remarkable victories in the 1854 elections. Their showing spelled doom for the Whigs, as party members deserted in droves to the Know-Nothings. With perhaps a million voters enrolled in its lodges in every state of the Union, Know-Nothing leaders confidently predicted in 1855 that they would elect the next president.

Yet only a year later—by the end of 1856—the party had collapsed as quickly as it had risen. Inexperienced leaders failed to enact the party's reform platform; but in the end, rising sectional tensions destroyed the party when it adopted a proslavery platform for the elections of 1856. Northern party members then flocked to the other new party, the Republicans. This party, unlike the Know-Nothings, had no base in the South. It intended to elect a president by sweeping the free states, which controlled a majority of the electoral votes.

**The Republicans and Bleeding Kansas** >> At first, the Republican Party made little headway in the North. Although it attracted a variety of Whigs, anti-Nebraska Democrats, and Free Soilers, many moderate Whigs and Democrats viewed the party as too radical.

^ As Kansas became a battleground over whether slavery would expand into the new territories, proslavery and antislavery factions armed themselves for open conflict. This free-state battery stands with its howitzer at the ready.

Those attitudes changed on the heels of the alarming developments in Kansas. Most early settlers migrated to Kansas for the same reason other white Americans headed west: the chance to prosper in a new land. But Stephen Douglas's idea of popular sovereignty transformed the new settlement into a referendum on slavery in the territories. A race soon developed between northerners and southerners to settle Kansas first. To the proslavery residents of neighboring Missouri, free-state communities like Lawrence seemed ominous threats. "We are playing for a mighty stake," former senator David Rice Atchison of Missouri insisted. "If we win, we carry slavery to the Pacific Ocean; if we fail, we lose Missouri, Arkansas and Texas and all the territories; the game must be played boldly."

When the first Kansas elections were held in 1854 and 1855, Missourians poured over the border, seized the polls, and stuffed the ballot boxes. This massive fraud tarnished popular sovereignty at the outset and greatly aroused public opinion in the North. It also provided proslavery forces with a commanding majority in the Kansas legislature, where they enacted a strict legal code designed to intimidate antislavery settlers. This Kansas Code limited such time-honored rights as freedom of speech, impartial juries, and fair elections. Mobilized into action, the free-staters in the fall of 1855 organized a separate government, drafted a state constitution prohibiting slavery, and asked Congress to admit Kansas as a free state. In such a polarized situation, violence quickly broke out between the two factions, which culminated in the raid on Lawrence in May 1856 (see the chapter introduction).

KANSAS
SOUTHERN CHIVALRY— ARGUMENT VERSUS CLUB'S.

^ The caning of Senator Charles Sumner of Massachusetts by Representative Preston S. Brooks of South Carolina inflamed public opinion. In this northern cartoon the fallen Sumner, a martyr to free speech, raises his pen against Brooks's club. Rushing to capitalize on the furor, printmakers did not know what the obscure Brooks looked like and thus had to devise ingenious ways of portraying the incident. In this print, Brooks's face is hidden by his raised arm. ©Bettmann/Getty Images

**The Caning of Charles Sumner** >> Only a few days before the proslavery attack on Lawrence, Republican senator Charles Sumner of Massachusetts delivered a scathing speech, "The Crime against Kansas." Sumner passionately condemned slavery and deliberately insulted the state of South Carolina and one of its senators. Preston S. Brooks, a member of Congress from South Carolina, was outraged that Sumner had insulted his relative and mocked his state.

Several days later, on May 22, Brooks strode into the Senate after it had adjourned, went up to Sumner, who was seated at his desk, and proceeded to beat him over the head with a cane. The cane shattered into three pieces from the violence of the attack, but Brooks, swept up in the emotion of the moment, furiously continued hitting Sumner until the senator collapsed unconscious, drenched in blood.

Northerners were electrified to learn that a senator of the United States had been beaten unconscious in the Senate chamber. What caused them even greater consternation was southern reaction—for in his own region, Preston Brooks was lionized as a hero. Instantly, the Sumner caning breathed life into the fledgling Republican Party. Its claims about "Bleeding Kansas" and the Slave Power now seemed credible.

**The Election of 1856** >> In the face of the storm over Kansas, the Democrats turned to James Buchanan of Pennsylvania as their presidential nominee. Buchanan's supreme qualification was having the good fortune to have been out of the country as minister to England when the Kansas-Nebraska Act was passed. The American Party, split badly by the Kansas issue, nominated former president Millard Fillmore.

The Republicans chose John C. Frémont, a western explorer who had helped liberate California during the Mexican War. The party's platform denounced slavery as a "relic of barbarism" and demanded that Kansas be admitted as a free state. Throughout the summer the party hammered away on Bleeding Sumner and Bleeding Kansas.

A number of basic principles guided the Republican Party, one of which was the ideal of free labor. Slavery degraded labor, Republicans argued, and would inevitably drive free labor out of the territories. Condemning the South as a stagnant, hierarchical, and economically backward region, Republicans praised the North as a fluid society of widespread opportunity where enterprising individuals could improve their lot. Stopping the expansion of slavery, in Republican eyes, would preserve this heritage of opportunity and economic independence for white Americans. Republicans also appealed to former Know-Nothings by criticizing the Catholic Church, particularly its political activity, and by being much more favorable to temperance.

Also important was the moral opposition to slavery, strengthened by such works as Harriet Beecher Stowe's *Uncle Tom's Cabin*. Republican speakers and editors stressed that slavery was a moral wrong, that it was incompatible with the ideals of the Republic and Christianity. "Never forget," Republican leader Abraham Lincoln declared on one occasion, "that we have before us this whole matter of the right and wrong of slavery in this Union, though the immediate question is as to its spreading out into new Territories and States."

More negatively, Republicans gained support by shifting their attacks from slavery itself to the Slave Power, or the political influence of the planter class. Pointing to the Sumner assault and the incidents in Kansas, Republicans contended that the Slave Power had set out to destroy the liberties of white northerners. Just as the nation's founders had battled against tyranny, aristocracy, and minority rule in the Revolution, so the North confronted the unrepublican Slave Power. "If our government, for the sake of Slavery, is to be perpetually the representative of a minority," argued the *Cincinnati Commercial*, "it may continue republican in form, but the substance of its republicanism has departed."

In the election Buchanan all but swept the South (losing only Maryland to Fillmore) and won enough free states to push him over the top. Still, the violence in Kansas and Sumner's caning nearly lofted Frémont into the presidency. Had he carried Pennsylvania plus one more free state, he would have been elected. For the first time in American history, an antislavery party based entirely in the North threatened to elect a president and snap the bonds of union.

 **REVIEW**

What events led the political realignment of the 1850s to favor the Know-Nothings at first? What events led the Republicans to emerge as the more powerful party?

# THE WORSENING CRISIS

James Buchanan was one of the most experienced men ever elected president: he had served in Congress, in the cabinet, and in the foreign service. Moderates in both sections hoped that the new president would thwart Republicans in the North and secessionists of the Deep South, popularly known as "fire-eaters." Throughout his career, however, Buchanan had taken the southern position on sectional matters, and he proved insensitive to the concerns of northern Democrats. Moreover, on March 6, 1857, only two days after Buchanan's inauguration, the Supreme Court rendered one of the most controversial decisions in its history.

**The *Dred Scott* Decision** >> The owner of a Missouri slave named Dred Scott had taken him to live for several years in Illinois, a free state, and in what is now Minnesota, where slavery had been banned by the Missouri Compromise. Eventually the owner returned with Scott to Missouri. Scott sued for his freedom on the grounds that his residence in a free state and a free territory had made him free, and his case ultimately went to the Supreme Court. Two northern justices joined all five southern members in ruling 7 to 2 that Scott remained a slave. The majority opinion was written by Chief Justice Roger Taney of Maryland.

Wanting to strengthen the judicial protection of slavery, Taney ruled that African Americans could not be and never had been citizens of the United States. Instead, he insisted that they were "regarded as beings of an inferior order" at the time the Constitution was adopted, "so far inferior that they had no rights which the white man was bound to respect." In addition, the Court ruled that the Missouri Compromise was unconstitutional. Congress, it declared, had no power to ban slavery from any territory of the United States.

While southerners rejoiced at this result, Republicans denounced the Court for rejecting their party's main principle, that Congress should prohibit slavery in all territories. "We know the court . . . has often over-ruled its own decisions," Abraham Lincoln observed, "and we shall do what we can to have it over-rule this." For Republicans, the decision foreshadowed the spread of slavery throughout the West and even the nation.

But the decision also was a blow to Stephen Douglas's moderate solution of popular sovereignty. If Congress had no power to prohibit slavery in a territory, how could it authorize a territorial legislature to do so? Although the Court did not rule on this point, the clear implication of the *Dred Scott* decision was that popular sovereignty was also unconstitutional. The Court, in effect, had endorsed John C. Calhoun's radical view that slavery was legal in all the territories. In so doing, the Court, which had intended to settle the question of slavery in the territories, instead pushed the political debate toward new extremes.

Although the nation grappled with the *Dred Scott* decision, an economic depression aggravated sectional conflict. The Panic of 1857 was nowhere near as severe as the depression of 1839–1843. But the psychological results were far-reaching, for the South remained relatively untouched. With the price of cotton and other southern commodities still high, southern secessionists hailed the panic as proof that an independent southern nation could survive economically. Insisting that cotton sustained the international economy, James Henry Hammond, a senator from South Carolina, boasted: "No, you dare not make war on cotton. No power on earth dares to make war on it. Cotton is king."

## The Lecompton Constitution

>> Although the *Dred Scott* decision and economic depression weakened the bonds of the Union, Kansas remained at the center of the political stage. In June 1857, when the territory elected delegates to draft a state constitution, free-staters boycotted the election, giving proslavery forces control of the convention that met in Lecompton. The delegates promptly drafted a constitution that made slavery legal. Even more boldly, they scheduled a referendum in which voters could not vote against either the constitution or slavery. Once again, free-staters boycotted the election, and the Lecompton constitution was approved.

President Buchanan had pledged earlier that there would be a free and fair vote on the Lecompton constitution. But the outcome offered Buchanan the unexpected opportunity to create one additional slave state and thereby satisfy his southern supporters by pushing the Lecompton constitution through Congress. This was too much for Douglas, who broke party ranks and denounced the Lecompton constitution as a fraud. Although the administration prevailed in the Senate without Douglas's support, the House rejected the constitution. In a compromise, Congress returned the constitution to Kansas for another vote. This time it was decisively defeated, 11,300 to 1,788. No doubt remained that as soon as Kansas had sufficient population, it would come into the Union as a free state.

The attempt to force slavery on the people of Kansas drove many conservative northerners into the Republican Party. And Douglas now found himself assailed by the southern wing of his party. On top of that, in the summer of 1858, he faced a desperate fight for reelection to the Senate in his race against Republican Abraham Lincoln.

## The Lincoln-Douglas Debates

>> "He is the strong man of his party . . . and the best stump speaker, with his droll ways and dry jokes, in the West," Douglas commented when he learned of Lincoln's nomination to oppose him. "He is as honest as he is shrewd, and if I beat him my victory will be hardly won." Tall (6 feet 4 inches) and gangly, Lincoln had an awkward manner as he spoke, yet his logic and sincerity carried the audience with him. His sentences had none of the oratorical flourishes common in that day. "If we could first know *where* we are, and *whither* we are tending, we could then better judge *what* to do, and *how* to do it," Lincoln began, in accepting his party's nomination for senator in 1858. He then commented on a proverb from the Bible:

> "A house divided against itself cannot stand." I believe this government cannot endure, permanently half *slave* and half *free*. I do not expect the Union to be *dissolved*—I do not expect the house to *fall*—but I *do* expect it will cease to be divided. It will become *all* one thing, or *all* the other. Either the *opponents* of slavery, will arrest the further spread of it, and place it where the public mind shall rest in the belief that it is in the course of ultimate extinction; or its *advocates* will push it forward, till it shall become alike lawful in all the States, *old* as well as *new—North* as well as *South.*

The message echoed through the hall and across the pages of the national press.

Born in the slave state of Kentucky, Lincoln had grown up mostly in southern Indiana and central Illinois. Yet his intense ambition lifted him above the backwoods from which he came. He compensated for a lack of schooling through disciplined self-education, and he became a shrewd courtroom lawyer of respectable social standing. Known for his sense of humor, he was nonetheless subject to fits of acute depression.

Lincoln's first love was always politics. A fervent admirer of Henry Clay and his economic program, Lincoln became a Whig and then, after the party's collapse, joined the Republicans and became one of their key leaders in Illinois. He challenged Douglas to discuss the issues of slavery and the sectional controversy in a series of seven debates.

In the campaign Douglas sought to portray Lincoln as a radical who preached sectional warfare. The nation *could* endure half slave and half free, Douglas declared, as long as states and territories were left alone to regulate their own affairs. Lincoln countered by insisting that the spread of slavery was a blight on the Republic. Even though Douglas had voted against the Lecompton constitution, he could not be counted on to oppose slavery's expansion, for he admitted that he didn't care whether slavery was voted "down or up."

In the debate held at Freeport, Illinois, Lincoln asked Douglas how under the *Dred Scott* decision the people of a territory could lawfully exclude slavery before statehood. Douglas answered, with what became known as the **Freeport Doctrine**, that slaveowners would never bring their slaves into an area where slavery was not legally protected. Therefore, Douglas explained, if the people of a territory refused to pass a slave code, slavery would never be established there.

**Freeport Doctrine** Stephen A. Douglas's response to Lincoln (at Freeport, Illinois) that even though the *Dred Scott* decision forbade Congress from banning slavery in any territory, a territorial government might effectively do so by refusing to pass a slave code.

^ Superb debaters, Douglas (*left*) and Lincoln (*right*) nevertheless had very different speaking styles. The deep-voiced Douglas was constantly on the attack, drawing on his remarkable memory and showering points like buckshot in all directions. Lincoln, who had a high-pitched voice, developed his arguments more carefully and methodically, relying on his sense of humor and unmatched ability as a storyteller to drive home his points.
(Douglas) Source: Library of Congress, Prints and Photographs Division [LC-USZ61-2039]
(Lincoln) Source: Library of Congress, Prints and Photographs Division [LC-USZ62-7992]

In a close race, the legislature elected Douglas to another term in the Senate.[1] But on the national scene, southern Democrats angrily repudiated him and condemned the Freeport Doctrine. And although Lincoln lost, his impressive performance marked him as a possible presidential contender for 1860.

**The Beleaguered South** >> While northerners increasingly feared that the Slave Power was conspiring to extend slavery into the free states, southerners worried that the "Black Republicans" would hem them in and undermine their political power.

The very factors that brought prosperity during the 1850s stimulated the South's sense of crisis. As the price of slaves rose sharply, the proportion of southerners who owned slaves had dropped almost a third since 1830. At the same time, California and Kansas had been closed to southern slaveholders—unfairly, in their eyes. Finally, Douglas's clever claim that a territory could effectively outlaw slavery using the Freeport Doctrine seemed to negate the *Dred Scott* decision that slavery was legal in all the territories.

Several possible solutions to the South's internal crisis had failed. Agricultural reform to restore wornout lands had made significant headway only in Virginia and Maryland. Elsewhere the rewards of a single-crop economy were too great to persuade southern farmers to adopt new methods. Another alternative—bringing industry to the South—had also failed to take root. Finally, private military expeditions in Latin America, which were designed to strengthen the South by adding slave territory to the United States, came to naught.

The South's growing sense of isolation made this crisis more acute. By the 1850s slavery had been abolished throughout most of the Americas, and in the United States the South's political power was steadily shrinking. Only the expansion of slavery and the admission of new slave states held any promise of preserving the South's political power and protecting its way of life. "The truth is," fumed one Alabama politician, "the South is excluded from the common territories of the Union. The right of expansion claimed to be a necessity of her continued existence, is practically and effectively denied the South."

**REVIEW**

How did the *Dred Scott* decision and Stephen A. Douglas's Freeport Doctrine affect the debate over whether slavery could exist in the territories?

# THE ROAD TO WAR

In 1857 John Brown—the abolitionist firebrand—had returned to the East from Kansas, consumed with the idea of attacking slavery in the South itself. Financed by a number of prominent northern reformers, Brown gathered 21 followers, including 5 free blacks, in hope of fomenting a slave insurrection. On the night of October 16, 1859, his band

[1] State legislatures elected senators until 1913, when the Seventeenth Amendment was adopted. Although Lincoln and Douglas both campaigned for the office, Illinois voters actually voted for candidates for the legislature who were pledged to one of the senatorial candidates.

seized the unguarded federal armory at Harpers Ferry in Virginia. But no slaves rallied to Brown's standard: few lived in the area to begin with. Before long the raiders found themselves surrounded and holed up in the town. Charging with bayonets fixed, federal troops commanded by Colonel Robert E. Lee soon captured Brown and his raiders. On December 2, 1859, Virginia hanged Brown for treason.

Brown's raid at Harpers Ferry was yet another blow weakening the forces of compromise within the nation. Although the invasion itself was a dismal failure, the old man knew how to bear himself with a martyr's dignity. Republicans made haste to denounce Brown's raid, lest they be tarred as radicals, but other northerners were less cautious. Ralph Waldo Emerson described Brown as a "saint, whose martyrdom will make the gallows as glorious as the cross." While only a minority of northerners endorsed Brown, southerners were shocked by such displays of sympathy. "I have always been a fervid Union man," one North Carolina resident wrote, "but I confess the endorsement of the Harpers Ferry outrage has shaken my fidelity and I am willing to take the chances of every probable evil that may arise from disunion, sooner than submit any longer to Northern insolence and Northern outrage."

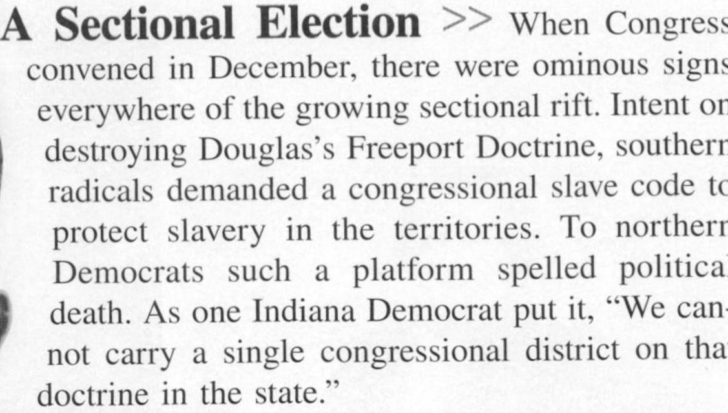

^ John Brown
©FPG/Getty Images

## A Sectional Election

>> When Congress convened in December, there were ominous signs everywhere of the growing sectional rift. Intent on destroying Douglas's Freeport Doctrine, southern radicals demanded a congressional slave code to protect slavery in the territories. To northern Democrats such a platform spelled political death. As one Indiana Democrat put it, "We cannot carry a single congressional district on that doctrine in the state."

At the Democratic National Convention in April, southern radicals boldly pressed their demand for a federal slave code. Instead the convention adopted the Douglas platform upholding popular sovereignty, whereupon the delegations from eight southern states walked out. The convention finally reassembled two months later and nominated Douglas. At this point most of the remaining southern Democrats departed and, together with those delegates who had seceded earlier, nominated Vice President John C. Breckinridge of Kentucky on a platform supporting a federal slave code. The last major national party had shattered.

The Republicans turned to Abraham Lincoln, a moderate on slavery who was strong in his home state of Illinois and the other doubtful states that the party had failed to carry in 1856. Republicans also sought to broaden their appeal by adding to their platform several economic planks that endorsed a moderately protective tariff, a homestead bill, and a northern transcontinental railroad.

The election that followed was really two contests in one. In the North, which had a majority of the electoral votes, only Lincoln and Douglas had any chance to carry a state. In the South the race pitted Breckinridge against John Bell of Tennessee, the candidate of the new Constitutional Union Party. Although Lincoln received less than 40 percent of the popular vote and had virtually no support in the South, he won 180 electoral votes, 27 more than needed

DAY BOOK
TRIBUNE
TRIBUNE BUILDING
BAKER & GODWIN PRINTERS

<< A torchlight parade in New York City staged by the Republican Wide-Awake Club, 1860. Most members were young white men in their late teens and early twenties. For their parades they carried torches and wore black capes and military-style caps. In remarkably few years, the Republicans' new sectional party sensed victory within its reach in the presidential election.

Source: Library of Congress, Prints and Photographs Division [LC-USZ62-59401]

| Candidate (Party) | Electoral Vote (%) | Popular Vote (%) |
|---|---|---|
| Abraham Lincoln (Republican) | 180 (59) | 1,865,908 (40) |
| J. C. Breckinridge (Southern Democratic) | 72 (24) | 848,019 (18) |
| John Bell (Constitutional Union) | 39 (13) | 590,631 (13) |
| Stephen A. Douglas (Northern Democratic) | 12 (4) | 1,375,157 (29) |
| Nonvoting territories | | |

## MAP 15.3: ELECTION OF 1860

Although Lincoln did not win a majority of the popular vote, he still would have been elected even if the votes for all three of his opponents had been combined, because he won a clear majority in every state he carried except California, Oregon, and New Jersey (whose electoral votes he split with Douglas).

for election. For the first time, the nation had elected a president who headed a completely sectional party and who was committed to stopping the expansion of slavery.

**Secession** >> Although the Republicans had not won control of either house of Congress, Lincoln's election struck many southerners as a blow of terrible finality. Lincoln had been lifted into office on the strength of the free states alone. It was not unrealistic, many fire-eaters argued, to believe that he would use federal aid to encourage the border states to free their slaves voluntarily. Once slavery disappeared there, and new states were added, the necessary three-fourths majority would exist to approve a constitutional amendment abolishing slavery. Or perhaps Lincoln might send other John Browns into the South to stir up more slave insurrections. The *Montgomery* (Alabama) *Mail* accused Republicans of intending "to free the negroes and force amalgamation between them and the children of the poor men of the South."

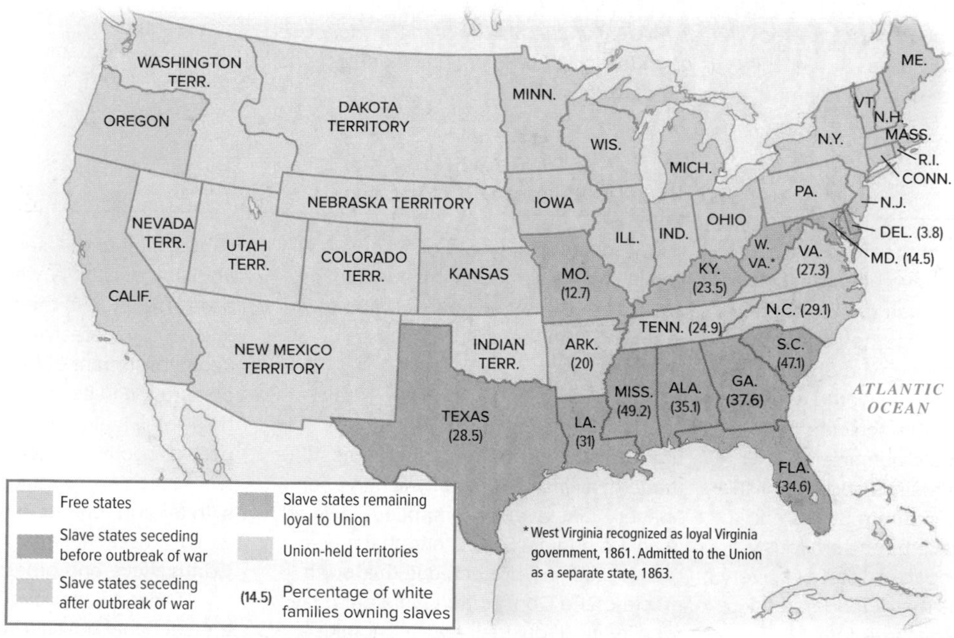

WASHINGTON TERR.
OREGON
DAKOTA TERRITORY
MINN.
WIS.
MICH.
N.Y.
ME.
VT.
N.H.
MASS.
R.I.
CONN.
N.J.
PA.
NEBRASKA TERRITORY
IOWA
NEVADA TERR.
UTAH TERR.
COLORADO TERR.
KANSAS
ILL.
IND.
OHIO
W. VA.*
VA. (27.3)
DEL. (3.8)
MD. (14.5)
MO. (12.7)
KY. (23.5)
CALIF.
N.C. (29.1)
TENN. (24.9)
NEW MEXICO TERRITORY
INDIAN TERR.
ARK. (20)
S.C. (47.1)
MISS. (49.2)
ALA. (35.1)
GA. (37.6)
ATLANTIC OCEAN
TEXAS (28.5)
LA. (31)
FLA. (34.6)
Free states
Slave states remaining loyal to Union
Slave states seceding before outbreak of war
Union-held territories
Slave states seceding after outbreak of war
(14.5) Percentage of white families owning slaves
*West Virginia recognized as loyal Virginia government, 1861. Admitted to the Union as a separate state, 1863.


## MAP 15.4: THE PATTERN OF SECESSION

Led by South Carolina, the Deep South seceded between Lincoln's election in November and his inauguration in March. The Upper South did not secede until after the firing on Fort Sumter. The four border slave states never seceded and remained in the Union throughout the war. As the map indicates, secession sentiment was strongest in states where the highest percentage of white families owned slaves. *What factors explain the hesitation of the Upper South to secede?*

# *Many* HISTORIES

## Slavery and Secession

*The two highest officials of the Confederacy provide contrasting opinions on slavery's relation to the Civil War. The first, Alexander Stephens, delivered his remarks (which came to be known as the "Cornerstone Speech") in Savannah, Georgia, shortly after being elected vice president of the new government. Jefferson Davis, president of the Confederacy, published his reflections after the war.*

### DOCUMENT 1
### Alexander Stephens: Slavery Is the Cornerstone

The new Constitution [of the Confederate States of America] has put at rest forever all the agitating questions relating to our peculiar institutions—African slavery as it exists among us—the proper *status* of the negro in our form of civilization. *This was the immediate cause of the late rupture and present revolution.* JEFFERSON, in his forecast, had anticipated this, as the "rock upon which the old Union would split." He was right. What was conjecture with him, is now a realized fact. But whether he fully comprehended the great truth upon which that rock stood and stands, may be doubted. *The prevailing ideas entertained by him and most of the leading statesmen at the time of the formation of the Old Constitution were, that the enslavement of the African was in violation of the laws of nature; that it was wrong in principle, socially, morally and politically.* It was an evil they knew not well how to deal with but the general opinion of the men of that day was that, somehow or other, in the order of Providence, the institution would be evanescent and pass away. This idea, though not incorporated in the Constitution, was the prevailing idea at the time. . . . *Those ideas, however, were fundamentally wrong. They rested upon the assumption of the equality of races. This was an error.* It was a sandy foundation, and the idea of a Government built upon it—when the "storm came and the wind blew, it fell."

*Our new Government is founded upon exactly the opposite ideas; its foundations are laid, its cornerstone rests, upon the great truth that the negro is not equal to the white man; that slavery, subordination to the superior race, is his natural and moral condition. This, our new Government, is the first, in the history of the world, based upon this great physical philosophical and moral truth. . . .*

It is the first Government ever instituted upon principles in strict conformity to nature, and the ordination of Providence, in furnishing the materials of human society. Many Governments have been founded upon the principles of certain classes; but the classes thus enslaved, were of the same race, and in violation of the laws of nature. Our system commits no such violation of nature's laws. The negro by nature, or by the curse against Canaan, is fitted for that condition which he occupies in our system. . . . The substratum of our society is made of the material fitted by nature for it, and by experience we know that it is the best, not only for the superior but for the inferior race, that it should be so.

*Source:* Stephens, Alexander, "Speech Delivered March 21, 1861 Savannah, Georgia," in *The Rebellion Record*, Moore, Frank, ed. New York, NY: G. P. Putnam, 1868, pp. 45–46.

### DOCUMENT 2
### Jefferson Davis: Slavery Did Not Cause the Civil War

The reader of many of the treatises on these events, which have been put forth as historical . . . might naturally enough be led to the conclusion that the controversies which arose between the States, and the war in which they culminated, were caused by efforts on the one side to extend and perpetuate human slavery, and on the other to resist it and establish human liberty. The Southern States and Southern people have been sedulously represented as "propagandists" of slavery, and the Northern as the defenders and champions of universal freedom. . . .

I have not attempted, and shall not permit myself to be drawn into any discussion of the merits or demerits of slavery as an ethical or even as a political question. It would be foreign to my purpose, irrelevant to my subject and would only serve—as it has invariably served in the hands of its agitators—to "darken counsel" and divert attention from the genuine issues involved. . . .

As a mere historical fact, we have seen that African servitude among us—confessedly the mildest and most humane of all institutions to which the name "slavery" has ever been applied—existed in all the original States, and that it was recognized and protected in the fourth article of the Constitution. Subsequently, for climatic, industrial, and economical—not moral or sentimental—reasons, it was abolished in the Northern, while it continued to exist in the Southern States. . . . Eleven years after the agitation on the Missouri [Compromise of 1820], when the subject first took a sectional shape, the abolition of slavery was proposed and earnestly debated in the Virginia Legislature, and its advocates were so near the accomplishment of their purpose, that a declaration in its favor was defeated only by a small majority. . . . At a still later period, abolitionist lecturers and teachers were mobbed, assaulted, and threatened with tar and feather in New York, Pennsylvania, Massachusetts, New Hampshire, Connecticut, and other States. . . .

These facts prove incontestably that the sectional hostility which exhibited itself in 1820, on the application of Missouri for admission into the Union, which again broke out on the proposition for the annexation of Texas in 1844, and which reappeared after the Mexican war . . . was not the consequence of any difference on the abstract question of slavery. It was the offspring of sectional rivalry and political ambition. It would have manifested itself just as certainly if slavery had existed in all the States, or if there had not been a negro in America. . . . It was not slavery that threatened a rupture in 1832 [during the nullification crisis], but the unjust and unequal operation of a protective tariff. . . .

The truth remains intact and incontrovertible, that the existence of African servitude was in no wise the cause of the conflict, but only an incident. In the later controversies that arose, however, its effect in operating as a lever upon the passions, prejudices, or sympathies of mankind, was so potent that it has been spread, like a thick cloud, over the whole horizon of historical truth.

*Source:* Davis, Jefferson, "Slavery Did Not Cause the Civil War," *The Rise and Fall of the Confederate Government.* New York, NY: D. Appleton and Co., 1881, pp. 77–80.

**THINKING CRITICALLY**

*What does Stephens mean by "the curse against Canaan"? How do Davis and Stephens differ in discussing the underlying causes of the Civil War? Does the date when each man delivered his opinion suggest a reason for the attitudes toward slavery and the reasons for secession? What evidence would you seek to decide the question of whether the dispute over slavery was the primary motivation for seceding?*

Secession seemed the only alternative left to protect southern rights. South Carolina, which had challenged federal authority in the nullification crisis of the 1830s, was determined to force the other southern states to act. On December 20, 1860, a popular convention unanimously passed a resolution seceding from the Union. The rest of the Deep South followed, and on February 7, 1861, the states stretching from South Carolina to Texas organized the Confederate States of America and elected Jefferson Davis president.

^ When news of secession spread, some southern white women wore decorative cockades made of woven palmetto leaves and silk.
©American Civil War Museum, Richmond, Virginia/Katherine Wetzel, photographer

But the Upper South and the border states declined to secede, hoping that once again Congress could patch together a settlement. Senator John Crittenden of Kentucky proposed extending to California the old Missouri Compromise line of 36°30′. Slavery would be prohibited north of this line and given federal protection south of it in all territories, including any acquired in the future. Furthermore, Crittenden proposed an "unamendable amendment" to the Constitution, forever safeguarding slavery in states where it already existed.

But the Crittenden Compromise was doomed for the simple reason that the two groups who were required to make concessions—Republicans and secessionists—had no interest in doing so. "We have just carried an election on principles fairly stated to the people," Lincoln wrote in opposing the compromise. "Now we are told in advance, the government shall be broken up, unless we surrender to those we have beaten, before we take the offices. If we surrender, it is the end of us, and of the government."

**The Outbreak of War >>** As he prepared to become president, Lincoln pondered what to do about secession. In his inaugural address on March 4, he sought to reassure southerners that he did not intend, "directly or indirectly, to interfere with the institution of slavery in the States where it exists." But echoing Andrew Jackson in the nullification crisis, he maintained that "the Union of these states is perpetual," and he announced that he intended to "hold, occupy and possess" federal property and collect customs duties under the tariff. He closed by calling for a restoration of the "bonds of affection" that united all Americans.

The new president hoped for time to work out a solution, but on his first day in office he was given a dispatch from Major Robert Anderson, commander of the federal garrison at Fort Sumter in Charleston harbor. Sumter was one of the few remaining federal outposts in the South. Anderson informed the government that he was almost out of food and that, unless resupplied, he would have to surrender. For a month Lincoln looked for a way out, but he finally sent a relief expedition. As a conciliatory gesture, he notified the governor of South Carolina that supplies were being sent and that if the fleet were allowed to pass, only food, and not men, arms, or ammunition, would be landed.

The burden of decision now shifted to Jefferson Davis. From his point of view, secession was a constitutional right, and the Confederacy was not a bogus but a legitimate government. To allow the United States to hold property and maintain military forces within the Confederacy would destroy its claim of independence. Davis therefore instructed the Confederate commander at Charleston to demand the immediate surrender of Fort Sumter and, if refused, to open fire. When Anderson declined the ultimatum, Confederate batteries began shelling the fort on April 12 at 4:30 a.m. Some 33 hours later Anderson surrendered. A wave of indignation swept across the North in response. When Lincoln called for 75,000 volunteers to put down the rebellion, four states in the Upper South, led by Virginia, also seceded. Matters had passed beyond compromise.

**The Roots of a Divided Nation** >> And so the Union was broken. After 70 years, the forces of sectionalism and separatism had finally outpulled the ties binding "these United States." Why did affairs come to such a pass?

In some ways, the revolution in markets, improving transportation networks, and increasingly sophisticated systems of credit and finance all served to tie the nation together. The cotton planter who rode the steamship *Fashion* along the Alabama River ("Time's money! Time's money!") was wearing ready-made clothes manufactured in New York from southern cotton. Chauncey Jerome's clocks from Connecticut were keeping time not only for commercial planters but also for Lowell mill workers such as Mary Paul, who learned to measure her lunch break in minutes. Farmers in both Tennessee and Iowa were interested in the price of wheat in New York, for it affected the profits that could be made shipping their grain by the new railroad lines. American society had become far more specialized and far more interdependent since the days of the self-sufficient farmer of the 1780s.

But a specialized economy had not brought unity. For the North, specialization meant more factories, more cities and towns, and a higher percentage of urban workers. Industry affected midwestern farmers as well, for their steel plows and McCormick reapers allowed them to farm larger holdings and required greater capital investment in the new machinery. For its part, the South was transformed by the Industrial Revolution too, as textile factories made cotton the booming mainstay of its economy. But for all its growth, the region remained largely a rural society. Its prosperity stemmed from expansion westward into new areas of cotton production, not new forms of production or technology.

Above all, the intensive labor required to produce cotton, rice, and sugar made slavery an inseparable part of the southern way of life—"so intimately mingled with our social conditions," as one Georgian admitted, "that it would be impossible to eradicate it." An increasing number of northerners viewed slavery as evil, not so much out of high-minded sympathy toward slaves but as a labor system that threatened the republican ideals of white American society.

It fell to the political system to try to resolve sectional conflict, through a system of national parties that represented various interest groups and promoted democratic debate. But the political system had critical weaknesses. The American process of electing a president gave the winning candidate a state's entire electoral vote, regardless of the margin of victory. That procedure made a northern sectional party possible, since the Republicans could never have carried an election on the basis of a popular vote alone. In addition, since 1844 the Democratic Party had required a two-thirds vote to nominate its presidential candidate. Unintentionally, this requirement made it difficult to pick any truly forceful leader and gave the South a veto over the party's candidate. Yet the South, by itself, could not elect a president.

The nation's republican heritage also contributed to the political system's vulnerability. Ever since the Revolution, when Americans accused the king and Parliament of deliberately plotting to deprive them of their liberties, Americans were on the watch for political conspiracies. For their part, Republicans emphasized the existence of the Slave Power bent on eradicating northern rights. Southerners, however, accused the Black Republicans of conspiring to destroy southern equality. Each side viewed itself as defending the country's republican tradition from an internal threat.

 **REVIEW**

Why did Lincoln's election cause some southern states to secede from the Union? Which southern states did not secede until later, and why?

But in the end the threat to the Union came not from within but from beyond its borders. As the United States expanded in the 1840s it incorporated vast new territories, becoming a truly continental republic. And that forced the Union, in absorbing new lands, to define itself anew. If the American frontier had not swept so quickly toward the Pacific, the nation might have been able to postpone the day of reckoning on slavery until some form of gradual emancipation could be adopted. But the luxury of time was not available. The new territories became the battlegrounds for two contrasting ways of life, with slavery at the center of the debate. Elsewhere in the world the push toward abolition grew louder, whether of serfdom in eastern Europe or of slavery across the globe. Americans who saw the issue in moral terms joined that chorus. They saw no reason why the abolition of slavery should be postponed.

In 1850 supporters and opponents of slavery were still willing to compromise on how "the peculiar institution" could expand into the new territories. But a decade later, many Americans both North and South had come to accept the idea of an irrepressible conflict between two societies, one based on freedom, the other on slavery, in which only one side could ultimately prevail. At stake, it seemed, was control of the nation's future. Four years later, as a weary Abraham Lincoln looked back to the beginning of the conflict, he noted, "Both parties deprecated war, but one of them would make war rather than let the nation survive, and the other would accept war rather than let it perish, and the war came."

## Make a Case

Was the Civil War an "irrepressible conflict," as Senator William Seward of New York insisted, or could it have been avoided?

# CHAPTER SUMMARY

In the 1850s the slavery issue reemerged in national politics and increasingly disrupted the party system, leading to the outbreak of war in 1861.

- Fundamental economic changes heightened sectional tensions in the 1850s.
  - The construction of a vast railroad network reoriented western trade from the South to the East.
  - A tide of new immigrants swelled the North's population (and hence its political power) at the expense of the South, thereby stimulating southern fears.
- The old Jacksonian party system was shattered by the nativist movement and by renewed controversy over the expansion of slavery.
  - In the Kansas-Nebraska Act, Senator Stephen A. Douglas tried to defuse the slavery debate by incorporating popular sovereignty (the idea that the people of a territory should decide the status of slavery there). This act effectively repealed the Missouri Compromise.
  - Popular sovereignty failed in the Kansas Territory, where fighting broke out between proslavery and antislavery partisans.
  - Sectional violence reached a climax in May 1856 with the proslavery attack on Lawrence, Kansas, and the caning of Senator Charles Sumner of Massachusetts by Representative Preston S. Brooks of South Carolina.
- Sectional tensions sparked the formation of a new antislavery Republican Party, and the party system realigned along sectional lines.
  - The Supreme Court's *Dred Scott* decision, the Panic of 1857, the congressional struggle over the proslavery Lecompton constitution, and John Brown's attack on Harpers Ferry in 1859 strengthened the two sectional extremes.
- In 1860 Abraham Lincoln became the first Republican to be elected president.
  - Following Lincoln's triumph, the seven states of the Deep South seceded.
  - When Lincoln sent supplies to the Union garrison in Fort Sumter in Charleston harbor, Confederate batteries bombarded the fort into submission.
  - The North rallied to Lincoln's decision to use force to restore the Union, and in response the four states of the Upper South seceded.

## Additional Reading

The problem of the coming of the Civil War has attracted considerable historical attention over the years. John Ashworth, *The Republic in Crisis* (2012), is a lucid, recent interpretation. The political aspects of the conflict also take center stage in Michael F. Holt's brief and incisive work, *The Fate of Their Country: Politicians, Slavery Extension, and the Coming of the Civil War* (2004). Holt stresses the self-interest of the political leaders and plays down the larger structural economic and social factors. A contrasting and similarly brief study can be found in Don E. Fehrenbacher, *Sectional Crises and Southern Constitutionalism* (1995).

The heavy immigration during these years is explored in Raymond L. Cohn, *Mass Migration under Sail* (2009). For slavery's mounting implications for American politics, see Eric Foner, *The Fiery Trial* (2010).

Paul Quigley's *Shifting Grounds* (2012) puts the idea of southern nationalism in a broad spatial context. The most thorough examination of the blend of factors that produced the Republican Party is William E. Gienapp, *The Origins of the Republican Party, 1852–1856* (1987). Eric Foner's classic *Free Soil, Free Labor, Free Men* (1970) focuses on the ideas of Republican Party leaders. For the turbulent history of Kansas in this period, see Nicole Etcheson, *Bleeding Kansas* (2006). The critical events of 1857 are the focal point of Kenneth M. Stampp's *America in 1857* (1990). William W. Freehling's two-volume work *The Road to Disunion* (1991, 2007) offers a broad perspective on the secessionist project; and Charles B. Dew provides a regional view by examining the role of the Secession Commissioners appointed by the Confederacy to persuade wavering southerners in *Apostles of Secession* (2001). Adam Goodheart's *1861: The Civil War Awakening* (2011) presents a rich portrait of the war's beginnings. For a discussion of the broader issues of why the South chose secession and fought the Civil War, see Gary W. Gallagher and Alan T. Nolan, eds., *The Myth of the Lost Cause and Civil War History* (2000); and James L. Huston, *The British Gentry, the Southern Planter, and the Northern Family Farmer* (2015).

16

# The Civil War and the Republic

## 1861–1865

Thousands of volunteers answered President Lincoln's call to preserve the Union, as this march in New York City on April 19, 1865, attests. Few thought the war would last long and engulf the nation in the struggle that transformed it. Only three months later, with the opening battle at Bull Run, did people begin to realize that the struggle might be brutal and grueling.



### >> An American Story

## A ROUT AT BULL RUN

"The war won't last sixty days!" Of that Jim Tinkham was confident. With dreams of a hero's return, Tinkham enlisted for three months in a Massachusetts regiment. Soon he was transferred to Washington, D.C., as part of the Union army being assembled by General Irvin McDowell to crush the rebellion. Tinkham was elated when in mid-July 1861 he was finally ordered to march toward the Confederates concentrated at Manassas Junction, 25 miles away.

The battle began at dawn on July 21, with McDowell commanding 30,000 troops against General Pierre Beauregard's 22,000. Tinkham did not arrive on the field until early afternoon.

^ The Civil War was the first conflict whose major battles routinely involved more than 100,000 troops, and casualties soared beyond the scale Americans experienced in the U.S.-Mexican War. The Battle of Antietam, fought in 1862, produced almost 23,000 casualties, the bloodiest single day of the war. A group of Confederate soldiers are shown where they fell along the Hagerstown Pike. Said one Union officer of the fighting: "Men, I cannot say fell; they were knocked out of the ranks by dozens."
Source: Library of Congress, Prints and Photographs Division [LC-DIG-cwpb-01097]

As his regiment pushed toward the front, he felt faint at his first sight of the dead and wounded, some mangled horribly. But he was soon caught up in the excitement of battle as he charged up Henry Hill. Suddenly the Confederate ranks broke, and exuberant Union troops shouted: "The war is over!"

The arrival of fresh troops, however, enabled the Confederates to regroup. Among the reinforcements who rushed to Henry Hill was 19-year-old Randolph McKim of Baltimore. A student at the University of Virginia, McKim joined the First Maryland Infantry as a private when Abraham Lincoln imposed martial law in his home state. "The cause of the South had become identified with liberty itself," he explained. The arrival of the First Maryland and other reinforcements in the late afternoon turned the tide of battle. The faltering Confederate line held, and Union troops began to withdraw.

But with retreat came confusion. Discipline dissolved and the army degenerated into a stampeding mob. As they fled, terrified troops threw away their equipment, shoved aside officers who tried to stop them, and raced frantically past the wagons and artillery pieces that clogged the road. All the next day in a drizzling rain, mud-spattered troops straggled into the capital in complete disorder. William Russell, an English reporter, asked one pale officer where they were coming from. "Well, sir, I guess we're all coming out of Virginny as far as we can, and pretty well whipped too," he replied. Joining the stampede was Jim Tinkham, who confessed he would have continued on to Boston if he had not been stopped by a guard in Washington.

The rout at Bull Run sobered the North. Gone were dreams of ending the war with one glorious battle. Gone was the illusion that 75,000 volunteers serving three months would be sufficient. As one perceptive observer noted, "We have undertaken to make war without in the least knowing how." Having cast off his earlier misconceptions, a newly determined Jim Tinkham reenlisted for a three-year hitch.

Still, it was not surprising that both sides underestimated the magnitude of the conflict. Warfare as it had evolved in Europe consisted largely of maneuverings that took relatively few lives, respected private property, and left civilians largely unharmed. The Civil War, however, was the first war whose major battles routinely involved more than 100,000 troops. This many combatants could be equipped only through the use of factory-produced weaponry, they could be moved and supplied only with the help of railroads, and they could be sustained only through the concerted efforts of civilian society as a whole. The morale of the population, the quality of political leadership, and the use of industrial and economic might were all critical to the outcome. <<

## THEMATIC TIMELINE

**1861**
Border states remain in the Union; Battle of Bull Run

Lincoln brings the Border States into the Union and begins a campaign to isolate the South (the Anaconda Plan) while invading its territory. General Grant makes progress in the West; McClellan falters in the east.

**1862**
Forts Henry and Donelson captured; Battle of Shiloh; New Orleans captured; McClellan's Peninsula campaign fails; Battle of Antietam; Lincoln suspends writ of habeas corpus throughout the Union; Battle of Fredericksburg

**1863**
Emancipation Proclamation issued; Union institutes conscription; Confederacy enacts general tax laws, initiates impressment; bread riots in the Confederacy; Battle of Gettysburg; Vicksburg captured; New York City draft riots

The war turns in the Union's favor in 1863 with victories at Gettysburg and Vicksburg. Lincoln puts Grant in command.

Wartime demands stress the home front in both the North and especially the South, ravaged by inflation and food shortages.

**1864**
Grant becomes Union general in chief; Grant's Virginia offensive; siege of Petersburg; fall of Atlanta; Lincoln reelected; Sherman's march to the sea

**1865**
Sherman's march through the Carolinas; Lee surrenders; Lincoln assassinated; Thirteenth Amendment ratified

As Grant lays siege to Lee's army at Richmond and Petersburg, Sherman cuts a path of destruction from Atlanta to Savannah. Their offensives compel the Confederacy's surrender.

# THE DEMANDS OF WAR

When the war began, the North had an enormous advantage in manpower and industrial capacity. The Union's population was 2.5 times larger; it contained more railroad track and rolling stock and possessed more than 10 times the industrial capacity.

From a modern perspective the South's attempt to resist against such odds seems hopeless. But the South enjoyed definite strategic advantages. To be victorious it did not need to invade the North—only to defend its own land and prevent the North from destroying its armies. Southern soldiers knew the topography of their home country better than Yankees, and a friendly population regularly supplied them with intelligence about Union troop movements.

The North, in contrast, had to invade and conquer the Confederacy and destroy the southern will to resist. To do so it would have to deploy thousands of soldiers to defend long supply lines in enemy territory, a situation that significantly reduced the northern advantage in manpower. Yet by 1865 Union forces had penetrated virtually every part of the 500,000 square miles of the Confederacy and were able to move almost at will. The Civil War demonstrated the capacity of a modern society to overcome the problems of distance and terrain with technology.

**Political Leadership** >> To sustain a commitment to total war required effective political leadership. This task fell on Abraham Lincoln and Jefferson Davis, presidents of the rival governments.

Jefferson Davis grew up in Mississippi accustomed to life's advantages. Educated at West Point, he had fought in the U.S.-Mexican War, had served as Franklin Pierce's secretary of war, and had become one of the South's leading advocates in the Senate. Although hardworking and committed, he was quarrelsome, resented criticism, and refused to work with those he disliked. "He cannot brook opposition or criticism," one member of the

| | Union | Confederacy | Union advantage |
|---|---|---|---|
| Total population | 23,300,000 | 9,100,000* | **2.5 to 1** |
| White male population (18–45 years) | 4,600,000 | 1,100,000 | **4.2 to 1** |
| Bank deposits | $207,000,000 | $47,000,000 | **4.4 to 1** |
| Value of manufactured goods | $1,730,000,000 | $156,000,000 | **11 to 1** |
| Railroad mileage | 22,000 | 9,000 | **2.4 to 1** |
| Shipping tonnage | 4,600,000 | 290,000 | **16 to 1** |
| Value of textiles produced | $181,000,000 | $10,000,000 | **18 to 1** |
| Value of firearms produced | $2,290,000 | 73,000 | **31 to 1** |
| Pig iron production (tons) | 951,000 | 37,000 | **26 to 1** |
| Coal production (tons) | 13,680,000 | 650,000 | **21 to 1** |
| Corn and wheat production (bushels) | 698,000,000 | 314,000,000 | **2.2 to 1** |
| Draft animals | 5,800,000 | 2,900,000 | **2 to 1** |
| Cotton production (bales) | 43,000 | 5,344,000 | **1 to 124** |

**Slaves accounted for 3,300,000, or 40 percent.*

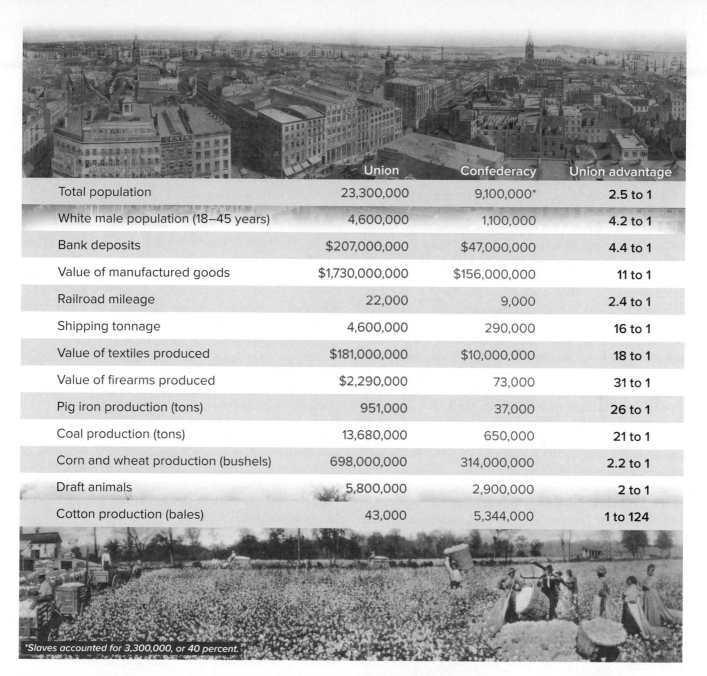

## RESOURCES OF THE UNION AND THE CONFEDERACY, 1861

Source: U.S. Census Bureau 1860 and Long, E. B., *The Civil War Day by Day,* New York, NY: Doubleday, 1971, p. 723.
*Photos:* (*top*): Source: Library of Congress, Prints and Photographs Division [LC-DIG-ppmsca-09854]
(*bottom*) Source: Library of Congress, Prints and Photographs Division [LC-USZ62-120480]

Confederate Congress testified, "and those who do not bow down before him have no chance of success with him."

Yet for all Davis's personal handicaps, he faced an institutional one even more daunting. The Confederacy had been founded on the ideology of states' rights. But to meet the demands of the war, Davis would need to increase the authority of the central government beyond anything the South had ever experienced.

When Lincoln took the oath of office, his national experience consisted of one term in the House of Representatives. But Lincoln was a shrewd judge of character and a superb politician. To achieve a common goal, he willingly overlooked withering criticism and personal slights. He was not easily humbugged, overawed, or flattered, and he never allowed personal feelings to blind him to his larger objectives. "No man knew better how to summon and dispose of political ability to attain great political ends," commented one associate.

"This is essentially a People's contest," Lincoln asserted at the start of the war, and few presidents have been better able to communicate with the average citizen. He regularly visited Union troops in camp, in the field, and in army hospitals. "The boys liked him," wrote Joseph Twichell, from a Connecticut regiment, "in fact his popularity with the army is and has been universal." Always Lincoln reminded the public that the war was being fought for the ideals of the Revolution and the Republic. It was a test, he remarked in his famous address at Gettysburg, of whether a nation "conceived in Liberty, and dedicated to the proposition that all men are created equal" could "long endure."

He also proved the more effective military leader. Jefferson Davis took his title of commander in chief literally, constantly interfering with his generals, but he failed to formulate an overarching strategy. In contrast, Lincoln clearly grasped the challenge confronting the Union. He accepted General Winfield Scott's proposal to blockade the Confederacy, cut off its supplies, and slowly strangle it into submission, just as an anaconda snake squeezes its prey. But unlike Scott, Lincoln realized that this "anaconda plan" was not enough: the South would also have to be invaded and defeated on at least two fronts. The first was the eastern theater in Virginia. A second front was in the West, where Union control of the Mississippi River would divide the Confederacy. Lincoln understood that the Union's superior manpower and matériel would become decisive only when the Confederacy was simultaneously threatened at many points. It took time before the president found generals able to execute this novel strategy.

**The Border States >>** When the war began, only Delaware of the border slave states was certain to remain in the Union. Lincoln's immediate political challenge was to retain the loyalty of Maryland, Kentucky, and Missouri. Maryland especially was crucial, for if it was lost, Washington itself would have to be abandoned.

Lincoln moved vigorously—even ruthlessly—to secure Maryland. He suppressed pro-Confederate newspapers and suspended the writ of **habeas corpus**, the right under the Constitution of an arrested person either to be charged with a specific crime or to be released. That done, he held without trial prominent Confederate sympathizers. Under these conditions Unionists won a complete victory in the fall state election.

**habeas corpus** the right that ensures the government cannot arbitrarily arrest and imprison a citizen without giving grounds for doing so.

As for Kentucky, which had proclaimed itself neutral, Lincoln forbade Union generals from occupying the state, preferring to wait for Unionist sentiment to assert itself. After Unionists won control of the legislature in the summer election, a Confederate army entered the state, giving Lincoln the opening he needed. He quickly sent in troops, and Kentucky stayed in the Union.

In Missouri, guerrilla warfare raged between Union and Confederate sympathizers throughout the war. But a Union victory in the state in March 1862 kept Missouri within the Union. In Virginia internal divisions led to the creation of a new border state, because the hilly western counties where slavery was weak refused to support the Confederacy. After adopting a congressionally mandated program of gradual emancipation, West Virginia was formally admitted to the Union in June 1863.

The Union scored an important triumph in holding the border states. The population of all five equaled that of the four states of the Upper South that had joined the Confederacy, and their production of military supplies—food, animals, and minerals—was greater. Furthermore, Maryland and West Virginia contained railroad lines critical to the defense of Washington, while Kentucky and Missouri gave the Union army access to the major river systems of the western theater, down which it launched the first successful invasions of the Confederacy.

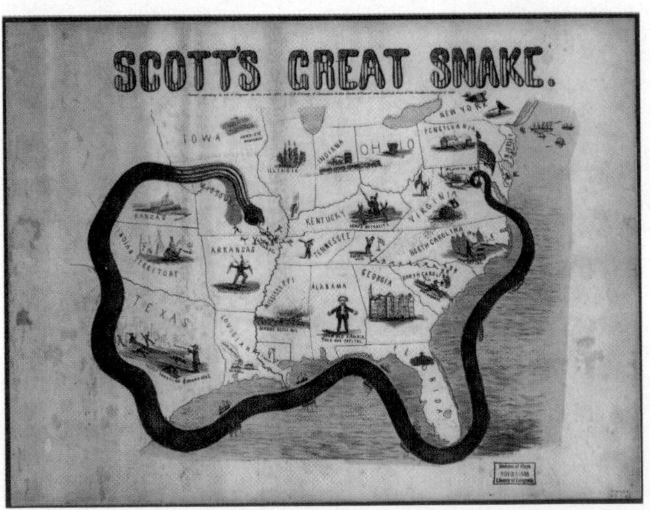
SCOTT'S GREAT SNAKE.
IOWA
OHIO
NEW YORK
KENTUCKY
TENNESSEE
VIRGINIA
ARKANSAS
TEXAS
ALABAMA
GEORGIA

^ General Winfield Scott's "anaconda plan" called for a naval blockade to squeeze the Confederacy, like an anaconda snake. Ships are sketched next to the snake in this cartoon from 1861. But Lincoln realized that the war would have to be taken to the interior of the Confederate States, in the eastern theater of battle (Virginia, the Carolinas, and Georgia) as well as in the western theater, beyond the Appalachian Mountains.
Source: Library of Congress, Geography and Map Division [G3701.S5 1861 .E4 CW 11]

**REVIEW**

How was Lincoln's leadership demonstrated in the opening months of the war? What leadership qualities did Jefferson Davis lack?

# OPENING MOVES

After the Confederate victory at Bull Run, Congress authorized a much larger army of long-term volunteers, and Lincoln named 34-year-old George McClellan, a West Point graduate and former railroad executive, to be the new commander. Energetic and ambitious, he spent the next eight months directing the much-needed task of organizing and drilling the Army of the Potomac.

**Blockade and Isolate** >> Although the U.S. Navy began the war with only 42 ships available to blockade 3,550 miles of Confederate coastline, by the spring of 1862 it had taken control of key islands off the coasts of the Carolinas and Georgia, to use as supply bases. The navy also began building powerful gunboats to operate on the rivers. In April 1862 Flag Officer David G. Farragut ran a gauntlet of Confederate shore batteries to capture New Orleans, the Confederacy's largest port. Memphis, another important river city, fell to Union forces in June.

Small, fast ships continued to slip through the blockade, but southern trade suffered badly nonetheless. As a countermeasure the Confederacy converted the wooden USS *Merrimack* (rechristened the *Virginia*) into an ironclad gunboat. In March 1862 a Union ironclad, the *Monitor*, battled it to a standoff, and the Confederates scuttled the *Virginia* when they evacuated Norfolk in May. After that, the Union's naval supremacy was secure.

The Confederacy looked to diplomacy as another means to lift the blockade. With cotton so vital to European economies, especially Great Britain's, southerners believed Europe would formally recognize the Confederacy and come to its aid. Indeed, the governments of France and Great Britain both seemed to favor the South. Leaders in the two countries dismissed the notion that this was a war to end slavery; after all, Lincoln himself denied it. Stripped of that larger purpose, the conflict seemed to many observers across the Atlantic only a futile and increasingly savage effort to force southerners back into a union they abhorred. Most concretely, the war crippled the global distribution of cotton, something French and British industry remained desperately dependent upon. The two powers contemplated intervention or at least formal recognition of the Confederacy—prospects that terrified Lincoln and thrilled Davis. But France and Britain hesitated to act until Confederate armies demonstrated that they could win the war. Meanwhile, new supplies of cotton from Egypt and India enabled the British textile industry to recover. In the end, Europe's great powers refused to recognize the Confederacy, and the South was left to stand or fall on its own resources.

**Grant in the West** >> In the western war theater the first decisive Union victory was won by a short, shabbily dressed, cigar-chomping general named Ulysses S. Grant. An undistinguished student at West Point, Grant eventually had resigned his commission. He had failed at everything he had tried in civilian life, and when the war broke out, he was a store clerk in Galena, Illinois. Almost

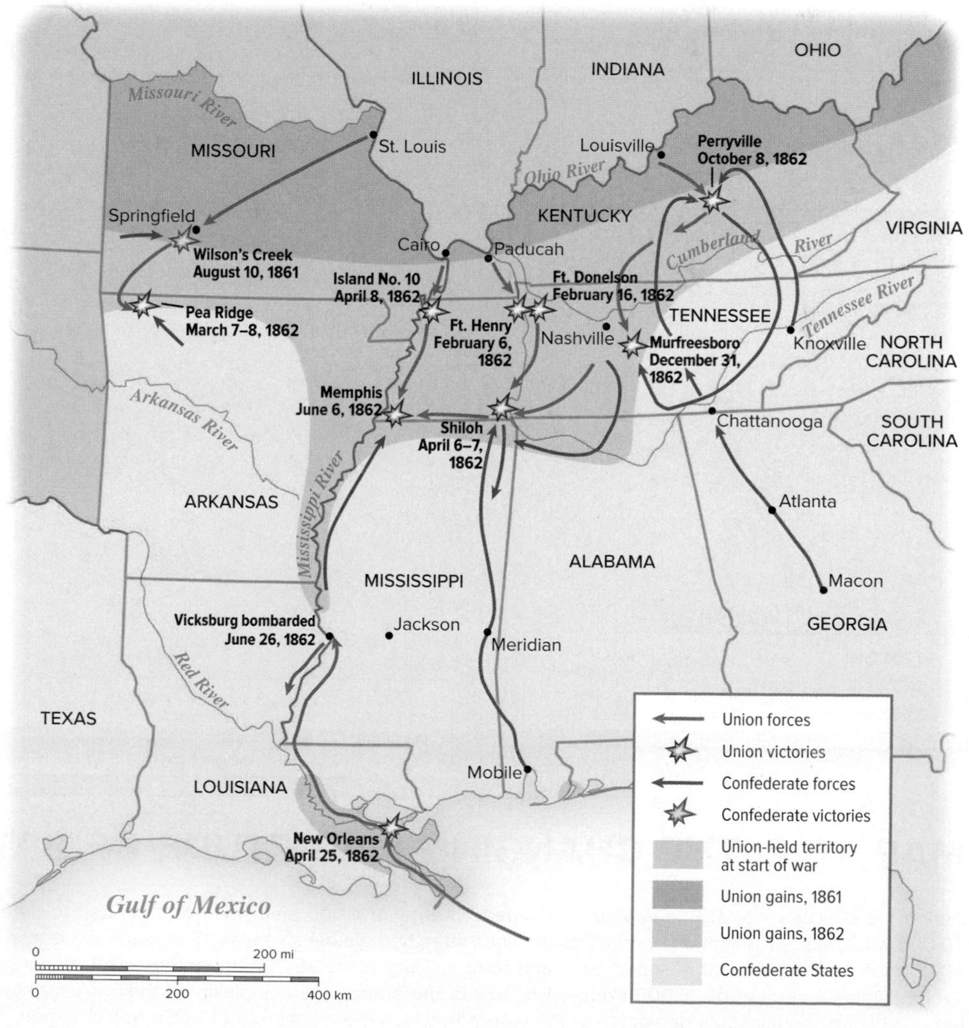

ILLINOIS
INDIANA
OHIO
Missouri River
MISSOURI
St. Louis
Louisville
Perryville
October 8, 1862
Ohio River
KENTUCKY
VIRGINIA
Springfield
Wilson's Creek
August 10, 1861
Cairo
Paducah
Cumberland River
Island No. 10
April 8, 1862
Ft. Donelson
February 16, 1862
Pea Ridge
March 7–8, 1862
TENNESSEE
Tennessee River
Ft. Henry
February 6, 1862
Nashville
Murfreesboro
December 31, 1862
Knoxville
NORTH CAROLINA
Arkansas River
Memphis
June 6, 1862
Shiloh
April 6–7, 1862
Chattanooga
SOUTH CAROLINA
ARKANSAS
Mississippi River
Atlanta
ALABAMA
MISSISSIPPI
Macon
Vicksburg bombarded
June 26, 1862
Jackson
GEORGIA
Meridian
Red River
TEXAS
Mobile
LOUISIANA
New Orleans
April 25, 1862
Gulf of Mexico
0
200 mi
0
200
400 km
Union forces
Union victories
Confederate forces
Confederate victories
Union-held territory at start of war
Union gains, 1861
Union gains, 1862
Confederate States


## MAP 16.1: THE WAR IN THE WEST, 1861–1862

Grant's push southward stalled after his costly victory at Shiloh; nevertheless, by the end of 1862 the Union had secured Kentucky and Missouri, as well as most of Confederate Tennessee and the upper and lower stretches of the Mississippi River. *How did Grant use the geography of the South to plan his campaign in the West?*

39, he promptly volunteered, and two months later became a brigadier general.

Grant's quiet, self-effacing manner gave little indication of his military ability or iron determination. He had a flair for improvising, was alert to seize any opening, and remained extraordinarily calm and clear-headed in battle. Most important, Grant grasped that hard fighting, not fancy maneuvering, would bring victory. "The art of war is simple," he once explained. "Find out where your enemy is, get at him as soon as you can and strike him as hard as you can, and keep moving on."

Grant realized that rivers were avenues into the interior of the Confederacy, and in February 1862, supported by Union gunboats, he captured Fort Henry on the Tennessee River and Fort Donelson on the Cumberland. These victories forced the Confederates to withdraw from Kentucky and middle Tennessee. Grant continued south with 40,000 men, but he was surprised on April 6 by General Albert Johnston at Shiloh, just north of the Tennessee-Mississippi border. Johnston was killed in the day's fierce fighting, but by nightfall his army had driven the Union troops back to the Tennessee River, where they huddled numbly as a cold rain fell.

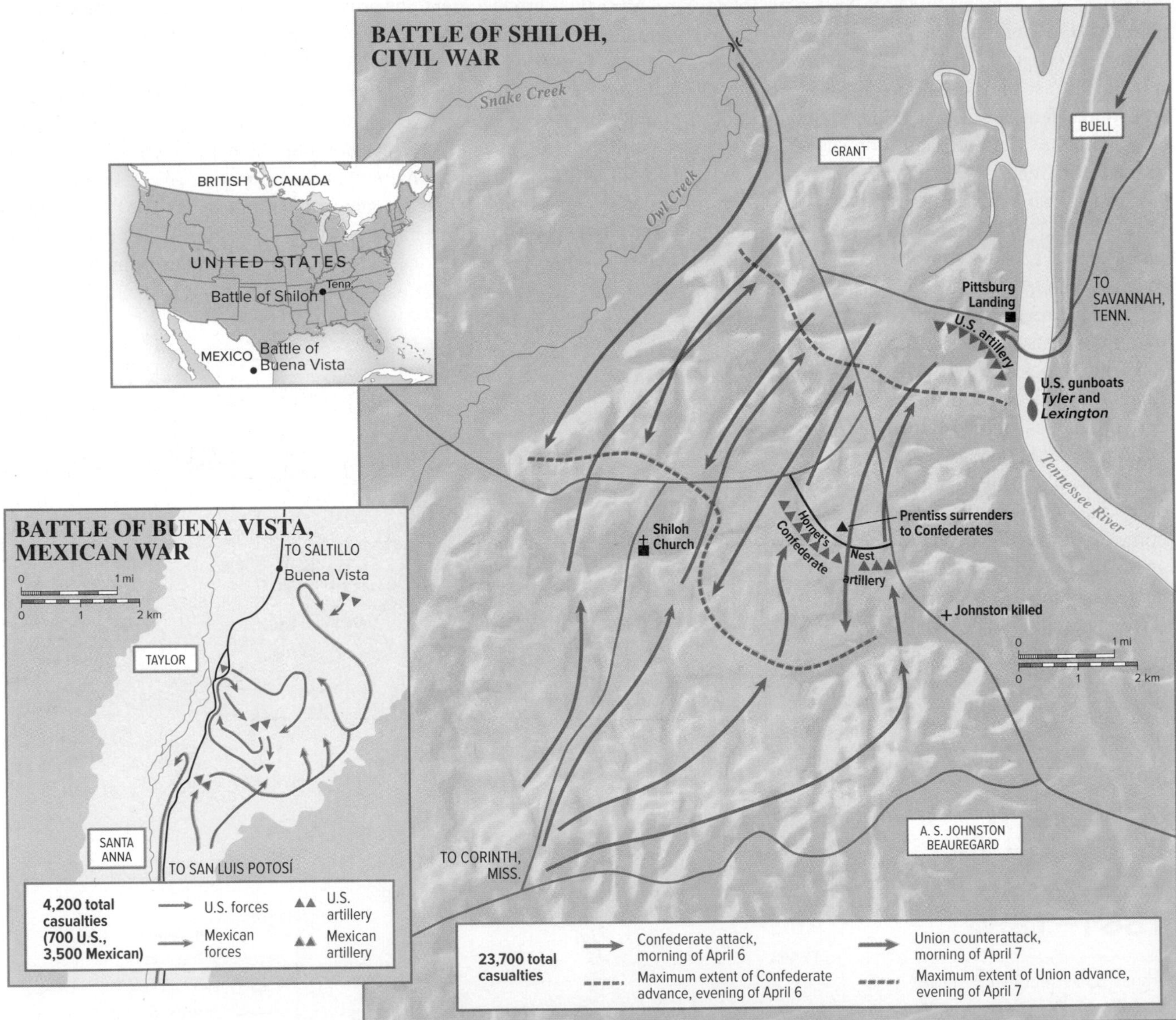

BATTLE OF SHILOH, CIVIL WAR
Snake Creek
Owl Creek
GRANT
BUELL
Pittsburg Landing
TO SAVANNAH, TENN.
U.S. artillery
U.S. gunboats Tyler and Lexington
Tennessee River
Shiloh Church
Hornet's Nest
Confederate artillery
Prentiss surrenders to Confederates
Johnston killed
0 1 mi
0 1 2 km
TO CORINTH, MISS.
A. S. JOHNSTON BEAUREGARD
23,700 total casualties
Confederate attack, morning of April 6
Maximum extent of Confederate advance, evening of April 6
Union counterattack, morning of April 7
Maximum extent of Union advance, evening of April 7
BRITISH CANADA
UNITED STATES
Tenn.
Battle of Shiloh
MEXICO
Battle of Buena Vista
BATTLE OF BUENA VISTA, MEXICAN WAR
TO SALTILLO
Buena Vista
0 1 mi
0 1 2 km
TAYLOR
SANTA ANNA
TO SAN LUIS POTOSÍ
4,200 total casualties (700 U.S., 3,500 Mexican)
U.S. forces
Mexican forces
U.S. artillery
Mexican artillery


## MAP 16.2: THE CHANGING MAGNITUDE OF BATTLE

During the Mexican War at Buena Vista, the American army of 4,800 men was overextended to defend a two-mile line against 15,000 Mexicans. At Shiloh, in contrast, battle lines stretched almost six miles. (The maps are drawn to the same scale.) Against 40,000 Confederates Grant galloped back and forth, rallying some 35,000 troops organized under five subordinates and coordinating the overnight reinforcement of 25,000 troops. The size of the armies, the complexity of their organization, the length of the battle lines, and the number of casualties all demonstrate the extent to which the magnitude of battle had changed.

William Tecumseh Sherman, one of Grant's subordinates, found the general standing under a dripping tree, his coat collar drawn up against the damp, puffing on a cigar. Sherman was about to suggest retreat, but something in Grant's eyes, lighted by the glow of his stogie, made him hesitate. So he said only, "Well, Grant, we've had the devil's own day, haven't we?" "Yes," the Union commander replied quietly. "Lick 'em tomorrow, though." And he did. With the aid of reinforcements, which he methodically ferried across the river all night, Grant counterattacked the next morning and drove the Confederates from the field.

But victory came at a high price, for Shiloh inflicted more than 23,000 casualties. The Confederacy would not yield easily. "At Shiloh," Grant wrote afterward, "I gave up all idea of saving the Union except by complete conquest."

**Eastern Stalemate** >> Grant's victories did not silence his critics, who charged that he drank too much. But Lincoln was unmoved. "I can't spare this man. He fights." That was a quality in short supply in the East, where General McClellan directed operations.

McClellan looked like a general, but beneath his arrogance and bravado lay a self-doubt that rendered him excessively cautious. As the months dragged on and McClellan did nothing but train and plan, Lincoln's frustration grew. "If General McClellan does not want to use the army I would like to *borrow* it," he remarked sarcastically. Where McClellan was cautious and defensive, the aristocratic Robert E. Lee was daring and ever alert to assume the offensive. His first name, one of his colleagues commented, should have been Audacity: "He will take more chances, and take them quicker than any other general in this country."

In the Seven Days' battles, McClellan successfully parried the attacks of Lee and Thomas "Stonewall" Jackson, a deeply religious Calvinist whose rigorous discipline honed his troops to a hard edge. But McClellan, ever cautious, pulled the Union army back until it was under the protection of Union gunboats. Frustrated, Lincoln ordered the Peninsula campaign abandoned and formed a new army under John Pope. After Lee mauled Pope at the Second Battle of Bull Run in August, Lincoln restored McClellan to command.

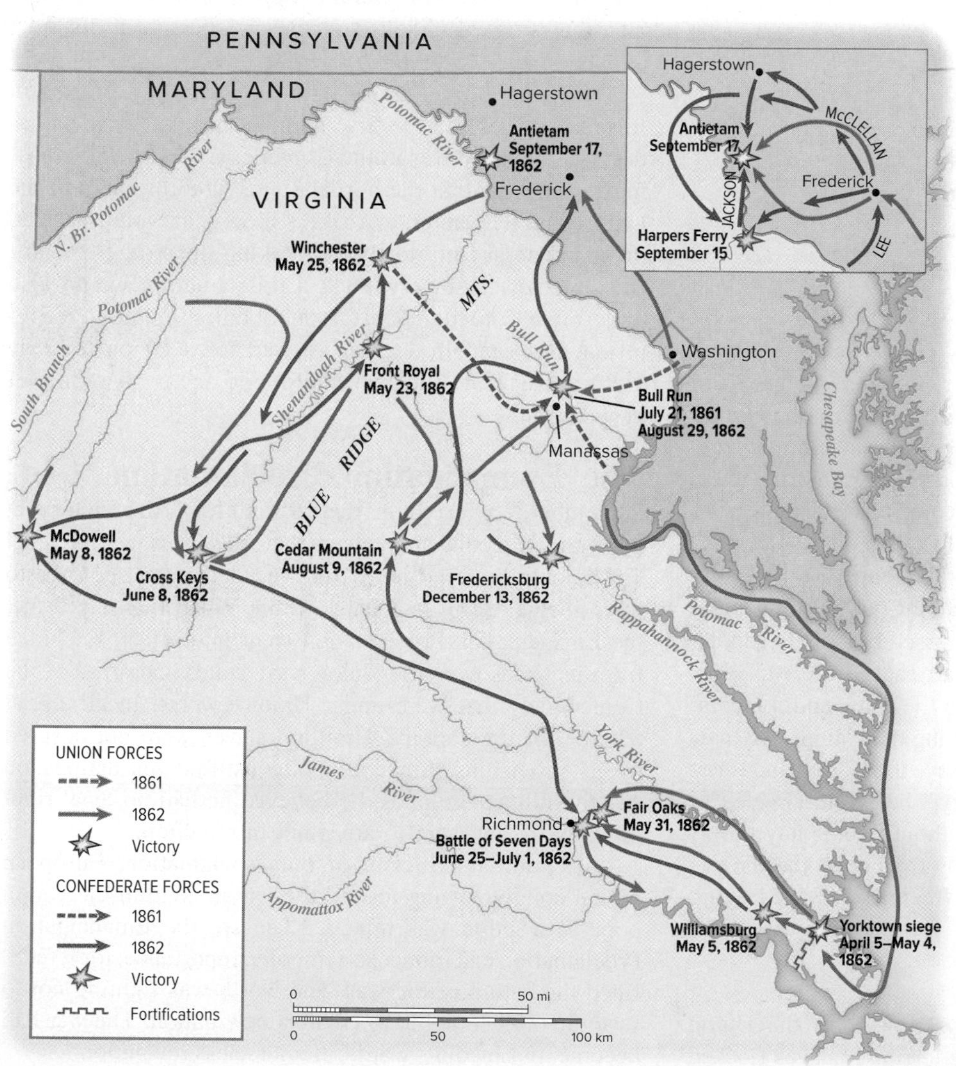

PENNSYLVANIA
MARYLAND
VIRGINIA
Hagerstown
Antietam September 17, 1862
Frederick
Potomac River
N. Br. Potomac
Potomac River
South Branch
Winchester May 25, 1862
MTS.
Bull Run
Washington
Shenandoah River
Front Royal May 23, 1862
Bull Run July 21, 1861 August 29, 1862
Manassas
BLUE RIDGE
Chesapeake Bay
McDowell May 8, 1862
Cross Keys June 8, 1862
Cedar Mountain August 9, 1862
Fredericksburg December 13, 1862
Rappahannock River
Potomac River
York River
James River
Richmond
Battle of Seven Days June 25–July 1, 1862
Fair Oaks May 31, 1862
Appomattox River
Williamsburg May 5, 1862
Yorktown siege April 5–May 4, 1862
Antietam September 17
McCLELLAN
JACKSON
LEE
Harpers Ferry September 15
UNION FORCES
1861
1862
Victory
CONFEDERATE FORCES
1861
1862
Victory
Fortifications
0
50 mi
0
50
100 km


## MAP 16.3: THE WAR IN THE EAST, 1861–1862

McClellan's campaign against Richmond failed when Joseph Johnston surprised him at Fair Oaks. Taking command of the Army of Northern Virginia, Lee drove back McClellan in the Seven Days' battles, then won a resounding victory over Pope in the Second Battle of Bull Run. He followed this up by invading Maryland. McClellan checked his advance at Antietam. The Army of the Potomac's devastating defeat at Fredericksburg ended a year of frustration and failure for the Union in the eastern theater. *What does this map tell us about the relative naval power of the two sides?*

Now Lee looked to strike a decisive victory for the Confederacy. He invaded the North, hoping to detach Maryland and isolate Washington. By good fortune McClellan learned of Lee's battle plan when two Union soldiers stumbled on a discarded "Special Order 191" wrapped around three cigars. But even with this advantage McClellan managed only to launch a series of badly coordinated assaults near Antietam Creek on September 17. Lee repulsed the attack—barely—but his daring plan to invade the North had been blocked, and he retreated back to Virginia. Nearly 5,000 soldiers were killed and another 18,000 wounded, making it the bloodiest single day in American history. When McClellan allowed Lee's army to escape back into Virginia, an exasperated Lincoln permanently relieved him of command.

In the winter of 1862 Union morale sank to an all-time low. General Ambrose Burnside, who assumed McClellan's place, took little more than a month to demonstrate his utter incompetence at the Battle of Fredericksburg. The Union's disastrous defeat there prompted Lincoln to put "Fighting Joe" Hooker in charge. In the West, Grant had emerged as the dominant figure, but the Army of the Potomac still lacked a capable commander, the deaths kept mounting, and no end to the war was in sight.

REVIEW

How did Grant's strategies in the western theater of the war contrast with McClellan's in the eastern theater?

# EMANCIPATION

In 1858 Abraham Lincoln had proclaimed that the United States must eventually become either all slave or all free. When the war began, however, the president refused to make emancipation a Union war aim. He feared the social upheaval that such a revolutionary step would cause, and he did not want to alarm the wavering border slave states.

Republican radicals such as Senator Charles Sumner and newspaper editor Horace Greeley pressed Lincoln to adopt a policy of emancipation. Slavery had caused the war, they argued; its destruction would hasten the war's end. Lincoln, however, placed first priority on saving the Union. "My paramount object in this struggle is to save the Union, and is not either to save or to destroy slavery," he wrote Greeley in 1862. "If I could save the Union without freeing any slave I would do it, and if I could save it by freeing all the slaves I would do it, and if I could save it by freeing some and leaving others alone, I would also do that." For the first year of the war, this remained Lincoln's policy.

**Moving toward Freedom** >> As the Union army began to occupy Confederate territory, slaves flocked to the Union lines. In May 1861 the army adopted the policy of declaring runaway slaves "**contraband** of war" and refused to return them to their rebel owners. In the Confiscation Act of August 1861, Congress provided that slaves used for military purposes by the Confederacy would become free if they fell into Union hands. For a year Lincoln accepted that position but would go no further. When two of his generals, acting on their own authority, abolished slavery in their districts, he countermanded their orders.

> **contraband** goods seized by a government during wartime, when the goods were being used by an enemy nation or being shipped to an enemy nation by a neutral nation. The term was applied during the Civil War to escaped slaves who fled behind Union lines.

By 1862 opinion was clearly shifting. In July Congress passed the Second Confiscation Act, which declared that the slaves of anyone who supported the rebellion would be freed if they came into federal custody. Unlike with the first act, it did not matter whether the slaves had been used for military purposes. Lincoln signed this bill, then proceeded to ignore it. Instead, he encouraged the border states to undertake programs of gradual emancipation, warning them that the war was likely to destroy slavery of its own momentum.

When the border states rebuffed Lincoln's efforts, on July 22 he presented to his cabinet a proposed proclamation freeing the slaves in the Confederacy. He was increasingly confident that the border states would remain in the Union, and he wanted to strike a blow that would weaken the Confederacy militarily. By making the struggle one of freedom versus slavery, such a proclamation would also undermine Confederate efforts to obtain diplomatic recognition. But Lincoln decided to wait for a Union military victory, so that his act would not seem like one of desperation.

**The Emancipation Proclamation** >> On September 22, 1862, in the aftermath of the victory at Antietam, Lincoln announced that all slaves within rebel lines would be freed unless the seceded states returned to their allegiance by January 1, 1863. When that day came, the Emancipation Proclamation went into effect. Excluded from its terms were the Union slave states and areas of the Confederacy that were under Union control. In all, about 830,000 of the nation's 4 million slaves were not covered by its provisions. Since Lincoln justified his actions on strictly military grounds, he believed he had no legal right to apply the measure to areas not in rebellion.

After initial criticism of the Proclamation, European public opinion swung toward the Union. Within the Union popular reaction was mixed. Even so, the Emancipation Proclamation had immense symbolic importance, for it redefined the nature of the war. The North was fighting not to save the old Union but to create a new nation. The war had become, in Lincoln's words, "remorseless revolution."

WATCH MEETING DEC.31.1862
WAITING FOR THE HOUR.
Ent'd according to Act of Congress, A. D. 1863, by W. T. Carlton, in the Clerk's Office of the District Court of the District of Mass.

^ Many African American churches held "watch night meetings" every New Year's Eve, to welcome in the new year. With the Emancipation Proclamation set to go into effect January first, these sessions took on special significance in December 1862.
Source: Library of Congress, Prints and Photographs Division [LC-DIG-ppmsca-10980]

Early in the conflict slaves concluded that emancipation would be one consequence of a Union victory. Perhaps as many as half a million—one-seventh of the total slave population of the Confederacy—fled to Union lines. The ex-slaves, called "freedmen," ended up living in refugee or contraband camps that were overcrowded and disease-ridden and provided only the most basic shelter and food.

Convinced that freed slaves would not work on their own initiative, the U.S. government put some contrabands to work assisting the army. Their wages were well below those paid white citizens for the same work. In the Mississippi valley, where two-thirds of the freedpeople under Union control were located, most were forced to work on plantations leased or owned by loyal planters. They worked for little more than room and board, and the conditions often approximated slavery.

**African Americans' Civil War** >> Under the pressure of war, slavery disintegrated. Well before federal troops entered an area, slaves undermined the institution by openly challenging white authority and claiming greater personal freedom. One experienced overseer reported in frustration that the "slaves will do only what pleases them, go out in the morning when it suits them, come in when they please, etc."

**Black Soldiers** >> In adopting the policy of emancipation, Lincoln also announced that African Americans would be accepted into the navy and, more controversially,

^ Black men, including runaway slaves, joined the Union army and navy beginning in 1863. As soldiers, former slaves developed a new sense of pride and confidence. At his first roll call, recruit Elijah Marrs recalled, "I felt freedom in my bones."
©Corbis via Getty Images

the army. Resistance to accepting black volunteers in the army remained especially strong in the Midwest. Black northerners themselves were divided over whether to enlist, but Frederick Douglass spoke for the vast majority when he argued that once a black man had served in the army, there was "no power on earth which can deny that he has earned the right of citizenship in the United States."

In the end, nearly 200,000 black Americans served in the Union forces, about 10 percent of the Union's total military manpower. Some, including two of Douglass's sons, were free, but most were former slaves who enlisted after escaping to Union lines. As a concession to the racism of white troops, blacks served in segregated units under white officers. Not until June 1864 did Congress grant equal pay to African American soldiers.

Assigned at first to the most undesirable duties, black soldiers successfully lobbied for the chance to fight. They deeply impressed white troops with their courage under fire. "I have been one of those men who never had much confidence in colored troops fighting," one Union officer admitted, "but these doubts are now all removed, for they fought as bravely as any troops in the Fort." In the end 37,000 African American servicemen gave their lives, a rate of loss significantly higher than that among white soldiers. So dismal were conditions in their camps that compared with whites, three times the number of black soldiers died from disease. Yet black recruits had good reasons to fight fiercely: they knew that the freedom of their race hung in the balance, they hoped to win civil rights at home by their performance on the battlefield, they resented racist sneers about their loyalty and ability, and they knew that capture might mean death.

 **REVIEW**

What steps took the North along the path from a war to save the Union to a war in which emancipation became a central goal?

# THE CONFEDERATE HOME FRONT

"How shall we subsist this winter?" John Jones wondered in the fall of 1862. A clerk in the War Department in Richmond, Jones found it increasingly difficult to make ends meet. "I cannot afford to have more than an ounce of meat daily for each member of my family of six," he recorded in 1864. By the end of the year inflation had taken such a toll that a month's supply of food and fuel was costing him $762, a sum sufficient to have supported his family for a year in peacetime. "This is war, terrible war!" The conflict's privations fell most heavily on the Confederacy, where the demands of war fundamentally transformed the southern economy, society, and government.

**The New Economy >>** With the Union blockade tightening, the production of foodstuffs became crucial. More and more plantations switched from cotton to raising grain and livestock. Even so, food production declined. In the last two years of the war the shortage was serious.

The Union blockade also made it impossible to rely on European manufactured goods. So the Confederate War Department built and ran factories, took over the region's mines, and regulated private manufacturers so as to increase the production of war goods. Although the Confederacy never became industrially self-sufficient, its accomplishments were impressive. In fact, the Confederacy sustained itself far better in industrial goods than it did in agricultural produce. It was symbolic that when Lee surrendered, his troops had sufficient guns and ammunition to continue, but they had not eaten in two days.

**New Opportunities for Southern Women >>** Southern white women took an active role in the war. Some gained notoriety as spies; others smuggled military supplies into the South. Many knitted and sewed clothes for soldiers. Perhaps most important, with so many men fighting, women took charge of agricultural production. On plantations the mistress often supervised the slaves as well as the wrenching shift from cotton to foodstuffs. "All this attention to farming is uphill work with me," one South Carolina woman confessed to her army husband.

Another example of southern white women was Emily Lyles Harris, the wife of a small slaveowner in upcountry South Carolina. When her husband joined the army in 1862, she was left to care for her seven children as well as supervise the slaves and manage the farm. Despite the disruptions of wartime, she succeeded remarkably, one year producing the largest crop of oats in the neighborhood and always making enough money for her family to live decently. She took little pride, however, in her achievements. "I shall never get used to being left as the head of affairs at home," she confessed. "The burden is very heavy." Although she pushed on, by 1865 she openly hoped for defeat.

**Confederate Finance and Government >>** The most serious domestic problem the Confederate government faced was finance, for which officials at Richmond never developed a satisfactory program. Only in 1863 did the government begin levying a **graduated income tax** (from 1 to 15 percent) and a series

**graduated income tax** tax based on a percentage of an individual's income, the percentage increasing as total income increases.

## Historian's TOOLBOX

### Face Value?

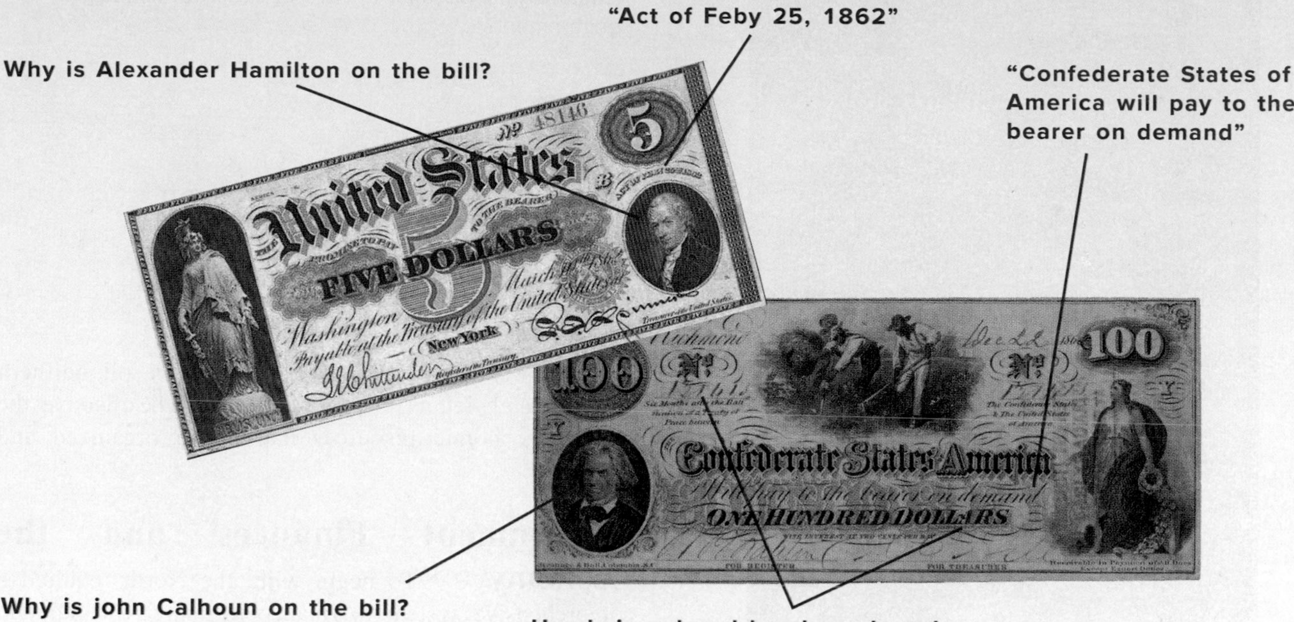
"Act of Feby 25, 1862"
Why is Alexander Hamilton on the bill?
"Confederate States of America will pay to the bearer on demand"
Why is john Calhoun on the bill?
Hand-signed and hand-numbered
United States
FIVE DOLLARS
Confederate States America
ONE HUNDRED DOLLARS
100

A government at war can survive only if it maintains its credit—not only with its bankers but with its citizens. Both the Union and the Confederacy issued paper money to finance the war, and by examining the bills' designs, historians can appreciate the efforts to portray the issuers as creditworthy. The Union note uses Alexander Hamilton to vouch for its reliability—the republic's first treasury secretary, who during the 1790s stabilized the nation's shaky finances. It announces the act of Congress that allows the government to issue the notes: the Legal Tender Act, passed February 25, 1862. And the intricate engraving and red treasury seal made the bill harder to counterfeit. The Confederacy had more difficulty issuing bills because few skilled engravers lived in the South. To help prevent counterfeiting, the Confederacy followed the older tradition of signing each bill individually, employing as many as 200 secretaries to do the tedious work. (The Union's signatures were printed.) But by war's end so many Confederate notes had been issued that they were carted about in wheelbarrows to pay the hugely inflated prices for goods. In the end mere symbols of credit could not obliterate the realities on the ground.

### THINKING CRITICALLY

*The fine print located above the Confederate promise to "pay on demand" reads "Six months after a ratification of a Treaty of Peace between The Confederate States & The United States of America." What effect does this condition have? Who are the people portrayed at the center of the Confederate bill? Why choose to include them?*

(*Left*) ©American Numismatic Association, Edward C. Rochette Money Museum (Fr-61 [face]); (*right*) Source: Library of Congress, Prints and Photographs Division [LC-USZ62-125842]

of excise taxes. Most controversial, the government resorted to a tax-in-kind on farmers that, after exempting a certain portion, took one-tenth of their crops. Even more unpopular was the policy of impressment, which allowed the army to seize private property for its own use, often with little or no compensation.

Above all, the Confederacy financed the war effort simply by printing paper money not backed by specie, some $1.5 billion, which amounted to three times more than the federal government issued. The result was runaway inflation, so that by 1865 a Confederate dollar was worth only 1.7 cents in gold and prices had soared to 92 times their prewar base. Prices were highest in Richmond, where flour sold for $275 a barrel by early 1864 and coats for $350 each. Shortages led to widespread suffering, and even looting.

In politics even more than finance, the Confederacy exercised far greater powers than those of the federal government before 1861. Indeed, Jefferson Davis strove to meet the demands of war by transforming the South into a centralized, national state. He sought to limit state authority over military units, and in April 1862 the Confederacy passed the first national **conscription** law in American history. The same year, the

**conscription** compulsory enrollment for military service, as opposed to voluntary enlistment.

Southern women aided the war effort in a variety of ways, but in addition to the often unexpected jobs they performed, the shadow of death was never far away. This Confederate woman wears a black mourning dress and a brooch showing a Confederate soldier (her dead husband?) and holds her son in her lap. Source: Library of Congress, Prints and Photographs Division [LC-DIG-ppmsca-37270]

Confederate Congress authorized Davis to invoke martial law and suspend the writ of habeas corpus.

Critics protested that Davis was destroying states' rights, the driving principle of the Confederacy. Intent on preserving states' traditional powers, Confederate governors obstructed the draft and retained military supplies. When President Davis suspended the writ of habeas corpus, his own vice president, Alexander H. Stephens, accused him of aiming at a dictatorship. Davis used those powers for a limited time and only with the permission of Congress, yet in practice it made little difference whether the writ was suspended or not. With disloyalty a greater problem than in the Union, the Confederate army arrested thousands of civilians.

But the Confederate draft, more than any other measure, produced an outcry. As one Georgia leader complained, "It's a notorious fact if a man has influential friends—or a little money to spare—he will never be enrolled." Most controversially, the draft exempted from service one white man on every plantation with 20 or more slaves (later reduced to 15). This law was designed to preserve control of the slave population, but more and more non-slaveholders complained that it was a rich man's war and a poor man's fight.

In what ways did the Confederacy, which championed states' rights, become a more centralized, national government?

# THE UNION HOME FRONT

Since the war was fought mostly on southern soil, northern civilians rarely felt its effects directly. Yet to be effective, the North's economic resources had to be organized and mobilized.

**Government Finances and the Economy** >> To begin with, the North required a comprehensive system to finance its massive campaign. Taxing the populace was one obvious means, and taxes paid for 21 percent of Union war expenses, compared with only 1 percent of the Confederacy's. In August 1861 Congress levied the first federal income tax, 3 percent on all incomes over $800 a year. When that, along with increased tariff duties, proved insufficient, Congress enacted a comprehensive tax law in 1862 that for the first time brought the tax collector into every northern household.

The government also borrowed heavily, through the sale of $2.2 billion in **bonds**. It financed the rest of the war's cost by issuing paper money. In all, the Union printed $431 million in greenbacks (so named because of their color on one side). Congress also instituted a national banking system, allowing nationally chartered banks to issue notes backed by U.S. bonds. By taxing state bank notes out of circulation, Congress for the first time created a uniform national currency.

**bonds** certificates of debt issued by a government or corporation promising to repay the buyers their original investment, plus interest, by a specified date of maturity.

During the war the Republican-controlled Congress encouraged economic development. Tariffs to protect industry from foreign competition rose to an average rate of 47 percent, compared to 19 percent in 1860. To encourage development of the West, the Homestead Act of 1862 granted 160 acres of public land—the size of the traditional American family farm—to anyone (including women) who settled and improved the land for five years. In addition, the Land Grant College Act of 1862 donated the proceeds from certain land sales to finance public colleges and universities. This aid was especially crucial in promoting higher education in the West.

^ The superiority of northern industry was an important factor in the war's eventual outcome. Here molten ore is cast into cannons at a foundry in West Point, New York. This factory produced 3,000 cannons during the war.


## A Rich Man's War >>

Over the course of the war the government purchased more than $1 billion worth of goods and services. In response to this heavy demand, the economy boomed and business and agriculture prospered. Since prices rose faster than wages, workers' real income dropped almost 30 percent, which meant that the working class paid a disproportionate share of financing the war.

The Republican belief that government should play a major role in the economy also fostered a cozy relationship between business and politics, inviting corruption. In the rush to profit from government contracts, some suppliers sold inferior goods at inflated prices. Uniforms made of "shoddy"—bits of unused thread and recycled cloth—were fobbed off in such numbers that the word became an adjective describing inferior quality.

Stocks and dividends rose with the economy, speculation during the last two years of the war became particularly feverish, and the fortunes made went toward the purchase of showy luxuries. Like Richmond, Washington became the symbol of this moral decay. Prostitution, drinking, and corruption reached epidemic proportions in the capital, and social festivities became the means to shut out the numbing horror of the casualty lists.

## Women and the Workforce >>

Even more than in the South, the war opened new opportunities for northern women. Countless wives ran farms while their husbands were away at war. One traveler in Iowa reported, "I met more women driving teams on the road and saw more at work in the fields than men." The war also stimulated the shift to mechanization: by 1865 three times as many reapers and harvesters were in use as in 1861. Beyond the farm, women filled approximately 100,000 new jobs in industry. As in the South, they also worked as clerks in the expanding government bureaucracy.

The war allowed women to enter and eventually dominate the profession of nursing. Led by Drs. Emily and Elizabeth Blackwell, Dorothea Dix, and Mary Ann Bickerdyke, women fought the bureaucratic inefficiency of the army medical corps. Their service in the hospital wards reduced the hostility to women in medicine.

One nurse was Clara Barton, who later founded the Red Cross. During the Battle of Fredericksburg, she worked in a battlefield hospital. She later recalled that as she rose from the side of one soldier, "I wrung the blood from the bottom of my clothing, before I could step, for the weight about my feet." She steeled herself at the sight of amputated arms and legs casually tossed in piles outside the front door as the surgeons cut away. Sleeping in a tent nearby, she drove herself to the brink of exhaustion until the last patients were transferred to permanent hospitals.

## Civil Liberties and Dissent >>

In mobilizing the northern war effort, Lincoln did not hesitate to curb dissenters. Shortly after the firing on Fort Sumter, he suspended the writ of habeas corpus in specified areas, which allowed the indefinite detention of anyone suspected of disloyalty or activity against the war. Although the Constitution permitted such suspension in time of rebellion or invasion, Lincoln did so without consulting Congress (unlike President Davis), and he used his power far more broadly, expanding it in 1862 to cover the entire North for cases involving antiwar activities. The president also decreed that those arrested under its provisions could be tried in a military court. Eventually more than 20,000 individuals were arrested, most never brought to trial.

## Make a Case

Was Lincoln justified in suspending habeas corpus? Did events vindicate his decision?

Democrats attacked Lincoln as a tyrant bent on destroying the Constitution. After the war the Supreme Court, in *Ex parte Milligan* (1866), struck down the military conviction of a civilian accused of plotting to free Confederate prisoners of war. The Court ruled that as long as the regular courts remained open, civilians could not be tried by military tribunals.

Republicans labeled northern Democrats who opposed the war **Copperheads**, conjuring up the image of a venomous snake waiting to strike the Union. Copperheads constituted the extreme peace wing of the Democratic Party. They condemned the draft as an attack on individual freedom and an instrument of special privilege. According to the provisions enacted in 1863, a person would be exempt from the present draft by paying a commutation fee of $300, about a year's wages for a worker or an ordinary farmer. Or those drafted could hire a substitute, the cost of which was beyond the reach of all but the wealthy. In July 1863 largely Irish workers in New York City rose in anger against the draft. By the time order was restored four days later, at least 105 people had been killed, the worst loss of life from any riot in American history.

**Copperheads** derogatory term used by Republicans to label northern Democrats who opposed the war policies of the Lincoln administration and advocated a negotiated peace.

REVIEW

How did the war affect women in the workforce? How were civil liberties compromised?

# GONE TO BE A SOLDIER

Marcus Spiegel, the son of a rabbi, came to the United States after the German revolution of 1848 failed. A naturalized citizen when the war began, Spiegel considered it his duty to preserve the Union for his children, so he enlisted and eventually rose to the rank of colonel. He did not go to war to end slavery and flatly proclaimed that black people were not "worth fighting for." But after seeing slavery firsthand, his views changed, and by 1864 he was "in favor of doing away with the institution of Slavery." He assured his wife that "this is no hasty conclusion but a deep conviction." A few weeks later Spiegel died while fighting in Louisiana.

By war's end about 2 million men had served the Union cause and another million the Confederate. They were mostly young, with almost 40 percent of entering soldiers 21 years of age or younger. They were not drawn disproportionately from the poor, and in both North and South, farmers and farm laborers accounted for the largest number of recruits.

**Camp Life >>** The near-holiday atmosphere of the war's early months soon gave way to dull routine. While discipline remained lax by modern standards, Union and Confederate soldiers alike chaffed under supervision. Men from rural areas, accustomed to the freedom of the farm, complained about the endless recurrence of reveille, roll call, and drill. "When this war is over," one Rebel promised, "I will whip the man that says 'fall in' to me." Troops in neither army cared for the spit and polish of regular army men. "They keep us very strict here," noted one Illinois soldier. "It is the most like a prison of any place I ever saw."

On average, soldiers spent 50 days in camp for every day in battle. Camp life was often unhealthy as well as unpleasant. Poor sanitation, miserable food, exposure, and primitive medical care contributed to widespread sickness and disease. It was a common belief that if a fellow went to the hospital, "you might as well say good bye." Conditions were even worse in the Confederate hospitals, for the Union blockade produced a shortage of medical supplies. Twice as many soldiers died from dysentery, typhoid, and other diseases as from wounds.

The boredom of camp life, the horrors of battle, and the influence of an all-male society all loosened morals. Swearing and heavy drinking were common and gambling was pervasive, especially immediately after payday. Prostitutes flooded the camps of both armies. Yet with death so near, some soldiers also sought solace in religion, especially in Confederate camps. A wave of revivals swept their ranks during the last two winters of the war, producing between 100,000 and 200,000 conversions. Significantly, the first major revivals occurred after the South's twin defeats at Vicksburg and Gettysburg. Then, too, as battle after battle thinned Confederate ranks, the prospect of death loomed increasingly large.

**Carnage at the Front >>** Most obviously, Americans at the front produced death and bore witness to it on a staggering scale. Upwards of three-quarters of a million men died in the war. The conflict lasted 1,458 days, claiming more than 500 lives each day on average. But of course the war's carnage did not unfold gradually. The scale of the violence increased as the conflict ground on, and much of the dying came in staggering, appalling surges at places thereafter synonymous with death—places like Bull Run, Shiloh, Antietam, Gettysburg.

Technological advances in the tools of destruction helped account for staggering losses. Smoothbore muskets, which at first served as the basic infantry weapon, gave way to the rifle, so named because of the grooves etched into the barrel to give a bullet spin. A new bullet, the minié ball, allowed the rifle to be easily loaded, and the invention of the percussion cap rendered it serviceable in wet weather. More important, the new weapon had an effective range of 400 yards—up to four times greater than that of the old musket. As a result, soldiers fought each other from greater distances and hit

^ Reveille rouses drowsy Union soldiers on a wintry morning as a drummer boy warms his hands. Instead of the glory they expected, reveille, roll call, and drill constituted Civil War soldiers' usual camp routine. A hired black laborer is already at work as the troops awaken.


their targets far more frequently. Battles took much longer to fight and produced vastly more casualties. Under such conditions, the defense became a good deal stronger than the offense. The larger artillery pieces also adopted rifled barrels, but they lacked good fuses and accurate sighting devices and could not effectively support attacking troops at distance. Artillery remained a deadly defensive weapon, however, one that devastated advancing infantry at close range. More than 100 regiments on both sides suffered in excess of 50 percent casualties in a single battle.

Soldiers struggled to convey to those back home the gruesome truths of combat. "No tongue can tell, no mind can conceive, no pen portray the horrible sights I witnessed this morning," a Union soldier wrote after Antietam. And still they tried. An Indiana soldier at Perryville (7,600 casualties): "It was an awful sight to see there men torn all to pieces with cannon balls and bom shells[.] [T]he dead and wounded lay thick in all directions." An Ohio soldier at Antietam (23,000 casualties), two days after the fighting: "The smell was offul . . . there was about 5 or 6,000 dead bodes decaying over the field. . . . I could have walked on the boddees all most from one end too the other." A Georgian, the day after Chancellorsville (30,000 casualties): "It looked more like a slaughter pen than anything else. . . . The shrieks and groans of the wounded . . . was heart rending beyond all description." A Maine soldier who fought at Gettysburg (50,000 casualties): "I have Seen . . . men rolling in their own blood, Some Shot in one place, Some another . . . our dead lay in the road and the Rebels in their hast to leave dragged both their baggage wagons and artillery over them and they lay mangled and torn to pieces so that Even friends could not tell them. You can form no idea of a battlefield."

Surrounded by the wreckage of war, amid the sounds and smells and sight of thousands of dead or dying men, soldiers who fell on the battlefield struggled to die as they thought they should. If they made it to a camp hospital, they might

^ Field hospitals were often makeshift, like this house where the surgeon operates in front on a table. The only anesthetic is to the right of the patient's head: a bottle of whiskey. Often, wounded soldiers lay untended or waited so long for help that their open wounds teemed with maggots "as though a swarm of bees had settled" on them. Confederate Walter Lenoir had his wounded leg sawn off below the knee and then endured a 20-mile ride in a rude farm wagon, every jolt causing "a pang which felt as if my stump was thrust into liquid fire."
Source: Library of Congress, Prints and Photographs Division [LC-USZ62-46779]

look to exhausted nurses, doctors, or aides to stay with them in their final moments. They might give comrades or outright strangers messages for kin—parents, wives, siblings, and children they knew they would never see again. Many tens of thousands simply died where they fell; some immediately, others more slowly, and some others granted final moments with treasured photographs or with letters from people they loved. Survivors became hardened through horror. "The daily sight of blood and mangled bodies," observed a Rhode Island soldier, "so blunted their finer sensibilities as almost to blot out all love, all sympathy from the heart."

**The Business of Grief** >> This multitude of war dead forced immense tasks upon the living. Millions of people across the country would spend years and lifetimes grieving as a consequence of the war. They wanted to know how their loved ones died, wanted to know where their bodies were, and, increasingly, wanted to retrieve those bodies and bury them closer to home. The railroad network and the new practice of embalming made this heartfelt desire possible for the first time in the history of warfare. Volunteers like Clara Barton organized to help grieving families locate the bodies of their fallen soldiers. A feverish alliance of shipping agents and undertakers emerged to meet demand. Embalmers propped up the preserved corpses of unknown dead in shop windows to advertise their services. Responding to popular pressure, the U.S. government pledged to help in the task of identification and recovery—eventually spending $4 million to identify the resting places of half the Union's fallen soldiers and to rebury most of them. Not until 1906 would the national government assume the same responsibilities for Confederate dead. Instead, such tasks fell to state governments and, after the war, to civic organizations like the Daughters of the Confederacy.

 REVIEW

How did the experience of battle evolve during the war?

# THE UNION'S TRIUMPH

In the spring of 1863 matters still looked promising for Robert E. Lee, the general who had so ably led the Confederates in Virginia. At the battle of Chancellorsville, he won another brilliant victory. But during the fighting Stonewall Jackson was accidentally shot by his own men and died a few days later—a grievous setback for the Confederacy. Determined to invade the North and take the offensive, Lee invaded Pennsylvania in June with an army of 75,000. Lincoln's newest general, George Gordon Meade, warily shadowed the Confederates. On the first of July, advance parties from the two armies accidentally collided at the town of Gettysburg, and the war's greatest battle ensued.

**The Battle of Gettysburg** >> The iconic battle unfolded over the course of three bloody days, July 1–3. Confederate forces enjoyed some successes at first, before either side had all its troops in position, and these successes left Lee emboldened. He instructed General Richard Ewell, in command of Stonewall Jackson's corps, to seize a critical Union position called Cemetery Ridge, "if practicable." Jackson would have taken this for an order and charged his men up the hill. But Ewell, far more cautious, took Lee's wording as a suggestion rather than a command and decided against an attack. Some historians point to this inaction as the critical missed opportunity in the battle.

By day two most Union and Confederate troops had reached Gettysburg. Northern forces arrayed themselves in a formidable defensive line—so formidable that Lee's top subordinate urged him to withdraw and find a more defensible position somewhere to the east. Lee refused, and desperate fighting raged for a second day. The rebels won some close-fought engagements, but failed to consolidate them for lack of coordination. By dusk both sides had endured great casualties, but the robust Union lines held. Again Lee was urged to withdraw. Again he refused. Convinced that he had left Union men bloodied and demoralized, he decided to mass his forces for a coordinated attack on Meade's center the following day. It would prove to be the costliest mistake of his military career.

Day three opened with some surprising Union victories, including one led by a dashing 23-year-old General named George Armstrong Custer. Not until early afternoon did Lee's plan become clear. Around 1 p.m. he gave the order and the sky exploded as massed Confederate artillery blasted away at the Union center. Meade responded in kind, and for an hour Gettysburg was a deafening furnace of explosions and shattering bodies. Then, one by one, the Union guns fell silent. Convinced that he had disabled Meade's artillery and believing victory was at hand, Lee ordered three Confederate divisions to take the Union positions. Remembered as "Pickett's Charge," after General George Pickett, the effort started off confidently with some 12,500 Confederate soldiers marching up to Cemetery Ridge. But the silencing of artillery had been a ruse; once the Confederate infantrymen were well advanced, union cannons roared back to life and began blasting them to pieces. Meade's soldiers poured musket and rifle fire into the cratering Confederate charge,

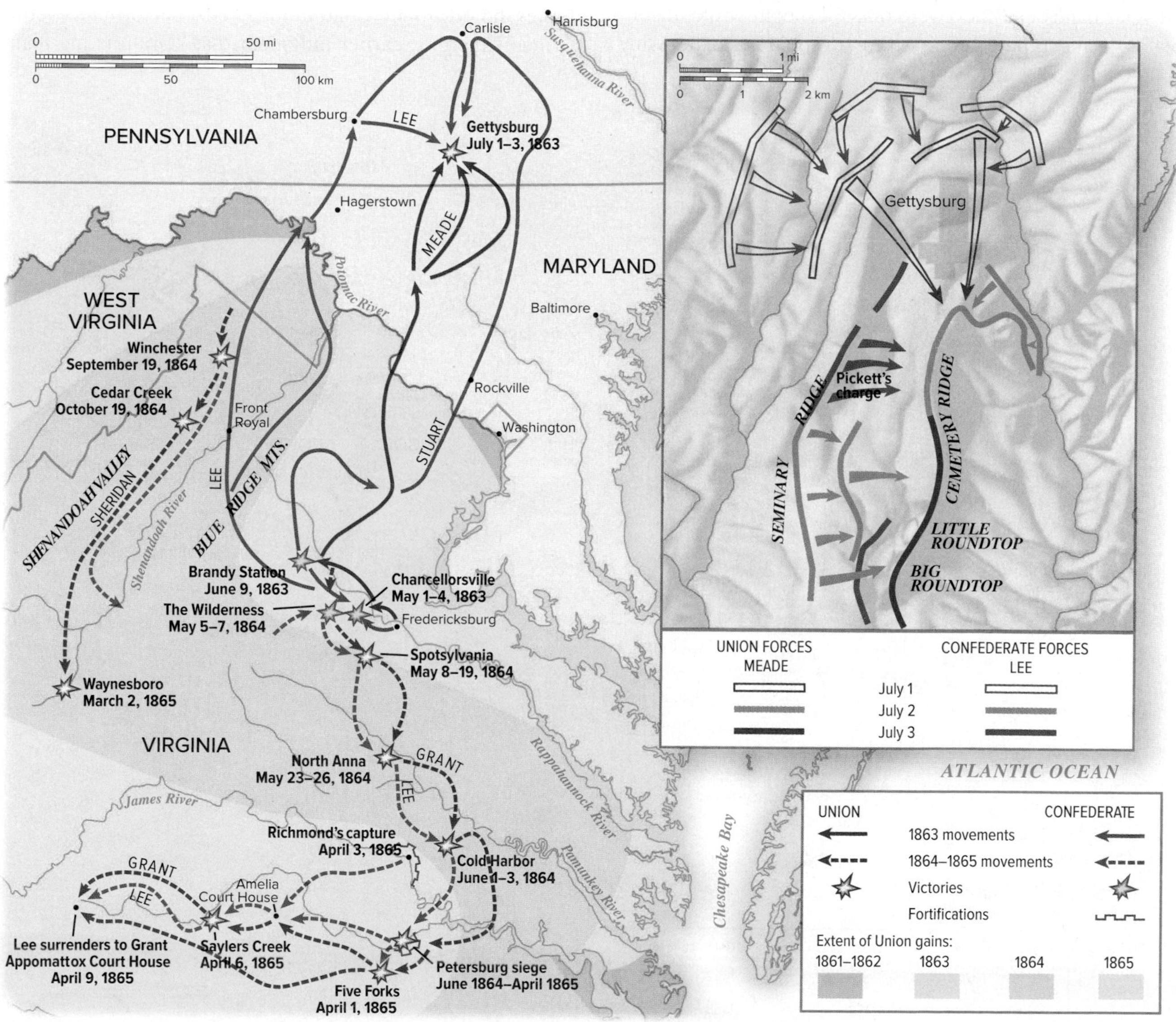

PENNSYLVANIA
MARYLAND
WEST VIRGINIA
VIRGINIA
Carlisle
Harrisburg
Chambersburg
Gettysburg July 1–3, 1863
Hagerstown
Baltimore
Rockville
Washington
Winchester September 19, 1864
Cedar Creek October 19, 1864
Front Royal
Brandy Station June 9, 1863
Chancellorsville May 1–4, 1863
The Wilderness May 5–7, 1864
Fredericksburg
Spotsylvania May 8–19, 1864
Waynesboro March 2, 1865
North Anna May 23–26, 1864
Richmond's capture April 3, 1865
Cold Harbor June 1–3, 1864
Amelia Court House
Lee surrenders to Grant Appomattox Court House April 9, 1865
Saylers Creek April 6, 1865
Five Forks April 1, 1865
Petersburg siege June 1864–April 1865
LEE
MEADE
STUART
GRANT
SHERIDAN
SHENANDOAH VALLEY
BLUE RIDGE MTS.
Susquehanna River
Potomac River
Shenandoah River
James River
Rappahannock River
Pamunkey River
Chesapeake Bay
ATLANTIC OCEAN
Gettysburg
Pickett's charge
SEMINARY RIDGE
CEMETERY RIDGE
LITTLE ROUNDTOP
BIG ROUNDTOP
UNION FORCES MEADE
CONFEDERATE FORCES LEE
July 1
July 2
July 3
UNION
CONFEDERATE
1863 movements
1864–1865 movements
Victories
Fortifications
Extent of Union gains:
1861–1862
1863
1864
1865
0 50 mi
0 50 100 km
0 1 mi
0 1 2 km


## MAP 16.4: THE WAR IN THE EAST, 1863–1865

Lee won his most brilliant victory at Chancellorsville, then launched a second invasion of the North, which ended in defeat at Gettysburg. In 1864 Grant delivered a series of blows against Lee's outnumbered forces in Virginia. Despite staggering losses, Grant pressed on. (Note the casualties listed from mid-May to mid-June of 1864; Grant lost nearly 60,000 men, equal to Lee's total strength.) In April 1865, too weak to defend Richmond any longer, Lee surrendered at Appomattox Court House.

*Which battles showed the steepest losses for Grant?*

with horrible results. "Pickett's division just seemed to melt away in the blue musketry smoke which now covered the hill," one Confederate officer wrote. "Nothing but stragglers came back."

Indeed, only half of the men in the charge returned to Lee's lines, leaving the great general distraught. "It's all my fault," he exclaimed. "You must help me. All good men must rally." But there would be no rally. Lee managed to get most of his surviving men back across the Potomac, barely. Lincoln implored Meade to throw his army at the retreating Confederates and finish them. But Meade's men were battered, bloody, and exhausted; and their general would do little more than harry Lee's retreat. "We had only to stretch forth our hands and they were ours," Lincoln wrote, inconsolably. "And nothing I could say or do could make the Army move." Gettysburg did not end the war. But it did rob Lee of more than 25,000 men—a third of his force. Never again would he be in a position to take the fight to the North.

**Lincoln Finds His General** >> To the west, Grant had been trying for months to capture Vicksburg, a Rebel stronghold on the Mississippi. In a daring maneuver, he left behind his supply lines and marched inland, feeding his army from the produce of Confederate farms. On July 4 the city surrendered. With the fall of Port Hudson, Louisiana, four days later, the Mississippi was completely in Union hands, thus dividing the Confederacy.

Grant followed up this victory by rescuing Union forces holed up in Chattanooga. His performance confirmed Lincoln's earlier judgment that "Grant is my man,

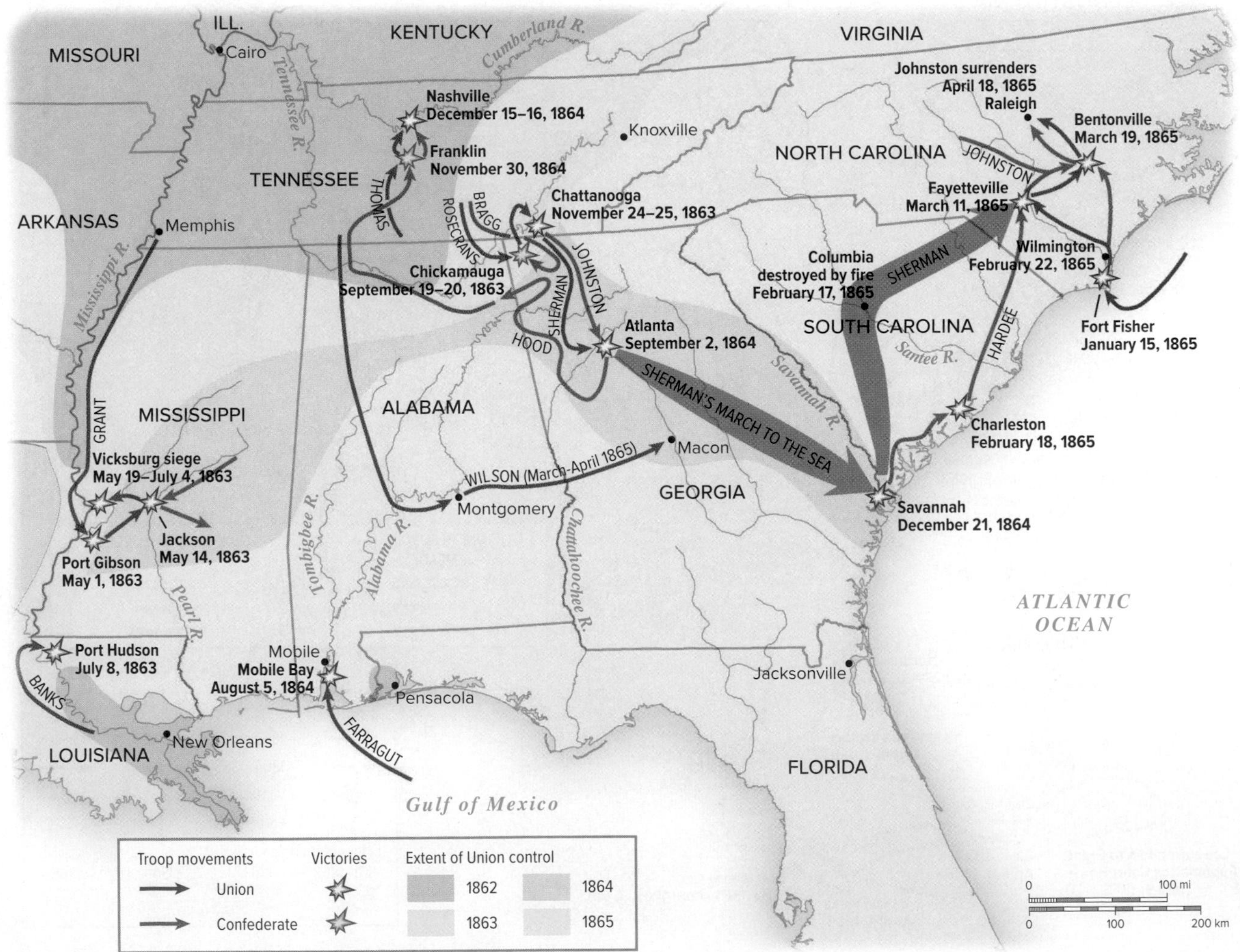

ILL.
MISSOURI
Cairo
KENTUCKY
Cumberland R.
VIRGINIA
Tennessee R.
Nashville
December 15–16, 1864
Knoxville
Johnston surrenders
April 18, 1865
Raleigh
Bentonville
March 19, 1865
Franklin
November 30, 1864
TENNESSEE
NORTH CAROLINA
JOHNSTON
THOMAS
ROSECRANS
BRAGG
Chattanooga
November 24–25, 1863
Fayetteville
March 11, 1865
ARKANSAS
Memphis
Mississippi R.
Chickamauga
September 19–20, 1863
JOHNSTON
SHERMAN
HOOD
Columbia
destroyed by fire
February 17, 1865
SHERMAN
Wilmington
February 22, 1865
Atlanta
September 2, 1864
SOUTH CAROLINA
Fort Fisher
January 15, 1865
Santee R.
HARDEE
Savannah R.
SHERMAN'S MARCH TO THE SEA
GRANT
MISSISSIPPI
ALABAMA
Charleston
February 18, 1865
Vicksburg siege
May 19–July 4, 1863
Macon
WILSON (March–April 1865)
Montgomery
GEORGIA
Savannah
December 21, 1864
Jackson
May 14, 1863
Port Gibson
May 1, 1863
Tombigbee R.
Alabama R.
Chattahoochee R.
Pearl R.
ATLANTIC
OCEAN
Port Hudson
July 8, 1863
Mobile
Mobile Bay
August 5, 1864
Pensacola
Jacksonville
BANKS
New Orleans
LOUISIANA
FARRAGUT
FLORIDA
Gulf of Mexico
Troop movements
Union
Confederate
Victories
Extent of Union control
1862
1863
1864
1865
0
100 mi
0
100
200 km


## MAP 16.5: THE WAR IN THE WEST, 1863–1865

The Union continued its war of mobility in the western theater, bringing more Confederate territory under its control. After Grant captured Vicksburg, the entire Mississippi River lay in Union hands. His victories at Lookout Mountain and Missionary Ridge, near Chattanooga, ended the Confederate threat to Tennessee. In 1864 Sherman divided the Confederacy by seizing Atlanta and marching across Georgia; then he turned north. When Joseph Johnston surrendered, several weeks after Lee's capitulation at Appomattox, the war was effectively over.

and I am his the rest of the war." In March 1864 Lincoln brought Grant east and placed him in command of all the Union armies.

Grant recognized that in the past Union forces had "acted independently and without concert, like a balky team, no two ever pulling together." He intended to change that. While he launched a major offensive against Lee in Virginia, William Tecumseh Sherman, who replaced Grant as commander of the western army, would drive a diagonal wedge through the Confederacy from Tennessee across Georgia. Grant instructed Sherman to "get into the interior of the enemy's country so far as you can, inflicting all the damage you can against their war resources."

In May and June 1864 Grant tried to maneuver Lee out of the trenches and into an open battle. But Lee was too weak to win head-on, so he opted for a strategy of attrition, hoping to inflict such heavy losses that the northern will would break. It was a strategy that nearly worked, for Union casualties were staggering. In a month of fierce fighting, the Army of the Potomac lost 60,000 men. Yet at the end of the campaign Grant's reinforced army was larger than when it started, whereas Lee's was significantly weaker.

Unable to break Lee's lines, Grant settled into a siege of Petersburg, which guarded Richmond's last remaining rail link to the south. In the west, meanwhile, the gaunt and grizzled Sherman fought his way by July to the outskirts of Atlanta, which was heavily defended and gave no sign of capitulating. "Our all depends on that army at Atlanta," wrote Mary Chesnut in August, based on her conversations with Confederate leaders in Richmond. "If that fails us, the game is up."

## War in the Balance >>

As the Union war machine swept more and more northerners south to their death, and with Grant and Sherman bogged down in Virginia and Georgia, Lincoln's chances for reelection in 1864 seemed slim. Yet the president rejected any suggestion to postpone the election, an act that he believed would be to lose democracy itself. At the Republican National Convention, he made certain that the Republican platform called for adoption of a constitutional amendment abolishing slavery. To balance the ticket he selected Andrew Johnson, the military governor of Tennessee and a prowar Democrat, as his running mate. The two men ran under the label of the "Union" party.

The Democrats nominated George McClellan, the former Union commander. Their platform called for an armistice and a peace conference. Warned that a cessation of fighting would lead to disunion, McClellan partially repudiated this position, insisting that "the Union is the one condition of peace—we ask no more." In private he made it clear that if elected he intended to restore slavery. Late in August, Lincoln was still gloomy about his prospects, as well as those of the Union. But Admiral David Farragut won a dramatic victory at Mobile Bay, and in early September, Sherman captured Atlanta. As Secretary of State Seward gleefully noted, "Sherman and Farragut have

^ The war's greatest generals, Ulysses S. Grant (*left*) and Robert E. Lee (*right*), confronted each other in the eastern theater during the last year of the war. A member of a distinguished Virginia family, the tall, impeccably dressed Lee was every inch the aristocratic gentleman. Grant, a short, slouched figure with a stubby beard, dressed indifferently, but his determination is readily apparent in this picture, taken at his field headquarters in 1864.
(left) Source: Library of Congress, Prints and Photographs Division [LC-USZ61-903]; (right) ©Library of Congress/Corbis/VCG via Getty Images

knocked the bottom out of the Chicago [Democratic] nominations."

Polling an impressive 55 percent of the popular vote, Lincoln won 212 electoral votes to McClellan's 21. Eighteen states allowed soldiers to vote in the field, and Lincoln received nearly 80 percent of their ballots. One lifelong Democrat described the sentiment in the army: "I had rather stay out here a lifetime (much as I dislike it) than consent to a division of our country." Jefferson Davis remained defiant, but the last hope of a Confederate victory was gone.

Equally important, the election of 1864 ended any doubt that slavery would be abolished in the reconstructed Union. The Emancipation Proclamation had not put an end to the question, for its legal status remained unclear. Lincoln argued that as a war measure, it would have no standing once peace returned; and in any case, it had not freed slaves in the border states or those parts of the Confederacy already under Union control.

In 1864 the Senate approved an amendment to the Constitution that freed all slaves without compensating their owners. The measure passed the House on January 31, 1865. By December enough states had ratified the Thirteenth Amendment to make it part of the Constitution.

**The Twilight of the Confederacy** >> For the Confederacy the outcome of the 1864 election had a terrible finality. In March 1865 the Confederate Congress authorized recruiting 300,000 slaves for military service. When he signed the bill, Davis announced that freedom would be given to those who volunteered and to their families. That same month he offered through a special envoy to abolish slavery in exchange for British diplomatic recognition. A Mississippi paper denounced this proposal as "a total abandonment of the chief object of this war." The British rejected the offer, and the war ended before any slaves were mustered into the Confederate army, but the demands of war had forced Confederate leaders to forsake the Old South's most important values and institutions.

In the wake of Lincoln's reelection the Confederate will to resist disintegrated. As Sherman pushed deeper into the Confederacy, the war came home to southern civilians as never before. "We haven't got nothing in the house to eat but a little bit o meal," wrote the wife of one Alabama soldier in December 1864. "Try to get off and come home and fix us all up some and then you can go back. . . . If you put off a-coming, 'twont be no use to come, for we'll all . . . [be] in the grave

U.S. Gun Boat Cimerone
U.S TROOPS BURNING "The COLE HOUSE" and PLANTATION. OPPOSITE HARRISON'S
LANDING JAMES RIVER on the night of 1st August 1862

^ General William Sherman demonstrated the tactics of unrestricted war in the autumn of 1864. "Destroyed all we could not eat . . . burned their cotton and gins . . . burned and twisted their railroads," wrote one of Sherman's soldiers. This drawing, done by a Union private, depicts a similar destructive raid on a plantation along Virginia's James River in 1862, and by the spring of 1865 Confederate armies were increasingly unable to resist Union might.
©Virginia Historical Society, Richmond, Virginia

yard." He deserted. In the last months of the fighting, over half the Confederacy's soldiers were absent without leave.

After the fall of Atlanta, Sherman imitated Grant's strategy by abandoning his supply lines for an audacious 300-mile march to the sea. The goal was to deprive Lee's army of the supplies it desperately needed to continue and to break the southern will to resist. Or as he bluntly put it, "to whip the Rebels, to humble their pride, to follow them to their recesses, and make them fear and dread us."

Moving in four columns, Sherman's army covered about 10 miles a day, cutting a path of destruction 50 miles wide. Sherman estimated that his men did $100 million in damage, of which $20 million was necessary to supply his army and the rest was wanton destruction. After he captured Savannah, he turned north and wreaked even greater havoc in South Carolina.

By December the interior of the Confederacy was essentially conquered. Only Lee's army remained, entrenched around Petersburg. As Grant extended his lines, Lee's troops were forced to evacuate Richmond. Westward Grant doggedly pursued the Army of Northern Virginia, until the weary gentleman from Virginia finally asked for terms. On April 9, 1865, Lee surrendered at Appomattox Court House. As the vanquished foe mounted his horse, Grant saluted by raising his hat; Lee raised his respectfully and rode off at a slow trot. The guns were quiet.

Remaining resistance throughout the Confederacy collapsed within a matter of weeks. Visiting the captured

^ Lincoln's funeral procession.
Source: Library of Congress, Prints and Photographs Division [LC-DIG-cwpbh-03254]

city of Richmond on April 4, Lincoln was enthusiastically greeted by the black population. He looked "pale, haggard, utterly worn out," noted one observer. The lines in his face showed how much the war had aged him in only four years. Often his friends had counseled rest, but Lincoln had observed that "the tired part of me is inside and out of reach." The burden, he confessed, was almost too much to bear.

Back in Washington the president received news of Lee's surrender with relief. The evening of April 14, Lincoln, seeking a welcome escape, went to a comedy at Ford's Theater. In the midst of the performance John Wilkes Booth, a famous actor and Confederate sympathizer, slipped into the presidential box and shot him. Lincoln died the next morning. As he had called on his fellow citizens to do in his Gettysburg Address, the sixteenth president had given his "last full measure of devotion" to the Republic.

REVIEW

What decisions by Grant and Lincoln led the Union to victory?

The assassination left a tiredness in the nation's bones—a tiredness "inside" and not easily within reach. In every way the conflict had produced fundamental changes. There was, of course, the carnage. Historians now believe that upwards of 800,000 men lost their lives, as many or more than as in all the other wars the nation has fought from the Revolution through Vietnam combined. In material terms, the conflict cost an estimated $20 billion, more than 11 times the total amount spent by the federal government from 1789 to 1861. Even without adding the market value of freed slaves, southern wealth declined 43 percent, transforming what had been the richest section in the nation (on a white per-capita basis) into the poorest.

The Civil War reordered not only the national economy but also economic relations worldwide. Manufacturers were forced to supply the army on an unprecedented scale over great distances. One consequence was the creation of truly national industries in flour milling, meatpacking, clothing and shoe manufacture, and machinery making.

People across the globe felt the effects of the war, particularly because of changes in the cotton trade. In 1860 the South was supplying more than three-quarters of all cotton imported by Britain, France, Germany, and Russia. When the war cut off that supply, India, Egypt, and Brazil all opened new cotton fields. The effect of the trade on Egypt was so great, historians of that nation rank the American Civil War along with the construction of the Suez Canal as the most crucial events in its nineteenth-century history.

Politically, the war dramatically changed the balance of power. The South lost its substantial influence, as did the Democratic Party, while the Republicans emerged in a dominant position. The Union's military victory also signaled the triumph of nationalism. The war destroyed the idea that the Union was a voluntary confederacy of sovereign states, as John C. Calhoun and others had argued, and that the states had the right to secede.

In the short run, the price was disillusionment and bitterness. The war's corrosive effect on morals corrupted American life and politics, destroyed idealism, and severely crippled humanitarian reform. Millennialism and perfectionism were victims of the war's appalling slaughter, forsaken for a new emphasis on practicality, order, materialism, and science.

The remorseless logic of war did push to the fore one ideal of the previous decades: the abolition of slavery. In 1865 the United States joined the ranks of those nations that had embraced emancipation: Britain in 1833, Portugal (1836), Sweden (1847), Denmark and France (1848), and Holland (1863). (Spain would not relent until 1886.) Without war to force the issue, slavery in the United States might have continued for decades.

George Ticknor, a prominent critic of the day, reflected on the changes that had shaken the nation. The war, it seemed to him, had left "a great gulf between what happened before it in our century and what has happened since. . . . It does not seem to me as if I were living in the country in which I was born."

# CHAPTER SUMMARY

The Civil War's outcome depended not just on armies but also on the mobilization of society's human, economic, and intellectual resources.

- Confederate president Jefferson Davis's policy of concentrating power in the government at Richmond, along with the resort to a draft and impressment of private property, provoked strong protests from many southerners.
- Abraham Lincoln's suspension of habeas corpus and interference with civil liberties were equally controversial, but Lincoln skillfully kept the border states in the Union.
- Lincoln at first resisted pressure to make emancipation a Union war aim, but he eventually issued the Emancipation Proclamation, which transformed the meaning of the war.
- African Americans helped undermine slavery and contributed vitally to the Union's military victory.
- On the home front, women confronted new responsibilities and enjoyed new occupational opportunities.
- Confederate financial and tax policies and the tightening Union blockade increased hardships within the Confederacy.
- Technology, particularly the use of rifles and rifled artillery, revolutionized the tactics of warfare.
- The Union victory at Gettysburg and Lincoln's choice of Grant to lead Union forces marked the turning point of the war. Union success relied in part on the strategy of bringing the war home to the South's civilian population.

## Additional Reading

Good single-volume histories of the Civil War are James M. McPherson's *Battle Cry of Freedom* (1988); and Mark Neely's *The Civil War and the Limits of Destruction* (2007). For the evolution of the Union's strategy toward southern civilians, see Mark Grimsley, *The Hard Hand of War* (1995).

The best biography of Lincoln is David Donald, *Lincoln* (1995). William E. Gienapp, *Abraham Lincoln and Civil War America* (2002), is concise and focuses on the presidential years. The president's complex thinking on slavery is the subject of Eric Foner's masterful book *The Fiery Trial* (2010). For the contradictions of the southern project, see Stephanie McCurry, *Confederate Reckoning* (2010). Drew Gilpin Faust, *Mothers of Invention* (1996), is an imaginative study of slave-holding women; Edward Ayers, *In the Presence of Mine Enemies* (2003), examines the consequences of war in Virginia and Pennsylvania. For the northern home front, see J. Matthew Gallman, *The North Fights the Civil War* (1994). Chandra Manning, in *What This Cruel War Was Over* (2007), argues that Union rank and file widely believed in emancipation as early as the end of 1861. Drew Gilpin Faust, *This Republic of Suffering* (2008), brilliantly explores how death, grieving, and belief were changed by this most deadly of wars; and Martha Hodes, *Mourning Lincoln* (2015), delves into the ways that ordinary people, North and South, responded to the president's assassination. For Britain's critical role in the diplomacy of the Civil War, see Amanda Foreman's *A World on Fire* (2011); and for that conflict's global significance, read Don H. Doyle's *The Cause of All Nations* (2015).

# 17 Reconstructing the Union

## 1865–1877

Artist Alfred Waud sketched these African American soldiers greeting loved ones after being mustered out of the army in Arkansas. The war's end brought both joy and uncertainty about what was to come.

Source: Library of Congress, Prints and Photographs Division [LC-USZC4-13286]

## >> An American Story

# A SECRET SALE AT DAVIS BEND

Joseph Davis had had enough. Well on in years and financially ruined by the war, he decided to sell his Mississippi plantations Hurricane and Brierfield to Benjamin Montgomery and his sons in November 1866. Selling a plantation was common enough after the war, but this transaction was bound to attract attention, since Joseph Davis was the elder brother of

Jefferson Davis. Indeed, before the war the ex-Confederate president had operated Brierfield as his own plantation, even though his brother retained legal title to it. But the sale was unusual for another reason—so unusual that the parties involved agreed to keep it secret. The plantation's new owners were black, and Mississippi law prohibited African Americans from owning land.

Though a slave, Benjamin Montgomery had been the business manager of the two Davis plantations before the war. He had also operated a store on Hurricane Plantation with his own line of credit in New Orleans. In 1863 Montgomery fled to the North, but when the war was over, he returned to Davis Bend, where the federal government had confiscated the Davis plantations and was leasing plots of the land to black farmers. Montgomery quickly emerged as the leader of the African American community at the Bend.

Then, in 1866, President Andrew Johnson pardoned Joseph Davis and restored his lands. Davis was now over 80 years old and lacked the will and stamina to rebuild, yet unlike many ex-slaveholders, he felt bound by obligations to his former slaves. Convinced that with encouragement African Americans could succeed in freedom, he sold his land secretly to Benjamin Montgomery. Only when the law prohibiting African Americans from owning land was overturned in 1867 did Davis publicly confirm the sale to his former slave.

For his part, Montgomery undertook to create a model society at Davis Bend based on mutual cooperation. He rented land to black farmers, hired others to work his own fields, sold supplies on credit, and ginned and marketed the crops. The work was hard indeed: Davis Bend's farmers faced the destruction caused by the war, several disastrous floods, insects, droughts, and declining cotton prices. Yet before long, cotton production exceeded that of the prewar years. The Montgomerys eventually acquired 5,500 acres, which made them reputedly the third-largest planters in the state, and they won national and international awards for the quality of their cotton. Their success demonstrated what African Americans, given a fair chance, might accomplish.

The experiences of Benjamin Montgomery were not those of most black southerners, who did not own land or have a powerful white benefactor. Yet all African Americans shared Montgomery's dream of economic independence. As one black veteran noted: "Every colored man will be a slave, and feel himself a slave until he can raise him own bale of cotton and put him own mark upon it and say this is mine!" Blacks could not gain effective freedom simply through a proclamation of emancipation. They needed economic power, including their own land that no one could unfairly take away. And political power too, if the legacy of slavery was to be overturned.

How would the Republic be reunited, now that slavery had been abolished? War, in its blunt way, had roughed out the contours of a solution, but only in broad terms. The North, with its industrial might, would be the driving force in the nation's economy and retain the dominant political voice. But would African Americans receive effective power? How would North and South readjust their economic and political relations? These questions lay at the heart of the problem of Reconstruction. <<

## THEMATIC TIMELINE

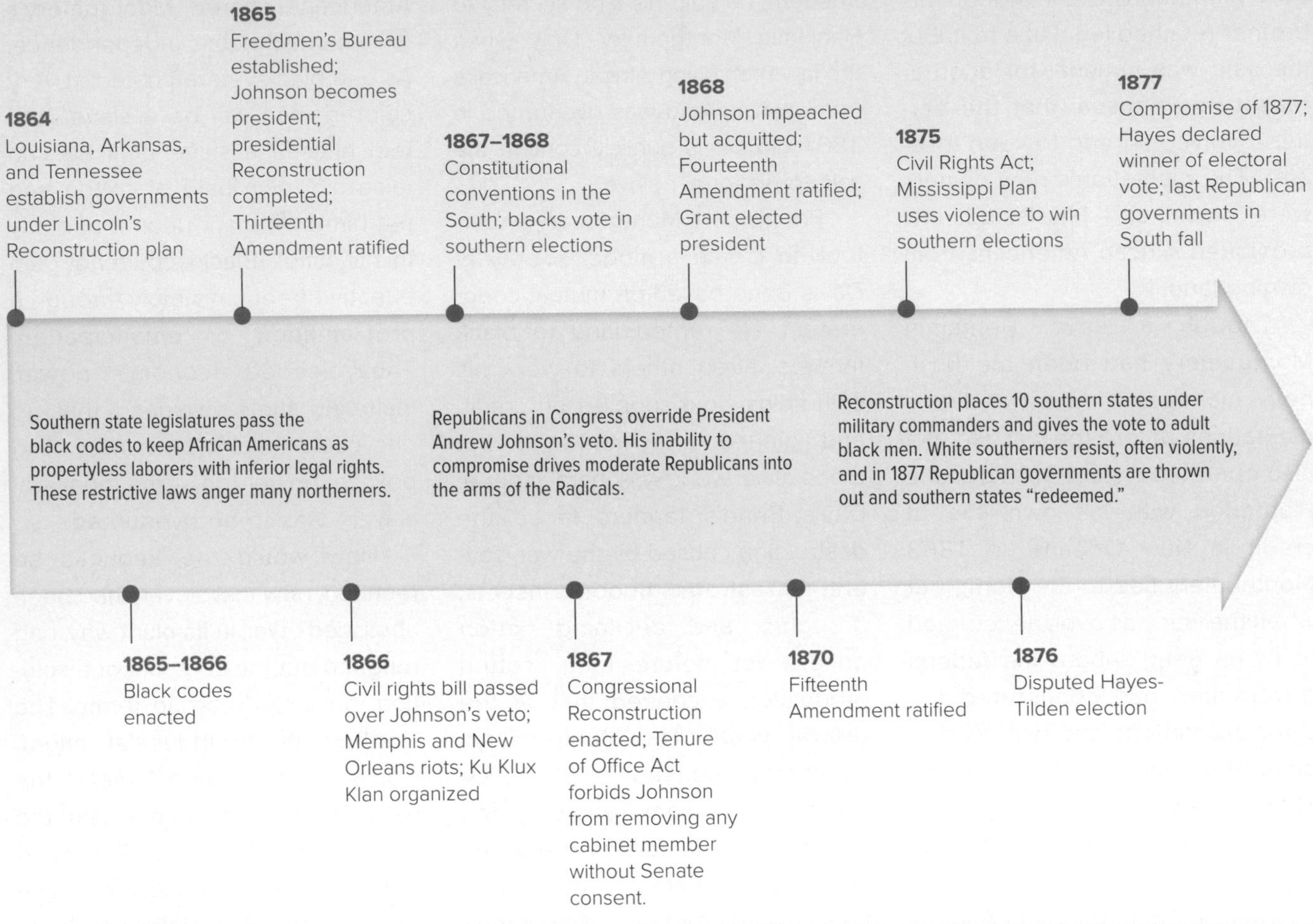
1864
Louisiana, Arkansas, and Tennessee establish governments under Lincoln's Reconstruction plan
1865
Freedmen's Bureau established; Johnson becomes president; presidential Reconstruction completed; Thirteenth Amendment ratified
1867–1868
Constitutional conventions in the South; blacks vote in southern elections
1868
Johnson impeached but acquitted; Fourteenth Amendment ratified; Grant elected president
1875
Civil Rights Act; Mississippi Plan uses violence to win southern elections
1877
Compromise of 1877; Hayes declared winner of electoral vote; last Republican governments in South fall
Southern state legislatures pass the black codes to keep African Americans as propertyless laborers with inferior legal rights. These restrictive laws anger many northerners.
Republicans in Congress override President Andrew Johnson's veto. His inability to compromise drives moderate Republicans into the arms of the Radicals.
Reconstruction places 10 southern states under military commanders and gives the vote to adult black men. White southerners resist, often violently, and in 1877 Republican governments are thrown out and southern states "redeemed."
1865–1866
Black codes enacted
1866
Civil rights bill passed over Johnson's veto; Memphis and New Orleans riots; Ku Klux Klan organized
1867
Congressional Reconstruction enacted; Tenure of Office Act forbids Johnson from removing any cabinet member without Senate consent.
1870
Fifteenth Amendment ratified
1876
Disputed Hayes-Tilden election

# PRESIDENTIAL RECONSTRUCTION

Throughout the war Abraham Lincoln had considered Reconstruction his responsibility. Elected with less than 40 percent of the popular vote in 1860, he was acutely aware that once the states of the Confederacy were restored to the Union, the Republicans would be weakened unless they ceased to be a sectional party. By a generous peace, Lincoln hoped to attract former Whigs in the South, who supported many of the Republicans' economic policies, and build up a southern wing of the party.

**Lincoln's 10 Percent Plan** >> Lincoln outlined his program in a Proclamation of **Amnesty** and Reconstruction, issued in December 1863. When a minimum of 10 percent of the qualified voters from 1860 took a **loyalty oath** to the Union, they could organize a state government. The new state constitution had to abolish slavery and provide for black education, but Lincoln did not insist that high-ranking Confederate leaders be barred from public life.

**amnesty** general pardon granted by a government, usually for political crimes.

**loyalty oath** oath of fidelity to the state or to an organization.

Lincoln indicated that he would be generous in granting pardons to Confederate leaders and did not rule out compensation for slave property. Moreover, while he privately advocated limited black suffrage in the disloyal southern states, he did not demand social or political equality for black Americans. In Louisiana, Arkansas, and Tennessee he recognized pro-Union governments that allowed only white men to vote.

The Radical Republicans found Lincoln's approach much too lenient. Strongly antislavery, Radical members of Congress had led the struggle to make emancipation a war aim. Now they led the fight to guarantee the rights of former slaves, or freedpeople. The Radicals believed that it was the duty of Congress, not the president, to set the terms under

EX. C.S.A.

<< The mood of white southerners at the end of the war was mixed. Many, like the veteran caricatured here by northern cartoonist Thomas Nast, remained hostile. Others, like Texas captain Samuel Foster, came to believe that the institution of slavery "had been abused, and perhaps for that abuse this terrible war . . . was brought upon us as a punishment."

Source: Library of Congress, Prints and Photographs Division [LC-USZ62-131562]

which states would regain their rights in the Union. Though the Radicals often disagreed on other matters, they were united in a determination to readmit southern states only after slavery had been ended, black rights protected, and the power of the planter class destroyed.

Under the direction of Senator Benjamin Wade of Ohio and Representative Henry Winter Davis of Maryland, Congress formulated a much stricter plan of Reconstruction. The Wade-Davis bill required half the white adult males to take an oath of allegiance before drafting a new state constitution, and it restricted political power to the hardcore Unionists. Lincoln vetoed this approach, but as the war drew to a close, he appeared ready to make concessions to the Radicals, such as placing the defeated South temporarily under military rule. Then Booth's bullet found its mark, and Lincoln's final approach to Reconstruction would never be known.

## Reconstruction under Andrew Johnson >>

In the wake of defeat, the immediate reaction among white southerners was one of shock, despair, and hopelessness. Some former Confederates were openly antagonistic. A North Carolina innkeeper remarked bitterly that Yankees had stolen his slaves, burned his house, and killed all his sons, leaving him only one privilege: "To hate 'em. I got up at half-past four in the morning, and sit up till twelve at night, to hate 'em." Most Confederate soldiers were less defiant, having had their fill of war. Even among hostile civilians the feeling was widespread that the South must accept northern terms. A South Carolina paper admitted that "the conqueror has the right to make the terms, and we must submit."

This psychological moment was critical. To prevent a resurgence of resistance, the president needed to lay out in unmistakable terms what white southerners had to do to regain their old status in the Union. Perhaps even a clear and firm policy would not have been enough. But with Lincoln's death, the executive power had come to rest in far less capable hands.

Andrew Johnson, the new president, had been born in North Carolina and eventually moved to Tennessee, where he worked as a tailor. Barely able to read and write when he married, he rose to political power by portraying himself as the champion of the people against the wealthy planter class. "Some day I will show the stuck-up aristocrats who is running the country," he vowed as he began his political career. Although he accepted emancipation as one consequence of the war, Johnson lacked any concern for the welfare of African Americans. "Damn the negroes," he said during the war, "I am fighting these traitorous aristocrats, their masters." After serving in Congress and as military governor of Tennessee following its occupation by Union forces, Johnson, a Democrat, was tapped by Lincoln in 1864 as his running mate on the rechristened "Union" ticket.

A JOHNSON
TAILOR

^ Andrew Johnson was a staunch Unionist, but his contentious personality and inflexibility masked a deep-seated insecurity, which was rooted in his humble background. As a young man, he worked and lived in this rude tailor shop in Greeneville, Tennessee.

(left) Source: Library of Congress, Prints and Photographs Division [LC-BH-832-2417]; (right) Source: Library of Congress, Prints and Photographs Division [LC-USZ62-130976]

The Radicals expected Johnson to uphold their views on Reconstruction, and on assuming the presidency he spoke of prosecuting Confederate leaders and breaking up planters' estates. Unlike most Republicans, however, Johnson strongly supported states' rights, and his political shortcomings sparked conflicts almost immediately. Scarred by his humble origins, he became tactless and inflexible when challenged or criticized, alienating even those who sought to work with him.

Johnson moved to return the southern states to the Union quickly. He prescribed a loyalty oath that most white southerners would have to take to regain their civil and political rights and to have their property, except for slaves, restored. High Confederate officials and those with property worth over $20,000 had to apply for individual pardons. Once a state drafted a new constitution and elected state officers and members of Congress, Johnson promised to revoke martial law and recognize the new state government. Suffrage was limited to white citizens who had taken the loyalty oath. This plan was similar to Lincoln's, though more lenient. Only informally did Johnson stipulate that the southern states were to renounce their ordinances of secession, repudiate the Confederate debt, and ratify the Thirteenth Amendment abolishing slavery, which had been passed by Congress in January 1865 and was in the process of being ratified by the states. (It became part of the Constitution in December.)

## The Failure of Johnson's Program

>> The southern delegates who met to construct new governments were in no mood to follow Johnson's recommendations. Several states merely repealed instead of repudiating their ordinances of secession, rejected the Thirteenth Amendment, or refused to repudiate the Confederate debt.

Nor did the new governments allow African Americans any political rights or provide in any effective way for black education. In addition, each state passed a series of laws, often modeled on its old slave code, that applied only to African Americans. These **"black codes"** did give African Americans some rights that had not been granted to slaves. They legalized marriages from slavery and allowed black southerners to hold and sell property and to sue and be sued in state courts. Yet their primary intent was to keep African Americans as propertyless agricultural laborers with inferior legal rights. The new freedpeople could not serve on juries, testify against whites, or work as they pleased. Mississippi prohibited them from buying or renting farmland, and most states ominously provided that black people who were vagrants could be arrested and hired out to landowners. Many northerners were incensed by the restrictive black codes, which violated their conception of freedom.

**black codes** laws passed by southern states in 1865 and 1866, modeled on the slave codes in effect before the Civil War. The codes did grant African Americans some rights not enjoyed by slaves, but their primary purpose was to keep African Americans as propertyless agricultural laborers.

Southern voters under Johnson's plan also defiantly elected prominent Confederate military and political leaders to office. At this point, Johnson could have called for new elections or admitted that a different program of Reconstruction was needed. Instead, he caved in. For all his harsh rhetoric, he shrank from the prospect of social upheaval, and as the lines of ex-Confederates waiting to see him lengthened, he began issuing special pardons almost as fast as they could be printed. Publicly Johnson put on a bold face, announcing that Reconstruction had been successfully completed. But many members of Congress were deeply alarmed, and the stage was set for a serious confrontation.

## Johnson's Break with Congress

>> The new Congress was by no means of one mind. A small number of Democrats and a few conservative Republicans backed the president's program of immediate and unconditional restoration. At the other end of the spectrum, a larger group of Radical Republicans, led by Thaddeus Stevens, Charles Sumner, Benjamin Wade, and others, was bent on remaking southern society in the image of the North. Reconstruction must "revolutionize Southern institutions, habits, and manners," insisted Representative Stevens, "or all our blood and treasure have been spent in vain."

As a minority the Radicals needed the aid of the moderate Republicans, the largest bloc in Congress. Led by William Pitt Fessenden and Lyman Trumbull, the moderates had no desire to foster social revolution or promote racial equality in the South. But they wanted to keep Confederate leaders from reassuming power, and they were convinced that the former slaves needed federal protection. Otherwise, Trumbull declared, the freedpeople would "be tyrannized over, abused, and virtually reenslaved."

^ Thaddeus Stevens, Radical Republican leader in the House. Source: Library of Congress, Prints and Photographs Division [LC-USZ62-63460]

The central issue dividing Johnson and the Radicals was the place of African Americans in American society. Johnson accused his opponents of seeking "to Africanize the southern half of our country," while the Radicals championed civil and political rights for African Americans. The only way to maintain loyal governments and develop a Republican party in the South, Radicals argued, was to give black men the ballot. Moderates agreed that the new southern governments were too harsh toward African Americans, but they feared that too great an emphasis on black civil rights would alienate northern voters.

In December 1865, when southern representatives to Congress appeared in Washington, a majority in Congress voted to exclude them. Congress also appointed a joint committee, chaired by Senator Fessenden, to look into Reconstruction.

The growing split with the president became clearer after Congress passed a bill extending the life of the Freedmen's Bureau. Created in March 1865, the bureau provided emergency food, clothing, and medical care to war refugees (including white southerners) and took charge of settling freedpeople on abandoned lands. The new bill gave the bureau the added responsibilities of supervising special courts to resolve disputes involving freedpeople and establishing schools for black southerners. Although this bill passed with virtually unanimous Republican support, Johnson vetoed it.

Johnson also vetoed a civil rights bill designed to overturn the more flagrant provisions of the black codes. The law made African Americans citizens of the United States and granted them the right to own property, make contracts, and have access to courts as parties and witnesses. (The law did not go so far as to grant freedpeople the right to vote.) For most Republicans Johnson's action was the last straw, and in April 1866 Congress overrode his veto. Congress then approved and promptly overrode the president's veto of a slightly revised Freedmen's Bureau bill in July. Johnson's refusal to compromise drove the moderates into the arms of the Radicals.

**The Fourteenth Amendment** >> To prevent unrepentant Confederates from taking over the reconstructed state governments and denying African Americans basic freedoms, the Joint Committee on Reconstruction proposed an amendment to the Constitution, which passed both houses of Congress with the necessary two-thirds vote in June 1866.

The amendment guaranteed repayment of the national war debt and prohibited repayment of the Confederate debt. To counteract the president's wholesale pardons, it disqualified prominent Confederates from holding office. Because moderates balked at giving the vote to African Americans, the amendment merely gave Congress the right to reduce the representation of any state that did not have impartial male suffrage. The practical effect of this provision, which Radicals labeled a "swindle," was to allow northern states to retain white suffrage, since unlike southern states they had few African Americans in their populations and thus would not be penalized.

The amendment's most important provision, Section 1, defined an American citizen as anyone born in the United States or naturalized, thereby automatically making African Americans citizens. Section 1 also prohibited states from abridging "the privileges or immunities" of citizens, depriving "any person of life, liberty, or property, without due process of law," or denying "any person . . . equal protection of the laws." The framers of the amendment probably intended to prohibit laws that applied to one race only, such as the black codes, or that made certain acts felonies when committed by black but not white people, or that decreed different penalties for the same crime when committed by white and black lawbreakers. The framers probably did not intend to prevent segregation (the legal separation of the races) in schools and public places.

Johnson denounced the amendment and urged southern states not to ratify it. Ironically, of the seceded states only the president's own state ratified the amendment, and Congress readmitted Tennessee with no further restrictions. The telegram sent to Congress by a longtime foe of Johnson, officially announcing Tennessee's approval, ended with this sardonic salutation: "Give my respects to the dead dog in the White House."

**The Election of 1866** >> When Congress blocked his policies, Johnson undertook a speaking tour of the East and Midwest in the fall of 1866 to drum up popular support. But the president found it difficult to convince northern audiences that white southerners were fully repentant. Only months earlier white mobs in Memphis and New Orleans had attacked black residents and killed nearly 100 in two major race riots. "The negroes now know, to their sorrow, that it is best not to arouse the fury of the white man," boasted one Memphis newspaper. When the president encountered hostile audiences during his northern campaign, he made matters only worse by trading insults and proclaiming that the Radicals were traitors.

SCENES IN MEMPHIS, TENNESSEE, DURING THE RIOT—BURNING A FREEDMEN'S SCHOOL-HOUSE.

In 1866 white mobs in Memphis and New Orleans attacked African Americans in two major riots. Here rioters set fire to a schoolhouse used by freedpeople.

Source: Library of Congress, Prints and Photographs Division [LC-USZ62-111152]

**bloody shirt** campaign tactic of "waving the bloody shirt" invoked the deaths and casualties from the Civil War as a reason to vote for Republicans as the party of the Union rather than Democrats, who had often opposed the war.

Not to be outdone, the Radicals vilified Johnson as a traitor aiming to turn the country over to former rebels. Resorting to the tactic of "waving the **bloody shirt**," they appealed to voters by reviving bitter memories of the war. In a classic example of such rhetoric, Governor Oliver Morton of Indiana proclaimed that "every bounty jumper, every deserter, every sneak who ran away from the draft calls himself a Democrat. Every 'Son of Liberty' who conspired to murder, burn, rob arsenals and release rebel prisoners calls himself a Democrat. In short, the Democratic party may be described as a common sewer."

Voters soundly repudiated Johnson, as the Republicans won more than a two-thirds majority in both houses of Congress. The Radicals had reached the height of their power, propelled by genuine alarm among northerners that Johnson's policies would lose the fruits of the Union's victory. Johnson was a president virtually without a party.

 **REVIEW**

What were Lincoln's and Andrew Johnson's approaches to Reconstruction, and why did Congress reject Johnson's approach?

# CONGRESSIONAL RECONSTRUCTION

With a clear mandate in hand congressional Republicans passed their own program of Reconstruction, beginning with the first Reconstruction Act in March 1867. Like all later pieces of Reconstruction legislation, it was repassed over Johnson's veto.

Placing the 10 unreconstructed states under military commanders, the act provided that in enrolling voters, officials were to include black adult males but not former Confederates, who were barred from holding office under the Fourteenth Amendment. Delegates to the state conventions were to frame constitutions that provided for black suffrage and disqualified prominent ex-Confederates from office. The first state legislatures to meet under the new constitution were required to ratify the Fourteenth Amendment. Once these steps were completed and Congress approved the new state constitution, a state could send representatives to Congress.

White southerners found these requirements so insulting that officials took no steps to register voters. Congress then enacted a second Reconstruction Act, also in March, ordering the local military commanders to put the machinery of Reconstruction into motion. Johnson's efforts to limit the power of military commanders produced a third act, passed in July, that upheld their superiority in all matters. When the first election was held in Alabama to ratify the new state constitution, whites boycotted it in sufficient numbers to prevent a majority of voters from participating. Undaunted, Congress passed the fourth Reconstruction Act (March 1868), which required ratification of the constitution by only a majority of those voting rather than those who were registered.

By June 1868 Congress had readmitted the representatives of seven states. Texas, Virginia, and Mississippi did not complete the process until 1869. Georgia finally followed in 1870.

## Post-Emancipation Societies in the Americas

>> With the exception of Haiti's revolution (1791–1804), the United States was the only society in the Americas in which the destruction of slavery was accomplished by violence. But the United States, uniquely among these societies, enfranchised former slaves almost immediately after the emancipation. Thus, in the United States, former masters and slaves battled for control of the state in ways that did not occur in other post-emancipation societies. In most of the Caribbean, property requirements

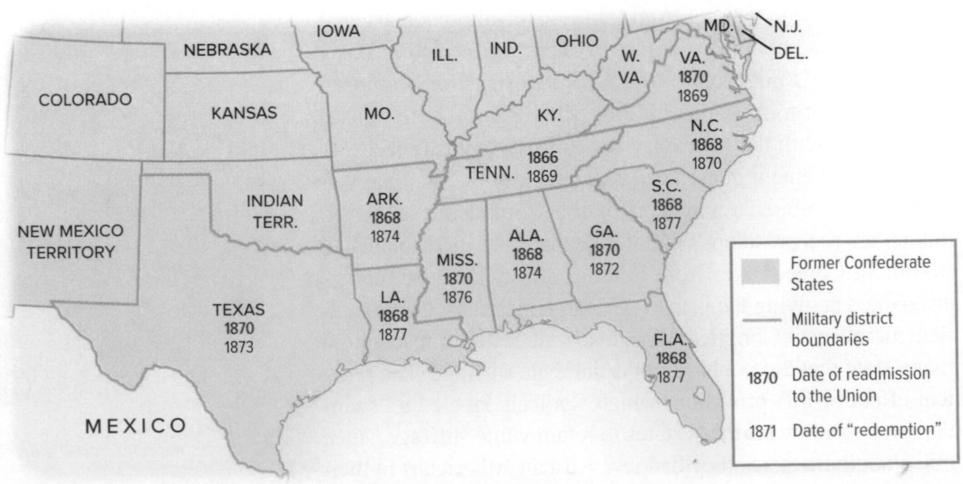
IOWA
NEBRASKA
ILL.
IND.
OHIO
MD.
N.J.
DEL.
W. VA.
VA. 1870 1869
COLORADO
KANSAS
MO.
KY.
N.C. 1868 1870
TENN. 1866 1869
INDIAN TERR.
ARK. 1868 1874
S.C. 1868 1877
NEW MEXICO TERRITORY
ALA. 1868 1874
GA. 1870 1872
MISS. 1870 1876
LA. 1868 1877
TEXAS 1870 1873
FLA. 1868 1877
MEXICO
Former Confederate States
Military district boundaries
1870 Date of readmission to the Union
1871 Date of "redemption"

**MAP 17.1: THE SOUTHERN STATES DURING RECONSTRUCTION**

for voting left the planters in political control. Jamaica, for example, with a population of 500,000 in the 1860s, had only 3,000 voters.

Moreover, in reaction to political efforts to mobilize disenfranchised black peasants, Jamaican planters dissolved the assembly and reverted to being a Crown colony governed from London. Of the sugar islands, all but Barbados adopted the same policy, thereby blocking the potential for any future black peasant democracy. Nor did any of these societies have the counterparts of the Radical Republicans, a group of outsiders with political power that promoted the fundamental transformation of the post-emancipation South. These comparisons highlight the radicalism of Reconstruction in the United States, which alone saw an effort to forge an interracial democracy.

**The Land Issue** >> While the political process of Reconstruction proceeded, Congress debated whether land should be given to former slaves to foster economic independence. At a meeting with Secretary of War Edwin Stanton near the end of the war, African American leaders had declared: "The way we can best take care of ourselves is to have land, and till it by our own labor." The Second Confiscation Act of 1862 had authorized the government to seize and sell the property of supporters of the rebellion. In June 1866, however, President Johnson ruled that confiscation laws applied only to wartime.

After more than a year of debate, Congress rejected all proposals to give land to former slaves. Given Americans' strong belief in self-reliance, little sympathy existed for the idea that government should support any group. In addition, land redistribution represented an attack on property rights, another cherished American value. "A division of rich men's lands amongst the landless," argued the *Nation*, a Radical journal, "would give a shock to our whole social and political system from which it would hardly recover without the loss of liberty." By 1867 land reform was dead.

**Impeachment** >> Throughout 1867 Congress routinely overrode Johnson's vetoes, but the president undercut congressional Reconstruction in other ways. He interpreted the new laws narrowly and removed military commanders who vigorously enforced them. Congress responded by restricting his power to issue orders to military commanders in the South. It also passed the Tenure of Office Act, which forbade Johnson to remove any member of the cabinet without the Senate's consent. The intention of this law was to prevent him from firing Secretary of War Edwin Stanton, the only remaining Radical in the cabinet.

When Johnson tried to dismiss Stanton in February 1868, the House of Representatives angrily approved articles of impeachment. The articles focused on the violation of the Tenure of Office Act, but the charge with the most substance was that Johnson had acted to systematically obstruct Reconstruction legislation. In the trial before the Senate, his lawyers argued that a president could be impeached only for an indictable crime, which Johnson clearly had not committed. The Radicals countered that impeachment applied to political offenses, not merely criminal acts. In May 1868 the Senate voted 35 to 19 to convict, one vote short of the two-thirds majority needed. The seven Republicans who joined the Democrats in voting for acquittal were uneasy about using impeachment as a political weapon.

 REVIEW

What was Congress's approach to Reconstruction, and why did it not include a provision for giving land to former slaves?

# RECONSTRUCTION IN THE SOUTH

As the power of the Radicals in Congress waned, the fate of Reconstruction increasingly hinged on developments in the southern states themselves. Power in these states rested with the new Republican parties, representing a coalition of black and white southerners and transplanted northerners.

**Black and White Republicans** >> Once African Americans received the right to vote, black men constituted as much as 80 percent of the Republican voters in the South. They steadfastly opposed the Democratic Party with its appeal to white supremacy. But during Reconstruction, African Americans never held office in proportion to their voting strength. No African American was ever elected governor. And only in South Carolina, where more than 60 percent of the population was black, did they control even one house of the state legislature. Between 15 and 20 percent of the state officers and 6 percent of members of Congress (2 senators and 15 representatives) were black. Only in South Carolina did black officeholders approach their proportion of the population.

Those who held office came from the top levels of African American society. Among state and federal officeholders, perhaps 80 percent were literate, and over a quarter had been free before the war, both marks of distinction in the black community. Their occupations also set them apart: many were professionals (mostly clergy), and of the third who were farmers, nearly all owned land. In their political and social values, African American leaders were more conservative than the rural black population, and they showed little interest in land reform.

Black citizens were a majority of the voters only in South Carolina, Mississippi, and Louisiana. Thus in most of the South the Republican Party had to secure white votes to stay in power. Opponents scornfully labeled white southerners

^ Hiram Revels, a minister and educator, became the first African American to serve in the U.S. Senate, representing Mississippi. Later he served as president of Alcorn University.
Source: Library of Congress, Prints and Photographs Division [LC-DIG-cwpbh-03275]

**scalawags** white southerners who supported the Republican Party.

who allied with the Republican Party **scalawags**, yet an estimated quarter of white southerners at one time voted Republican. They were primarily Unionists from the upland counties and hill areas and largely yeoman farmers. Such voters were attracted by Republican promises to rebuild the South, restore prosperity, create public schools, and open isolated areas to the market with railroads.

The other group of white Republicans in the South were known as **carpetbaggers**. Originally from the North, they allegedly had arrived with all their worldly possessions stuffed in a carpetbag, ready to loot and plunder the defeated South. Some did, certainly, but northerners moved south for a variety of reasons. Though carpetbaggers made up only a small percentage of Republican voters, they controlled almost a third of the offices in the South. More than half of all southern Republican governors and nearly half of Republican members of Congress were originally northerners.

**carpetbaggers** northern white Republicans who came to live in the South after the Civil War. Most were veterans of the Union army; many were teachers, Freedmen's Bureau agents, or investors in cotton plantations.

The Republican Party in the South had difficulty maintaining unity. Scalawags were especially susceptible to the race issue and social pressure. "Even my own kinspeople have turned the cold shoulder to me because I hold office under a Republican administration," testified a Mississippi white Republican. As black southerners pressed for greater recognition, white southerners increasingly defected to the Democrats. Carpetbaggers, in contrast, were less sensitive to race, although most felt that their black allies should be content with minor offices. The animosity between scalawags and carpetbaggers, which grew out of their rivalry for party honors, was particularly intense.

**Reforms under the New State Governments** >> The new southern state constitutions enacted several significant reforms. They devised fairer systems of legislative representation and made many previously appointive offices elective. The Radical state governments also assumed some responsibility for social welfare and established the first statewide systems of public schools in the South.

Although all the new constitutions proclaimed the principle of equality and granted black adult males the right to vote, on social relations they were much more cautious. No state outlawed segregation, and South Carolina and Louisiana were the only ones that required integration in public schools (a mandate that was almost universally ignored). Sensitive to status, mulattoes pushed for prohibition of social discrimination, but white Republicans refused to adopt such a radical policy.

**Economic Issues and Corruption** >> With the southern economy in ruins at the end of the war, problems of economic reconstruction were severe. The new Republican governments encouraged industrial development by providing subsidies, loans, and even temporary exemptions from taxes. These governments also largely rebuilt the southern railroad system, offering lavish aid to railroad corporations. In the two decades after 1860, the region doubled its manufacturing establishments, yet the South steadily slipped further behind the booming industrial economy of the North.

The expansion of government services offered temptations for corruption. Southern officials regularly received bribes and kickbacks for awarding railroad charters, franchises, and other contracts. The railroad grants and new social services such as schools also left state governments in debt, even though taxes rose in the 1870s to four times the rate in 1860.

Corruption, however, was not only a southern problem but a national one. During these years, the Democratic Tweed Ring in New York City alone stole more money than all the southern Radical governments combined. Moreover, corruption was hardly limited to southern Republicans: many Democrats and white business leaders participated.

Louisiana governor Henry Warmoth, a carpetbagger, told a congressional committee: "Everybody is demoralizing down here. Corruption is the fashion."

Corruption in Radical governments existed, but southern Democrats exaggerated its extent for partisan purposes. They opposed honest Radical regimes just as bitterly as notoriously corrupt ones. In the eyes of most white southerners, the real crime of the Radical governments was that they allowed black citizens to hold some offices and tried to protect the civil rights of black Americans. Race was white conservatives' greatest weapon. And it would prove the most effective means to undermine Republican power in the South.

**REVIEW**

What roles did African Americans, southern whites, and northern whites play in the Reconstruction governments of the South?

# BLACK ASPIRATIONS

Emancipation came to slaves in different ways and at different times. Betty Jones's grandmother was told about the Emancipation Proclamation by another slave while they were hoeing corn. Mary Anderson received the news from her master near the end of the war when Sherman's army invaded North Carolina. Whatever the timing, freedom meant a host of precious blessings to people who had been in bondage all their lives.

**Experiencing Freedom** >> The first impulse was to think of freedom as a contrast to slavery. Emancipation immediately released slaves from the most oppressive aspects of bondage—the whippings, the breakup of families, the sexual exploitation. Freedom also meant movement, the right to travel without a pass or white permission. Above all, freedom meant that African Americans' labor would be for their own benefit. One Arkansas freedman, who earned his first dollar working on a railroad, recalled that when he was paid, "I felt like the richest man in the world."

Freedom included finding a new place to work. Changing jobs was one concrete way to break the psychological ties of slavery. Even planters with reputations for kindness sometimes saw most of their former hands depart. The cook who left a South Carolina family, despite the offer of higher wages than her new job's, explained: "I must go. If I stays here I'll never know I'm free."

Symbolically, freedom meant having a full name. African Americans now adopted last names, most commonly the name of the first master in the family's oral history as far back as it could be recalled. Most, however, retained their first name, especially if the name had been given to them by their parents (as was most often the case). Whatever the name, black Americans insisted on making the decision themselves.

**The Black Family** >> African Americans also sought to strengthen the family in freedom. Since slave marriages had not been recognized as legal, thousands of former slaves insisted on being married again by proper authorities, even though this was not required by law. Those who had been forcibly separated in slavery and later remarried confronted the dilemma of which spouse to take. Laura Spicer, whose husband had been sold away in slavery, wrote him after the war seeking to resume their marriage. In a series of wrenching letters, he explained that he had thought her dead, had remarried, and had a new family. "You know it never was our wishes to be separated from each other, and it never was our fault. I had rather anything to had happened to me most than ever have been parted from you and the children," he wrote. "As I am, I do not know which I love best, you or Anna." Declining to return, he closed, "Laura, truly, I have got another wife, and I am very sorry."

As in white families, black husbands deemed themselves the head of the family and acted legally for their wives. They often insisted that their wives would not work in the fields as they had in slavery. "The [black] women say they never mean to do any more outdoor work," one planter reported, "that white men support their wives and they mean that their husbands shall support them." In negotiating contracts, a father also demanded the right to control his children and their labor. All these changes were designed to insulate the black family from white control.

**The Schoolhouse and the Church** >> In freedom, the schoolhouse and the black church became essential institutions in the black community. "My Lord, Ma'am, what a great thing learning is!" a South Carolina freedman told a northern teacher. "White folks can do what they likes, for they know so much more than we." At first, northern churches and missionaries, working with the Freedmen's Bureau, set up black schools in the South. Tuition at these schools represented 10 percent or more of a laborer's monthly wages, yet these schools were full. Eventually, states established public school systems, which by 1867 enrolled 40 percent of African American children.

Black adults, who often attended night classes, had good reasons for seeking literacy. They wanted to be able to read the Bible, to defend their newly gained civil and political rights, and to protect themselves from being cheated. Both races saw that education would undermine the servility that slavery had fostered.

The teachers in the Freedmen's Bureau schools were primarily northern middle-class white women sent south by northern missionary societies. "I feel that it is a precious

^ When Beale Street Baptist Church was founded by African Americans after the Civil War, the congregation was so poor, it met in a brush arbor—a canopy of leaves and branches held up by log poles. But the Memphis church grew by leaps and bounds as freedpeople flocked to the city. Their contributions to the weekly collection plate financed the building of this stately church, whose tower featured a statue of John the Baptist. By the early 1880s, Memphis boasted more black than white Protestant churches.
Source: Library of Congress, Prints and Photographs Division [HABS TENN,79-MEMPH,7—1]

privilege," Esther Douglass wrote, "to be allowed to do something for these poor people." Many saw themselves as peacetime soldiers, struggling to make emancipation a reality. Indeed, hostile white southerners sometimes destroyed black schools and threatened and even murdered white teachers. Then there were the everyday challenges: low pay, run-down buildings, few books, classes of 100 or more children. By 1869 most teachers in these Freedmen's Bureau schools were black, trained by the bureau.

Most slaves had attended white churches or services supervised by whites. Once free, African Americans quickly established their own congregations led by black preachers. Mostly Methodist and Baptist, black churches were the only major organizations in the African American community controlled by blacks themselves. A white missionary reported that "the Ebony preacher who promises perfect independence from White control and direction carried the colored heart at once." Just as in slavery, religion offered African Americans a place of refuge in a hostile white world and provided them with hope, comfort, and a means of self-identification.

**New Working Conditions** >> As a largely propertyless class, blacks in the postwar South had no choice but to work for white landowners. Except for paying wages, whites wanted to retain the old system of labor, including close supervision, gang labor, and physical punishment. Determined to remove all emblems of servitude, African Americans refused to work under these conditions, and they demanded time off to devote to their own interests. Because of shorter hours and the withdrawal of children and women from the fields, blacks' output declined by an estimated 35 percent in freedom. They also refused to live in the old slave quarters located near the master's house and instead erected cabins on distant parts of the plantation. Wages initially were $5 or $6 a month plus provisions and a cabin; by 1867, they had risen to an average of $10 a month.

These changes eventually led to the rise of sharecropping. Under this arrangement African American families farmed discrete plots of land and then at the end of the year divided the crop, normally on an equal basis, with the white landowner. Sharecropping had higher status and offered greater personal freedom than being a wage laborer. "I am not working for wages," one black farmer declared in defending his right to leave the plantation at will, "but am part owner of the crop and as [such,] I have all the rights that you or any other man has." Although black per-capita agricultural income increased 40 percent in freedom, sharecropping was a harshly exploitative system in which black families often sank into perpetual debt.

The task of supervising the transition from slavery to freedom on southern plantations fell to the Freedmen's Bureau, a unique experiment in social policy supported by the federal government. Assigned the task of protecting freedpeople's economic rights, approximately 550 local agents regulated working conditions in southern agriculture after the war. The racial attitudes of Bureau agents varied widely, as did their commitment and competence.

Most agents required written contracts between white planters and black laborers, specifying wages and the conditions of employment. Although agents sometimes intervened to protect freedpeople from unfair treatment, they also provided important help to planters. They insisted that black laborers not leave at harvesttime, they arrested those who violated their contracts or refused to sign new ones at the beginning of the year, and they preached the need to be orderly and respectful. Because of such attitudes, freedpeople increasingly complained that Bureau agents were mere tools of the planter class. One observer reported: "Doing justice seems to mean seeing that the blacks don't break contracts and compelling them to submit cheerfully."

The primary means of enforcing working conditions were the Freedmen's Courts, which Congress created in 1866 in order to avoid the discrimination African Americans received in state courts. These new courts functioned as

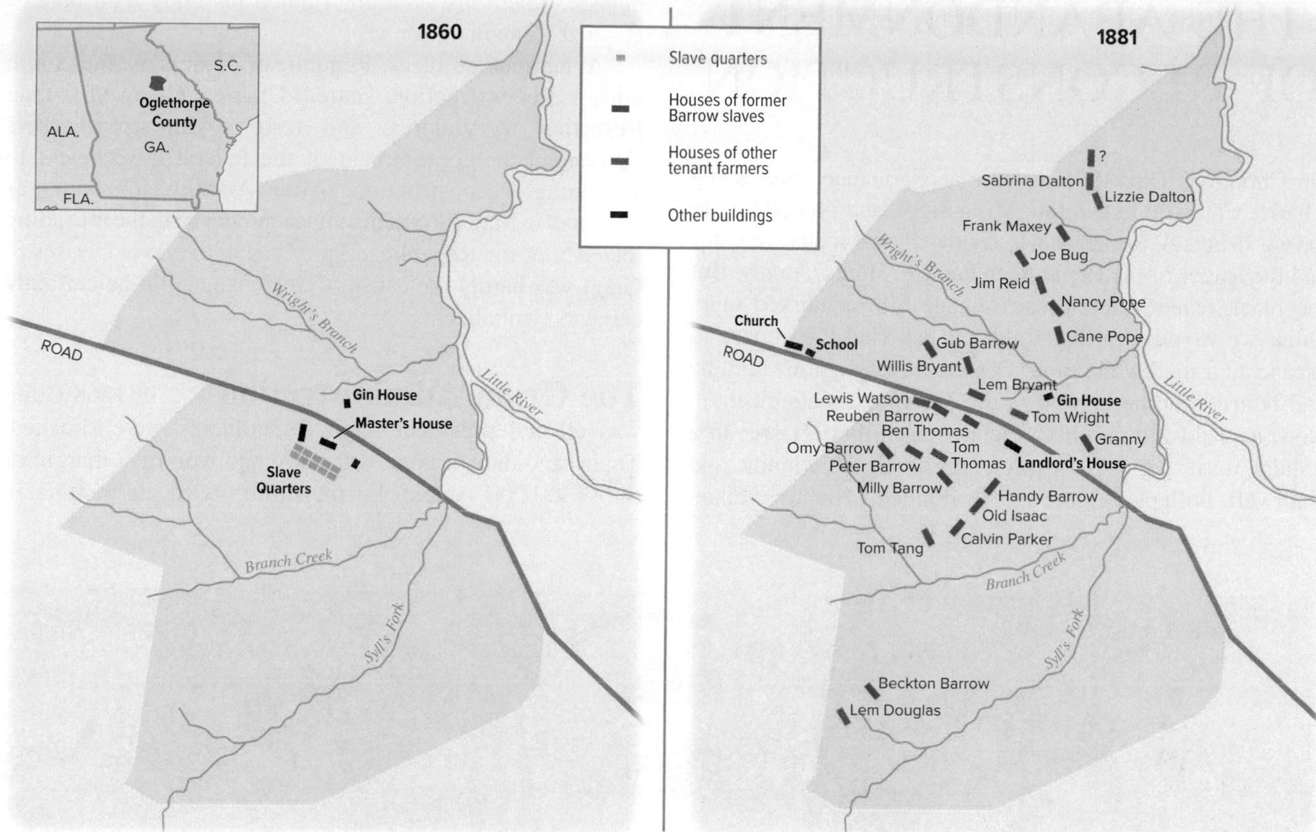
1860
S.C.
Oglethorpe County
ALA.
GA.
FLA.
Wright's Branch
ROAD
Little River
Gin House
Master's House
Slave Quarters
Branch Creek
Syll's Fork
Slave quarters
Houses of former Barrow slaves
Houses of other tenant farmers
Other buildings
1881
?
Sabrina Dalton
Lizzie Dalton
Frank Maxey
Joe Bug
Jim Reid
Nancy Pope
Wright's Branch
Church
School
Gub Barrow
Cane Pope
ROAD
Willis Bryant
Lem Bryant
Gin House
Lewis Watson
Reuben Barrow
Tom Wright
Ben Thomas
Granny
Omy Barrow
Tom Thomas
Landlord's House
Peter Barrow
Milly Barrow
Handy Barrow
Old Isaac
Calvin Parker
Tom Tang
Little River
Branch Creek
Syll's Fork
Beckton Barrow
Lem Douglas

## MAP 17.2: GEORGIA PLANTATION AFTER THE WAR

After emancipation, sharecropping became the dominant form of agricultural labor in the South. Black families no longer lived in the old slave quarters but dispersed to separate plots of land that they farmed themselves. At the end of the year, each sharecropper turned over part of the crop to the white landowner.

*What accounts for the difference between where slave families lived before the war and where the families of freedpeople lived by 1881?*

military tribunals, and often the agent was the entire court. The sympathy black laborers received varied from state to state. But since Congress was opposed to creating any permanent welfare agency, it shut down the Freedmen's Bureau, and by 1872 it had gone out of business. Despite its mixed record, it was the most effective agency in protecting blacks' civil and political rights. Its disbanding signaled the beginning of the northern retreat from Reconstruction.

**Planters and a New Way of Life** >> Planters and other white southerners faced emancipation with dread. "All the traditions and habits of both races had been suddenly overthrown," a Tennessee planter recalled, "and neither knew just what to do, or how to accommodate themselves to the new situation." Slavery had been a complex institution that welded black and white southerners together in intimate relationships. The old ideal of a paternalistic planter, which required blacks to act subservient and grateful, gave way to an emphasis on strictly economic relationships. Only with time did planters develop new norms to judge black behavior.

After the war, however, planters increasingly embraced the ideology of segregation. Since emancipation significantly reduced the social distance between the races, white southerners sought psychological separation and kept dealings with African Americans to a minimum. By the time Reconstruction ended, white planters had developed a new way of life based on the institutions of sharecropping and segregation, and undergirded by a militant white supremacy.

While most planters kept their land, they did not regain the economic prosperity of the prewar years. Cotton prices began a long decline, and southern per-capita income suffered as a result. By 1880 the value of southern farms had slid 33 percent below the level of 1860.

**REVIEW**

In what ways were the church and the school central to African American hopes after the Civil War?

# THE ABANDONMENT OF RECONSTRUCTION

On Christmas Day 1875 a white acquaintance approached Charles Caldwell in Clinton, Mississippi, and invited him to have a drink. A former slave, Caldwell was a state senator and the leader of the Republican Party in Hinds County. But the black leader's fearlessness made him a marked man. Only two months earlier, Caldwell had fled the county to escape an armed white mob. Despite threats against him, he had returned home to vote in the November state election. Now, as Caldwell and his "friend" raised their glasses in a holiday toast, a gunshot exploded through the window and Caldwell collapsed, mortally wounded. He was taken outside, where his assassins riddled his body with bullets. He died alone in the street.

A number of black Republican leaders in the South during Reconstruction shared Charles Caldwell's fate. Resorting to violence and terror, white southerners challenged the commitment of the federal government to sustaining Reconstruction. After Andrew Johnson was acquitted in May 1868 at his impeachment trial, the crusading idealism of the Republican Party began to wane. Ulysses S. Grant was hardly the cause of this change, but he certainly came to symbolize it.

**The Grant Administration** >> In 1868 Grant was elected president—and Republicans were shocked. Their candidate, a great war hero, had won by a margin of only 300,000 votes. Furthermore, with an estimated

THE FIFTEENTH AMENDMENT.
CELEBRATED MAY 19th 1870.

^ The Fifteenth Amendment, ratified in 1870, secured the right of African American males to vote as free citizens. In New York, black citizens paraded in support of Ulysses S. Grant for president (*center*). But citizenship was only one component of what African Americans insisted were central aspects of their freedom. What other features of a free life does the poster champion?
Source: Library of Congress, Prints and Photographs Division [LC-DIG-ppmsca-34808]

450,000 black Republican votes cast in the South, a majority of whites had voted Democratic. The election helped convince Republican leaders that an amendment securing black suffrage throughout the nation was necessary.

In February 1869 Congress sent the Fifteenth Amendment to the states for ratification. It forbade any state to deny the right to vote on grounds of race, color, or previous condition of servitude. It did not forbid literacy and property requirements, as some Radicals wanted, because the moderates feared that only a conservative version of the amendment could be ratified. As a result, when the amendment was ratified in March 1870, loopholes remained that eventually allowed southern states to **disenfranchise** African Americans.

**disenfranchise** deny a citizen's right to vote.

Advocates of women's suffrage were bitterly disappointed when Congress refused to outlaw voting discrimination on the basis of sex as well as race. The Women's Loyal League, led by Elizabeth Cady Stanton and Susan B. Anthony, had pressed for first the Fourteenth and then the Fifteenth Amendment to recognize that women had a civic right to vote. But even most Radicals were unwilling to back women's suffrage, contending that black rights had to be ensured first. As a result, the Fifteenth Amendment divided the feminist movement. Although disappointed that women were not included in its provisions, Lucy Stone and the American Woman Suffrage Association urged ratification. Stanton and Anthony, however, denounced the amendment and organized the National Woman Suffrage Association to work for passage of a new amendment giving women the ballot. The division hampered the women's rights movement for decades to come.

When Ulysses S. Grant was a general, his quiet manner and well-known resolution served him well. As president he proved much less certain of his goals and therefore less effective at corralling politicians than at maneuvering troops.

A series of scandals wracked his administration, so much so that "Grantism" soon became a code word in American politics for corruption, cronyism, and venality. Although Grant did not profit personally, he remained loyal to his friends and displayed little zeal to root out wrongdoing. Nor was Congress immune from the lowered tone of public life. In such a climate ruthless state machines, led by men who favored the status quo, came to dominate the party.

As corruption in both the North and the South worsened, reformers became more interested in cleaning up government than in protecting black rights. Congress in 1872 passed an amnesty act, allowing many more ex-Confederates to serve in southern governments. That same year, liberal Republicans broke with the Republican Party and nominated for president Horace Greeley, the editor of the *New York Tribune*. A one-time Radical, Greeley had become disillusioned with Reconstruction and urged a restoration of home rule in the South as well as adoption of civil service reform.

WHISKEY
RING
NAVY
RING
THIRD
TERM
CORRUPTION


^ Grant swings from a trapeze while supporting a number of associates accused of corruption. Secretary of the Navy George M. Robeson (*top center*) was accused of accepting bribes for awarding Navy contracts; Secretary of War William W. Belknap (*top right*) was forced to resign for selling Indian post traderships; and the president's private secretary, Orville Babcock (*bottom right*), was implicated in the Whiskey Ring scandal. Although not personally involved in the scandals, Grant was reluctant to dismiss from office supporters accused of wrongdoing.
Source: Library of Congress, Prints and Photographs Division [LC-USZCN4-322]

Democrats decided to back the Liberal Republican ticket. The Republicans renominated Grant, who, despite the defection of a number of prominent Radicals, won an easy victory.

# Make a Case

If the North won the war, how well did it win the peace?

## Growing Northern Disillusionment >>

During Grant's second term Congress passed the Civil Rights Act of 1875, the last major piece of Reconstruction legislation. This law prohibited racial discrimination in public accommodations, transportation, places of amusement, and juries. At the same time, Congress rejected a ban on segregation in public schools, which was almost universally practiced in the North as well as the South. The federal government made little attempt to enforce the law, however, and in 1883 the Supreme Court struck down its provisions, except the one relating to juries.

Despite passage of the Civil Rights Act, many northerners were growing disillusioned with Reconstruction. They were repelled by the corruption of the southern governments, they were tired of the violence and disorder that accompanied elections in the South, and they had little faith in black Americans. William Dodge, a wealthy New York capitalist and an influential Republican, wrote in 1875 that the South could never develop its resources "till confidence in her state governments can be restored, and this will never be done by federal bayonets." It had been a mistake, he went on, to make black southerners feel "that the United States government was their special friend, rather than those . . . among whom they must live and for whom they must work. We have tried this long enough," he concluded. "Now let the South alone."

As the agony of the war became more distant, the Panic of 1873, which precipitated a severe four-year depression, diverted public attention to economic issues. Battered by the panic and the corruption issue, the Republicans lost a shocking 77 seats in Congress in the 1874 elections, and along with them control of the House of Representatives for the first time since 1861.

"The truth is our people are tired out with the worn out cry of 'Southern outrages'!!" one Republican concluded. "Hard times and heavy taxes make them wish the 'ever lasting nigger' were in hell or Africa." More and more, Republicans spoke about cutting loose the unpopular southern governments.

## The Triumph of White Supremacy >>

Meanwhile, southern Democrats set out to overthrow the remaining Radical governments. Already, white Republicans in the South felt heavy pressure to desert their party. To poor white southerners who lacked social standing, the Democratic appeal to racial solidarity offered special comfort. The large landowners and other wealthy groups that led southern Democrats objected less to black southerners voting, since they were confident that if outside influences were removed, they could control the black vote.

Democrats also resorted to economic pressure to undermine Republican power. In heavily black counties, newspapers published the names of black residents who cast Republican ballots and urged planters to discharge them. But terror and violence provided the most effective means to overthrow the radical regimes. A number of paramilitary organizations broke up Republican meetings, terrorized white and black Republicans, assassinated Republican leaders, and prevented black citizens from voting. The most notorious of these organizations was the Ku Klux Klan, which along with similar groups functioned as an unofficial arm of the Democratic Party.

In the war for supremacy, contesting control of the night was paramount to both southern whites and blacks. Before emancipation masters regulated the nighttime hours, with a system of passes and patrols that chased slaves who went hunting or tried to sneak a visit to a family member at a neighboring plantation. For slaves the night provided precious free time: to read, to meet for worship, school, or dancing. During Reconstruction African Americans actively took back the night for a host of activities, including torchlight political parades and meetings of such organizations as the Union League. Part of the Klan's mission was to recoup this contested ground and to limit the ability of African Americans to use the night as they pleased. When indirect threats of violence were not enough (galloping through black neighborhoods rattling fences with lances), beatings and executions were undertaken—again, facilitated by the dark of night.

What became known as the Mississippi Plan was inaugurated in 1875, when Democrats decided to use as much violence as necessary to carry the state election. Local papers trumpeted, "Carry the election peaceably if we can, forcibly if we must." Recognizing that northern public opinion had grown sick of repeated federal intervention in southern elections, the Grant administration rejected the request of Republican governor Adelbert Ames for troops to stop the violence. Bolstered by terrorism, the Democrats swept the election in Mississippi. Violence and intimidation prevented as many as 60,000 black and white Republicans from voting, converting the normal Republican majority into a Democratic majority of 30,000. Mississippi had been "redeemed."

## The Disputed Election of 1876 >>

The 1876 presidential election was crucial to the final overthrow of Reconstruction. The Republicans nominated Ohio governor Rutherford B. Hayes to oppose Samuel J. Tilden, governor of New York. Once again violence prevented an estimated quarter of a million Republican votes from being cast in the South. Tilden had a clear majority of 250,000 in the popular vote, but the outcome in the Electoral College was in doubt because both parties claimed South Carolina, Florida, and Louisiana, the only reconstructed states still in Republican hands.

To arbitrate the disputed returns, Congress established a 15-member electoral commission. By a straight party vote of 8 to 7, the commission awarded the disputed electoral votes—and the presidency—to Hayes.

## *Historian's* TOOLBOX

### Dressed to Kill

Klan members drawn for *Harper's Weekly* magazine.

These three Klansmen were arrested in Tishomingo County, Mississippi, for attempted murder.

Why wear a hooded mask? Might there be more than one reason?

The costumes of Ku Klux Klan night riders—pointed hoods and white sheets—have become a staple of history books. But why use such outlandish disguises? To hide the identity of members, according to some accounts, or to terrorize freedpeople into thinking they were being menaced by Confederate ghosts. Historian Elaine F. Parsons has suggested that KKK performances took their cues from American popular culture; they took the costumes of Mardi Gras and similar carnivals, as well as minstrel shows. In behaving like carnival revelers, KKK members may have hoped to fool northern authorities into viewing the night rides as humorous pranks, not a threat to Radical rule. For southern white Democrats the theatrical night rides helped overturn the social order of Reconstruction, just as carousers at carnivals disrupted the night. The ritual garb provided seemingly innocent cover for what was truly a campaign of terror and intimidation that often turned deadly.

#### THINKING CRITICALLY

*In what ways do these disguises affect the people who wear them? Assess how the combination of horror and jest might have worked in terms of the different groups perceiving the Klan's activities: white northerners, white southerners, and African American southerners. In terms of popular culture, do modern horror films sometimes combine both terror and humor?*

(*left, right*) Source: Library of Congress, Prints and Photographs Division [LC-USZ62-119565]; (middle) Source: Library of Congress, Prints and Photographs Division [LC-USZ62-49988]

When angry Democrats threatened a filibuster to prevent the electoral votes from being counted, key Republicans met with southern Democrats and reached an informal understanding, later known as the Compromise of 1877. Hayes's supporters agreed to withdraw federal troops from the South and not oppose the new Democratic state governments. For their part, southern Democrats dropped their opposition to Hayes's election and pledged to respect African Americans' rights.

Without federal support, the last Republican southern governments collapsed, and Democrats took control of the remaining states of the Confederacy. By 1877 the entire South was in the hands of the **Redeemers**, as they called themselves. Reconstruction and Republican rule had come to an end.

**Redeemers** southerners who came to power in southern state governments between 1875 and 1877, claiming to have "redeemed" the South from Reconstruction. The Redeemers looked to undo many of the changes wrought by the Civil War.

## Racism and the Failure of Reconstruction >> Reconstruction failed for a multitude of reasons. The reforming impulse behind the Republican Party of the 1850s had been battered and worn down by the war. The new materialism of industrial America inspired a jaded cynicism in many Americans. In the South, African American voters and leaders inevitably lacked a certain amount of education and experience; elsewhere, Republicans were divided over policies and options.

Yet beyond these obstacles, the sad fact remains that the ideals of Reconstruction were most clearly defeated by a deep-seated racism that permeated American life. Racism stimulated white southern resistance, undercut northern support for black rights, and eventually made northerners willing to write off Reconstruction, and with it the welfare of African Americans. Although Congress could pass a constitutional amendment abolishing slavery, it could not overturn at a stroke the social habits of two centuries.

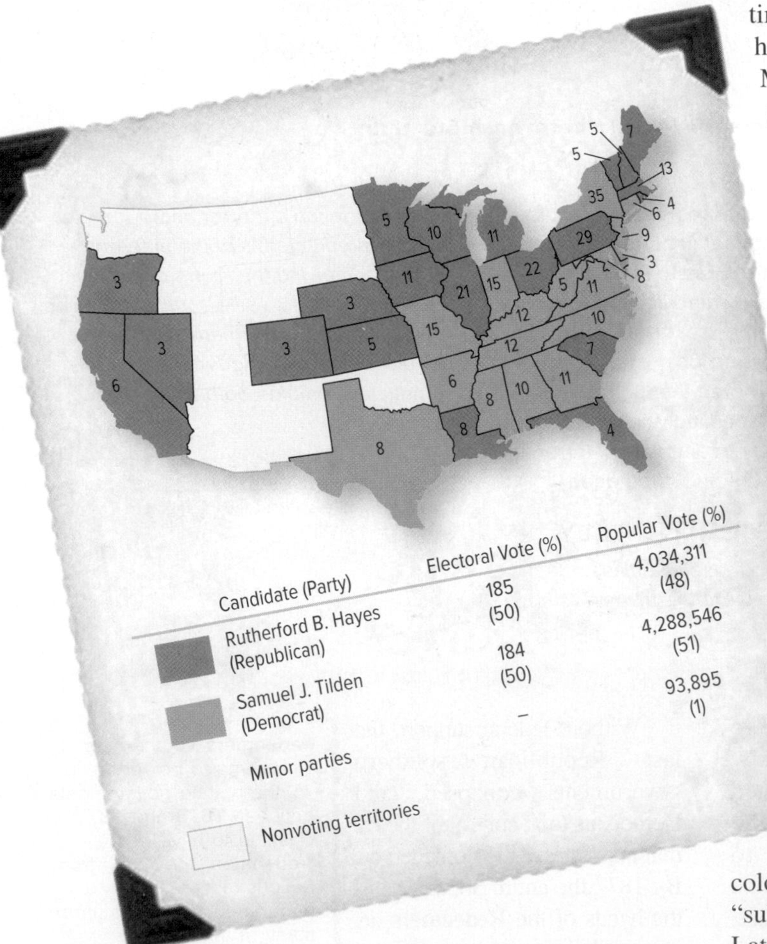
Candidate (Party)
Electoral Vote (%)
Popular Vote (%)
Rutherford B. Hayes (Republican)
185 (50)
4,034,311 (48)
Samuel J. Tilden (Democrat)
184 (50)
4,288,546 (51)
Minor parties
–
93,895 (1)
Nonvoting territories

MAP 17.3: ELECTION OF 1876

**REVIEW**

What factors in the North and the South led the federal government to abandon Reconstruction in the South?

With the overthrow of Reconstruction, the white South had won back some of the power it had lost in 1865—but not all. In the longer term, the political equations of power had been changed. Even under Redeemer governments, African Americans did not return to the social position they had occupied before the war. They were no longer slaves, and black southerners who walked dusty roads in search of family members, sent their children to school, or worshiped in their own black churches knew what a momentous change this was. Even under the exploitative sharecropping system, black income rose significantly in freedom. Then, too, the guarantees of "equal protection" and "due process of law" had been written into the Constitution and would be available for later generations to use in championing once again the Radicals' goal of racial equality.

But this was a struggle left to future reformers. For the time being, the clear trend was away from change or hope—especially for former slaves like Benjamin Montgomery and his sons, the owners of the old Davis plantations in Mississippi. In the 1870s bad crops, lower cotton prices, and falling land values undermined the Montgomerys' financial position, and in 1875 Jefferson Davis sued to have the sale of Brierfield invalidated. Following the overthrow of Mississippi's Radical government, a white conservative majority of the court awarded Brierfield to Davis in 1878. The Montgomerys lost Hurricane as well.

The waning days of Reconstruction were times filled with such ironies: of governments "redeemed" by violence, of Fourteenth Amendment rights being used by conservative courts to protect not black people but giant corporations, of reformers taking up other causes. Increasingly, the industrial North focused on an economic task: integrating both the South and the West into the Union. In the case of both regions, northern factories sought to use southern and western raw materials to produce goods and to find national markets for those products. Indeed, during the coming decades European nations also scrambled to acquire natural resources and markets. In the onrushing age of imperialism, Western nations would seek to dominate newly acquired colonies in Africa and Asia, with the same disregard for their "subject peoples" that was seen with African Americans, Latinos, and Indians in the United States.

Disowned by its northern supporters and unmourned by public opinion, Reconstruction was over.

# CHAPTER SUMMARY

Presidents Abraham Lincoln and Andrew Johnson and the Republican-dominated Congress each developed a program of Reconstruction to quickly restore the Confederate States to the Union.

- Lincoln's 10 percent plan required that 10 percent of qualified voters from 1860 swear an oath of loyalty to begin organizing a state government.
- Following Lincoln's assassination, Andrew Johnson changed Lincoln's terms and lessened Reconstruction's requirements.
- The more radical Congress repudiated Johnson's state governments and eventually enacted its own program of Reconstruction, which included the principle of black suffrage.
  - Congress passed the Fourteenth and Fifteenth Amendments and also extended the life of the Freedmen's Bureau, a unique experiment in social welfare.
  - Congress rejected land reform, however, which would have provided the freedpeople with a greater economic stake.
  - The effort to remove Johnson from office through impeachment failed.
- The Radical governments in the South, led by black and white southerners and transplanted northerners, compiled a mixed record on matters such as racial equality, education, economic issues, and corruption.
- Reconstruction was a time of both joy and frustration for former slaves.
  - Former slaves took steps to reunite their families and establish black-controlled churches.
  - They evidenced a widespread desire for land and education.
  - Black resistance to the old system of labor led to the adoption of sharecropping.
  - The Freedmen's Bureau fostered these new working arrangements and also the beginnings of black education in the South.
- Northern public opinion became disillusioned with Reconstruction during the presidency of Ulysses S. Grant.
- Southern whites used violence, economic coercion, and racism to overthrow the Republican state governments.
- In 1877 Republican leaders agreed to end Reconstruction in exchange for Rutherford B. Hayes's election as president.
- Racism played a key role in the eventual failure of Reconstruction.

## Additional Reading

Historians' views of Reconstruction have dramatically changed over the past half century. Modern studies offer a more sympathetic assessment of Reconstruction and the experience of African Americans. Indicative of this trend is Eric Foner, *Reconstruction* (1988), and his briefer treatment (with photographic essays by Joshua Brown) *Forever Free: The Story of Emancipation and Reconstruction* (2005). Michael Les Benedict treats the clash between Andrew Johnson and Congress in *The Impeachment and Trial of Andrew Johnson* (1973). Political affairs in the South during Reconstruction are examined in Dan T. Carter, *When the War Was Over* (1985); and Thomas Holt, *Black over White* (1977), an imaginative study of black political leadership in South Carolina. Hans Trefousse, *Thaddeus Stevens: Nineteenth-Century Egalitarian* (1997), provides a sympathetic reassessment of the influential Radical Republican. Mark W. Summers, *A Dangerous Stir* (2009), deftly examines the ways in which fear and paranoia shaped Reconstruction.

Leon Litwack, *Been in the Storm So Long* (1979), sensitively analyzes the transition of enslaved African Americans to freedom. Heather Andrea Williams, *Self-Taught: African American Education in Slavery and Freedom* (2005), illustrates the black drive for literacy and education. James L. Roark, *Masters without Slaves* (1977), discusses former slaveholders' adjustment to the end of slavery. The dialectic of black-white relations is charted from the antebellum years through Reconstruction and beyond in Steven Hahn, *A Nation under Our Feet: Black Political Struggles in the Rural South from Slavery to the Great Migration* (2003). Two excellent studies of changing labor relations in southern agriculture are Julie Saville, *The Work of Reconstruction* (1995); and John C. Rodrigue, *Reconstruction in the Cane Fields* (2001). For contrasting views of the Freedmen's Bureau, see George R. Bentley, *A History of the Freedmen's Bureau* (1955)—favorable—and Donald Nieman, *To Set the Law in Motion* (1979)—critical. William Gillette, *Retreat from Reconstruction, 1869–1879* (1980), focuses on national politics and the end of Reconstruction; while Michael Perman, *The Road to Redemption* (1984), looks at developments in the South. Heather Cox Richardson explores the postwar context in the North in *The Death of Reconstruction* (2004), and considers Reconstruction in the West in *West from Appomattox* (2008).

# Appendix

- The Declaration of Independence
- The Constitution of the United States of America

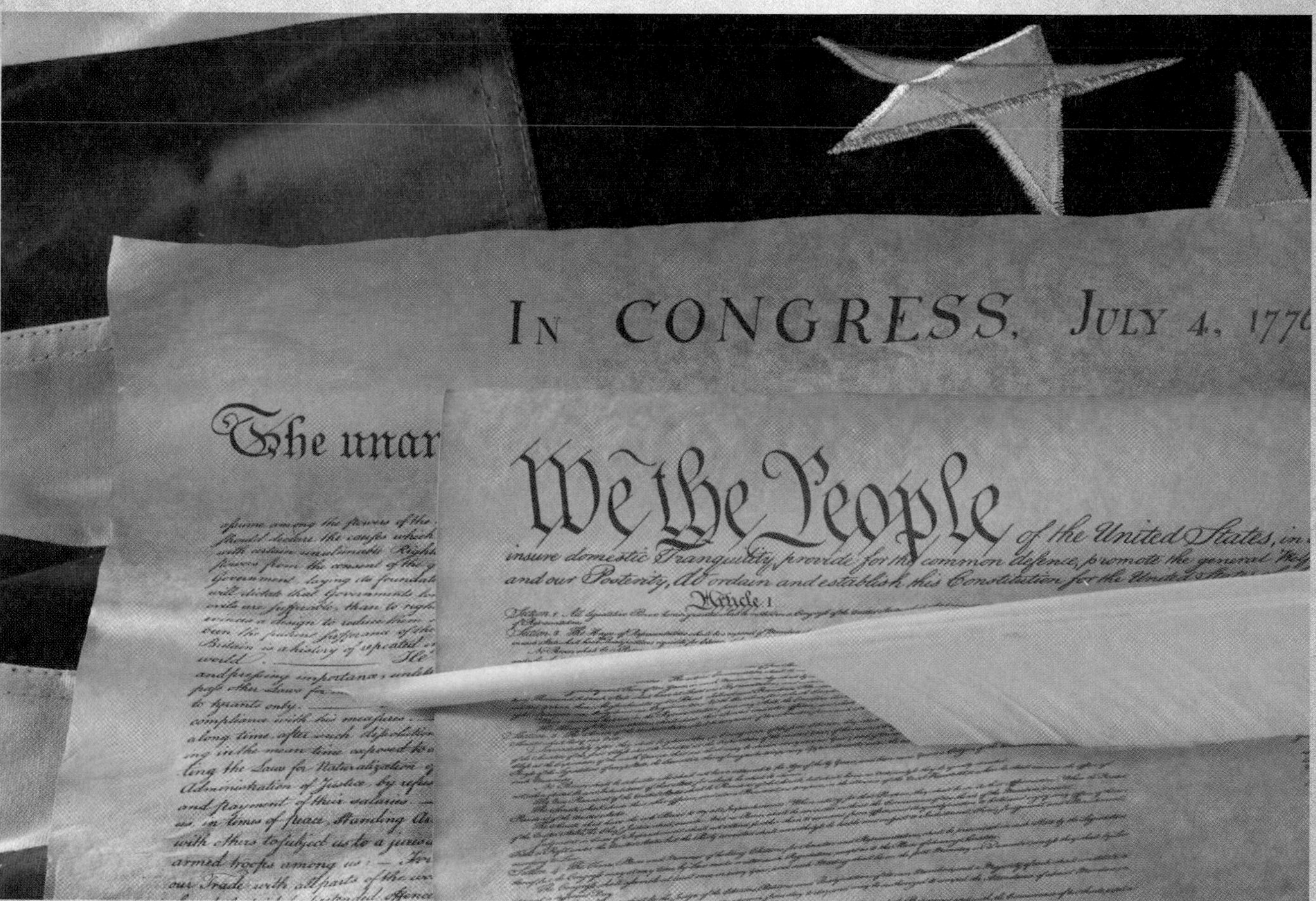
IN CONGRESS, JULY 4,
We the People
of the United States,
Article 1

©Tetra Images/Corbis RF

# The Declaration of Independence

## IN CONGRESS, JULY 4, 1776

### The Unanimous Declaration of the Thirteen United States of America

When, in the course of human events, it becomes necessary for one people to dissolve the political bands which have connected them with another, and to assume, among the powers of the earth, the separate and equal station to which the laws of nature and of nature's God entitle them, a decent respect to the opinions of mankind requires that they should declare the causes which impel them to the separation.

We hold these truths to be self-evident, that all men are created equal; that they are endowed by their Creator with certain unalienable rights; that among these, are life, liberty, and the pursuit of happiness. That, to secure these rights, governments are instituted among men, deriving their just powers from the consent of the governed; that, whenever any form of government becomes destructive of these ends, it is the right of the people to alter or to abolish it, and to institute a new government, laying its foundation on such principles, and organizing its powers in such form, as to them shall seem most likely to effect their safety and happiness. Prudence, indeed, will dictate that governments long established, should not be changed for light and transient causes; and, accordingly, all experience hath shown, that mankind are more disposed to suffer, while evils are sufferable, than to right themselves by abolishing the forms to which they are accustomed. But, when a long train of abuses and usurpations, pursuing invariably the same object, evinces a design to reduce them under absolute despotism, it is their right, it is their duty, to throw off such government and to provide new guards for their future security. Such has been the patient sufferance of these colonies, and such is now the necessity which constrains them to alter their former systems of government. The history of the present King of Great Britain is a history of repeated injuries and usurpations, all having, in direct object, the establishment of an absolute tyranny over these States. To prove this, let facts be submitted to a candid world:

He has refused his assent to laws the most wholesome and necessary for the public good.

He has forbidden his governors to pass laws of immediate and pressing importance, unless suspended in their operation till his assent should be obtained; and, when so suspended, he has utterly neglected to attend to them.

He has refused to pass other laws for the accommodation of large districts of people, unless those people would relinquish the right of representation in the legislature; a right inestimable to them, and formidable to tyrants only.

He has called together legislative bodies at places unusual, uncomfortable, and distant from the depository of their public records, for the sole purpose of fatiguing them into compliance with his measures.

He has dissolved representative houses repeatedly for opposing, with manly firmness, his invasions on the rights of the people.

He has refused, for a long time after such dissolutions, to cause others to be elected; whereby the legislative powers, incapable of annihilation, have returned to the people at large for their exercise; the state remaining, in the meantime, exposed to all the danger of invasion from without, and convulsions within.

He has endeavored to prevent the population of these States; for that purpose, obstructing the laws for naturalization of foreigners, refusing to pass others to encourage their migration hither, and raising the conditions of new appropriations of lands.

He had obstructed the administration of justice, by refusing his assent to laws for establishing judiciary powers. He has made judges dependent on his will alone, for the tenure of their offices, and the amount and payment of their salaries.

He has erected a multitude of new offices, and sent hither swarms of officers to harass our people, and eat out their substance.

He has kept among us, in time of peace, standing armies, without the consent of our legislatures.

He has affected to render the military independent of, and superior to, the civil power.

He has combined, with others, to subject us to a jurisdiction foreign to our Constitution, and unacknowledged by our laws; giving his assent to their acts of pretended legislation:

For quartering large bodies of armed troops among us:

For protecting them by a mock trial, from punishment, for any murders which they should commit on the inhabitants of these States:

For cutting off our trade with all parts of the world:

For imposing taxes on us without our consent:

For depriving us, in many cases, of the benefit of trial by jury:

For transporting us beyond seas to be tried for pretended offences:

For abolishing the free system of English laws in a neighboring province, establishing therein an arbitrary government, and enlarging its boundaries, so as to render it at once an example and fit instrument for introducing the same absolute rule into these colonies:

For taking away our charters, abolishing our most valuable laws, and altering, fundamentally, the powers of our governments:

For suspending our own legislatures, and declaring themselves invested with power to legislate for us in all cases whatsoever.

He has abdicated government here, by declaring us out of his protection, and waging war against us.

He has plundered our seas, ravaged our coasts, burnt our towns, and destroyed the lives of our people.

He is, at this time, transporting large armies of foreign mercenaries to complete the works of death, desolation, and tyranny, already begun, with circumstances of cruelty and perfidy scarcely paralleled in the most barbarous ages, and totally unworthy the head of a civilized nation.

He has constrained our fellow citizens, taken captive on the high seas, to bear arms against their country, to become the executioners of their friends, and brethren, or to fall themselves by their hands.

He has excited domestic insurrections amongst us, and has endeavored to bring on the inhabitants of our frontiers, the merciless Indian savages, whose known rule of warfare is an undistinguished destruction of all ages, sexes, and conditions.

In every stage of these oppressions, we have petitioned for redress, in the most humble terms; our repeated petitions have been answered only by repeated injury. A prince, whose character is thus marked by every act which may define a tyrant, is unfit to be the ruler of a free people.

Nor have we been wanting in attention to our British brethren. We have warned them, from time to time, of attempts made by their legislature to extend an unwarrantable jurisdiction over us. We have reminded them of the circumstances of our emigration and settlement here. We have appealed to their native justice and magnanimity, and we have conjured them, by the ties of our common kindred, to disavow these usurpations, which would inevitably interrupt our connections and correspondence. They, too, have been deaf to the voice of justice and consanguinity. We must, therefore, acquiesce in the necessity which denounces our separation, and hold them as we hold the rest of mankind, enemies in war, in peace, friends.

We, therefore, the representatives of the United States of America, in general Congress assembled, appealing to the Supreme Judge of the world for the rectitude of our intentions, do, in the name, and by the authority of the good people of these colonies, solemnly publish and declare, that these united colonies are, and of right ought to be, free and independent states: that they are absolved from all allegiance to the British Crown, and that all political connection between them and the state of Great Britain is, and ought to be, totally dissolved; and that, as free and independent states, they have full power to levy war, conclude peace, contract alliances, establish commerce, and to do all other acts and things which independent states may of right do. And, for the support of this declaration, with a firm reliance on the protection of Divine Providence, we mutually pledge to each other our lives, our fortunes, and our sacred honor.

The foregoing Declaration was, by order of Congress, engrossed, and signed by the following members:

**JOHN HANCOCK**

**NEW HAMPSHIRE**
Josiah Bartlett
William Whipple
Matthew Thornton

**MASSACHUSETTS BAY**
Samuel Adams
John Adams
Robert Treat Paine
Elbridge Gerry

**RHODE ISLAND**
Stephen Hopkins
William Ellery

**CONNECTICUT**
Roger Sherman
Samuel Huntington
William Williams
Oliver Wolcott

**NEW YORK**
William Floyd
Philip Livingston
Francis Lewis
Lewis Morris

**NEW JERSEY**
Richard Stockton
John Witherspoon
Francis Hopkinson
John Hart
Abraham Clark

**PENNSYLVANIA**
Robert Morris
Benjamin Rush
Benjamin Franklin
John Morton
George Clymer
James Smith
George Taylor
James Wilson
George Ross

**DELAWARE**
Caesar Rodney
George Read
Thomas M'Kean

**MARYLAND**
Samuel Chase
William Paca
Thomas Stone
Charles Carroll, of Carrollton

**VIRGINIA**
George Wythe
Richard Henry Lee
Thomas Jefferson
Benjamin Harrison
Thomas Nelson, Jr.
Francis Lightfoot Lee
Carter Braxton

**NORTH CAROLINA**
William Hooper
Joseph Hewes
John Penn

**SOUTH CAROLINA**
Edward Rutledge
Thomas Heyward, Jr.
Thomas Lynch, Jr.
Arthur Middleton

**GEORGIA**
Button Gwinnett
Lyman Hall
George Walton

*Resolved,* That copies of the Declaration be sent to the several assemblies, conventions, and committees, or counsils of safety, and to the several commanding officers of the continental troops; that it be proclaimed in each of the United States, at the head of the army.

# The Constitution of the United States of America[1]

We the People of the United States, in Order to form a more perfect Union, establish Justice, insure domestic Tranquility, provide for the common defence, promote the general Welfare, and secure the Blessings of Liberty to ourselves and our Posterity, do ordain and establish this CONSTITUTION for the United States of America.

## ARTICLE I

**SECTION 1.** All legislative Powers herein granted shall be vested in a Congress of the United States, which shall consist of a Senate and House of Representatives.

**SECTION 2.** The House of Representatives shall be composed of Members chosen every second Year by the People of the several States, and the Electors in each State shall have the Qualifications requisite for Electors of the most numerous Branch of the State Legislature. No Person shall be a Representative who shall not have attained to the Age of twenty-five Years, and been seven Years a Citizen of the United States, and who shall not, when elected, be an Inhabitant of that State in which he shall be chosen.

[Representatives and direct Taxes[2] shall be apportioned among the several States which may be included within this Union, according to their respective Numbers, which shall be determined by adding to the whole Number of free Persons, including those bound to Service for a Term of Years, and excluding Indians not taxed, three fifths of all other Persons.][3] The actual Enumeration shall be made within three Years after the first Meeting of the Congress of the United States, and within every subsequent Term of ten Years, in such Manner as they shall by Law direct. The Number of Representatives shall not exceed one for every thirty Thousand, but each State shall have at Least one Representative; and until such enumeration shall be made, the State of New Hampshire shall be entitled to chuse three, Massachusetts eight, Rhode-Island and Providence Plantations one, Connecticut five, New York six, New Jersey four, Pennsylvania eight, Delaware one, Maryland six, Virginia ten, North Carolina five, South Carolina five, and Georgia three. When vacancies happen in the Representation from any State, the Executive Authority thereof shall issue Writs of Election to fill such Vacancies. The House of Representatives shall chuse their Speaker and other Officers; and shall have the sole Power of Impeachment.

**SECTION 3.** The Senate of the United States shall be composed of two Senators from each State, chosen by the Legislature thereof, for six Years; and each Senator shall have one Vote.

Immediately after they shall be assembled in Consequence of the first Election, they shall be divided as equally as may be into three Classes. The Seats of the Senators of the first Class shall be vacated at the Expiration of the second Year, of the second Class at the Expiration of the fourth Year, and of the third Class at the Expiration of the sixth Year, so that one-third may be chosen every second Year; and if Vacancies happen by Resignation, or otherwise, during the Recess of the Legislature of any State, the Executive thereof may make temporary Appointments until the next Meeting of the Legislature, which shall then fill such Vacancies. No Person shall be a Senator who shall not have attained to the Age of thirty Years, and been nine Years a Citizen of the United States, and who shall not, when elected, be an Inhabitant of that State for which he shall be chosen.

The Vice President of the United States shall be President of the Senate, but shall have no vote, unless they be equally divided.

The Senate shall chuse their other Officers, and also a President pro tempore, in the absence of the Vice President, or when he shall exercise the Office of President of the United States.

The Senate shall have the sole Power to try all Impeachments. When sitting for that purpose they shall be on Oath or Affirmation. When the President of the United States is tried, the Chief Justice shall preside: And no person shall be convicted without the Concurrence of two thirds of the Members present.

Judgment in Cases of Impeachment shall not extend further than to removal from Office, and disqualification to hold and enjoy any Office of honor, Trust, or Profit under the United States: but the Party convicted shall nevertheless be liable and subject to Indictment, Trial, Judgment, and Punishment, according to Law.

1 This version follows the original Constitution in capitalization and spelling. It is adapted from the text published by the United States Department of the Interior, Office of Education.

2 Altered by the Sixteenth Amendment.

3 Negated by the Fourteenth Amendment.

**SECTION 4.** The Times, Places and Manner of holding Elections for Senators and Representatives, shall be prescribed in each State by the Legislature thereof; but the Congress may at any time by Law make or alter such Regulations, except as to the Places of Chusing Senators. The Congress shall assemble at least once in every Year, and such Meeting shall be on the first Monday in December, unless they shall by Law appoint a different Day.

**SECTION 5.** Each House shall be the Judge of the Elections, Returns and Qualifications of its own Members, and a Majority of each shall constitute a Quorum to do Business; but a smaller number may adjourn from day to day, and may be authorized to compel the Attendance of absent Members, in such Manner, and under such Penalties, as each House may provide.

Each House may determine the Rules of its Proceedings, punish its Members for disorderly Behaviour, and, with the Concurrence of two thirds, expel a Member. Each House shall keep a Journal of its Proceedings, and from time to time publish the same, excepting such Parts as may in their Judgment require Secrecy; and the Yeas and Nays of the Members of either House on any question shall, at the Desire of one fifth of those Present, be entered on the Journal.

Neither House, during the Session of Congress, shall, without the Consent of the other, adjourn for more than three days, nor to any other Place than that in which the two Houses shall be sitting.

**SECTION 6.** The Senators and Representatives shall receive a Compensation for their Services, to be ascertained by Law, and paid out of the Treasury of the United States. They shall in all Cases, except Treason, Felony, and Breach of the Peace, be privileged from Arrest during their Attendance at the Session of their respective Houses, and in going to and returning from the same; and for any Speech or Debate in either House, they shall not be questioned in any other Place. No Senator or Representative shall, during the Time for which he was elected, be appointed to any civil Office under the Authority of the United States, which shall have been created, or the Emoluments whereof shall have been increased, during such time; and no Person holding any Office under the United States shall be a Member of either House during his continuance in Office.

**SECTION 7.** All Bills for raising Revenue shall originate in the House of Representatives; but the Senate may propose or concur with Amendments as on other bills. Every Bill which shall have passed the House of Representatives and the Senate, shall, before it become a Law, be presented to the President of the United States; If he approve he shall sign it, but if not he shall return it, with his Objections, to that House in which it shall have originated, who shall enter the Objections at large on their Journal, and proceed to reconsider it. If after such Reconsideration two thirds of that House shall agree to pass the bill, it shall be sent, together with the objections, to the other House, by which it shall likewise be reconsidered, and if approved by two thirds of that House, it shall become a Law. But in all such Cases the Votes of both Houses shall be determined by Yeas and Nays, and the Names of the Persons voting for and against the Bill shall be entered on the Journal of each House respectively. If any Bill shall not be returned by the President within ten Days (Sundays excepted) after it shall have been presented to him, the Same shall be a Law, in like Manner as if he had signed it, unless the Congress by their Adjournment prevent its Return, in which Case it shall not be a Law. Every Order, Resolution, or Vote to which the Concurrence of the Senate and House of Representatives may be necessary (except on a question of Adjournment) shall be presented to the President of the United States; and before the Same shall take Effect, shall be approved by him, or being disapproved by him, shall be repassed by two thirds of the Senate and House of Representatives, according to the Rules and Limitations prescribed in the Case of a Bill.

**SECTION 8.** The Congress shall have Power To lay and collect Taxes, Duties, Imposts and Excises, to pay the Debts and provide for the common Defence and general Welfare of the United States; but all Duties, Imposts and Excises shall be uniform throughout the United States;

To borrow money on the credit of the United States;

To regulate Commerce with foreign Nations, and among the several States, and with the Indian Tribes;

To establish an uniform rule of Naturalization, and uniform Laws on the subject of Bankruptcies throughout the United States; To coin Money, regulate the Value thereof, and of foreign Coin, and fix the Standard of Weights and Measures;

To provide for the Punishment of counterfeiting the Securities and current Coin of the United States;

To establish Post Offices and post Roads; To promote the Progress of Science and useful Arts, by securing for limited Times to Authors and Inventors the exclusive Right to their respective Writings and Discoveries;

To constitute Tribunals inferior to the Supreme Court;

To define and punish Piracies and Felonies committed on the high Seas, and Offenses against the Law of Nations;

To declare War, grant Letters of Marque and Reprisal, and make Rules concerning Captures on Land and Water;

To raise and support Armies, but no Appropriation of Money to that Use shall be for a longer Term than two Years;

To provide and maintain a Navy;

To make Rules for the Government and Regulation of the land and naval forces;

To provide for calling forth the Militia to execute the Laws of the Union, suppress Insurrections and repel Invasions;

To provide for organizing, arming, and disciplining the Militia, and for government such Part of them as may be employed in the Service of the United States, reserving to the States respectively, the Appointment of the Officers, and the Authority of training the Militia according to the discipline prescribed by Congress;

To exercise exclusive Legislation in all Cases whatsoever, over such District (not exceeding ten Miles square) as may, by Cession of particular States, and the acceptance of Congress, become the Seat of the Government of the United States, and to exercise like Authority over all Places purchased by the Consent of the Legislature of the State in which the Same shall be, for the Erection of Forts, Magazines, Arsenals, Dockyards, and other needful Buildings;—And

To make all Laws which shall be necessary and proper for carrying into Execution the foregoing Powers, and all other Powers vested by this Constitution in the Government of the United States, or in any Department or Officer thereof.

**SECTION 9.** The Migration or Importation of such Persons as any of the States now existing shall think proper to admit, shall not be prohibited by the Congress prior to the Year one thousand eight hundred and eight, but a tax or duty may be imposed on such Importation, not exceeding ten dollars for each Person.

The privilege of the Writ of Habeas Corpus shall not be suspended, unless when in Cases of Rebellion or Invasion the public Safety may require it.

No bill of Attainder or ex post facto Law shall be passed.

No capitation, or other direct, Tax shall be laid unless in Proportion to the Census or Enumeration herein before directed to be taken.

No Tax or Duty shall be laid on Articles exported from any State.

No Preference shall be given by any Regulation of Commerce or Revenue to the Ports of one State over those of another: nor shall Vessels bound to, or from, one State, be obliged to enter, clear, or pay Duties in another.

No Money shall be drawn from the Treasury, but in Consequence of Appropriations made by Law; and a regular Statement and Account of the Receipts and Expenditures of all public Money shall be published from time to time.

No Title of Nobility shall be granted by the United States: And no Person holding any Office of Profit or Trust under them, shall, without the Consent of the Congress, accept of any present, Emolument, Office, or Title, of any kind whatever, from any King, Prince, or foreign State.

**SECTION 10.** No State shall enter into any Treaty, Alliance, or Confederation; grant Letters of Marque and Reprisal; coin Money; emit Bills of Credit; make any Thing but gold and silver Coin a Tender in Payment of Debts; pass any Bill of Attainder, ex post facto Law, or Law impairing the Obligation of Contracts, or grant any Title of Nobility.

No State shall, without the Consent of the Congress, lay any Imposts or Duties on Imports or Exports, except what may be absolutely necessary for executing its inspection Laws; and the net Produce of all Duties and Imposts, laid by any State on Imports or Exports, shall be for the use of the Treasury of the United States; and all such Laws shall be subject to the Revision and Control of the Congress.

No state shall, without the Consent of Congress, lay any duty of Tonnage, keep Troops, or Ships of War in time of Peace, enter into any Agreement or Compact with another State, or with a foreign Power, or engage in War, unless actually invaded, or in such imminent Danger as will not admit of delay.

# ARTICLE II

**SECTION 1.** The executive Power shall be vested in a President of the United States of America. He shall hold his Office during the Term of four years, and, together with the Vice President, chosen for the same Term, be elected, as follows:

Each State shall appoint, in such Manner as the Legislature thereof may direct, a Number of Electors, equal to the whole Number of Senators and Representatives to which the State may be entitled in the Congress: but no Senator or Representative, or Person holding an Office of Trust or Profit under the United States, shall be appointed an Elector.

[The Electors shall meet in their respective States, and vote by Ballot for two persons, of whom one at least shall not be an Inhabitant of the same State with themselves. And they shall make a List of all the Persons voted for, and of the Number of Votes for each; which List they shall sign and certify, and transmit sealed to the Seat of the Government of the United States, directed to the President of the Senate. The President of the Senate shall, in the Presence of the Senate and House of Representatives, open all the Certificates, and the Votes shall then be counted. The Person having the greatest Number of Votes shall be the President, if such Number be a Majority of the whole Number of Electors appointed; and if there be more than one who have such Majority, and have an equal Number of Votes, then the House of Representatives shall immediately chuse by Ballot one of them for President; and if no Person have a Majority, then from the five highest on the List the said House shall in like Manner chuse the President. But in chusing the President, the Votes shall be taken by States, the Representation from each State having one Vote; a quorum for this Purpose shall consist of a Member or Members from two-thirds of the States, and a Majority of all the States shall be necessary to a Choice. In every Case, after the Choice of the President, the Person having the greatest Number of Votes of the Electors shall be the Vice President. But if there should remain two or more who have equal votes, the Senate shall chuse from them by Ballot the Vice President.][4]

4 Revised by the Twelfth Amendment.

The Congress may determine the Time of chusing the Electors, and the Day on which they shall give their Votes; which Day shall be the same throughout the United States.

No person except a natural-born Citizen, or a Citizen of the United States, at the time of the Adoption of this Constitution, shall be eligible to the Office of President; neither shall any Person be eligible to that Office who shall not have attained to the Age of thirty-five years, and been fourteen Years a Resident within the United States.

In Case of the Removal of the President from Office, or of his Death, Resignation, or Inability to discharge the Powers and Duties of the said Office, the same shall devolve on the Vice President, and the Congress may by Law provide for the Case of Removal, Death, Resignation, or Inability, both of the President and Vice President, declaring what Officer shall then act as President, and such Officer shall act accordingly, until the disability be removed, or a President shall be elected.

The President shall, at stated Times, receive for his Services a Compensation, which shall neither be increased nor diminished during the Period for which he shall have been elected, and he shall not receive within that Period any other Emolument from the United States, or any of them.

Before he enter on the execution of his Office, he shall take the following Oath or Affirmation:—"I do solemnly swear (or affirm) that I will faithfully execute the Office of President of the United States, and will, to the best of my Ability, preserve, protect, and defend the Constitution of the United States."

**SECTION 2.** The President shall be Commander in Chief of the Army and Navy of the United States, and of the Militia of the several States, when called into the actual Service of the United States; he may require the Opinion, in writing, of the principal Officer in each of the executive Departments, upon any subject relating to the Duties of their respective Offices, and he shall have Power to Grant Reprieves and Pardons for Offenses against the United States, except in Cases of Impeachment.

He shall have Power, by and with the Advice and Consent of the Senate, to make Treaties, provided two-thirds of the Senators present concur; and he shall nominate, and by and with the Advice and Consent of the Senate, shall appoint Ambassadors, other public Ministers and Consuls, Judges of the supreme Court, and all other Officers of the United States, whose Appointments are not herein otherwise provided for, and which shall be established by Law: but the Congress may by Law vest the Appointment of such inferior Officers, as they think proper, in the President alone, in the Courts of Law, or in the Heads of Departments.

The President shall have Power to fill up all Vacancies that may happen during the Recess of the Senate, by granting Commissions which shall expire at the End of their next Session.

**SECTION 3.** He shall from time to time give to the Congress Information of the State of the Union, and recommend to their Consideration such Measures as he shall judge necessary and expedient; he may, on extraordinary occasions, convene both Houses, or either of them, and in Case of Disagreement between them, with respect to the Time of Adjournment, he may adjourn them to such Time as he shall think proper; he shall receive Ambassadors and other public Ministers; he shall take care that the Laws be faithfully executed, and shall Commission all the Officers of the United States.

**SECTION 4.** The President, Vice President and all civil Officers of the United States, shall be removed from Office on Impeachment for, and Conviction of, Treason, Bribery, or other high Crimes and Misdemeanors.

# ARTICLE III

**SECTION 1.** The judicial Power of the United States, shall be vested in one supreme Court, and in such inferior Courts as the Congress may from time to time ordain and establish. The Judges, both of the supreme and inferior Courts, shall hold their Offices during good Behaviour, and shall, at stated Times, receive for their Services, a Compensation, which shall not be diminished during their Continuance in Office.

**SECTION 2.** The judicial Power shall extend to all Cases, in Law and Equity, arising under this Constitution, the Laws of the United States, and Treaties made, or which shall be made, under their Authority;—to all Cases affecting ambassadors, other public ministers and consuls;—to all cases of admiralty and maritime Jurisdiction;—to Controversies to which the United States shall be a Party;—to Controversies between two or more States;—between a State and Citizens of another State;[5]—between Citizens of different States—between Citizens of the same State claiming Lands under Grants of different States, and between a State, or the Citizens thereof, and foreign States, Citizens, or Subjects. In all Cases affecting Ambassadors, other public Ministers and Consuls, and those in which a State shall be Party, the supreme Court shall have original Jurisdiction. In all the other Cases before mentioned, the supreme Court shall have appellate Jurisdiction, both as to Law and Fact, with such Exceptions, and under such Regulations as the Congress shall make.

The trial of all Crimes, except in Cases of Impeachment, shall be by Jury; and such Trial shall be held in the State where the said Crimes shall have been committed; but when not committed within any State, the Trial shall be at such Place or Places as the Congress may by Law have directed.

5 Qualified by the Eleventh Amendment.

**SECTION 3.** Treason against the United States, shall consist only in levying War against them, or in adhering to their Enemies, giving them Aid and Comfort. No Person shall be convicted of Treason unless on the Testimony of two Witnesses to the same overt Act, or on Confession in open Court.

The Congress shall have power to declare the Punishment of Treason, but no Attainder of Treason shall work Corruption of Blood, or Forfeiture except during the Life of the Person attainted.

# ARTICLE IV

**SECTION 1.** Full Faith and Credit shall be given in each State to the public Acts, Records, and judicial Proceedings of every other State. And the Congress may by general Laws prescribe the Manner in which such Acts, Records and Proceedings shall be proved, and the Effect thereof.

**SECTION 2.** The Citizens of each State shall be entitled to all Privileges and Immunities of Citizens in the several States.

A Person charged in any State with Treason, Felony, or other Crime, who shall flee from Justice, and be found in another State, shall on demand of the executive Authority of the State from which he fled, be delivered up, to be removed to the State having Jurisdiction of the crime. No Person held to Service or Labour in one State, under the Laws thereof, escaping into another, shall, in Consequence of any Law or Regulation therein, be discharged from such Service or Labour, but shall be delivered up on Claim of the Party to whom such Service or Labour may be due.

**SECTION 3.** New States may be admitted by the Congress into this Union; but no new State shall be formed or erected within the Jurisdiction of any other State; nor any State be formed by the Junction of two or more States, or parts of States, without the Consent of the Legislatures of the States concerned as well as of the Congress. The Congress shall have Power to dispose of and make all needful Rules and Regulations respecting the Territory or other Property belonging to the United States; and nothing in this Constitution shall be so construed as to Prejudice any Claims of the United States, or of any particular State.

**SECTION 4.** The United States shall guarantee to every State in this Union a Republican Form of Government, and shall protect each of them against Invasion; and on Application of the Legislature, or of the Executive (when the Legislature cannot be convened) against domestic Violence.

# ARTICLE V

The Congress, whenever two-thirds of both Houses shall deem it necessary, shall propose Amendments to this Constitution, or, on the Application of the Legislatures of two-thirds of the several States, shall call a Convention for proposing Amendments, which, in either Case, shall be valid to all Intents and Purposes, as part of this Constitution, when ratified by the Legislatures of three-fourths of the several States, or by Conventions in three-fourths thereof, as the one or the other Mode of Ratification may be proposed by the Congress; Provided that no Amendment which may be made prior to the Year One thousand eight hundred and eight shall in any Manner affect the first and fourth Clauses in the Ninth Section of the first Article; and that no State, without its Consent, shall be deprived of its equal Suffrage in the Senate.

# ARTICLE VI

All Debts contracted and Engagements entered into, before the Adoption of this Constitution, shall be as valid against the United States under this Constitution, as under the Confederation.

This Constitution, and the Laws of the United States which shall be made in Pursuance thereof; and all Treaties made, or which shall be made, under the Authority of the United States, shall be the supreme Law of the Land; and the Judges in every State shall be bound thereby, any Thing in the Constitution or Laws of any State to the Contrary notwithstanding.

The Senators and Representatives before mentioned, and the Members of the several State Legislatures, and all executive and judicial Officers, both of the United States and of the several States, shall be bound by Oath or Affirmation to support this Constitution; but no religious Tests shall ever be required as a qualification to any Office or public Trust under the United States.

# ARTICLE VII

The Ratification of the Conventions of nine States shall be sufficient for the Establishment of this Constitution between the States so ratifying the same.

Done in Convention by the Unanimous Consent of the States present the Seventeenth Day of September in the Year of our Lord one thousand seven hundred and Eighty seven, and of the Independence of the United States of America the Twelfth. In Witness whereof We have hereunto subscribed our Names.[6]

6 These are the full names of the signers, which in some cases are not the signatures on the document.

**GEORGE WASHINGTON**
PRESIDENT AND DEPUTY FROM VIRGINIA

**NEW HAMPSHIRE**
John Langdon
Nicholas Gilman

**MASSACHUSETTS**
Nathaniel Gorham
Rufus King

**CONNECTICUT**
William Samuel Johnson
Roger Sherman

**NEW YORK**
Alexander Hamilton

**NEW JERSEY**
William Livingston
David Brearley
William Paterson
Jonathan Dayton

**PENNSYLVANIA**
Benjamin Franklin
Thomas Mifflin
Robert Morris
George Clymer
Thomas FitzSimons
Jared Ingersoll
James Wilson
Gouverneur Morris

**DELAWARE**
George Read
Gunning Bedford, Jr.
John Dickinson
Richard Bassett
Jacob Broom

**MARYLAND**
James McHenry
Daniel of St. Thomas
Jenifer
Daniel Carroll

**VIRGINIA**
John Blair
James Madison, Jr.

**NORTH CAROLINA**
William Blount
Richard Dobbs Spaight
Hugh Williamson

**SOUTH CAROLINA**
John Rutledge
Charles Cotesworth
Pinckney
Charles Pinckney
Pierce Butler

**GEORGIA**
William Few
Abraham Baldwin

*Articles in Addition to, and Amendment of, the Constitution of the United States of America, Proposed by Congress, and Ratified by the Legislatures of the Several States, Pursuant to the Fifth Article of the Original Constitution*[7]

# [AMENDMENT I]

Congress shall make no law respecting an establishment of religion, or prohibiting the free exercise thereof; or abridging the freedom of speech, or of the press; or the right of the people peaceably to assemble, and to petition the Government for a redress of grievances.

# [AMENDMENT II]

A well regulated Militia, being necessary to the security of a free State, the right of the people to keep and bear Arms shall not be infringed.

# [AMENDMENT III]

No Soldier shall, in time of peace, be quartered in any house, without the consent of the Owner, nor in time of war, but in a manner to be prescribed by law.

# [AMENDMENT IV]

The right of the people to be secure in their persons, houses, papers, and effects, against unreasonable searches and seizures, shall not be violated, and no Warrants shall issue, but upon probable cause, supported by Oath or affirmation, and particularly describing the place to be searched, and the persons or things to be seized.

7 This heading appears only in the joint resolution submitting the first ten amendments, known as the Bill of Rights.

# [AMENDMENT V]

No person shall be held to answer for a capital or otherwise infamous crime, unless on a presentment or indictment of a Grand Jury, except in cases arising in the land or naval forces, or in the Militia, when in actual service in time of War or public danger; nor shall any person be subject for the same offence to be twice put in jeopardy of life or limb; nor shall be compelled in any criminal case to be a witness against himself, nor be deprived of life, liberty, or property, without due process of law; nor shall private property be taken for public use, without just compensation.

# [AMENDMENT VI]

In all criminal prosecutions, the accused shall enjoy the right to a speedy and public trial, by an impartial jury of the State and district wherein the crime shall have been committed, which district shall have been previously ascertained by law, and to be informed of the nature and cause of the accusation; to be confronted with the witnesses against him; to have compulsory process for obtaining witnesses in his favour, and to have the Assistance of Counsel for his defence.

# [AMENDMENT VII]

In suits at common law, where the value in controversy shall exceed twenty dollars, the right of trial by jury shall be preserved, and no fact tried by a jury, shall be otherwise reexamined in any Court of the United States, than according to the rules of the common law.

# [AMENDMENT VIII]

Excessive bail shall not be required, nor excessive fines imposed, nor cruel and unusual punishments inflicted.

# [AMENDMENT IX]

The enumeration of the Constitution, of certain rights, shall not be construed to deny or disparage others retained by the people.

# [AMENDMENT X]

The powers not delegated to the United States by the Constitution, nor prohibited by it to the States, are reserved to the States respectively, or to the people. [Amendments I-X, in force 1791.]

# [AMENDMENT XI][8]

The Judicial power of the United States shall not be construed to extend to any suit in law or equity, commenced or prosecuted against one of the United States by Citizens of another State, or by Citizens or Subjects of any Foreign State.

# [AMENDMENT XII][9]

The Electors shall meet in their respective States and vote by ballot for President and Vice-President, one of whom, at least, shall not be an inhabitant of the same State with themselves; they shall name in their ballots the person voted for as President, and in distinct ballots the person voted for as Vice-President, and they shall make distinct lists of all persons voted for as President, and of all persons voted for as Vice-President, and of the number of votes for each, which lists they shall sign and certify, and transmit sealed to the seat of the government of the United States, directed to the President of the Senate;—The President of the Senate shall, in the presence of the Senate and House of Representatives, open all the certificates and the votes shall then be counted;—The person having the greatest number of votes for President, shall be the President, if such number be a majority of the whole number of Electors appointed; and if no person have such majority, then from the persons having the highest numbers not exceeding three on the list of those voted for as President, the House of Representatives shall choose immediately, by ballot, the President. But in choosing the President, the votes shall be taken by states, the representation from each state having one vote; a quorum for this purpose shall consist of a member or members from two-thirds of the states, and a majority of all the states shall be necessary to a choice. And if the House of Representatives shall not choose a President whenever the right of choice shall devolve upon them, before the fourth day of March next following, then the Vice-President shall act as President, as in the case of the death or other constitutional disability of the President.—The person having the greatest number of votes as Vice-President, shall be the Vice-President, if such number be a majority of the whole number of Electors appointed, and if no person have a majority, then from the two highest numbers on the list, the Senate shall choose the Vice-President; a quorum for the purpose shall consist of two-thirds of the whole number of Senators, and a majority of the whole number shall be necessary to a choice. But no person constitutionally ineligible to the office of President shall be eligible to that of Vice-President of the United States.

# [AMENDMENT XIII][10]

**SECTION 1.** Neither slavery nor involuntary servitude, except as a punishment for crime whereof the party shall have been duly convicted, shall exist within the United States, or any place subject to their jurisdiction.

**SECTION 2.** Congress shall have power to enforce this article by appropriate legislation.

# [AMENDMENT XIV][11]

**SECTION 1.** All persons born or naturalized in the United States, and subject to the jurisdiction thereof, are citizens of the United States and of the State wherein they reside. No State shall abridge the privileges or immunities of citizens of the United States; nor shall any State deprive any person of life, liberty, or property, without due process of

8 Adopted in 1798.

9 Adopted in 1804.

10 Adopted in 1865.

11 Adopted in 1868.

law; nor deny to any person within its jurisdiction the equal protection of the laws.

SECTION 2. Representatives shall be apportioned among the several States according to their respective numbers, counting the whole number of persons in each State, excluding Indians not taxed. But when the right to vote at any election for the choice of electors for President and Vice-President of the United States, Representatives in Congress, the Executive and Judicial officers of a State, or the members of the Legislature thereof, is denied to any of the male inhabitants of such State, being twentyone years of age, and citizens of the United States, or in any way abridged, except for participation in rebellion, or other crime, the basis of representation therein shall be reduced in the proportion which the number of such male citizens shall bear to the whole number of male citizens twenty-one years of age in such State.

SECTION 3. No person shall be a Senator or Representative in Congress, or elector of President and Vice-President, or hold any office, civil or military, under the United States, or under any State, who, having previously taken an oath, as a member of Congress, or as an officer of the United States, or as a member of any State legislature, or as an executive or judicial officer of any State, to support the Constitution of the United States, shall have engaged in insurrection or rebellion against the same, or given aid or comfort to the enemies thereof. But Congress may by a vote of two-thirds of each House, remove such disability.

SECTION 4. The validity of the public debt of the United States, authorized by law, including debts incurred for payment of pensions and bounties for services in suppressing insurrection or rebellion, shall not be questioned. But neither the United States nor any State shall assume or pay any debts or obligation incurred in aid of insurrection or rebellion against the United States, or any claim for the loss or emancipation of any slave; but all such debts, obligations, and claims shall be held illegal and void.

SECTION 5. The Congress shall have the power to enforce, by appropriate legislation, the provisions of this article.

# [AMENDMENT XV][12]

SECTION 1. The right of citizens of the United States to vote shall not be denied or abridged by the United States or by any State on account of race, color, or previous condition of servitude.

12 Adopted in 1870.

SECTION 2. The Congress shall have power to enforce this article by appropriate legislation.

# [AMENDMENT XVI][13]

The Congress shall have power to lay and collect taxes on incomes, from whatever source derived, without apportionment among the several States, and without regard to any census or enumeration.

# [AMENDMENT XVII][14]

The Senate of the United States shall be composed of two Senators from each State, elected by the people thereof, for six years; and each Senator shall have one vote. The electors in each State shall have the qualifications requisite for electors of the most numerous branch of the State legislatures.

When vacancies happen in the representation of any State in the Senate, the executive authority of such State shall issue writs of election to fill such vacancies: Provided, That the legislature of any State may empower the executive thereof to make temporary appointments until the people fill the vacancies by election as the legislature may direct. This amendment shall not be so construed as to affect the election or term of any Senator chosen before it becomes valid as part of the Constitution.

# [AMENDMENT XVIII][15]

SECTION 1. After one year from the ratification of this article the manufacture, sale, or transportation of intoxicating liquors within, the importation thereof into, or the exportation thereof from the United States and all territory subject to the jurisdiction thereof for beverage purposes is hereby prohibited.

SECTION 2. The Congress and the several States shall have concurrent power to enforce this article by appropriate legislation.

SECTION 3. This article shall be inoperative unless it shall have been ratified as an amendment to the Constitution by the legislatures of the several States, as provided in the Constitution, within seven years from the date of the submission hereof to the States by the Congress.

13 Adopted in 1913.

14 Adopted in 1913.

15 Adopted in 1918.

# [AMENDMENT XIX][16]

The right of citizens of the United States to vote shall not be denied or abridged by the United States or by any State on account of sex.

Congress shall have power to enforce this article by appropriate legislation.

# [AMENDMENT XX][17]

**SECTION 1.** The terms of the President and Vice-President shall end at noon on the 20th day of January, and the terms of Senators and Representatives at noon on the 3d day of January, of the years in which such terms would have ended if this article had not been ratified; and the terms of their successors shall then begin.

**SECTION 2.** The Congress shall assemble at least once in every year, and such meeting shall begin at noon on the 3d day of January, unless they shall by law appoint a different day.

**SECTION 3.** If, at the time fixed for the beginning of the term of the President, the President elect shall have died, the Vice-President elect shall become President. If a President shall not have been chosen before the time fixed for the beginning of his term or if the President elect shall have failed to qualify, then the Vice-President elect shall act as President until a President shall have qualified; and the Congress may by law provide for the case wherein neither a President elect nor a Vice-President elect shall have qualified, declaring who shall then act as President, or the manner in which one who is to act shall be selected, and such person shall act accordingly until a President or Vice-President shall have qualified.

**SECTION 4.** The Congress may by law provide for the case of the death of any of the persons from whom the House of Representatives may choose a President whenever the right of choice shall have devolved upon them, and for the case of the death of any of the persons from whom the Senate may choose a Vice-President whenever the right of choice shall have devolved upon them.

**SECTION 5.** Sections 1 and 2 shall take effect on the 15th day of October following the ratification of this article.

**SECTION 6.** This article shall be inoperative unless it shall have been ratified as an amendment to the Constitution by the legislatures of three-fourths of the several States within seven years from the date of its submission.

16 Adopted in 1920.

17 Adopted in 1933.

# [AMENDMENT XXI][18]

**SECTION 1.** The eighteenth article of amendment to the Constitution of the United States is hereby repealed.

**SECTION 2.** The transportation or importation into any State, Territory, or possession of the United States for delivery or use therein of intoxicating liquors, in violation of the laws thereof, is hereby prohibited.

**SECTION 3.** This article shall be inoperative unless it shall have been ratified as an amendment to the Constitution by conventions in the several States, as provided in the Constitution, within seven years from the date of the submission hereof to the States by the Congress.

# [AMENDMENT XXII][19]

No person shall be elected to the office of the President more than twice, and no person who has held the office of President, or acted as President, for more than two years of a term to which some other person was elected President shall be elected to the office of the President more than once.

But this Article shall not apply to any person holding the office of President when this Article was proposed by the Congress, and shall not prevent any person who may be holding the office of President, or acting as President, during the term within which this Article becomes operative from holding the office of President or acting as President during the remainder of such term.

This article shall be inoperative unless it shall have been ratified as an amendment to the Constitution by the legislatures of three-fourths of the several states within seven years from the date of its submission to the states by the Congress.

# [AMENDMENT XXIII][20]

**SECTION 1.** The District constituting the seat of Government of the United States shall appoint in such manner as the Congress may direct:

18 Adopted in 1933.

19 Adopted in 1951.

20 Adopted in 1961.

A number of electors of President and Vice-President equal to the whole number of Senators and Representatives in Congress to which the District would be entitled if it were a State, but in no event more than the least populous State; they shall be in addition to those appointed by the States, but they shall be considered, for the purpose of the election of President and Vice-President, to be electors appointed by a State; and they shall meet in the District and perform such duties as provided by the twelfth article of amendment.

SECTION 2. The Congress shall have power to enforce this article by appropriate legislation.

# [AMENDMENT XXIV][21]

SECTION 1. The right of citizens of the United States to vote in any primary or other election for President or Vice-President, for electors for President or Vice-President, or for Senator or Representative in Congress, shall not be denied or abridged by the United States or any state by reason of failure to pay any poll tax or other tax.

SECTION 2. The Congress shall have the power to enforce this article by appropriate legislation.

# [AMENDMENT XXV][22]

SECTION 1. In case of the removal of the President from office or of his death or resignation, the Vice-President shall become President.

SECTION 2. Whenever there is a vacancy in the office of the Vice President, the President shall nominate a Vice President who shall take office upon confirmation by a majority vote of both Houses of Congress.

SECTION 3. Whenever the President transmits to the President Pro Tempore of the Senate and the Speaker of the House of Representatives his written declaration that he is unable to discharge the powers and duties of his office, and until he transmits to them a written declaration to the contrary, such powers and duties shall be discharged by the Vice-President as Acting President.

SECTION 4. Whenever the Vice-President and a majority of either the principal officers of the executive departments or of such other body as Congress may by law provide, transmit to the President Pro Tempore of the Senate and the Speaker of the House of Representatives their written declaration that the President is unable to discharge the powers and duties of his office, the Vice President shall immediately assume the powers and duties of the office as Acting President.

Thereafter, when the President transmits to the President Pro Tempore of the Senate and the Speaker of the House of Representatives his written declaration that no inability exists, he shall resume the powers and duties of his office unless the Vice President and a majority of either the principal officers of the executive departments or of such other body as Congress may by law provide, transmit within four days to the President Pro Tempore of the Senate and the Speaker of the House of Representatives their written declaration that the President is unable to discharge the powers and duties of his office. Thereupon Congress shall decide the issue, assembling within forty-eight hours for that purpose if not in session. If the Congress, within twenty-one days after receipt of the latter written declaration, or, if Congress is not in session, within twenty-one days after Congress is required to assemble, determines by two-thirds vote of both Houses that the President is unable to discharge the powers and duties of his office, the Vice President shall continue to discharge the same as Acting President; otherwise, the President shall resume the powers and duties of his office.

# [AMENDMENT XXVI][23]

SECTION 1. The right of citizens of the United States, who are eighteen years of age or older, to vote shall not be denied or abridged by the United States or by any State on account of age.

SECTION 1. The Congress shall have power to enforce this article by appropriate legislation.

# [AMENDMENT XXVII][24]

No law, varying the compensation for the services of the Senators and Representatives, shall take effect, until an election of Representatives shall have intervened.

21 Adopted in 1964.

22 Adopted in 1967.

23 Adopted in 1971.

24 Adopted in 1992.

# Index

## A



## B

## C

## D



## E



## F

## G



## H



## I



## J

# K



# L



# M

# Q



# R



# S

## T



## U

## V



## W

## Z

## Real Writing for a Real World Context

*Real Writing* helps you tackle the challenges of writing by guiding you through the process, step by step. In addition to sample writing from the classroom and workplace, you'll also get practice exercises, writing prompts, and graphics that will help you understand all of the basics you need. This book includes the essays and assignments you need in order to do your classwork. Using this book will provide you with the best opportunity to succeed in your course.

## Did your instructor assign *LaunchPad Solo for Readers and Writers*?

**macmillanhighered.com/readwrite**

Launch PadSolo
for Readers and Writers

*Real Writing* includes cross-references to *LaunchPad Solo for Readers and Writers* with video, audio, and practice activities that give you immediate feedback. If your book did not come packaged with an access code, you can purchase access to ***LaunchPad Solo for Readers and Writers*** at **macmillanhighered.com/readwrite**.

---

Real Writing
e-book

**Value-priced options.** For less than the cost of the print book, you can purchase this text as an e-book that will work with computers, tablets, or e-readers. For details, visit **macmillanhighered.com/catalog/ebookpartners**.

BUDGET BOOKS

**Why choose Loose-leaf?**

Cost: Priced 35% less than a bound book.

Ease: Bring only the chapter you need to class and take notes right on the pages!

Organization: Integrate lecture notes and other course materials right into your binder.



macmillanhighered.com

bedford
ST. MARTIN'S

macmillan education

ISBN 978-1-319-00321-0

90000
9 781319 003210

# Useful Editing and Proofreading Marks

The marks and abbreviations below are those typically used by instructors when marking papers (add any alternate marks used by your instructor in the left-hand column), but you can also mark your own work or that of your peers with these helpful symbols.

| Alternate symbol | Standard symbol | How to revise or edit (numbers in boldface are chapters where you can find help) |
|---|---|---|
| | *adj* | Use correct adjective form **Ch. 21** |
| | *adv* | Use correct adverb form **Ch. 21** |
| | *agr* | Correct subject-verb agreement or pronoun agreement **Chs. 18 and 20** |
| | *awk* | Awkward expression: edit for clarity **Ch. 18** |
| | *cap* or triple underline [example] | Use capital letter correctly **Ch. 34** |
| | *case* | Use correct pronoun case **Ch. 20** |
| | *cliché* | Replace overused phrase with fresh words **Ch. 27** |
| | *coh* | Revise paragraph or essay for coherence **Ch. 5** |
| | *coord* | Use coordination correctly **Ch. 23** |
| | *cs* | Comma splice: join the sentences correctly **Ch. 17** |
| | *dev* | Develop your paragraph or essay more completely **Chs. 3 and 4** |
| | *dm* | Revise to avoid a dangling modifier **Ch. 22** |
| | *frag* | Attach the fragment to a sentence or make it a sentence **Ch. 16** |
| | *fs* | Fused sentence: join the two sentences correctly **Ch. 17** |
| | *ital* | Use italics **Ch. 32** |
| | *lc* or diagonal slash [Example] | Use lowercase **Ch. 34** |
| | *mm* | Revise to avoid a misplaced modifier **Ch. 22** |
| | *pl* | Use the correct plural form of the verb **Ch. 19** |
| | *ref* | Make pronoun reference clear **Ch. 20** |
| | *ro* | Run-on sentence; join the two sentences correctly **Ch. 17** |
| | *sp* | Correct the spelling error **Ch. 29** |
| | *sub* | Use subordination correctly **Ch. 23** |
| | *sup* | Support your point with details, examples, or facts **Ch. 4** |
| | *tense* | Correct the problem with verb tense **Ch. 19** |
| | *trans* | Add a transition **Ch. 5** |
| | *w* | Delete unnecessary words **Ch. 27** |
| | *wc* | Reconsider your word choice **Ch. 27** |
| | ? | Make your meaning clearer **Ch. 5** |
| | ^ , | Use comma correctly **Ch. 30** |
| | ; : ( ) - — | Use semicolon / colon / parentheses / hyphen / dash correctly **Ch. 33** |
| | " " (with carets) | Use quotation marks correctly **Ch. 32** |
| | ^ | Insert something |
| | ℘ [exaample] | Delete something |
| | ∽ [words example] | Change the order of letters or words |
| | ¶ | Start a new paragraph |
| | # [examplewords] | Add a space |
| | ⁀ [ex ample] | Close up a space |

Launch PadSolo
for Readers and Writers

## Missing something?

Instructors may assign the online materials that accompany this text. To access them, visit **macmillanhighered.com/readwrite**.

# Inside *LaunchPad Solo for Readers and Writers*

| | Video | LearningCurve | Pre/Post MC | Quizbank |
|---|---|---|---|---|
| **Welcome** | | | | |
| Teaching and Learning Advice | | | | |
| **Diagnostics** | | | | |
| Grammar | | | ● | |
| Reading | | | ● | |
| **Reading** | ● | | | |
| Topics and Main Ideas | ● | ● | ● | ● |
| Topic Sentences and Supporting Details | ● | ● | ● | ● |
| Patterns of Organization | ● | ● | ● | |
| Vocabulary | ● | ● | ● | |
| Active Reading | ● | | ● | |
| Critical Reading | ● | ● | ● | |
| Interpretive Reading | ● | | ● | |
| Reading Tutorials | ● | | | |
| 25 Reading Quizzes | | | ● | |
| **Writing Process** | ● | | | |
| Purpose, Audience, and Topic | ● | | ● | |
| Prewriting | ● | | ● | |
| Thesis Statements | ● | | ● | ● |
| Drafting | ● | | ● | ● |
| Revising | ● | | ● | |
| Editing | ● | | ● | |
| Digital Writing Tutorials | ● | | | |
| **Integrated Reading and Writing** | ● | | | |
| Argument | ● | ● | ● | |
| Summarizing | ● | | ● | ● |
| **Research** | ● | | | |
| Working with Sources | ● | ● | ● | ● |
| Documentation Guides | | | | |
| Search and Citation Tutorials | ● | | | |
| **Grammar: Parts of Speech** | ● | ● | ● | ● |
| **Grammar: Basic Sentences** | ● | ● | ● | ● |
| **Grammar: Style and Mechanics** | ● | ● | ● | ● |
| **Grammar: Resources for Multilingual Writers** | | ● | | ● |

## U



## V



## W



## Y



## Z

## Q

## N



## O



## P

## F



## G

## D



## E

# Index

## A



## B

# Brief Contents

# Real Writing

*with Readings*

Seventh Edition

# Real Writing

## with Readings

### Paragraphs and Essays for Success in College, Work, and Everyday Life

**Susan Anker**

with **Nicole Aitken**
Illinois Central College

Bedford/St.Martin's
A Macmillan Education Imprint
Boston • New York

**For Bedford/St. Martin's**

*Vice President, Editorial, Macmillan Higher Education Humanities:* Edwin Hill
*Editorial Director for Literature and Music:* Karen S. Henry
*Publisher for Composition, Business and Technical Writing, and Developmental Writing:* Leasa Burton
*Executive Editor:* Vivian Garcia
*Senior Developmental Editor:* Jill Gallagher
*Production Editors:* Annette Pagliaro Sweeney, Louis C. Bruno Jr.
*Publishing Services Manager:* Andrea Cava
*Senior Production Supervisor:* Jennifer Wetzel
*Project Management:* Graphic World, Inc.
*Director of Rights and Permissions:* Hilary Newman
*Senior Art Director:* Anna Palchik
*Text Design:* Claire Seng-Niemoeller
*Cover Design:* William Boardman
*Cover Art:* © Murray Lee / Getty Images
*Composition:* Graphic World, Inc.
*Printing and Binding:* LSC Communications



Manufactured in the United States of America.
0 9 8 7
f e d c

*For information, write:* Bedford/St. Martin's, 75 Arlington Street, Boston, MA 02116 (617-399-4000)

ISBN 978-1-319-00319-7 (Student Edition)
ISBN 978-1-319-00321-0 (Loose-leaf Edition)

**Acknowledgments**

COURTESY OF JIM ANKER

## A note to students from Susan Anker

For the last twenty years or so, I have traveled the country talking to students about their goals and, more important, about the challenges they face on the way to achieving those goals. Students always tell me that they want good jobs and that they need a college degree to get those jobs. I designed *Real Writing* with those goals in mind — strengthening the writing, reading, and editing skills needed for success in college, at work, and in everyday life.

Here is something else: good jobs require not only a college degree but also a college education—knowing not only how to read and write but how to think critically and learn effectively. So that is what I stress here, too. It is worth facing the challenges. All my best wishes to you, in this course and in all your future endeavors.

## A note to students from Nicole Aitken

COURTESY OF NICOLE AITKEN

I've been working in both the university and community college environments since 2001, and I've had the opportunity to be a student in all different types of situations as well, including a large university, a small private college, and community colleges. I understand how your surroundings affect the way you learn and how important it is to be comfortable in those surroundings. What you bring with you to the classroom is as important to the learning experience as the material you learn in that classroom.

What does that mean? It means that you, as a student, have something to say and something to contribute. Every day you are thinking, reading, and writing in a critical way that is valuable to the college classroom, but you may not be aware of how to access those thoughts or skills in a meaningful way just yet. Although this book may introduce you to some new words and concepts, chances are good that many of these concepts or methods are ones you use regularly. Every day you are writing. You are texting, emailing, and sending messages, and you are communicating through written or spoken language. When you read or hear someone speak to you, you are analyzing what was said or written and interpreting those words; that is all a part of thinking critically and being a receptive audience.

Come to the classroom ready to share what you already know and understand that a concept we may call by a new and foreign term is actually something that may already be commonplace to you. Let's share our knowledge and ideas. While this book can guide you and help you make the choices you need to be successful in your careers and in college, you are also already an expert: you are the expert in your life, your technologies, and your own experiences. A writing community asks that we all share our experiences to increase the knowledge of the group: join our writing community and increase our collective knowledge.

## A note to students from Susan Anker

For the last twenty years or so, I have traveled the country talking to students about their goals and, more important, about the challenges they face on the way to achieving those goals. Students always tell me that they want good jobs and that they need a college degree to get those jobs. I designed *Real Writing* with these goals in mind—strengthening the writing, reading, and editing skills needed for success in college, at work, and in everyday life.

Here is something else: good jobs require not only a college degree but also a college education—knowing not only how to [illegible] but how to think critically and learn [illegible]. [illegible] It is worth facing the challenges. All my [illegible] and in all your future endeavors.

## A note to students from Nicole Aitken

I've been working in both the university and community college environments since 20[illegible], and I've had the opportunity [illegible] student in all different types of [illegible] as well, including [illegible]

[illegible] community colleges. I [illegible]

[illegible] the way you learn and how [illegible] and your surroundings. What you bring with you to the [illegible] [illegible] the learning experience [illegible] the material you learn in the classroom.

[illegible] that it means that [illegible] to contribute. Every day [illegible] and [illegible] way that is valuable to [illegible] [illegible] how to access those thoughts or skills in [illegible] introduce you to some [illegible] that [illegible] of these concepts or methods [illegible] writing. You are texting, emailing, and sending messages, and you [illegible] or spoken language. When you read or hear someone speak to you, you [illegible] or written and interpreting those words that is all a part of thinking critically and being a receptive audience.

[illegible] already know [illegible] that a concept we [illegible] term is actually something that may already [illegible] to you [illegible] and ideas. While this book can guide you and help you make the choices you need to be successful in your career and in college, you are also already an expert. You are the expert in your [illegible], and your own experiences. A writing community asks that we all share our experiences to increase the knowledge of the group; join our writing community and increase our collective knowledge!

# Contents

# Thematic Contents

# Preface

The first aim of *Real Writing with Readings* has always been to communicate to students that good writing skills are both *essential* and *attainable*. When they have this, perspective, students can start fresh, reframing the writing course for themselves not as an irrelevant hoop to jump through but as a central gateway — a potentially life-changing opportunity, worthy of their best efforts. In large and small ways, this book is designed to help students prepare for their futures. It connects the writing class to their other courses, to their real lives, and to the expectations of the larger world.

*Real Writing* underscores this powerful message in its initial chapter, "Critical Thinking, Reading, and Writing"; in its practical advice on writing different kinds of essays; and in its step-by-step grammar sections, which build confidence and proficiency by focusing first on the most serious errors students commonly make. A diverse collection of both student and professional readings further encourages students to see the big picture, giving them a context for what they are learning. Profiles of Success provide inspirational portraits of former students, now in the workplace, who reflect on the varied, important ways they use writing in their work. These profiles are accompanied by real samples of the kinds of writing these professionals use in the workplace.

*Real Writing* shares this practical, real-world approach with its companion texts — *Real Essays, Real Skills,* and *Real Reading and Writing,* an integrated reading and writing text. All four books put writing in a real-world context and link writing skills to students' own goals in and beyond college.

## *Core Features*

Successful and popular features of earlier editions of *Real Writing* have been carried over to this edition, with revisions based on suggestions from many insightful instructors and students.

**A Comprehensive Teaching and Learning Package:** *Real Writing* combines carefully curated readings, writing samples, writing assignments, grammar instruction, critical thinking and reading coverage, and online practice in one convenient volume, allowing instructors to focus on their students.

**Writing Practice:** Not only does *Real Writing* feature a number of student model paragraphs and essays, workplace writing, and professional readings, it asks students to write their own paragraphs and essays in multiple assignments throughout the book. These assignments aid students in translating their writing skills to the real world, asking them to practice concepts through the

**WRITING ABOUT IMAGES**

Study the photograph below, and complete the following steps.

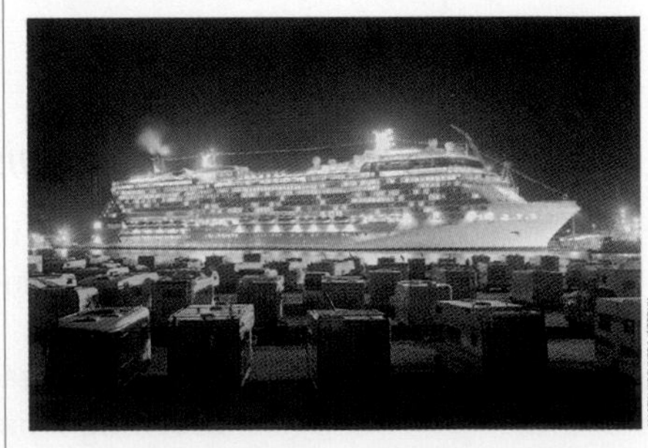

MARTIN KIRCHNER/laif/REDUX

1. **Read the image** Ask yourself: What details does the photographer focus on? How do the colors and lights affect you as a viewer? What main impression does the picture make? (For more information on reading images, see Chapter 1.)
2. **Write an illustration** The photograph shows a luxury liner whose bright, colorful lights attract onlookers and potential customers. Write an illustration paragraph or essay about businesses that draw customers with colorful displays, loud music, or some other appeal to the senses. Include the types of details you examined in step 1.

### Profile of Success

#### Process Analysis in the Real World

COURTESY OF STEVE BARRETT

**Monique Rizer**
Chief of Staff

**Background** I was the oldest of six children, and before my mother married my stepfather, she was on welfare. She homeschooled me for five years until I begged her to let me go to a public high school. There I made friends with some people who expected to go to college, and I realized I wanted to go, too. I started at Green River Community College, but just then my parents' financial situation got really bad, and the eight of us had to move to a trailer. I stopped going to school until I met my future husband, who was going to a community college and encouraged me to go back. Several months later, I became pregnant with my first son. I was determined to stay in college, so I completed one year at Highline Community College. That summer, I had my son, got married, and found loans to transfer to Pacific Lutheran University. While there, I received a Gates Millennium Scholarship, which made continuing college possible. Although I moved a few times, I graduated from college and went on to graduate school. After I finished graduate school, I had another son.

**Degrees/Colleges** B.A., Gonzaga University; M.S., Syracuse University

**Employer** Be the Change, Inc.

**Writing at Work** Writing is the one skill I use every day at work. As chief of staff, I'm responsible for supporting our fundraising efforts, managing our board, leading staff meetings, and other special projects. So, I am often writing to staff within the organization, my leadership, our board members, or people outside our organization with whom we are developing a relationship. I usually communicate through e-mail and I've learned it's so important to keep an e-mail short and to the point, but also friendly. Write, "Good morning" or write "Thank you" or "My best." These are small ways to keep e-mail communication personal through what can be a very impersonal technology, especially with people you don't see very often. Also, when I have to e-mail someone with a criticism or difficult message, I always try to start that e-mail with a positive note or thanks. Finally, I think very carefully about sending an e-mail when a phone call or face-to-face conversation is better. We rely on e-mail and text a lot, and we have to really try to keep those writing forums professional. But sometimes a phone call or a face-to-face conversation is more appropriate depending on the message or purpose. As I've grown in my career, I find my writing to be more important. I also have been responsible for hiring new staff and I pay close attention to how they represent themselves in writing.

I represent my leaders often in writing and so I'm very careful about what I am writing and how it will reflect on them and my organization. Sometimes I'll also write or edit something in the voice of my leadership as well. So, reading their writing and learning their "voice" has become an important skill along with writing. Finally, I draft my writing and have someone look it over or let it sit and look at it later—even a few minutes—just to get some distance and look at it with fresh eyes. Getting some distance or having a fresh view almost always improves my writing.

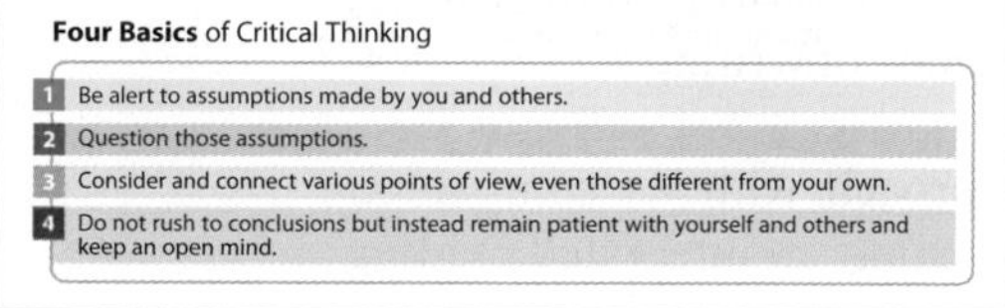

**Four Basics** of Critical Thinking

1. Be alert to assumptions made by you and others.
2. Question those assumptions.
3. Consider and connect various points of view, even those different from your own.
4. Do not rush to conclusions but instead remain patient with yourself and others and keep an open mind.

**2PR** The Critical Reading Process

**P**review the text.

**R**ead the text, looking for the main idea and support.

**P**ause to question and interpret the text, taking notes as you read.

**R**eview the text and your notes, and **R**espond to it.

lens of tasks they will need to complete in college and beyond, such as analyzing monthly expenses, evaluating instructors, and creating a résumé. Each rhetorical mode chapter also features a step-by-step writing guide and checklist that students can refer to when completing their writing assignments.

**Profiles of Success:** These profiles feature former students who regularly use writing in their careers, highlighting their background and the ways in which they use writing beyond the classroom. These inspirational stories give students an idea of the diverse range of careers in which writing skills are valuable — from auto technician to chief of police — and how they, too, can hope to reach their career goals.

**The Four Basics and Four Most Serious Errors:** This approach breaks the writing process down into logical steps, focusing on the four basics of each rhetorical mode as well as the four most serious errors in grammar. This lets students digest information at their own pace, helping them really understand each concept before starting a new one.

**2PR Critical Reading Process:** Appearing throughout the book, this process helps students tackle readings using critical thinking skills, asking them to preview, read, pause, review, and respond to each reading. Students can use this process not only with the readings in this course, but those in all of their college courses.

## *New to This Edition*

This edition includes carefully developed new features to help students become better readers and writers in college and beyond.

**Expanded Reading Coverage:** Every chapter in Parts 1 and 2 of the book features Learning Objectives, Key Terms, and a Reading Roadmap that help students zero in on the skills they should be learning in each chapter. Reflecting on the Journey, at the end of these chapters, allows students to track their own progress on those skills. Together, these new features help students become stronger readers by pointing them precisely where they need to focus.

**Updated Readings:** This new edition features new relevant and relatable readings on themes such as military service, climate change, the language of hip-hop, and issues of class and gender. Nearly all of the student writing and Profiles of

Success came to us from our users — instructors and students who have used the book in their own classrooms.

**Emphasis on Situational Writing:** Real writing samples from the workplace, including a police report, a blog post, a professional and student résumé, an auto repair form, and a program e-mail showcase the various ways in which students will use writing skills beyond the classroom, encouraging them to apply what they learn in their future college courses and in their daily lives.

Calysta Will
555 N. Oak Terrace, Normal, IL 60052 | (111) 555-5678 | cwill@ilstu.edu

**Education**
Bachelor of Arts | May 2015 | Illinois State University
Major: Public Relations
Lorenze de' Medici University | Spring 2013 | Florence, Italy

**Skills & Abilities**
*Communication and computer skills*
Microsoft Word and Power Point: Proficient
Excel: Intermediate
Spanish: Proficient
Italian: Basic, conversational, and reading

**Leadership**
Social Chair, Public Relations Student Society of America, Illinois State University
August 2014–May 2015

**Experience**
Academic Peer Advisor | Illinois State University—University College | May 2014–Present
- Advise first-year students with academic planning and major exploration in partnership with a University College Professional Advisor
- Assist in the delivery of University College programs and services
- Maintain accurate, detailed record of all advising contacts

Marketing and Communications Intern | Special Olympics Illinois | January–May 2014
- Created various publications for Special Olympics events
- Planned and executed Special Olympics events
- Facilitated creative projects to be featuring Special Olympics Illinois athletes
- Supported and promoted accomplishments of Special Olympics athletes

Communications Intern | Illinois State University Dean of Students | January–May 2014
- Conducted research to define needs of members of the Student Government Association
- Reconstructed operations manual for Student Government Association
- Edited and condensed various documents included in the operations manual

Peer Instructor | Illinois State University Success 101 Program | August 2012–January 2014
- Provided academic support to first-year students
- Created lesson plans focused on important skills necessary to being successful in higher education
- Planned and facilitated social events for students

**Redesigned Interior:** A streamlined design allows students to focus on the most important elements of the text, getting rid of the clutter of additional features while still being visually appealing.

**A Slimmer Book:** Working from instructor feedback, this edition has been carefully edited to sharpen the instructional content, making the concepts easier for students to absorb and simpler for instructors to teach. Writing process chapters have been condensed, and all readings are now integrated into the rhetorical modes chapters instead of appearing in a separate chapter at the end of the book.

## *Support for Instructors and Students*

*Real Writing* is accompanied by comprehensive teaching and learning support.

### STUDENT RESOURCES

***LaunchPad Solo for Readers and Writers*** includes multimedia content and assessments, including diagnostics on grammar and reading and LearningCurve adaptive quizzing, organized into pre-built, curated units for easy assigning and monitoring of student progress. For critical reading practice, twenty-five reading selections with quizzes are also included. Get all our great resources and activities in one fully customizable space online; then assign and mix our resources with yours. *LaunchPad Solo for Readers and Writers* **can be packaged at a significant discount.** Order ISBN 978-1-319-03616-4 to ensure your students can take full advantage. Visit **macmillanhighered.com/readwrite** for more information.

***LearningCurve for Readers and Writers:*** LearningCurve, Bedford/St. Martin's adaptive quizzing program, quickly learns what students already know and helps them practice what they don't yet understand. Game-like quizzing motivates students to engage with their course, and reporting tools help teachers discern their students' needs.

With LearningCurve, students receive as much practice as they need to master a given concept and are provided with immediate feedback and links back to online instruction. A personalized study plan with suggestions for further practice

completes Bedford's plan to give your students just what they need to be successful in the college classroom. To order *LearningCurve for Readers and Writers* packaged with *Real Writing*, please use the following package ISBN: 978-1-319-03615-7.

**Please note:** *LearningCurve for Readers and Writers* is included with *LaunchPad Solo for Readers and Writers.*

**The *Bedford/St. Martin's Planner*** includes everything that students need to plan and use their time effectively, with advice on preparing schedules and to-do lists plus blank schedules and calendars (monthly and weekly). The planner fits easily into a backpack or purse, so students can take it everywhere. Free when packaged with the print text. ISBN: 978-0-312-57447-5

***The Bedford/St. Martin's ESL Workbook,* Second Edition,** by Sapna Gandhi-Rao, Maria McCormack, and Elizabeth Trelenberg provides ESL students with a broad range of exercises. This outstanding resource covers grammatical issues for multilingual students with varying English-language skills and cultural backgrounds. To reinforce each lesson, instructional introductions are followed by examples and exercises. ISBN: 978-0-312-54034-0

### E-BOOK OPTIONS

***Real Writing* e-book.** Available in several formats for use with computers, tablets, and e-readers — visit **macmillanhighered.com/catalog/ebookpartners** for more information.

### FREE INSTRUCTOR RESOURCES

**The *Instructor's Annotated Edition of Real Writing*** gives practical page-by-page advice on teaching with *Real Writing* and answers to exercises. It includes discussion prompts, strategies for teaching ESL students, ideas for additional classroom activities, suggestions for using other print and media resources, and cross-references useful to teachers at all levels of experience. ISBN: 978-1-319-00323-4

***Instructor's Manual for Real Writing*** provides helpful information and advice on teaching integrated reading and writing. It includes sample syllabi, reading levels scores, tips on building students' critical thinking skills, resources for teaching nonnative speakers and speakers of nonstandard dialects, ideas for assessing students' writing and progress, and up-to-date suggestions for using technology in the writing classroom and lab. Available for download; see **macmillanhighered .com/realwriting/catalog**.

***Teaching Developmental Reading: Historical, Theoretical, and Practical Background Readings,* Second Edition,** is a professional development resource edited by Sonya L. Armstrong, Norman A. Stahl, and Hunter R. Boylan. It offers a wealth of readings from the historical foundations of the developmental reading field to the latest scholarship. ISBN: 978-1-4576-5895-2

***Teaching Developmental Writing: Background Readings,* Fourth Edition**, is a professional resource edited by Susan Naomi Bernstein, former co-chair of the Conference on Basic Writing. It offers essays on topics of interest to basic writing instructors, along with editorial apparatus pointing out practical applications for the classroom. ISBN: 978-0-312-60251-2

***The Bedford Bibliography for Teachers of Basic Writing,* Third Edition** (also available online at **macmillanhighered.com/basicbib**), has been compiled by members of the Conference on Basic Writing under the general editorship of Gregory R. Glau and Chitralekha Duttagupta. This annotated list of books, articles, and periodicals was created specifically to help teachers of basic writing find valuable resources. ISBN: 978-0-312-58154-1

### ORDERING INFORMATION

To order any of these ancillaries for *Real Writing* contact your local Bedford/St. Martin's sales representative; send an e-mail to **sales_support@macmillan.com**; or visit our Web site at **macmillanhighered.com**.

## *Acknowledgments*

Like every edition that preceded it, this book grew out of a collaboration with teachers and students across the country and with the talented staff of Bedford/St. Martin's. I am grateful for everyone's thoughtful contributions.

### REVIEWERS

I would like to thank the following instructors for their many good ideas and suggestions for this edition. Their insights were invaluable.

Lauren Birdsong, Atlantic Cape Community College
Polly Hawk, Kansas City Kansas Community College
Vickie Kelly, Hinds Community College
Loren Kleinman, Passaic County Community College
Rebekah Lewis, Miami Dade College, North Campus
Katherine Lott, College of Southern Maryland
Sonya McCoy-Wilson, Atlanta Technical College
Susan Monroe, Housatonic Community College
John Mravik, Elgin Community College
Clarence Nero, Baton Rouge Community College
Lonetta Oliver, St. Louis Community College — Florissant Valley
Regina Peters, Blinn College
Anne Marie Prendergast, Bergen Community College
Tara Ronda, Atlantic Cape Community College
Lori Smalley, Greenville Technical College
Lisa Tittle, Hartford Community College
Debbie Wilke, Daytona State College

### STUDENTS

Many current and former students have helped shape this edition of *Real Writing* and I am grateful for all their contributions.

Among the students who provided paragraphs and essays for the book are Jelani Lynch, Arianna Morgan, Casandra Palmer, Alessandra Cepeda, Brian Healy, Charton Brown, Daniel Bird, Lorenza Mattazi, Kelly Hultgren, Corin Costas, Said Ibrahim, Armand Powell-Archie, Caitlin Prokop, Stephanie Alaimo, and Mark Koester.

### CONTRIBUTORS

Art researcher Connie Gardner, working with Martha Friedman, assisted with finding and obtaining permission for the many new, thought-provoking images included in the book.

Kathleen Karcher, working with Kalina Ingham, successfully completed the large and essential task of clearing text permissions.

I am also deeply grateful to designer Claire Seng-Niemoeller, who freshened the look of the book's interior.

### BEDFORD/ST. MARTIN'S

I have been extremely fortunate to work with the incredibly talented staff of Bedford/St. Martin's, whose perceptiveness, hard work, and dedication to everything they do are without parallel.

Thanks to Edwin Hill, Vice President of Humanities for Macmillan Education; Leasa Burton, Publisher for Composition; and Vivian Garcia, Executive Editor for Developmental English. Editorial assistant Eliza Kritz helped with innumerable tasks, from running review programs to assisting with manuscript preparation. We were very fortunate to have Annette Pagliaro Sweeney and Louis Bruno, production editors, shepherding *Real Writing* through production, as well as Matt Rosenquist at Graphic World. Overseeing and thoughtfully contributing to all aspects of the design was Anna Palchik, senior art director. Thanks to Billy Boardman for his work on the cover design. I must also extend tremendous gratitude to the sales and marketing team. Christina Shea, senior marketing manager, has been a great advocate for all my books and has helped me to forge greater connections with the developmental market and to stay up to date on its needs. And I continue to be deeply thankful for the hard work and smarts of all the sales managers and representatives.

This book would not have reached its fullest potential without the input and attention it received, from the earliest stages of development, from executives and long-time friends in the Boston office. Thanks also to my editor, Jill Gallagher, for developing this edition.

As he has in the past, to my great good fortune, my husband Jim Anker provides assurance, confidence, steadiness, and the best companionship throughout the projects and the years. His surname is supremely fitting.

— *Susan Anker*

In addition to the names already mentioned, I wanted to thank Alexis Walker, former Executive Editor for Developmental Studies at Bedford/St. Martin's, for asking me to be involved in this project. Although it was initially a bit of a surprise to be

contacted to work on this project, it has been a very insightful and rewarding experience. It was a delight to collaborate with Alexis and Martha Bustin, my initial contacts at Bedford/St. Martin's, and I am grateful for their trust in letting me work with Susan Anker's time-tested materials. I would also like to acknowledge Jill Gallagher, who walked me through the book's development. Jill was certainly one of the most valuable assets to me in this process, and I owe her a great debt of thanks. She has made the process of editing this book one of pure joy and discovery; her assistance and insights were undoubtedly crucial to the finished product.

I need to also express my gratitude to colleagues, students, and friends who stepped in and assisted me along the way whenever I asked for help. There were several people in the Department of English, Humanities, and Language Studies at Illinois Central College as well as friends and colleagues working in developmental studies and transfer-level courses who were willing to provide any assistance I needed. I also need to thank the friends and colleagues who offered up writing samples within a day when asked. I'm blessed to have such a strong group of writers and colleagues ready to step up and offer their work and support.

Finally, I want to thank my family. My husband, Brian Aitken, has been endlessly patient and supportive through this entire process. There have been quite a few times when his encouragement has been my rock, and that was certainly crucial to my success. I also thank my amazing daughters, Katie and Hope, who have adjusted their schedules at times to allow me to work on this book. I hope that they will see this work as something that they can be proud of as well, since they are the reason I work so hard on everything I do. Thank you to my entire family for supporting me and believing in me; you are all a blessing to me.

*—Nicole Aitken*

contributed to work on this project. It has been a very insightful and rewarding experience. It was a delight to collaborate with Nicol and Martha Burton, my friend and contacts at Bedford/St. Martin's, and I am grateful for their trust in letting me work with [illegible] materials. I would also like to acknowledge Jill Gallagher, who walked me through the book's development. Jill was certainly one of the most valuable assets to me in this process, and I owe her a great debt of thanks. She has made the process of editing this book one of much joy and discovery; her assistance and insights were undoubtedly crucial to the finished product.

Extending my thanks further, my gratitude to colleagues, students, and friends who [illegible] along the way whenever I asked for help. There were several people in the Department of English, [illegible] and Language Studies [illegible] friends and colleagues working in developmental studies [illegible] who were willing to provide any assistance [illegible]. I also need to thank the friends and colleagues who offered their writing samples [illegible]. I am blessed to have such a strong group of writers and colleagues [illegible] and offer their work and support.

Finally, I need to thank my family. My husband, Brian Aitken, has been endlessly patient and supportive through this entire process. There have been quite a few times when my encouragement has been my rock, and that was certainly [illegible]. I also thank my [illegible] daughters, Katie and Hope, who have [illegible] to work on this book. I hope that they [illegible] will be proud of its result, since they are the [illegible]. Thank you to my entire family for [illegible] and [illegible] me.

—Nicole Aitken

# Part 1

# How to Write Paragraphs and Essays

"I write ideas and summaries. Writing is a tool in my creative process."

Tate Brown-S., student

# 1

# Critical Thinking, Reading, and Writing

## Making Connections

## READING ROADMAP

### Learning Objectives

**Chapter Goal:** Learn how to become a prepared and active student as well as a critical thinker, reader, and writer.

**Tools to Achieve the Goal:**

- Student Preparedness Checklist (p. 5)
- Four Basics of Critical Thinking (p. 11)
- 2PR: The Critical Reading Process (p. 13)
- Writing Critically about Readings (p. 21)
- Writing Critically about Visuals (p. 25)
- Problem Solving (p. 28)

### Key Terms

Skim Chapter 1 before reading. Find these words or terms in **bold** type. Put a check mark next to each once you locate it.

____ critical thinking
____ making connections
____ assumptions
____ biases, critical reading
____ boldface
____ guiding question
____ main idea
____ purpose
____ support
____ summary
____ analysis
____ synthesis
____ evaluation
____ Z pattern

### Guided Reading for Chapter 1

Fill out the following chart before you begin reading. For each skill, write what you know about the skill and what you would like to know upon completing the chapter. At the end of the chapter, you will be asked to share what you learned about each skill.

| Skill | When I have used this skill | What I want to know about this skill |
|---|---|---|
| Preparing for success | | |
| Thinking critically | | |
| Using the critical reading process | | |
| Writing critically about readings | | |
| Writing critically about visuals | | |
| Problem solving | | |

Visit **LaunchPad Solo for Readers and Writers > Reading** for more tutorials, videos, and practice with critical reading.

## Understanding College Success

If you are reading this chapter, you probably just started a college writing course, and you might not know what to expect. What will the teacher require? What will class be like? How do I get through it—and all my courses—successfully?

Students come to college from all walks of life and with different types of experiences and backgrounds. What may be common knowledge to you about how to be a successful student may be a new idea to another student, or it could even be a strategy that one of your classmates used at one time but has forgotten. Before starting any course, it is important not only to purchase your supplies and attend class but also to put yourself into a mind-set that will help create a successful college experience for you.

In the first section of this chapter, you will learn about common expectations that many college writing instructors have of their students. Some of these expectations may be familiar to you, and some may be new. It is important not only to be aware of these expectations, but also to set goals for yourself for the semester. Setting goals helps you focus your time in the classroom and identify what you want to learn in this class. The writing classroom, however, is a bit different from other classes you may enroll in because a writing class is a writing community. At times, you may find the experience of sharing your writing uneasy or uncomfortable, but learning to work with others to brainstorm, draft, revise, and edit papers will help you become a stronger writer. By understanding your role in that community and how that community will help you grow as a writer and a student, you will be better equipped to prepare for the semester and become a more successful student.

### *Becoming a Prepared and Active Student*

All students can benefit from thinking carefully about the strategies that will help them become successful in class. During the first week of class, your instructor should distribute a syllabus or some other document with expectations and policies. Not all policies and expectations will be the same because every instructor and every course is different, but most share the baseline expectations outlined here. You should be aware of them as you start this course because your instructor will expect you to understand and adhere to them throughout the semester.

#### PRACTICE 1 Learn more about your own preparedness

Take a few minutes to go through the list of items on the next page that make a student more prepared and mentally ready to engage with the course. How many of these items are ones that you already employ? Why have you chosen to use them? If you haven't used one of them, why not? Would you be willing to try? Why or why not?

After writing about your own preferences, interview one or two other students in the class—preferably those who are not sitting in the same general area as you. What did they write in their own responses? Why did they make the choices they did? What does this tell you about the way different people learn and participate in a class?

## Student Preparedness Checklist

| Item | What it means | Do you do this? |
|---|---|---|
| *Treat your course as seriously as you would a job.* | Your boss does not *give* you money—you *earn* it, through hard work and professional behavior. Likewise, your instructor does not *give* you a grade. You *earn* the grade you get. Think of your coursework as a job that can lead to bigger and better things—if you work hard and perform well. | |
| *Come to class on time, and stay until your instructor dismisses you.* | Again, going to class is like going to a job—you have to come and go on the boss's schedule, not your own. When you arrive late or leave early, you not only disrupt other students, you might miss instructions for the day's work, and you may miss additional instructions for homework to prepare for the next day. | |
| *Come to class prepared.* | You have to do your homework or expect to fail. Even if you have never regularly done homework before and have managed to pass, you will not pass in college. You will also likely have points taken off for late homework. Some instructors may even ask you to leave class or count you as absent if you do not have your homework completed. | |
| *Connect to others in class.* | Students often sit in the same places for each class. Exchange names, phone numbers, and e-mail addresses with at least one student who sits near you. That way, if you miss a class, you can find out from that person what you missed. You might also want to study with that person. | |
| *Let your instructor know if you know you are going to miss class, and contact him or her about the work you missed.* | Be a good communicator. Instructors can help you make up what you have missed—but only if you have made a connection and communicate in a clear, respectful way. Send an e-mail or call your instructor to find out what you missed, and make sure you write in clear language—not texting language. | |
| *Read the syllabus carefully and hang onto it the entire semester.* | Your instructor will expect you to know what the homework is and when assignments are due: Your syllabus will tell you. Always bring your syllabus to class, in case your instructor announces updates or reminders. | |
| *Get to know your instructor.* | Communication is important. If you get a low grade or do not understand something, ask in class, via e-mail, or visit your instructor during office hours. It is up to you to take steps to clear up anything you do not understand. | |
| *Participate in class: ask questions, answer questions, and make comments.* | Do not be afraid of making a stupid comment or giving the wrong answer. That is part of the learning process. Plus, many instructors grade on participation. ► | |

| Item | What it means | Do you do this? |
|---|---|---|
| ***Listen and take notes.*** | When the instructor is talking, listen carefully, but do not try to write down every word he or she says. To figure out what you should make a note of, look at the instructor. Important points are often signaled with a hand gesture, a note on the board, or a change in the tone of the instructor's voice. | |
| ***Don't hide.*** | The further back in the classroom you sit, or the closer you are to a back corner, the more tempting it is to let your mind wander or to stop focusing on class material. If you want to keep your mind focused on the task at hand, try to get a seat near the front of the class. | |
| ***Schedule your time wisely.*** | If you choose to wait until the last minute to work on a large project, you will either not be able to finish or you will do a bad job and get a bad grade. Part of being a successful student is the ability to schedule your time. | |

## *Setting Goals*

You may already know what kind of degree you want to pursue in college and what type of job you want in the future. With these long-term goals in mind, you also need shorter-term goals—steps that help you get where you want to go. To be successful in any course, it is important to identify both your long-term and short-term goals. These goals give you a reason to attend class and a tangible goal to work toward. Consider each of the following as you start this new semester.

### PRACTICE 2 Look ahead to writing goals

List at least four writing goals—skills you want to learn, practice, or improve in this course. Be as specific as possible. For example, "Learn to write better" is too general to help you focus on what you need to do. A better example could be "Learn how to write clear thesis statements." Throughout the course, refer to these goals, changing or updating them as needed. As you progress through the semester, you may find that your goals become more specific. The list will give you a way to reflect on the skills and abilities that you are actively developing.

1. ______________________________

2. ______________________________

3. ______________________________

4. ______________________________

**PRACTICE 3** **Look ahead to reading goals**

Identify at least four reading goals—skills you want to learn, practice, or improve in this course. Be as specific as possible. For some people, this is not as easy to identify or articulate as their writing goals because we don't often think about our reading as a process. Do your best to think about what happens when you, personally, sit down to read. Do you need to work on limiting distractions when you read? Do your best to identify what, exactly, you would like to improve. Then, throughout the course, refer to this list of skills and abilities to help you refine what you've learned.

1. ______________________________

2. ______________________________

3. ______________________________

4. ______________________________

**PRACTICE 4** **Looking ahead to degree goals**

Whether or not you have decided what you want to major in, you should still ask yourself some questions now. Which majors interest me? Which courses would I need to take to complete the major(s) that interest me? What are the required core courses that every student must take to graduate, and when should I take those courses?

Course requirements for each major are listed in the college bulletin and on the college Web site. It's a good idea, though, to sit down with your academic adviser as soon as possible to plan a sequence of courses. If you are like most students, you are juggling a lot of important priorities, and having a plan to reach your goals will help you achieve them. Write your tentative plans in the spaces provided.

**I (might) want to major in** ______________________________.

**Courses I will need for that major** (If you do not know your major yet, list the courses required for all students.)

______________________________

______________________________

______________________________

______________________________

______________________________

______________________________

______________________________

**Number of courses I can take next term** ______________________

**Courses I should take if they fit into my schedule** (Remember, certain courses have other courses as prerequisites.)

______________________

## PRACTICE 5 Looking ahead to career goals

You may or may not know what your career goals are at this point. Even if you do not yet have clear goals, try answering the following questions to jump-start your thinking.

What field might I like to work in after completing my college coursework?

______________________

What kinds of additional degrees or certifications might I need to obtain to work in that field? (If you need additional coursework beyond your current degree or certificate program, list them here.)

______________________

______________________

In this field, how is writing used? (Reports? Memos? Charts?)

______________________

______________________

In this field, how is reading used? (Computer records? Articles? Guidebooks?)

______________________

______________________

## *Becoming a Critical Thinker*

"To be successful, be a critical thinker." This statement is becoming more and more common, and it is true. College courses require critical thinking. Workplaces require it. Life requires it. The good news is, you already practice critical thinking, and it is a skill you can strengthen, as you will learn in this chapter.

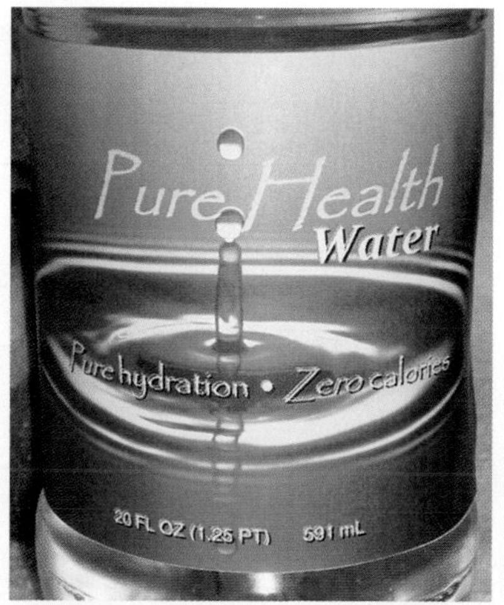
Pure Health
Water
Pure hydration • Zero calories
20 FL OZ (1.25 PT) 591 mL
COURTESY OF BETH CASTRODALE

Take a closer look at a type of critical thinking with which you are already familiar: making judgments about what to buy, or not to buy, based on product labels and advertising. First, **study** the picture to the right. **Ask yourself:**

- Why did the designers of this label make the choices that they did?

- What textual and visual elements of the label suggest health and purity?
- **Make a connection** to your daily life: Are you any more likely to purchase Pure Health Water or any type of bottled water based on this label? Why or why not?

Now, **study** this advertisement from Tappening, an environmental group. **Ask yourself:**

- What is this ad's main message?
- What is the message behind the **boldface** note in the lower left corner of the ad?
- **Make a connection** to the previous label: How would the creator of the Tappening ad respond to the way the bottled-water company presents its product?

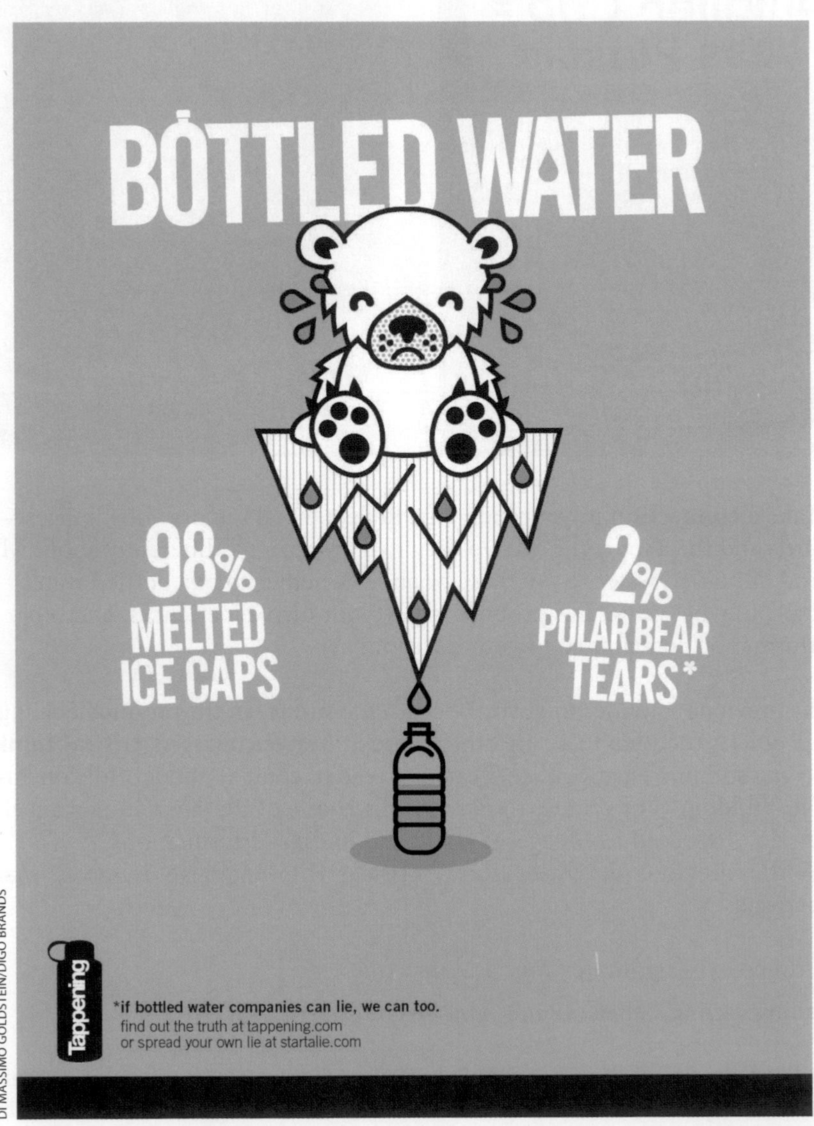
BOTTLED WATER
98% MELTED ICE CAPS
2% POLAR BEAR TEARS*
Tappening
*if bottled water companies can lie, we can too.
find out the truth at tappening.com
or spread your own lie at startalie.com

DI MASSIMO GOLDSTEIN/DIGO BRANDS

- **Make a connection** to your daily life: Does the Tappening ad make bottled water any less appealing to you? Why or why not?

Finally, **study** the labels below. **Ask yourself:**

- What do these bottled-water labels say about the companies that produced them?
- **Make a connection** to the previous advertisement: How do these labels respond to the main message of the Tappening advertisement?

Smaller Cap =
Less Plastic
Our Eco-Slim cap is part of our ongoing effort to reduce our impact on the environment. This cap contains an average of 37% less plastic than our previous cap.
WE CAN ALL MAKE A DIFFERENCE. PLEASE RECYCLE.
WARNING: Cap is a small part and poses a CHOKING HAZARD, particularly for children.

COURTESY OF BETH CASTRODALE

CA CASH REFUND
plantbottle
*up to 30% made from plants
100% recyclable plastic bottle

COURTESY OF BETH CASTRODALE

- **Make a connection** to your daily life: Reflect on all the previous images—the labels and the Tappening ad. Do they make you think differently about what kind of bottled water to purchase or about whether to buy bottled water at all? In what ways have product labels, your own experiences, and other information contributed to your decision?

The previous activities took you beneath the surface of the product labeling and beyond quick reactions to it. In other words, they encouraged **critical thinking**, actively questioning what you see, hear, and read to come to thoughtful conclusions about it. Building your critical thinking skills is one of the most important things you can do to succeed in college, at work, and in everyday situations.

As the previous activities show, critical thinking also involves **making connections**

- between existing impressions and new ones
- among various beliefs, claims, and bits of information.

In the following sections, we will take a closer look at critical thinking strategies. Also, we will explore the connections among critical thinking, reading, and writing.

# What Is Critical Thinking?

Imagine you are the supervisor at a small, family-owned business. Recently, one of the owners hired a new employee that you are asked to train during your shift. When the shift begins, the new employee still has not shown up. In fact, she shows up fifteen minutes late. When she does finally arrive, her uniform is a bit sloppy, and she doesn't seem in any hurry to find you or anyone else so that she can start her shift.

What do you think to yourself about this person? What assumptions have you made about her? What kind of employee will she be? Why do you think that?

Everything you know is based on a first impression—an assumption or guess. You don't have any facts, but you are using what you see on the surface to judge this new employee's overall performance. This is something everyone does from time to time; however, in college we need to learn to move beyond assumptions and quick judgments and to think more critically. Critical thinking asks us to explore the reasons behind something and not to rely on our snap judgments and assumptions.

### **Four Basics** of Critical Thinking

1. Be alert to assumptions made by you and others.
2. Question those assumptions.
3. Consider and connect various points of view, even those different from your own.
4. Do not rush to conclusions but instead remain patient with yourself and others and keep an open mind.

**Assumptions**—ideas or opinions that we do not question and that we automatically accept as true—can get in the way of clear, critical thinking. Here are some assumptions you would probably make about the new employee:

> The new employee is careless because she is late.
>
> The new employee is sloppy because her uniform is a mess.
>
> The new employee is unreliable because she didn't contact anyone before coming in late.
>
> The new employee will not be a good employee because she didn't immediately apologize for her tardiness.

In college, work, and everyday life, we often hold assumptions that we are not even aware of. By identifying these assumptions, stating them, and questioning them, we stand a better chance of seeing reality and acting more effectively.

In the case of the new employee, perhaps she had not realized her shift started fifteen minutes before she arrived. Perhaps she thought she was fifteen minutes early. In that case, she would have had plenty of time to straighten out her uniform and introduce herself. She still should have double-checked the schedule and straightened her uniform before entering the workplace, but it's possible that all, or at least some, of these assumptions are entirely incorrect.

When questioning assumptions, it can help to try to get a bit of distance from them. Imagine what people with entirely different points of view might say. You might even try disagreeing with your own assumptions. Take a look at the following examples.

## Questioning Assumptions

| Situation | Assumption | Questions |
|---|---|---|
| **COLLEGE:** I saw from the syllabus that I need to write five essays for this course. | This course may be too difficult for me. | Other students have passed this course; what makes me think I cannot?<br>What obstacles might be getting in my way?<br>What might be some ways around those obstacles?<br>What have others done in this situation? |
| **WORK:** Two of my coworkers just got raises. | My own raise is just around the corner. | Did my coworkers accomplish anything I did not?<br>When were their last raises, and when was mine? |
| **EVERYDAY LIFE:** My friend has been acting strangely toward me lately. | I must have done something wrong. | Is it possible it has nothing to do with me?<br>Maybe he is going through something really difficult in his life. |

**Tip** In every situation, try to be open to different points of view. Listen and think before responding or coming to any conclusions. Although you may not agree with other points of view, you can learn from them.

You need to be aware not only of your own assumptions but also of those in what you read, see, and hear. For example, bottled-water labels and advertising might suggest directly or indirectly that bottled water is better than tap water. Think carefully about the evidence they provide to support this assumption. What other sources of information could be consulted to either support, disprove, or call into question this assumption? However confidently a claim is made, never assume it is 100% correct and cannot be questioned.

### PRACTICE 6 Thinking critically

What assumptions are behind each of the images on pages 8–10? Write down as many as you can identify. Then, write down questions about these assumptions, considering different points of view.

In addition to assumptions, be aware of **biases**, one-sided and sometimes prejudiced views that may blind you to the truth of a situation. Here is just one example:

> No one older than age fifty can pick up new skills quickly.

Others could contradict this extreme statement with their own experiences, exceptions, and insights or with additional information that could show reality is more nuanced or complicated than this statement allows.

Be on the lookout for bias in your own views and in whatever you read, see, and hear. When a statement seems one-sided or extreme, ask yourself what facts or points of view might have been omitted.

## What Is Critical Reading?

**Critical reading** is paying close attention as you read and asking yourself questions about the author's purpose, his or her main idea, the support he or she gives, and how good that support is. It is important to think critically as you read, looking out for assumptions and biases (both the writer's and your own). You should also consider whether you agree or disagree with the points being made.

Here are the four steps of the critical reading process:

### 2PR The Critical Reading Process

**Preview** the text.

**Read** the text, looking for the main idea and support.

**Pause** to question and interpret the text, taking notes as you read.

**Review** the text and your notes, and **Respond** to it.

### 2PR *Preview the Text*

Before reading any piece of writing, skim the whole thing, using the following steps.

#### READ THE TITLE, HEADNOTE, AND INTRODUCTORY PARAGRAPHS

The title of a chapter, an article, or any other document usually gives you some idea of what the topic is. Some documents are introduced by headnotes, which summarize or provide background about the selection. If there is a headnote, read it. Whether or not there is a headnote, writers often introduce their topic and main idea in the first paragraphs, so read those and make a note stating what you think is the main idea.

#### READ HEADINGS, KEY WORDS, AND DEFINITIONS

Textbooks and magazine articles often include headings to help readers follow the author's ideas. These headings (such as "Preview the Text" above) tell you what the important subjects are within the larger piece of writing.

Any terms in **boldface** type are especially important. In textbooks, writers often use boldface for key words that are important to the topic.

#### LOOK FOR SUMMARIES, CHECKLISTS, AND CHAPTER REVIEWS

Many textbooks (such as this one) include features that summarize or list main ideas. Review summaries, checklists, or chapter reviews to make sure you have understood the main ideas.

### READ THE CONCLUSION

Writers usually review their main idea in their concluding paragraphs. Read the conclusion, and compare it with the note you made after you read the introduction and thought about what the main idea might be.

### ASK A GUIDING QUESTION

As the final step in your preview of a text, ask yourself a **guiding question**—a question you think the text might answer. This question will give you a purpose for reading and help keep you focused. Sometimes, you can turn the title into a guiding question. For example, read the title of this chapter, and write a possible guiding question.

## 2PR *Read the Text: Find the Main Idea and Support*

After previewing, begin reading carefully for meaning, trying especially to identify a writer's main idea and the support for that idea.

### MAIN IDEA AND PURPOSE

For more on main ideas, see Chapter 3.

The **main idea** of a text is the central idea the author wants to communicate. The main idea is related to the writer's **purpose**, which can be to explain, to demonstrate, to persuade, or to entertain. Writers often introduce their main idea early, so read the first few paragraphs with special care. After reading the first paragraph (or more, depending on the length of the reading selection), stop and write down—in your own words—what you think the main idea is. If the writer has stated the main idea in a single sentence, double-underline it.

#### PRACTICE 7 Finding the main idea

Read each of the following paragraphs. Then, write the main idea in your own words in the spaces provided.

1. Making a plan for your college studies is a good way to reach your academic goals. The first step to planning is answering this question: "What do I want to be?" If you have only a general idea—for example, "I would like to work in the health-care field"—break this large area into smaller, more specific subfields. These subfields might include working as a registered nurse, a nurse practitioner, or a physical therapist. The second step to planning is to meet with an academic adviser to talk about the classes you will need to take to get a degree or certificate in your chosen field. Then, map out the courses you will be taking over the next couple of semesters. Throughout the process, bear in mind the words of student mentor Ed Powell: "Those who fail to plan, plan to fail." A good plan boosts your chances of success in college and beyond.

   **Main idea:** ______________________________

   ______________________________

2. Networking is a way businesspeople build connections with others to get ahead. Building connections in college also is well worth the effort. One way to build connections is to get to know some of your classmates and to exchange names, phone numbers, and e-mail addresses with them. That way, if you cannot make it to a class, you will know someone who can tell you what you missed. You can also form study groups with these other students. Another way to build connections is to get to know your instructor. Make an appointment to visit your instructor during his or her office hours. When you go, ask questions about material you are not sure you understood in class or problems you have with other course material. You and your instructor will get the most out of these sessions if you bring examples of specific assignments with which you are having trouble.

   **Main idea:** ______________________________

   ______________________________

### SUPPORT

**Support** is the details that show, explain, or prove the main idea. The author might use statistics, facts, definitions, and scientific results for support. Or he or she might use memories, stories, comparisons, quotations from experts, and personal observations.

For more on support, see Chapter 4.

**PRACTICE 8** **Identifying support**

Go back to Practice 7 (p. 14), and underline the support for the main ideas of each passage in the practice.

Not all support that an author offers in a piece of writing is good support. When you are reading, ask yourself: What information is the author including to help me understand or agree with the main idea? Is the support (evidence) valid and convincing? If not, why not?

## 2PR *Pause to Think*

Taking notes and asking questions as you read will help you understand the author's points and develop a thoughtful response. As you read, do the following:

- Double-underline or write the main idea in the margin.
- Note the major support points by underlining them.
- Note ideas that you agree with by placing a check mark next to them (✓).
- Note ideas that you do not agree with or that surprise you with an ✗ or !, and ideas you do not understand with a question mark (?).
- Note any examples of an author's or expert's bias.
- Jot any additional notes or questions in the margin.
- Consider how parts of the reading relate to the main idea.

## 2PR Review and Respond

After reading, it is important to take a few minutes to look back and review. Go over your guiding question, your marginal notes, and your questions—and *connect yourself to what you have read.* Consider, "What interested me? What did I learn? How does it fit with what I know from other sources?" When you have reviewed your reading in this way and fixed it well in your mind and memory, it is much easier to respond in class discussions and writing assignments. To write about a text, you need to generate and organize your ideas, draft and revise your response, and, above all, use your critical thinking skills (see p. 11).

### *A Critical Reader at Work*

Read the following piece. The notes in the margins show how one student applied the process of critical reading to an essay on bottled water.

Amanda Jacobowitz

# A Ban on Water Bottles: A Way to Bolster the University's Image

Amanda Jacobowitz is a student at Washington University and a columnist for the university's publication *Student Life,* in which the following essay appeared.

**Guiding question:** What does the author think about the ban on bottled water?

*Larger main idea (not stated directly): (1) the ban is ineffective, and (2) there are better ways to protect the environment.*

1 Lately, I am always thirsty. Always! I could not figure out why until I realized that the bottled water I had purchased continuously throughout my day had disappeared. At first I was just confused. Where did all the water bottles go? Then I learned the simple explanation: The University banned water bottles in an effort to be environmentally friendly.

*Why not just drink from a water fountain? You don't have to have a bottle.*

2 Ideally, given the ban on selling water bottles, every student on campus should now take the initiative to carry a water bottle, filling it up throughout the day at the water fountains on campus. Realistically, we know this has not and will not happen. I have tried to bring a water bottle with me to classes—I do consider myself somewhat environmentally conscious—but have rarely succeeded in this effort. Instead, although I have never been too much of a soda drinker, I find myself reaching for a bottle of Coke out of pure convenience. We can't buy bottled water, but we can buy soda, juice, and other drinks, many of which come in plastic bottles. I am sure that for most people—particularly those who give very little thought to being environmentally conscientious—convenience prevails and they purchase a drink other than water. Wonderful result. The University can pride itself on being more environmentally friendly, with the fallback that its students will be less healthy!

*Examples of other common forms of waste*

3 Even if students are not buying unhealthy drinks, any benefit from the reduction of plastic water bottles could easily be offset by its alternatives.

Students are not using their hands to drink water during meals. They are using plastic cups—cups provided by the University at every eatery on campus. Presumably no person picks up a cup, drinks their glass of water, and then saves that same cup for later in the day. That being said, how many plastic cups are used by a single student, in a single day? How many cups are used by the total campus-wide population daily, yearly? This plastic cup use must equate to an exorbitant amount of waste as well.

*Examples of other common forms of waste*

4 My intent is not to have the University completely roll back the water bottle ban, nor is my intent for the University to level the playing field by banning all plastic drink bottles. I'm simply questioning the reasons for specifically banning bottled water of all things. Why not start with soda bottles—decreasing the environmental impact, as well as the health risks? There are also many other ways to help the environment that seem to be so easily overlooked.

*Examples of other ways to protect the environment*

5 Have you ever noticed a patch of grass on campus that's not perfectly green? I can't say that I have. The reason: the sprinklers. Now, I admit that I harbor some animosity when it comes to the campus sprinklers; I somehow always manage to mistakenly and inadvertently walk right in their path, the spray of water generously dousing my feet. However, my real problem with the sprinklers is the waste of water they represent. Do we really need our grass to be green at all times?

6 The landscaping around our beloved Danforth University Center (Gold LEED Certified) is irrigated with the use of rainwater. There is a 50,000-gallon rainwater tank below the building to collect rain! I admit, this is pretty impressive, but what about the rest of the campus? What water is used to irrigate and keep green the rest of our 169 acres on the Danforth campus?

*Town/city water, I assume.*

7 I understand that being environmentally conscious is difficult to do, particularly at an institutional level. I applaud the Danforth University Center and other environmental efforts the University has initiated. However, I can't help but wonder if the University's ban on the sale of water bottles is more about appearance and less about decreasing the environmental impact of our student body. The water bottle ban has become a way to build the school's public image: We banned water bottles; we are working hard to be environmentally friendly! In reality, given the switch to plastic cups and the switch to other drinks sold in plastic bottles, is the environmental impact of the ban that significant? Now that the ban has been implemented, I certainly don't see the University retracting it. However, I hope that in the future the University focuses less on its public image and more on the environment itself when instituting such dramatic changes.

*Is it really about public image? What would a university administrator say?*

**PRACTICE 9** **Making connections**

Look back at the images on pages 8–10. Then, review the reading by Amanda Jacobowitz. What assumptions does she make about bottled water? What evidence, if any, is provided to support these assumptions? On the basis of your observations, would you like to see bottled water not banned or banned at your college? Why or why not?

## Read Real-World Documents Critically

Careless reading in your everyday life can cause minor problems such as a ruined recipe, but it can also have more serious consequences. For example, if you overlook the fine print in a loan offer, you might end up agreeing to a high interest rate and, therefore, more debt.

To read real-world documents closely and carefully, try the **2PR** strategy, especially for longer documents. Also, when you see a document or sign that makes a claim, ask yourself: Does this claim look too good to be true? If so, why?

### PRACTICE 10 Reading real-world documents

Working by yourself or with other students, read the following documents from college and everyday life, and answer the critical reading questions.

1. What is the writer's purpose? ______________________________
______________________________
______________________________
______________________________
______________________________
2. Is the writer biased? ______________________________
3. What are the key words or major claims? ______________________________
______________________________
4. What is in the fine print? ______________________________
______________________________
5. What do you think of what you have read? Why? Does anything seem odd, unrealistic, or unreliable? Give specific examples. ______________________________
______________________________

**College: An E-mailed Advertisement**

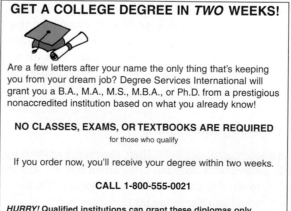

**GET A COLLEGE DEGREE IN *TWO* WEEKS!**

Are a few letters after your name the only thing that's keeping you from your dream job? Degree Services International will grant you a B.A., M.A., M.S., M.B.A., or Ph.D. from a prestigious nonaccredited institution based on what you already know!

**NO CLASSES, EXAMS, OR TEXTBOOKS ARE REQUIRED**

for those who qualify

If you order now, you'll receive your degree within two weeks.

**CALL 1-800-555-0021**

***HURRY!* Qualified institutions can grant these diplomas only because of a legal loophole that may be closed within weeks.**

**Everyday Life: Electric Bill**

| Account Number |
|---|
| 12 8 0000005360 0 80 2106 178 H |

| Please Pay By |
|---|
| Oct. 26, 2014 |

| Please Pay Amount |
|---|
| $53.60 |

NSTAR Electric

MOVING? PLEASE LET US KNOW. OTHERWISE YOU MAY BE RESPONSIBLE FOR ENERGY USE AFTER YOU MOVE.

Service Provided To:

## Electric Bill Summary

| Account Number | 106 178 |
|---|---|

| Please Pay By | Please Pay Amount |
|---|---|
| October 26, 2014 | $53.60 |

| Current Bill Date | Next Meter Read Date |
|---|---|
| October 8, 2014 | November 6, 2014 |

**Electric Bill Comparison**

| | Current Month | Last Month | Last Year |
|---|---|---|---|
| **Electric Charges** | **$53.60** | **$64.11** | |
| Total Electricity Use (kWh) | 265 | 324 | |
| Delivery Charges (per kWh) *Cost to deliver electricity to your home.* | 10.8¢ | 10.4¢ | |
| **Delivery Charges Total** | **$28.75** | **$33.72** | |
| Generation Charges (per kWh) *Cost to purchase electricity on your behalf.* | 9.3¢ | 9.3¢ | |
| **Generation Total** | **$24.85** | **$30.39** | |

**Bill Analysis**

| | | |
|---|---|---|
| Billing Days | 28 | 29 |
| Avg. Daily Electric Use (kWh) | 9.4 | 11.1 |
| Avg. Daily Temp (degrees) | 64 | 73 |

**Highlights From This Month's Billing Period**

*September 5, 2014 to October 3, 2014*

| | |
|---|---|
| Amount of Your Last Bill | $64.11 |
| Payment - Thank You | -$64.11 |
| Previous Balance | $0.00 |
| Adjustments | $0.00 |
| Delivery Charges Total | $28.75 |
| Generation Charges | $24.85 |
| Total Charges for Electricity | $53.60 |
| **Please Pay Amount** | **$53.60** |

**Your Electricity Use By Month At A Glance**

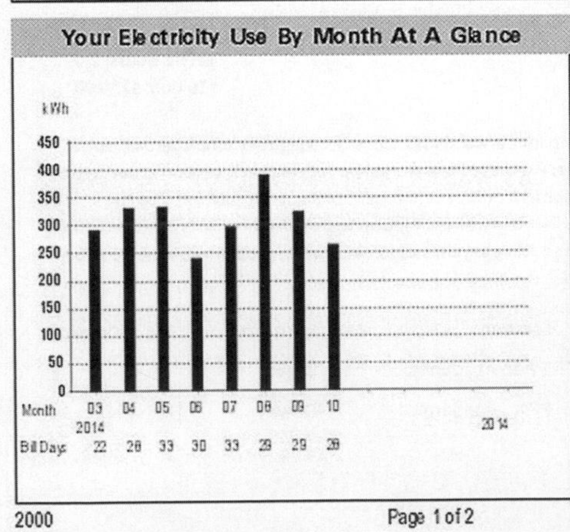

kWh
450
400
350
300
250
200
150
100
50
0
Month 03 04 05 06 07 08 09 10
2014
2014
Bill Days 22 28 33 30 33 29 29 28


NSTAR Green is an exciting option available for residential and small business customers looking to support renewable energy in the region and reduce greenhouse gas emissions.

By signing up, you can choose to have all (NSTAR Green 100) or half (NSTAR Green 50) of your electric use support wind energy. There is an additional premium for NSTAR Green.

More information about NSTAR Green, including pricing and an online enrollment form, is available on NSTAR.com.

**www.nstar.com**

**800-592-2000**

2000 Page 1 of 2

**Everyday Life: Nutrition Label**

Nutrition Facts
Serving Size 2/3 cup (51g)
Servings Per Container About 9
Cereal with 1/2 cup Skim Milk
Amount Per Serving Cereal
Calories 240 280
Calories from Fat 70 70
% Daily Value**
Total Fat 8g* 12% 12%
Saturated Fat 2.5g 13% 13%
Trans Fat 0g
Cholesterol 0mg 0% 0%
Sodium 50mg 2% 5%
Total Carbohydrate 37g 12% 14%
Dietary Fiber 3g 12% 12%
Sugars 13g
Protein 4g 8% 16%
Vitamin A 0% 4%
Vitamin C 0% 0%
Calcium 2% 15%
Iron 6% 6%

CHRIS SADOWSKI/GETTY IMAGES

**College: Course Catalog**

BUS 121

PRINCIPLES OF CUSTOMER SERVICE

Credit Hours: 3.0
*Tuition: $375.00

This course focuses on the importance of customer service, perception, and satisfaction, and the application of various customer relation systems in the marketplace. The course is designed to promote an understanding of the principles of customer service in general and how the application of customer service specifically contributes to positive customer perception and the success of business. Emphasis is placed on the importance of excellence in service to retain customers and gain a competitive advantage.

| Class # | Days | Time | Location | Instructor | Details |
|---|---|---|---|---|---|
| 2996 | wed | 06:00-08:50 pm | Technology Cent | Dewey | Lecture |

BUS 151

JOB ORIENTATION

Credit Hours: 2.0
*Tuition: $250.00

This course employs a series of activities designed to identify and improve skills sought by employers of job candidates and current employees in the workplace. Presented in a workshop format, each session is devoted to one or more group activities focused on the development and/or refinement of a specific job skill. The class culminates in group presentations that require the members of each group to use all of the skills practiced during the course. Targeted skills include, but are not limited to: communication; teamwork; problem-solving; decision-making; and data analysis and presentation.

| Class # | Days | Time | Location | Instructor | Details |
|---|---|---|---|---|---|
| 1288 | mon | 06:00-07:15 pm | E Peo Academic | Dewey | Lecture |
| 1288 | mon | 06:00-07:15 pm | E Peo Academic | Dewey | Lecture |

COURTESY OF ILLINOIS CENTRAL COLLEGE

# What Is Writing Critically about Readings?

Being able to write critically about what you read is a key college skill because it shows your deep understanding of course content. When you write critically about readings, you summarize, analyze, synthesize, and evaluate, and, in doing so, you answer the following questions.

## Reading and Writing Critically

### Summarize

- What is important about the text?
- What is the purpose, the big picture?
- What are the main ideas and key support?

### Analyze

- What elements have been used to convey the main idea?
- Do any elements raise questions? Do any key points seem missing or undeveloped?

### Synthesize

- What do other sources say about the topic of the text?
- How does your own (or others') experience affect how you see the topic?
- What new point(s) might you make by bringing together all the different sources and experiences?

### Evaluate

- Based on your application of summary, analysis, and synthesis, what do you think about the material you have read?
- Is the work successful? Does it achieve its purpose?
- Does the author show any biases? If so, do they make the piece more effective or less effective?

## *Summary*

A **summary** is a condensed, or shortened, version of something—often, a longer piece of writing, a movie or television show, a situation, or an event. In writing a summary, you give the main ideas and key support in your own words.

The following is an excerpt from the *Textbook of Basic Nursing* by Caroline Bunker Rosdahl and Mary T. Kowalski. It comes from a chapter that discusses some of the stresses that families can face, including divorce.

> Adults who are facing separation from their partners—and a return to single life—may feel overwhelmed. They may become preoccupied with their own feelings, thereby limiting their ability to handle the situation effectively or to be strong for their children. The breakdown of the family system may require a restructuring of responsibilities, employment, childcare, and housing

arrangements. Animosity between adults may expose children to uncontrolled emotions, arguments, anger, and depression.

Children may feel guilt and anxiety over their parents' divorce, believing the situation to be their fault. They may be unable to channel their conflicting emotions effectively. Their school performance may suffer, or they may engage in misbehavior. Even when a divorce is handled amicably, children may experience conflicts about their loyalties and may have difficulties making the transition from one household to another during visitation periods. . . .

Experts estimate that approximately 50% of all children whose parents divorce will experience another major life change within 3 years: remarriage. The arrival of a stepparent in the home presents additional stressors for children. Adapting to new rules of behavior, adjusting to a new person's habits, and sharing parents with new family members can cause resentment and anger. When families blend children, rivalries and competition for parental attention can lead to repeated conflicts.

Now, here is a summary of the textbook excerpt. The main idea is double-underlined, and the support points are underlined.

Although divorce seriously affects the people who are splitting up, Rosdahl and Kowalski point out that the couple's children face equally difficult consequences, both immediately and in the longer term. In the short term, according to the authors, children may blame themselves for the split or feel that their loyalty to both parents is divided. These negative emotions can affect their behavior at school and elsewhere. Later on, if one or both of the parents remarry, the children may have trouble adjusting to the new family structure.

## Analysis

An **analysis** breaks down the points or parts of something and considers how they work together to make an impression or convey a main idea. When writing an analysis, you might also consider points or parts that seem to be missing or that raise questions in your mind.

Here is an analysis of the excerpt from the *Textbook of Basic Nursing*. The main idea is double-underlined, and the support points are underlined.

We all know that divorce is difficult for the people who are splitting up, but Rosdahl and Kowalski pay special attention to the problems faced by children of divorce, both right after the split and later on. The authors mention several possible outcomes of divorce on children, including emotional and behavioral difficulties and trouble in school. They also discuss the stresses that remarriage can create for children.

The authors rightly emphasize the negative effects that divorce can have on children. However, I found myself wondering what a divorcing couple could do to help their children through the process. Also, how might parents and stepparents

help children adjust to a remarriage? I would like to examine these questions in a future paper.

[Note how the writer raises questions about the textbook excerpt.]

## *Synthesis*

A **synthesis** pulls together information from additional sources or experiences to make a new point. Here is a synthesis of the textbook material on divorce. Because the writer wanted to address some of the questions she raised in her analysis, she incorporated additional details from published sources and from people she interviewed. Her synthesis of this information helped her arrive at a fresh conclusion.

In the *Textbook of Basic Nursing*, Rosdahl and Kowalski focus on the problems faced by children of divorce, both right after the split and later on. According to the authors, immediate problems can include emotional and behavioral difficulties and trouble in school. Later on, parents' remarriage can create additional stresses for children. Although the authors discuss the impact of divorce on all parties, they do not suggest ways in which parents or stepparents might help children through the process of divorce or remarriage. However, other sources, as well as original research on friends who have experienced divorce as children or adults, provide some additional insights into these questions. First source

A Web site produced by the staff at the Mayo Clinic recommends that parents come together to break the news about their divorce to their children. The Web site also suggests that parents keep the discussion brief and free of "ugly details." In addition, parents should emphasize that the children are in no way to blame for the divorce and that they are deeply loved. As the divorce proceeds, neither parent should speak negatively about the other parent in the child's presence or otherwise try to turn the child against the ex-spouse. Finally, parents should consider counseling for themselves or their children if any problems around the divorce persist. Second source

The Web site of the University of Missouri Extension addresses the problems that can arise for children after their parents remarry. Specifically, the Web site describes several things that stepparents can do to make their stepchildren feel more comfortable with them and the new family situation. One strategy is to try to establish a friendship with the children before assuming the role of a parent. Later, once stepparents have assumed a more parental role, they should make sure they and their spouse stand by the same household rules and means of discipline. With time, the stepparents might also add new traditions for holidays and other family gatherings to help build new family bonds while respecting the old ones. Third source

To these sources, I added interviews with three friends—two who are children of divorce and one who is both a divorced parent and a stepparent. The children of divorce said that they experienced many of the same difficulties and stresses that Rosdahl and Kowalski described. Interestingly, though, they also reported that they Fourth source

felt guilty, even though their parents told them not to, just as the Mayo Clinic experts recommend. As my friend Kris said, "For a long time after the divorce, every time me and my dad were together, he seemed distracted, like he wished I wasn't there. I felt bad that I couldn't just vanish." Dale, the stepparent I interviewed, liked the strategies suggested by the University of Missouri Extension, and he had actually tried some of these approaches with his own stepchildren. However, as Dale told me, "When you're as busy as most parents and kids are these days, you can let important things fall by the wayside—even time together. That's not good for anyone."

Fresh conclusion

Thinking back on Kris's and Dale's words and everything I've learned from the other sources, I have come to conclude that divorced parents and stepparents need to make sure they build "together time" with their own children and/or stepchildren into every day. Even if this time is just a discussion over a meal or a quick bedtime story, children will remember it and appreciate it. This approach would help with some of the relationship building that the University of Missouri Extension recommends. It would also improve communication, help children understand that they are truly loved by *all* their parents, and assist with the process of postdivorce healing.

**Works Cited**

Leigh, Sharon, Maridith Jackson, and Janet A. Clark. "Foundations for a Successful Stepfamily." U of Missouri Extension, Apr. 2007. Web. 13 Oct. 2015.

Mayo Clinic Staff. "Children and Divorce: Helping Kids after a Breakup." *Mayo Clinic.* Mayo Clinic, 14 May 2011. Web. 12 Oct. 2015.

Rosdahl, Caroline Bunker, and Mary T. Kowalski. *Textbook of Basic Nursing.* 9th ed. Philadelphia: Lippincott Williams & Wilkins, 2008. 92. Print.

## *Evaluation*

An **evaluation** is your *thoughtful* judgment about something based on what you have discovered through your summary, analysis, and synthesis. To evaluate something effectively, apply the questions from the Reading and Writing Critically box on page 21. You will want to refer to these questions as you work through later chapters of this book and through readings from other college courses.

Here is an evaluation of the excerpt from the *Textbook of Basic Nursing:*

In just a few paragraphs, Rosdahl and Kowalski give a good description of the effects of divorce, not only on the former spouses but also on their children. The details that the authors provide help to clearly communicate the difficulties that such children face. In the short term, these difficulties can include emotional and behavioral problems and trouble in school. In the longer term, if one or both of a child's parents remarry, the child faces the stress of dealing with a new and different family. Although the authors do not specifically address ways that parents and stepparents can ease children into divorce and/or new families, other sources—such as the Web sites of the University of Missouri Extension and the Mayo Clinic, as well as people I interviewed—do get into these issues. In the end, I think that Rosdahl and Kowalski present a good

overview of their subject in a short piece of writing that was part of a larger discussion on family stresses.

**PRACTICE 11** **Making connections**

As you work through this exercise, refer to the Reading and Writing Critically box on page 21.

1. **Summary:** Summarize Amanda Jacobowitz's essay on pages 16–17.
2. **Analysis:** Whether you agree or disagree with Jacobowitz, write a paragraph analyzing the points she presents.
3. **Synthesis:** Read additional opinion pieces or blog postings about bottled water. In one paragraph, state your position on the subject according to your reading of these materials. Also, explain the range of opinions on the subject.
4. **Evaluation:** Write a paragraph that evaluates Jacobowitz's essay.

## What Is Writing Critically about Visuals?

Images play a huge role in our lives today, and it is important to think critically about them just as you would about what you read or hear. Whether the image is a Web site, a photograph or illustration, a graphic, or an advertisement, you need to be able to "read" it. You can apply the same critical reading skills of summary, analysis, synthesis, and evaluation to read a visual.

Look carefully at the advertisement from Tappening on page 9. Then, consider how to read a visual using the critical thinking skills you have learned.

### *Summary*

To summarize a visual, ask yourself what the big picture is: What is going on? What is the main impression or message (the main idea)? What is the purpose? How is this purpose achieved (the support)? To answer these questions, consider some strategies used in visuals.

#### DOMINANT ELEMENTS

Artists, illustrators, and advertisers may place the most important object in the center of an image. Or, they may design visuals using a **Z pattern**, with the most important object in the top left and the second most important object in the bottom right. In English and many other languages, people read printed material from left to right and from top to bottom, and the Z pattern takes advantage of that pattern. Because of these design strategies, the main idea of a visual can often be determined by looking at the center of the image or at the top left or bottom right.

#### FIGURES AND OBJECTS

The person who creates an image has a purpose (main idea) and uses visual details to achieve (or support) that purpose. In a photograph, illustration, or painting, details about the figures and objects help create the impression the artist wants to

convey. (Here, the term *figures* refers to people, animals, or other forms that can show action or emotion.) When studying any image, ask yourself the following questions:

- Are the figures from a certain period in history?
- What kind of clothes are they wearing?
- What are the expressions on their faces? How would I describe their attitudes?
- Are the figures shown realistically, or are they shown as sketches or cartoons?
- What important details about the figures does the creator of the image want me to focus on?

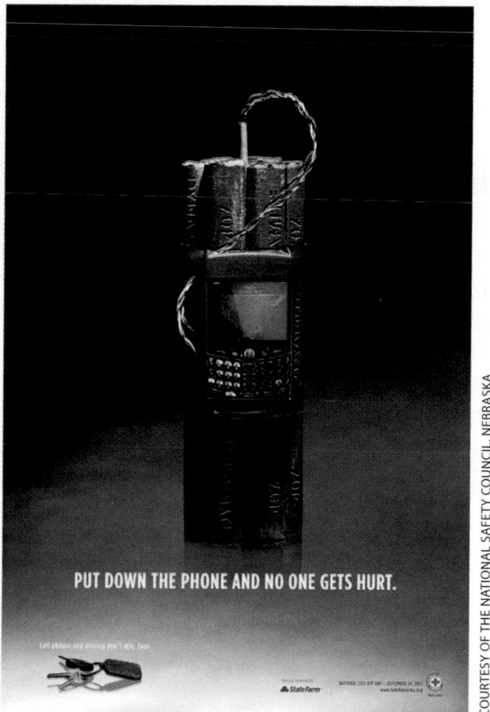
PUT DOWN THE PHONE AND NO ONE GETS HURT.

COURTESY OF THE NATIONAL SAFETY COUNCIL, NEBRASKA

**PRACTICE 12** **Summarizing a visual**

Focus on the public service announcement from the Nebraska Safety Council above, and answer the following questions.

1. What is the big picture? What is going on? ____________________

   ____________________________________________

2. What is at the center of the ad? ____________________

3. What is the ad's purpose? ______________________________

______________________________

4. What details do you notice about the ad? Include as many as you can.

______________________________

______________________________

______________________________

## *Analysis*

To analyze a visual, focus on the parts of it (figures, objects, type), and ask yourself how they contribute to the message or main impression. Consider the background, the use of light and dark, and the various elements' colors, contrasts, textures, and sizes.

### PRACTICE 13 Analyzing a visual

Focus on the public service announcement from the Nebraska Safety Council on page 26, and answer the following questions.

1. What elements are placed in large type? Why? ______________________________

______________________________

______________________________

______________________________

2. How do all the features in the ad contribute to the main impression? ______

______________________________

______________________________

## *Synthesis*

To synthesize your impressions of a visual, ask yourself what the message seems to be, using your summary and analysis skills. Consider how this message relates to what else you know from experience and observation.

### PRACTICE 14 Synthesizing your impressions of a visual

Focus on the public service announcement from the Nebraska Safety Council on page 26, and answer the following questions.

1. What is the ad's central message? ______________________________

______________________________

2. How does this message relate to what you already know or have heard or experienced? ________________________________

### *Evaluation*

To evaluate an image, ask yourself how effective it is in achieving its purpose and conveying its main idea or message. What do you think of the image, using your summary, analysis, and synthesis skills? Consider any biases or assumptions that may be working in the image.

**PRACTICE 15** **Evaluating a visual**

Focus on the public service announcement from the Nebraska Safety Council on page 26, and answer the following questions.

1. What do you think about the ad, especially its visual elements? ________

________________________________

________________________________

2. Does the creator of the ad seem to have any biases? Why or why not?

________________________________

________________________________

3. Is the ad effective, given its purpose and the main idea it is trying to make? Why or why not? ________________________________

________________________________

________________________________

## What Is Problem Solving?

In college, at work, and in everyday life, we often need to "read" situations to make important decisions about them. This process, known as problem solving, can also involve summarizing, analyzing, synthesizing, and evaluating. Let's look at key steps in the process.

1. Summarize the problem.

   Try to describe it in a brief statement or question.

   **EXAMPLE:** My ten-year-old car needs a new transmission, which will cost at least $1000. Should I keep the car or buy a new one?

2. Analyze the problem.

   Consider possible ways to solve it, examining any questions or assumptions you might have.

**EXAMPLES**

*Assumption:* I need to have a reliable car.

*Question:* Is this assumption truly justified?

*Answer:* Yes. I can't get to school or work without a reliable car. I live more than fifteen miles from each location, and there is no regular public transportation to either place from my home.

**POSSIBLE SOLUTIONS**

- Pay for the transmission repair.
- Buy a new car.

3. Synthesize information about the problem.

   Consult various information sources to get opinions about the possible solutions.

   **EXAMPLES**

   - My mechanic
   - Friends who have had similar car problems
   - Car advice from print or Web sources
   - My past experience with car repairs and expenses

4. Evaluate the possible solutions, and make a decision.

   You might consider the advantages and disadvantages of each possible solution. Also, when you make your decision, you should be able to give reasons for your choice.

   **EXAMPLES (considering only advantages and disadvantages)**

- Pay for the transmission repair.

  *Advantage:* This option would be cheaper than buying a new car.

  *Disadvantage:* The car might not last much longer, even with the new transmission.

- Buy a new car.

  *Advantage:* I will have a reliable car.

  *Disadvantage:* This option is much more expensive than paying for the repair.

**FINAL DECISION:** Pay for the transmission repair.

**REASONS:** I do not have money for a new car, and I do not want to take on more debt. Also, two mechanics told me that my car should run for three to five more years with the new transmission. At that point, I will be in a better position to buy a new car.

### PRACTICE 16 Solving a problem

Think of a problem you are facing now—in college, at work, or in your everyday life. On a separate sheet of paper, summarize the problem. Next, referring to the previous steps, write down and analyze possible solutions,

considering different sources of information. Then, write down your final decision or preferred solution, giving reasons for your choice.

## Chapter Review

1. What are the four basics of critical thinking? ______________________________

______________________________

______________________________

2. What are the four major steps of the critical reading process? ______________________________

______________________________

3. Why is it important to read real-world documents critically? ______________________________

______________________________

4. What are the four major steps of writing critically about readings and visuals?

______________________________

5. Without looking back in the chapter, define the task of synthesizing in your own words. ______________________________

______________________________

## REFLECTING ON THE JOURNEY

### Skills Learned

Now that you've completed the chapter, share what you've learned about each skill by completing the following chart.

| Skill | What I learned about this skill |
|---|---|
| Preparing for success | |
| Thinking critically | |
| Using the critical reading process | |
| Writing critically about readings | |
| Writing critically about visuals | |
| Problem solving | |

# 2

# Writing Basics

## Audience, Purpose, and Process

## READING ROADMAP

### Learning Objectives

**Chapter Goal:** Learn what audience and purpose are and how they affect the writing process.

**Tools to Achieve the Goal:**

- Four Basics of Good Writing (p. 32)
- Understand Audience and Purpose (p. 32)
- Understand the Writing Process (p. 36)
- Understand Grading Criteria (p. 37)
- Relationship between Paragraphs and Essays (p. 38)

### Key Terms

Skim Chapter 2 before reading. Find these words or terms in **bold** type. Put a check mark next to each once you locate it.

____ audience
____ purpose
____ paragraph
____ topic sentence
____ main idea
____ body
____ support sentences
____ concluding sentence
____ essay
____ introduction
____ thesis
____ support paragraphs
____ conclusion
____ writing process
____ rubric

### Guided Reading for Chapter 2

Fill out the following chart before you begin reading. For each skill, write what you know about the skill and what you would like to know upon completing the chapter. At the end of the chapter, you will be asked to share what you learned about each skill.

| Skill | When I have used this skill | What I want to know about this skill |
|---|---|---|
| Identify a specific audience | | |
| Identify a specific purpose | | |
| Consider the needs and expectations of the audience | | |
| Use a clear writing process to develop and revise a draft | | |
| Make a clear, definite point | | |
| Provide support that shows, explains, or proves the main idea | | |
| Read and understand a rubric | | |

Four elements are key to good writing. Keep them in mind whenever you write.

**Four Basics** of Good Writing

1. It considers what the audience knows and needs.
2. It fulfills the writer's purpose.
3. It includes a clear, definite point.
4. It provides support that shows, explains, or proves the main idea.

LaunchPadSolo
Visit **LaunchPad Solo for Readers and Writers > Writing Process > Purpose, Audience, and Topic** for more practice with writing basics.

This chapter discusses the four basics in more detail. It also outlines the writing process, previewing steps that are covered more thoroughly in the next three chapters. Finally, it gives you some typical grading criteria and shows how they are applied to assess unsatisfactory, satisfactory, and excellent paragraphs.

# Understand Audience and Purpose

Your **audience** is the person or people who will read what you write. In college, your audience is usually your instructors. Whenever you write, always have at least one real person in mind as a reader. Think about what that person already knows and what he or she will need to know to understand your main idea.

Your **purpose** is your reason for writing. Let's take a look at some different audiences and purposes.

## Audience and Purpose

| Type of writing | Audience | Purpose | Tips |
|---|---|---|---|
| **College:** A research essay about the environmental effects of "fracking": fracturing rock layers to extract oil or natural gas | The professor of your environmental science class | • To complete an assignment according to your professor's instructions and any research methods discussed in class<br>• To show what you have learned about the topic | When writing to fulfill a course assignment, never make assumptions such as, "My instructor already knows this fact, so what's the point of mentioning it?" By providing plenty of relevant examples and details, you demonstrate your knowledge of a subject and make your writing more effective. |
| **Work:** An e-mail to coworkers about your company's new insurance provider | Fellow workers | To make sure that coworkers understand all the important details about the new provider | Define or explain any terminology or concepts that will not be familiar to your audience. |
| **Everyday Life:** A text message to your recreational softball league informing them about a time change for this week's game | The members of your softball team | To make sure your team knows what time to show up for their game this week | Although informal, texting still requires you to provide all the necessary information and to make sure you don't assume that everyone on that list understands every texting abbreviation. You may need to spell out some of the words you may not usually spell out with your friends. |

The tone and content of your writing will vary depending on your audiences and purposes. Read the following three notes, which describe the same situation but are written for different audiences and purposes.

**Situation:** Marta woke up one morning feeling strange, and her face was swollen and red. Marta immediately called her doctor's office and made an appointment. Marta's mother was coming to stay with Marta's children in a few minutes, so Marta asked a neighbor to watch the children until her mother got there. Marta then texted her mother explaining why she had already left. When she got to the doctor's office, she was feeling better, and, since the doctor was running late, she decided not to wait. The nurse asked her to write a brief description of her symptoms for the doctor to read later. Before leaving the doctor's office, however, Marta also wanted to make sure that her office knew that she would be at work sooner than she expected. She sent a quick e-mail to her office to let them know she would be there on time.

### Marta's text to her mother

*Nt feelng well; going 2 DR. I'm OK. Don't wry. Thx for watching kds 4 me.*

### Marta's note to the doctor

*When I woke up this morning, my face was swollen, especially around the eyes, which were almost shut. My lips and skin were red and dry, and my face was itchy. However, the swelling seemed to go down quickly.*

### Marta's e-mail to work

*Mrs. Smith,*
*After calling in this morning to let you know that I would be a bit late due to a potential illness, I realized that I am now feeling better and will manage to make it in to work on time. I am leaving the doctor's office right now and should be at the office very shortly. I apologize for any inconvenience this may cause and will make sure to make up for any missed time.*
*Sincerely,*
*Marta*

## PRACTICE 1 Comparing Marta's notes

Read Marta's three notes, and answer the following questions.

1. How does Marta's note to her mother differ from the one to the doctor?

   How does the one to the doctor differ from the one to work? ____________

   ____________________________________________

   ____________________________________________

   ____________________________________________

   ____________________________________________

2. How do the different audiences and purposes affect what the notes say (the content) and how they say it (the tone)? ______________________________

______________________________

______________________________

______________________________

______________________________

______________________________

3. Which note has more detail, and why? ______________________________

______________________________

As these examples show, we communicate with family members and friends differently than we communicate with people in authority (like employers, instructors, or other professionals)—or we should. Marta's text to her mother is extremely informal; it not only uses incomplete sentences but also incomplete words because the two women know each other well and are used to speaking casually to each other. Because Marta's purpose is to get quick information to her mother and to reassure her, she does not need to provide a lot of details. On the other hand, Marta's note to her doctor is more formal, with complete sentences, because the relationship is more formal. Also, the note to the doctor is more detailed because the doctor will be making treatment decisions based on it. Finally, the e-mail to work is the most formal because it requires Marta to be professional and businesslike. Anything less would not be acceptable in that environment.

In college, at work, and in your everyday life, when you are speaking or writing to someone in authority for a serious purpose, use formal English; people will take you seriously.

### PRACTICE 2 Writing for a formal audience

A student, Terri Travers, sent the following e-mail to a friend to complain about not getting into a criminal justice course. Rewrite the e-mail as if you were Terri and you were writing to Professor Widener. The purpose is to ask whether the professor would consider allowing you into the class given that you signed up early and have the necessary grades.

To: Miles Rona

Fr: Terri Travers

Subject: Bummin

Seriously bummin that I didn't get into Prof Widener's CJ class. U and Luis said it's the best ever, lol. Wonder why I didn't . . . I signed up early and I have the grades. Sup w/that?

C ya,

TT

## *Understand Paragraph and Essay Form*

In this course (and in the rest of college), you will write paragraphs and essays. Each kind of writing has a basic structure.

### PARAGRAPH FORM

A **paragraph** has three necessary parts: the topic sentence, the body, and the concluding sentence.

| Paragraph Part | Purpose of the Paragraph Part |
|---|---|
| 1. The **topic sentence** | states the **main idea**. The topic sentence is often the first sentence of the paragraph. |
| 2. The **body** | supports (shows, explains, or proves) the main idea with **support sentences** that contain facts and details. |
| 3. The **concluding sentence** | reminds readers of the main idea and often makes an observation. |

Read the paragraph that follows with the paragraph parts labeled.

Following a few basic strategies can help you take better notes, an important skill for succeeding in any course. First, start the notes for each class session on a fresh page of your course notebook, and record the date at the top of the page. Next, to improve the speed of your note taking, abbreviate certain words, especially ones your instructor uses regularly. For example, abbreviations for a business course might include *fncl* for financial, *svc* for service, and *mgt* for management. However, don't try to write down every word your instructor says. Instead, look for ways to boil down extended explanations into short phrases. For instance, imagine that a business instructor says the following: "A profit-and-loss statement is a report of an organization's revenue and expenses over a specific financial period. Often, P-and-L's are used to determine ways to boost revenue or cut costs, with the goal of increasing profitability." The note taker might write down something like, "P&L: rpt of revenue + expenses over a specific period. Used to boost rev or cut costs." Although you do not need to record every word of a lecture, listen for clues that indicate that your instructor is making a point important enough to write down. At such times, the instructor might raise his or her voice, or he or she might introduce key information with such phrases as "It's important to remember" or "Bear in mind." In addition, if the instructor has made a certain point more than once, it is a good indication that this point is important. By carefully listening to and recording information from your instructor, you are not just getting good notes to study later; you are already beginning to seal this information into your memory.

Topic sentence

Body (with support sentences)

Concluding sentence

### ESSAY FORM

An **essay** is a piece of writing that examines a topic in more depth than a paragraph. A short essay may have four or five paragraphs, totaling three hundred to six hundred words. A long essay may be many pages long, depending on what the essay needs to accomplish, such as persuading someone to do something, using research to make a point, or explaining a complex concept.

An essay has three necessary parts: the introduction, the body, and the conclusion.

| Essay Part | Purpose of the Essay Part |
|---|---|
| 1. The **introduction** | states the main idea, or **thesis**, generally in a single, strong statement. The introduction may be a single paragraph or multiple paragraphs. |
| 2. The **body** | supports (shows, explains, or proves) the main idea. It generally has at least three **support paragraphs**, each containing facts and details that develop the main idea. Each support paragraph has a topic sentence that supports the thesis statement. |
| 3. The **conclusion** | reminds readers of the main idea and makes an observation. Often, it also summarizes and reinforces the support. |

| Paragraph | | Essay |
|---|---|---|
| Topic sentence | → | Thesis statement |
| Support sentences | → | Support paragraphs |
| Concluding sentence | → | Conclusion |

The diagram on pages 38–39 shows how the parts of an essay correspond to the parts of a paragraph.

## Understand the Writing Process

The chart that follows shows the four stages of the **writing process**. These are all the steps you need to follow to write well. The rest of the chapters in Part 1 cover every stage except editing (presented later in the book). You will practice each stage, see how another student completed the process, and write your own paragraph or essay. Keep in mind that you may not always go in a straight line through the four stages; instead, you might circle back to earlier steps to further improve your writing.

Some writing strategies—such as finding and exploring a topic, coming up with a main idea, and revising—are similar for both paragraphs and essays. In these cases, this book discusses the strategies for paragraphs and essays together. (See Chapters 3, 4, and 5.) However, other activities, such as supporting main ideas or drafting individual parts of paragraphs or essays, are somewhat different for the two

**The Writing Process**

**Generate ideas**

**Consider:** What is my purpose in writing? Given this purpose, what interests me? Who will read this paper? What do they need to know?

- Find and explore your topic (Chapter 3).
- Make your point (Chapter 3).
- Support your point (Chapter 4).

**Draft**

**Consider:** How can I organize my ideas effectively and show my readers what I mean?

- Arrange your ideas, and make an outline (Chapter 5).
- Write a draft, including an introduction that will interest your readers, a strong conclusion, and a title (Chapter 5).

**Revise**

**Consider:** How can I make my draft clearer or more convincing to my readers? How do I avoid plagiarism? How do I meet the requirements of the grading rubric?

- Look for ideas that do not fit (Chapter 5).
- Look for ideas that could use more detailed support (Chapter 5).
- Connect ideas with transitional words and sentences (Chapter 5).

**Edit**

**Consider:** What errors could confuse my readers and weaken my point?

- Find and correct errors in grammar (Chapters 15-26).
- Look for errors in word use (Chapters 27 and 28), spelling (Chapter 29), and punctuation and capitalization (Chapters 30–34).

types of writing. In those cases, this book makes greater distinctions between paragraphs and essays.

## Understand Grading Criteria

Your instructor may use a **rubric**—a list of the elements on which your papers will be graded. If your instructor uses a rubric, it may be included in the course syllabus, and you should refer to it each time you write. Also, use the rubric to revise your writing.

# Relationship between Paragraphs and Essays

For more on the important features of writing, see the Four Basics of Good Writing on page 32.

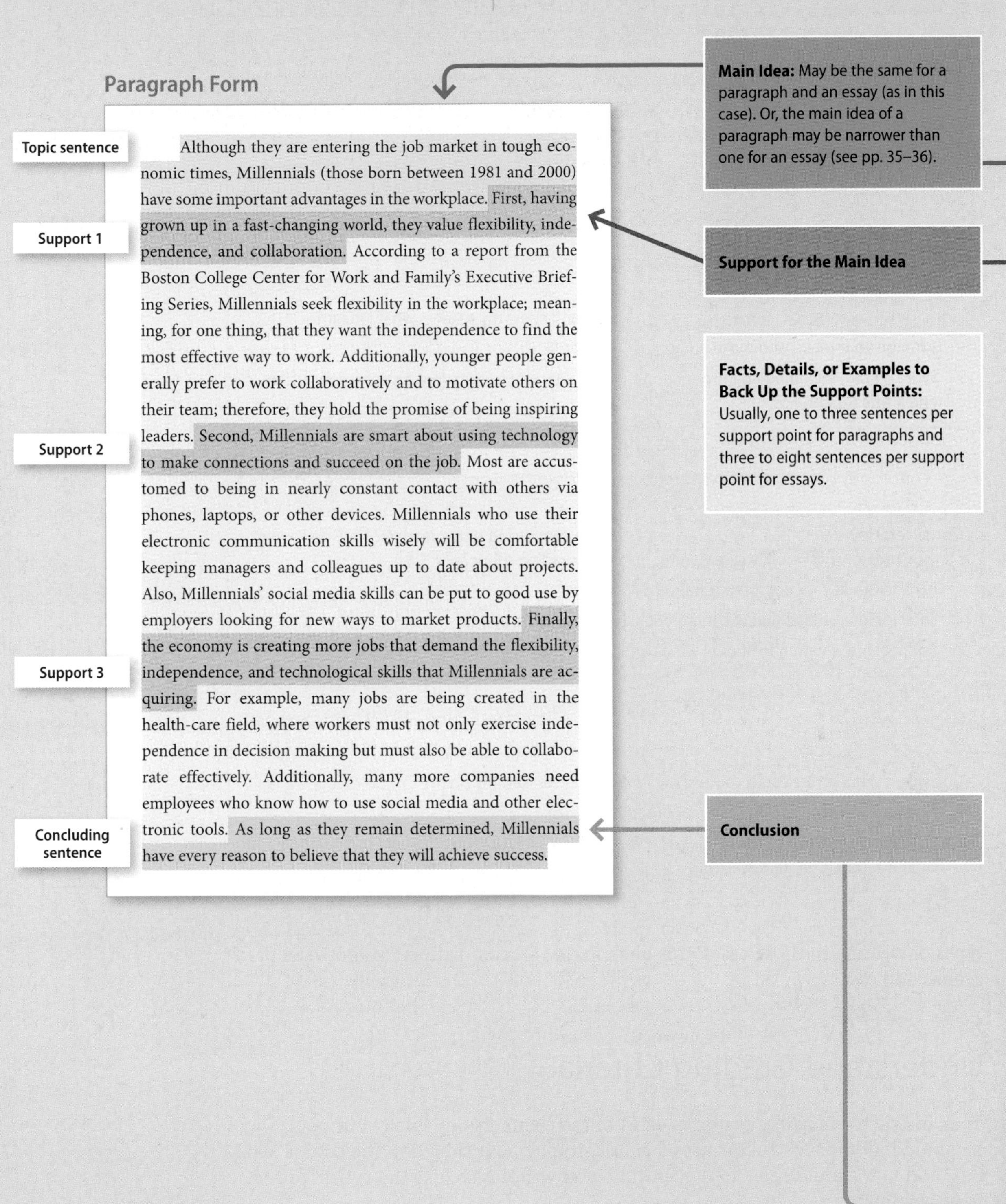
Paragraph Form
Topic sentence
Although they are entering the job market in tough economic times, Millennials (those born between 1981 and 2000) have some important advantages in the workplace. First, having grown up in a fast-changing world, they value flexibility, independence, and collaboration. According to a report from the Boston College Center for Work and Family's Executive Briefing Series, Millennials seek flexibility in the workplace; meaning, for one thing, that they want the independence to find the most effective way to work. Additionally, younger people generally prefer to work collaboratively and to motivate others on their team; therefore, they hold the promise of being inspiring leaders. Second, Millennials are smart about using technology to make connections and succeed on the job. Most are accustomed to being in nearly constant contact with others via phones, laptops, or other devices. Millennials who use their electronic communication skills wisely will be comfortable keeping managers and colleagues up to date about projects. Also, Millennials' social media skills can be put to good use by employers looking for new ways to market products. Finally, the economy is creating more jobs that demand the flexibility, independence, and technological skills that Millennials are acquiring. For example, many jobs are being created in the health-care field, where workers must not only exercise independence in decision making but must also be able to collaborate effectively. Additionally, many more companies need employees who know how to use social media and other electronic tools. As long as they remain determined, Millennials have every reason to believe that they will achieve success.
Support 1
Support 2
Support 3
Concluding sentence
Main Idea: May be the same for a paragraph and an essay (as in this case). Or, the main idea of a paragraph may be narrower than one for an essay (see pp. 35–36).
Support for the Main Idea
Facts, Details, or Examples to Back Up the Support Points: Usually, one to three sentences per support point for paragraphs and three to eight sentences per support point for essays.
Conclusion

## Essay Form

Introductory paragraph

1

Fairly often, I hear older people saying that Millennials (those born between 1981 and 2000) are spoiled, self-centered individuals who have much less to contribute to the workplace than previous generations did. Based on my own experiences an[d] I must disagree. Although they are entering the job market in tough economic times, Millennials have some important advantages in the workpla[ce].

Thesis statement

Topic sentence 1

First, having grown up in a fast-changing world, they value flexibility, independence, and collaboration. Unlike their parents and grandparents, Millennials never knew a world without personal computers, and the youngest of them never knew a world without the Internet or ever-changing models of smartphones. They are used to rapid change, and most of them have learned to adapt to it. Consequently, Millennials, for the most part, expect workplaces to adapt to them. According to a report from the Boston College Center for Work and Family's Executive Briefing Series (EBS), Millennials seek flexibility in the workplace—for example, in when and where they work. This attitude

2

does not mean that they are looking out for themselves alone. Instead, they want the independence to find the most effective and productive way to work. Additionally, according to the EBS report, Millennials are more likely than older workers to reject old-fashioned business hierarchies in which managers tell lower-ranking employees what to do, and there is no give-and-take. In general, younger people prefer to work collaboratively and to do what they can to motivate others on their team; therefore, they hold the promise of being inspiring leaders.

Topic sentence 2

Second, Millennials are smart about using technology to make connections and succeed on the job. Most of them are accustomed to being in nearly constant contact with others via phones, laptops, or other devices. Although some people fear that [con]nectedness can be a distraction in the workp[lace, these] technologies can be used productively and allow effective multitasking. For instance, over the course of a day, Millennials who have learned to use their electronic communication skills wisely will be comfortable

Support paragraphs

3

keeping managers and colleagues up to date about projects and responding to questions and requests as they arise. Furthermore, most Millennials are open to continuing such electronic exchanges during evenings and weekends if they feel they are collaborating with colleagues to meet an important goal. Also, many Millennials are skilled in using social media to reach out to and remain connected with others; in fact, some people refer to them as "the Facebook generation." Employers can put these skills to good use as they look for new ways to market their products and find new customers.

Topic sentence 3

Finally, the economy is creating more jobs that demand the flexibility, independence, and technological skills that Millennials are acquiring. For example, many jobs are being created in the health-care field, where workers, such as nurses and physician assistants, must not only exercise independence in decision making but must also be able to collaborate effectively. Additionally, many more companies need employees who know how to use social media and

4

other electronic tools for marketing purposes. Similarly, Millennials with social media skills may have an advantage in finding work in the marketing and advertising industries specifically. There is also always a need for independent-minded people to create new businesses and innovations. Thus, Millennials can play a valuable role in helping the economy grow.

As long as they remain determined and confident, Millennials have every reason to believe that they will achieve career success. According to the EBS report and other sources, meaningful, challenging work is more important to this generation than having a high salary. In the long term, workers with those types of values will always be in demand.

Concluding paragraph

The following sample rubric shows you some of the elements you may be graded on. Many rubrics include how each element is weighted; because that practice differs among instructors and courses, the example does not specify percentages of importance or points.

## Sample Rubric

| Element | Grading criteria | Point range |
|---|---|---|
| Appropriateness | • Did the student follow the assignment directions? | 0–5 |
| Main idea | • Does the paper clearly state a strong main idea in a complete sentence? | 0–10 |
| Support | • Is the main idea developed with specific support, including specific details and examples?<br>• Is enough support presented to make the main idea evident to the reader?<br>• Is all the support directly related to the main idea? | 0–10 |
| Organization | • Is the writing logically organized?<br>• Does the student use transitions (e.g., *also, for example, sometimes,* and *so on*) to move the reader from one point to another? | 0–10 |
| Conclusion | • Does the conclusion remind the reader of the main point?<br>• Does it make an observation based on the support? | 0–5 |
| Grammar | • Is the writing free of the four most serious errors? (See Chapters 16–19)<br>• Is the sentence structure clear?<br>• Does the student choose words that clearly express his or her meaning?<br>• Are the words spelled correctly?<br>• Is the punctuation correct? | 0–10 |

The paragraph that follows shows how rubrics are applied to a piece of writing. For a key to the correction symbols used, see the Useful Editing and Proofreading Marks chart at the back of this book.

**Assignment:** Write a paragraph about something you enjoy doing. Make sure you give enough details about the activity so that a reader who knows little about it will have an idea of why you enjoy it.

### Paragraph

*tense* *tense*
In my spare time, I enjoy talking with my friend Karen. I know Karen since we ten,
*tense* *frag*
so we have growed up together and been through many things. Like a sister. We can

talk about anything. Sometimes we talk about problems. Money problems, problems
frag frag
with men. When I was in a difficult relationship, for example. Now we both have
sp sp tense
children and we talk about how to raise them. Things are diffrent then when we kids.
wc
Talking with a good friend helps me make good decisions and patience. Especially
frag punc
now that my son is a teenager. We also talk about fun things, like what were going
run-on
to do on the weekend, what clothes we buy. We tell each other good jokes and make
each other laugh. These conversations are as important as talking about problems.

**Analysis of paragraph:** This paragraph would receive an average grade (not an A or B), for the following reasons.

## Sample Rubric

| Element | Grading criteria | Point: Comment |
|---|---|---|
| Appropriateness | • Did the student follow the assignment directions? | 5/5: Yes. |
| Main idea | • Does the paper clearly state a strong main idea in a complete sentence? | 10/10: Yes. |
| Support | • Is the main idea developed with specific support, including specific details and examples?<br>• Is there enough support to make the main idea evident to the reader?<br>• Is all the support directly related to the main idea? | 5/10: The paragraph has some support and detail, but it could use more. |
| Organization | • Is the writing logically organized?<br>• Does the student use transitions (e.g., *also, for example, sometimes,* and *so on*) to move the reader from one point to another? | 6/10: The student uses a few transitions (*sometimes, when, for example, now*). |
| Conclusion | • Does the conclusion remind the reader of the main idea?<br>• Does it make an observation based on the support? | 3/5: The conclusion relates back to the main idea, but the observation is weak. |
| Grammar | • Is the writing free of the four most serious errors? (See Chapters 16–19.)<br>• Is the sentence structure clear?<br>• Does the student choose words that clearly express his or her meaning?<br>• Are the words spelled correctly?<br>• Is the punctuation correct? | 6/10: The writing has some major grammar errors.<br>**TOTAL POINTS: 35/50** |

### PRACTICE 3 Analyzing the paragraph

Referring to the sample paragraph, answer the following questions.

1. Which sentence is the topic sentence? ______
2. Underline some of the added details that make Paragraph 3 stronger than the first two paragraphs, and note those details here. ______
3. Circle the transitions, and write them here. ______
4. In what way is the last sentence a good concluding sentence? ______

## Chapter Review

1. In your own words, define *audience*. ______
2. In college, who is your audience likely to be? ______
3. What are the stages of the writing process? ______
4. Think of other courses in which you have written papers or taken tests. What purposes has that writing had? ______
5. What are four of the elements often evaluated in rubrics? ______

# REFLECTING ON THE JOURNEY

## Skills Learned

Now that you've completed the chapter, share what you've learned about each skill by completing the following chart.

| Skill | What I learned about this skill |
|---|---|
| Identify a specific audience | |
| Identify a specific purpose | |
| Consider the needs and expectations of the audience | |
| Use a clear writing process to develop and revise a draft | |
| Make a clear, definite point | |
| Provide support that shows, explains, or proves the main idea | |
| Read and understand a rubric | |

# 3

# Finding Your Topic and Writing Your Thesis Statement

## Making a Point

### Learning Objectives

**Chapter Goal:** Learn how to identify, narrow, and explore your topic and then learn how to write thesis statements and topic sentences.

**Tools to Achieve the Goal:**

- Understand What a Topic Is (p. 45)
- Practice Narrowing a Topic (p. 45)
- Practice Exploring Your Topic (p. 48)
- Write Your Own Topic and Ideas (p. 52)
- Understand What a Topic Sentence and a Thesis Statement Are (p. 52)
- Practice Developing a Good Topic Sentence or Thesis Statement (p. 55)
- Write Your Own Topic Sentence or Thesis Statement (p. 64)

## READING ROADMAP

### Key Terms

Skim Chapter 3 before reading. Find these words or terms in **bold** type. Put a check mark next to each once you locate it.

____ topic
____ narrow
____ prewriting techniques
____ freewriting
____ listing
____ brainstorming
____ peer review
____ clustering
____ mapping
____ main idea
____ topic sentence
____ thesis statement
____ peer review

### Guided Reading for Chapter 3

Fill out the following chart before you begin reading. For each skill, write what you know about the skill and what you would like to know upon completing the chapter. At the end of the chapter, you will be asked to share what you learned about each skill.

| Skill | When I have used this skill | What I want to know about this skill |
|---|---|---|
| Understand the difference between a topic and a main idea | | |
| Explore and narrow a topic | | |
| Write a thesis statement | | |
| Write topic sentences | | |

## Understand What a Topic Is

A **topic** is who or what you are writing about. It is the subject of your paragraph or essay.

**LaunchPadSolo**
Visit **LaunchPad Solo for Readers and Writers > Writing Process** for more tutorials, videos, and practice with prewriting, topics, and main ideas.

**Questions for finding a good topic**

- Does this topic interest me? If so, why do I care about it?
- Do I know something about the topic? Do I want to know more?
- Can I get involved with some part of the topic? Is it relevant to my life in some way?
- Is the topic specific enough for the assignment (a paragraph or a short essay)?

Choose one of the following topics or one of your own and focus on one part of it that you are familiar with. (For example, focus on one personal goal or a specific problem of working students that interests you.)

| | |
|---|---|
| Music/group I like | Sports |
| Problems of working students | My favorite vacation |
| An activity/group I am involved in | A personal goal |
| My proudest moment | A time when I took a big risk |
| An issue in the news | My ideal job |
| Relationships | A current trend |

**PRACTICE 1** **Finding a good topic**

Ask the "Questions for Finding a Good Topic" about the topic you have chosen. If you answer "no" to any of them, keep looking for another topic or modify the topic.

**My topic:** ______________________________

______________________________

With the general topic you have chosen in mind, read this chapter and complete all the practices. When you finish the chapter, you will have found a good topic to write about and explored ideas related to it.

## Practice Narrowing a Topic

If your instructor assigns a general topic, it may at first seem uninteresting, unfamiliar, or too general. It is up to you to find a good, specific topic based on the general one. Whether the topic is your own or assigned, you next need to narrow and explore it. To **narrow** a general topic, focus on the smaller parts of it until you find one that is interesting and specific.

Here are some ways to narrow a general topic.

## DIVIDE IT INTO SMALLER CATEGORIES

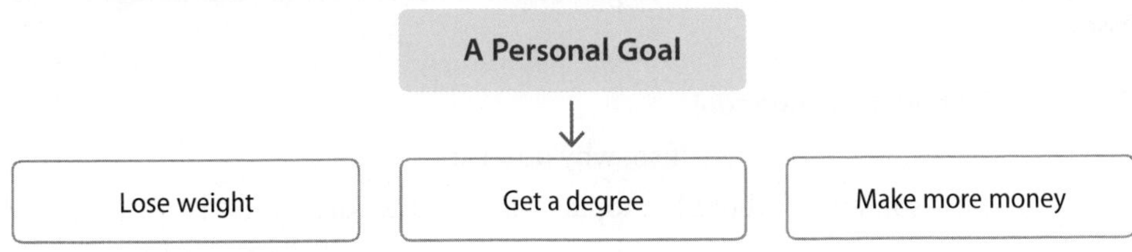
A Personal Goal
Lose weight
Get a degree
Make more money

## THINK OF SPECIFIC EXAMPLES FROM YOUR LIFE

**General Topic** **Crime**

Stolen identities (how does it happen?)

When I had my wallet stolen by two kids (how? what happened?)

The e-mail scam that my grandmother lost money in (how did it work?)

**General Topic** **Social media**

Twitter (which feeds do I follow regularly? what do I get from them?)

Facebook (what features are fun or useful? what feels like a waste of time?)

Instagram (why do people feel the need to document their every move with pictures and post them online?)

## THINK OF SPECIFIC EXAMPLES FROM CURRENT EVENTS

**General Topic** **Job-creation ideas**

Tax breaks for businesses

Training of future entrepreneurs in growth areas, like solar or wind energy

A special fund for public projects that will employ many people

**General Topic** **Heroism**

The guy who pulled a stranger from a burning car

My aunt, who volunteers at a homeless shelter for ten hours a week

## QUESTION YOUR ASSUMPTIONS

Questioning assumptions—an important part of critical thinking (see Chapter 1)—can be a good way to narrow a topic. First, identify any assumptions you have about your topic. Then, question them, playing "devil's advocate"; in other words, imagine

what someone with a different point of view might say. For example, imagine that your general topic is the pros or cons of letting kids play video games.

| Possible assumptions | Questions |
|---|---|
| Video game pros:<br>Kids get rewarded with good scores for staying focused. →<br>Video games can teach some useful skills. → | Does staying focused on a video game mean that a kid will stay focused on homework or in class?<br>Like what? How am I defining "useful"? |
| Video game cons:<br>They make kids more violent. →<br>They have no real educational value. → | Is there really any proof for that? What do experts say?<br>Didn't my niece say that some video game helped her learn to read? |

Next, ask yourself what assumptions and questions interest you the most. Then, focus on those interests.

When you have found a promising topic for a paragraph or essay, be sure to test it by using the Questions for Finding a Good Topic at the beginning of this chapter. You may need to narrow and test your ideas several times before you find a topic that will work for the assignment.

A topic for an essay can be a little broader than one for a paragraph because essays are longer than paragraphs and allow you to develop more ideas. But be careful: Most of the extra length in an essay should come from developing ideas in more depth (giving more examples and details, explaining what you mean), not from covering a broader topic.

Read the following examples of how a general topic was narrowed to a more specific topic for an essay and an even more specific topic for a paragraph.

| General topic | | Narrowed essay topic | | Narrowed paragraph topic |
|---|---|---|---|---|
| Internships | → | How internships can help you get a job | → | One or two important things you can learn from an internship |
| Social media | → | Popularity of social media among preteens | → | Should there be an age limit to use social media? |
| A personal goal | → | Getting healthy | → | Eating the right foods |
| A great vacation | → | A family camping trip | → | What I learned on our family camping trip to Michigan |

**PRACTICE 2** **Narrowing a general topic**

Use one of the four methods on page 47 to narrow your topic. Then, ask yourself the Questions for Finding a Good Topic. Write your narrowed topic below.

**My narrowed topic:** ______________________________________________

______________________________________________

## Practice Exploring Your Topic

**Tip** Scholar and writer Mina Shaughnessy said that a writer "gets below the surface of a topic." When it comes to exploring a topic, what do you think getting "below the surface" means?

**Prewriting techniques** can give you ideas at any time during your writing: to find a topic, to get ideas for what you want to say about it, and to support your ideas. Ask yourself: What interests me about this topic? What do I know? What do I want to say? Then, use one or more of the prewriting techniques to find the answers. No one uses all those techniques; writers choose the ones that work best for them.

**Prewriting Techniques**

- Freewriting
- Listing/brainstorming
- Discussing
- Clustering/mapping
- Using the Internet
- Keeping a journal

When prewriting, your goal is to come up with as many ideas as possible. Do not say, "Oh, that's stupid" or "That won't work." Just get your brain working by writing down all the possibilities.

A student, Chelsea Wilson, was assigned to write a short essay. She chose to write on the general topic of a personal goal, which she narrowed to "Getting a college degree." The following pages show how she used the first five prewriting techniques to explore her topic.

### *Freewriting*

**Tip** If you are writing on a computer, try a kind of freewriting called "invisible writing." Turn the monitor off, or adjust the screen so that you cannot see what you are typing. Then, write quickly for five minutes without stopping. After five minutes, read what you have written. You may be surprised by the ideas that you can generate this way.

**Freewriting** is like having a conversation with yourself, on paper. To freewrite, just start writing everything you can think of about your topic. Write nonstop for five minutes. Do not go back and cross anything out, and do not worry about using correct grammar or spelling; just write. Here is Chelsea's freewriting:

*So I know I want to get a college degree even though sometimes I wonder if I ever can make it because it's so hard with work and my two-year-old daughter and no money and a car that needs work. I can't take more than two courses at a time and even then I hardly get a chance to sleep if I want to do any of the assignments or study. But I have to think I'll get a better job because this one at the restaurant is driving me nuts and doesn't pay much so I have to work a lot with a boss I can't stand and still wonder how I'm gonna pay the bills. I know life can be better if I can just manage to become a nurse. I'll make more money and can live anywhere I want because everyplace needs nurses. I won't have to work at a job where I am not respected by anyone. I want respect, I know I'm hardworking and smart and good with people and deserve better than this. So does my daughter. No one in my family has ever graduated from college even though my sister took two courses, but then she stopped. I know I can do this, I just have to make a commitment to do it and not look away.*

## *Listing/Brainstorming*

**Listing** (or **brainstorming**) is when you list all the ideas about your topic that you can think of. Write as many as you can in five minutes without stopping.

GETTING A COLLEGE DEGREE

*want a better life for myself and my daughter*
*want to be a nurse and help care for people*
*make more money*
*not have to work so many hours*
*could live where I want in a nicer place*
*good future and benefits like health insurance*
*get respect*
*proud of myself, achieve, show everyone*
*be a professional, work in a clean place*

## *Discussing*

Many people find it helpful to discuss ideas with another person before they write. As they talk, they get more ideas and immediate feedback.

If you and your discussion partner both have writing assignments, first explore one person's topic and then explore the other's. The person whose topic is being explored is the interviewee; the other person is the interviewer. The interviewer should ask questions about anything that seems unclear and should let the interviewee know what sounds interesting. In addition, the interviewer should identify and try to question any assumptions the interviewee seems to be making (see page 46). The interviewee should give thoughtful answers and keep an open mind. He or she should also take notes.

**Tip** If you find that talking about your ideas with someone is a good way to get going, you might want to ask another student to be your regular partner and discuss ideas before beginning any paragraph or essay assignment.

Part of learning to be a successful writer is learning how to become a part of a writing community. Most composition classes will use a process called peer review at some point. **Peer review** asks a fellow student to read your paper and respond as a reader and writer, but it can also occur without a finished paper. To create a successful peer review experience, keep the following in mind:

- Know what questions you want to ask your peer. Try to avoid simple yes or no questions because they may not give you enough information to move forward in your writing process.
- Don't feel shy about asking for help. If you don't understand something or you are having trouble with something, ask about it during the peer review process. Your peers may have the same writing assignment that you do, so they may be able to explain it to you in a way that makes more sense. If not, you may feel better knowing someone else is also confused and the two of you can ask for clarification from the instructor.
- When responding to another person's paper, avoid being overly harsh and critical with your word choices. The purpose is to give helpful feedback in a constructive manner. However, you should also avoid being too general or too positive. Telling other writers that "everything looks good" doesn't help them improve their paper.
- Most important, when you receive feedback on your paper or your ideas, try to think about them objectively. It is up to you what ideas you choose to use or how you want to revise or approach your assignment. Peer review is a process meant to help you and give you an additional set of eyes.

By keeping these factors in mind, the peer review process can be beneficial for all involved and help create a supportive writing community within the classroom and beyond.

**PRACTICE 3** **Exploring your narrowed topic**

Use two or three prewriting techniques to explore your narrowed topic.

## *Clustering/Mapping*

**Tip** For online mapping tools, visit **http://bubbl.us**.

**Clustering**, also called **mapping**, is like listing except that you arrange your ideas visually. Start by writing your narrowed topic in the center. Then, answer the following questions around the narrowed topic: Why? What interests me? and What do I want to say? Using Chelsea's clustering below as a model, write three answers to these questions. Keep branching out from the ideas until you feel you have fully explored your topic. Note that when Chelsea filled in "Why?" "What interests me?" and "What do I want to say?" she had lots of reasons and ideas that she could use in her writing assignment.

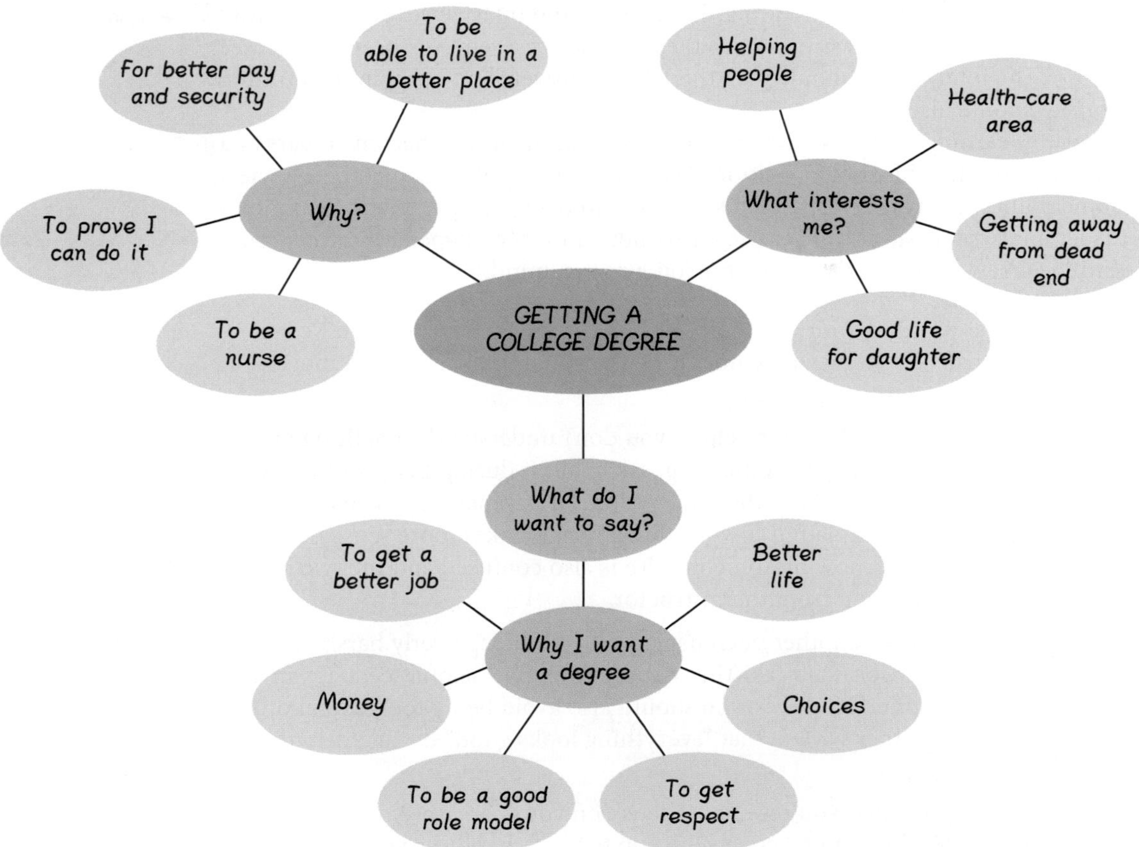
GETTING A COLLEGE DEGREE
Why?
For better pay and security
To be able to live in a better place
To prove I can do it
To be a nurse
What interests me?
Helping people
Health-care area
Getting away from dead end
Good life for daughter
What do I want to say?
Why I want a degree
To get a better job
Better life
Money
Choices
To be a good role model
To get respect

## Using the Internet

Go to www.google.com and type in specific key words about your topic. The search will provide more results than you can use, but it will help you with ideas for your paper. Be sure to make your search terms as specific as possible so that the results are targeted and relevant to your topic. For example, Chelsea typed in "reasons to get a college degree" and got lots of information about aspects of her topic that she did not know much about, such as what a college degree is worth. Make notes about important or useful ideas you get from the Internet.

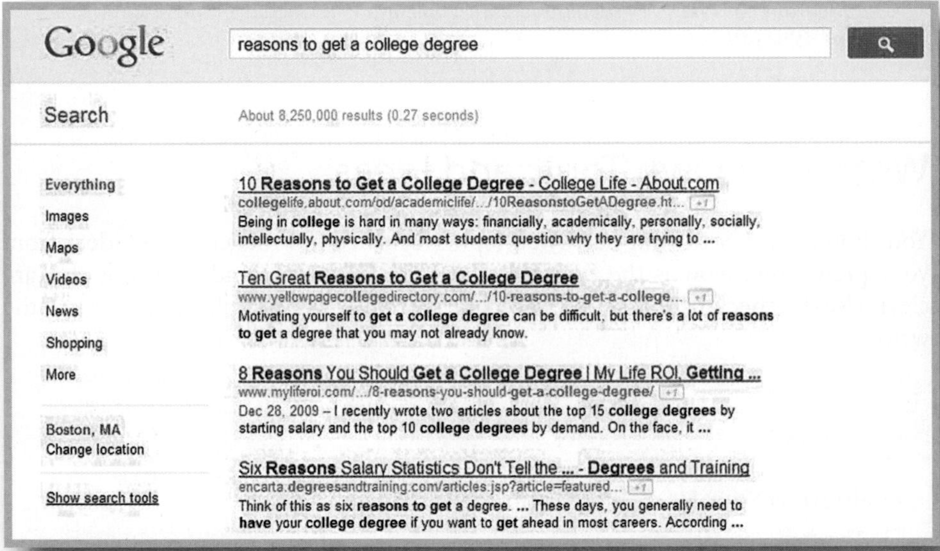
Google
reasons to get a college degree
Search
About 8,250,000 results (0.27 seconds)
Everything
Images
Maps
Videos
News
Shopping
More
Boston, MA
Change location
Show search tools
10 Reasons to Get a College Degree - College Life - About.com
collegelife.about.com/od/academiclife/.../10ReasonstoGetADegree.ht...
Being in college is hard in many ways: financially, academically, personally, socially, intellectually, physically. And most students question why they are trying to ...
Ten Great Reasons to Get a College Degree
www.yellowpagecollegedirectory.com/.../10-reasons-to-get-a-college...
Motivating yourself to get a college degree can be difficult, but there's a lot of reasons to get a degree that you may not already know.
8 Reasons You Should Get a College Degree | My Life ROI. Getting ...
www.myliferoi.com/.../8-reasons-you-should-get-a-college-degree/
Dec 28, 2009 – I recently wrote two articles about the top 15 college degrees by starting salary and the top 10 college degrees by demand. On the face, it ...
Six Reasons Salary Statistics Don't Tell the ... - Degrees and Training
encarta.degreesandtraining.com/articles.jsp?article=featured...
Think of this as six reasons to get a degree. ... These days, you generally need to have your college degree if you want to get ahead in most careers. According ...

## Keeping a Journal

Setting aside a few minutes on a regular schedule to write in a journal will give you a great source of ideas when you need them. What you write does not need to be long or formal. You can use a journal in several ways:

- To record and explore your personal thoughts and feelings
- To comment on things that happen, to you personally or in politics, in your neighborhood, at work, in college, and so on
- To explore situations you do not understand (as you write, you may figure them out)
- To keep track of your opinions on movies you have seen, tv shows you watch, music you've listened to, or books you have read.

One student, Jack, did all these things in the following journal entry.

**Tip** If you start keeping a journal, you might use some of the strategies described by writer Joan Didion. She says, "I write entirely to find out what I'm thinking, what I'm looking at, what I see and what it means. What I want and what I fear."

*Been feeling a little confused about school lately. Doing OK in my classes and still liking the construction tech program. But having some doubts. Elena, another student in my English class, is studying to be a solar tech in a new program at the school. She's going to learn how to install and repair solar energy systems at a facility near campus, and that's pretty cool. Solar seems kind of sci-fi, and I love sci-fi movies. But seriously I'm truly interested in the technology, and some of the skills I've been learning in construction tech would probably transfer. And maybe I'd have a better chance of getting a job in solar energy since it's a field that seems to be growing? Not sure, but something to investigate. Bottom line: I can't get this new idea out of my mind, even though I thought I was sure about construction tech. I guess I'll keep talking with Elena about the solar tech program. And maybe I should meet with one of the instructors in the program? Or visit the solar facility?*

## Write Your Own Topic and Ideas

You should have both your narrowed topic (recorded in Practice 2) and ideas from your prewriting. Now is the time to make sure your topic and ideas about it are clear. Use the checklist that follows to make sure you have completed this step of the writing process.

**CHECKLIST**

### Evaluating Your Narrowed Topic

- ☐ This topic interests me.
- ☐ My narrowed topic is specific.
- ☐ I can write about it in a paragraph or an essay (whichever you have been assigned).
- ☐ I have generated some things to say about this topic.

Now that you have focused your topic, you are ready to create a clear and forceful thesis statement and topic sentences.

## Understand What a Topic Sentence and a Thesis Statement Are

Every good piece of writing has a **main idea**—what the writer wants to get across to the readers about the topic or the writer's position on that topic. A **topic sentence** (for a paragraph) and a **thesis statement** (for an essay) express the writer's main idea. To see the relationship between the thesis statement of an essay and the topic sentences of paragraphs that support a thesis statement, see the diagram on pages 56–57.

In many paragraphs, the main idea is expressed in either the first or last sentence. In essays, the thesis statement is usually one sentence (often the first or last) in an introductory paragraph that contains several other sentences related to the main idea.

A good topic sentence or thesis statement has several basic features.

**Basics of a good topic sentence or thesis statement**

- It fits the size of the assignment.
- It states a single main idea or position about a topic.
- It is specific.
- It is something you can show, explain, or prove.
- It is forceful.

**Weak** Giving children chores teaches them responsibility, and I think doing chores as a kid made me a better adult.

[This statement has more than one point (how chores teach responsibility and how they made the writer a better adult); it is not specific (what is "responsibility"? what does it mean to be a "better adult"?); and it is not forceful (the writer says, "I think").]

**Good** Giving children chores teaches them the responsibilities of taking care of things and completing assigned tasks.

Being assigned chores as a child helped teach me the important adult skills of teamwork and attention to detail.

One way to write a topic sentence for a paragraph or a thesis statement for an essay is to use this basic formula as a start:

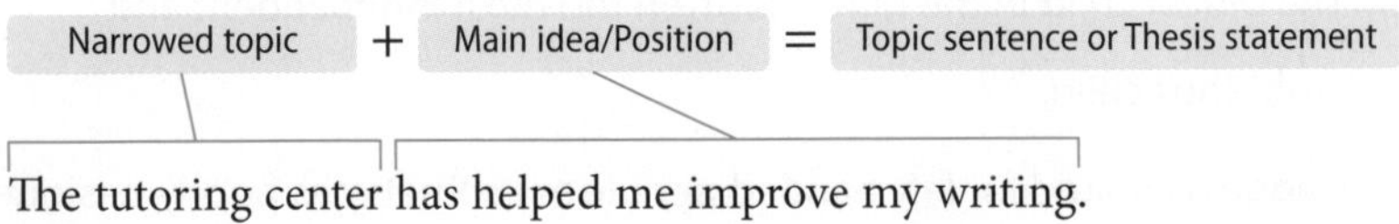
Narrowed topic
+
Main idea/Position
=
Topic sentence or Thesis statement
The tutoring center has helped me improve my writing.

If you have trouble coming up with a main idea or position, look back over the prewriting you did. For example, when the student Chelsea Wilson looked over her prewriting about getting a college degree (see pp. 48–50), she realized that several times she had mentioned the idea of more options for employment, living places, and chances to go on and be a nurse. She could also have chosen to focus on the topic of respect or on issues relating to her young daughter, but she was most drawn to write about the idea of *options*. Here is how she stated her main idea:

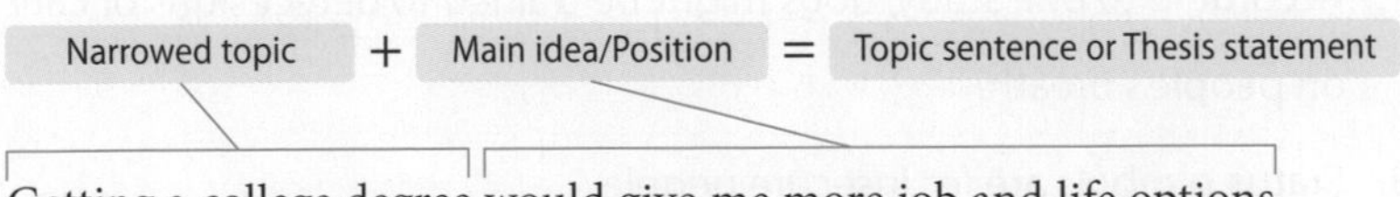
Narrowed topic
+
Main idea/Position
=
Topic sentence or Thesis statement
Getting a college degree would give me more job and life options.

### PRACTICE 4 Finding the topic sentence and main idea

Read the paragraph that follows, and underline the topic sentence. In the spaces below the paragraph, identify the narrowed topic and the main idea.

A recent survey reported that employers consider communication skills more critical to success than technical skills. Employees can learn technical skills on the job and practice them every day. But they need to bring well-developed communication skills to the job. They need to be able to make themselves understood to colleagues, both in speech and in writing. They need to be able to work cooperatively as part of a team. Employers cannot take time to teach communication skills, but without them an employee will have a hard time.

Narrowed Topic: ______________________________

Main Idea: ______________________________

______________________________

### PRACTICE 5 Identifying topics and main ideas

In each of the following sentences, underline the topic and double-underline the main idea about the topic.

**Example:** **Rosie the Riveter was the symbol of working women during World War II.**

1. Discrimination in the workplace is alive and well.
2. The oldest child in the family is often the most independent and ambitious child.
3. Gadgets created for left-handed people are sometimes poorly designed.
4. Presidential campaigns bring out dirty politics.
5. Walking away from a mortgage has become a financial survival strategy for some homeowners.
6. The magazine *Consumer Reports* can help you decide which brands or models are the best value.
7. According to one study, dogs might be trained to detect signs of cancer on people's breath.
8. Status symbols are for insecure people.

9. Some song lyrics have serious messages about important social issues.
10. The Puritans came to America to escape religious intolerance, but they were intolerant themselves.

As you get further along in your writing, you may go back several times to revise the topic sentence or thesis statement based on what you learn as you develop your ideas. Look at how one student revised the example sentence on page 53 to make it more detailed:

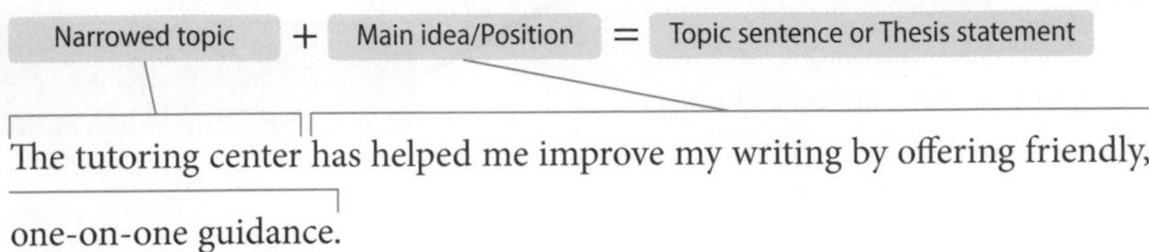
Narrowed topic
+
Main idea/Position
=
Topic sentence or Thesis statement
The tutoring center has helped me improve my writing by offering friendly, one-on-one guidance.

## Practice Developing a Good Topic Sentence or Thesis Statement

The explanations and practices in this section, organized according to the "basics" described previously, will help you write good topic sentences and thesis statements.

### *It Fits the Size of the Assignment*

As you develop a topic sentence or thesis statement, think carefully about the length of the assignment.

Sometimes, a main-idea statement can be the same for a paragraph or essay.

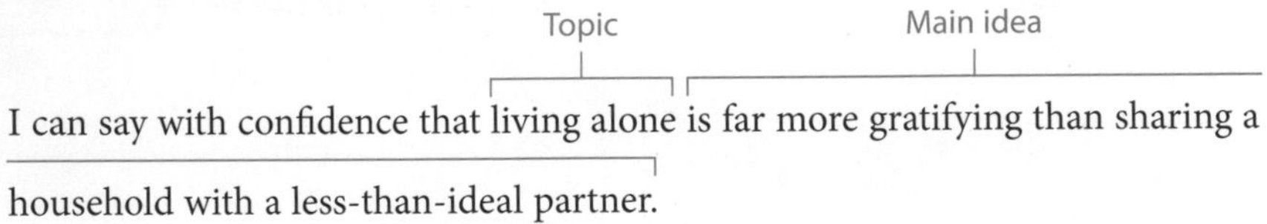
Topic
Main idea
I can say with confidence that living alone is far more gratifying than sharing a household with a less-than-ideal partner.

If the writer had been assigned a paragraph, she might follow the main idea with support sentences and a concluding sentence like those in the "paragraph" diagram on pages 56–57.

If the writer had been assigned an essay, she might develop the same support, but instead of writing single sentences to support her main idea, she would develop each support point into a paragraph. The support sentences she wrote in a paragraph might be topic sentences for support paragraphs. (For more on providing support, see Chapter 4.)

Often, however, a topic sentence for a paragraph is much narrower than a thesis statement for an essay, simply because a paragraph is shorter and allows less development of ideas.

## Relationship between Paragraphs and Essays

For more on the important features of writing, see the Four Basics of Good Writing on page 32.

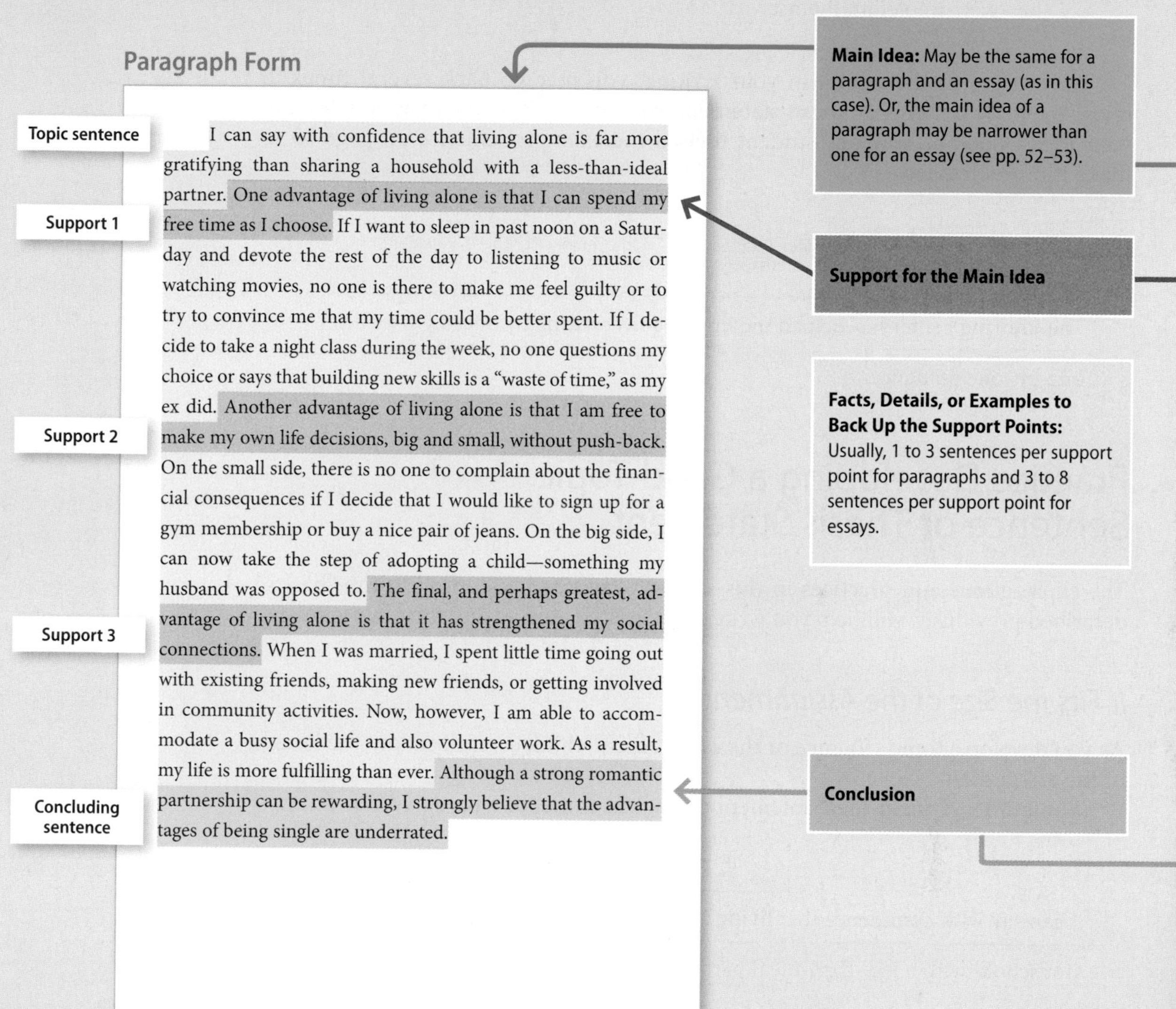
Paragraph Form
Topic sentence
Support 1
Support 2
Support 3
Concluding sentence
I can say with confidence that living alone is far more gratifying than sharing a household with a less-than-ideal partner. One advantage of living alone is that I can spend my free time as I choose. If I want to sleep in past noon on a Saturday and devote the rest of the day to listening to music or watching movies, no one is there to make me feel guilty or to try to convince me that my time could be better spent. If I decide to take a night class during the week, no one questions my choice or says that building new skills is a "waste of time," as my ex did. Another advantage of living alone is that I am free to make my own life decisions, big and small, without push-back. On the small side, there is no one to complain about the financial consequences if I decide that I would like to sign up for a gym membership or buy a nice pair of jeans. On the big side, I can now take the step of adopting a child—something my husband was opposed to. The final, and perhaps greatest, advantage of living alone is that it has strengthened my social connections. When I was married, I spent little time going out with existing friends, making new friends, or getting involved in community activities. Now, however, I am able to accommodate a busy social life and also volunteer work. As a result, my life is more fulfilling than ever. Although a strong romantic partnership can be rewarding, I strongly believe that the advantages of being single are underrated.
Main Idea: May be the same for a paragraph and an essay (as in this case). Or, the main idea of a paragraph may be narrower than one for an essay (see pp. 52–53).
Support for the Main Idea
Facts, Details, or Examples to Back Up the Support Points: Usually, 1 to 3 sentences per support point for paragraphs and 3 to 8 sentences per support point for essays.
Conclusion

## Essay Form

1

Introductory paragraph

As a young woman, I saw being single as a temporary—and undesirable—condition. When, at twenty-four, I married, I considered myself extremely lucky. That was until I spent years in an increasingly unsatisfying relationship that ultimately ended in divorce. Since the divorce, however, my life h

Thesis statement

for the better in many ways. I can now say with confidence that living alone is far more gratifying than sharing a household with a less-than-ideal

Topic sentence 1

One advantage of living alone is that I can spend my free time as I choose. If I want to sleep in past noon on a Saturday and devote the rest of the day to listening to music or watching movies, no one is there to make me feel guilty or to try to convince me that my time could be better spent. If I decide to take a night class during the week, no one questions my choice or says that building new skills is a "waste of time," as my ex did. Also, when I am able to take vacation days, I can spend them relaxing at home, visiting out-of-state family members, or doing something more adventurous. In other words, I can set my own agenda, all the time.

2

Another advantage of living alone i

Topic sentence 2

free to make my own life decisions, big

without push-back. On the small side, there is no one to complain about the financial consequences if I decide that I would like to sign up for a gym membership or buy a nice pair of jeans. On the big

Support paragraphs

now take the step of adopting a child—som

husband was opposed to. I realize that making all my own decisions requires personal responsibility and the ability to take some risks. But, to me, the benefits of independence far outweigh the challenges.

Topic sentence 3

The final, and perhaps greatest, advantage of living alone is that it has strengthened my social connections. When I was married, I spent little time going out with existing friends, making new friends, or getting involved in community activities. If I did not spend nearly all of my free time with my husband, he would complain. Now, however, I am able to accommodate a busy social life and also volunteer work in my community. As a result, my life is more fulfilling than ever.

3

Although a strong romantic partnership can be rewarding, I strongly believe that the advantages of being single are underrated. Consequentl

Concluding paragraph

like to offer one piece of advice to partner

Do not feel sorry for your single friends. One day, you may join their ranks and find that you have never been happier.

Consider how one general topic could be narrowed into an essay topic and into an even more specific paragraph topic.

| General topic | | Narrowed essay topic | | Narrowed paragraph topic |
|---|---|---|---|---|
| Internships | → | How internships can help you get a job | → | One or two important things you can learn from an internship |

**Possible thesis statement (essay)** The skills and connections you gain through a summer internship can help you get a good job after graduation.

[The essay would discuss several benefits of internships, describing the various skills they can teach and the professional connections they can offer to interns.]

**Possible topic sentence (paragraph)** A summer internship is a good way to test whether a particular career is right for you.

[The paragraph would focus on one benefit of internships: They are a way to test out a career. The paragraph might go on to discuss signs that a certain type of work is or is not passing the test.]

### PRACTICE 6 Writing sentences to fit the assignment

Using the following example as a guide, write a thesis statement for the narrowed essay topic and a topic sentence for the narrowed paragraph topic.

**Example:**

**Topic: Sports**

**Narrowed for an essay: Competition in school sports**

**Narrowed for a paragraph: User fees for school sports**

**Possible thesis statement (essay):** *Competition in school sports has reached dangerous levels.*

**Possible topic sentence (paragraph):** *This year's user fees for participation in school sports are too high.*

1. **Topic:** Public service opportunities

   **Narrowed for an essay:** Volunteering at a homeless shelter

   **Narrowed for a paragraph:** My first impression of the homeless shelter

   **Possible thesis statement** (essay): ______________________________

   ______________________________________________

   **Possible topic sentence** (paragraph): ______________________________

   ______________________________________________

2. **Topic:** A personal goal

   **Narrowed for an essay:** Getting healthy

   **Narrowed for a paragraph:** Eating the right foods

   **Possible thesis statement** (essay): ______________________________

   ______________________________________________________________

   **Possible topic sentence** (paragraph): ___________________________

   ______________________________________________________________

3. **Topic:** A great vacation

   **Narrowed for an essay:** A family camping trip

   **Narrowed for a paragraph:** A lesson I learned on our family camping trip

   **Possible thesis statement** (essay): ______________________________

   ______________________________________________________________

   **Possible topic sentence** (paragraph): ___________________________

   ______________________________________________________________

Some topic sentences or thesis statements are too broad for either a short essay or a paragraph. A main idea that is too broad is impossible to show, explain, or prove within the space of a paragraph or short essay.

**Too broad** Art is important.

[How could a writer possibly support such a broad concept in a paragraph or essay?]

**Narrower** Art instruction for young children has surprising benefits.

A topic sentence or thesis statement that is too narrow leaves the writer with little to write about. There is little to show, explain, or prove.

**Too narrow** Buy rechargeable batteries.

[OK, so now what?]

**Broader** Choosing rechargeable batteries over conventional batteries is one action you can take to reduce your effect on the environment.

### PRACTICE 7 Writing topic sentences that are neither too broad nor too narrow

In the following five practice items, three of the topic sentences are either too broad or too narrow, and two of them are OK. In the space to the left of each item, write "B" for too broad, "N" for too narrow, or "OK" for just right.

Rewrite the three weak sentences to make them broader or narrower as needed.

**Example:** B **Life can be tough for soldiers when they come home.**

*We are not providing our returning soldiers with enough help in readjusting to civilian life.*

1. ____ I take public transportation to work.

2. ____ Because of state and national education budget cuts, schools are having to lay off teachers and cut important programs.

3. ____ College is challenging.

4. ____ I would like to be successful in life.

5. ____ Having a positive attitude improves people's ability to function, improves their interactions with others, and reduces stress.

## *It Contains a Single Main Idea*

Your topic sentence or thesis statement should focus on only one main idea. Two main ideas can split and weaken the focus of the writing.

### TOPIC SENTENCE WITH TWO MAIN IDEAS

High schools should sell healthy food instead of junk food, and they should start later in the morning.

The two main ideas are underlined. Although both are good main ideas, together they split both the writer's and the readers' focus. The writer would need to give reasons to support each idea, and the ideas are completely different.

### TOPIC SENTENCE WITH A SINGLE MAIN IDEA

High schools should sell healthy food instead of junk food.

OR

High schools should start later in the morning.

**PRACTICE 8** **Writing sentences with a single main idea**

In each of the following sentences, underline the main idea(s). Identify the sentences that have more than a single main idea by marking an ✗ in the space provided to the left of that item. Put a check mark (✓) next to sentences that have a single main idea.

**Example:** _✗_ **Shopping at secondhand stores is a fun way to save money, and you can meet all kinds of interesting people as you shop.**

1. ____ My younger sister, the baby of the family, was the most adventurous of my four siblings.
2. ____ Servicing hybrid cars is a growing part of automotive technology education, and dealers cannot keep enough hybrids in stock.
3. ____ My brother, Bobby, is incredibly creative, and he takes in stray animals.
4. ____ Pets can actually bring families together, and they require lots of care.
5. ____ Unless people conserve voluntarily, we will deplete our water supply.

## *It Is Specific*

A good topic sentence or thesis statement gives readers specific information so that they know exactly what the writer's main idea is.

**General** Students are often overwhelmed.

[How are students overwhelmed?]

**Specific** Working college students have to learn how to juggle many responsibilities.

One way to make sure your topic sentence or thesis statement is specific is to make it a preview of what you are planning to say in the rest of the paragraph or essay. Just be certain that every point you preview is closely related to your main idea.

**Preview:** Working college students have to learn how to juggle many responsibilities: doing a good job at work, getting to class regularly and on time, being alert in class, and doing the homework assignments.

**Preview:** I have a set routine every Saturday morning that includes sleeping late, going to the gym, and shopping for food.

**PRACTICE 9** **Writing sentences that are specific**

In the space below each item, revise the sentence to make it more specific. There is no one correct answer. As you read the sentences, think about what would make them more understandable to you if you were about to read a paragraph or essay on the topic.

**Example: Marriage can be a wonderful thing.** *Marriage to the right person can add love, companionship, and support to life.*

1. My job is horrible.

_______________

2. Working with others is rewarding.

_______________

3. I am a good worker.

_______________

4. This place could use a lot of improvement.

_______________

5. My science class was challenging.

_______________

## *It Is an Idea You Can Show, Explain, or Prove*

If a main idea is so obvious that it does not need support or if it states a simple fact, you will not have much to say about it.

**Obvious** The Toyota Prius is a top-selling car.

Many people like to take vacations in the summer.

**Revised** Because of rising gas costs and concerns about the environmental impact of carbon emissions, the Toyota Prius is a top-selling car.

The vast and incredible beauty of the Grand Canyon draws crowds of visitors each summer.

**Fact** Employment of medical lab technicians is projected to increase by 14 percent between 2008 and 2018.

Three hundred cities worldwide have bicycle-sharing programs.

**Revised** Population growth and the creation of new types of medical tests mean the employment of lab technicians should increase by 14 percent between 2008 and 2018.

Bicycle-sharing programs are popular, but funding them long-term can be challenging for cities with tight budgets.

**PRACTICE 10** **Writing sentences with ideas you can show, explain, or prove**

Revise the following sentences so that they contain an idea you could show, explain, or prove.

**Example: Leasing a car is popular.**

*Leasing a car has many advantages over buying one.*

1. Texting while driving is dangerous.

   ______________________________

2. My monthly rent is $750.

   ______________________________

3. Health insurance rates rise every year.

   ______________________________

4. Many people in this country work for minimum wage.

   ______________________________

5. Technology is becoming increasingly important.

   ______________________________

## *It Is Forceful*

A good topic sentence or thesis statement is forceful. Do not say you *will* make a point; just make it. Do not say "I think." Just state your point.

**Weak** In my opinion, everyone should exercise.

**Forceful** Everyone should exercise to reduce stress, maintain a healthy weight, and feel better overall.

**Weak** I think student fees are much too high.

**Forceful** Student fees need to be explained and justified.

**PRACTICE 11** **Writing forceful sentences**

Rewrite each of the following sentences to make them more forceful. Also, add details to make the sentences more specific.

**Example: Jason's Market is the best.**

*Jason's Market is clean, organized, and filled with quality products.*

1. I will prove that drug testing in the workplace is an invasion of privacy.

   ______________________________

2. This school does not allow cell phones in class. ______________________

______________________________________________

3. I strongly think I deserve a raise. ______________________

______________________________________________

4. Nancy should be the head of the Students' Association. ______________________

______________________________________________

______________________________________________

5. I think my neighborhood is nice. ______________________

______________________________________________

## Write Your Own Topic Sentence or Thesis Statement

If you have worked through this chapter, you should have a good sense of how to write a topic sentence or thesis statement that includes the five features of a good one (see p. 53).

Before writing your own topic sentence or thesis statement, consider the process that Chelsea Wilson used. First, she narrowed her topic.

**General Topic:** *a personal goal*
**Narrowed topic (for a paragraph):** *why I want to get a nursing degree*
**Narrowed topic (for an essay):** *the many benefits of getting a college degree*

Then, she did prewriting to get ideas about her topic.

**For a paragraph:** *why I want to get a nursing degree*
*make more money*
*get a better job*
*become a respected professional*
*live where I want*
**For an essay:** *the many benefits of getting a college degree*
*get a job as a nurse*
*make more money*
*be a good role model for my daughter*
*be proud of myself*

Next, she was ready to write the statement of her main idea.

**Topic sentence (paragraph):** *My goal is to get a nursing degree.*
**Thesis statement (essay):** *My goal is to get a college degree.*

Finally, Chelsea revised this statement to make it more forceful.

**Topic sentence:** *My goal is to become a registered nurse.*

**Thesis statement:** *I am committed to getting a college degree because it will give me many good job and life options.*

You may want to change the wording of your topic sentence or thesis statement later, but following a sequence like Chelsea's should start you off with a good basic statement of your main idea.

**WRITING ASSIGNMENT**

Write a topic sentence or thesis statement using the narrowed topic you developed earlier in the chapter or one of the following topics (which you will have to narrow).

| | |
|---|---|
| Community service | A holiday or family tradition |
| A controversial issue | A strong belief |
| Dressing for success | Bullying |
| Movies | Exciting experiences |
| Saving money | Juggling many responsibilities |
| Interviewing for jobs | Friendship |
| Music | Learning/teaching cooking skills |

After writing your topic sentence or thesis statement, complete the checklist that follows.

**CHECKLIST**

### Evaluating Your Main Idea

- ☐ It is a complete sentence.
- ☐ It fits the assignment.
- ☐ It includes my topic and the main idea I want to make about it.
- ☐ It states a single main idea.
- ☐ It is specific.
- ☐ It is something I can show, explain, or prove.
- ☐ It is forceful.

Coming up with a good working topic sentence or thesis statement is the foundation of the writing you will do. Now that you know what you want to say, you are ready to learn more about how to show, explain, and prove your main idea to others. The next chapter, "Supporting Your Point," helps you make a strong case, consider what your readers need to know, and provide sufficient details and examples in your paragraph or essay.

## Chapter Review

1. What are four questions that can help you find a good topic? ____________________

2. How can you narrow a topic that is too broad or general? ____________________

3. What are some prewriting techniques? ____________________

4. Write for one minute on "Topics I would like to know more about."

5. The main idea of a piece of writing is ____________________

6. One way to write a topic sentence or a thesis statement is to include the narrowed topic and ____________________

7. The basics of a good topic sentence or thesis statement are ____________________

8. Write for one minute about "What questions I should ask my instructor."

## REFLECTING ON THE JOURNEY

### Skills Learned

Now that you've completed the chapter, share what you've learned about each skill by completing the following chart.

| Skill | What I learned about this skill |
|---|---|
| Understand the difference between a topic and a main idea | |
| Explore and narrow a topic | |
| Write a thesis statement | |
| Write topic sentences | |

# 4

# Supporting Your Point

## Finding Details, Examples, and Facts

## READING ROADMAP

### Learning Objectives

**Chapter Goal:** Learn to support your main idea by presenting strong evidence and details.

**Tools to Achieve the Goal:**

- Key Features of Good Support (p. 68)
- Three Quick Strategies for Generating Support (p. 70)
- Write Your Own Support (p. 72)

### Key Terms

Skim Chapter 4 before reading. Find these words or terms in **bold** type. Put a check mark next to each once you locate it.

____ support
____ primary support points
____ secondary support

### Guided Reading for Chapter 4

Fill out the following chart before you begin reading. For each skill, write what you know about the skill and what you would like to know upon completing the chapter. At the end of the chapter, you will be asked to share what you learned about each skill.

| Skill | When I have used this skill | What I want to know about this skill |
|---|---|---|
| Write primary support points | | |
| Write secondary support points | | |
| Generate support | | |
| Relate support directly to the main idea | | |

# Understand What Support Is

**Support** is the collection of examples, facts, or evidence that shows, explains, or proves your main idea. **Primary support points** are the major ideas that back up your main idea, and **secondary support** gives details to back up your primary support.

## *Key Features of Good Support*

Without support, you *state* the main idea, but you do not *make* the main idea. Consider these unsupported statements:

> The amount shown on my bill is incorrect.
>
> I deserve a raise.
>
> I need a vacation.

The statements may be true, but without good support, they are not convincing. If you sometimes get papers back with the comment "You need to support/develop your ideas," the suggestions in this chapter will help you.

Also, keep in mind that the same point repeated several times is not support. It is just repetition.

| | |
|---|---|
| **Repetition, Not Support** | The amount shown on my bill is incorrect. You overcharged me. It didn't cost that much. The total is wrong. |
| **Support** | The amount shown on my bill is incorrect. I ordered the bacon-cheeseburger plate, which is $6.99 on the menu. On the bill, the order is correct, but the amount is $16.99. |

As you develop support for your main idea, make sure it has these three features.

**Tip** Showing involves providing visual details or other supporting observations. Explaining involves offering specific examples or illustrating aspects of the main idea. Proving involves providing specific evidence, sometimes from outside sources.

**Basics of good support**

- It relates directly to your main idea. Remember that the purpose of support is to show, explain, or prove your main idea.
- It considers your readers and what they will need to know.
- It gives readers enough specific details, particularly through examples, so that they can see what you mean.

## *Support in Paragraphs versus Essays*

Again, primary support points are the major ideas that back up your main idea. In paragraphs, your main idea is expressed in a topic sentence. In both paragraphs and essays, it is important to add enough details (secondary support) about the primary support to make the main idea clear to readers.

In the following paragraph, the topic sentence is underlined twice, the primary support is underlined once, and the details for each primary support point are in italics.

> When I first enrolled in college, I thought that studying history was a waste of time. But after taking two world history classes, I have come to the conclusion that these courses count for far more than some credit hours in my college record. First, learning about historical events has helped me put important current events in perspective. *For instance, by studying the history of migration around the world, I have learned that immigration has been going on for hundreds of years. In addition, it is common in many countries, not just the United States. I have also learned about ways in which various societies have debated immigration, just as Americans are doing today.* Second, history courses have taught me about the power that individual people can have, even under very challenging circumstances. *I was especially inspired by the story of Toussaint L'Ouverture, a former slave who, in the 1790s, led uprisings in the French colony of Saint-Domingue, transforming it into the independent nation of Haiti. Although L'Ouverture faced difficult odds, he persisted and achieved great things.* The biggest benefit of taking history courses is that they have encouraged me to dig more deeply into subjects than I ever have before. *For a paper about the lasting influence of Anne Frank,*[1] *I drew on quotations from her famous diary, on biographies about her, and on essays written by noted historians. The research was fascinating, and I loved piecing together the various facts and insights to come to my own conclusions.* To sum up, I have become hooked on history, and I have a feeling that the lessons it teaches me will be relevant far beyond college.

1. **Anne Frank (1929-1945):** a German Jewish girl who fled to the Netherlands with her family after Adolf Hitler, leader of the Nazi Party, became chancellor of Germany. In 1944, Anne and her family were arrested by the Nazis, and she died in a concentration camp the following year.

In an essay, each primary support point, along with its supporting details, is developed into a separate paragraph. (See the diagram on pages 56–57.) Specifically, each underlined point in the previous paragraph could be turned into a topic sentence that would be supported by the italicized details. However, in preparing an essay on the preceding topic, the writer would want to add more details and examples for each primary support point. Here are some possible additions:

- **For primary support point 1:** more connections between history and current events (one idea: the rise and fall of dictators in past societies and in the modern Middle East)
- **For primary support point 2:** more examples of influential historical figures (one idea: the story of Joan of Arc, who, in the fifteenth century, led the French to victories over English armies)
- **For primary support point 3:** more examples of becoming deeply engaged in historical subjects (one idea: fascination with reprinted diaries or letters of World War II soldiers)

# Practice Supporting a Main Idea

## *Generate Support*

To generate support for the main idea of a paragraph or essay, try one or more of the following strategies.

**Three quick strategies for generating support**

1. *Circle an important word or phrase* in your topic sentence (for a paragraph) or thesis statement (for an essay), and write about it for a few minutes. As you work, refer back to your main idea to make sure you're on the right track.
2. *Reread your topic sentence or thesis statement, and write down the first thought you have.* Then, write down your next thought. Keep going.
3. *Use a prewriting technique* (freewriting, listing, discussing, clustering, and so on) while thinking about your main idea and your audience. Write for three to five minutes without stopping.

**PRACTICE 1 Generating supporting ideas**

Choose one of the following sentences, or your own topic sentence or thesis statement, and use one of the three strategies to generate support just mentioned. Because you will need a good supply of ideas to support your main idea, try to find at least a dozen possible supporting ideas. Keep your answers because you will use them in later practices in this chapter.

1. Some television shows challenge my way of thinking instead of numb my mind.
2. Today there is no such thing as a "typical" college student.
3. Learning happens not only in school but throughout a person's life.
4. Practical intelligence can't be measured by grades.
5. I am an excellent candidate for the job.

## *Select the Best Primary Support*

After you have generated possible support, review your ideas; then, select the best ones to use as primary support. Here you take control of your topic, shaping the way readers will see it and the main idea you are making about it. These ideas are *yours*, and you need to sell them to your audience.

The following steps can help.

**Tip** For a diagram showing the relationship between topic sentences and support in paragraphs, and thesis statements and support in essays, see pages 56–57 of Chapter 3.

1. Carefully read the ideas you have generated.
2. Select three to five primary support points that will be clearest and most convincing to your readers, providing the best examples, facts, and observations to support your main idea. If you are writing a paragraph, these points will become the primary support for your topic sentence. If

you are writing an essay, they will become topic sentences of the individual paragraphs that support your thesis statement.

3. Cross out ideas that are not closely related to your main idea.
4. If you find that you have crossed out most of your ideas and do not have enough left to support your main idea, use one of the three strategies from page 70 to find more.

**PRACTICE 2** **Selecting the best support**

Refer to your response to Practice 1 (p. 70). Of your possible primary support points, choose three to five that you think will best show, explain, or prove your main idea to your readers. Write your three to five points in the space provided.

_______________

_______________

## *Add Secondary Support*

Once you have selected your best primary support points, you need to flesh them out for your readers. Do this by adding **secondary support**, specific examples, facts, and observations to back up your primary support points.

**PRACTICE 3** **Adding secondary support**

Using your answers to Practice 2, choose three primary support points, and write them in the spaces indicated below. Then, read each of them carefully, and write down at least three supporting details (secondary support) for each one. For examples of secondary support, see the example paragraph on page 69.

Primary support point 1:

_______________

Supporting details: _______________

_______________

Primary support point 2:

_______________

Supporting details: _______________

_______________

Primary support point 3:

_______________

Supporting details: _______________

_______________

## Write Your Own Support

Before developing your own support for a main idea, look at how Chelsea developed support for her paragraph.

**Topic sentence:** *My goal is to get a nursing degree.*

First, she did some prewriting (using the listing technique) and selected the best primary support points, while eliminating ones she didn't think she would use.

### Primary support points

GETTING AN LPN DEGREE

*nurses help people and I want to do that*
*jobs all over the country*
*good jobs with decent pay*
~~*good setting, clean*~~
*a profession, not just a job*
*opportunity, like RN*
*bigger place, more money*
*treated with respect*
*role model*
*pride in myself and my work, what I've done*
~~*good benefits*~~
~~*nice people to work with*~~
*may get paid to take more classes—chance for further professional development*
~~*uniform so not lots of money for clothes*~~
~~*I'll be something*~~

Chelsea noticed that some of her notes were related to the same subject, so she arranged them into related clusters, with the smaller points indented under the larger ones.

### Organized list of support points

*good job*
- *decent pay*
- *jobs all over the country*

*a profession, not just a job*
- *treated with respect*
- *opportunity for the future (like RN)*
- *maybe get paid to take more classes?*

*pride/achievement*
- *a job that helps people*
- *I would take pride in my hard work*
- *I'd be a role model*

Then, she took the notes she made and organized them into primary support and supporting details. Notice how she changed and reorganized some of her smaller points.

**Primary support:** *Being an LPN is an excellent job.*

**Supporting details:** *The pay is regular and averages about $40,000 a year.*

*I could afford to move to a bigger and better place with more room for my daughter and work fewer hours.*

**Primary support:** *Nursing is a profession, not just a job.*

**Supporting details:** *Nurses help care for people, an important job, giving to the world.*

*Future opportunities, like becoming an RN with more money and responsibility.*

*People respect nurses.*

**Primary support:** *Being a nurse will be a great achievement for me.*

**Supporting details:** *I will have worked hard and met my goal.*

*I will respect myself and be proud of what I do.*

*I will be a good role model for my daughter.*

**WRITING ASSIGNMENT**

Develop primary support points and supporting details using your topic sentence or thesis statement from Chapter 3 or one of the following topic sentences/thesis statements.

Wearing seatbelts in cars should be/should not be mandatory

The drinking age should/should not be lowered.

Going to college is/is not essential.

People who do not speak "proper" English are discriminated against.

Most people in the United States could/could not live without technology today.

After developing your support, complete the following checklist.

**CHECKLIST**

### Evaluating Your Support

- ☐ It is directly related to my main idea.
- ☐ It uses examples, facts, and observations that will make sense to my readers.
- ☐ It includes enough specific details to show my readers exactly what I mean.

Once you have pulled together your primary support points and secondary supporting details, you are ready for the next step: drafting a paragraph or essay based on a plan. For more information, go on to the next chapter.

## Chapter Review

1. Support points are examples, facts, or evidence that __________, __________, or __________ your main idea.
2. Three basics of good support are: ____________________________________________
3. To generate support, try these three strategies: ____________________________________________
4. When you have selected your primary support points, what should you then add? ____________________________________________
5. Write for one minute about "What questions I should ask my instructor."

## REFLECTING ON THE JOURNEY

### Skills Learned

Now that you've completed the chapter, share what you've learned about each skill by completing the following chart.

| Skill | What I learned about this skill |
|---|---|
| Write primary support points | |
| Write secondary support points | |
| Generate support | |
| Relate support directly to the main idea | |

# 5

# Drafting and Revising

## The Writing Process

## READING ROADMAP

### Learning Objectives

**Chapter Goal:** Learn how to draft a full paragraph or essay and revise and edit it.

**Tools to Achieve the Goal:**

- Basics of a Good Draft (p. 76)
- Sample Outline for a Paragraph and Essay (p. 79)
- Basics of a Good Introduction (p. 84)
- Basics of a Good Conclusion (p. 86)
- Tips for Revising Your Writing (p. 91)
- Checklist for Revision (pp. 91–92)
- Special Note on Plagiarism (pp. 98–100)

### Key Terms

Skim Chapter 5 before reading. Find these words or terms in **bold** type. Put a check mark next to each once you locate it.

____ draft
____ order
____ space order
____ time order
____ order of importance
____ outline
____ concluding sentence
____ title
____ revising
____ editing
____ unity
____ coherence
____ transitions
____ key word
____ plagiarism

### Guided Reading for Chapter 5

Fill out the following chart before you begin reading. For each skill, write what you know about the skill and what you would like to know upon completing the chapter. At the end of the chapter, you will be asked to share what you learned about each skill.

| Skill | When I have used this skill | What I want to know about this skill |
|---|---|---|
| Use an outline to draft a paragraph or essay | | |
| Draft a paragraph or essay with a thesis statement and/or topic sentences | | |
| Draft an effective introduction | | |
| Draft an effective conclusion | | |
| Revise for unity, coherence, and detail | | |
| Avoid plagiarism | | |

LaunchPadSolo

Visit **LaunchPad Solo for Readers and Writers > Writing Process** for more tutorials, videos, and practice with drafting and revising.

## Understand What a Draft Is

A **draft** is the first whole version of all your ideas put together in a piece of writing. Do the best job you can in drafting but know that you can make changes later.

**Basics of a good draft**

- It has a topic sentence (for a paragraph) and a thesis statement (for an essay) that states a clear main idea.
- It has a logical organization of ideas.
- It has primary and secondary support that shows, explains, or proves the main idea.
- It has a conclusion that makes an observation about the main idea.
- It follows standard paragraph form (see p. 35) or standard essay form (see p. 36).

Two good first steps to drafting a paragraph or essay are (1) to arrange the ideas that you have generated in an order that makes sense and (2) to write out a plan for your draft. We will look at these steps next.

## Arrange Your Ideas

In writing, **order** means the sequence in which you present your ideas: what comes first, what comes next, and so on. There are three common ways of ordering—arranging—your ideas: time order (also called chronological order), space order, and order of importance.

Read the paragraph examples that follow. In each paragraph, the topic sentences are underlined twice, the primary support points are underlined once, and the secondary support is in italics.

### *Use Time Order to Write about Events*

Use **time order** (chronological order) to arrange points according to when they happened. Time order works best when you are writing about events. You can go from

- First to last or last to first
- Most recent to least recent or least recent to most recent

**Example using time order**

Officer Meredith Pavlovic's traffic stop of August 23, 2011, was fairly typical of an investigation and arrest for drunk driving. First, at around 12:15 a.m. that day, she noticed that the driver of a blue Honda Civic was acting suspiciously. *The car was weaving between the fast and center lanes of Interstate 93 North near exit 12. In addition, it was proceeding at approximately 45 mph in a 55 mph zone.* Therefore, Officer Pavlovic took the second step of pulling the driver over for a closer investigation. *The driver's license told Officer Pavlovic that the driver was twenty-six-year-old Paul Brownwell. Brownwell's red eyes, slurred speech, and alcohol-tainted breath told Officer Pavlovic that Brownwell was very drunk.* But she had to be absolutely sure. Thus, as a next step, she tested his balance and blood alcohol level. *The results were that Brownwell could barely get out of the car, let alone stand on one foot. Also, a Breathalyzer test showed that his blood alcohol level was 0.13, well over the legal limit of 0.08.* These results meant an arrest for Brownwell, an unfortunate outcome for him, but a lucky one for other people on the road at that time.

What kind of time order does the author use? ______________________________

## *Use Space Order to Describe Objects, Places, or People*

Use **space order** to arrange ideas so that your readers picture your topic the way you see it. Space order usually works best when you are writing about a physical object or place or a person's appearance. You can move from

- Top to bottom or bottom to top
- Near to far or far to near
- Left to right or right to left
- Back to front or front to back

**Example using space order**

I was gazing at my son's feet, in awe. There were ten toes, and they were no bigger than my fingernail. *How could something so small be moving so quickly?* Staring at those little toes squirming around as I tried to put socks on them, I had to laugh because the chubby little tree trunks that his dad and I call legs decided to get in on the action. Those full kicks that I had felt for the past several months and that had felt like someone performing kung-fu on my internal organs were now free and he clearly enjoyed that open space. Nothing, however, could prepare me for that tubby little belly. *So small, round, and smooth – yet it bounced up and down with each giggle, burp, and cry.* Two large sausage-like appendages turned into arms with long, slender fingers and fingernails that were no larger than the head of a pin, or so it appeared. But what did all that matter when the true beauty perched right atop his non-existent neck: *that gorgeous, round head covered with brown peach fuzz, sticking up in all directions.* Add all the pieces together, and all you see is love.

What type of space order does the example use? ______________________________

### *Use Order of Importance to Emphasize a Particular Point*

Use **order of importance** to arrange points according to their significance, interest, or surprise value. Usually, save the most important point for last.

**Example using order of importance**

Many parents today do not realize that there is a serious problem in their own home: prescription drug abuse. Unfortunately, we live in a day and age where the answer for many different problems is a prescription drug of some type. *We are prescribed drugs for pain, illness, mental disorders, sleep disorders, and even sexual problems.* With so many different disorders or problems that need treatment today, it is likely that any household has at least two or three active prescriptions at any one time, but who is actually using and taking those pills? News reports have shown that adults do not typically think to take the same precautions with prescriptions as they would with other dangerous substances, *namely weapons like guns or knives*; however, pills are just as deadly and far more addicting. If you are not keeping your prescriptions locked up, you are not keeping your home and your children safe.

What is the writer's most important point? ______________________________

__________________________________________________

## Make a Plan

**Tip** Try using the cut-and-paste function on your computer to experiment with different ways to order support for your main idea. Doing so will give you a good sense of how your final paragraph or final essay will look.

When you have decided how to order your primary support points, it is time to make a more detailed plan for your paragraph or essay. A good, visual way to plan a draft is to arrange your ideas in an outline. An **outline** lists the topic sentence (for a paragraph) or thesis statement (for an essay), the primary support points for the topic sentence or thesis statement, and secondary supporting details for each of the support points. It provides a map of your ideas that you can follow as you write.

### *Outlining Paragraphs*

Look at the outline Chelsea Wilson created with the support she wrote. She had already grouped together similar points and put the more specific details under the primary support (see p. 72). When she thought about how to order her ideas, the only way that made sense to her was by importance. If she had been telling the steps she would take to become a nurse, time order would have worked well. If she had been describing a setting where nurses work, space order would have been a good choice. However, because she was writing about why she wanted to get a college degree and become a nurse, she decided to arrange her reasons in order of importance. Notice that Chelsea also strengthened her topic sentence and made changes in her primary support and secondary support. At each stage, her ideas and the way she expressed them changed as she got closer to what she wanted to say.

**Sample outline for a paragraph**

**Topic sentence:** *Becoming a nurse is a goal of mine because it offers so much that I value.*

**Primary support 1:** *It is a good and practical job.*

**Supporting details:** *Licensed practical nurses make an average of $40,000 per year. That amount is much more than I make now. With that salary, I could move to a better place with my daughter and give her more, including more time.*

**Primary support 2:** *Nursing is a profession, not just a job.*

**Supporting details:** *It helps people who are sick and in need. Being an LPN offers great opportunities, like the chance to go on to become a registered nurse, with more money and responsibility. People respect nurses.*

**Primary support 3:** *I will respect and be proud of myself for achieving my goal through hard work.*

**Supporting details:** *I will be a good role model for my daughter. I will help her and others, but I will also be helping myself by knowing that I can accomplish good things.*

**Conclusion:** *Reaching my goal is important to me and worth the work.*

## *Outlining Essays*

The outline that follows is for a typical five-paragraph essay, in which three body paragraphs (built around three topic sentences) support a thesis statement. The thesis statement is included in an introductory paragraph; the fifth paragraph is the conclusion. However, essays may include more or fewer than five paragraphs, depending on the size and complexity of the topic.

This example is a "formal" outline form, with letters and numbers to distinguish between primary supporting and secondary supporting details. Some instructors require this format. If you are making an outline just for yourself, you might choose to write a less formal outline, simply indenting the secondary supporting details under the primary support rather than using numbers and letters.

**Sample outline for a five-paragraph essay**

**Thesis statement** (part of introductory paragraph 1)

A. **Topic sentence for support point 1** (paragraph 2)
   1. Supporting detail 1 for support point 1
   2. Supporting detail 2 for support point 1 (and so on)

B. **Topic sentence for support point 2** (paragraph 3)
   1. Supporting detail 1 for support point 2
   2. Supporting detail 2 for support point 2 (and so on)

C. **Topic sentence for support point 3** (paragraph 4)
   1. Supporting detail 1 for support point 3
   2. Supporting detail 2 for support point 3 (and so on)

**Concluding paragraph** (paragraph 5)

**PRACTICE 1** **Making an outline**

Reread the paragraph on pages 76–77 that illustrates time order of organization. Then, make an outline for it in the space provided.

**Topic sentence:** ______________________________

______________________________

**Primary support 1:** ______________________________

______________________________

1. **Supporting detail:** ______________________________

   ______________________________

2. **Supporting detail:** ______________________________

   ______________________________

**Primary support 2:** ______________________________

______________________________

1. **Supporting detail:** ______________________________

   ______________________________

2. **Supporting detail:** ______________________________

   ______________________________

   ______________________________

**Primary support 3:** ______________________________

______________________________

1. **Supporting detail:** ______________________________

   ______________________________

2. **Supporting detail:** ______________________________

   ______________________________

## Practice Writing a Draft Paragraph

As you write your paragraph, you will need to go through the steps in the following sections. Also, refer to the Basics of a Good Draft on page 76.

### *Write a Draft Using Complete Sentences*

Write your draft with your outline in front of you. Be sure to include your topic sentence, and express each point in a complete sentence. As you write, you may want to add support or change the order. It is OK to make changes from your outline as you write.

Read the following paragraph, annotated to show the various parts of the paragraph.

**Parabens: Widely Used Chemicals Spark New Cautions** — Title

Parabens, preservatives used in many cosmetics and personal-care products, are raising concerns with more and more consumers. In some people, parabens cause allergic reactions, but the effects of these chemicals may be more than skin deep. After being applied to the face or body, parabens can enter the bloodstream, where they have been found to mimic the hormone estrogen. Because long-term exposure to estrogen can increase the risk of breast cancer, researchers have tried to determine whether there is any link between parabens and breast cancer. So far, the findings have been inconclusive. One study found parabens in the breast cancer tissue of some research subjects. However, the study was small, and based on its results, it cannot be said that parabens actually cause cancer. Nevertheless, some consumers wish to reduce their use of paraben-containing products or to avoid them altogether. To do so, they carefully read the labels of personal-care products, looking out for ingredients like butylparaben, ethylparaben, methylparaben, isopropyl, and propylparaben. All these chemicals are parabens. Consumers who do not wish to give up parabens entirely might consider avoiding only those paraben-containing products, like lotions and makeup, that stay on the skin for an extended period. Products that are rinsed away quickly, like shampoos and soaps, do not have as much time to be absorbed through the skin.

Topic sentence

Support

Although paragraphs typically begin with topic sentences, they may also begin with a quote, an example, or a surprising fact or idea. The topic sentence is then presented later in the paragraph. For examples of various introductory techniques, see pages 83–86.

**Tip** For more on topic sentences, see Chapter 3.

## *Write a Concluding Sentence*

A **concluding sentence** refers back to the main idea and makes an observation based on what you have written. The concluding sentence does not just repeat the topic sentence.

In the preceding paragraph, the main idea, expressed in the topic sentence, is "Parabens, preservatives used in many cosmetics and personal-care products, are raising concerns with more and more consumers."

A good conclusion might be, "Given the growing concerns about parabens and uncertainties about their potential dangers, more research is clearly needed." This sentence **refers back to the main idea** by repeating the words *parabens* and *concerns*. It **makes an observation** by stating, "more research is clearly needed."

Concluding paragraphs for essays are discussed on pages 86–87.

### PRACTICE 2 Writing concluding sentences

Read the following paragraphs, and write a concluding sentence for each one.

1. One of the most valuable ways parents can help children is to read to them. Reading together is a good way for parents and children to relax,

and it is sometimes the only "quality" time they spend together during a busy day. Reading develops children's vocabulary. They understand more words and are likely to learn new words more easily than children who are not read to. Also, hearing the words aloud helps children's pronunciation and makes them more confident with oral language. In addition, reading at home increases children's chances of success in school because reading is required in every course in every grade.

Possible concluding sentence: ______________________________

______________________________

______________________________

2. Almost everyone uses certain memory devices, called mnemonics. One of them is the alphabet song. If you want to remember what letter comes after j, you will probably sing the alphabet song in your head. Another is the "Thirty days hath September" rhyme that people use when they want to know how many days are in a certain month. Another mnemonic device is the rhyme "In 1492, Columbus sailed the ocean blue."

Possible concluding sentence: ______________________________

______________________________

# Practice Writing a Draft Essay

The basics of a good essay draft are all listed on page 76. In addition,

- The essay should include an introductory paragraph that draws readers in and includes the thesis statement.
- The topic sentences for the paragraphs that follow the introduction should directly support the thesis statement. In turn, each topic sentence should be backed by enough support.
- The conclusion should be a full paragraph rather than a single sentence.

Let's start by looking at topic sentences and support for them.

## *Write Topic Sentences, and Draft the Body of the Essay*

When you start to draft your essay, use your outline to write complete sentences for your primary support points. These sentences will serve as the topic sentences for the body paragraphs of your essay.

**PRACTICE 3** **Writing topic sentences**

Each thesis statement that follows has support points that could be topic sentences for the body paragraphs of an essay. For each support point, write a topic sentence.

**Example**

**Thesis statement: My daughter is showing definite signs of becoming a teenager.**

**Support point: constantly texting friends**

**Topic sentence:** *She texts friends constantly, even when they are sitting with her while I'm driving them.*

**Support point: doesn't want me to know what's going on**

**Topic sentence:** *She used to tell me everything, but now she is secretive and private.*

**Support point: developing an "attitude"**

**Topic sentence:** *The surest and most annoying sign that she is becoming a teenager is that she has developed a definite "attitude."*

**Thesis statement:** The Latin American influence is evident in many areas of U.S. culture.

**Support point:** Spanish language used in lots of places

**Topic sentence:** ______________________________

**Support point:** lots of different kinds of foods

**Topic sentence:** ______________________________

**Support point:** new kinds of music and popular musicians

**Topic sentence:** ______________________________

Drafting topic sentences for your essay is a good way to start drafting the body of the essay (the paragraphs that support each of these topic sentences). As you write support for your topic sentences, refer back to your outline, where you listed supporting details. (For an example, see Chelsea Wilson's outline on page 79.) Turn these supporting details into complete sentences, and add additional support if necessary. (Prewriting techniques can help here; see Chapter 3.) Don't let yourself get stalled if you are having trouble with one word or sentence. Just keep writing. Remember that a draft is a first try; you will have time later to improve it.

## *Write an Introduction*

The introduction to your essay captures your readers' interest and presents the main idea. Ask yourself: How can I sell my essay to readers? You need to market your main idea.

**Basics of a good introduction**

- It should catch readers' attention.
- It should present the thesis statement of the essay, usually in the first or the last sentence of an introductory paragraph.
- It should give readers a clear idea of what the essay will cover.

Here are some common kinds of introductions that spark readers' interest. In each one, the introductory technique is in boldface. These introductions are not the only ways to start essays, but they should give you some useful models.

## OPEN WITH A QUOTATION

A good, short quotation definitely gets people interested. It must lead naturally into your main idea, however, and not be there just for effect. If you start with a quotation, make sure you tell the reader who the speaker is.

> **"Never before had I truly felt such an extreme sense of estrangement and alienation,"** [a Vanderbilt student] says of his first few months. **"I quickly realized that although I may look the part, my cultural and socio-economic backgrounds were vastly different from those of my predominantly white, affluent peers. I wanted to leave."**
>
> —Liz Riggs, "What It's Like to Be the First Person in Your Family to Go to College"

## GIVE AN EXAMPLE, OR TELL A STORY

People like stories, so opening an essay with a brief story or example often draws readers in.

> **The bank called today, and I told them my deposit was in the mail, even though I hadn't written a check yet.** It'd been a rough day. The baby I'm pregnant with decided to do aerobics on my lungs for two hours, our three-year-old daughter painted the living-room couch with lipstick, the IRS put me on hold for an hour, and I was late to a business meeting because I was tired.
>
> —Stephanie Ericsson, "The Ways We Lie"

## START WITH A SURPRISING FACT OR IDEA

Surprises capture people's interest. The more unexpected and surprising something is, the more likely people are to notice it.

> **In some places, towns essentially shut down in the afternoon while everyone goes home for a siesta.** Unfortunately, in the U.S.—more bound to our corporate lifestyles than our health—a mid-day nap is seen as a luxury and, in some cases, a sign of pure laziness. But before you feel guilty about that weekend snooze or falling asleep during a movie, rest assured that napping is actually good for you and a completely natural phenomena in the circadian (sleep-wake cycle) rhythm.
>
> —Elizabeth Renter, "Napping Can Dramatically Increase Learning, Memory, Awareness, and More"

### OFFER A STRONG OPINION OR POSITION

The stronger the opinion, the more likely it is that your readers will pay attention. Don't write wimpy introductions. Make your point and shout it!

> **Yes, money can buy happiness, but probably not in the way you imagined.** Spending it on yourself may not do much for your spirits, but spending it on others will make you happier, according to a report from a team of social psychologists in the new issue of *Science*.
>
> —John Tierney, "Yes, Money Can Buy Happiness"

### ASK A QUESTION

A question needs an answer, so if you start your introduction with a question, your readers will need to read on to get the answer.

> **At the end of a tour of Catskill Animal Sanctuary last year, a visitor who'd just been kissed by cows and held chickens in his lap said to me, "OK. I get it. How do I start?"**
>
> —Kathy Stevens, "Ten Tips for Easing into Plant-Based Eating"

**Tip** If you get stuck while writing your introductory statement, try one or more of the prewriting techniques described in Chapter 3 on pages 48–52.

#### PRACTICE 4 Marketing your main idea

As you know from advertisements, a good writer can make just about anything sound interesting. For each of the following topics, write an introductory statement using the technique indicated. Some of these topics are purposely dull to show you that you can make an interesting statement about almost any subject, if you put your mind to it.

**Example**

**Topic:** **Reality TV**

**Technique:** **Question**

*Exactly how many recent top-selling songs have been recorded by former contestants of reality TV singing contests?*

1. **Topic:** Credit cards

   **Technique:** Surprising fact or idea

   ______________________________

2. **Topic:** Role of the elderly in society

   **Technique:** Question

   ______________________________

3. **Topic:** Stress

   **Technique:** Quote (You can make up a good one.)

   ______________________________________________

**PRACTICE 5** **Identifying strong introductions**

In a newspaper or magazine, an online news site, an advertising flier—or anything written—find a strong introduction. Bring it to class and explain why you chose it as an example.

## *Write a Conclusion*

When they have finished the body of their essay, some writers believe their work is done—but it isn't quite finished. Remember that people usually remember best what they see, hear, or read last. Use your concluding paragraph to drive your main idea home one final time. Make sure your conclusion has the same energy as the rest of the essay, if not more.

**Basics of a good essay conclusion**

- It refers back to the main idea.
- It sums up what has been covered in the essay.
- It makes a further observation or point.

In general, a good conclusion creates a sense of completion. It brings readers back to where they started, but it also shows them how far they have come.

One of the best ways to end an essay is to refer directly to something in the introduction. If you asked a question, re-ask and answer it. If you started a story, finish it. If you used a quote, use another one—maybe a quote by the same person or maybe one by another person on the same topic. Or, use some of the same words you used in your introduction. Look again at one of the introductions you read earlier, and notice how the writer concluded her essay. Pay special attention to the text in boldface.

**Ericsson's introduction**

The bank called today, and I told them my deposit was in the mail, even though I hadn't written a check yet. It'd been a rough day. The baby I'm pregnant with decided to do aerobics on my lungs for two hours, our three-year-old daughter painted the living-room couch with lipstick, the IRS put me on hold for an hour, and I was late to a business meeting because I was tired.

— Stephanie Ericsson, "The Ways We Lie"

**Ericsson's conclusion**

**Maybe if I don't tell the bank the check's in the mail I'll be less tolerant of the lies told to me every day.** A country song I once heard said it all for me, "You've got to stand for something or you'll fall for anything."

— Stephanie Ericsson, "The Ways We Lie"

**PRACTICE 6** **Finding good introductions and conclusions**

In a newspaper or magazine or anything written, find a piece of writing that has a strong introduction and conclusion. (You may want to use what you found for Practice 5.) Answer the questions that follow.

1. What method of introduction is used? ______________________
2. What does the conclusion do? (Restate the main idea? Sum up the support? Make a further observation?) ______________________
______________________
3. How are the introduction and the conclusion linked? ______________________
______________________

## *Title Your Essay*

Even if your **title** is the last part of the essay you write, it is the first thing readers read. Use your title to get your readers' attention and to tell them, in a brief way, what your paper is about. Use vivid, strong, specific words.

### Basics of a good essay title

- It makes people want to read the essay.
- It hints at the main idea (thesis statement), but it does not repeat it.

One way to find a good title is to consider the type of essay you are writing. If you are writing an argument (as you will in Chapter 14), state your position in your title. If you are telling your readers how to do something (as you will in Chapter 9), try using the term *steps* or *how to* in the title. This way, your readers will know immediately not only what you are writing about but how you will discuss it.

**Tip** Center your title at the top of the page before the first paragraph. Do not put quotation marks around it or underline it.

**PRACTICE 7** **Titling an essay**

Reread the paragraphs on pages 86–87, and write an alternate title for the essay that they belong to.

Ericsson's introduction/conclusion: ______________________

## Write Your Own Draft Paragraph or Essay

Before you draft your own paragraph, read Chelsea Wilson's annotated draft. It is based on her outline from page 79.

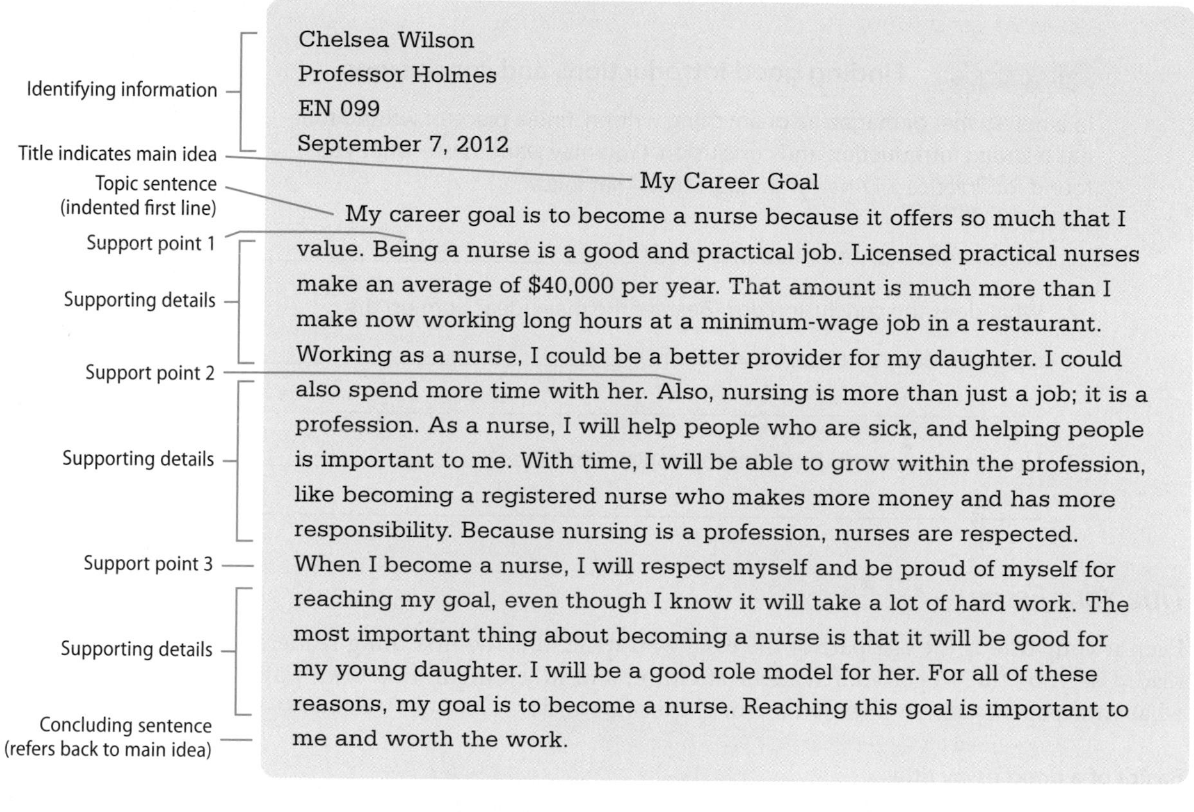

Identifying information
Title indicates main idea
Topic sentence (indented first line)
Support point 1
Supporting details
Support point 2
Supporting details
Support point 3
Supporting details
Concluding sentence (refers back to main idea)

Chelsea Wilson
Professor Holmes
EN 099
September 7, 2012

My Career Goal

My career goal is to become a nurse because it offers so much that I value. Being a nurse is a good and practical job. Licensed practical nurses make an average of $40,000 per year. That amount is much more than I make now working long hours at a minimum-wage job in a restaurant. Working as a nurse, I could be a better provider for my daughter. I could also spend more time with her. Also, nursing is more than just a job; it is a profession. As a nurse, I will help people who are sick, and helping people is important to me. With time, I will be able to grow within the profession, like becoming a registered nurse who makes more money and has more responsibility. Because nursing is a profession, nurses are respected. When I become a nurse, I will respect myself and be proud of myself for reaching my goal, even though I know it will take a lot of hard work. The most important thing about becoming a nurse is that it will be good for my young daughter. I will be a good role model for her. For all of these reasons, my goal is to become a nurse. Reaching this goal is important to me and worth the work.

**WRITING ASSIGNMENT** **Paragraph**

Write a draft paragraph using what you have developed in previous chapters or one of the following topic sentences. If you use one of the topic sentences below, you may want to revise it to fit what you want to say.

Being a good __________ requires __________.

I can find any number of ways to waste my time.

So many decisions are involved in going to college.

The most important thing to me in life is __________.

After writing your draft paragraph, complete the following checklist.

**CHECKLIST**

### Evaluating Your Draft Paragraph

- ☐ It has a clear, confident topic sentence that states my main idea.
- ☐ Each primary support point is backed up with supporting details, examples, or facts.

- ☐ The support is arranged in a logical order.
- ☐ The concluding sentence reminds readers of my main idea and makes an observation.
- ☐ The title reinforces the main idea.
- ☐ All the sentences are complete, consisting of a subject and verb, and expressing a complete thought.
- ☐ The draft is properly formatted:
  - My name, my instructor's name, the course, and the date appear in the upper left corner.
  - The first sentence of the paragraph is indented, and the text is double-spaced (for easier revision).
- ☐ I have followed any other formatting guidelines provided by my instructor.

Before you draft your own essay, read Chelsea Wilson's annotated draft of her essay.

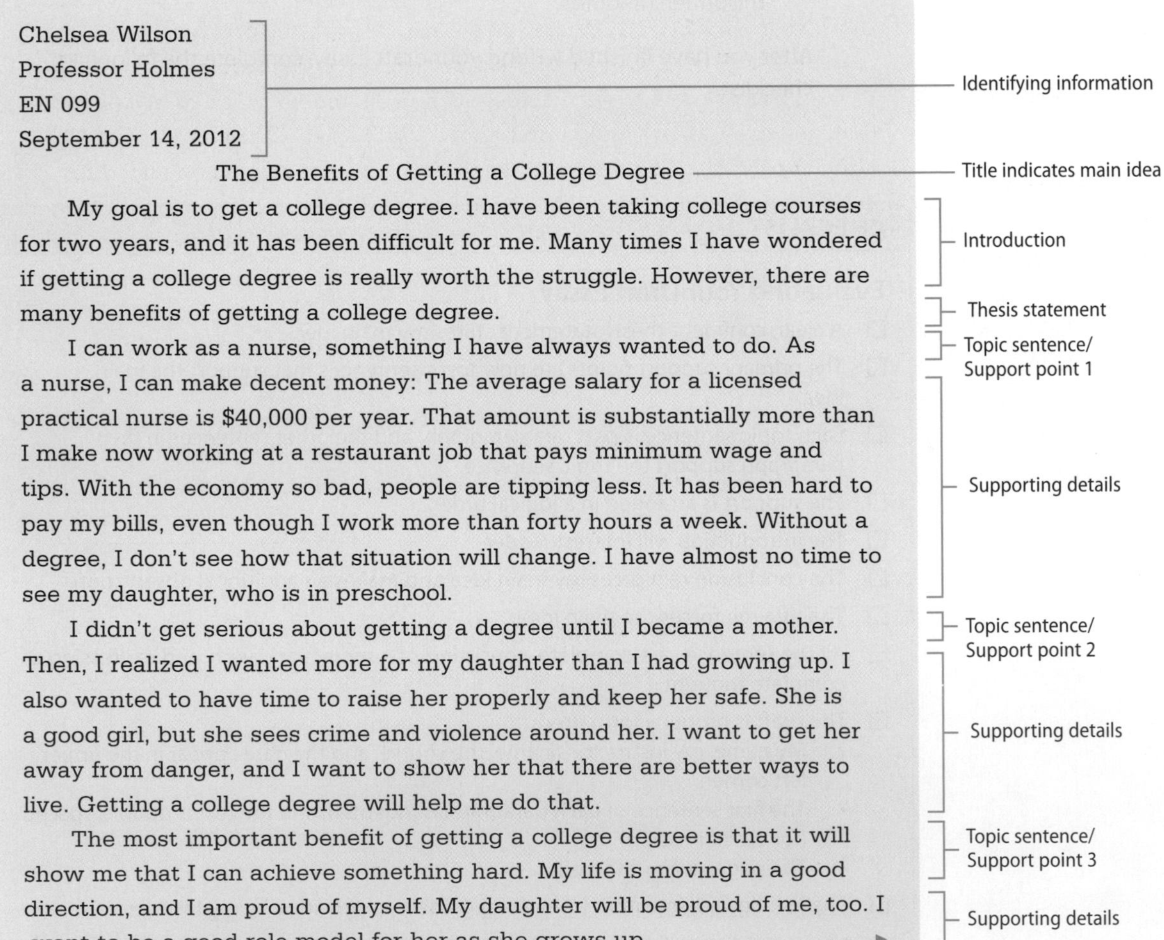

Chelsea Wilson
Professor Holmes
EN 099
September 14, 2012

The Benefits of Getting a College Degree

My goal is to get a college degree. I have been taking college courses for two years, and it has been difficult for me. Many times I have wondered if getting a college degree is really worth the struggle. However, there are many benefits of getting a college degree.

I can work as a nurse, something I have always wanted to do. As a nurse, I can make decent money: The average salary for a licensed practical nurse is $40,000 per year. That amount is substantially more than I make now working at a restaurant job that pays minimum wage and tips. With the economy so bad, people are tipping less. It has been hard to pay my bills, even though I work more than forty hours a week. Without a degree, I don't see how that situation will change. I have almost no time to see my daughter, who is in preschool.

I didn't get serious about getting a degree until I became a mother. Then, I realized I wanted more for my daughter than I had growing up. I also wanted to have time to raise her properly and keep her safe. She is a good girl, but she sees crime and violence around her. I want to get her away from danger, and I want to show her that there are better ways to live. Getting a college degree will help me do that.

The most important benefit of getting a college degree is that it will show me that I can achieve something hard. My life is moving in a good direction, and I am proud of myself. My daughter will be proud of me, too. I want to be a good role model for her as she grows up. ▸


Identifying information
Title indicates main idea
Introduction
Thesis statement
Topic sentence/ Support point 1
Supporting details
Topic sentence/ Support point 2
Supporting details
Topic sentence/ Support point 3
Supporting details

Conclusion

Because of these benefits, I want to get a college degree. It will give me the chance to earn a better living, it will give my daughter and me a better life, and I will be proud of myself.

**WRITING ASSIGNMENT** **Essay**

Write a draft essay using what you have developed in previous chapters or one of the following thesis statements. If you choose one of the thesis statements that follow, you may want to modify it to fit what you want to say.

Being successful at __________________ requires __________________.

Doing ____________________ gave me a great deal of pride in myself.

Training for a (job/marathon/sport/performance) requires a lot of discipline.

Some of the differences between men and women create misunderstandings.

After you have finished writing your draft essay, complete the following checklist.

**CHECKLIST**

## Evaluating Your Draft Essay

- ☐ A clear, confident thesis statement states my main idea.
- ☐ The primary support points are now topic sentences that support the main idea.
- ☐ Each topic sentence is part of a paragraph, and the other sentences in the paragraph support the topic sentence.
- ☐ The support is arranged in a logical order.
- ☐ The introduction will interest readers.
- ☐ The conclusion reinforces my main idea and makes an additional observation.
- ☐ The title reinforces the main idea.
- ☐ All the sentences are complete, consisting of a subject and verb, and expressing a complete thought.
- ☐ The draft is properly formatted:
  - My name, my instructor's name, the course, and the date appear in the upper left corner.
  - The first sentence of each paragraph is indented, and the text is double-spaced (for easier revision).
  - The pages are numbered.
- ☐ I have followed any other formatting guidelines provided by my instructor.

Give yourself some time away from your draft, at least a few hours and preferably a day or two. Taking a break will allow you to return to your writing later with a fresher eye and more energy for revision, resulting in a better piece of writing—and a better grade. After your break, you will be ready to take the next step: revising your draft.

## Understand What Revision Is

When you finish a draft, you probably wish that you were at the end: You don't want to have to look at it again. But a draft is just the first whole version, a rough cut; it is not the best you can do to represent yourself and your ideas. After taking a break, you need to look at the draft with fresh eyes to revise and edit it.

**Revising** is making your ideas clearer, stronger, and more convincing. When revising, you are evaluating how well you have made your point.

**Editing** is finding and correcting problems with grammar, word usage, punctuation, and capitalization. When editing, you are evaluating the words, phrases, and sentences you have used.

Most writers find it difficult to revise and edit well if they try to do both at once. It is easier to solve idea-level problems first (by revising) and then to correct smaller, word-level ones (by editing). This chapter focuses on revising. For editing help, use Chapters 15 through 34.

**Tips for revising your writing**

- Wait a few hours or, if possible, a couple of days before starting to revise.
- Read your draft aloud, and listen for places where the writing seems weak or unclear.
- Read critically and ask yourself questions, as if you were reading through someone else's eyes.
- Write notes about changes to make. For small things, like adding a transition (pp. 96–97), you can make the change on the draft. For other things, like adding or getting rid of an idea or reordering your support points, make a note in the margin.
- Get help from a tutor at the writing center, or get feedback from a friend (see the following section for information on peer review).

**Tip** For more on reading critically, see Chapter 1.

Even the best writers do not get everything right the first time. So, if you finish reading your draft and have not found anything that could be better, you are not reading carefully enough or are not asking the right questions. Use the following checklist to help you make your writing better.

**CHECKLIST**

### Revising Your Writing

- ☐ If someone else just read my topic sentence or thesis statement, what would he or she think the paper is about? Would the main point make a lasting impression? What would I need to do to make it more interesting? ▸

**Tip** Add transitions as you read to help move from one idea to the next.

- ☐ Does each support point really relate to my main idea? What more could I say about the topic so that someone else will see it my way? Is any of what I have written weak? If so, should I delete it?
- ☐ What about the way the ideas are arranged? Should I change the order so that the writing makes more sense or has more effect on a reader?
- ☐ What about the ending? Does it just droop and fade away? How could I make it better?
- ☐ If, before reading my paragraph or essay, someone knew nothing about the topic or disagreed with my position, would what I have written be enough for him or her to understand the material or be convinced by my argument?

## Practice Revising for Unity, Detail, and Coherence

You may need to read what you have written several times before deciding what changes would improve it. Remember to consider your audience and your purpose and to focus on three areas: unity, detail, and coherence.

### *Revise for Unity*

**Unity** in writing means that all the points you make are related to your main idea; they are *unified* in support of it. As you draft a paragraph or an essay, you may detour from your main idea without even being aware of it, as the writer of the following paragraph did with the underlined sentences. The diagram after the paragraph shows what happens when readers read the paragraph.

First, double-underline the main idea in the paragraph that follows to help you see where the writer got off-track.

> If you want to drive like an elderly person, use a cell phone while driving. A group of researchers from the University of Utah tested the reaction times of two groups of people—those between the ages of sixty-five to seventy-four and those who were eighteen to twenty-five—in a variety of driving tasks. All tasks were done with hands-free cell phones. That part of the study surprised me because I thought the main problem was using only one hand to drive. I hardly ever drive with two hands, even when I'm not talking to anyone. Among other results, braking time for both groups slowed by 18 percent. A related result is that the number of rear-end collisions doubled. The study determined that the younger drivers were paying as much—or more—attention to their phone conversations as they were to what was going on around them on the road. The elderly drivers also experienced longer reaction times and more accidents, pushing most of them into the category of dangerous driver. This study makes a good case for turning off the phone when you buckle up.

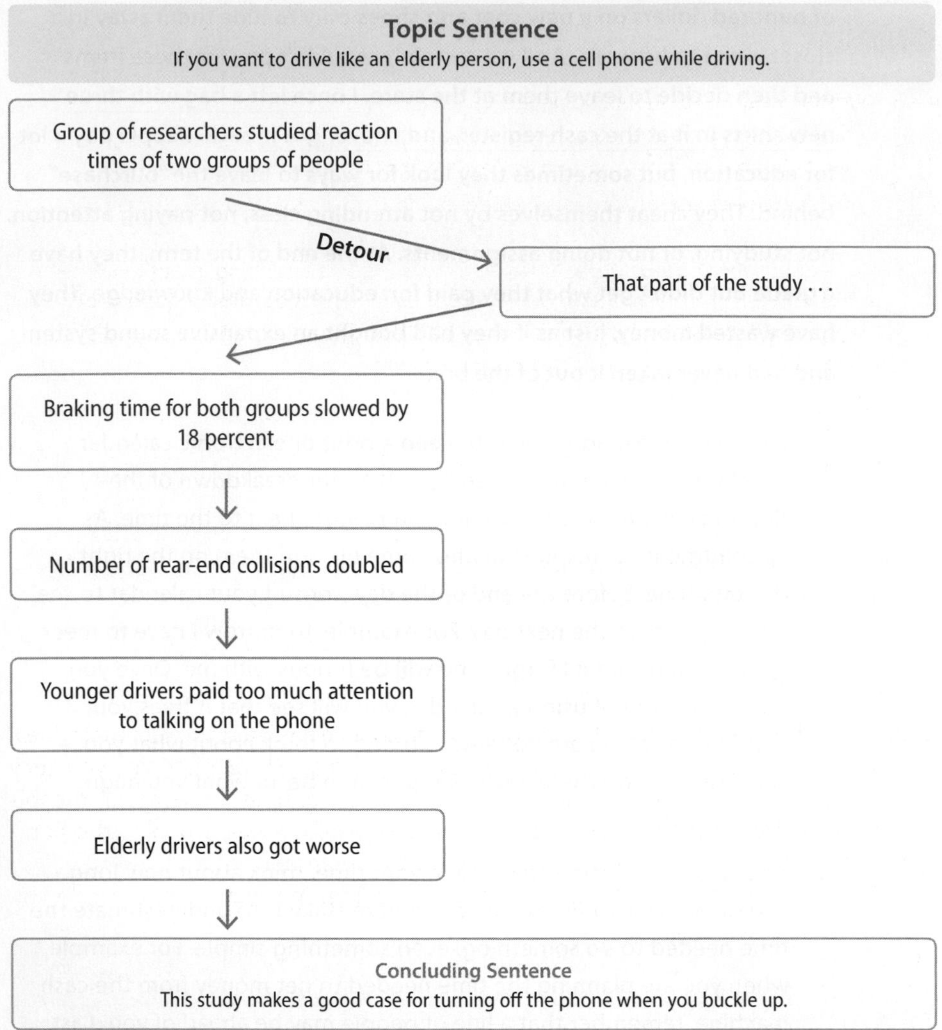
Topic Sentence
If you want to drive like an elderly person, use a cell phone while driving.
Group of researchers studied reaction times of two groups of people
Detour
That part of the study . . .
Braking time for both groups slowed by 18 percent
Number of rear-end collisions doubled
Younger drivers paid too much attention to talking on the phone
Elderly drivers also got worse
Concluding Sentence
This study makes a good case for turning off the phone when you buckle up.

Detours weaken your writing because readers' focus is shifted from your main idea. As you revise, check to make sure your paragraph or essay has unity.

**PRACTICE 8** **Revising for unity**

Each of the following paragraphs contains a sentence that detours from the main idea. First, double-underline the main idea. Then, underline the detour in each paragraph.

**Example: "Education is one of the few things people are willing to pay for and not get." When we buy something expensive, we make sure we take it home and use it. For example, we wouldn't think of spending a couple**

**of hundred dollars on a new coat and shoes only to hide them away in a closet never to be worn. And we certainly wouldn't pay for those items and then decide to leave them at the store. I once left a bag with three new shirts in it at the cash register, and I never got it back. People pay a lot for education, but sometimes they look for ways to leave the "purchase" behind. They cheat themselves by not attending class, not paying attention, not studying, or not doing assignments. At the end of the term, they have a grade but didn't get what they paid for: education and knowledge. They have wasted money, just as if they had bought an expensive sound system and had never taken it out of the box.**

1. One way to manage time is to keep a print or electronic calendar or schedule. It should have an hour-by-hour breakdown of the day and evening, with space for you to write next to the time. As appointments or responsibilities come up, add them on the right day and time. Before the end of the day, consult your calendar to see what's going on the next day. For example, tomorrow I have to meet Kara at noon, and if I forget, she will be furious with me. Once you are in the habit of using a calendar, you will see that it frees your mind because you are not always trying to think about what you're supposed to do, where you're supposed to be, or what you might have forgotten.

2. As you use a calendar to manage your time, think about how long certain activities will take. A common mistake is to underestimate the time needed to do something, even something simple. For example, when you are planning the time needed to get money from the cash machine, remember that a line of people may be ahead of you. Last week in the line I met a woman I went to high school with. When you are estimating time for a more complex activity, such as reading a chapter in a textbook, block out more time than you think you will need. If you finish in less time than you have allotted, so much the better.

## *Revise for Detail and Support*

When you revise a paper, look carefully at the support you have developed. Will readers have enough information to understand and be convinced by the main idea?

In the margin or between the lines of your draft (which should be double-spaced), note ideas that seem weak or unclear. As you revise, build up your support by adding more details.

**PRACTICE 9** **Revising for detail and support**

Read the following paragraphs, double-underline the main idea, and add at least three additional support points or supporting details. Write them in the spaces provided under each paragraph, and indicate where they should go in the paragraph by writing in a caret (^) and the number.

**Example: Sojourner Truth was a brave woman who helped educate people about the evils of slavery. She was a slave herself in New York** ^1**.** ^2 **After she had a religious vision, she traveled from place to place giving speeches about how terrible it was to be a slave.** ^3 **But even after the Emancipation Proclamation was signed in 1863, slave owners did not follow the laws. Sojourner Truth was active in the Civil War, nursing soldiers and continuing to give speeches. She was active in the fight for racial equality until her death in 1883.**

1. *and was not allowed to learn to read or write*
2. *Sojourner Truth ran away from her owner because of his cruelty.*
3. *Although she was beaten for her beliefs, she continued her work and was part of the force that caused Abraham Lincoln to sign the Emancipation Proclamation freeing the slaves.*

1. Sports fans can turn from normal people into destructive maniacs. After big wins, a team's fans sometimes riot. Police have to be brought in. Even in school sports, parents of the players can become violent. People get so involved watching the game that they lose control of themselves and are dangerous.

   1. ______
   2. ______
   3. ______

2. If a friend is going through a hard time, try to be as supportive as you can. For one thing, ask if you can help out with any errands or chores. Also, find a time when you can get together in a quiet, nonstressful place. Here, the two of you can talk about the friend's difficulties or just spend time visiting. Let the friend decide how the time is spent. Just knowing that you are there for him or her will mean a lot.

   1. ______
   2. ______
   3. ______

## *Revise for Coherence*

**Coherence** in writing means that all your support connects to form a whole. In other words, you have provided enough "glue" for readers to see how one point leads to another.

A good way to improve coherence is to use **transitions**—words, phrases, and sentences that connect your ideas so that your writing moves smoothly from one point to the next. The table on pages 96–97 shows some common transitions and what they are used for.

Here are two paragraphs, one that does not use transitions and one that does. Read them and notice how much easier the second paragraph is to follow because of the underlined transitions.

**No transitions**

It is not difficult to get organized—it takes discipline to stay organized. All you need to do is follow a few simple ideas. You must decide what your priorities are and do these tasks first. You should ask yourself every day: What is the most important task I have to accomplish? Make the time to do it. To be organized, you need a personal system for keeping track of things. Making lists, keeping records, and using a schedule help you remember what tasks you need to do. It is a good idea not to let belongings and obligations stack up. Get rid of possessions you do not need, put items away every time you are done using them, and do not take on more responsibilities than you can handle. Getting organized is not a mystery; it is just good sense.

**Transitions added**

It is not difficult to get organized—although it takes discipline to stay organized. All you need to do is follow a few simple ideas. You must decide what your priorities are and do these tasks first. For example, you should ask yourself every day: What is the most important task I have to accomplish? Then, make the time to do it. To be organized, you also need a personal system for keeping track of things. Making lists, keeping records, and using a schedule help you remember what tasks you need to do. Finally, it is a good idea not to let belongings and obligations stack up. Get rid of possessions you do not need, put items away every time you are done using them, and do not take on more responsibilities than you can handle. Getting organized is not a mystery; it is just good sense.

### Common Transitional Words and Phrases

**Indicating space**

| | | | |
|---|---|---|---|
| above | below | near | to the right |
| across | beside | next to | to the side |
| at the bottom | beyond | opposite | under |
| at the top | farther/further | over | where |
| behind | inside | to the left | |

| **Indicating time** | | | |
|---|---|---|---|
| after | eventually | meanwhile | soon |
| as | finally | next | then |
| at last | first | now | when |
| before | last | second | while |
| during | later | since | |
| **Indicating importance** | | | |
| above all | in fact | more important | most important |
| best | in particular | most | worst |
| especially | | | |
| **Signaling examples** | | | |
| for example | for instance | for one thing | one reason |
| **Signaling additions** | | | |
| additionally | and | as well as | in addition |
| also | another | furthermore | moreover |
| **Signaling contrast** | | | |
| although | however | nevertheless | still |
| but | in contrast | on the other hand | yet |
| even though | instead | | |
| **Signaling causes or results** | | | |
| as a result | finally | so | therefore |
| because | | | |

## PRACTICE 10 Adding transitions

Read the following paragraphs. In each blank, add a transition that would smoothly connect the ideas. In each case, there is more than one correct answer.

### Example

**LifeGem, a Chicago company, has announced that it can turn cremated human ashes into high-quality diamonds.** After **cremation, the ashes are heated to convert their carbon to graphite.** Then**, a lab wraps the graphite around a tiny diamond piece and again heats it and pressurizes it.** After **about a**

**week of crystallizing, the result is a diamond.** ___Because of___ **the time and labor involved, this process can cost as much as $20,000.** ___Although___ **the idea is very creative, many people will think it is also very weird.**

1. Frida Kahlo (1907–1954) is one of Mexico's most famous artists. From an early age, she had an eye for color and detail. __________, it was not until she was seriously injured in a traffic accident that she devoted herself to painting. _________ her recovery, she went to work on what would become the first of many self-portraits. ___________, she married the famous muralist Diego Rivera. __________ Rivera was unfaithful to Kahlo, their marriage was difficult. ____________, Kahlo continued to develop as an artist and produce great work. Rivera may have summed up Kahlo's paintings the best, describing them as "acid and tender, hard as steel and delicate and fine as a butterfly's wing, lovable as a beautiful smile, and profound and cruel as the bitterness of life."
2. Many fast-food restaurants are adding healthier foods to their menus. ____________, several kinds of salads are now on most menus. These salads offer fresh vegetables and roasted, rather than fried, chicken. __________, be careful of the dressings, which can be very high in calories. _______, avoid the huge soft drinks that have large amounts of sugar. _________, skip the french fries. They are high in fat and calories and do not have much nutritional value.

Another way to give your writing coherence is to repeat a **key word**—a word that is directly related to your main idea. For example, in the paragraphs on page 96, the writer repeats the word *organized* several times. Repetition of a key word is a good way to keep your readers focused on your main idea, but make sure you don't overdo it.

### NOTE: AVOIDING PLAGIARISM

In all the writing you do, it is important to avoid **plagiarism**—using other people's words as your own or handing in information you gather from another source as your own. Your instructors are aware of plagiarism and know how to look for it. Writers who plagiarize, either on purpose or by accident, risk failing a course or losing their jobs and damaging their reputations.

To avoid plagiarism, take careful notes on every source (books, interviews, television shows, Web sites, and so on) you might use in your writing. When recording information from sources, take notes in your own words, unless you plan to use direct quotations. In that case, make sure to record the quotation word for word. Also, include quotation marks around it, both in your notes and in your paper. When you use material from other sources—whether you directly quote or put information in your own words (paraphrase)—you must name and give citation information about these sources.

## Revise Your Own Paragraph

On page 88, you read Chelsea's draft paragraph. Reread that now as if it were your own, asking yourself the questions in the Checklist for Revising Your Writing on pages 91–92. Work either by yourself or with a partner or a small group to answer the questions about Chelsea's draft. Then, read Chelsea's revised paragraph that follows, and compare the changes you suggested with those she made. Make notes on the similarities and differences to discuss with the rest of the class.

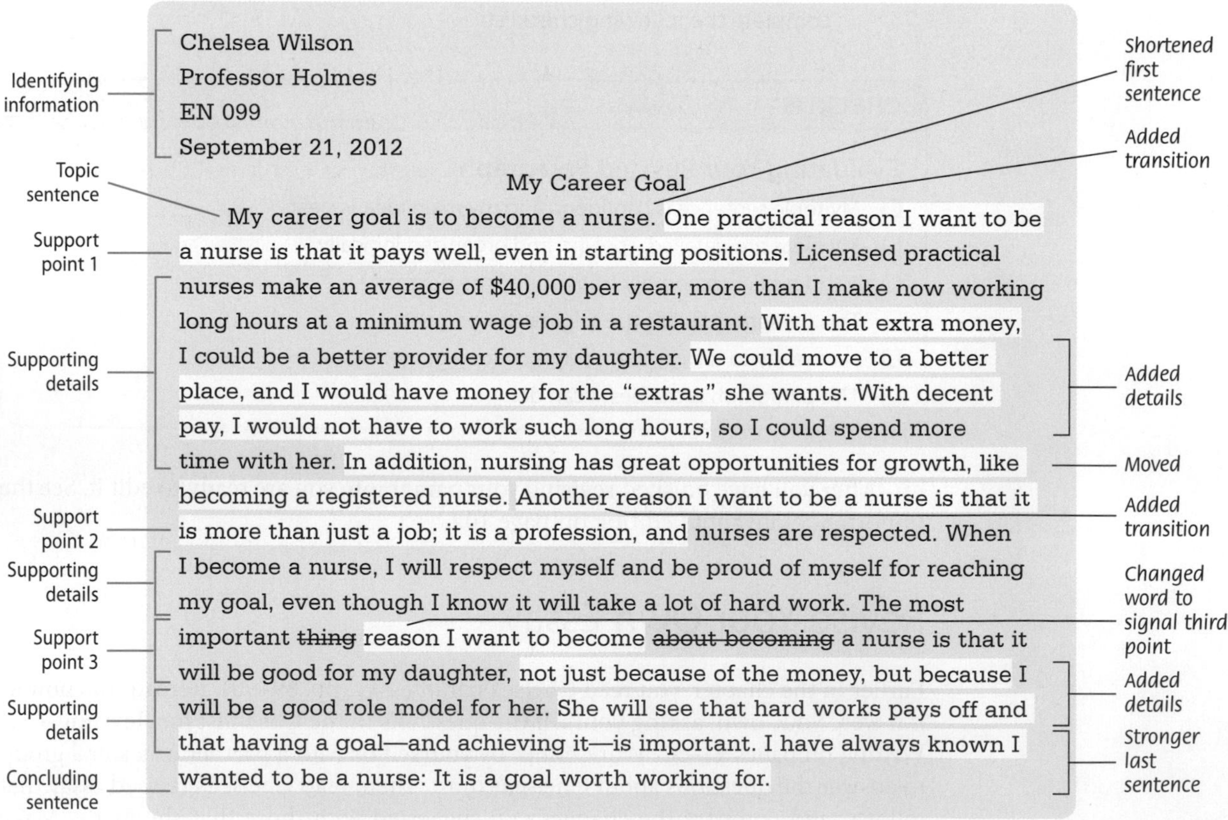

Chelsea Wilson
Professor Holmes
EN 099
September 21, 2012

My Career Goal

My career goal is to become a nurse. One practical reason I want to be a nurse is that it pays well, even in starting positions. Licensed practical nurses make an average of $40,000 per year, more than I make now working long hours at a minimum wage job in a restaurant. With that extra money, I could be a better provider for my daughter. We could move to a better place, and I would have money for the "extras" she wants. With decent pay, I would not have to work such long hours, so I could spend more time with her. In addition, nursing has great opportunities for growth, like becoming a registered nurse. Another reason I want to be a nurse is that it is more than just a job; it is a profession, and nurses are respected. When I become a nurse, I will respect myself and be proud of myself for reaching my goal, even though I know it will take a lot of hard work. The most important ~~thing~~ reason I want to become ~~about becoming~~ a nurse is that it will be good for my daughter, not just because of the money, but because I will be a good role model for her. She will see that hard works pays off and that having a goal—and achieving it—is important. I have always known I wanted to be a nurse: It is a goal worth working for.

Identifying information
Topic sentence
Support point 1
Supporting details
Support point 2
Supporting details
Support point 3
Supporting details
Concluding sentence
Shortened first sentence
Added transition
Added details
Moved
Added transition
Changed word to signal third point
Added details
Stronger last sentence

**PRACTICE 11** **Revising a paragraph**

1. What major changes did you suggest for Chelsea's draft in response to the Checklist for Revising Your Writing?

______________________________________________

______________________________________________

2. Did Chelsea make any of the suggested changes? Which ones?

______________________________________________

______________________________________________

3. Did Chelsea make any changes that were not suggested? Which ones? Were they good changes?

______________________________________________

______________________________________________

**WRITING ASSIGNMENT** **Paragraph**

Revise the draft paragraph you wrote on page 88. After revising your draft, complete the following checklist.

**CHECKLIST**

**Evaluating Your Revised Paragraph**

- ☐ My topic sentence is confident, and my main idea is clear.
- ☐ My ideas are detailed, specific, and organized logically.
- ☐ My ideas flow smoothly from one to the next.
- ☐ This paragraph fulfills the original assignment.
- ☐ I am ready to turn in this paragraph for a grade.
- ☐ This paragraph is the best I can do.

After you have finished revising your paragraph, you are ready to edit it. See the Important Note about editing on page 102.

## Revise Your Own Essay

Earlier in the chapter, you read Chelsea's draft essay (pp. 89–90). Reread that now as if it were your own, asking yourself the questions in the Checklist for Revising Your Writing on pages 91–92. Work either by yourself or with a partner or a small group to answer the questions about Chelsea's draft. Then, read Chelsea's revised essay that follows, and compare the changes you suggested with those that she made. Make notes on the similarities and differences to discuss with the rest of the class.

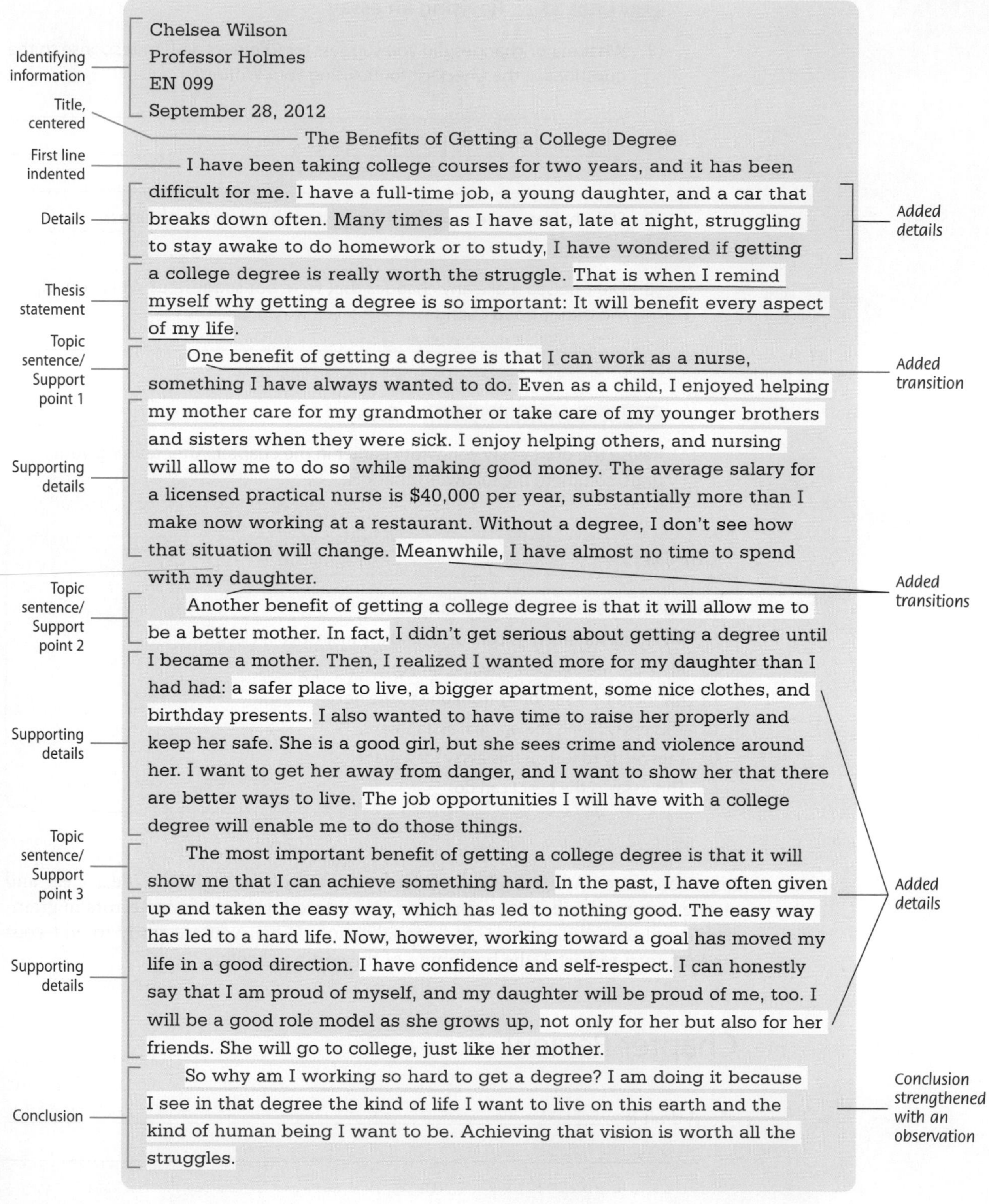
Identifying information
Title, centered
First line indented
Details
Thesis statement
Topic sentence/ Support point 1
Supporting details
Topic sentence/ Support point 2
Supporting details
Topic sentence/ Support point 3
Supporting details
Conclusion
Added details
Added transition
Added transitions
Added details
Conclusion strengthened with an observation

Chelsea Wilson
Professor Holmes
EN 099
September 28, 2012

The Benefits of Getting a College Degree

I have been taking college courses for two years, and it has been difficult for me. I have a full-time job, a young daughter, and a car that breaks down often. Many times as I have sat, late at night, struggling to stay awake to do homework or to study, I have wondered if getting a college degree is really worth the struggle. That is when I remind myself why getting a degree is so important: It will benefit every aspect of my life.

One benefit of getting a degree is that I can work as a nurse, something I have always wanted to do. Even as a child, I enjoyed helping my mother care for my grandmother or take care of my younger brothers and sisters when they were sick. I enjoy helping others, and nursing will allow me to do so while making good money. The average salary for a licensed practical nurse is $40,000 per year, substantially more than I make now working at a restaurant. Without a degree, I don't see how that situation will change. Meanwhile, I have almost no time to spend with my daughter.

Another benefit of getting a college degree is that it will allow me to be a better mother. In fact, I didn't get serious about getting a degree until I became a mother. Then, I realized I wanted more for my daughter than I had had: a safer place to live, a bigger apartment, some nice clothes, and birthday presents. I also wanted to have time to raise her properly and keep her safe. She is a good girl, but she sees crime and violence around her. I want to get her away from danger, and I want to show her that there are better ways to live. The job opportunities I will have with a college degree will enable me to do those things.

The most important benefit of getting a college degree is that it will show me that I can achieve something hard. In the past, I have often given up and taken the easy way, which has led to nothing good. The easy way has led to a hard life. Now, however, working toward a goal has moved my life in a good direction. I have confidence and self-respect. I can honestly say that I am proud of myself, and my daughter will be proud of me, too. I will be a good role model as she grows up, not only for her but also for her friends. She will go to college, just like her mother.

So why am I working so hard to get a degree? I am doing it because I see in that degree the kind of life I want to live on this earth and the kind of human being I want to be. Achieving that vision is worth all the struggles.

**PRACTICE 12** **Revising an essay**

1. What major changes did you suggest for Chelsea's draft in response to the questions in the Checklist for Revising Your Writing?

 ______________________________________

 ______________________________________

 ______________________________________

2. Did Chelsea make any of the suggested changes? Which ones?

 ______________________________________

3. Did Chelsea make any changes that were not suggested? Which ones? Were they good changes?

 ______________________________________

**WRITING ASSIGNMENT** **Essay**

Revise the draft essay you wrote earlier in the chapter. After revising your draft, complete the following checklist.

**CHECKLIST**

### Evaluating Your Revised Essay

- ☐ My thesis statement is confident, and my main idea is clear.
- ☐ My ideas are detailed, specific, and organized logically.
- ☐ My ideas flow smoothly from one to the next.
- ☐ This essay fulfills the original assignment.
- ☐ I am ready to turn in this essay for a grade.
- ☐ This essay is the best I can do.

**Important note:** After you have revised your writing to make the ideas clear and strong, you need to edit it to eliminate any distracting or confusing errors in grammar, word use, punctuation, and capitalization. When you are ready to edit your writing, turn to Part 3, the beginning of the editing chapters.

# Chapter Review

1. A draft is ______________________________________

 ______________________________________

2. List the basic features of a good draft paragraph or essay: ____________
____________
____________
____________
____________
____________

3. Three ways to order ideas are ________, ________, and ________.

4. Making an ________ is a useful way to plan your draft.

5. Five ways to start an essay are
____________
____________
____________
____________
____________

6. Three features of a good essay conclusion are
____________
____________
____________

7. Two basic features of a good essay title are
____________
____________

8. Revising is ____________
____________

9. Three basic features of useful feedback are
____________
____________

10. As you revise, make sure your paragraph or essay has these three things: ________, ________, and ________.

11. ________ means that all the points you make are related to your main idea.

12. Coherence means ____________

13. An important way to ensure coherence in your writing is to ______________________________

______________________________________________________________________

14. Transitions are ______________________________________________________

______________________________________________________________________

15. Write for one minute about "What questions I should ask my instructor."

## REFLECTING ON THE JOURNEY

### Skills Learned

Now that you've completed the chapter, share what you've learned about each skill by completing the following chart.

| Skill | What I learned about this skill |
|---|---|
| Use an outline to draft a paragraph or essay | |
| Draft a paragraph or essay with a thesis statement and/or topic sentences | |
| Draft an effective introduction | |
| Draft an effective conclusion | |
| Revise for unity, coherence, and detail | |
| Avoid plagiarism | |

# Part 2

# Writing Different Kinds of Paragraphs and Essays



"I write school essays, performance reviews, and letters to my daughter."

–Sam M., student

# 6

# Narration

## Writing That Tells Important Stories

### Learning Objectives

**Chapter Goal:** Learn how to write a narrative paper.

**Tools to Achieve the Goal:**

- Four Basics of Good Narration (p. 108)
- Diagram: Paragraphs and Essays in Narration (pp. 112–13)
- Common Transitions in Narration (p. 115)
- Sample Narration Paragraph and Rubric (pp. 116–17)
- Student Narration Paragraph: Jelani Lynch, *My Turnaround* (p. 118)
- Student Narration Essay: Arianna Morgan, *The Time I Almost Lost My Baby Brother* (p. 119)
- Profile of Success and Workplace Narration: Alice Adoga (p. 121)
- Professional Narration Essay: Amy Tan, *Fish Cheeks* (p. 123)
- Checklist: How to Write Narration (p. 127)

## READING ROADMAP

### Key Terms

Skim Chapter 6 before reading. Find these words or terms in **bold** type. Put a check mark next to each once you locate it.

____ narration
____ main idea
____ support
____ time (chronological) order
____ transitions

### Guided Reading for Chapter 6

Fill out the following chart before you begin reading. For each skill, write what you know about that skill and what you would like to know upon completing the chapter. At the end of the chapter, you will be asked to share what you learned about each skill.

| Skill | When I have used this skill | What I want to know about this skill |
|---|---|---|
| Write a story about myself or someone else | | |
| Write a clear thesis statement or main idea for a narrative | | |
| Generate support for a narrative paper | | |
| Relate support directly to the main idea of the paper | | |
| Read and analyze a narrative paper | | |

LaunchPadSolo
Visit **LaunchPad Solo for Readers and Writers > Reading > Patterns of Organization** for more tutorials, videos, and practice with patterns of organization.

# Understand What Narration Is

**Narration** is writing that tells the story of an event or an experience.

### Four Basics of Good Narration

1. It reveals something of importance to the writer (the main idea).
2. It includes all the major events of the story (primary support).
3. It brings the story to life with details about the major events (secondary support).
4. It presents the events in a clear order, usually according to when they happened.

In the following paragraph, the numbers and colors correspond to the Four Basics of Good Narration.

4 Events in time order

1 Last year, a writing assignment I hated produced the best writing I have done. 2 When my English teacher told us that our assignment would be to do a few hours of community service and write about it, I was furious. 3 I am a single mother, I work full time, and I am going to school—isn't that enough? 2 The next day, I spoke to my teacher during her office hours and told her that I was already so busy I could hardly make time for homework, never mind housework. My own life was too full to help with anyone else's life. 3 She said that she understood perfectly and that the majority of her students had lives as full as mine. Then, she explained that the service assignment was just for four hours and that other students had enjoyed both doing the assignment and writing about their experiences. She said they were all surprised and that I would be, too. 2 After talking with her, I decided to accept my fate. The next week, I went to the Community Service Club and was set up to spend a few hours at an adult day-care center near where I live. A few weeks later, I went to the Creative Care Center in Cocoa Beach, not knowing what to expect. 3 I found friendly, approachable people who had so many stories to tell about their long, full lives. 2 The next thing I knew, I was taking notes because I was interested in these people: 3 their marriages, life during the Depression, the wars they fought in, their children, their joys and sorrows. I felt as if I was experiencing everything they lived while they shared their history with me. 2 When it came time to write about my experience, I had more than enough to write about: 3 I wrote the stories of the many wonderful elderly people I had talked with. 2 I got an A on the paper, and beyond that accomplishment, I made friends whom I will visit on my own, not because of an assignment but because I value them.

You can use narration in many practical situations.

| | |
|---|---|
| **College** | In a lab course, you are asked to tell what happened in an experiment. |
| **Work** | Something goes wrong at work, and you are asked to explain to your boss—in writing—what happened. |
| **Everyday life** | In a letter of complaint about service you received, you need to tell what happened that upset you. |

In college, the word *narration* probably will not appear in writing assignments. Instead, an assignment might ask you to *describe* the events, *report* what happened, or *retell* what happened. Words or phrases that call for an *account of events* are situations that require narration.

## Main Idea in Narration

In narration, the **main idea** is what is important about the story—to you and to your readers. To help you discover the main idea for your own narration, complete the following sentence:

**Main idea in narration** **What is important to me about the experience is . . .**

The topic sentence (paragraph) or thesis statement (essay) usually includes the topic and the main idea the writer wants to make about the topic. Let's look at a topic sentence first.

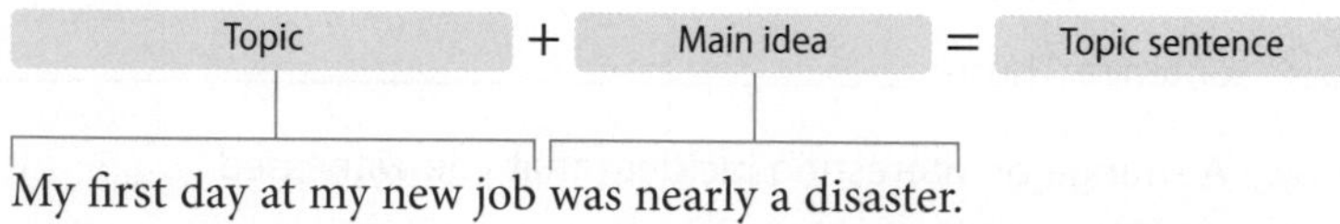
Topic
+
Main idea
=
Topic sentence
My first day at my new job was nearly a disaster.

Remember that a topic for an essay can be a little broader than one for a paragraph.

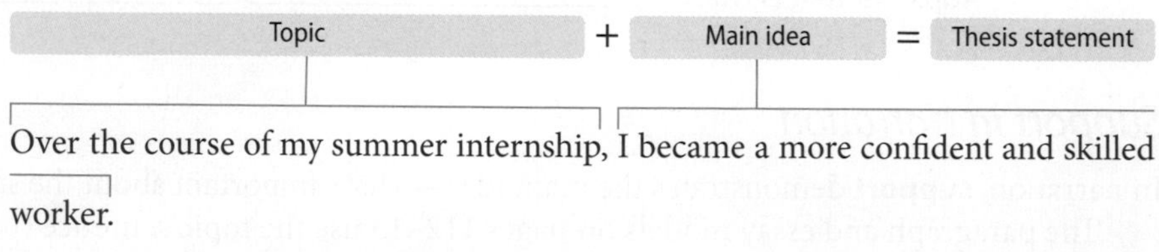
Topic
+
Main idea
=
Thesis statement
Over the course of my summer internship, I became a more confident and skilled worker.

Whereas the topic sentence is focused on just one workday, the thesis statement considers a season-long internship.

**Tip** Sometimes, the same main idea can be used for a paragraph and an essay, but the essay must develop this idea in more detail. (See pp. 68–69.)

**PRACTICE 1** **Writing a main idea**

Look at the example narration paragraph on page 108. Fill in the diagram with the paragraph's topic sentence.

Topic | Main idea

**PRACTICE 2** **Deciding on a main idea**

For each of the following topics, write a main idea for a narration. Then, write a sentence that includes your topic and your main idea. This sentence would be your topic sentence (paragraph) or thesis statement (essay).

**Example:**

**Topic: A fight I had with my sister**

**Important because:** *it taught me something*

**Main idea:** *learned it is better to stay cool*

**Topic sentence/Thesis:** *After a horrible fight with my sister, I learned the value of staying calm.*

1. Topic: A powerful, funny, or embarrassing experience

   Important because: ____________________

   Main idea: ____________________

   Topic sentence/Thesis: ____________________

2. Topic: A strange or interesting incident that you witnessed

   Important because: ____________________

   Main idea: ____________________

   Topic sentence/Thesis: ____________________

## *Support in Narration*

**Tip** In an essay, the major events may form the topic sentences of paragraphs. The details supporting the major events then make up the body of these paragraphs.

In narration, **support** demonstrates the main idea—what's important about the story.

The paragraph and essay models on pages 112–13 use the topic sentence (paragraph) and thesis statement (essay) from the Main Idea section of this chapter. (The thesis statement has been revised slightly.) Both models include the support used in

all narration writing—major events backed up by details about the events. In the essay model, however, the major support points (events) are topic sentences for individual paragraphs.

## CHOOSING MAJOR EVENTS

When you tell a story to a friend, you can include events that are not essential to the story. In contrast, when you are writing a narration, you need to give more careful thought to which events you will include, selecting only those that most clearly demonstrate your main idea.

### PRACTICE 3 Choosing major events

Choose two items from Practice 2, and write down the topic sentence or thesis statement you came up with for each. Then, for each topic sentence/thesis statement, write three events that would help you make your main idea.

**Example:**

**Topic: A fight I had with my sister**

**Topic sentence/Thesis:** *After a horrible fight with my sister, I learned the value of staying calm.*

**Events:** *We disagreed about who was going to have the family party.*

*She made me so mad that I started yelling at her, and I got nasty.*

*I hung up on her, and now we're not talking.*

1. Topic: A powerful, funny, or embarrassing experience

   Topic sentence/Thesis: ______________________

   ______________________

   ______________________

   Events: ______________________

   ______________________

   ______________________

   ______________________

2. Topic: A strange or interesting incident that you witnessed

   Topic sentence/Thesis: ______________________

   Events: ______________________

## Paragraphs vs. Essays in Narration

For more on the important features of narration, see the Four Basics of Good Narration on page 108.

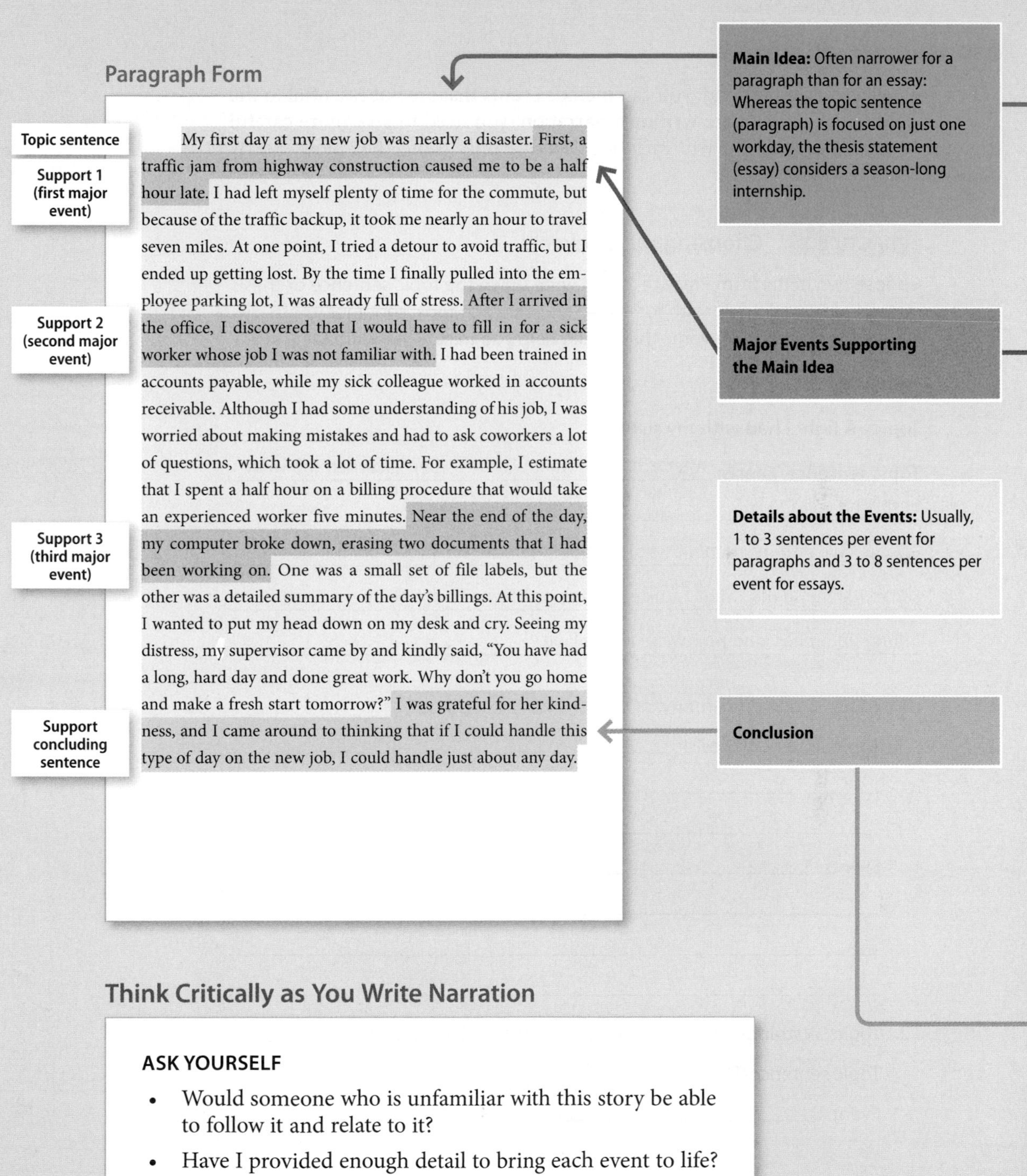
Paragraph Form
Topic sentence
Support 1 (first major event)
Support 2 (second major event)
Support 3 (third major event)
Support concluding sentence
My first day at my new job was nearly a disaster. First, a traffic jam from highway construction caused me to be a half hour late. I had left myself plenty of time for the commute, but because of the traffic backup, it took me nearly an hour to travel seven miles. At one point, I tried a detour to avoid traffic, but I ended up getting lost. By the time I finally pulled into the employee parking lot, I was already full of stress. After I arrived in the office, I discovered that I would have to fill in for a sick worker whose job I was not familiar with. I had been trained in accounts payable, while my sick colleague worked in accounts receivable. Although I had some understanding of his job, I was worried about making mistakes and had to ask coworkers a lot of questions, which took a lot of time. For example, I estimate that I spent a half hour on a billing procedure that would take an experienced worker five minutes. Near the end of the day, my computer broke down, erasing two documents that I had been working on. One was a small set of file labels, but the other was a detailed summary of the day's billings. At this point, I wanted to put my head down on my desk and cry. Seeing my distress, my supervisor came by and kindly said, "You have had a long, hard day and done great work. Why don't you go home and make a fresh start tomorrow?" I was grateful for her kindness, and I came around to thinking that if I could handle this type of day on the new job, I could handle just about any day.
Main Idea: Often narrower for a paragraph than for an essay: Whereas the topic sentence (paragraph) is focused on just one workday, the thesis statement (essay) considers a season-long internship.
Major Events Supporting the Main Idea
Details about the Events: Usually, 1 to 3 sentences per event for paragraphs and 3 to 8 sentences per event for essays.
Conclusion

### Think Critically as You Write Narration

**ASK YOURSELF**

- Would someone who is unfamiliar with this story be able to follow it and relate to it?
- Have I provided enough detail to bring each event to life?

## Essay Form

Introductory paragraph

1

Several of my friends question whether summer internships are really worthwhile, especially if the pay is low or nonexistent. However, the right internship definitely pays off professionally in the l[ong run], even if it doesn't financially in the short run. The proof is in my own summer marketing internship, which made me a far more confident and skilled worker.

Thesis statement

During the first two weeks of the internship, I received thorough training in every part of my job. For example, my immediate superviso[r spent two] full days going over everything I would [need to know to] help with e-mail campaigns, online marketing efforts, and other promotions. She even had me draft a promotional e-mail for a new product and gave me feedback about how to make the message clearer and more appealing. I also spent a lot of time with other staffers, who taught me everything from how to use the photocopier and printers to how to pull together marketing and sales materials for executive meetings. Most impressive, the president of the company took some time out of a busy afternoon to answer my questions about

Topic sentence 1 (first major event)

2

how he got started in his career and what he sees as the keys to success in the marketing field. As I explained to a friend, I got a real "insider's view" of [the company] and its leadership.

Topic sentence 2 (second major event)

Next, I got hands-on experience with listening to customers and addressing their needs. Specifically, I sat in on meetings with new clients and listened to them describe products and services they would like the company's help in promoting. They also discussed the message they would like to get across about their businesses. After the meetings, I sat in on brainstorming sessions with other staffers in which we came up with as many ideas as we could about campaigns to address the clients' needs. At first, I didn't think anyone would care about my ideas, but others listened to them respectfully and even ended up including some of them in the marketing plans that were sent back to the clients. I learned later that some of m[y ideas would] be included in the actual promotional ca[mpaigns].

Topic sentence 3 (third major event)

By summer's end, I had advanced my skills so much that I was asked to return next summer. My

3

supervisor told me that she was pleased not only with all I had learned about marketing but also with the responsibility I took for every aspect of my job. I did not roll my eyes about having to make photocopies or help at the reception desk, nor did I seem intimidated by bigger, more meaningful tasks. Although I'm not guaranteed a full-time job at the company after graduation, I think my chances are good. Even if I don't end up working there long term, I am grateful for how the job has helped me grow.

Concluding paragraph

In the end, the greatest benefit of the internship might be the confidence it gave me. I have learned that no matter how challenging the task before me—at work or in real life—I can succeed at it by getting the right information and input on anything unfamiliar, working effectively with others, and truly dedicating myself to doing my best. My time this past summer was definitely well spent.

## GIVING DETAILS ABOUT THE EVENTS

When you write a narration, include examples and details that will make each event easier to visualize and understand. You want your readers to share your point of view and see the same message in the story that you do.

### PRACTICE 4 Giving details about the events

Write down the topic sentence or thesis statement for each item from Practice 3. Then, write the major events in the spaces provided. Give a detail about each event.

**Example:**

**Topic sentence/Thesis:** *After a horrible fight with my sister, I learned the value of staying calm.*

**Event:** *We disagreed about who was going to have the family party.*

**Detail:** *Even though we both work, she said she was too busy and I would have to do it.*

**Event:** *She made me so mad, I started yelling at her, and I got nasty.*

**Detail:** *I brought up times in the past when she had tried to pass responsibilities off on me, and I told her I was sick of being the one who did everything.*

**Event:** *I hung up on her, and now we are not talking.*

**Detail:** *I feel bad, and I know I will have to call her sooner or later because she is my sister. I do love her, even though she is a pain sometimes.*

1. Topic sentence/Thesis: ______________________________

______________________________

Event: ______________________________

Detail: ______________________________

______________________________

Event: ______________________________

Detail: ______________________________

______________________________

Event: ______________________________

Detail: ______________________________

______________________________

2. Topic sentence/Thesis: ______________________________

______________________________

Event: ______________________________

Detail: ______________________________

______________________________

Event: ______________________________

Detail: ______________________________

______________________________

Event: ______________________________

Detail: ______________________________

______________________________

## *Organization in Narration*

Narration usually presents events in the order in which they happened, which is referred to as **time (chronological) order**. As shown in the paragraph and essay models on pages 112–13, a narration starts at the beginning of the story and describes events as they unfolded.

**Transitions** move readers from one event to the next.

**Tip** For more on time order, see pages 76–77.

### Common Transitions in Narration

| | | | |
|---|---|---|---|
| after | eventually | meanwhile | since |
| as | finally | next | soon |
| at last | first | now | then |
| before | last | once | when |
| during | later | second | while |

**PRACTICE 5** **Using transitions in narration**

Read the paragraph that follows, and fill in the blanks with time transitions.

Some historians believe that as many as four hundred women disguised themselves as men so that they could serve in the U.S. Civil War (1861–1865). One of the best known of these women was Sarah Emma Edmonds. ________ the war began, Edmonds, an opponent of slavery, felt driven to join the Union Army, which fought for the free states. ________ President Abraham Lincoln asked for

army volunteers, she disguised herself as a man, took the name Frank Thompson, and enlisted in the infantry. __________ her military service, Edmonds worked as a male nurse and a messenger. _________ serving as a nurse, she learned that the Union general needed someone to spy on the Confederates. ________ extensive training, Edmonds took on this duty and, disguised as a slave, went behind enemy lines. Here, she learned about the Confederates' military strengths and weaknesses. _____________, she returned to the Union side and went back to work as a nurse. In 1863, Edmonds left the army after developing malaria. She was worried that hospital workers would discover that she was a woman. As a result of her departure, "Frank Thompson" was listed as a deserter. In later years, Edmonds, under her real name, worked to get a veteran's pension and to get the desertion charge removed from her record. __________, in 1884, a special act of Congress granted her both of these wishes.

## Evaluate Narration

To become a more successful writer, it is important not only to understand the Four Basics of Good Narration but to read and evaluate examples as well. In this section, you will have the opportunity to use a sample rubric to analyze or evaluate the samples of narrative writing provided. By using this rubric, you will gain a better understanding of how the components of good narration work together to create a successful paragraph or essay. Additionally, reading examples of narration will help you write your own.

Read the following sample narration paragraph. Using the Four Basics of Good Narration and the sample grading rubric, decide what grade this paragraph would earn. Explain your answer.

**Assignment:** Write a paragraph about one moment that made a significant difference in your week. You should use clear transitions to indicate the passage of time, and you should use enough detail to bring the story to life for your reader.

**As I was driving to work the other day, I noticed that it was starting to rain. Normally, that would not be a problem, but on this day it was. I had no windshield wipers. They had broken the previous week and I had not had enough money to fix them yet. Although the rain never became overly heavy, it was enough to be annoying. Perhaps I should consider putting in new wipers when I get home. Without good windshield wipers, I am putting both myself and others in danger in poor weather.**

**Analysis of Sample Paragraph:**

**Sample rubric**

| Element | Grading criteria | Point: Comment |
|---|---|---|
| **Appropriateness** | • Did the student follow the assignment directions? | ____/5: |
| **Main idea** | • Does the paper clearly state a strong main idea in a complete sentence? | ____/10: |
| **Support** | • Is the main idea developed with specific support, including specific details and examples?<br>• Is there enough support to make the main idea evident to the reader?<br>• Is all the support directly related to the main idea? | ____/10: |
| **Organization** | • Is the writing logically organized?<br>• Does the student use transitions (*also, for example, sometimes,* and so on) to move the reader from one point to another? | ____/10: |
| **Conclusion** | • Does the conclusion remind the reader of the main idea?<br>• Does it make an observation based on the support? | ____/5: |
| **Grammar** | • Is the writing free of the Four Most Serious Errors? (See Chapters 16–19.)<br>• Is the sentence structure clear?<br>• Does the student choose words that clearly express his or her meaning?<br>• Are the words spelled correctly?<br>• Is the punctuation correct? | ____/10: |
| | | TOTAL POINTS: ____/50 |

# Read and Analyze Narration

The first two examples of narrative writing here come from students Jelani Lynch and Arianna Morgan. In the third example, a Profile of Success, Alice Adoga shows how she uses narration in her field of social work. The final example is a narration essay by Amy Tan, a professional writer. As you read these selections, pay attention to the vocabulary, and answer the questions in the margin. They will help you read critically.

*Student Narration Paragraph*

Jelani Lynch

# My Turnaround

**integrity:** honesty; having a sound moral code

**mentor:** a counselor, a teacher, an adviser

**Predict** What will Jelani's paragraph explain?

**Reflect** Have you ever made a decision that changed your life?

**Summarize** How did meeting Shawn change Jelani's life?

**Vocabulary development** Underline these words as you read Jelani's paragraph: *integrity, mentor.*

1 Before my big turnaround, my life was headed in the wrong direction. I grew up in the city and had a typical sad story: broken home, not much money, gangs, and drugs. In this world, few positive male role models are available. I played the game "Street Life": running the streets, stealing bikes, robbing people, carrying a gun, and selling drugs. The men in my neighborhood did not have regular jobs; they got their money outside the system. No one except my mother thought school was worth much. I had a history of poor school performance, a combination of not showing up and not doing any work when I did. My pattern of failure in that area was pretty strong. When I was seventeen, though, things got really bad. I was arrested for possession of crack cocaine. I was kicked out of school for good. During this time, I realized that my life was not going the way I wanted it to be. I was headed nowhere, except a life of crime, violence, and possibly early death. I knew that way of life, because I was surrounded by people who had chosen that direction. I did not want to go there anymore. When I made that decision, my life started to change. First, I met Shawn Brown, a man who had had the same kind of life I did. He got out of that life, though, by graduating from high school and college and getting a good job. He has a house, a wife, and children, along with great clothes. Shawn became my role model, showing me that with honesty, integrity, and hard work I could live a much better life. Since meeting Shawn, I have turned my life around. I started taking school seriously and graduated from high school, something I thought I would never do. Working with Shawn, I have read books and learned I enjoy writing. I have met the mayor of Boston and got a summer job at the State House. I have been part of an educational video and had many opportunities to meet and work with people who are successful. Now, I am a mentor with Diamond Educators, and I work with other young, urban males to give them a role model and help them make good choices. Now, I have a bright future with goals and plans. I have turned my life around and know I will be a success.

1. Underline the topic sentence.
2. What is important about the story? ______________________________

______________________________________________

______________________________________________

3. Number the major events.
4. Circle the transitions.
5. Does Jelani's paragraph follow the Four Basics of Good Narration (p. 108)? Be ready to give specific reasons for your answer. ______________

______________________________

______________________________

*Student Narration Essay*

Arianna Morgan

# The Time I Almost Lost My Baby Brother

Arianna is a student at Illinois Central College pursuing a degree in Theater. She is currently employed by Right at School, and she is the site manager of Dunlap Grade. Arianna explains, This was one of my favorite essays I got to write. The writing process wasn't very difficult for me. I just wrote a story about a moment when I thought I was going to lose someone very close to me, and I revised it once. The day I wrote about was one of the hardest days of my life. I have never been more connected to a paper than I was with this one. When I wrote this, I wasn't just typing words onto a paper. Every word came from my heart, and I'm glad other people get to experience this moment with me now.

**Predict** What situation do you think Morgan's family faced?

**Vocabulary development** Underline these words as you see them in Morgan's essay: *Stevens-Johnson syndrome, Staph*

**Stevens-Johnson syndrome:** a rare disorder characterized by flu-like symptoms followed by painful blisters and rashes on the skin that then shed and die. This syndrome requires immediate hospital treatment and an often lengthy recovery.

**Staph:** short for *Staphylococcus*, a bacterium that can cause pus formations, especially in the skin and mucus membranes.

1 Just like any other summer day it was very warm and sunny out and I had stayed with my aunt and uncle the night prior. My Aunt Rosa and I were on our way home after going to the store, but when we walked inside, my uncle was standing in the kitchen, and I could tell by looking at him that something was wrong. He looked at me and said, "Grandpa called; they think they know what is wrong with Bryce. The doctors say that he has a 30 percent chance of living." Those words rang in my ears; I couldn't believe what was just said. We were just staring at him. None of us could comprehend the words my uncle just spoke. All of our minds were going crazy, but no one could speak, and we wished it could have been one of us rather than Bryce.

2 I just stood there because I could not believe what my uncle had just said, and I was thinking of what I could do to help my baby brother. Unfortunately, there was nothing I could do, and, as a big sister, that's the worst feeling, so I kept shaking my head as we were all crying. How could this happen to him? He was just fine and healthy last week. I didn't understand.

**Reflect** Have you ever had an experience that made you feel overwhelmed and powerless? What did you do to work through that situation or try to deal with it?

**Summarize** What particular ideas went through Arianna's mind as she tried to process the new information about her brother?

3 After what seemed like hours, I realized that I couldn't even create any words and I just had this blank stare with every kind of emotion running through my mind and body. Why did he have to get sick? Inside I was so angry. Why couldn't it have been one of the older kids? Someone more grown up could have fought it off, but he couldn't because he was so small. Terrified and alone, I just wanted to hold him in my arms again and tell him how much I loved him. I was so sad, hurt, and upset. This could not happen; I would not lose my little brother.

4 At this point I couldn't take it anymore. The tears and sadness were too much. Slamming the door behind me, I stormed out of the back door, bawling. All I could hear was my aunt yelling for me to come back in, but I couldn't because I was thinking to myself, "I just need fresh air and time alone to figure out what is going on." I could not even pray—which is something that I've always done when I had no one else to turn to. Everything around me made me upset. I wanted to hit something or scream at the top of my lungs, but I knew it wouldn't help.

5 My aunt came outside, but I kept running down the driveway until I couldn't run anymore. As I fell to my knees, my eyes filled with tears and I was sitting there crying like a little baby. Would I have to bury my baby brother? Would I have to be strong for my mom and little sister? Was I strong enough to do this? My aunt tried to pick me up off the ground, but I couldn't breathe, let alone get up. I couldn't feel anything other than the fact that I was in a deep dark black hole, and no one could do anything to pull me out.

6 My baby brother was going to die. I wouldn't be able to laugh or play with him ever again. All I wanted was to see my older brother and sister. I needed to see them, to hug them, and to tell them how much I loved both of them. Finally, my aunt picked me up and we went inside so I could calm down.

7 The doctors were wrong but we didn't find this out until much later. Bryce didn't have Stevens-Johnson syndrome; he had a staph infection and the doctors let us know later that he was going to live, but he would be in the hospital for a week or so.

8 After almost losing my brother so much changed. I learned to appreciate my family and everyone in it, and I don't take things for granted anymore. My baby brother is five years old now, and he's alive, healthy, and he's growing up into a little man. Any time I get annoyed with him I think about when I almost lost him, and I am just thankful he's here with us. Since this was such a life-changing experience, this moment will be a time I will always remember.

1. Underline the topic sentence.

2. What is important about the story? ______________________________

______________________________________________

______________________________________________

______________________________________________

# Profile of Success

## Narration in the Real World

COURTESY OF ALICE ADOGA

**Alice Adoga**
Family Service Specialist

**Background:** In January 2007, I moved from West Africa, Nigeria, to the United States at the age of eighteen to live with my stepmom and three siblings. Before my departure from Nigeria, I knew my life was going to change a great deal. However, I had no idea what these changes would be. In the fall of 2007, I was admitted into the twelfth grade at Franklin High School after taking many Standards of Learning Tests. Many were surprised that I could speak English or even articulate well. Not only did I have to deal with cultural differences, I also had to adjust to the educational system of this country. In my English classes, I was lacking in grammar and I had difficulties writing research papers. I was always self-conscious about my writing and panicked when asked to write a paper. After graduating from high school in 2008, I decided to further my education at Paul D. Camp Community College (PDCCC). While at PDCCC, I had to take developmental English, and I struggled through most English classes during my freshman year in college. I worked very closely with all my English teachers and professors in high school and college. I also had several tutors assist me with my papers. Although my grammar has improved, I am still learning how to be a better writer today. I have always had a passion for education. I believe that knowledge is power. The many challenges I faced all these years have sparked my zeal to continue my academic journey no matter what it takes. I am currently seeking my master's degree online at Liberty University in Human Services Counseling with concentration in crisis response and trauma.

**Degrees/Colleges:** A.S., Paul D. Camp Community College; B.S. Psychology, George Mason University

**Employer:** City of Franklin Department of Social Services

**Writing at work:** My writing at work is an objective narrative of reports from mandated reporters and clients' documentation during intake assessment or investigations. My job requires accurate documentation of interactions with clients during interviews and any interactions carried out with child victims and anyone involved. Reports made to our agency need to be documented in the Online Automated Structured Information System (OASIS). Part of my job is to write out accurately what has been reported to me during interviews and investigation to help give the reader a better picture of what took place during the incident. After interviews with a client, I write a descriptive narrative of what was said to me without inclusion of personal thoughts or opinions.

3. Double underline the major events.
4. Does Arianna's essay follow the Four Basics of Good Narration (p. 108)? Be ready to give specific reasons for your answer. ______________________

______________________

______________________

*Workplace Narration*

# Incident Descriptions (Hypothetical Example)

1 Caller, Ms. Joyce Baton, stated that she knows that Courtney Moses is leaving her seven-year-old daughter, Lilian Moses, at home alone in the evening several nights of the week and all day during the weekends without any food. Also, the apartment has been without power for the past three weeks. Caller informed this worker that she noted several times over the past month that Lilian has come over to their house after school and near dinner time to see their daughter, Melody Baton. Caller informed this worker that Lilian and her daughter Melody go to the same school and ride the same bus to and from school. Whenever she stops by their house, Lilian asks if she can join Melody for dinner because, "Mom doesn't have anything for me to eat." Ms. Baton stated that her daughter and Lilian "hang out" after school, and sometimes Lilian stays over for dinner. Ms. Baton says she always makes Lilian call her mother to get permission, and she has even talked with Ms. Moses about Lilian's frequent dinner requests. Ms. Baton reports that Ms. Moses does not mind that Lilian stays over and profusely thanks her for letting Lilian eat dinner with them. When this first began, Ms. Baton thought Lilian just didn't like what was being offered at home. However, Ms. Baton said she recently began to notice that Lilian "wolfs her food down" when she eats and is always finished earlier than her family. She has told her on a few occasions that, "we don't have any food left."

2 Ms. Baton stated that Melody is in the same class as Lilian. Melody told her that Lilian did not have food in her lunch bag several times last week. She also told her that Lilian asks other kids for food at school and on the bus. Ms. Baton has been to the Moses's home but has not been comfortable talking with Ms. Moses about the lack of food. Ms. Baton is concerned because her daughter has come home every day this week and reported that Lilian was begging for food. She has begun putting extra sandwiches and fruit in her daughter's lunch to share with Lilian. Ms. Baton informed this worker that she saw Lilian and her daughter get on the bus this morning. They use the same bus stop. Lilian is currently at All Kings Elementary School. The address is 1539 Lakeview Drive, Franklin, Virginia 23851. Ms. Baton stated that she wants to remain anonymous because no one knows she is calling us. She believes Ms. Moses knows about Lilian's behavior.

1. What is your main impression of what is happening in the Moses home?

   ____________________________________________

   ____________________________________________

2. Underline the primary details that support the main impression.

3. Double underline or circle any secondary details that help tell the story and give more information to the reader.

4. How is the description organized? ______________________

## *Professional Narration Essay*

Amy Tan

# Fish Cheeks

Amy Tan was born in Oakland, California, in 1952, several years after her mother and father emigrated from China. She studied at San Jose City College and later San Jose State University, receiving a B.A. with a double major in English and linguistics. In 1973, she earned an M.A. in linguistics from San Jose State University. In 1989, Tan published her first novel, *The Joy Luck Club*, which was nominated for the National Book Award and the National Book Critics Circle Award. Tan's other books include *The Kitchen God's Wife* (1991), *The Hundred Secret Senses* (1995), *Saving Fish from Drowning* (2005), and *The Valley of Amazement* (2013). Her short stories and essays have been published in the *Atlantic, Grand Street, Harper's,* the *New Yorker,* and other publications.

In the following essay, Tan uses narration to describe an experience that taught her an important lesson.

**Vocabulary development** Underline these words as you read the narration essay: *prawns, appalling, clamor, murmured, belched.*

**prawns:** shrimp or shrimp-like creatures
**appalling:** horrifying
**clamor:** noise
**murmured:** spoke in low tones
**belched:** burped

1 I fell in love with the minister's son the winter I turned fourteen. He was not Chinese, but as white as Mary in the manger. For Christmas I prayed for this blond-haired boy, Robert, and a slim new American nose.

2 When I found out that my parents had invited the minister's family over for Christmas dinner, I cried. What would Robert think of our shabby Chinese Christmas? What would he think of our noisy Chinese relatives who lacked proper American manners? What terrible disappointment would he feel upon seeing not a roasted turkey and sweet potatoes but Chinese food?

**Predict** Based on the second paragraph, what do you think will happen?

3 On Christmas Eve I saw that my mother had outdone herself in creating a strange menu. She was pulling black veins out of the backs of fleshy prawns. The kitchen was littered with appalling mounds of raw food: A slimy rock cod with bulging eyes that pleaded not to be thrown into a pan of hot oil. Tofu, which looked like stacked wedges of rubbery white sponges. A bowl soaking dried fungus back to life. A plate of squid, their backs crisscrossed with knife markings so they resembled bicycle tires.

4 And then they arrived—the minister's family and all my relatives in a clamor of doorbells and rumpled Christmas packages. Robert grunted hello, and I pretended he was not worthy of existence.

**Reflect** Name an event during which you tried to make a good impression on someone.

5 Dinner threw me into despair. My relatives licked the ends of their chopsticks and reached across the table, dipping them into the dozen or so plates of food. Robert and his family waited patiently for platters to be passed to them. My relatives murmured with pleasure when my mother brought out the whole steamed fish. Robert grimaced. Then my father poked his chopsticks just below the fish eye and plucked out the soft meat. "Amy, your favorite," he said, offering me the tender fish cheek. I wanted to disappear.

6 At the end of the meal my father leaned back and belched loudly, thanking my mother for her fine cooking. "It's a polite Chinese custom to show you are satisfied," explained my father to our astonished guests. Robert was looking down at his plate with a reddened face. The minister managed to muster up a quiet burp. I was stunned into silence for the rest of the night.

**Reflect** Have you ever felt different on the outside than you did on the inside?

7 After everyone had gone, my mother said to me, "You want to be the same as American girls on the outside." She handed me an early gift. It was a miniskirt in beige tweed. "But inside you must always be Chinese. You must be proud you are different. Your only shame is to have shame."

8 And even though I didn't agree with her then, I knew that she understood how much I had suffered during the evening's dinner. It wasn't until many years later—long after I had gotten over my crush on Robert—that I was able to fully appreciate her lesson and the true purpose behind our particular menu. For Christmas Eve that year, she had chosen all my favorite foods.

**Tip** For reading advice, see Chapter 1.

1. What is Tan's purpose for writing? ______________________________

______________________________________________

______________________________________________

2. Does she achieve it? ______________________________

3. In your own words, state her main idea. ______________________________

______________________________________________

______________________________________________

4. How has Tan organized her essay? ____________. Circle the transitional words and phrases that indicate this order.

Respond to one of the following assignments in a paragraph or essay.

1. Have you ever been embarrassed by your family or by others close to you? Write about the experience, and describe what you learned from it.
2. Write about a time when you felt different from other people. How did you react at the time? Have your feelings about the situation changed since then? If so, how?

3. Write about an experience that was uncomfortable at the time but funny later. Explain how you came to see humor in the situation.

## Write Your Own Narration

In this section, you will write your own narration based on one of the following assignments. For help, refer to the "How to Write Narration" checklist on page 127.

**ASSIGNMENT OPTIONS** **Writing about college, work, and everyday life**

Write a narration paragraph or essay on one of the following topics or on one of your own choice.

**College**

- Tell the story of how a teacher made a difference in your life.
- Write about a time when you achieved success or experienced a difficulty or success in school.
- Interview a college graduate about his or her educational experience. Questions might include the following: "Why did you go to college?" "What were your biggest challenges?" and "What were your greatest accomplishments?" Then, write that person's story.

**Work**

- Write about a situation or incident that made you decide to leave a job.
- Imagine a successful day or a frustrating day at your current or previous job. Then, tell the story of that day, including examples of successes.
- Write your own work history, guided by a statement that you would like to make about this history or your work style. Here is one example: "Being a people person has helped me in every job I have ever had." You might imagine that you are interviewing with a potential employer.

**Everyday life**

- Write about an experience that triggered a strong emotion: happiness, sadness, fear, anger, regret.
- Find a campus community service club that offers short-term assignments. Take an assignment and write about your experience.
- Tell the story of a community issue that interests you. One example is plans to create a bike lane on a major road. Discuss how the issue arose, and describe key developments. Research details by visiting a local newspaper's Web site.

## ASSIGNMENT OPTIONS Reading and writing critically

Complete one of the following assignments, which ask you to apply the critical thinking, reading, and writing skills discussed in Chapter 1.

**Tip** For a reminder of how to summarize, analyze, synthesize, and evaluate, see the Reading and Writing Critically box on page 21.

### WRITING CRITICALLY ABOUT READINGS

Both Alice Adoga's "Incident Descriptions" (p. 122) and Celia Hyde's "Police Report" (p. 165) require the writer to carefully and deliberately tell a specific story, recording only the facts. Review both of these pieces. Then, follow these steps:

1. **Summarize** Briefly summarize the works, listing major events.
2. **Analyze** List any types of examples or details you wish had been included in Adoga's or Hyde's reports. Also, write down any questions that the pieces raise for you.
3. **Synthesize** Using examples from either Adoga's and Hyde's stories and from your own experience, write about an observation in your own life. Choose an event that was significant and write about it clearly and with detail.
4. **Evaluate** Which piece do you think is more effective? Why? To write your evaluation, look back on your responses to step 2.

### WRITING ABOUT IMAGES

Study the photograph below, and complete the following steps.

PAUL BRADBURY/GETTY IMAGES

1. **Read the image** Ask yourself: What details does the photographer focus on? What seems to be the photo's message? (For more information on reading images, see Chapter 1.)
2. **Write a narration** Write a narration paragraph or essay about what has happened (or is happening) in the photograph. Be as creative as you like, but be sure to include details and reactions from step 1.

**WRITING TO SOLVE A PROBLEM**

Read or review the discussion of problem solving in Chapter 1 (pp. 28–30). Then, consider the following problem:

**You have learned that a generous scholarship is available for low-income, first-generation college students. You really need the money to cover day-care expenses while you are taking classes (in fact, you had thought you would have to stop going to college for a while). Many people have been applying. Part of the application is to write about yourself and why you deserve the scholarship.**

**Assignment:** Write a paragraph or essay that tells your story and why you should be considered for the scholarship. Think about how you can make your story stand out. You might start with the following sentence:

**Even though you will be reading applications from many first-generation college students, my story is a little different because** ______________________

______________________________________________________________.

**Tip** Such scholarships really do exist. Go online or to the college financial aid office to find out about them. If you are pleased with what you have written for this assignment, you could use it as part of your application.

**CHECKLIST**

## How to Write Narration

| Steps | Details |
|---|---|
| ☐ Narrow and explore your topic. See Chapter 3. | • Make the topic more specific.<br>• Prewrite to get ideas about the narrowed topic. |
| ☐ Write a topic sentence (paragraph) or thesis statement (essay). See Chapter 3. | • State what is most important to you about the topic and what you want your readers to understand. |
| ☐ Support your point. See Chapter 4. | • Come up with examples and details to explain your main idea to readers. |
| ☐ Write a draft. See Chapter 5. | • Make a plan that puts events or examples in a logical order.<br>• Include a topic sentence (paragraph) or thesis statement (essay) and all the supporting events, examples, and details. |
| ☐ Revise your draft. See Chapter 5. | • Make sure it has *all* the Four Basics of Good Narration.<br>• Make sure you include transitions to move readers smoothly from one event or example to the next. |
| ☐ Edit your revised draft. See Parts 3 through 6. | • Correct errors in grammar, spelling, word use, and punctuation. |

## Chapter Review

1. Narration is writing that ______________________________
2. List the Four Basics of Good Narration. ______________________________
______________________________
______________________________
______________________________
3. The topic sentence in a narration paragraph or the thesis statement in a narration essay usually includes what two things? ______________________________
4. What type of organization do writers of narration usually use? ______________________________
______________________________
5. List five common transitions for this type of organization. ______________________________
6. Write sentences using the following vocabulary words: *integrity, mentor, prawns, appalling*, *clamor*, *murmured*, and *belched*. ______________________________
______________________________
______________________________

## REFLECTING ON THE JOURNEY

### Skills Learned

Now that you've completed the chapter, share what you've learned about each skill by completing the following chart.

| Skill | What I learned about this skill |
|---|---|
| Write a story about myself or someone else | |
| Write a clear thesis statement or main idea for a narrative | |
| Generate support for a narrative paper | |
| Relate support directly to the main idea of the paper | |
| Read and analyze a narrative paper | |

7

# Illustration

## Writing That Gives Examples

### Learning Objectives

**Chapter Goal:** Learn how to write an illustration paper.

**Tools to Achieve the Goal:**

- Four Basics of Good Illustration (p. 130)
- Diagram: Paragraphs and Essays in Illustration (pp. 134–35)
- Sample Illustration Paragraph and Rubric (pp. 137–38)
- Student Illustration Paragraph: Casandra Palmer, *Gifts from the Heart* (p. 138)
- Student Illustration Essay: Sarah Bigler, *High School Is Not Preparing Us for College* (p. 139)
- Profile of Success and Workplace Illustration: John D'Urso (p. 141)
- Professional Illustration Essay: Andrea Whitmer, *When Poor People Have Nice Things* (p. 143)
- Checklist: How to Write Illustration (p. 149)

## READING ROADMAP

### Key Terms

Skim Chapter 7 before reading. Find these words or terms in **bold** type. Put a check mark next to each once you locate it.

____ illustration
____ main idea
____ support
____ order of importance
____ time order
____ transitions

### Guided Reading for Chapter 7

Fill out the following chart before you begin reading. For each skill, write what you know about that skill and what you would like to know upon completing the chapter. At the end of the chapter, you will be asked to share what you learned about each skill.

| Skill | When I have used this skill | What I want to know about this skill |
|---|---|---|
| Write a paper with one specific idea | | |
| Identify the best possible support details to show, explain, or prove the main idea | | |
| Provide examples to support the main idea | | |
| Provides enough details and examples to get the idea across to the readers | | |

Visit **LaunchPad Solo for Readers and Writers > Reading > Patterns of Organization** for more tutorials, videos, and practice with patterns of organization.

# Understand What Illustration Is

**Illustration** is writing that uses examples to support a point.

## **Four Basics** of Good Illustration

1. It has a point.
2. It gives specific examples that show, explain, or prove the point.
3. It gives details to support the examples.
4. It uses enough examples to get the point across to the reader.

In the following paragraph, the numbers and colors correspond to the Four Basics of Good Illustration.

**4** Enough examples to get the point across to the reader

**1** Many people would like to serve their communities or help with causes that they believe in, but they do not have much time and do not know what to do. Now, the Internet provides people with ways to help that do not take much time or money. **2** Web sites now make it convenient to donate online. With a few clicks, an organization of your choice can receive your donation or money from a sponsoring advertiser. For example, if you are interested in helping rescue unwanted and abandoned animals, you can go to www.theanimalrescuesite.com. **3** When you click as instructed, a sponsoring advertiser will make a donation to help provide food and care for the 27 million animals in shelters. Also, a portion of any money you spend in the site's online store will go to providing animal care. **2** If you want to help fight world hunger, go to www.thehungersite.com **3** and click daily to have sponsor fees directed to hungry people in more than seventy countries via the Mercy Corps, Feeding America, and Millennium Promise. Each year, hundreds of millions of cups of food are distributed to one billion hungry people around the world. **2** Other examples of click-to-give sites are www.thechildhealthsite.com, www.theliteracysite.com, and www.breastcancersite.com. **3** Like the animal-rescue and hunger sites, these other sites have click-to-give links, online stores that direct a percentage of sales income to charity, and links to help you learn about causes you are interested in. One hundred percent of the sponsors' donations go to the charities, and you can give with a click every single day. Since I have found out about these sites, I go to at least one of them every day. **1** I have learned a lot about various problems, and every day, I feel as if I have helped a little.

It is hard to explain anything without using examples, so you use illustration in almost every communication situation.

| | |
|---|---|
| **College** | An exam question asks you to explain and give examples of a concept. |
| **Work** | Your boss asks you to tell her what office equipment needs to be replaced and why. |
| **Everyday life** | You complain to your landlord that the building superintendent is not doing his job. The landlord asks for examples. |

In college, the words *illustration* and *illustrate* may not appear in writing assignments. Instead, you might be asked to *give examples of* ______ or to *be specific about* ______. Regardless of an assignment's wording, to be clear and effective, most types of writing require specific examples. Include them whenever they help you make your point.

## *Main Idea in Illustration*

In illustration, the **main idea** is the message you want your readers to receive and understand. To help you discover your main idea, complete the following sentence:

**Main idea in illustration** **What I want readers to know about this topic is . . .**

The topic sentence (in a paragraph) or thesis statement (in an essay) usually includes the topic and the main idea the writer wants to make about the topic. Let's look at a topic sentence first.

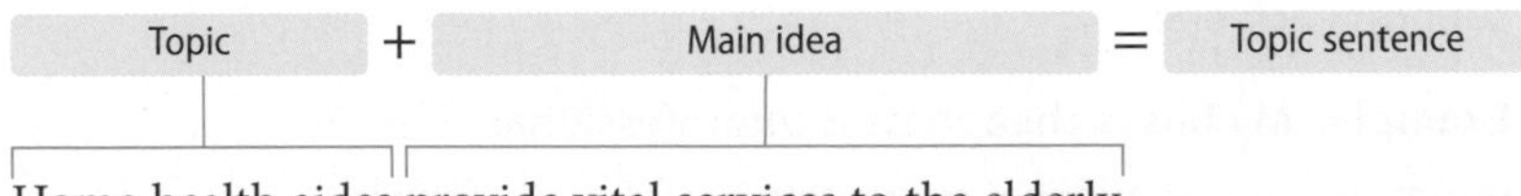
Topic
+
Main idea
=
Topic sentence

Home health aides provide vital services to the elderly.

Remember that a thesis statement for an essay can be a little broader than a paragraph topic.

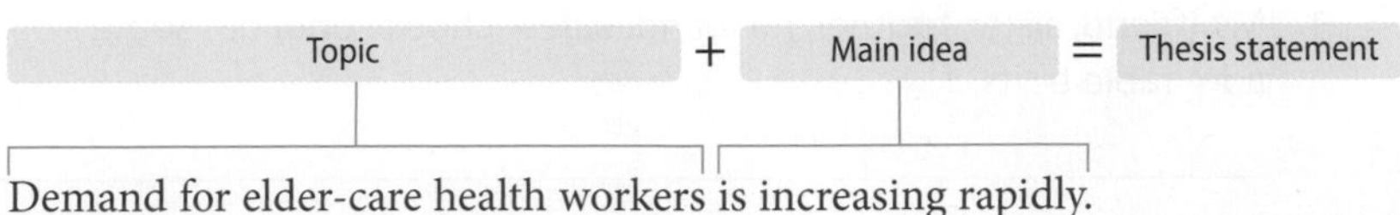
Topic
+
Main idea
=
Thesis statement

Demand for elder-care health workers is increasing rapidly.

Whereas the topic sentence is focused on just home health aides, the thesis statement considers elder-care careers in general.

**Tip** Sometimes, the same main idea can be used for a paragraph and an essay, but the essay must develop this point in more detail. (See pp. 68–69.)

**PRACTICE 1** **Forming a main idea**

Each of the items in this practice is a narrowed topic. Think about each of them, and write a main idea about each topic in the space provided.

**Example: The words to songs I like** *relate closely to experiences I have had.*

1. A few moments alone ______
2. A course I am taking ______
3. The busiest time at work ______
4. Being a parent of a newborn baby ______
5. Working with other people ______

## *Support in Illustration*

The paragraph and essay models on pages 134–35 use the topic sentence (paragraph) and thesis statement (essay) from the Main Idea section of this chapter. Both models include the **support** used in all illustration writing: examples backed up by details about the examples. In the essay model, however, the major support points (examples) are topic sentences for individual paragraphs.

To generate good detailed examples, use one or more of the prewriting techniques discussed in Chapter 3. First, write down all the examples that come into your mind. Then, review your examples, and choose the ones that will best communicate your point to your readers.

**PRACTICE 2** **Supporting your main idea with examples**

Read the following main ideas, and give three examples you might use to support each one.

**Example: My boss's cheapness is unprofessional.**

*makes us bring in our own calculators*

*makes us use old, rusted paper clips*

*will not replace burned-out light bulbs*

1. My (friend, sister, brother, husband, wife—choose one) has some admirable traits.

______

______

______

______

2. This weekend is particularly busy.

______________________________________________

______________________________________________

______________________________________________

**PRACTICE 3** **Giving details about the examples**

In the spaces provided, copy your main ideas and examples from Practice 2. Then, for each example, write a detail that further shows, explains, or proves what you mean.

**Example:**

**Main idea: My boss's cheapness is unprofessional.**

**Example:** *makes us bring in our own calculators*

**Detail:** *Some people do not have a calculator.*

**Example:** *makes us use old, rusted paper clips*

**Detail:** *They leave rust marks on important documents.*

**Example:** *will not replace burned-out light bulbs*

**Detail:** *The dim light leads to more errors.*

1. Main idea: ______________________________________________

 Example: ______________________________________________

 Detail: ______________________________________________

 Example: ______________________________________________

 Detail: ______________________________________________

 Example: ______________________________________________

 Detail: ______________________________________________

2. Main idea: ______________________________________________

 Example: ______________________________________________

 Detail: ______________________________________________

 Example: ______________________________________________

 Detail: ______________________________________________

 Example: ______________________________________________

 Detail: ______________________________________________

# Paragraphs vs. Essays in Illustration

For more on the important features of illustration, see the Four Basics of Good Illustration on page 130.

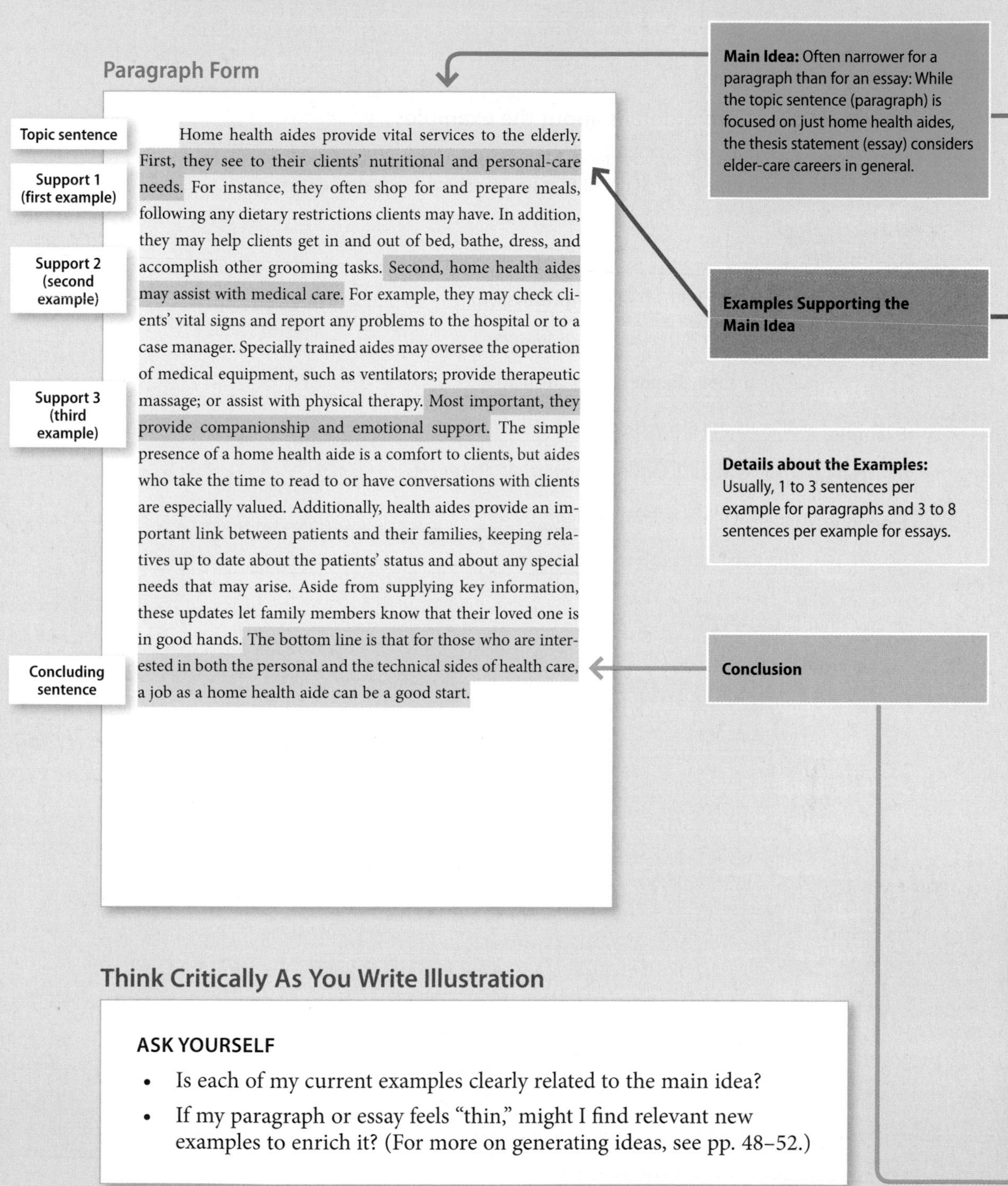
Main Idea: Often narrower for a paragraph than for an essay: While the topic sentence (paragraph) is focused on just home health aides, the thesis statement (essay) considers elder-care careers in general.
Examples Supporting the Main Idea
Details about the Examples: Usually, 1 to 3 sentences per example for paragraphs and 3 to 8 sentences per example for essays.
Conclusion
Topic sentence
Support 1 (first example)
Support 2 (second example)
Support 3 (third example)
Concluding sentence

## Paragraph Form

Home health aides provide vital services to the elderly. First, they see to their clients' nutritional and personal-care needs. For instance, they often shop for and prepare meals, following any dietary restrictions clients may have. In addition, they may help clients get in and out of bed, bathe, dress, and accomplish other grooming tasks. Second, home health aides may assist with medical care. For example, they may check clients' vital signs and report any problems to the hospital or to a case manager. Specially trained aides may oversee the operation of medical equipment, such as ventilators; provide therapeutic massage; or assist with physical therapy. Most important, they provide companionship and emotional support. The simple presence of a home health aide is a comfort to clients, but aides who take the time to read to or have conversations with clients are especially valued. Additionally, health aides provide an important link between patients and their families, keeping relatives up to date about the patients' status and about any special needs that may arise. Aside from supplying key information, these updates let family members know that their loved one is in good hands. The bottom line is that for those who are interested in both the personal and the technical sides of health care, a job as a home health aide can be a good start.

## Think Critically As You Write Illustration

**ASK YOURSELF**

- Is each of my current examples clearly related to the main idea?
- If my paragraph or essay feels "thin," might I find relevant new examples to enrich it? (For more on generating ideas, see pp. 48–52.)

## Essay Form

Introductory paragraph

1

During these difficult economic times, many students are looking to pursue careers in expanding fields with good long-term prospects. On

**Thesis statement**

they should seriously consider is elder care. Because the U.S. population is aging, demand for workers who specialize in the health of the elderly is increasing rapidly.

One set of workers in great demand consists of physical therapists, who help elderly patients improve their mobility and retain their independence. Some of these therapists are based at hospitals or nu

**Topic sentence 1 (first example)**

ties, others at clinics or private offices. Re where they work, they provide a variety of services to elderly patients, from helping stroke sufferers relearn how to walk and perform other daily activities to showing others how to live a more active life. Physical therapists can also help patients injured in falls reduce their reliance on painkillers, which can become less effective over time and in certain cases even addictive. According to the U.S. Department of Labor, employment of physical therapists will grow by 30 percent

2

over the next ten years, largely because of the increasing number of elderly Americans.

Also in demand are nutritionists who specialize in older people's dietary needs. These pr

**Topic sentence 2 (second example)**

may plan meals and provide nutrition advi pitals, nursing homes, and other institutions, or they may counsel individual patients on how to eat more healthfully or on how to prepare meals that meet certain dietary restrictions. For instance, elderly patients suffering from heart disease may need to eat foods that are low in salt and saturated fat. Other patients might have to avoid foods that interfere with the absorption of certain medications. Although the market for nutritionists is not expected to grow as quickly as that for physical therapists, it is projected

**Topic sentence 3 (third example)**

steadily as the population continues to age.

The highest-demand workers are those who provide at-home health care to the elderly. One subset of these workers consists of home nurses, who often provide follow-up care after patients are released from a hospital or other medical facility. These nurses help

3

patients transition from an institutional setting while making sure they continue to receive high-quality care. For instance, they track patients' vital signs, administer and monitor medications, and carry out specific tasks required to manage particular diseases. Another subset of home health workers is made up of home health aides, who assist nurses and other professionals with medical care, see to clients' nutritional and personal-care needs, and provide companionship and emotional support. Both home health aides and nurses provide an important link between patients and their families, keeping relatives up to date about the patients' status and about any special needs that may arise. In addition to supplying key information, these updates let family members know that their loved one is in good hands. Because of home health-care workers' vital role in serving the expanding elderly population, their employment is expected to grow significantly: c 30 to 40 percent over the next ten years.

Concluding paragraph

Given the growing demand for elder-care workers, people pursuing these professions stand an excel-

4

lent chance of getting jobs with good long-term outlooks. Based on what I have learned about these professions, the best candidates are those who have a strong interest in health or medicine, a willingness to work hard to get the necessary qualifications, and, perhaps most important, an ability to connect with and truly care for others.

## *Organization in Illustration*

**Tip** For more on order of importance and time order, see pages 76–78.

Illustration often uses **order of importance**, saving the most powerful example for last. This strategy is used in the paragraph and essay models on pages 134–35. Or, if the examples are given according to when they happened, it might be organized by **time order**.

**Transitions** in illustration let readers know that you are introducing an example or moving from one example to another.

### Common Transitions in Illustration

| | | | |
|---|---|---|---|
| also | first, second, and so on | for one thing/ for another | the most/the least |
| another | for example | in addition | one example/ another example |
| finally | for instance | | |

**PRACTICE 4** **Using transitions in illustration**

Read the paragraph that follows, and fill in the blanks with transitions.

Greek myths include many heroes, such as the great warriors Achilles and Herakles. ____________, the myths describe several monsters that tested the heroes' strength. ____________ of these frightening creatures was the Hydra, a water serpent with many heads. When a warrior cut off one of these heads, two or more would sprout up in its place. ________________ of these mythical monsters was the Gorgons, three sisters who had snakes for hair. Any person who looked into the Gorgons' eyes would turn to stone. __________ terrifying monster was Cerberus, a three-headed dog with snapping jaws. He guarded the gates to the underworld, keeping the living from entering and the dead from leaving. Fortunately, some heroes' cleverness equaled the monsters' hideousness. ____________, Herakles discovered that by applying a torch to the wounds of the Hydra, he could prevent the creature from growing more heads. ______, Orpheus, a famous mythical musician, soothed Cerberus by plucking the strings of a lyre. In this way, Orpheus got past the beast and entered the underworld, from which he hoped to rescue his wife.

## Evaluate Illustration

To become a more successful writer, it is important not only to understand the Four Basics of Good Illustration but to read and evaluate examples as well. In this section, you will have the opportunity to use a sample rubric to analyze or evaluate the samples of illustration provided. By using this rubric, you will gain a better understanding of how the components of good illustration work together to create a successful paragraph or essay. Additionally, reading examples of illustration will help you write your own.

Read the following sample illustration paragraph. Using the Four Basics of Good Illustration (p. 130) and the sample grading rubric, decide what grade this paragraph would earn. Explain your answer.

**Assignment:** Write a paragraph explaining why any one particular extracurricular activity is important.

**When I mention "marching band," it's pretty clear that most of my readers have already tuned out. In fact, I think that a lot of people reading this may not even consider it a true activity because it does not involve physical exercise, like any number of sporting activities; intense intellectual thought, as a chess or math team may require; or even individual performance, as you may see in theater. But to feel this way is to overlook activities like choir and band that not only keep students involved and out of trouble, but also help them learn leadership and teamwork skills that they may not find in other activities. As a member of a large group, every member of that group is always counting on them, so while it seems like it may be a "safety" activity where one can hide, I believe it is a significant and important activity.**

**Analysis of Sample Paragraph:**

**Sample rubric**

| Element | Grading criteria | Point: Comment |
|---|---|---|
| Appropriateness | • Did the student follow the assignment directions? | ____/5: |
| Main idea | • Does the paper clearly state a strong main idea in a complete sentence? | ____/10: |
| Support | • Is the main idea developed with specific support, including specific details and examples?<br>• Is there enough support to make the main idea evident to the reader?<br>• Is all the support directly related to the main idea? | ____/10: |

►

| Element | Grading criteria | Point: Comment |
|---|---|---|
| Organization | • Is the writing logically organized?<br>• Does the student use transitions (*also, for example, sometimes*, and so on) to move the reader from one point to another? | ____/10: |
| Conclusion | • Does the conclusion remind the reader of the main idea?<br>• Does it make an observation based on the support? | ____/5: |
| Grammar | • Is the writing free of the Four Most Serious Errors? (See Chapters 16–19.)<br>• Is the sentence structure clear?<br>• Does the student choose words that clearly express his or her meaning?<br>• Are the words spelled correctly?<br>• Is the punctuation correct? | ____/10: |
| | | **TOTAL POINTS: ____/50** |

# Read and Analyze Illustration

Reading examples of illustration will help you write your own. First, two pieces of student work, a paragraph and an essay, are featured as examples. Next, the Profile of Success is paired with writing from the real world. In this profile, John D'Urso shows how he uses illustration in his work as an automobile technician. The final example is an illustration essay by Andrea Whitmer, a professional writer. As you read these selections, pay attention to the vocabulary, and answer the questions in the margin. They will help you read critically.

## *Student Illustration Paragraph*

Casandra Palmer

## Gifts from the Heart

**Predict** After reading the title, what do you think the paragraph will be about?

**Reflect** Have you ever received a gift that made you laugh or cry?

1 In our home, gift exchanges have always been meaningful items to us. We do not just give things so that everyone has lots of presents. Each item has a purpose, such as a need or something that someone has desired for a long time. Some things have been given that may have made the other person laugh or cry. I remember one Christmas, our daughter Hannah had her boyfriend, who looked a lot like Harry Potter, join us. We wanted to include him, but we did not know him well, so it was hard to know what to give him. We decided to get Hannah a Harry Potter poster and crossed

out the name Harry Potter. In place of Harry Potter, we put her boyfriend's name. Everyone thought it was funny, and we were all laughing, including Hannah's boyfriend. It was a personal gift that he knew we had thought about. For some reason, Hannah did not think it was so funny, but she will still remember it. Another meaningful gift came from watching the movie *Titanic* with my other daughter, Tabitha. We both cried hard and hugged each other. She surprised me by getting a necklace that resembled the gem known as "Heart of the Ocean." I was so touched that she gave me something to remind me of the experience we shared. These special moments have left lasting impressions on my heart.

1. Double-underline the **topic sentence**.
2. Underline the **examples** that support the main idea.
3. Circle the **transitions**.
4. Does the paragraph have the Four Basics of Good Illustration (p. 130)? Why or why not? ________________________________

   ________________________________________
5. Does the paragraph use a particular kind of organization, like time, space, or importance? Does that choice help the paragraph's effectiveness or not?

   ________________________________________

   ________________________________________

## *Student Illustration Essay*

Sarah Bigler

# High School Is Not Preparing Us for College

Sarah Bigler is a political science major and editor of *The Daily Eastern News* at Eastern Illinois University in Charleston, IL.

**Vocabulary development** Underline these words as you see them in Sarah's essay: *hype, myriad, tedious.*

**hype:** exaggerated or extravagant claim

**myriad:** a countless or extremely great number

**tedious:** too long, slow, or dull

**Predict** Before reading the article, what do you think some of Bigler's reasons may be? Why do you think she would say that high school doesn't prepare students for college?

1 When I first got to college I heard the same thing over and over again from professors in all of my general education classes.

2 "How do you not know this?" "What are they teaching you in high school?"

3 As a freshman, I would sort of shrug and didn't have an answer for them. I remembered analyzing a lot of literature, and vaguely remember triangles in math and dates from history. As a senior, I totally understand my professors' point. I even feel bad for them now.

**Reflect** In your own experience as a student, have you ever felt the "gap" that Bigler discusses? How did or does it affect you?

4 The problem everyone misses is that there's a gap in high school teaching and college teaching. High school is supposed to prepare you for college; it doesn't. It prepares you for getting into college and for little else.

5 My high school teachers used to warn us whenever we felt they were being unfairly strict that college professors wouldn't compromise with us and that we had no idea what we were in for. I don't know why they were trying to scare us, but that wasn't true. I'm a transfer student, and neither of the schools I've been to have lived up to the terrifying hype.

6 They also told us that high school was preparation for the type of study we'd experience in college. That's definitely not true. High school was all about learning for the myriad tests the government requires. It was about passing the SAT and ACT and getting a high enough GPA to apply to the particular college you wanted.

**Reflect** Bigler says that high school is just about "getting through." What does she mean? Do you agree with this statement?

7 Basically, high school was just about getting through. It was a way station between grade school and college.

8 It wasn't about learning and knowledge, it was about memorization of facts. I look back and wonder the same thing my professors do, because it seems nothing I learned back then has an impact on my day-to-day life now.

9 The public school system is failing us. They teach without explaining why something is important. They don't instill a sense that education is an important factor in our lives. They teach us names and dates and numbers without showing us how they will affect our decisions and ability to get good jobs in the future.

10 Take writing for an example. The way grammar is taught is tedious and mind-numbing, especially when there are just random sentences lined up on a page and covered in red markings. Every high school student complains about having to take grammar and learn all of the awful exceptions to every grammar and spelling rule in the English language.

**Reflect** Think about your chosen field or the career you would like to have. How is writing used in that field?

11 But every job that requires a college degree in America will expect a good level of writing competence. Even mathematicians and scientists have to be able to write cover letters for their resumes, research grant proposals, and reports for their bosses.

12 No one bothered to explain that in my high school English class, and no type of writing outside of a grocery list requires someone to line up random sentences in order.

13 But in college, the emphasis is on learning and thinking. I've had dozens of teachers emphasize critical thinking in their classes, and advisers, counselors, professors and parents suddenly want students to think for themselves. It's a huge change from high school, where students are expected to follow rules and lessons blindly.

14 Sometimes the instinct to just get by has been so embedded in students that they don't even make a serious effort in their chosen majors. These are the classes that students are supposed to feel passionately about and that they assumedly want to use for the rest of their lives.

**Reflect** Do you agree with Bigler's explanation about why students do not write well?

15 To use my grammar example again, I've even seen evidence of students majoring in English and journalism who do not take grammar seriously. I'm wondering why they chose those majors if they don't care about making their writing more clear and professional.

16 High school should be a time to prepare for college and for the real world. The teenage years are the beginning of finding out who each person is and what he or she wants to do with his or her life. High schools should

be promoting individuality and should be working off a more college-like atmosphere, instead of just herding teenagers through.

1. Double underline the **topic sentence.**
2. Underline the **examples** that Bigler uses to support her point.
3. Does Bigler use enough examples to make her point clear? ________________
4. Does Bigler's essay follow the Four Basics of Good Illustration (p. 130)? ________

## Profile of Success

### Illustration in the Real World

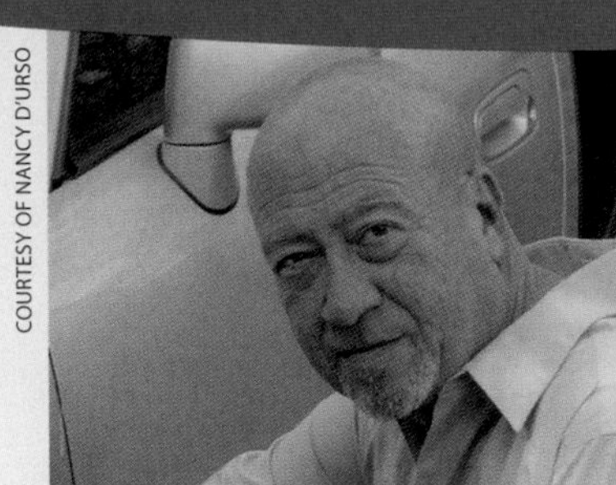
COURTESY OF NANCY D'URSO

**John D'Urso**

Automobile Technician

**Background** I grew up in Warwick, Rhode Island. I was an only child, so many things came easy for me. School was not one of those things. I had no intention of continuing my education after high school, so I enrolled in the vocational program and chose auto shop as my major. I excelled and graduated at the top of my class.

After being out of school for twenty-three years, I enrolled at Rhode Island College and chose career and technical education as my major. In my previous life as a technician, I wrote reports to illustrate the repairs needed and the consequences of not performing those repairs to the service writer, who then communicated this information to customers. But as a college student, my writing skills had to become more intense to satisfy the many professors I was now dealing with in my quest for an undergraduate degree in teaching.

I graduated in 2002 and became an assistant professor at New England Tech, where I used writing to illustrate the different methods and procedures used to repair today's automobile to my many students. As an instructor, I illustrated different nomenclature and parts both with writing and drawings.

**Writing at Work** In my forty-one years in the automotive field I have always viewed the pen to be one of the most important and most used tools in my toolbox. As a technician, I used writing to illustrate repairs needed. I also used writing to illustrate repairs I had performed so I could get paid. The flat rate system pays by the repair, so the more writing I did to illustrate the work I was doing, the more I got paid.

In my tenure as an assistant professor in the automotive department I used writing in all of its forms. Because of the many different levels of students' knowledge we were seeing, it became important to be able to communicate at different levels as well. I also found myself including writing as a requirement in my courses and letting students know that writing will always be a necessary part of their life.

In my current position as a mobile fleet service technician, I serve as the service writer, the parts person, and the repair person.

I use illustration on repair orders to explain and document repairs needed and to explain and document repairs performed. I also use it to show labor charges and how they break down for the different procedures and explain the parts used to complete the repair. All of this illustrative writing must be very detailed so that the customer, who may not have knowledge of all the different parts and procedures, will more clearly understand what they are paying for.

## Workplace Illustration

**Tasca Mobile Fleet Work Order**

Date: 8/26/14 LOF (Lube, Oil & Filter) Due: 53,775
Plate: P28-6789 Company: Simmons Oil
Miles: 66,192 Trucks: 1
VIN: IFTF3TCIU66894

**Repair Requested:**

LOF, Air filter, TPMS (Tire Pressure Monitoring System) light on, R/S (right-side) mirror broken

| Rotor Measurement | Pad Measurement | Tire Spec |
|---|---|---|
| LF 5 MM—RF 5 MM<br>LR 7 MM—RR 6 MM | LF 6 MM—RF 6 MM<br>LR 2 MM—RR 2 MM | LF 2 MM—RF 2 MM<br>LR 8 MM—RR 7 MM |

**Repair Completed:**

LOF

TPMS light on. Found R/F (right front) TPMS sensor broken inside.
Replaced and programmed sensor and both front tires under Spec replaced.
TPMS12x1 reprogram

Found air filter dirty. Replaced.

R/S mirror broken. Replaced.

Found rear brakes and L/F ball joints bad. Tech did not have time to repair.
Set up services on September 2, 2014 at 7 a.m.

1. Based on the work order above, what repairs were made on the vehicle?

______________________________

______________________________

______________________________

______________________________

2. For any work order, the technician needs to provide evidence (support) to demonstrate why something needs to be repaired or replaced. Where do you see that in this work order?

_______________

_______________

_______________

3. What is the purpose of the memo? _______________

_______________

_______________

## *Professional Illustration Essay*

Andrea Whitmer

# When Poor People Have Nice Things

Andrea Whitmer is a freelance writer and blogger. Most of her writing attempts to help others—mothers in particular—find the humor in everyday situations. She also hopes to share her hard-earned wisdom with others so that they can learn from and, possibly, not make some of the same choices she did. This essay first appeared on her blog, So Over This, in June of 2012.

**Vocabulary development** Underline these words as you see them in Andrea's essay: *graphic, circulating, indignant, scrounging.*

**graphic:** diagrams, pictures, charts
**circulating:** to pass from place to place or person to person
**indignant:** a feeling or expressing of extreme disgust
**scrounging:** attempt to gather something by looking carefully or asking for the help of others.

**Predict** What will Whitmer's essay be about?

1 There's a graphic circulating on some of my friends' Facebook profiles that really gets on my nerves. I told myself I wouldn't write about it, but I saw it again last night and I just can't help myself. The graphic says, "Maybe someday I'll be able to afford an iPhone like the person in front of me at the grocery store. The one paying with FOOD STAMPS!"

2 Anytime that picture (or something similar) is posted, it gets about 50 "likes" and a long string of comments from indignant people who have personally witnessed a poor person owning something of value. The rage is evident—how dare someone on food stamps have a smartphone! Why should they even be allowed to have a phone at all? Our tax dollars blah blah blah blah . . .

3 Here's the thing: We can all think of at least one person who games the system. After working as a therapist for almost 7 years, I can think of quite a few. But no one knows the life situation of every single person on the planet, no matter how much they think they do.

**Reflect** Has there ever been a time in your own life where you had to make a difficult financial decision? What factors did you consider before making that decision?

4 A good friend of mine got fired from her job just days after her husband was laid off. Both of them had iPhones on his parents' plan, which cost them $50 a month total. Now what makes the most sense—breaking that contract at hundreds of dollars, or scrounging up the $50 a month in hopes that one or both of them would find another job soon? They didn't have to sign up for assistance—they were both lucky to get jobs before their emergency fund was drained—but if they had, they would have been in the grocery checkout line with iPhones in their pockets.

**I Speak From Experience**

**Reflect** When you read about Whitmer's experience, what is your immediate assumption? Why?

5 The only assistance I've ever personally used was Medicaid for my son at two different times during his life. But I will tell you—during both of those times, I had cable TV. I had Internet access at home. This last time, I had an iPhone (gasp!). I also owned several items that could have been pawned or sold for a decent amount of money.

6 Was I living it up? No. Not even close. But as someone with two college degrees and tons of ambition, I also never planned to continue collecting that assistance forever. Why should I empty my house of all the things I bought with my own money, only to have to buy them again when the crisis was over? That really doesn't make sense.

**Reflect** Have any of Whitmer's examples affected your initial assumption?

7 Now, I could understand it if I had a Lamborghini or two in my garage. But when you're used to a fairly middle-class existence and something happens to you (no matter what it is), you assume that your situation will improve at some point. It's not like the poverty police come take all your stuff in the middle of the night. You still own all the things you did before. If you had nice clothes, you'll still have nice clothes. If your cousin bought you an expensive handbag last Christmas, you'll still have that handbag. No one drops off a tattered, dirty wardrobe for you to put on before you leave your house.

**I Know What You're Thinking**

8 I can just hear the comments now. "Well, I know someone who did X and Y," or "I saw a lady buy Z at the mall." I know. I've seen it too. That's not the point.

**Reflect** Has there ever been a time where someone has judged you without knowing you? Or have you judged someone else and found out you were incorrect?

9 The point is, some people are in situations that we know nothing about. Some people own nice things from a better time in their lives and choose to keep those things during a setback. And some people make choices after becoming poor that we wouldn't personally make. Talking smack about those people on Facebook isn't doing anything to eradicate poverty or to change the fact that there is widespread abuse of our current system.

10 If you get upset when you see a poor person with nice things like smartphones, all I ask is that you consider this:

> Maybe they just got laid off last month and they already owned the iPhone.
>
> Maybe a family member pays the phone bill.

Maybe they're picking up groceries for a disabled neighbor with the neighbor's food stamp card.

Maybe the phone was a gift and it's on a prepaid plan.

Maybe you should worry less about what someone else has and more about yourself.

11 To many people, I could be considered "poor" right now (even though my bills are paid and I'm saving money). And guess what? I own several nice things. Some of you will judge me for that, and there's nothing I can do about it. But I will continue to be disgusted when people criticize another person's choices, especially when they can't possibly know the full set of circumstances.

**Evaluate** Based on Whitmer's observations, do you think we have become too comfortable making judgments based only on appearance?

1. In your own words, state Whitmer's main idea. ______________________________________________
______________________________________________
______________________________________________
______________________________________________.
2. Underline the examples Whitmer provides to support her main idea.
3. What type of order is the author using? ______________________________.
4. What do you think of this essay? Do you have a better understanding of why some people may appear to have nicer things than they can afford? __________
______________________________________________
______________________________________________.

**Tip** For reading advice, see Chapter 1.

Respond to one of the following assignments in a paragraph or essay.

1. Write about a time when someone made a snap judgment about you. This could be because of where you work, how you speak, or how you dress. How did you find out about it? How did it make you feel? How close to being accurate was it? Why do you think that person made those assumptions?
2. With social networking and its primary focus on images and short text, it has become easier than ever to publicly humiliate or bully others. Do you think that social networking has created more bullying and caused more harm than there was before media like Facebook, Instagram, Twitter, and other platforms existed?
3. In your opinion, why is it important to question our assumptions about other people? How can that benefit both ourselves and other people?

# Write Your Own Illustration

In this section, you will write your own illustration based on one of the following assignments. For help, refer to the How to Write Illustration checklist on page 149.

**ASSIGNMENT OPTIONS** **Writing about college, work, and everyday life**

Write an illustration paragraph, essay, or other document (as described below) on one of the following topics or on one of your own choice.

**College**

- Describe your goals for this course, making sure to explain the benefits of achieving each goal.
- If you are still deciding on a degree program or major, identify at least two areas of study that interest you. To get some ideas, you might refer to a course catalog. Also, consider visiting a counselor at your college's guidance office or career center. The counselor might be able to recommend some study programs to you based on your goals and interests. Next, write about the areas of study that appeal to you the most, giving examples of what you would learn and explaining how each of your choices matches your goals and interests.
- Produce a one- or two-page newsletter for other students in your class on one of the following topics. Make sure to describe each club, opportunity, and event in enough detail for readers. Also, include contact information, as well as hours and locations for events and club meetings.
  - Student clubs
  - Volunteer opportunities
  - Upcoming campus events (such as lectures, movies, and sports events)
  - Upcoming events in the larger community

**Work**

- What is the best or worst job you have ever had? Give examples of what made it the best or worst job.
- Thinking like a television producer, find a category of jobs—such as "dirty jobs," the name of a popular cable show—that a TV audience would find strange and interesting. Then, give examples of jobs in the category. (Examples of professions covered in the show *Dirty Jobs* include maggot farming, camel ranching, and bologna making.) Give enough details about each job to make it clear why that job is unusual. To get some ideas, you might type "strange jobs" into a search engine.
- Think of the job you would most like to have after graduation. Then, write a list of your skills—both current ones and ones you will be building in college—that are relevant to the job. To identify skills you will be building

through your degree program, you might refer to a course catalog. To identify relevant work skills, consider your past or present jobs as well as internships or other work experiences you would like to have before graduation. Finally, write a cover letter explaining why you are the best candidate for your ideal job. Be sure to provide several examples of your skills, referring to the list that you prepared.

**Everyday life**

- Write about stresses in your life or things that you like about your life. Give plenty of details for each example.
- Give examples of memories that have stayed with you for a long time. For each memory, provide enough details so that readers will be able to share your experience.
- Identify at least three public improvements you think would benefit a significant number of people in your community, such as the addition of sidewalks in residential areas to encourage exercise. These improvements should not include changes, such as the creation of a boat dock on a local lake, that would benefit only a small portion of the community. Then, in a letter to the editor of your local paper, describe each suggested improvement in detail, and explain why it would be an asset to the community.

## ASSIGNMENT OPTIONS Reading and writing critically

Complete one of the following assignments, which ask you to apply the critical thinking, reading, and writing skills discussed in Chapter 1.

### WRITING CRITICALLY ABOUT READINGS

Both Andrea Whitmer's *When Poor People Have Nice Things* (pp. 143–45) and Joshua Boyce's *Conditioning* (pp. 277–78) illustrate the assumptions that people make about others around them on a daily basis. Read or review both of these pieces, and then follow these steps:

1. **Summarize** Briefly summarize the works, listing major examples.
2. **Analyze** What questions do the essays raise for you? Are there any other issues you wish they had covered?
3. **Synthesize** Using examples from both Whitmer's and Boyce's essays and from your own experience, discuss why we make these assumptions about others or how it feels to have others make assumptions about you.
4. **Evaluate** Which essay, Whitmer's or Boyce's, do you think is more effective? Why? Does the writers' use of clear examples get their points across? Why or why not? In writing your evaluation, you might look back on your responses to step 2.

**Tip** For a reminder of how to summarize, analyze, synthesize, and evaluate, see the Reading and Writing Critically box on page 21.

## WRITING ABOUT IMAGES

Study the photograph below, and complete the following steps.

EQUINOX

MARTIN KIRCHNER/laif/REDUX

1. **Read the image** Ask yourself: What details does the photographer focus on? How do the colors and lights affect you as a viewer? What main impression does the picture make? (For more information on reading images, see Chapter 1.)

2. **Write an illustration** The photograph shows a luxury liner whose bright, colorful lights attract onlookers and potential customers. Write an illustration paragraph or essay about businesses that draw customers with colorful displays, loud music, or some other appeal to the senses. Include the types of details you examined in step 1.

## WRITING TO SOLVE A PROBLEM

Read or review the discussion of problem solving in Chapter 1 (pp. 28–30). Then, consider the following problem.

> Your college is increasing its tuition by $500 next year, and you do not think that you can continue. You have done well so far, and you really want to get a college degree.

**Assignment** Rather than just giving up and dropping out next year, as many students do, working in a small group or on your own, make a list of resources

you could consult to help you, and explain how they might help. You might want to start with the following sentence:

> Before dropping out of school for financial reasons, students should consult ____________________ because ____________________.

***For a paragraph:*** Name your best resource, and give examples of how this person or office might help you.

***For an essay:*** Name your three best resources, and give examples of how they might help you.

**CHECKLIST**

## How to Write Illustration

| Steps | Details |
|---|---|
| ☐ Narrow and explore your topic. See Chapter 3. | • Make the topic more specific.<br>• Prewrite to get ideas about the narrowed topic. |
| ☐ Write a topic sentence (paragraph) or thesis statement (essay). See Chapter 3. | • State what you want your readers to understand about your topic. |
| ☐ Support your point. See Chapter 4. | • Come up with examples and details to show, explain, or prove your main idea to readers. |
| ☐ Write a draft. See Chapter 5. | • Make a plan that puts examples in a logical order.<br>• Include a topic sentence (paragraph) or thesis statement (essay) and all the supporting examples and details. |
| ☐ Revise your draft. See Chapter 5. | • Make sure it has *all* the Four Basics of Good Illustration.<br>• Make sure you include transitions to move readers smoothly from one example to the next. |
| ☐ Edit your revised draft. See Parts 3 through 6. | • Correct errors in grammar, spelling, word use, and punctuation. |

## Chapter Review

1. Illustration is writing that ______________________________
2. What are the Four Basics of Good Illustration? ______________________________

   ______________________________

   ______________________________

   ______________________________
3. Write sentences using the following vocabulary words: *hype, myriad, tedious, graphic, circulating, indignant,* and *scrounging*. ______________________________

   ______________________________

   ______________________________

## REFLECTING ON THE JOURNEY

### Skills Learned

Now that you've completed the chapter, share what you've learned about each skill by completing the following chart.

| Skill | What I learned about this skill |
|---|---|
| Write a paper with one specific idea | |
| Identify the best possible support details to show, explain, or prove the main idea | |
| Provide examples to support the main idea | |
| Provide enough details and examples to get the idea across to the readers | |

# 8

# Description

## Writing That Creates Pictures in Words

READING ROADMAP

### Learning Objectives

**Chapter Goal:** Learn how to write a descriptive paper.

**Tools to Achieve the Goal:**

- Four Basics of Good Description (p. 152)
- Diagram: Paragraphs and Essays in Description (pp. 156–57)
- Sample Description Paragraph and Rubric (p. 160)
- Student Description Paragraph: Alessandra Cepeda, *Bird Rescue* (p. 161)
- Student Description Essay: Brian Healy, *First Day in Fallujah* (p. 162)
- Profile of Success and Workplace Description: Celia Hyde (p. 165)
- Professional Description Essay: Oscar Hijuelos, *Memories of New York City Snow* (p. 166)
- Checklist: How to Write Description (p. 171)

### Key Terms

Skim Chapter 8 before reading. Find these words or terms in **bold** type. Put a check mark next to each once you locate it.

____ description
____ main idea
____ support
____ order of time
____ order of space
____ order of importance
____ transitions

### Guided Reading for Chapter 8

Fill out the following chart before you begin reading. For each skill, write what you know about that skill and what you would like to know upon completing the chapter. At the end of the chapter, you will be asked to share what you learned about each skill.

| Skill | When I have used this skill | What I want to know about this skill |
|---|---|---|
| Write a paper using descriptive detail | | |
| Describe something using the five senses | | |
| Generate support for a description paper | | |
| Relate support and description details directly to the main idea of the paper | | |

LaunchPadSolo
Visit **LaunchPad Solo for Readers and Writers > Reading > Patterns of Organization** for more tutorials, videos, and practice with patterns of organization.

## Understand What Description Is

**Description** is writing that creates a clear and vivid impression of a person, place, or thing, often by appealing to the physical senses.

### **Four Basics** of Good Description

1. It creates a main impression—an overall effect, feeling, or image—about the topic.
2. It uses specific examples to support the main impression.
3. It supports those examples with details that appeal to the five senses: sight, hearing, smell, taste, and touch.
4. It brings a person, place, or physical object to life for the reader.

In the following student paragraph, the numbers and colors correspond to the Four Basics of Good Description.

Scars are stories written on a person's skin and sometimes on his heart. **1** My scar is not very big or very visible. **2** It is only about three inches long and an inch wide. It is on my knee, so it is usually covered, unseen. **3** It puckers the skin around it, and the texture of the scar itself is smoother than my real skin. It is flesh-colored, almost like a raggedy bandage. The story on my skin is a small one. **1** The story on my heart, though, is much deeper. **2** It was night, very cold, **3** my breath pluming into the frigid air. I took deep breaths that smelled like winter, piercing through my nasal passages and into my lungs as I walked to my car. I saw a couple making out against the wall of a building I was nearing. **2** I smiled and thought about them making their own heat. **3** I thought I saw steam coming from them, but maybe I imagined that. As I got near, I heard a familiar giggle: my girlfriend's. Then I saw her scarlet scarf, one I had given her, along with soft red leather gloves. I turned and ran, before they could see me. There was loud pounding in my ears, from the inside, sounding and feeling as if my brain had just become the loudest bass I had ever heard. My head throbbed, and slipping on some ice, I crashed to the ground, landing on my hands and knees, ripping my pants. I knew my knee was bleeding, even in the dark. I didn't care: **4** That scar would heal. The other one would take a lot longer.

Being able to describe something or someone accurately and in detail is important in many situations.

**College** On a physical therapy test, you describe the symptoms you observed in a patient.

**Work** You write a memo to your boss describing how the office could be arranged for increased efficiency.

**Everyday life** You describe something you lost to the lost-and-found clerk at a store.

In college assignments, the word *describe* may mean *tell about* or *report*. When an assignment asks you to actually describe a person, place, or thing, however, you will need to use the kinds of specific descriptive details discussed later in this chapter.

## *Main Idea in Description*

In description, the **main idea** is the main impression you want to create for your readers. To help you discover your main idea, complete the following sentence:

**Main idea in description** **What is most interesting, vivid, and important to me about this topic is . . .**

If you do not have a main impression about your topic, think about how it smells, sounds, looks, tastes, or feels.

### PRACTICE 1 Finding a main impression

For the following general topics, jot down impressions that appeal to you, and circle the one you would use as a main impression. Base your choice on what is most interesting, vivid, and important to you.

**Example:**

**Topic: A vandalized car**

**Impressions:** *wrecked, smashed, damaged, battered*

1. Topic: A fireworks display

   Impressions: ______________________________

2. Topic: A football player

   Impressions: ______________________________

3. Topic: The room you are in

   Impressions: ______________________________

The topic sentence (paragraph) or thesis statement (essay) in description usually contains both your narrowed topic and your main impression. Here is a topic sentence for a description paragraph:

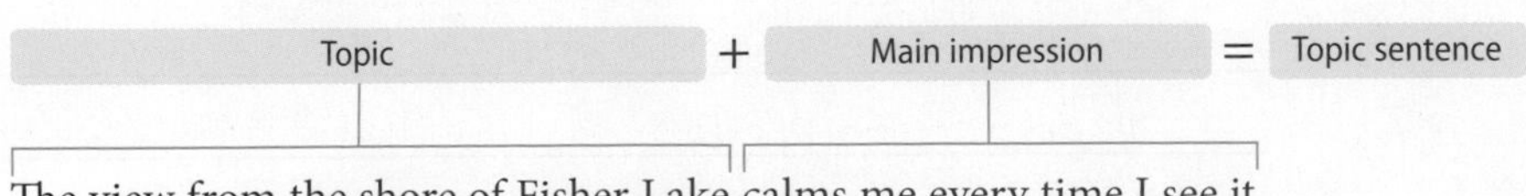
Topic
+
Main impression
=
Topic sentence
The view from the shore of Fisher Lake calms me every time I see it.

Remember that a topic for an essay can be a little broader than one for a paragraph.

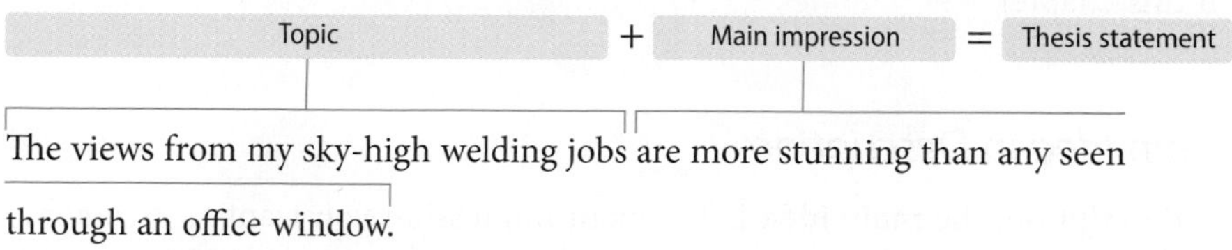
Topic
+
Main impression
=
Thesis statement

The views from my sky-high welding jobs are more stunning than any seen through an office window.

**Tip** Sometimes, the same main idea can be used for a paragraph and an essay, but the essay must develop this point in more detail. (See pp. 68–69.)

Whereas the topic sentence is focused on just one location and view, the thesis statement sets up descriptions of different views from different sites.

To be effective, your topic sentence or thesis statement should be specific. You can make it specific by adding details that appeal to the senses.

### PRACTICE 2 Writing a statement of your main impression

For two of the items from Practice 1, write the topic and your main impression. Then, write a statement of your main impression. Finally, revise the statement to make the main impression sharper and more specific.

**Example:**

**Topic/main impression:** *A vandalized car/battered*

**Statement:** *The vandalized car on the side of the highway was battered.*

**More specific:** *The shell of a car on the side of the road was dented all over, apparently from a bat or club, and surrounded by broken glass.*

1. Topic/main impression: ______________________

   Statement: ______________________

   More specific: ______________________

2. Topic/main impression: ______________________

   Statement: ______________________

   More specific: ______________________

## *Support in Description*

In description, **support** consists of the specific examples and details that help readers experience the sights, sounds, smells, tastes, and textures of your topic. Your description should get your main impression across to readers. Here are some qualities to consider.

| Sight | Sound | Smell |
|---|---|---|
| Colors? | Loud/soft? | Sweet/sour? |
| Shapes? | Piercing/soothing? | Sharp/mild? |
| Sizes? | Continuous/off and on? | Good? (Like what?) |
| Patterns? | Pleasant/unpleasant? (How?) | Bad? (Rotten?) |
| Shiny/dull? | | New? (New what? Leather? Plastic?) |
| Does it look like anything else? | Does it sound like anything else? | Old? |
| | | Does it smell like anything else? |

| Taste | Touch |
|---|---|
| Good? (What does "good" taste like?) | Hard/soft? |
| Bad? (What does "bad" taste like?) | Liquid/solid? |
| Bitter/sugary? Metallic? | Rough/smooth? |
| Burning? Spicy? | Hot/cold? |
| Does it taste like anything else? | Dry/oily? |
| | Textures? |
| | Does it feel like anything else? |

**Tip** When writing descriptions, consider this advice from writer Rhys Alexander: "Detail makes the difference between boring and terrific writing. It's the difference between a pencil sketch and a lush oil painting. As a writer, words are your paint. Use all the colors."

The paragraph and essay models on pages 156–57 use the topic sentence (paragraph) and thesis statement (essay) from the Main Idea section of this chapter. Both models include the support used in all descriptive writing—examples that communicate the writer's main impression, backed up by specific sensory details. In the essay model, however, the major support points (examples) are topic sentences for individual paragraphs.

### PRACTICE 3 Finding details to support a main impression

Read the statements on page 158, and write four sensory details you might use to support the main impression.

**Example: The physical sensations of a day at the beach are as vivid as the visual ones.**

a. *softness of the sand*

b. *push and splash of waves*

c. *chill of the water*

d. *smoothness of worn stones and beach glass*

# Paragraphs vs. Essays in Description

For more on the important features of description, see the Four Basics of Good Description on page 152.

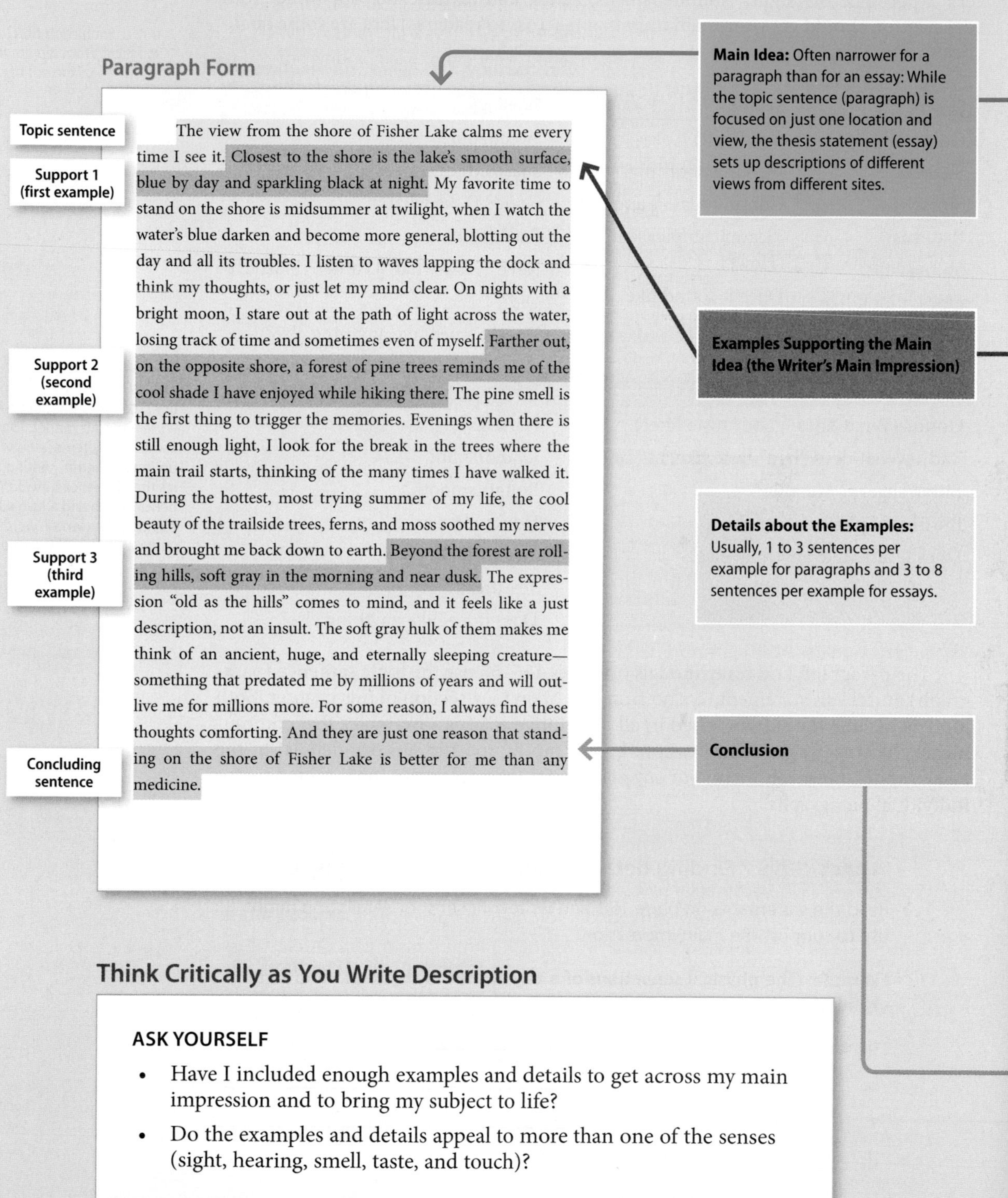

Paragraph Form
Topic sentence
Support 1 (first example)
Support 2 (second example)
Support 3 (third example)
Concluding sentence
The view from the shore of Fisher Lake calms me every time I see it. Closest to the shore is the lake's smooth surface, blue by day and sparkling black at night. My favorite time to stand on the shore is midsummer at twilight, when I watch the water's blue darken and become more general, blotting out the day and all its troubles. I listen to waves lapping the dock and think my thoughts, or just let my mind clear. On nights with a bright moon, I stare out at the path of light across the water, losing track of time and sometimes even of myself. Farther out, on the opposite shore, a forest of pine trees reminds me of the cool shade I have enjoyed while hiking there. The pine smell is the first thing to trigger the memories. Evenings when there is still enough light, I look for the break in the trees where the main trail starts, thinking of the many times I have walked it. During the hottest, most trying summer of my life, the cool beauty of the trailside trees, ferns, and moss soothed my nerves and brought me back down to earth. Beyond the forest are rolling hills, soft gray in the morning and near dusk. The expression "old as the hills" comes to mind, and it feels like a just description, not an insult. The soft gray hulk of them makes me think of an ancient, huge, and eternally sleeping creature—something that predated me by millions of years and will outlive me for millions more. For some reason, I always find these thoughts comforting. And they are just one reason that standing on the shore of Fisher Lake is better for me than any medicine.
Main Idea: Often narrower for a paragraph than for an essay: While the topic sentence (paragraph) is focused on just one location and view, the thesis statement (essay) sets up descriptions of different views from different sites.
Examples Supporting the Main Idea (the Writer's Main Impression)
Details about the Examples: Usually, 1 to 3 sentences per example for paragraphs and 3 to 8 sentences per example for essays.
Conclusion


## Think Critically as You Write Description

**ASK YOURSELF**

- Have I included enough examples and details to get across my main impression and to bring my subject to life?
- Do the examples and details appeal to more than one of the senses (sight, hearing, smell, taste, and touch)?

| Element | Grading criteria | Point: Comment |
|---|---|---|
| Conclusion | • Does the conclusion remind the reader of the main idea?<br>• Does it make an observation based on the support? | ____/5: |
| Grammar | • Is the writing free of the four most serious errors? (See Chapters 16-19.)<br>• Is the sentence structure clear?<br>• Does the student choose words that clearly express his or her meaning?<br>• Are the words spelled correctly?<br>• Is the punctuation correct? | ____/10: |
| | | **TOTAL POINTS: ____/50** |

## Read and Analyze Description

Reading examples of description will help you write your own. The first two examples are by students; one is a shorter paragraph, and the second is a longer essay. In the third example, the Profile of Success, police chief Celia Hyde shows how she uses description in a crime scene report. Last is an example of a professional description essay by Oscar Hijuelos. As you read, pay attention to the vocabulary, and answer the questions in the margin. They will help you read critically.

### *Student Description Paragraph*

Alessandra Cepeda

## Bird Rescue

1 When the owner opened the empty storage unit, we could not believe that any living creature could have survived under such horrible conditions. The inside was complete darkness, with no windows and no ventilation. The air hit us with the smell of rot and decay. A flashlight revealed three birds, quiet and huddled in the back corner. They were quivering and looked sickly. Two of the birds had injured wings, hanging from them uselessly at odd angles, obviously broken. They were exotic birds that should have had bright and colorful feathers, but the floor of the unit was covered in the feathers they had molted. We entered slowly and retrieved the abused birds. I cried at how such beautiful and helpless creatures had been mistreated. We adopted two of them, and our Samantha is now eight years old, with beautiful green feathers topped off with a brilliant blue and red head. She

talks, flies, and is a wonderful pet who is dearly loved and, I admit, very spoiled. She deserves it after such a rough start to her life.

1. Double-underline the topic sentence.
2. What main impression does the writer create? ______________________

______________________

______________________

3. Underline the sensory details (sight, sound, smell, taste, texture) that create the main impression.
4. Does the paragraph have the Four Basics of Good Description (p. 152)? Why or why not? ______________________

______________________

wasteland: an area that is uncultivated and barren or devastated by natural disasters or war

squandered: wasted; not used to good advantage

battalion: an army unit

craters: shallow, bowl-shaped depressions on a surface, caused by an impact or explosion

torso: the trunk of a human body

severed: cut or divided

fog of war: a term describing the general uncertainty that soldiers experience during military operations

objective: a goal or target

wrath: strong, fierce anger; angry vengeance

relentless: steady; persistent; unyielding

grenades: handheld explosives

trance: a dazed or bewildered condition; a state seemingly between sleeping and waking.

tracer rounds: ammunition containing a substance that causes bullets or rounds to trail

**Predict** What type of experience will Healy be describing?

## *Student Description Essay*

Brian Healy

# First Day in Fallujah

Brian Healy served in Iraq and later pursued a degree in business management at Florida Community College. Although a typical writing process includes submitting a piece to several rounds of revision, Healy decided to "revise this essay as little as possible." He says, "I felt that given the topic, I should go with what I first wrote so that it would show more dirty truth than be polished to perfection." He values the role of emotion in writing and exhorts others not to "write for the sake of writing, [but to] write because you are passionate about it."

**Vocabulary development** Underline these words as you read them in Healy's essay: *wasteland, squandered, battalion, craters, torso, severed, fog of war, objective, wrath, relentless, grenades, trance, tracer rounds*

1 The year was 2004, and I was a young, 21-year-old U.S. Marine corporal on my second tour of Iraq. I had been in the country for five months and was not enjoying it any more than I had the first time. From the first time I set foot in Iraq, I perceived it as a foul-smelling wasteland where my youth and, as I would soon find out, my innocence were being squandered. I had been in a number of firefights, roadside bomb attacks, and mortar and rocket attacks; therefore, I had thought I had seen it all. So when the word came down that my battalion was going to Fallujah to drive through the center of the city, I was as naïve as a child on the first day of school. The lesson of that first day would be taught with blood, sweat, and tears, learned through pain and suffering, and never forgotten.

2 At 2:00 in the morning on November 10, the voice of my commander pierced the night: "Mount up!" Upon hearing these words, I boarded the Amtrak transport. I heard a loud "clank, clank," the sound of metal hitting metal as the ramp closed and sealed us in. Sitting shoulder to shoulder, we had no more room to move than sardines in a pitch-dark can. The diesel fumes choked our lungs and burned our throats. There was a sudden jolt as the metal beast began to move, and with each bump and each turn, I was thrown from side to side inside the beast's belly with only the invisible bodies of my comrades to steady myself. I thought back to my childhood, to a time of carefree youth. I thought how my father would tell me how I was the cleanest of his sons. I chuckled as I thought, "If only he could see me now, covered in sweat and dirt and five days away from my last shower."

**Reflect** What specific sounds, sights, and feelings does Healy use when describing transportation? Why does he want the reader to be able to feel like they are sharing this experience with him?

3 I was violently jerked back into the present with three thunderous explosions on the right side of the Amtrak vehicle. We continued to move faster and faster with more intensity and urgency than before. My heart was racing, pounding as if it were trying to escape from my chest when we came to a screeching halt.

**Reflect** Have you ever had an experience where you were anxious about something because you did not know what was about to happen? What did it feel like? Use your five senses to describe.

4 With the same clank that sealed us in, the ramp dropped and released us from our can. I ran out of the Amtrak nearly tripping on the ramp. There was no moon, no streetlight, nothing to pierce the blanket of night. Therefore, seeing was almost completely out of the question. However, what was visible was a scene that I will never forget. The massive craters from our bombs made it seem as if we were running on the surface of the moon. More disturbing were the dead bodies of those enemies hit with the bombs. Their bodies were strewn about in a frenzied manner: a leg or arm here, torso there, a head severed from its body. Trying to avoid stepping on them was impossible. Amidst all this and the natural "fog of war," we managed to get our bearings and move toward our objective. We were able to take the entrance to a government complex located at the center of the city, and we did so in fine style. "Not so tough," we all thought. We would not have to wait long until we would find out how insanely foolish we were.

5 As the sun began to rise, there were no morning prayers, no loudspeakers, and no noise at all. This, of course, was odd since we had become accustomed to the sounds of Iraq in the morning. However, this silence did not last long and was shattered as the enemy released hell's wrath upon us. The enemy was relentless in its initial assault but was unable to gain the advantage and was slowly pushed back.

6 As the day dragged on, the enemy fought us in an endless cycle of attack and retreat. There was no time to relax as rocket-propelled grenades whistled by our heads time and time again. Snipers' bullets skipped off the surface of the roof we were on. While some bullets tore through packs, radios, and boots and clothing, a lucky few found their mark and ripped through flesh like a hot knife through butter.

**Reflect** Healy takes a lot of time to describe the evening, the day, and the afternoon. Why does he do this? What may be about to happen?

7 Suddenly, there was a deafening crack as three 82-millimeter mortars rained upon us, throwing me to the ground. The dust blacked out the sun and choked my lungs. I began to rise only to be thrown back down by a rocket-propelled grenade whizzing just overhead, narrowly missing my face. At this point, it seemed clear to me that there was no end to this enemy. In the windows, out the doorways, through alleyways, and down streets, they would run. We would kill one, and another would pop up in his stead, as if some factory just out of sight was producing more and more men to fight us.

**Reflect** Healy says that his friends had become "old men" in one day. How did that happen? What caused it?

8 As the sun fell behind the horizon, the battle, which had so suddenly started, ended just as swiftly. The enemy, like moths to light, were nowhere to be seen. The rifles of the Marines, which were so active that day, were silent now. We were puzzled as to why it was so quiet. My ears were still ringing from that day's events when the order came down to hole up for the night. There was no sleep for me that night; the events of the day made sure of that. I sat there that cold November night not really thinking of anything. I just sat in a trance, listening to small firefights of the battle that were still raging: a blast of machine gun fire, tracer rounds, and air strikes. Artillery flying through the air gave the appearance of a laser light show. Explosions rattling the earth lit my comrades' faces. As I looked over at them, I did not see my friends from earlier in the day; instead, I was looking at old men who were wondering what the next day would bring. I wondered if I would survive the next day.

**Reflect** What effect does this essay have on you?

**Reflect** Have you ever had an experience that made you feel frightened or overwhelmed? What did you do to work through that situation or try to deal with it?

**Summarize** What particular ideas went through Healey's mind as he found himself in the middle of the firefight?

9 The battle for Fallujah would rage on for another three weeks. The Marines of the First Battalion Eighth Marine Regiment would continue to fight with courage and honor. As each day of the battle passed, I witnessed new horrors and acts of bravery, of which normal men are not capable. However, none of those days would have the impact on me that that first day did.

10 The battle is over, but for the men who were there, it will never end. It is fought every day in their heads and in voices of friends long gone, all the while listening to the screams and taunts of people who know nothing of war but would call these men terrorists.

1. What is the main impression of Healy's essay? ______________________________

______________________________________________

______________________________________________

2. Underline the sensory details.

3. Circle any transitional words or phrases Healy uses.

4. What senses does Healy use in his essay? ______________________________

______________________________________________

5. Is Healy's paper organized by space, time, or importance? ______________

# Profile of Success

## Description in the Real World

**Celia Hyde**
Chief of Police

**Background** When I graduated from high school, I was not interested in academics. I took some courses at a community college but then dropped out to travel. After traveling and trying several colleges, I returned home. The police chief in town was a family friend and encouraged me to think about law enforcement. I entered that field and have been there since.

**College** Greenfield Community College, Mt. Wachusett Community College, Fort Lauderdale Community College, Western New England College

**Employer** Town of Bolton, Massachusetts

**Writing at work** As chief of police, I do many kinds of writing: policies and procedures for the officers to follow; responses to attorneys' requests for information; letters, reports, and budgets; interviews with witnesses; statements from victims and criminals; accident reports. In all of the writing I do, detail, clarity, and precision are essential. I have to choose my words carefully to avoid any confusion or misunderstanding.

### *Workplace Description*

The following report is one example of the descriptive reports Celia writes.

**Report, breaking and entering scene**

**Response to burglar alarm, 17:00 hours**

The house at 123 Main Street is situated off the road with a long, narrow driveway and no visible neighbors. The dense fir trees along the drive block natural light, though it was almost dusk and getting dark. There was snow on the driveway from a recent storm. I observed one set of fresh tire marks entering the driveway and a set of footprints exiting it.

The homeowner, Mr. Smith, had been awakened by the sounds of smashing glass and the squeaking of the door as it opened. He felt a cold draft from the stairway and heard a soft shuffle of feet crossing the dining room. Smith descended the stairs to investigate and was met at the bottom by the intruder, who shoved him against the wall and ran out the front door.

While awaiting backup, I obtained a description of the intruder from Mr. Smith. The subject was a white male, approximately 25–30 years of age and 5′9″–5′11″ in height. He had jet-black hair of medium length, and it was worn slicked back from his forehead. He wore a salt-and-pepper, closely shaved beard and had a birthmark on his neck the size of a dime. The subject was wearing a black nylon jacket with some logo on it in large white letters, a blue plaid shirt, and blue jeans.

1. What is your **main impression** of the scene and of the intruder? ____________

____________________________________________

2. Underline the **details** that support the main impression.

3. What senses do the details appeal to? ____________________

4. How is the description organized? ____________________

*Professional Description Essay*

Oscar Hijuelos

# Memories of New York City Snow

circa: [taken] around
aloft: high
trestles: support structures
girded: reinforced
burlesque houses: theaters that offer live, often humorous performances and/or strip-tease acts
palatial: palace-like
perilous: dangerous
nary: not even
stint: brief job
toque: hat
to the hilt: completely, to the maximum extent possible
nostalgia: a longing for something from the past
connotation: meaning or association
inaccessible divinity: unreachable god

Oscar Hijuelos, the son of Cuban immigrants, was born in New York City in 1951. After receiving undergraduate and master's degrees from the City University of New York, he took a job at an advertising firm and wrote fiction at night. Since then, he has published numerous novels. His first, *The Mambo Kings Play Songs of Love* (1989), was awarded the Pulitzer Prize for fiction, making Hijuelos the first Hispanic writer to receive this honor. His most recent novels include *A Simple Habana Melody* (2002), *Dark Dude* (2008), and *Beautiful Maria of My Soul* (2010). Hijuelos has also published a memoir, *Thoughts without Cigarettes* (2011).

The following essay was taken from the anthology *Metropolis Found* (2003). In it, Hijuelos describes a New York City winter from the perspective of new immigrants, noting the emotions that the season inspired in them.

**Vocabulary development** Underline these words as you read the description essay: *circa, aloft, trestles, girded, burlesque houses, palatial, perilous, nary, stint, toque, to the hilt, nostalgia, connotation, inaccessible divinity*

**Predict** Why might snow be significant to the author's father and godfather?

1 For immigrants of my parents' generation, who had first come to New York City from the much warmer climate of Cuba in the mid-1940s, the very existence of snow was a source of fascination. A black-and-white photograph that I have always loved, circa 1948, its surface cracked like that of a thawing ice-covered pond, features my father, Pascual, and my godfather, Horacio, fresh up from **Oriente Province**,[1] posing in a snow-covered meadow in Central Park. Decked out in long coats, scarves, and black-rimmed hats, they are holding, in their be-gloved hands, a huge chunk of hardened snow. Trees and their straggly witch's hair branches, glimmering with ice and frost, recede into the distance behind them. They stand on a field of whiteness, the two men seemingly afloat in midair, as if they were being held aloft by the magical substance itself.

1. **Oriente Province:** a former province of Cuba, in the eastern part of the country

2 That they bothered to have this photograph taken—I suppose to send back to family in Cuba—has always been a source of enchantment for me. That something so common to winters in New York would strike them as an object of exotic admiration has always spoken volumes about the newness—and innocence—of their

immigrants' experience. How thrilling it all must have seemed to them, for their New York was so very different from the small town surrounded by farms in eastern Cuba that they hailed from. Their New York was a fanciful and bustling city of endless sidewalks and unimaginably high buildings; of great bridges and twisting outdoor elevated train trestles; of walkup tenement houses with mysteriously dark basements, and subways that burrowed through an underworld of girded tunnels; of dancehalls, burlesque houses, and palatial department stores with their complement of Christmas Salvation Army Santa Clauses on every street corner. Delightful and perilous, their New York was a city of incredibly loud noises, of police and air raid sirens and factory whistles and subway rumble; a city where people sometimes shushed you for speaking Spanish in a public place, or could be unforgiving if you did not speak English well or seemed to be of a different ethnic background. (My father was once nearly hit by a garbage can that had been thrown off the rooftop of a building as he was walking along La Salle Street in upper Manhattan.)

3 Even so, New York represented the future. The city meant jobs and money. Newly arrived, an aunt of mine went to work for Pan Am; another aunt, as a Macy's saleslady. My own mother, speaking nary a word of English, did a stint in the garment district as a seamstress. During the war some family friends, like my godfather, were eventually drafted, while others ended up as factory laborers. Landing a job at the Biltmore Men's Bar, my father joined the hotel and restaurant workers' union, paid his first weekly dues, and came home one day with a brand new white chef's toque in hand. Just about everybody found work, often for low pay and ridiculously long hours. And while the men of that generation worked a lot of overtime, or a second job, they always had their day or two off. Dressed to the hilt, they'd leave their uptown neighborhoods and make an excursion to another part of the city—perhaps to one of the grand movie palaces of Times Square or to beautiful Central Park, as my father and godfather, and their ladies, had once done, in the aftermath of a snowfall.

**Reflect** What main impression do these descriptions of the city create?

4 Snow, such as it can only fall in New York City, was not just about the cold and wintry differences that mark the weather of the north. It was about a purity that would descend upon the grayness of its streets like a heaven of silence, the city's complexity and bustle abruptly subdued. But as beautiful as it could be, it was also something that provoked nostalgia; I am certain that my father would miss Cuba on some bitterly cold days. I remember that whenever we were out on a walk and it began to snow, my father would stop and look up at the sky, with wonderment—what he was seeing I don't know. Perhaps that's why to this day my own associations with a New York City snowfall have a mystical connotation, as if the presence of snow really meant that some kind of inaccessible divinity had settled his breath upon us.

**Reflect** What types of weather do you associate with particular feelings or moods?

1. Double-underline the **thesis statement**.
2. Underline the **sensory details** (sight, sound, smell, taste, texture).

**Tip** For reading advice, see Chapter 1.

3. Circle the **transitions**.
4. Does the essay create a clear picture of New York City in the winter? Why or why not? ______________________________

Respond to one of the following assignments in a paragraph or essay.

1. Describe a place that is important to you or associated with significant memories. It might be a city, a favorite park, a friend's or relative's home, or a vacation spot.
2. Describe an outdoor scene from your favorite season. You might work from a personal photograph taken during that season.
3. Describe a person who has played a major role in your life. Try to include sensory details that go beyond the person's appearance. For instance, you might describe the sight of his or her usual surroundings, the sound of his or her voice, or the texture of a favorite piece of clothing.

# Write Your Own Description

In this section, you will write your own description based on one of the following assignments. For help, refer to the How to Write Description checklist on page 171.

**ASSIGNMENT OPTIONS** **Writing about college, work, and everyday life**

Write a description paragraph or essay on one of the following topics or on one of your own choice.

**College**

- Describe the sights, sounds, smells, and tastes in the cafeteria or another dining spot on campus.
- Find a place where you can get a good view of your campus (for instance, a window on an upper floor of one of the buildings). Then, describe the scene using space order (p. 158).
- Think back on a place or scene on campus that has made a strong sensory impression on you. Then, describe the place or scene with specific examples and details, and explain why it made such an impression on you.

**Work**

- Describe your workplace, including as many sensory details as you can.
- Describe your boss or a colleague you work with closely. First, think of the main impression you get from this person. Then, choose details that would make your impression clear to readers.
- Have you ever worked with anyone who creates a mess in their office environment? If so, describe the person's workspace and/or messes in detail.

**Everyday life**

- Describe a favorite photograph, using as many details as possible. For a good example of a photograph description, see the first paragraph of Oscar Hijuelos's essay (p. 166).
- Describe a holiday celebration from your past, including as many sensory details as possible. Think back on the people who attended, the food served, the decorations, and so on.
- Visit an organization that serves your community, such as an animal shelter or a food pantry. During your visit, take notes about what you see. Later, write a detailed description of the scene.

## ASSIGNMENT OPTIONS Reading and writing critically

Complete one of the following assignments, which ask you to apply the critical thinking, reading, and writing skills discussed in Chapter 1.

### WRITING CRITICALLY ABOUT READINGS

Both Oscar Hijuelos's "Memories of New York City Snow" (p. 166) and Amy Tan's "Fish Cheeks" (p. 123) describe scenes from the past. Read or review both of these pieces, and then follow these steps:

1. **Summarize** Briefly summarize the works, listing major examples and details.
2. **Analyze** Tan uses humor to make her point, whereas Hijuelos's essay is more serious. Why do you think the authors might have chosen these different approaches?
3. **Synthesize** Using examples from both Tan's and Hijuelos's essays and from your own experience, discuss the types of details that make certain things in our lives (such as an event or a photograph) so memorable.
4. **Evaluate** Which essay, Tan's or Hijuelos's, do you think is more effective? Why? In writing your evaluation, you might look back on your responses to step 2.

**Tip** For a reminder of how to summarize, analyze, synthesize, and evaluate, see the Reading and Writing Critically box on page 21.

### WRITING ABOUT IMAGES

Study the photographs on page 170, and complete the following steps.

1. **Read each image** Ask yourself: What part of the photograph draws your attention the most, and why? What main impression does each picture create, and what details contribute to this impression? (For more information on reading images, see Chapter 1.)
2. **Write a description** Write a paragraph or essay that describes each photograph and explains the main impression it gives. Include the details and reactions from step 1.

ALEX E. PROIMOS/GETTY IMAGES

DENNIS OSWALD/GETTY IMAGES

## WRITING TO SOLVE A PROBLEM

Read or review the discussion of problem solving in Chapter 1 (pp. 28–30). Then, consider the following problem:

**An abandoned house on your street is a safety hazard for the children in the neighborhood. Although you and some of your neighbors have called the local Board of Health, nothing has been done. Finally, you and your neighbors decide to write to the mayor.**

**Assignment** Working in a small group or on your own, write to the mayor describing why this house is a safety hazard. Thoroughly describe the house (outside and inside). Imagine a place that is not just ugly; it must also pose safety problems to children. You might start with the following sentence:

**Not only is the abandoned house at 45 Main Street an eyesore, but it is also** ____________________________________.

***For a paragraph:*** Describe in detail one room on the first floor of the house or just the exterior you can see from the street.

***For an essay:*** Describe in detail at least three rooms in the house or the exterior you can see if you walk entirely around the house.

**CHECKLIST**

## How to Write Description

| Steps | Details |
|---|---|
| ☐ Narrow and explore your topic. See Chapter 3. | • Make the topic more specific.<br>• Prewrite to get ideas about the narrowed topic. |
| ☐ Write a topic sentence (paragraph) or thesis statement (essay). See Chapter 3. | • State what is most interesting, vivid, and important about your topic. |
| ☐ Support your point. See Chapter 4. | • Come up with examples and details that create a main impression about your topic. |
| ☐ Write a draft. See Chapter 5 | • Make a plan that puts examples in a logical order.<br>• Include a topic sentence (paragraph) or thesis statement (essay) and all the supporting examples and details. |
| ☐ Revise your draft. See Chapter 5. | • Make sure it has *all* the Four Basics of Good Description.<br>• Make sure you include transitions to move readers smoothly from one detail to the next. |
| ☐ Edit your revised draft. See Parts 3 through 6. | • Correct errors in grammar, spelling, word use, and punctuation |

# Chapter Review

1. Description is writing that ______________________________

______________________________

2. What are the Four Basics of Good Description?

______________________________

______________________________

______________________________

______________________________

3. The topic sentence in a description paragraph or the thesis statement in a description essay includes what two elements? ______________________________

______________________________

4. Write sentences using the following vocabulary words: *objective, wrath, relentless, grenades, trance, girded, circa, aloft, trestle, nary, connotation, aloft, palatial, perilous, stint, nostalgia.* ______________________________

______________________________

## REFLECTING ON THE JOURNEY

### Skills Learned

Now that you've completed the chapter, share what you've learned about each skill by completing the following chart.

| Skill | What I learned about this skill |
|---|---|
| Write a paper using descriptive detail | |
| Describe something using the five senses | |
| Generate support for a descriptive paper | |
| Relate support and descriptive details directly to the main idea of the paper | |

# 9

# Process Analysis

## Writing That Explains How Things Happen

### Learning Objectives

**Chapter Goal:** Learn how to write a process analysis paper.

**Tools to Achieve the Goal:**

- Four Basics of Good Process Analysis (p. 174)
- Diagram: Paragraphs and Essays in Process Analysis (pp. 178–79)
- Sample Process Analysis Paragraph and Rubric (p. 180)
- Student Process Analysis Paragraph: Charlton Brown, *Buying a Car at Auction* (pp. 181–82)
- Student Process Analysis Essay: Daniel Bird, *What's Appropriate: How to Talk to Children about Disasters* (pp. 182–84)
- Profile of Success and Workplace Process Analysis: Monique Rizer (p. 184)
- Professional Process Analysis Essay: Kathy Stevens, *10 Tips to Ease into Plant-Based Eating* (pp. 186–88)
- Checklist: How to Write Process Analysis (pp. 192–93)

## READING ROADMAP

### Key Terms

Skim Chapter 9 before reading. Find these words or terms in **bold** type. Put a check mark next to each once you locate it.

_____ process analysis
_____ purpose
_____ main idea
_____ support
_____ time order
_____ transitions

### Guided Reading for Chapter 9

Fill out the following chart before you begin reading. For each skill, write what you know about that skill and what you would like to know upon completing the chapter. At the end of the chapter, you will be asked to share what you learned about each skill.

| Skill | When I have used this skill | What I want to know about this skill |
|---|---|---|
| Describe the steps of a process | | |
| Include all of the significant steps in a process | | |
| Generate support for a process analysis paper | | |
| Relate support directly to the main idea of the paper in a logical order | | |
| Read and analyze a process analysis paper | | |

## Understand What Process Analysis Is

LaunchPadSolo

Visit **LaunchPad Solo for Readers and Writers > Reading > Patterns of Organization** for more tutorials, videos, and practice with patterns of organization.

**Process analysis** either explains how to do something (so that your readers can do it) or explains how something works (so that your readers can understand it).

### **Four Basics** of Good Process Analysis

1. It tells readers what process the writer wants them to know about and makes a point about it.
2. It presents the essential steps in the process.
3. It explains the steps in detail.
4. It presents the steps in a logical order (usually time order).

In the following paragraph, the numbers and colors correspond to the Four Basics of Good Process Analysis.

4 Time order is used.

The poet Dana Gioia once said, "Art delights, instructs, consoles. It educates our emotions." 1 Closely observing paintings, sculpture, and other forms of visual art is a great way to have the type of experience that Gioia describes, and following a few basic steps will help you get the most from the experience. 2 First, choose an art exhibit that interests you. 3 You can find listings for exhibits on local museums' Web sites or in the arts section of a newspaper. Links on the Web sites or articles in a newspaper may give you more information about the exhibits, the artists featured in them, and the types of work to be displayed. 2 Second, go to the museum with an open mind and, ideally, with a friend. 3 While moving through the exhibit, take time to examine each work carefully. As you do so, ask yourself questions: What is my eye most drawn to, and why? What questions does this work raise for me, and how does it make me feel? How would I describe it to someone over the phone? Ask your friend the same questions, and consider the responses. You might also consult an exhibit brochure for information about the featured artists and their works. 2 Finally, keep your exploration going after you have left the museum. 3 Go out for coffee or a meal with your friend. Trade more of your thoughts and ideas about the artwork, and discuss your overall impressions. If you are especially interested in any of the artists or their works, you might look for additional information or images on the Internet, or you might consult books at the library. Throughout the whole experience, put aside the common belief that only artists or cultural experts "get" art. The artist Eugène Delacroix described paintings as "a bridge between the soul of the artist and that of the spectator." Trust your ability to cross that bridge and come to new understandings.

You use process analysis in many situations:

| | |
|---|---|
| **College** | In a science course, you explain photosynthesis. |
| **Work** | You write instructions to explain how to operate something (the copier, the fax machine). |
| **Everyday life** | You write out a recipe for an aunt. |

In college, a writing assignment may ask you to *describe the process of*, but you might be asked to *describe the stages of* ________ or *explain how* ________ *works*. Whenever you need to identify and explain the steps or stages of anything, you will use process analysis.

## *Main Idea in Process Analysis*

In process analysis, your **purpose** is to explain how to do something or how something works. Your **main idea** should tell readers what process you are describing and what you want readers to know about it.

To help you discover the main idea for your process analysis, complete the following sentence:

| | |
|---|---|
| **Main idea in process analysis** | **What I want readers to know about this process is that . . .** |

Here is an example of a topic sentence for a paragraph:

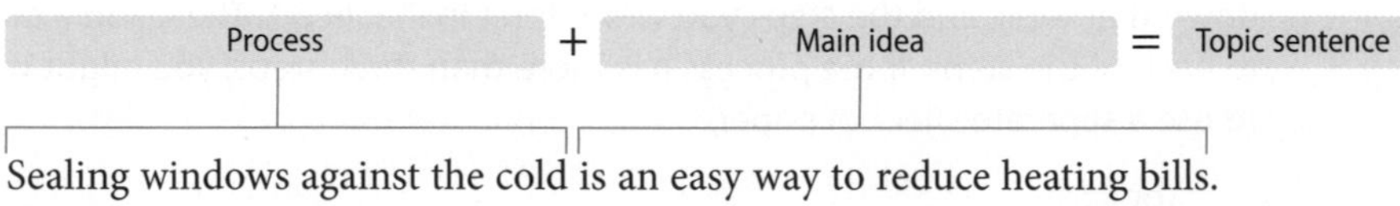
Process
+
Main idea
=
Topic sentence
Sealing windows against the cold is an easy way to reduce heating bills.

Remember that the topic for an essay can be a little broader than one for a paragraph.

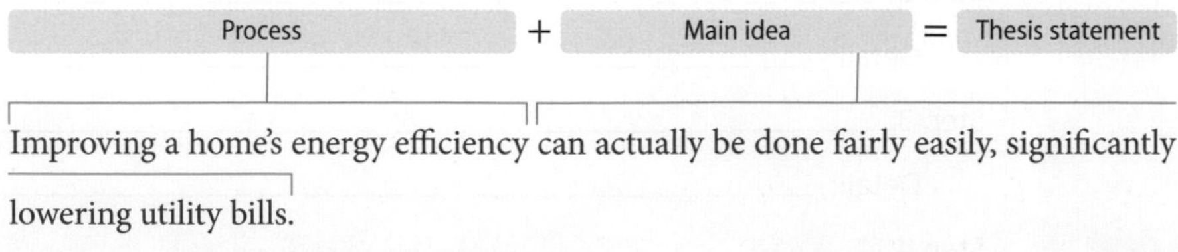
Process
+
Main idea
=
Thesis statement
Improving a home's energy efficiency can actually be done fairly easily, significantly lowering utility bills.

Whereas the topic sentence focuses on just one method to improve energy efficiency, the thesis statement sets up a discussion of multiple methods.

**Tip** Sometimes, the same main idea can be used for a paragraph and an essay, but the essay must develop this point in more detail. (See pp. 68–69.)

## *Support in Process Analysis*

The paragraph and essay models on pages 178–79 use the topic sentence (paragraph) and thesis statement (essay) from the Main Idea section of this chapter. Both models include the **support** used in all writing about processes: the steps in the process backed up by details about these steps. In the essay model, however, the major support points (steps) are topic sentences for individual paragraphs.

### PRACTICE 1 Finding and choosing the essential steps

For each of the following topics, write the essential steps in the order you would perform them.

1. Making (your favorite food) is simple.

 ________________________________________

 ________________________________________

2. I think I could teach anyone how to ____________________.

 ________________________________________

3. Operating a ______________ is ______________.

 ________________________________________

 ________________________________________

### PRACTICE 2 Adding details to essential steps

Choose one of the topics from Practice 1. In the spaces that follow, first copy down that topic and the steps you wrote for it in Practice 1. Then, add a detail to each of the steps. If the process has more than three steps, you might want to use a separate sheet of paper.

Topic: ____________________________________

Step 1: ____________________________________

Detail: ____________________________________

Step 2: ____________________________________

Detail: ____________________________________

Step 3: ____________________________________

Detail: ____________________________________

Step 4: ____________________________________

Detail: ____________________________________

**Tip** If you have written a narration paragraph already, you will notice that narration and process analysis are alike in that they both usually present events or steps in time order—the order in which they occur. The difference is that narration reports what happened, whereas process analysis describes how to do something or how something works.

## *Organization in Process Analysis*

Process analysis is usually organized by **time order** because it explains the steps of the process in the order in which they occur. This is the strategy used in the paragraph and essay models on pages 178–79.

**Transitions** move readers smoothly from one step to the next.

**Tip** For more on time order, see pages 76–77.

### Common Transitions in Process Analysis

| | | | |
|---|---|---|---|
| after | eventually | meanwhile | since |
| as | finally | next | soon |
| at last | first | now | then |
| before | last | once | when |
| during | later | second | while |

**PRACTICE 3 Using transitions in process analysis**

Read the paragraph that follows, and fill in the blanks with transitions.

Scientists have discovered that, like something from a zombie movie, a mind-controlling fungus attacks certain carpenter ants. ________, as if following the fungus's orders, the ants help their invader reproduce. The process begins when an ant is infected. ________, the ant begins to act strangely. For instance, instead of staying in its home high in the trees, it drops to the forest floor. ________ wandering, it searches for a cool, moist place. ________ the zombie-ant finds the right place, it clamps its jaws to a leaf and dies. ____________, the fungus within the ant grows until it bursts from the insect's head, and more ants are infected. By studying this process, researchers may find better ways to control the spread of carpenter ants.

# Evaluate Process Analysis

To become a more successful writer, it is important not only to understand the Four Basics of Good Process Analysis but to read and evaluate examples as well. In this section, you will have the opportunity to use a sample rubric to analyze or evaluate the samples of process analysis writing provided. By using this rubric, you will gain a better understanding of how the components of good process analysis work

## Paragraphs vs. Essays in Process Analysis

For more on the important features of process analysis, see the Four Basics of Good Process Analysis on page 174.

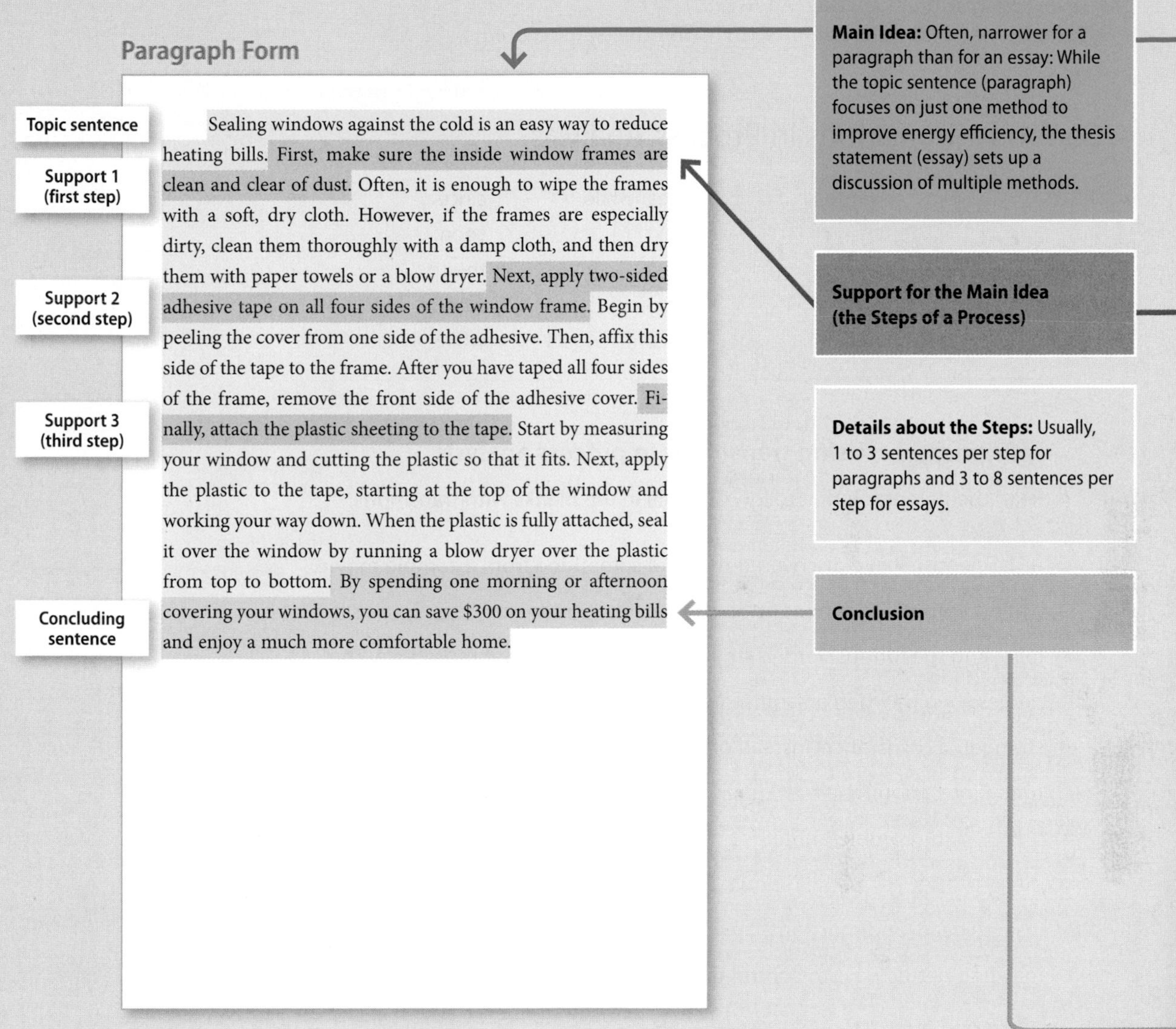
Paragraph Form
Topic sentence
Support 1 (first step)
Support 2 (second step)
Support 3 (third step)
Concluding sentence
Sealing windows against the cold is an easy way to reduce heating bills. First, make sure the inside window frames are clean and clear of dust. Often, it is enough to wipe the frames with a soft, dry cloth. However, if the frames are especially dirty, clean them thoroughly with a damp cloth, and then dry them with paper towels or a blow dryer. Next, apply two-sided adhesive tape on all four sides of the window frame. Begin by peeling the cover from one side of the adhesive. Then, affix this side of the tape to the frame. After you have taped all four sides of the frame, remove the front side of the adhesive cover. Finally, attach the plastic sheeting to the tape. Start by measuring your window and cutting the plastic so that it fits. Next, apply the plastic to the tape, starting at the top of the window and working your way down. When the plastic is fully attached, seal it over the window by running a blow dryer over the plastic from top to bottom. By spending one morning or afternoon covering your windows, you can save $300 on your heating bills and enjoy a much more comfortable home.
Main Idea: Often, narrower for a paragraph than for an essay: While the topic sentence (paragraph) focuses on just one method to improve energy efficiency, the thesis statement (essay) sets up a discussion of multiple methods.
Support for the Main Idea (the Steps of a Process)
Details about the Steps: Usually, 1 to 3 sentences per step for paragraphs and 3 to 8 sentences per step for essays.
Conclusion

### Think Critically as You Write Process Analysis

**ASK YOURSELF**

- Have I included all the steps necessary for others to complete or understand the process?
- Would any information from experts make my description of the process clearer?

## Essay Form

1

Many people are intimidated by the work necessary to make their homes more energ[y] **Thesis statement** and they do not see it as a do-it-yourself job. However, improving a home's energy efficiency can actually be done fairly easily, significantly lowering utility bills.

First, seal air leaks around windows and doors. To seal air leaks around windows, apply cau **Topic sentence 1 (first step)** window frames and walls. Also, if you fashioned windows that are not weather-proof, cover them with plastic before the cold temperatures set in. This process involves affixing two-sided adhesive tape to the window frames and then attaching plastic sheeting, which is sealed with the use of a blow dryer. Next, look for drafty spots around doors. Many air leaks at the top or sides of doors can be sealed with adhesive-backed foam strips. Leaks under doors can be stopped with foam draft guards. Alternatively, a rolled-up blanket, rug, or towel can keep the cold from coming in. All of these measures can save up to $600 per season on heating bills.

2

Second, install water-saving shower heads and faucet aerators. These fixtures are inexpens **Topic sentence 2 (second step)** available in most hardware stores. Also, th to install. First, unscrew the old shower or faucet head. Then, follow the package instructions for affixing the new shower head or aerator. In some cases, you might have to use pipe tape or a rubber washer to ensure a good seal. After this step, run the water to make sure there are no leaks. If you find any leaks, use pliers to tighten the seal. In time, you will discover that the new shower heads and aerators will cut your w **Topic sentence 3 (third step)** and the cost of water heating by up to 50 p

Finally, look for other places where energy efficiency could be increased. One simple improvement is to replace traditional light bulbs with compact fluorescent bulbs, which use up to 80 percent less energy. Also, make sure your insulation is as good as it can be. Many utilities now offer free assessments of home insulation, identifying places where it is missing or inadequate. In some cases, any necessary insulation improvements may be subsidized by the utilities or by

3

government agencies. It is well worth considering such improvements, which, in the case of poorly insulated homes, can save thousands of dollars a year, quickly covering any costs. Although some people prefer to have professionals blow insulating foam into their walls, it is not difficult to add insulation to attics, where a large amount of heat can be lost c **Concluding paragraph** months.

Taking even one of these steps can make a significant financial difference in your life and also reduce your impact on the environment. My advice, though, is to improve your home's energy efficiency as much as possible, even if it means doing just a little at a time. The long-term payoff is too big to pass up.

together to create a successful paragraph or essay. Additionally, reading examples of process analysis will help you write your own.

Read the following sample process analysis paragraph. Using the Four Basics of Good Process Analysis and the sample grading rubric, decide what grade this paragraph would earn. Explain your answer.

**Assignment** Please write a paragraph about how to take better notes when reading and studying. You should make sure that your instructions are careful and deliberate: what steps should be taken, what is involved in each step, and in what order a student should proceed.

**Learning to take effective notes in class can be very easy once a student understands what they need to do. Too often, a student will start taking notes as they read. This becomes a problem because the student does not know what the main idea or most significant ideas of the reading are because they have not read the entire assignment yet. In order to avoid extra work or overly lengthy notes it is best to preview the reading: look at the title, any subheadings, and any bold or italicized words. After previewing, read the entire article from start to finish. Once you have completed those two steps, highlight or underline. In this way, your notes will be clearer and easier to read. It is also less likely they will contain too much extra information.**

**Analysis of Sample Paragraph:**

**Sample rubric**

| Element | Grading criteria | Point: Comment |
|---|---|---|
| **Appropriateness** | • Did the student follow the assignment directions? | ____/5: |
| **Main Idea** | • Does the paper clearly state a strong main idea in a complete sentence? | ____/10: |
| **Support** | • Is the main idea developed with specific support, including specific details and examples?<br>• Is there enough support to make the main idea evident to the reader?<br>• Is all the support directly related to the main idea? | ____/10: |
| **Organization** | • Is the writing logically organized?<br>• Does the student use transitions (*also, for example, sometimes,* and so on) to move the reader from one point to another? | ____/10: |

| Element | Grading criteria | Point: Comment |
|---|---|---|
| Conclusion | • Does the conclusion remind the reader of the main idea?<br>• Does it make an observation based on the support? | ____/5: |
| Grammar | • Is the writing free of the four most serious errors? (See Chapters 16-19.)<br>• Is the sentence structure clear?<br>• Does the student choose words that clearly express his or her meaning?<br>• Are the words spelled correctly?<br>• Is the punctuation correct? | ____/10: |
| | | TOTAL POINTS: ____/50 |

## Read and Analyze Process Analysis

Reading examples of process analysis will help you write your own. The first two examples of process analysis are a paragraph from a student writer and a student essay. In the Profile of Success, Monique Rizer outlines a process she uses in her career, and the final example is a professional essay by Kathy Stevens. As you read, pay attention to the vocabulary, and answer the questions in the margin. They will help you read critically.

### *Student Process Analysis Paragraph*

Charlton Brown

# Buying a Car at an Auction

**legitimate:** lawful; genuine; real

**savvy:** knowledgeable; well informed

**bid:** an offer, in this case, of a price

**thorough:** complete; detailed

**Vocabulary development** Underline these words as you read: *legitimate, savvy, bid,* and *thorough.*

**Predict** What preparation do you think Charlton will say buyers need before attending a car auction?

1 Buying a car at an auction is a good way to get a cheap car, but buyers need to be prepared. First, decide what kind of vehicle you want to buy. Then, find a local auction. Scams are common, though, so be careful. Three top sites that are legitimate are www.gov-auctions.org, www.carauctioninc.com, and www.seizecars.com. When you have found an auction and a vehicle you are interested in, become a savvy buyer. Make sure you know the car's actual market value. You can find this out from Edmunds.com, Kellybluebook.com, or NADA (the National Automobile Dealers Association).

Because bidding can become like a competition, decide on the highest bid you will make, and stick to that. Do not get drawn into the competition. On the day of the auction, get to the auction early so that you can look at the actual cars. If you do not know about cars yourself, bring someone who does with you to the auction so that he or she can examine the car. Next, begin your thorough examination. Check the exterior; especially look for any signs that the car has been in an accident. Also, check the windshield because many states will not give an inspection sticker to cars with any damage to the windshield. Check the interior and try the brakes. Start the engine and listen to how it sounds. Check the heat and air conditioning, the CD player, and all other functions. As a final check before the bidding, look at the car's engine and transmission. Finally, get ready to place your bid, and remember, do not go beyond the amount you settled on earlier. Good luck!

**Summarize** What steps are necessary to buy a car at auction?

1. Double-underline the **topic sentence**.
2. What is Charlton's **main idea**? ______________________________
3. Underline the **major steps**.
4. Circle the words that signal when Charlton moves from one step to the next.
5. Does Charlton's paragraph follow the Four Basics of Good Process Analysis (p. 174)? Why or why not? ______________________________

*Student Process Analysis Essay*

Daniel Bird

## What's Appropriate: How to Talk to Children about Disasters

**news cycle:** 24-hour investigation and reporting

**graphically:** giving a clear and effective picture

**screen time:** the amount of time someone spends in front of technology: television, tablets, computers, cell phones, etc.

**severity:** harshness or intensity

**adjunct:** an employee, typically at a college or university, without full-time status

**therapeutic:** treating or curing

**dynamics:** motivating or driving forces

Daniel Bird is a student at Skyline College in California. His focus is journalism. The following essay was published in the school newspaper, the *Skyline View*, in May 2013.

**Vocabulary Development** Underline these words as you read: *news cycle, graphically, screen time, severity, adjunct, therapeutic,* and *dynamics.*

**Predict** Before reading the article, what do you think may be some ways to help a child handle a disaster?

1 Sandy Hook Elementary. The Boston Marathon. Hurricane Sandy.

2 Whether natural disasters or acts of terrorism, these horrific events have been told and retold within the constant news cycle. Being an adult and

trying to take all of the distressing news in is difficult enough, but for a child it could be life-shattering. The child in your life, be it son, daughter, cousin, niece, nephew, will need your help.

**Reflect** Before reading any further, what are your own initial thoughts or reactions when you think of these events?

3 The first step you should take in order to help the child in your life is to scale down all of the information for them to take in. Keep everything age appropriate, meaning don't give them information they cannot understand. For younger children, tell them generally what happened (not graphically), for older children give them more details, but not graphic ones.

**Identify** Bird refers to providing information that is "age appropriate." What specific ideas or events would you share to a younger child? Why limit those ideas or events? What might an older child be able to understand more clearly?

4 Secondly, you want to limit their screen time, meaning turn off the media that they can see. You may want to see what the newest information is, but while that news comes in, older information is being replayed on the constant news cycle. Sylvia Ford, Early Childhood Education professor at Skyline told me about her opinion of news images and children.

5 "They don't benefit from graphic images," Ford said.

**Reflect** If you were asked to turn off your technology or limit your screen time, especially after a disaster, would you be able to do it? Explain your answer.

6 We still see these images because according to her, "blood sells." After a traumatic event, children will knowingly be out of their routine. It is the family's job to make sure we are able to protect and help our loved ones process at this time. Depending on the severity of the disaster, parents should alter their routine in order to adjust them to what has happened. It may be best for an immediate family member to spend extra time with them.

**Reflect** What does Ford mean when she says "blood sells?" Do you agree or disagree with this statement?

7 Parents and family should not feel completely alone with their issues around this subject. The National Association for the Education of Young Children (NAEYC) has specific instructions on how to explain disasters to children. Children benefit from physical comfort, and comfort around them. Comfort is extremely important at this point in time.

8 Adjunct faculty and Early Childhood Education Professor Shawna Whitney told me families need to plan for a disaster in the same way as you would an emergency. This includes making a plan, have a kit filled with comforting items (favorite toy, fuzzy pajamas, etc.). Adults being prepared will help the children as best as possible.

9 Helping your children can often be a therapeutic without having to have a long discussion. Sometimes the most effective thing to do for children is to escape what has immediately happened.

10 "Getting them involved in an activity that's a little bit distracting right after, when they might be particularly fearful," Early Childhood Education Program Supervisor Cece Rebele said. "Use things like puppets and books that might explain it at their level of understanding."

**Identify** Other than books or puppets, what may be some other ways to help a child deal with a disaster?

11 Dynamics within an area often change after a disaster. This includes all of the helpers that come out to aid those in need such as firefighters, police officers, Red Cross volunteers, etc. Make sure to discuss who these people are and what jobs they do. Let your children know that these people are always there to help them if they need it.

12 Having children in your family does not mean you are the parents; most of us have younger siblings, cousins, nieces, or nephews and talking to them as someone who is not their parent is important. While most parents

COURTESY OF STEVE BARRETT

**Monique Rizer**

Chief of Staff

# *Profile of Success*

## Process Analysis in the Real World

**Background** I was the oldest of six children, and before my mother married my stepfather, she was on welfare. She homeschooled me for five years until I begged her to let me go to a public high school. There I made friends with some people who expected to go to college, and I realized I wanted to go, too. I started at Green River Community College, but just then my parents' financial situation got really bad, and the eight of us had to move to a trailer. I stopped going to school until I met my future husband, who was going to a community college and encouraged me to go back. Several months later, I became pregnant with my first son. I was determined to stay in college, so I completed one year at Highline Community College. That summer, I had my son, got married, and found loans to transfer to Pacific Lutheran University. While there, I received a Gates Millennium Scholarship, which made continuing college possible. Although I moved a few times, I graduated from college and went on to graduate school. After I finished graduate school, I had another son.

**Degrees/Colleges** B.A., Gonzaga University; M.S., Syracuse University

**Employer** Be the Change, Inc.

**Writing at Work** Writing is the one skill I use every day at work. As chief of staff, I'm responsible for supporting our fundraising efforts, managing our board, leading staff meetings, and other special projects. So, I am often writing to staff within the organization, my leadership, our board members, or people outside our organization with whom we are developing a relationship. I usually communicate through e-mail and I've learned it's so important to keep an e-mail short and to the point, but also friendly. Write, "Good morning" or write "Thank you" or "My best." These are small ways to keep e-mail communication personal through what can be a very impersonal technology, especially with people you don't see very often. Also, when I have to e-mail someone with a criticism or difficult message, I always try to start that e-mail with a positive note or thanks. Finally, I think very carefully about sending an e-mail when a phone call or face-to-face conversation is better. We rely on e-mail and text a lot, and we have to really try to keep those writing forums professional. But sometimes a phone call or a face-to-face conversation is more appropriate depending on the message or purpose. As I've grown in my career, I find my writing to be more important. I also have been responsible for hiring new staff and I pay close attention to how they represent themselves in writing.

I represent my leaders often in writing and so I'm very careful about what I am writing and how it will reflect on them and my organization. Sometimes I'll also write or edit something in the voice of my leadership as well. So, reading their writing and learning their "voice" has become an important skill along with writing. Finally, I draft my writing and have someone look it over or let it sit and look at it later—even a few minutes—just to get some distance and look at it with fresh eyes. Getting some distance or having a fresh view almost always improves my writing.

are able to talk to them one on one, other older family members should be prepared to. Use the tips listed above and speak to the parents if you feel the child may need more answers.

13 "Books with disasters in them that way she could be more aware of what might happen," sophomore Brittney Jacobs said about talking with her four-year-old sister about a disaster.

14 Your child wants to be reassured that they're going to be alright, and that even though bad things happen we still go on with our lives. If your child doesn't respond to verbal communication, don't get discouraged. Ask them to use puppets, books, or even a song to communicate what they feel.

1. Double underline the topic sentence.
2. Underline the steps and ways to encourage or comfort a child that Bird outlines in this article.
3. Does Bird use enough examples to make his point clear? ______

   ______
4. Does Bird's essay follow the Four Basics of Good Process Analysis (p. 174)?

   ______

## *Workplace Process Analysis*

The following is an example of an e-mail Rizer would send to her staff.

Dear team,

Thank you for your time and effort to help make the staff retreat a success. It was amazing to see how much interest there was during your presentations.

How did you feel the day went? I would love to get your thoughts.

After such a successful retreat, there are some concrete steps we need to take to keep the positive momentum going. Some can wait until our next monthly meeting, but some are immediate.

Here's what's coming up:

**Monthly in-person leadership meetings:** We'd like to start meeting in person as a leadership team every month. We can rotate between our two office locations and build around existing schedules.

**Task Force:** We scratched the surface on collaborating around a new project. Leadership would like you three to lead this continued conversation and recommend folks from your teams to support. We will discuss more in December.

**Asset mapping:** Several of the staff commitments referenced our organization assets, grassroots relationships, communication functions, etc. We'd like your recommendations for who should do this work in a short-term work group.

Finally, please incorporate the feedback from the meeting and share your updates. Please have those updates by **end of day Dec. 1.**

Again, we appreciate your time, thoughts, and work as we move forward.

Best,

Monique

1. What is the purpose being outlined in the e-mail above? ______

   ______
2. How does Rizer ensure that everyone understands this process? ______

   ______

3. Where did the information for this e-mail come from, and how does she create a process for moving forward? ______________________________

______________________________

______________________________

______________________________

*Professional Process Analysis Essay*

Kathy Stevens

# Ten Tips to Ease into Plant-Based Eating

Kathy Stevens is the founder and director of one of the nation's leading sanctuaries for animals, Catskill Animal Sanctuary. Although she is a vegan herself, she understands that not everyone is comfortable with the idea behind a vegan lifestyle and the seemingly enormous changes that are required to eat food that does not consist of any animal products at all. Her overwhelming message in all of her writing and speaking engagements is "kindness to all."

In the following process analysis essay, which appeared in the *Huffington Post* in April 2014, Stevens presents a step-by-step process to help people learn to add more plant-based foods into their diet without feeling deprived.

**vegan:** one who refrains from consuming animal products, including but not limited to, meat, eggs, butter, and milk

**laden:** heavily loaded or weighted down

**cuisine:** a style of cooking practices that is often associated with a particular culture

**Predict** What are some reasons or steps that Stevens may use to help people ease into a plant-based diet?

**Vocabulary development** Underline these words as you read: *vegan, laden,* and *cuisine.*

1 At the end of a tour of Catskill Animal Sanctuary last year, a visitor who'd just been kissed by cows and held chickens in his lap said to me, "OK. I get it. How do I start?" The question came up again last night, when I was discussing my most recent post with my dad. "I've been eating one way for a long time," he said. "It's hard to change."

2 Not if you do it one step at a time, I said to him. In legions, Americans are opening their eyes, minds, and hearts to the personal, environmental, and ethical horrors of growing animals to feed humans. Moving toward a kinder and healthier way of eating needn't feel drastic if you simply *ease into it.* Here are ten tips for doing just that!

**1. Eat vegan in the a.m.**

3 Oatmeal. Berries and granola with almond milk. English muffin with jam and nondairy butter. Fruit and soy-yogurt smoothies. Green smoothies. Toast with peanut butter. Lots of your favorite cereals—Chex, Corn Flakes, and Special K, for starters—are vegan. Pancakes (there's no difference in taste between vegan pancakes and the ones you're used to). Tofu scramble and vegan sausage: Can you say yum?

4 Now come on . . . was that hard?

**2. Switch to nondairy milk.**

5 From soy to coconut to rice to almond, plant-based milks abound! With fewer calories and no cholesterol, they're arguably healthier. And the impact on animals if America went nondairy is staggering! Here's the math: In 2010, the average American drank more than 20 gallons of milk, which translates to more than 6 billion gallons of milk annually. If each cow produces 2,500 gallons, it takes 2.5 million cows to produce the milk America consumes. If we switched to nondairy milk, 2.5 million animals each year would be spared a life that consists of forcible impregnation, growth hormones and antibiotics, the stealing of their babies immediately after birth, intensive confinement and milk production for much of their lives, and slaughter at just a few years old when their wracked bodies are worn out. Many cows are too broken to stand when they arrive at the slaughterhouse. As "downed cows," they are simply shoved onto a pile and left to die.

**Reflect** How much of this information do you think the general population is aware of? Why might that be?

**3. Go Meatless Mondays.**

6 Cut back at dinner by joining the Meatless Mondays movement. If all Americans participated in this popular trend, 1.4 billion animals per year would be spared.

**4. Bake without animal products**

7 The reasons to bake without eggs and dairy abound. First, a single egg contains more than half the recommended maximum intake of cholesterol for a healthy person. Second, many believe that the egg and dairy industries are the cruelest industries that have ever existed. Finally, you can't taste the difference between a vegan quiche, cake, or cookie and one laden with butter and eggs. Get started here!

**Identify** What key steps to the plant-based eating process are outlined in this paragraph?

**5. Try one new vegan product a week.**

8 If you don't want to give up the taste and texture of meat and dairy, *you don't have to*. You won't like all of these foods, but when you find ones you do, use them as substitutes in your meat and dairy-based recipes. Here are some favorites: Trader Joe's vegan Meatless Meatballs, Field Roast Frankfurters, Gardein Beefless Burger, Beyond Meat Beef-free Crumbles, Tofurky Deli Slices, Daiya cheese, Treeline soft cheeses, Kite-hill cheese, Whole Soy yogurt, Almond Dream yogurt.

**6. Ditch McDonald's.**

9 McDonald's is the largest buyer of eggs in North America, and purchases its eggs from hens kept in battery cages. Grinding up all newborn male chicks is a standard industry practice. Another? Leaving dead birds in cages for months at a time. According to an undercover investigator at a McDonald's egg supplier, "[Dead] birds . . . were left in the cages . . . decomposing for weeks or months at a time . . . with birds who were still alive and laying eggs for human

consumption." Think conditions at McDonald's beef, chicken, and fish suppliers are any better?

**Reflect** How likely is it that someone would make these choices or substitutions? Why do you think that?

10 Choose Loving Hut, Native Foods, Moe's, or Chipotle instead for more humane options. Loving Hut and Native Foods, 100 percent vegan fast food chains, may not be as widespread as McDonald's, but their presence is growing. Loving Hut is now in more than forty locations across the United States, and Native Foods plans on adding 200 new restaurants in the next five years. Moe's and Chipotle also have many delicious vegan options. Fill your Moe's burrito with tofu or beans, or try the tasty new Chipotle Sofritas, a burrito with organic braised tofu.

**7. When choosing restaurants or recipes, think ethnic.**

11 America created the meat- and dairy-based diet that is making us all sick and fat. Most other cuisines are healthier than ours; the ones that seem to have a tremendous number of delicious plant-based choices are Indian, Japanese, Greek, Chinese, Thai, Spanish, and Mexican, so eat the foods you already love that happen to be vegan! There are also hundreds, literally, of vegan cookbooks on the market. Check Amazon or the cooking section of your favorite bookstore. My current favorite is *Big Vegan*.

**8. Give up one animal a month.**

12 If you're a typical American eater, you likely eat chickens, cows, pigs, and fish all the time. You drink milk and eat eggs. All these animals suffer mightily for the benefit of our taste buds. Cutting out one animal per month is a painless way to do a whole lot of good for the animals, your health, and the planet we all share.

**9. Make friends!**

13 Join a meet-up group and see how "seasoned" vegans live—it's helpful, inspiring . . . and fun!

**10. Visit an animal sanctuary.**

**Reflect** Have you ever followed any of the steps described in this essay?

14 *Huh?* Yep. In my view, this might be the most important tip of all. Catskill Animal Sanctuary is just two hours from Manhattan, an hour from Albany, four from Boston. We're also in the exquisite mid–Hudson Valley, a prime vacation destination. Most important, hundreds of animals, including some free-rangers who may hop into your car when you pull up to the barn, are here to work their way into your hearts. We open for the season in April—I will be there with a big smile on my face, as will Arthur the goat. Hope to see you soon. And if you can't get to CAS, find a reputable sanctuary near you. **Fair warning: Be prepared to fall in love, and be prepared for a new way of eating to begin feeling much easier than you ever imagined.**

1. The second paragraph contains the **thesis statement**. Double-underline it.

2. Now, look at this sentence from the last paragraph: **"Be prepared to fall in love, and be prepared for a new way of eating to begin feeling much easier than you ever imagined."** Does this sentence imply that people can skip steps 1 through 9 and only experience step 10 in their process of moving toward a vegan lifestyle? Explain your answer. ______________________________

3. Rather than using typically transitional words, Stevens chooses to number each step in the process. Why do you think she chose that organizational strategy? ______________________________

4. Does this essay follow the Four Basics of Good Process Analysis (p. 174)? Why or why not? ______________________________

**Tip** For reading advice, see Chapter 1.

Respond to one of the following assignments in a paragraph or essay.

1. Identify another process that many people are a part of daily (pumping gas, taking long showers, leaving lights on around the house) which could be changed easily if there was a simple reminder or process in place to change those behaviors. Then, write that process.
2. Although Stevens is a vegan, she describes herself as "passionate but patient," meaning that she never forces her ideas on someone else, no matter how frustrating it may be to her. Identify another process that you find frustrating, and write a detailed description of it.
3. Describe to a beginner how to do something that you do well.

# Write Your Own Process Analysis

In this section, you will write your own process analysis based on one of the following assignments. For help, refer to the How to Write Process Analysis checklist on pages 192–93.

## ASSIGNMENT OPTIONS Writing about college, work, and everyday life

Write a process analysis paragraph or essay on one of the following topics or on one of your own choice.

**College**

- Describe the process of preparing for an exam.
- Attend a tutoring session at your college's writing center. Afterward, describe the process: What specific things did the tutor do to help you? Also, explain what you learned from the process.
- Interview a college graduate about how he or she achieved success in school. During the interview, ask about the steps of specific processes. For example, one question might be, "What steps did you follow to take good notes?" After the interview, describe the processes in writing.

**Work**

- Describe how to make a positive impression at a job interview.
- Think of a challenging task you had to accomplish at work. What steps did you go through to complete it?
- Identify a job that you would like to have after graduation. Then, investigate the process of getting this job, including the courses you need to take, any exams or certifications that are required, the search stage, and the interview. To gather information, visit the Web site of your college's career center. Better yet, make an appointment to speak with a career counselor. After you have completed your research, describe the process in writing.

**Everyday life**

- Describe the process of making something, such as a favorite meal, a set of shelves, or a sweater.
- Think of a challenging process that you have completed successfully, such as fixing a leak under the sink, applying for a loan, or finding a good deal on a car or an apartment. Describe the steps specifically enough so that someone else could complete the process just as successfully.
- Take part in a community activity, such as a fund-raising event for a charity, a neighborhood cleanup, or food preparation at a homeless shelter. Then, describe the process you went through.

## ASSIGNMENT OPTIONS Reading and writing critically

Complete one of the following assignments, which ask you to apply the critical thinking, reading, and writing skills discussed in Chapter 1.

### WRITING CRITICALLY ABOUT READINGS

Although both Charlton Brown's "Buying a Car at Auction" (pp. 181–82) and Kathy Steven's "Ten Tips for Easing into Plant-Based Eating" (pp. 186–89)

describe processes, Steven's process analysis is listed out step by step. Read or review both of these pieces, and then follow these steps:

1. **Summarize** Briefly summarize the works, listing steps in the processes described.
2. **Analyze** Are there any other steps or details that the authors might have included?
3. **Synthesize** Using examples from both Brown's and Steven's writings and from your own experience, discuss (1) processes that would be easier to outline step by step and (2) processes that are easier to describe in full paragraphs.
4. **Evaluate** Which piece, Brown's or Steven's, do you think is more effective? Why? In writing your evaluation, you might look back on your responses to step 2.

**Tip** For a reminder of how to summarize, analyze, synthesize, and evaluate, see the Reading and Writing Critically box on page 21.

## WRITING ABOUT IMAGES

Apple pie
classic recipe
ingredients
flour
200gr type 00
sugar
70gr powdered
butter
150gr
eggs
200gr type 00
apricot marmalade
150gr
lemon
1
icing sugar
2 spoons
salt
a pinch
apples
450gr
difficulty
low
preparation
40 min
cooking
30 min
cost
low
dose for
10 people
preparation
Mix flour, diced butter and a pinch of salt. You can use an mixer to mix the ingredients.
Add eggs, sugar, grated lemon peel and lemon juice. Wrap the dough with plastic and put it inthe fridge for one hour.
Stretch the dough with a rolling pin and put a large disk in a buttered baking pan.
Peel and cut apples. Fill the dough with marmalade and apple slices. Fold in the borders of the dough. Cook in preheated oven at 60°C for 180 minutes.

ELENABSL/ SHUTTERSTOCK

Study this visual recipe for apple pie, and complete the following steps.

1. **Read the images** Ask yourself: How is the process broken apart into a step-by-step process? What changes do you notice from illustration to illustration? What is the purpose of showing this process? (For more information on reading images, see Chapter 1.) Is it as simple to read and comprehend this visual process as it would be if there were detailed written instructions? Why or why not?
2. **Write a process analysis** Write a paragraph or essay that describes the process shown in this illustration. In your description, include the changes you observed in step 1.

### WRITING TO SOLVE A PROBLEM

Read or review the discussion of problem solving in Chapter 1 (pp. 28–30). Then, consider the following problem.

**Midway through a course you are taking, your instructor asks the class to tell her how she could improve the course. You have not been happy with the class because the instructor is always late, comes in seeming rushed and tense, and ends up releasing class late because of material she forgot to cover. During class, she uses PowerPoint slides and reads to the class from them, seldom adding new information. Then, after handing out an assignment for students to work on, she returns to her desk to grade papers. You are afraid to ask questions about the lecture or assignment because the instructor does not seem overly helpful. You want to tell the instructor how the course could be better, but you do not want to offend her.**

**Assignment** Working in a small group or on your own, write to your instructor about how she could improve the course. Think of how the class could be structured differently so that you could learn more. Begin with how the class could start. Then, describe how the rest of the class period could proceed, suggesting specific activities if you can. State your suggestions in positive terms. For example, instead of telling the instructor what *not* to do, make suggestions using phrases like *you could, we could,* or *the class could*. Be sure to use formal English. You might start in this way:

**Several simple changes might improve our learning. At the start of each class,** ____________________

At the end, remember to thank your instructor for asking for students' suggestions.

### CHECKLIST

#### How to Write Process Analysis

| Steps | Details |
|---|---|
| ☐ Narrow and explore your topic<br>See Chapter 3. | • Make the topic more specific.<br>• Prewrite to get ideas about the narrowed topic and how you will explain the steps to your audience.<br>• Make sure your topic can be covered in the space given. |

| Steps | Details |
|---|---|
| ☐ Write a topic sentence (paragraph) or thesis statement (essay) See Chapter 3. | • Decide what you want readers to know about the process you are describing. |
| ☐ Support your point See Chapter 4. | • Include the steps in the process, and explain the steps in detail. |
| ☐ Write a draft See Chapter 5. | • Make a plan that puts the steps in a logical order (often chronological).<br>• Include a topic sentence (paragraph) or thesis statement (essay) and all the supporting details about each step. |
| ☐ Revise your draft See Chapter 5. | • Make sure it has *all* the Four Basics of Good Process Analysis.<br>• Read to make sure all the steps are present.<br>• Make sure you include transitions to move readers smoothly from one step to the next. |
| ☐ Edit your revised draft See Parts 3 through 6. | • Correct errors in grammar, spelling, word use, and punctuation. |

# Chapter Review

1. Process analysis is writing that ______________________________

______________________________

2. What are the Four Basics of Good Process Analysis?

______________________________

______________________________

______________________________

______________________________

3. Write sentences using the following vocabulary words: *legitimate, savvy, bid, thorough, vegan, laden, cuisine.* ______________________________

______________________________

______________________________

# REFLECTING ON THE JOURNEY

## Skills Learned

Now that you've completed the chapter, share what you've learned about each skill by completing the following chart.

| Skill | What I learned about this skill |
|---|---|
| Describe the steps of a process | |
| Include all of the significant steps in a process | |
| Generate support for a process analysis paper | |
| Relate support directly to the main idea of the paper in a logical order | |
| Read and analyze a process analysis paper | |

# 10

# Classification

## Writing That Sorts Things into Groups

READING ROADMAP

### Learning Objectives

**Chapter Goal:** Learn how to write a classification paper.

**Tools to Achieve the Goal:**

- Four Basics of Good Classification (p. 196)
- Diagram: Paragraphs and Essays in Classification (pp. 202–03)
- Sample Classification Paragraph and Rubric (p. 204)
- Student Classification Paragraph: Lorenza Mattazi, *All My Music* (p. 205)
- Student Classification Essay: Kelly Hultgren, *Pick Up the Phone to Call, Not Text* (p. 206)
- Profile of Success and Workplace Classification: Grant Grebner (p. 208)
- Professional Classification Essay: Stephanie Ericsson, *The Ways We Lie* (p. 209)
- Checklist: How to Write Classification (p. 215)

### Key Terms

Skim Chapter 10 before reading. Find these words or terms in **bold** type. Put a check mark next to each once you locate it.

____ classification
____ organizing principle
____ space order (or order of importance)
____ support
____ time order
____ transitions

### Guided Reading for Chapter 10

Fill out the following chart before you begin reading. For each skill, write what you know about that skill and what you would like to know upon completing the chapter. At the end of the chapter, you will be asked to share what you learned about each skill.

| Skill | When I have used this skill | What I want to know about this skill |
|---|---|---|
| Group items into categories | | |
| Identify similarities and differences | | |
| Generate detailed examples of what a category may contain | | |
| Relate examples or explanations to categories | | |
| Read and analyze a classification paper | | |

Visit **LaunchPad Solo for Readers and Writers > Reading > Patterns of Organization** for more tutorials, videos, and practice with patterns of organization.

## Understand What Classification Is

**Classification** is writing that organizes, or sorts, people or items into categories. It uses an **organizing principle**: *how* the people or items are sorted. The organizing principle is directly related to the purpose for classifying. For example, you might sort clean laundry (your purpose) using one of the following organizing principles: by ownership (yours, your roommate's) or by where it goes (the bedroom, the bathroom).

### **Four Basics** of Good Classification

1. It makes sense of a group of people or items by organizing them into categories.
2. It has a purpose for sorting the people or items.
3. It categorizes using a single organizing principle.
4. It gives detailed explanations or examples of what fits into each category.

In the following paragraph, the numbers and colors correspond to the Four Basics of Good Classification.

1 In researching careers I might pursue, I have learned that there are three major types of workers, 2 each having different strengths and preferences. 3 The first type of worker is a big-picture person, who likes to look toward the future and think of new businesses, products, and services. 4 Big-picture people might also identify ways to make their workplaces more successful and productive. Often, they hold leadership positions, achieving their goals by assigning specific projects and tasks to others. Big-picture people may be drawn to starting their own businesses, or they might manage or become a consultant for an existing business. 3 The second type of worker is a detail person, who focuses on the smaller picture, whether it be a floor plan in a construction project, a spreadsheet showing a business's revenue and expenses, or data from a scientific experiment. 4 Detail people take pride in understanding all the ins and outs of a task and doing everything carefully and well. Some detail people prefer to work with their hands, doing such things as carpentry or electrical wiring. Others prefer office jobs, such as accounting or clerical work. Detail people may also be drawn to technical careers, such as scientific research or engineering. 3 The third type of worker is a people person, who gets a lot of satisfaction from reaching out to others and helping meet their needs. 4 A people person has good social skills and likes to get out in the world to use them. Therefore, this type of worker is unlikely to be happy sitting behind a desk. A successful people person often shares qualities of the other types of workers; for example, he or she may show leadership potential. In addition, his or her job may require careful attention to detail. Good jobs for a

people person include teaching, sales, nursing, and other health-care positions. Having evaluated my own strengths and preferences, I believe that I am equal parts big-picture person and people person. I am happy to see that I have many career options.

You use classification anytime you want to organize people or items.

| | |
|---|---|
| **College** | In a health class, you are asked to group foods into the correct category based on the food pyramid. |
| **Work** | For a sales presentation, you classify the kinds of products your company produces. |
| **Everyday life** | You classify your typical monthly expenses to make a budget. |

In college, writing assignments probably will not use the word *classification*. Instead, you might be asked to *describe the types of* ________ or *explain the types or kinds of* ________. You might also be asked, *How is* ________ *organized?* or *What are the parts of* ________*?* These are the words and phrases that signal that you need to sort things into categories.

## *Main Idea in Classification*

The **main idea** in classification uses a single **organizing principle** to sort items in a way that serves your purpose. The categories should help you achieve your purpose.

To help you discover the organizing principle for your classification, complete the following sentences:

| | |
|---|---|
| **Main idea in classification** | **My purpose for classifying my topic is to explain to ________________ readers.**<br>**It would make most sense to my readers if I sorted this topic by . . .** |

### PRACTICE 1 Using a single organizing principle

For each topic that follows, one of the categories does not fit the same organizing principle as the rest. Circle the letter of the category that does not fit, and, in the space provided, write the organizing principle that the rest follow.

**Example:**

**Topic: Sports**

**Categories:**

**a. Basketball (b.) Gymnastics c. Football d. Baseball**

**Organizing principle:** *sports played on a team/sports using balls*

1. Topic: Relatives

   Categories:

   a. Aunts b. Uncles c. Sisters d. Nieces

   Organizing principle: ______________________

2. Topic: Jobs

   Categories:

   a. Weekly b. Hourly c. Monthly d. Summer

   Organizing principle: ______________________

3. Topic: Animals

   Categories:

   a. Dogs b. Cats c. Rabbits d. Whales

   Organizing principle: ______________________

Sometimes, it helps to think of classification in diagram form. Here is a diagram of the paragraph on pages 196–97.

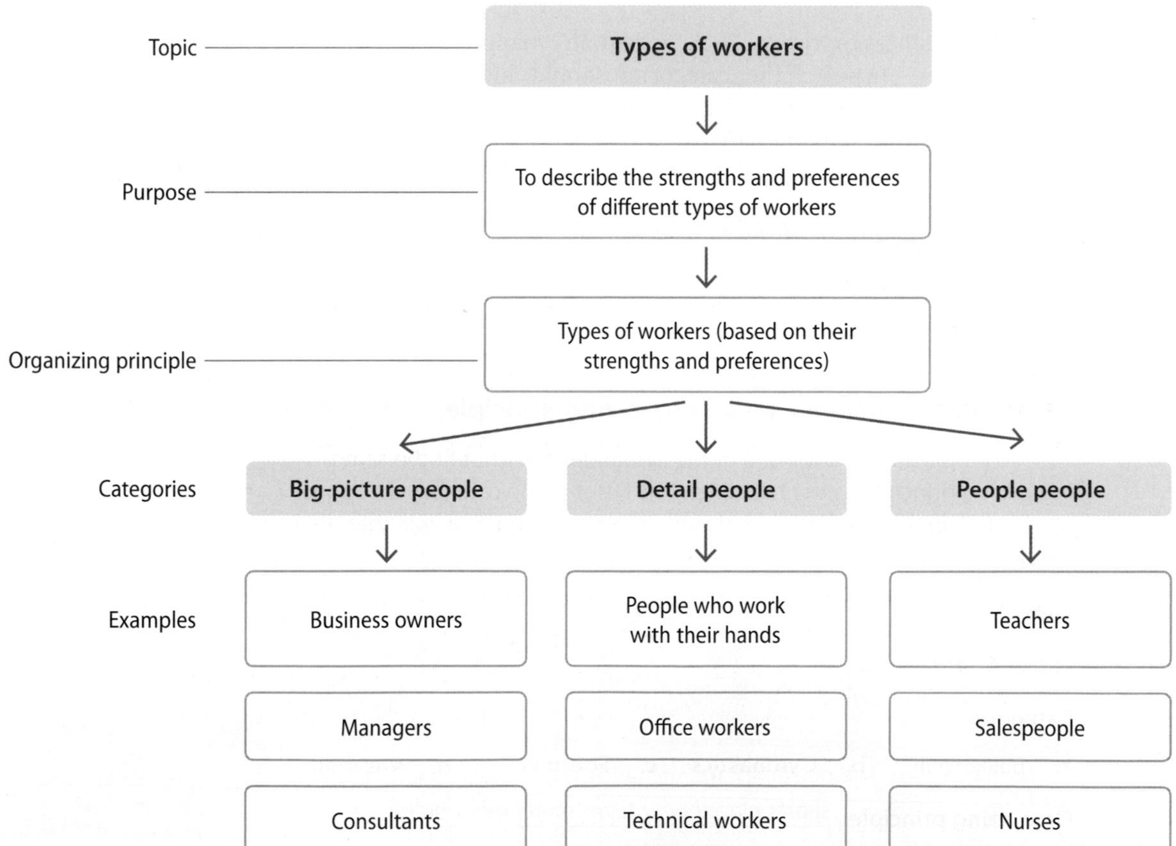
Topic
Types of workers
Purpose
To describe the strengths and preferences of different types of workers
Organizing principle
Types of workers (based on their strengths and preferences)
Categories
Big-picture people
Detail people
People people
Examples
Business owners
People who work with their hands
Teachers
Managers
Office workers
Salespeople
Consultants
Technical workers
Nurses

In classification, the main idea may or may not state the organizing principle directly. Look at the following examples:

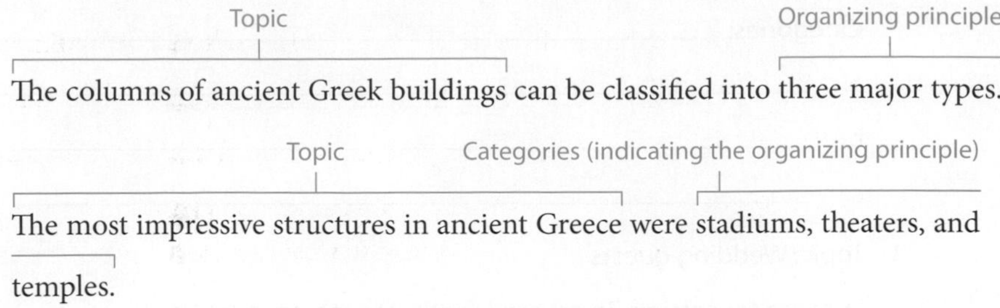
Topic
Organizing principle
Topic
Categories (indicating the organizing principle)

The columns of ancient Greek buildings can be classified into three major types.

The most impressive structures in ancient Greece were stadiums, theaters, and temples.

In both main ideas, the organizing principle is *types* of things—columns in the case of the paragraph and buildings in the case of the essay. The thesis statement does not state this principle directly, however. Instead, the categories—stadiums, theaters, and temples—make the principle clear.

Also, notice that the topic for the essay is broader than the one for the paragraph. Whereas the topic sentence focuses on just one part of ancient Greek buildings—the columns—the thesis statement considers entire groups of structures.

Make sure that the categories in your classification serve your purpose. In the previous thesis statement, the categories serve the purpose of presenting impressive structures in ancient Greece.

**Tip** Sometimes, the same main idea can be used for a paragraph and an essay, but the essay must develop this point in more detail. (See pp. 68–69.)

### PRACTICE 2 Choosing categories

In the items that follow, you are given a topic and a purpose for sorting. For each item, list three categories that serve your purpose. (There are more than three correct categories for each item.)

**Example:**

**Topic: Pieces of paper in my wallet**

**Purpose for sorting: To get rid of what I do not need**

**Categories:**

**a.** *Things I need to keep in my wallet*

**b.** *Things I can throw away*

**c.** *Things I need to keep, but not in my wallet*

1. Topic: College courses

   Purpose for sorting: To decide what I will register for

   Categories: ______________________

   a. ______________________

   b. ______________________

   c. ______________________

2. Topic: Stuff in my notebook

   Purpose for sorting: To organize my schoolwork

   Categories: ______________________________

   a. ______________________________

   b. ______________________________

   c. ______________________________

3. Topic: Wedding guests

   Purpose for sorting: To arrange seating at tables

   Categories: ______________________________

   a. ______________________________

   b. ______________________________

   c. ______________________________

4. Topic: Tools for home repair

   Purpose for sorting: To make them easy to find when needed

   Categories: ______________________________

   a. ______________________________

   b. ______________________________

   c. ______________________________

## *Support in Classification*

The paragraph and essay models on pages 202–03 use the topic sentence (paragraph) and thesis statement (essay) from the Main Idea section of this chapter. Both models include the **support** used in all classification writing: categories backed up by explanations or examples of each category. In the essay model, however, the major support points (categories) are topic sentences for individual paragraphs.

## *Organization in Classification*

**Tip** For more on the orders of organization, see pages 76–78.

Classification can be organized in different ways (**time order**, **space order**, or **order of importance**) depending on its purpose.

| Purpose | Likely Organization |
|---|---|
| to explain changes or events over time | time |
| to describe the arrangement of people/items in physical space | space |
| to discuss parts of an issue or problem, or types of people or things | importance |

Order of importance is used in the essay model on page 203.

As you write your classification, use **transitions** to move your readers smoothly from one category to another.

### Common Transitions in Classification

| | |
|---|---|
| another | for instance |
| another kind | last |
| first, second, third, and so on | one example/another example |
| for example | |

**PRACTICE 3** **Using transitions in classification**

Read the paragraph that follows, and fill in the blanks with transitions. You are not limited to the ones listed in the preceding box.

Every day, I get three kinds of e-mail: work, personal, and junk. The __________ of e-mail, work, I have to read carefully and promptly. Sometimes, the messages are important ones directed to me, but mostly they are group messages about meetings, policies, or procedures. ____________________, it seems as if the procedure for leaving the building during a fire alarm is always changing. ____________________ of e-mail, personal, is from friends or my mother. These I read when I get a chance, but I read them quickly and delete any that are jokes or messages that have to be sent to ten friends for good luck. ____________________ of e-mail is the most common and most annoying: junk. I get at least thirty junk e-mails a day, advertising all kinds of things that I do not want, such as life insurance or baby products. Even when I reply asking that the company stop sending me these messages, they keep coming. Sometimes, I wish e-mail did not exist.

## Evaluate Classification

Read the sample classification paragraph on page 204. Using the Four Basics of Good Classification and the sample grading rubric, decide what grade this paragraph would earn. Explain your answer.

**Assignment** Write a paragraph that classifies the types of classes a student usually has to pass to earn a degree in a particular field.

# Paragraphs vs. Essays in Classification

For more on the important features of classification, see the Four Basics of Good Classification on page 196.

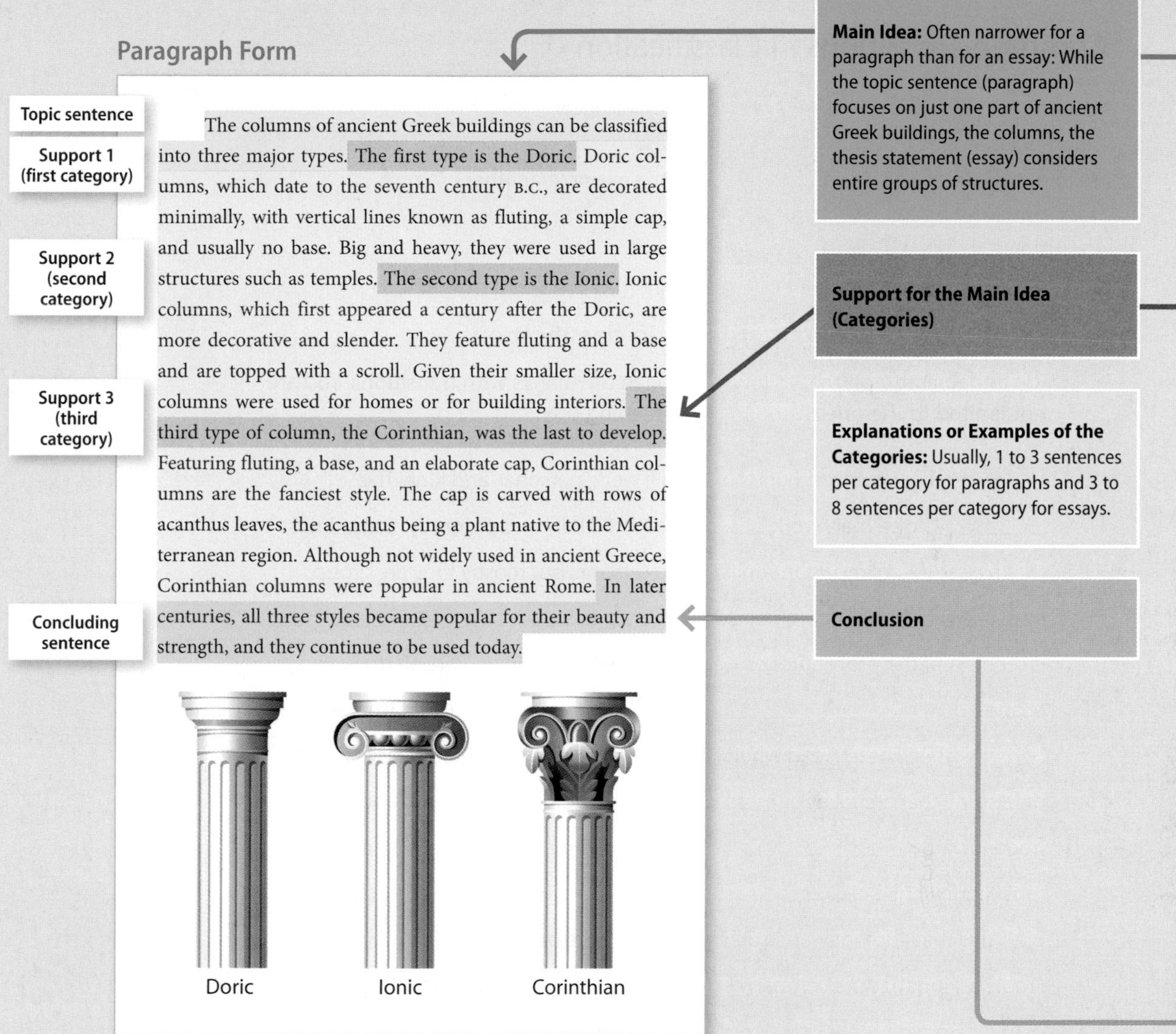
Paragraph Form
Topic sentence
Support 1 (first category)
Support 2 (second category)
Support 3 (third category)
Concluding sentence
Main Idea: Often narrower for a paragraph than for an essay: While the topic sentence (paragraph) focuses on just one part of ancient Greek buildings, the columns, the thesis statement (essay) considers entire groups of structures.
Support for the Main Idea (Categories)
Explanations or Examples of the Categories: Usually, 1 to 3 sentences per category for paragraphs and 3 to 8 sentences per category for essays.
Conclusion
Doric
Ionic
Corinthian

The columns of ancient Greek buildings can be classified into three major types. The first type is the Doric. Doric columns, which date to the seventh century B.C., are decorated minimally, with vertical lines known as fluting, a simple cap, and usually no base. Big and heavy, they were used in large structures such as temples. The second type is the Ionic. Ionic columns, which first appeared a century after the Doric, are more decorative and slender. They feature fluting and a base and are topped with a scroll. Given their smaller size, Ionic columns were used for homes or for building interiors. The third type of column, the Corinthian, was the last to develop. Featuring fluting, a base, and an elaborate cap, Corinthian columns are the fanciest style. The cap is carved with rows of acanthus leaves, the acanthus being a plant native to the Mediterranean region. Although not widely used in ancient Greece, Corinthian columns were popular in ancient Rome. In later centuries, all three styles became popular for their beauty and strength, and they continue to be used today.

## Think Critically As You Write Classification

**ASK YOURSELF**

- Will readers be clear about my organizing principle even if my main idea doesn't state it directly?
- Do the categories that make up the support for my main idea go with my organizing principle? If not, does it make sense to rethink the categories, the organizing principle, or both?
- Are all the explanations or examples for each category relevant?

hypothetical guy liked her and then assumed he didn't based only on his texting frequency. What if the poor guy was having phone issues or was working? You're just getting started; don't expect him to drop the whole world just to send back a response to your simple "hey" text message.

5 This example addresses some aspects of texting: You don't know what the person is physically doing, and you cannot tell the person's mood (emoticons do not count). Therefore, one of every student's favorite forms of interaction is inherently deceiving. At the start of a relationship, why do we communicate and subsequently put so much emphasis on texting, when it's not a reliable way to get to know someone?

**Reflect** Have you ever made an incorrect assumption about a texter based on his or her message or a lack of response to one of your own texts?

6 As I mentioned before, texting can be a deal-breaker. Let's classify some different types of texters and how they can create problems.

7 First up, we have Lazy Texters. Lazy Texters often initiate the conversation and then leave the responsibility of carrying on the conversation with the other person, rarely asking questions and usually responding with one-word answers.

**Identify** Underline the different types of texters Hultgren describes.

8 Then we have the Minimalists. Minimalists make their texts short and concise, and they often take longer to respond. They are also notorious for ignoring people, but you would never know this, because you didn't call. This leads us to another bittersweet characteristic of texting: You really don't know if someone has seen your text or not (unless you have Blackberry Messenger; then, your cover is blown).

9 The next type is the Stage Five Clinger, who will constantly blow up your phone wanting to know what you're doing, where you're going, and where you live. This texter sometimes sends text after text, even when you're not responding. Creepy.

10 A less creepy yet still consistent type of texter is the Text-a-holic. They are constantly texting, and they experience separation anxiety when away from their phones.

11 The use of texting to get acquainted with someone is really just a small portion of humanity's increasing problem of becoming socially inept. I said socially inept, not social-networking inept, as in not being able to communicate with someone face to face. The next time you meet someone and get that warm and fuzzy feeling in your tummy, break through the technological barricade and get to know the person in person. And, please refrain from sending the emoticon with hearts for its eyes.

**Reflect** Do you plan to take any of Hultgren's advice? Why or why not?

1. Double-underline the **topic sentence**.
2. What **categories** of texters does Kelly write about? ______________________

   ______________________________________________
3. Circle the **transitions**.
4. Does the paragraph have the Four Basics of Good Classification (p. 196)? Why or why not? ______________________
5. What kind of organization does Kelly use? ______________________

COURTESY OF DAVID CROSSETT

**Grant Grebner**

Professor of Agriculture

# *Profile of Success*

## Classification in the Real World

**Background** I studied animal science at the University of Illinois where I earned both my bachelor's and master's degrees. After college, I returned to our family farm where I worked on our diversified grain and livestock operation with two brothers. Today as a professor of agriculture, I find that both my education and my real-world experiences on the farm help me provide a better classroom and learning experience for my students since I can share both textbook and real-life examples through personal experience and knowledge.

**Degrees/Colleges** B.S., Animal Science, University of Illinois—Urbana-Champaign; M.S., Non-Ruminant Nutrition, University of Illinois—Urbana-Champaign

**Employer** Professor and Teaching Chair, Agriculture, Illinois Central College

**Writing at work** My writing is extensive and varied at work. On a daily basis, I write e-mails to students, colleagues, and administrators. I also write to agricultural businesses and farmers to seek their assistance by providing worksite locations for student interns or by providing a laboratory experience for one of our agriculture classes. In addition, I write e-mails or letters to respond to high school students who express an interest in our programs. Other writing includes thank you letters or notes to the many people who support our various classes and activities.

We learn about the ways to categorize beef cattle breeds in our introductory animal science course. Students in this course learn to identify eighty breeds in five different species of livestock. Being able to classify these breeds makes them easier to learn and distinguish.

### *Workplace Classification*

# Classification of Cattle

Beef cattle can be divided into two basic classifications, *Bos taurus* and *Bos indicus*. Cattle are not native to the Western Hemisphere.

The *Bos taurus* cattle originated in the British Isles and western continental Europe and offer high-quality meat. *Bos taurus* also have strong milking ability to nourish their calves. Examples of *Bos taurus* cattle include the breeds of Angus and Hereford.

*Bos indicus* originated in south-central Asia and are recognizable by the large hump at the top of their shoulder as well as their large, pendulous ears. They are known for heat tolerance and hardiness and are most commonly utilized in the arid conditions of the southwestern United States. Examples include the Brahman and Santa Gertrudis breeds.

A breed can be described as animals of common genetic origin that possess distinguishing characteristics that are passed on from parent to offspring. Currently, more than 80 breeds of beef cattle can be registered in the United States.

1. Double-underline the **main idea** of the article.
2. What categories does Grant break the cattle into? ________________________________________
3. Does the article have the Four Basics of Good Classification (p. 196)? ________________________________________

## *Professional Classification Essay*

Stephanie Ericsson

# The Ways We Lie

Stephanie Ericsson was born in 1953 and raised in San Francisco. She has lived in a variety of places, including New York, Los Angeles, London, Mexico, the Spanish island of Ibiza, and Minnesota, where she currently resides. Ericsson's life took a major turn when her husband died suddenly; she was two months pregnant at the time. She began a journal to help her cope with the grief and loss, and she later used her writing to help others with similar struggles. An excerpt from her journal appeared in the *Utne Reader*, and her writings were later published in a book titled *Companion through the Darkness: Inner Dialogues on Grief* (1993).

In "The Ways We Lie," which also appeared in the *Utne Reader* and is taken from her follow-up work, *Companion into the Dawn: Inner Dialogues on Loving* (1994), Ericsson continues her search for truth by examining and classifying our daily lives.

**Vocabulary Development** Underline these words as you read: *haggard, minimize, confrontation, indulge, keels, travails, hedging, penance, misdemeanors, frank, arrogance, pittance, facades, plethora, ecclesiastical, pedophilia, diocese, context, coperpetrator, nanoseconds, obliterated, refute, sleight, pious, embellish, shrouds,* and *reticent.*

**Guiding question** As you read this essay, pay attention to the examples Ericsson provides. What examples of lying can you think of from your own experience?

1 The bank called today, and I told them my deposit was in the mail, even though I hadn't written a check yet. It'd been a rough day. The baby I'm pregnant with decided to do aerobics on my lungs for two hours, our three-year-old daughter painted the living-room couch with lipstick, the IRS put me on hold for an hour, and I was late to a business meeting because I was tired.

2 I told my client that the traffic had been bad. When my partner came home, his haggard face told me his day hadn't gone any better than mine, so when he asked,

**haggard:** drawn, worn out
**minimize:** to reduce
**confrontation:** an argumentative meeting
**indulge:** to become involved in
**keels:** falls over
**travails:** painful efforts; tribulations
**hedging:** avoiding the question
**penance:** a penalty to make up for an action
**misdemeanors:** minor violations of rules
**frank:** honest; direct
**arrogance:** belief in one's superiority
**pittance:** a small amount
**facades:** masks
**plethora:** excess
**ecclesiastical:** relating to a church
**pedophilia:** sexual abuse of children
**diocese:** a district or churches under the guidance of a bishop
**context:** a surrounding situation
**coperpetrator:** the helper of a person who commits an action
**nanoseconds:** billionths of a second
**obliterated:** wiped out
**refute:** to deny
**sleight:** a skillful trick
**pious:** religious
**embellish:** to decorate
**shrouds:** covers, conceals
**reticent:** reserved; silent; reluctant

"How was your day?" I said, "Oh, fine," knowing that one more straw might break his back. A friend called and wanted to take me to lunch. I said I was busy. Four lies in the course of a day, none of which I felt the least bit guilty about.

3 We lie. We all do. We exaggerate, we minimize, we avoid confrontation, we spare people's feelings, we conveniently forget, we keep secrets, we justify lying to the big-guy institutions. Like most people, I indulge in small falsehoods and still think of myself as an honest person. Sure I lie, but it doesn't hurt anything. Or does it?

4 I once tried going a whole week without telling a lie, and it was paralyzing. I discovered that telling the truth all the time is nearly impossible. It means living with some serious consequences: The bank charges me $60 in overdraft fees, my partner keels over when I tell him about my travails, my client fires me for telling her I didn't feel like being on time, and my friend takes it personally when I say I'm not hungry. There must be some merit to lying.

5 But if I justify lying, what makes me any different from slick politicians or the corporate robbers who raided the S&L industry? Saying it's OK to lie one way and not another is hedging. I cannot seem to escape the voice deep inside me that tells me: When someone lies, someone loses.

6 What far-reaching consequences will I, or others, pay as a result of my lie? Will someone's trust be destroyed? Will someone else pay *my* penance because I ducked out? We must consider the *meaning of our actions*. Deception, lies, capital crimes, and misdemeanors all carry meanings. *Webster's* definition of *lie* is specific:

1. a false statement or action especially made with the intent to deceive;
2. anything that gives or is meant to give a false impression.

7 A definition like this implies that there are many, many ways to tell a lie. Here are just a few.

### The White Lie

**Reflect** Think of another common human behavior. Break it into categories, and give examples for each category.

**Identify** In the first two paragraphs, the author provides four examples of lies she has told. Put an X by these examples.

**Reflect** Do you agree that there "must be some merit to lying"? Why or why not?

8 The white lie assumes that the truth will cause more damage than a simple, harmless untruth. Telling a friend he looks great when he looks like hell can be based on a decision that the friend needs a compliment more than a frank opinion. But, in effect, it is the liar deciding what is best for the lied to. Ultimately, it is a vote of no confidence. It is an act of subtle arrogance for anyone to decide what is best for someone else.

9 Yet not all circumstances are quite so cut and dried. Take, for instance, the sergeant in Vietnam who knew one of his men was killed in action but listed him as missing so that the man's family would receive indefinite compensation instead of the lump-sum pittance the military gives widows and children. His intent was honorable. Yet for twenty years this family kept their hopes alive, unable to move on to a new life.

### Facades

10 We all put up facades to one degree or another. When I put on a suit to go to see a client, I feel as though I am putting on another face, obeying the expectation

that serious businesspeople wear suits rather than sweatpants. But I'm a writer. Normally, I get up, get the kid off to school, and sit at my computer in my pajamas until four in the afternoon. When I answer the phone, the caller thinks I'm wearing a suit (although the UPS man knows better).

11 But facades can be destructive because they are used to seduce others into an illusion. For instance, I recently realized that a former friend was a liar. He presented himself with all the right looks and the right words and offered lots of new consciousness theories, fabulous books to read, and fascinating insights. Then I did some business with him, and the time came for him to pay me. He turned out to be all talk and no walk. I heard a plethora of reasonable excuses, including in-depth descriptions of the big break around the corner. In six months of work, I saw less than a hundred bucks. When I confronted him, he raised both eyebrows and tried to convince me that I'd heard him wrong, that he'd made no commitment to me. A simple investigation into his past revealed a crowded graveyard of disenchanted former friends.

### Ignoring the Plain Facts

12 In the sixties, the Catholic Church in Massachusetts began hearing complaints that Father James Porter was sexually molesting children. Rather than relieving him of his duties, the ecclesiastical authorities simply moved him from one parish to another between 1960 and 1967, actually providing him with a fresh supply of unsuspecting families and innocent children to abuse. After treatment in 1967 for pedophilia, he went back to work, this time in Minnesota. The new diocese was aware of Father Porter's obsession with children, but they needed priests and recklessly believed treatment had cured him. More children were abused until he was relieved of his duties a year later. By his own admission, Porter may have abused as many as a hundred children.

13 Ignoring the facts may not in and of itself be a form of lying, but consider the context of this situation. If a lie is *a false action done with the intent to deceive*, then the Catholic Church's conscious covering for Porter created irreparable consequences. The church became a coperpetrator with Porter.

**Identify** Underline the main idea of this paragraph. What example does Ericsson use to support it?

**Summarize** In your own words, summarize the example in this paragraph in one or two sentences.

### Stereotypes and Clichés

14 Stereotype and cliché serve a purpose as a form of shorthand. Our need for vast amounts of information in nanoseconds has made the stereotype vital to modern communication. Unfortunately, it often shuts down original thinking, giving those hungry for truth a candy bar of misinformation instead of a balanced meal. The stereotype explains a situation with just enough truth to seem unquestionable.

15 All the *isms*—racism, sexism, ageism, et al.—are founded on and fueled by the stereotype and the cliché, which are lies of exaggeration, omission, and ignorance. They are always dangerous. They take a single tree and make it a landscape. They destroy curiosity. They close minds and separate people. The single mother on

welfare is assumed to be cheating. Any black male could tell you how much of his identity is obliterated daily by stereotypes. Fat people, ugly people, beautiful people, old people, large-breasted women, short men, the mentally ill, and the homeless all could tell you how much more they are like us than we want to think. I once admitted to a group of people that I had a mouth like a truck driver. Much to my surprise, a man stood up and said, "I'm a truck driver, and I never cuss." Needless to say, I was humbled.

**Predict** Pause just as you start the "Out-and-Out Lies" section. How do you think Ericsson might define such lies?

### Out-and-Out Lies

16 Of all the ways to lie, I like this one the best, probably because I get tired of trying to figure out the real meanings behind things. At least I can trust the bald-faced lie. I once asked my five-year-old nephew, "Who broke the fence?" (I had seen him do it.) He answered, "The murderers." Who could argue?

17 At least when this sort of lie is told it can be easily confronted. As the person who is lied to, I know where I stand. The bald-faced lie doesn't toy with my perceptions—it argues with them. It doesn't try to refashion reality; it tries to refute it. *Read my lips* . . . No sleight of hand. No guessing. If this were the only form of lying, there would be no such thing as floating anxiety or the adult-children of alcoholics movement.

18 These are only a few of the ways we lie. Or are lied to. As I said earlier, it's not easy to entirely eliminate lies from our lives. No matter how pious we may try to be, we will still embellish, hedge, and omit to lubricate the daily machinery of living. But there is a world of difference between telling functional lies and living a lie. Martin Buber once said, "The lie is the spirit committing treason against itself." Our acceptance of lies becomes a cultural cancer that eventually shrouds and reorders reality until moral garbage becomes as invisible to us as water is to a fish.

19 How much do we tolerate before we become sick and tired of being sick and tired? When will we stand up and declare our *right* to trust? When do we stop accepting that the real truth is in the fine print? Whose lips do we read this year when we vote for president? When will we stop being so reticent about making judgments? When do we stop turning over our personal power and responsibility to liars?

**Reflect** Think back on your answer to the question on page 210 about whether lying ever has any merit. Have your views on this issue changed? Why or why not?

20 Maybe if I don't tell the bank the check's in the mail I'll be less tolerant of the lies told to me every day. A country song I once heard said it all for me: "You've got to stand for something or you'll fall for anything."

1. Double underline the thesis statement.
2. How many categories does Ericsson use to classify types of lying? What does she call those categories? ______________________________

   ______________________________

3. Do you agree with these categories? If not, which ones don't seem to be labeled appropriately or should she create a new category for some of the examples? ______

4. How does Ericsson organize her essay? ______

5. What is Ericsson's attitude toward lying? What examples in the essay support your answer? ______

# Write Your Own Classification

In this section, you will write your own classification based on one of the following assignments. For help, refer to the How to Write Classification checklist on page 216.

**ASSIGNMENT OPTIONS** **Writing about college, work, and everyday life**

Write a classification paragraph or essay on one of the following topics or on one of your own choice.

**College**

- Classify the types of resources available in your college's library, giving examples of things in each category. If you don't have time to visit the library, spend time looking at its Web site. (Some library Web sites include virtual tours.)
- Classify the course requirements for your program into different categories, such as easy, challenging, and very challenging. Your purpose could be to help a future student in the program understand what to expect.
- Classify the types of students at your college, giving explanations and examples for each category. You might classify students by such things as their interests, their level of dedication to school, and their backgrounds (for example, *older students returning to college* and *young students*).

**Work**

- Classify the different types of bosses or employees, giving explanations and examples for each category.
- Classify the types of skills you need in your current job or a job you held in the past. Give explanations and examples for each category of skill.
- Look back at the paragraph on pages 196–97 that illustrates the Four Basics of Good Classification. Based on your own experiences, think of at least two other ways in which workers might be classified. In writing about your classification, give examples of the types of jobs these workers would like and dislike.

**Everyday life**

- Using Lorenza Mattazi's paragraph as a guide (see p. 205), classify the types of music you enjoy.
- Write about the types of challenges you face in your everyday life, giving explanations and examples for each category.
- Find out about social-service volunteer opportunities in your community. Write about the types of opportunities that are available. Or research an organization that interests you, and write about the kinds of things it does.

## ASSIGNMENT OPTIONS Reading and writing critically

Complete one of the following assignments, which ask you to apply the critical thinking, reading, and writing skills discussed in Chapter 1.

### WRITING CRITICALLY ABOUT READINGS

Both Stephanie Ericsson's "The Ways We Lie" (pp. 209–12) and Kelly Hultgren's "Pick Up the Phone to Call, Not Text" (pp. 206–07) describe certain behaviors (lying or stretching the truth in certain circumstances and refusing to call a person and speak to them). Read or review both of these essays, and then follow these steps:

**Tip** For a reminder of how to summarize, analyze, synthesize, and evaluate, see the Reading and Writing Critically box on page 21.

1. **Summarize** Briefly summarize the works, listing examples they include.
2. **Analyze** Are there any other examples or details that the authors might have provided?
3. **Synthesize** Using examples from both Ericsson's and Hultgren's essays and from your own experience, discuss various types of behaviors, annoying or endearing, and explain why you feel that way about them.
4. **Evaluate** Which piece, Ericsson's or Hultgren's, do you think is more effective? Why? In writing your evaluation, you might look back on your responses to step 2.

### WRITING ABOUT IMAGES

Study the visual below, and complete the following steps.

KRISTIAN SEKULIC/GETTY IMAGES

1. **Read the image** Ask yourself: What purpose does the visual serve? How do the faces, clothing, and positions of the bodies in it help viewers understand how people feel in this image? (For more information on reading images, see Chapter 1.)

2. **Write a classification** Write a paragraph or essay classifying the types of behaviors that send signals to others. The signals can be from a pet or from a person. You might include or expand on the types of behaviors described in the visual.

### WRITING TO SOLVE A PROBLEM

Read or review the discussion of problem solving in Chapter 1 (pp. 28–30). Then, consider the following problem.

**You need a car loan. The loan officer gives you an application that asks for your monthly income and expenses. Because you find yourself short on money every month, you realize that you need to see how you spend your money. You decide to make a monthly budget that categorizes the kinds of expenses you have.**

**Assignment:** Working with a group or on your own, break your monthly expenses into categories, thinking of everything that you spend money on. Then, review the expenses carefully to see which ones might be reduced. Next, write a classification paragraph or essay for the loan officer that classifies your monthly expenses, with examples, and ends with one or two suggestions about how you might reduce your monthly spending. You might start with this sentence:

**My monthly expenses fall into __________ basic categories: ____________, ____________, and ____________.**

## Chapter Review

1. Classification is writing that ______________________________
2. The organizing principle is ______________________________
3. What are the Four Basics of Good Classification?

______________________________

______________________________

______________________________

______________________________

4. Write sentences using the following vocabulary words: *discourse, inept, keels, travails, hedging, facades, perpetrator*, and *reticent*. ____________________

______________________________

______________________________

CHECKLIST

## How to Write Classification

| Steps | Details |
|---|---|
| ☐ Narrow and explore your topic. See Chapter 3. | • Make the topic more specific.<br>• Prewrite to get ideas about the narrowed topic. |
| ☐ Write a topic sentence (paragraph) or thesis statement (essay). See Chapter 3. | • State your topic and your organizing principle or categories. |
| ☐ Support your point. See Chapter 4. | • Come up with explanations/examples to support each category. |
| ☐ Write a draft. See Chapter 5. | • Make a plan that puts the categories in a logical order.<br>• Include a topic sentence (paragraph) or thesis statement (essay) and all the supporting categories with explanations and examples. |
| ☐ Revise your draft. See Chapter 5. | • Make sure it has *all* the Four Basics of Good Classification.<br>• Make sure you include transitions to move readers smoothly from one category to the next. |
| ☐ Edit your revised draft. See Parts 3 through 6. | • Correct errors in grammar, spelling, word use, and punctuation. |

# REFLECTING ON THE JOURNEY

## Skills Learned

Now that you've completed the chapter, share what you've learned about each skill by completing the following chart.

| Skill | What I learned about this skill |
|---|---|
| Group items into categories | |
| Identify similarities and differences to create groups | |
| Generate detailed examples of what a category may contain | |
| Relate examples or explanations to categories | |
| Read and analyze a classification paper | |

11

# Definition

## Writing That Tells What Something Means

### Learning Objectives

**Chapter Goal:** Learn how to write a definition paper.

**Tools to Achieve the Goal:**

- Four Basics of Good Definition (p. 219)
- Diagram: Paragraphs and Essays in Definition (pp. 222–23)
- Student Definition Paragraph: Corin Costas, *What Community Involvement Means to Me* (pp. 226–27)
- Student Definition Essay: Vidette Editorial Board, *ISU Restroom Change Shows Commitment to Diversity* (pp. 227–30)
- Profile of Success and Workplace Definition: Moses Maddox (pp. 228–29)
- Professional Definition Essay: Elizabeth Renter, *Napping Can Dramatically Increase Memory, Learning, Awareness, and More* (pp. 232–33)
- Checklist: How to Write Definition (p. 236)

## READING ROADMAP

### Key Terms

Skim Chapter 11 before reading. Find these words or terms in **bold** type. Put a check mark next to each once you locate it.

____ definition
____ main idea
____ support
____ order of importance
____ transitions

### Guided Reading for Chapter 11

Fill out the following chart before you begin reading. For each skill, write what you know about that skill and what you would like to know upon completing the chapter. At the end of the chapter, you will be asked to share what you learned about each skill.

| Skill | When I have used this skill | What I want to know about this skill |
|---|---|---|
| Define a word or concept | | |
| Provide examples to explain the definition of a word or concept | | |
| Provide enough details to support the definition of a word or concept | | |
| Read, analyze, and evaluate a definition | | |

# Understand What Definition Is

**Definition** is writing that explains what a term or concept means.

**Four Basics** of Good Definition

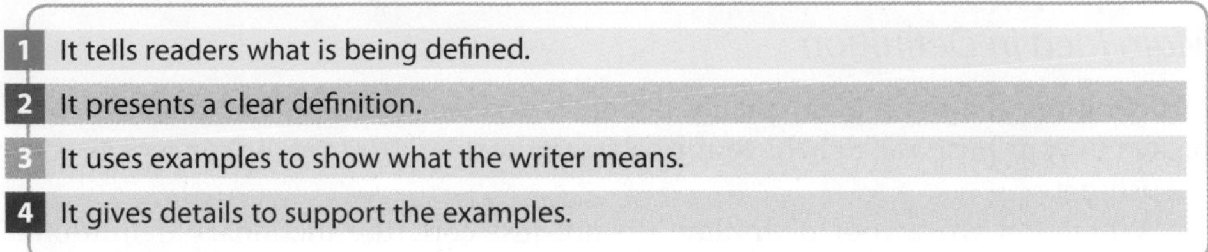

1. It tells readers what is being defined.
2. It presents a clear definition.
3. It uses examples to show what the writer means.
4. It gives details to support the examples.

LaunchPadSolo

Visit **LaunchPad Solo for Readers and Writers > Reading > Patterns of Organization** for more tutorials, videos, and practice with patterns of organization.

In the following paragraph, the numbers and colors correspond to the Four Basics of Good Definition.

A [1] stereotype [2] is a conventional idea or image that is simplistic—and often wrong, particularly when it is applied to people or groups of people. Stereotypes can prevent us from seeing people as they really are because stereotypes blind us with preconceived notions about what a certain type of person is like. [3] For example, I had a stereotyped notion of Native Americans until I met my friend Daniel, a Chippewa Indian. [4] I thought all Indians wore feathers and beads, had long black hair, and avoided all contact with non–Native Americans because they resented their land being taken away. Daniel, however, wears jeans and T-shirts, and we talk about everything—even our different ancestries. After meeting him, I understood that my stereotype of Native Americans was completely wrong. [3] Not only was it wrong, but it set up an us-them concept in my mind that made me feel that I, as a non–Native American, would never have anything in common with Native Americans. My stereotype would not have allowed me to see any Native American as an individual: I would have seen him or her as part of a group that I thought was all alike, and all different from me. From now on, I won't assume that any individual fits my stereotype; I will try to see that person as I would like them to see me: as myself, not a stereotyped image.

You can use definition in many practical situations.

| | |
|---|---|
| **College** | On a math exam, you are asked to define *exponential notation.* |
| **Work** | On a job application, you are asked to choose one word that describes you and explain why. |
| **Everyday life** | In a relationship, you define for your partner what you mean by *commitment* or *communication.* |

**Tip** Once you have a basic statement of your definition, try revising it to make it stronger, clearer, or more interesting.

In college, writing assignments may include the word *define*, but they might also use phrases such as *explain the meaning of* ________ and *discuss the meaning of* ________. In these cases, use the strategies discussed in this chapter to complete the assignment.

## Main Idea in Definition

In definition, the **main idea** usually defines a term or concept. The main idea is related to your purpose: to help your readers understand the term or concept as you are using it.

When you write your definition, do not just copy the dictionary definition; write it in your own words as you want your readers to understand it. To help you, you might first complete the following sentence:

**Main idea in definition** **I want readers to understand that this term means . . .**

Then, based on your response, write a topic sentence (paragraph) or thesis statement (essay). These main-idea statements can take the following forms.

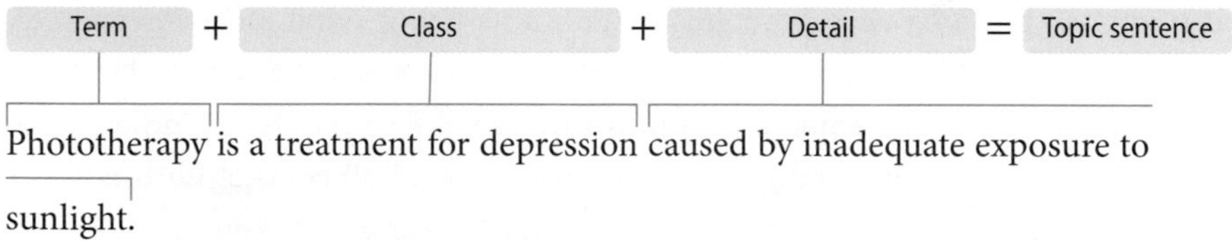
Term
+
Class
+
Detail
=
Topic sentence
Phototherapy is a treatment for depression caused by inadequate exposure to sunlight.

In this example, "Class" is the larger group the term belongs to. Main-idea statements do not have to include a class, however. For example:

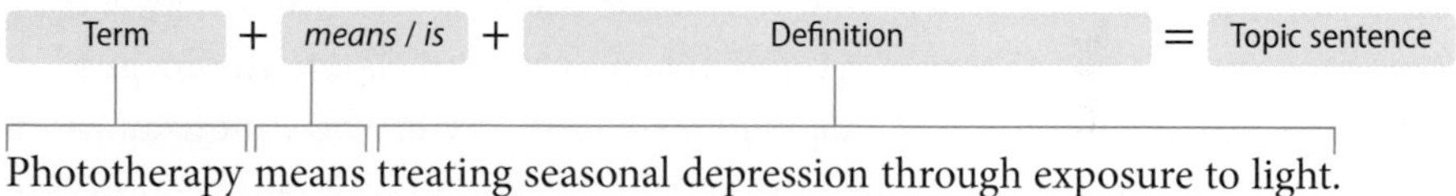
Term
+
means / is
+
Definition
=
Topic sentence
Phototherapy means treating seasonal depression through exposure to light.

Now, look at this thesis statement about a related topic.

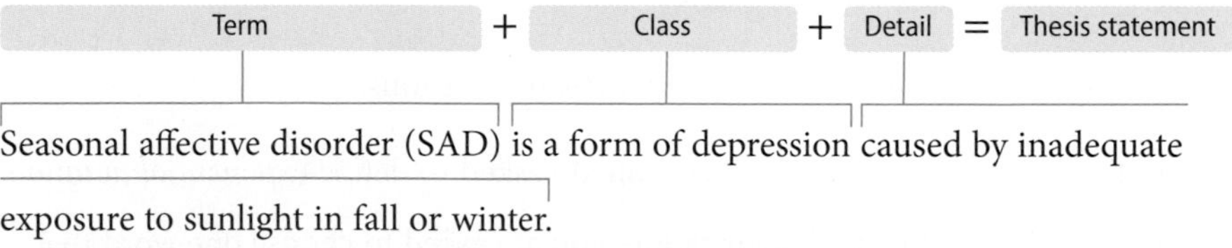
Term
+
Class
+
Detail
=
Thesis statement
Seasonal affective disorder (SAD) is a form of depression caused by inadequate exposure to sunlight in fall or winter.

**Tip** Sometimes, the same main idea can be used for a paragraph and an essay, but the essay must develop this point in more detail. (See pp. 68–69.)

The thesis statement is broader in scope than the topic sentences because it sets up a discussion of the larger subject of seasonal affective disorder. In contrast, the topic sentences consider one particular treatment for this disorder (phototherapy).

**PRACTICE 1** **Writing a statement of your definition**

For each of the following terms, write a definition statement using the pattern indicated in brackets. You may need to use a dictionary.

**Example:**

**Cirrhosis [term + class + detail]:**

*Cirrhosis is a liver disease often caused by alcohol abuse.*

1. Stress [term + class + detail]: ______________________________
2. Vacation [term + *means* /*is* + definition]: ______________________________
3. Confidence [term + class + detail]: ______________________________
4. Conservation [term + *means* /*is* + definition]: ______________________________
5. Marriage [term + *means* /*is* + definition]: ______________________________

## *Support in Definition*

The paragraph and essay models on pages 222–23 use one topic sentence (paragraph) and the thesis statement (essay) from the Main Idea section in this chapter. Both models include the **support** used in all definition writing: examples that explain what a term or concept means backed up by details about these examples. In the essay model, however, the major support ideas (examples) are topic sentences for individual paragraphs.

**PRACTICE 2** **Selecting examples and details to explain the definition**

List three examples or pieces of information you could use to explain each of the following definitions.

**Example:**

**Insomnia means sleeplessness.**

a. *hard to fall asleep*

b. *wake up in the middle of the night*

c. *wake up without feeling rested in the morning*

*(Continued on page 224.)*

# Paragraphs vs. Essays in Definition

For more on the important features of definition, see the Four Basics of Good Definition on page 219.

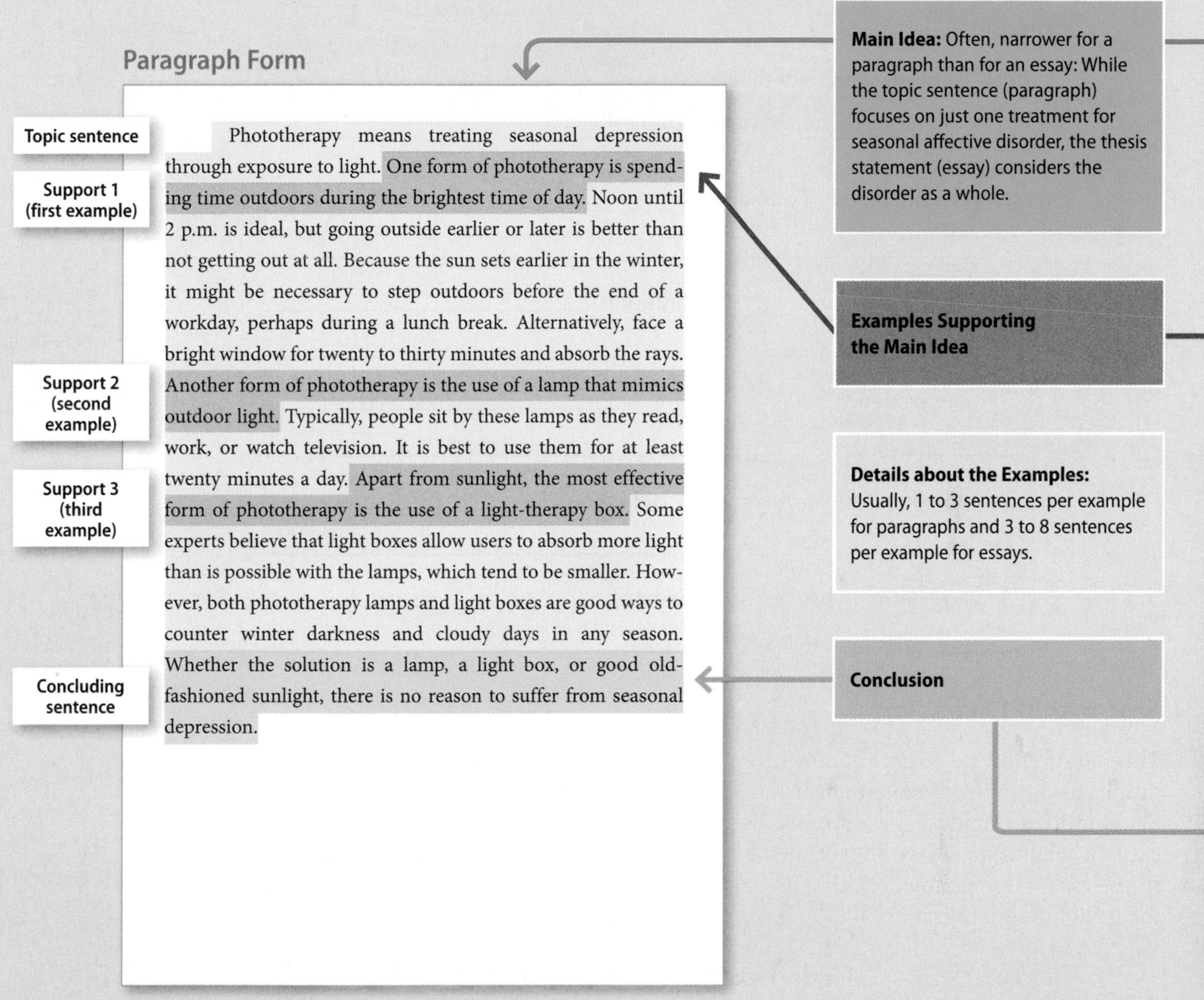

Paragraph Form
Topic sentence
Support 1 (first example)
Support 2 (second example)
Support 3 (third example)
Concluding sentence
Phototherapy means treating seasonal depression through exposure to light. One form of phototherapy is spending time outdoors during the brightest time of day. Noon until 2 p.m. is ideal, but going outside earlier or later is better than not getting out at all. Because the sun sets earlier in the winter, it might be necessary to step outdoors before the end of a workday, perhaps during a lunch break. Alternatively, face a bright window for twenty to thirty minutes and absorb the rays. Another form of phototherapy is the use of a lamp that mimics outdoor light. Typically, people sit by these lamps as they read, work, or watch television. It is best to use them for at least twenty minutes a day. Apart from sunlight, the most effective form of phototherapy is the use of a light-therapy box. Some experts believe that light boxes allow users to absorb more light than is possible with the lamps, which tend to be smaller. However, both phototherapy lamps and light boxes are good ways to counter winter darkness and cloudy days in any season. Whether the solution is a lamp, a light box, or good old-fashioned sunlight, there is no reason to suffer from seasonal depression.
Main Idea: Often, narrower for a paragraph than for an essay: While the topic sentence (paragraph) focuses on just one treatment for seasonal affective disorder, the thesis statement (essay) considers the disorder as a whole.
Examples Supporting the Main Idea
Details about the Examples: Usually, 1 to 3 sentences per example for paragraphs and 3 to 8 sentences per example for essays.
Conclusion


## Think Critically As You Write Definition

### ASK YOURSELF

- Have I examined different definitions of this term or concept? (If not, research them and consider broadening or narrowing your definition based on what you learn.)
- Would someone who is unfamiliar with this term or concept understand it based on my definition and my supporting details and examples?

## Essay Form

Thesis statement

1

Seasonal affective disorder (SAD) is a form of depression caused by inadequate exposure to sunlight in fall or winter. It can seriously affect the daily life of those who suffer from it.

Topic sentence 1 (first example)

One consequence of SAD is sleepiness and a lack of energy. SAD sufferers may find that they [...]ing longer yet are still drowsy during the day [...] during the afternoon. Connected to the drowsiness may be moodiness and an inability to concentrate. The latter effect can result in poorer performance at work and at other tasks. Those affected by SAD may also find that they move more slowly than usual and that all types of physical activity are more challenging than they used to be. All these difficulties can be a source of frustration, sometimes worsening the depression. Another consequence of SAD is loss of interest in work, hobbies, and other activities. To some ex[...] symptoms may be connected to a lack of ene[...] however, the feelings run deeper than that. Activities that once lifted one's spirits may have the opposite effect. For instance, a mother who at one time never

Topic sentence 2 (second example)

2

missed her child's soccer games might now see attending them as a burden. Someone who was once a top performer at work may find that it is all he or she can do to show up in the morning. Such changes in one's outlook can contribute to a feeling of hopelessness.

Topic sentence 3 (third example)

The most serious consequence of SAD is withdrawal from interactions with others. SA[...] may find that they are no longer intereste[...] out with friends, and they may turn down requests to get together for movies, meals, or social events. They may even withdraw from family members, engaging less frequently in conversation or even spending time alone in their room. Furthermore, they may postpone or cancel activities, such as vacation trips, that might require them to interact with family for hours at a time. Withdrawal symptoms may also extend to the workplace, with SAD sufferers becoming less vocal at meetings or avoiding lunches or conversations with colleagues. Concern that family members or coworkers may be noticing such personality changes can cause or worsen anxiety in those with SAD.

Concluding paragraph

3

Because the effects of SAD can be so significant, it is important to address them as soon as possible. Fortunately, there are many good therapies for the condition, from drug treatment to greater exposure to sunlight, whether real or simulated through special lamps or light boxes. Often, such treatments have SAD sufferers feeling better quickly.

1. A good workout makes you feel better.

   a. ______________________________

   b. ______________________________

   c. ______________________________

2. A real friend is not just someone for the fun times.

   a. ______________________________

   b. ______________________________

   c. ______________________________

3. A family is a group you always belong to, no matter what.

   a. ______________________________

   b. ______________________________

   c. ______________________________

4. Beauty is an important element in life that a viewer needs to be always looking for, even in unlikely places.

   a. ______________________________

   b. ______________________________

   c. ______________________________

## *Organization in Definition*

**Tip** For more on order of importance, see page 78.

The examples in definition are often organized by **order of importance**, meaning that the example that will have the most effect on readers is saved for last. This strategy is used in the paragraph and essay models on pages 222–23.

**Transitions** in definition move readers from one example to the next. Here are some transitions you might use in definition, although many others are possible, too.

### Common Transitions in Definition

| | |
|---|---|
| alternately | first, second, third, and so on |
| another; one/another | for example |
| another kind | for instance |

**PRACTICE 3** **Using transitions in definition**

Read the paragraph that follows, and fill in the blanks with transitions. You are not limited to the ones listed in the preceding box.

Each year, *Business Week* publishes a list of the most family-friendly companies to work for. The magazine uses several factors to define the

organizations as family-friendly. _______ factor is whether the company has flextime, allowing employees to schedule work hours that better fit family needs. ______________, a parent might choose to work from 6:30 a.m. to 2:30 p.m. to be able to spend time with children. _____________, a parent might split his or her job with a colleague, so each person thus has more time for child care. __________________ factor is whether family leave programs are encouraged. In addition to maternity leaves, ______________, does the company encourage paternity leaves and leaves for care of elderly parents? Increasingly, companies are trying to become more family-friendly to attract and keep good employees.

## Evaluate Definition

Read the following sample definition paragraph. Using the Four Basics of Good Definition and the sample grading rubric, decide what grade this paragraph would earn. Explain your answer.

**Assignment** Define one character trait that you would look for in a best friend.

**Finding a best friend isn't always easy because it's important to make sure to know the person well. When I first meet a person and begin to spend time with them, I want to make sure that we have enough in common to be good friends. If we can't agree on places to go or what to do, then that may mean that we do not really share enough interests to spend a lot of time together. What if I always want to go to sporting events and they always want to go to a movie? That makes it hard for us to hang out because we just don't find the same things entertaining. Therefore, if we are not spending a lot of time together, then we probably are not a great fit as best friends.**

**Analysis of Sample Paragraph:**

**Sample rubric**

| Element | Grading criteria | Point: Comment |
|---|---|---|
| **Appropriateness** | • Did the student follow the assignment directions? | _____/5: |
| **Main idea** | • Does the paper clearly state a strong main idea in a complete sentence? | _____/10: |
| **Support** | • Is the main idea developed with specific support, including specific details and examples?<br>• Is there enough support to make the main idea evident to the reader?<br>• Is all the support directly related to the main idea? | _____/10: |

▸

| Element | Grading criteria | Point: Comment |
|---|---|---|
| **Organization** | • Is the writing logically organized according to a basic principle (order of importance)?<br>• Does the student use transitions (*also, for example, sometimes,* and so on) to move the reader from one point to another? | ____/10: |
| **Conclusion** | • Does the conclusion remind the reader of the main idea? | ____/5: |
| **Grammar** | • Is the writing free of the four most serious errors? (See Chapters 16–19.)<br>• Is the sentence structure clear?<br>• Does the student choose words that clearly express his or her meaning?<br>• Are the words spelled correctly?<br>• Is the punctuation correct? | ____/10: |
| | | **TOTAL POINTS: ____/50** |

## Read and Analyze Definition

Reading examples of definition will help you write your own. The first example is a student paragraph by Corin Costas about a community service group in which he is involved. An essay by the Vidette Editorial Board explores a controversial issue on campus. In the Profile of Success, Moses Maddox describes how he uses definition in his career. Finally, a professional essay by Elizabeth Renter defines "napping" and how it can positively affect a person's performance in everyday life. As you read these pieces, pay attention to the vocabulary, and answer the questions in the margin. They will help you read critically.

### *Student Definition Paragraph*

Corin Costas

## What Community Involvement Means to Me

SHOCWAVES is a student organization at Bunker Hill Community College. SHOCWAVES stands for Students Helping Our Community with Activities, and its mission is to get students involved with the community—to become part of it by actively working in it in positive ways. Each year, SHOCWAVES is assigned a budget by the Student Activities Office, and it spends that budget in activities that help the community in a variety of ways. Some of the money is spent, for example, in fund-raising events for community causes. We have

money to plan and launch a fund-raiser, which raises far more than we spend. In the process, other students and members of the community also become involved in the helping effort. We get to know lots of people, and we usually have a lot of fun—all while helping others. Recently, we have worked as part of the Charles River Cleanup, the Walk for Hunger, collecting toys for sick and needy children, and Light One Little Candle. While SHOCWAVES's mission is to help the community, it also benefits its members. Working in the community, I have learned so many valuable skills, and I always have something I care about to write about for my classes. I have learned about budgeting, advertising, organizing, and managing. I have also developed my creativity by coming up with new ways to do things. I have networked with many people, including people who are important in the business world. SHOCWAVES has greatly improved my life, and my chances for future success.

1. Double-underline the **topic sentence**.
2. Underline the **examples** of what SHOCWAVES does for the community.
3. Double-underline the sentence that makes a final observation about the topic.
4. Does this paragraph follow the Four Basics of Good Definition (p. 219)? Why or why not? ______________________________

______________________________

*Student Definition Essay*

# ISU's Restroom Change Shows Commitment to Diversity

The following article is an editorial published by the Illinois State University student newspaper, *The Daily Vidette.*

**Vocabulary development** Underline these words as you read: *garner, dubbing, baffled, rendition, dismay, transgender, bewilderment, empathize, profound,* and *ideology.*

**garner:** to gather, collect, or hoard
**dubbing:** to give a nickname
**baffled:** frustrated or confused
**rendition:** an interpretation
**dismay:** to alarm or dishearten
**transgender:** a person appearing to or attempting to be of the opposite sex
**bewilderment:** confused
**empathize:** sympathize
**profound:** going beyond what is obvious
**ideology:** the belief that guides a group

1 When Illinois State University changed their "Family Restroom" signs to "All Gender," they most likely did not expect the switch to garner national attention. As it turns out, however, Fox News has a keen eye for such changes.

**Predict** Why might such a change create headlines nationwide? What do you think the article will be about?

2 Dubbing the new signs as a product of the "P.C. Police," Fox News was both confused and even amused by the concept of such a restroom.

**Reflect** What do you think Fox News meant by the term, "P.C. Police?"

3 The news channel was so baffled by the idea that it even took to the streets asking random people outside of the studio if they understood the meaning of the "All Gender" sign.

4 A Fox News representative carried a large rendition of the sign, a figure that is half male and half female, and gave those they interviewed twenty

COURTESY OF MOSES MADDOX

**Moses Maddox**

Fellowship Specialist at The Mission Continues

# *Profile of Success*

## Definition in the Real World

**Background** When I was pursuing my degree, I struggled with writing. It wasn't that I didn't enjoy writing, but with my program being in social sciences I had concentrations in sociology, political science, and history, and I also pursued a minor in philosophy because, well, why not? The struggle with having four different focuses was that all four subjects had different tones in writing. When writing a paper in history, you had to present facts and analysis of those facts, and there was little room for personality or creativity beyond the presentation of those facts. In philosophy, one had to be careful of what one was writing so that one didn't commit any logical fallacies. In philosophy, it will take you four pages to write something that would be one page in history because you have to be careful that the reader understands your premise before you get to your point. It was a tough learning experience to get a "C" on a history paper because I "didn't write a history paper." That happened a lot. What I learned through experiences like that was to understand my audience. Sometimes people just want the facts and your presentation of those facts; however, in my current position, if I just presented facts, it would impact how seriously a person would take this program. I have also learned how to find my voice through my writing. I was encouraged by my professors to experiment, to look at writing as my true expression of self. People will forget what you've said, but what you write can last forever. I was taught to write so that if someone one hundred years from now read something I'd written, they would get a sense of who I am, as though I was able to communicate with a person in the future. Writing is that powerful.

**Degrees/Colleges** B.A. Social Sciences with Philosophy Minor from California State University, San Marcos; A.A. Arts & Humanities, Social & Behavioral Sciences, Sociology from Palomar College, San Marcos, CA

seconds to see if they could determine its meaning. Likely to their dismay, not only were none of the people confused by the signs, but even the child that was asked completely understood what the sign was supposed to mean.

5 The reaction by Fox News really should not be surprising. The program has a long history of being insensitive to the transgender community as well as any group they perceive as "different."

**Identify** The writers claim that FOX News reacted without empathy when it reported this story. What specific examples do the writers give to support that claim?

6 Their laughter and utter bewilderment of ISU's new direction only reflects their inability to understand diversity or to empathize with other cultures. Complete disconnect.

7 Such a reaction, though, is not tolerable, especially in this day and age. As we attempt to push our country into a more progressive and an all-encompassing state, such attitudes simply have no place. If anything, Illinois State should be lauded for its attempt to create a more understanding community.

8 In the Fox News segment, Heather Nauert claimed that ISU students didn't ask for these changes. This is true to some extent, but the reality is we

**Writing at work** What I do at The Mission Continues is manage returning post-9/11 veterans as they navigate through their six-month Fellowships. A Fellowship with The Mission Continues resembles more of an executive internship where Fellows pick the nonprofit organization they want to serve, but as they pick that organization, it has to fulfill some sort of qualitative and quantitative goals. That means that they have to fulfill a professional goal, a continued education goal, or a continued service goal, and they have to generate data. What Fellows accomplish throughout their Fellowships serves as resume fodder for many of them, who have a ton of leadership experience from the military but do not necessarily have the relevant work experience to be marketable in the civilian job market.

Veterans are really good at the "how" part of life. If you give military members a job to do, they will do it and do it well. However, if you ask them why they are doing the job, many don't know the answer. My position is to facilitate our curriculum, where we focus on personal and professional development through goal setting, finding allies, identifying role models, identifying driving force, and creating personal mission statements. The overarching goal is for our veterans to be in a place where they can go out into the world and understand what they are looking for in a career and understand how their military experience applies to the nonmilitary world. We feel that service is a vehicle through a successful transition, and my job is to hold the Fellows accountable for the goals that they set and push them to explore their inner selves so that they can move on and find joy in their lives.

As such, writing is a huge part of my job. Although the writing is mainly conversational in tone, creating the correct message is important. Things such as punctuation are important because there is a difference between "You're doing a great job." and "You're doing a great job!" It is part of the job to remain positive, as well as approachable, in all of my interactions. In covering rather deep philosophical conversations, if one approaches the topic in a completely academic tone, then people will check out. If one approaches it in a conversational tone, people are more receptive. One e-mail—in fact, one sentence—can mean the difference between a successful Fellowship or someone giving up completely. So focusing on writing is one of the key competencies of my work.

did not need to. To be a student at Illinois State means entering an inclusive community, one that tries to recognize the perspectives of all people.

9 The changes themselves may be small, as they only affect 10 restrooms, but their meaning is incredibly profound. They represent an attitude that is held by the university: Everyone is welcome and ISU is committed to the needs of every student. Such an ideology shouldn't be confusing to anyone.

10 Ideally, these changes will inspire other universities to do the same. This country suffers a lack of empathy for the transgender community, and introducing gender-neutral restrooms could be an important step in creating such understanding.

11 Even for those that do object to the philosophy behind a gender-neutral restroom, it is not as if the changes will dramatically affect anyone in a negative way. Again, the "All-Gender" restrooms make up only a small portion of those found on campus and will still function in the same way that the "Family Restrooms" did.

**Identify** What exactly, is an "All-Gender" restroom, and why did ISU believe it was an important change to make on the campus?

12 Ultimately, though, these new restrooms are the beginning of a bold new direction that ISU is taking. Regardless of the opinions of Fox News,

these changes make ISU a better university. Students here should be proud that their university is truly a school for everyone.

1. What is the term being defined in this essay? ______________________________

   ______________________________

   ______________________________

2. Underline the specific examples the article gives to support the inclusion of this type of facility on campus.

3. Circle any transitions used throughout the paper.

4. Does this article meet all the requirements of the Four Basics of Good Definition on p. 219? ______________________________

## *Workplace Definition*

The following is an e-mail Moses sent out to his clients at The Mission Continues.

Hello Fellows,

First: amazing work! Thanks each and every single one of you for getting me your written assignments on time. Your candid responses have let me know that you are taking this seriously and have given me a look into the impact you all want to make. All of your goals are achievable, and all of your fears can be overcome!

In Month 2, we talk more about overcoming fear and identifying allies. In a few minutes, I will share some tips and tricks to get the most out of Month 2. First, I want to recap the two main terms I went over with all of you in Month 1:

**Eudaimonia:** gotta love the work that goes into "well-being" or "being well." My goal for all of you is to find your joy and be well.

**10,000 Hours:** Malcolm Gladwell stated that it takes 10,000 hours of deliberate practice to become an expert at something. The actual research (attached) suggests that it takes 10 years. I think most of us have agreed that achieving 10,000 hours of deliberate practice helps you master the basics. We have also agreed that for many of you, due to your time in the military, you have devoted more than 10,000 hours of your life to service, and your Fellowships add to your tally.

**Month 2:**

Month 2 is less intimidating, but just as deep. Here are the terms that I enjoyed researching, and the stuff we will talk about over the month.

**Mental Rehearsal:** The best way to face your fears is to think about them, visualize the worst-case scenario, and then in your visualization, come up with a way to solve your worst-case scenario. In philosophy, we call this a thought experiment. Einstein famously used thought experimentation during his development of the theory of special relativity. Long story short, with enough practice, mental rehearsal can be a great tool.

**Finding Allies:** You will read (or have read) an excerpt from Reid Hoffman from his book *The Start-Up of You*. The summary I attached is basically a CliffsNotes version of the book. Also, *How to Win Friends and Influence People* was mentioned, and I included the entire book mainly because it is such an amazing and enlightening read.

Remember that no person is an island, so when you are thinking about your allies, the reading states that "allies can be friends, spouses, colleagues, family, supervisors, mentors," which I agree with. However, don't pick your spouse as an ally just because he or she is there. Choose allies that share your goals, offer something of their own, and are willing to be helped. Also remember that an ally is:

- Someone you consult regularly for advice.
- Someone with whom you share opportunities and collaborate.

Cheers,
Mo

1. Double-underline the **topic sentence**.
2. Maddox includes many terms and definitions in his e-mail. Define each of the following using context clues:

   Eudaimonia: ______________________________

   Thought experiment: ______________________________

   ______________________________

   Allies: ______________________________

   ______________________________

3. Maddox notes that, "allies can be friends, spouses, colleagues, family, supervisors, mentors;" however, he also warns his readers about choosing someone just because they are close in proximity. Why do you think he does this? What does he want his readers to do as they choose an ally? ______________________________

   ______________________________

   ______________________________

   ______________________________

   ______________________________

4. Maddox notes that he is always aware of his audience and how they will perceive his work. Who do you think he is writing to in this e-mail? What clues do you see that help you identify that reader? ______________________________

   ______________________________

   ______________________________

*Professional Definition Essay*

Elizabeth Renter

# Napping Can Dramatically Increase Learning, Memory, Awareness, More . . .

**siesta:** a midday or afternoon rest or nap (from Spanish)
**circadian rhythm:** the body's natural sleep-wake cycle
**affirmed:** to confirm
**reboot:** to restart
**defragged:** to improve performance
**grogginess:** dazed and weakened by lack of sleep

Elizabeth Renter is a freelance writer and editor whose works have appeared in *The Huffington Post, FOX Health, Lifehacker*, and *Natural Society*, among other publications. After graduating from Bellevue University with a B.S. in Criminal Justice Administration, she now writes a variety of articles that are typically focused on topics of social justice/injustice and natural living.

The following essay, which appeared in *Natural Society* in 2014, outlines and defines the benefits of napping.

**Vocabulary development** Underline these words as you read: *siesta, circadian rhythm, affirmed, reboot, defragged,* and *grogginess.*

## How Long to Nap

**10 to 20 Minutes**
This power nap is ideal for a boost in alertness and energy, experts say. This length usually limits you to the lighter stages of non-rapid eye movement (NREM) sleep, making it easier to hit the ground running after waking up.

**30 Minutes**
Some studies show sleeping this long may cause sleep inertia, a hangover-like groggy feeling that lasts for up to 30 minutes after waking up, before the nap's restorative benefits become apparent.

**60 Minutes**
This nap is best for improvement in remembering facts, faces and names. It includes slow-wave sleep, the deepest type. The downside: some grogginess upon waking up.

**90 Minutes**
This is a full cycle of sleep, meaning the lighter and deeper stages, including REM (rapid eye movement) sleep, typically likened to the dreaming stage. This leads to improved emotional and procedural memory (i.e. riding a bike, playing the piano) and creativity. A nap of this length typically avoids sleep inertia, making it easier to wake up.

**Summarize** In your own words, describe how napping is beneficial for a person.

**Predict** Before reading the article, what reasons can you think of that may support the idea that napping is good for a person?

1 In some places, towns essentially shut down in the afternoon while everyone goes home for a siesta. Unfortunately, in the U.S.—more bound to our corporate lifestyles than our health—a mid-day nap is seen as a luxury and, in some cases, a sign of pure laziness. But before you feel guilty about that weekend snooze or falling asleep during a movie, rest assured that napping is actually good for you and a completely natural phenomena in the circadian (sleep-wake cycle) rhythm.

2 As our day wears on, even when we get enough sleep at night, our focus and alertness degrade. While this can be a minor inconvenience in modern times, it may have meant life or death for our ancestors. Whether you are finishing up a project for work or hunting for your livelihood, a nap can rekindle your alertness and have your neurons back up and firing on high in as little as 15 to 20 minutes.

3 Big name (and high-dollar) companies recognize this. Google and Apple are just a few that allow employees to have naptime. Studies have affirmed that short naps can improve awareness and productivity. Plus, who wouldn't love a boss that lets you get a little shut-eye before the afternoon push?

4 A study from the University of Colorado Boulder found that children who missed their afternoon nap showed less joy and interest, more anxiety, and poorer problem-solving skills than other children. The same can be seen in adults that benefit from napping.

5 Researchers with Berkeley found an hour nap to dramatically increase learning ability and memory. Naps sort of provide a reboot, where the short-term memory is cleared out and our brain becomes refreshed with new defragged space.

6 Experts say a 10 to 20 minute "power nap" is best for refreshing your mind and increasing energy and alertness. The sleep isn't as deep as longer naps, which allows you to get right back at your day upon waking.

7 A 30-minute nap can lead to 30 minutes of grogginess, as you are often waking just as your body enters the deeper stages of sleep. You'll experience some of that same fogginess if you sleep for an hour, but 60-minute naps are good for memory boosting.

8 The longest naps—around 90 minutes—are good for those people who just don't get enough sleep at night. It's a complete sleep cycle and can improve emotional memory and creativity.

9 Naps are good for you—physically and mentally. But don't sacrifice night time zzz's for an afternoon snooze; take your nap in addition to a good night's sleep.

**Reflect** How often do you actually feel rested in the morning? What causes you to feel sleepy or why are you often awake too long to be well rested?

**Reflect** Many people believe that these kinds of "perks" offered by companies such as Google and Apple are a step forward and lead to healthy, happy workers, while others believe it is a waste of time and hurts productivity. What is your opinion: would such a policy be taken advantage of, or would it improve work quality?

**Identify** Looking at the previous two studies and the infographic, what is the ideal naptime? Why?

1. Double-underline the **thesis statement**.
2. Circle the **transitions** used to introduce examples.
3. Do the writers provide enough examples to demonstrate why napping is a benefit? If not, where could more examples be added? ____________________

   ______________________________________________
4. Look back at the final paragraph. Why do you suppose the authors chose to conclude in that way? ____________________

   ______________________________________________

   ______________________________________________

**Tip** For reading advice, see Chapter 1.

Respond to one of the following assignments in a paragraph or essay.

1. Are you the type of person who needs a nap to make it through your day, or are you one who either can't or won't nap? What are your reasons for your answer? (In other words, if you "need" a nap, why and how does it help you? If you choose not to nap, why not? What happens if you do try to nap?)
2. Napping isn't the only way that humans attempt to make up for "lost time." Can you think of any other parts of our day or our life where we try to catch up for something we missed? For example, cramming for a test rather than creating a schedule for studying in advance.
3. Define "full night's sleep" and provide reasons and examples to support making time to sleep at night, rather than napping during the day.

## Write Your Own Definition

In this section, you will write your own definition based on one of the following assignments. For help, refer to the How to Write Definition checklist on page 236.

**ASSIGNMENT OPTIONS** **Writing about college, work, and everyday life**

Write a definition paragraph or essay on one of the following topics or on one of your own choice.

**College**

- How would you define effective study habits and noneffective study habits? Give examples to explain your definition.
- Identify a difficult or technical term from a class you are taking. Then, define the term, and give examples of different ways in which it might be used.
- Define *learning,* not only in terms of school but in terms of all the ways in which it can occur. You might start by writing down the different types of learning that go on both in school and in other settings. Then, (1) write a main idea that defines learning in a broader way, and (2) support your definition with the examples you came up with.

**Work**

- Define a satisfying job, giving explanations and examples.
- If you have ever held a job that used unusual or interesting terminology, write about some of the terms used, what they meant, and their function on the job.
- In many businesses, it's common for workers to use jargon, which can be defined either as insider language or as vague, empty, or overused expressions. Some examples are "going the extra mile," "being on the same page," and "thinking outside the box." Give examples of work jargon that you've heard of, provide definitions, and explain why the jargon is vague or ineffective. Then, for each expression, suggest more specific words.

**Everyday life**

- What does it mean to be a good friend? Provide a definition, giving explanations and examples.
- What does it mean to be a good parent? Provide a definition, giving explanations and examples.
- Ask three (or more) people to tell you what they think *community service* means. Take notes on their responses, and then write a paragraph or an essay combining their definitions with your own.

## ASSIGNMENT OPTIONS Reading and writing critically

Complete one of the following assignments, which ask you to apply the critical thinking, reading, and writing skills discussed in Chapter 1.

### WRITING CRITICALLY ABOUT READINGS

Both Kathy Stevens's "Ten Tips to Ease into Plant-Based Eating" (p. 186) and Elizabeth Renter's "Napping Can Dramatically Increase Memory, Learning, Awareness, and More" (p. 232) define a situation (eating and napping) and explain that definition through evidence and examples. Read or review both of these essays, and then follow these steps:

1. **Summarize** Briefly summarize the works, listing examples they include.
2. **Analyze** What questions do the essays raise for you?
3. **Synthesize** Using examples from both essays and from your own experience, describe ways in which you have redefined a common term or concept for your own life. For example, just as one can nap for different lengths with different outcomes, consider how eating many small meals during a day may affect a person.
4. **Evaluate** Which essay do you think is more effective? Why? In writing your evaluation, look back on your responses to step 2.

**Tip** For a reminder of how to summarize, analyze, synthesize, and evaluate, see the Reading and Writing Critically box on page 21.

### WRITING ABOUT IMAGES

Study the photograph to the right, and complete the following steps.

1. **Read the image** A phobia is a fear, and one that many people share is coulrophobia: a fear of clowns. You could explain to a friend your fear of clowns, or you could show your friend the picture to the right. What makes this photograph such a striking visual definition? (For more on reading images, see Chapter 1.)
2. **Write a definition** Write a paragraph or essay that explains what a visual definition is. To support your definition, use examples of any types of images you are familiar with—signs, advertisements, photographs, and so on.

SAMULI SULTANEN/GETTY IMAGES

## WRITING TO SOLVE A PROBLEM

Read or review the discussion of problem solving in Chapter 1 (pp. 28–30). Then, consider the following problem.

**A recent survey asked business managers what skills or traits they value most in employees. The top five responses were (1) motivation, (2) interpersonal skills, (3) initiative, (4) communication skills, and (5) maturity.**

**You have a job interview next week, and you want to be able to present yourself well. Before you can do that, though, you need to have a better understanding of the five skills and traits noted above and what examples you might be able to give to demonstrate that you have them.**

**Assignment** Working in a group or on your own, come up with definitions of three of the five terms, and think of some examples of how the skills or traits

### CHECKLIST

#### How to Write Definition

| Steps | Details |
|---|---|
| ☐ Narrow and explore your topic. See Chapter 3. | • Make the topic more specific.<br>• Prewrite to get ideas about the narrowed topic. |
| ☐ Write a topic sentence (paragraph) or thesis statement (essay). See Chapter 3. | • State the term that you are focusing on, and provide a definition for it. |
| ☐ Support your point. See Chapter 4. | • Come up with examples and details to explain your definition. |
| ☐ Write a draft. See Chapter 5. | • Make a plan that puts the examples in a logical order.<br>• Include a topic sentence (paragraph) or thesis statement (essay) and all the supporting examples and details. |
| ☐ Revise your draft. See Chapter 5. | • Make sure it has *all* the Four Basics of Good Definition.<br>• Make sure you include transitions to move readers smoothly from one example to the next. |
| ☐ Edit your revised draft. See Parts 3 through 6. | • Correct errors in grammar, spelling, word use, and punctuation. |

could be used at work. Then, do one of the following assignments. You might begin with the following sentence:

**I am a person who is (or has)** ______________________________________________
______________________________________________________________________.

***For a paragraph:*** Choose one of the terms, and give examples of how you have demonstrated the trait.

***For an essay:*** Write about how you have demonstrated the three traits.

## Chapter Review

1. Definition is writing that ______________________________________________

2 What are the Four Basics of Good Definition?

______________________________________________________________________

______________________________________________________________________

______________________________________________________________________

______________________________________________________________________

3. Write sentences using the following vocabulary words: *garner, dubbing, rendition, dismay, empathize, profound, ideology.* ______________________________

______________________________________________________________________

## REFLECTING ON THE JOURNEY

### Skills Learned

Now that you've completed the chapter, share what you've learned about each skill by completing the following chart.

| Skill | What I learned about this skill |
|---|---|
| Define a word or concept | |
| Provide examples to explain the definition of a word or concept | |
| Provide enough details to support the definition of a word or concept | |
| Read, analyze, and evaluate a definition | |

# 12

# Comparison and Contrast

## Writing That Shows Similarities and Differences

## READING ROADMAP

### Learning Objectives

**Chapter Goal:** Learn how to write compare-and-contrast documents.

**Tools to Achieve the Goal:**

- Four Basics of Good Comparison and Contrast (p. 239)
- Sample Comparison and Contrast Paragraph and Rubric (pp. 247–48)
- Student Comparison/Contrast Paragraph: Said Ibrahim, *Eyeglasses vs. Laser Surgery: Benefits and Drawbacks* (p. 249)
- Student Comparison/Contrast Essay: Armand Powell-Archie, *Pirate vs. Poet* (pp. 250–251)
- Profile of Success and Workplace Comparison and Contrast: Darin Adams (p. 252)
- Professional Comparison/Contrast Essay: John Tierney, *Yes, Money Can Buy Happiness* (pp. 257–58)
- Checklist: How to Write Good Comparison and Contrast (p. 262)

### Key Terms

Skim Chapter 12 before reading. Find these words or terms in **bold** type. Put a check mark next to each once you locate it.

____ comparison
____ contrast
____ main idea
____ support
____ point by point
____ whole to whole
____ order of importance
____ transitions

### Guided Reading for Chapter 12

Fill out the following chart before you begin reading. For each skill, write what you know about that skill and what you would like to know upon completing the chapter. At the end of the chapter, you will be asked to share what you learned about each skill.

| Skill | When I have used this skill | What I want to know about this skill |
|---|---|---|
| Compare two or more objects to identify similarities | | |
| Contrast two or more objects to identify differences | | |
| Identify topics that have enough in common to be compared or contrasted | | |
| Present logical points to support the comparison or contrast | | |
| Arrange points in a logical order | | |
| Read and analyze compare and contrast documents | | |

# Understand What Comparison and Contrast Are

**Comparison** is writing that shows the similarities among subjects—people, ideas, situations, or items; **contrast** shows the differences. In conversation, people often use the word *compare* to mean either compare or contrast, but as you work through this chapter, the terms will be separated.

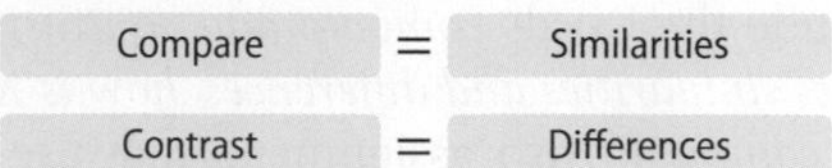
Compare = Similarities
Contrast = Differences

**LaunchPadSolo**

Visit **LaunchPad Solo for Readers and Writers > Reading > Patterns of Organization** for more tutorials, videos, and practice with patterns of organization.

## **Four Basics** of Good Comparison and Contrast

1. It uses subjects that have enough in common to be compared or contrasted in a useful way.
2. It serves a purpose—to help readers make a decision, to help them understand the subjects, or to show your understanding of the subjects.
3. It presents several important, parallel points of comparison and contrast.
4. It arranges points in a logical order.

In the following paragraph, written for a biology course, the numbers and colors correspond to the Four Basics of Good Comparison and Contrast.

**Tip** This paragraph uses point-by-point organization. For more information, see page 244.

1 Although frogs and toads are closely related, 2 they differ in appearance, habitat, and behavior. 3 The first major difference is in the creatures' physical characteristics. Whereas most frogs have smooth, slimy skin that helps them move through water, toads tend to have rough, bumpy skin suited to drier surroundings. Also, whereas frogs have long, muscular hind legs that help them leap away from predators or toward food, most toads have shorter legs and, therefore, less ability to move quickly. Another physical characteristic of frogs and toads is their bulging eyes, which help them see in different directions. This ability is important because neither creature can turn its head to look for food or spot a predator. However, frogs' eyes may protrude more than toads'. The second major difference between frogs and toads is their choice of habitat. Frogs tend to live in or near ponds, lakes, or other sources of water. In contrast, toads live mostly in drier areas, such as gardens, forests, and fields. But, like frogs, they lay their eggs in water. The third major difference between frogs and toads concerns their behavior. Whereas frogs may be active during the day or at night, most toads keep a low profile until nighttime. Some biologists believe that it is nature's way of making up for toads' inability to escape from danger as quickly as frogs can. At night, toads are less likely to be spotted by predators. Finally, although both frogs and toads tend to live by themselves, toads, unlike frogs, may form groups while they are hibernating. Both creatures can teach us a lot about how animals adapt to their environments, and studying them is a lot of fun.

4 Points arranged in a logical order

| | |
|---|---|
| **College** | In a pharmacy course, you compare and contrast the side effects of two drugs prescribed for the same illness. |
| **Work** | You are asked to contrast this year's sales with last year's. |
| **Everyday life** | At the supermarket, you contrast brands of the same food to decide which to buy. |

In college, writing assignments may include the words *compare and contrast,* but they might also use phrases such as *discuss similarities and differences, how is X like (or unlike) Y?,* or *what do X and Y have in common?* Also, assignments may use only the word *compare.*

## *Main Idea in Comparison and Contrast*

The **main idea** should state the subjects you want to compare or contrast and help you achieve your purpose. (See the second of the Four Basics of Good Comparison and Contrast, p. 239.)

To help you discover your main idea, complete the following sentence:

| | |
|---|---|
| **Main idea in comparison and contrast** | **I want my readers to ______________ after reading my comparison or contrast.** |

Then, write a topic sentence (paragraph) or thesis statement (essay) that identifies the subjects and states the main idea you want to make about them. Here is an example of a topic sentence for a paragraph:

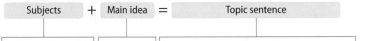

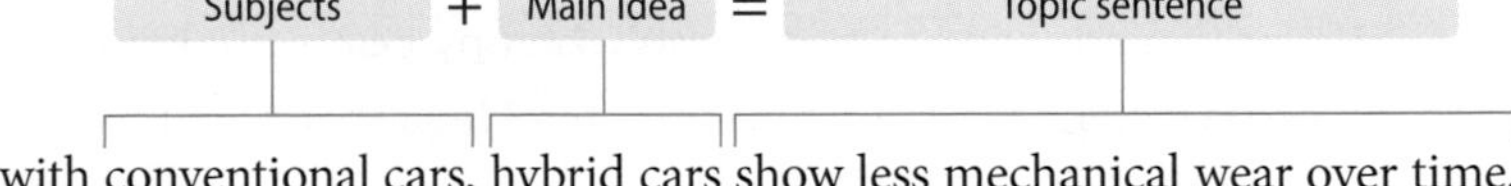
Subjects
+
Main idea
=
Topic sentence

Compared with conventional cars, hybrid cars show less mechanical wear over time.

[Purpose: to help readers understand mechanical differences between conventional cars and hybrids.]

Remember that the topic for an essay can be a little broader than one for a paragraph.

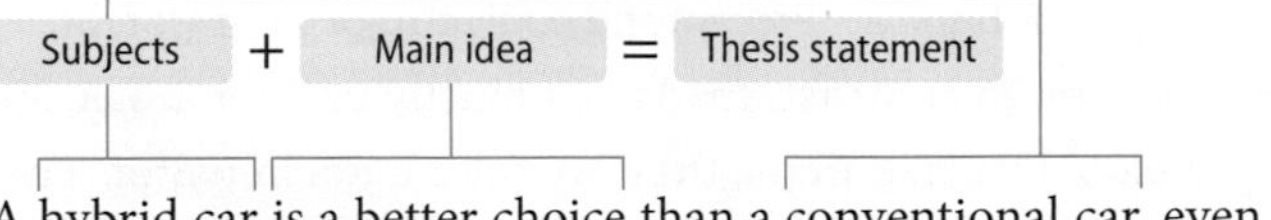
Subjects
+
Main idea
=
Thesis statement

A hybrid car is a better choice than a conventional car, even one with low gas mileage.

[Purpose: to help readers decide which type of car to buy.]

**Tip** Sometimes, the same main idea can be used for a paragraph and an essay, but the essay must develop this point in more detail. (See pp. 68–69.)

Whereas the topic sentence focuses on the mechanical advantages of hybrid cars, the thesis statement sets up a broader discussion of these cars' benefits.

## *Support in Comparison and Contrast*

The paragraph and essay models on pages 242–43 use the topic sentence (paragraph) and thesis statement (essay) from the Main Idea section in this chapter. Both models include the **support** used in all comparison and contrast writing: points of comparison/contrast backed up by details. In the essay model, however, the points of comparison/contrast are topic sentences for individual paragraphs.

The support in comparison/contrast should show how your subjects are the same or different. To find support, many people make a list with two columns, one for each subject, with parallel points of comparison or contrast.

**TOPIC SENTENCE/THESIS STATEMENT:** The two credit cards I am considering offer different financial terms.

| **Big card** | **Mega card** |
|---|---|
| no annual fee | $35 annual fee |
| $1 fee per cash advance | $1.50 fee per cash advance |
| 30 days before interest charges begin | 25 days before interest charges begin |
| 15.5% finance charge | 17.9% finance charge |

Choose points that will be convincing and understandable to your readers. Explain your points with facts, details, or examples.

### PRACTICE 1 Finding points of contrast

Each of the following items lists some points of contrast. Fill in the blanks with more points.

**Example:**

**Contrast hair lengths**

| **Long hair** | **Short hair** |
|---|---|
| **takes a long time to dry** | **dries quickly** |
| **can be worn a lot of ways** | *only one way to wear it* |
| *does not need to be cut often* | **needs to be cut every five weeks** |
| **gets tangled, needs brushing** | *low maintenance* |

1. Contrast sports

| Baseball | Soccer |
|---|---|
| runs = points | goals = points |
| __________ | ball is kicked |
| __________ | __________ |

*(Continued on page 244.)*

## Paragraphs vs. Essays in Comparison and Contrast

For more on the important features of comparison and contrast, see the Four Basics of Good Comparison and Contrast on page 239.

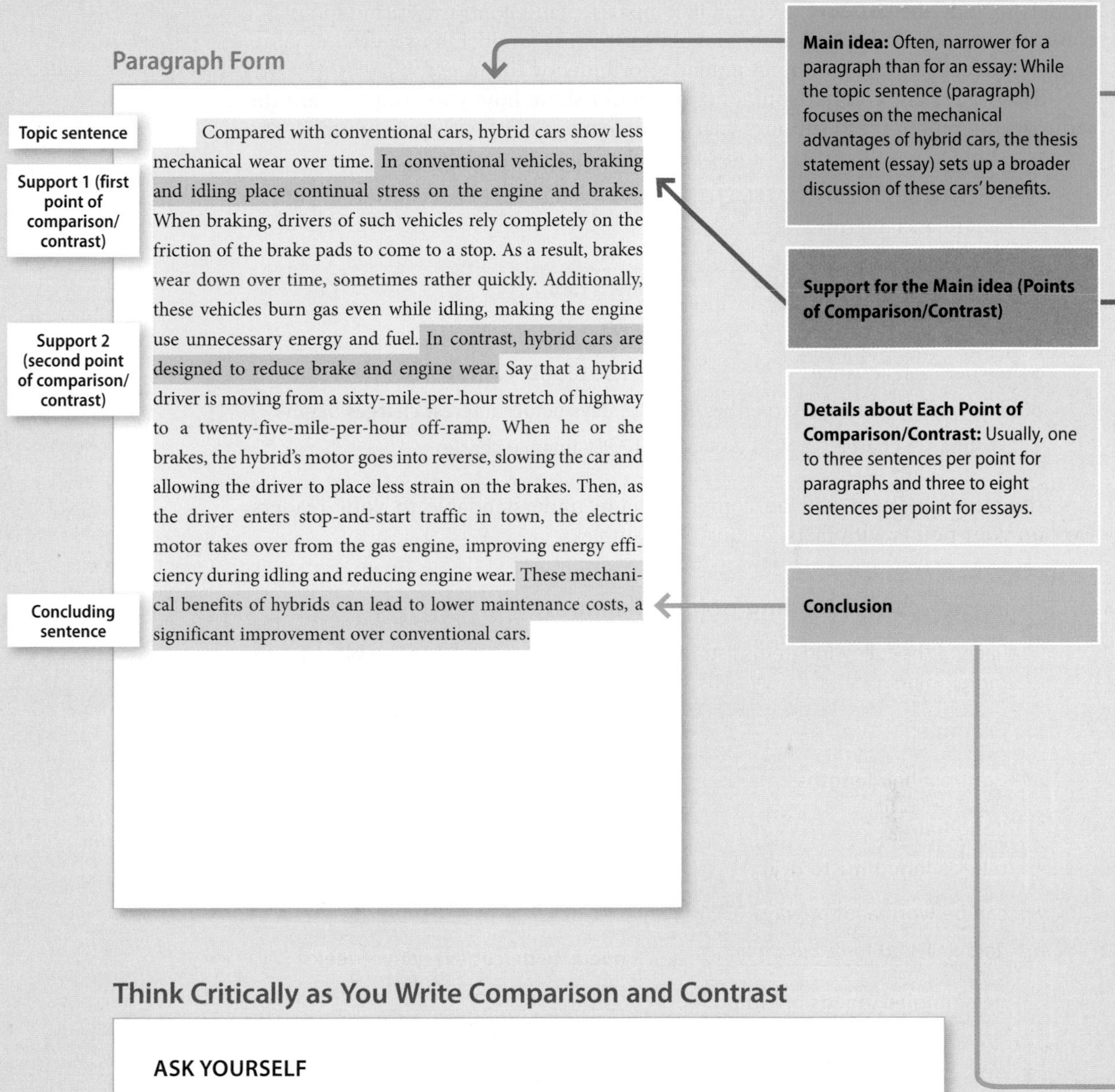

Paragraph Form
Topic sentence
Support 1 (first point of comparison/contrast)
Support 2 (second point of comparison/contrast)
Concluding sentence
Compared with conventional cars, hybrid cars show less mechanical wear over time. In conventional vehicles, braking and idling place continual stress on the engine and brakes. When braking, drivers of such vehicles rely completely on the friction of the brake pads to come to a stop. As a result, brakes wear down over time, sometimes rather quickly. Additionally, these vehicles burn gas even while idling, making the engine use unnecessary energy and fuel. In contrast, hybrid cars are designed to reduce brake and engine wear. Say that a hybrid driver is moving from a sixty-mile-per-hour stretch of highway to a twenty-five-mile-per-hour off-ramp. When he or she brakes, the hybrid's motor goes into reverse, slowing the car and allowing the driver to place less strain on the brakes. Then, as the driver enters stop-and-start traffic in town, the electric motor takes over from the gas engine, improving energy efficiency during idling and reducing engine wear. These mechanical benefits of hybrids can lead to lower maintenance costs, a significant improvement over conventional cars.
Main idea: Often, narrower for a paragraph than for an essay: While the topic sentence (paragraph) focuses on the mechanical advantages of hybrid cars, the thesis statement (essay) sets up a broader discussion of these cars' benefits.
Support for the Main idea (Points of Comparison/Contrast)
Details about Each Point of Comparison/Contrast: Usually, one to three sentences per point for paragraphs and three to eight sentences per point for essays.
Conclusion


### Think Critically as You Write Comparison and Contrast

**ASK YOURSELF**

- Have I provided all the information needed to fulfill my purpose: to help readers make a decision or to understand the subjects being compared or contrasted? (This information includes all the important similarities or differences between the subjects, as well as details about these similarities or differences.)
- If my information about similarities or differences feels "thin," might consulting outside sources help me find new details?

Introductory paragraph

1

For the past two years, while trying to keep my dying 1999 Chevy on the road, these words have popped into my head every time I have thought about purchasing a hybrid car. But now that I **Thesis statement** some research, I am finally convinced: A hybrid car is a better choice than a conventional car, even one with low gas mileage.

The first advantage of hybrid cars over conventional cars is that buyers can get tax breaks and other hybrid-specific benefits. Although federal **Topic sentence 1 (first point of comparison/contrast)** for hybrid purchasers expired in 2010, sev including Colorado, Louisiana, Maryland, Mexico, continue to offer such credits. Also, in Arizona, Florida, and several other states, hybrid drivers are allowed to use the less congested high-occupancy vehicle (HOV) lanes even if the driver is the only person on board. Additional benefits for hybrid drivers include longer warranties than those offered for conventional cars and, in some states and cities, rebates, reduced licensing fees, and free parking. None of these benefits are offered to drivers of conventional cars.

2

The second advantage of hybrid cars over conventional cars is that they save money over the long term. In addition to using less fuel, hybrid **Topic sentence 2 (second point of comparison/contrast)** mechanical wear over time, reducing m costs. When braking, drivers of convention completely on the friction of the brake pads to come to a stop. As a result, brakes wear down over time, sometimes rather quickly. Additionally, these vehicles burn gas even while idling, making the engine use unnecessary energy and fuel. In contrast, when hybrid drivers hit the brakes, the car's motor goes into reverse, slowing the car and allowing the driver to place less strain on the brakes. Then, as the driver enters stop-and-start traffic in town, the electric motor **Topic sentence 3 (third point of comparison/contrast)** from the gas engine, improving energy during idling and reducing engine wear.

The most important benefit of hybrid cars over conventional cars is that they have a lower impact on the environment. Experts estimate that each gallon of gas burned by conventional motor vehicles produces 28 pounds of carbon dioxide ($CO_2$), a greenhouse gas

3

that is a major contributor to global warming. Because hybrid cars use about half as much gas as conventional vehicles, they reduce pollution and greenhouse gases by at least 50 percent. Some experts estimate that they reduce such emissions by as much as 80 percent. The National Resources Defense Council says that if hybrid vehicles are widely adopted, annual reductions in emissions could reach 450 million metric tons by the year 2050. This reduction would be equa **Concluding paragraph** 82.5 million cars off the road.

Although hybrid cars are more expensive than conventional cars, they are well worth it. From an economic standpoint, they save on fuel and maintenance costs. But, to me, the best reasons for buying a hybrid are ethical: By switching to such a vehicle, I will help reduce my toll on the environment. So goodbye, 1999 Chevy, and hello, Toyota Prius!

2. Contrast pets

| **Dogs** | **Cats** |
|---|---|
| bark | ________ |
| ________ | independent |
| ________ | ________ |

**PRACTICE 2** **Finding points of comparison**

Each of the following items lists some points of comparison. Fill in the blanks with more.

1. Compare sports

| **Baseball** | **Soccer** |
|---|---|
| team sport | team sport |
| ________ | ________ |
| ________ | ________ |

2. Compare pets

| **Dogs** | **Cats** |
|---|---|
| shed fur | ________ |
| common household pet | ________ |
| ________ | ________ |

## *Organization in Comparison and Contrast*

Comparison/contrast can be organized in one of two ways: A **point-by-point** organization presents one point of comparison or contrast between the subjects and then moves to the next point. (See the essay model on page 243.) A **whole-to-whole** organization presents all the points of comparison or contrast for one subject and then all the points for the next subject. (See the paragraph model on page 242.) Consider which organization will best explain the similarities or differences to your readers. Whichever organization you choose, stay with it throughout your writing.

**PRACTICE 3** **Organizing a comparison/contrast**

The first outline that follows is for a comparison paper using a whole-to-whole organization. Reorganize the ideas and create a new outline (outline 2) using a point-by-point organization. The first blank has been filled in for you. The third outline is for a contrast paper using a point-by-point organization. Reorganize

the ideas, and create a new outline (outline 4) using a whole-to-whole organization. The first blank in outline 4 has been filled in for you.

1. Comparison paper using whole-to-whole organization

   Main idea: My daughter is a lot like I was at her age.

   a. Me

      Not interested in school

      Good at sports

      Hard on myself

   b. My daughter

      Does well in school but doesn't study much or do more than the minimum

      Plays in a different sport each season

      When she thinks she has made a mistake, she gets upset with herself

2. Comparison paper using point-by-point organization

   Main idea: My daughter is a lot like I was at her age.

   a. Interest in school

      Me: ______________________________

      My daughter: ______________________________

   b. ______________________________

      Me: ______________________________

      My daughter: ______________________________

   c. ______________________________

      Me: ______________________________

      My daughter: ______________________________

3. Contrast paper using point-by-point organization

   Main idea: My new computer is a great improvement over my old one.

   a. Weight and portability

      New computer: ______________________________

      Old computer: ______________________________

   b. ______________________________

      New computer: ______________________________

      Old computer: ______________________________

c. ______________________

New computer: ______________________

Old computer: ______________________

4. Contrast paper using whole-to-whole organization

   Main idea: My new phone is a great improvement over my old one.

   a. New phone

      *More apps*

      ______________________

      ______________________

   b. Old phone

      ______________________

      ______________________

      ______________________

**Tip** For more on order of importance, see page 78.

Comparison/contrast is often organized by **order of importance**, meaning that the most important point is saved for last. This strategy is used in the essay model on page 243.

**Transitions** in comparison/contrast move readers from one subject to another and from one point of comparison or contrast to the next.

## Common Transitions in Comparison and Contrast

| Comparison | Contrast |
|---|---|
| both | in contrast |
| like/unlike | most important difference |
| most important similarity | now/then |
| one similarity/another similarity | one difference/another difference |
| similarly | unlike |
| | while |

### PRACTICE 4 Using transitions in comparison and contrast

Read the paragraph that follows, and fill in the blanks with transitions. You are not limited to the ones listed in the preceding box.

Modern coffee shops share many similarities with the coffeehouses that opened hundreds of years ago in the Middle East and Europe.

_______________ is that the coffeehouses of history, like modern cafés, were popular places to socialize. In sixteenth-century Constantinople (now Istanbul, Turkey) and in seventeenth- and eighteenth-century London, customers shared stories, information, and opinions about current events, politics, and personal matters. The knowledge shared at London coffeehouses led customers to call these places "Penny Universities," a penny being the price of admission. ___________________ is that the old coffeehouses, like today's coffee shops, were often places of business. However, although most of today's coffee-shop customers work quietly on their laptops, customers of the old shops openly, and sometimes loudly, discussed business and sealed deals. In fact, for more than seventy years, traders for the London Stock Exchange operated out of coffeehouses. ____________________ similarity between the old coffeehouses and modern coffee shops is that they both increased the demand for coffee and places to drink it. In 1652, a former servant from western Turkey opened the first coffeehouse in London. As a result of its popularity, many more coffeehouses soon sprouted up all over the city, and within a hundred years there were more than 500 coffeehouses in London. ___________, in recent years the popularity of Starbucks, and its shops, spread rapidly throughout the United States.

## Evaluate Comparison and Contrast

Read the following sample comparison and contrast paragraph. Using the Four Basics of Good Comparison and Contrast and the sample grading rubric, decide what grade this paragraph would earn. Explain your answer.

**Assignment** Describe one significant difference between your classes in high school and ones you are enrolled in at college.

**High school and college are completely different in many ways. When I was in high school, I didn't have a lot of choices about what courses I wanted to take and I didn't really need to think about what classes I was taking because it didn't really apply to my future or job or anything. When I got to college I found out that everything was different. Although a lot of classes were required. Some of them were choices that I got to make on my own. The biggest change is the amount of homework, time I have to spend on it all.**

*Student Comparison/Contrast Essay*

Armand Powell-Archie

# Pirate vs. Poet

**valiant:** possessing or showing determination or courage
**convey:** transport or carry
**hostile:** unfriendly
**articulate:** express an idea clearly and coherently
**hail:** one's home or origin
**harassing:** to disturb persistently; to torment
**vulgar:** indecent or obscene
**brash:** hasty

Armand Powell-Archie is a twenty-year-old communications student. Aside from school, Armand is an aspiring writer who is passionate about music and composes both poetry and song lyrics. He also works with children at an after-school program and for UPS as a preloader. He wrote this essay as an assignment for his English class and said it was "very easy" because most of his conversations are about music and hip-hop. He says, "For me to actually compose the essay, I gathered all my thoughts and feelings, and from there everything flowed naturally. It's all genuine and authentic."

**Vocabulary development** Underline these words as you read: *valiant, convey, hostile, articulate, hail, harassing, vulgar,* and *brash.*

**Predict** What may the author use to compare or contrast these two musicians?

1 In the genre of hip-hop, there have been many artists, or emcees (as they're known in the genre), to step behind a microphone and make valiant efforts to convey messages to the people. Personally, however, there are two individuals who convey a message deeper than the average person and stand on a higher podium to do so because their messages are more efficient. Nas and The Notorious B.I.G. (also known as Biggie, Biggie Smalls, Frank White, etc.) are vocal prophets, and anybody willing to lend their ears for three minutes can easily understand why.

2 Both Biggie and Nas bring a unique, unmatched, and unparalleled style to the hip-hop community and to the world of music. Through tough times such as being raised by struggling single mothers, being financially limited, and growing up in hostile environments, both artists are thoroughly able to articulate their experiences to the point where you practically envision their hardships and feel them as your own. Both of these greats hail from the Empire State (New York) and grew up in the seventies and eighties. Not only did they grown up during the crack epidemic, which had a significant role in the lives of both Nas and B.I.G., facing financial tribulations, both men sold drugs including crack to earn some sort of profit.

**Reflect** It is clear that the writer believes that the background of each person plays a significant role in his music. Do you agree with that assessment? Why or why not?

3 With the drug game comes the responsibility of being armed to protect themselves and their product, but also being paranoid as a result of the life they live. Their paranoia comes from the worry of somebody trying to handle them in the street and from law enforcement trying to lock them up. Law enforcement in these times were best known for harassing young black men. All of this came with the territory of drug dealing and hustling, which both men were well aware of and were able to share in the stores they told. But with the many similarities these emcees share, there are just as many differences to differentiate them.

4 If you were to sit down and listen to a story from both Biggie and Nas, you'd probably be more amazed and astonished listening to that story from Biggie's perspective. With vivid yet vulgar language, the Notorious B.I.G. can vocally illustrate a brash, blunt, and straight to the point picture. The Bed-Stuy, Brooklyn, native possesses a delivery so very forceful and

hard-hitting like a brick through a windshield. Although at times his stories consisted of his lavish come up, his many escapades, and how much of a Casanova he was, Biggie viewed the world through a more pessimistic lens.

5 His debut album titled *Ready to Die* is ironically how Frank White lived his life, enjoying and working every day like it was his last. With songs like *Suicidal Thoughts* and *Things Done Changed* he stresses to us both intentionally and unintentionally his reasoning for being so volatile. Biggie Smalls tells the story exactly how he sees it. His raw wit and his rugged style makes it easier for me to label him the Pirate.

6 Now if you're listening to that same story narrated by Nas, you'd be more intrigued and fascinated than anything else. "God's Son," as he's well known, uses colorful and descriptive vocabulary that creates an image of both triumph and hope. Through his frustrations of being poor, black, and a target for police brutality, the Queens, New York, representative displays vocal and lyrical finesse to spread his message. His deep thought process and his compassion for the people make him relatable to a politician; however, his policies won't suit everybody: Only people who have shared the same struggle as he such as the thugs, the gangsters, the frustrated, and those who wish to find a way.

**Identify** Looking at the previous and following paragraphs, what similarities do the two men share? What differences are there?

7 Nas is a combination of a political activist and a cold-blooded criminal, which ultimately makes it easy for him to be labeled a Political Gangster. However, his intellect is prominent, and he uses phrases to make us sit back and reflect "people fear what they don't understand/hate what they can't conquer guess it's just the theory of man." His style is sharp, clever, and crisp, and even with his thug persona he remains polished and punctual. While Biggie is known for telling it how it is in black and white, Nas shares what he envisions and what he hopes to see. Songs like "The World Is Yours,' "If I Ruled the World," and "Rule" solidify and confirm that. Nas's intellect, his wordplay, and his overall way of expression make it easy for me to label him the Poet.

8 From whomever you hear the story, you are guaranteed to have a thorough understanding of what's being told. Both Nas and the Notorious give clear insight to the daily and everyday struggles of somebody living in the inner city. They also portray the message of a man in America—just trying to make his own way for both he and his family. A shared message one being told from the angle of a Pirate. "If I said it I meant it, bite my tongue for no one call me evil or unbelievable." And the other being told from the angle of a Poet "we should take time to think, bombs and war leave mankind extinct." Although Biggie is our Pirate and Nas is our Poet, it can easily be inferred that both individuals are profound prophets in the world of music and inspiration to anybody who can relate.

**Summarize** Briefly restate the main ideas of this essay.

1. Underline the topic sentence.

2. What are the main criteria being compared and contrasted in this article?

COURTESY OF DARIN ADAMS

**Darin Adams**
Claims Representative

# *Profile of Success*

## Comparison and Contrast in the Real World

**Background** I almost didn't graduate high school on time, and the only reason I was able to walk was due to an English teacher that was gracious enough to allow me to redo an assignment. When I graduated high school, I left with a GPA of 1.83, which at the time was the lowest GPA allowable by the state. I initially went to Hawkeye Community College when I graduated and had to take developmental classes because of my low GPA. I failed horribly and decided to join the military. After my time in the military, I went back to college and had the best English teacher one could ever have. She laid the foundation for my success throughout the remainder of my life.

I studied Liberal Arts at Hawkeye Community College and transferred to the University of Northern Iowa to finish out my education. I graduated in 2013 with my degree in criminology with a cumulative GPA of 3.07. I finished my education in 3.5 years while working 35+ hours a week at PepsiCo, serving in the U.S. Army Reserve, and somehow finding time to be a husband.

**Degrees/Colleges** A.A., Hawkeye Community College; B.A., University of Northern Iowa

**Writing at work** I work for the Social Security Administration as a claims representative. My job in some ways is hard to describe because the scope of work is pretty vast. I'm a mix between a lawyer, disability examiner, benefits expert, fraud/waste/misuse criminal investigator, and in some situations also a judge.

On a day-to-day basis, I help the public with the process of applying for benefits and ensuring they are entitled to benefits according to state/local/federal laws. The scope of benefits that I process are Retirement, Survivors, Hospital Insurance, Disability, and Auxiliary (children/spouses) Benefits. In addition to my daily tasks, there are other workloads where I use what I learned in college. When I'm looking at a case of fraud/waste/misuse of benefits, I have to look back to my training as a criminologist and ensure I'm following the law correctly. If I do find fraud/waste/misuse, I have to make the determination if the case should be moved forward for official criminal action or if the case should be subject to administrative sanctions. If the case is subject to administrative sanctions, I have to look at which parties are liable and sanction them accordingly. On a typical day, I will communicate with the public via letters, e-mails, and other forms of written correspondence.

3. Does the author use enough examples to make his point clear? ____________

____________________________________________

4. Does this essay follow the Four Basics of Good Comparison and Contrast (p. 239)? ____________________________________________

### *Workplace Comparison and Contrast*

The following is Darin's professional résumé, which he used to secure his job at the Social Security Administration.

1111 Newcastle Road
Newburg, IA
(111) 500-0123
adams@uni.edu
Darin Adams

**Education**

B.A. Criminology: December 2013
University of Northern Iowa, Cedar Falls, IA
A.A. Liberal Arts: May 2012
Hawkeye Community College, Waterloo, IA

**Experience**

**Assistant Manager, Wal-Mart, Marshalltown, IA**
**May 2013–Present**

- Manage 150 employees in a constantly changing diverse operational environment.
- Utilize and train conflict resolution solutions to assist in managing customer complaints, concerns, and suggestions.
- Facilitated the hiring, termination, coaching, development, and promotion of a wide range of associates in multiple management positions.
- Train more than 30 associates with tasks relevant to their career choices.

**Merchandiser, Pepsi Beverages Company, Waterloo, IA**
**March 2010–April 2013**

- Trained a group of high-performing merchandisers to perform as a team, operate independently, and incorporate the values of Pepsi Beverages Company.
- Arranged and coordinated displays to showcase Pepsi products to increase product visibility and drive bottom-line sales.
- Resolved customer and client complaints on-site to reduce workload on salesmen and the PepsiCo warehouse.

**Computer Administrator U.S. Army Reserve, Fort McCoy, WI**
**December 2009–June 2013**

- Managed a computer network of 100 terminals used by multiple U.S. Army Reserve Battalions.
- Ensured the 11th of the 100th Military Intelligence Battalion had the resources necessary to accomplish USAR missions.

**Yellow Ribbon Program Coordinator, Fort McCoy, WI**
**December 2009–June 2013**

- Designed and coordinated biannual presentations detailing the complexity and vast number of VA resources available to service members and veterans.
- Developed and managed multiple Yellow Ribbon Program sessions for soldiers of the 11th of the 100th and multiple other battalions at Fort McCoy, Wisconsin.

**Infantryman, U.S. Army, Fort Wainwright, AK**
**January 2005–December 2009**

- Performed duties as a Team Leader during drills and live combat; aided in the mobilization of vehicles, troops, weaponry, equipment, and assisted in reconnaissance missions, use, maintenance, and storage of various combat weaponry and equipment.
- Maintained the operational capability of more than $4 million worth of military equipment with zero inventory loss and constant operational use.
- Lead a team of communication experts to ensure the communication capability over 60 km of land space in hostile territory.

**Volunteerism and Leadership**

**Employer Representative, Employer Support of the Guard and Reserve, Department of Defense**
**June 2013–Present**

- Coordinate multiple training sessions for Wal-Mart assistant managers, comanagers, and store mangers covering the Uniformed Services Employment and Reemployment Rights Act.
- Setup multiple on-the-job training locations at Wal-Mart stores for veterans to use their education benefits to attain their career goals.
- Coordinate a mentorship program for veterans pursuing educational and career goals within Wal-Mart.

**Committee Member, Veteran Student Services Committee, University of Northern Iowa**
**January 2011–May 2013**

- Created the first veterans scholarship called Boots to Books at the University of Northern Iowa, which is funded for the next several years to provide a $1000 scholarship to student veterans.
- Assisted in developing specialized brochures that were targeted at veteran recruitment and resulted in showcasing the resources, facilities, and empowering faculty at the university.
- Secured the support of dozens of businesses and nonprofits in the Waterloo/Cedar Valley area for the Veteran Upward Bound Program Grant.
- Worked with faculty, university leadership, and student government to secure a student center for veterans on campus.

**Member, UNI Proud, University of Northern Iowa**
**September 2012–May 2013**

- Coordinated the first NOH8 at My School photo shoot in the United States with more than 500 participants.
- Facilitated the creation of the first lesbian-gay-bisexual-transgender (LGBT) Scholarship at the University of Northern Iowa.
- Drove an initiative to create an LGBT Center at UNI that opened in December 2013.
- Raised private capital to bring a speaker to UNI to discuss the ramifications of the repeal of Don't Ask, Don't Tell and his military service.

**SVA Hawkeye Community College Chapter, Hawkeye Community College**
**January 2010–May 2012—Founder and President**

- Founded the first Veterans Club at Hawkeye Community College and was elected as the first president.
- Grew the Veterans Club to be the largest student group at Hawkeye Community College.
- Partnered with the UNI Veterans Association during September 2011 to assist in the development of their organization, and developed resources to assist UNI and the veterans on their campus.
- Facilitated an open discussion with Senator Tom Harkin regarding the Post 9/11 GI Bill and resources for veterans at universities and at the Veterans Administration.

**Student Veteran Advisor, Veterans Task Force, Hawkeye Community College**
**December 2009–May 2012**

- Coordinated with Hawkeye Community College Grant Office to assist in the pursuit of grants for veterans.
- Identified areas of opportunity for Hawkeye regarding the veteran population at the institution.
- Coordinated a veterans forum to identify the needs of veterans at Hawkeye Community College with the participation of 35% of student veterans on campus.

**Skills** Proficient in Microsoft Office, Adobe Acrobat, Android Operating System, Active Directory, VA Once; knowledgeable on veteran employment programs and veteran education programs.

**Decorations** The Diversity Matters Award from the University of Northern Iowa, Combat Infantrymen's Badge, Two Army Commendation Medals, Three Good Conduct Medals, Presidential Unit Citation

**References** Available on request.

The next résumé is an example of a student résumé, from Calysta Will, a student at Illinois State University.

**Calysta Will**

**555 N. Oak Terrace, Normal, IL 60052 | (111) 555-5678 | cwill@ilstu.edu**

**Education**

Bachelor of Arts | May 2015 | Illinois State University

Major: Public Relations

Lorenze de' Medici University | Spring 2013 | Florence, Italy

**Skills & Abilities**

*Communication and computer skills*

Microsoft Word and Power Point: Proficient

Excel: Intermediate

Spanish: Proficient

Italian: Basic, conversational, and reading

**Leadership**

Social Chair, Public Relations Student Society of America, Illinois State University
August 2014–May 2015

**Experience**

Academic Peer Advisor | Illinois State University—University College | May 2014–Present

- Advise first-year students with academic planning and major exploration in partnership with a University College Professional Advisor
- Assist in the delivery of University College programs and services
- Maintain accurate, detailed record of all advising contacts

Marketing and Communications Intern | Special Olympics Illinois | January–May 2014

- Created various publications for Special Olympics events
- Planned and executed Special Olympics events
- Facilitated creative projects to be featuring Special Olympics Illinois athletes
- Supported and promoted accomplishments of Special Olympics athletes

Communications Intern | Illinois State University Dean of Students | January–May 2014

- Conducted research to define needs of members of the Student Government Association
- Reconstructed operations manual for Student Government Association
- Edited and condensed various documents included in the operations manual

Peer Instructor | Illinois State University Success 101 Program | August 2012–January 2014

- Provided academic support to first-year students
- Created lesson plans focused on important skills necessary to being successful in higher education
- Planned and facilitated social events for students

1. What are the main similarities between the two résumés? What about the differences? ______________________________

______________________________

______________________________

2. According to the Four Basics of Good Comparison and Contrast, there are only a few possible purposes. What is the purpose of these résumés?

______________________________

______________________________

______________________________

3. Does the article have the Four Basics of Good Comparison and Contrast (p. 239)?

______________________________

______________________________

4. What organization does each résumé use, and is it effective? ______________

______________________________

______________________________

## *Professional Comparison/Contrast Essay*

John Tierney

# Yes, Money Can Buy Happiness . . .

John Tierney is a columnist for the Science Times section of the *New York Times*. He has also written for many other science publications such as *Discovery*, *Hippocrates*, and *Science 86*. According to his biography, "he's using TierneyLab to check out new research and rethink conventional wisdom about science and society. The Lab's work is guided by two founding principles: Just because an idea appeals to a lot of people doesn't mean it's wrong. But that's a good working theory."

This essay originally appeared in his TierneyLab column in the *New York Times* in 2008.

**Vocabulary development** Underline these words as you read: *correlated, prosocially,* and *derive.*

**correlated:** to be related in some sense
**prosocially:** good for society
**derive:** to trace from a source

1 Yes, money can buy happiness, but probably not in the way you imagined. Spending it on yourself may not do much for your spirits, but spending it on others will make you happier, according to a report from a team of social psychologists in the new issue of *Science*.

2 The researchers confirmed the joys of giving in three separate ways. First, by surveying a national sample of more than 600 Americans, they found that spending more on gifts and charity correlated with greater happiness, whereas spending more

money on oneself did not. Second, by tracking 16 workers before and after they received profit-sharing bonuses, the researchers found that that the workers who gave more of the money to others ended up happier than the ones who spent more of it on themselves. In fact, how the bonus was spent was a better predictor of happiness than the size of the bonus.

3 The final bit of evidence came from an experiment in which 46 students were given either $5 or $20 to spend by the end of the day. The ones who were instructed to spend the money on others—they bought toys for siblings, treated friends to meals and made donations to the homeless—were happier at the end of the day than the ones who were instructed to spend the money on themselves.

4 "These experimental results," the researchers conclude, "provide direct support for our causal argument that spending money on others promotes happiness more than spending money on oneself." The social psychologists—Elizabeth Dunn and Lara Aknin of the University of British Columbia, Vancouver, and Michael Norton of Harvard Business School—also conclude that "how people choose to spend their money is at least as important as how much money they make."

5 I asked Dr. Dunn if she had any advice for Lab readers on how much to spend on others. Her reply:

> I think even minor changes in spending habits can make a difference. In our experiment with college students, we found that spending just $5 prosocially had a substantial effect on happiness at the end of the day. But I wouldn't say that there's some fixed amount that everyone should spend on others. Rather, the best bet might be for people to think about whether they can push themselves to devote just a little more of their money to helping others.

6 But why wouldn't people be doing that already? Because most people don't realize the personal benefits of charity, according to Dr. Dunn and her colleagues. When the researchers surveyed another group of students, they found that most of the respondents predicted that personal spending would make them happier than spending the money on other people.

7 Perhaps that will change as word of these experiments circulates—although that prospect raises another question, which I put to Dr. Dunn: If people started giving away money chiefly in the hope of making themselves happier, as opposed to wanting to help others, would they still derive the same happiness from it?

8 "This is a fascinating question," she replied. "I certainly hope that telling people about the emotional benefits of prosocial spending doesn't completely erase these benefits; I would hate to be responsible for the downfall of joyful prosocial behavior."

9 Do you have any theories on the joys of giving? Any reports of your own experiments? Or any questions you'd like to ask the researchers? Dr. Dunn, in keeping with the results of her experiments, has generously offered to provide some answers free of charge.

Tip For reading advice, see Chapter 1.

1. Double-underline the **thesis statement**.
2. What type of organization does this essay use (point by point or whole to whole)? ______
3. Why do you suppose each group of people had different outcomes from spending money? ______
4. Why is it that even though spending money on others makes people happier, more people don't give to charity? ______

Respond to one of the following assignments in a paragraph or essay.

1. The main idea of the article involves our intent: whether we spend money on others or ourselves, we feel differently about the experience. Why do you suppose the students instructed to spend money on others felt better than those who spent it on themselves?
2. In paragraph 8, Tierney asks Dr. Dunn if people would still feel happy when spending money on others if they knew that it would make them happier? What do you think? Explain your answer.

# Write Your Own Comparison and Contrast

In this section, you will write your own comparison and contrast based on one of the following assignments. For help, refer to the How to Write Comparison and Contrast checklist on page 262.

**ASSIGNMENT OPTIONS** **Writing about college, work, and everyday life**

Write a comparison/contrast paragraph or essay on one of the following topics or on one of your own choice.

**College**

- Describe similarities and differences between high school and college, and give examples.
- Compare two approaches you have used to study, such as studying in a group and studying on your own using notes or other aids. Explain whether you prefer one approach over the other or like to use both methods.
- If you are still deciding on a major area of study, see if you can sit in on a class or two in programs that interest you. Then, compare and contrast the classes. If this process helped you decide on a program, explain the reasons for your choice.

**Work**

- Compare a job you liked with one you did not like, and give reasons for your views.
- Have you had experience working for both a bad supervisor and a good one? If so, compare and contrast their behaviors, and explain why you preferred one supervisor to another.
- Work styles tend to differ from employee to employee. For instance, some like to work in teams, whereas others prefer to complete tasks on their own. Some like specific directions on how to do things, whereas others want more freedom. Contrast your own work style with someone else's, whose approach and preferences are quite different from yours.

**Everyday life**

- Compare your life now with the way you would like it to be in five years.
- Have your experiences changed how you see your surroundings? If so, discuss your experiences, and give examples.
- Participate in a cleanup effort in your community, and then compare and contrast how the area looked before the cleanup with how it looked afterward.

## ASSIGNMENT OPTIONS Reading and writing critically

Complete one of the following assignments, which ask you to apply the critical thinking, reading, and writing skills discussed in Chapter 1.

### WRITING CRITICALLY ABOUT READINGS

**Tip** For a reminder of how to summarize, analyze, synthesize, and evaluate, see the Reading and Writing Critically box on page 21.

Both Amy Tan's "Fish Cheeks" (p. 123) and Liz Riggs "What It's Like to Be the First Person in Your Family to Go to College" (p. 278) present an unfamiliar scene or a time that the writer felt concerned about fitting in. Read or review both of these pieces, and then follow these steps:

1. **Summarize** Briefly summarize the works, listing major events.
2. **Analyze** What questions do the pieces raise for you?
3. **Synthesize** Sometimes we approach new experiences tentatively, as in Riggs's piece, and other times we are embarrassed by them, as in Tan's. Using examples from these writings and from your own experience, discuss which types of changes are positive, which types are negative, and why.
4. **Evaluate** Which piece did you connect with more, and why? In writing your evaluation, you might look back on your responses to step 2.

### WRITING ABOUT IMAGES

Study the photographs on page 261, and complete the following steps.

1. **Read the images** Ask yourself: What details are you drawn to in each photograph? What differences do you notice as you move from the 1973 model to the 1985 model and from these cell-phone ancestors to the 1991–2014 phones? (For more on reading images, see Chapter 1.)

2. **Write a comparison and contrast** Choose two or more of the photographs to compare and contrast, and write a paragraph or essay about the changing looks of mobile phones. You might want to address how changes in mobile phones represent larger changes in society and culture. Also, answer this question: What do you think phones will look like in another ten years? In writing your comparison/contrast, include the details and differences you identified in step 1.

## ANCESTORS OF MODERN CELL PHONES, 1973 AND 1985

ERIC RISBERG/AP PHOTO

© SCIENCE AND SOCIETY/SUPERSTOCK

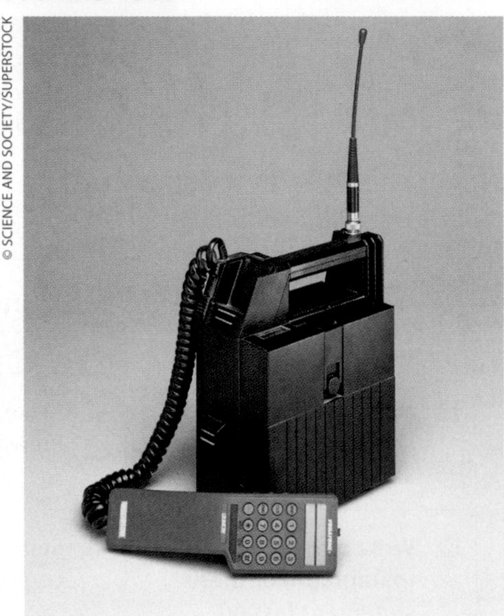

**Above left:** Martin Cooper, chairman and CEO of ArrayComm, holds a Motorola DynaTAC, a 1973 prototype of the first handheld cellular telephone. Thirty years before this photograph was taken, on April 2, 2003, the first call was made from a cellular phone.
**Above right:** The Vodafone mobile phone, introduced in 1985. Marketed by Racal-Vodac Limited, this phone was aimed at busy professionals and regular travelers, for portable use or for use in their cars. This phone came with a battery charger and an antenna for use in areas with poor reception.

## CELL PHONES FROM 1991 TO 2011

MARTIN SHIELDS/PHOTO RESEARCHERS, INC.

**Brands from left to right:** Motorola (1991), Nokia (1999), LG (2005/2006), and Motorola Droid 2 Global (2011).

MARTYN LANDI/PA WIRE URN:20980472 (PRESS ASSOCIATION VIA AP IMAGES)

The Apple iPhone 6 (2014).

## WRITING TO SOLVE A PROBLEM

Read or review the discussion of problem solving in Chapter 1 (pp. 28–30). Then, consider the following problem:

**You need a new smartphone, and you want the best one for your money. Before ordering, you do some research.**

**Assignment** Consult a Web site that rates smartphones, such as www.pcworld.com. Identify three features covered by the ratings, and make notes about why each feature is important to you. Then, choose a model based on these features. Finally, write a contrast paragraph or essay that explains your decision and contrasts your choice versus another model. Make sure to support your choice based on the three features you considered.

### CHECKLIST

### How to Write Comparison and Contrast

| Steps | Details |
|---|---|
| ☐ **Narrow and explore your topic.** See Chapter 3. | • Make the topic more specific.<br>• Prewrite to get ideas about the narrowed topic. |
| ☐ **Write a topic sentence (paragraph) or thesis statement (essay).** See Chapter 3. | • State the main idea you want to make in your comparison/contrast. |
| ☐ **Support your point.** See Chapter 4. | • Come up with points of comparison/contrast and with details about each one. |
| ☐ **Write a draft.** See Chapter 5. | • Make a plan that sets up a point-by-point or whole-to-whole comparison/contrast.<br>• Include a topic sentence (paragraph) or thesis statement (essay) and all the support points. |
| ☐ **Revise your draft.** See Chapter 5. | • Make sure it has *all* the Four Basics of Good Comparison and Contrast.<br>• Make sure you include transitions to move readers smoothly from one subject or comparison/contrast point to the next. |
| ☐ **Edit your revised draft.** See Parts 3 through 6. | • Correct errors in grammar, spelling, word use, and punctuation. |

## Chapter Review

1. What are the Four Basics of Good Comparison and Contrast? ______

2. The topic sentence (paragraph) or thesis statement (essay) in comparison/contrast should include what two parts? ______

3. What are the two ways to organize comparison/contrast? ______

4. In your own words, explain the two ways of organizing comparison/contrast.

5. Write sentences using the following vocabulary words: *laser, reasonably, forgo, valiant, convey, hostile, articulate, hail, harassing, vulgar, brash, correlated, prosocially,* and *derive.* ______

# REFLECTING ON THE JOURNEY

## Skills Learned

Now that you've completed the chapter, share what you've learned about each skill by completing the following chart.

| Skill | What I learned about this skill |
|---|---|
| Compare two or more objects to identify similarities | |
| Contrast two or more objects to identify differences | |
| Identify topics that have enough in common to be compared or contrasted | |
| Present logical points to support the comparison or contrast | |
| Arrange points in a logical order | |
| Read and analyze compare-and-contrast documents | |

13

# Cause and Effect

## Writing That Explains Reasons or Results

### Learning Objectives

**Chapter Goal:** Learn how to write a good cause-and-effect paper

**Tools to Achieve the Goal:**

- Four Basics of Good Cause-and-Effect (p. 266)
- Sample Cause-and-Effect Paragraph and Grading Rubric (pp. 272–73)
- Student Cause-and-Effect Paragraph: Caitlin Prokop, *A Difficult Decision with a Positive Outcome* (p. 274)
- Student Cause-and-Effect Essay: Stephanie Alaimo and Mark Koester, *The Backdraft of Technology* (pp. 275–76)
- Profile of Success and Workplace Cause and Effect: Joshua Boyce (p. 277)
- Professional Cause-and-Effect Essay: Liz Riggs, *What It's Like to Be the First Person in Your Family to Go to College* (pp. 278–81)
- Checklist: How to Write Cause-and-Effect (p. 284)

### READING ROADMAP

Skim Chapter 13 before reading. Find these words or terms in **bold** type. Put a check mark next to each once you locate it.

____ cause
____ effect
____ main idea
____ support
____ transitions

### Guided Reading for Chapter 13

Fill out the following chart before you begin reading. For each skill, write what you know about that skill and what you would like to know upon completing the chapter. At the end of the chapter, you will be asked to share what you learned about each skill.

| Skill | When I have used this skill | What I want to know about this skill |
|---|---|---|
| Identify the causes of events | | |
| Identify the effects of events | | |
| Express causes, effects, or both through writing | | |
| Provide specific examples to support those causes and effects | | |
| Read and analyze cause and effect | | |

LaunchPadSolo
Visit **LaunchPad Solo for Readers and Writers > Reading > Patterns of Organization** for more tutorials, videos, and practice with patterns of organization.

# Understand What Cause and Effect Are

A **cause** is what made an event happen. An **effect** is what happens as a result of the event.

### **Four Basics** of Good Cause and Effect

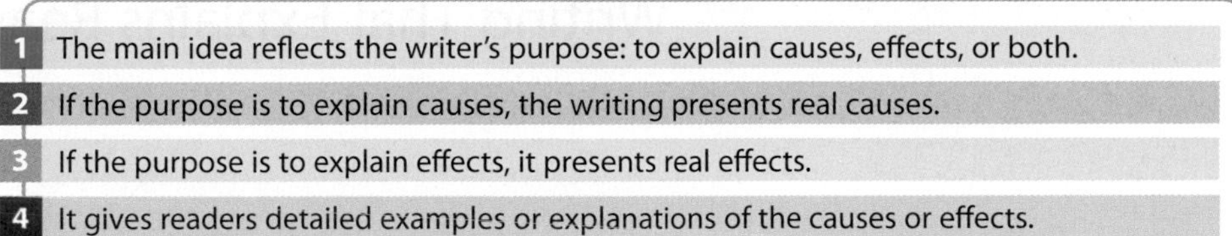
1 The main idea reflects the writer's purpose: to explain causes, effects, or both.
2 If the purpose is to explain causes, the writing presents real causes.
3 If the purpose is to explain effects, it presents real effects.
4 It gives readers detailed examples or explanations of the causes or effects.

In the following paragraph, the numbers and colors correspond to the Four Basics of Good Cause and Effect.

1 Although the thought of writing may be a source of stress for college students, researchers have recently found that it can also be a potent stress reliever. In the winter of 2008, during a time when many people catch colds or the flu or experience other symptoms of ill health, two psychologists conducted an experiment with college students to find out if writing could have positive effects on their minds and/or their bodies. After gathering a large group of college students, a mix of ages, genders, and backgrounds, the psychologists explained the task. The students were asked to write for only two minutes, on two consecutive days, about their choice of three kinds of experiences: a traumatic experience, a positive experience, or a neutral experience (something routine that happened). The psychologists did not give more detailed directions about the kinds of experiences, rather just a bad one, a good one, or one neither good nor bad. A month after collecting the students' writing, the psychologists interviewed each of the students and asked them to report any symptoms of ill health, such as colds, flu, headaches, or lack of sleep. 3 What the psychologists found was quite surprising. 4 Those students who had written about emotionally charged topics, either traumatic or positive, all reported that they had been in excellent health, avoiding the various illnesses that had been circulating in the college and the larger community. The students who had chosen to write about routine, day-to-day things that didn't matter to them reported the ill health effects that were typical of the season, such as colds, flu, poor sleep, and coughing. From these findings, the two psychologists reported that writing about things that are important to people actually has a positive effect on their health. Their experiment suggests the value to people of regularly recording their reactions to experiences, in a journal of some sort. If writing can keep you well, it is worth a good try. The mind-body connection continues to be studied because clearly each affects the other.

When you are writing about causes and effects, make sure that you do not confuse something that happened before an event with a real cause or something that happened after an event with a real effect. For example, if you have pizza on Monday and get the flu on Tuesday, eating the pizza is not the cause of the flu just because it happened before you got the flu, nor is the flu the effect of eating pizza. You just happened to get the flu the next day.

You use cause and effect in many situations.

| | |
|---|---|
| **College** | In a nutrition course, you are asked to identify the consequences (effects) of poor nutrition. |
| **Work** | Sales are down in your department or branch, and you have to explain the cause. |
| **Everyday life** | You explain to your child why a certain behavior is not acceptable by warning him or her about the negative effects of that behavior. |

In college, writing assignments might include the words *discuss the causes (or effects) of*, but they might also use phrases such as *explain the results of*, *discuss the impact of*, and *how did X affect Y?* In all these cases, use the strategies discussed in this chapter.

## *Main Idea in Cause and Effect*

The **main idea** introduces causes, effects, or both. To help you discover your main idea, complete the following sentence:

**Main idea in cause and effect** **(Your topic) causes (or caused) . . .**
**(Your topic) resulted in (or results in) . . .**

Here is an example of a topic sentence for a paragraph:

Topic + Main idea (effect of regular exercise) = Topic sentence

Regular exercise improves cardiovascular health.

Remember that the main idea for an essay can be a little broader than one for a paragraph.

**Tip** If the writer wanted to explore causes, he or she might look into the factors that motivate people to exercise.

Topic + Main idea (effect of regular exercise) = Thesis statement

Regular exercise provides more physical and mental benefits than any medication could offer.

**Tip** Sometimes, the same main idea can be used for a paragraph and an essay, but the essay must develop this point in more detail. (See pp. 68–69.)

Whereas the topic sentence focuses on just one major benefit of regular exercise, the thesis statement considers multiple benefits.

**PRACTICE 1** **Stating your main idea**

For each of the following topics, make notes about possible causes and effects on a separate sheet of paper. Then, in each of the spaces below, write a sentence that states a main idea. First, look at the following example.

**Example:**

**Topic: Bankruptcy**

**Main idea:** *Although many different kinds of people declare bankruptcy each year, the causes of bankruptcy are often the same.*

1. Topic: A fire in someone's home

   Main idea: ______________________

2. Topic: An "A" in this course

   Main idea: ______________________

3. Topic: Waking up late in the morning

   Main idea: ______________________

## *Support in Cause and Effect*

The paragraph and essay models on pages 270–71 use the topic sentence (paragraph) and thesis statement (essay) from the Main Idea section of this chapter. Both models include the **support** used in all cause-effect writing: statements of cause or effect backed up by detailed explanations or examples. In the essay plan, however, the major support points (statements of cause/effect) are topic sentences for individual paragraphs.

**PRACTICE 2** **Giving examples and details**

Write down two causes or two effects for two of the three topics from Practice 1. Then, give an example or detail that explains each cause or effect.

**Example:**

**Topic: Bankruptcy**

**Cause 1:** *Overspending*

**Example/Detail:** *bought a leather jacket I liked and charged it*

**Cause 2:** *Poor budgeting*

**Example/Detail:** *not tracking monthly expenses versus income*

1. Topic: A fire in someone's home

   Cause/Effect 1: ______________________

   Example/Detail: ______________________

   Cause/Effect 2: ______________________

   Example/Detail: ______________________

2. Topic: An "A" in this course

   Cause/Effect 1: ______________________________

   Example/Detail: ______________________________

   Cause/Effect 2: ______________________________

   Example/Detail: ______________________________

3. Topic: Waking up late in the morning

   Cause/Effect 1: ______________________________

   Example/Detail: ______________________________

   Cause/Effect 2: ______________________________

   Example/Detail: ______________________________

## *Organization in Cause and Effect*

Cause and effect can be organized in a variety of ways, depending on your purpose.

**Tip** For more on the different orders of organization, see pages 76–78.

| Main Idea | Purpose | Organization |
|---|---|---|
| The "Occupy" protests of 2011 brought attention to the economic difficulties faced by low- and middle-income citizens. | To explain the effects of the protests | Order of importance, saving the most important effect for last |
| A desire to remain at a protest site for an extended period led "Occupy" protesters to create miniature towns, with food service, libraries, and more. | To describe the places where protesters camped out | Space order |
| The "Occupy" protests in New York City inspired other protests throughout the country. | To describe the spread of the protest movement over time | Time order |

**NOTE:** If you are explaining both causes and effects, you would present the causes first and the effects later.

Use **transitions** to move readers smoothly from one cause to another, from one effect to another, or from causes to effects. Because cause and effect can use any method of organization depending on your purpose, the following list shows just a few of the transitions you might use.

### Common Transitions in Cause and Effect

| | |
|---|---|
| also | more important/serious cause or effect |
| as a result | most important/serious cause or effect |
| because | one cause/effect; another cause or effect |
| the final cause or effect | a primary cause; a secondary cause |
| the first, second, third cause or effect | a short-term effect; a long-term effect |

# Paragraphs vs. Essays in Cause and Effect

For more on the important features of cause and effect, see the Four Basics of Good Cause and Effect on page 266.

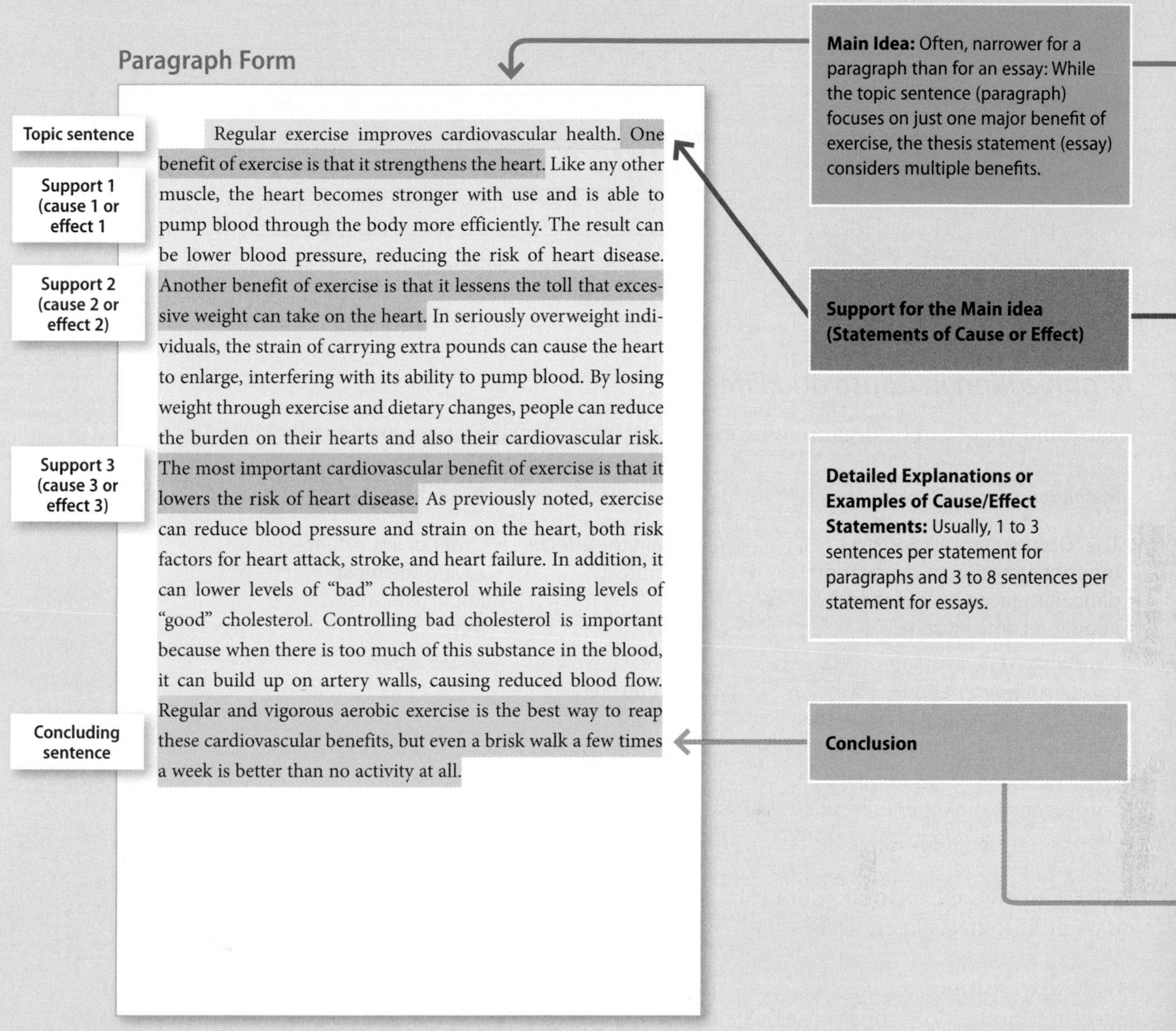

Paragraph Form
Topic sentence
Support 1 (cause 1 or effect 1
Support 2 (cause 2 or effect 2)
Support 3 (cause 3 or effect 3)
Concluding sentence
Regular exercise improves cardiovascular health. One benefit of exercise is that it strengthens the heart. Like any other muscle, the heart becomes stronger with use and is able to pump blood through the body more efficiently. The result can be lower blood pressure, reducing the risk of heart disease. Another benefit of exercise is that it lessens the toll that excessive weight can take on the heart. In seriously overweight individuals, the strain of carrying extra pounds can cause the heart to enlarge, interfering with its ability to pump blood. By losing weight through exercise and dietary changes, people can reduce the burden on their hearts and also their cardiovascular risk. The most important cardiovascular benefit of exercise is that it lowers the risk of heart disease. As previously noted, exercise can reduce blood pressure and strain on the heart, both risk factors for heart attack, stroke, and heart failure. In addition, it can lower levels of "bad" cholesterol while raising levels of "good" cholesterol. Controlling bad cholesterol is important because when there is too much of this substance in the blood, it can build up on artery walls, causing reduced blood flow. Regular and vigorous aerobic exercise is the best way to reap these cardiovascular benefits, but even a brisk walk a few times a week is better than no activity at all.
Main Idea: Often, narrower for a paragraph than for an essay: While the topic sentence (paragraph) focuses on just one major benefit of exercise, the thesis statement (essay) considers multiple benefits.
Support for the Main idea (Statements of Cause or Effect)
Detailed Explanations or Examples of Cause/Effect Statements: Usually, 1 to 3 sentences per statement for paragraphs and 3 to 8 sentences per statement for essays.
Conclusion


## Think Critically As You Write Cause and Effect

**ASK YOURSELF**

- Have I examined a variety of possible causes and/or effects related to my topic? (If not, research them, and consider revising your main idea and support based on what you learn.)
- Am I certain that my causes are real causes and my effects real effects? (For help with answering this question, see p. 267.)

## Essay Form

Introductory paragraph

1

Most people know how hard it is to start and stick with an exercise program. However, there is a good reason to build a significant amount [Thesis statement] activity into every week: Regular exercise provides more physical and mental benefits than any medication could offer.

First, exercise helps people achieve and maintain a healthy weight. A nutritious diet [Topic sentence 1 (cause 1 or effect 1)] excessive in calories has a greater effect loss than exercise does. However, regular exercise—ideally, interspersed throughout the day—can make an important contribution. For instance, people trying to lose weight might walk to work or to other destinations instead of driving. Or, they might take the stairs to their office instead of the elevator. If they go the gym at the end of the day, so much [Topic sentence 2 (cause 2 or effect 2)] Added up, all these efforts can make a dif

Second, exercise boosts mood and energy levels. For example, exercise causes the body to release endorphins, chemicals that give us a sense of well-being, even happiness. Accordingly, exercise can help

2

reduce stress and combat depression. In addition, because exercise can make people look and feel more fit, it can improve their self-esteem. Finally, by improving strength and endurance, exercise gives individuals more energy to go about their lives.

The most important benefit of exercise is that it can help prevent disease. For example, ex [Topic sentence 3 (cause 3 or effect 3)] improve the body's use of insulin and, as lier, help people maintain a healthy weight. Therefore, it can help prevent or control diabetes. Additionally, exercise can lower the risk of heart attacks, strokes, and heart failure. For instance, exercise strengthens the heart muscle, helping it pump blood more efficiently and reducing high blood pressure, a heart disease risk factor. Also, exercise can lower levels of "bad" cholesterol while raising levels of "good" cholesterol. Controlling levels of bad cholesterol is important because when there is too much of this substance in the blood, it can build up in the walls of arteries, possibly blocking blood flow. Finally, some research suggests that regular exercise

3

can reduce the risk of certain cancers, including breast, colon, and lung cancer.

Concluding paragraph

In my own life, exercise has made a huge difference. Before starting a regular exercise program, I was close to needing prescription medications to lower my blood pressure and cholesterol. Thanks to regular physical activity, however, both my blood pressure and cholesterol levels are now in the normal range, and I have never felt better. Every bit of time spent at the gym or exchanging a ride in an elevator for a walk up the stairs has been well worth it.

**PRACTICE 3** **Using transitions in cause and effect**

Read the paragraph that follows, and fill in the blanks with transitions.

Recently, neuroscientists, who have long been skeptical about meditation, confirm that it has numerous positive outcomes. ______________ is that people who meditate can maintain their focus and attention longer than people who do not. This ability to stay "on task" was demonstrated among students who had been practicing meditation for several weeks. They reported more effective studying and learning because they were able to pay attention. ________________ positive outcome was the ability to relax on command. Many people lead busy, stressful lives with multiple pressures on them—family responsibilities, work duties, financial worries, and uncertainties about the future. While meditating, people learned how to reduce their heart rates and blood pressure so that they could relax more easily in all kinds of situations. ________________________ outcome was a thickening of the brain's cortex. Meditators' cortexes were uniformly thicker than nonmeditators'. Because the cortex enables memorization and the production of new ideas, this last outcome is especially exciting, particularly in fighting Alzheimer's disease and other dementias.

## Evaluate Cause and Effect

Read the following sample cause-and-effect paragraph. Using the Four Basics of Good Cause and Effect and the sample grading rubric, decide what grade this paragraph would earn. Explain your answer.

**Assignment** Write a paragraph that identifies one reason (cause) that may have resulted in a poor grade on a test (effect).

**Failing grades on a test can have any number of causes. For example, lack of sleep. Sleep is important to help a student perform well on tests. If tired may cause the student to not pay attention or read questions. Tired may also cause misunderstanding. When you know you have a test coming, you need to make sure that you have more than enough rest in order to focus.**

**Analysis of Sample Paragraph:**

**Sample rubric**

| Element | Grading criteria | Point: Comment |
|---|---|---|
| **Appropriateness** | • Did the student follow the assignment directions? | ____/5: |
| **Main idea** | • Does the paper clearly state a strong main idea in a complete sentence? | ____/10: |
| **Support** | • Is the main idea developed with specific support, including specific details and examples?<br>• Is there enough support to make the main idea evident to the reader?<br>• Is all the support directly related to the main idea? | ____/10: |
| **Organization** | • Does the writer clearly demonstrate how one behavior causes the end result?<br>• Does the student use transitions (*also, for example, sometimes,* and so on) to move the reader from one point to another? | ____/10: |
| **Conclusion** | • Does the conclusion remind the reader of the main idea? | ____/5: |
| **Grammar** | • Is the writing free of the four most serious errors? (See Chapters 16–19.)<br>• Is the sentence structure clear?<br>• Does the student choose words that clearly express his or her meaning?<br>• Are the words spelled correctly?<br>• Is the punctuation correct? | ____/10: |
| | | **TOTAL POINTS: ____/50** |

## Read and Analyze Cause and Effect

Reading examples of cause and effect will help you write your own. The first example is a student cause-and-effect paragraph, followed by a student essay written about the effects of modern technology. The Profile of Success and workplace cause-and-effect essay are by blogger Joshua Boyce, and the final essay is by professional writer Liz Riggs.

*Student Cause-and-Effect Paragraph*

Caitlin Prokop

## A Difficult Decision with a Positive Outcome

**accompany:** to be with; to go with

**cherish:** to value highly

**Vocabulary development** Underline these words as you read: *accompany* and *cherish.*

When my mother made the decision to move back to New York, I made the choice to move in with my dad so that I could finish high school. This decision affected me in a positive way because I graduated with my friends, built a better relationship with my father, and had the chance to go to college without leaving home. Graduating with my friends was important to me because I have known most of them since we were in kindergarten. It was a journey through childhood that we had shared, and I wanted to finish it with them. Accomplishing the goal of graduating from high school with my close friends, those who accompanied me through school, made me a stronger and more confident person. Another good outcome of my difficult decision was the relationship I built with my dad. We never saw eye to eye when I lived with both of my parents. For example, we stopped talking for five months because I always sided against him with my mom. Living together for the past five years has made us closer, and I cherish that closeness we have developed. Every Thursday is our day, a day when we talk to each other about what is going on in our lives, so that we will never again have a distant relationship. A third good outcome of my decision is that I can go to Brevard Community College, which is right down the street. In high school, I had thought that I would want to go away to college, but then I realized that I would miss my home. By staying here, I have the opportunity to attend a wonderful college that is preparing me for transferring to a four-year college and finding a good career. I have done some research and believe I would like to become a police officer, a nurse, or a teacher. Through the school, I can do volunteer work in each of these areas. Right now, I am leaning toward becoming a teacher, based on my volunteer work in a kindergarten class. There, I can explore what grades I want to teach. In every way, I believe that my difficult decision was the right one, giving me many opportunities that I would not have had if I had moved to a new and unfamiliar place.

1. Double-underline the **topic sentence**.
2. Does Caitlin write about causes or effects? ______________________
3. Circle the **transitions** Caitlin uses to move readers from one point to the next.
4. Does Caitlin's paragraph include the Four Basics of Good Cause and Effect?

   Why or why not? ______________________

   ______________________

5. Have you made a difficult decision that turned out to be a good one? Why and how? ______

## *Student Cause-and-Effect Essay*

Stephanie Alaimo and Mark Koester

# The Backdraft of Technology

Stephanie Alaimo and Mark Koester both graduated from DePaul University of Chicago. Alaimo was a Spanish major who volunteered as an English tutor. She is now studying sociology at the University of California, San Diego. Koester majored in philosophy and taught English in Hangzhou, China, after graduation. He is now developing software in China as an entrepreneur.

**Vocabulary development** Underline these words as you read: *miscellaneous, automated, entry level,* and *mechanization.*

**miscellaneous:** random; an assortment

**automated:** controlled by a machine

**entry level:** a job at the lowest level of experience in any field

**mechanization:** the process of doing work with machinery

**Guiding question** Do Stephanie and Mark present causes, effects, or both in their essay? Keep track of them while you read.

1 You have picked up the bread and the milk and the day's miscellaneous foodstuffs at your local grocery store. The lines at the traditional, human-operated checkouts are a shocking two customers deep. Who wants to wait? Who would wait when we have society's newest upgrade in not having to wait: the self-checkout?

2 Welcome to the automated grocery store. "Please scan your next item," a repetitively chilling, mechanical voice orders you.

3 If you have yet to see it at your nearest grocer, a new technological advance has been reached. Instead of waiting for some minimally waged, minimally educated, and, most likely, immigrant cashier to scan and bag your groceries for you, you can now do it yourself. In a consumer-driven, hyperactive, "I want" world, an increase in speed is easily accepted thoughtlessly. We're too busy. But, in gaining efficiency and ease, a number of jobs have been lost, particularly at the entry level, and a moment of personal, human engagement with actual people has vanished.

**Predict** Before reading the rest of the paper, consider what you may already know about this topic. What are some of the reasons Stephanie and Mark may use to support their thesis?

4 It seems easy enough to forget about the consequences when you are rushed and your belly is grumbling. The previously utilized checkout lanes at local grocery stores and super, mega, we-have-everything stores are now routinely left unattended during the peak hours. In these moments, your options are using the self-checkout or waiting for a real human being. Often in a hurried moment we choose the easiest, fastest, and least mentally involved option without much consideration.

5 We forget to consider that with the aid of the self-checkout, at least two jobs have been lost. As a result, a human cashier and grocery bagger are now waiting in the unemployment line. Furthermore, self-checkout

machines are probably not manufactured in the United States, thus shipping more jobs overseas. And sadly, the job openings are now shrinking by putting consumers to work. The wages from these jobs are stockpiled by those least in need—corporations and those who own them.

**Identify** What specific information do Stephanie and Mark supply about self-checkouts? Are they a cause of the problem of unemployment or an effect? Explain your answer.

6 The mechanization of the service industry has been occurring throughout our lifetimes. Gas stations were once full-service. Human bank tellers, instead of ATMs, handled simple cash withdrawals. Even video stores are being marginalized from people ordering online from companies like Netflix. And did you know that you can now order a pizza for delivery online without even talking to a person?

7 Sure, these new robots and computers reduce work, which could potentially be a really good thing. But these mechanizations have only increased profit margins for large corporations and have reduced the need to hire employees. Jobs are lost along with means of providing for one's self and family.

8 For those who find the loss of grocery store labor to be meaningless and, quite frankly, beyond impacting their future lives as accountants or lawyers, it does not seem to be entirely implausible that almost any job or task could become entirely technologically mechanized and your elitist job market nuked.

**Reflect** Have you seen negative publicity about self-checkouts? Has it made you consider whether you choose to use them, or did you ignore it? Explain your answer.

9 We are a society trapped in a precarious fork in the road. We can either eliminate the time and toil of the human workload and still allow people to have jobs and maintain the same standard of living, though working less, or, in a darker scenario, we can eliminate human work in terms of actual human jobs and make the situation of the lower classes more tenuous. Is it our goal to reduce the overall time that individuals spend laboring? Or is it our goal to increase corporate profits at the loss of many livelihoods?

10 At present, corporations and their executives put consumers to work, cut the cost of labor through the use of technology such as self-checkouts and ATMs, and profit tremendously. But a host of workers are now scrambling to find a way to subsist. To choose the self-checkout simply as a convenience cannot be morally justified unless these jobs remain.

**Summarize** Briefly restate the main ideas of this essay.

11 The choices we make on a daily basis affect the whole of our society. Choosing convenience often translates to eliminating actual jobs that provide livelihoods and opportunities to many. Think before you simply follow the next technological innovation. Maybe it could be you in their soon-to-be-jobless shoes. Say "No!" to self-checkout.

1. Underline the **topic sentence**.
2. Do the authors use enough examples and detail to demonstrate the causes and effects in the essay? ______________________
3. Does this essay follow the Four Basics of Good Cause and Effect (p. 266)?
______________________

# Profile of Success

## Cause and Effect in the Real World

**Joshua Boyce**
Blogger

**Background** I grew up in poverty and graduated from high school not knowing how to read, write, or do any math beyond simple arithmetic. This occurred because I was wrongfully placed in special education at an early age. Upon completion of high school, I attended Job Corps. There I learned how to weld and moved to Vicksburg, Mississippi. Shortly after moving, I met Dr. Nettle, a local minister. He taught me how to read and encouraged me to pursue my GED.

After getting my GED, I enrolled full time at a two-year college where I graduated with honors. Then I attended a four-year institution and received my B.S. degree in exercise science. Currently, I am a fitness trainer and blogger. My blog, "Slim Chance Motivation," is aimed at inspiring others to dream and pursue their goals no matter what the odds are.

**Degrees/Colleges** A.A. Degree/Hinds Community College; B.S./Mississippi College

**Writing at work** This blog post reveals the harmful effect of wrong conditioning and challenges people to make steps to recondition their mind.

### *Workplace Cause and Effect: Conditioning*

> "If you make a man feel that he is inferior, you do not have to compel him to accept an inferior status, for he will seek it himself. If you make a man think that he is justly an outcast, you do not have to order him to the back door. He will go without being told; and if there is no back door, his very nature will demand one."
>
> —Dr. Carter G. Woodson

1 Dr. Woodson's quote paints a good picture of the effect of conditioning. In athletics, conditioning is important. It is the combination of physical and mental training with the right nutritional plan. The right conditioning program makes a difference between experiencing the sweet taste of victory or the bitterness of defeat, and the same applies to people and their goals.

2 I was conditioned to accept failure, and this mindset wreaked havoc in my life for many years. This became even more evident when I was in Job Corp. No matter how many welding processes or techniques I learned, I still had this strong internal feeling that I was going to fail. My conditioning was preventing me from believing in my ability to weld even though I had all the proof that suggested differently.

3 There are still many enslaved by this conditioning. It leads to the acceptance of going to prison instead of college or trade school. It forces you into submission to a mindless, backbreaking job. It causes fear in doing the most simple of tasks. I have been, and I have watched too many individuals, be held down by this conditioning.

4 I was reconditioned to think otherwise by two important factors. (1) **People**—Mr. Beard, my Job Corp welding instructor, saw my ability to weld and often helped me to shake the doubts. (2) **Interpretation**—With the help of Mr. Beard, I was able to understand and accept that it was not luck but my ability to perform a task well that was producing the result. With people and good discernment, I was able to decrease the doubts and increase my confidence.

5 In the end, it is still a battle, one you cannot win on your own. I needed help, and you will also. So to make a slim chance a chance, I had to be reconditioned, and so will you.

1. Underline the main idea of the article.
2. What is Boyce's **purpose?** ______________________________

______________________________

______________________________

3. Identify and list the **effects of being conditioned or not being conditioned.**

______________________________

______________________________

4. Identify and list the causes that lead to these effects. ______________________________

______________________________

______________________________

## *Professional Cause-and-Effect Essay*

Liz Riggs

# What It's Like to Be the First Person in Your Family to Go to College

Liz Riggs in a writer and teacher who lives in Nashville, Tennessee. Her work has appeared in *The Atlantic*, *The Huffington Post*, and *Relevant* magazine, to name just a few. This piece first appeared in *The Atlantic* in January 2014.

**Vocabulary development** Underline these words as you read: *immigrant, rigorous, estrangement, alienation, remedial, formidable, influx,* and *lag.*

**immigrant:** a person who comes to live permanently in a foreign country
**rigorous:** rigidly severe or harsh
**estrangement:** unfriendly or hostile
**alienation:** withdrawn from the rest of the world
**remedial:** intended to correct or improve one's skill
**formidable:** causing fear, apprehension, or dread
**influx:** flowing inward
**lag:** to fail to maintain a desired pace

**Guiding question** As you read the article, try to identify potential causes and effects for the way Harry felt during his time at school.

1 When Harry arrived at Vanderbilt University in 2008, he became the first person in his family to attend college. His parents were immigrants from Nicaragua,

and he had attended a so-called "academically and economically disadvantaged" high school on the North side of Miami. Even after completing a rigorous IB [international baccalaureate] program as a high-school student and receiving a scholarship, he arrived on campus feeling like an outsider.

2 "Never before had I truly felt such an extreme sense of estrangement and alienation," he says of his first few months. "I quickly realized that although I may look the part, my cultural and socio-economic backgrounds were vastly different from those of my predominantly white, affluent peers. I wanted to leave."

**Reflect** Have you ever found yourself in a situation where you felt you didn't belong or understand what was going on around you?

3 Harry opted to stay at Vanderbilt, but he found acclimating to the school's cultural climate to be extremely difficult. His scholarship covered books, tuition, and housing—but it didn't cover little costs like dorm move-in needs and travel costs home for breaks—expenses his classmates could typically afford that exacerbated his feelings of alienation. Eventually, he found refuge in the school's theatre department and student government.

4 "There were very few Latinos that I could connect with," he says. "[But], I got very involved in extra-curricular activities in hopes of meeting people. . . . It was in each of these organizations that I met older students that informally mentored me. . . . I would ask questions shamelessly and learn about their experiences.

5 Harry's difficult adjustment is just one example of the many obstacles first-generation and minority students confront each year that don't typically plague their second- and third-generation peers. Extensive studies show that low-income and first-generation students are more likely to be academically behind, sometimes several years in core subjects. They're more likely to live at home or off-campus. They're less likely to have gained AP [advanced placement] credit and more likely to have to take uncredited remedial courses. And they're more likely to face serious financial hurdles.

**Identify** What specific causes are identified in the previous paragraph that explain why a first-generation student may have difficulty when they begin their college education?

6 These challenges are sometimes so formidable that studies say that only 8 percent of low-income (many of whom are first-generation) students will graduate college by age 25. Social integration is only one piece of the puzzle for these students, and for Harry—like many other students—combating this transition can be easier with the help of older peers, teachers and guiding professors who act as mentors. While the definition of "mentor" varies, there are both informal and formal structures that have the potential to influence first-generation college persistence and graduation. Armed with this understanding, many secondary and post-secondary institutions have created programming to better support and mentor first-generation students.

**Reflect** Do you think students would benefit from the types of mentoring and counseling these schools provide? Explain.

7 In Chicago, The Noble Network of Charter Schools collects extensive data on their alumni to determine what students need in order to persist and graduate from college. Last year, nine of the campuses graduated seniors and each of these nine schools has a college counselor and an alumni coordinator—allowing students to have extensive support through the college application, matriculation, and transition process.

8 "It's very intentionally called college counseling," Matt Niksch, Noble's Chief College Officer, tells me. "They're not kids anymore, [and] a lot of it is about helping young adults determine the right choice for them."

9 Noble schools look to a college's institutional minority graduation rate as a predictor of student success, but even these statistics can't always foresee what different students will face.

**Reflect** In the previous paragraphs, the author identifies many causes of student success or a lack of success. Have you ever found yourself in one of these situations? What did you do about it?

10 Caroline Kelly, a college counselor at Noble's Pritzker College Prep, categorizes the challenges into "different buckets. One is financial, one is motivation, one is family, one is academics, and one is social integration."

11 Many first-generation students, like Harry, struggle socially when they arrive on a college campus only to find that they have trouble identifying with their wealthier peers, or they feel a distinct "otherness" that they didn't experience in high school. Others adjust socially but find themselves paying for their education for the first time in their lives.

12 "In high school your education was given to you for free in most cases," says Mac, a current junior at the University of Illinois at Urbana Champaign. Mac is an alumnus of a traditional public school on the Southside of Chicago, where he participated in OneGoal, a teacher-led college persistence program for low-income students that provides school-based support for students over the course of three years. OneGoal teachers begin work with students during their junior year of high school and bridge the gap between high school and college with a curriculum that continues into each student's first-year of college.

13 Despite the influx of programs on high-school and college campuses, many programs still lag in hard graduation numbers.

14 "College becomes a major expense. I have to focus a lot more on how I will pay for school before attending school each semester," he says. He has had support from the program since his junior year in high school, when OneGoal teachers helped him prepare for standardized tests, research and apply for schools and apply for financial aid. His OneGoal teacher even drove him to college on move-in day. "Before OneGoal I don't feel that college was even on my radar," he says.

15 "There's just a huge financial gap," says Thomas Dickson, the Director of Teacher Recruitment for OneGoal.

**Identify** Out of all the causes Riggs identifies, which do you believe is the biggest hurdle for first generation college students and why?

16 Since its official launch in 2007, 87 percent of OneGoal's high school graduates have enrolled in college, and of those who have enrolled, 85 percent are persisting in college or have graduated with a college degree.

17 OneGoal has many look-alike organizations in other cities, some of which are school-based (KIPP Through College, Achievement First's Alumni Program) and others that are independent companies such as College Forward—a non-profit college-coaching organization based in Texas that boasts 78 percent of their students as still enrolled or graduated, or InsideTrack, a for-profit coaching organization aimed at increasing college enrollment and graduation rates.

18 Despite the influx of programs on high-school and college campuses, many programs still lag in hard graduation numbers.

19 "Our four-year college graduation numbers are not even close to where we want them to be," Angela Montagna, Noble's Director of External Affairs, says. Noble says 88 percent of their students make it from their first to their second year, but don't always make it to graduation.

20 Though there isn't significant research that measures all mentoring relationships and their effects on college persistence, there is some research showing the positive effects of mentoring relationships on young kids. Colleges across the country are implementing mentoring initiatives for first-generation college students in attempts to combat the staggeringly low graduation rates.

21 And, while a degree is the ultimate goal for many parents, teachers and students, there are other results that are perhaps more important for first-generation college students, Noble's Matt Niksch says.

22 "A lot of [students] talk about college as the goal. But we also don't want them to forget that really the goal is: We want them to have happy, successful, choice-filled lives."

**Summarize** What is the author's main idea in this article?

1. Double-underline the **thesis statement**.
2. Does this essay present causes, effects, or both? Explain how you came to your conclusion. ______________________________
3. Does this essay follow the Four Basics of Good Cause and Effect (p. 266)? Why or why not? ______________________________

Respond to one of the following assignments in a paragraph or essay.

**Tip** For reading advice, see Chapter 1.

1. At the beginning of her essay, Riggs writes about situations that may cause a student to feel uncomfortable or alienated at college because of their background. Write about a time when your past created an uncomfortable situation and how you managed to work through it.
2. In paragraph 10, Caroline Kelly identifies some causes of difficulty as a student enters college: financial, motivation, family, academics, and social integration. Which of these causes can be controlled by a student? In other words, to be

successful, students can change the effect that some of these have on their life: which would those be?

3. In paragraph 20, Riggs presents some research that shows how mentoring can have a positive effect on both children and college students. Why do you think that is?

## Write Your Own Cause and Effect

In this section, you will write your own cause-and-effect paragraph or essay based on one of the following assignments. For help, refer to the How to Write Cause and Effect checklist on page 284.

**ASSIGNMENT OPTIONS** **Writing about college, work, and everyday life**

Write a cause-and-effect paragraph or essay on one of the following topics or on one of your own choice.

**College**

- Write about the causes, effects, or both of not studying for an exam.
- If you have chosen a major or program of study, explain the factors behind your decision. How do you think this choice will shape your future?
- Why do some people stay in college, while others drop out? Interview one or two college graduates about the factors behind their decision to stay in school. Also, ask them how staying in school and graduating has affected their lives. Then, write about the causes and effects they describe.

**Work**

- Write about the causes, effects, or both of stress at work.
- Identify a friend or acquaintance who has been successful at work. Write about the factors behind this person's success.
- Write about the causes, effects, or both of having a good or bad attitude at work.

**Everyday life**

- Think of a possession that has great personal meaning for you. Then, write about why you value the possession, and give examples of its importance in your life.
- Try to fill in this blank: "__________ changed my life." Your response can be an event, an interaction with a particular person, or anything significant to you. It can be something positive or negative. After you fill in the blank, explain how and why this event, interaction, or time had so much significance.
- Arrange to spend a few hours at a local soup kitchen or food pantry, or on another volunteer opportunity that interests you. (You can use a search engine to find volunteer opportunities in your area.) Write about how the experience affected you.

**ASSIGNMENT OPTIONS** **Reading and writing critically**

Complete one of the following assignments, which ask you to apply the critical thinking, reading, and writing skills discussed in Chapter 1.

## WRITING CRITICALLY ABOUT READINGS

Jelani Lynch's "My Turnaround" (p. 118), Caitlin Prokop's "A Difficult Decision with a Positive Outcome" (p. 274), and Liz Riggs's "What It's Like to Be the First Person in Your Family to Go to College" (p. 278) talk about taking control of one's life. Read or review these pieces, and then follow these steps:

1. **Summarize** Briefly summarize the works, listing major examples.
2. **Analyze** What questions do these pieces raise for you? Are there any other issues you wish they had covered?
3. **Synthesize** Using examples from Lynch, Prokop's, and Riggs's writings and from your own experience, discuss different ways—big and small—in which people can take control of their lives.
4. **Evaluate** Which of the pieces had the deepest effect on you? Why? In writing your evaluation, you might look back on your responses to step 2.

**Tip** For a reminder of how to summarize, analyze, synthesize, and evaluate, see the Reading and Writing Critically box on page 21.

## WRITING ABOUT IMAGES

Sometimes, using language is not an effective means of communication. This can happen when a child is too young to speak, a person does not feel comfortable with written or spoken language (perhaps he or she is learning a new language and is not comfortable speaking or writing publicly), or when something, for instance, pain, makes it difficult to speak or write. Study the following images and then answer the following questions.

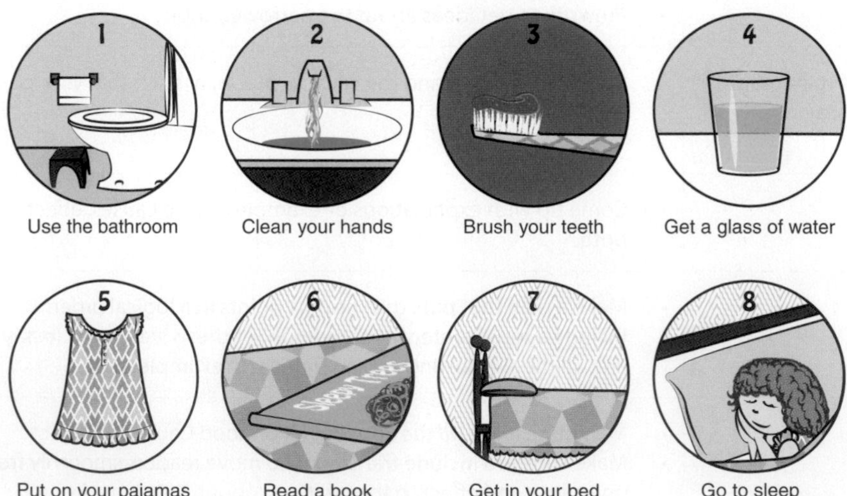
1
Use the bathroom
2
Clean your hands
3
Brush your teeth
4
Get a glass of water
5
Put on your pajamas
6
Read a book
7
Get in your bed
8
Go to sleep

It's important to make a bedtime ritual that helps children prepare to go to sleep each night.

1. **Read the images** Ask yourself: Why is it a good idea to use a series of images, instead of a single image, to help the "reader" identify what they want to say? (For more information on reading images, see Chapter 1.)

2. **Write a cause-and-effect paragraph or essay** Identify another situation in which using images to explain the cause-and-effect relationship between two situations, feelings, or actions would be as helpful or more helpful than written directions/instructions.

## WRITING TO SOLVE A PROBLEM

Read or review the discussion of problem solving in Chapter 1 (pp. 28–30). Then, consider the following problem.

**You have learned of a cheating ring at school that uses cell phones to give test answers to students taking the test. A few students in your math class, who are also friends of yours, think that this scheme is a great idea and are planning to cheat on a test you will be taking next week. You decide not to participate, partly because you fear getting caught, but also because you think that cheating is wrong. Now you want to convince your friends not to cheat, because you don't want them to get caught and possibly kicked out of school. How do you make your case?**

*(Continued on page 285.)*

### CHECKLIST

#### How to Write Cause and Effect

| Steps | Details |
|---|---|
| ☐ Narrow and explore your topic.<br>See Chapter 3. | • Make the topic more specific.<br>• Prewrite to get ideas about the narrowed topic. |
| ☐ Write a topic sentence (paragraph) or thesis statement (essay).<br>See Chapter 3. | • State your subject and the causes, effects, or both that your paper will explore. |
| ☐ Support your point.<br>See Chapter 4. | • Come up with explanations or examples of the causes, effects, or both. |
| ☐ Write a draft.<br>See Chapter 5. | • Make a plan that puts the support points in a logical order.<br>• Include a topic sentence (paragraph) or thesis statement (essay) and all the supporting explanations and examples. |
| ☐ Revise your draft.<br>See Chapter 5. | • Make sure it has *all* the Four Basics of Good Cause and Effect.<br>• Make sure you include transitions to move readers smoothly from one cause and effect to the next. |
| ☐ Edit your revised draft.<br>See Parts 3 through 6. | • Correct errors in grammar, spelling, word use, and punctuation. |

**Assignment** Working in a group or on your own, list the various effects of cheating—both immediate and long term—you could use to convince your friends. Then, write a cause-and-effect paragraph or essay that identifies and explains some possible effects of cheating. You might start with this sentence:

**Cheating on tests or papers is not worth the risks.**

## Chapter Review

1. A cause is ______________________________
2. An effect is ______________________________
3. What are the Four Basics of Good Cause and Effect? ______________________________
______________________________
______________________________
______________________________
4. Write sentences using the following vocabulary words: *cherish, motives, immigrant, rigorous, estrangement, alienation, remedial, formidable, influx, lag.* ______________________________
______________________________
______________________________
______________________________

## REFLECTING ON THE JOURNEY

### Skills Learned

Now that you've completed the chapter, share what you've learned about each skill by completing the following chart.

| Skill | What I learned about this skill |
|---|---|
| Identify the causes of events | |
| Identify the effects of events | |
| Express causes, effects, or both through writing | |
| Provide specific examples to support those causes and effects | |
| Read and analyze cause and effect | |

# 14

# Argument

## Writing That Persuades

## READING ROADMAP

### Learning Objectives

**Chapter Goal:** Learn how to write an argument paper.

**Tools to Achieve the Goal:**

- Four Basics of Good Argument (p. 287)
- Diagram: Paragraphs and Essays in Argument (pp. 290–92)
- Sample Paragraph and Rubric (pp. 299–300)
- Profile of Success and Workplace Argument: Stacie Brown (pp. 301–02)
- Professional Argument Essay: John Hawkins, *5 Scientific Reasons that Global Warming Isn't Happening* (pp. 303–05)
- Professional Argument Essay: The Environmental Protection Agency, *Climate Change is Happening* (pp. 305–07)
- Checklist: How to Write Argument (p. 310)

### Key Terms

Skim Chapter 14 before reading. Find these words or terms in **bold** type. Put a check mark next to each once you locate it.

_____ argument
_____ main idea
_____ support
_____ reasons
_____ evidence
_____ assumptions
_____ order of importance
_____ transitions

### Guided Reading for Chapter 14

Fill out the following chart before you begin reading. For each skill, write what you know about that skill and what you would like to know upon completing the chapter. At the end of the chapter, you will be asked to share what you learned about each skill.

| Skill | When I have used this skill | What I want to know about this skill |
|---|---|---|
| Identify an argument | | |
| Identify strong points, evidence, and support for an argument | | |
| Consider opposing views | | |
| Read and analyze argument | | |

# Understand What Argument Is

**Argument** is writing that takes a position on an issue and gives supporting evidence to persuade someone else to accept, or at least consider, the position. Argument is also used to convince someone to take (or not take) an action.

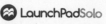

LaunchPadSolo

Visit **LaunchPad Solo for Readers and Writers > Reading > Patterns of Organization** for more tutorials, videos, and practice with patterns of organization.

## **Four Basics** of Good Argument

1 It takes a strong and definite position.

2 It gives good reasons and supporting evidence to defend the position.

3 It considers opposing views.

4 It has enthusiasm and energy from start to finish.

In the following paragraph, the numbers and colors correspond to the Four Basics of Good Argument.

1 Even though I write this blog post on an 88-degree day, I am truly glad that I stopped using my air conditioner, and I urge you to follow my lead. 2 For one thing, going without air conditioning can save a significant amount of money. Last summer, this strategy cut my electricity costs by nearly $2,000, and I am on my way to achieving even higher savings this summer. For another thing, living without air conditioning reduces humans' effect on the environment. Agricultural researcher Stan Cox estimates that air conditioning creates 300 million tons of carbon dioxide ($CO_2$) emissions each year. This amount, he says, is the equivalent of every U.S. household buying an additional car and driving it 7,000 miles annually. Because $CO_2$ is one of the greenhouse gases responsible for trapping heat in our atmosphere, reducing $CO_2$ emissions is essential to curbing climate change. The final reason for going without air conditioning is that it is actually pretty comfortable. The key to staying cool is keeping the blinds down on south-facing windows during the day. It is also a good idea to open windows throughout the home for cross ventilation while turning on ceiling fans to improve air circulation. 3 Although some people argue that using fans is just as bad as switching on the air conditioner, fans use far less electricity. In closing, let me make you a promise: The sooner you give up air conditioning, the sooner you will get comfortable with the change—and the sooner you and the planet will reap the rewards.

4 Argument is enthusiastic and energetic.

Knowing how to make a good argument is one of the most useful skills you can develop.

| | |
|---|---|
| **College** | You argue for or against makeup exams for students who do not do well the first time. |
| **Work** | You need to leave work an hour early one day a week for twelve weeks to take a course. You persuade your boss to allow you to do so. |
| **Everyday life** | You try to negotiate a better price on an item you want to buy. |

In college, writing assignments might include questions or statements such as the following: *Do you agree or disagree with ________? Defend or refute ________. Is ________ fair and just?* In all these cases, use the strategies discussed in this chapter.

## Main Idea in Argument

Your **main idea** in argument is the position you take on the issue (or topic) about which you are writing. When you are free to choose an issue, choose something that matters to you. When you are assigned an issue, try to find some part of it that matters to you. You might try starting with a "should" or "should not" sentence:

**Main idea in argument** **College football players should/should not be paid.**

If you have trouble seeing how an issue matters, talk about it with a partner or write down ideas about it using the following tips.

**Tips for Building Enthusiasm and Energy**

- Imagine yourself arguing your position with someone who disagrees.
- Imagine that your whole grade rests on persuading your instructor to agree with your position.
- Imagine how this issue could affect you or your family personally.
- Imagine that you are representing a large group of people who care about the issue very much and whose lives will be forever changed by it. It is up to you to win their case.

In argument, the topic sentence (in a paragraph) or thesis statement (in an essay) usually includes the issue/topic and your position about it. Here is an example of a topic sentence for a paragraph:

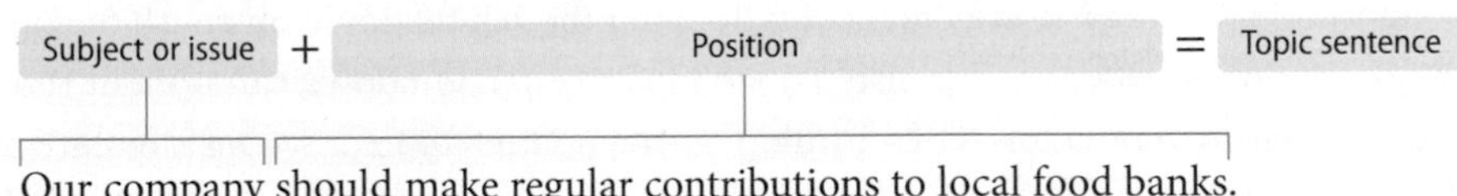
Subject or issue
+
Position
=
Topic sentence
Our company should make regular contributions to local food banks.

Remember that the main idea for an essay can be a little broader than one for a paragraph.

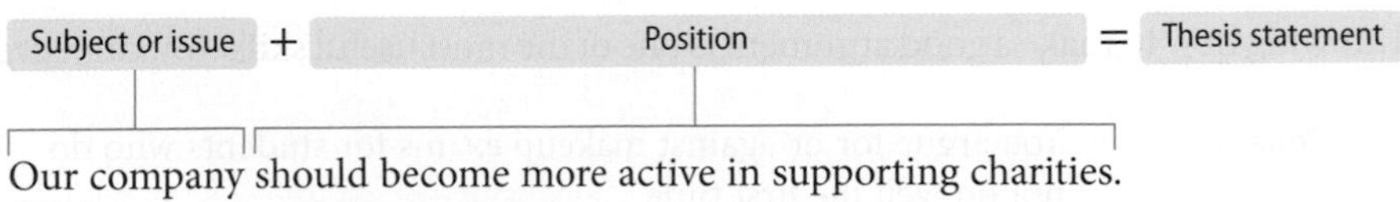
Subject or issue
+
Position
=
Thesis statement
Our company should become more active in supporting charities.

**Tip** Sometimes, the same main idea can be used for a paragraph and an essay, but the essay must develop this point in more detail. (See pp. 68–69.)

Whereas the topic sentence focuses on just one type of charitable organization, the thesis statement sets up a discussion of different ways to help different charities.

**PRACTICE 1** **Writing a statement of your position**

Write a statement of your position for each item.

**Example:**

**Issue: Prisoners' rights**

**Position statement:** *Prisoners should not have more rights and privileges than law-abiding citizens.*

1. Issue: Lab testing on animals

   Position statement: ______________________________

2. Issue: Wearing seatbelts.

   Position statement: ______________________________

3. Issue: Athletes' salaries

   Position statement: ______________________________

4. Issue: Treadmill desks

   Position statement: ______________________________

5. Issue: GMOs

   Position statement: ______________________________

## *Support in Argument*

The paragraph and essay models on pages 290–91 use the topic sentence (paragraph) and thesis statement (essay) from the Main Idea section of this chapter. Both models include the **support** used in all argument writing: the **reasons** for the

**Tip** For more on evidence, see page 292.

## Paragraphs vs. Essays in Argument

For more on the important features of argument, see the Four Basics of Good Argument on page 287.

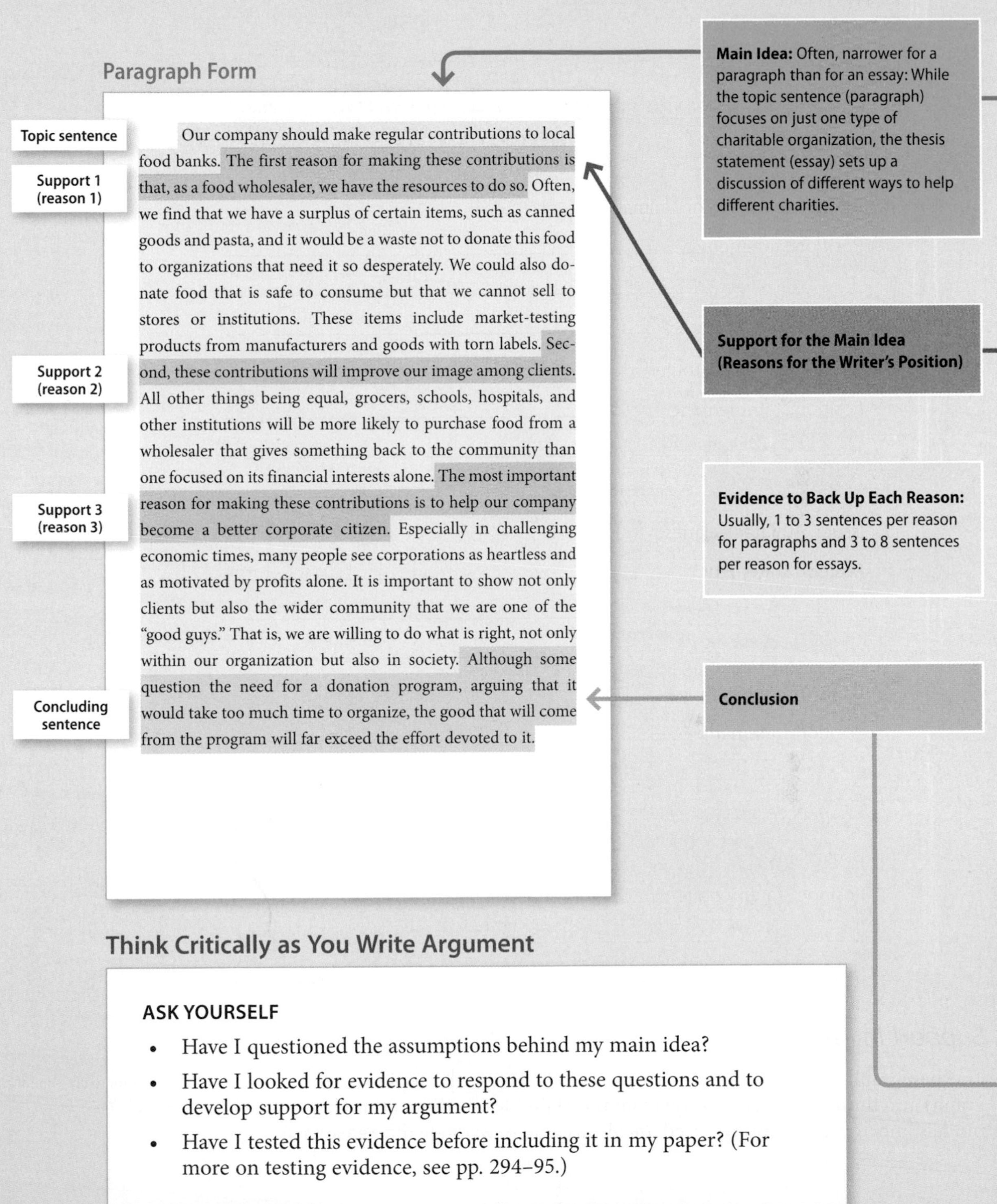

Paragraph Form
Topic sentence
Support 1 (reason 1)
Support 2 (reason 2)
Support 3 (reason 3)
Concluding sentence
Our company should make regular contributions to local food banks. The first reason for making these contributions is that, as a food wholesaler, we have the resources to do so. Often, we find that we have a surplus of certain items, such as canned goods and pasta, and it would be a waste not to donate this food to organizations that need it so desperately. We could also donate food that is safe to consume but that we cannot sell to stores or institutions. These items include market-testing products from manufacturers and goods with torn labels. Second, these contributions will improve our image among clients. All other things being equal, grocers, schools, hospitals, and other institutions will be more likely to purchase food from a wholesaler that gives something back to the community than one focused on its financial interests alone. The most important reason for making these contributions is to help our company become a better corporate citizen. Especially in challenging economic times, many people see corporations as heartless and as motivated by profits alone. It is important to show not only clients but also the wider community that we are one of the "good guys." That is, we are willing to do what is right, not only within our organization but also in society. Although some question the need for a donation program, arguing that it would take too much time to organize, the good that will come from the program will far exceed the effort devoted to it.
Main Idea: Often, narrower for a paragraph than for an essay: While the topic sentence (paragraph) focuses on just one type of charitable organization, the thesis statement (essay) sets up a discussion of different ways to help different charities.
Support for the Main Idea (Reasons for the Writer's Position)
Evidence to Back Up Each Reason: Usually, 1 to 3 sentences per reason for paragraphs and 3 to 8 sentences per reason for essays.
Conclusion


### Think Critically as You Write Argument

**ASK YOURSELF**

- Have I questioned the assumptions behind my main idea?
- Have I looked for evidence to respond to these questions and to develop support for my argument?
- Have I tested this evidence before including it in my paper? (For more on testing evidence, see pp. 294–95.)

Introductory paragraph

1

At the last executive meeting, we discussed several possible ways to improve our company's marketing and advertising and to increase employee morale. Since attending the meeting, I have become convinc effort would help in those areas and more: Our company should become more active in supporting charities.

Thesis statement

First, giving time and money to community organizations is a good way to promote our organization. This approach has worked well for several o petitors. For example, Lanse Industries is v for sponsoring Little League teams throughout the city. Its name is on the back of each uniform, and banners promoting Lanse's new products appear on the ball fields. Lanse gets free promotion of these efforts through articles in the local papers, and according to one company source quoted in the *Hillsburg Gazette*, Lanse's good works in the community have boosted its sales by 5 to 10 percent. Another competitor, Great Deals, has employees serve meals at soup kitchens over the holidays and at least once during the spring or summer. It, too, has gotten great publicity from these efforts,

Topic sentence 1 (reason 1)

2

including a spot on a local TV news show. It is time for our company to start reaping these kinds of benefits.

Second, activities like group volunteering will help employees feel more connected to one another and to their community. Kay Rodriguez, a manag Deals and a good friend of mine, organize pany's group volunteering efforts at the soup kitchens, and she cannot say enough good things about the results. Aside from providing meals to the needy, the volunteering has boosted the morale of Great Deals employees because they understand that they are supporting an important cause in their community. Kay has also noticed that as employees work together at the soup kitchens, they form closer bonds. She says, "Some of these people work on different floors and rarely get to see each other during the work week. Or they just do not have time to talk. But while they work together on the volunteering, I see real connections forming." I know that some members of our executive committee might think it would be too time-consuming to organize companywide volunteering efforts. Kay assures

Topic sentence 2 (reason 2)

3

me, however, that this is not the case and that the rewards of such efforts far exceed the costs in time.

The most important reason for supporting charities is that it is the right thing to do. As a business that depends on the local comm large share of revenue and employees, I believe we owe that community something in return. If our home city does not thrive, how can we? By giving time and money to local organizations, we provide a real service to people, and we present our company as a good and caring neighbor instead of a faceless corporation that could not care less if local citizens went hungry, had trash and graffiti in their parks, or couldn't afford sports teams for their kids. We could make our community proud to have us around.

Topic sentence 3 (reason 3)

Concluding paragraph

I realize that our main goal is to run a profitable and growing business. I do not believe, however, that this aim must exclude doing good in the community. In fact, I see these two goals moving side by side, and hand in hand. When companies give back to local citizens, their businesses benefit, the community benefits, and everyone is pleased by the results.

writer's position backed up by **evidence**. In the essay model, however, the major support points (reasons) are topic sentences for individual paragraphs.

A good way to find strong support for an argument is to return to some of the critical-thinking strategies you learned about in Chapter 1. Let's take another look at the basics.

**Four Basics** of Critical Thinking

1. Be alert to assumptions made by you and others.
2. Question those assumptions.
3. Consider and connect various points of view, even those different from your own.
4. Do not rush to conclusions; instead, remain patient with yourself and others, and keep an open mind.

When writing, you may apply some of these basics while working on an argument paper for English class. Consider the following:

> While working at a local restaurant, your attention is drawn to something on the TV over the restaurant's bar. On the TV, a political commentator and a doctor were debating whether a tax on soda would help reduce obesity.
>
> You are in favor of just about any reasonable approach to fighting obesity, although you are uncertain about a tax on soda (and other sugary beverages) and whether it would work. Even the doctor on TV seemed a little unsure.
>
> After finishing your shift and thinking more about the issue, you begin to see how the pros of such a tax might outweigh the cons but decide to sleep on the issue before coming to any final conclusions. Here is the working main idea as you may write it down in a notebook before going to bed.
>
> **Main idea** Taxing sugary drinks might be a good way to reduce obesity.

### QUESTIONING ASSUMPTIONS TO BUILD EVIDENCE

**Tip** Consider this advice from actor Alan Alda:

*"Begin challenging your own assumptions. Your assumptions are your windows on the world. Scrub them off every once in a while, or the light won't come in."*

The next step in this process is to use key critical-thinking strategies to explore the main idea in more depth. Specifically, it is important to identify some of the **assumptions** (unquestioned ideas or opinions) behind that main idea. You may want to write them down on one half of a sheet of notebook paper. One way to examine these assumptions is to try to put yourself in the shoes of someone opposed to beverage taxes. Then, write these questions on the other half of the notebook paper.

| Assumptions behind main idea | Questions about assumptions |
|---|---|
| Sugary drinks, like soda, energy drinks, and sweetened tea, can make people fat. | But why target sugary drinks instead of other junk food? Aren't french fries just as bad for the waistline as soda is? |
| Taxes on sugary drinks would make people less likely to buy these beverages. | Really? It's easy for me to say that this tax would work because I'm not a big fan of these drinks. But if they taxed coffee, the taxes would have to be pretty big to break my four-cups-a-day habit. |

| Assumptions behind main idea | Questions about assumptions |
| --- | --- |
| *The tax revenues would benefit the public.* | *How much difference would they really make?* |

To answer these questions, you will typically need to turn to some sources recommended by a college librarian, draw on results from an Internet search, and include information from your own experiences and observations. Through those methods, you may gather the following four types of evidence used most often in support of arguments.

- *Facts:* Statements or observations that can be proved. Statistics—real numbers from actual studies—can be persuasive factual evidence.
- *Examples:* Specific information or experiences that support your position.
- *Expert opinions:* The opinions of people considered knowledgeable about your topic because of their educational or work background, their research into the topic, or other qualifications. It is important to choose these sources carefully. For example, an economics professor might be knowledgeable about the possible benefits and drawbacks of beverage taxes. He or she probably wouldn't be the best source of information on the health effects of soda, however.
- *Predictions:* Forecasts of the possible outcomes of events or actions. These forecasts are the informed views of experts, not the best guesses of nonexperts.

The following chart shows the evidence that could be pulled together to address assumptions and questions about them. (Your original questions can be revised and expanded as you explore your topic further.)

**Tip** When looking for evidence about assumptions, always seek the most reliable sources of information.

| Assumptions/questions to investigate | Evidence in response |
| --- | --- |
| To what degree do sugary drinks contribute to obesity? | **Fact:** According to the Centers for Disease Control and Prevention, about half of all Americans get a major portion of their daily calories from sweetened beverages.<br>**Fact:** In the *Journal of Pediatrics,* Robert Murray reported that one-fourth of U.S. teenagers drink as many as four cans of soda or fruit drinks a day, each one containing about 150 calories. That translates to a total of 600 calories a day, the equivalent of an additional meal.<br>**Expert opinion:** Dr. Richard Adamson, senior scientific consultant for the American Beverage Association, says, "Blaming one specific product or ingredient as the root cause of obesity defies common sense. Instead, there are many contributing factors, including regular physical activity." |
| Do sugary drinks deserve to be targeted more than other dietary factors that can contribute to obesity? | **Example (from Jess's personal experience):** My brother, his wife, and their three kids are all big soda drinkers, and they are all overweight. They also eat lots of junk food, however, so it is hard to tell how much the soda is to blame for their weight.<br>**Fact:** The Center for Science in the Public Interest says that sugary beverages are more likely to cause weight gain than solid foods are. After eating solid food, people tend to reduce their consumption of other calorie sources. Unlike solid foods, however, sugary beverages do not make people feel full. Therefore, they may add on calories to satisfy their hunger. |

| Assumptions/questions to investigate | Evidence in response |
|---|---|
| To what degree would taxes on sugary drinks discourage people from buying these beverages and also reduce obesity? | **Expert opinion/fact:** Several researchers say that the taxes would have to be pretty significant to affect consumer behavior. The average national tax on a 12-ounce bottle of soda is 5 cents, and that has not provided enough discouragement.<br>**Prediction:** In the *New England Journal of Medicine,* Kelly D. Brownell says that a penny-per-ounce tax on sugary beverages could reduce consumption of these beverages by more than 10 percent. |
| Would the taxes have any other benefits? | **Prediction:** Kelly D. Brownell says that by reducing the consumption of sugary beverages, the taxes could help cut public expenditures on obesity. Each year, about $79 billion goes toward the health-care costs of overweight and obese individuals. Approximately half of these costs are paid by taxpayers.<br>**Expert opinion:** Brownell also believes that the tax revenues could and should be used for programs to prevent childhood obesity. |

**PRACTICE 2** **Deepening the search for evidence**

Come up with at least one other question that could be raised about the sugary drinks tax issue. Then, list the type(s) of evidence (such as personal examples, an expert opinion from a scientific study, or a prediction from a business leader) that could help answer the question.

**Question(s):** ______________________________

______________________________

**Type(s) of evidence:** ______________________________

In the process of investigating your assumptions, it is important to gather not only good support but also some opposing views (one of the Four Basics of Good Argument). One of the opposing views, from Dr. Richard Adamson of the American Beverage Association, may make you stop and evaluate the credibility or bias of the source. Because he represents the interests of the beverage industry, he might not offer a completely balanced opinion on the health effects of sweetened drinks, but you may decide that as long as you mentioned his affiliation with the beverage industry, his point might be worth including in the paper.

In reviewing your evidence, consider the following tips as well:

### Testing evidence

- Consider your audience's view of the issue. Are audience members likely to agree with you, to be uncommitted, or to be hostile? Then, make sure your evidence would be convincing to a typical member of your audience.

- Reread your evidence from an opponent's perspective, looking for ways to knock it down. Anticipate your opponent's objections, and include evidence to answer them.
- Do not overgeneralize. Statements about what everyone else does or what always happens are easy to disprove. It is better to use facts (including statistics), specific examples, expert opinions, and informed predictions.
- Make sure you have considered every important angle of the issue.
- Reread the evidence to make sure it provides good support for your position. Also, the evidence must be relevant to your argument.

**PRACTICE 3** **Reviewing the evidence**

For each of the following positions, one piece of evidence is weak: It does not support the position. Circle the letter of the weak evidence, and, in the space provided, state why it is weak.

**Example:**

**Position: Advertisements should not use skinny models.**

**Reason: Skinny should not be promoted as ideal.**

**a. Three friends of mine became anorexic trying to get skinny.**

**(b.) Everyone knows that most people are not that thin.**

**c. A survey of girls shows that they think that they should be as thin as models.**

**d. People can endanger their health trying to fit the skinny "ideal" promoted in advertisements.**

**Not strong evidence because** *"everyone knows" is not strong evidence; everyone obviously doesn't know that.*

1. Position: People who own guns should not be allowed to keep them at home.

   Reason: It is dangerous to keep a gun in the house.

   a. Guns can go off by accident.

   b. Keeping guns at home has been found to increase the risk of home suicides and adolescent suicides.

   c. Just last week, a story in the newspaper told about a man who, in a fit of rage, took his gun out of the drawer and shot his wife.

   d. Guns can be purchased easily.

   Not strong evidence because ______________________________

   ______________________________

2. Position: Schoolchildren in the United States should go to school all year.

   Reason: Year-round schooling promotes better learning.

   a. All my friends have agreed that we would like to end the long summer break.
   b. A survey of teachers across the country showed that children's learning improved when they had multiple shorter vacations rather than entire summers off.
   c. Many children are bored and restless after three weeks of vacation and would be better off returning to school.
   d. Test scores improved when a school system in Colorado went to year-round school sessions.

   Not strong evidence because ______________________________

   ______________________________________________

3. Position: The "three strikes and you're out" law that forces judges to send people to jail after three convictions should be revised.

   Reason: Basing decisions about sentencing on numbers alone is neither reasonable nor fair.

   a. A week ago, a man who stole a slice of pizza was sentenced to eight to ten years in prison because it was his third conviction.
   b. The law makes prison overcrowding even worse.
   c. Judges always give the longest sentence possible anyway.
   d. The law too often results in people getting major prison sentences for minor crimes.

   Not strong evidence because ______________________________

   ______________________________________________

After reviewing the evidence, you may need to refine the initial position.

**Revised main idea** To help address the obesity crisis, states should place significant taxes on sugary beverages.

Notice the removal of the word *might* that was part of the original main idea. Having done some research, you now believe strongly that the taxes are a good idea—as long as they are high enough to make a significant dent in consumption.

Before writing a paper, create a rough outline stating the main idea and the major support points—the reasons for the position expressed in the main idea. The reasons are based on the evidence you gathered.

### Rough outline

**Main idea:** To help address the obesity crisis, states should place significant taxes on sugary beverages.

**Support/reasons:**

Sugary drinks are a major contributor to obesity.

As long as they are significant, taxes on these drinks could reduce consumption.

The taxes could fund programs targeting childhood obesity.

### WRITING THE CONCLUSION

Your conclusion is your last opportunity to convince readers of your position. Make it memorable and forceful. Remind readers of the stand you are taking and the rightness of this stand, even in the face of opposing views.

Before writing your conclusion, imagine that you are an attorney making a final, impassioned appeal to the judge in an important case. Then, put this energy into words with a conclusion that drives your point home. (See a sample conclusion on p. 298.)

## *Organization in Argument*

Most arguments are organized by **order of importance**, starting with the least important evidence and saving the most convincing reason and evidence for last.

**Tip** For more on order of importance, see page 78.

Use **transitions** to move your readers smoothly from one supporting reason to another. Here are some of the transitions you might use in your argument.

### Common Transitions in Argument

| | |
|---|---|
| above all | more important |
| also | most important |
| best of all | one fact/another fact |
| especially | one reason/another reason |
| for example | one thing/another thing |
| in addition | remember |
| in fact | the first (second, third) point |
| in particular | worst of all |
| in the first (second, third) place | |

The sample that follows uses order of importance to organize the argument in favor of taxes on sugary drinks. The transitions are highlighted in bold.

You will notice that this draft doesn't incorporate all the evidence from the chart on pages 293–94; instead, it includes only the evidence believed to offer the strongest support for the main idea. It also includes an opposing view.

To help address the obesity crisis, states should place significant taxes on sugary beverages, such as soda, sweetened tea and fruit juices, and energy drinks. These drinks are a good target for taxation because they are a major contributor to obesity. According to the Centers for Disease Control and Prevention, about half of all Americans get a major portion of their daily calories from sweetened beverages. **In addition**, the *Journal of Pediatrics* reports that one-fourth of U.S. teenagers get as many as 600 calories a day from soda or fruit drinks. This consumption is the equivalent of an additional meal. **Another reason to tax sugary drinks is that** such taxation could reduce consumption. However, it is important that these taxes be significant because taxes of just a few additional pennies per can or bottle probably wouldn't deter consumers. According to Kelly D. Brownell, director of the Rudd Center for Food Policy and Obesity, a penny-per-ounce tax on sugary beverages could cut consumption of these beverages by more than 10 percent. It could also reduce the estimated $79 billion of taxpayer money spent each year on health care for overweight and obese individuals. **The most important reason to tax sugary drinks is that** the money from such taxes could be used to prevent future cases of obesity. As Brownell notes, the taxes could fund antiobesity programs aimed at educating children about healthy diets and encouraging them to exercise. Some people who are opposed to taxing sugary beverages, such as Dr. Richard Adamson of the American Beverage Association, argue that it is unfair to blame one product for our expanding waistlines. It is true that overconsumption of soda and other sweetened beverages is just one cause of obesity. Nevertheless, targeting this one cause could play a vital, lasting role in a larger campaign to bring this major health crisis under control.

### PRACTICE 4 Using transitions in argument

The following argument essay encourages students to get involved in service work during college. It was written by Jorge Roque, an Iraq War veteran and Miami-Dade College student who is vice president of a service fraternity.

After reading Jorge's essay, fill in the blanks with transitions. You are not limited to the ones listed in the box on page 297.

Even for the busiest student, getting involved in service organizations is worth the time and effort it takes. At one point, after I had returned from Iraq, was homeless, and was experiencing posttraumatic stress disorder, I was referred to Veteran Love, a nonprofit organization that helps disabled ex-soldiers, and it helped me when I needed it most. When I was back on track, I knew that I wanted to help others. I was working and going to school with little extra time, but getting involved has been important in ways I had not expected.

______________________________________________________________

________ you meet many new people and form a new and larger network of friends and colleagues. You also learn new skills, like organization, project management, communication, teamwork, and public speaking. The practical experience I have now is more than I could have gotten from a class, and I have met people who want to help me in my career.

______________________________________________________________

________________ you help other people and learn about them. You feel as if you have something valuable to give. You also feel part of something larger than yourself. So often, students are not connected to meaningful communities and work, and service helps you while you help others.

______________________________________________________ service work makes you feel better about yourself and your abilities. What I am doing is important and real, and I feel better than I ever have because of my service involvement. If you get involved with community service of any kind, you will become addicted to it. You get more than you could ever give.

# Evaluate Argument

To become a more successful writer, it is important not only to understand the Four Basics of Good Argument but also to read and evaluate examples. In this section, you will have the opportunity to use a sample rubric to analyze or evaluate the samples of argument writing provided. By using this rubric, you will gain a better understanding of how the components of good argument work together to create a successful paragraph or essay.

Read the following sample argument paragraph. Using the Four Basics of Good Argument and the sample grading rubric, decide what grade this paragraph would earn. Explain your answer.

**Assignment** Concealed carry laws are becoming increasingly controversial, especially when people feel as though their rights are being restricted or that they are in danger. Write a paragraph that takes a position on the question: Should students be allowed to carry a concealed weapon on a college campus? Support your argument with specific examples and evidence.

**College students should be allowed to carry concealed weapons on campus if they are legally permitted to do so. To have a firearm legally, people are required to apply for a FOID card (Firearms Owner Identification) and subject themselves to a background check. This process is meant to ensure that the people who are allowed to carry these weapons have no history of violence or mental illness that may create future problems. Although there has not been a security issue at my own campus, I would**

**like to know that I have the option to protect myself if a situation like this occurred. In addition, the legal age for owning specific firearms is eighteen or twenty-one, depending on what type of gun a person chooses to carry. I am safer with a weapon than without.**

**Analysis of Sample Paragraph:**

Sample rubric

| Element | Grading criteria | Point: Comment |
|---|---|---|
| Appropriateness | • Did the student follow the assignment directions? | ____/5: |
| Main idea | • Does the paper clearly state a strong main idea in a complete sentence? | ____/10: |
| Support | • Is the main idea developed with specific support, including specific details and examples?<br>• Is there enough support to make the main idea evident to the reader?<br>• Is all the support directly related to the main idea?<br>• Is there a counterargument present at some point? | ____/10: |
| Organization | • Is the writing logically organized?<br>• Does the student use transitions (*also, for example, sometimes,* and so on) to move the reader from one point to another? | ____/10: |
| Conclusion | • Does the conclusion remind the reader of the main idea?<br>• Does it make an observation based on the support? | ____/5: |
| Grammar | • Is the writing free of the four most serious errors? (See Chapters 16–19.)<br>• Is the sentence structure clear?<br>• Does the student choose words that clearly express his or her meaning?<br>• Are the words spelled correctly?<br>• Is the punctuation correct? | ____/10: |
| | | TOTAL POINTS: ____/50 |

# Profile of Success

## Argument in the Real World

COURTESY OF STACIE BROWN

**Stacie Brown**

Legal Assistant

**Background** I grew up in an exceptionally small town (population 99) where it was easy for me to excel in high school—and I did—because all the teachers would know why I didn't do well if I didn't. After my dad died during my senior year of high school, though, school was just something I had to finish.

After high school, I couldn't settle on anything because everything seemed useless or pointless. Hoping to find my way, I enrolled in Blinn College for the first time. I ended up dropping two classes and failing the other two, one of which was English 1301. A few years later, I enrolled in a veterinary technician course, but I soon decided that also wasn't for me.

I started dating my husband a while after that and soon became pregnant. Twenty-five years old, no career plan, no college degree, baby on the way—I knew I had to get my act together. With support from family and friends, I enrolled in college for the third time.

While at Blinn College, a few encouraging teachers helped me to realize my potential, and I started writing again. (I had put the pen down after my dad died.) Indeed, I graduated Blinn College with honors. My long-term goal is to become a novelist.

After getting my associate's degree, I started my career in the administrative field as a legal assistant, and I get to use my writing and editing skills every day to communicate with clients, attorneys, courts, and other business entities. I am now situated to pursue my passion. My career has taught me that everyone has at least one remarkable story. It's up to me to write it.

**Degrees/Colleges** Associate of Applied Science, Blinn College

**Writing at Work** I write business e-mails, letters, memos, legal pleadings, and other legal documents. Working with clients often involves discussing uncomfortable or difficult topics. Addressing issues related to billing are necessary not only for a business to succeed but also for building a strong, successful attorney-client relationship. Many times, an attorney needs to communicate with not only a client but also the client's family member—and family members can be quite inexorable. One must respond in a firm but tactful manner.

# Read and Analyze Argument

In this section, the Profile of Success illustrates how Stacie Brown uses argument in her job in a legal office. Next, two professional articles present different positions in the debate surrounding climate change. The first one makes the claim that climate change is not a problem and is not occurring at present. The second article, a piece by the Environmental Protection Agency of the United States, argues that climate change is a very real threat to the environment. Both articles present a clear position and evidence to support that position. By reading two perspectives on the same issue, you can start to understand your own position on the subject. All good arguments start with some degree of research to see what has already been written on the topic and to better inform the writer. Read these selections, pay attention to the vocabulary, and answer the questions in the margin. They will help you read critically.

## *Workplace Argument*

The following is an example of an e-mail pertaining to billing.

Dear John Doe:

We recently sent your most recent invoice (November 2014) to the address we have in our file: 555 No Name Street, Anywhere, Texas 55555. It was returned to us as "not deliverable as addressed, unable to forward." As a result, I am e-mailing your November 2014 invoice, which is attached. If the mailing address we have on file is incorrect, please notify our office immediately of your correct mailing address.

Additionally, when we last spoke about payment arrangements, you agreed to send a money order once you received your tax return, which you indicated would be in ten to twelve days. It has been six months since that phone conversation, and our office has yet to receive payment of any kind. As you are aware, our office policy dictates that attorneys may not continue work for a client for which there is no money left in the Trust account. This means that any pending or future issues related to your case will not be considered until your balance is paid in full.

If you believe there has been an error in receiving payment, please contact our office to discuss. Otherwise, please consider this e-mail a formal demand for payment in full. If your payment is not received within fifteen days from the date of this e-mail, our office will have no choice but to begin formal collection actions. These actions will, of course, increase the amount owed to this office. I sincerely hope this will not be necessary.

Thank you,
Stacie
Stacie Brown
Legal Assistant
Law Firm
555 No Name Street
Anywhere, Texas 55555
Phone: 555.555.5555
Fax: 555.555.5556
E-mail: emailaddress@domain.net

1. Double-underline the **thesis statement**.
2. Circle the **transitions** that introduce the different reasons supporting the argument.
3. Underline the parts of the e-mail that present each supporting reason for the argument.
4. Does this workplace sample follow the Four Basics of Good Argument (p. 287)?

   Why or why not? ______________________________

*Professional Argument Essay 1: Climate Change Is Not Happening*

John Hawkins

# 5 Scientific Reasons That Global Warming Isn't Happening

John Hawkins is a well-known writer and political commentator. Not only does Hawkins write for publications such as *The Huffington Post*, *Washington Examiner*, and *The Hill*, he also makes numerous regular appearances on ABC News, MSNBC, and C-Span. Throughout his career, he has spent a great deal of time interviewing and working with conservatives and he is the founder of Rightroots group, an organization that raises money to fund conservative political candidates nationwide.

This piece first appeared on TownHall.com on February 18, 2014.

**Vocabulary development** Underline these words as you read: *hinging, unverifiable, skeptical, assertion, upswing, consensus, mainstream, talking point, tipping point, troposphere,* and *hasty.*

**Guiding question** As you read this essay, identify what specific evidence the writer uses to support the main argument.

**hinging:** that something is based on or dependent on

**unverifiable:** not able to determine the truth of

**skeptical:** showing doubt

**assertion:** a positive statement, often without support

**upswing:** a marked increase or improvement

**consensus:** general agreement

**mainstream:** the dominant tendency

**talking point:** a fact that supports only one side

**tipping point:** the point at which a minor development becomes a major crisis

**troposphere:** the lowest layer of the atmosphere

**hasty:** moving or acting quickly

1 How did global warming discussions end up hinging on what's happening with polar bears, unverifiable predictions of what will happen in a hundred years, and whether people are "climate deniers" or "global warming cultists"? If this is a scientific topic, why aren't we spending more time discussing the science involved? Why aren't we talking about the evidence and the actual data involved? Why aren't we looking at the predictions that were made and seeing if they match up to the results? If this is such an open and shut case, why are so many people who care about science skeptical? Many Americans have long since thought that the best scientific evidence available suggested that man wasn't causing any sort of global warming. However, now, we can go even further and suggest that the planet isn't warming at all.

**Predict** What reasons can you think of that may support the foregoing argument?

2 There hasn't been any global warming since 1997: If nothing changes in the next year, we're going to have kids who graduate from high school who will have never seen any "global warming" during their lifetimes. That's right; the temperature of the planet has essentially been flat for 17 years. This isn't a controversial assertion either. Even the former Director of the Climate Research Unit (CRU) of the University of East Anglia, Phil Jones, admits that it's true. Since the planet was cooling from 1940 to 1975 and the upswing in temperature afterward only lasted 22 years, a 17-year pause is a big deal. It also begs an obvious question: How can we be experiencing global warming if there's no actual "global warming"?

3 There is no scientific consensus that global warming is occurring and caused by man: Questions are not decided by "consensus." In fact, many scientific theories that were once widely believed to be true were made irrelevant by new evidence.

**Reflect** What have you noticed about our climate? Is it becoming warmer or colder? Does that affect you?

Just to name one of many, many examples, in the early seventies, scientists believed global cooling was occurring. However, once the planet started to warm up, they changed their minds. Yet, the primary "scientific" argument for global warming is that there is a "scientific consensus" that it's occurring. Setting aside the fact that's not a scientific argument, even if that ever was true (and it really wasn't), it's certainly not true anymore. Over 31,000 scientists have signed on to a petition saying humans aren't causing global warming. More than 1000 scientists signed on to another report saying there is no global warming at all. There are tens of thousands of well-educated, mainstream scientists who do not agree that global warming is occurring at all, and people who share their opinion are taking a position grounded in science.

**Identify** What significance does the amount of Arctic ice have on the planet?

4 Arctic ice is up 50% since 2012: The loss of Arctic ice has been a big talking point for people who believe global warming is occurring. Some people have even predicted that all of the Arctic ice would melt by now because of global warming. Yet, Arctic ice is up 50% since 2012. How much Arctic ice really matters is an open question since the very limited evidence we have suggests that a few decades ago, there was less ice than there is today, but the same people who thought the drop in ice was noteworthy should at least agree that the increase is important as well.

5 Climate models showing global warming have been wrong over and over: These future projections of what global warming will do to the planet have been based on climate models. Essentially, scientists make assumptions about how much of an impact different factors will have; they guess how much of a change there will be and then they project changes over time. Unfortunately, almost all of these models showing huge temperature gains have turned out to be wrong.

**Reflect** How credible are the sources that the author is using? What makes you say that?

6 Former NASA scientist Dr. Roy Spencer says that climate models used by government agencies to create policies "have failed miserably." Spencer analyzed 90 climate models against surface temperature and satellite temperature data, and found that more than 95 percent of the models "have over-forecast the warming trend since 1979, whether we use their own surface temperature dataset (HadCRUT4), or our satellite dataset of lower tropospheric temperatures (UAH)."

**Identify** Can you clearly summarize what the author means by "garbage in, garbage out?" Do you agree with his statement?

7 There's an old saying in programming that goes, "Garbage in, garbage out." In other words, if the assumptions and data you put into the models are faulty, then the results will be worthless. If the climate models that show a dire impact because of global warming aren't reliable—and they're not—then the long-term projections they make are meaningless.

8 Predictions about the impact of global warming have already been proven wrong: The debate over global warming has been going on long enough that we've had time to see whether some of the predictions people made about it have panned out in the real world. For example, Al Gore predicted all the Arctic ice would be gone by 2013. In 2005, the *Independent* ran an article saying that the Arctic had entered a death spiral.

9 Scientists fear that the Arctic has now entered an irreversible phase of warming which will accelerate the loss of the polar sea ice that has helped to keep the climate stable for thousands of years. . . . The greatest fear is that the Arctic has reached a "tipping point" beyond which nothing can reverse the continual loss of sea ice and with it the massive land glaciers of Greenland, which will raise sea levels dramatically. Of course, the highway is still there.

10 Meanwhile, Arctic ice is up 50% since 2012. James Hansen of NASA fame predicted that the West Side Highway in New York would be under water by now because of global warming.

11 If the climate models and the predictions about global warming aren't even close to being correct, wouldn't it be more scientific to reject hasty action based on faulty data so that we can further study the issue and find out what's really going on?

**Tip** For reading advice, see Chapter 1.

1. Double-underline the **thesis statement.**
2. In your own words, what is the main idea of this article? ______________
3. Briefly summarize the article, making sure to include all main ideas. ______________
4. Does the author consider counterarguments? What are they? ______________

Respond to one of the following assignments in a paragraph or essay.

1. According to the author, what are the definitions of *global warming* and *global cooling*? What evidence does the author provide to support his claims that either one is or is not happening currently? Is enough evidence provided to support those claims?
2. In paragraph 9, Hawkins writes about Arctic ice and the claim that global warming and climate change has created an inevitable tipping point for our planet. Do you agree or disagree with this claim? Explain your answer.

## *Professional Argument Essay 2: Climate Change Is Happening*

Environmental Protection Agency

# Climate Change Is Happening

The U.S. Environmental Protection Agency (EPA) was formed in 1970 in response to concern about pollution and how it might be affecting the country. By creating this government agency, federal research, monitoring, standard-setting, and enforcement activities

**potentially:** possible but not happening yet
**climate:** the general weather conditions of a region, averaged over a series of years
**carbon dioxide:** a colorless, odorless, fireproof gas, present in the atmosphere and formed during breathing, usually obtained from coal or natural gas
**deforestation:** to clear of trees
**adapted:** to adjust or modify

connected to pollution and the environment have been consolidated to "work for a cleaner, healthier environment for the American People."

The following article was posted on the EPA's Web site under the heading "Climate Change: Basic Information" on March 18, 2014.

**Vocabulary development** Underline these words as you read: *potentially, climate, carbon dioxide, deforestation,* and *adapted.*

**Guiding question** According to the EPA, how is climate change affecting humans?

1 Our Earth is warming. Earth's average temperature has risen by 1.4°F over the past century, and is projected to rise another 2 to 11.5°F over the next hundred years. Small changes in the average temperature of the planet can translate to large and potentially dangerous shifts in climate and weather.

**Predict** After reading the first paragraph, what types of evidence do you expect to see in this article? For example: Do you think the agency will rely on statistics and facts? Personal experiences? Data trends over decades or centuries? Why do you think this?

2 The evidence is clear. Rising global temperatures have been accompanied by changes in weather and climate. Many places have seen changes in rainfall, resulting in more floods, droughts, or intense rain, as well as more frequent and severe heat waves. The planet's oceans and glaciers have also experienced some big changes—oceans are warming and becoming more acidic, ice caps are melting, and sea levels are rising. As these and other changes become more pronounced in the coming decades, they will likely present challenges to our society and our environment.

3 Humans are largely responsible for recent climate change. Over the past century, human activities have released large amounts of carbon dioxide and other greenhouse gases into the atmosphere. The majority of greenhouse gases come from burning fossil fuels to produce energy, although deforestation, industrial processes, and some agricultural practices also emit gases into the atmosphere.

**Reflect** Have you experienced extreme weather (cold, hot, wet, dry) in the past few years? Does that weather fit the general climate of your area? Why or why not?

4 Greenhouse gases act like a blanket around Earth, trapping energy in the atmosphere and causing it to warm. This phenomenon is called the greenhouse effect and is natural and necessary to support life on Earth. However, the buildup of greenhouse gases can change Earth's climate and result in dangerous effects to human health and welfare and to ecosystems.

**Identify** What specific choices is the article referring to?

5 The choices we make today will affect the amount of greenhouse gases we put in the atmosphere in the near future and for years to come.

### Climate Change Affects Everyone

**Identify** The EPA says that humans are able to adapt to changing conditions. What evidence does the agency give to support that claim?

6 Our lives are connected to the climate. Human societies have adapted to the relatively stable climate we have enjoyed since the last ice age, which ended several thousand years ago. A warming climate will bring changes that can affect our water supplies, agriculture, power and transportation systems, the natural environment, and even our own health and safety.

7 Some changes to the climate are unavoidable. Carbon dioxide can stay in the atmosphere for nearly a century, so Earth will continue to warm in the coming

decades. The warmer it gets, the greater the risk for more severe changes to the climate and Earth's system. Although it's difficult to predict the exact impacts of climate change, what's clear is that the climate we are accustomed to is no longer a reliable guide for what to expect in the future.

8 We can reduce the risks we will face from climate change. By making choices that reduce greenhouse gas pollution, and preparing for the changes that are already underway, we can reduce risks from climate change. Our decisions today will shape the world our children and grandchildren will live in.

**Summarize** Write a brief summary about what you read.

**Tip** For reading advice, see Chapter 1.

1. Double-underline the **thesis statement.**
2. What is the main idea of this article? ______________________________

   ______________________________
3. What counterarguments do you see in this article? ______________________________

   ______________________________
4. How does the EPA think humans have affected climate change? ______________________________

   ______________________________

Respond to one of the following assignments in a paragraph or essay.

1. What do humans do that cause climate change? Do you think we would alter our behavior to save the planet? Explain your answer.
2. In paragraph 2, the EPA notes extreme weather patterns that could be connected to global warming. Do you agree with this connection or not? Explain your answer.

# Write Your Own Argument

In this section, you will write your own argument based on one of the following assignments. For help, refer to the How to Write Argument checklist on page 310.

**ASSIGNMENT OPTIONS** **Writing about college, work, and everyday life**

Write an argument paragraph or essay on one of the following topics or on one of your own choice.

**College** • Take a position on a controversial issue on your campus. If you need help coming up with topics, you might consult the campus newspaper.

→

- Argue for or against the use of standardized tests or placement tests. Make sure to research different positions on the tests to support your argument and address opposing views. Many schools use placement tests for incoming students to determine what courses they are prepared to take. If your school has one, think about what it tested and how it affected your schedule or the courses you have to take. One Web site you might consult is standardizedtests.procon.org.
- Within the past few years, the media have started to discuss student loans and how they often cause a college student to enter the workforce deeply in debt. Does it cost too much to attend college? Is there a way, other than student loans, for a potential student to be able to afford a college education? Take one clear position on the issue and support that position with evidence.

**Work**

- Argue for a change in company policy such as a new chain of command, clearer job descriptions, or more transparency in the hiring process.
- Argue for something that you would like to get at work, such as a promotion, a raise, or a flexible schedule. Explain why you deserve what you are asking for, and give specific examples.
- Argue for an improvement in your workplace, such as the addition of a bike rack, new chairs in the break room, or a place to swap books or magazines. Make sure your request is reasonable in cost and will be beneficial to a significant number of employees.

**Everyday life**

- Take a position on a controversial issue in your community.
- Choose a community organization that you belong to, and write about why it is important. Try to persuade your readers to join.
- Oscar Wilde (1854–1900), a famous Irish writer, once commented, "Most people are other people. Their thoughts are someone else's opinions, their lives a mimicry,[1] their passions a quotation." Write an argument that supports or opposes Wilde's views, giving reasons and examples for your position.

1. **mimicry:** an imitation of something else

## ASSIGNMENT OPTIONS Reading and writing critically

Complete one of the following assignments, which ask you to apply the critical thinking, reading, and writing skills discussed in Chapter 1.

### WRITING CRITICALLY ABOUT READINGS

The article from *The Daily Vidette* titled "ISU Restroom Change Shows Commitment to Diversity" (p. 227) and John Tierney's essay, "Yes, Money Can Buy Happiness" (p. 257) both take a strong position on an issue. That position can be expressed either implicitly (it requires you to use clues in the paper to

determine the position) or explicitly (it is clearly identified). Read or review these pieces, and then follow these steps:

1. **Summarize** Briefly summarize the two works, listing major examples and details.
2. **Analyze** What features of argument do you see in each essay?
3. **Synthesize** Using examples from one or both of the two essays and from your own experience, describe the features that make an argument successful and convincing. Think of features beyond those in the Four Basics of Good Argument.
4. **Evaluate** In your opinion, are strongly focused arguments or subtler arguments more effective? Or do both types of writing have a place? Explain your answer.

**Tip** For a reminder of how to summarize, analyze, synthesize, and evaluate, see the Reading and Writing Critically box on page 21.

### WRITING ABOUT IMAGES

The following image illustrates the concept of climate change as it affects animals, not just humans.

SMETEK/GETTY IMAGES

Study the photograph, and complete the following steps.

1. **Read the image** Ask yourself: What details are you drawn to, and why? What emotions or reactions does the melting glacier or stranded animals bring about in you? (For more information on reading images, see Chapter 1.)

2. **Write an argument** Write a paragraph or essay in which you respond to this image and discuss the argument you think it is making. How effective do you find the visual argument? Is it a good way to convey the effects of climate change? Why or why not? Include the details and reactions from step 1.

### WRITING TO SOLVE A PROBLEM

Read or review the discussion of problem solving in Chapter 1 (pp. 28–30). Then, consider the following problem.

**Your friend/child/relative has just turned sixteen and is planning to drop out of high school. He has always done poorly, and if he drops out, he can increase his hours at the restaurant where he works. You think that this idea is terrible for many reasons.**

*(Continued on page 311.)*

### CHECKLIST

#### How to Write Argument

| Steps | Details |
|---|---|
| ☐ Narrow and explore your topic. See Chapter 3. | • Make the topic more specific.<br>• Prewrite to get ideas about the narrowed topic. |
| ☐ Write a topic sentence (paragraph) or thesis statement (essay). See Chapter 3. | • State your position on your topic. |
| ☐ Support your point. See Chapter 4. | • Come up with reasons and evidence to back up your position. |
| ☐ Write a draft. See Chapter 5. | • Make a plan that puts the reasons in a logical order.<br>• Include a topic sentence (paragraph) or thesis statement (essay) and all the reasons and supporting evidence. |
| ☐ Revise your draft. See Chapter 5. | • Make sure it has *all* the Four Basics of Good Argument.<br>• Make sure you include transitions to move readers smoothly from one reason to the next. |
| ☐ Edit your revised draft. See Parts 3 through 6. | • Correct errors in grammar, spelling, word use, and punctuation. |

**Assignment** In a group or on your own, come up with various reasons in support of your decision. Consider, too, your friend's/child's/relative's possible objections to your argument, and account for them. Then, write an argument paragraph or essay to persuade him to complete high school. Give at least three solid reasons, and support your reasons with good evidence or examples. You might start with the following sentence:

**There are so many important reasons to stay in school and get your high school diploma.**

## Chapter Review

1. Argument is writing ______________________________
______________________________________________
2. What are the Four Basics of Good Argument?
______________________________________________
______________________________________________
______________________________________________
______________________________________________
3. The topic sentence (paragraph) or thesis statement (essay) in an argument should include what two elements? ______________________________
______________________________________________
4. What three types of information make good evidence? ______________________________
______________________________________________
5. Why do you need to be aware of opposing views? ______________________________
______________________________________________
6. Write sentences using the following vocabulary words: *hinging, unverifiable, skeptical, assertion, upswing, consensus, mainstream, talking point, tipping point, hasty, potentially, climate, deforestation*, and *adapted.* ______________________________
______________________________________________
______________________________________________
______________________________________________
______________________________________________
______________________________________________

# REFLECTING ON THE JOURNEY

## Skills Learned

Now that you've completed the chapter, share what you've learned about each skill by completing the following chart.

| Skill | What I learned about this skill |
|---|---|
| Identify an argument | |
| Identify strong points, evidence, and support for an argument | |
| Consider opposing views | |
| Read and analyze argument | |

# Part 3

# The Four Most Serious Errors



"I write directions, instructions, captions for photographs, and descriptions of my art."

—Ali K., student

15

# The Basic Sentence

## The Four Most Serious Errors

This part of the book focuses first on the four grammar errors that people most often notice.

**The Four Most Serious Errors**

1. Fragments (Chapter 16)
2. Run-ons (Chapter 17)
3. Problems with subject-verb agreement (Chapter 18)
4. Problems with verb form and tense (Chapter 19)

If you can edit your writing to correct these four errors, your grades will improve.

This chapter reviews the basic sentence elements you will need to understand to find and fix the four most serious errors.

LaunchPadSolo

Visit **LaunchPad Solo for Readers and Writers > Grammar > Parts of Speech and Basic Sentences** for more tutorials, videos, and practice with crafting paragraphs.

## GRAMMAR & MECHANICS ROADMAP

### An Overview

**This Chapter Identifies the Following Trouble Spots**

- The four most important grammar errors to find and fix
- The basic elements of a sentence
- Essential grammar terms, including the parts of speech
- Prepositional phrases
- Different types of verbs
- Complete thoughts

**Tools to Address the Trouble Spots**

- List of the Four Most Serious Errors (p. 315)
- The Seven Basic Parts of Speech (p. 316)
- The Basic Sentence (p. 317)
- List of Common Linking Verbs (p. 320)
- List of Common Helping Verbs (p. 320)
- Complete Thoughts (p. 322)
- Six Basic English Sentence Patterns (p. 322)

# The Parts of Speech

There are seven basic parts of speech:

1. **Noun:** names a person, place, thing, or idea (for information on making nouns plural, see p. 490). A **noun phrase** is a group of words that includes a noun, or a word that functions as a noun, and any surrounding article and modifiers.

   Jaime dances.

**Tip** In the examples in this chapter, subjects are underlined once, and verbs are underlined twice.

2. **Pronoun:** replaces a noun in a sentence. *He, she, it, we,* and *they* are pronouns.

   She dances.

**Tip** For a definition of *subject,* see page 317.

3. **Verb:** tells what action the subject does or links a subject to another word that describes it.

   Jaime **dances**. [The verb *dances* is what the subject, Jaime, does.]

   She **is** a dancer.
   [The verb *is* links the subject, Jaime, to a word that describes her, *dancer*.]

4. **Adjective:** describes a noun or a pronoun (can also be a participle, a verb that functions as a noun).

   Jaime is **thin**. [The adjective *thin* describes the noun *Jaime*.]

   She is **graceful**. [The adjective *graceful* describes the pronoun *She*.]

**Tip** Some grammar experts consider **interjections** to be a part of speech. Interjections are words or phrases that are often used to convey emotion—for example, "Ouch!", "Oh no!", and "Good grief!"

5. **Adverb:** describes an adjective, a verb, or another adverb. Adverbs often end in *-ly*.

   Jaime is **extremely** graceful. [The adverb *extremely* describes the adjective *graceful*.]

   She practices **often**. [The adverb *often* describes the verb *practices*.]

   Jaime dances **quite** beautifully.
   [The adverb *quite* describes another adverb, *beautifully*.]

6. **Preposition:** connects a noun, pronoun, or verb with information about it. *Across, around, at, in, of, on,* and *out* are prepositions (there are many others).

   Jaime practices **at** the studio.
   [The preposition *at* connects the verb *practices* with the noun *studio*.]

7. **Conjunction:** connects words to each other. An easy way to remember the seven common conjunctions is to connect them in your mind to **FANBOYS**: *for, and, nor, but, or, yet, so.*

   The studio is expensive **but** good.

**Tip** For more on coordinating conjunctions, see pages 409–11. For more on subordinating conjunctions (dependent words), see page 413.

# The Basic Sentence

A **sentence** is the basic unit of written communication. A complete sentence in written standard English must have these three elements:

- A **subject**
- A **verb**
- A **complete thought**

## Subjects

The **subject** of a sentence is the person, place, thing, or idea that a sentence is about. The subject of a sentence can be a noun or a pronoun. For a list of common pronouns, see page 382.

To find the subject, ask yourself, **Whom or what is the sentence about?**

**Person as subject** Isaac arrived last night.
[***Whom*** is the sentence about? *Isaac*]

**Thing as subject** The restaurant has closed.
[***What*** is the sentence about? The *restaurant*]

A **compound subject** consists of two or more subjects joined by *and, or,* or *nor*.

**Two subjects** Kelli and Kate love animals of all kinds.

**Several subjects** The baby, the cats, and the dog play well together.

The subject of a sentence is *never* in a **prepositional phrase**, a word group that begins with a preposition and ends with a noun or pronoun, called the **object of a preposition**.

Preposition
Subject | Object of preposition

Your dinner is in the oven.

Prepositional phrase

| Preposition | Object | Prepositional phrase |
|---|---|---|
| from | the bakery | from the bakery |
| to | the next corner | to the next corner |
| under | the table | under the table |

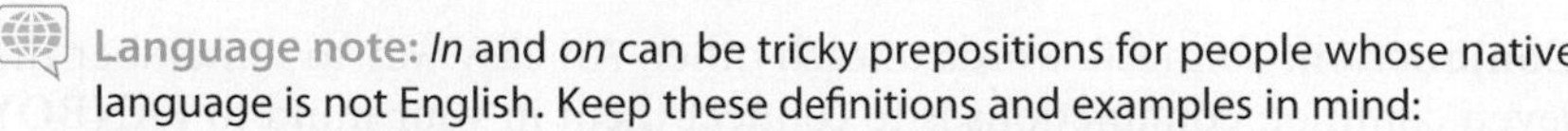

**Language note:** *In* and *on* can be tricky prepositions for people whose native language is not English. Keep these definitions and examples in mind:

***in*** = inside of (in the box, in the office) or at a certain time (in January, in the fall, in three weeks)

***on*** = on top of (on the table, on my foot), located in a certain place (on the page, on Main Street), or at a certain time (on January 31)

If you have trouble deciding which prepositions to use, see Chapter 26.

**Tip** For common prepositional phrases, see Chapter 26.

See if you can identify the subject of the following sentence:

One of my best friends races cars.

Although you might think that the word *friends* is the subject, it isn't. *One* is the subject. The word *friends* cannot be the subject because it is in the prepositional phrase *of my best friends*. When you are looking for the subject of a sentence, cross out the prepositional phrase.

**Prepositional Phrase Crossed Out**

One ~~of the students~~ won the science prize.

The rules ~~about the dress code~~ are very specific.

**Language note:** The example sentences use the word *the* before the noun (*the rules, the dress code*). *The, a,* and *an* are called *articles*. If you have trouble deciding which article to use with which nouns, see Chapter 26.

### PRACTICE 1 Identifying subjects and prepositional phrases

In each of the following sentences, cross out any prepositional phrases, and underline the subject of the sentence.

**Example:** **Coupons ~~from newspapers and Web sites~~ are just one way to save money.**

1. A friend from my neighborhood packs her lunch every day.
2. Sandwiches in her workplace cafeteria cost five dollars.
3. Restaurants near her job charge even more.
4. Therefore, sandwiches from her own kitchen are saving my friend twenty-five dollars or more each week.
5. Savings in gasoline expenses are also possible.
6. Everything in the trunk of a car increases the car's weight and gasoline usage.

7. Recently, a hiker down the street cleaned out his trunk.
8. The amount of old hiking gear in the trunk was surprisingly large.
9. The result of his cleanup was greatly reduced gasoline expenses.
10. Savings during just one week reached thirty dollars.

## *Verbs*

Every sentence has a **main verb**, the word or words that tell what the subject does or that link the subject to another word that describes it. There are three kinds of verbs: action verbs, linking verbs, and helping verbs.

**Tip** Verbs do not always immediately follow the subject: Other words may come between the subject and the verb. **Example:** The boy who came in first won a prize.

### ACTION VERBS

An **action verb** tells what action the subject performs.

To find the main action verb in a sentence, ask yourself: **What action does the subject perform?**

**Action verbs** The band played all night.
The alarm rings loudly.

### LINKING VERBS

A **linking verb** connects (links) the subject to another word (or group of words) that describes the subject. Linking verbs show no action. The most common linking verb is *be* (*am, is, are,* and so on). Other linking verbs, such as *seem* and *become,* can usually be replaced by a form of the verb *be,* and the sentence will still make sense.

To find linking verbs, ask yourself: **What word joins the subject and the words that describe the subject?**

**Linking verbs** The bus is late.

My new shoes look shiny. (My new shoes are shiny.)

The milk tastes sour. (The milk is sour.)

Some words can be used as either action verbs or linking verbs, depending on how the verb is used in a particular sentence.

**Action verb** Justine smelled the flowers.

**Linking verb** The flowers smelled wonderful.

## Common Linking Verbs

| Forms of *be* | Forms of *seem* and *become* | Forms of sense verbs |
|---|---|---|
| am | seem, seems, seemed | look, looks, looked |
| are | become, becomes, became | appear, appears, appeared |
| is | | smell, smells, smelled |
| was | | taste, tastes, tasted |
| were | | feel, feels, felt |

 **Language note:** The verb *be* cannot be left out of sentences in English.

**Incorrect** Tonya well now.

**Correct** Tonya is well now.

### HELPING VERBS

A **helping verb** joins the main verb in a sentence to form the **complete verb (also known as a verb phrase—the main verb and all of its helping verbs)**. The helping verb is often a form of the verb *be, have,* or *do*. A sentence may have more than one helping verb along with the main verb.

Helping verb + Main verb = Complete verb

Sharon was listening to the radio as she was studying for the test.
[The helping verb is *was*; the complete verbs are *was listening* and *was studying*.]

I am saving my money for a car.

Colleen might have borrowed my sweater.

You must pass this course before taking the next one.

You should stop smoking.

## Common Helping Verbs

| Forms of *be* | Forms of *have* | Forms of *do* | Other |
|---|---|---|---|
| am | have | do | can |
| are | has | does | could |
| been | had | did | may |
| being | | | might |
| is | | | must |
| was | | | should |
| were | | | will |
| | | | would |

Before you begin Practice 2, look at these examples to see how action, linking, and helping verbs are different.

**Action verb** Kara graduated last year.
[The verb *graduated* is an action that Kara performed.]

**Linking verbs** Kara is a graduate.
[The verb *is* links Kara to the word that describes her: *graduate*. No action is performed.]

**Helping verb** Kara is graduating next spring.
[The helping verb *is* joins the main verb *graduating* to make the complete verb *is graduating*, which tells what action the subject is taking.]

### PRACTICE 2 Identifying the verb (action, linking, or helping verb + main verb)

In the following sentences, underline each subject and double-underline each verb. Then, identify each verb as an action verb, a linking verb, or a helping verb + a main verb.

*Helping verb + main verb*
**Example: Bowling was created a long time ago.**

1. The ancient Egyptians invented bowling.
2. Dutch settlers were responsible for bowling's introduction to North America.
3. They bowled outdoors on fields of grass.
4. One area in New York City is called Bowling Green because the Dutch bowled there in the 1600s.
5. The first indoor bowling alley in the United States opened in 1840 in New York.
6. Indoor bowling soon became popular across the country.
7. The largest bowling alley in the United States offers more than a hundred lanes.
8. Visitors to Las Vegas can bowl there.
9. Most people would not think of bowling as more popular than basketball.
10. However, more Americans participate in bowling than in any other sport.

## *Complete Thoughts*

A **complete thought** is an idea, expressed in a sentence that makes sense by itself, without additional words. An incomplete thought leaves readers wondering what's going on.

| | |
|---|---|
| **Incomplete thought** | because my alarm did not go off |
| **Complete thought** | I was late because my alarm did not go off. |
| **Incomplete thought** | the people who won the lottery |
| **Complete thought** | The people who won the lottery were old. |

To determine whether a thought is complete, ask yourself: **Do I have to ask a question to understand?**

| | |
|---|---|
| **Incomplete thought** | in my wallet<br>[You would have to ask a question to understand, so it is not a complete thought.] |
| **Complete thought** | My ticket is in my wallet. |

## *Six Basic English Sentence Patterns*

In English, there are six basic sentence patterns, some of which you have just worked through in this chapter. Although there are other patterns, they build on these six.

1. **Subject-Verb (S-V).** This pattern is the most basic one, as you have already seen.

   S V
   Babies cry.

2. **Subject-Linking Verb-Noun (S-LV-N)**

   S LV N
   They are children.

3. **Subject-Linking Verb-Adjective (S-LV-ADJ)**

   S LV ADJ
   Parents are tired.

4. **Subject-Verb-Adverb (S-V-ADV)**

   S V ADV
   They sleep poorly.

5. **Subject-Verb-Direct Object (S-V-DO).** A *direct object* directly receives the action of the verb.

   S V DO
   Teachers give tests. [The *tests* are given.]

6. **Subject-Verb-Direct Object-Indirect Object.** An *indirect object* does not directly receive the action of the verb.

S V DO IO
Teachers give tests to students. [The *tests* are given; the *students* are not.]

This pattern can also have the indirect object before the direct object.

S V IO DO
Teachers give students tests.

**PRACTICE 3** **Identifying basic sentence patterns**

Using the sentence pattern indicated, write a sentence for each of the following items.

1. (Subject-verb-direct object) ______________________________
______________________________
2. (Subject-linking verb-noun) ______________________________
______________________________
3. (Subject-verb-adverb) ______________________________
______________________________
4. (Subject-verb-direct object-indirect object) ______________________________
______________________________
5. (Subject-verb-indirect object-direct object) ______________________________
______________________________

**PRACTICE 4** **Identifying complete sentences**

In this essay, underline the subject of each sentence, and double-underline the verb. Correct five incomplete thoughts.

(1) Space travel fascinates my grandpa Bill. (2) He watches every space movie at least a dozen times. (3) Before 1996, he never even thought about the moon, Mars, or beyond. (4) He was too old to be an astronaut. (5) Now, however, he is on board a satellite. (6) It analyzes particles in the atmosphere. (7) He has the company of millions of other people. (8) And me, too. (9) Truthfully, only our names travel to Mars or beyond. (10) We are happy with that.

(11) In 1996, the Planetary Society flew the names of members into space. (12) Using the Mars *Pathfinder*. (13) At first, individuals signed a paper. (14) Then, Planetary Society members put the signatures into electronic form. (15) Now, people submit names on the Internet. (16) By filling out a form. (17) The names go on a microchip. (18) One spacecraft to the moon had more than a million names on board. (19) Some people have placed their names on a spacecraft going past Pluto and out of our solar system. (20) Their names are on a CD. (21) Which could survive for billions of years.

(22) Grandpa and I feel good about our journey into space. (23) In a way, we will travel to places only dreamed about. (24) After signing up, we received colorful certificates to print out. (25) To tell about our mission. (26) My certificate hangs on my wall. (27) My grandpa and I travel proudly into space.

## Chapter Review

1. List the seven parts of speech. ______________________________
______________________________
2. A sentence must have three things: ______________________________
______________________________
3. A __________ is the person, place, or thing that a sentence is about.
4. A prepositional phrase is ______________________________
______________________________
5. Write an example of a prepositional phrase (not from one of the examples presented earlier): ______________________________
6. An action verb tells ______________________________
7. A linking verb ______________________________
______________________________
8. A helping verb ______________________________
______________________________

# 16

# Fragments

## Incomplete Sentences

## Understand What Fragments Are

Visit **LaunchPad Solo for Readers and Writers > Grammar > Basic Sentences** for more tutorials, videos, and practice with crafting paragraphs.

A **fragment** is a group of words that is missing one or more parts of a complete sentence: a subject, a verb, or a complete thought.

**Sentence** I was hungry, so I ate some cold pizza and drank a soda.

**Fragment** I was hungry, so I ate some cold pizza. *And drank a soda.*
[*And drank a soda* contains a verb (*drank*) but no subject.]

**Language note:** Remember that any idea that ends with a period needs a subject and verb to be complete. As a quick review, a subject is the person, place, or thing that a sentence is about. A verb tells what the subject does, links the subject to another word that describes it, or "helps" another verb form a complete verb.

## GRAMMAR & MECHANICS ROADMAP

### An Overview

**This Chapter Identifies the Following Trouble Spots**

- Fragments that start with a preposition
- Fragments that start with a dependent word
- Fragments that start with *-ing* words
- Fragments that start with *to* and a verb
- Fragments that are examples or explanations

**Tools to Address the Trouble Spots**

## *In the Real World, Why Is It Important to Correct Fragments?*

People outside the English classroom notice fragments and consider them major mistakes.

**Situation:** Justina is interested in starting a blog to establish an online presence and attract potential employers. Here is part of an e-mail that Justina sent to a popular blogger:

> I am getting in touch with you about starting a blog on dress design. Because I have heard about the success you have had with your fashion blog. For a long time, I have designed and sewn many dresses for myself and my friends, and I have a good sense of style. On my blog, I would like to share sewing tips and patterns based on my dress designs. Which should appeal to many readers. I would like to ask your opinion about many things. Especially about how to write clear, interesting blog posts. I have to admit that my dream would be for my blog to catch the eye of a major fashion house looking for talent. To come up with new looks for its dress line. Could we set up a time to talk in person?

**YOUR TURN**

What are your thoughts about Justina's e-mail?

Does Justina present herself professionally in her e-mail?

How could grammar and spelling mistakes in an e-mail potentially affect Justina's future as a blogger?

What can Justina do to improve her e-mail?

# Find and Correct Fragments

To find fragments in your own writing, look for the five trouble spots in this chapter. They often signal fragments.

When you find a fragment in your own writing, you can usually correct it in one of two ways.

**Basic Ways to Correct a Fragment**

- Add what is missing (a subject, a verb, or both).
- Attach the fragment to the sentence before or after it.

**PRACTICE 1** **Finding fragments**

Find and underline the four fragments in Justina's e-mail.

## *1. Fragments That Start with Prepositions*

Whenever a preposition starts what you think is a sentence, check for a subject, a verb, and a complete thought. If the group of words is missing any of these three elements, it is a fragment.

**Tip** Remember that the subject of a sentence is *never* in a prepositional phrase (see p. 317).

**Fragment** I pounded as hard as I could. *Against the door.*
[*Against the door* lacks both a subject and a verb.]

**Tip** In the examples in this chapter, subjects are underlined once, and verbs are underlined twice.

Correct a fragment that starts with a preposition by connecting it to the sentence either before or after it. If you connect such a fragment to the sentence after it, put a comma after the fragment to join it to the next sentence.

### Common Prepositions

| | | | | |
|---|---|---|---|---|
| about | before | for | on | until |
| above | behind | from | out | up |
| across | below | in | outside | upon |
| after | beneath | inside | over | with |
| against | beside | into | past | within |
| along | between | like | since | without |
| among | by | near | through | |
| around | down | next to | to | |
| at | during | of | toward | |
| because of | except | off | under | |

## *2. Fragments That Start with Dependent Words*

A **dependent word** (also called a **subordinating conjunction**) is the first word in a dependent clause (a clause is a group of words that has a subject and a verb).

**Sentence with a dependent word** We arrived late *because* the bus was delayed.
[*Because* is a dependent word introducing the dependent clause *because the bus was delayed.*]

A dependent clause cannot be a sentence because it does not express a complete thought, even though it has a subject and a verb. Whenever a dependent word starts what you think is a sentence, stop to check for a subject, a verb, and a complete thought.

**Fragment** *Since I moved.* I have eaten out every day.
[*Since I moved* has a subject (*I*) and a verb (*moved*), but it does not express a complete thought.]

**Corrected** Since I moved, I have eaten out every day.

## Common Dependent Words

| | | |
|---|---|---|
| after | if/if only | until |
| although | now that | what (whatever) |
| as/as if/as though | once | when (whenever) |
| as long as/as soon as | since | where (wherever) |
| because | so that | whether |
| before | that | which |
| even if/even though | though | while |
| how | unless | who/whose |

When a word group starts with *who, whose,* or *which,* it is not a complete sentence unless it is a question.

**Fragment** That woman is the police officer. *Who gave me a ticket last week.*

**Question** *Who* gave you a ticket last week?

**Fragment** He is the goalie. *Whose team is so bad.*

**Question** *Whose* team are you on?

**Fragment** Sherlene went to the HiHo Club. *Which serves alcohol.*

**Question** *Which* club serves alcohol?

Correct a fragment that starts with a dependent word by connecting it to the sentence before or after it. If the dependent clause is joined to the sentence after it, put a comma after the dependent clause.

**Tip** For more on commas with dependent clauses, see Chapters 23 and 30.

### PRACTICE 2 Correcting fragments that start with prepositions or dependent words

In the following items, circle any prepositions or dependent words that start a word group. Then, correct each fragment by connecting it to the sentence before or after it.

**Example:** **The fire at the Triangle Waist Company in New York City marked a turning point. In U.S. labor history.**

1. Before the fire occurred, on March 25, 1911. Labor activists had raised complaints against the company, a maker of women's blouses.
2. The activists demanded shorter hours and better wages. For the company's overworked and underpaid sewing-machine operators.

3. The owners refused these requests, however. Because they placed profits over their employees' welfare.
4. When activists demanded better safety measures, such as sprinkler systems. The owners again refused to do anything.
5. On the day of the fire. A scrap bin on the eighth floor of the blouse factory ignited by accident.
6. Although workers threw buckets of water on the flames. Their efforts could not keep the fire from spreading to other floors.
7. Without access to safe or unlocked exits. Many workers died in the smoke and flames or jumped to their deaths.
8. One hundred and forty-six workers had lost their lives. By the end of this tragic day.
9. After news of the tragedy spread. The public reacted with outrage and greater demands for better working conditions.
10. Within a few years of the fire. Legislatures in New York and other states passed laws to improve workplace safety and worker rights.

### PRACTICE 3 Correcting fragments that start with prepositions or dependent words

Read the following paragraph, and circle the ten fragments that start with prepositions or dependent words. Then, correct the fragments.

Staying focused at an office job can be difficult. Because of these jobs' many distractions. After making just a few changes. Workers will find that they are less distracted and more productive. A good first step is to clear away clutter, such as old files. From their desktop screen. Once that screen is cleared. It is helpful to make a list of the most important tasks for the day. It is best for workers to do brain-demanding tasks when they are at their best. Which is often the start of the day. Workers can take on simpler tasks, like filing. When they are feeling less energetic. While they are doing something especially challenging. Workers might want to disconnect themselves from the Internet and turn off their personal cell phones. Although it is tempting to look at social media sites and answer e-mails and phone calls immediately. They are among the worst workplace distractions. Since social media is

particularly distracting. It is important to avoid it while at work. Because it is not an appopriate work activity. Some people set a special electronic folder. For personal e-mails. They check this folder only while they are on break or between tasks. Finally, it is important for workers to remember the importance of breaks. Which recharge the mind and improve its focus.

## 3. *Fragments That Start with* -ing *Verb Forms*

An ***-ing* verb form** (also called a **gerund**) is the form of a verb that ends in *-ing: walking, writing, running*. Sometimes, an *-ing* verb form is used at the beginning of a complete sentence.

**Sentence** Walking is good exercise.

[The *-ing* verb form *walking* is the subject; *is* is the verb. The sentence expresses a complete thought.]

Sometimes, an *-ing* verb form introduces a fragment. When an *-ing* verb form starts what you think is a sentence, stop and check for a subject, a verb, and a complete thought.

**Fragment** I ran as fast as I could. *Hoping to get there on time.*

[*Hoping to get there on time* lacks a subject, and it does not express a complete thought.]

Correct a fragment that starts with an *-ing* verb form either by adding whatever sentence elements are missing (usually a subject and a helping verb) or by connecting the fragment to the sentence before or after it. Usually, you will need to put a comma before or after the fragment to join it to the complete sentence.

### PRACTICE 4 Correcting fragments that start with *-ing* verb forms

Circle any *-ing* verb that appears at the beginning of a word group in the paragraph. Then, read the word group to see if it has a subject and a verb and expresses a complete thought. Not *all* the word groups that start with an *-ing* verb are fragments, so read carefully. In the space provided, record the numbers of the word groups that are fragments. Then, correct each fragment either by adding the missing sentence elements or by connecting it to the sentence before or after it.

Which word groups are fragments? ____________

(1) People sometimes travel long distances in unusual ways trying to set new world records. (2) Walking is one unusual way to set records. (3) In 1931, Plennie Wingo set out on an ambitious journey. (4) Walking backward

around the world. (5) Wearing sunglasses with rearview mirrors, he started his trip early one morning. (6) After eight thousand miles, Wingo's journey was interrupted by a war in Pakistan. (7) Ending his ambitious journey. (8) Hans Mullikan spent more than two years in the late 1970s traveling to the White House by crawling from Texas to Washington, D.C. (9) Taking time out to earn money as a logger and a Baptist minister. (10) Alvin Straight, suffering from poor eyesight, traveled across the Midwest on a lawn mower. (11) Looking for his long-lost brother.

## 4. *Fragments That Start with* to *and a Verb*

When what you think is a sentence begins with *to* and a verb (called the *infinitive* form of the verb), you need to make sure it is not a fragment.

**Fragment** Each day, I check freecycle.org. *To see if it has anything I need.*

**Corrected** Each day, I check freecycle.org to see if it has anything I need.

If a word group begins with *to* and a verb, it must have another verb; if not, it is not a complete sentence. When you see a word group that begins with *to* and a verb, first check to see if there is another verb. If there is no other verb, the word group is a fragment.

**Sentence** *To run* a complete marathon was my goal.
[*To run* is the subject; *was* is the verb.]

**Fragment** Cheri got underneath the car. *To change the oil.*
[No other verb appears in the word group that begins with *to change*.]

**Language note:** Do not confuse the infinitive (*to* before the verb) with *that*.

**Incorrect** My brother wants *that* his girlfriend cook.

**Correct** My brother wants his girlfriend *to cook.*

To correct a fragment that starts with *to* and a verb, join it to the sentence before or after it, or add the missing sentence elements.

### PRACTICE 5 Correcting fragments that start with *to* and a verb

Circle any *to*-plus-verb combination that appears at the beginning of a sentence in the paragraph. Then, read the word group to see if it has a subject and a verb and expresses a complete thought. Not *all* the word groups that start with *to* and a verb are fragments, so read carefully. In the space provided, record the numbers of the word groups that are fragments. Then, correct each

fragment either by adding the missing sentence elements or by connecting it to the sentence before or after it.

Which word groups are fragments? ___________

(1) For people older than twenty-five, each hour spent watching TV lowers life expectancy by nearly twenty-two minutes. (2) This finding is the result of Australian researchers' efforts. (3) To investigate the health effects of TV viewing. (4) To put it another way, watching an hour of television is about the same as smoking two cigarettes. (5) The problem is that most people are inactive while watching TV. (6) They are not doing anything, like walking or playing sports. (7) To strengthen their heart and maintain a healthy weight. (8) Fortunately, it is possible. (9) To counteract some of TV's negative health effects. (10) To increase their life expectancy by three years. (11) People need to exercise just fifteen minutes a day. (12) To accomplish this goal, they might exchange a ride in an elevator for a climb up the stairs. (13) Or they might walk around the block during a lunch break at work.

## 5. *Fragments That Are Examples or Explanations*

As you edit your writing, pay special attention to groups of words that are examples or explanations of information you presented in the previous sentence. They may be fragments.

**Fragment** More and more people are reporting food allergies. *For example, allergies to nuts or milk.*

**Fragment** My body reacts to wheat-containing foods. *Such as bread or pasta.*
[*For example, allergies to nuts or milk* and *Such as bread or pasta* are not complete thoughts.]

This last type of fragment is harder to recognize because there is no single word or kind of word to look for. The following words may signal a fragment, but fragments that are examples or explanations do not always start with these words.

especially for example like such as

When a group of words gives an example or explanation connected to the previous sentence, stop to check it for a subject, a verb, and a complete thought.

**Tip** *Such as* and *like* do not often begin complete sentences.

**Fragment** I have found great things at freecycle.org. *Like a nearly new computer.*

**Fragment** Freecycle.org is a good site. *Especially for household items.*

**Fragment** It lists many gently used appliances. *Such as DVD players.*
[*Like a nearly new computer, Especially for household items,* and *Such as DVD players* are not complete thoughts.]

Correct a fragment that starts with an example or explanation by connecting it to the sentence before or after it. Sometimes, you can add whatever sentence elements are missing (a subject, a verb, or both) instead. When you connect the fragment to a sentence, you may need to change some punctuation. For example, fragments that are examples are often set off by a comma.

**PRACTICE 6** **Correcting fragments that are examples or explanations**

Circle word groups that are examples or explanations. Then, read the word group to see if it has a subject and verb and expresses a complete thought. In the space provided, record the numbers of the word groups that are fragments. Then, correct each fragment either by adding the missing sentence elements or by connecting it to the sentence before or after it.

Which word groups are fragments? _______________

(1) Being a smart consumer can be difficult. (2) Especially when making a major purchase. (3) At car dealerships, for example, important information is often in small type. (4) Like finance charges or preparation charges. (5) Advertisements also put negative information in small type. (6) Such as a drug's side effects. (7) Credit-card offers often use tiny, hard-to-read print for the terms of the card. (8) Like interest charges and late fees, which can really add up. (9) Phone service charges can also be hidden in small print. (10) Like limits on text messaging and other functions. (11) Especially now, as businesses try to make it seem as if you are getting a good deal, it is important to read any offer carefully.

# Edit for Fragments

Use the chart on page 336, Finding and Fixing Fragments, to help you complete the practices in this section and edit your own writing.

**PRACTICE 7** **Correcting various fragments**

In the following items, circle each word group that is a fragment. Then, correct fragments by connecting them to the previous or next sentence or by adding the missing sentence elements.

**Example:** **With the high cost of producing video games. Game publishers are turning to a new source of revenue.** [handwritten correction: ", game"]

1. To add to their income. Publishers are placing advertisements in their games.

2. Sometimes, the ads show a character using a product. For example, drinking a specific brand of soda to earn health points.
3. One character, a race-car driver, drove his ad-covered car. Across the finish line.
4. When a warrior character picked up a sword decorated with an athletic-shoe logo. Some players complained.
5. Worrying that ads are distracting. Some publishers are trying to limit the number of ads per game.
6. But most players do not seem to mind seeing ads in video games. If there are not too many of them.
7. These players are used to seeing ads in all kinds of places. Like grocery carts and restroom walls.
8. For video game publishers. The goal is making a profit, but most publishers also care about the product.
9. To strike a balance between profitable advertising and high game quality. That is what publishers want.
10. Doing market research. Will help publishers find that balance.

**PRACTICE 8** **Editing paragraphs for fragments**

Find and correct the ten fragments in the following paragraphs.

1. Ida Lewis was born on February 25, 1842, in Newport, Rhode Island. Her father, Hosea, had been a coast pilot but was transferred to the Lighthouse Service. Although he was in failing health. In 1853, he was appointed lighthouse keeper at Lime Rock in Newport. Many lighthouse keepers were forced to leave family behind when they assumed their duties. Because the lighthouses were in remote locations and the living situations were poor. At first, Lime Rock had only a shed. For the keeper and a temporary lantern for light. Appropriate housing was constructed in 1857, and Hosea moved his family to Lime Rock.
2. Hosea was completely disabled by a stroke. In only a few months. Ida, who was already caring for an ill sister, took care of her father and the lighthouse as well. Keeping the lighthouse lamp lit. At sunset, the lamp

had to be filled with oil and refilled at midnight. The reflectors needed constant polishing, and the light had to be extinguished in the morning. Since schools were on the mainland, Ida rowed her brothers and sisters to school every day. Strengthening her rowing ability, which ultimately saved many lives. In 1872, Hosea died, and Ida's mother was appointed keeper. Even though Ida did all the work. Finally, in 1879, Ida became the keeper and received a salary of $500 a year.

3. She was the best-known lighthouse keeper because of her many rescues. Some called her "The Bravest Woman in America." Saving eighteen lives during her time of service. In 1867, during a storm, sheepherders had gone into the water after a lost sheep. Ida saved both the sheep and the sheepherders. She became famous, and many important people came to see her. For example, President Ulysses S. Grant. All the ships anchored in the harbor tolled their bells. To honor her after her death. Later, the Rhode Island legislature changed the name of Lime Rock to Ida Lewis Rock, the first and only time this honor was awarded.

### PRACTICE 9 Editing fragments and using formal English

Your friend wants to send this thank-you note to an employer who interviewed her for a job. She knows that the note has problems and has asked for your help. Correct the fragments in the note. Then, edit the informal English in it.

**Tip** For more advice on using formal English, see Chapter 26. For advice on choosing appropriate words, see Chapter 27.

Dear Ms. Hernandez,

(1) Thank you so much for taking the time. (2) To meet with me this past Wednesday. (3) I am more psyched than ever about the administrative assistant position at Fields Corporation. (4) Learning more about the stuff I would need to do. Was very cool. (5) Also, I enjoyed meeting you and the other managers. (6) With my strong organizational skills, professional experience, and friendly personality. (7) I'm sure that I would be awesome for the job. (8) Because I'm totally jazzed about the position. (9) I hope you will keep me in mind. (10) Please let me know if you need any other info.

(11) Like references or a writing sample.

(12) Thank U much,

Sincerely,

Terri Hammons

**PRACTICE 10** **Editing Justina's e-mail**

Look back at Justina's e-mail on page 326. You may have already underlined the fragments in her e-mail; if not, do so now. Next, using what you have learned in this chapter, correct each fragment in the e-mail.

**PRACTICE 11** **Editing your own writing for fragments**

Edit fragments in a piece of your own writing—a paper for this course or another one, or something you have written for work or your everyday life. Use the chart below to help you.

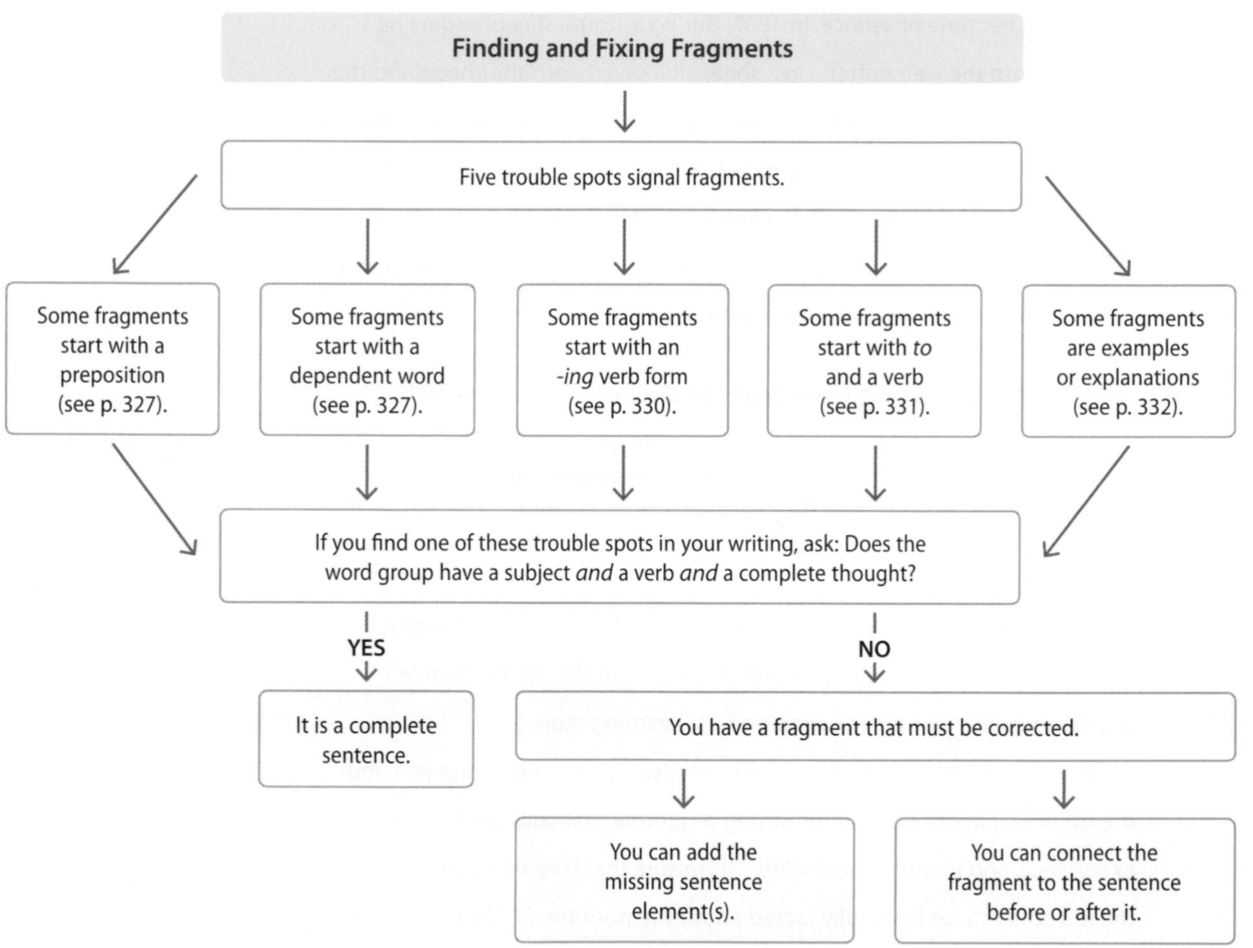
Finding and Fixing Fragments
Five trouble spots signal fragments.
Some fragments start with a preposition (see p. 327).
Some fragments start with a dependent word (see p. 327).
Some fragments start with an *-ing* verb form (see p. 330).
Some fragments start with *to* and a verb (see p. 331).
Some fragments are examples or explanations (see p. 332).
If you find one of these trouble spots in your writing, ask: Does the word group have a subject *and* a verb *and* a complete thought?
YES
NO
It is a complete sentence.
You have a fragment that must be corrected.
You can add the missing sentence element(s).
You can connect the fragment to the sentence before or after it.

# Chapter Review

1. A *sentence* is a group of words that has three elements: a ________, a ________, and a ____________________.

2. A ____________ seems to be a complete sentence but is only a piece of one. It lacks a ____________, a ________, or a ____________________.

3. What are the five trouble spots that signal possible fragments?

   ______________________________________________________________

   ______________________________________________________________

   ______________________________________________________________

   ______________________________________________________________

   ______________________________________________________________

4. What are the two basic ways to correct fragments?

   ______________________________________________________________

   ______________________________________________________________

# 17

# Run-Ons

## Two Sentences Joined Incorrectly

Visit **LaunchPad Solo for Readers and Writers > Grammar > Basic Sentences** for more tutorials, videos, and practice with crafting paragraphs.

## Understand What Run-Ons Are

A sentence is also called an independent clause, a group of words with a subject and a verb that expresses a complete thought. Sometimes, two independent clauses can be joined to form one larger sentence.

**Sentence with two independent clauses**

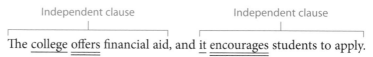

Independent clause | Independent clause

The college offers financial aid, and it encourages students to apply.

## GRAMMAR & MECHANICS ROADMAP

### An Overview

**This Chapter Identifies the Following Trouble Spots**

- Run-ons
- Fused sentences
- Comma splices

**Tools to Address Trouble Spots**

A **run-on** is two complete sentences (independent clauses) joined incorrectly as one sentence. There are two kinds of run-ons: **fused sentences** and **comma splices**.

A **fused sentence** is two complete sentences joined without a coordinating conjunction (*for, and, nor, but, or, yet, so*) or any punctuation.

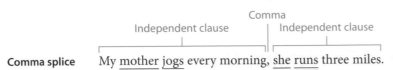

No punctuation

Independent clause | Independent clause

**Fused sentence** Exercise is important it has many benefits.

A **comma splice** is two complete sentences joined by only a comma.

Comma

Independent clause | Independent clause

**Comma splice** My mother jogs every morning, she runs three miles.

When you join two sentences, use the proper punctuation.

**Corrections** Exercise is important; it has many benefits.

My mother jogs every morning; she runs 3 miles.

**Tip** To find and correct run-ons, you need to be able to identify a complete sentence. For a review, see Chapter 15.

**Tip** In the examples throughout this chapter, subjects are underlined once, and verbs are underlined twice.

## *In the Real World, Why Is It Important to Correct Run-Ons?*

People outside the English classroom notice run-ons and consider them major mistakes.

**Situation:** Naomi is applying to a special program for returning students at Cambridge College. Here is one of the essay questions on the application, followed by a paragraph from Naomi's answer.

**Statement of Purpose:** In two hundred words or less, describe your intellectual and professional goals and how a Cambridge College education will assist you in achieving them.

> For many years, I did not take control of my life, I just drifted without any goals. I realized one day as I met with my daughter's guidance counselor that I hoped my daughter would not turn out like me. From that moment, I decided to do something to help myself and others. I set a goal of becoming a teacher. To begin on that path, I took a math course at night school, then I took another in science. I passed both courses with hard work, I know I can do well in the Cambridge College program. I am committed to the professional goal I finally found it has given new purpose to my whole life.

**YOUR TURN**

What are your thoughts about Naomi's essay?

If you were a college official looking at applications, how would you perceive Naomi as a potential student? Why?

What kind of error is Naomi making most often? How does it affect the text (in other words, can you still easily read and comprehend what she wants to say? Is it harder to understand certain ideas or thoughts?)?

How would you correct Naomi's essay?

## Find and Correct Run-Ons

To find run-ons, focus on each sentence in your writing, one at a time, looking for fused sentences and comma splices. Pay special attention to sentences longer than two lines. By spending this extra time, your writing will improve.

**PRACTICE 1 Finding run-ons**

Find and underline the four run-ons in Naomi's writing on page 339.

Once you have found a run-on, there are five ways to correct it.

**Five Ways to Correct Run-Ons**

1. **Add a period.**

   I saw the man. He did not see me. (*he* corrected to *He*)

2. **Add a semicolon.**

   I saw the man; he did not see me.

3. **Add a semicolon, a conjunctive adverb, and a comma.**

   I saw the man; *however,* he did not see me.

4. **Add a comma and a coordinating conjunction.**

   I saw the man, *but* he did not see me.

5. **Add a dependent word.**

   *When* I saw the man, he did not see me.

## Add a Period

You can correct run-ons by adding a period to make two separate sentences. After adding the period, capitalize the letter that begins the new sentence. Reread your two sentences to make sure they each contain a subject, a verb, and a complete thought.

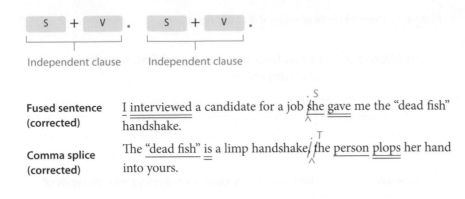

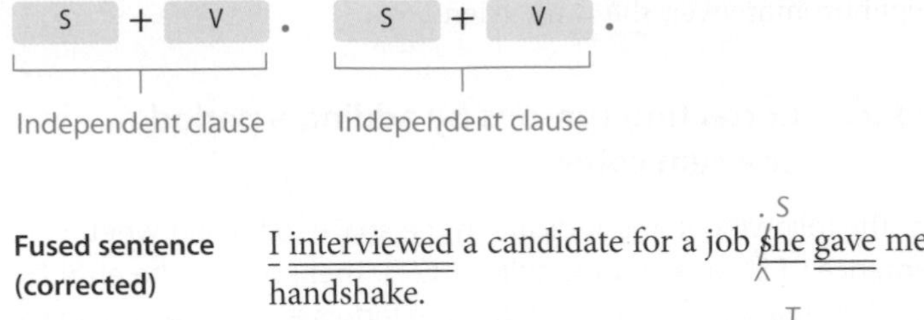
S + V .
Independent clause
S + V .
Independent clause

**Fused sentence (corrected)** I interviewed a candidate for a job. She gave me the "dead fish" handshake.

**Comma splice (corrected)** The "dead fish" is a limp handshake. The person plops her hand into yours.

## Add a Semicolon

A second way to correct run-ons is to use a semicolon (;) to join the two sentences. Use a semicolon only when the two sentences express closely related ideas and the words on each side of the semicolon can stand alone as a complete sentence. Do not capitalize the word that follows a semicolon unless it is the name of a specific person, place, or thing that is usually capitalized—for example, Mary, New York, or the Eiffel Tower.

**Fused sentence (corrected)** Slouching creates a terrible impression; it makes a person seem uninterested, bored, or lacking in self-confidence.

**Comma splice (corrected)** It is important in an interview to hold your head up; it is just as important to sit up straight.

## Add a Semicolon, a Conjunctive Adverb, and a Comma

A third way to correct run-ons is to add a semicolon followed by a **conjunctive adverb** and a comma.

### Common Conjunctive Adverbs

| | | | |
|---|---|---|---|
| consequently | indeed | moreover | still |
| finally | instead | nevertheless | then |
| furthermore | likewise | otherwise | therefore |
| however | meanwhile | similarly | |

Conjunctive adverb
Semicolon | Comma

I stopped by the market; however, it was closed.

Conjunctive adverb
Semicolon | Comma

Sharon is a neighbor; moreover, she is my friend.

**PRACTICE 2** **Correcting run-ons by adding a period or a semicolon**

For each of the following items, indicate in the space to the left whether it is a fused sentence ("FS") or a comma splice ("CS"). Then, correct the error by adding a period or a semicolon. Capitalize the letters as necessary to make two sentences.

**Example:** __FS__ **Being a farmer can mean dealing with all types of challenges ; one of the biggest ones comes from the sky.**

1. ____ Farmers have been trying to keep hungry birds out of their crops for centuries, the first scarecrow was invented for this reason.
2. ____ Some farmers have used a variety of chemicals, other farmers have tried noise, such as small cannons.
3. ____ Recently, a group of berry farmers tried something new they brought in bigger birds called falcons.
4. ____ Small birds such as starlings love munching on berries each year they destroy thousands of dollars' worth of farmers' berry crops.
5. ____ Because these starlings are frightened of falcons, they fly away when they see these birds of prey in the fields they need to get to where they feel safe.
6. ____ Using falcons to protect their crops saves farmers money, it does not damage the environment either.
7. ____ A falconer, or a person who raises and trains falcons, keeps an eye on the birds during the day he makes sure they only chase away the starlings instead of killing them.
8. ____ Falcons are used for protection in other places as well, they are used in vineyards to keep pests from eating the grapes.

9. ____ In recent years, the falcons have also been used in landfills to scatter birds and other wildlife some have even been used at large airports to keep flocks of birds out of the flight path of landing airplanes.

10. ____ Although a falconer's services are not cheap, they cost less than some other methods that farmers have tried for example, putting nets over a berry field can often cost more than $200,000.

## *Add a Comma and a Coordinating Conjunction*

A fourth way to correct run-ons is to add a comma and a **coordinating conjunction**: a link that joins independent clauses to form one sentence. The seven coordinating conjunctions are *and, but, for, nor, or, so,* and *yet.* Some people remember these words by thinking of **FANBOYS:** *for, and, nor, but, or, yet, so.*

To correct a fused sentence this way, add a comma and a coordinating conjunction. A comma splice already has a comma, so just add a coordinating conjunction that makes sense in the sentence.

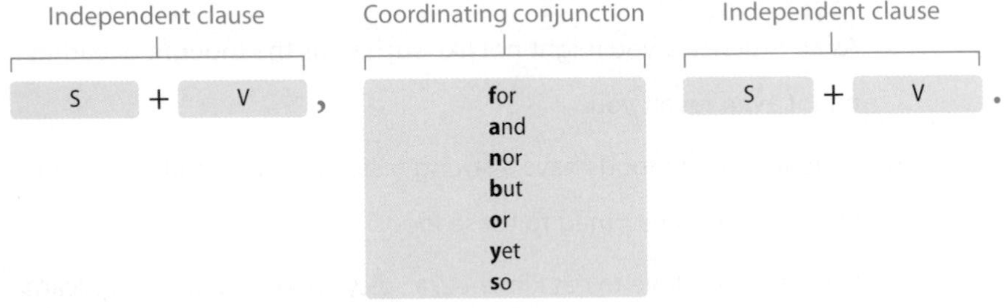

Independent clause
Coordinating conjunction
Independent clause
S + V ,
for
and
nor
but
or
yet
so
S + V .

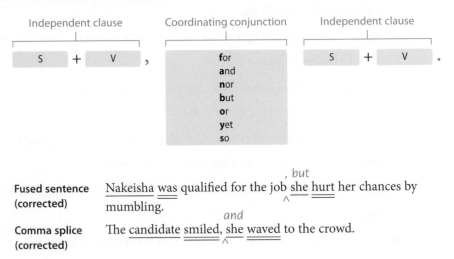

**Tip** Notice that the comma does not follow the conjunction. The comma follows the word before the conjunction.

**Fused sentence (corrected)** Nakeisha was qualified for the job *, but* she hurt her chances by mumbling.

**Comma splice (corrected)** The candidate smiled, *and* she waved to the crowd.

Coordinating conjunctions need to connect two independent clauses. They are not used to join a dependent and an independent clause.

**Incorrect** Although we warned Min-li to wear a seatbelt, **but** she never did.

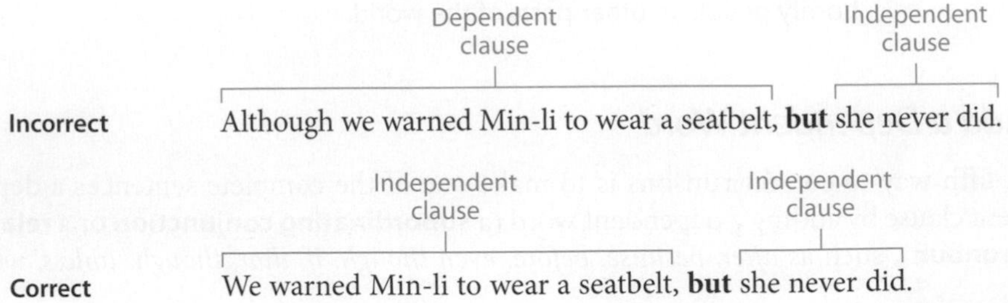

Dependent clause
Independent clause
Independent clause
Independent clause


**Correct** We warned Min-li to wear a seatbelt, **but** she never did.

**PRACTICE 3** **Correcting run-ons by adding a comma and/or a coordinating conjunction**

Correct each of the following run-ons by adding a comma, if necessary, and an appropriate coordinating conjunction. First, underline the subjects, and double-underline the verbs.

**Example:** **Most Americans do not like the idea of eating certain kinds of food, *and* most of us would probably reject horse meat.**

1. In most cultures, popular foods depend on availability and tradition people tend to eat old familiar favorites.
2. Sushi shocked many Americans thirty years ago, today some young people in the United States have grown up eating raw fish.
3. In many societies, certain foods are allowed to age this process adds flavor.
4. Icelanders bury eggs in the ground to rot for months, these aged eggs are considered a special treat.
5. As an American, you might not like such eggs the thought of eating them might even revolt you.
6. In general, aged foods have a strong taste, the flavor is unpleasant to someone unaccustomed to those foods.
7. Many Koreans love to eat kimchee, a spicy aged cabbage, Americans often find the taste odd and the smell overpowering.
8. Herders in Kyrgyzstan drink kumiss this beverage is made of aged horse's milk.
9. Americans on a visit to Kyrgyzstan consider themselves brave for tasting kumiss, local children drink it regularly.
10. We think of familiar foods as normal, favorite American foods might horrify people in other parts of the world.

## *Add a Dependent Word*

A fifth way to correct run-ons is to make one of the complete sentences a dependent clause by adding a dependent word (a **subordinating conjunction** or a **relative pronoun**), such as *after, because, before, even though, if, that, though, unless, when,*

*who,* and *which.* (For a more complete list of these words, see the graphic below.) Choose the dependent word that best expresses the relationship between the two clauses.

Turn an independent clause into a dependent one when it is less important than the other clause or explains it, as in the following sentence:

> *When I get to the train station,* I will call Josh.

The italicized clause is dependent (subordinate) because it just explains when the most important part of the sentence—calling Josh—will happen. It begins with the dependent word *when.*

Because a dependent clause is not a complete sentence (it has a subject and verb but does not express a complete thought), it can be joined to a sentence without creating a run-on. When the dependent clause is the second clause in a sentence, you usually do not need to put a comma before it unless it is showing contrast.

**Two sentences**

Halloween was originally a religious holiday. People worshipped the saints.

**Dependent clause: no comma needed**

Halloween was originally a religious holiday *when people worshipped the saints.*

**Dependent clause showing contrast: comma needed**

Many holidays have religious origins, *although some celebrations have moved away from their religious roots.*

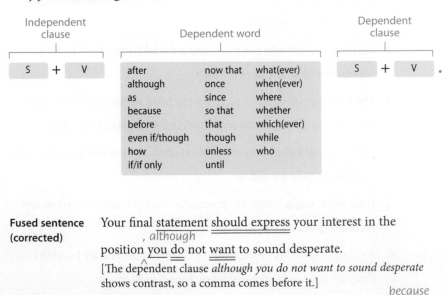

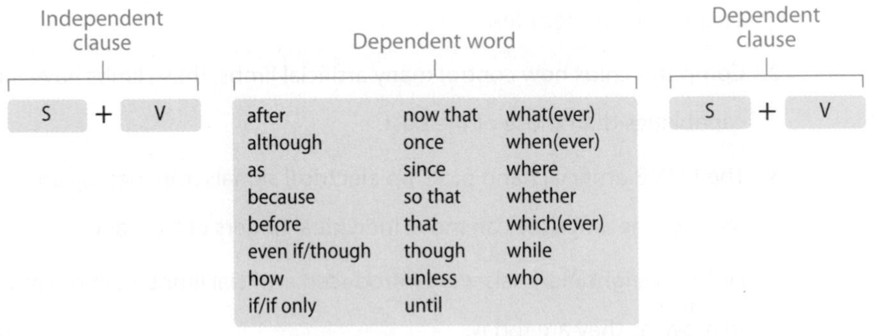
Independent clause
S + V
Dependent word
after
although
as
because
before
even if/though
how
if/if only
now that
once
since
so that
that
though
unless
until
what(ever)
when(ever)
where
whether
which(ever)
while
who
Dependent clause
S + V .

**Fused sentence (corrected)** Your final statement should express your interest in the position ^, although^ you do not want to sound desperate.

[The dependent clause *although you do not want to sound desperate* shows contrast, so a comma comes before it.]

**Comma splice (corrected)** It is important to end an interview on a positive note~~,~~ ^because^ that final impression is what the interviewer will remember.

You can also put the dependent clause first. When the dependent clause comes first, be sure to put a comma after it.

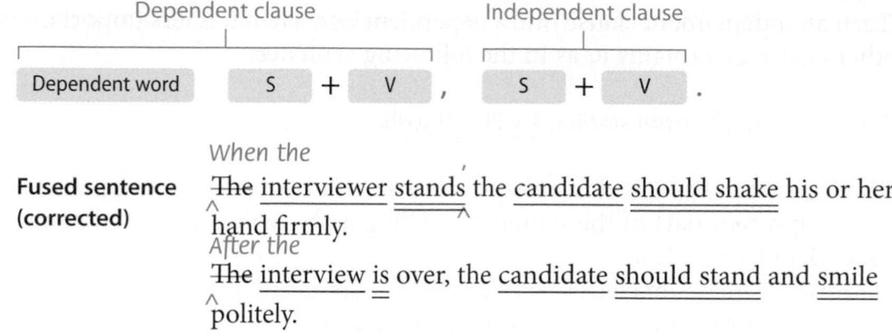
Dependent clause
Independent clause
Dependent word
S + V ,
S + V .

**Fused sentence (corrected)** ~~The~~ *When the* interviewer stands, the candidate should shake his or her hand firmly.

~~The~~ *After the* interview is over, the candidate should stand and smile politely.

## PRACTICE 4 Correcting run-ons by adding a dependent word

Correct run-ons by adding a dependent word to make a dependent clause. First, underline the subjects, and double-underline the verbs. Although these run-ons can be corrected in different ways, in this exercise, correct by adding dependent words. You may want to refer to the graphic on page 345.

**Example:** *When many* **~~Many~~ soldiers returned from Iraq and Afghanistan missing arms or legs, demand for better artificial limbs increased.**

1. Computer chips were widely used artificial limbs remained largely unchanged for decades.
2. Computer chips now control many artificial limbs, these limbs have more capabilities than those of the past.
3. The i-LIMB artificial hand picks up electrical signals from nearby arm muscles the amputee can move individual fingers of the hand.
4. Lighter-weight materials were introduced artificial limbs were not as easy to move as they are today.
5. Now, the C-Leg artificial leg is popular it is lightweight, flexible, and technically advanced.
6. A C-Leg user wants to jog, bike, or drive instead of walk he or she can program the leg for the necessary speed and motion.
7. Major advances have been made in artificial limbs, researchers believe the technology has not reached its full potential.

8. Many will not be satisfied the human brain directly controls the motion of artificial limbs.
9. A thought-controlled artificial arm is being tested on patients, that time may not be far off.
10. The artificial arm passes those tests it may be introduced to the market within the next few years.

### *A Word That Can Cause Run-Ons: Then*

Many run-ons are caused by the word *then*. You can use *then* to join two sentences, but if you add it without the correct punctuation or added words, your sentence will be a run-on. Often, writers use just a comma before *then*, but that makes a comma splice.

**Comma splice** I picked up my laundry, then I went home.

Some of the methods you have just practiced can be used to correct errors caused by *then*. These methods are shown in the following examples.

I picked up my laundry. Then I went home.

I picked up my laundry; then I went home.

I picked up my laundry, and then I went home.

I picked up my laundry before I went home.
[dependent word *before* added to make a dependent clause]

## Edit for Run-Ons

Use the chart on page 351, Finding and Fixing Run-Ons, to help you complete the practices in this section and edit your own writing.

**PRACTICE 5** **Correcting various run-ons**

In the following items, correct any run-ons. Use each method of correcting such errors—adding a period; adding a semicolon; adding a semicolon, a conjunctive adverb, and a comma; adding a comma and a coordinating conjunction; or adding a dependent word—at least once.

**Example:** Although some ~~**Some**~~ **people doubt the existence of climate change, few can deny that the weather has become more extreme and dangerous.**

1. More than nine hundred tornadoes tore through the United States in 2013, hundreds of people lost their lives.
2. That same year, parts of the Midwest experienced severe flooding droughts in Texas cost farmers upward of 8 billion.
3. Some cities are taking steps to adapt to environmental changes, they are focusing on the biggest threats.
4. Global temperatures are rising, sea levels are also rising—a threat to coastal regions.
5. As a result, some coastal cities are planning to build protective walls, others are raising roadbeds.
6. Extreme heat is another major problem, urban planners are studying different ways to address it.
7. New York City is painting some rooftops white, light and heat will be reflected away from the city.
8. In Chicago, landscapers are planting heat-tolerant trees, these trees should help cool the environment and reduce flooding during heavy rains.
9. All these efforts are encouraging most parts of the United States are doing little or nothing to plan for ongoing environmental changes.
10. One study reports that only fourteen states are undertaking such planning the threats of severe weather remain.

### PRACTICE 6 Editing paragraphs for run-ons

Find and correct the run-ons you underlined in Naomi's paragraph in Practice 1.

### PRACTICE 7 Editing paragraphs for run-ons

Find and correct the six run-ons in the following paragraphs.

(1) For the first time, monster-size squid were filmed while still in the wild. (2) The images were caught on camera in the North Pacific Ocean the

site is located just off the coast of southeastern Japan. (3) A team of Japanese scientists followed a group of sperm whales to locate the rare squids the whales like to eat the eight-legged creatures. (4) Wherever the whales went, the squids were likely to be found as well.

(5) From aboard their research ship, the team located the squids thousands of feet under the water, the scientists lowered bait over the side to attract them. (6) Next, they sent down cameras alongside the bait to catch images of these bizarre animals as soon as they appeared.

(7) The Dana octopus squid, also known as *Taningia danae,* often grows to the size of a human being or even larger. (8) Its eight arms are covered in suckers, as most squid species are, these particular types of arms end in catlike claws. (9) Two of the arms contain special organs on the ends called photophores. (10) These photophores produce flashing bursts of light they are designed to lure and capture prey. (11) The burst of light stuns other creatures, giving a squid a chance to capture and eat its victim. (12) When the squid isn't hunting, it still glows. (13) Experts believe that squids remain lighted as a way of communicating with other squids about potential dangers or as a way of attracting mates. (14) These lights appear eerie, the scientists were glad for them, as the lights made the giant squids slightly easier to find and finally film.

### PRACTICE 8 Editing run-ons and using formal English

Your brother has been overcharged for an MP3 player he ordered online, and he is about to send this e-mail to the seller's customer-service department. Help him by correcting the run-ons. Then, edit the informal English.

**Tip** For more advice on using formal English, see Chapter 26. For advice on choosing appropriate words, see Chapter 27.

(1) I'm writing 2U cuz I was seriously ripped off for the Star 3 MP3 player I ordered from your Web site last week. (2) U listed the price as $50 $150 was charged to my credit card. (3) Check out any competitors' sites, U will see that no one expects people 2 cough up that much cash for the Star model, the prices are never higher than $65. (4) I overpaid big bucks on this, I want my money back as soon as possible.

(5) Seriously bummin',

Chris Langley

**PRACTICE 9** **Editing your own writing for run-ons**

Edit run-ons in a piece of your own writing—a paper for this course or another one, or something you have written for work or your everyday life. Use the chart on page 345 to help you.

## Chapter Review

1. A sentence can also be called an ____________________.
2. A ________________ is two complete sentences joined without any punctuation.
3. A ________________ is two complete sentences joined by only a comma.
4. What are the five ways to correct run-ons?

   ________________________________________

   ________________________________________

   ________________________________________

   ________________________________________

   ________________________________________
5. What word in the middle of a sentence may signal a run-on? ________________
6. What are the seven coordinating conjunctions? ____________________

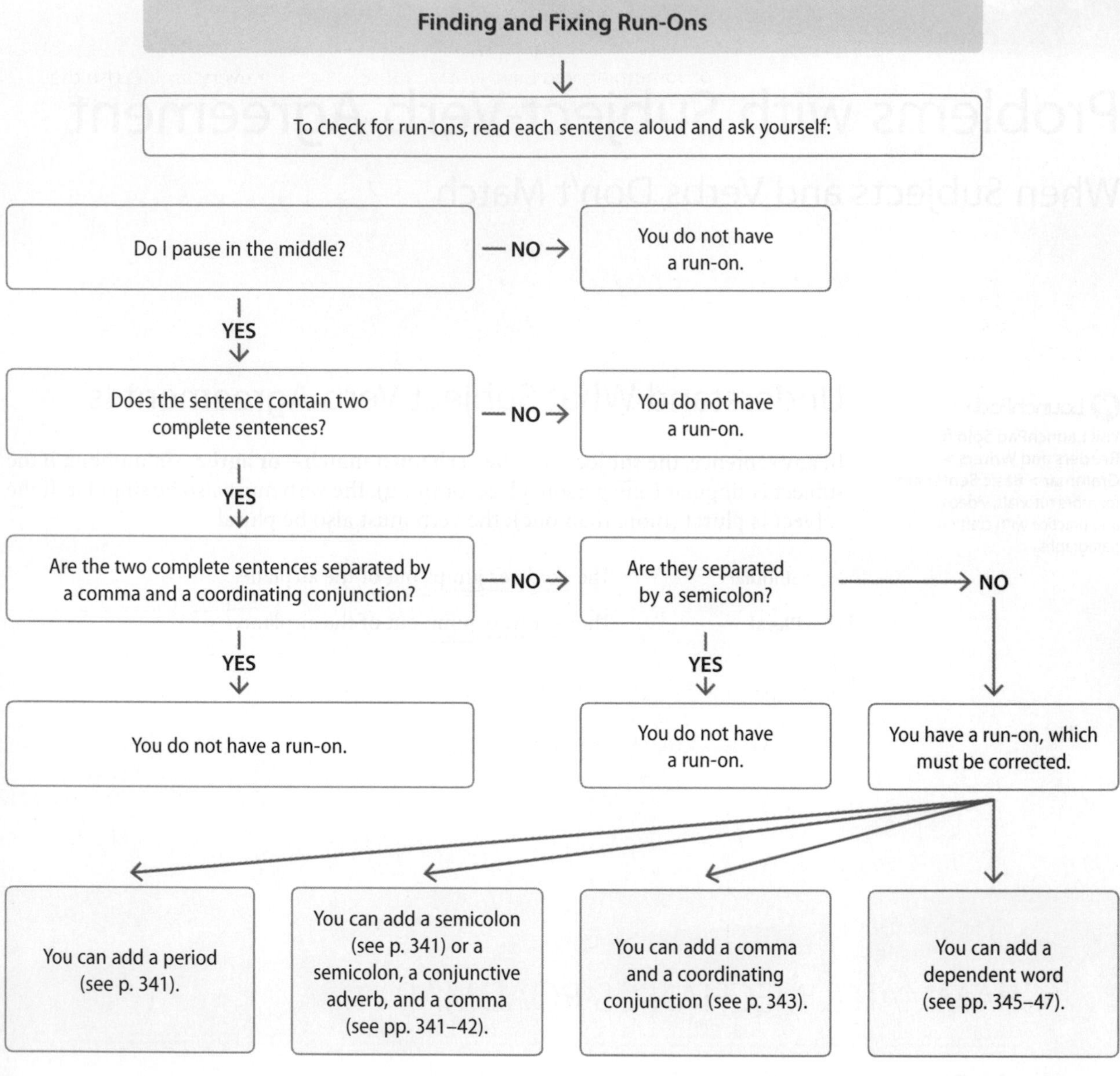
Finding and Fixing Run-Ons
To check for run-ons, read each sentence aloud and ask yourself:
Do I pause in the middle?
NO
You do not have a run-on.
YES
Does the sentence contain two complete sentences?
NO
You do not have a run-on.
YES
Are the two complete sentences separated by a comma and a coordinating conjunction?
NO
Are they separated by a semicolon?
NO
YES
You do not have a run-on.
YES
You do not have a run-on.
You have a run-on, which must be corrected.
You can add a period (see p. 341).
You can add a semicolon (see p. 341) or a semicolon, a conjunctive adverb, and a comma (see pp. 341–42).
You can add a comma and a coordinating conjunction (see p. 343).
You can add a dependent word (see pp. 345–47).

18

# Problems with Subject-Verb Agreement

## When Subjects and Verbs Don't Match

LaunchPadSolo

Visit **LaunchPad Solo for Readers and Writers > Grammar > Basic Sentences** for more tutorials, videos, and practice with crafting paragraphs.

## Understand What Subject-Verb Agreement Is

In any sentence, the **subject and the verb must match—or agree—**in number. If the subject is singular (one person, place, or thing), the verb must also be singular. If the subject is plural (more than one), the verb must also be plural.

| | |
|---|---|
| **Singular** | The skydiver jumps out of the airplane. |
| **Plural** | The skydivers jump out of the airplane. |

GRAMMAR & MECHANICS ROADMAP

### An Overview

#### This Chapter Identifies the Following Trouble Spots

- Agreement problems when using the verb forms *Be*, *Have*, or *Do*
- Agreement problems when using words between the subject and the verb
- Agreement problems with a compound subject
- Agreement problems when the subject is an indefinite pronoun
- Agreement problems when the verb comes before the subject

#### Tools to Address the Trouble Spots

- Understand What Subject-Verb Agreement Is (p. 352)
- Forms of *be* verbs (p. 354)
- Forms of *have* verbs (p. 354)
- Forms of *do* verbs (p. 354)
- List of indefinite pronouns (p. 357)
- Edit for agreement problems exercises (p. 359)
- Finding and fixing agreement problems flowchart (p. 362)

## Regular Verbs, Present Tense

| | Singular | | Plural |
|---|---|---|---|
| **First person** | I walk. | no *-s* | We walk. |
| **Second person** | You walk. | | You walk. |
| **Third person** | He (she, it) walks. | all end in *-s* | They walk. |
| | Joe walks. | | Joe and Alice walk. |
| | The student walks. | | The students walk. |

**Tip** In the examples throughout this chapter, subjects are underlined, and verbs are double-underlined.

**Regular verbs** (with forms that follow standard English patterns) have two forms in the present tense: one that ends in *-s* and one that has no ending. The third-person subjects—*he, she, it*—and singular nouns always use the form that ends in *-s*. First-person subjects (*I*), second-person subjects (*you*), and plural subjects use the form with no ending.

### *In the Real World, Why Is It Important to Correct Errors in Subject-Verb Agreement?*

People outside the English classroom notice subject-verb agreement errors and consider them major mistakes.

**Situation:** Regina Toms wrote the following brief report about a company employee whom she was sending to the employee assistance program. These programs help workers with various problems, such as alcoholism or mental illness, that may affect their job performance.

> Mr. XXX, who has been a model employee of the company for five years, have recently behaved in ways that is inappropriate. For example, last week he was rude when a colleague asked him a question. He has been late to work several times and has missed work more often than usual. When I spoke to him about his behavior and asked if he have problems, he admitted that he had been drinking more than usual. I would like him to speak to someone who understand more about this than I do.

**YOUR TURN**

Did you immediately notice Regina's errors in subject-verb agreement in her report? Which ones were most obvious? Which ones did you miss?

How does a problem with subject-verb agreement affect the reader's understanding of the material?

Rewrite the report fixing all of Regina's errors.

## Find and Correct Errors in Subject-Verb Agreement

To find problems with subject-verb agreement in your own writing, look for five trouble spots that often signal these problems.

### 1. *The Verb Is a Form of* Be, Have, *or* Do

The verbs *be, have,* and *do* do not follow the rules for forming singular and plural forms; they are **irregular verbs**.

#### Forms of the Verb *Be*

| Present Tense | Singular | Plural |
|---|---|---|
| First person | I am | we are |
| Second person | you are | you are |
| Third person | she, he, it is | they are |
| | the student is | the students are |
| **Past tense** | | |
| First person | I was | we were |
| Second person | you were | you were |
| Third person | she, he, it was | they were |
| | the student was | the students were |

#### Forms of the Verb *Have*, Present Tense

| | Singular | Plural |
|---|---|---|
| First person | I have | we have |
| Second person | you have | you have |
| Third person | she, he, it has | they have |
| | the student has | the students have |

#### Forms of the Verb *Do*, Present Tense

| | Singular | Plural |
|---|---|---|
| First person | I do | we do |
| Second person | you do | you do |
| Third person | she, he, it does | they do |
| | the student does | the students do |

These verbs cause problems for writers who in conversation use the same form in all cases: *He do the cleaning; they do the cleaning.* People also sometimes use the word *be* instead of the correct form of *be: She be on vacation.*

In college and at work, use the correct forms of the verbs *be, have,* and *do* as shown in the charts on page 354.

They ~~is~~ *are* sick today.

Joan ~~have~~ *has* the best jewelry.

Carlos ~~do~~ *does* the laundry every Wednesday.

**PRACTICE 1** **Identifying problems with subject-verb agreement**

Find and underline the four problems with subject-verb agreement in Regina Toms's report on page 353.

## 2. *Words Come between the Subject and the Verb*

When the subject and verb are not directly next to each other, it is more difficult to find them to make sure they agree. Most often, either a prepositional phrase or a dependent clause comes between the subject and the verb.

### PREPOSITIONAL PHRASE BETWEEN THE SUBJECT AND THE VERB

A **prepositional phrase** starts with a preposition and ends with a noun or pronoun: I took my bag *of books* and threw it *across the room.*

**The subject of a sentence is never in a prepositional phrase.** When you are looking for the subject of a sentence, you can cross out any prepositional phrases.

**Tip** For a list of common prepositions, see page 327.

A volunteer ~~in the Peace Corps~~ (serve/serves) two years.

### DEPENDENT CLAUSE BETWEEN THE SUBJECT AND THE VERB

A **dependent clause** has a subject and a verb, but it does not express a complete thought. When a dependent clause comes between the subject and the verb, it usually starts with the word *who, whose, whom, that,* or *which.*

**The subject of a sentence is never in a dependent clause.** When you are looking for the subject of a sentence, you can cross out any dependent clauses.

The coins ~~that I found last week~~ (seem/seems) valuable.

**PRACTICE 2** **Making subjects and verbs agree when they are separated by a dependent clause**

In each of the following sentences, cross out any dependent clauses. Then, correct any problems with subject-verb agreement. If the subject and the verb agree, write "OK" next to the sentence.

*have*

**Example: My cousins, ~~who immigrated to this country from Ecuador,~~ has ^ jobs in a fast-food restaurant.**

1. The restaurant that hired my cousins are not treating them fairly.
2. People who work in the kitchen has to report to work at 7:00 a.m.
3. The boss who supervises the morning shift tells the workers not to punch in until 9:00 a.m.
4. The benefits that full-time workers earn have not been offered to my cousins.
5. Ramón, whose hand was injured slicing potatoes, need to have physical therapy.
6. No one who works with him has helped him file for worker's compensation.
7. The doctors who cleaned his wound and put in his stitches at the hospital expects him to pay for the medical treatment.
8. The managers who run the restaurant insists that he is not eligible for medical coverage.
9. My cousins, whose English is not yet perfect, feels unable to leave their jobs.
10. The restaurant that treats them so badly offers the only opportunity for them to earn a living.

## *3. The Sentence Has a Compound Subject*

A **compound subject** is two (or more) subjects joined by *and, or,* or *nor.*

**Tip** Whenever you see a compound subject joined by *and,* try replacing it in your mind with *they*.

**And/Or Rule:** If two subjects are joined by *and,* use a plural verb. If two subjects are joined by *or* (or *nor*), they are considered separate, and the verb should agree with whatever subject it is closer to.

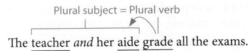

Plural subject = Plural verb

The teacher *and* her aide grade all the exams.

Subject *or* Singular subject = Singular verb

Either the teacher *or* her aide grades all the exams.

Subject *or* Plural subject = Plural verb

The teacher *or* her aides grade all the exams.

Subject *nor* Plural subject = Plural verb

Neither the teacher *nor* her aides grade all the exams.

## 4. *The Subject Is an Indefinite Pronoun*

An **indefinite pronoun** replaces a general person, place, or thing or a general group of people, places, or things. Indefinite pronouns are often singular, although there are some exceptions, as shown in the following chart.

| | |
|---|---|
| **Singular** | Everyone wants the semester to end. |
| **Plural** | Many want the semester to end. |
| **Singular** | Either of the meals is good. |

Often, an indefinite pronoun is followed by a prepositional phrase or dependent clause. Remember that the verb of a sentence must agree with the subject of the sentence, and the subject of a sentence is *never in a prepositional phrase or dependent clause.* To choose the correct verb, cross out the prepositional phrase or dependent clause.

Everyone ~~in all the classes~~ (want/wants) the term to end.

Several ~~who have to take the math exam~~ (is/are) studying together.

### Indefinite Pronouns

| **Always singular** | | | **May be singular or plural** |
|---|---|---|---|
| another | everybody | no one | all |
| anybody | everyone | nothing | any |
| anyone | everything | one (of) | none |
| anything | much | somebody | some |
| each (of)* | neither (of)* | someone | |
| either (of)* | nobody | something | |

*When one of these words is the subject, mentally replace it with *one*. *One* is singular and takes a singular verb.

## 5. *The Verb Comes before the Subject*

In most sentences, the subject comes before the verb. Two kinds of sentences often reverse the usual subject-verb order: questions and sentences that begin with *here* or *there*. In these two types of sentences, check carefully for errors in subject-verb agreement.

### QUESTIONS

In questions, the verb or part of the verb comes before the subject. To find the subject and verb, you can turn the question around as if you were going to answer it.

Where is the bookstore?/The bookstore is . . .

Are you excited?/You are excited.

 **Language note:** For reference charts showing how to form questions, see pages 450–51 and pages 452–55, in Chapter 26.

**Note:** Sometimes the verb in a sentence appears before the subject even in sentences that are not questions:

Most inspiring of all were her speeches on freedom.

### SENTENCES THAT BEGIN WITH *HERE* OR *THERE*

When a sentence begins with *here* or *there*, the subject often follows the verb. Turn the sentence around to find the subject and verb.

Here is your key to the apartment./Your key to the apartment is here.

*There* are four keys on the table./Four keys are on the table.

**PRACTICE 3** **Correcting a sentence when the verb comes before the subject**

Correct any problem with subject-verb agreement in the following sentences. If a sentence is already correct, write "OK" next to it.

**Example: What electives ~~do~~ the school offer?** (*does*)

1. What are the best reason to study music?
2. There is several good reasons.
3. There is evidence that music helps students with math.
4. What is your favorite musical instrument?
5. Here is a guitar, a saxophone, and a piano.

6. There is very few people with natural musical ability.
7. What time of day does you usually practice?
8. There is no particular time.
9. What musician does you admire most?
10. Here are some information about the importance of regular practice.

# Edit for Subject-Verb Agreement Problems

Use the chart on page 362, Finding and Fixing Problems with Subject-Verb Agreement, to help you complete the practices in this section and edit your own writing.

## PRACTICE 4 Correcting various subject-verb agreement problems

In the following sentences, identify any verb that does not agree with its subject. Then, correct the sentence using the correct form of the verb.

**Example: Some twenty-somethings in Washington, D.C., ~~wakes~~ [wake] before dawn to read the news.**

1. They does so not out of interest in current events.
2. Instead, their jobs in government and business requires them to read and summarize the latest information related to these jobs.
3. Each of their bosses need this information early in the morning to be prepared for the day.
4. For example, a politician who introduces new legislation want to know the public's reaction as soon as possible.
5. Learning of new complaints about such legislation by 8 a.m. give the politician time to shape a thoughtful response for a 10 a.m. news conference.
6. What is the benefits of the reading-and-summarizing job?
7. There is several, according to the young people who do such work.
8. Information and power goes together, some of them say.

9. A reputation for being in-the-know help them rise through the ranks at their workplaces.
10. Also, they has a chance to build skills and connections that can lead to other jobs.

### PRACTICE 5 Editing paragraphs for subject-verb agreement

Find and correct six problems with subject-verb agreement in the following paragraphs.

(1) You probably does not have a mirror at your computer desk, but if you did, you might notice something about yourself you had not been aware of before. (2) As you sit there, hour after hour, your shoulders are rounded, your back is slumped, and your posture are awful.

(3) Do not worry; you are not alone. (4) Most students spend hours in front of a computer monitor with terrible posture. (5) Then, they make things worse by getting up and heading off to school with painfully heavy backpacks on their backs. (6) Young people who carry a heavy burden is forced to hunch forward even more to balance the weight, adding strain to already seriously fatigued muscles. (7) Everyone who studies these trends are concerned.

(8) The study of people and their surroundings is known as *ergonomics*. (9) Improperly slouching at the computer and toting around a heavy backpack are both examples of poor ergonomics. (10) These bad habits is two causes of chronic back pain that can interfere with school, work, and sports. (11) Everyone, according to experts, need to sit up straight while at the computer, take frequent breaks to get up and walk around, and carry less in his or her backpack.

### PRACTICE 6 Editing subject-verb agreement errors and using formal English

**Tip** For more advice on using formal English, see Chapter 26. For advice on choosing appropriate words, see Chapter 27.

A friend of yours has been turned down for a course because of high enrollment, even though she registered early. She knows that her e-mail to the instructor teaching the course has a few problems in it. Help her by correcting any subject-verb agreement errors. Then, edit the informal English in the e-mail.

(1) Hey Prof Connors,

(2) I am e-mailing you to make sure you gets the e-mail I sent before about registering for your Business Writing course this semester.

(3) IMHO, it is one of the best classes this college offers. (4) I does not miss the deadline; I signed up on the first day, in fact. (5) I plans to graduate with a degree in business and economics, so your class is important to me. (6) Could you please check yur class roster to see if I was somehow skipped or missed? (7) I would sure appreciate it a ton, LOL. (8) Plz let me know what you finds out. (9) If I cannot get into your class this semester, I will have to rearrange my schedule so that I can takes it next semester instead. (10) I look forward to taking your class and learning all about business writing. (11) You rocks, prof.

(12) Sincerely,

Cameron Taylor

**PRACTICE 7** **Editing Regina's report**

Look back at Regina Toms's report on page 353. You may have already underlined the subject-verb agreement errors; if not, do so now. Next, using what you have learned in this chapter, correct each error.

**PRACTICE 8** **Editing your own writing for subject-verb agreement**

Edit for subject-verb agreement problems in a piece of your own writing—a paper for this course or another one, or something you have written for work or your everyday life. Use the chart on page 362 to help you.

# Chapter Review

1. The __________ and the ________ in a sentence must agree (match) in terms of number. They must both be __________, or they must both be plural.
2. Five trouble spots can cause errors in subject-verb agreement:
   - When the verb is a form of ______, ________, or ______.
   - When a ____________________ or a __________________ comes between the subject and the verb.
   - When the sentence has a ____________ subject joined by *and, or,* or *nor*.
   - When the subject is an ___________ pronoun.
   - When the _______ comes ________ the subject.

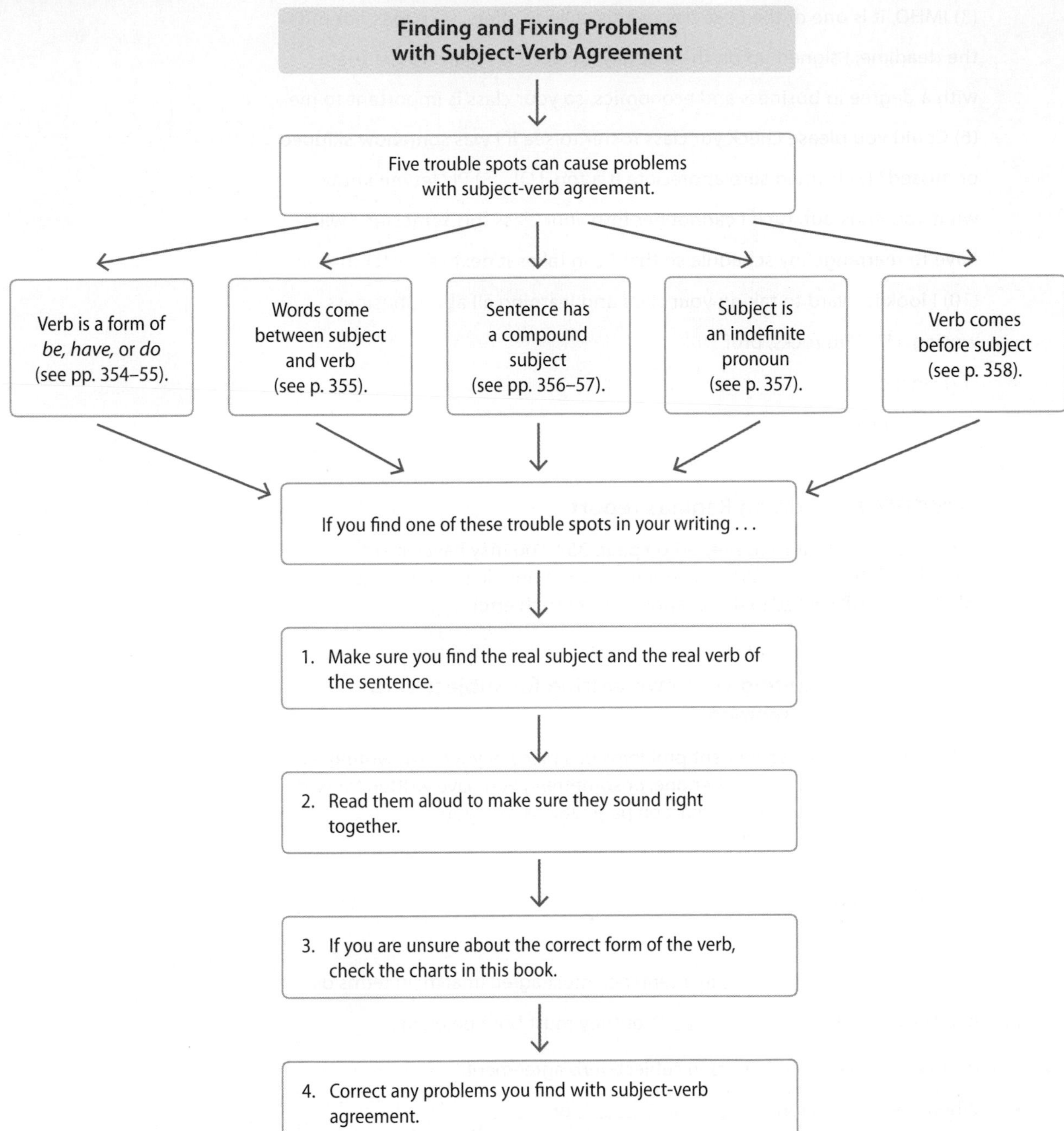
Finding and Fixing Problems with Subject-Verb Agreement
Five trouble spots can cause problems with subject-verb agreement.
Verb is a form of *be, have,* or *do* (see pp. 354–55).
Words come between subject and verb (see p. 355).
Sentence has a compound subject (see pp. 356–57).
Subject is an indefinite pronoun (see p. 357).
Verb comes before subject (see p. 358).
If you find one of these trouble spots in your writing . . .
1. Make sure you find the real subject and the real verb of the sentence.
2. Read them aloud to make sure they sound right together.
3. If you are unsure about the correct form of the verb, check the charts in this book.
4. Correct any problems you find with subject-verb agreement.

19

# Verb Tense

## Using Verbs to Express Different Times

## Understand What Verb Tense Is

**Verb tense** tells *when* an action happened or will happen: in the past, in the present, or in the future. Verbs change their **base form** or use the helping verbs *have, be,* or *will* to indicate different tenses.

| | |
|---|---|
| **Present tense** | Rick hikes every weekend. |
| **Past tense** | He hiked 10 miles last weekend. |
| **Future tense** | He will hike again on Saturday. |

**LaunchPadSolo**

Visit **LaunchPad Solo for Readers and Writers > Grammar > Basic Sentences** for more tutorials, videos, and practice with crafting paragraphs.

## GRAMMAR & MECHANICS ROADMAP

### An Overview

#### This Chapter Identifies the Following Trouble Spots

- Regular verb problems with present-tense endings
- Regular verb problems with past-tense endings
- Regular verb problems with past-participle endings
- Irregular verb problems in the present tense
- Irregular verb problems in the past tense
- Irregular verb problems in the past-participle tense
- Irregular verb problems in the past-perfect tense

#### Tools to Address the Trouble Spots


- Understanding verb tense (p. 363)
- Present tense endings for regular verbs (p. 365)
- Past-tense endings for regular verbs (p. 366)
- Past-participle endings for regular verbs (p. 366)
- List of irregular verbs (pp. 366–69)
- Verb forms of *be* and *have* (p. 369)
- Edit for Verb Problems exercises (p. 374)
- Chapter Review (p. 376)
- Finding and fixing verb tenses flowchart (p. 377)

 **Language note:** Remember to include needed endings on present-tense and past-tense verbs, even if they are not noticed in speech.

| | |
|---|---|
| **Present tense** | Nate listen**s** to his new iPod wherever he go**es**. |
| **Past tense** | Nate listen**ed** to his iPod while he walk**ed** the dog. |

## *In the Real World, Why Is It Important to Use the Correct Verb Tense?*

People outside the English classroom notice errors in verb tense and consider them major mistakes.

**Situation:** Cal is a summer intern in the systems division of a large company. He would like to get a part-time job there during the school year because he is studying computer science and knows that the experience would help him get a job after graduation. He sends this e-mail to his supervisor.

> I have work hard since coming to Technotron and learn many new things. Mr. Joseph tell me that he like my work and that I shown good motivation and teamwork. As he know, I spended many hours working on a special project for him. I would like to continue my work here beyond the summer. Therefore, I hope that you will consider me for future employment.
>
> Sincerely,
>
> Cal Troppo

**YOUR TURN**

What are your thoughts about Cal's e-mail?

Does Cal present himself professionally in this e-mail?

How could verb errors affect Cal's potential career or how he is perceived as an applicant for a job?

What can Cal do to improve his e-mail? Rewrite it so it has no verb errors.

**Tip** To find and correct problems with verbs, you need to be able to identify subjects and verbs. For a review, see Chapter 15. Some students have a tendency to forget these basic sentence parts unless they are often reinforced; make sure to go over them again if you haven't done so recently.

# Practice Using Correct Verbs

This section will teach you about verb tenses and give you practice with using them. The best way to learn how to use the various verb tenses correctly, however, is to read, write, and speak them as often as possible.

**PRACTICE 1** **Identifying verb errors**

Find and underline the seven verb errors in Cal's e-mail.

## *Regular Verbs*

Most verbs in English are **regular verbs** that follow standard rules about what endings to use to express time.

### PRESENT-TENSE ENDINGS: -*S* AND NO ENDING

The **present tense** is used for actions that are happening at the same time that they are being written about (the present) and for things that happen all the time. Present-tense, regular verbs either end in -*s* or have no ending added.

**Tip** A complete verb, also known as a verb phrase, is made up of the main verb and all of its helping verbs.

| *-s* ending | No ending |
|---|---|
| jumps | jump |
| walks | walk |
| lives | live |

Use the -*s* ending when the subject is *he, she, it,* or the name of one person or thing. Use no ending for all other subjects.

### Regular Verbs in the Present Tense

| | Singular | Plural |
|---|---|---|
| **First person** | I jump. | We jump. |
| **Second person** | You jump. | You jump. |
| **Third person** | She (he, it) jumps. | They jump. |
| | The child jumps. | The children jump. |

**Tip** For more about making verbs match subjects, see Chapter 18.

Do not confuse the simple present tense with the **present progressive**, which is used with a form of the helping verb *be* to describe actions that are in progress right now.

**Tip** In the examples throughout this chapter, subjects are underlined, and verbs are double-underlined.

| | |
|---|---|
| **Simple present** | I eat a banana every day. |
| **Present progressive** | I am eating a banana. |

 **Language note:** Some languages do not use progressive tenses. If you have trouble using progressive tenses, see Chapter 26.

### ONE REGULAR PAST-TENSE ENDING: -ED

**Tip** If a verb already ends in *-e*, just add *-d*: dance/danced. If a verb ends in *-y*, usually the *-y* changes to *-i* when *-ed* is added: *spy/spied; try/tried.*

The **past tense** is used for actions that have already happened. An *-ed* ending is needed on all regular verbs in the past tense.

| | Present tense | Past tense |
|---|---|---|
| **First person** | I avoid her. | I avoided her. |
| **Second person** | You help me. | You helped me. |
| **Third person** | He walks quickly. | He walked quickly. |

### ONE REGULAR PAST-PARTICIPLE ENDING: -ED

**Tip** The modal auxiliary verbs are *can, could, may, might, must, shall, should, will,* and *would.*

The **past participle** is a verb that is used with a helping verb (also called a modal auxiliary), such as *have* or *be*. For all regular verbs, the past-participle form is the same as the past-tense form: It uses an *-ed* ending. (To learn about when past participles are used, see pp. 371–73.)

| Past tense | Past participle |
|---|---|
| My kids watched cartoons. | They have watched cartoons before. |
| George visited his cousins. | He has visited them every year. |

## *Irregular Verbs*

**Irregular verbs** do not follow the simple rules of regular verbs, which have just two present-tense endings (*-s* or *-es*) and two past-tense endings (*-d* or *-ed*). Irregular verbs show past tense with a change in spelling, although some irregular verbs, such as *cost, hit,* and *put,* do not change their spelling. The most common irregular verbs are *be* and *have* (see p. 369). As you write and edit, use the following chart to make sure you use the correct form of irregular verbs.

**Note:** What is called "present tense" in the chart that follows is sometimes called the "base form of the verb."

### Irregular Verbs

| Present tense (base form of verb) | Past tense | Past participle (used with helping verb) |
|---|---|---|
| be (am/are/is) | was /were | been |
| become | became | become |
| begin | began | begun |
| bite | bit | bitten |
| blow | blew | blown |
| break | broke | broken |
| bring | brought | brought |
| build | built | built |
| buy | bought | bought |

| Present tense (base form of verb) | Past tense | Past participle (used with helping verb) |
|---|---|---|
| catch | caught | caught |
| choose | chose | chosen |
| come | came | come |
| cost | cost | cost |
| dive | dived, dove | dived |
| do | did | done |
| draw | drew | drawn |
| drink | drank | drunk |
| drive | drove | driven |
| eat | ate | eaten |
| fall | fell | fallen |
| feed | fed | fed |
| feel | felt | felt |
| fight | fought | fought |
| find | found | found |
| fly | flew | flown |
| forget | forgot | forgotten |
| get | got | gotten |
| give | gave | given |
| go | went | gone |
| grow | grew | grown |
| have/has | had | had |
| hear | heard | heard |
| hide | hid | hidden |
| hit | hit | hit |
| hold | held | held |
| hurt | hurt | hurt |
| keep | kept | kept |
| know | knew | known |
| lay | laid | laid |
| lead | led | led |
| leave | left | left |
| let | let | let |
| lie | lay | lain |
| light | lit | lit |
| lose | lost | lost |
| make | made | made |
| mean | meant | meant |
| meet | met | met |

►

| Present tense (base form of verb) | Past tense | Past participle (used with helping verb) |
|---|---|---|
| pay | paid | paid |
| put | put | put |
| quit | quit | quit |
| read | read | read |
| ride | rode | ridden |
| ring | rang | rung |
| rise | rose | risen |
| run | ran | run |
| say | said | said |
| see | saw | seen |
| seek | sought | sought |
| sell | sold | sold |
| send | sent | sent |
| shake | shook | shaken |
| show | showed | shown |
| shrink | shrank | shrunk |
| shut | shut | shut |
| sing | sang | sung |
| sink | sank | sunk |
| sit | sat | sat |
| sleep | slept | slept |
| speak | spoke | spoken |
| spend | spent | spent |
| stand | stood | stood |
| steal | stole | stolen |
| stick | stuck | stuck |
| sting | stung | stung |
| strike | struck | struck, stricken |
| swim | swam | swum |
| take | took | taken |
| teach | taught | taught |
| tear | tore | torn |
| tell | told | told |
| think | thought | thought |
| throw | threw | thrown |
| understand | understood | understood |

| Present tense (base form of verb) | Past tense | Past participle (used with helping verb) |
|---|---|---|
| wake | woke | woken |
| wear | wore | worn |
| win | won | won |
| write | wrote | written |

### PRESENT TENSE OF BE AND HAVE

The present tense of the verbs *be* and *have* is irregular, as shown in the following chart.

## Present Tense of *Be* and *Have*

| ***Be*** | | ***Have*** | |
|---|---|---|---|
| I am | we are | I have | we have |
| you are | you are | you have | you have |
| he, she, it is | they are | he, she, it has | they have |
| the editor is | the editors are | | |
| Beth is | Beth and Christina are | | |

### PAST TENSE OF BE

The past tense of the verb *be* is tricky because it has two forms: *was* and *were.*

## Past Tense of *Be*

| | Singular | Plural |
|---|---|---|
| **First person** | I was | we were |
| **Second person** | you were | you were |
| **Third person** | she, he, it was | they were |
| | the student was | the students were |

**PRACTICE 2** **Using irregular verbs in the past tense**

In the following paragraph, replace any incorrect present-tense verbs with the correct past tense of the verb. If you are unsure of the past-tense forms of irregular verbs, refer to the chart on pages 366–69.

(1) For years, Homer and Langley Collyer are known for their strange living conditions. (2) Neighbors who passed by the brothers' New York City townhouse see huge piles of trash through the windows. (3) At night, Langley roamed the streets in search of more junk. (4) In March 1947, an anonymous caller tells the police that someone had died in the Collyers' home. (5) In response, officers break through a second-floor window and tunneled through mounds of newspapers, old umbrellas, and other junk. (6) Eventually, they find the body of Homer Collyer, who seemed to have died of starvation. (7) But where was Langley? (8) In efforts to locate him, workers spend days removing trash from the house—more than one hundred tons' worth in total. (9) They bring a strange variety of items to the curb, including medical equipment, bowling balls, fourteen pianos, and the frame of a Model T car. (10) In early April, a worker finally discovered Langley's body. (11) It lies just 10 feet from where Homer had been found. (12) Apparently, Langley died while bringing food to his disabled brother. (13) As he tunneled ahead, a pile of trash falls on him and crushed him. (14) This trash was part of a booby trap that Langley had created to stop intruders. (15) Not long after the brothers' deaths, the city demolished their former home. (16) In 1965, community leaders do something that might have surprised Homer and Langley: Where the trash-filled home once stands, workers created a neat and peaceful park. (17) In the 1990s, this green space becomes the Collyer Brothers Park.

For irregular verbs, the past participle is often different from the past tense.

| | Past tense | Past participle |
|---|---|---|
| **Regular verb** | I walked home. | I have walked home before. |
| **Irregular verb** | I drove home. | I have driven home before. |

It is difficult to predict how irregular verbs form the past participle. Until you are familiar with them, find them in the chart on pages 366–69.

## *Past Participles*

A **past participle**, by itself, cannot be the main verb of a sentence. When a past participle is combined with another verb, called a **helping verb**, however, it can be used to make the present perfect tense and the past perfect tense.

**Tip** For more about using perfect-tense verbs, see Chapter 26.

*Have/Has* + Past participle = Present perfect tense

The **present perfect** tense is used for an action that began in the past and either continues into the present or was completed at some unknown time in the past.

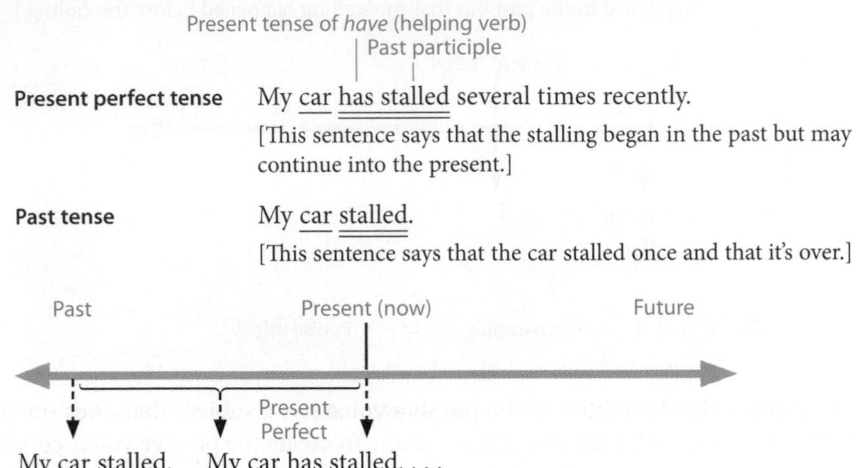
Present tense of *have* (helping verb)
Past participle
**Present perfect tense** My car has stalled several times recently.
[This sentence says that the stalling began in the past but may continue into the present.]
**Past tense** My car stalled.
[This sentence says that the car stalled once and that it's over.]
Past
Present (now)
Future
Present Perfect
My car stalled.
My car has stalled. . . .

## Present Perfect Tense

| | **Singular** | **Plural** |
|---|---|---|
| **First person** | I have laughed. | We have laughed. |
| **Second person** | You have laughed. | You have laughed. |
| **Third person** | She /he /it has laughed. | They have laughed. |
| | The baby has laughed. | The babies have laughed. |

**Language note:** Be careful not to leave out *have* when it is needed for the present perfect. Time-signal words such as *since* and *for* may mean that the present perfect is required.

**Incorrect** I drive since 1985. We wait for 2 hours.

**Correct** I **have** driven since 1985. We **have** waited for 2 hours.

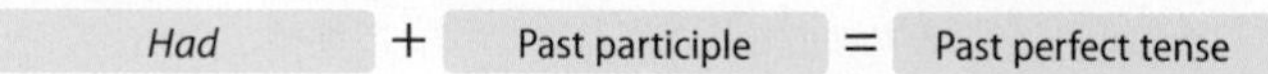
*Had* + Past participle = Past perfect tense

Use *had* plus the past participle to make the **past perfect tense**. The past perfect tense is used for an action that began in the past and ended before some other past action.

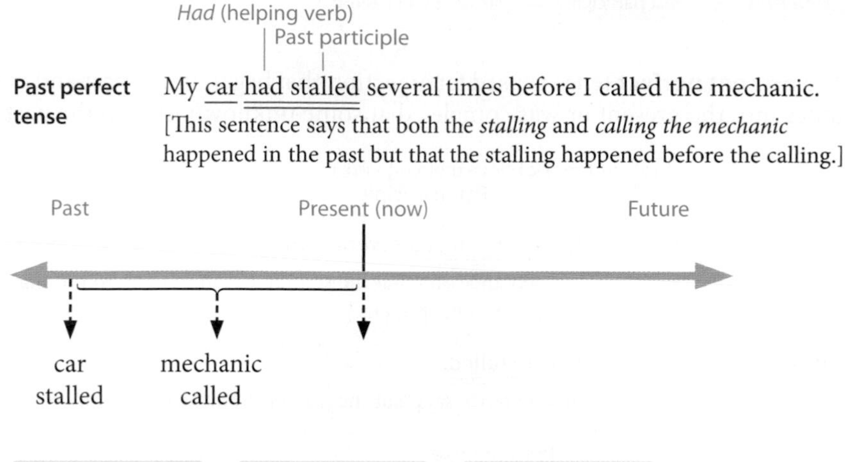
*Had* (helping verb)
Past participle
Past
Present (now)
Future
car stalled
mechanic called

**Past perfect tense** My car had stalled several times before I called the mechanic.

[This sentence says that both the *stalling* and *calling the mechanic* happened in the past but that the stalling happened before the calling.]

*Be* + Past participle = Passive voice

A sentence that is written in the **passive voice** has a subject that does not perform an action. Instead, the subject is acted on. To create the passive voice, combine a form of the verb *be* with a past participle.

Form of *be* (helping verb)
Past participle

**Passive** The newspaper was thrown onto the porch.

[The subject, *newspaper,* did not throw itself onto the porch. Some unidentified person threw the newspaper.]

Most sentences should be written in the **active voice**, which means that the subject performs the action.

**Active** The delivery person threw the newspaper onto the porch.

[The subject, *delivery person,* performed the action: He or she threw the newspaper.]

Use the passive voice when no one person performed the action, when you do not know who performed the action, or when you want to emphasize the receiver of the action. When you know who performed the action, it is usually preferable to identify the actor.

**Active** The bandleader chose Kelly to do a solo.

**Passive** Kelly was chosen to do a solo.

[If you wanted to emphasize Kelly's being chosen rather than the bandleader's choice, you might decide to use the passive voice.]

**PRACTICE 3** **Changing the passive voice to the active voice**

Rewrite the following sentences, changing them from the passive voice to the active voice.

*The legislature cut funding*
**Example:** ~~**Funding**~~ **for animal shelters** ~~**was cut by the legislature.**~~

1. Some shelters were going to be closed by the owners.
2. What would become of the animals was unknown.
3. A campaign was started by animal lovers.
4. Interviews were given by the owners and volunteers at shelters.
5. The animals were filmed by news teams.
6. The stories were aired on all the local television stations.
7. A protest was staged by animal lovers across the state.
8. Fund-raisers of all sorts were held.
9. Some funds were restored by the legislature.
10. Enough money was raised to keep the shelters open.

## *Consistency of Verb Tense*

**Consistency of verb tense** means that all actions in a sentence that happen (or happened) at the same time are in the same tense. If all the actions happen in the present or happen all the time, use the present for all verbs in the sentence. If all the actions happened in the past, use the past tense for all verbs.

Past tense — Present tense

**Inconsistent** The movie started just as we take our seats.

[The actions both happened at the same time, but *started* is in the past tense, and *take* is in the present tense.]

Past tense — Present tense

**Consistent, past tense** The movie started just as we took our seats.

[The actions *started* and *took* both happened in the past, and both are in the past tense.]

Use different tenses only when you are referring to different times.

My daughter hated math as a child, but now she loves it.

[The sentence uses two tenses because the first verb (*hated*) refers to a past condition, whereas the second verb (*loves*) refers to a present one.]

**PRACTICE 4** **Using consistent verb tense**

In each of the following sentences, double-underline the verbs, and correct any unnecessary shifts in verb tense. Write the correct form of the verb in the blank space provided.

**Example:** _have_ **Although some people dream of having their picture taken by a famous photographer, not many ~~had~~ the chance.**

1. __________ Now, special stores in malls take magazine-quality photographs of anyone who wanted one.
2. __________ The founder of one business got the idea when she hear friends complaining about how bad they looked in family photographs.
3. __________ She decide to open a business to take studio-style photographs that did not cost a lot of money.
4. __________ Her first store included special lighting and offers different sets, such as colored backgrounds and outdoor scenes.
5. __________ Now, her stores even have makeup studios for people who wanted a special look for their pictures.

# Edit for Verb Problems

Use the chart on page 377, Finding and Fixing Verb-Tense Errors, to help you complete the practices in this section and edit your own writing.

**PRACTICE 5** **Correcting various verb problems**

In the following sentences, find and correct any verb problems.

**Example: Sheena ~~be~~ tired of the tattoo on her left shoulder.** (is)

1. Sheena had never consider a tattoo until several of her friends got them.
2. Sheena was twenty-two when she goes to the tattoo parlor.
3. After looking at many designs, she choose a purple rose design, which she gave to the tattoo artist.
4. Her sister liked the tattoo, but her mother faints.
5. Like Sheena, many people who now reached their thirties want to get rid of their old tattoos.

6. A few years ago, when a person decides to have a tattoo removed, doctors had to cut out the design.
7. That technique leaved scars.
8. Today, doctors using laser light to break up the ink molecules in the skin.
9. Six months ago, Sheena start to have treatments to remove her tattoo.
10. The procedure hurted every time she saw the doctor, but she hoped it would be worth the pain.

## PRACTICE 6 Editing paragraphs for verb problems

Find and correct seven problems with verb tense in the following paragraphs.

(1) When you thought about a farm, you probably imagine acres of cornfields and stalls full of noisy animals. (2) Although that is an understandable vision, it may not be a particularly accurate one in the near future. (3) Some experts believes that farms of the future will be found inside the top floors of a city's tallest skyscrapers. (4) This concept have been referred to as "vertical gardening."

(5) Indoor city gardening not only would help make places become more self-sufficient but also could provide new uses for the variety of abandoned buildings that are finded scattered throughout large cities. (6) Experts has suggested that the water used for these small farms and gardens could be recycled from indoor fishponds. (7) False sunlight could be created through the use of artificial lights. (8) Thermostats could control the indoor temperatures.

(9) Although this technology is not currently available, architects has been toying with possible designs. (10) In the future, farms will most likely include everything from solar panels and windmills to generators that run on biofuels. (11) It is about five to ten years before all these ideas will be commonplace.

**PRACTICE 7** **Editing verb problems and using formal English**

Your sister has a bad case of laryngitis and wants to bring a note about her condition to her doctor. Help her by correcting the verb problems in the note. Then, edit the informal English.

(1) What's up, Doc Kerrigan?

(2) Your assistant ask me to tell you about my symptoms, so I will describe them as well as I can. (3) I becomed sick about a day ago. (4) Now, my throat hurt every time I swallowed, and I cannot speak. (5) Also, I has a high fever, and I be wicked tired. (6) I do not think I has ever feeled so crappy before. (7) I looked forward to seeing you during my appointment.

(8) Thanks mucho,

Corrine Evans

**PRACTICE 8** **Editing your own writing for verb problems**

Edit verb-tense problems in a piece of your own writing—a paper for this course or another one, or something you have written for work or your everyday life. Use the chart on page 377 to help you.

# Chapter Review

1. Verb ________ indicates when the action in a sentence happens (past, present, or future).
2. What are the two present-tense endings for regular verbs? ________________
3. How do regular verbs in the past tense end? __________
4. The past participle is used with a _________ verb.
5. Verbs that do not follow the regular pattern for verbs are called __________.
6. An action that started in the past but might continue into the present uses the ________________.
7. An action that happened in the past before something else that happened in the past uses the ________________.
8. You should usually avoid using the _________ voice, which has a subject that performs no action but is acted upon.
9. Verb tenses are consistent when actions that happen at the same _______ are in the same _______.

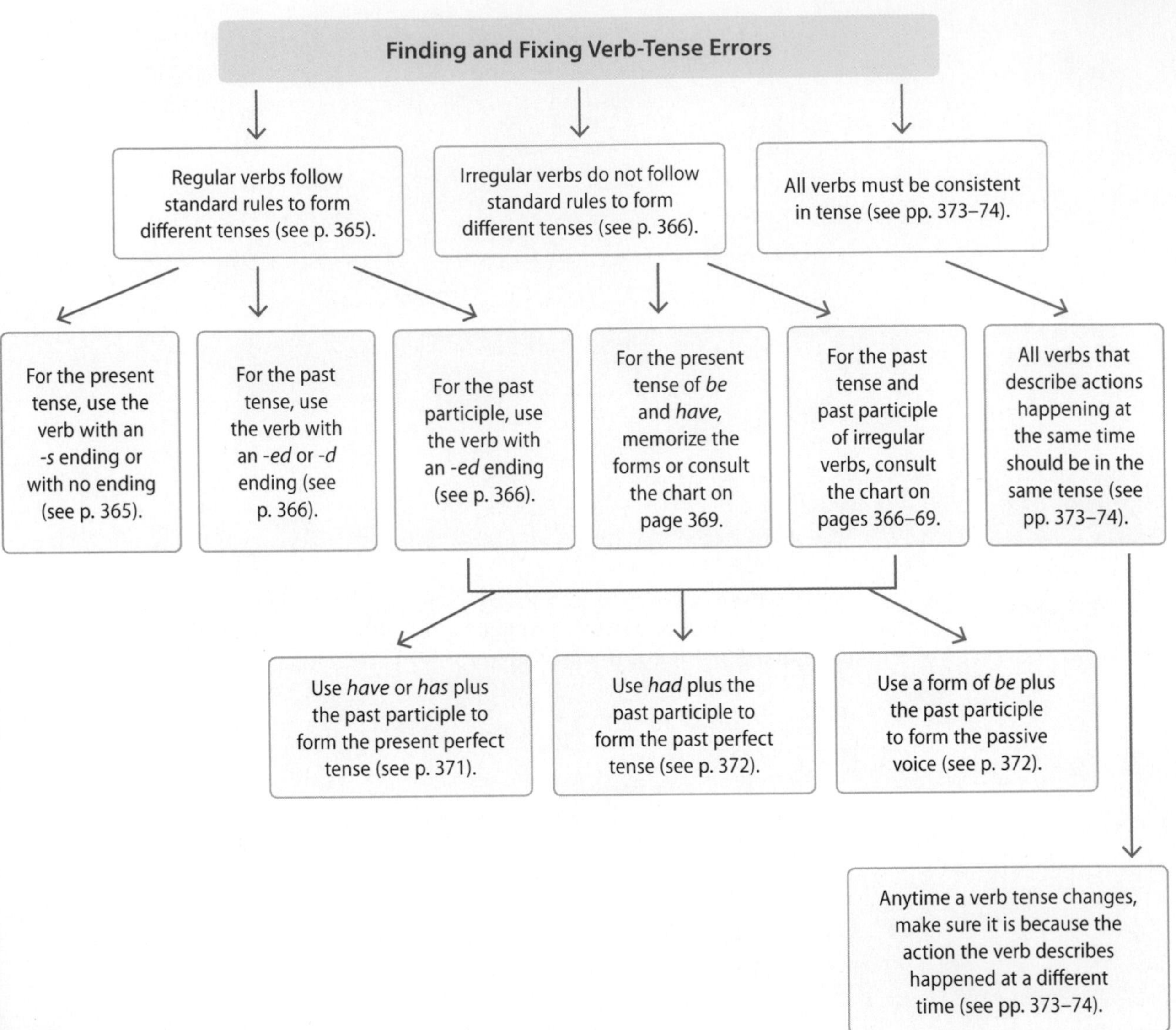
Finding and Fixing Verb-Tense Errors
Regular verbs follow standard rules to form different tenses (see p. 365).
Irregular verbs do not follow standard rules to form different tenses (see p. 366).
All verbs must be consistent in tense (see pp. 373–74).
For the present tense, use the verb with an -s ending or with no ending (see p. 365).
For the past tense, use the verb with an -ed or -d ending (see p. 366).
For the past participle, use the verb with an -ed ending (see p. 366).
For the present tense of be and have, memorize the forms or consult the chart on page 369.
For the past tense and past participle of irregular verbs, consult the chart on pages 366–69.
All verbs that describe actions happening at the same time should be in the same tense (see pp. 373–74).
Use have or has plus the past participle to form the present perfect tense (see p. 371).
Use had plus the past participle to form the past perfect tense (see p. 372).
Use a form of be plus the past participle to form the passive voice (see p. 372).
Anytime a verb tense changes, make sure it is because the action the verb describes happened at a different time (see pp. 373–74).

# Part 4

# Other Grammar Concerns

"I write to persuade and to make connections."

—John F., student

# 20

# Pronouns

## Using Substitutes for Nouns

## Understand What Pronouns Are

A **pronoun** is used in place of a noun or other pronoun mentioned earlier. Pronouns enable you to avoid repeating those nouns or other pronouns mentioned earlier.

Sheryl got into ~~Sheryl's~~ her car.

I like Mario. ~~Mario~~ He is a good dancer.

The noun or pronoun that a pronoun replaces is called the **antecedent**. In most cases, a pronoun refers to a specific antecedent nearby.

I picked up my new glasses. They are cool.

(Antecedent: glasses; Pronoun replacing antecedent: They)

**LaunchPadSolo**

Visit **LaunchPad Solo for Readers and Writers > Grammar > Parts of Speech** for more tutorials, videos, and practice with crafting paragraphs.

## GRAMMAR & MECHANICS ROADMAP

### An Overview

**This Chapter Identifies the Following Trouble Spots**

- Pronoun agreement
- Indefinite pronouns
- Collective nouns
- Vague and ambiguous pronouns
- Subject, object, and possessive pronouns
- Point of view pronouns

**Tools to Address the Trouble Spots**

# Practice Using Pronouns Correctly

## *Identify Pronouns*

Before you practice finding and correcting common pronoun errors, it is helpful to practice identifying pronouns.

### Common Pronouns

| Personal pronouns | Possessive pronouns | Indefinite pronouns | |
|---|---|---|---|
| I | my | all | much |
| me | mine | any | neither (of) |
| you | your/yours | anybody | nobody |
| she/he | hers/his | anyone | none (of) |
| her/him | hers/his | anything | no one |
| it | its | both | nothing |
| we | our/ours | each (of) | one (of) |
| us | our/ours | either (of) | some |
| they | their/theirs | everybody | somebody |
| them | their/theirs | everyone | someone |
| | | everything | something |
| | | few (of) | |

**PRACTICE 1** **Identifying pronouns**

In each of the following sentences, circle the pronoun, underline the noun it refers to, and draw an arrow from the pronoun to the noun.

**Example:** **People can have a hard time seeing stars at night if they live in or near a big city.**

1. Each night, the stars fill the skies, but in many large cities, they are impossible to see.
2. The huge amount of light coming from homes, businesses, and streets creates a type of pollution, and it makes seeing the stars difficult.
3. The average night sky has approximately 2,500 stars in it, and they can be seen with the human eye.

4. In many neighborhoods, however, only two hundred or three hundred stars can be spotted, whereas in a big city, only about a dozen of them can be seen.
5. The International Dark Sky Association focuses on reducing light pollution as its main goal and has several recommendations.
6. Pointing lights down toward the ground instead of allowing them to shine up toward the sky is one suggestion.
7. To help battle light pollution, some cities and towns have passed laws limiting what lights they will allow.
8. Experts have been studying light pollution, and they have reported that it can affect many things, including wildlife and even human health.
9. Migrating birds sometimes fly over brightly lit cities and, confused by the unnatural light, fly in circles until they become exhausted.
10. Too much light has also been shown to be harmful to humans, and studies are being done to determine just how this overexposure affects them.

## *Check for Pronoun Agreement*

A pronoun must agree with (match) the noun or pronoun it refers to in number. It must be either singular (one) or plural (more than one).

If a pronoun is singular, it must also match the noun or pronoun it refers to in gender (*he, she,* or *it*).

**Consistent** Magda sold *her* old television set.
[*Her* agrees with *Magda* because both are singular and feminine.]

**Consistent** The Wilsons sold *their* old television set.
[*Their* agrees with *the Wilsons* because both are plural.]

Watch out for singular, general nouns. If a noun is singular, the pronoun that refers to it must be singular as well.

**Inconsistent** Any student can tell you what *their* least favorite course is.
[*Student* is singular, but the pronoun *their* is plural.]

**Consistent** Any student can tell you what *his* or *her* least favorite course is.
[*Student* is singular, and so are the pronouns *his* and *her*.]

To avoid using the awkward phrase *his or her*, make the subject plural when you can.

**Consistent** Most students can tell you what *their* least favorite course is.

Two types of words often cause errors in pronoun agreement: indefinite pronouns and collective nouns.

## *Indefinite Pronouns*

An **indefinite pronoun** does not refer to a specific person, place, or thing: It is general. Indefinite pronouns often take singular verbs. Whenever a pronoun refers to an indefinite pronoun, check for agreement.

The monks got up at dawn. Everybody had ~~their~~ his chores for the day.

### Indefinite Pronouns

| Always singular | | | May be plural or singular |
|---|---|---|---|
| another | everyone | nothing | all |
| anybody/anyone | everything | one (of) | any |
| anything | much | somebody | none |
| each (of) | neither (of) | someone | some |
| either (of) | nobody | something | |
| everybody | no one | | |

**Note:** Many people object to the use of only the masculine pronoun *he* when referring to a singular indefinite pronoun, such as *everyone*. Although grammatically correct, using the masculine form alone to refer to an indefinite pronoun is considered sexist. Here are two ways to avoid this problem:

1. Use *his or her*.

   Someone posted *his or her* e-mail address to the Web site.

2. Change the sentence so that the pronoun refers to a plural noun or pronoun.

   Some students posted *their* e-mail addresses to the Web site.

**PRACTICE 2** **Using indefinite pronouns**

Circle the correct pronoun or group of words in parentheses.

(1) Anyone who wants to start (their/his or her) own business had better be prepared to work hard. (2) One may find, for example, that (his or her/

their) work is never done. (3) Something is always waiting, with (its/their) own peculiar demands. (4) Nothing gets done on (their/its) own. (5) Anybody who expects to have more freedom now that (he or she no longer works/they no longer work) for a boss may be disappointed. (6) After all, when you work as an employee for a company, someone above you makes decisions as (they see/he or she sees) fit. (7) When you are your own boss, no one else places (themselves/himself or herself) in the position of final responsibility.

(8) Somebody starting a business may also be surprised by how much tax (they/he or she) must pay. (9) Each employee at a company pays only about half as much toward social security as what (they/he or she) would pay if self-employed. (10) Neither medical nor dental coverage can be obtained as inexpensively as (it/they) can when a person is an employee at a corporation.

## *Collective Nouns*

A **collective noun** names a group that acts as a single unit.

### Common Collective Nouns

| | | |
|---|---|---|
| audience | company | group |
| class | crowd | jury |
| college | family | society |
| committee | government | team |

Collective nouns are usually singular, so when you use a pronoun to refer to a collective noun, it is also usually singular.

The team had ~~their~~ its sixth consecutive win of the season.

If the people in a group are acting as individuals, however, the noun is plural and should be used with a plural pronoun.

The class brought *their* papers to read.

## *Make Pronoun Reference Clear*

In an **ambiguous pronoun reference**, the pronoun could refer to more than one noun.

**Ambiguous** Enrico told Jim that *he* needed a better résumé.
[Did Enrico tell Jim that Enrico himself needed a better résumé? Or did Enrico tell Jim that Jim needed a better résumé?]

**Edited** Enrico advised Jim to revise his résumé.

**Ambiguous** I put the glass on the shelf, even though it was dirty.
[Was the glass dirty? Or was the shelf dirty?]

**Edited** I put the dirty glass on the shelf.

In a **vague pronoun reference**, the pronoun does not refer clearly to any particular person, place, or thing. To correct a vague pronoun reference, use a more specific noun instead of the pronoun.

**Vague** When Tom got to the clinic, they told him it was closed.
[Who told Tom the clinic was closed?]

**Edited** When Tom got to the clinic, the nurse told him it was closed.

**Vague** Before I finished printing my report, it ran out of paper.
[What ran out of paper?]

**Edited** Before I finished printing my report, the printer ran out of paper.

### PRACTICE 3 Avoiding ambiguous or vague pronoun references

Edit each sentence to eliminate ambiguous or vague pronoun references. Some sentences may be revised in more than one way.

**Example: I am always looking for good advice on controlling my weight, but ~~they~~ *experts* have provided little help.**

1. My doctor referred me to a physical therapist, and she said that I needed to exercise more.
2. I joined a workout group and did exercises with the members, but it did not solve my problem.
3. I tried a lower-fat diet along with the exercising, but it did not really work either.
4. They used to say that eliminating carbohydrates is the easiest way to lose weight.
5. Therefore, I started eating fats again and stopped consuming carbs, but this was not a permanent solution.
6. Although I lost weight and loved eating fatty foods, it did not keep me from eventually gaining the weight back.
7. Last week, I overheard my Uncle Kevin talking to my brother, and he explained how he stayed slender even while traveling a lot.

8. Uncle Kevin eats fruit and vegetables instead of junk food while traveling, and it has kept off the pounds.
9. He says that it is not hard to pack carrots or apples for a trip, so anyone can do this.
10. I now try to plan better, eat less at each meal, and ignore all diet books, and I hope it works.

In a **repetitious pronoun reference**, the pronoun repeats a reference to a noun rather than replacing the noun.

The nurse at the clinic ~~he~~ told Tom that it was closed.

The newspaper~~,~~ ~~it~~ says that the new diet therapy is promising.

**PRACTICE 4** **Avoiding repetitious pronoun references**

Correct any repetitious pronoun references in the following sentences.

**Example: Car commercials ~~they~~ want viewers to believe that buying a certain brand of car will bring happiness.**

1. Young people they sometimes take advertisements too literally.
2. In a beer advertisement, it might suggest that drinking alcohol makes people more attractive and popular.
3. People who see or hear an advertisement they have to think about the message.
4. Parents should help their children understand why advertisements they do not show the real world.
5. A recent study, it said that parents can help kids overcome the influence of advertising.

## *Use the Right Type of Pronoun*

Three important types of pronouns are **subject pronouns**, **object pronouns**, and **possessive pronouns**. Notice their uses in the following sentences.

Object pronoun | Subject pronoun

The dog barked at *him*, and *he* laughed.

Possessive pronoun

As Josh walked out, *his* phone started ringing.

**Tip** Never put an apostrophe in a possessive pronoun.

## Pronoun Types

| | Subject | Object | Possessive |
|---|---|---|---|
| **First-person singular/plural** | I/we | me/us | my, mine/our, ours |
| **Second-person singular/plural** | you/you | you/you | your, yours/your, yours |
| **Third-person singular** | he, she, it<br>who | him, her, it<br>whom | his, her, hers, its<br>whose |
| **Third-person plural** | they<br>who | them<br>whom | their, theirs<br>whose |

**Language note:** Notice that pronouns have gender (*he/she, him/her, his/her/hers*). The pronoun must agree with the gender of the noun to which it refers.

**Incorrect** Carolyn went to see *his* boyfriend.

**Correct** Carolyn went to see *her* boyfriend.

Also, notice that English has different forms for subject and object pronouns, as shown in the previous chart.

Read the following sentence, and replace the underlined nouns with pronouns. Notice that all the pronouns are different.

When Andreas made an A on Andreas's final exam, Andreas was proud of himself, and the teacher congratulated Andreas.

### SUBJECT PRONOUNS

**Subject pronouns** serve as the subject of a verb.

*You* live next door to a coffee shop.
*I* opened the door too quickly.

### OBJECT PRONOUNS

**Tip** For a list of common prepositions, see page 327.

**Object pronouns** either receive the action of a verb or are part of a prepositional phrase.

**Object of the verb** Jay gave *me* his watch.

**Object of the preposition** Jay gave his watch to *me*.

## POSSESSIVE PRONOUNS

**Possessive pronouns** show ownership.

Dave is *my* uncle.

Three trouble spots make it difficult to know which type of pronoun to use; compound subjects and objects, comparisons, and sentences that need *who* or *whom*.

## OTHER TYPES OF PRONOUNS

**Intensive pronouns** emphasize a noun or other pronoun. **Reflexive pronouns** are used when the performer of an action is also the receiver of the action. Both types of pronouns end in *-self* or *-selves*.

**Reflexive** He taught *himself* how to play the guitar.

**Intensive** The club members *themselves* have offered to support the initiative.

**Relative pronouns** refer to a noun already mentioned, and introduce a group of words that describe this noun (*who, whom, whose, which, that*).

Tomatoes, *which* are popular worldwide, were first grown in South America.

**Interrogative pronouns** are used to begin questions (*who, whom, whose, which, what*).

*What* did the senator say at the meeting?

**Demonstrative pronouns** specify which noun is being referred to (*this, these, that, those*).

Use *this* simple budgeting app, not *that* complicated one.

**Reciprocal pronouns** refer to individuals when the antecedent is plural (*each other, one another*).

My friend and I could not see *one another* in the crowd.

## PRONOUNS USED WITH COMPOUND SUBJECTS AND OBJECTS

A **compound subject** has more than one subject joined by *and* or *or*. A **compound object** has more than one object joined by *and* or *or*.

**Compound subject** *Chandler and I* worked on the project.

**Compound object** My boss gave the assignment to *Chandler and me.*

**Tip** When you are writing about yourself and someone else, always put yourself after everyone else. *My friends and I went to a club*, not *I and my friends went to a club.*

To decide which type of pronoun to use in a compound construction, try leaving out the other part of the compound and the *and* or *or*. Then, say the sentence aloud to yourself.

**Tip** Many people make the mistake of using *I* in the phrase *between you and I*. The correct pronoun with *between* is the object *me*.

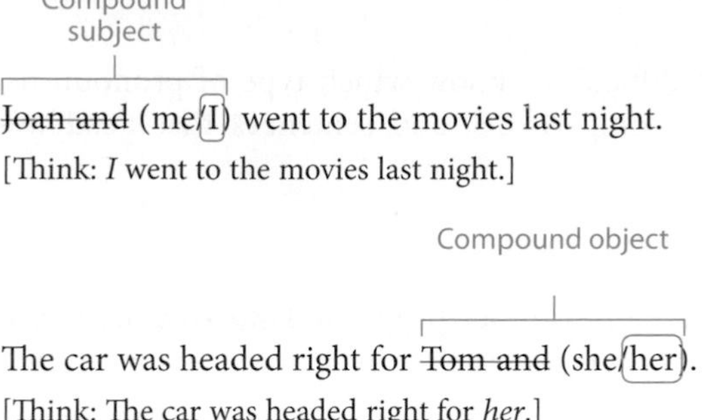
Compound subject
~~Joan and~~ (me/I) went to the movies last night.
[Think: *I* went to the movies last night.]
Compound object
The car was headed right for ~~Tom and~~ (she/her).
[Think: The car was headed right for *her*.]

If a pronoun is part of a compound object in a prepositional phrase, use an object pronoun.

Compound object

I will keep that information just between you and (I/me).

[*Between you and me* is a prepositional phrase, so an object pronoun, *me*, is required.]

**PRACTICE 5** **Editing pronouns in compound constructions**

Correct any pronoun errors in the following sentences. If a sentence is already correct, write a "C" next to it.

**Example: Marie Curie made several major contributions to science, but in 1898, ~~her~~** *she* **and her husband, Pierre Curie, announced their greatest achievement: the discovery of radium.**

1. Before this discovery, Marie and Pierre understood that certain substances gave off rays of energy, but them and other scientists were just beginning to learn why and how.
2. Eventually, the Curies made a discovery that intrigued they and, soon afterward, hundreds of other researchers.
3. Two previously unknown elements, radium and polonium, were responsible for the extra radioactivity; fascinated by this finding, Marie began thinking about the consequences of the work that she and her husband had done.

4. As them and other researchers were to discover, radium was especially valuable because it could be used in X-rays and for other medical purposes.
5. Marie was deeply moved when, in 1903, the scientific community honored she and Pierre with the Nobel Prize in physics.

## PRONOUNS USED IN COMPARISONS

Using the right type of pronoun in comparisons is particularly important because using the wrong type changes the meaning of the sentence. Editing comparisons can be tricky because they often imply (suggest the presence of) words that are not actually included in the sentence.

Bob trusts Donna more than *I.*

[This sentence means that Bob trusts Donna more than I trust her. The implied words are *trust her.*]

Bob trusts Donna more than *me.*

[This sentence means that Bob trusts Donna more than he trusts me. The implied words are *he trusts.*]

**Tip** To find comparisons, look for the word *than* or *as.*

To decide whether to use a subject or object pronoun in a comparison, try adding the implied words and saying the sentence aloud.

The registrar is much more efficient than (us/we).

[Think: The registrar is much more efficient than *we are.*]

Susan rides her bicycle more than (he/him).

[Think: Susan rides her bicycle more than *he does.*]

**Tip** Add the additional words to the comparison when you speak and write. Then, others will not think you are incorrect.

## CHOOSING BETWEEN *WHO* AND *WHOM*

*Who* is always a subject; *whom* is always an object. If a pronoun performs an action, use the subject form *who.* If a pronoun does not perform an action, use the object form *whom.*

**Who = subject** I would like to know *who* delivered this package.

**Whom = object** He told me to *whom* I should report.

**Tip** In the examples here, subjects are underlined, and verbs are double-underlined.

In sentences other than questions, when the pronoun (*who* or *whom*) is followed by a verb, use *who.* When the pronoun (*who* or *whom*) is followed by a noun or pronoun, use *whom.*

**Tip** *Whoever* is a subject pronoun; *whomever* is an object pronoun.

The pianist (who/whom) played was excellent.

[The pronoun is followed by the verb *played.* Use *who.*]

The pianist (who/whom) I saw was excellent.

[The pronoun is followed by another pronoun: *I.* Use *whom.*]

### *Make Pronouns Consistent in Person*

**Person** is the point of view a writer uses—the perspective from which he or she writes. Pronouns may be in first person (*I* or *we*), second person (*you*), or third person (*he, she,* or *it*). (See the chart on p. 388.)

| | |
|---|---|
| **Inconsistent** | As soon as *a shopper* walks into the store, *you* can tell it is a weird place.<br>[The sentence starts with the third person (*a shopper*) but shifts to the second person (*you*).] |
| **Consistent, singular** | As soon as *a shopper* walks into the store, *he* or *she* can tell it is a weird place. |
| **Consistent, plural** | As soon as *shoppers* walk into the store, *they* can tell it is a weird place. |

## Edit for Pronouns

### PRACTICE 6 Correcting various pronoun problems

In the following sentences, find and correct problems with pronoun use. You may be able to revise some sentences in more than one way, and you may need to rewrite some sentences to correct errors.

**Example:** ~~**Everyone with a busy schedule has**~~ *Students with busy schedules have* **probably been tempted to take shortcuts on their coursework.**

1. My class received its term paper grades yesterday.
2. My friend Gene and me were shocked to see that he had gotten an F on his paper.
3. I usually get better grades than him, but he does not usually fail.
4. Mr. Padilla, the instructor, who most students consider strict but fair, scheduled an appointment with Gene.
5. When Gene went to the department office, they told him where to find Mr. Padilla.
6. Mr. Padilla told Gene that he did not think he had written the paper.
7. The paper it contained language that was unusual for Gene.
8. The instructor said that you could compare Gene's in-class writing with this paper and see differences.

9. Mr. Padilla, whom had typed some passages from Gene's paper into a search engine, found two online papers containing sentences that were also in Gene's paper.
10. Gene told Mr. Padilla that he had made a terrible mistake.
11. Gene told my girlfriend and I later that he did not realize that borrowing sentences from online sources was plagiarism.
12. We looked at the paper, and you could tell that parts of it did not sound like Gene's writing.
13. Anyone doing Internet research must be especially careful to document their sources, as Gene now knows.
14. The department decided that they would not suspend Gene from school.
15. Mr. Padilla will let Gene take the class again and will help him avoid accidental plagiarism, and Gene said that no one had ever been more relieved than him to hear that news.

**PRACTICE 7** **Editing paragraphs for pronoun problems**

Find and correct seven errors in pronoun use in the following paragraphs.

(1) Ask anyone who has moved to a city, and they will tell you: At first, life can feel pretty lonely. (2) Fortunately, it is possible to make friends just about anywhere. (3) One good strategy is to get involved in a group that interests you, such as a sports team or arts club. (4) In many cases, a local baseball team or theater group will open their arms to new talent. (5) Joining in on practices, games, or performances is a great way to build friendships with others whom have interests like yours. (6) Also, most community organizations are always in need of volunteers. (7) It is a great way to form new friendships while doing something positive for society.

(8) Getting a pet or gardening, it is another great way to meet new people. (9) In many cities, you can walk down the street for a long time and never be greeted by another person. (10) If you are walking a dog, though, it is likely that others will say hello. (11) Some may even stop to talk with you and pet your dog. (12) Also, gardeners tend to draw other gardeners. (13) If you are

planting flowers and other flower growers stop by to chat, them and you will have plenty to talk about.

(14) To sum up, newcomers to any city do not have to spend all their nights alone in front of the TV. (15) You have plenty of opportunities to get out and feel more connected.

**PRACTICE 8** **Editing your own writing for pronoun problems**

Edit pronoun errors in a piece of your own writing—a paper for this course or another one, or something you have written for work or your everyday life. Use the chart on page 395 to help you.

## Chapter Review

1. Pronouns replace ________ or other ___________ in a sentence.
2. A pronoun must agree with (match) the noun or pronoun it replaces in __________ and _________.
3. In an _____________ pronoun reference, the pronoun could refer to more than one noun.
4. Subject pronouns serve as the subject of a verb. Write a sentence using a subject pronoun. ____________________________________________________________
____________________________________________________________________
5. What are two other types of pronouns? ______________________________________
6. What are three trouble spots in pronoun use?
____________________________________________________________________
____________________________________________________________________
____________________________________________________________________

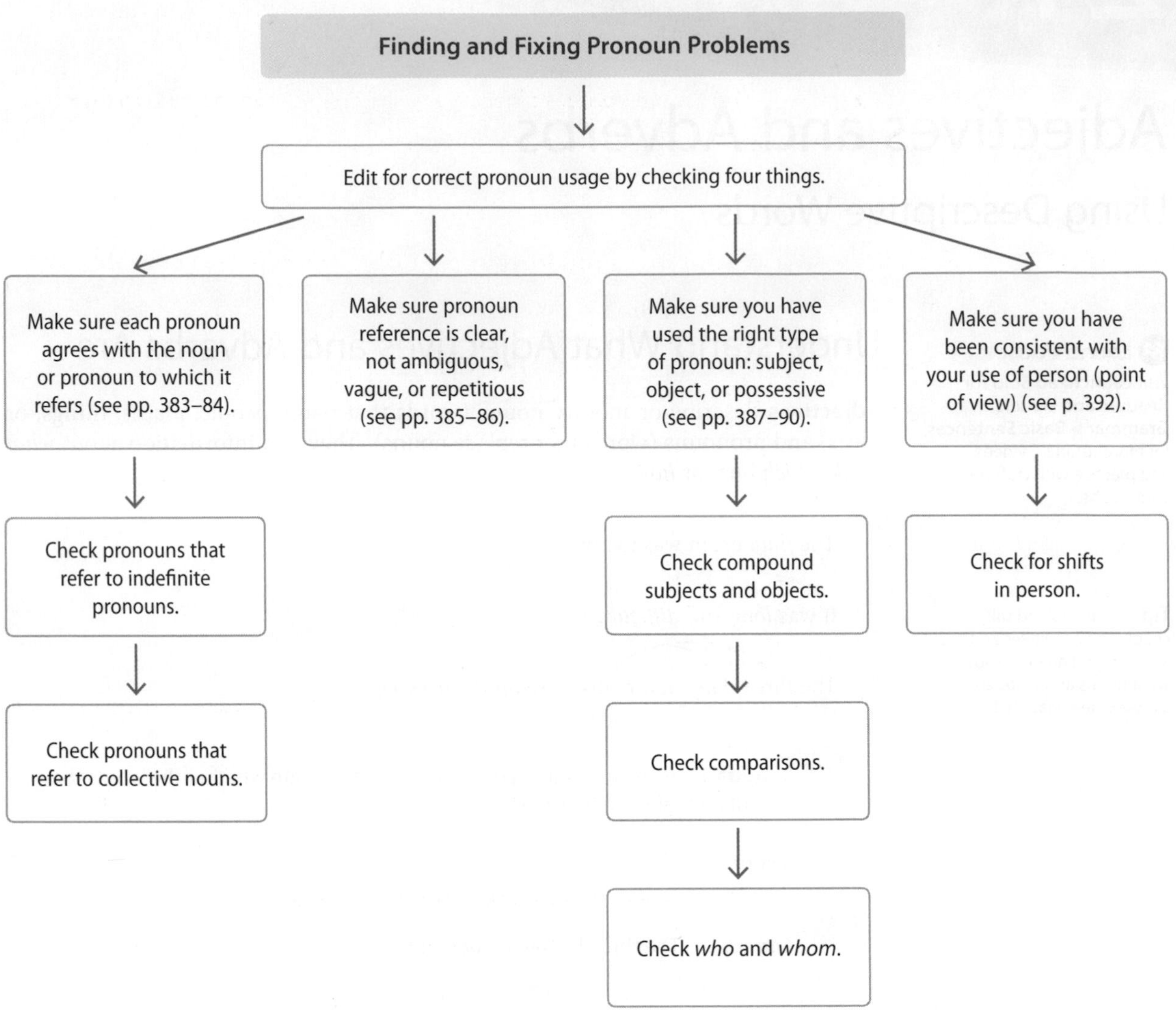
Finding and Fixing Pronoun Problems
Edit for correct pronoun usage by checking four things.
Make sure each pronoun agrees with the noun or pronoun to which it refers (see pp. 383–84).
Check pronouns that refer to indefinite pronouns.
Check pronouns that refer to collective nouns.
Make sure pronoun reference is clear, not ambiguous, vague, or repetitious (see pp. 385–86).
Make sure you have used the right type of pronoun: subject, object, or possessive (see pp. 387–90).
Check compound subjects and objects.
Check comparisons.
Check *who* and *whom*.
Make sure you have been consistent with your use of person (point of view) (see p. 392).
Check for shifts in person.

# 21

# Adjectives and Adverbs

## Using Descriptive Words

Visit **LaunchPad Solo for Readers and Writers > Grammar > Basic Sentences** for more tutorials, videos, and practice with crafting paragraphs.

**Tip** To understand this chapter on adjectives and adverbs, you need to know what nouns and verbs are. For a review, see Chapter 15.

## Understand What Adjectives and Adverbs Are

**Adjectives** describe or modify nouns (words that name people, places, things, or ideas) and pronouns (words that replace nouns). They add information about *what kind, which one,* or *how many.*

The *final* exam was today.

It was *long* and *difficult.*

The *three shiny new* coins were on the dresser.

**Language note:** In English, adjectives do not indicate whether the words they describe are singular or plural.

**Incorrect** The three babies are *adorables.*

[The adjective *adorables* should not end in *-s.*]

**Correct** The three babies are *adorable.*

## GRAMMAR & MECHANICS ROADMAP

### An Overview

**This Chapter Identifies the Following Trouble Spots**

- Choosing between adjectives and adverbs
- Using adjectives and adverbs in comparisons
- Using *good, well, bad,* and *badly*

**Tools to Address the Trouble Spots**

- Understand What Adjectives and Adverbs Are (p. 396)
- Forming Comparatives and Superlatives (p. 399)
- Edit for Adjectives and Adverbs exercises (p. 400)
- Chapter Review (p. 401)
- Editing for Correct Usage of Adjectives and Adverbs flowchart (p. 401)

**Adverbs** describe or modify verbs (words that tell what happens in a sentence), adjectives, or other adverbs. They add information about *how, how much, when, where, why*, or *to what extent*.

| | |
|---|---|
| **Modifying verb** | Sharon *enthusiastically* accepted the job. |
| **Modifying adjective** | The *very* young lawyer handled the case. |
| **Modifying another adverb** | The team played *surprisingly* well. |

Adjectives usually come before the words they modify; adverbs come before or after. You can use more than one adjective or adverb to modify a word.

**Language note:** The *-ed* and *-ing* forms of adjectives are sometimes confused. Common examples include *bored/boring, confused/confusing, excited/exciting*, and *interested/interesting*.

Often, the *-ed* form describes a person's reaction, whereas the *-ing* form describes the thing to which a person is reacting.

| | |
|---|---|
| **Incorrect** | Janelle is interesting in ghosts and ghost stories. |
| **Correct** | Janelle is interested in ghosts and ghost stories. |
| **Correct** | Janelle finds ghosts and ghost stories interesting. |

# Practice Using Adjectives and Adverbs Correctly

## *Choosing between Adjectives and Adverbs*

Many adverbs are formed by adding *-ly* to the end of an adjective.

| adjective | adverb |
|---|---|
| She received a *quick* answer. | Her sister answered *quickly*. |
| Our *new* neighbors just got married. | The couple is *newly* married. |
| That is an *honest* answer. | Please answer *honestly*. |

To decide whether to use an adjective or an adverb, find the word being described. If that word is a noun or pronoun, use an adjective. If it is a verb, adjective, or another adverb, use an adverb.

**PRACTICE 1** **Choosing between adjectives and adverbs**

In each sentence, underline the word in the sentence that is being described or modified. Then, circle the correct word in parentheses.

**Example** **People are (common/commonly) aware that smoking causes health risks.**

1. Many smokers are (stubborn/stubbornly) about refusing to quit.
2. Others who are thinking about quitting may decide (sudden/suddenly) that the damage from smoking has already been done.
3. In such cases, the (typical/typically) smoker sees no reason to stop.
4. The news about secondhand smoke may have made some smokers stop (quick/quickly) to save the health of their families.
5. Research now shows that pet lovers who smoke can have a (terrible/terribly) effect on their cats.
6. Cats who live with smokers (frequent/frequently) develop cancer.
7. Veterinarians point out that the cats of smokers may smell (strong/strongly) of smoke.
8. Cats like to have their fur (clean/cleanly), and they lick the fur to groom themselves.
9. When they are grooming, cats may inhale a (large/largely) dose of tobacco smoke.
10. Perhaps some smokers who believe that it is too late for their own health will (serious/seriously) consider quitting for the sake of their pets.

## *Using Adjectives and Adverbs in Comparisons*

To compare two people, places, or things, use the **comparative** form of adjectives or adverbs. Comparisons often use the word *than.*

Carol ran *faster* than I did.

Johan is *more intelligent* than his sister.

To compare three or more people, places, or things, use the **superlative** form of adjectives or adverbs.

Carol ran the *fastest* of all the women runners.

Johan is the *most intelligent* of the five children.

If an adjective or adverb is short (one syllable), add the endings *-er* to form the comparative and *-est* to form the superlative. Also use this pattern for adjectives that end in *-y* (but change the *-y* to *-i* before adding *-er* or *-est*).

For all other adjectives and adverbs, add the word *more* to make the comparative and the word *most* to make the superlative.

**Tip** Some people refer to the correct use of comparatives and superlatives as *appropriate degree forms.*

### Forming Comparatives and Superlatives

| Adjective or adverb | Comparative | Superlative |
|---|---|---|
| **Adjectives and adverbs of one syllable** | | |
| tall | taller | tallest |
| fast | faster | fastest |
| **Adjectives ending in -y** | | |
| happy | happier | happiest |
| silly | sillier | silliest |
| **Other adjectives and adverbs** | | |
| graceful | more graceful | most graceful |
| gracefully | more gracefully | most gracefully |
| intelligent | more intelligent | most intelligent |
| intelligently | more intelligently | most intelligently |

Use either an ending (*-er* or *-est*) or an extra word (*more* or *most*) to form a comparative or superlative—not both at once.

This park is known for the ~~most~~ greatest hiking trails.

## *Using* Good, Well, Bad, *and* Badly

Four common adjectives and adverbs have irregular forms: *good, well, bad,* and *badly.*

**Tip** *Irregular* means not following a standard rule.

### Forming Irregular Comparatives and Superlatives

| | Comparative | Superlative |
|---|---|---|
| **Adjective** | | |
| good | better | best |
| bad | worse | worst |
| **Adverb** | | |
| well | better | best |
| badly | worse | worst |

People often get confused about whether to use *good* or *well*. *Good* is an adjective, so use it to describe a noun or pronoun. *Well* is an adverb, so use it to describe a verb or an adjective.

| | |
|---|---|
| **Adjective** | She has a *good* job. |
| **Adverb** | He works *well* with his colleagues. |

*Well* can also be an adjective to describe someone's health: I am not *well* today.

## Edit for Adjectives and Adverbs

### PRACTICE 2 Editing paragraphs for correct adjectives and adverbs

Find and correct seven adjective and adverb errors in the following paragraphs.

(1) Every day, many people log on to play one of the popularest computer games of all time, *World of Warcraft*. (2) This multiplayer game was first introduced by Blizzard Entertainment in 1994 and has grown quick ever since. (3) More than 11 million players participate in the game every month, according to the recentest figures.

(4) Computer game experts call *World of Warcraft* a "massively multiplayer online role-playing game," or MMORPG for short. (5) Players of this game select a realm in which to play. (6) They choose from among four differently realms. (7) Each realm has its own set of rules and even its own language. (8) Players also choose if they want to be members of the Alliance or the Horde, which are groups that oppose each other. (9) Each side tends to think that it is gooder than the other one.

(10) In *World of Warcraft*, questing is one of the funnest activities. (11) Questing players undertake special missions or tasks to earn experience and gold. (12) The goal is to trade these earnings for better skills and equipment. (13) Players must proceed careful to stay in the game and increase their overall power and abilities.

### PRACTICE 3 Editing your own writing for correct adjectives and adverbs

Edit a piece of your own writing for correct use of adjectives and adverbs. It can be a paper for this course or another one, or choose something you have written for work or your everyday life. Use the chart on page 401 to help you.

## Chapter Review

1. Adjectives modify ________ and __________.
2. Adverbs modify ________, ___________, or ______________.
3. Many adverbs are formed by adding an _____ ending to an adjective.
4. The comparative form of an adjective or adverb is used to compare how many people, places, things, or ideas? _______
5. The superlative form of an adjective or adverb is used to compare how many people, places, things, or ideas? ______________
6. What four words have irregular comparative and superlative forms?

_______________________________________________

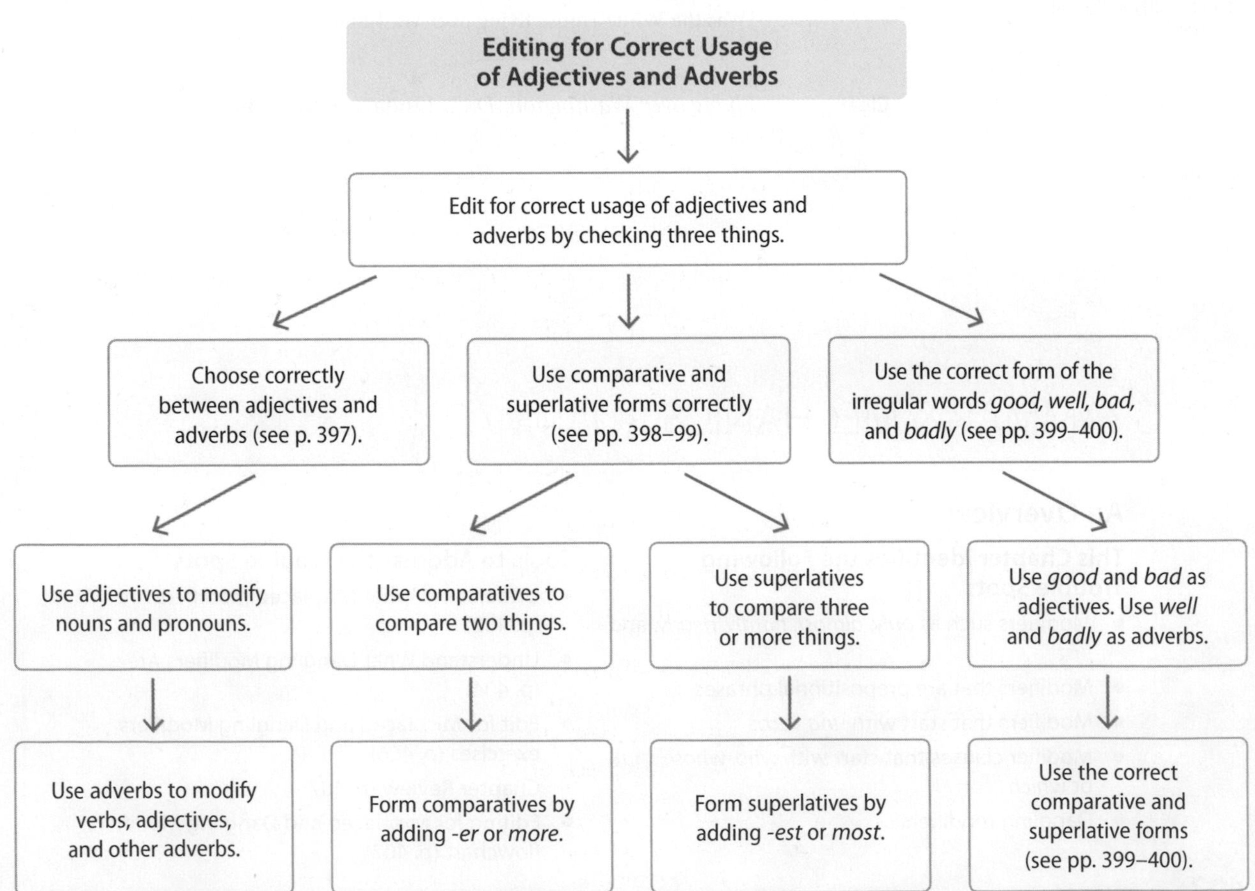
Editing for Correct Usage of Adjectives and Adverbs
Edit for correct usage of adjectives and adverbs by checking three things.
Choose correctly between adjectives and adverbs (see p. 397).
Use comparative and superlative forms correctly (see pp. 398–99).
Use the correct form of the irregular words *good, well, bad,* and *badly* (see pp. 399–400).
Use adjectives to modify nouns and pronouns.
Use adverbs to modify verbs, adjectives, and other adverbs.
Use comparatives to compare two things.
Form comparatives by adding *-er* or *more.*
Use superlatives to compare three or more things.
Form superlatives by adding *-est* or *most.*
Use *good* and *bad* as adjectives. Use *well* and *badly* as adverbs.
Use the correct comparative and superlative forms (see pp. 399–400).

# 22

# Misplaced and Dangling Modifiers

## Avoiding Confusing Descriptions

LaunchPadSolo

Visit **LaunchPad Solo for Readers and Writers > Grammar > Basic Sentences** for more tutorials, videos, and practice with crafting paragraphs.

**Tip** For a review of basic sentence elements, see Chapter 15.

## Understand What Misplaced Modifiers Are

**Modifiers** are words or word groups that describe other words in a sentence. Modifiers should be near the words they modify; otherwise, the sentence can be unintentionally funny. A **misplaced modifier**, because it is in the wrong place, describes the wrong word or words.

**Misplaced** Linda saw the White House *flying over Washington, D.C.*
[Was the White House flying over Washington?]

**Clear** *Flying over Washington, D.C.*, Linda saw the White House.

## GRAMMAR & MECHANICS ROADMAP

### An Overview

**This Chapter Identifies the Following Trouble Spots**

- Modifiers such as *only, almost, hardly, nearly,* and *just*
- Modifiers that are prepositional phrases
- Modifiers that start with *-ing* verbs
- Modifier clauses that start with *who, whose, that,* or *which*
- Dangling modifiers

**Tools to Address the Trouble Spots**

To correct a misplaced modifier, place the modifier as close as possible to the word or words it modifies, often directly before it.

> Wearing my bathrobe,
> I went outside to get the paper. ~~wearing my bathrobe.~~

Four constructions often lead to misplaced modifiers.

1. Modifiers such as *only, almost, hardly, nearly,* and *just.* These words need to be immediately before—not just close to—the words or phrases they modify.

   > only
   > I ~~only~~ found two old photos in the drawer.
   >
   > [The intended meaning is that just two photos were in the drawer.]

   > almost
   > Joanne ~~almost~~ ate the whole cake.
   >
   > [Joanne actually ate; she did not "almost" eat.]

   > nearly
   > Thomas ~~nearly~~ spent 2 hours waiting for the bus.
   >
   > [Thomas spent close to 2 hours waiting; he did not "nearly" spend them.]

2. Modifiers that are prepositional phrases.

   > from the cash register
   > The cashier found money on the floor. ~~from the cash register.~~

   > in plastic cups
   > Jen served punch to the seniors. ~~in plastic cups.~~

3. Modifiers that start with *-ing* verbs.

   > Using jumper cables,
   > Darlene started the car. ~~using jumper cables.~~
   >
   > [The car was not using jumper cables; Darlene was.]

   > Wearing flip-flops,
   > Javier climbed the mountain. ~~wearing flip-flops.~~
   >
   > [The mountain was not wearing flip-flops; Javier was.]

4. Modifier clauses that start with *who, whose, that,* or *which.*

   > that was infecting my hard drive
   > Joel found the computer virus attached to an e-mail message. ~~that was infecting my hard drive.~~
   >
   > [The e-mail did not infect the hard drive; the virus did.]

   > who was crying
   > The baby on the bus ~~who was crying~~ had curly hair.
   >
   > [The bus was not crying; the baby was.]

## Practice Correcting Misplaced Modifiers

### PRACTICE 1 Correcting misplaced modifiers

Find and correct misplaced modifiers in the following sentences.

**Example** **I write things in my blog that I used to ~~only~~ tell ^only my best friends.**

1. I used to write about all kinds of personal things and private observations in a diary.
2. Now, I nearly write the same things in my blog.
3. Any story might show up in my blog that is entertaining.
4. The video I was making was definitely something I wanted to write about in my blog of my cousin Tim's birthday.
5. I had invited to the birthday party my loudest, wildest friends wanting the video to be funny.
6. We jumped off tables, had mock swordfights, and almost used ten cans of whipped cream in a food fight.
7. Unfortunately, the battery in the smartphone died that I was using to make the video.
8. I told my friends that I would write a blog post about the party anyway apologizing to them.
9. I explained how I would include the funny story about the failed video session in the blog post.
10. My friends hardly said that they could wait until we tried again to make the video.

## Understand What Dangling Modifiers Are

A **dangling modifier** "dangles" because the word or word group it modifies is not in the sentence. Dangling modifiers usually appear at the beginning of a sentence and seem to modify the noun or pronoun that immediately follows them, but they are really modifying another word or group of words.

**Dangling** *Rushing to class,* the books fell out of my bag.
[The books were not rushing to class.]

**Clear** *Rushing to class*, I dropped my books.

There are two basic ways to correct dangling modifiers. Use the one that makes more sense. One way is to add the word being modified immediately after the opening modifier so that the connection between the two is clear.

I on my bike
Trying to eat a hot dog, ~~my bike~~ swerved.
^ ^

Another way is to add the word being modified in the opening modifier itself.

While I was trying
~~Trying~~ to eat a hot dog, my bike swerved.
^

## Practice Correcting Dangling Modifiers

### PRACTICE 2 Correcting dangling modifiers

Find and correct any dangling modifiers in the following sentences. If a sentence is correct, write a "C" next to it. It may be necessary to add new words or ideas to some sentences.

Because I had invited
**Example: ~~Inviting~~ my whole family to dinner, the kitchen was filled with all kinds of food.**
^

1. Preparing a big family dinner, the oven suddenly stopped working.
2. In a panic, we searched for Carmen, who can solve any problem.
3. Trying to help, the kitchen was crowded.
4. Looking into the oven, the turkey was not done.
5. Discouraged, the dinner was about to be canceled.
6. Staring out the window, a pizza truck went by.
7. Using a credit card, Carmen ordered six pizzas.
8. With one quick phone call, six large pizzas solved our problem.
9. Returning to the crowd in the kitchen, family members still surrounded the oven.
10. Delighted with Carmen's decision, cheers filled the room.

## Edit for Misplaced and Dangling Modifiers

**PRACTICE 3** **Editing paragraphs for misplaced and dangling modifiers**

Find and correct any misplaced or dangling modifiers in the following paragraphs.

(1) Carrying overfilled backpacks is a common habit, but not necessarily a good one. (2) Bulging with books, water bottles, and sports equipment and weighing an average of fourteen to eighteen pounds, students' backs can gradually become damaged. (3) Because they have to plan ahead for the whole day and often need books, extra clothes, and on-the-go meals, backpacks get heavier and heavier. (4) An increasing number of medical professionals, primarily physical therapists, are seeing young people with chronic back problems.

(5) Researchers have recently invented a new type of backpack. from the University of Pennsylvania and the Marine Biological Laboratory. (6) Designed with springs, the backpack moves up and down as a person walks. (7) This new backpack creates energy, which is then collected and transferred to an electrical generator. (8) Experiencing relief from the wear and tear on muscles, the springs make the pack more comfortable.

(9) What is the purpose of the electricity generated by these new backpacks? (10) Needing electricity for their night-vision goggles, the backpacks could solve a problem. for soldiers. (11) Soldiers could benefit from such an efficient energy source to power their global positioning systems and other electronic gear. (12) Instead of being battery operated, the soldiers could use the special backpacks and would not have to carry additional batteries. (13) For the average student, these backpacks might one day provide convenient energy for video games, television, and music players, all at the same time. (14) Designed with this technology, kids would just have to look both ways before crossing the street.

**PRACTICE 4** **Editing your own writing for misplaced and dangling modifiers**

Edit a piece of your own writing for misplaced and dangling modifiers. It can be a paper for this course or another one, or it could be something you have written for work or your everyday life. You may want to use the chart on page 407.

# Chapter Review

1. __________ are words or word groups that describe other words in a sentence.
2. A ______________ describes the incorrect word or word group because it is in the wrong place in a sentence.
3. When an opening modifier does not modify any word in the sentence, it is a ______________.
4. Which four constructions often lead to misplaced modifiers?

______________________________

______________________________

______________________________

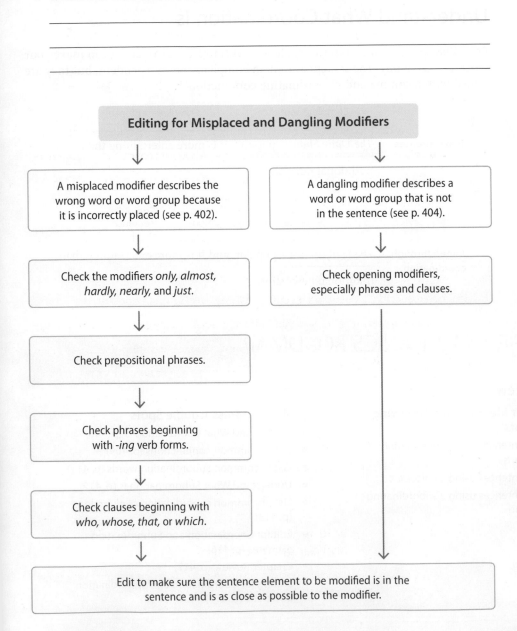

**Editing for Misplaced and Dangling Modifiers**

A misplaced modifier describes the wrong word or word group because it is incorrectly placed (see p. 402).

↓

Check the modifiers *only, almost, hardly, nearly,* and *just*.

↓

Check prepositional phrases.

↓

Check phrases beginning with *-ing* verb forms.

↓

Check clauses beginning with *who, whose, that,* or *which*.

A dangling modifier describes a word or word group that is not in the sentence (see p. 404).

↓

Check opening modifiers, especially phrases and clauses.

↓

Edit to make sure the sentence element to be modified is in the sentence and is as close as possible to the modifier.

# 23

# Coordination and Subordination

## Joining Sentences with Related Ideas

Visit **LaunchPad Solo for Readers and Writers > Grammar > Basic Sentences** for more tutorials, videos, and practice with crafting paragraphs.

**Tip** To understand this chapter, you need to be familiar with basic sentence elements. For a review, see Chapter 15.

## Understand What Coordination Is

**Coordination** is used to join two sentences with related ideas, and it can make your writing less choppy. The sentences remain complete and independent, but they are joined with a comma and a coordinating conjunction.

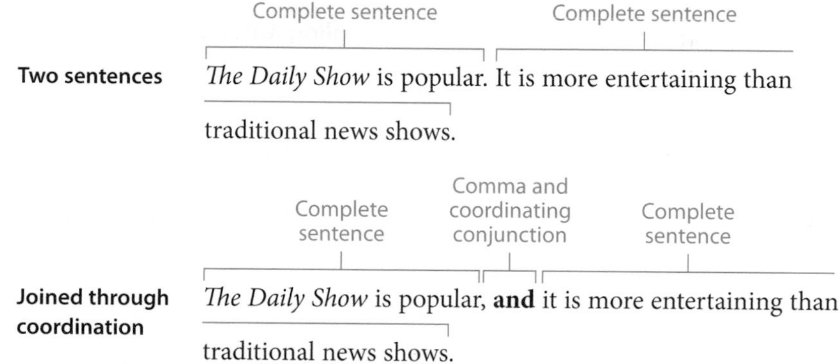

Complete sentence
Complete sentence
Two sentences
*The Daily Show* is popular. It is more entertaining than traditional news shows.
Complete sentence
Comma and coordinating conjunction
Complete sentence
Joined through coordination
*The Daily Show* is popular, **and** it is more entertaining than traditional news shows.


## GRAMMAR & MECHANICS ROADMAP

### An Overview

**This Chapter Identifies the Following Trouble Spots**

- Joining sentences using coordinating conjunctions
- Joining sentences using semicolons
- Joining sentences using a subordinating conjunction

**Tools to Address Trouble Spots**

# Practice Using Coordination

## *Using Coordinating Conjunctions*

**Conjunctions** join words, phrases, or clauses. **Coordinating conjunctions** join ideas of equal importance. (You can remember them by thinking of FANBOYS—*for, and, nor, but, or, yet, so*.) To join two sentences through coordination, put a comma and one of these conjunctions between the sentences. Choose the conjunction that makes the most sense for the meaning of the two sentences.

| Complete sentence | , for<br>, and<br>, nor<br>, but<br>, or<br>, yet<br>, so | Complete sentence |
|---|---|---|
| Wikipedia is a popular encyclopedia | , for<br>[*For* indicates a reason or cause.] | it is easily available online. |
| The encyclopedia is open to all | , and<br>[*And* simply joins two ideas.] | anyone can add information to it. |
| Often, inaccurate entries cannot be stopped | , nor<br>[*Nor* indicates a negative.] | is there any penalty for them. |
| People have complained about errors | , but<br>[*But* indicates a contrast.] | the mistakes may or may not be fixed. |
| Some people delete information | , or<br>[*Or* indicates alternatives.] | they add their own interpretations. |
| Many people know that Wikipedia is flawed | , yet<br>[*Yet* indicates a contrast or possibility.] | they continue to use it. |
| Wikipedia now has trustees | , so<br>[*So* indicates a result.] | perhaps it will be monitored more closely. |

**Tip** For more on the use of commas, see Chapter 30.

### PRACTICE 1 Combining sentences with coordinating conjunctions

Combine each pair of sentences into a single sentence by using a comma and a coordinating conjunction. In some cases, there may be more than one correct answer.

**Example: In business, e-mails can make a good or bad impression~~.~~** *, so people* **~~People~~ should mind their e-mail manners.**

1. Many professionals use e-mail to keep in touch with clients and contacts. They must be especially careful not to offend anyone with their e-mail messages.
2. However, anyone who uses e-mail should be cautious. It is dangerously easy to send messages to the wrong person.
3. Employees may have time to send personal messages from work. They should remember that employers often have the ability to read their workers' messages.
4. R-rated language and jokes may be deleted automatically by a company's server. They may be read by managers and cause problems for the employee sending or receiving them.
5. No message should be forwarded to everyone in a sender's address book. Senders should ask permission before adding someone to a mass-mailing list.
6. People should check the authenticity of mailings about lost children, dreadful diseases, and terrorist threats before passing them on. Most such messages are hoaxes.
7. Typographical errors and misspellings in e-mail make the message appear less professional. Using all capital letters—a practice known as *shouting*—is usually considered even worse.
8. People who use e-mail for business want to be taken seriously. They should make their e-mails as professional as possible.

## *Using Semicolons*

A **semicolon** is a punctuation mark that can join two sentences through coordination. Use semicolons *only* when the ideas in the two sentences are closely related. Do not overuse semicolons.

3. These tools allow people to search a wide range of records with key words. Researchers can gather details about their ancestors' lives much more quickly and efficiently.
4. Recently, people have started using social-networking tools to find out about living and dead relatives. Some of them are getting more information even more quickly.
5. One researcher, Lauren Axelrod, used Ancestry.com to gather some information on the birth mother of her husband, who had been adopted. Using this information, she searched for his birth mother on Facebook.
6. The entire search, wich ended successfully, took only 2 hours. In less than a week, Axelrod's husband was talking on the phone with his birth mother.
7. Not everyone thinks that genealogy research has to be a purely serious hobby. Some people see it as a great way to have fun.
8. In the online Family Village Game, players create characters, or avatars, representing their ancestors. Using genealogical records, they add background information on these ancestors.
9. Players have a lot of fun creating the characters and their worlds. They get additional genealogical information by following the research suggestions provided by the game.
10. Some parents play Family Village Game with their children. The children see their connection to the past.

## Understand What Subordination Is

Like coordination, **subordination** is a way to join short, choppy sentences with related ideas into a longer sentence. With subordination, you put a dependent word (such as *after*, *although*, *because*, or *when*) in front of one of the sentences, which then becomes a dependent clause and is no longer a complete sentence.

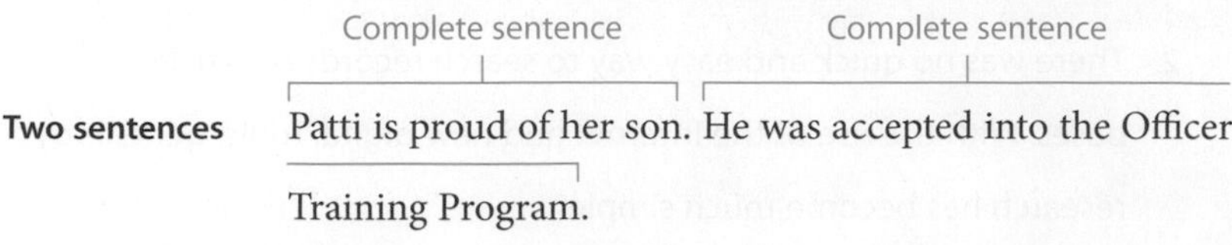
Complete sentence
Complete sentence
**Two sentences**
Patti is proud of her son. He was accepted into the Officer Training Program.

| Complete sentence | ; | Complete sentence |
|---|---|---|
| Antarctica is a mystery | ; | few people know much about it. |
| Its climate is extreme | ; | few people want to endure it. |
| My cousin went there | ; | he loves to explore the unknown. |

A semicolon alone does not tell readers much about the relationship between the two ideas. To give more information about the relationship, use a **conjunctive adverb** after the semicolon. Put a comma after the conjunctive adverb.

**Tip** When you connect two sentences with a conjunctive adverb, the statement following the semicolon remains a complete thought. If you use a subordinating word such as *because,* however, the second statement becomes a dependent clause, and a semicolon is not needed: *The desert is cold at night because sand does not store heat well.*

| Complete sentence | ; also,<br>; as a result,<br>; besides,<br>; furthermore,<br>; however,<br>; in addition,<br>; in fact,<br>; instead,<br>; moreover,<br>; still,<br>; then,<br>; therefore, | Complete sentence |
|---|---|---|
| Antarctica is largely unexplored | ; as a result, | it is unpopulated. |
| It receives little rain | ; also, | it is incredibly cold. |
| It is a huge area | ; therefore, | scientists are becoming more interested in it. |

## PRACTICE 2 Combining sentences with semicolons and conjunctive adverbs

Combine each pair of sentences by using a semicolon and a conjunctive adverb. In some cases, there may be more than one correct answer.

**Example: More and more people are researching their family history, or genealogy~~. This~~** ; in fact, this **type of research is now considered one of the fastest-growing hobbies in North America.**

1. Before the Internet, genealogy researchers had to contact public offices to get records of ancestors' births, marriages, occupations, and deaths. Some visited libraries to search for old newspaper articles mentioning the ancestors.

2. There was no quick and easy way to search records or article databases. With the rise of the Internet and new digital tools, genealogy research has become much simpler.

| Complete sentence | ; | Complete sentence |
|---|---|---|
| Antarctica is a mystery | ; | few people know much about it. |
| Its climate is extreme | ; | few people want to endure it. |
| My cousin went there | ; | he loves to explore the unknown. |

A semicolon alone does not tell readers much about the relationship between the two ideas. To give more information about the relationship, use a **conjunctive adverb** after the semicolon. Put a comma after the conjunctive adverb.

**Tip** When you connect two sentences with a conjunctive adverb, the statement following the semicolon remains a complete thought. If you use a subordinating word such as *because,* however, the second statement becomes a dependent clause, and a semicolon is not needed: *The desert is cold at night because sand does not store heat well.*

| Complete sentence | ; also,<br>; as a result,<br>; besides,<br>; furthermore,<br>; however,<br>; in addition,<br>; in fact,<br>; instead,<br>; moreover,<br>; still,<br>; then,<br>; therefore, | Complete sentence |
|---|---|---|
| Antarctica is largely unexplored | ; as a result, | it is unpopulated. |
| It receives little rain | ; also, | it is incredibly cold. |
| It is a huge area | ; therefore, | scientists are becoming more interested in it. |

## PRACTICE 2 Combining sentences with semicolons and conjunctive adverbs

Combine each pair of sentences by using a semicolon and a conjunctive adverb. In some cases, there may be more than one correct answer.

**Example: More and more people are researching their family history, or genealogy. This type of research is now considered one of the fastest-growing hobbies in North America.** (handwritten edit: "; in fact, this" replacing ". This")

1. Before the Internet, genealogy researchers had to contact public offices to get records of ancestors' births, marriages, occupations, and deaths. Some visited libraries to search for old newspaper articles mentioning the ancestors.

2. There was no quick and easy way to search records or article databases. With the rise of the Internet and new digital tools, genealogy research has become much simpler.

3. These tools allow people to search a wide range of records with key words. Researchers can gather details about their ancestors' lives much more quickly and efficiently.
4. Recently, people have started using social-networking tools to find out about living and dead relatives. Some of them are getting more information even more quickly.
5. One researcher, Lauren Axelrod, used Ancestry.com to gather some information on the birth mother of her husband, who had been adopted. Using this information, she searched for his birth mother on Facebook.
6. The entire search, wich ended successfully, took only 2 hours. In less than a week, Axelrod's husband was talking on the phone with his birth mother.
7. Not everyone thinks that genealogy research has to be a purely serious hobby. Some people see it as a great way to have fun.
8. In the online Family Village Game, players create characters, or avatars, representing their ancestors. Using genealogical records, they add background information on these ancestors.
9. Players have a lot of fun creating the characters and their worlds. They get additional genealogical information by following the research suggestions provided by the game.
10. Some parents play Family Village Game with their children. The children see their connection to the past.

## Understand What Subordination Is

Like coordination, **subordination** is a way to join short, choppy sentences with related ideas into a longer sentence. With subordination, you put a dependent word (such as *after*, *although*, *because*, or *when*) in front of one of the sentences, which then becomes a dependent clause and is no longer a complete sentence.

Complete sentence | Complete sentence

**Two sentences** Patti is proud of her son. He was accepted into the Officer Training Program.

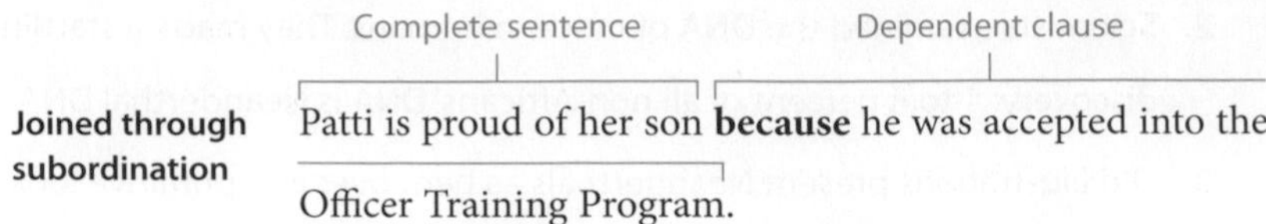

Complete sentence
Dependent clause
Joined through subordination
Patti is proud of her son **because** he was accepted into the Officer Training Program.


## Practice Using Subordination

To join two sentences through subordination, use a **subordinating conjunction**. Choose the conjunction that makes the most sense with the two sentences. Here are some of the most common subordinating conjunctions.

| Complete sentence | Subordinating conjunctions | | Dependent clause |
|---|---|---|---|
| | after | now that | |
| | although | once | |
| | as | since | |
| | as if | so that | |
| | because | unless | |
| | before | until | |
| | even if/ though | when | |
| | | whenever | |
| | if | where | |
| | if only | while | |
| I love music | because | | it makes me relax. |
| It is hard to study at home | when | | my children want my attention. |

When a dependent clause ends a sentence, it usually does not need to be preceded by a comma unless it is showing a contrast.

When the dependent clause begins a sentence, use a comma to separate it from the rest of the sentence.

| Subordinating conjunction | Dependent clause | , | Complete sentence |
|---|---|---|---|
| When | I eat out | , | I usually have steak. |
| Although | it is harmful | , | young people still smoke. |

### PRACTICE 3 Combining sentences through subordination

Combine each pair of sentences into a single sentence by using an appropriate subordinating conjunction either at the beginning of or between the two sentences. Use a conjunction that makes sense with the two sentences, and add commas where necessary.

**Example:** *If someone* **~~Someone~~ told you that you share DNA with humans' extinct relatives, the Neanderthals~~. You~~** *, you* **might be surprised.**

1. In fact, scientists have found that mating between humans and Neanderthals occurred. Groups of humans migrated north and east from Africa.

2. Scientists examined the DNA of modern humans. They made a startling discovery: 1 to 4 percent of all non-Africans' DNA is Neanderthal DNA.
3. Old illustrations present Neanderthals as bent over and primitive looking. It may be hard to believe that humans would want to mate with them.
4. However, a Neanderthal man got a good shave and a nice set of clothes. He might pass for a modern man.
5. Researchers are learning more about Neanderthals. Many mysteries remain.
6. Researchers continue their investigations. They are trying to answer one key question: What are the specific genetic differences between humans and Neanderthals?
7. They have started sequencing the entire Neanderthal genome. They can answer this question.
8. The genome is the entire set of genetic material for an organism. Comparing the Neanderthal genome to the human one might help researchers identify a number of differences between the two species.
9. These differences have yet to be identified. Scientists are growing more and more certain about the answer to one question: Why did Neanderthals become extinct?
10. Humans mated with Neanderthals. They also contributed to Neanderthals' extinction, either by killing them or by outcompeting them for food and other resources.

## PRACTICE 4 Combining sentences through coordination and subordination

Join each of the following sentence pairs in two ways, first by coordination and then by subordination.

**Example: Rick has many talents. He is still deciding what to do with his life.**

**Joined by coordination:** *Rick has many talents, but he is still deciding what to do with his life.*

**Joined by subordination:** *Although Rick has many talents, he is still deciding what to do with his life.*

1. Rick rides a unicycle. He can juggle four oranges.

   Joined by coordination: ______________________________

   ______________________________

   Joined by subordination: ______________________________

   ______________________________

2. A trapeze school opened in our town. Rick signed up immediately.

   Joined by coordination: ______________________________

   ______________________________

   Joined by subordination: ______________________________

   ______________________________

3. Rick is now at the top of his class. He worked hard practicing trapeze routines.

   Joined by coordination: ______________________________

   ______________________________

   Joined by subordination: ______________________________

   ______________________________

4. Rick asks me for career advice. I try to be encouraging.

   Joined by coordination: ______________________________

   ______________________________

   Joined by subordination: ______________________________

   ______________________________

5. He does not want to join the circus. He could study entertainment management.

   Joined by coordination: ______________________________

   ______________________________

   Joined by subordination: ______________________________

   ______________________________

# Edit for Coordination and Subordination

**PRACTICE 5** **Editing paragraphs for coordination and subordination**

In the following paragraphs, combine the six pairs of underlined sentences. For three of the sentence pairs, use coordination. For the other three sentence pairs, use subordination. Do not forget to punctuate correctly, and keep in mind that there may be more than one way to combine each sentence pair.

(1) Washington, D.C., was the first city in the United States to offer a public bicycle-sharing program. (2) The idea has been popular in Europe for years. (3) In fact, Paris has more than twenty thousand bikes available for people to rent and ride around the city. (4) Called Capital Bikeshare, the Washington program costs citizens $7 a day, $25 a month, or $75 a year to join. (5) For that fee, they have access to more than one thousand bikes available at 110 stations set up all over Washington and in Arlington, Virginia. (6) After using the bikes, people must return them to one of the stations. (7) Other riders might be waiting for one. (8) Regular users have come to depend on Capital Bikeshare for short trips and errands. (9) The popularity of the program is growing.

(10) Throughout the United States, cycling has become much more popular in recent years. (11) Gasoline prices have increased. (12) A number of other cities are now considering bike-sharing programs. (13) Studies show that these programs can reduce city traffic by 4 to 5 percent. (14) Some companies are already creating similar programs to encourage their employees to exercise more and drive less. (15) Company leaders are aware that fit employees and a healthier environment are important goals to achieve. (16) It means that the company spends a little extra time, money, and effort to start and run a bike-sharing program.

**PRACTICE 6** **Editing your own writing for coordination and subordination**

Edit a piece of your own writing for coordination and subordination. It can be a paper for this course or another one, or it can be something you have written for work or your everyday life. You may want to use the chart on page 417.

## Chapter Review

1. What are the two ways to join sentences through coordination?

   ______________________________________________

   ______________________________________________

2. Use a semicolon *only* when the sentences are ______________.

3. Write two sentences using coordination. ______________________

   ______________________________________________

4. With subordination, you put a ______________ in front of one of two related sentences.

5. Write two sentences using subordination. ______________________

   ______________________________________________

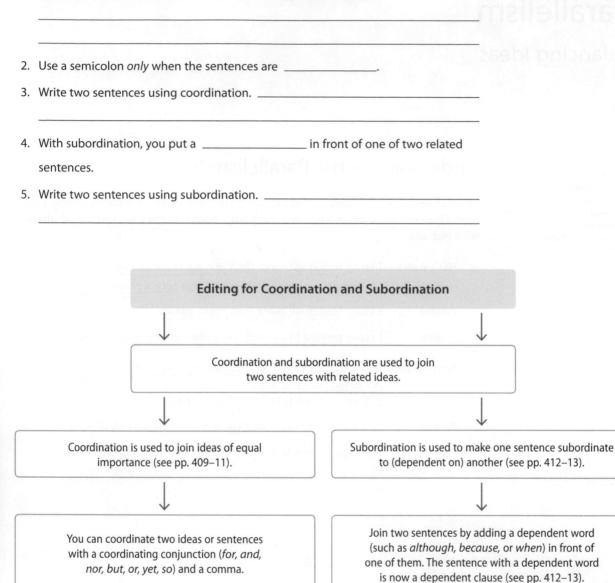

**Editing for Coordination and Subordination**

↓

Coordination and subordination are used to join two sentences with related ideas.

↓

Coordination is used to join ideas of equal importance (see pp. 409–11).

↓

You can coordinate two ideas or sentences with a coordinating conjunction (*for, and, nor, but, or, yet, so*) and a comma.

or

You can coordinate two ideas or sentences with a semicolon or with a semicolon and a conjunctive adverb (such as *also, however,* or *instead*) followed by a comma.

↓

Subordination is used to make one sentence subordinate to (dependent on) another (see pp. 412–13).

↓

Join two sentences by adding a dependent word (such as *although, because,* or *when*) in front of one of them. The sentence with a dependent word is now a dependent clause (see pp. 412–13).

↓

If the complete sentence comes before the dependent clause, a comma is usually not needed. If the complete sentence comes after the dependent clause, add a comma after the dependent clause.

# 24

# Parallelism

## Balancing Ideas

Visit **LaunchPad Solo for Readers and Writers > Grammar > Basic Sentences** for more tutorials, videos, and practice with crafting paragraphs.

## Understand What Parallelism Is

**Parallelism** in writing means that similar parts in a sentence have the same structure: Their parts are balanced. Use nouns with nouns, verbs with verbs, and phrases with phrases.

| | |
|---|---|
| **Not parallel** | I enjoy basketball more than playing video games. [*Basketball* is a noun, but *playing video games* is a phrase.] |
| **Parallel** | I enjoy basketball more than video games. |
| **Parallel** | I enjoy playing basketball more than playing video games. |
| **Not parallel** | Last night, I worked, studied, and was watching television. [Verbs must be in the same tense to be parallel. *Was watching* has a different structure from *worked* and *studied.*] |
| **Parallel** | Last night, I worked, studied, and watched television. |
| **Parallel** | Last night, I was working, studying, and watching television. |

## GRAMMAR & MECHANICS ROADMAP

### An Overview

**This Chapter Identifies the Following Trouble Spots**

- Parallelism in pairs and lists
- Parallelism in comparisons
- Parallelism with certain paired words

**Tools to Address Trouble Spots**

**Not parallel** This weekend, we can go to the beach or walking in the mountains.
[*To the beach* should be paired with another prepositional phrase: *to the mountains.*]

**Parallel** This weekend, we can go to the beach or to the mountains.

**Tip** To understand this chapter, you need to be familiar with basic sentence elements, such as nouns and verbs. For a review, see Chapter 15.

# Practice Writing Parallel Sentences

## *Parallelism in Pairs and Lists*

When two or more items in a series are joined by *and* or *or,* use a similar form for each item.

**Not parallel** The professor assigned readings, practices to do, and a paper.

**Parallel** The professor assigned readings, practices, and a paper.

**Not parallel** The story was in the newspaper, on the radio, and the television.
[*In the newspaper* and *on the radio* are prepositional phrases. *The television* is not.]

**Parallel** The story was in the newspaper, on the radio, and on the television.

**PRACTICE 1** **Using parallelism in pairs and lists**

In each sentence, underline the parts of the sentence that should be parallel. Then, edit the sentence to make it parallel.

**Example: Coyotes roam the western mountains, the central plains, and ~~they are in the~~ *suburbs* ~~suburbs~~ of the East Coast ~~of the United States.~~**

1. Wild predators, such as wolves, are vanishing because people hunt them and are taking over their land.
2. Coyotes are surviving and they do well in the modern United States.
3. The success of the coyote is due to its varied diet and adapting easily.
4. Coyotes are sometimes vegetarians, sometimes scavengers, and sometimes they hunt.
5. Today, they are spreading and populate the East Coast for the first time.
6. The coyotes' appearance surprises and is worrying many people.
7. The animals have chosen an area that is more populated and it's not as wild as their traditional home.

8. Coyotes can adapt to rural, suburban, and even living in a city.
9. One coyote was identified, tracked, and they captured him in Central Park in New York City.
10. Suburbanites are getting used to the sight of coyotes and hearing them.

## *Parallelism in Comparisons*

Comparisons often use the word *than* or *as*. When you edit for parallelism, make sure the items on either side of those words have parallel structures.

| | |
|---|---|
| **Not parallel** | Taking the bus downtown is as fast as the drive there. |
| **Parallel** | Taking the bus downtown is as fast as driving there. |
| **Not parallel** | To admit a mistake is better than denying it. |
| **Parallel** | To admit a mistake is better than to deny it.<br>Admitting a mistake is better than denying it. |

Sometimes you need to add or delete a word or two to make the parts of a sentence parallel.

| | |
|---|---|
| **Not parallel** | A tour package is less expensive than arranging every travel detail yourself. |
| **Parallel, word added** | *Buying* a tour package is less expensive than arranging every travel detail yourself. |
| **Not parallel** | The sale price of the shoes is as low as paying half of the regular price. |
| **Parallel, words dropped** | The sale price of the shoes is as low as half of the regular price. |

### PRACTICE 2 Using parallelism in comparisons

In each sentence, underline the parts of the sentence that should be parallel. Then, edit the sentence to make it parallel.

**Example: Leasing a new car may be less expensive than ~~to buy~~ buying one.**

1. Car dealers often require less money down for leasing a car than for the purchase of one.
2. The monthly payments for a leased car may be as low as paying for a loan.
3. You should check the terms of leasing to make sure they are as favorable as to buy.

4. You may find that to lease is a safer bet than buying.
5. You will be making less of a financial commitment by leasing a car than to own it.
6. Buying a car may be better than a lease on one if you plan to keep it for several years.
7. A used car can be more economical than getting a new one.
8. However, maintenance of a new car may be easier than taking care of a used car.
9. A used car may not be as impressive as buying a brand-new vehicle.
10. To get a used car from a reputable source can be a better decision than a new vehicle that loses value the moment you drive it home.

## *Parallelism with Certain Paired Words*

Certain paired words, called **correlative conjunctions**, link two equal elements and show the relationship between them. Here are the paired words:

| | | |
|---|---|---|
| both . . . and | neither . . . nor | rather . . . than |
| either . . . or | not only . . . but also | |

Make sure the items joined by these paired words are parallel.

**Not parallel** Bruce wants *both* freedom *and* to be wealthy.
[*Both* is used with *and*, but the items joined by them are not parallel.]

**Parallel** Bruce wants *both* freedom *and* wealth.

**Parallel** Bruce wants *both* to have freedom *and* to be wealthy.

**Not parallel** He can *neither* fail the course and quitting his job is also impossible.

**Parallel** He can *neither* fail the course *nor* quit his job.

### PRACTICE 3 Using parallelism with certain paired words

In each sentence, circle the paired words, and underline the parts of the sentence that should be parallel. Then, edit the sentence to make it parallel. You may need to change one of the paired elements to make the sentence parallel.

**Example: A cell phone can be either a lifesaver or ~~it can be annoying~~.** *an annoyance*

1. Twenty years ago, most people neither had cell phones nor did they want them.

2. Today, cell phones are not only used by people of all ages but also are carried everywhere.

3. Cell phones are not universally popular: Some commuters would rather ban cell phones on buses and trains than being forced to listen to other people's conversations.

4. No one denies that a cell phone can be both useful and convenience is a factor.

5. A motorist stranded on a deserted road would rather have a cell phone than to walk to the nearest gas station.

6. When cell phones were first introduced, some people feared that they either caused brain tumors or they were a dangerous source of radiation.

7. Most Americans today neither worry about radiation from cell phones nor other injuries.

8. The biggest risk of cell phones is either that drivers are distracted by them or people getting angry at someone talking too loudly in public on a cell phone.

9. Cell phones probably do not cause brain tumors, but some experiments on human cells have shown that energy from the phones may both affect people's reflexes and it might alter the brain's blood vessels.

10. Some scientists think that these experiments show that cell phone use might have not only physical effects on human beings but it also could influence mental processes.

### PRACTICE 4 Completing sentences with paired words

For each sentence, complete the correlative conjunction, and add more information. Make sure the structures on both sides of the correlative conjunction are parallel.

**Example: I am both impressed by your company** *and enthusiastic to work for you*.

1. I could bring to this job not only youthful enthusiasm ______________________________.

2. I am willing to work either in your main office ______________________________________________.

3. My current job neither encourages initiative ______________________.

4. I would rather work in a challenging job ______________________.

5. In college, I learned a lot both from my classes ______________________.

# Edit for Parallelism

## PRACTICE 5 Editing paragraphs for parallelism problems

Find and correct five parallelism errors in the following paragraphs.

(1) On a mountainous island between Norway and the North Pole is a special underground vault. (2) It contains neither gold and currency. (3) Instead, it is full of a different kind of treasure: seeds. (4) They are being saved for the future in case something happens to the plants that people need to grow for food.

(5) The vault has the capacity to hold 4.5 million types of seed samples. (6) Each sample contains an average of five hundred seeds, which means that up to 2.25 billion seeds can be stored in the vault. (7) To store them is better than planting them. (8) Stored, they are preserved for future generations to plant. (9) On the first day that the vault's storage program began, 268,000 different seeds were deposited, put into sealed packages, and collecting into sealed boxes. (10) Some of the seeds were for maize (corn), and others were for rice, wheat, and barley.

(11) Although some people call it the "Doomsday Vault," many others see it as a type of insurance policy against starvation in the case of a terrible natural disaster. (12) The vault's location keeps it safe from floods, earthquakes, and storming. (13) Carefully storing these seeds will help ensure not only that people have food to eat important crops never go extinct.

## PRACTICE 6 Editing your own writing for parallelism

Edit a piece of your own writing for parallelism. It can be a paper for this course or another one, or it can be something you have written for work or your everyday life. You may want to use the chart on page 424.

## Chapter Review

1. Parallelism in writing means that ______________________________________________.

2. In what three situations do problems with parallelism most often occur? ______________________________________________

3. What are two pairs of correlative conjunctions? ______________________________________________

4. Write two sentences using parallelism. ______________________________________________

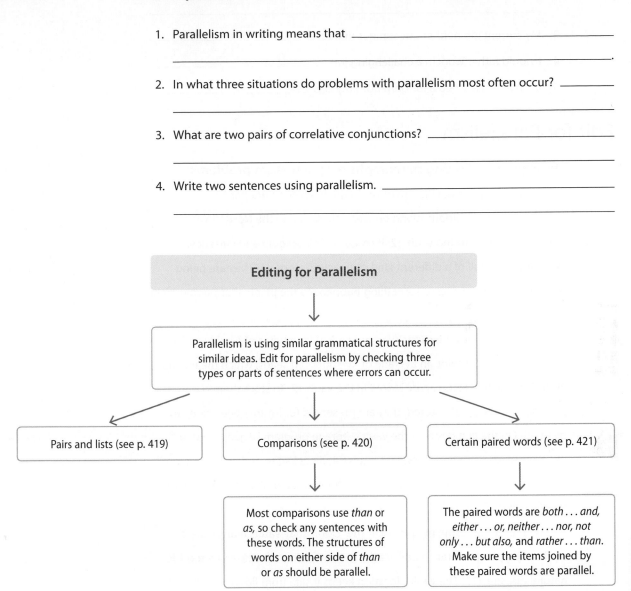

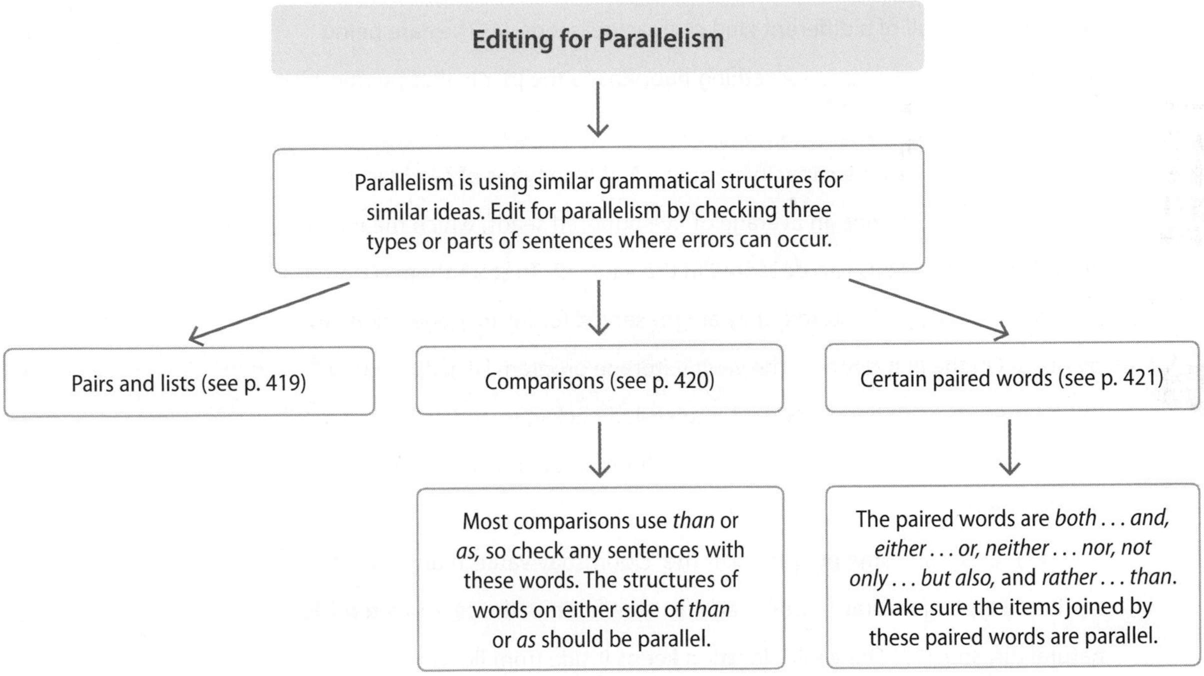

**Editing for Parallelism**

↓

Parallelism is using similar grammatical structures for similar ideas. Edit for parallelism by checking three types or parts of sentences where errors can occur.

Pairs and lists (see p. 419)

Comparisons (see p. 420)

↓

Most comparisons use *than* or *as*, so check any sentences with these words. The structures of words on either side of *than* or *as* should be parallel.

Certain paired words (see p. 421)

↓

The paired words are *both . . . and, either . . . or, neither . . . nor, not only . . . but also,* and *rather . . . than.* Make sure the items joined by these paired words are parallel.

# 25

# Sentence Variety

## Putting Rhythm in Your Writing

## Understand What Sentence Variety Is

Visit **LaunchPad Solo for Readers and Writers > Grammar > Style and Mechanics** for more tutorials, videos, and practice with crafting paragraphs.

**Sentence variety** means using different sentence patterns and lengths to give your writing good rhythm and flow. Notice how the first of the following examples does not have any rhythm.

**With short, simple sentences**

Many people do not realize how important their speaking voice and style are. Speaking style can make a difference, particularly in a job interview. What you say is important. How you say it is nearly as important. Your speaking voice creates an impression. Mumbling is a bad way of speaking. It makes the speaker appear sloppy and lacking in confidence. Mumbling also makes it difficult for the interviewer to hear what is being said. Talking too fast is another bad speech behavior. The speaker runs his or her ideas together. The interviewer cannot follow them or distinguish what is important. A third common bad speech behavior concerns verbal "tics." Verbal tics are empty filler phrases like "um,"

## GRAMMAR & MECHANICS ROADMAP

### An Overview

**This Chapter Identifies the Following Trouble Spots**

- Starting sentences with adverbs
- Joining ideas using an *-ing* verb
- Joining ideas using a past participle
- Joining ideas using an appositive
- Joining ideas using an adjective clause

**Tools to Address Trouble Spots**

"like," and "you know." Practice for an interview. Sit up straight. Look the person to whom you are speaking directly in the eye. Speak up. Slow down. One good way to find out how you sound is to leave yourself a voice-mail message. If you sound bad to yourself, you need practice speaking aloud. Do not let poor speech behavior interfere with creating a good impression.

**With sentence variety**
Many people do not realize how important their speaking voice and style are, particularly in a job interview. What you say is important, but how you say it is nearly as important in creating a good impression. Mumbling is a bad way of speaking. Not only does it make the speaker appear sloppy and lacking in confidence, but mumbling also makes it difficult for the interviewer to hear what is being said. Talking too fast is another bad speech behavior. The speaker runs his or her ideas together, and the interviewer cannot follow them or distinguish what is important. A third common bad speech behavior is called verbal "tics," empty filler expressions such as "um," "like," and "you know." When you practice for an interview, sit up straight, look the person to whom you are speaking directly in the eye, speak up, and slow down. One good way to find out how you sound is to leave yourself a voice-mail message. If you sound bad to yourself, you need practice speaking aloud. Do not let poor speech behavior interfere with creating a good impression.

## Practice Creating Sentence Variety

Most writers tend to write short sentences that start with the subject, so this chapter focuses on techniques for starting with something other than the subject and for writing a variety of longer sentences. Two additional techniques for achieving sentence variety—coordination and subordination—are covered in Chapter 23.

### *Start Some Sentences with Adverbs*

**Tip** For more about adverbs, see Chapter 22.

**Adverbs** are words that describe verbs, adjectives, or other adverbs; they often end with *-ly*. As long as the meaning is clear, adverbs can be placed at the beginning of a sentence instead of in the middle. Adverbs at the beginning of a sentence are usually followed by a comma.

| | |
|---|---|
| **Adverb in middle** | Stories about haunted houses *frequently* surface at Halloween. |
| **Adverb at beginning** | *Frequently*, stories about haunted houses surface at Halloween. |
| **Adverb in middle** | These stories *often* focus on ship captains lost at sea. |
| **Adverb at beginning** | *Often*, these stories focus on ship captains lost at sea. |

**PRACTICE 1** **Starting sentences with an adverb**

Edit each sentence so that it begins with an adverb.

**Example:** ~~**Rabies unfortunately**~~ **remains a problem in the United States.** [inserted: *Unfortunately, rabies*]

1. Rabies once was a major threat to domestic pets in this country.
2. The disease is now most deadly to wildlife such as raccoons, skunks, and bats.
3. People frequently fail to have their pets vaccinated against rabies.
4. They believe mistakenly that their dogs and cats are no longer in danger.
5. An oral vaccine that prevents rabies in raccoons and skunks has been developed, thankfully.

**PRACTICE 2** **Writing sentences that start with an adverb**

Write three sentences that start with an adverb. Use commas as necessary. Choose among the following adverbs: *often, sadly, amazingly, luckily, lovingly, aggressively, gently, frequently, stupidly.*

1. ______________________________________________
2. ______________________________________________
3. ______________________________________________

## *Join Ideas Using an -ing Verb*

One way to combine sentences is to add *-ing* to the verb in the less important of the two sentences and to delete the subject, creating a phrase.

| | |
|---|---|
| **Two sentences** | A pecan roll from our bakery is not a health food. It contains 800 calories. |
| **Joined with *-ing* verb form** | *Containing* 800 calories, a pecan roll from our bakery is not a health food. |

You can add the *-ing* phrase to the beginning or the end of the other sentence, depending on what makes more sense.

The fat content is also high. ~~It equals~~ the fat in a huge country breakfast. [inserted: *, equaling*]

If you add the *-ing* phrase to the beginning of a sentence, you will usually need to put a comma after it. If you add the phrase to the end of a sentence, you will

usually need to put a comma before it. A comma should *not* be used only when the *-ing* phrase is essential to the meaning of the sentence.

| | |
|---|---|
| **Two sentences** | Experts examined the effects of exercise on arthritis patients. The experts found that walking, jogging, or swimming could reduce pain. |
| **Joined without commas** | Experts examining the effects of exercise on arthritis patients found that walking, jogging, or swimming could reduce pain. [The phrase *examining the effects of exercise on arthritis patients* is essential to the meaning of the sentence.] |

**Tip** For more on finding and correcting dangling modifiers, see Chapter 22, and for more on joining ideas, see Chapter 23.

If you put a phrase starting with an *-ing* verb at the beginning of a sentence, be sure the word that the phrase modifies follows immediately. Otherwise, you will create a dangling modifier.

| | |
|---|---|
| **Two sentences** | I ran through the rain. My raincoat got all wet. |
| **Dangling modifier** | Running through the rain, my raincoat got all wet. |
| **Edited** | Running through the rain, I got my raincoat all wet. |

### PRACTICE 3 Joining ideas using an *-ing* verb

Combine each pair of sentences into a single sentence by using an *-ing* verb. Add or delete words as necessary.

**Example: Some people read faces amazingly well~~.~~, interpreting ~~They interpret~~ nonverbal cues that other people miss.**

1. A recent study tested children's abilities to interpret facial expressions. The study made headlines.
2. Physically abused children participated in the study. They saw photographs of faces changing from one expression to another.
3. The children told researchers what emotion was most obvious in each face. The children chose among fear, anger, sadness, happiness, and other emotions.
4. The study also included nonabused children. They served as a control group for comparison with the other children.
5. All the children in the study were equally good at identifying most emotions. They all responded similarly to happiness or fear.

6. Battered children were especially sensitive to one emotion on the faces. These children identified anger much more quickly than the other children could.
7. The abused children have learned to look for anger. They protect themselves with this early-warning system.
8. Their sensitivity to anger may not help the abused children later in life. It perhaps hurts them socially.
9. The abused children tend to run from anger they observe. They have difficulty connecting with people who exhibit anger.
10. The human brain works hard to acquire useful information. It often hangs on to the information after its usefulness has passed.

**PRACTICE 4** **Joining ideas using an *-ing* verb**

Write two sets of sentences, and join them using an *-ing* verb form.

**Example:**

**a.** *Carol looked up.*

**b.** *She saw three falling stars in the sky.*

**Combined:** *Looking up, Carol saw three falling stars in the sky.*

1. a. ______________________________

   b. ______________________________

   Combined: ______________________________

2. a. ______________________________

   b. ______________________________

   Combined: ______________________________

## *Join Ideas Using a Past Participle*

Another way to combine sentences is to use a past participle (often, a verb ending in *-ed*) to turn the less important of the two sentences into a phrase.

**Tip** For more on helping verbs, see Chapters 15 and 19. Chapter 19 also covers past participles.

| | |
|---|---|
| **Two sentences** | Henry VIII was a powerful English king. He is *remembered* for his many wives. |
| **Joined with a past participle** | *Remembered* for his many wives, Henry VIII was a powerful English king. |

Past participles of irregular verbs do not end in *-ed*; they take different forms.

| | |
|---|---|
| **Two sentences** | Tim Treadwell was *eaten* by a grizzly bear. He showed that wild animals are unpredictable. |
| **Joined with a past participle** | *Eaten* by a grizzly bear, Tim Treadwell showed that wild animals are unpredictable. |

Notice that sentences can be joined this way when one of them has a form of *be* along with a past participle (*is remembered* in the first Henry VIII example and *was eaten* in the first Tim Treadwell example).

To combine sentences this way, delete the subject and the *be* form from the sentence that has the *be* form and the past participle. You now have a phrase that can be added to the beginning or the end of the other sentence, depending on what makes more sense.

Subject | *be* form | Past participle | Pronoun changed to a noun

D / , *Henry VIII*

~~Henry VIII was~~ determined to divorce one of his wives/ ~~He~~ created the Church of England because Catholicism does not allow divorce.

**Tip** If you put a phrase starting with a past participle at the beginning of a sentence, be sure the word that the phrase modifies follows immediately. Otherwise, you will create a dangling modifier.

If you add a phrase that begins with a past participle to the beginning of a sentence, put a comma after it. If you add the phrase to the end of the sentence, put a comma before it.

## PRACTICE 5 Joining ideas using a past participle

Combine each pair of sentences into a single sentence by using a past participle.

*Forced* / , *the oil*

**Example:** ~~**The oil company was forced**~~ **to take the local women's objections seriously/ ~~The~~ company had to close for ten days during their protest.**

1. The women of southern Nigeria were angered by British colonial rule in 1929. They organized a protest.
2. Nigeria is now one of the top ten oil-producing countries. The nation is covered with pipelines and oil wells.
3. The oil is pumped by American and other foreign oil companies. The oil often ends up in wealthy Western economies.
4. The money from the oil seldom reaches Nigeria's local people. The cash is stolen by corrupt rulers in many cases.

5. The Nigerian countryside is polluted by the oil industry. The land then becomes a wasteland.
6. Many Nigerians are insulted by the way the oil industry treats them. They want the oil companies to pay attention to their problems.
7. Local Nigerian women were inspired by the 1929 women's protests. They launched a series of protests against the oil industry in the summer of 2002.
8. The women prevented workers from entering or leaving two oil company offices. The offices were located in the port of Warri.
9. Workers at the oil company were concerned about the women's threat to take off their clothes. Many workers told company officials that such a protest would bring a curse on the company and shame to its employees.
10. The company eventually agreed to hire more local people and to invest in local projects. The projects are intended to supply electricity and provide the villagers with a market for fish and poultry.

## PRACTICE 6 Joining ideas using a past participle

Write two sets of sentences, and join them with a past participle.

**Example:**

**a.** *Chris is taking intermediate accounting.*

**b.** *It is believed to be the most difficult course in the major.*

**Combined:** *Chris is taking intermediate accounting, believed to be the most difficult course in the major.*

1. a. ______

   b. ______

   Combined: ______

2. a. ______

   b. ______

   Combined: ______

## *Join Ideas Using an Appositive*

An **appositive** is a noun or noun phrase that renames a noun or pronoun. Appositives can be used to combine two sentences into one.

**Tip** Usually, you will want to turn the less important of the two sentences into an appositive.

| | |
|---|---|
| **Two sentences** | Brussels sprouts can be roasted for a delicious flavor. They are a commonly disliked food. |
| **Joined with an appositive** | Brussels sprouts, a commonly disliked food, can be roasted for a delicious flavor. |
| | [The phrase *a commonly disliked food* renames the noun *brussels sprouts.*] |

Notice that the sentence that renames the noun was turned into a noun phrase by dropping the subject and the verb (*They* and *are*). Also, commas set off the appositive.

### PRACTICE 7 Joining ideas using an appositive

Combine each pair of sentences into a single sentence by using an appositive. Be sure to use a comma or commas to set off the appositive.

*, perhaps the most famous work clothes in the world,*

**Example: Levi's jeans ^ have looked the same for well over a century. ~~They are perhaps the most famous work clothes in the world.~~**

1. Jacob Davis was a Russian immigrant working in Reno, Nevada. He was the inventor of Levi's jeans.
2. Davis came up with an invention that made work clothes last longer. The invention was the riveted seam.
3. Davis bought denim from a wholesaler. The wholesaler was Levi Strauss.
4. In 1870, he offered to sell the rights to his invention to Levi Strauss for the price of the patent. Patents then cost about $70.
5. Davis joined the firm in 1873 and supervised the final development of its product. The product was the famous Levi's jeans.
6. Davis oversaw a crucial design element. The jeans all had orange stitching.
7. The curved stitching on the back pockets was another choice Davis made. It also survives in today's Levi's.
8. The stitching on the pockets has been a trademark since 1942. It is very recognizable.

9. During World War II, Levi Strauss temporarily stopped adding the pocket stitches because they wasted thread. It was a valuable resource.
10. Until the war ended, the pocket design was added with a less valuable material. The company used paint.

## *Join Ideas Using an Adjective Clause*

An **adjective clause** is a group of words with a subject and a verb that describes a noun. An adjective clause often begins with the word *who, which,* or *that,* and it can be used to combine two sentences into one.

**Tip** For more about adjectives, see Chapter 21.

| | |
|---|---|
| **Two sentences** | Lauren has won many basketball awards. She is captain of her college team. |
| **Joined with an adjective clause** | Lauren, *who is captain of her college team,* has won many basketball awards. |

To join sentences this way, use *who, which,* or *that* to replace the subject in a sentence that describes a noun in the other sentence. You now have an adjective clause that you can move so that it follows the noun it describes. The sentence with the more important idea (the one you want to emphasize) should become the main clause. The less important idea should be in the adjective clause.

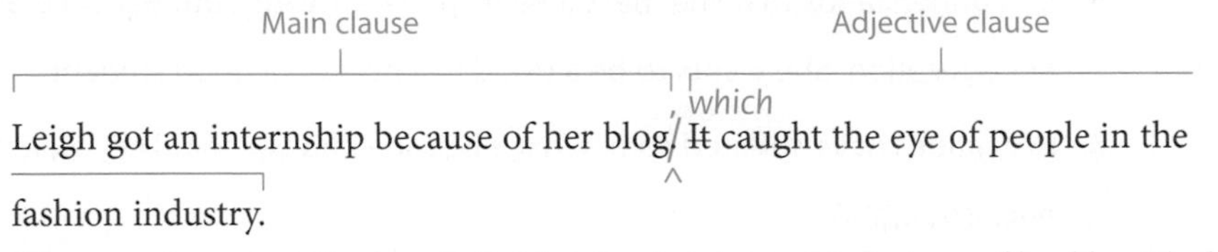
Main clause
Adjective clause
, which
Leigh got an internship because of her blog. It caught the eye of people in the fashion industry.

[The more important idea here is that Leigh got an internship because of her blog. The less important idea is that the blog caught the eye of people in the fashion industry.]

**Tip** Use *who* to refer to a person, *which* to refer to places or things (but not to people), and *that* for places or things.

**NOTE:** If an adjective clause can be taken out of a sentence without completely changing the meaning of the sentence, put commas around it.

Lauren, *who is captain of her college team,* has won many basketball awards.

[The phrase *who is captain of her college team* adds information about Lauren, but it is not essential.]

If an adjective clause is an essential part of a sentence, do not put commas around it.

Lauren is an award-winning basketball player who overcame childhood cancer.

[*Who overcame childhood cancer* is an essential part of this sentence.]

## PRACTICE 8 Joining ideas using an adjective clause

Combine each pair of sentences into a single sentence by using an adjective clause beginning with *who, which,* or *that*.

*, who has been going to college for the past three years,*
**Example: My friend Erin ^ had her first child last June. ~~She has been going to college for the past three years.~~**

1. While Erin goes to classes, her baby boy stays at a day-care center. The day-care center costs Erin about $100 a week.
2. Twice when her son was ill, Erin had to miss her geology lab. The lab is an important part of her grade for that course.
3. Occasionally, Erin's parents come up and watch the baby while Erin is studying. They live about 70 miles away.
4. Sometimes Erin feels discouraged by the extra costs. The costs have come from having a child.
5. She believes that some of her professors are not very sympathetic. These professors are the ones who have never been parents themselves.
6. Erin understands that she must take responsibility for both her child and her education. She wants to be a good mother and a good student.
7. Her grades have suffered somewhat since she had her son. They were once straight A's.
8. Erin wants to graduate with honors. She hopes to go to graduate school someday.
9. Her son is more important than an A in geology. He is the most important thing to her.
10. Erin still expects to have a high grade point average. She has simply given up expecting to be perfect.

## PRACTICE 9 Joining ideas using an adjective clause

Fill in the blank in each of the following sentences with an appropriate adjective clause. Add commas, if necessary.

**Example: The firefighters** ___*who responded to the alarm*___ **entered the burning building.**

1. A fire ______________________________ began in our house in the middle of the night.
2. The members of my family ______________________________ were all asleep.
3. My father ______________________________ was the first to smell smoke.
4. He ran to our bedrooms ______________________________ and woke us up with his shouting.
5. The house ______________________________ was damaged, but everyone in my family reached safety.

# Edit for Sentence Variety

**PRACTICE 10** **Editing paragraphs for sentence variety**

Create sentence variety in the following paragraphs by joining at least two sentences in each of the paragraphs. Use several of the techniques covered in this chapter. More than one correct answer is possible.

(1) Few people would associate the famous English poet and playwright William Shakespeare with prison. (2) However, Shakespeare has taken on an important role in the lives of certain inmates. (3) They are serving time at the Luther Luckett Correctional Complex in Kentucky. (4) These inmates were brought together by the Shakespeare Behind Bars program. (5) They spend nine months preparing for a performance of one of the great writer's plays.

(6) Recently, prisoners at Luckett performed *The Merchant of Venice*. (7) It is one of Shakespeare's most popular plays. (8) Many of the actors identified with Shylock. (9) He is a moneylender who is discriminated against because he is Jewish. (10) When a rival asks Shylock for a loan to help a friend, Shylock drives a hard bargain. (11) He demands a pound of the rival's flesh if the loan is not repaid. (12) One inmate shared his views of this play with a newspaper reporter. (13) The inmate said, "It deals with race. It deals with discrimination. It deals with gambling, debt, cutting people. It deals with it all. And we were all living that someway, somehow."

(14) Through the Shakespeare performances, the inmates form bonds not only with the characters but also with one another. (15) Additionally,

they are able to explore their own histories and their responsibility for the crimes they committed. (16) Many feel changed by their experience on the stage. (17) One actor was affected deeply by his role in *The Merchant of Venice.* (18) He said, "You feel like you're in a theater outside of here. You don't feel the razor wire."

**PRACTICE 11** **Editing your own writing for sentence variety**

Add more sentence variety to a piece of your own writing—a paper for this course or another one, or choose something you have written for work or your everyday life. You may want to use the chart on page 437.

# Chapter Review

1. Having sentence variety means ______________________________________________

______________________________________________.

2. If you tend to write short, similar-sounding sentences, what five techniques should you try? ______________________________________________

______________________________________________

______________________________________________.

3. An ____________ is a noun or noun phrase that renames a noun.

4. An ____________ clause often starts with *who,* __________, or __________. It describes a noun or pronoun.

5. Use commas around an adjective clause when the information in it is (essential/not essential) to the meaning of the sentence.

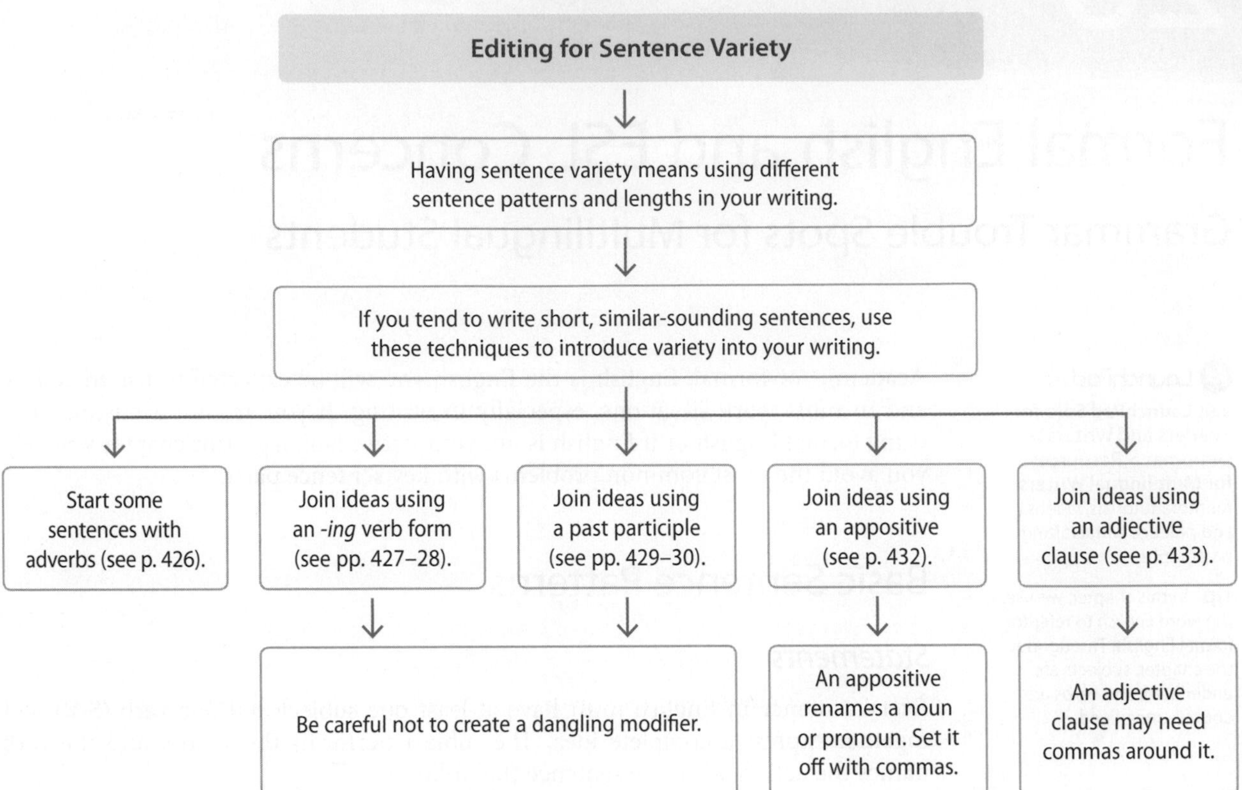
Editing for Sentence Variety
Having sentence variety means using different sentence patterns and lengths in your writing.
If you tend to write short, similar-sounding sentences, use these techniques to introduce variety into your writing.
Start some sentences with adverbs (see p. 426).
Join ideas using an -ing verb form (see pp. 427–28).
Join ideas using a past participle (see pp. 429–30).
Join ideas using an appositive (see p. 432).
Join ideas using an adjective clause (see p. 433).
Be careful not to create a dangling modifier.
An appositive renames a noun or pronoun. Set it off with commas.
An adjective clause may need commas around it.

# 26

# Formal English and ESL Concerns

## Grammar Trouble Spots for Multilingual Students

Visit **LaunchPad Solo for Readers and Writers > Grammar > Resources for Multilingual Writers** for more tutorials, videos, and practice with crafting paragraphs.

**Tip** In this chapter, we use the word *English* to refer to formal English. Throughout the chapter, subjects are underlined, and verbs are double-underlined.

Academic, or formal, English is the English you will be expected to use in college and in most work situations, especially in writing. If you are not accustomed to using formal English or if English is not your native language, this chapter will help you avoid the most common problems with key sentence parts.

## Basic Sentence Patterns

### *Statements*

Every sentence in English must have at least one subject and one verb **(S-V)** that together express a complete idea. The subject performs the action, and the verb names the action, as in the sentence that follows.

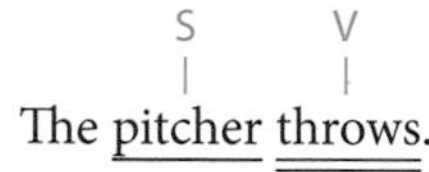

GRAMMAR & MECHANICS ROADMAP

**An Overview**

**This Chapter Identifies the Following Trouble Spots**

- Sentence patterns and word order
- Pronouns
- Negatives
- Questions
- *There is* and *there are*
- Confusing subject and object pronouns
- Verbs
- Articles
- Count and noncount nouns
- Prepositions

**Tools to Address Trouble Spots**

- Understand Basic Sentence Patterns (p. 438)
- List of common negatives and helping verbs (pp. 440–41)
- List of Pronoun Types (p. 444)
- Coverage of verbs and verb tenses (p. 445)
- List of Modal (Helping) Verbs (pp. 452–55)
- List of verbs commonly followed by a gerund or infinitive (pp. 457–58)
- List of Count and Noncount Nouns (p. 460)
- Common verb/preposition combinations (p. 462)
- Chapter Review (p. 463)

Other English sentence patterns build on that structure. One of the most common patterns is subject-verb-object **(S-V-O)**.

S V O

The pitcher throws the ball.

There are two kinds of objects.

**Direct objects** receive the action of the verb.

S V DO

The pitcher throws the ball.

[The ball directly receives the action of the verb *throws*.]

**Indirect objects** do not receive the action of the verb. Instead, the action is performed *for* or *to* the person.

S V IO DO

The pitcher throws me the ball.

**PRACTICE 1** **Sentence patterns**

Label the subject (S), verb (V), direct object (DO), and indirect object (IO), if any, in the following two sentences.

1. John sent the letter.

2. John sent Beth the letter.

Another common sentence pattern is subject-verb-prepositional phrase. In standard English, the prepositional phrase typically follows the subject and verb.

**Tip** For more on the parts of sentences, see Chapter 15.

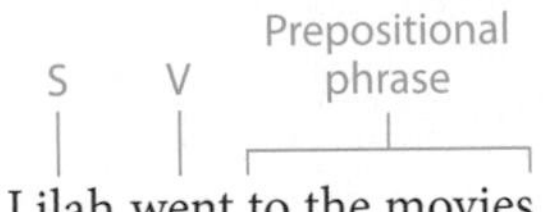
S
V
Prepositional phrase

Lilah went to the movies.

**PRACTICE 2** **Using correct word order**

Read each of the sentences that follow. If the sentence is correct, write "C" in the blank to the left of it. If it is incorrect, write "I"; then, rewrite the sentence using correct word order.

**Example:** __I__ **My friend to me gave a present.**

**Revision:** *My friend gave me a present.*

1. ____ Presents I like very much.

Revision: ______________________________________

2. ____ To parties I go often.

Revision: ______________________________

3. ____ To parties, I always bring a present.

Revision: ______________________________

4. ____ At my parties, people bring me presents, too.

Revision: ______________________________

5. ____ Always write to them a thank-you note.

Revision: ______________________________

## *Negatives*

To form a negative statement, use one of the words listed here, often with a helping verb such as *can/could, does/did, has/have*, or *should/will/would.*

| never | nobody | no one | nowhere |
|---|---|---|---|
| no | none | not | |

Notice in these examples that the word *not* comes *after* the helping verb.

**Sentence** Dina can sing.

**Negative** Dina ~~no can~~ sing. [cannot]

**Sentence** The store sells cigarettes.

**Negative** The store ~~no~~ sell~~s~~ cigarettes. [does not]

**Sentence** Bruce will call.

**Negative** Bruce ~~no~~ will call. [not]

**Sentence** Caroline walked.

**Negative** Caroline ~~no~~ did walk. [not]

**Tip** For more on helping verbs and their forms, see Chapter 15.

The helping verb cannot be omitted in expressions using *not.*

**Incorrect** The store *not sell* cigarettes.

**Correct** The store *does not sell* cigarettes.
[*Does,* a form of the helping verb *do,* must come before *not.*]

**Correct** The store *is not selling* cigarettes.
[*Is,* a form of *be,* must come before *not.*]

### Common Helping Verbs

| Forms of *be* | Forms of *have* | Forms of *do* | Other verbs |
|---|---|---|---|
| am | have | do | can |
| are | has | does | could |
| is | had | did | may |
| been | | | might |
| being | | | must |
| was | | | should |
| were | | | will |
| | | | would |

Double negatives are not standard in English.

**Incorrect** Shane *does not have no* ride.

**Correct** Shane *does not have a* ride.

**Correct** Shane *has no* ride.

When forming a negative in the simple past tense, use the past tense of the helping verb *do*.

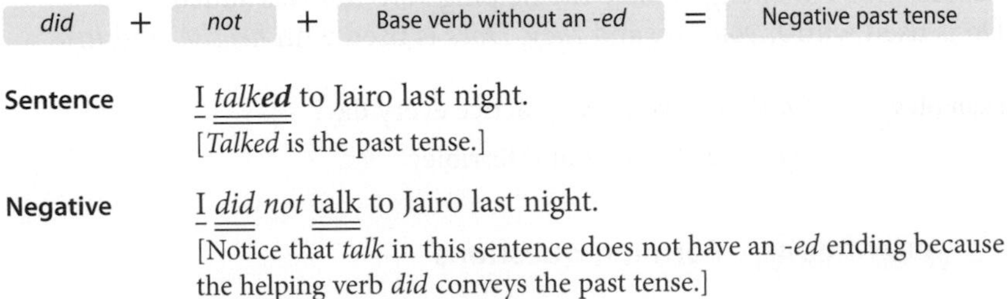

*did* + *not* + Base verb without an *-ed* = Negative past tense

**Sentence** I ***talked*** to Jairo last night.
[*Talked* is the past tense.]

**Negative** I *did not* talk to Jairo last night.
[Notice that *talk* in this sentence does not have an *-ed* ending because the helping verb *did* conveys the past tense.]

**PRACTICE 3** **Forming negatives**

Rewrite the sentences to make them negative.

**Example: Hassan's son is ^not talking now.**

1. He can say several words.
2. Hassan remembers when his daughter started talking.
3. He thinks it was at the same age.
4. His daughter was an early speaker.
5. Hassan expects his son to be a talkative adult.

## Questions

**Tip** Sometimes the verb appears before the subject in sentences that are not questions: *Behind the supermarket is the sub shop.*

To turn a statement into a question, move the helping verb so that it comes before the subject. Add a question mark (**?**) to the end of the question.

**Statement** Johan *can go* tonight.

**Question** *Can* Johan go tonight?

If the only verb in the statement is a form of *be,* it should be moved before the subject.

**Statement** Jamie *is* at work.

**Question** *Is* Jamie at work?

If the statement does not contain a helping verb or a form of *be,* add a form of *do* and put it before the subject. Be sure to end the question with a question mark (**?**).

| | | |
|---|---|---|
| **Statement** | Norah sings in the choir. | Tyrone goes to college. |
| **Question** | *Does* Norah sing in the choir? | *Does* Tyrone go to college? |
| **Statement** | The building burned. | The plate broke. |
| **Question** | *Did* the building burn? | *Did* the plate break? |

Notice that the verb changed once the helping verb *did* was added.

*Do* is used with *I, you, we,* and *they*. *Does* is used with *he, she,* and *it*.

**Examples** *Do* [I/you/we/they] practice every day?
*Does* [he/she/it] sound terrible?

### PRACTICE 4 Forming questions

Rewrite the sentences to make them into questions.

**Example:** ^Does **Brad knows how to cook.** ^?

1. He makes dinner every night for his family.
2. He goes to the grocery store once a week.
3. He uses coupons to save money.
4. Brad saves a lot of money using coupons.

## There Is *and* There Are

English sentences often include *there is* or *there are* to indicate the existence of something.

> *There* is a man at the door.
> [You could also say, *A man is at the door.*]
> *There* are many men in the class.
> [You could also say, *Many men are in the class.*]

When a sentence includes the words *there is* or *there are*, the verb (*is*, *are*) comes before the noun it goes with (which is actually the subject of the sentence). The verb must agree with the noun in number. For example, the first sentence above uses the singular verb *is* to agree with the singular noun *man*, and the second sentence uses the plural verb *are* to agree with the plural noun *men*.

In questions, *is* or *are* comes before *there*.

| | |
|---|---|
| **Statements** | *There* is plenty to eat. |
| | *There* are some things to do. |
| **Questions** | Is *there* plenty to eat? |
| | Are *there* some things to do? |

# Pronouns

**Pronouns** replace nouns or other pronouns in a sentence so that you do not have to repeat them. There are three types of pronouns: subject pronouns, object pronouns, and possessive pronouns.

**Tip** For more on pronouns, see Chapter 20.

**Subject pronouns** serve as the subject of the verb (and remember that every English sentence *must* have a subject).

> Rob is my cousin. ~~Rob~~ He lives next to me.

**Object pronouns** receive the action of the verb or are part of a prepositional phrase.

> Rob asked *me* for a favor.
> [The object pronoun *me* receives the action of the verb *asked*.]
> Rob lives next door *to me*.
> [*To me* is the prepositional phrase; *me* is the object pronoun.]

**Possessive pronouns** show ownership.

> Rob is *my* cousin.

Use the following chart to check which type of pronoun to use.

## Pronoun Types

| Subject | | Object | | Possessive | |
|---|---|---|---|---|---|
| **Singular** | **Plural** | **Singular** | **Plural** | **Singular** | **Plural** |
| I | we | me | us | my/mine | our/ours |
| you | you | you | you | your/yours | your/yours |
| he/she/it | they | him/her/it | them | his/her/hers/its | theirs |

**Relative Pronouns**

who, which, that

The singular pronouns *he/she, him/her,* and *his/hers* show gender. *He, him,* and *his* are masculine pronouns; *she, her,* and *hers* are feminine.

Here are some examples of common pronoun errors, with corrections.

### *Confusing Subject and Object Pronouns*

Use a subject pronoun for the word that *performs* the action of the verb, and use an object pronoun for the word that *receives* the action.

Tashia is a good student. ~~Her~~ ^She gets all A's.

[The pronoun performs the action *gets,* so it should be the subject pronoun, *she.*]

Tomas gave the keys to ~~she~~ ^her. Banh gave the coat to ~~he~~ ^him.

[The pronoun receives the action of *gave,* so it should be the object pronoun, *her* or *him.*]

### *Confusing Gender*

Use masculine pronouns to replace masculine nouns, and use feminine pronouns to replace feminine nouns.

Nick is sick. ~~She~~ ^He has the flu.

[*Nick* is a masculine noun, so the pronoun must be masculine.]

The jacket belongs to Jane. Give it to ~~him~~ ^her.

[*Jane* is feminine, so the pronoun must be feminine.]

### Leaving Out a Pronoun

Some sentences use the pronoun *it* as the subject or object. Do not leave *it* out of the sentence.

It is ~~Is~~ a holiday today.

Maria will bring the food. It will ~~Will~~ be delicious.

I tried calamari last night and liked it very much.

### Using a Pronoun to Repeat a Subject

A pronoun *replaces* a noun, so do not use both a subject noun and a pronoun.

My father ~~he~~ is very strict.
[*Father* is the subject noun, so the sentence should not also have the subject pronoun *he*.]

The bus ~~it~~ was late.
[*Bus* is the subject noun, so the sentence should not also have the subject pronoun *it*.]

### Using Relative Pronouns

The words *who, which,* and *that* are **relative pronouns**. Use relative pronouns in a clause that gives more information about the subject.

- Use *who* to refer to a person or people.

  The man *who* lives next door plays piano.
- Use *which* or *that* to refer to nonliving things.

  The plant, *which* was a gift, died.

  The phone *that* I bought last week is broken.

## Verbs

Verbs have different tenses to show when something happened: in the past, present, or future.

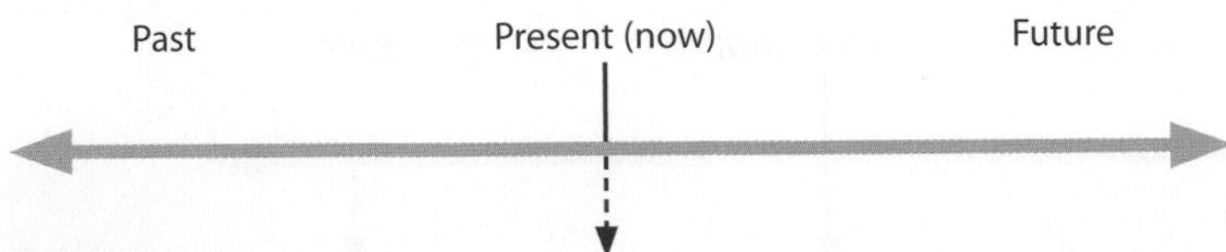
Past
Present (now)
Future

This section contains time lines, examples, and common errors for the simple and perfect tenses; coverage of progressive tenses; and more. See Chapter 19 for full coverage of the simple tenses and the perfect tenses, as well as practice exercises.

## *The Simple Tenses*

### SIMPLE PRESENT

Use the simple present to describe situations that exist now.

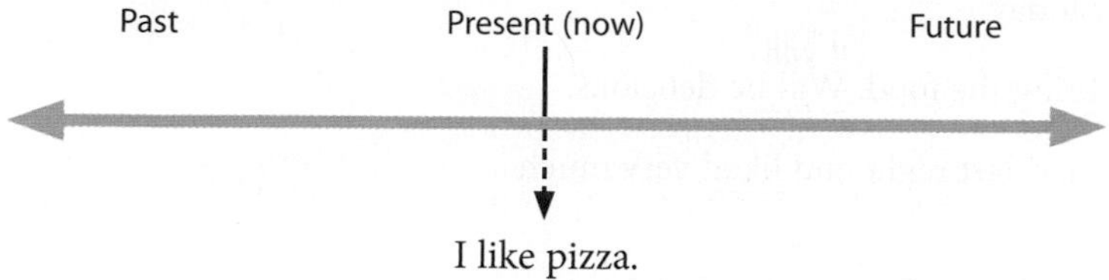
Past
Present (now)
Future
I like pizza.

I/You/We/They like pizza.

She/He likes pizza.

The third-person singular (*she/he*) of regular verbs ends in *-s* or *-es*. For irregular verb endings, see pages 366–69.

### SIMPLE PAST

Use the simple past to describe situations that began and ended in the past.

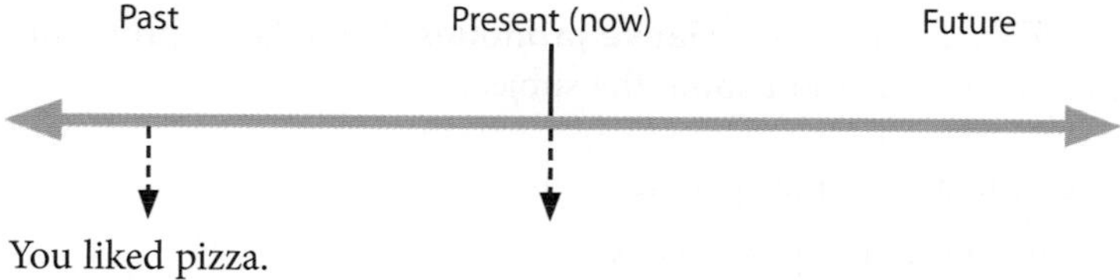
Past
Present (now)
Future
You liked pizza.

I/You/She/He/We/They like**d** pizza.

For regular verbs, the simple past is formed by adding either *-d* or *-ed* to the verb. For the past forms of irregular verbs, see the chart on pages 366–69.

### SIMPLE FUTURE

Use the simple future to describe situations that will happen in the future. It is easier to form than the past tense. Use this formula for forming the future tense.

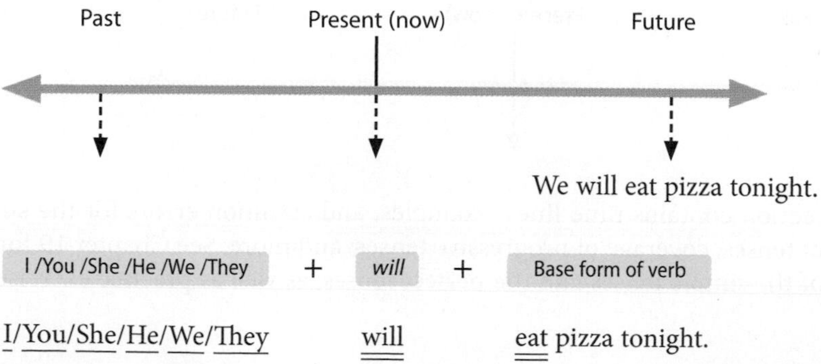
Past
Present (now)
Future
We will eat pizza tonight.
I /You /She /He /We /They + *will* + Base form of verb
I/You/She/He/We/They will eat pizza tonight.

### COMMON ERRORS IN USING SIMPLE TENSES

Following are some common errors in using simple tenses.

**Simple present.** Forgetting to add *-s* or *-es* to verbs that go with third-person singular subjects (*she/he/it*)

**Tip** The subject and the verb must agree in number. For more on subject-verb agreement, see Chapter 18.

| | |
|---|---|
| **Incorrect** | She know the manager. |
| **Correct** | She know**s** the manager. |

**Simple past.** Forgetting to add *-d* or *-ed* to regular verbs

| | |
|---|---|
| **Incorrect** | Gina work late last night. |
| **Correct** | Gina work**ed** late last night. |

Forgetting to use the correct past forms of irregular verbs (see the chart of irregular verb forms on pages 366–69)

| | |
|---|---|
| **Incorrect** | Gerard speaked to her about the problem. |
| **Correct** | Gerard **spoke** to her about the problem. |

Forgetting to use the base verb without an ending for negative sentences

**Tip** Double negatives (*Johnetta will **not** call **no one***) are not standard in English. One negative is enough (*Johnetta will **not** call **anyone***).

| | |
|---|---|
| **Incorrect** | She does not wants money for helping. |
| **Correct** | She does not **want** money for helping. |

## The Perfect Tenses

### PRESENT PERFECT

Use the present perfect to describe situations that started in the past and either continue into the present or were completed at some unknown time in the past.

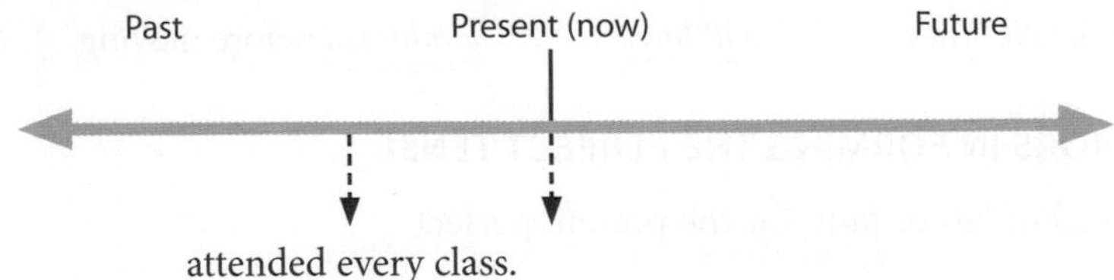
Past
Present (now)
Future
attended every class.

To form the present perfect tense, use this formula:

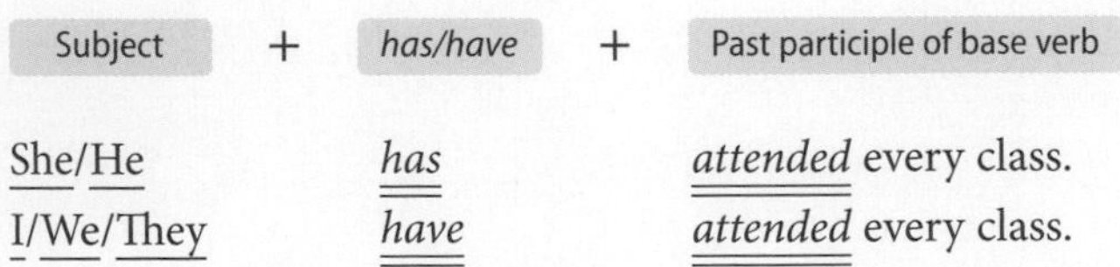
Subject + has/have + Past participle of base verb
She/He has attended every class.
I/We/They have attended every class.

Notice that *I/We/They* use *have* and that *She/He* use *has.*

#### PAST PERFECT

Use the past perfect to describe situations that began and ended before some other situation happened.

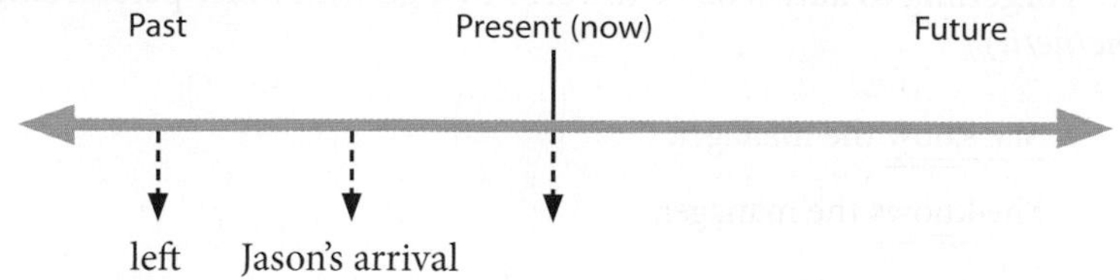
Past
Present (now)
Future
left
Jason's arrival

To form the past perfect tense, use this formula:

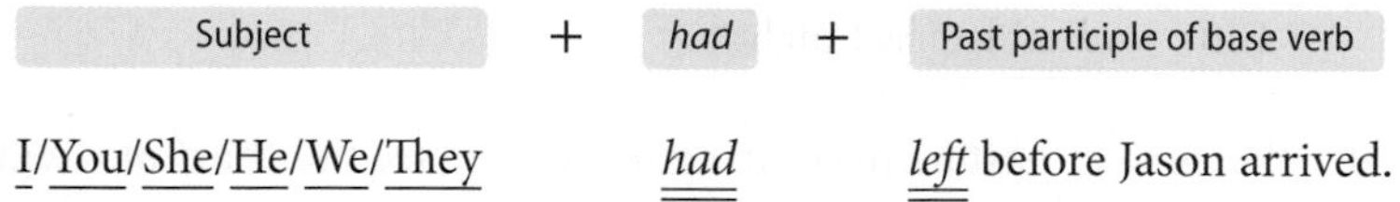
Subject
+
*had*
+
Past participle of base verb
I/You/She/He/We/They
*had*
*left* before Jason arrived.

#### FUTURE PERFECT

Use the future perfect to describe situations that begin and end before another situation begins.

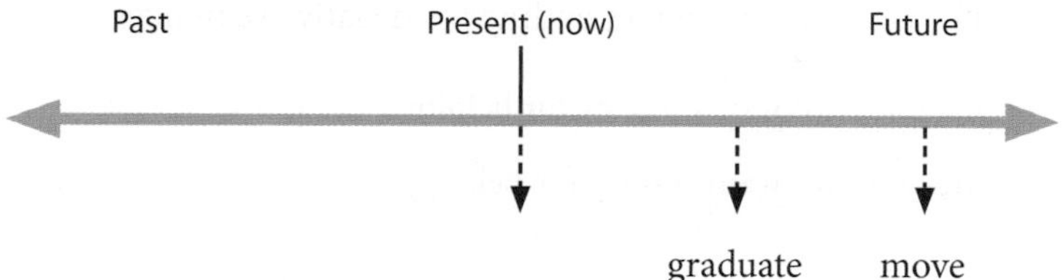
Past
Present (now)
Future
graduate
move

Use this formula to form the future perfect tense:

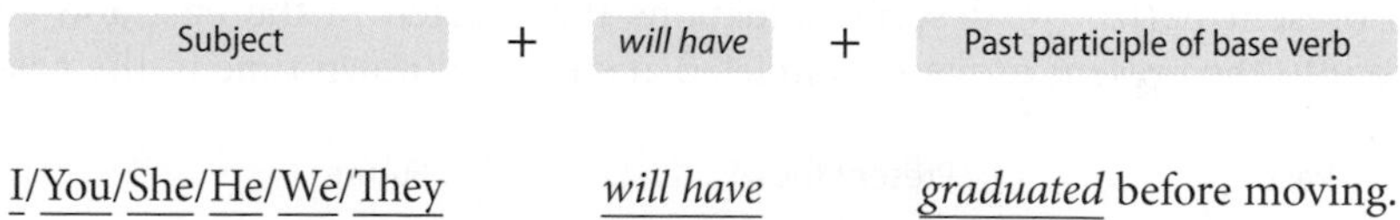
Subject
+
*will have*
+
Past participle of base verb
I/You/She/He/We/They
*will have*
*graduated* before moving.

#### COMMON ERRORS IN FORMING THE PERFECT TENSE

Using *had* instead of *has* or *have* for the present perfect

| | |
|---|---|
| **Incorrect** | We **had** lived here since 2003. |
| **Correct** | We **have** lived here since 2003. |

Forgetting to use past participles (with *-d* or *-ed* endings for regular verbs)

**Incorrect** She has attend every class.

**Correct** She has attend**ed** every class.

Using *been* between *have* or *has* and the past participle of a base verb

**Incorrect** I have **been** attended every class.

**Correct** I have attended every class.

**Incorrect** I will have **been** graduated before I move.

**Correct** I will have graduated before I move.

## *The Present Progressive Tenses*

The progressive tense is used to describe ongoing actions in the present, past, or future. Following are some common errors in using the present progressive tense.

Forgetting to add *-ing* to the verb

**Incorrect** I am type now.
She/he is not type now.

**Correct** I am typ**ing** now.
She/he is not typ**ing** now.

Forgetting to include a form of *be* (*am/is/are*)

**Incorrect** He typing now.
They typing now.

**Correct** He **is** typing now.
They **are** typing now.

Forgetting to use a form of *be* (*am/is/are*) to start questions

**Incorrect** They typing now?

**Correct** **Are** they typing now?

The following charts show how to use the present, past, and future progressive tenses in regular statements, negative statements, and questions.

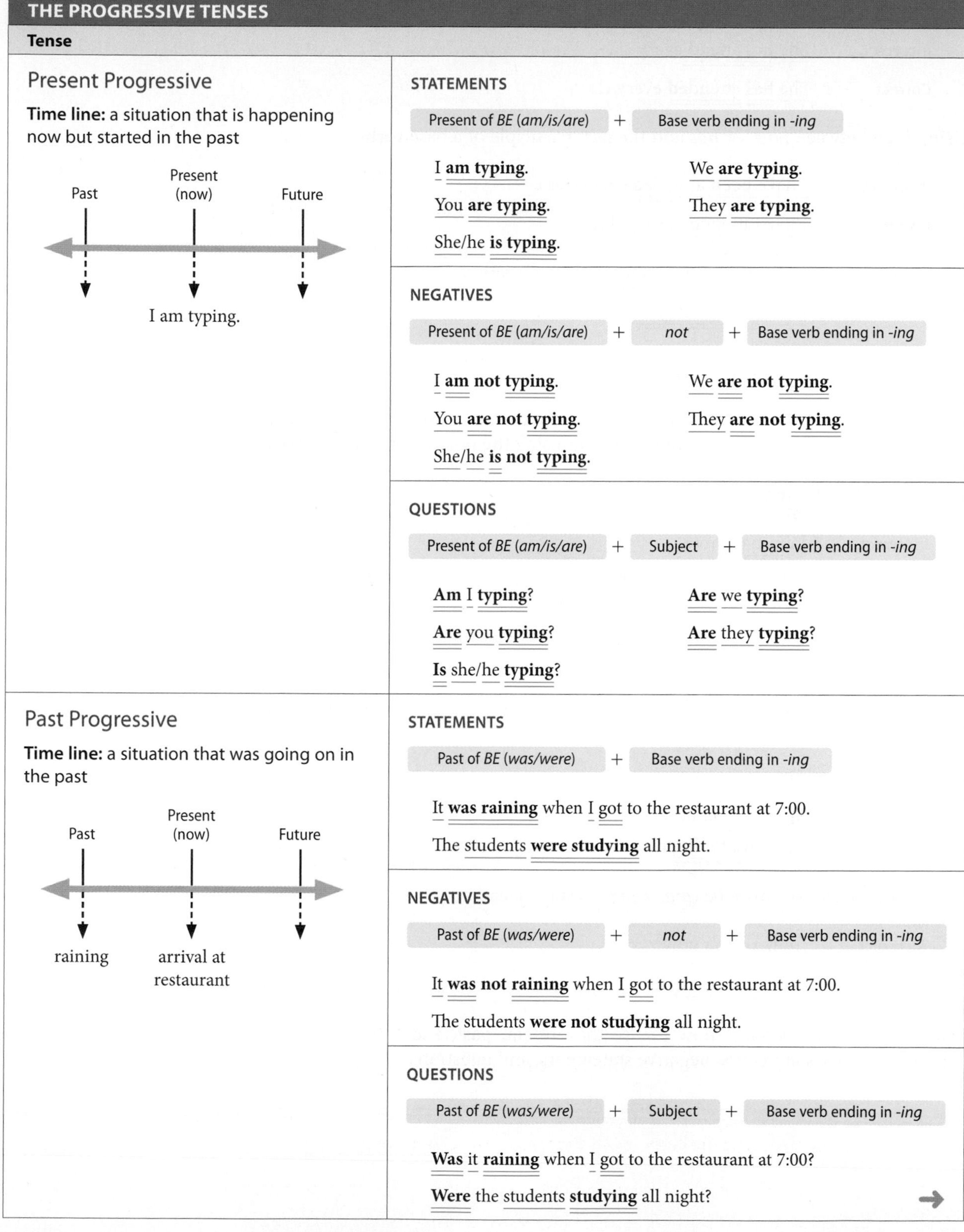

**THE PROGRESSIVE TENSES**

| Tense | |
|---|---|
| **Present Progressive**<br>**Time line:** a situation that is happening now but started in the past<br>Past — Present (now) — Future<br>I am typing. | **STATEMENTS**<br>Present of *BE* (*am/is/are*) + Base verb ending in *-ing*<br>I **am typing**. We **are typing**.<br>You **are typing**. They **are typing**.<br>She/he **is typing**. |
| | **NEGATIVES**<br>Present of *BE* (*am/is/are*) + *not* + Base verb ending in *-ing*<br>I **am not typing**. We **are not typing**.<br>You **are not typing**. They **are not typing**.<br>She/he **is not typing**. |
| | **QUESTIONS**<br>Present of *BE* (*am/is/are*) + Subject + Base verb ending in *-ing*<br>**Am** I **typing**? **Are** we **typing**?<br>**Are** you **typing**? **Are** they **typing**?<br>**Is** she/he **typing**? |
| **Past Progressive**<br>**Time line:** a situation that was going on in the past<br>Past — Present (now) — Future<br>raining — arrival at restaurant | **STATEMENTS**<br>Past of *BE* (*was/were*) + Base verb ending in *-ing*<br>It **was raining** when I got to the restaurant at 7:00.<br>The students **were studying** all night. |
| | **NEGATIVES**<br>Past of *BE* (*was/were*) + *not* + Base verb ending in *-ing*<br>It **was not raining** when I got to the restaurant at 7:00.<br>The students **were not studying** all night. |
| | **QUESTIONS**<br>Past of *BE* (*was/were*) + Subject + Base verb ending in *-ing*<br>**Was** it **raining** when I got to the restaurant at 7:00?<br>**Were** the students **studying** all night? |

→

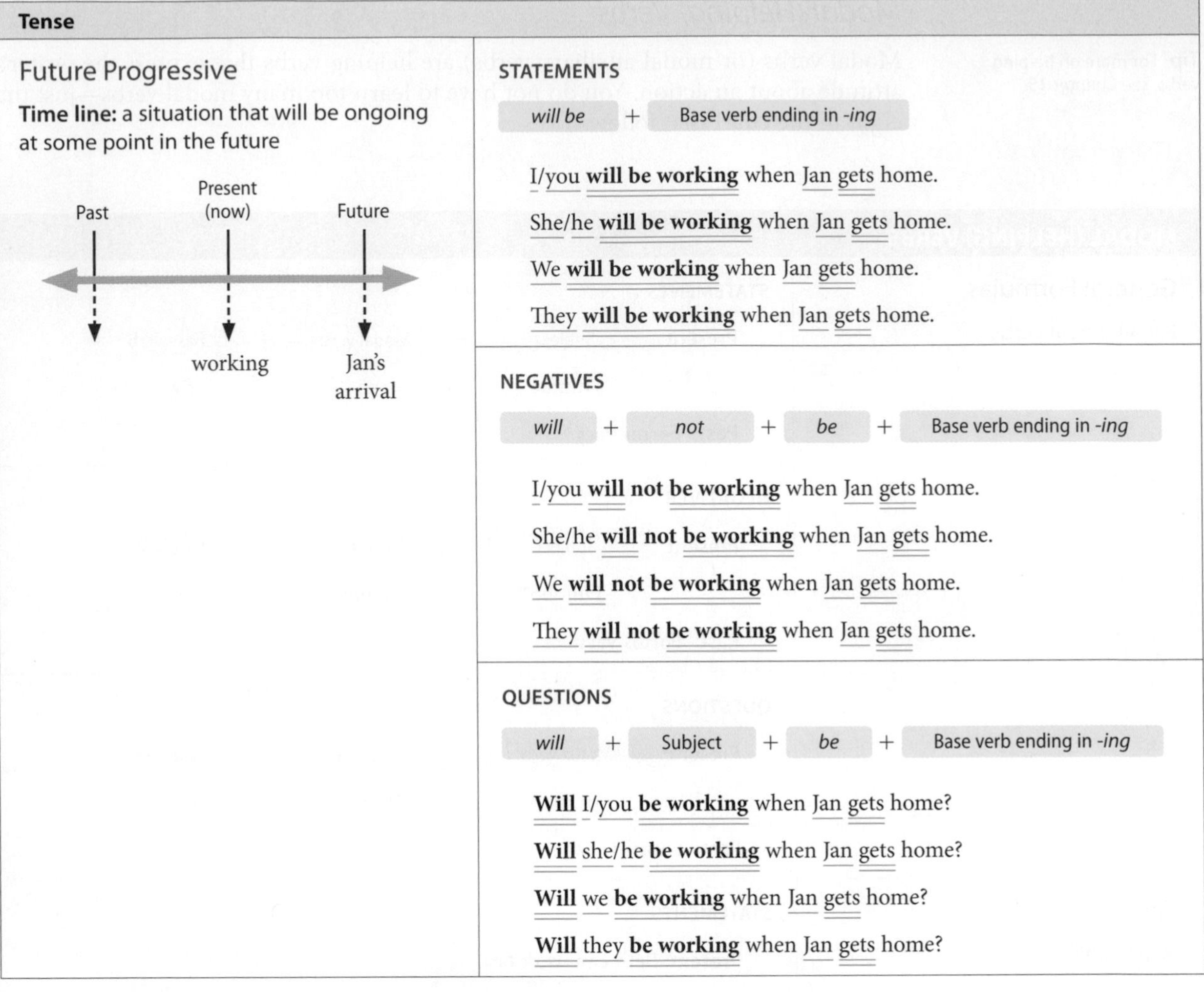

| Tense | |
|---|---|
| **Future Progressive**<br>**Time line:** a situation that will be ongoing at some point in the future<br><br>Past — Present (now) — Future<br>working — Jan's arrival | **STATEMENTS**<br>*will be* + Base verb ending in *-ing*<br><br>I/you **will be working** when Jan gets home.<br>She/he **will be working** when Jan gets home.<br>We **will be working** when Jan gets home.<br>They **will be working** when Jan gets home. |
| | **NEGATIVES**<br>*will* + *not* + *be* + Base verb ending in *-ing*<br><br>I/you **will not be working** when Jan gets home.<br>She/he **will not be working** when Jan gets home.<br>We **will not be working** when Jan gets home.<br>They **will not be working** when Jan gets home. |
| | **QUESTIONS**<br>*will* + Subject + *be* + Base verb ending in *-ing*<br><br>**Will** I/you **be working** when Jan gets home?<br>**Will** she/he **be working** when Jan gets home?<br>**Will** we **be working** when Jan gets home?<br>**Will** they **be working** when Jan gets home? |

## PRACTICE 5 Forming negative statements and questions

Rewrite the following sentences as indicated.

1. Betsy is golfing today. *Make the sentence a question:*

   ______________________________

2. It was snowing when we got up. *Make the sentence a negative statement:*

   ______________________________

3. You are going to the mall. *Make the sentence a question:*

   ______________________________

4. They are losing the game. *Make the sentence a negative statement:*

   ______________________________

5. Meriam was eating when you arrived. *Make the sentence into a question:*

   ______________________________

## Modal (Helping) Verbs

**Tip** For more on helping verbs, see Chapter 15.

Modal verbs (or modal auxiliary verbs) are helping verbs that express the writer's attitude about an action. You do not have to learn too many modal verbs—just the eight in the chart that follows.

| MODAL (HELPING) VERBS | |
|---|---|
| General Formulas<br>For all modal verbs | **STATEMENTS**<br>**Present:** Subject + Modal verb + Base verb<br>Dumbo can fly.<br>**Past:** Forms vary. |
| | **NEGATIVES**<br>**Present:** Subject + Modal verb + *not* + Base verb<br>Dumbo cannot fly.<br>**Past:** Forms vary. |
| | **QUESTIONS**<br>**Present:** Modal verb + Subject + Base verb<br>Can Dumbo fly?<br>**Past:** Forms vary. |
| Can<br>Means *ability* | **STATEMENTS**<br>**Present:** Beth **can** work fast.<br>**Past:** Beth **could** work fast. |
| | **NEGATIVES**<br>**Present:** Beth **can**not work fast.<br>**Past:** Beth **could** not work fast. |
| | **QUESTIONS**<br>**Present:** **Can** Beth work fast?<br>**Past:** **Could** Beth work fast? |

→

| MODAL (HELPING) VERBS | |
|---|---|
| **Could**<br>Means *possibility*. It can also be the past tense of *can*. | **STATEMENTS**<br>**Present:** Beth **could** work quickly if she had more time.<br>**Past:** Beth **could** have worked quickly if she had had more time. |
| | **NEGATIVES**<br>*Can* is used for present negatives. (See above.)<br>**Past:** Beth **could** not have worked quickly. |
| | **QUESTIONS**<br>**Present:** **Could** Beth work quickly?<br>**Past:** **Could** Beth have worked quickly? |
| **May**<br>Means *permission*<br>For past-tense forms, see *might*. | **STATEMENTS**<br>**Present:** You **may** borrow my car. |
| | **NEGATIVES**<br>**Present:** You **may** not borrow my car. |
| | **QUESTIONS**<br>**Present:** **May** I borrow your car? |
| **Might**<br>Means *possibility*. It can also be the past tense of *may*. | **STATEMENTS**<br>**Present** (with *be*): Lou **might** be asleep.<br>**Past** (with *have* + past participle of *be*): Lou **might** have been asleep.<br>**Future:** Lou **might** sleep. |
| | **NEGATIVES**<br>**Present** (with *be*): Lou **might** not be asleep.<br>**Past** (with *have* + past participle of *be*): Lou **might** not have been asleep.<br>**Future:** Lou **might** not sleep. |
| | **QUESTIONS**<br>*Might* in questions is very formal and not often used. → |

**MODAL (HELPING) VERBS**

| | |
|---|---|
| Must<br>Means *necessary* | STATEMENTS<br>**Present:** We **must** try.<br>**Past** (with *have* + past participle of base verb): We **must** have tried.<br>**Past** (with *had* + *to* + base verb): We **had to** try. |
| | NEGATIVES<br>**Present:** We **must** not try.<br>**Past** (with *have* + past participle of base verb): We **must** not have tried. |
| | QUESTIONS<br>**Present:** **Must** we try?<br>Past-tense questions with *must* are unusual. |
| Should<br>Means *duty* or *expectation* | STATEMENTS<br>**Present:** They **should** call.<br>**Past** (with *have* + past participle of base verb): They **should** have called. |
| | NEGATIVES<br>**Present:** They **should** not call.<br>**Past** (with *have* + past participle of base verb): They **should** not have called. |
| | QUESTIONS<br>**Present:** **Should** they call?<br>**Past** (with *have* + past participle of base verb): **Should** they have called? |
| Will<br>Means *intend to* (future)<br>For past-tense forms, see *would.* | STATEMENTS<br>**Future:** I **will** succeed. |
| | NEGATIVES<br>**Future:** I **will** not succeed. |
| | QUESTIONS<br>**Future:** **Will** I succeed? |

→

| MODAL (HELPING) VERBS | |
|---|---|
| Would<br>Means *prefer* or used to start a future request. It can also be the past tense of *will*. | STATEMENTS<br>**Present:** I **would** like to travel.<br>**Past** (with *have* + past participle of base verb):<br>I **would** have traveled if I had had the money. |
| | NEGATIVES<br>**Present:** I **would** not like to travel.<br>**Past** (with *have* + past participle of base verb):<br>I **would** not have traveled if it had not been for you. |
| | QUESTIONS<br>**Present:** **Would** you like to travel?<br>*Or* to start a request: **Would** you help me?<br>**Past** (with *have* + past participle of base verb):<br>**Would** you have traveled with me if I had asked you? |

## COMMON ERRORS WITH MODAL VERBS

Following are some common errors in using modal verbs.

Using more than one helping verb

**Incorrect** They **will can** help.

**Correct** They **will** help. (future intention)

They **can** help. (are able to)

Using *to* between the modal verb and the main (base) verb

**Incorrect** Emilio **might to** come with us.

**Correct** Emilio **might** come with us.

Using *must* instead of *had to* to form the past tense

**Incorrect** She **must** work yesterday.

**Correct** She **had to** work yesterday.

Forgetting to change *can* to *could* to form the past negative

**Incorrect** Last night, I **can**not sleep.

**Correct** Last night, I **could** not sleep.

Forgetting to use *have* with *could/should/would* to form the past tense

**Incorrect** Tara **should** called last night.

**Correct** Tara **should have** called last night.

Using *will* instead of *would* to express a preference in the present tense

**Incorrect** I **will** like to travel.

**Correct** I **would** like to travel.

## PRACTICE 6 Using the correct tense

Fill in the blanks with the correct form of the verbs in parentheses, adding helping verbs as needed. Refer to the verb charts if you need help.

**Example:** ___Have___ **you** ___heard___ **(hear) of volcano boarding?**

(1) In a November 5, 2002, article in *National Geographic Today,* Zoltan Istvan __________ (report) on a new sport: volcano boarding. (2) Istvan first ______ (get) the idea in 1995, when he ____________ (sail) past Mt. Yasur, an active volcano on an island off the coast of Australia. (3) For centuries, Mt. Yasur __________ (have) the reputation of being a dangerous volcano. (4) For example, it regularly _______ (spit) out lava bombs. (5) These large molten rocks _______ often ________ (strike) visitors on the head.

(6) There is a village at the base of Mt. Yasur. (7) When Istvan arrived with his snowboard, the villagers ______ not ________ (know) what to think. (8) He ________ (make) his way to the volcano, ________ (hike) up the highest peak, and rode his board all the way down. (9) After he __________ (reach) the bottom, Istvan admitted that volcano boarding is more difficult than snowboarding. (10) Luckily, no lava bombs ______ (fall) from the sky, although the volcano _____________ (erupt) seconds before his descent. (11) Istvan hopes that this new sport _____________ (become) popular with snowboarders around the world.

## *Gerunds and Infinitives*

A **gerund** is a verb form that ends in *-ing* and acts as a noun. An **infinitive** is a verb form that is preceded by the word *to*. Gerunds and infinitives cannot be the main verbs in sentences; each sentence must have another word that is the main verb.

**Gerund** Mike loves **swimming**.
[*Loves* is the main verb, and *swimming* is a gerund.]

**Infinitive** Mike loves **to run**.
[*Loves* is the main verb, and *to run* is an infinitive.]

How do you decide whether to use a gerund or an infinitive? The decision often depends on the main verb in a sentence. Some verbs can be followed by either a gerund or an infinitive.

### Verbs That Can Be Followed by Either a Gerund or an Infinitive

| | | | |
|---|---|---|---|
| begin | hate | remember | try |
| continue | like | start | |
| forget | love | stop | |

Sometimes, using a gerund or an infinitive after one of these verbs results in the same meaning.

**Tip** To improve your ability to write and speak standard English, read print or online articles, and listen to television and radio news programs. Also, reading articles aloud will help your pronunciation.

**Gerund** Joan likes **playing** the piano.

**Infinitive** Joan likes **to play** the piano.

Other times, however, the meaning changes depending on whether you use a gerund or an infinitive.

**Infinitive** Carla stopped **helping** me.
[This wording means Carla no longer helps me.]

**Gerund** Carla stopped **to help** me.
[This wording means Carla stopped what she was doing and helped me.]

## Verbs That Are Followed by a Gerund

| | | | |
|---|---|---|---|
| admit | discuss | keep | risk |
| avoid | enjoy | miss | suggest |
| consider | finish | practice | |
| deny | imagine | quit | |

The politician risked **losing** her supporters.

Sophia considered **quitting** her job.

## Verbs That Are Followed by an Infinitive

| | | | |
|---|---|---|---|
| agree | decide | need | refuse |
| ask | expect | offer | want |
| beg | fail | plan | |
| choose | hope | pretend | |
| claim | manage | promise | |

Aunt Sally wants **to help**.

Cal hopes **to become** a millionaire.

Do not use the base form of the verb when you need a gerund or an infinitive.

**Incorrect, base verb** *Swim* is my favorite activity.

[*Swim* is the base form of the verb, not a noun; it cannot be the subject of the sentence.]

**Correct, gerund** *Swimming* is my favorite activity.

[*Swimming* is a gerund that can be the subject of the sentence.]

**Incorrect, base verb** My goal is *graduate* from college.

**Correct, gerund** My goal is *graduating* from college.

**Correct, infinitive** My goal is *to graduate* from college.

**Incorrect, base verb** I need *stop* at the store.

[*Need* is the verb, so there cannot be another verb that shows the action of the subject, *I*.]

**Correct, infinitive** I need *to stop* at the store.

**PRACTICE 7** **Using gerunds and infinitives**

Read the paragraphs, and fill in the blanks with either a gerund or an infinitive as appropriate.

**Example: If you want** ___*to be*___ **(be) an actor, be aware that the profession is not all fun and glamour.**

(1) When you were a child, did you pretend ________ (be) famous people? (2) Did you imagine __________ (play) roles in movies or on television? (3) Do you like _________ (take) part in plays? (4) If so, you might want __________ (make) a career out of acting.

(5) Be aware of some drawbacks, however. (6) If you hate __________ (work) with others, acting may not be the career for you. (7) Also, if you do not enjoy ___________ (repeat) the same lines over and over, you will find acting dull. (8) You must practice ___________ (speak) lines to memorize them. (9) Despite these drawbacks, you will gain nothing if you refuse ________ (try). (10) Anyone who hopes ____________ (become) an actor has a chance at succeeding through hard work and determination.

# Articles

**Articles** announce a noun. English uses only three articles—***a***, ***an***, and ***the***—and the same articles are used for both masculine and feminine nouns.

## *Definite and Indefinite Articles*

*The* is a **definite article** and is used before a specific person, place, or thing. *A* and *an* are **indefinite articles** and are used with a person, place, or thing whose specific identity is not known.

**Definite article** *The* car crashed into the building.
[A specific car crashed into the building.]

**Indefinite article** *A* car crashed into the building.
[Some car, we don't know which one exactly, crashed into the building.]

When the word following the article begins with a vowel (*a, e, i, o, u*), use *an* instead of *a*.

*An* old car crashed into the building.

To use the correct article, you need to know what count and noncount nouns are.

## *Count and Noncount Nouns*

**Count nouns** name things that can be counted, and they can be made plural, usually by adding *-s* or *-es*. **Noncount nouns** name things that cannot be counted, and they are usually singular. They cannot be made plural.

| | |
|---|---|
| **Count noun/singular** | I got a **ticket** for the concert. |
| **Count noun/plural** | I got two **tickets** for the concert. |
| **Noncount noun** | The Internet has all kinds of **information**.<br>[You would not say, *The Internet has all kinds of informations*.] |

Here is a brief list of several count and noncount nouns. In English, all nouns are either count or noncount.

| Count | Noncount | |
|---|---|---|
| apple/apples | beauty | milk |
| chair/chairs | flour | money |
| dollar/dollars | furniture | postage |
| letter/letters | grass | poverty |
| smile/smiles | grief | rain |
| tree/trees | happiness | rice |
| | health | salt |
| | homework | sand |
| | honey | spaghetti |
| | information | sunlight |
| | jewelry | thunder |
| | mail | wealth |

Use the chart that follows to determine when to use ***a, an, the***, or no article.

### Articles with Count and Noncount Nouns

| Count nouns | | Article used |
|---|---|---|
| Singular | | |
| Specific | → | *the*<br>**I want to read the book on taxes that you recommended.**<br>[The sentence refers to one particular book: the one that was recommended.]<br>**I cannot stay in the sun very long.**<br>[There is only one sun.] |
| Not specific | → | *a* or *an*<br>**I want to read a book on taxes.**<br>[It could be any book on taxes.] |

►

| Count nouns | | Article used |
|---|---|---|
| Plural | | |
| Specific | → | *the*<br>**I enjoyed the books that we read.**<br>[The sentence refers to a particular group of books: the ones that we read.] |
| Not specific | → | no article or *some*<br>**I usually enjoy books.**<br>[The sentence refers to books in general.]<br>**She found some books.**<br>[I do not know which books she found.] |

| Noncount nouns | | Article used |
|---|---|---|
| Singular | | |
| Specific | → | *the*<br>**I put away the food that we bought.**<br>[The sentence refers to particular food: the food that we bought.] |
| Not specific | → | no article or *some*<br>**There is food all over the kitchen.**<br>[The reader does not know what food the sentence refers to.]<br>**Give some food to the neighbors.**<br>[The sentence refers to an indefinite quantity of food.] |

## Prepositions

A **preposition** is a word (such as *of, above, between,* or *about*) that connects a noun, pronoun, or verb with information about it. The correct preposition to use is often determined by common practice rather than by the preposition's actual meaning.

**Tip** For more on prepositions, see Chapter 15.

### *Prepositions after Adjectives*

Adjectives are often followed by prepositions. Here are some common examples.

| | | |
|---|---|---|
| afraid of | full of | scared of |
| ashamed of | happy about | sorry about/sorry for |
| aware of | interested in | tired of |
| confused by | proud of | |
| excited about | responsible for | |

Peri is afraid ~~to~~ ^of walking alone.

We are happy ~~of~~ ^about Dino's promotion.

### *Prepositions after Verbs*

Many verbs consist of a verb plus a preposition. The meaning of these combinations is not usually the meaning that the verb and the preposition would each have on its own. Often, the meaning of the verb changes completely depending on which preposition is used with it.

> You must **take out** the trash. [*take out* = bring to a different location]
>
> You must **take in** the exciting sights of New York City. [*take in* = observe]

Here are a few common verb/preposition combinations.

| | |
|---|---|
| call in (telephone) | You can *call in* your order. |
| call off (cancel) | They *called off* the party. |
| call on (ask for a response) | The teacher always *calls on* me. |
| drop in (visit) | *Drop in* the next time you are around. |
| drop off (leave behind) | Juan will *drop off* the car for service. |
| drop out (quit) | Many students *drop out* of school. |
| fight against (combat) | He tried to *fight against* the proposal. |
| fight for (defend) | We will *fight for* our rights. |
| fill out (complete) | Please *fill out* the form. |
| fill up (make full) | Do not *fill up* with junk food. |
| find out (discover) | Did you *find out* the answer? |
| give up (forfeit) | Do not *give up* your chance to succeed. |
| go by (visit, pass by) | I may *go by* the store on my way home. |
| go over (review) | Please *go over* your notes before the test. |
| grow up (mature) | All children *grow up*. |
| hand in (submit) | Please *hand in* your homework. |
| lock up (secure) | *Lock up* the apartment before leaving. |
| look up (check) | *Look up* the meaning in the dictionary. |
| pick out (choose) | *Pick out* a good apple. |
| pick up (take or collect) | Please *pick up* some drinks. |
| put off (postpone) | Do not *put off* starting your paper. |
| sign in (register) | *Sign in* when you arrive. |
| sign out (borrow) | You can *sign out* a book from the library. |
| sign up (register for) | I want to *sign up* for the contest. |
| think about (consider) | Simon *thinks about* moving. |
| turn in (submit) | Please *turn in* your homework. |

**PRACTICE 8** **Editing paragraphs for preposition problems**

Edit the following paragraphs to make sure the correct prepositions are used.

**Example: At some point, many people think ~~out~~ *about* having a more flexible work schedule.**

(1) If they are responsible in child care, they might want to get home from work earlier than usual. (2) Or they might be interested on having one workday a week free for studying or other activities. (3) Employees shouldn't be afraid to asking a supervisor about the possibility of a flexible schedule. (4) For instance, the supervisor might be willing to allow the employee to do 40 hours of work in four days instead of five days. (5) Or a worker who wants to leave a little earlier than usual might give out half of a lunch hour to do so.

(6) The wide use of computers also allows for flexibility. (7) For example, busy parents might use their laptops to work from home a day or two a week. (8) They can stay in touch with the office by e-mailing supervisors or coworkers, or they might call on.

(9) Often, employers who allow more flexibility find in that they benefit, too. (10) Workers are happy on having more control over their own time; therefore, they are less stressed out and more productive than they would have been on a fixed schedule.

## Chapter Review

1. What is a pronoun? ______________________________

   What are the three types of pronouns in English? ____________________

2. Rewrite this sentence in the simple past and the simple future:

   Melinda picks flowers every morning.

   Past: ______________________________

   Future: ______________________________

3. Rewrite this sentence so that it uses the perfect tense correctly:

   They have call an ambulance. ______________________________

4. Using the progressive tenses, first rewrite this sentence as a question:

   Chris is learning Spanish.

   Then, rewrite the question in the past tense and in the future tense.

   Question: ______________________________

   Past: ______________________________

   Future: ______________________________

5. Rewrite these sentences so that they use the modal verb correctly:

   Jennifer should to help her mother. ______________________________

   Yesterday, I cannot work. ______________________________

6. What is a gerund? ______________________________

   Write a sentence with a gerund in it. ______________________________

   ______________________________

7. What is an infinitive? ______________________________

   Write a sentence with an infinitive in it. ______________________________

   ______________________________

8. Give an example of a count noun. ______________________________

   Give an example of a noncount noun. ______________________________

9. What is a preposition? ______________________________

   ______________________________

   Write a sentence using a preposition. ______________________________

   ______________________________

# Part 5

# Word Use



"I write presentations for work and school."

—Katie F., student

# 27

# Word Choice

## Using the Right Words

## Understand the Importance of Choosing Words Carefully

In conversation, you show much of your meaning through facial expression, tone of voice, and gestures. In writing, you have only the words on the page to make your point, so you must choose them carefully. If you use vague or inappropriate words, your readers may not understand you.

Two resources will help you find the best words for your meaning: a dictionary and a thesaurus.

LaunchPadSolo
Visit **LaunchPad Solo for Readers and Writers > Grammar > Style and Mechanics** for more tutorials, videos, and practice with crafting paragraphs.

### *Dictionary*

Dictionaries give you all kinds of useful information about words: spelling, division of words into syllables, pronunciation, parts of speech, other forms of words, definitions, and examples of use. Following is a sample dictionary entry.

**Tip** A number of good dictionaries are now available free online. An excellent resource is at **www.dictionary.com.**

Spelling and end-of-line division | Pronunciation | Parts of speech | Other forms

**con • crete** (kon′krēt, kong′-, kon-krēt′), *adj., n., v.* **-cret • ed, -cret • ing,** — Definition
*adj.* **1.** constituting an actual thing or instance; real; perceptible; substantial: — Example
*concrete proof.* **2.** pertaining to or concerned with realities or actual instances

## GRAMMAR & MECHANICS ROADMAP

### An Overview

**This Chapter Identifies the Following Trouble Spots**

- Choosing the correct word
- Vague and abstract words
- Slang
- Wordy language
- Clichés

**Tools to Address Trouble Spots**


- Dictionary (p. 467)
- Thesaurus (p. 468)
- List of Vague and Abstract Words (p. 468)
- List of Common Wordy Expressions (p. 471)
- List of Common Clichés (p. 472)
- Edit for Word Choice exercises (p. 474)
- Chapter Review (p. 475)
- Editing for Word Choice flowchart (p. 475)

> rather than abstractions; particular as opposed to general: *concrete proposals.* **3.** referring to an actual substance or thing, as opposed to an abstract quality: The words *cat, water,* and *teacher* are concrete, whereas the words *truth, excellence,* and *adulthood* are abstract.
>
> — *Random House Webster's College Dictionary*

### *Thesaurus*

**Tip** To look up words online in both a dictionary and a thesaurus, go to the free online resource **www.merriam-webster.com**.

A thesaurus gives **synonyms** (words that have the same meaning) for the word you look up. Use a thesaurus when you cannot find the right word for what you mean. Be careful, however, to choose a word that has the precise meaning you intend. Following is a sample thesaurus entry.

> **Concrete,** *adj.* 1. Particular, specific, single, certain, special, unique, sole, peculiar, individual, separate, isolated, distinct, exact, precise, direct, strict, minute; definite, plain, evident, obvious; pointed, emphasized; restrictive, limiting, limited, well-defined, clear-cut, fixed, finite; determining, conclusive, decided.
>
> —J. I. Rodale, *The Synonym Finder*

## Practice Avoiding Four Common Word-Choice Problems

**Tip** For tools to build your vocabulary, try the word games at **www.dictionary.com**.

Four common problems with word choice may make it hard for readers to understand your point.

### *Vague and Abstract Words*

Vague and abstract words are too general. They do not give your readers a clear idea of what you mean. Here are some common vague and abstract words.

#### Vague and Abstract Words

| | | | |
|---|---|---|---|
| a lot | cute | nice | stuff |
| amazing | dumb | OK (okay) | terrible |
| awesome | good | old | thing |
| bad | great | pretty | very |
| beautiful | happy | sad | whatever |
| big | huge | small | young |

When you see one of these words or another general word in your writing, replace it with a concrete or more specific word or description. A **concrete** word names something that can be seen, heard, felt, tasted, or smelled. A **specific** word names a particular person or quality. Compare these two sentences:

| | |
|---|---|
| **Vague and abstract** | An old man crossed the street. |
| **Concrete and specific** | An eighty-seven-year-old priest stumbled along Main Street. |

The first version is too general to be interesting. The second version creates a clear, strong image. Some words are so vague that it is best to avoid them altogether.

| | |
|---|---|
| **Vague and abstract** | It is awesome.<br>[This sentence is neither concrete nor specific.] |

### PRACTICE 1 Avoiding vague and abstract words

In the following sentences, underline any words that are vague or abstract. Then, edit each sentence by replacing the vague or abstract words with concrete, specific ones. You may invent details or base them on brief online research into physician assistant careers.

**Example: It would be cool to be a physician assistant (PA).** *It would be rewarding to be a physician assistant (PA).*

1. I am drawn to this career because it would let me do neat things for others. ______

2. I know that becoming a PA would require tons of work. ______

3. Also, each day in the classroom or clinic would be long. ______

4. Furthermore, I would have to be able to tolerate some rough sights. ______

5. However, I would learn a lot. ______

6. And in meetings with patients, I would be able to apply my great listening skills. ______

7. All this stuff would be interesting. ______________________

______________________

8. I am confident that my PA education would have a good outcome. ______

______________________

9. Also, my starting salary would be decent. ______________________

______________________

10. Getting accepted into a PA program would be awesome. ____________

______________________

## *Slang*

**Slang**, informal and casual language, should be used only in informal situations. Avoid it when you write, especially for college classes or at work. Use language that is appropriate for your audience and purpose.

| Slang | Edited |
|---|---|
| S'all good. | Everything is going well. |
| Dawg, I don't deserve this grade. | Professor, I don't deserve this grade. |

### PRACTICE 2 Avoiding slang

In the following sentences, underline any slang words. Then, edit the sentences by replacing the slang with language appropriate for a formal audience and purpose. Imagine that you are writing to a boss where you work.

**Example:** ~~Yo,~~ *(Hello,)* **Randy, I need to talk** ~~at~~ *(to)* **you for a minute.**

1. That reference letter you wrote for me was really awesome sweet.
2. I am grateful because the one my English instructor did for me sucked.
3. She said that I thought I was all that, but that is not true.
4. I would be down with doing a favor for you in return if you need it.
5. Maybe you and I could hang sometime one of these weekends?
6. I know that we cannot be best buds, but we could shoot some hoops or something.
7. You could let me know whazzup when I see you at work next week.
8. If you are too stressed, do not go all emo on me.
9. Just chill out, and forget about it.
10. Text me when you get a mo.

## *Wordy Language*

People sometimes use too many words to express their ideas. They may think that using more words will make them sound smart, but too many words can weaken a writer's point.

**Wordy** I am not interested *at this point in time.*

**Edited** I am not interested now.
[The phrase *at this point in time* uses five words to express what could be said in one word: *now*.]

### Common Wordy Expressions

| Wordy | Edited |
|---|---|
| As a result of | Because |
| Due to the fact that | Because |
| In spite of the fact that | Although |
| It is my opinion that | I think (*or just make the point*) |
| In the event that | If |
| The fact of the matter is that | (*Just state the point.*) |
| A great number of | Many |
| At that time | Then |
| In this day and age | Now |
| At this point in time | Now |
| In this paper, I will show that . . . | (*Just make the point; do not announce it.*) |
| Utilize | Use |

### PRACTICE 3 Avoiding wordy language

In the following sentences, underline the wordy or repetitive language. Then, edit each sentence to make it more concise. Some sentences may contain more than one wordy phrase.

**Example: Sugar substitutes are a popular diet choice for people ~~of all ages~~ when they are searching for ways to ~~cut down on all~~** *reduce* **the calories they ingest ~~on a daily basis~~** *each day***.**

1. It is a well-known fact that dieting is difficult for most people.
2. Due to the fact that people are trying to cut calories, sugar substitutes are used in sodas, snacks, and other products.
3. The fact of the matter is that these substitutes provide a sweet taste, but without the calories of sugar or honey.

4. A great number of researchers have stated at this time that such substitutes are not necessarily safe or healthy to use in large quantities.
5. Some of the current experts on the matter are of the opinion that sugar substitutes can cause cancer, allergies, and other serious health problems.
6. At this point in time, other experts on the same subject believe that using these substitutes maintains a person's addiction to sugar and leads people to eat more junk food.
7. Despite these warnings, negative evaluations, and critical opinions from the experts, nearly 200 million people consume sugar-free or low-calorie products each year.
8. In this day and age, people are consuming an average of four of these items each day.
9. In spite of the fact that people know sugar is bad for them, their tastes will probably not change anytime in the near future.
10. It is my opinion that it would be better if people just learned to consume foods that do not contain sweeteners of any kind.

## Clichés

**Clichés** are phrases used so often that people no longer pay attention to them. To get your point across and to get your readers' attention, replace clichés with fresh and specific language.

| Clichés | Edited |
|---|---|
| I cannot *make ends meet.* | I do not have enough money to live on. |
| My uncle *worked his way up the corporate ladder.* | My uncle started as a shipping clerk but ended up as a regional vice president. |
| This roll is *as hard as a rock.* | This roll is so hard I could bounce it. |

### Common Clichés

as big as a house
as light as a feather
better late than never
break the ice
crystal clear
a drop in the bucket
easier said than done
few and far between
hell on earth
last but not least
no way on earth
110 percent
playing with fire
spoiled brat
starting from scratch
sweating blood/bullets
too little, too late
24/7
work like a dog

**PRACTICE 4 Avoiding clichés**

In the following sentences, underline the clichés. Then, edit each sentence by replacing the clichés with fresh and specific language.

Tip Hundreds of clichés exist. To check if you have used one, go to **www.clichesite.com.**

**Example: Riding a bicycle 100 miles a day can be ~~hell on earth~~** *excruciating* **unless you are willing to ~~give 110 percent~~** *work extremely hard***.**

1. You have to persuade yourself to sweat blood and work like a dog for up to 10 hours.
2. There's no way on earth you can do it without extensive training.
3. Staying on your bike until the bitter end, of course, is easier said than done.
4. It is important to keep the fire in your belly and keep your goal of finishing the race crystal clear in your mind.
5. No matter how long it takes you to cross the finish line, remind yourself that it's better late than never.
6. Even if you are not a champion racer, training for a bike race will keep you fit as a fiddle.
7. It may take discipline to make yourself train, but you should keep your nose to the grindstone.
8. Bike racers should always play it safe by wearing helmets.
9. When you train for road racing, keep an eye peeled for cars.
10. You do not want to end up flat on your back in the hospital or six feet under!

**A final note:** Language that favors one gender over another or that assumes that only one gender performs a certain role is called *sexist*. Such language should be avoided.

Tip See Chapter 20 for more advice on using pronouns.

**Sexist** A doctor should politely answer *his* patients' questions.

[Not all doctors are male, as suggested by the pronoun *his*.]

**Revised** A doctor should politely answer *his or her* patients' questions.

*Doctors* should politely answer *their* patients' questions.

[The first revision changes *his* to *his or her* to avoid sexism. The second revision changes the subject to a plural noun (*Doctors*) so that a genderless pronoun (*their*) can be used. Usually, it is preferable to avoid *his or her*.]

## Edit for Word Choice

### PRACTICE 5 Editing paragraphs for word choice

Find and edit six examples of vague or abstract language, slang, wordy language, or clichés in the following paragraphs.

(1) Imagine spending almost two weeks living in the coolest home in the world. (2) That is what scientist Lloyd Godson did when he lived at the bottom of a lake in Australia for thirteen days. (3) Although there is no way on earth I would want to do that, it sure sounds fascinating.

(4) Godson's home was an 8-by-11-foot-long yellow steel box that he dubbed the BioSUB. (5) His air supply came from the algae plants growing inside the BioSUB. (6) Divers brought him food, water, and other junk through a manhole built in the bottom of his underwater home. (7) To keep busy, he rode on an exercise bicycle, which created electricity for him to recharge his laptop and run the lights for his plants. (8) He used his computer to talk to students all over the world and to watch movies.

(9) Godson paid for this experiment with money he had won in the "Live Your Dream" contest. (10) At this point in time, I have to say that for most people, the BioSUB home would be less appealing than a regular, aboveground room, apartment, or house. (11) Indeed, by the time his two weeks were over, Godson was ready to come up, feel the sunshine and wind on his face again, and "smell the roses."

### PRACTICE 6 Editing your own writing for word choice

Edit a piece of your own writing for word choice. It can be a paper for this course or another one, or choose something you have written for work or your everyday life. You may want to use the chart on page 475.

## Chapter Review

1. What two resources will help you choose the best words to get your ideas across in writing? ________________
2. What are four common word-choice problems? ________________
3. Replace vague and abstract words with ________ and ________ words.
4. When is it appropriate to use slang in college writing or in writing at work? ________
5. Give two examples of wordy expressions. ________________

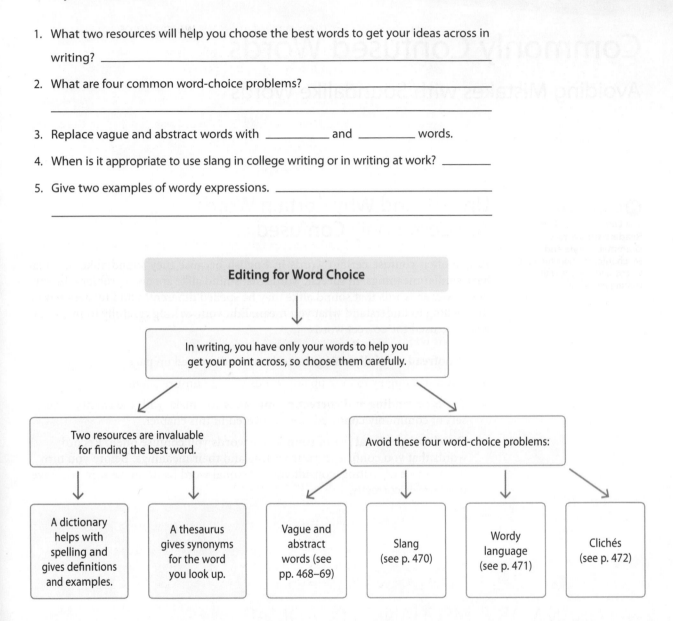

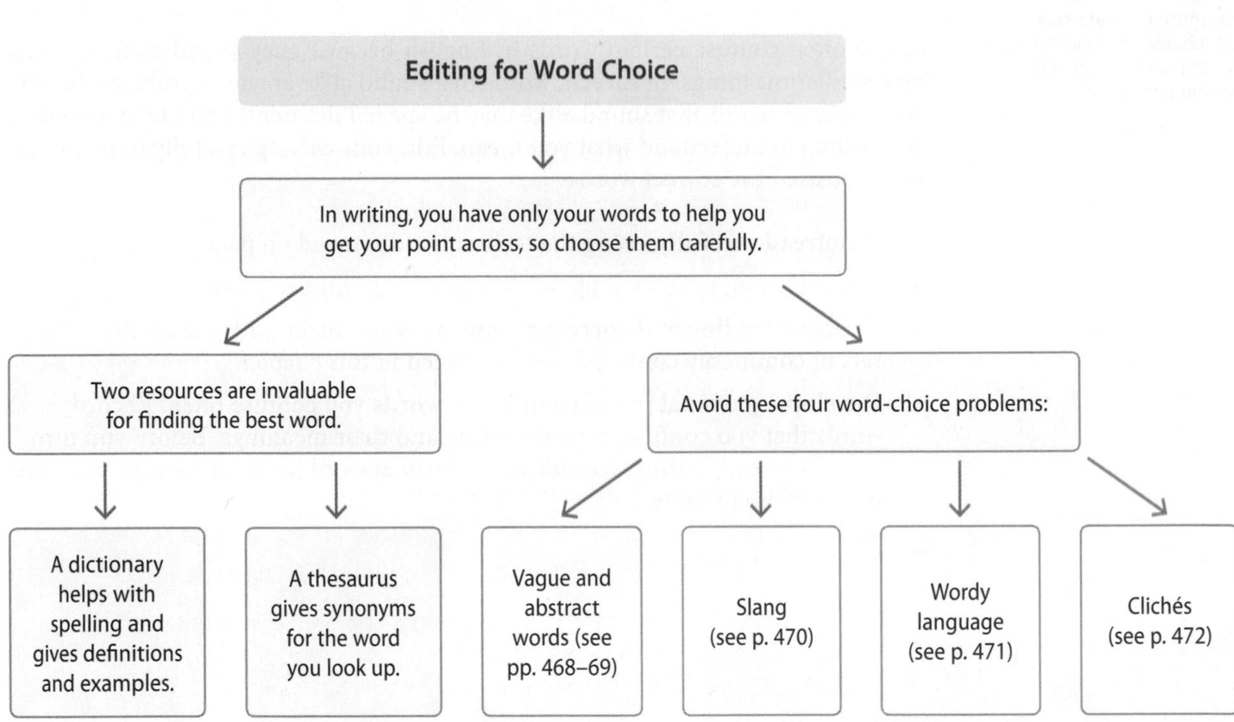
Editing for Word Choice
In writing, you have only your words to help you get your point across, so choose them carefully.
Two resources are invaluable for finding the best word.
Avoid these four word-choice problems:
A dictionary helps with spelling and gives definitions and examples.
A thesaurus gives synonyms for the word you look up.
Vague and abstract words (see pp. 468–69)
Slang (see p. 470)
Wordy language (see p. 471)
Clichés (see p. 472)

# 28

# Commonly Confused Words

## Avoiding Mistakes with Soundalike Words

LaunchPadSolo

Visit **LaunchPad Solo for Readers and Writers > Grammar > Style and Mechanics** for more tutorials, videos, and practice with crafting paragraphs.

## Understand Why Certain Words Are Commonly Confused

People often confuse certain words in English because they sound alike and may have similar meanings. In speech, words that sound alike are not a problem. In writing, however, words that sound alike may be spelled differently, and readers rely on the spelling to understand what you mean. Edit your writing carefully to make sure you have used the correct words.

- **Proofread carefully,** using the techniques discussed on page 487.
- **Use a dictionary** to look up any words you are unsure about.
- **Focus on finding and correcting mistakes** you make with the twenty-seven sets of commonly confused words covered in this chapter.
- **Develop a personal list of soundalike words** you confuse often. Record words that you confuse in your writing and their meanings. Before you turn in any piece of writing, consult your personal word list to make sure you have used words correctly.

## GRAMMAR & MECHANICS ROADMAP

### An Overview

**This Chapter Identifies the Following Trouble Spots**

- 27 sets of commonly confused words

**Tools to Address Trouble Spots**

- Definition of each set of words and how they should be used (p. 477)
- Edit for Commonly Confused Words exercises (p. 484)
- Chapter Review (p. 485)

# Practice Using Commonly Confused Words Correctly

Study the different meanings and spellings of these twenty-seven sets of commonly confused words. Complete the sentence after each set of words, filling in each blank with the correct word.

**Tip** Some commonly confused words sound similar but not exactly alike, such as *conscience* and *conscious*, *loose* and *lose*, and *of* and *have*. To avoid confusing these words, practice pronouncing them correctly.

## A/AN/AND

**a:** used before a word that begins with a consonant sound

*A* friend of mine just won the lottery.

**an:** used before a word that begins with a vowel sound

*An* old friend of mine just won the lottery.

**and:** used to join two words

My friend *and* I went out to celebrate.

*A* friend *and* I ate at *an* Italian restaurant.

Other lottery winners were _____ algebra teacher _______ bowling team.

## ACCEPT/EXCEPT

**accept:** to agree to receive or admit (verb)

I will *accept* the job offer.

**except:** but, other than

All the stores are closed *except* the Quik-Stop.

I *accept* all the job conditions *except* the low pay.

Do not _______ gifts from clients _______ those who are also personal friends.

## ADVICE/ADVISE

**advice:** opinion (noun)

I would like your *advice* before I make a decision.

**advise:** to give an opinion (verb)

Please *advise* me what to do.

Please *advise* me what to do; you always give me good *advice*.

If you do not like my _______, please _______ me how to proceed.

## AFFECT/EFFECT

**affect:** to make an impact on, to change something (verb)

The whole city was *affected* by the hurricane.

**Tip** Thinking "*the* effect" will help you remember that *effect* is a noun.

**effect:** a result (noun)

What *effect* will the hurricane have on the local economy?

Although the storm will have many negative *effects*, it will not *affect* the price of food.

The _______ of the disaster will _______ many people.

## ARE/OUR

**are:** a form of the verb *be*

The workers *are* about to go on strike.

**our:** a pronoun showing ownership

The children played on *our* porch.

My relatives *are* staying at *our* house.

______ new neighbors ______ moving in today.

## BY/BUY/BYE

**by:** next to, before, or past

Meet me *by* the entrance.

Make sure the bill is paid *by* the fifteenth of the month.

The motorcycle raced *by* me.

**buy:** to purchase (verb)

I would like to *buy* a new laptop.

**bye:** an informal way to say *goodbye*

"Bye, Grandma!"

I said "______" from the window as we drove ______our friends, who were standing next to the house I wanted to ______.

**Tip** Remember that one of the words is *con-science*; the other is not.

## CONSCIENCE/CONSCIOUS

**conscience:** a personal sense of right and wrong (noun)

Jake's *conscience* would not allow him to cheat.

**conscious:** awake, aware (adjective)

The coma patient is now *conscious*.

I am *conscious* that it is getting late.

The judge was *conscious* that the accused had acted according to his *conscience* even though he had broken the law.

The man said that he was not __________ that what he had done was illegal, or his __________ would not have let him do it.

### FINE/FIND

**fine:** of high quality (adjective); feeling well (adjective); a penalty for breaking a law (noun)

This jacket is made of *fine* leather.

After a day in bed, Jacob felt *fine*.

The *fine* for exceeding the speed limit is $50.

**find:** to locate, to discover (verb)

Did Clara *find* her glasses?

I *find* gardening to be a *fine* pastime.

Were you able to ______ a place to store your ______ jewelry?

### ITS/IT'S

**its:** a pronoun showing ownership

The dog chased *its* tail.

**it's:** a contraction of the words *it is*

*It's* about time you got here.

*It's* very hard for a dog to keep *its* teeth clean.

______ no surprise that the college raised _____ tuition.

**Tip** If you are not sure whether to use *its* or *it's* in a sentence, try substituting *it is*. If the sentence does not make sense with *it is*, use *its*.

### KNEW/NEW/KNOW/NO

**knew:** understood; recognized (past tense of the verb *know*)

I *knew* the answer, but I could not think of it.

**new:** unused, recent, or just introduced (adjective)

The building has a *new* security code.

**know:** to understand; to have knowledge of (verb)

I *know* how to bake bread.

**no:** used to form a negative

I have *no* idea what the answer is.

I never *knew* how much a *new* car costs.

The ______ teacher _______ many of her students already.

There is _____ way Tom could _______ where Celia is hiding.

I _______ that there is _____ cake left.

### LOOSE/LOSE

**loose:** baggy; relaxed; not fixed in place (adjective)

In hot weather, people tend to wear *loose* clothing.

**lose:** to misplace; to forfeit possession of (verb)

Every summer, I *lose* about three pairs of sunglasses.

If the ring is too *loose* on your finger, you might *lose* it.

I ______ my patience with the ______ rules on Wall Street.

## MIND/MINE

**mind:** to object to (verb); the thinking or feeling part of one's brain (noun)

Toby does not *mind* if I borrow his tool chest.

Estela has a good *mind,* but often she does not use it.

**mine:** belonging to me (pronoun); a source of ore and minerals (noun)

That coat is *mine.*

My uncle worked in a coal *mine* in West Virginia.

That writing problem of *mine* was on my *mind.*

If you do not ______, the gloves you just took are ______.

## OF/HAVE

**of:** coming from; caused by; part of a group; made from (preposition)

The leader *of* the band played bass guitar.

**have:** to possess (verb; also used as a helping verb)

I *have* one more course to take before I graduate.

I should *have* started studying earlier.

The president *of* the company should *have* resigned.

Sidney could ______ been one _____ the winners.

**Note:** Do not use *of* after *would*, *should*, *could*, and *might*. Use *have* after those words (*would have*, *should have*).

## PASSED/PAST

**passed:** went by or went ahead (past tense of the verb *pass*)

We *passed* the hospital on the way to the airport.

**past:** time that has gone by (noun); gone by, over, just beyond (preposition)

In the *past*, I was able to stay up all night and not be tired.

I drove *past* the burning warehouse.

This *past* school year, I *passed* all my exams.

Trish ______ me as we ran ______ the 1-mile marker.

### PEACE/PIECE

**peace:** no disagreement; calm

Could you quiet down and give me a little *peace*?

**piece:** a part of something larger

May I have a *piece* of that pie?

The feuding families found *peace* after they sold the *piece* of land.

To keep the ________, give your sister a _______ of candy.

### PRINCIPAL/PRINCIPLE

**principal:** main (adjective); head of a school or leader of an organization (noun)

Brush fires are the *principal* risk in the hills of California.

Ms. Edwards is the *principal* of Memorial Elementary School.

Corinne is a *principal* in the management consulting firm.

**principle:** a standard of beliefs or behaviors (noun)

Although tempted, she held on to her moral *principles.*

The *principal* questioned the delinquent student's *principles.*

The __________ problem is that you want me to act against my __________.

### QUIET/QUITE/QUIT

**quiet:** soft in sound; not noisy (adjective)

The library was *quiet.*

**quite:** completely; very (adverb)

After cleaning all the windows, Alex was *quite* tired.

**quit:** to stop (verb)

She *quit* her job.

After the band *quit* playing, the hall was *quite quiet.*

If you would ______ shouting and be _______, you would find that the scenery is _______ pleasant.

### RIGHT/WRITE

**right:** correct; in a direction opposite from left (adjective)

You definitely made the *right* choice.

When you get to the stoplight, make a *right* turn.

**write:** to put words on paper (verb)

Will you *write* your phone number for me?

Please *write* the *right* answer in the space provided.

You were _______ to _______ to the senator.

#### SET/SIT

**set:** a collection of something (noun); to place an object somewhere (verb)

Paul has a complete *set* of Johnny Cash records.

Please *set* the package on the table.

**sit:** to rest in a chair or other seat-like surface; to be located in a particular place

I need to *sit* on the sofa for a few minutes.

The shed *sits* between the house and the garden.

If I *sit* down now, I will not have time to *set* the plants outside.

Before you _____ on that chair, _____the magazines on the floor.

#### SUPPOSE/SUPPOSED

**suppose:** to imagine or assume to be true

I *suppose* you would like something to eat.

*Suppose* you won a million dollars.

**supposed:** past tense of *suppose*; intended

Karen *supposed* Thomas was late because of traffic.

I *suppose* you know that Rita was *supposed* to be home by 6:30.

I _________ you want to leave soon because we are __________ to arrive before the guests.

#### THAN/THEN

**than:** a word used to compare two or more people, places, or things

It is colder inside *than* outside.

**then:** at a certain time; next in time

I got out of the car and *then* realized the keys were still in it.

Clara ran more miles *than* she ever had before, and *then* she collapsed.

Back _______, I smoked more _______ three packs a day.

#### THEIR/THERE/THEY'RE

**Tip** If you are not sure whether to use *their* or *they're*, substitute *they are*. If the sentence does not make sense, use *their*.

**their:** a pronoun showing ownership

I borrowed *their* clippers to trim the hedges.

**there:** a word indicating location or existence

Just put the keys *there* on the desk.

*There* are too many lawyers.

**they're:** a contraction of the words *they are*

*They're* about to leave.

*There* is a car in *their* driveway, which indicates that *they're* home.

_______ beach house is empty except for the one week that ________ vacationing _______.

### THOUGH/THROUGH/THREW

**though:** however; nevertheless; in spite of (conjunction)

*Though* he is short, he plays great basketball.

**through:** finished with (adjective); from one side to the other (preposition)

I am *through* arguing with you.

The baseball went right *through* the window.

**threw:** hurled; tossed (past tense of the verb *throw*)

She *threw* the basketball.

Even *though* it was illegal, she *threw* the empty cup *through* the window onto the road.

________ she did not really believe it would bring good luck, Jan _______ a penny _________ the air into the fountain.

### TO/TOO/TWO

**to:** a word indicating a direction or movement (preposition); part of the infinitive form of a verb

Please give the message *to* Sharon.

It is easier *to* ask for forgiveness than *to* get permission.

**too:** also; more than enough; very (adverb)

I am tired *too*.

Dan ate *too* much and felt sick.

That dream was *too* real.

**two:** the number between one and three (noun)

The lab had only *two* computers.

They went *to* a restaurant and ordered *too* much food for *two* people.

When Marty went _____ pay for his meal, the cashier charged him ______ times, which was ______ bad.

### USE/USED

**use:** to employ or put into service (verb)

How do you plan to *use* that blueprint?

**Tip** Writing *use to* instead of *used to* is a common error. Train yourself not to make that mistake.

**used:** past tense of the verb *use*. *Used to* can indicate a past fact or state, or it can mean "familiar with."

He *used* his lunch hour to do errands.

He *used* to go for a walk during his lunch hour.

She *used* to be a chef, so she knows how to *use* all kinds of kitchen gadgets.

She is also *used* to improvising in the kitchen.

Tom _______ the prize money to buy a boat; his family hoped he would _______ the money for his education, but Tom was _______ to getting his way.

### WHO'S/WHOSE

**Tip** If you are not sure whether to use *whose* or *who's*, substitute *who is*. If the sentence does not make sense, use *whose*.

**who's:** a contraction of the words *who is*

*Who's* at the door?

**whose:** a pronoun showing ownership

*Whose* car is parked outside?

*Who's* the person *whose* car sank in the river?

The student _______ name is first on the list is the one _______ in charge.

### YOUR/YOU'RE

**Tip** If you are not sure whether to use *your* or *you're*, substitute *you are*. If the sentence does not make sense, use *your*.

**your:** a pronoun showing ownership

Did you bring *your* wallet?

**you're:** a contraction of the words *you are*

*You're* not telling me the whole story.

*You're* going to have *your* third exam tomorrow.

_______ teacher says that _______ good with numbers.

## Edit for Commonly Confused Words

**PRACTICE 1** **Editing paragraphs for commonly confused words**

Edit the following paragraphs to correct eighteen errors in word use.

1 More and more women are purchasing handguns, against the advise of law enforcement officers. 2 Few of these women are criminals or plan to commit crimes. 3 They no the risks of guns, and they except those risks. 4 They buy weapons primarily because their tired of feeling like victims. 5 They do not want to contribute too the violence in are society, but they also realize that women are the victims of violent attacks far to often. 6 Many women loose

they're lives because they cannot fight off there attackers. 7 Some women have made a conscience decision to arm themselves for protection.

8 But does buying a gun make things worse rather then better? 9 Having a gun in you're house makes it three times more likely that someone will be killed there—and that someone is just as likely to be you or one of your children as a criminal. 10 Most young children cannot tell the difference between a real gun and a toy gun when they fine one. 11 Every year, their are tragic examples of children who accidentally shoot and even kill other youngsters while they are playing with guns. 12 A mother who's children are injured while playing with her gun will never again think that a gun provides piece of mind. 13 Reducing the violence in are society may be a better solution.

**PRACTICE 2** **Editing your own writing for commonly confused words**

Edit a piece of your own writing for commonly confused words. It can be a paper for this course or another one, or choose something you have written for work or your everyday life.

## Chapter Review

1. What are four strategies you can use to avoid confusing words that sound alike or have similar meanings? ______________________________________________

______________________________________________

______________________________________________

______________________________________________

2. What are the top five commonly confused words on your personal list? __________

______________________________________________

# 29

# Spelling

## Using the Right Letters

LaunchPadSolo

Visit **LaunchPad Solo for Readers and Writers > Grammar > Style and Mechanics** for more tutorials, videos, and practice with crafting paragraphs.

## Finding and Correcting Spelling Mistakes

Some extremely smart people are poor spellers. Unfortunately, spelling errors are easy for readers to spot, and they make a bad impression. Learn to find and correct spelling mistakes in your writing by using the following strategies.

### *Use a Dictionary*

**Tip** Online dictionaries, such as **www.merriam-webster.com**, can help you spell because they often allow you to type in an incorrectly spelled word and get the correct spelling.

When proofreading your papers, consult a dictionary whenever you are unsure about the spelling of a word. *Checking a dictionary is the single most important thing you can do to improve your spelling.*

### *Use a Spell Checker—with Caution*

Use a spell checker after you have completed a piece of writing but before you print it out. This word-processing tool finds and highlights a word that may be misspelled, suggests other spellings, and gives you the opportunity to change the spelling of the word.

## GRAMMAR & MECHANICS ROADMAP

### An Overview

**This Chapter Identifies the Following Trouble Spots**

- Common spelling mistakes

**Tools to Address Trouble Spots**

However, never rely on a spell checker to do your editing for you. It ignores anything it recognizes as a word, so it will not help you find misused words or misspellings that are also words. For example, a spell checker would not highlight any of the problems in these phrases:

| | |
|---|---|
| Just *to* it. | (Correct: Just *do* it.) |
| pain in the *nick* | (Correct: pain in the *neck*) |
| my writing *coarse* | (Correct: my writing *course*) |

### *Use Proofreading Techniques*

Use some of the following proofreading techniques to focus on the spelling of one word at a time. Try them all. Then, decide which ones work best for you.

- Print out your paper before proofreading. (Many writers find it easier to detect errors on paper than on a computer screen.)
- Put a piece of paper under the line that you are reading.
- Proofread your paper backward, one word at a time.
- Print out a version of your paper that looks noticeably different: Make the words larger, make the margins larger, triple-space the lines, or make all these changes.
- Read your paper aloud. This strategy will help you if you tend to leave out words.
- Exchange papers with a partner and proofread each other's papers, identifying only possible misspellings.

### *Make a Personal Spelling List*

Set aside a section of your course notebook for your spelling list. Every time you edit a paper, write down the words that you misspelled. Every couple of weeks, go back to your spelling list to see whether your problem words have changed. Are you misspelling fewer words in each paper?

For each word on your list, create a memory aid or silly phrase to help you remember the correct spelling. For example, if you often misspell *a lot*, you could remember that "*a lot* is a lot of words."

## Strategies for Becoming a Better Speller

Here are three good strategies for becoming a better speller.

### *Master Commonly Confused Words*

Chapter 28 covers twenty-seven sets of words that are commonly confused because they sound similar, such as *write* and *right*. If you can master these commonly confused words, you will avoid many spelling mistakes.

## *Learn Six Spelling Rules*

If you can remember the following six rules, you can correct many of the spelling errors in your writing.

First, here is a quick review of vowels and consonants.

**Vowels:** *a, e, i, o,* and *u*

**Consonants:** *b, c, d, f, g, h, j, k, l, m, n, p, q, r, s, t, v, w, x,* and *z*

**The letter *y*** can be either a vowel or a consonant. It is a vowel when it sounds like the *y* in *fly* or *hungry*. It is a consonant when it sounds like the *y* in *yellow*.

**Rule 1.** "*I* before *e*, except after *c*. Or when sounded like *a*, as in *neighbor* or *weigh*."

Many people repeat this rhyme to themselves as they decide whether a word is spelled with an *ie* or an *ei*.

p**ie**ce (*i* before *e*)

rec**ei**ve (except after *c*)

**ei**ght (sounds like *a*)

**Exceptions:** *either, neither, foreign, height, seize, society, their, weird*

**Rule 2. Drop the final *e*** when adding an ending that begins with a vowel.

hop**e** + ing = hoping

imagin**e** + ation = imagination

**Keep the final *e*** when adding an ending that begins with a consonant.

achiev**e** + ment = achiev**e**ment

definit**e** + ly = definit**e**ly

**Exceptions:** *argument, awful, judgment, simply, truly,* and others

**Rule 3.** When adding an ending to a word that ends in *y*, **change the *y* to *i*** when a consonant comes before the *y*.

| | |
|---|---|
| lone**ly** + est = lonel**i**est | apolo**gy** + ize = apolo**g**ize |
| hap**py** + er = happ**i**er | like**ly** + hood = likel**i**hood |

**Do not change the *y*** when a vowel comes before the *y*.

| | |
|---|---|
| b**oy** + **ish** = boyish | surv**ey** + **or** = surveyor |
| p**ay** + **ment** = payment | b**uy** + **er** = buyer |

**Exceptions:**

1. When adding *-ing* to a word ending in *y*, always keep the *y*, even if a consonant comes before it: stu**dy** + ing = stud**y**ing.
2. Other exceptions include *daily, dryer, said*, and *paid*.

**Rule 4.** When adding an ending that starts with a vowel to a one-syllable word, follow these rules.

**Double the final consonant** only if the word ends with a consonant-vowel-consonant.

| | |
|---|---|
| **trap** + ed = tra**pp**ed | **knit** + ed = kni**tt**ed |
| **drip** + ed = dri**pp**ed | **fat** + er = fa**tt**er |

**Do not double the final consonant** if the word ends with some other combination.

| Vowel-vowel-consonant | Vowel-consonant-consonant |
|---|---|
| cl**ean** + est = cle**an**est | sl**ick** + er = sli**ck**er |
| p**oor** + er = poo**r**er | t**each** + er = tea**ch**er |
| cl**ear** + ed = clea**r**ed | l**ast** + ed = la**st**ed |

**Rule 5.** When adding an ending that starts with a vowel to a word with two or more syllables, follow these rules.

**Double the final consonant** only if the word ends with a consonant-vowel-consonant and the stress is on the last syllable.

sub**mit** + ing = submi**tt**ing

**prefer** + ed = prefe**rr**ed

**Do not double the final consonant** in other cases.

underst**and** + ing = understan**d**ing

**offer** + ed = offe**r**ed

**Rule 6. Add** ***-s*** to most nouns to form the plural, including words that end in *o* preceded by a vowel.

| Most words | Words that end in vowel plus *o* |
|---|---|
| book + **s** = books | vid**eo** + **s** = videos |
| college + **s** = colleges | ster**eo** + **s** = stereos |

**Add** ***-es*** to words that end in *o* preceded by a consonant and words that end in *s, sh, ch,* or *x.*

| Words that end in consonant plus *o* | Words that end in *s, sh, ch,* or *x* |
|---|---|
| pota**to** + **es** = potat**oes** | cla**ss** + **es** = cla**sses** |
| he**ro** + **es** = her**oes** | pu**sh** + **es** = pu**shes** |
| | ben**ch** + **es** = ben**ches** |
| | fa**x** + **es** = fa**xes** |

## *Exceptions When Forming Plurals*

A **compound noun** is formed when two nouns are joined, with a hyphen (*in-law*), a space (*life vest*), or no space (*keyboard, stockpile*). Plurals of compound nouns are generally formed by adding an *-s* to the end of the last noun (*in-laws, life vests*) or to the end of the combined word (*keyboards, stockpiles*). Some hyphenated compound words such as *mother-in-law* or *hole-in-one* form plurals by adding an *-s* to the chief word (*mothers-in-law, holes-in-one*).

Some words form plurals in different ways, as in the list below.

### Different Types of Plurals

| Singular | Plural | Singular | Plural |
|---|---|---|---|
| analysis | analyses | louse | lice |
| bacteria | bacterium | loaf | loaves |
| bison | bison | medium | media |
| cactus | cacti | man | men |
| calf | calves | mouse | mice |
| child | children | phenomenon | phenomena |
| deer | deer | roof | roofs |
| die | dice | sheep | sheep |
| foot | feet | shelf | shelves |
| focus | foci | tooth | teeth |
| goose | geese | thief | thieves |
| half | halves | vertebra | vertebrae |
| hoof | hooves | wife | wives |
| knife | knives | wolf | wolves |
| leaf | leaves | woman | women |

## *Consult a List of Commonly Misspelled Words*

Use a list like the one that follows as an easy reference to check your spelling.

### One Hundred Commonly Misspelled Words

absence
achieve
across
aisle
a lot
already
analyze
answer
appetite
argument
athlete
awful
basically
beautiful
beginning
believe
business
calendar
career
category
chief
column
coming
commitment
conscious
convenient
cruelty
daughter
definite
describe
develop
dictionary
different
disappoint
dollar
eighth
embarrass
environment
especially
exaggerate
excellent/excellence
exercise
fascinate
February
finally
foreign
friend
government
grief
guidance
harass
height
humorous
illegal
immediately
independent
interest
jewelry
judgment
knowledge
license
lightning
loneliness
marriage
meant
muscle
necessary
ninety
noticeable
occasion
perform
physically
prejudice
probably
psychology
receive
recognize
recommend
restaurant
rhythm
roommate
schedule
scissors
secretary
separate
sincerely
sophomore
succeed
successful
surprise
truly
until
usually
vacuum
valuable
vegetable
weight
weird
writing
written

## Chapter Review

1. What are two important tools for finding and correcting spelling mistakes?

   ______________________________________________

   ______________________________________________

2. What three strategies can you use to become a better speller? ____________

   ______________________________________________

   ______________________________________________

# Part 6

# Punctuation and Capitalization



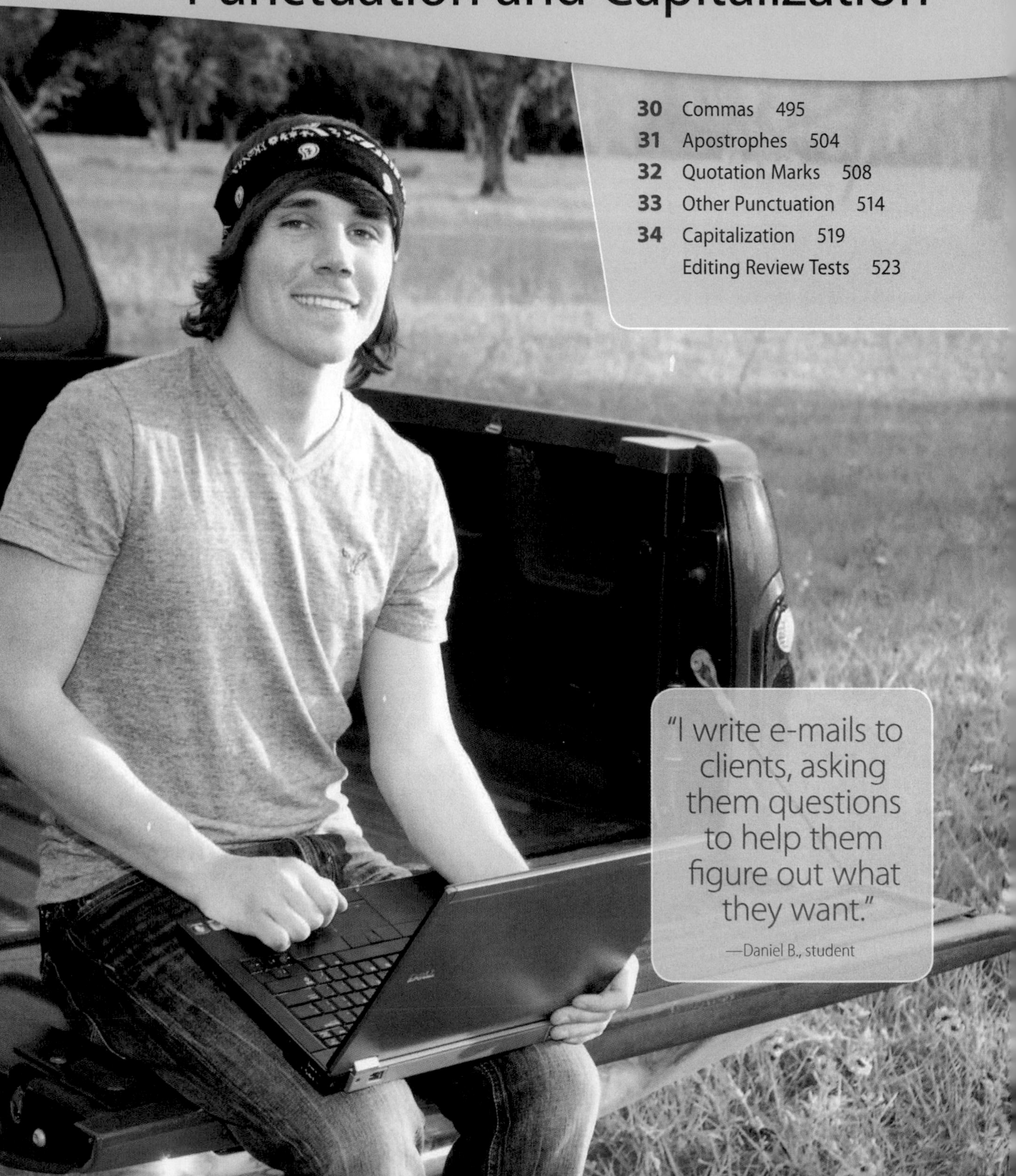

"I write e-mails to clients, asking them questions to help them figure out what they want."

—Daniel B., student

# 30

# Commas 

## Understand What Commas Do

**Commas (,)** are punctuation marks that help readers understand a sentence. Read the following three sentences aloud. How does the use of commas change the meaning?

| | |
|---|---|
| **No comma** | When you call Sarah I will start cooking. |
| **One comma** | When you call Sarah, I will start cooking. |
| **Two commas** | When you call, Sarah, I will start cooking. |

To get your intended meaning across to your readers, it is important that you understand when and how to use commas.

**LaunchPadSolo**
Visit **LaunchPad Solo for Readers and Writers > Grammar > Style and Mechanics** for more tutorials, videos, and practice with crafting paragraphs.

## GRAMMAR & MECHANICS ROADMAP

### An Overview

**This Chapter Identifies the Following Trouble Spots**

- Commas between items in a series
- Commas between coordinate adjectives
- Commas in compound sentences
- Commas after introductory words
- Commas around appositives and interrupters
- Commas around adjective clauses
- Commas with quotation marks
- Commas with dates
- Commas with addresses
- Commas with names

**Tools to Address Trouble Spots**


- Understand What Commas Do (p. 495)
- List of coordinating conjunctions (p. 497)
- Understand introductory words and phrases (p. 497)
- Understand appositives and interrupters (p. 498)
- Identify adjective clauses (p. 500)
- Edit for Commas exercises (p. 502)
- Chapter Review (p. 503)

# Practice Using Commas Correctly

## *Commas between Items in a Series*

Use commas to separate the items in a series (three or more items), including the last item in the series, which usually has *and* before it.

Item , Item , Item , and Item

To get from South Dakota to Texas, we will drive through *Nebraska*, *Kansas*, and *Oklahoma*.

We can *sleep in the car*, *stay in a motel*, or *camp outside*.

As I drive, I see many beautiful sights, such as *mountains*, *plains*, and *prairies*.

**Tip** How does a comma change the way you read a sentence aloud? Many readers pause when they come to a comma.

**Note:** Writers do not always use a comma before the final item in a series (this comma is known as the Oxford comma or serial comma). In college writing, however, it is best to include it.

## *Commas between Coordinate Adjectives*

**Coordinate adjectives** are two or more adjectives that independently modify the same noun and are separated by commas.

Conor ordered a *big*, *fat*, *greasy* burger.

The diner food was *cheap*, *unhealthy*, and *delicious*.

Do *not* use a comma between the final adjective and the noun it describes.

**Incorrect** Joelle wore a *long*, *clingy*, *red*, dress.

**Correct** Joelle wore a *long*, *clingy*, *red* dress.

**Cumulative adjectives** describe the same noun but are not separated by commas because they form a unit that describes the noun. You can identify cumulative adjectives because separating them by *and* does not make any sense.

The store is having its *last storewide clearance* sale.

[Putting *and* between *last* and *storewide* and between *storewide* and *clearance* would make an odd sentence: The store is having its *last* and *storewide* and *clearance* sale. The adjectives in the sentence are cumulative adjectives and should not be separated by commas.]

In summary:

- **Do** use commas to separate two or more **coordinate adjectives**.
- **Do not** use commas to separate **cumulative adjectives**.

## Commas in Compound Sentences

A **compound sentence** contains two complete sentences joined by a coordinating conjunction: *and, but, for, nor, or, so, yet*. Use a comma before the joining word to separate the two complete sentences.

**Tip** Remember the coordinating conjunctions with *FANBOYS: for, and, nor, but, or, yet,* and *so*. For more information, see Chapter 23.

Sentence , *and, but, for, nor, or, so, yet* Sentence.

I called my best friend, and she agreed to drive me to work.

I asked my best friend to drive me to work, but she was busy.

I can take the bus to work, or I can call another friend.

Language note: A comma alone cannot separate two sentences in English. Doing so creates a run-on (see Chapter 17).

## Commas after Introductory Words

Use a comma after an introductory word, phrase, or clause. The comma lets your readers know when the main part of the sentence is starting.

Introductory word or word group , Main part of sentence.

| | |
|---|---|
| **Introductory word** | *Yesterday*, I went to the game. |
| **Introductory phrase** | *By the way*, I do not have a babysitter for tomorrow. |
| **Introductory clause** | *While I waited outside*, Susan went backstage. |

### PRACTICE 1 Using commas after introductory word groups

In each item, underline introductory words or word groups. Then, add commas after introductory word groups where they are needed. If a sentence is already correct, put a "C" next to it.

**Example:** **In the 1960s, John Mackey became famous for his speed and strength as a tight end for the Baltimore Colts football team.**

1. In his later years the National Football League Hall-of-Famer was in the news for another reason: He suffered from dementia possibly linked to the head blows he received on the football field.

2. According to medical experts, repeated concussions can severely damage the brain over time, and they are especially harmful to young people, whose brains are still developing.

3. Based on these warnings and on stories like John Mackey's athletic associations, coaches, and parents of young athletes are taking new precautions.
4. For example more football coaches are teaching players to tackle and block with their heads up, reducing the chance that they will receive a blow to the top of the head.
5. Also when players show signs of a concussion—such as dizziness, nausea, or confusion—more coaches are taking them out of the game.
6. Ideally coaches then make sure injured players receive immediate medical attention.
7. Once concussion sufferers are back home, they should take a break from sports until the symptoms of their injury are gone.
8. During their recovery they should also avoid any activity that puts too much stress on the brain; these activities can include playing video games, studying, and driving.
9. When concussion sufferers feel ready to get back into the game a doctor should confirm that it is safe for them to do so.
10. As a result of these new precautions young athletes may avoid experiencing anything like the long, difficult decline of John Mackey, who died in 2011.

## *Commas around Appositives and Interrupters*

**Tip** For more on appositives, see Chapter 25

An **appositive** comes directly before or after a noun or pronoun and renames it.

Lily, *a senior*, will take her nursing exam this summer.

The prices are outrageous at Beans, *the local coffee shop.*

An **interrupter** is an aside or transition that interrupts the flow of a sentence and does not affect its meaning.

My sister, *incidentally*, has good reasons for being late.

Her child had a fever, *for example.*

Putting commas around appositives and interrupters tells readers that these elements give extra information but are not essential to the meaning of a sentence. If an appositive or interrupter is in the middle of a sentence, set it off with a pair of commas, one before and one after. If an appositive or interrupter comes at the

beginning or end of a sentence, separate it from the rest of the sentence with one comma.

*By the way*, your proposal has been accepted.

Your proposal, *by the way*, has been accepted.

Your proposal has been accepted, *by the way*.

**Note:** Sometimes, an appositive is essential to the meaning of a sentence. When a sentence would not have the same meaning without the appositive, the appositive should not be set off with commas.

The actor *Leonardo DiCaprio* has never won an Oscar.

[The sentence *The actor has never won an Oscar* does not have the same meaning.]

### PRACTICE 2 Using commas to set off appositives and interrupters

Underline all the appositives and interrupters in the following sentences. Then, use commas to set them off.

**Example: Harry, an attentive student, could not hear his teacher because the radiator in class made a constant rattling.**

1. Some rooms in fact are full of echoes, dead zones, and mechanical noises that make it hard for students to hear.
2. The American Speech-Language-Hearing Association experts on how noise levels affect learning abilities has set guidelines for how much noise in a classroom is too much.
3. The association recommends that background noise the constant whirring or whining sounds made by radiators, lights, and other machines be no more than thirty-five decibels.
4. That level thirty-five decibels is about as loud as a whispering voice 15 feet away.
5. One study found a level of sixty-five decibels the volume of a vacuum cleaner in a number of classrooms around the country.
6. Other classroom noises came for example from ancient heating systems, whirring air-conditioning units, rattling windows, humming classroom computers, buzzing clocks, and the honking of traffic on nearby streets.
7. An increasing number of school districts are beginning to pay more attention to acoustics the study of sound when they plan new schools.

8. Some changes such as putting felt pads on the bottoms of chair and desk legs to keep them from scraping against the floor are simple and inexpensive.
9. Other changes however can be costly and controversial; these changes include buying thicker drapes, building thicker walls, or installing specially designed acoustic ceiling tiles.
10. School administrators often parents themselves hope that these improvements will result in a better learning environment for students.

## *Commas around Adjective Clauses*

An **adjective clause** is a group of words that begins with *who, which,* or *that*; has a subject and a verb; and describes a noun right before it in a sentence.

If an adjective clause can be taken out of a sentence without completely changing the meaning of the sentence, put commas around the clause.

Lily, *who is my cousin*, will take her nursing exam this summer.

Beans, *which is the local coffee shop*, charges outrageous prices.

I complained to Mr. Kranz, *who is the shop's manager.*

If an adjective clause is essential to the meaning of a sentence, do not put commas around it. You can tell whether a clause is essential by taking it out and seeing if the meaning of the sentence changes significantly, as it would if you took the clauses out of the following examples.

The only grocery store *that sold good bread* went out of business.

Students *who do internships* often improve their hiring potential.

Salesclerks *who sell liquor to minors* are breaking the law.

| Noun | Adjective clause essential to meaning | Rest of sentence. |
|---|---|---|
| Noun , | Adjective clause not essential to meaning , | Rest of sentence. |

### PRACTICE 3 Using commas to set off adjective clauses

In each item, underline the adjective clauses. Then, put commas around these clauses where they are needed. Remember that if an adjective clause is essential to the meaning of a sentence, commas are not necessary. If a sentence is already correct, put a "C" next to it.

**Example: Daniel Kish, who has been blind since the age of one, has changed many people's ideas about what blind people can and cannot do.**

1. Kish who runs the organization World Access for the Blind regularly rides his bike down busy streets and goes on long hikes.
2. His system for "seeing" his surroundings which is known as echolocation uses sound waves to create mental pictures of buildings, cars, trees, and other objects.
3. As Kish bikes around his neighborhood or hikes to sites that are deep in the wilderness, he clicks his tongue and listens to the echoes.
4. The echoes which differ depending on the distance and physical features of nearby objects allow him to map his surroundings in his mind.
5. This mental map which he constantly revises as he moves ahead helps him avoid running into cars, trees, and other obstacles.
6. Researchers who recently investigated Kish's echolocation made some interesting discoveries.
7. They found that Kish's visual cortex which is the part of the brain that processes visual information was activated during his sessions of mapping with sound.
8. This finding which received a lot of attention in the scientific community suggests that Kish's way of seeing the world is indeed visual.
9. Other blind people who have been trained in echolocation have learned to be as active and independent as Kish is.
10. The successes that they and Kish have achieved offer additional proof that blindness does not equal helplessness.

## *Other Uses for Commas*

### COMMAS WITH QUOTATION MARKS

**Quotation marks** are used to show that you are repeating exactly what someone said. Use commas to set off the words inside quotation marks from the rest of the sentence.

**Tip** For more on quotation marks, see Chapter 32.

"Let me see your license," demanded the police officer.

"Did you realize," she asked, "that you were going 80 miles per hour?"

I exclaimed, "No!"

Notice that a comma never comes directly after a quotation mark.

When quotations are not attributed to a particular person, commas may not be necessary.

"Pretty is as pretty does" never made sense to me.

### COMMAS IN ADDRESSES

Use commas to separate the elements of an address included in a sentence. However, do not use a comma before a zip code.

My address is 2512 Windermere Street, Jackson, Mississippi 40720.

If a sentence continues after a city-state combination or after a street address, put a comma after the state or the address.

I moved here from Detroit, Michigan, when I was eighteen.

I've lived at 24 Heener Street, Madison, since 1989.

### COMMAS IN DATES

Separate the day from the year with a comma. If you give just the month and year, do not separate them with a comma.

My daughter was born on November 8, 2004.

The next conference is in August 2014.

If a sentence continues after the date, put a comma after the date.

On April 21, 2013, the contract will expire.

### COMMAS WITH NAMES

Put a comma after (and sometimes before) the name of someone being addressed directly.

Don, I want you to come look at this.

Unfortunately, Marie, you need to finish the report by next week.

### COMMAS WITH *YES* OR *NO*

Put a comma after the word *yes* or *no* in response to a question.

Yes, I believe that you are right.

## Edit for Commas

**PRACTICE 4** **Editing paragraphs for commas**

Edit the following paragraphs by adding commas where they are needed.

(1) By the end of 2011, communities in California Texas Washington and several other states had banned the use of plastic bags. (2) One grocery

store chain Whole Foods Market was an early leader in restricting the use of these bags. (3) As of April 22 2008 Whole Foods stopped asking customers if they wanted paper bags or plastic bags. (4) The store which cares about environmental issues now offers only paper bags made from recycled paper.

(5) The president of Whole Foods stated "We estimate we will keep 100 million new plastic grocery bags out of our environment between Earth Day and the end of this year." (6) The company also sells cloth bags, hoping to encourage shoppers to bring their own reusable bags with them when they go shopping.

(7) Experts believe that plastic bags do a great deal of damage to the environment. (8) They clog drains harm wildlife and take up an enormous amount of space in the nation's landfills. (9) According to the experts it takes more than a thousand years for a plastic bag to break down, and Americans use 100 billion of them every single year.

**PRACTICE 5** **Editing your own writing for commas**

Edit a piece of your own writing for comma usage. It can be a paper for this course or another one, or something you have written for work or your everyday life.

## Chapter Review

1. A comma (,) is a ________________ that helps readers understand a sentence.
2. How do you use commas in these three situations?

   In a series of items, ________________________________.

   In a compound sentence, ________________________________

   ________________________________.

   With introductory words, ________________________________

   ________________________________.
3. An appositive comes before or after a noun or pronoun and ________________

   ________________________________.
4. An interrupter is an ________________ that interrupts the flow of a sentence.
5. Put commas around an adjective clause when it is ________________ to the meaning of a sentence.

# 31

# Apostrophes 

Visit **LaunchPad Solo for Readers and Writers > Grammar > Style and Mechanics** for more tutorials, videos, and practice with crafting paragraphs.

## Understand What Apostrophes Do

An **apostrophe (')** is a punctuation mark that either shows ownership (*Susan's*) or indicates that a letter has been intentionally left out to form a contraction (*I'm, that's, they're*).

## Practice Using Apostrophes Correctly

### *Apostrophes to Show Ownership*

**Add -*'s* to a singular noun to show ownership even if the noun already ends in -*s*.**

> *Karen's* apartment is on the South Side.
>
> *James's* roommate is looking for him.

GRAMMAR & MECHANICS ROADMAP

**An Overview**

**This Chapter Identifies the Following Trouble Spots**

- Apostrophes to show ownership
- Apostrophes in contractions
- Apostrophes with letters, numbers, and time

**Tools to Address Trouble Spots**

- Understand What Apostrophes Do (p. 504)
- List of Possessive Pronouns (p. 505)
- List of Common Contractions (p. 506)
- Edit for Apostrophes exercises (p. 507)
- Chapter Review (p. 507)

**If a noun is plural and ends in *-s*, just add an apostrophe. If it is plural but does not end in *-s*, add *-'s*.**

My *books'* covers are falling off.

[More than one book]

The *twins'* father was building them a playhouse.

[More than one twin]

The *children's* toys were broken.

The *men's* locker room is being painted.

**Tip** Use apostrophes to show ownership for abbreviations: *The NBA's playoff system has changed.*

**The placement of an apostrophe makes a difference in meaning.**

My *sister's* six children are at my house for the weekend.

[One sister who has six children]

My *sisters'* six children are at my house for the weekend.

[Two or more sisters who together have six children]

**Do not use an apostrophe to form the plural of a noun.**

Gina went camping with her *sister/s* and their children.

All the *highway/s* to the airport are under construction.

**Do not use an apostrophe with a possessive pronoun.** These pronouns already show ownership (possession).

Is that bag *your/s*? No, it is *our/s*.

## Possessive Pronouns

| | | | |
|---|---|---|---|
| my | his | its | their |
| mine | her | our | theirs |
| your | hers | ours | whose |
| yours | | | |

The single most common error with apostrophes and pronouns is confusing *its* (a possessive pronoun) with *it's* (a contraction meaning "it is"). Whenever you write *it's*, test correctness by replacing it with *it is* and reading the sentence aloud to hear if it makes sense.

## Apostrophes in Contractions

**Tip** Ask your instructor if contractions are acceptable in papers.

A **contraction** is formed by joining two words and leaving out one or more of the letters. When writing a contraction, put an apostrophe where the letter or letters have been left out.

*She's* on her way. = *She is* on her way.

*I'll* see you there. = *I will* see you there.

**Tip** To shorten the full year to only the final two numbers, replace the first two numbers: The year 2016 becomes '16.

Be sure to put the apostrophe in the correct place.

It *doesn't* really matter.

### Common Contractions

| | |
|---|---|
| aren't = are not | she'll = she will |
| can't = cannot | she's = she is, she has |
| couldn't = could not | there's = there is |
| didn't = did not | they'd = they would, they had |
| don't = do not | they'll = they will |
| he'd = he would, he had | they're = they are |
| he'll = he will | they've = they have |
| he's = he is, he has | who'd = who would, who had |
| I'd = I would, I had | who'll = who will |
| I'll = I will | who's = who is, who has |
| I'm = I am | won't = will not |
| I've = I have | wouldn't = would not |
| isn't = is not | you'd = you would, you had |
| it's = it is, it has | you'll = you will |
| let's = let us | you're = you are |
| she'd = she would, she had | you've = you have |

## Apostrophes with Letters, Numbers, and Time

**Use -'s to make letters and numbers plural.** The apostrophe prevents confusion or misreading.

In Scrabble games, there are more *e's* than any other letter.

In women's shoes, size *8's* are more common than size *10's*.

**Use an apostrophe or -'s in certain expressions in which time nouns are treated as if they possess something.**

She took four *weeks'* maternity leave after the baby was born.

This *year's* graduating class is huge.

## Edit for Apostrophes

**PRACTICE 1** **Editing paragraphs for apostrophes**

Edit the following paragraphs by adding two apostrophes where needed and crossing out five incorrectly used apostrophes.

(1) Have you noticed many honeybee's when you go outside? (2) If not, it is'nt surprising. (3) For reasons that scientists still don't quite understand, these bees have been disappearing all across the country. (4) This mass disappearance is a problem because bees are an important part of growing a wide variety of flowers, fruits, vegetables, and nuts as they spread pollen from one place to another.

(5) In the last year, more than one-third, or billions, of the honeybees in the United States' have disappeared. (6) As a consequence, farmers have been forced either to buy or to rent beehives for their crops. (7) Typically, people who are in the bee business ship hives to farmers fields by truck. (8) The hives often have to travel hundreds of miles.

(9) Scientist's have been trying to find out what happened to the once-thriving bee population. (10) They suspect that either a disease or chemicals harmed the honeybee's.

**PRACTICE 2** **Editing your own writing for apostrophes**

Edit a piece of your own writing for apostrophes. It can be a paper for this course or another one, or choose something you have written for work or your everyday life.

## Chapter Review

1. An apostrophe (') is a punctuation mark that either shows ____________ or indicates that a letter or letters have been intentionally left out to form a ____________.
2. To show ownership, add _____ to a singular noun, even if the noun already ends in *-s*. For a plural noun, add an ____________ alone if the noun ends in *-s*; add _____ if the noun does not end in *-s*.
3. Do not use an apostrophe with a ____________ pronoun.
4. Do not confuse *its* and *it's*. *Its* shows ____________; *it's* is a ____________ meaning "it is."
5. A ____________________ is formed by joining two words and leaving out one or more of the letters.

# 32

# Quotation Marks 

Visit **LaunchPad Solo for Readers and Writers > Grammar > Style and Mechanics** for more tutorials, videos, and practice with crafting paragraphs.

## Understand What Quotation Marks Do

**Quotation marks (" ")** always appear in pairs. Quotation marks have two common uses in college writing:

- They are used with direct quotations, which exactly repeat, word for word, what someone said or wrote. (Nick said, "You should take the downtown bus.")
- They are used to set off **titles**. (My favorite song is "Sophisticated Lady.")

## Practice Using Quotation Marks Correctly

### *Quotation Marks for Direct Quotations*

When you write a direct quotation, use quotation marks around the quoted words. Quotation marks tell readers that the words used are exactly what was said or written.

1. "I do not know what she means," I said to my friend Lina.
2. Lina asked, "Do you think we should ask a question?"

## GRAMMAR & MECHANICS ROADMAP

### An Overview

**This Chapter Identifies the Following Trouble Spots**

- Quotation marks for direct quotations
- Quotation marks for certain titles

**Tools to Address the Trouble Spots**

3. “Excuse me, Professor Soames,” I called out, “but could you explain that again?”
4. “Yes,” said Professor Soames. “Let me make sure you all understand.”
5. After further explanation, Professor Soames asked, “Are there any other questions?”

When you are writing a paper that uses outside sources, use quotation marks to indicate where you quote the exact words of a source.

> We all need to become more conscientious recyclers. A recent editorial in the *Bolton Common* reported, “When recycling volunteers spot-checked bags that were supposed to contain only newspaper, they found a collection of nonrecyclable items such as plastic candy wrappers, aluminum foil, and birthday cards.”

When quoting, writers usually use words that identify who is speaking, such as *I said to my friend Lina* in the first example in the “Quotation Marks for Direct Quotations” section. The identifying words can come after the quoted words (example 1), before them (example 2), or in the middle of them (example 3). Here are some guidelines for capitalization and punctuation.

**Guidelines for Capitalization and Punctuation**

- Capitalize the first letter in a complete sentence that is being quoted, even if it comes after some identifying words (example 2 on the previous page).
- Do not capitalize the first letter in a quotation if it is not the first word in a complete sentence (*but* in example 3).
- If it is a complete sentence and it is clear who the speaker is, a quotation can stand on its own (second sentence in example 4).
- Identifying words must be attached to a quotation; they cannot be a sentence on their own.
- Use commas to separate any identifying words from quoted words in the same sentence.
- Always put quotation marks after commas and periods. Put quotation marks after question marks and exclamation points if they are part of the quoted sentence.

Quotation mark — Quotation mark

Lina asked, “Do you think we should ask a question?”

Comma — Question mark

**Tip** For more on commas with quotation marks, see Chapter 30.

- If a question mark or exclamation point is part of your own sentence, put it after the quotation mark.

Quotation mark — Quotation mark

What did she mean when she said, “All tests are graded on a curve”?

Comma — Question mark

## *Setting Off a Quotation within Another Quotation*

Sometimes, when you quote someone directly, part of what that person said quotes words that someone else said or wrote. Put single quotation marks (‘ ’) around the quotation within a quotation so that readers understand who said what.

> The student handbook says, "Students must be given the opportunity to make up work missed for legitimate reasons."
>
> Terry told his instructor, "I am sorry I missed the exam, but that is not a reason to fail me for the term. Our student handbook says, ‘Students must be given the opportunity to make up work missed for legitimate reasons,’ and I have a good reason."

### PRACTICE 1 Punctuating direct quotations

Edit the following sentences by adding quotation marks and commas where needed.

**Example: A radio journalist asked a nurse at a critical-care facility, "Do you believe that the medical community needlessly prolongs the life of the terminally ill?"**

1. If I could answer that question quickly the nurse replied I would deserve an honorary degree in ethics.
2. She added But I see it as the greatest dilemma we face today.
3. How would you describe that dilemma? the reporter asked the nurse.
4. The nurse said It is a choice of when to use our amazing medical technology and when not to.
5. The reporter asked So there are times when you would favor letting patients die on their own?
6. Yes the nurse replied I would.
7. The reporter asked Under what circumstances should a patient be allowed to die?
8. I cannot really answer that question because so many variables are involved the nurse replied.
9. Is this a matter of deciding how to allocate scarce resources? the reporter asked.
10. In a sense, it is the nurse replied. As a colleague of mine says, We should not try to keep everyone alive for as long as possible just because we can.

### *No Quotation Marks for Indirect Quotations*

When you report what someone said or wrote but do not use the person's exact words, you are writing an **indirect quotation.** Do not use quotation marks for indirect quotations. Indirect quotations often begin with the word *that.*

| **Indirect quotation** | **Direct quotation** |
|---|---|
| Sam said that there was a fire downtown. | Sam said, "There was a fire downtown." |
| The police told us to move along. | "Move along," directed the police. |
| Tara told me that she is graduating. | Tara said, "I am graduating." |

**PRACTICE 2** **Punctuating direct and indirect quotations**

Edit the following sentences by adding quotation marks where needed and crossing out quotation marks that are used incorrectly. If a sentence is already correct, put a "C" next to it.

**Example: Three days before her apartment was robbed, Jocelyn told a friend, "I worry about the safety of this building."**

1. Have you complained to the landlord yet? her friend asked.
2. Not yet, Jocelyn replied, although I know I should.
3. Jocelyn phoned the landlord and asked him to install a more secure lock on the front door.
4. The landlord said that "he believed that the lock was fine the way it was."
5. When Jocelyn phoned the landlord after the burglary, she said, I know this burglary would not have happened if that lock had been installed.
6. I am sorry, the landlord replied, but there is nothing I can do about it now.
7. Jocelyn asked a tenants' rights group whether she had grounds for a lawsuit.
8. The person she spoke to said that "she probably did."
9. If I were you, the person said, I would let your landlord know about your plans.
10. When Jocelyn told her landlord of the possible lawsuit, he said that he would reimburse her for the stolen items.

### *Quotation Marks for Certain Titles*

When you refer to a short work such as a magazine or newspaper article, a chapter in a book, a short story, an essay, a song, or a poem, put quotation marks around the title of the work.

| | |
|---|---|
| **Newspaper article** | "Volunteers Honored for Service" |
| **Short story** | "The Awakening" |
| **Essay** | "Why Are We So Angry?" |

Usually, titles of longer works, such as novels, books, magazines, newspapers, movies, television programs, and albums, are italicized. The titles of sacred books such as the Bible or the Koran are neither underlined nor surrounded by quotation marks.

| | |
|---|---|
| **Book** | *To Kill a Mockingbird* |
| **Newspaper** | *Washington Post* |

Do not italicize or capitalize the word *the* before the name of a newspaper or magazine, even if it is part of the title: I saw that article in the *New York Times*. But do capitalize *The* when it is the first word in titles of books, movies, and other sources.

If you are writing a paper with many outside sources, your instructor will probably refer you to a particular system of citing sources. Follow that system's guidelines when you use titles in your paper.

**Note:** Do not enclose the title of a paragraph or an essay that you have written in quotation marks when it appears at the beginning of your paper. Do not italicize it either.

## Edit for Quotation Marks

**PRACTICE 3** **Editing paragraphs for quotation marks**

Edit the following paragraphs by adding twelve sets of quotation marks where needed and crossing out the two sets of incorrectly used quotation marks. Correct any errors in punctuation.

(1) When Ruiz first came into my office, he told me that he was a poor student. (2) I asked, What makes you think that?

(3) Ruiz answered, I have always gotten bad grades, and I do not know how to get any better. (4) He shook his head. (5) I have just about given up.

(6) I told him that "there were some resources on campus he could use and that we could work together to help him."

(7) "What kind of things are you talking about?" asked Ruiz. (8) What exactly will I learn?

(9) I said, There are plenty of programs to help you. (10) You really have no excuse to fail.

(11) Can you be a little more specific? he asked.

(12) Certainly, I said. (13) I told him about the survival skills program. (14) I also pulled out folders on study skills, such as managing time, improving memory, taking notes, and having a positive attitude. (15) Take a look at these, I said.

(16) Ruiz said, No, I am not interested in that. (17) And I do not have time.

(18) I replied, "That is your decision, Ruiz, but remember that education is one of the few things that people are willing to pay for and not get." (19) I paused and then added, It sounds to me like you are wasting the money you spent on tuition. (20) Why not try to get what you paid for?

(21) Ruiz thought for a moment, while he looked out the window, and finally told me that "he would try."

(22) Good, I said. (23) I am glad to hear it.

**PRACTICE 4** **Editing your own writing for quotation marks**

Edit a piece of your own writing for quotation marks. It can be a paper for this course or another one, or choose something you have written for work or your everyday life.

## Chapter Review

1. Quotation marks look like ______. They always appear in (pairs/threes).
2. A direct quotation exactly _________ what someone (or some outside source) said or wrote. (Use/Do not use) quotation marks around direct quotations.
3. An indirect quotation ______________________________________________. (Use/Do not use) quotation marks with indirect quotations.
4. To set off a quotation within a quotation, use _________________________.
5. Put quotation marks around the titles of short works such as (give four examples) ______________________________________________________________.
6. For longer works such as magazines, novels, books, newspapers, and so on, _________ the titles.

# 33

# Other Punctuation 

LaunchPadSolo
Visit **LaunchPad Solo for Readers and Writers > Grammar > Style and Mechanics** for more tutorials, videos, and practice with crafting paragraphs.

## Understand What Punctuation Does

Punctuation helps readers understand your writing. If you use punctuation incorrectly, you send readers a confusing—or, even worse, a wrong—message. This chapter covers five punctuation marks that people sometimes use incorrectly because they are not quite sure what these marks are supposed to do.

## GRAMMAR & MECHANICS ROADMAP

### An Overview

**This Chapter Identifies the Following Trouble Spots**

- Semicolons
- Parenthesis
- Dash
- Hyphen

**Tools to Address Trouble Spots**

# Practice Using Punctuation Correctly

## *Semicolon ;*

### SEMICOLONS TO JOIN CLOSELY RELATED SENTENCES

Use a semicolon to join two closely related sentences into one sentence.

> In an interview, hold your head up and do not slouch; it is important to look alert.
>
> Make good eye contact; looking down is not appropriate in an interview.

**Language note:** Using a comma instead of a semicolon to join two sentences would create a run-on (see Chapter 17).

### SEMICOLONS WHEN ITEMS IN A LIST CONTAIN COMMAS

Use semicolons to separate items in a list that itself contains commas. Otherwise, it is difficult for readers to tell where one item ends and another begins.

> For dinner, Bob ate an order of onion rings; a 16-ounce steak; a baked potato with sour cream, bacon bits, and cheese; a green salad; and a huge bowl of ice cream with fudge sauce.

Because one item, *a baked potato with sour cream, bacon bits, and cheese*, contains its own commas, all items need to be separated by semicolons.

## *Colon :*

### COLONS BEFORE LISTS

Use a colon after an independent clause to introduce a list. An independent clause contains a subject, a verb, and a complete thought. It can stand on its own as a sentence.

> The software conference fair featured a vast array of products:
> financial-management applications, games, educational CDs, college-application programs, and so on.

### COLONS BEFORE EXPLANATIONS OR EXAMPLES

Use a colon after an independent clause to let readers know that you are about to provide an explanation or example of what you just wrote.

> The conference was overwhelming: too much hype about too many things.

One of the most common misuses of colons is to use them after a phrase instead of an independent clause. Watch out especially for colons following the phrases *such as* and *for example.*

**Tip** See Chapter 30 (Commas), Chapter 31 (Apostrophes), and Chapter 32 (Quotation Marks) for coverage of these punctuation marks. For more information on using semicolons to join sentences, see Chapter 23.

**Incorrect** Tonya enjoys sports that are sometimes dangerous. For example: white-water rafting, wilderness skiing, rock climbing, and motorcycle racing.

**Correct** Tonya enjoys sports that are sometimes dangerous: white-water rafting, wilderness skiing, rock climbing, and motorcycle racing.

**Incorrect** Jeff has many interests. They are: bicycle racing, sculpting, and building musical instruments.

**Correct** Jeff has many interests: bicycle racing, sculpting, and building musical instruments.

### COLONS IN BUSINESS CORRESPONDENCE AND BEFORE SUBTITLES

Use a colon after a greeting (called a *salutation)* in a business letter and after the standard heading lines at the beginning of a memorandum.

Dear Mr. Hernandez:

To: Pat Toney

From: Susan Anker

Colons should also be used before subtitles—for example, "Running a Marathon: The Five Most Important Tips."

## Parentheses ( )

Use parentheses to set off information that is not essential to the meaning of a sentence. Parentheses are always used in pairs and should be used sparingly.

My grandfather's most successful invention (and also his first) was the electric blanket.

When he died (at the age of ninety-six), he had more than 150 patents registered.

## Dash --

Dashes can be used like parentheses to set off additional information, particularly information that you want to emphasize. Make a dash by writing or typing two hyphens together. Do not put extra spaces around a dash.

The final exam--worth 25 percent of your total grade--will be next Thursday.

A dash can also indicate a pause, much like a comma does.

My uncle went on long fishing trips--without my aunt and cousins.

## *Hyphen -*

### HYPHENS TO JOIN WORDS THAT FORM A SINGLE DESCRIPTION

Writers often join two or more words that together form a single description of a person, place, or thing. To join the words, use a hyphen.

> Being a stockbroker is a high-risk career.
>
> Jill is a lovely three-year-old girl.

When writing out two-word numbers from twenty-one to ninety-nine, put a hyphen between the two words.

> Seventy-five people participated in the demonstration.

### HYPHENS TO DIVIDE A WORD AT THE END OF A LINE

Use a hyphen to divide a word when part of the word must continue on the next line.

> Critics accused the tobacco industry of increasing the amounts of nico-
> tine in cigarettes to encourage addiction and boost sales.

If you are not sure where to break a word, look it up in a dictionary. The word's main entry will show you where you can break the word: *dic • tio • nary*. If you still are not confident that you are putting the hyphen in the correct place, do not break the word; write it all on the next line.

**Tip** Most word-processing programs automatically put an entire word on the next line rather than hyphenating it. When you write by hand, however, you need to hyphenate correctly.

# Edit for Other Punctuation Marks

**PRACTICE 1** **Editing paragraphs for other punctuation marks**

Edit the following paragraphs by adding semicolons, colons, parentheses, dashes, and hyphens when needed. In some places, more than one type of punctuation may be acceptable.

(1) When John Wood was on a backpacking trip to Nepal in 1998, he discovered something he had not expected only a few books in the nation's schools. (2) He knew that if the students did not have the materials they needed, it would be much harder for them to learn. (3) They did not need high tech supplies as much as they needed old fashioned books. (4) Wood decided that he would find a way to get those books.

(5) Two years later, Wood founded Room to Read, an organization dedicated to shipping books to students who needed them. (6) Since then, the group has donated more than three million books. (7) One of Wood's first shipments was carried to students on the back of a yak. (8) Many others arrived in a Cathay Pacific Airlines plane.

(9) Along with the books, Room to Read has also built almost three hundred schools and has opened five thousand libraries. (10) Different companies donate books to the organization Scholastic, Inc., recently sent 400,000 books to Wood's group. (11) Money to fund all these efforts comes through various fund-raisers read-a-thons, auctions, and coin drives.

**PRACTICE 2** **Editing your own writing for punctuation**

Edit a piece of your own writing for semicolons, colons, parentheses, dashes, and hyphens. It can be a paper for this course or another one, or choose something you have written for work or your everyday life. You may want to try more than one way to use these punctuation marks in your writing.

## Chapter Review

1. Semicolons (;) can be used to ______________________________
   and to ______________________________.
2. Colons (:) can be used in what three ways? ______________________________
   ______________________________
   ______________________________
   ______________________________
3. A colon in a sentence must always be used after an ______________________________.
4. Parentheses ( ) set off information that is ______________ to a sentence.
5. ______________ also set off information in a sentence, usually information that you want to emphasize.
6. Hyphens (-) can be used to join two or more words that together ______________ ______________ and to __________ a word at the end of a line.

# 34

# Capitalization

## Using Capital Letters

## Understand Three Rules of Capitalization

LaunchPadSolo

Visit **LaunchPad Solo for Readers and Writers > Grammar > Style and Mechanics** for more tutorials, videos, and practice with crafting paragraphs.

Capital letters (A, B, C, etc.) are generally bigger than lowercase letters (a, b, c, etc.), and they may have a different form. To avoid the most common errors of capitalization, follow these three rules:

**Capitalize the first letter**

- Of every new sentence.
- In names of specific people, places, dates, and things (also known as proper nouns).
- Of important words in titles.

## Practice Capitalization

### *Capitalization of Sentences*

Capitalize the first letter of each new sentence, including the first word of a direct quotation.

> The superintendent was surprised.
>
> He asked, "What is going on here?"

## GRAMMAR & MECHANICS ROADMAP

### An Overview

**This Chapter Identifies the Following Trouble Spots**

- Capitalization of sentences
- Capitalization of names of specific people, places, dates, and things
- Capitalization of titles

**Tools to Address Trouble Spots**

- Understanding capitalization (p. 519)
- Chapter Review (p. 522)

## *Capitalization of Names of Specific People, Places, Dates, and Things*

The general rule is to capitalize the first letter in names of specific people, places, dates, and things. Do not capitalize a generic (common) name such as *college* as opposed to the specific name: *Carroll State College*. Look at the examples for each group.

### PEOPLE

Capitalize the first letter in names of specific people and in titles used with names of specific people.

| Specific | Not specific |
|---|---|
| Jean Heaton | my neighbor |
| Professor Fitzgerald | your math professor |
| Dr. Cornog | the doctor |
| Aunt Pat, Mother | my aunt, your mother |

The name of a family member is capitalized when the family member is being addressed directly: Happy Birthday, *Mother*. In other instances, do not capitalize: It is my *mother's* birthday.

The word *president* is not capitalized unless it comes directly before a name as part of that person's title: *President* Barack Obama.

### PLACES

Capitalize the first letter in names of specific buildings, streets, cities, states, regions, and countries.

| Specific | Not specific |
|---|---|
| Bolton Town Hall | the town hall |
| Arlington Street | our street |
| Dearborn Heights | my hometown |
| Arizona | this state |
| the South | the southern region |
| Spain | that country |

Do not capitalize directions in a sentence.

Drive *south* for five blocks.

### DATES

Capitalize the first letter in the names of days, months, and holidays. Do not capitalize the names of the seasons (winter, spring, summer, fall).

| Specific | Not specific |
|---|---|
| Wednesday | tomorrow |
| June 25 | summer |
| Thanksgiving | my birthday |

 Language note: Some languages, such as Spanish, French, and Italian, do not capitalize days, months, and languages. In English, such words must be capitalized.

**Incorrect** I study russian every monday, wednesday, and friday from january through may.

**Correct** I study **Russian** every **Monday**, **Wednesday**, and **Friday** from **January** through **May**.

### ORGANIZATIONS, COMPANIES, AND GROUPS

| Specific | Not specific |
|---|---|
| Taft Community College | my college |
| Microsoft | that software company |
| Alcoholics Anonymous | the self-help group |

### LANGUAGES, NATIONALITIES, AND RELIGIONS

| Specific | Not specific |
|---|---|
| English, Greek, Spanish | my first language |
| Christianity, Buddhism | your religion |

The names of languages should be capitalized even if you aren't referring to a specific course.

I am taking psychology and *Spanish*.

### COURSES

| Specific | Not specific |
|---|---|
| Composition 101 | a writing course |
| Introduction to Psychology | my psychology course |

COMMERCIAL PRODUCTS

| Specific | Not specific |
|---|---|
| Diet Pepsi | a diet cola |
| Skippy peanut butter | peanut butter |

## *Capitalization of Titles*

**Tip** For more on punctuating titles, see Chapter 32. For a list of common prepositions, see page 327.

When you write the title of a book, movie, television program, magazine, newspaper, article, story, song, paper, poem, and so on, capitalize the first word and all important words. The only words that do not need to be capitalized (unless they are the first word) are *the, a, an,* coordinating conjunctions (*and, but, for, nor, or, so, yet*), and prepositions.

> *I Love Lucy* was a long-running television program.
>
> Both *USA Today* and the *New York Times* are popular newspapers.
>
> "Once More to the Lake" is one of Chuck's favorite essays.

# Chapter Review

1. Capitalize the __________ of every new sentence.
2. Capitalize the first letter in names of specific _________, _________, _________, and _________.
3. Capitalize the first word and all ______________ in titles.

Name ____________________ Section ____________________

# Editing Review Test 1

## The Four Most Serious Errors (Chapters 15–19)

1

Directions: Each of the underlined word groups contains one or more errors. As you locate and identify each error, write its item number on the appropriate line below. Then, edit the underlined word groups to correct the errors. If you need help, turn back to the chapters indicated.

Two fragments ____________________ Two verb problems ____________________

Two run-ons ____________________ Four subject-verb agreement errors ____________________

1 Every time you step outside, you are under attack. 2 Which you may not know what is hitting you, but the attack is truly happening. 3 Invisible storms of sky dust rain down on you all the time. 4 It does not matter if the sun is shining and the sky are bright blue. 5 The dust is still there.

6 Sky dust consist of bug parts, specks of hair, pollen, and even tiny chunks of comets. 7 According to experts, 6 million pounds of space dust settle on the earth's surface every year. 8 You will never notice it, scientists, however, are collecting it in order to learn more about weather patterns and pollution. 9 Using sophisticated equipment like high-tech planes and sterile filters to collect dust samples.

10 Dan Murray, a geologist at the University of Rhode Island, has began a new project that invites students and teachers to help collect samples of cosmic dust. 11 Murray says that collecting the dust particles are quite simple. 12 It starts with a researcher setting up a small, inflatable swimming pool. 13 Next, this investigator leaves the pool out in the open for 48 hours. 14 Finally, the researcher uses a special type of tape to pick up whatever have settled over time. 15 The tape is put into a beaker of water to dissolve a microscope is used to analyze what comes off the tape. 16 The information finded there will help scientists predict insect seasons, measure meteor showers, or even catch signs of global warming.

Name ______________________ Section ______________________

2

# Editing Review Test 2

## The Four Most Serious Errors (Chapters 15–19)

Directions: Each of the underlined word groups contains one or more errors. As you locate and identify each error, write its item number on the appropriate line below. Then, edit the underlined word groups to correct the errors. If you need help, turn back to the chapters indicated.

Two fragments ______________________ Two verb problems ______________________

Three run-ons ______________________ Three subject-verb agreement errors ______________________

1 Most people spend many hours a day indoors, so windows and natural light is important to their health. 2 Light helps people feel connected to the world around them. 3 However, traditional windows allow the loss of heat in winter and of cool air in summer; the result is high energy costs to maintain office buildings and homes at comfortable temperatures. 4 Architects and designers knowed this fact, so they have developed energy-efficient "smart windows." 5 Shifting from clear to dark and back again. 6 Some smart windows change from clear to dark with a touch of a button others change automatically in response to the intensity of the outside light.

7 Their design and engineering make smart windows *chromogenic,* or able to change colors. 8 Smart windows shifts to darker colors when they are given a small electrical charge. 9 The darker the room, the more it remains cool the sun does not warm it. 10 Smart windows take only a minute or so to darken.

11 Although these smart windows save energy, they may not be ready for the market. 12 For a few more years. 13 At present, designers face some resistance from potential customers who distrust the technology. 14 Another obstacle is the price tag, this new technology remains expensive. 15 To deal with both of these issues, developers are starting small. 16 They were creating motorcycle and ski helmets with face masks that switch between dark and clear. 17 They hopes that handy products like these helmets will help the new technology gain wide acceptance.

Name ______________________________ Section ______________

# Editing Review Test 3

3

## The Four Most Serious Errors (Chapters 15–19)
## Other Grammar Concerns (Chapters 20–26)

**Directions:** Each of the underlined word groups contains one or more errors. As you locate and identify each error, write its item number on the appropriate line below. Then, edit the underlined word groups to correct the errors. If you need help, turn back to the chapters indicated.

| | |
|---|---|
| Two fragments ______________ | Two verb problems ______________ |
| One run-on ______________ | Two pronoun errors ______________ |
| One adjective error ______________ | One parallelism error ______________ |
| Two subject-verb agreement errors ______________ | |

1 Flying an airplane across the Atlantic Ocean may have been a miracle almost a century ago, but today it be quite commonplace. 2 When a man named Maynard Hill decided to do it, however, most people told him that he simply could not be done. 3 Giving it a try despite everyone's doubts. 4 His persistence was rewarded when TAM-5, his 11-pound model airplane, flew from Canada to Ireland in approximately 39 hours. 5 TAM-5's flight sat world records not only for the longest distance but also for the longest time ever flown by this type of airplane. 6 Following the same path as the first nonstop flight across the ocean in 1919.

7 This successful trip was not Hill's first attempt, by any means. 8 He started its project a decade ago, and he lost several planes trying to complete the journey. 9 Finally, in August 2003, he made a fifth attempt. 10 He tossed the TAM-5 into the air once airborne, it was guided by remote control on the ground. 11 It was the most best version he had made. 12 It soared to a cruising altitude of almost a thousand feet, and at that point a computerized autopilot took over.

13 For days, the flight crew watched the clock, followed the TAM-5's progress, and hopes for the best. 14 A crowd of fifty people waited on the shore in Ireland to watch the TAM-5's landing. 15 When the plane appeared on the horizon, a cheer went up. 16 Today, model plane enthusiasts remembers his feat. 17 Even though the plane were made out of nothing more than balsa wood, fiberglass, and plastic film, it flew right into history that August afternoon.

Name ______________________ Section ______________________

4

# Editing Review Test 4

## The Four Most Serious Errors (Chapters 15–19)
## Other Grammar Concerns (Chapters 20–26)

Directions: Each of the underlined word groups contains one or more errors. As you locate and identify each error, write its item number on the appropriate line below. Then, edit the underlined word groups to correct the errors. If you need help, turn back to the chapters indicated.

| | |
|---|---|
| Two fragments ______ | One run-on ______ |
| One subject-verb agreement error ______ | One pronoun error ______ |
| One misplaced/dangling modifier ______ | Two coordination/ subordination errors ______ |
| One use of inappropriately informal or casual language ______ | |

1 Early on May 1, 2011, Sohaib Athar, an IT consultant in Pakistan, was surprised to hear helicopters flying over his house. 2 Soon, he sent a Twitter message about it: "Helicopter hovering above Abbottabad at 1 a.m. (is a rare event)." 3 He continued to tweet about what he was hearing for the next half hour, attracting many Twitter followers.

4 Because he didn't know it at the time, Athar became the first person to publicize the raid in which Osama bin Laden was captured and assassinated. 5 For this reason, Athar also became one of the most famous of a growing number of so-called citizen journalists. 6 Unlike most traditional news gatherers, citizen journalists aren't trained in journalism. 7 They follow events and trends that interest them, but they send their observations to others through Facebook, Twitter, and other social media.

8 Certain media critics argue, however, that if someone tweets about something newsworthy, they don't necessarily deserve to be called a journalist. 9 That is the view of Dan Miller, a reporter who had the following reaction to Athar's famous reports: "Wondering on Twitter why there are helicopters flying around your neighborhood isn't journalism." 10 According to Miller, traditional media, not Athar, got the 411 about bin Laden's capture out to the whole world. 11 Not to just some Twitter followers.

12 Others say that Athar provided a more valuable service. 13 For example, he communicated with people who were following him and tried to answer their questions, he sought out other sources of information and shared them. 14 Also, tried to analyze what he observed himself and what he learned from other sources.

15 Whether or not Athar deserves to be called a journalist, one thing is clear: More people is feeling driven to tweet, text, or blog from their particular corners of the world.

Name ______________________ Section ______________

# Editing Review Test 5

5

## The Four Most Serious Errors (Chapters 15–19)
## Other Grammar Concerns (Chapters 20–26)
## Word Use (Chapters 27–29)

**Directions:** Each of the underlined word groups contains one or more errors. As you locate and identify each error, write its item number on the appropriate line below. Then, edit the underlined word groups to correct the errors. If you need help, turn back to the chapters indicated.

One run-on ______________

One word-choice error ______________

One adjective error ______________

One subject-verb agreement error ______________

Two commonly confused word errors ______________

One verb problem ______________

Two pronoun errors ______________

One spelling error ______________

One misplaced/dangling modifier ______________

1 How do you celebrate the New Year? 2 Some people watch television on New Year's Eve so that he can see the glittering ball drop in New York's Times Square. 3 Others invite friends and family over to celebrate with special foods or fireworks.

4 The New Year are celebrated all over the world in a variety of ways. 5 For example, in Australia, people spended the day in fun, outdoor activities, such as picnics, trips to the beach, and rodeos. 6 After all, it is summertime there in January. 7 In Spain, people eat a dozen grapes at midnight. 8 They eat one each time the clock chimes because she believe that it will bring good luck for the New Year. 9 The people of Denmark have the unusualest tradition. 10 On New Year's Eve, they throw old dishes at the doors of their friends' homes. 11 If you find a lot of broken junk in front of your house in the morning, you are well liked. 12 Wearing all new clothes is the way many Koreans celebrate the start of the New Year. 13 In Germany, people leave food on there plates, this practice is meant to ensure that their kitchens will be full of food for the coming New Year.

14 Not all countries celebrate the New Year on January 1. 15 Setting off firecrackers, the holiday is celebrated later by the Chinese people. 16 The date of the Chinese New Year depends on the lunar calander and usually falls somewhere between January 21 and February 20. 17 The Chinese often have a big parade with colorful floats of dancing dragons. 18 The mythical creatures are supposed to be cymbals of wealth and long life.

**Name** ______________________ **Section** ______________

6

# Editing Review Test 6

## The Four Most Serious Errors (Chapters 15–19)
## Other Grammar Concerns (Chapters 20–26)
## Word Use (Chapters 27–29)

**Directions:** Each of the underlined word groups contains one or more errors. As you locate and identify each error, write its item number on the appropriate line below. Then, edit the underlined word groups to correct the errors. If you need help, turn back to the chapters indicated.

| | |
|---|---|
| One run-on ______ | One use of inappropriately informal or casual language ______ |
| One subject-verb agreement error ______ | One verb problem ______ |
| One parallelism error ______ | One pronoun error ______ |
| Two commonly confused word errors ______ | Two spelling errors ______ |

1 The idea of being able to unlock your car, turn on a light, or starting your computer just by waving your hand sounds like something out of a science-fiction novel. 2 Thanks to advancements in technology, the futuristic idea has became a reality. 3 Some people are all ready able to accomplish routine actions in this unusual way. 4 They do not have special powers they have special computer chips embedded inside their bodies. 5 These high-tech chips help people do daily tasks with little or no effort.

6 Known as RFIDs, which stands for "radio frequency identification devices," the chips are way small. 7 They are as tiny as a peice of rice, have small antennas that send signals, and can be painlessly implanted and worn under the skin. 8 Health-care workers uses the chips in a variety of life-saving ways. 9 For example, emergency medical workers can scan the chips in accident victims to determine his blood type or allergies.

10 For security reasons, some parents have their children wear RFIDs on backpacks, bracelets, or ID tags. 11 Through a cell-phone signal, the chips automatically let the parents know when their children have reached and left school or other destinations. 12 Even some pets are now equipped with these computer chips. 13 If the pet runs away or gets lost, than its owners can track down their pet more easily by using the chip. 14 Although many people think that these chips have great potental, others worry that the government will eventually use them to spy on people.

Name ______________________ Section ______________________

# Editing Review Test 7

7

## The Four Most Serious Errors (Chapters 15–19)
## Other Grammar Concerns (Chapters 20–26)
## Word Use (Chapters 27–29)
## Punctuation and Capitalization (Chapters 30–34)

Directions: Each of the underlined word groups contains one or more errors. As you locate and identify each error, write its item number on the appropriate line below. Then, edit the underlined word groups to correct the errors. If you need help, turn back to the chapters indicated.

| | |
|---|---|
| One run-on ______ | One verb problem ______ |
| One apostrophe error ______ | One pronoun error ______ |
| One adverb error ______ | One quotation mark error ______ |
| One subject-verb agreement error ______ | One capitalization error ______ |
| One comma error ______ | One semicolon error ______ |

1 In response to the ongoing economic crisis, more high schools are teaching financial literacy: how to create a budget, save money, and stay out of debt. 2 Although most experts agree that teaching these skills is a good idea, some recommend that such education begin more earlier—even in preschool. 3 This way, young people have more time to learn good habit's, save money, and plan for their financial future.

4 The Moonjar is one Tool for teaching children good money skills. 5 It consists of three tin boxes; each of which is labeled "spend," "save," or "share." 6 Children are encouraged to divide allowances or gifts of money equally among the boxes. 7 As the weeks pass by, they watch their savings grow, helping them see the benefits of saving money over time, they also learn discipline about spending. 8 For example a child who is shopping with a parent might ask for a pack of candy or a small toy. 9 The parent can reply, "Do you have enough money in your spend box"? 10 Exchanges like that one help the child understand the consequences of financial decisions; if they spend money on one item now, less money will be available for other purchases in the future.

11 Mary Ryan Karges, who is in charge of sales for Moonjar LLC, recommend that financial skills be emphasized as much as other basic skills taught to young children. 12 She says, "If we teach save, spend, share with the same vigor that we teach stop, look, listen, we won't run into so many financial problems." 13 Once children have seed the benefits of good financial choices, they are on their way to a better future.

Name ______________________________ Section ______________

# 8 Editing Review Test 8

## The Four Most Serious Errors (Chapters 15–19)
## Other Grammar Concerns (Chapters 20–26)
## Word Use (Chapters 27–29)
## Punctuation and Capitalization (Chapters 30–34)

Directions: Each of the underlined word groups contains one or more errors. As you locate and identify each error, write its item number on the appropriate line below. Then, edit the underlined word groups to correct the errors. If you need help, turn back to the chapters indicated.

One run-on ____________
One pronoun error ____________
One comma error ____________
One apostrophe error ____________
One use of inappropriately informal or casual language ____________
One capitalization error ____________
One semicolon error ____________
One verb problem ____________
One adverb error ____________
One spelling error ____________
One parallelism error ____________
One hyphen error ____________

1 If it seems as though places in the United States are more crowded lately; it might be because the country's population recently hit three hundred million. 2 The nation has the third-largest population in the world. 3 Only China and India have more people. 4 Experts belief that by 2043 there will be four hundred million people in the United States.

5 The country is growing rapidly because people are having more babies more people are moving to the United States. 6 The northeast is the most populated area within the country. 7 It took fifty two years for the country's population to go from one hundred million to two hundred million. 8 It took only thirty-nine years to rise from two hundred million to its current three hundred million. 9 If experts statistics are correct, it will take even less time for the population of the United States to reach four hundred million.

10 Some people worry that the United States is growing too quick. 11 Researchers predict some super scary possibilitys. 12 They state that if the population grows too large, it will stress available land, deplete water resources, and it can increase air pollution. 13 Its concerns are valid ones; in the meantime, the population just keeps growing. 14 Although this country is large future generations may be squeezed in more tightly than the present generation can imagine.

Name ______________________________ Section ______________

# Editing Review Test 9

9

## The Four Most Serious Errors (Chapters 15–19)
## Other Grammar Concerns (Chapters 20–26)
## Word Use (Chapters 27–29)
## Punctuation and Capitalization (Chapters 30–34)

**Directions:** Each of the underlined word groups contains one or more errors. As you locate and identify each error, write its item number on the appropriate line below. Then, edit the underlined word groups to correct the errors. If you need help, turn back to the chapters indicated.

One fragment ______________
One run-on ______________
One pronoun error ______________
One parallelism error ______________
One commonly confused word error ______________
One spelling error ______________
One hyphen error ______________
One semicolon error ______________
One parenthesis error ______________
One word-choice error ______________

1 Whenever you have to write a paper, a letter, or any other document for work or school, you probably head toward the computer. 2 In this day and age, most people reach for keyboards faster than they pick up pens. 3 At one elementary school in Scotland, however, the principle, Bryan Lewis, is taking a different approach. 4 He believes that neat handwriting is still an important skill, so he has his students write not only by hand but also with old fashioned fountain pens.

5 Fountain pens were used in schools long ago and lately have been regaining popularity because they are refillable. 6 A writer using a fountain pen dips the point into a little ink bottle. 7 Drawing ink up into the barrel of the pen, as needed. 8 Today, a writer simply throws an empty pen away; and gets a new one.

9 So far, Principal Lewis is pleased with the results of his experimint. 10 He reports that students are taking more care with their work, their self-esteem has improved as well. 11 He stresses to teachers all over the world that the ability to produce legible handwriting remains a necessary skill. 12 Lewis is happy with the improvement he sees in his students' writing (and in his own writing, too. 13 He knows that computers are here to stay and that it will not disappear. 14 However, he believes that the practice with fountain pens helps students focus, write faster, and they can feel proud of themselves.

Name ____________________ Section ____________________

# 10 Editing Review Test 10

## The Four Most Serious Errors (Chapters 15–19)
## Other Grammar Concerns (Chapters 20–26)
## Word Use (Chapters 27–29)
## Punctuation and Capitalization (Chapters 30–34)

**Directions:** Each of the underlined word groups contains one or more errors. As you locate and identify each error, write its item number on the appropriate line below. Then, edit the underlined word groups to correct the errors. If you need help, turn back to the chapters indicated.

One subject-verb agreement error ________
One pronoun error ________
One coordination/subordination error ________
One colon error ________
One commonly confused word error ________
One spelling error ________
One comma error ________
One semicolon error ________
One apostrophe error ________

1 When Shaun Ellis decided that he wanted to learn more about wolves, he made a radical life change. 2 He decided to live with the wolves yet imitate their wild lifestyle as closely as he possibly could. 3 For eighteen months, he lived with three wolf pups that had been abandoned. 4 He pretended to be its mother in many ways. 5 He worked to teach them the skills they would need to survive in the wild. 6 It certainly was not an easy way to live. 7 Ellis shared an outdoor pen with the pups, and it had no heat or beding. 8 To keep warm on the cold nights, he had to snuggle with the young wolves.

9 To communicate with them, Ellis learned how to: growl, snarl, and howl. 10 He also learned how to use body positions and facial expressions in order to get a message across to the animals. 11 While living with the wolves, he also try to eliminate any emotion because animals do not feel things as human beings do. 12 This mans transition back to regular life was quite difficult for him.

13 Ellis's unorthodox methods have earned him criticism from his colleagues; but he firmly believes that his techniques led to valuable knowledge about wolves. 14 He has founded, the Wolf Pack Management organization in England. 15 Its goal is to get captive wolves released back into the wild and than use what was learned to help the animals avoid future conflicts with humans.

# Appendix

## Problem Solving in Writing

Some writing assignments, both in English and in other subjects, will require you to use problem-solving skills. Such assignments will ask you to read and analyze a problem to develop possible solutions, often by synthesizing information from various sources.

Problem-solving skills are necessary not only in college but also—and even more so—in the work world. Often, managers assign a team to work on and pose possible solutions to a problem that the organization faces. Also, problem-solving skills will help you in your everyday life when you run into a situation that you want to change.

Each of the chapters in Part 2 includes problem-based writing assignments ("Writing to Solve a Problem"). These assignments offer you the opportunity to solve real-world problems by working alone or as part of a team. Use the following section to complete those assignments or to address any problem you may face in college, at work, or in your everyday life.

### *Problem Solving*

Problem solving is the process of identifying a problem and figuring out a reasonable solution.

Problems range from minor inconveniences like finding a rip in the last clean shirt you have when you're running late to more serious problems such as being laid off from your job. Although such problems disrupt our lives, they also give us opportunities to tackle difficult situations with confidence.

Too often, people are paralyzed by problems because they don't have strategies for attacking them. However, backing away from a problem rarely helps solve it. When you know how to approach a challenging situation, you are better able to take charge of your life.

Problem solving consists of five basic steps, which can be used effectively by both individuals and groups of people.

## The Problem-Solving Process

### Understand the problem.

You should be able to say or write it in a brief statement or question.

**EXAMPLE:** Your ten-year-old car needs a new transmission, which will cost at least $1500. Do you keep the car or buy a new one?

### Identify people or information that can help you solve the problem (resources).

**EXAMPLES**

- Your mechanic
- Friends who have had similar car problems
- Car advice from print or Web sources

### List the possible solutions.

**EXAMPLES**

- Pay for the transmission repair.
- Buy a new car.

### Evaluate the possible solutions.

1. Identify the steps each solution would require.
2. List possible obstacles for each solution (like money or time constraints).
3. List the advantages and disadvantages of the solutions.

**EXAMPLES (considering only advantages and disadvantages):**

- Pay for the transmission repair.

  *Advantage:* This would be cheaper than buying a new car.

  *Disadvantage:* The car may not last much longer, even with the new transmission.
- Buy a new car.

  *Advantage:* You will have a reliable car.

  *Disadvantage:* This option is much more expensive.

### Choose the most reasonable solution.

Choose the solution that is realistic—the simpler the better. Be able to give reasons for your choice.

*Solution:* Pay for the transmission repair.

*Reasons:* You do not have money for a new car, and you do not want to assume more debt. Opinions from two mechanics indicate that your car should run for three to five more years with the new transmission. At that point, you will be in a better position to buy a new car.

# Acknowledgments

Sarah Bigler. "High School Is Not Preparing Us for College." *Daily Eastern News,* October 10, 2010. Reprinted by permission.

Daniel Bird. "What's Appropriate: How to Talk to Children about Disasters." *The Skyline View,* May 16, 2013. Reprinted by permission.

Environmental Protection Agency. "Climate Change Is Happening." Courtesy of the Environmental Protection Agency.

Stephanie Ericsson. "The Ways We Lie." Copyright © 1992 by Stephanie Ericsson. Originally published by the *Utne Reader.* Reprinted by permission of Dunham Literary as agents for the author.

John Hawkins. "5 Scientific Reasons That Global Warming Isn't Happening." *Townhall.com,* February 18, 2014. Reprinted by permission.

Oscar Hijuelos. "Memories of New York City Snow." *Metropolis Found: New York Is Book Country 25th Anniversary Collection* (New York: New York Is Book Country, 2003). Copyright © 2003 by Oscar Hijuelos. Reprinted with the permission of the Jennifer Lyons Literary Agency, LLC for the author.

Kelly Hultgren. "Pick Up the Phone to Call, Not Text." Dailywildcat.com, August 31, 2011.

Amanda Jacobowitz. "A Ban on Water Bottles: A Way to Bolster the University's Image." Posted by Amanda Jacobowitz on April 28, 2010. Forum Staff Columnists.

Elizabeth Renter. "Napping Can Dramatically Increase Learning, Memory, Awareness, and More." *Natural Society,* March 17, 2014. Reprinted by permission. Illustration courtesy of Remie Geoffroi. www.remgeo.com.

Liz Riggs. "What It's Like to Be the First Person in Your Family to Go to College." *The Atlantic,* January 13, 2014. Reprinted by permission.

Caroline Bunker Rosdahl and Mary T. Kowalski. Excerpt from *Textbook of Basic Nursing,* 9th ed. © 2008 Wolters Kluwer Health | Lippincott Williams & Wilkins.

Kathy Stevens. "Ten Tips for Easing into Plant-Based Eating." *Huffington Post,* April 18, 2014. Reprinted by permission.

Amy Tan. "Fish Cheeks." © 1987 by Amy Tan. First appeared in *Seventeen* Magazine. Reprinted by permission of the author and the Sandra Dijkstra Literary Agency.

John Tierney. "Yes, Money Can Buy Happiness." *The New York Times,* March 20, 2008. © 2008 *The New York Times.* All rights reserved. Used by permission and protected by the laws of the United States. The printing, copying redistribution, or transmission of the material without express permission is prohibited.

Vidette Editorial Board. "ISU's Restroom Change Shows Commitment to Diversity." *Vidette,* July 14, 2014. Used by permission.

Andrea Whitmer. "When Poor People Have Nice Things." sooverthis.com, June 18, 2012. Reprinted by permission.